Enhance your learning experience with the accompanying interactive e-book, featuring video clips, exercises, quizzes and more!

Visit **www.wileyopenpage.com** to access your interactive e-book.

INCLUDES INTERACTIVE E-BOOK
LOOK FOR THIS ICON AS YOUR GUIDE TO THE EMBEDDED MEDIA

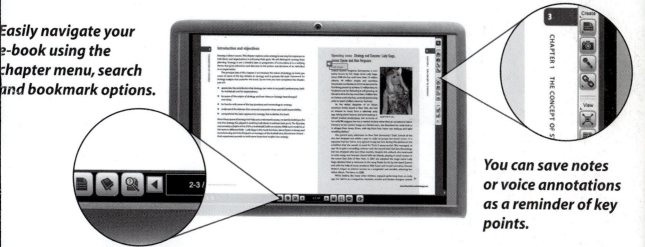

Easily navigate your e-book using the chapter menu, search and bookmark options.

You can save notes or voice annotations as a reminder of key points.

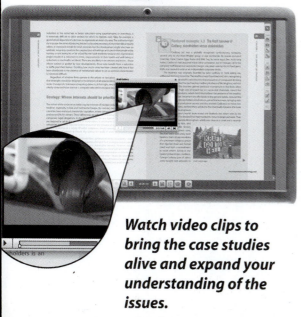

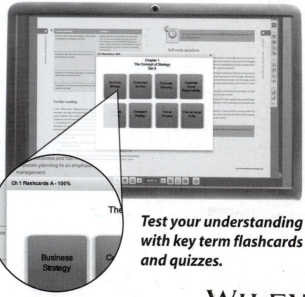

Watch video clips to bring the case studies alive and expand your understanding of the issues.

Test your understanding with key term flashcards and quizzes.

WILEY

CONTEMPORARY
STRATEGY
ANALYSIS
TEXT AND CASES

CONTEMPORARY STRATEGY ANALYSIS
TEXT AND CASES

EIGHTH EDITION

ROBERT M. GRANT

WILEY

ISBN 9781119941897 (pbk)
ISBN 9781118600221 (iebk)
ISBN 9781118591062 (ebk)
ISBN 9781118591055 (ebk)
ISBN 9781118560426 (ebk)

A catalogue record for this book is available from the British Library

Set in 10/12pt ITC Garamond Std by MPS Limited, Chennai, India
Printed in Italy by Printer Trento S.r.l.

FSC
www.fsc.org
MIX
Paper from
responsible sources
FSC® C015829

To Sue

BRIEF CONTENTS

CONTENTS

PREFACE TO EIGHTH EDITION

Contemporary Strategy Analysis equips managers and students of management with the concepts, frameworks, and techniques needed to make better strategic decisions. My goal is a strategy text that reflects the dynamism and intellectual rigor of this fast-developing field of management and takes account of the strategic management practices of leading-edge companies.

Contemporary Strategy Analysis endeavors to be both rigorous and relevant. While embodying the latest thinking in the strategy field, it aims to be accessible to students from different backgrounds and with varying levels of experience. I achieve this accessibility by combining clarity of exposition, concentration on the fundamentals of value creation, and an emphasis on practicality.

This eighth edition maintains the book's focus on the essential tasks of strategy: identifying the sources of superior business performance and formulating and implementing a strategy that exploits these sources of superior performance. At the same time, the content of the book has been revised to reflect recent developments in the business environment and in strategy research and to take account of feedback from instructors.

Distinctive features of the eighth edition include a:

- broader approach to value creation that takes account of the value that is created for stakeholders other than the firm's shareholders (Chapter 2);
- stronger emphasis on the role of complementary products, especially in technology-based industries (Chapters 4 and 9);
- more systematic treatment of resource and capability analysis that is structured around a practical approach to undertaking an analysis of resources and capabilities;
- more integrated treatment of strategy implementation; while the book maintains its emphasis on integrating strategy formulation with strategy implementation, Chapters 6 and 14 offer a systematic approach to strategy execution;
- new chapter on external growth strategies through mergers, acquisitions, and alliances (Chapter 15), which are important to firms as they navigate a challenging and unpredictable business world.

There is little in *Contemporary Strategy Analysis* that is original: I have plundered mercilessly the ideas, theories, and evidence of fellow scholars. My greatest debts are to my colleagues and students at the business schools where this book has been developed and tested, notably Georgetown University and Bocconi University. I have also benefitted from feedback and suggestions from professors and students in the many other schools where *Contemporary Strategy Analysis* has been adopted. I look forward to continuing my engagement with users.

I am grateful for the professionalism and enthusiasm of the editorial, production, and sales and marketing teams at John Wiley & Sons, Ltd, especially to Steve Hardman, Deb Egleton, Claire Jardine, Peter Hudson, Kelly Simmons, Juliet Booker, and Tim Bettsworth—I couldn't wish for better support!

Robert M. Grant

GUIDE TO
WEB RESOURCES

Visit **www.contemporarystrategyanalysis.com** for access to all the teaching and learning resources available for this textbook.

Instructors will find:

- Instructor's manual
- Case teaching notes
- PowerPoint slides
- Test bank
- Case video clips   *NEW TO THIS EDITION*

Students will find:

- Self-test quizzes
- Author video clips
- Glossary flashcards   *NEW TO THIS EDITION*

You can also access your interactive e-book at **www.wileyopenpage.com** using the scratch code included on the inside-front cover of the printed book. Video clips, quizzes, and flashcards are embedded throughout the e-book for easy access:

 Simply click on the "Play" icon located at relevant parts of the text.

Refer to the advert at the front of this book for more information.

I

INTRODUCTION

1 The Concept of Strategy

> Strategy is the great work of the organization. In situations of life or death, it is the Tao of survival or extinction. Its study cannot be neglected.
>
> —SUN TZU, *THE ART OF WAR*

> To shoot a great score you need a clever strategy.
>
> —RORY MCILROY, *GOLF MONTHLY*, MAY 19, 2011

OUTLINE

Introduction and Objectives

Strategy is about achieving success. This chapter explains what strategy is and why it is important to success, both for organizations and individuals. We will distinguish strategy from planning. Strategy is not a detailed plan or program of instructions; it is a unifying theme that gives coherence and direction to the actions and decisions of an individual or an organization.

The principal task of this chapter will be to introduce the basic framework for strategy analysis that underlies this book. I will introduce the two basic components of strategy analysis: analysis of the external environment of the firm (mainly industry analysis) and analysis of the internal environment (primarily analysis of the firm's resources and capabilities).

By the time you have completed this chapter, you will be able to:

◆ appreciate the contribution that strategy can make to successful performance, both for individuals and for organizations, and recognize the key characteristics of an effective strategy;

◆ comprehend the basic framework of strategy analysis that underlies this book;

◆ become familiar with how our thinking about business strategy has evolved over the past 60 years;

◆ be capable of identifying and describing the strategy of a business enterprise;

◆ understand how strategy is made within organizations;

◆ gain familiarity with the challenges of strategy making among not-for-profit organizations.

Since the purpose of strategy is to help us to win, we start by looking at the role of strategy in success.

The Role of Strategy in Success

Strategy Capsules 1.1 and 1.2 describe the careers of two individuals, Queen Elizabeth II and Lady Gaga, who have been outstandingly successful in leading their organizations. Although these two remarkable women operate within vastly different arenas, can their success be attributed to any common factors?

For neither of these successful women can success be attributed to overwhelmingly superior resources. For all of Queen Elizabeth's formal status as reigning monarch, she has very little real power and, in most respects, is a servant of the British government led by the prime minister. Lady Gaga is clearly a creative and capable entertainer, but few would claim that she has outstanding talents as a vocalist, musician, or songwriter.

Nor can their success be attributed either exclusively or primarily to luck. Indeed, Queen Elizabeth has experienced a succession of difficulties and tragedies, while Lady Gaga has experienced setbacks (e.g., the cancelation of her first recording contract). Their ability to respond to events with flexibility and clarity of direction has been central to their success.

My contention is that common to both the 60-year successful reign of Queen Elizabeth II and the short but remarkable career of Lady Gaga is the presence of a soundly formulated and effectively implemented strategy. While these strategies did not exist as explicit plans, for both Queen Elizabeth and Lady Gaga we can observe a consistency of direction based on a clear understanding of desired goals and a keen awareness of how to maneuver into a position of advantage.

In the vast array of formal and informal activities that Elizabeth Windsor has performed as queen, she has given herself a clearly defined role in relation to the people of the UK and the Commonwealth countries. This role has combined the traditional notions of being a figurehead for the nation, a symbol of British family and cultural life, and an exemplar of service and professional dedication. Yet this constancy has also embraced flexibility to respond to the unexpected.

Lady Gaga's remarkable success in the three years up to the beginning of 2012 reflects a career strategy that uses music as her gateway, but she has then built a celebrity status by combining the generic tools of star creation—shock value, fashion leadership, and media presence—with a uniquely differentiated image that has captured the imagination and affection of teenagers and young adults throughout the world.

We can go further. What do these examples tell us about the characteristics of a strategy that are conducive to success? In both stories, four common factors stand out (Figure 1.1):

- *Goals that are consistent and long term*: Both Queen Elizabeth and Lady Gaga display a focused commitment to career goals that they have pursued steadfastly.
- *Profound understanding of the competitive environment*: The ways in which both Elizabeth II and Gaga define their roles and pursue their careers reveal a deep and insightful appreciation of the external environments in which they operate. Queen Elizabeth has been alert both to the changing political environment in which the monarchy is situated and to the mood and needs of the British people. Lady Gaga's business model and strategic positions show a keen awareness of the changing economics of the music business, the marketing potential of social networking, and the needs of Generation Y.
- *Objective appraisal of resources*: Both Queen Elizabeth and Lady Gaga have been adept at recognizing and deploying the resources at their disposal. Both, too, have been aware of the limits of those resources and drawn upon the resources of others—Queen Elizabeth through her family, the royal household, and a network of loyal supporters; Lady Gaga upon the variety of talents in her Haus of Gaga.
- *Effective implementation*: Without effective implementation, the best-laid strategies are of little use. Critical to the success of Queen Elizabeth and Lady Gaga has been their effectiveness as leaders and the creation of loyal, supportive organizations to provide decision support and operational implementation.

STRATEGY CAPSULE 1.1
Queen Elizabeth II and the House of Windsor

June 2012 marked the diamond jubilee of the reign of Queen Elizabeth II: for 60 years she had been the ruling monarch of the United Kingdom of Great Britain and Northern Ireland.

At her birth on April 21, 1926, hereditary monarchies were common throughout the world. Apart from the British Empire, 45 countries had this form of government. By 2012, the forces of democracy, modernity, and reform had reduced these to 26—mostly small autocracies such as Bahrain, Qatar, Oman, Kuwait, Bhutan, and Lesotho. Monarchies had also survived in Denmark, Sweden, Norway, the Netherlands, and Belgium, but these royal families had lost most of their wealth and privileges.

By contrast, the British royal family retains considerable wealth—the Queen's personal net worth was estimated by *Forbes* magazine at $450 million—in addition, she and her family have use of palaces and real estate owned by the nation and receive annual government funding of £7.9 million ($12 million). Despite having no political power, she has formal status as head of state, head of the Church of England, and head of the armed forces. Despite the winding down of the British Empire, the Queen retains her role as head of the Commonwealth and is head of state of 15 other countries, including Canada and Australia. In addition, she has created a strong informal role. According to her

website, she "has a less formal role as Head of Nation" where she "acts as a focus for national identity, unity and pride; gives a sense of stability and continuity; officially recognises success and excellence; and supports the ideal of voluntary service" (www.royal.gov.uk).

How has Queen Elizabeth been able to retain not just the formal position of the monarchy but also its status, influence, and wealth despite the challenges of the past 60 years? These challenges include the social and political changes which have swept away most of the privileges conferred by hereditary status (including the exclusion of most hereditary lords from the House of Lords, Britain's upper chamber of Parliament) and the internal challenges presented by such a famously dysfunctional family—including the failed marriages of most of her family members and the controversy that surrounded the life and death of her daughter-in-law, Diana, Princess of Wales.

At the heart of Elizabeth's sustaining of the British monarchy has been her single-minded devotion to what she regards as her duties to the monarchy and to the nation. Throughout her 60-year reign she has cultivated the role of leader of her nation—a role that she has not compromised by pursuit of personal or family interests. In pursing this role she has recognized the need for political neutrality—even when she has personally disagreed with her prime ministers (notably

These observations about the role of strategy in success can be made in relation to most fields of human endeavor. Whether we look at warfare, chess, politics, sport, or business, the success of individuals and organizations is seldom the outcome of a purely random process. Nor is superiority in initial endowments of skills and resources typically the determining factor. Strategies that build on these four elements almost always play an influential role.

Look at the "high achievers" in any competitive area. Whether we review the world's political leaders, the CEOs of the Fortune 500, or our own circles of friends with Margaret Thatcher's "socially divisive" policies and Tony Blair's commitment of British troops to Iraq and Afghanistan).

Her leadership embodies a set of values—both British and Christian—which are directed toward sustaining British traditions and promoting British influence, British culture, and British values within the wider world. The Commonwealth provides a key focus for her promotion of British influence: she has made multiple visits to each of the 54 Commonwealth nations, including 26 to Canada and 16 to Australia.

Maintaining her popularity with the British people and the status of the royal family has required adaptation to the wrenching changes of her era. Recognizing the growing unacceptability of hereditary privilege and the traditional British class system, she has repositioned the royal family from being the leader of the ruling class to an embodiment of the nation as a whole. To make her and her family more inclusive and less socially stereotyped she cultivated involvement with popular culture, with ordinary people engaged in social service and charitable work, and, most recently, endorsing the marriage of her grandson William to Kate Middleton—the first member of the royal family to marry outside the ranks of the aristocracy.

In broadening the popular appeal of the monarchy, she has been adept at exploiting new media. Television has provided an especially powerful medium for communicating both with her subjects and with a wider global audience. The Queen's web page appeared in 1997, in 2009 she joined Twitter, and in 2010 Facebook. Throughout her reign, her press and public relations strategy has been carefully managed by a group of top professionals who report to her private secretary.

While respecting tradition and protocol, she adapts in the face of pressing circumstances. The death of her daughter-in-law, Diana, created difficult tensions between her responsibilities as a grandmother and her need to show leadership to a grieving nation. In responding to this time of crisis she departed from several established traditions: including bowing to the coffin of her ex-daughter-in-law as it passed the palace.

In pursuing her role of monarch, Elizabeth has drawn upon the resources available to her. First and foremost of these has been the underlying desire of the British people for continuity and their inherent distrust of their political leaders. By positioning herself above the political fray and emphasizing her lineage—including the prominent public role of her mother until her death in 2002—she reinforces the legitimacy of herself, her family, and the institution they represent. She has also exploited her powers of patronage, using her formal position to cultivate informal relationships both with political leaders such as Nelson Mandela and with individuals such as the Australian entertainer Rolf Harris, who obtained the rare privilege of painting her portrait.

The success of Elizabeth's 60-year reign is indicated by the popular support for her personally and for the institution of the monarchy. Outside of Northern Ireland, the UK lacks any significant republican movement; republicanism is also weak in Canada and Australia.

and acquaintances, those who have achieved outstanding success in their careers are seldom those who possessed the greatest innate abilities. Success has gone to those who managed their careers most effectively, typically by combining these four strategic factors. They are goal focused; their career goals have taken primacy over the multitude of life's other goals—friendship, love, leisure, knowledge, spiritual fulfillment—which the majority of us spend most of our lives juggling and reconciling. They know the environments within which they play and tend to be fast learners in terms of recognizing the paths to advancement. They know themselves well in

STRATEGY CAPSULE 1.2

Lady Gaga and the Haus of Gaga

Stefani Joanne Angelina Germanotta, better known as Lady Gaga, is the most successful popular entertainer to emerge in the 21st century. Since releasing her first album, *The Fame*, in 2008 she has certified record sales of 42 million,[a] swept leading music awards including Grammy, MTV, and Billboards, completed a 201-concert world tour that grossed $227.4 million (the highest for any debut artist), and topped *Forbes Celebrity 100* list for 2011.

Since dropping out of NYU's Tisch School of the Arts in 2005, she has shown total commitment to advancing her musical career and developing her Lady Gaga persona. After initially working as a songwriter, she developed her own musical act and image. Her debut album and its follow up, *The Fame Monster*, yielded a succession of number-one hits during 2009 and 2010.

Gaga's music is a catchy mix of pop and dance, well suited to dance clubs and radio airplay. It features good melodies, Gaga's capable singing voice, and her reflections on society and life, but it is hardly exceptional or innovative: music critic Simon Reynolds described it as: "ruthlessly catchy, naughties pop glazed with Auto-Tune and undergirded with R&B-ish beats."[b]

However, music is only one element in the Lady Gaga phenomenon—her achievement is not so much as a singer or songwriter as in establishing a persona which transcends pop music. Like David Bowie and Madonna before her, Lady Gaga is famous for being Lady Gaga. To do this requires a multi-media, multi-faceted offering that comprises an integrated array of components including music, visual appearance, newsworthy events, a distinctive attitude and personality, and a set of values with which fans can identify.

Key among these is visual impact and theatricality. Her hit records were heavily promoted by the visually stunning music videos that accompanied them. *Paparazzi* and *Bad Romance* each won best video awards at the 2009 and 2010 Grammies; the latter is the second-most-downloaded YouTube video of all time. Most striking of all has been Lady Gaga's dress and overall appearance, which have set new standards in eccentricity, innovation, and impact. Individual outfits—her plastic bubble dress, meat dress, and "decapitated-corpse dress"—together with weird hairdos, extravagant hats, and extreme footwear (she met President Obama in 16-inch heels)—are as well known as her hit songs. The range of visual images she projects is so varied that her every appearance creates a buzz of anticipation as to her latest incarnation.

---

terms of both strengths and weaknesses. Finally, they implement their career strategies with commitment, consistency, and determination. As the late Peter Drucker observed: "we must learn how to be the CEO of our own careers."[1]

There is a downside, however. Focusing on a single goal may lead to outstanding success but may be matched by dismal failure in other areas of life. Many people who have reached the pinnacles of their careers have led lives scarred by poor relationships with friends and families and stunted personal development. These include Howard Hughes and Jean Paul Getty in business, Richard Nixon and Joseph Stalin in politics, Elvis Presley and Marilyn Monroe in entertainment, Mike Tyson and O. J. Simpson in sport, and Bobby Fischer in chess. Fulfillment in our personal lives is likely to require broad-based lifetime strategies.[2]

More than any other star, Lady Gaga has developed a business model that recognizes the realities of the post-digital world of entertainment. Like Web 2.0 pioneers such as Facebook and Twitter, Gaga has followed the model: first build market presence, and then think about monetizing that presence. Her record releases are accompanied, sometimes preceded, by music videos on YouTube. With 45 million Facebook fans, 15.8 million Twitter followers, and 1.9 billion YouTube views (as of November 16, 2011), Famecount crowned her "most popular living musician online." Her networking with fans includes Gagaville, an interactive game developed by Zynga, and The Backplane, a music-based social network.

Her emphasis on visual imagery reflects the ways in which her fame is converted into revenues. While record royalties are important, concerts are her primary revenue source. Her 2012 Born This Way Ball Tour promises to make her one of the world's highest-earning entertainers. Other revenue sources—product placement in videos and concerts, merchandizing deals, and her appointment as Polaroid's creative director—also link closely with her visual presence.

A distinctive feature of Gaga's market development is the emphasis she gives to building relations with her fans. The devotion of her fans—her "Little Monsters"—is based less on their desire to emulate her look as upon empathy with her values and attitudes. They recognize Gaga's images more as social statements of non-conformity than as fashion statements. In communicating her experiences of alienation and bullying at school and her values of individuality, sexual freedom, and acceptance of differences—reinforced through her involvement in charities and gay rights events—she has built a global fan base that is unusual in its loyalty and commitment. The sense of community is reinforced by tools such as the "Monster Claw" greeting and the "Manifesto of Little Monsters." As "Mother Monster," Gaga is spokesperson and guru for this community.[c]

Lady Gaga possesses talents as a singer, musician, and songwriter; however, her most outstanding abilities lie in her showmanship and theatricality. Modeled on Andy Warhol's "Factory," The Haus of Gaga is her creative workshop and augments her own capabilities. It includes manager Troy Carter, choreographer and creative director Laurieann Gibson, fashion director Nicola Formichetti, hair stylist Frederic Aspiras, stylist and designer Anna Trevelyan, fashion photographer Nick Night, makeup artist Tara Savelo, marketing director Bobby Campbell, and others involved in designing and producing songs, videos, concert sets, photo shoots, and the whole range of Gaga's public appearances.

Notes:

[a]http://en.wikipedia.org/wiki/List_of_best-selling_music_artists, accessed 14 Nov. 2011.

[b]Quoted in http://en.wikipedia.org/wiki/Lady_Gaga, accessed 14 November, 2011.

[c]I have drawn extensively upon Mauro Sala's BSc thesis, *The Strategy of Lady Gaga*, Bocconi University, Milan, June 2011.

FIGURE 1.1 Common elements in successful strategies

These same ingredients of successful strategies—clear goals, understanding the competitive environment, resource appraisal, and effective implementation—form the key components of our analysis of business strategy.

The Basic Framework for Strategy Analysis

Figure 1.2 shows the basic framework for strategy analysis that we shall use throughout the book. The four elements of a successful strategy shown in Figure 1.1 are recast into two groups—the firm and the industry environment—with strategy forming a link between the two. The firm embodies three of these elements: goals and values ("simple, consistent, long-term goals"), resources and capabilities ("objective appraisal of resources"), and structure and systems ("effective implementation"). The industry environment embodies the fourth ("profound understanding of the competitive environment") and is defined by the firm's relationships with competitors, customers, and suppliers.

This view of strategy as a link between the firm and its industry environment has close similarities with the widely used **SWOT framework**. However, as I explain in Strategy Capsule 1.3, a two-way classification of internal and external forces is superior to the four-way SWOT framework.

The task of business strategy, then, is to determine how the firm will deploy its resources within its environment and so satisfy its long-term goals, and how it will organize itself to implement that strategy.

Strategic Fit

Fundamental to this view of strategy as a link between the firm and its external environment is the notion of **strategic fit**. This refers to the consistency of a firm's strategy, first, with the firm's external environment and, second, with its internal environment, especially with its goals and values and resources and capabilities. A major reason for the decline and failure of some companies comes from their having a strategy that lacks consistency with either the internal or the external environment. The decline of Nokia (which lost over 90% of its stock market value in the four years up to July 2012) may be attributed to a strategy which failed to take account of a major change in its external environment: the growing consumer demand for smartphones. Other companies struggle to align their strategies to their internal resources and capabilities. A critical issue for Nintendo will be whether it possesses

FIGURE 1.2   The basic framework: Strategy as a link between the firm and its environment

STRATEGY CAPSULE 1.3
What's Wrong with SWOT?

Distinguishing between the external and the internal environment of the firm is common to most approaches to strategy analysis. The best-known and most widely used of these approaches is the "SWOT" framework, which classifies the various influences on a firm's strategy into four categories: Strengths, Weaknesses, Opportunities, and Threats. The first two—strengths and weaknesses—relate to the internal environment; the last two—opportunities and threats—relate to the external environment.

Which is better, a two-way distinction between internal and external influences or the four-way SWOT taxonomy? The key issue is whether it is sensible and worthwhile to classify internal factors into strengths and weaknesses and external factors into opportunities and threats. In practice, such distinctions are difficult.

Is Alex Ferguson a strength or a weakness for Manchester United Football Club? As the world's most experienced and successful soccer coach, he is a strength. As a 70-year-old man who has no obvious successor, he is a weakness.

Is global warming a threat or an opportunity for the world's automobile producers? By encouraging higher taxes on motor fuels and restrictions on car use, it is a threat. By encouraging consumers to switch to fuel-efficient and electric cars, it offers an opportunity for new sales.

The lesson here is that classifying external factors into opportunities and threats, and internal factors into strengths and weaknesses, is arbitrary. What is important is to carefully identify the external and internal forces that impact the firm, and then analyze their implications.

In this book I will follow a simple two-way classification of internal and external factors and avoid any superficial categorization into strengths or weaknesses, and opportunities or threats.

the financial and technological resources to continue to compete head-to-head with Sony and Microsoft in the market for video game consoles.

The concept of strategic fit also relates to the internal consistency among the different elements of a firm's strategy. Effective strategies are ones where functional strategies and individual decisions are aligned with one another to create a consistent strategic position and direction of development. This notion of internal fit is central to Michael Porter's conceptualization of the firm as an **activity system**. Porter states that "Strategy is the creation of a unique and differentiated position involving a different set of activities."[3] The key is how these activities fit together to form a consistent, mutually reinforcing system. Ryanair's strategic position is as Europe's lowest-cost airline providing no-frills flights to budget-conscious travelers. This is achieved by a set of activities which fit together to support that positioning (Figure 1.3).

The concept of strategic fit is one component of a set of ideas known as **contingency theory**. Contingency theory postulates that there is no single best way of organizing or managing. The best way to design, manage, and lead an organization depends upon circumstances—in particular the characteristics of that organization's environment.[4]

FIGURE 1.3 Ryanair's activity system

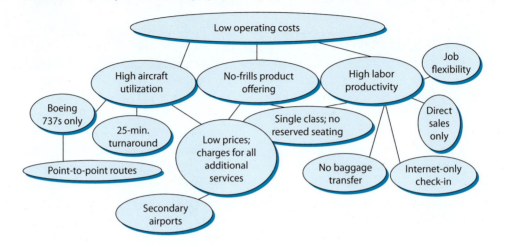

A Brief History of Business Strategy

Origins and Military Antecedents

Enterprises need business strategies for much the same reason that armies need military strategies—to give direction and purpose, to deploy resources in the most effective manner, and to coordinate the decisions made by different individuals. Many of the concepts and theories of business strategy have their antecedents in military strategy. The term *strategy* derives from the Greek word *strategia*, meaning "generalship." However, the concept of strategy did not originate with the Greeks: Sun Tzu's classic, *The Art of War*, from about 500 BC is regarded as the first treatise on strategy.[5]

Military strategy and business strategy share a number of common concepts and principles, the most basic being the distinction between strategy and tactics. Strategy is the overall plan for deploying resources to establish a favorable position; a tactic is a scheme for a specific action. Whereas tactics are concerned with the maneuvers necessary to win battles, strategy is concerned with winning the war. Strategic decisions, whether in military or business spheres, share three common characteristics:

- they are important
- they involve a significant commitment of resources
- they are not easily reversible.

Many of the principles of military strategy have been applied to business situations. These include the relative strengths of offensive and defensive strategies; the merits of outflanking over frontal assault; the roles of graduated responses to aggressive initiatives; the benefits of surprise; and the potential for deception, envelopment, escalation, and attrition.[6] At the same time, there are major differences between business competition and military conflict. The objective of war is (usually) to defeat the enemy. The purpose of business rivalry is seldom so aggressive: most business enterprises limit their competitive ambitions, seeking coexistence rather than the destruction of competitors.

The tendency for the principles of military and business strategy to develop along separate paths indicates the absence of a general theory of strategy. The publication of Von Neumann and Morgenstern's *Theory of Games* in 1944 gave rise to the hope that a general theory of competitive behavior would emerge. During the subsequent six decades, **game theory** has revolutionized the study of competitive interaction, not just in business but in politics, military conflict, and international relations as well. Yet, as we shall see in Chapter 4, game theory has achieved only limited success as a practical and broadly applicable general theory of strategy.[7]

From Corporate Planning to Strategic Management

The evolution of business strategy has been driven more by the practical needs of business than by the development of theory. During the 1950s and 1960s, senior executives experienced increasing difficulty in coordinating decisions and maintaining control in companies that were growing in size and complexity. While new techniques of discounted cash flow analysis allowed more rational choices over individual investment projects, firms lacked systematic approaches to their long-term development. **Corporate planning** (also known as *long-term planning*) was developed during the late 1950s to serve this purpose. Macroeconomic forecasts provided the foundation for the new corporate planning. The typical format was a five-year corporate planning document that set goals and objectives, forecasted key economic trends (including market demand, the company's market share, revenue, costs, and margins), established priorities for different products and business areas of the firm, and allocated capital expenditures. The diffusion of corporate planning was accelerated by a flood of articles and books addressing this new science.[8] The new techniques of corporate planning proved particularly useful for guiding the diversification strategies that many large companies pursued during the 1960s.[9] By the mid-1960s, most large US and European companies had set up corporate planning departments. Strategy Capsule 1.4 provides an example of this formalized corporate planning.

During the 1970s and early 1980s, confidence in corporate planning was severely shaken. Not only did diversification fail to deliver the anticipated synergies but the oil shocks of 1974 and 1979 ushered in a new era of macroeconomic instability, while increased international competition intensified as Japanese, Korean, and Southeast Asian firms stepped onto the world stage. The new turbulence meant that firms could no longer plan their investments and resource requirements three to five years ahead—they couldn't forecast that far ahead.

The result was a shift in emphasis from planning to strategy making, where the focus was less on the detailed management of a company's growth path as on market selection and positioning the company relative to its competitors in order to maximize the potential for profit. This transition from corporate planning to what became called *strategic management* involved a focus on competition as the central characteristic of the business environment, and on performance maximization as the primary goal of strategy.

This emphasis on strategy as a quest for performance directed attention to the sources of profitability. During the late 1970s and into the 1980s, attention focused on sources of profit within the industry environment. Michael Porter of Harvard Business School pioneered the application of industrial organization economics to

STRATEGY CAPSULE 1.4

Corporate Planning in a Large US Steel Company, 1965

The first step in developing long-range plans was to forecast the product demand for future years. After calculating the tonnage needed in each sales district to provide the "target" fraction of the total forecast demand, the optimal production level for each area was determined. A computer program that incorporated the projected demand, existing production capacity, freight costs, etc. was used for this purpose.

When the optimum production rate in each area was found, the additional facilities needed to produce the desired tonnage were specified. Then the capital costs for the necessary equipment, buildings, and layout were estimated by the chief engineer of the corporation and various district engineers. Alternative plans for achieving company goals were also developed for some areas, and investment proposals were formulated after considering the amount of available capital and the company debt policy. The vice president who was responsible for long-range planning recommended certain plans to the president and, after the top executives and the board of directors reviewed alternative plans, they made the necessary decisions about future activities.

Source: H. W. Henry, *Long Range Planning Processes in 45 Industrial Companies* (Englewood Cliffs, NJ: Prentice-Hall, 1967): 65.

analyzing the profit potential of different industries and markets.[10] Other studies examined the impact of market share and experience in determining how profits were distributed between the different firms in an industry.[11]

During the 1990s, the focus of strategy analysis shifted from the sources of profit in the external environment to the sources of profit within the firm. Increasingly the resources and capabilities of the firm became regarded as the main source of competitive advantage and the primary basis for formulating strategy.[12] This emphasis on what has been called the **resource-based view of the firm** represented a substantial shift in thinking about strategy. Rather than firms pursuing similar strategies, as in seeking attractive markets and favorable competitive positions, emphasis on internal resources and capabilities has encouraged firms to identify how they are *different* from their competitors and design strategies that exploit these differences.

During the 21st century, new challenges have continued to shape the principles and practice of strategy. Digital technologies have had a massive impact on the competitive dynamics of many industries, creating winner-take-all markets and standards wars.[13] Disruptive technologies[14] and accelerating rates of change have meant that strategy has become less and less about plans and more about creating options of the future,[15] fostering strategic innovation,[16] and seeking the "blue oceans" of uncontested market space.[17] The complexity of these challenges have meant that being self-sufficient is no longer viable for most firms—they increasingly depend upon other firms through outsourcing and strategic alliances.

The 2008–2009 financial crisis has had a major impact on firm strategy, encouraging new thinking about the purpose of business. Disillusion with the excesses and unfairness of market capitalism has renewed interest in corporate social responsibility, ethics, sustainability, and the role of legitimacy in long-term corporate success.[18]

FIGURE 1.4 Evolution of strategic management

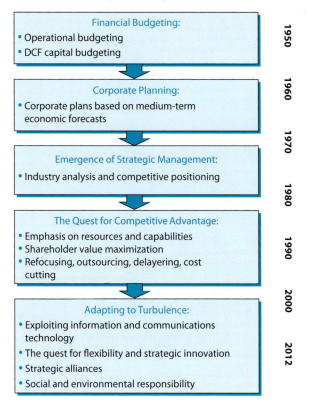

Figure 1.4 summarizes the main developments in strategic management since the mid-20th century.

Strategy Today

What Is Strategy?

In its broadest sense, strategy is the means by which individuals or organizations achieve their objectives. Table 1.1 presents a number of definitions of the term strategy. Common to most definitions is the notion that strategy is focused on achieving certain goals; that it involves allocating resources; and that it implies some consistency, integration, or cohesiveness of decisions and actions.

Yet, as we have seen, the conception of firm strategy has changed greatly over the past half-century. As the business environment has become more unstable and unpredictable, so strategy has become less concerned with detailed plans and more about guidelines for success. This is consistent with the examples that began this chapter. Neither Queen Elizabeth nor Lady Gaga appears to have had any detailed strategic plan, but both possessed clear ideas of what they wanted to achieve and how they would achieve it. This shift in emphasis from strategy as plan to strategy as direction does not imply any downgrading of the role of strategy. The more

TABLE 1.1 Some definitions of strategy

● Strategy: a plan, method, or series of actions designed to achieve a specific goal or effect.
—*Wordsmyth Dictionary* (http://www.wordsmyth.net)

● The determination of the long-run goals and objectives of an enterprise, and the adoption of courses of action and the allocation of resources necessary for carrying out these goals.
—Alfred Chandler, *Strategy and Structure*
(Cambridge, MA: MIT Press, 1962)

● Strategy is the pattern of objectives, purposes, or goals and the major policies and plans for achieving these goals, stated in such a way as to define what business the company is in or is to be in and the kind of company it is or is to be.
—Kenneth Andrews, *The Concept of Corporate Strategy*
(Homewood, IL: Irwin, 1971)

● Lost Boy: "Injuns! Let's go get 'em!"
 John Darling: "Hold on a minute. First we must have a strategy."
 Lost Boy: "Uhh? What's a strategy?"
 John Darling: "It's, er . . . it's a plan of attack."
—Walt Disney's *Peter Pan*

---

turbulent the environment, the more must strategy embrace flexibility and responsiveness. But it is precisely in these conditions that strategy becomes more, rather than less, important. When the firm is buffeted by unforeseen threats and where new opportunities are constantly appearing, then strategy becomes the compass that can navigate the firm through stormy seas.

Why Do Firms Need Strategy?

This transition from strategy as plan to strategy as direction raises the question of why firms (or any type of organization) need strategy. Strategy assists the effective management of organizations, first, by enhancing the quality of decision making, second, by facilitating coordination, and, third, by focusing organizations on the pursuit of long-term goals.

Strategy as Decision Support Strategy is a pattern or theme that gives coherence to the decisions of an individual or organization. But why can't individuals or organizations make optimal decisions in the absence of such a unifying theme? Consider the 1997 "man versus machine" chess epic in which Garry Kasparov was defeated by IBM's "Deep Blue" computer. Deep Blue did not need strategy. Its phenomenal memory and computing power allowed it to identify its optimal moves based on a huge decision tree.[19] Kasparov—although the world's greatest chess player—was subject to *bounded rationality*: his decision analysis was subject to the cognitive limitations that constrain all human beings.[20] For him, a strategy offered guidance that assisted positioning and helped create opportunities. Strategy improves decision making in several ways:

● It simplifies decision making by constraining the range of decision alternatives considered and acts as a *heuristic*—a rule of thumb that reduces the search required to find an acceptable solution to a decision problem.

- The strategy-making process permits the knowledge of different individuals to be pooled and integrated.
- It facilitates the use of analytic tools—the frameworks and techniques that we will encounter in the ensuing chapters of this book.

Strategy as a Coordinating Device The central challenge of management is coordinating the actions of different organizational members. Strategy acts as a communication device to promote coordination. Statements of strategy are a means by which the CEO can communicate the identity, goals, and positioning of the company to all organizational members. The strategic planning process acts as a forum in which views are exchanged and consensus developed; once formulated, strategy can be translated into goals, commitments, and performance targets that ensure that the organization moves forward in a consistent direction.

Strategy as Target Strategy is forward looking. It is concerned not only with how the firm will compete now but also with what the firm will become in the future. A key purpose of a forward-looking strategy is not only to establish a direction for the firm's development but also to set aspirations that can motivate and inspire members of the organization. Gary Hamel and C. K. Prahalad use the term **strategic intent** to describe this desired strategic position: "strategic intent creates an extreme misfit between resources and ambitions. Top management then challenges the organization to close the gap by building new competitive advantages."[21] The implication is that strategy should be less about fit and resource allocation and more about stretch and resource leverage.[22] Jim Collins and Jerry Porras make a similar point: US companies that have been sector leaders for 50 years or more—Merck, Walt Disney, 3M, IBM, and Ford—have all generated commitment and drive through setting "Big, Hairy, Ambitious Goals."[23] Striving, inspirational goals are found in most organizations' statements of vision and mission. One of the best known is that set by President Kennedy for NASA's space program: "before this decade is out, to land a man on the moon and return him safely to Earth."

Where Do We Find Strategy?

A company's strategy can be found in three places: in the heads of managers, in their articulations of strategy in speeches and written documents, and in the decisions through which strategy is enacted. Only the last two are observable.

Strategy has its origins in the thought processes of entrepreneurs and senior managers. For the entrepreneur the starting point of strategy is the idea for a new business. In most small companies, strategy remains in the heads of business proprietors: there is little need for any explicit statement of strategy. For large companies statements of strategy are found in board minutes and strategic planning documents, which are invariably confidential. However, most companies—public companies in particular—see value in communicating their strategy to employees, customers, investors, and business partners. Collis and Rukstad identify four types of statement through which companies communicate their strategies:

- The mission statement describes organizational purpose; it addresses "Why we exist."

- A statement of principles or values states "What we believe in and how we will behave."
- The vision statement projects "What we want to be."
- The strategy statement articulates the company's competitive game plan, which typically comprises statements of objectives, business scope, and advantage.[24]

These statements are typically found on the corporate pages of companies' websites. More detailed statements of strategy—including qualitative and quantitative medium-term targets—are often found in top management presentations to analysts, which are typically included in the "for investors" pages of company websites.

Detailed information on business scope (the products with which and the markets where the firm competes) and advantage (how it competes) can be found in a company's annual reports. For US corporations, the description of the business that forms Item 1 of the 10-K annual report to the Securities and Exchange Commission (SEC) is particularly informative about strategy.

Strategy Capsule 1.5 provides statements of strategy by McDonald's, the global fast-food giant, and Nokia, the world's largest supplier of wireless handsets.

Ultimately, strategy becomes enacted in the decisions and actions of an organization's members. Indeed, checking strategy statements against the actual decisions and behaviors is essential to close the gap between rhetoric and reality. As a reality check upon grandiose and platitudinous sentiments of vision and mission, it is useful to ask:

- Where is the company investing its money? Notes to financial statements provide detailed breakdowns of capital expenditure by region and by business segment.
- What technologies is the company developing? Identifying the patents that a company has filed (using the online databases of the US and EU patent offices) indicates the technological trajectory it is pursuing.
- What new products have been released, major investment projects initiated, and top management hired? These strategic decisions are typically announced in press releases.

To identify a firm's strategy it is necessary to draw upon multiple sources of information in order to build an overall picture of what the company says it is doing and what it is actually doing. We will return to this topic when we discuss *competitive intelligence* in Chapter 4.

Corporate and Business Strategy

Strategic choices can be distilled into two basic questions:

- Where to compete?
- How to compete?

The answers to these questions define the two major areas of a firm's strategy: **corporate strategy** and **business strategy**.

STRATEGY CAPSULE 1.5

Statements of Company Strategy: McDonald's and Nokia

MCDONALD'S CORPORATION PLAN TO WIN

Our entire System is unified by McDonald's Plan to Win—a clear set of actions involving the Company, our franchisees and our suppliers. This Plan is aimed at making McDonald's our customers' favorite place and way to eat by implementing the key drivers of an exceptional customer experience—people, products, price, place and promotion.

It's about having well-trained, friendly *people* working in our restaurants and the right *products* at a range of affordable prices. It's also about showcasing our restaurants as *places* that are clean, contemporary and welcoming, as well as creating promotions and marketing activities that resonate with key customer groups.

McDonald's Plan to Win is designed to support our strategy of growing sales at existing restaurants, rather than growing simply by opening more restaurants. Implementation of the Plan enables us to align our human and financial resources with our strategy for growth, and eliminate activities that are not focused on our customers or our restaurants.

Source: McDonald's Corporation *Summary Annual Report,* 2003, p. 5

NOKIA: OUR VISION AND STRATEGY

Nokia's mission is simple: Connecting People. Our goal is to build great mobile products that enable billions of people worldwide to enjoy more of what life has to offer. Our challenge is to achieve this in an increasingly dynamic and competitive environment . . .

Regaining leadership in the smartphone space. To help us achieve our mission, Nokia has formed a strategic partnership with Microsoft that will, we hope, see us regain lost ground in the smartphone market. Together, we intend to build a global ecosystem that surpasses anything currently in existence. The Nokia–Microsoft ecosystem will deliver differentiated and innovative products with unrivalled scale in terms of product breadth, geographical reach and brand identity.

Connecting the next billion. In feature phones, Nokia's strategy is to leverage its innovation and strength in growth markets to connect even more people to their first internet and application experience. By providing compelling, affordable and localized mobile experiences, particularly to emerging markets, our ambition is to bring the next billion online . . .

Source: Reproduced from http://www.nokia.com/global/about-nokia/about-us/about-us/ with permission from Nokia

Corporate strategy defines the scope of the firm in terms of the industries and markets in which it competes. Corporate strategy decisions include choice over diversification, vertical integration, acquisitions, and new ventures, and the allocation of resources between the different businesses of the firm.

Business strategy is concerned with how the firm competes within a particular industry or market. If the firm is to prosper within an industry, it must establish a

FIGURE 1.5   The sources of superior profitability

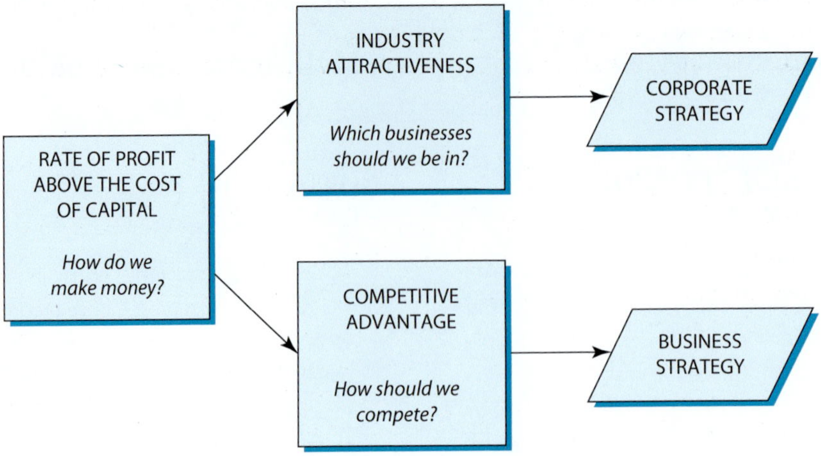

competitive advantage over its rivals. Hence, this area of strategy is also referred to as *competitive strategy*.

The distinction between corporate strategy and business strategy corresponds to the organizational structure of most large companies. Corporate strategy is the responsibility of the top management team and the corporate strategy staff. Business strategy is primarily the responsibility of divisional management.

This distinction between corporate and business strategy also corresponds to the primary sources of superior profit for a firm. As we have noted, the purpose of strategy is to achieve superior performance. Basic to this is the need to survive and prosper, which in turn requires that over the long term the firm earn a rate of return on its capital that exceeds its cost of capital. There are two possible ways of achieving this. First, by choosing to locate within industries where overall rates of return are attractive (corporate strategy). Second, by attaining a position of advantage vis-à-vis competitors within an industry, allowing it to earn a return that exceeds the industry average (Figure 1.5).

This distinction may be expressed in even simpler terms. The basic question facing the firm is "How do we make money?" The answer to this question corresponds to the two basic strategic choices we identified above: "Where to compete?" ("In which industries and markets should we be?") and "How should we compete?"

As an integrated approach to firm strategy, this book deals with both business and corporate strategy. However, my primary emphasis will be on business strategy. This is because the critical requirement for a company's success is its ability to establish competitive advantage. Hence, issues of business strategy precede those of corporate strategy. At the same time, these two dimensions of strategy are intertwined: the scope of a firm's business has implications for the sources of competitive advantage, and the nature of a firm's competitive advantage determines the range of businesses it can be successful in.

Describing Strategy

These same two questions—"Where is the firm competing?" and "How is it competing?"—also provide the basis upon which we can describe the strategy that a firm is pursuing. The *where* question has multiple dimensions. It relates to the products the firm supplies, the customers it serves, the countries and localities where it operates, and the vertical range of activities it undertakes.

Thus, Coca-Cola's strategy can be described in terms of these *where* and *how* choices. With regard to *where*:

- Coca-Cola competes in the soft drinks industry, where it supplies concentrate for its branded soda drinks (such as Coca-Cola, Sprite, Fanta, Tab, and Fresca) and supplies non-carbonated drinks (such as Minute Maid, Hi-C and Five Alive fruit juices, and Dasani bottled water).
- Geographically, Coca-Cola competes worldwide; its "big five" markets are the US, Mexico, Brazil, Japan, and China.
- In terms of vertical scope, Coca-Cola's main activities are product development, brand management, and the manufacture and distribution of concentrate. The production and distribution of its soft drinks are undertaken by its sister company, Coca-Cola Enterprises, and franchised local bottlers.

With regard to *how*, Coca-Cola pursues a differentiation strategy where it relies on brand image developed through heavy advertising and promotion. It seeks market share leadership through its mass marketing and through close relationships with the leading bottlers in every country where it does business.

However, strategy is not simply about "competing for today"; it is also concerned with "competing for tomorrow." This dynamic concept of strategy involves establishing objectives for the future and determining how they will be achieved. Future objectives relate to the overall purpose of the firm (mission), what it seeks to become (vision), and how it will meet specific performance targets.

In the case of Coca-Cola, this dynamic dimension of its strategy is outlined in terms of vision ("to refresh the world, to inspire moments of optimism and happiness, and to create value and make a difference"), mission (goals in relation to its six Ps: people, portfolio, planet, partners, profit, and productivity), and specific objectives (such as increasing system revenue to $200 billion by 2020 and doubling volume in terms of servings).[25]

These two dimensions of strategy—the static and the dynamic—are depicted in Figure 1.6. As we shall see in Chapter 8, reconciling these two dimensions of strategy—what Derek Abell calls "competing with dual strategies"—is one of the central dilemmas of strategic management.[26]

How Is Strategy Made? The Strategy Process

How companies make strategy and how they should make strategy are among the most hotly debated issues in strategic management. The corporate planning undertaken by large companies during the 1960s was a highly formalized approach to strategy making. Strategy may also emerge through adaptation to circumstances. In our opening discussion of Queen Elizabeth and Lady Gaga, I discerned a consistency and pattern to their career decisions that I identified as strategy, even though there is no evidence that either of them engaged in any systematic strategy making. Similarly, most successful companies are not products of grand designs. In August

FIGURE 1.6 Describing firm strategy: Competing in the present, preparing for the future

Strategy as Positioning	Strategy as Direction

• *Where are we competing?*
   -Product market scope
   -Geographical scope
   -Vertical scope
• *How are we competing?*
   -What is the basis of our
    competitive advantage?
	• *What do we want to become?*
	   -Vision statement
	• *What do we want to achieve?*
	   -Mission statement
	   -Performance goals
	• *How will we get there?*
	   -Guidelines for development
	   -Priorities for capital expenditure,
	    R & D
	   -Growth modes: organic growth,
	    M & A, alliances

COMPETING FOR THE PRESENT	*PREPARING FOR THE FUTURE*

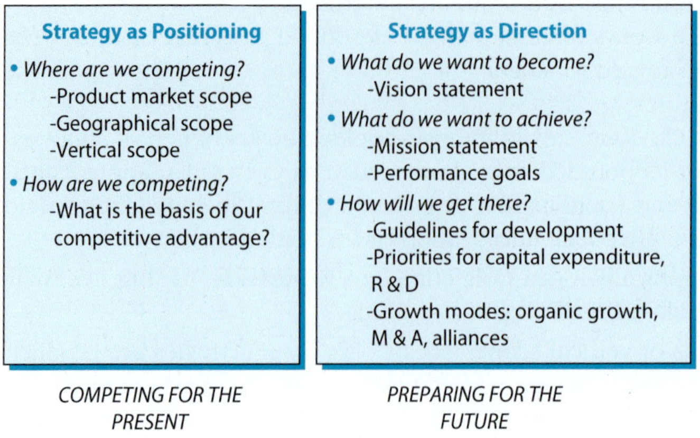

2011, Apple surpassed Exxon Mobil to become the world's most valuable company. Apple's success was based upon a strategy of creating consumer electronic products that integrated hardware, software, and design aesthetics to create a user experience characterized by accessibility and intuitive functionality. Apple began with Steve Jobs' recognition of the revolutionary potential of personal computing and the vision of creating a personal computer that would be cheap and easy to use. However, the strategy that would eventually make Apple one of the most successful companies of all time was a product of insight, intuition, experimentation, and events.

So, what does this mean for strategy making by companies and other types of organizations? Should managers seek to formulate strategy through a rational systematic process, or is the best approach in a turbulent world to respond to events while maintaining some sense of direction in the form of goals and guidelines?

Design versus Emergence

Henry Mintzberg is a leading critic of rational approaches to strategy design. He distinguishes intended, realized, and emergent strategies. **Intended strategy** is strategy as conceived of by the top management team. Even here, intended strategy is less a product of rational deliberation and more an outcome of negotiation, bargaining, and compromise among the many individuals and groups involved in the strategy-making process. However, **realized strategy**—the actual strategy that is implemented—is only partly related to that which was intended (Mintzberg suggests only 10–30% of intended strategy is realized). The primary determinant of realized strategy is what Mintzberg terms **emergent strategy**—the decisions that emerge from the complex processes in which individual managers interpret the intended strategy and adapt to changing circumstances.[27]

According to Mintzberg, rational design is not only an inaccurate account of how strategies are actually formulated but also a poor way of making strategy: "The notion that strategy is something that should happen way up there, far removed from the details of running an organization on a daily basis, is one of the great fallacies of conventional strategic management."[28] The emergent approaches to strategy making permit adaptation and learning through a continuous interaction between strategy formulation and strategy implementation in which strategy is constantly being adjusted and revised in the light of experience.

The debate between those who view strategy making as a rational, analytical process of deliberate planning (the *design school*) and those who envisage strategy making as an emergent process (the *emergence* or *learning school* of strategy) has centered on the case of Honda's successful entry into the US motorcycle market during the early 1960s.[29] The Boston Consulting Group lauded Honda for its single-minded pursuit of a global strategy based on exploiting economies of scale and learning to establish unassailable cost leadership.[30] However, subsequent interviews with the Honda managers in charge of its US market entry revealed a different story: a haphazard, experimental approach with little analysis and no clear plan.[31] As Mintzberg observes: "Brilliant as its strategy may have looked after the fact, Honda's managers made almost every conceivable mistake until the market finally hit them over the head with the right formula."[32]

In practice, strategy making almost always involves a combination of centrally driven rational design and decentralized adaptation. The design aspect of strategy comprises a number of organizational processes through which strategy is deliberated, discussed, and decided. In larger companies these include board meetings and a formalized process of strategic planning supplemented by more broadly participative events, such as strategy workshops. I will discuss processes of strategic planning more fully in Chapter 6.

At the same time, strategy is being continually enacted through decisions that are made by every member of the organization—by middle management especially. The decentralized, bottom-up process of strategy emergence often precedes more formalized top-down strategy formulation. Intel's historic decision to abandon memory chips and concentrate on microprocessors was initiated in the decisions taken by business unit and plant managers that were subsequently promulgated by top management as strategy.[33]

In all the companies I am familiar with, strategy making combines design and emergence—a process that I have referred to as "planned emergence."[34] The balance between the two depends greatly upon the stability and predictability of the organization's business environment. The Roman Catholic Church and La Poste, the French postal service, inhabit relatively stable environments; they can plan activities and resource allocations in some detail quite far into the future. For WikiLeaks, Zimbabwe Banking Corporation, or Somali pirate gangs, strategic planning will inevitably be restricted to a few guidelines; most strategic decisions must be responses to unfolding circumstances.

As the business environment becomes more turbulent and less predictable, so strategy making becomes less about detailed decisions and more about guidelines and general direction. Bain & Company advocates the use of strategic principles— "pithy, memorable distillations of strategy that guide and empower employees"—to combine consistent focus with adaptability and responsiveness.[35] McDonald's strategy statement in Strategy Capsule 1.5 is an example of such strategic principles. Similarly, Southwest Airlines encapsulates its strategy in a simple statement: "Meet customers' short-haul travel needs at fares competitive with the cost of automobile travel." Kathy Eisenhardt and Don Sull make a similar argument when they advocate "simple rules" as the basis for successful strategies in fast-moving businesses. For example, Lego evaluates new product proposals by applying a checklist of rules: "Does the product have the Lego look?" "Will children learn while having fun?" "Does it stimulate creativity?"[36]

We shall return to the role of rules and principles to guide an organization's evolution and coordinate the decisions of its many members in our final chapter, where we explore some of the implications of complexity theory for strategic management.

The Role of Analysis in Strategy Formulation

Despite the criticism of rational, analytical approaches to strategy formulation by Henry Mintzberg and others, the approach of this book is to emphasize analytic approaches to strategy formulation. This is not because I wish to downplay the role of intuition, creativity, or spontaneity—these qualities are essential ingredients of successful strategies. Nevertheless, whether strategy formulation is formal or informal, whether strategies are deliberate or emergent, systematic analysis is a vital input into the strategy process. Without analysis, strategic decisions are susceptible to power battles, individual whims, fads, and wishful thinking. Concepts, theories, and analytic tools are complements of, and not substitutes for, intuition and creativity. Their role is to provide frameworks for organizing discussion, processing information, and developing consensus.

This is not to endorse current approaches to strategy analysis. Strategic management is still a young field and the existing toolbox of concepts and techniques remains woefully inadequate. Our challenge is to do better. If existing analytical techniques do not adequately address the problems of strategy making and strategy implementation under conditions of uncertainty, technological change, and complexity, we need to augment and extend our analytical toolkit. In the course of this book, you will encounter concepts such as *real options*, *tacit knowledge*, *hypercompetition*, *complementarity*, and *complexity* that will help you address more effectively the challenges that firms are facing in today's turbulent business environment. We must also recognize the nature of *strategy analysis*. Unlike many of the analytical techniques in accounting, finance, market research, or production management, strategy analysis does not generate solutions to problems. It does not offer algorithms or formulae that tell us the optimal strategy to adopt. The strategic questions that companies face (like those that we face in our own careers and lives) are simply too complex to be programmed.

The purpose of strategy analysis is not to provide answers but to help us understand the issues. Most of the analytic techniques introduced in this book are frameworks that allow us to identify, classify, and understand the principal factors relevant to strategic decisions. Such frameworks are invaluable in allowing us to come to terms with the complexities of strategy decisions. In some instances, the most useful contribution may be in assisting us to make a start on the problem. By guiding us to the questions we need to answer and by providing a framework for organizing the information gathered, strategy analysis places us in a superior position to a manager who relies exclusively on experience and intuition. Finally, analytic frameworks and techniques can improve our flexibility as managers. The analysis in this book is general in its applicability; it is not specific to particular industries, companies, or situations. Hence, it can help increase our confidence and effectiveness in understanding and responding to new situations and new circumstances. By encouraging an in-depth understanding of fundamental issues concerning competitive advantage, customer needs, organizational capabilities, and the basis of competition, the concepts, frameworks, and techniques in this book will encourage rather than constrain innovation and flexibility.

Strategic Management of Not-For-Profit Organizations

When strategic management meant top-down, long-range planning, there was little distinction between business corporations and not-for-profit organizations: the techniques of forecast-based planning applied equally to both. As strategic management has become increasingly oriented toward the identification and exploitation of sources of profit, it has become more closely identified with for-profit organizations. So, can the concepts and tools of corporate and business strategy be applied to not-for-profit organizations?

The short answer is yes. Strategy is as important in not-for-profit organizations as it is in business firms. The benefits I have attributed to strategic management in terms of improved decision making, achieving coordination, and setting performance targets (see the section "Why Do Firms Need Strategy?" above) may be even more important in the non-profit sector. Moreover, many of the same concepts and tools of strategic analysis are readily applicable to not-for-profits—albeit with some adaptation. However, the not-for-profit sector encompasses a vast range of organizations. Both the nature of strategic planning and the appropriate tools for strategy analysis differ among these organizations.

The basic distinction here is between those not-for-profits that operate in competitive environments (most non-governmental, non-profit organizations) and those that do not (most government departments and government agencies). Among the not-for-profits that inhabit competitive environments we may distinguish between those that charge for the services they provide (most private schools, non-profit-making private hospitals, social and sports clubs, etc.) and those that provide their services free—most charities and NGOs (non-governmental organizations). Table 1.2 summarizes some key differences between each of these organizations with regard to the applicability of the basic tools of strategy analysis.

Among the tools of strategy analysis that are applicable to all types of not-for-profit organizations, those which relate to the role of strategy in specifying organizational goals and linking goals to resource-allocation decisions are especially important. For businesses, profit is always a key goal since it ensures survival and fuels development. But for not-for-profits, goals are typically complex. The mission of Harvard University is to "create knowledge, to open the minds of students to that knowledge, and to enable students to take best advantage of their educational opportunities." But how are these multiple objectives to be reconciled in practice? How should Harvard's budget be allocated between research and financial aid for students? Is Harvard's mission better served by investing in graduate or undergraduate education? The strategic planning process of not-for-profits needs to be designed so that mission, goals, resource allocation, and performance targets are closely aligned. Strategy Capsule 1.6 shows the strategic planning framework for the US State Department.

Similarly, most of the principles and tools of strategy implementation—especially in relation to organizational structure, management systems, techniques of performance management, and choice of leadership styles—are common to both for-profit and not-for-profit organizations.

In terms of the analysis of the external environment, there is little difference between the techniques of industry analysis applied to business enterprises and those relevant to not-for-profits that inhabit competitive environments and charge for their services. In many markets (theaters, sports clubs, vocational training) for-profits

TABLE 1.2 The applicability of the concepts and tools of strategic analysis to different types of not-for-profit organization

	Organizations in competitive environments that charge users	Organizations in competitive environments that provide free services	Organizations sheltered from competition
Examples	Royal Opera House Guggenheim Museum Stanford University	Salvation Army Habitat for Humanity Greenpeace Linux	UK Ministry of Defence European Central Bank New York Police Department World Health Organization
Analysis of goals and performance	Identification of mission, goals, and performance indicators and establishing consistency between them is a critical area of strategy analysis for all not-for-profits		
Analysis of the competitive environment	Main tools of competitive analysis are the same as for for-profit firms	Main arena for competition and competitive strategy is the market for funding	Not important. However, there is interagency competition for public funding
Analysis of resources and capabilities	Identifying and exploiting distinctive resources and capabilities critical to designing strategies that confer competitive advantage		Analysis of resources and capabilities essential for determining priorities and designing strategies
Strategy implementation	The basic principles of organizational design, performance management, and leadership are common to all organizational types		

STRATEGY CAPSULE 1.6

US State Department Strategic Plan, 2007–2012

MISSION

Advance freedom for the benefit of the American people and the international community by helping to build and sustain a more democratic, secure, and prosperous world composed of well-governed states that respond to the needs of their people, reduce widespread poverty, and act responsibly within the international system.

STRATEGIC GOALS

SG 1: Achieving Peace and Security

SG 2: Governing Justly and Democratically

SG 3: Investing In People

SG 4: Promoting Economic Growth and Prosperity

SG 5: Providing Humanitarian Assistance

SG 6: Promoting International Understanding

SG 7: Strengthening Consular and Management Capabilities

OPERATIONALIZING THE GOALS

These strategic goals were translated into a set of strategic priorities which were then operationalized through Mission Strategic Plans, Country Operational Plans, Bureau Strategic Plans, and a Department Performance Plan. Each of these plans was subject to an annual review.

Source: US Department of State and US Agency for International Development, *Strategic Plan for Fiscal Years 2007–2012*.

and not-for-profits may be in competition with one another. Indeed, for these types of not-for-profit organizations, the pressing need to break even in order to survive may mean that their strategies do not differ significantly from those of for-profit firms.

In the case of not-for-profits that do not charge users for the services they offer (mostly charities), competition does not really exist at the final market level: different homeless shelters in San Francisco cannot really be said to be competing for the homeless. However, these organizations compete for funding—raising donations from individuals, winning grants from foundations, or obtaining contracts from funding agencies. Competing in the market for funding is a key area of strategy for most not-for-profits.

The analysis of resources and capabilities is important to all organizations that inhabit competitive environments and must deploy their internal resources and capabilities to establish a competitive advantage; however, even for those organizations that are monopolists—many government departments and other public agencies—performance is enhanced by aligning strategy with internal strengths in resources and capabilities.

Summary

This chapter has covered a great deal of ground—I hope that you are not suffering from indigestion. If you are feeling a little overwhelmed, not to worry: we shall be returning to most of the themes and issues raised in this chapter in the subsequent chapters of this book.

The key lessons from this chapter are:

◆ Strategy is a key ingredient of success both for individuals and organizations. A sound strategy cannot guarantee success, but it can improve the odds. Successful strategies tend to embody four elements: clear, long-term goals; profound understanding of the external environment; astute appraisal of internal resources and capabilities; and effective implementation. These four elements form the primary analytic components of this book.

◆ Strategy is no longer concerned with detailed planning based upon forecasts; it is increasingly about direction, identity, and exploiting the sources of superior profitability.

◆ To describe the strategy of a firm (or any other type of organization) we need to recognize where the firm is competing, how it is competing, and the direction in which it is developing.

◆ Developing a strategy for an organization requires a combination of purpose-led planning (rational design) and a flexible response to changing circumstances (emergence).

◆ The principles and tools of strategic management have been developed primarily for business enterprises; however, they are also applicable to guiding the development and decision making of not-for-profit organizations, especially those that inhabit competitive environments.

Our next stage is to delve further into the basic strategy framework shown in Figure 1.2. As I have noted, the elements of this framework—goals and values, the industry environment, resources and capabilities, and structure and systems—comprise the basic components of strategy analysis. The next part of the book devotes separate chapters to each. We then deploy these tools in the analysis of competitive advantage (Part III), in the formulation and implementation of business strategies in different industry contexts (Part IV), and then in the development of corporate strategy (Part V). Figure 1.7 shows the framework for the book.

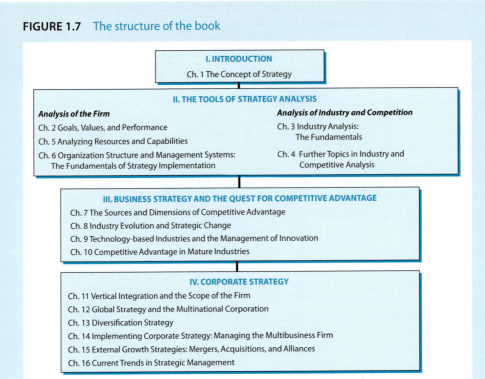

FIGURE 1.7   The structure of the book

I. INTRODUCTION

Ch. 1 The Concept of Strategy

II. THE TOOLS OF STRATEGY ANALYSIS

Analysis of the Firm

Ch. 2 Goals, Values, and Performance

Ch. 5 Analyzing Resources and Capabilities

Ch. 6 Organization Structure and Management Systems:
The Fundamentals of Strategy Implementation

Analysis of Industry and Competition

Ch. 3 Industry Analysis:
The Fundamentals

Ch. 4 Further Topics in Industry and
Competitive Analysis

III. BUSINESS STRATEGY AND THE QUEST FOR COMPETITIVE ADVANTAGE

Ch. 7 The Sources and Dimensions of Competitive Advantage

Ch. 8 Industry Evolution and Strategic Change

Ch. 9 Technology-based Industries and the Management of Innovation

Ch. 10 Competitive Advantage in Mature Industries

IV. CORPORATE STRATEGY

Ch. 11 Vertical Integration and the Scope of the Firm

Ch. 12 Global Strategy and the Multinational Corporation

Ch. 13 Diversification Strategy

Ch. 14 Implementing Corporate Strategy: Managing the Multibusiness Firm

Ch. 15 External Growth Strategies: Mergers, Acquisitions, and Alliances

Ch. 16 Current Trends in Strategic Management

Quizzes and flashcards to test yourself further are available in your interactive e-book at
www.wileyopenpage.com

Self-Study Questions

1. In relation to the four characteristics of successful strategies in Figure 1.1, assess the US government's strategy toward Iraq during 2002–12.

2. The discussion of the evolution of business strategy (see the section "From Corporate Planning to Strategic Management") established that the characteristics of a firm's strategic plans and its strategic planning process are strongly influenced by the volatility and unpredictability of its external environment. On this basis, what differences would you expect in the strategic plans and strategic planning processes of Coca-Cola Company and Facebook Inc.?

3. I have noted that a firm's strategy can be described in terms of the answers to two questions: "Where are we competing?" and "How are we competing?" Applying these two questions, provide a concise description of Lady Gaga's career strategy (see Strategy Capsule 1.2).

4. Using the framework of Figure 1.6, describe the strategy of the university or school you attend.

5. What is your career strategy for the next five years? To what extent does your strategy fit with your long-term goals, the characteristics of the external environment, and your own strengths and weaknesses?

Notes

1. P. F. Drucker, "Managing Oneself," *Harvard Business Review* (March/April 1999): 65–74.
2. Stephen Covey (in *The Seven Habits of Highly Effective People*, New York: Simon & Schuster, 1989) recommends that we develop lifetime mission statements based on the multiple roles that we occupy: in relation to our careers, our partners, our family members, our friends, and our spiritual lives.
3. M. E. Porter, "What is Strategy?" *Harvard Business Review* (November/December 1996): 61–78.
4. Major contributions to contingency theory include F. E. Fiedler's *Leader Attitudes and Group Effectiveness* (Urbana, IL: University of Illinois Press, 1958); and A. H. Van De Ven and R. Drazin's "The concept of fit in contingency theory" (*Research in Organizational Behavior* 7: 333–65, 1985).
5. Sun Tzu, *The Art of Strategy: A New Translation of Sun Tzu's Classic "The Art of War,"* trans. R. L. Wing (New York: Doubleday, 1988).
6. See R. Evered, "So What Is Strategy?" *Long Range Planning* 16, no. 3 (June 1983): 57–72; and E. Clemons and J. Santamaria, "Maneuver Warfare," *Harvard Business Review* (April 2002): 46–53.
7. On the contribution of game theory to business strategy analysis, see F. M. Fisher, "Games Economists Play: A Non-cooperative View," *RAND Journal of Economics* 20 (Spring 1989): 113–24; C. F. Camerer, "Does Strategy Research Need Game Theory?" *Strategic Management Journal* 12 (Winter 1991): 137–52; A. K. Dixit and B. J. Nalebuff, *The Art of Strategy: A Game Theorist's Guide to Success in Business and Life* (New York: W. W. Norton, 2008).
8. For example, D. W. Ewing, "Looking Around: Long-range Business Planning," *Harvard Business Review* (July/August 1956): 135–46; and B. Payne, "Steps in Long-range Planning," *Harvard Business Review* (March/April 1957): 95–101.
9. H. I. Ansoff, "Strategies for diversification," *Harvard Business Review* (September/October, 1957): 113–124.
10. M. E. Porter, *Competitive Strategy* (New York: Free Press, 1980).
11. See Boston Consulting Group, *Perspectives on Experience* (Boston: Boston Consulting Group, 1978) and studies using the PIMS (Profit Impact of Market Strategy) database, for example R. D. Buzzell and B. T. Gale, *The PIMS Principles* (New York: Free Press, 1987).
12. R. M. Grant, "The Resource-based Theory of Competitive Advantage: Implications for Strategy Formulation," *California Management Review* 33 (Spring 1991): 114–135; D. J. Collis and C. Montgomery, "Competing on Resources: Strategy in the 1990s," *Harvard Business Review* (July/August 1995): 119–128.
13. E. Lee, J. Lee, and J. Lee, "Reconsideration of the Winner-Take-All Hypothesis: Complex Networks and Local Bias," *Management Science* 52 (December 2006): 1838–48; C. Shapiro and H. R. Varian, *Information Rules* (Boston: Harvard Business School Press, 1998).
14. C. Christensen, *The Innovator's Dilemma* (Boston: Harvard Business School Press, 1997).
15. P. J. Williamson, "Strategy as options on the future," *Sloan Management Review* 40(3, 1999): 117–126.
16. C. Markides, "Strategic innovation in established companies," *Sloan Management Review* (June 1998): 31–42.
17. W. C. Kim and R. Mauborgne, "Creating new market space," *Harvard Business Review* (January/February 1999): 83–93.
18. Robert Peston, *The New Capitalism* (London: Hodder & Stoughton, 2010).
19. "Strategic Intensity: A Conversation with Garry Kasparov," *Harvard Business Review* (April 2005): 105–13.
20. The concept of bounded rationality was developed by Herbert Simon ("A Behavioral Model of Rational Choice," *Quarterly Journal of Economics* 69 (1955): 99–118.
21. G. Hamel and C. K. Prahalad, "Strategic Intent," *Harvard Business Review* (May/June 1989): 63–77.
22. G. Hamel and C. K. Prahalad, "Strategy as Stretch and Leverage," *Harvard Business Review* (March/April 1993): 75–84.
23. J. C. Collins and J. I. Porras, *Built to Last: Successful Habits of Visionary Companies* (New York: HarperCollins, 1995).
24. D. J. Collis and M. G. Rukstad, "Can You Say What Your Strategy Is?" *Harvard Business Review* (April 2008): 63–73.
25. http://www.thecoca-colacompany.com/ourcompany/mission_vision_values.html, accessed August 2, 2012).
26. D. F. Abell, *Managing with Dual Strategies* (New York: Free Press, 1993).
27. H. Mintzberg, "Patterns of Strategy Formulation," *Management Science* 24 (1978): 934–48; "Of Strategies: Deliberate and Emergent," *Strategic Management Journal* 6 (1985): 257–72.
28. H. Mintzberg, "The Fall and Rise of Strategic Planning," *Harvard Business Review* (January/February 1994): 107–14.
29. The two views of Honda are captured in two Harvard cases: Honda [A] and [B] (Boston: Harvard Business School, Cases 384049 and 384050, 1989).
30. Boston Consulting Group, *Strategy Alternatives for the British Motorcycle Industry* (London: Her Majesty's Stationery Office, 1975).
31. R. T. Pascale, "Perspective on Strategy: The Real Story Behind Honda's Success," *California Management Review* 26, no. 3 (Spring 1984): 47–72.
32. H. Mintzberg, "Crafting Strategy," *Harvard Business Review* (July/August 1987): 70.

33. R. A. Burgelman and A. Grove, "Strategic Dissonance," *California Management Review* 38 (Winter 1996): 8–28.

34. R. M. Grant, "Strategic Planning in a Turbulent Environment: Evidence from the Oil and Gas Majors," *Strategic Management Journal* 14 (June 2003): 491–517.

35. O. Gadiesh and J. Gilbert, "Transforming Corner-office Strategy into Frontline Action," *Harvard Business Review* (May 2001): 73–80.

36. K. M. Eisenhardt and D. N. Sull, "Strategy as Simple Rules," *Harvard Business Review* (January 2001): 107–16.

II

THE TOOLS OF STRATEGY ANALYSIS

2 Goals, Values, and Performance

> The strategic aim of a business is to earn a return on capital, and if in any particular case the return in the long run is not satisfactory, then the deficiency should be corrected or the activity abandoned for a more favorable one.
>
> —ALFRED P. SLOAN JR., PRESIDENT AND THEN CHAIRMAN OF
> GENERAL MOTORS, 1923 TO 1956.[1]

> Profits are to business as breathing is to life. Breathing is essential to life, but is not the purpose for living. Similarly, profits are essential for the existence of the corporation, but they are not the reason for its existence.
>
> —DENNIS BAKKE, FOUNDER AND FORMER CEO, AES CORPORATION

OUTLINE

Introduction and Objectives

Our framework for strategy analysis (Figure 1.2) comprises four components: the firm's goals and values, its resources and capabilities, its structure and management systems, and its industry environment. The chapters that form Part II of this book develop these four components of strategy analysis. We begin with goals and values of the firm and, by extension, the performance of the firm in attaining its goals.

As the opening quotations to this chapter indicate, there is fierce debate over the appropriate goals for business enterprises. In this chapter we will consider the extent to which the firm should pursue the interests of its owners, of its stakeholders, and of society as a whole. Our approach will be pragmatic. While acknowledging that firms possess multiple goals and, as reflected in their statements of mission and vision, that each firm has a unique purpose, we focus upon a single goal: the quest for value. This I interpret as the pursuit of profit over the lifetime of the firm. Hence, the focus of our strategy analysis is upon concepts and techniques that are concerned with identifying and exploiting the sources of profitability available to the firm. Our emphasis on profitability and value creation also means that we will draw upon some of the tools of financial analysis for the purposes of performance appraisal, performance diagnosis, and target setting.

Although profitability is the most useful indicator of firm performance, we shall acknowledge that firms are motivated by goals other than profit. Indeed, the companies that are most successful in generating profits over the long run are typically those motivated by other goals. Profit is the lifeblood of the organization, but it is not a goal that inspires organizational members to outstanding achievement. Moreover, for a firm to survive and generate profit over the long run requires responsiveness to the requirements of its social, political, and natural environments.

By the time you have completed this chapter, you will be able to:

- recognize that, while every firm has a distinct purpose, the common goal for all firms is creating value, and appreciate how the definition of value informs the debate over shareholder versus stakeholder goals for the firm;

- understand the relationship between profit, cash flow, and enterprise value;

- use the tools of financial analysis to appraise firm performance, diagnose the sources of performance problems, and set performance targets;

- appreciate how a firm's values, principles, and pursuit of corporate social responsibility can help define its strategy and support its creation of value;

- understand how real options contribute to firm value and the role of options thinking in strategy analysis.

Strategy as a Quest for Value

There is more to business than making money. For the entrepreneurs who create business enterprises, personal wealth appears to be a less important motivation than the wish for autonomy, the desire for achievement, and lust for excitement. Almost 80 years ago, the economist Joseph Schumpeter observed: "The entrepreneur–innovator's motivation includes such aspects as the dream to found a private kingdom, the will to conquer and to succeed for the sake of success itself, and the joy of creating and getting things done."[2] Business enterprises are creative organizations which offer individuals unsurpassed opportunity to make a difference in the world. Certainly, making money was not the goal that inspired Henry Ford to build a business that precipitated a social revolution:

> I will build a motor car for the great multitude ... It will be so low in price that no man making good wages will be unable to own one and to enjoy with his family the blessing of hours of pleasure in God's great open spaces ... When I'm through, everyone will be able to afford one, and everyone will have one.[3]

Each entrepreneur is inspired by a goal that is personal and unique—family cars for the multitude (Henry Ford), bringing the power of personal computing to the individual (Steve Jobs), reducing deaths from infection after surgery (Johnson & Johnson), or revolutionizing vacuum cleaning (James Dyson). In the case of established companies, Cynthia Montgomery argues that "forging a compelling organizational purpose" is the ongoing job of company leaders and the "crowning responsibility of the CEO."[4] Organizational purpose is articulated in companies' statements of mission and vision:

- Google's mission is "to organize the world's information and make it universally accessible and useful."
- "The IKEA vision is to create a better everyday life for the many people. We make this possible by offering a wide range of well-designed, functional home furnishing products at prices so low that as many people as possible will be able to afford them."
- "SAP strives to define and establish undisputed leadership in the emerging market for business process platform offerings and accelerate business innovation powered by IT for companies and industries worldwide."

Within this vast variety of organizational purposes, there is a common denominator: the desire, and the need, to create value. Value is the monetary worth of a product or asset. Hence, we can generalize by saying that the purpose of business is, first, to create value for customers and, second, to appropriate some of that customer value in the form of profit—thereby creating value for the firm.

Value can be created in two ways: by production and by commerce. Production creates value by physically transforming products that are less valued by consumers into products that are more valued by consumers—turning clay into coffee mugs, for example. Commerce creates value not by physically transforming products but by repositioning them in space and time. Trade involves transferring products from individuals and locations where they are less valued to individuals and locations where they are more valued. Similarly, speculation involves transferring products from a point in time where a product is valued less to a point in time where it is valued more. Thus, the essence of commerce is creating value through arbitrage across time and space.[5]

The difference between the value of a firm's output and the cost of its material inputs is its **value added**. Value added is equal to the sum of all the income paid to the suppliers of factors of production. Thus:

$$\text{Value Added} = \text{Sales revenue from output} - \text{Cost of material inputs}$$
$$= \text{Wages/Salaries} + \text{Interest} + \text{Rent} + \text{Royalties/License fees}$$
$$+ \text{Taxes} + \text{Dividends} + \text{Retained profit}$$

Value for Whom? Shareholders versus Stakeholders

The value added created by firms is distributed among different parties: employees (wages and salaries), lenders (interest), landlords (rent), government (taxes), and owners (profit). In addition, firms also create value for their customers to the extent that the satisfaction customers gain exceeds the price they pay (they derive **consumer surplus**). It is tempting, therefore, to think of the firm as operating for the benefit of multiple constituencies. This view of the business enterprise as a coalition of interest groups where top management's role to balance these different—often conflicting—interests is referred to as the **stakeholder approach to the firm**.[6]

The idea that the corporation should balance the interests of multiple stakeholders has a long tradition, especially in Asia and continental Europe. By contrast, most English-speaking countries have endorsed shareholder capitalism, where companies' overriding duty is to produce profits for owners. These differences are reflected in international differences in companies' legal obligations. In the US, Canada, the UK, and Australia, company boards are required to act in the interests of shareholders. In most continental European countries, companies are legally required to take account of the interests of employees, the state, and the enterprise as a whole.

There is an ongoing debate as to whether companies should operate exclusively in the interests of their owners or should also pursue the goals of multiple stakeholders. During the 1990s, "Anglo-Saxon" shareholder capitalism was in the ascendant—many continental European and Asian companies changed their strategies and corporate governance to reflect shareholder interests. However, during the 21st century, shareholder value maximization has become tainted by its association with short-termism, financial manipulation, excessive CEO compensation, and the failures of risk management that precipitated the 2008–2009 financial crisis.

Clearly, companies have legal and ethical responsibilities to employees, customers, society, and the natural environment. However, companies that adopt a stakeholder approach and seek to pursue the combined interests of multiple stakeholders face major problems in formulating and implementing their strategies. Taking account of multiple goals and specifying tradeoffs between them vastly increases the complexity of decision making.[7] Michael Jensen argues that, for all practical purposes, "multiple objectives is no objective."[8] The complexities of balancing the interests of different stakeholder groups can result in top management decision making becoming bogged down in political wrangling, indecisiveness, and lack of accountability.[9]

To simplify our analysis of strategy formulation I make the assumption that the primary goal of strategy is to maximize the value of the enterprise through seeking to maximize profits over the long term. Having extolled the virtues of business enterprises as creative institutions, how can I justify this unedifying focus on money making? I have three justifications:

- *Competition*: Competition erodes profitability. As competition increases, the interests of different stakeholders converge around the goal of survival. Survival requires that, over the long term, a firm earn a rate of profit that covers its cost of capital; otherwise, it will not be able to replace its assets. When weak demand and fierce international competition depress return on capital, few companies have the luxury of sacrificing profits for other goals.

- *The market for corporate control*: Management teams that fail to maximize the profits of their companies tend to be replaced by teams that do. In the "market for corporate control," companies that underperform financially suffer a declining share price, which attracts acquirers—both other public companies and private equity funds. Despite the admirable record of British chocolate maker Cadbury in relation to employees and local communities, its dismal return to shareholders between 2004 and 2009 meant that it was unable to resist acquisition by Kraft Foods. In addition, activist investors—both individuals and institutions—pressure boards of directors to dismiss CEOs who fail to create value for shareholders.[10]

- *Convergence of stakeholder interests*: There is likely to be more community of interests than conflict of interests among different stakeholders. Profitability over the long term requires loyalty from employees, trusting relationships with suppliers and customers, and support from governments and communities. Indeed, the instrumental theory of stakeholder management argues that pursuit of stakeholder interests is essential to creating competitive advantage, which in turn leads to superior financial performance.[11] As Michael Jensen observes: "In order to maximize value, corporate managers must not only satisfy, but enlist the support of, all corporate stakeholders—customers, employees, managers, suppliers, local communities." Empirical evidence shows that firms which take account of a broader set of interests, including that of society, achieve superior financial performance.[12]

Hence, the issue of whether firms should operate in the interests of shareholders or of all stakeholders matters more in principle than in practice. According to Jensen: "enlightened shareholder value maximization … is identical to enlightened stakeholder theory." We shall return to this issue later in this chapter when we consider explicitly the social and environmental responsibilities of firms.

What Is Profit?

Thus far, I have referred to firms' quest for profit in general terms. It is time to look more carefully at what we mean by **profit** and how it relates to value creation.

Profit is the surplus of revenues over costs available for distribution to the owners of the firm. But if profit maximization is to be a realistic goal, the firm must know what profit is and how to measure it; otherwise, instructing managers to maximize profit offers little guidance. What is the firm to maximize: total profit or rate of profit? Over what period? With what kind of adjustment for risk? And what is profit anyway—accounting profit, cash flow, or economic profit? These ambiguities become apparent once we compare the profit performance of companies. Table 2.1 shows that ranking companies by profitability depends critically on what profitability measure is used.

Accounting Profit and Economic Profit

A major problem of *accounting profit* is that it combines two types of returns: the normal return to capital, which rewards investors for the use of their capital, and **economic profit**, which is the surplus available after all inputs (including capital) have been paid for. Economic profit is a purer measure of profit which is a more precise measure of a firm's ability to generate surplus value. To distinguish economic profit from accounting profit, economic profit is often referred to as *rent* or *economic rent*.

A widely used measure of economic profit is **economic value added (EVA)**, devised and popularized by the consulting firm Stern Stewart & Company.[13] Economic value added is measured as follows:

$$\text{EVA} = \text{Net operating profit after tax (NOPAT)} - \text{Cost of capital}$$

where,

$$\text{Cost of capital} = \text{Capital employed} \times \text{Weighted average cost of capital (WACC)}.$$

Economic profit has two main advantages over accounting profit as a performance measure. First, it sets a more demanding performance discipline for managers. At many capital-intensive companies seemingly healthy profits disappear once cost of capital is taken into account. Second, it improves the allocation of capital between the different businesses of the firm by taking account of the real costs of more capital-intensive businesses (Strategy Capsule 2.1).

TABLE 2.1 The performance of some of the world's leading companies in terms of different profitability measures, 2010

Company	Market capitaliza- tion[a] ($ billion)	Net income[a] ($ billion)	ROS[b] (%)	ROE[c] (%)	ROA[d] (%)	Return to share- holders[e] (%)
ExxonMobil	354	30.5	15.2	20.7	17.5	10.1
Apple	338	14.0	31.2	29.3	29.0	53.1
PetroChina	226	22.9	10.6	15.3	11.7	−8.4
General Electric	155	11.6	12.7	9.8	18.9	23.9
JPMorgan Chase	108	17.4	28.5	9.9	11.8	2.3
Wal-Mart Stores	196	30.5	5.9	23.5	14.1	3.2
Volkswagen	64	9.1	7.5	32.9	3.6	123.2

Notes:
[a]Shares outstanding × closing price of shares on October 28, 2011.
[b]Return on sales = Pretax profit as a percentage of sales revenues.
[c]Return on equity = Net income as a percentage of year-end shareholder equity.
[d]Return on assets = Operating income as a percentage of year-end total assets.
[e]Dividend + share price appreciation during 2010.

STRATEGY CAPSULE 2.1

Economic Value Added at Diageo plc.

At Guinness-to-Johnny-Walker drinks giant Diageo, EVA transformed the way in which Diageo measured its performance, allocated its capital and advertising expenditures, and evaluated its managers.

Taking account of the costs of the capital tied up in slow-maturing, vintage drinks such as Talisker and Lagavulin malt whisky, Hennessey cognac, and Dom Perignon champagne showed that these high-margin drinks were often not as profitable as the company had believed. The result was that Diageo's advertising expenditures were reallocated toward Smirnoff vodka, Gordon's gin, Baileys, and other drinks that could be sold within weeks of distillation.

Once managers had to report profits after deduction of the cost of the capital tied up in their businesses, they took measures to reduce their capital bases and make their assets work harder. At Diageo's Pillsbury food business, the economic profit of every product and every major customer was scrutinized. The result was the elimination of many products and efforts to make marginal customers more profitable. Ultimately, EVA analysis resulted in Diageo selling Pillsbury to General Foods. This was followed by the sale of Diageo's Burger King chain to Texas Pacific, a private equity group.

Value-based management was extended throughout the organization by making EVA the primary determinant of the incentive pay earned by 1400 Diageo managers.

Sources: John McGrath, "Tracking Down Value," *Financial Times Mastering Management Review* (December 1998); www.diageo.com.

Linking Profit to Enterprise Value

There is also the problem of time. Once we consider multiple periods of time, then profit maximization means maximizing the net present value of the stream of profits over the lifetime of the firm.

Hence, profit maximization translates into maximizing the value of the firm. The value of the firm is calculated in the same way as any other asset: it is the *net present value* (NPV) of the returns that the asset generates. The relevant returns are the cash flows to the firm. Hence, firms are valued using the same *discounted cash flow* (DCF) methodology that we apply to the valuation of investment projects. Thus, the value of an enterprise (V) is the sum of its free cash flows (C) in each year t, discounted at the enterprise's cost of capital (r).[14] The relevant cost of capital is the weighted average cost of capital (r_{e+d}) that averages the cost of equity (r_e) and the cost of debt (r_d):

$$V = \sum_t \frac{C_t}{(1+r_{e+d})^t}$$

where C is measured as:

Net operating profit + Depreciation − Taxes − Investment in fixed and working capital

Thus, to maximize its value, a firm must maximize its future net cash flows while managing its risk to minimize its cost of capital.

This value-maximizing approach identifies cash flow rather than profit as the relevant performance measure for the value-maximizing firm. In practice, valuing companies by discounting economic profit gives the same result as by discounting net cash flows. The difference is in the treatment of the capital consumed by the business. The cash flow approach deducts capital at the time when the capital expenditure is made; the EVA approach follows the accounting convention of charging capital as it is consumed (through charging depreciation). In principle, a full DCF approach is the most satisfactory approach to valuing companies. In practice, for DCF analysis to be meaningful requires forecasting cash flows several years ahead, since cash flow for a single year is a poor indicator of underlying profitability (for instance profitable, fast-growing companies often have negative free cash flows). If financial forecasts can only be made for a few years out, then profit (net of depreciation) may offer a better basis for valuation than cash flow does.

The practical difficulties associated with DCF analysis have resulted in a search for alternative approaches to maximizing firm value that avoid the problems of forecasting cash flows or profits far into the future. McKinsey & Company argues that enterprise value depends upon three key variables: return on invested capital (ROIC), weighted average cost of capital (WACC), and growth of operating profit. Hence, creating enterprise value requires increasing ROIC, reducing WACC, and increasing the rate of growth of profits.[15]

What's Wrong with Shareholder Value Maximization?

How does maximizing the value of the firm (enterprise value) relate to the much-lauded goal of maximizing shareholder value? In 1958, Modigliani and Miller laid the foundations of modern financial theory by showing that the value of a company (the NPV of its stream profit) equals the market value of its securities: equity and debt.[16] Shareholder value is equal to enterprise value minus the value of the firm's debt. For most companies, maximizing enterprise value and maximizing shareholder value are roughly equivalent (i.e., they imply similar management decisions).

Shareholder value maximization may be interpreted in two ways:

- in terms of intrinsic value, shareholder value is the NPV of the stream of profits that accrue to owners (i.e., after the deduction of interest payments) discounted at the cost of equity;
- in terms of market value, shareholder value is the current stock market value of the firm's shares.[17]

So long as the stock market is reasonably efficient in valuing firm's future returns, current stock market valuation is a good indicator of intrinsic value. Hence, maximizing net profits over the life of the firm should also mean maximizing the stock market value of the firm. However, the experience of the past two decades suggests when top management focuses upon stock market value rather than profit over the life of the firm undesirable consequences follow. If stock markets are myopic, management may be encouraged to maximize short-term profits to the detriment of long-run profitability. This in turn may tempt top management to boost short-term earnings through financial manipulation rather than by growing the firm's operating profits. Such manipulation may include adjustments to financial structure, earnings smoothing, and the use of asset sales to flatter short-term reported profits. Hence, for shareholder value maximization to be aligned with the interests of long-term interests of shareholders and other stakeholders, it is vital that managers focus their attention not on their company's share price but on driving the profits that ultimately those share prices depend upon.

Our emphasis in this book will be on maximizing enterprise value rather than maximizing shareholder value. This is partly for convenience: distinguishing debt from equity is not always straightforward, due to the presence of preference stock and convertible debt, while junk bonds share the characteristics of both equity and debt. More importantly, focusing on the value of the enterprise as a whole supports our emphasis of the fundamental drivers of firm value in preference to the distractions and distortions that result from a preoccupation with stock market valuation.

Putting Performance Analysis into Practice

Our discussion so far has established that, while every business enterprise has a distinct purpose, profit earnings over the life of the business—enterprise value—is the best common indicator of the success of the business as a value-creating entity and offers the best guide to the selection of strategies for achieving business purpose.

So, how do we apply these principles to appraise and develop business strategies? There are four key areas where our analysis of profit performance can guide strategy: first, in appraising a firm's (or business unit's) performance; second, in diagnosing the sources of poor performance; third, in selecting strategies on the basis of their profit prospects; and, finally, setting performance targets.

Appraising Current and Past Performance

The first task of any strategy formulation exercise is to assess the current situation. This means identifying the current strategy of the firm and assessing how well that strategy is doing in terms of the financial performance of the firm. The next stage is diagnosis—identifying the sources of unsatisfactory performance. Thus, good strategic practice emulates good medical practice: first, assess the patient's state of health, and then determine the causes of any sickness.

Forward-Looking Performance Measures: Stock Market Value   If our goal is to maximize profit over the lifetime of the firm, then to evaluate the performance of a firm we need to look at its stream of profit (or cash flows) over the rest of its life. The problem, of course, is that we can only make reasonable estimates of these a few years ahead. For public companies stock market valuation represents the best available estimate of the NPV of future cash flows. Thus, to evaluate the performance of a firm in value creation we can compare the change in the market value of the firm relative to that of competitors over a period (preferably several years). Clearly, stock market valuation is an imperfect performance indicator—particularly in terms of its sensitivity to new information and its vulnerability to market psychology and disequilibrium—but it is the best indictor we have of intrinsic value.

Backward-Looking Performance Measures: Accounting Ratios   Because of the volatility of stock market values, evaluations of firm performance for the purposes of assessing the current strategy or evaluating management effectiveness tend to use accounting measures of performance. These are inevitably historical: financial reports appear at least three weeks after the period to which they relate. That said, many firms offer *earnings guidance*—forecasts of profit for the next 12 months (sometimes longer).

The McKinsey valuation framework identifies three drivers of enterprise value: rate of return on capital, cost of capital, and profit growth (see page 40). Among these, return on capital is the key indicator of the invested firm's effectiveness in generating profits from its assets. Hence, ROIC and its equivalent, return on capital employed (ROCE), or its closely related rate of return indicators, such as return on equity (ROE) and return on assets (ROA), are valuable performance indicators. Different profitability measures are related—the longer the period under consideration, the more they tend to converge.[18] Over shorter periods, the key issues are, first, to be aware of the limitations and biases inherent in any particular profitability measure and, second, to use multiple measures of profitability so that their consistency can be judged. The greatest of these limitations concerns the use of historical measures of performance to indicate the success of the firm in creating future profits. Table 2.2 outlines some widely used performance indicators.

TABLE 2.2   Profitability ratios

Ratio	Formula	Comments
Return on Invested Capital (ROIC)	$\dfrac{\text{Operating profit before interest after tax}}{\text{Fixed assets} + \text{Net current assets}}$	ROIC measures the return on the capital invested in the business. ROIC is also known as return on capital employed (ROCE). The numerator is operating profit or earnings (EBIT), and can be pre-tax or post-tax. The denominator can also be measured as equity plus debt.
Return on Equity (ROE)	$\dfrac{\text{Net income}}{\text{Shareholders' equity}}$	ROE measures the firm's success in using shareholders' capital to generate profits that are available for remunerating investors. Net income is often measured net of income from discontinued operations and before any special items.
Return on Assets (ROA)	$\dfrac{\text{Operating profit}}{\text{Total assets}}$	The numerator should correspond to the return on all the company's assets—e.g., operating profit, EBITDA (earnings before interest, tax, depreciation, and amortization), or EBIT (earnings before interest and tax).
Gross margin	$\dfrac{\text{Sales} - \text{Cost of bought-in goods and services}}{\text{Sales}}$	Gross margin measures the extent to which a firm adds value to the goods and services it buys in.
Operating margin	$\dfrac{\text{Operating profit}}{\text{Sales}}$	Operating margin and net margin measure a firm's ability to extract profit from its sales, but for appraising firm performance, these ratios reveal little because margins vary greatly between sectors according to capital intensity (see Table 2.1).
Net margin	$\dfrac{\text{Net income}}{\text{Sales}}$	

Notes:

Few accounting ratios have standard definitions, hence, it is advisable to be explicit about how you have calculated the ratio you are using. A general guideline for rate of return ratios is that the numerator should be the profits that are available to remunerate the owners of the assets in the denominator.

Profits are measured over a period of time (typically over a year). Assets are valued at a point of time. Hence, in rate of return calculations, assets, equity, and capital employed should to be averaged between the beginning and end of the period.

Interpreting probability ratios requires benchmarks. Comparisons over time tell us whether a profitability ratio is improving or deteriorating. Interfirm comparisons tell us how a firm is performing relative to a competitor, relative to its industry average, or relative to firms in general (e.g., relative to the Fortune 500, S&P 500, or FT 500). Another key benchmark is cost of capital. ROIC and ROCE should be compared with WACC, and ROE compared with the cost of equity capital.

Performance Diagnosis

If profit performance is unsatisfactory, we need to identify the sources of poor performance so that management can take corrective action. The main tool of diagnosis is disaggregation of return on capital in order to identify the fundamental *value drivers*. A starting point is to apply the Du Pont Formula to disaggregate return on invested capital into sales margin and capital turnover. We can then further disaggregate both sales margin and capital productivity into their component items (Figure 2.1). This points us toward the specific activities that are the sources of poor performance.

Strategy Capsule 2.2 compares the performance of UPS with that of FedEx. By disaggregating the overall return on assets, we can begin to pinpoint the sources of

FIGURE 2.1   Disaggregating return on capital employed

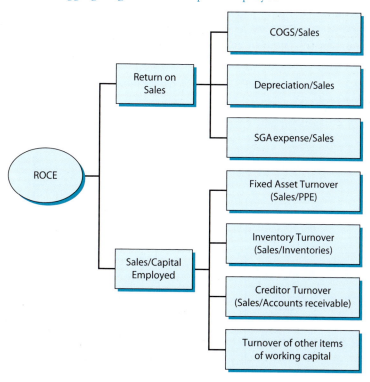

Notes:
ROCE: Return on capital employed.
COGS: Cost of goods sold.
PPE: Property, plant, and equipment.

For further discussion, see T. Koller *et al.*, *Valuation*, 5th edn (Chichester: John Wiley & Sons, Ltd, 2010).

STRATEGY CAPSULE 2.2
Diagnosing Performance: UPS vs. FedEx

Between 2006 and 2011, United Parcel Service (UPS), the world's leading package delivery company, has earned about double the return on invested capital as its closest rival, FedEx Corporation. What insights can financial analysis offer into the sources of this performance differential?

Disaggregating the companies' return on capital employed into sales margin and capital turnover shows that differences in ROCE can be attributed almost entirely to differences in return on sales—asset productivity (as indicated by capital turnover) is almost identical for the two companies. Disaggregation of capital turnover points to no significant differences between the two companies in the productivity with which individual assets are managed. See Figure 2.2.

However, disaggregation of ROS highlights major differences in the cost structure of the two companies:

UPS is more labor intensive with a much higher ratio of employee costs to sales. FedEx has much higher costs in terms of fuel, maintenance, depreciation, and "other."

These cost differences reflect differences in the composition of the two companies' business. UPS is more heavily involved in ground transportation (UPS has 100,000 vehicles; FedEx has 50,000), which tends to be more labor intensive. FedEx is more oriented toward air transportation (UPS has 527 aircraft; FedEx has 688). For FedEx, its express delivery segment was much less profitable than its ground delivery segment. However, the differences in business mix do not appear to completely explain the wide discrepancy in fuel, maintenance, and other costs between FedEx and UPS. The suspicion is that UPS has superior operational efficiency.

FIGURE 2.2 Analyzing why UPS (U) earns a higher return on capital employed (ROCE) than FedEx (F)

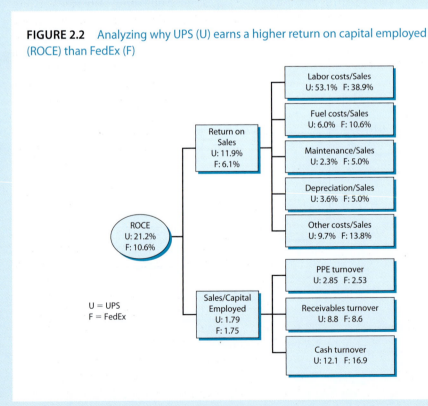

UPS's superior profitability. If we then combine the financial data with qualitative data on UPS's business strategy, its operations, its product strategy, the organizational issues it has faced, and the conditions in the world logistics and express delivery market, we can begin to diagnose why it has outperformed FedEx.

Can Past Performance Guide Strategies for the Future?

A probing diagnosis of a firm's recent performance—as outlined above—provides a useful input into strategy formulation. If we can establish why a company has been performing badly then we have a basis for corrective actions. These corrective actions are likely to be both strategic (i.e., focused on the medium to long term) and operational (focused on the short term). The worse a company's performance, the greater the need to concentrate on the short term. For companies teetering on the brink of bankruptcy—several of the world's airlines and some automotive companies—long-term strategy takes a back seat; survival is the dominant concern.

For companies that are performing well, financial analysis allows us to understand the sources of superior performance so that strategy can protect and enhance these determinants of success. For example, in the case of UPS (see Strategy Capsule 2.2), financial analysis points to the efficiency benefits that arise from being the US's biggest package delivery company and having an integrated system of collection and delivery that optimizes operational efficiency. The superior profitability of UPS's international business points to its ability to successfully enter foreign markets and integrate overseas operations within its global system.

However, analyzing the past only takes us so far. The world of business is one of constant change and the role of strategy is to help the firm to adapt to change. The challenge is to look into the future and identify factors that threaten performance or create new opportunities for profit. In making strategy recommendations to UPS, our financial analysis can tell us some of the reasons why UPS has been doing well up until now, but the key to sustaining UPS's performance is to recognize how its industry environment will be changing in terms of customer requirements, competition, technology, and energy costs and to assess UPS's capacity to adapt to these new conditions. While financial analysis is inevitably backward looking, strategic analysis allows us to look forward and understand some of the critical factors impacting a firm's success in the future.

Setting Performance Targets

We noted in Chapter 1 that an important role for strategic planning systems is to drive corporate performance through setting performance goals then monitoring results against targets. To be effective, performance targets need to be consistent with long-term goals, linked to strategy, and relevant to the tasks and responsibilities of individual organizational members. Company goals need to be actionable. A key problem of the stakeholder view is the difficulty of interpreting the goal of pursuing the interests of all stakeholders. Even the more precise goal of maximizing enterprise value may have little meaning outside the executive suite. Broad corporate goals need to be translated into specific objectives that are meaningful to managers further down the organization. The key is to establish performance targets that match the variables over which different managers exert influence. Thus, for the CEO, it may make sense to set the overall goal of maximizing enterprise value. For the chief operating officer and divisional heads, it makes sense to set more specific financial goals (such as maximizing ROCE on existing assets and investing in projects whose rate of return exceeds the cost of capital). More specific operating targets are preferable for functional, departmental, and unit managers. Thus, in a retailing company, store managers might be given targets with regard to sales per square foot and gross margins. Warehouse managers might be required to achieve target levels of inventory turns. Purchasing managers might be required to reduce the cost of goods purchased as a percentage of sales revenue. The chief financial officer might be required to minimize the average cost of capital and reduce cash balances.

The same procedure that we used to disaggregate return on capital for appraising past performance can be used to set performance targets appropriate to different levels and functions within the organization. Figure 2.3 uses the same breakout of the drivers of return on capital as Figure 2.1. The difference is that Figure 2.3 provides a basis for identifying the financial and operating ratios appropriate to managers at the different levels and in the different functions of the company.

Balanced Scorecards   The problem with any system of performance management is that the performance goals are long term (e.g., maximizing profits over the lifetime of the company), but to act as an effective control system performance targets need to be monitored over the short term. The problem with the above financially based approach of disaggregating profitability into its constituent ratios is that the short-term pursuit of financial targets is unlikely to result in long-term profit maximization. One

FIGURE 2.3   Linking value drivers to performance

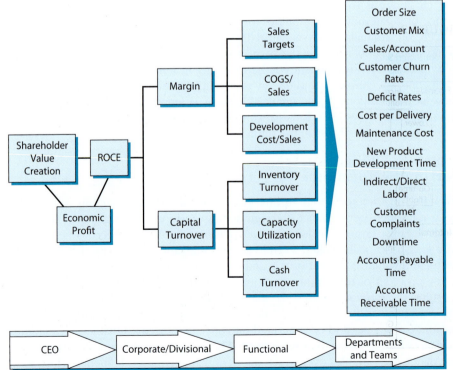

solution to this dilemma is to link the overall corporate goal of value maximization to strategic and operational targets to ensure that the pursuit of financial goals is not at the expense of the longer-term strategic position of the company. The most widely used method for doing this is the **balanced scorecard** developed by Robert Kaplan and David Norton.[19] The balanced scorecard methodology provides an integrated framework for balancing financial and strategic goals and cascading performance measures down the organization to individual business units and departments. The performance measures included in the balanced scorecard derive from answers to four questions:

- How do we look to shareholders? The financial perspective is composed of measures such as cash flow, sales and income growth, and return on equity.
- How do customers see us? The customer perspective comprises measures such as goals for new products, on-time delivery, and defect and failure levels.
- What must we excel at? The internal business perspective relates to internal business processes such as productivity, employee skills, cycle time, yield rates, and quality and cost measures.
- Can we continue to improve and create value? The innovation and learning perspective includes measures related to new product development cycle times, technological leadership, and rates of improvement.

By balancing a set of strategic and financial goals, the scorecard methodology allows the strategy of the business to be linked with the creation of shareholder value while providing a set of measurable targets to guide this process. Figure 2.4 shows the balanced scorecard for a US regional airline.

FIGURE 2.4   Balanced scorecard for a regional airline

Simplified Strategy Map	Performance Measures	Targets	Initiatives
Financial — Increase Profitability / Lower Cost / Increase Revenue	• Market Value • Seat Revenue • Plane Lease Cost	• 25% per year • 20% per year • 5% per year	• Optimize routes • Standardize planes
Customer — On-time Flights / More Customers / Low Prices	• FAA on-time arrival rating • Customer ranking • No. customers	• First in industry • 98% satisfaction • % change	• Quality management • Customer loyalty program
Internal — Improve turnaround time	• On Ground Time • On-Time Departure	• <25 Minutes • 93%	• Cycle time optimization program
Learning — Align Ground Crews	• % Ground crew stockholders • % Ground crew trained	• Year 1, 70% • Year 4, 90% • Year 6, 100%	• Stock ownership plan • Ground crew training

Source: Reproduced from www.balancedscorecard.org with permission.

Rethinking Performance Targets   Financial value drivers and balanced score-cards are systematic techniques of performance management based upon the assumption that, if overall goals can be disaggregated into precise, quantitative, time-specific targets, each member of the organization knows what is expected of him or her and is motivated toward achieving the targets set. However, a mounting body of evidence points to the unintended consequences of managing through performance targets. In particular, many of the companies that are the most effective long-term generators of profit and are best at creating shareholder value place little emphasis on financial goals. Why does the pursuit of profit so often fail to realize its goal? First, profit goals will only guide effective management action if managers know what determines profit. Obsession with profitability and shareholder return can blinker managers' perception of the real drivers of superior performance: in the case of Enron it helped fuel the destruction of all shareholder value.[20] Conversely, if companies focus their attention on the strategic drivers of competitive advantage, this can ultimately lead to superior long-term profitability. The general point—illustrated by the case of Boeing (Strategy Capsule 2.3)—is that *obliquity*, pursuing our goals indirectly, is often superior to a direct approach.[21]

There is also the danger that whenever broad, long-term goals are translated into time-specific performance metrics the performance targets become divorced from

---

STRATEGY CAPSULE 2.3
The Pitfalls of Pursuing Shareholder Value: Boeing

Boeing was one of the most financially successful members of the Dow Jones Industrial Index between 1960 and 1990. Yet Boeing gave little attention to financial management. CEO Bill Allen was interested in building great planes and leading the world market with them: "Boeing is always reaching out for tomorrow. This can only be accomplished by people who live, breathe, eat and sleep what they are doing." At a board meeting to approve Boeing's biggest ever investment, the 747, Allen was asked by non-executive director Crawford Greenwalt for Boeing's financial projections on the project. In response to Allen's vague reply, Greenwalt buried his head in his hands. "My God," he muttered, "these guys don't even know what the return on investment will be on this thing."

The change came in the mid-1990s when Boeing acquired McDonnell Douglas and a new management team of Harry Stonecipher and Phil Condit took over. Mr Condit proudly talked of taking the company into "a value-based environment where unit cost, return on investment, and shareholder return are the measures by which you'll be judged."

The result was lack of investment in major new civil aviation projects and diversification into defense and satellites. Under Condit, Boeing relinquished market leadership in passenger aircraft to Airbus, while faltering as a defense contractor due partly to ethical lapses by key executives. When Condit resigned on December 1, 2003, Boeing's stock price was 20% lower than when he was appointed.

Source: Adapted from John Kay, "Forget how the Crow Flies," *Financial Times Magazine* (January 17, 2004): 17–27, with permission.

the ultimate objective—as the Buddhist teaching warns us: "Mistaking the finger pointing at the moon for the moon itself." The widespread adoption of performance targets in the public sector has resulted in the propensity for agencies to "game the system" through neglecting what has not been targeted, manipulating data, and achieving targets but not improving the underlying performance that performance indicators are intended to reflect.[22]

Beyond Profit: Values and Corporate Social Responsibility

At the beginning of this chapter, I argued that, while every company has a distinct organizational purpose, the common goal for every business enterprise is to create value, and the best indicator of value creation is profit over the lifetime of the company—or, equivalently, maximizing enterprise value. Although the corporate scandals of the 21st century—from Enron in 2001 to Lehman Brothers in 2008—have discredited the pursuit of profit, in particular the principle of shareholder value maximization, I have justified the goal of long-run profit maximization as the most appropriate and practical goal for the firm.

This justification was based largely on the alignment which I perceived, first, between profits and the interests of society (reflecting Adam Smith's principle of the "invisible hand" which guides self-interest toward the common good) and, second, between the pursuit of stakeholder interests and earning profit over the long-term ("enlightened value maximization"). But what about when the pursuit of profit is not consistent with the social good or where it conflicts with ethics? How are such inconsistencies and conflicts to be managed? Is it sufficient to follow Milton Friedman's dictum that:

> There is one and only one social responsibility of business—to use its resources and engage in activities designed to increase its profits so long as it stays within the rules of the game, which is to say, engage in open and free competition without deception or fraud.[23]

Under this approach, it is the role of government to intervene in the economy where the pursuit of profit conflicts with the interest of society, using taxes and regulations to align profit incentives with social goals and legislation to criminalize unethical behavior. Conversely, others have argued that business enterprises should take the initiative to establish principles and values that extend beyond the limits of the law, and introduce strategies that are explicitly oriented toward the interests of society. Let us discuss each of these areas in turn.

Values and Principles

A sense of purpose—as articulated in statements of mission and vision—is often complemented by beliefs about how this purpose should be achieved. These organizational beliefs typically comprise a set of **values**—in the form of commitments to certain ethical precepts and to different stakeholder interests—and a set of principles to guide the decisions and actions of organizational members. Strategy Capsule 2.4 summarizes Shell's values and business principles.

STRATEGY CAPSULE 2.4

Royal Dutch Shell's Values and Principles

OUR VALUES

Shell employees share a set of core values—honesty, integrity and respect for people. We also firmly believe in the fundamental importance of trust, openness, teamwork and professionalism and pride in what we do.

PRINCIPLES

1   Economic. Long-term profitability is essential to achieving our business goals and to our continued growth…

2   Competition. Shell companies support free enterprise. We seek to compete fairly and ethically and within the framework of applicable competition laws…

3   Business integrity. Shell companies insist on honesty, integrity and fairness in all aspects of our business…

4   Political activities. Shell companies act in a socially responsible manner within the laws of the countries in which we operate in pursuit of our legitimate commercial objectives…

5   Health, safety, security and the environment. Shell companies have a systematic approach to health, safety, security and environmental management in order to achieve continuous performance improvement.

6   Local communities. Shell companies aim to be good neighbors by continuously improving the ways in which we contribute directly or indirectly to the general wellbeing of the communities within which we work…

7   Communication and engagement. Shell companies recognize that regular dialogue and engagement with our stakeholders is essential. We are committed to reporting of our performance by providing full relevant information to legitimately interested parties…

8   Compliance. We comply with all applicable laws and regulations of the countries in which we operate.

Source: Extracted from Royal Dutch Shell plc General Business Principles, 2008 with permission from Shell International.

At one level, statements of values and principles may be regarded as instruments of companies' external image management. Yet, to the extent that companies are consistent and sincere in their adherence to values and principles, these ideals can be a critical component of organizational identity and an important influence on employees' commitment and propensity to collaborate. To the extent that values are shared among organizational members, they form a central component of organizational culture.

The evidence that commitment to values and principles influences organizational performance is overwhelming. McKinsey & Company places "shared values" at the center of its "7-S framework."[24] Jim Collins and Jerry Porras argue that "core values" and "core purpose"—the organization's most fundamental reasons for being—unite to form an organization's "core ideology" which "defines an organization's timeless character" and is "the glue that holds the organization together."[25] They argue that when core ideology is put together with an "envisioned future" for the enterprise the result is a powerful sense of strategic direction that provides the foundation for long-term success.

Guidelines for Corporate Social Responsibility

The debate over the social responsibilities of companies has been both contentious and confused. Underlying the debate are different conceptions of the public corporation: "the property conception," which views the firm as a set of assets owned by the shareholders, and the "social entity conception," which views the firm as the community of individuals that is sustained and supported by its relationships with its social, political, economic, and natural environment.[26] While the "firm as property" view implies that management's sole responsibility is to operate in the interests of shareholders, the "firm as social entity" implies a responsibility to maintain the firm within its overall network of relationships and dependencies.

However, even from a pure efficacy viewpoint, it is clear that both poles of the spectrum of opinions are untenable. The proponents of the view that the sole purpose of the business enterprise is to make profit fail to recognize that to survive and earn profit an organization must maintain social legitimacy. The near-elimination of investment banks during the financial crisis of 2008-2009—including the transformation of Goldman Sachs and other investment banks into commercial banks—was caused less by their commercial failure as by a collapse of legitimacy. The phone hacking scandal that resulted in the closure of a British newspaper owned by Rupert Murdoch's News Corporation represented less than 1% of News Corp's revenues. However, in the five weeks after the scandal broke in July 2011, News Corp's market capitalization declined by 25%—a loss of $11 billion.

At the other end of the spectrum, the argument that the primary responsibility of business enterprises should be the pursuit of social goals is likely to be similarly dysfunctional. To extend Adam Smith's observation that it "is not from the benevolence of the butcher, the brewer or the baker, that we expect our dinner, but from their regard to their own interest,"[27] it is likely that if the butcher becomes an animal rights activist, the brewer joins the Temperance League, and the baker signs up to Weight Watchers none of us has much hope of getting dinner.

Somewhere in the middle of this spectrum therefore lies a region of sustainability where business enterprises are aligned with the requirements of their social and natural environment but have not lost touch either with their business purpose or with the need for financial viability. A number of contributions to the management literature have allowed us to define more precisely this intermediate region of sustainability and to outline the considerations that should guide the pursuit of social responsibility.

The key consideration here is survival through adaptation. The efficacy argument for **corporate social responsibility (CSR)** views the firm as embedded within an ecosystem of its social and natural environments, implying a congruence between the interests of the firm and those of the supporting ecosystem. Thus, according to former Shell executive Arie de Geus, long-living companies are those that build strong communities, have a strong sense of identity, commit to learning, and are sensitive to the world around them. In short, they recognize they are living organisms whose lifespans depend upon effective adaptation to a changing environment.[28]

This view of the firm jointly pursuing its own interests and those of its ecosystem has been developed by Michael Porter and Mark Kramer into guidelines for a focused and pragmatic approach to CSR.[29] Putting aside ethical arguments (what they call "the moral imperative"), they identify three reasons why CSR might also be in the interests of a company: the *sustainability* argument—CSR is in firms' interests due to a mutual interest in sustaining the ecosystem; the *reputation* argument—CSR enhances a firm's reputation with consumers and other third parties; and the *license-to-operate* argument—to conduct their businesses firms need the support of the constituencies upon which they depend. The critical task, in selecting which CSR initiatives firms should pursue is to identify specific intersections between the interests of the firm and those of society (i.e., projects and activities that create competitive advantage for the firm while generating positive social outcomes)—what they term *strategic CSR*.

In a subsequent article, Porter and Kramer develop their analysis of this intersection between corporate and social interests, which they call *shared value*: "creating economic value in a way which also creates value for society."[30] Shared value, they argue, is not about redistributing the value already created; it is about expanding the total pool of economic and social value. For example, fair trade is about the redistribution of value by paying farmers a higher price for their crops—in the case of Ivory Coast cocoa growers, it increases their incomes by 10–20%. By contrast, efforts by the major buyers to improve the efficiency of cocoa growing through improved growing methods, better quality control, and improved infrastructure can increase growers' incomes by 300%. Creating shared value involves reconceptualizing the firm's boundaries and its relationship with its environment. Rather than seeing itself as a separate entity which transacts with the external environment, the firm recognizes that it is co-dependent upon and intimately involved with its environment and the organizations and individuals it comprises. This offers three types of opportunity for shared value creation: reconceiving products and markets, redefining productivity within the value chain, and building local clusters of suppliers, distributors, and related businesses at the places where the firm does business.

This notion of shared value is embedded in **the bottom of the pyramid** initiatives—the potential for multinational companies to create profitable business and promote social and economic development through serving the world's poor—especially the four billion people living off less than $2 a day.[31] Again, the key is a switch of perception: rather than viewing the poor as victims or a burden, if multinationals recognize them as potential consumers, resilient workers, and creative entrepreneurs then a whole world of opportunity opens up.

Beyond Profit: Strategy and Real Options

So far, we have identified the value of the firm with the net present value (NPV) of its profit earnings (or free cash flows). But NPV is not the only source of value available to the firm. The simple idea that an option—the choice of whether to do something or not—has value has important implications for how we value firms. In recent years, the principles of option pricing have been extended from valuing financial securities to valuing investment projects and companies. The resulting field of **real option analysis** has emerged as one of the most important developments in financial theory over the past decade, with far-reaching implications for strategy analysis. The technical details of valuing real options are complex. However, the underlying principles are intuitive. Let me outline the basic ideas of real options theory and what they mean for strategy analysis.

Consider the investments that Royal Dutch Shell is making in joint-venture development projects to produce hydrogen for use in fuel cells. The large-scale use of fuel cells in transportation vehicles or for power generation seems unlikely within the foreseeable future. Shell's expenditure on these projects is small, but almost certainly these funds would generate a higher return if they were used in Shell's core oil and gas business. So, how can these investments—indeed, all of Shell's investments in renewable energy—be consistent with shareholder interests?

The answer lies in the option value of these investments. Shell is not developing a full-scale fuel cell business, and nor is it developing commercial-scale hydrogen production plants: it is developing technologies that could be used to produce hydrogen if fuel cells become widely used. By building know-how and intellectual property in this technology, Shell has created an *option*. If economic, environmental, or political factors restrict hydrocarbon use and if fuel cells advance to the point of technical and commercial viability, then Shell could exercise that option by investing much larger amounts in commercial-scale hydrogen production.

In a world of uncertainty, where investments, once made, are irreversible, flexibility is valuable. Instead of committing to an entire project, there is virtue in breaking the project into a number of phases, where the decision of whether and how to embark on the next phase can be made in the light of prevailing circumstances and the learning gained from the previous stage of the project. Most large companies have a "phases and gates" approach to product development in which the development process is split into distinct "phases," at the end of which the project is reassessed before being allowed through the "gate." Such a phased approach creates the options to continue the project, to abandon it, to amend it, or to wait. Venture capitalists clearly recognize the value of growth options. In September 2009, Twitter—which earned almost no revenue and burnt cash at the rate of about $10 million a month—raised over $100 million in investment, implying a company valuation of $1 billion. These investors were buying an option on Twitter's ability to find a way of monetizing its massive online presence and thereby establish a profitable business. The emphasis that venture capitalists place on *scalability*—the potential to scale up or replicate a business should the initial launch be successful—similarly acknowledges the value of growth options. Strategy Capsule 2.5 addresses the calculation of real option values.

Strategy as Options Management

For strategy formulation, our primary interest is how we can use the principles of option valuation to create shareholder value. There are two types of real option: growth options and flexibility options. *Growth options* allow a firm to make small initial investments in a number of future business opportunities but without committing to them. *Flexibility options* relate to the design of projects and plants that permit adaptation to different circumstances—flexible manufacturing systems allow different product models to be manufactured on a single production line. Individual projects can be designed to introduce both growth options and flexibility options. This means avoiding commitment to the complete project and introducing decision points at multiple stages, where the main options are to delay, modify, scale up, or abandon the project. Merck, an early adopter of option pricing, notes, "When you make an initial investment in a research project, you are paying an entry fee for a right, but you are not obligated to continue that research at a later stage."[32]

STRATEGY CAPSULE 2.5
Calculating Real Option Value

Application of real option value to investment projects and strategies has been limited by the complexity of the valuation techniques. Yet, even without getting into the mathematics needed to quantify option values, we can use the basic principles involved to understand the factors that determine option values and to recognize how projects and strategies can be designed in order to maximize their option values.

The early work on real option valuation adapted the Black–Scholes option-pricing formula developed for valuing financial options to the valuation of real investment projects.[a] Black–Scholes comprises six determinants of option value, each of which has an analogy in the valuation of a real option:

1 Stock price = The NPV of the project: a higher NPV increases option value

2 Exercise price = Investment cost: the higher the cost, the lower the option value

3 Uncertainty: for both financial and real options, uncertainty increases option value

4 Time to expiry: for both financial and real options, the longer the option lasts, the greater its value

5 Dividends = Decrease in the value of the investment over the option period: lowers option value

6 Interest rate: a higher interest rate increases option value by making deferral more valuable.[b]

However, the dominant methodology used for real option valuation is the binomial options pricing model. By allowing the sources of uncertainty and key decision points in a project to be modeled explicitly, the technique offers a more intuitive appreciation of the sources of option value. The analysis involves two main stages:

1 Create an event tree that shows the value of the project at each development period under two different scenarios.

2 Convert the event tree into a decision tree by identifying the key decision points on the event tree, typically the points where commitments of new funds to the project are required or where there is the option to defer development. Incremental project values at each stage can then be calculated for each decision point by working back from the final nodes of the decision tree (using a discount factor based upon the replicating portfolio technique). If the incremental project value at the initial stage exceeds the initial investment, proceed with the first phase, and similarly for each subsequent phase.[c]

Notes:

[a]See: F. Black and M. Scholes, "The Pricing of Options and Corporate Liabilities," *Journal of Political Economy* 81 (1993): 637–54.

[b]See: K. J. Leslie and M. P. Michaels, "The Real Power of Real Options," *McKinsey Quarterly Anthology: On Strategy* (Boston: McKinsey & Company, 2000). See also A. Dixit and R. Pindyck, "The Options Approach to Capital Investment," *Harvard Business Review* (May/June 1995): 105–15.

[c]This approach is developed in T. Copeland and P. Tufano, "A Real-world Way to Manage Real Options," *Harvard Business Review* (March 2004). See also T. Copeland, Developing Strategy Using Real Options (Monitor Company, October 2003).

In developing strategy, our main concern is with growth options. These might include:

- Platform investments. These are investments in core products or technologies that create a stream of additional business opportunities.[33] 3M's investment in nanotechnology offers the opportunity to create new products across a wide range of its businesses, from dental restoratives and drug-delivery systems to adhesives and protective coatings. Google's search engine and the huge internet traffic it draws has offered a platform for a large number of initiatives—not just search products but also a wide array of other software products and internet services (e.g., Gmail, Chrome, Android, Google+).[34]
- Strategic alliances and joint ventures, which are limited investments that offer options for the creation of whole new strategies.[35] Virgin Group has used joint ventures as the basis for creating a number of new businesses: with Stagecoach to create Virgin Rail, with AMP to create Virgin Money (financial services), with Deutsche Telecom to form Virgin Mobile. Shell has used joint ventures and alliances as a means of making initial investments in wind power, biodiesel fuel, solar power, and other forms of renewable energy.
- Organizational capabilities, which can also be viewed as options offering the potential to create competitive advantage across multiple products and businesses.[36] Apple's capability in combining hardware, software, aesthetics, and ergonomics to create products of exceptional user-friendliness has given it the option to expand into several new product areas: MP3 audio players, smartphones, tablet computers, and interactive TV.

Summary

Chapter 1 introduced a framework for strategy analysis that provides the structure for Part II of this book. This chapter has explored the first component of that framework—the goals, values, and performance of the firm.

We have explored in some depth the difficult, and still contentious, issue of the appropriate goals for the firm. While each firm has a specific business purpose, common to all firms is the desire, and the necessity, to create value. How that value is defined and measured distinguishes those who argue that the firms should operate primarily in the interests of owners (shareholders) from those who argue for a stakeholder approach. Our approach has been pragmatic: in practice there is widespread convergence between shareholder and stakeholder interests and, where they diverge, the pressure of competition limits the scope for pursuing stakeholder interests at the expense of profit, hence my conclusion that long-run profit—or its equivalent, enterprise value—is appropriate both as an indicator of firm performance and as a guide to strategy formulation. We explored the relationships between value, profit, and cash flow and saw how the failings of shareholder value maximization resulted primarily from its misapplication.

The application of financial analysis to the assessment of firm performance is an essential component of strategic analysis. Financial analysis creates a basis for strategy formulation, first, by appraising overall firm performance and, second, by diagnosing the sources of unsatisfactory performance. Combining financial analysis and strategic analysis allows us to establish performance targets for companies and their business units.

Finally, we looked beyond the limits of our useful, yet simplistic, profit-oriented approach to firm performance and business strategy. We looked, first, at how the principles of corporate social responsibility could be incorporated within a firm's strategy to enhance its creation of both social and shareholder value. Second, we extended our analysis of value maximization to take account of the fact that strategy creates enterprise value not only by generating profit but also by creating real options.

 Quizzes and flashcards to test yourself further are available in your interactive e-book at **www.wileyopenpage.com**

Self-Study Questions

1. Table 2.1 compares companies according to different profitability measures.

    a.   Which two of the six performance measures do you think are the most useful indicators of how well a company is being managed?

    b.   Is return on sales or return on equity a better basis on which to compare the performance of the companies listed?

    c.   Several companies are highly profitable yet have delivered very low returns to their shareholders. How is this possible?

2. India's Tata Group is a diversified group. Some of its largest companies are: Tata Steel, Tata Motors, Tata Consultancy Services (IT), Tata Power (electricity generation), Tata Chemicals, Tata Tea, Indian Hotels, and Tata Communications. How do you think Tata Group's recent adoption of EVA as a performance management tool is likely to influence the way in which it allocates investment among the companies listed above?

3. With regard to Strategy Capsule 2.2, what additional data would you seek and what additional analysis would you undertake to investigate further the reasons for UPS's superior profitability to FedEx?

4. The CEO of a chain of pizza restaurants wishes to initiate a program of CSR to be funded by a 5% levy on the company's operating profit. The board of directors, fearing a negative shareholder reaction, is opposed to the plan. What arguments might the CEO use to persuade the board that CSR might be in the interests of shareholders, and what types of CSR initiatives might the program include to ensure that this was the case?

5. Nike, a supplier of sports footwear and apparel, is interested in the idea that it could increase its stock market value by creating options for itself. What actions might Nike take that might generate option value?

Notes

1. A. P. Sloan, *My Years at General Motors* (New York: Doubleday, 1963).
2. J. A. Schumpeter, *The Theory of Economic Development* (Cambridge, MA: Harvard University Press 1934).
3. See www.abelard.org/ford.
4. C. A. Montgomery, "Putting Leadership Back into Strategy," *Harvard Business Review* (January 2008): 54–60.
5. In this chapter, I use the term *value* in two distinct senses. Here I am referring to *economic value*, which is worth as measured in monetary units. I shall also be discussing values as moral principles or standards of behavior.
6. T. Donaldson and L. E. Preston, "The stakeholder theory of the corporation," *Academy of Management Review* 20 (1995): 65–91.
7. J. Figuero, S. Greco, and M. Ehrgott, *Multiple Criteria Decision Analysis: State of the Art Surveys* (Berlin: Springer, 2005).
8. M. C. Jensen, "Value Maximization, Stakeholder Theory, and the Corporate Objective Function," *Journal of Applied Corporate Finance* 22 (Winter 2010): 34.
9. M. B. Lieberman and N. Balasubramanian ("Measuring Value Creation and Its Distribution among Stakeholders of the Firm," Anderson School, UCLA, June 2007) outline a method for estimating aggregate stakeholder value through calculating the sum of consumer and producer surplus. However, the complexity and multiple assumptions of their method render it impractical as a management tool.
10. J. Helwege, V. Intintoli, and A. Zhang, "Voting with Their Feet or Activism? Institutional Investors' Impact on CEO Turnover," *Journal of Corporate Finance* (forthcoming 2012).
11. T. M. Jones, "Instrumental Stakeholder Theory: A Synthesis of Ethics and Economics," *Academy of Management Review* 20 (1995): 404–37.
12. M. Orlitzky, F. L. Schmidt, and S. L. Rynes, "Corporate Social and Financial Performance: A Meta-Analysis," *Organization Studies* 24 (Summer 2003): 403–41.
13. See www.sternstewart.com. See also J. L. Grant, *Foundations of Economic Value Added*, 2nd edn (New York: John Wiley & Sons, Ltd, 2003).
14. The cost of equity capital is calculated using the capital asset pricing model: Firm X's cost of equity = the risk-free rate of interest + a risk premium. The risk premium is the excess of the stock market rate of return over the risk-free rate multiplied by Firm X's beta coefficient (its measure of systematic risk). See T. Koller, M. Goedhart, and D. Wessels, *Valuation: Measuring and Managing the Value of Companies*, 5th edn (Hoboken, NJ: John Wiley & Sons, Inc., 2010), Chapter 11.
15. T. Koller, M. Goedhart, D. Wessels, *Valuation: Measuring and Managing the Value of Companies*, 5th edn (Hoboken, NJ: John Wiley & Sons, Inc., 2010).
16. F. Modigliani and M. H. Miller, "The Cost of Capital, Corporation Finance, and the Theory of Investments," *American Economic Review* 48 (1958): 261–97.
17. This distinction is made by K. Kaiser and S. D. Young, "Blue Line Management: What Value Creation Really Means," Insead Working Paper 2009/37/FIN/AC.
18. J. A. Kay and C. Meyer, "On the Application of Accounting Rates of Return," *Economic Journal* 96 (1986): 199–207.
19. R. S. Kaplan and D. P. Norton, "The Balanced Scorecard: Measures that Drive Performance," *Harvard Business Review* (January/February 1992): 71–9; R. S. Kaplan and D. P. Norton, "Using the Balanced Scorecard as a Strategic Management System," *Harvard Business Review* (January/February 1996): 75–85.
20. S. Chatterjee, "Enron's Incremental Descent into Bankruptcy: A Strategic and Organizational Analysis," *Long Range Planning* 36 (2003): 133–49.
21. J. Kay, *Obliquity* (London: Profile Books, 2010).
22. G. Bevan and C. Hood, "What's Measured Is What Matters: Targets and Gaming in the English Public Health Care System," *Public Administration* 84 (2006): 517–538.
23. M. Friedman, *Capitalism and Freedom* (Chicago: University of Chicago Press, 1963).
24. L. Bryan, "Enduring Ideas: The 7-S Framework," *McKinsey Quarterly* (March 2008).
25. J. Collins and J. Porras, "Building Your Company's Vision," *Harvard Business Review* (September/October 1996): 65–77.
26. W. T. Allen, "Our Schizophrenic Conception of the Business Corporation," *Cardozo Law Review* 14 (1992): 261–81.
27. A. Smith, *An Inquiry into the Nature and Causes of the Wealth of Nations*, 5th edn (London: Methuen & Co., 1905), Chapter 2.
28. A. de Geus, "The Living Company," *Harvard Business Review* (March/April 1997): 51–9.
29. M. E. Porter and M. R. Kramer, "Strategy and Society: The Link between Competitive Advantage and Corporate Social Responsibility," *Harvard Business Review* (December 2006): 78–92.
30. M. E. Porter and M. R. Kramer, "Creating Shared Value," *Harvard Business Review* (January 2011): 62–77.
31. C. K. Prahalad and S. L. Hart, "The Fortune at the Bottom of the Pyramid," *strategy + business* 26 (2002): 54–67; T. London and S. L. Hart, "Reinventing Strategies for Emerging Markets: Beyond the Transnational Model," *Journal of International Business Studies* 35 (2004): 350–370.
32. N. Nichols, "Scientific Management at Merck: An Interview with CFO Judy Lewent," *Harvard Business Review* (January/February 1994): 89–105.

33. B. Kogut and N. Kulatilaka, "Options Thinking and Platform Investments: Investing in Opportunity," *California Management Review* (Winter 1994): 52–69.

34. A. Gower and M. A. Cusamano, "How Companies Become Platform Leaders," *Sloan Management Review* (Winter 2008): 28–35.

35. T. Chi, "Option to Acquire or Divest a Joint Venture," *Strategic Management Journal* 21 (2000) 665–87.

36. B. Kogut and N. Kulatilaka, "Capabilities as Real Options," *Organization Science* 12 (2001) 744–58; R. G. McGrath, W. Furrier, and A. Mendel, "Real Options as Engines of Choice and Heterogeneity," *Academy of Management Review* 29 (2004): 86–101.

3 Industry Analysis: The Fundamentals

> When a management with a reputation for brilliance tackles a business with a reputation for poor fundamental economics, it is the reputation of the business that remains intact.
>
> —WARREN BUFFETT, CHAIRMAN, BERKSHIRE HATHAWAY

> The reinsurance business has the defect of being too attractive-looking to new entrants for its own good and will therefore always tend to be the opposite of, say, the old business of gathering and rendering dead horses that always tended to contain few and prosperous participants.
>
> —CHARLES T. MUNGER, CHAIRMAN, WESCO FINANCIAL CORP

OUTLINE

Introduction and Objectives

In this chapter and the next we explore the external environment of the firm. In Chapter 1 we observed that profound understanding of the competitive environment is a critical ingredient of a successful strategy. We also noted that business strategy is essentially a quest for profit. The primary task for this chapter is to identify the sources of profit in the external environment. The firm's proximate environment is its industry environment; hence our environmental analysis will focus on the firm's industry surroundings.

Industry analysis is relevant both to corporate-level and business-level strategy.

◆ Corporate strategy is concerned with deciding which industries the firm should be engaged in and how it should allocate its resources among them. Such decisions require assessment of the attractiveness of different industries in terms of their profit potential. The main objective of this chapter is to understand how the competitive structure of an industry determines its profitability.

◆ Business strategy is concerned with establishing competitive advantage. By analyzing customer needs and preferences and the ways in which firms compete to serve customers, we identify the general sources of competitive advantage in an industry—what we call *key success factors*.

By the time you have completed this chapter, you will be able to:

◆ appreciate that the firm's industry represents the core of its external environment and understand that its characteristics and dynamics are essential components of strategy analysis;

◆ recognize the main structural features of an industry and understand how they impact the intensity of competition and overall level of profitability in the industry;

◆ apply industry analysis to explain the level of profitability in an industry and predict how profitability is likely to change in the future;

◆ develop strategies that (a) position the firm most favorably in relation to competition and (b) influence industry structure in order to enhance industry attractiveness;

◆ define the boundaries of the industry within which a firm is located;

◆ identify opportunities for competitive advantage within an industry (key success factors).

From Environmental Analysis to Industry Analysis

The business environment of the firm consists of all the external influences that impact its decisions and its performance. Given the vast number and range of external influences, how can managers hope to monitor, let alone analyze, environmental conditions? The starting point is some kind of system or framework for organizing information. Environmental influences can be classified by source, for example, into political, economic, social, and technological factors—what is known as *PEST analysis*. PEST analysis and similar approaches to macro-level environmental scanning can be useful in keeping a firm alert to what is happening in the world. The danger, however, is that continuous, systematic scanning and analysis of such a wide range of external influences is costly and may result in information overload.

The prerequisite for effective environmental analysis is to distinguish the vital from the merely important. To do this let us return to first principles in order to establish what features of a firm's external environment are relevant to its decisions. For the firm to make a profit it must create value for customers. Hence, it must understand its customers. Second, in creating value, the firm acquires goods and services from suppliers. Hence, it must understand its suppliers and manage relationships with them. Third, the ability to generate profitability depends on the intensity of competition among firms that vie for the same value-creating opportunities. Hence, the firm must understand competition. Thus, the core of the firm's business environment is formed by its relationships with three sets of players: customers, suppliers, and competitors. This is its industry environment.

This is not to say that macro-level factors such as general economic trends, changes in demographic structure, or social and political trends are unimportant for strategy analysis. These factors may be critical determinants of the threats and opportunities a company will face in the future. The key issue is how these more general environmental factors affect the firm's industry environment (Figure 3.1). Consider the threat of global warming. For most companies this is not an important strategic issue (at least, not for at least a decade). However, for those businesses most directly affected by changing weather patterns—farmers and insurance companies—and those subject to carbon taxes and environmental regulations—electricity generators and automobile producers—global warming is a vital issue. For these businesses, the key is to analyze the strategic implications of global warming for their particular industry. In the case of the automobile makers, what will be the impact on consumers and their preferences?

Will regulatory changes force a switch from private to public transportation? With regard to competition, will there be new entry by manufacturers of electric vehicles? Will the need for increased R & D cause the industry to consolidate?

If strategy is about identifying and exploiting sources of profit, then the starting point for industry analysis is the simple question "What determines the level of profit in an industry?"

In the last chapter we learned that for a firm to make profit it must create value for the customer. Value is created when the price the customer is willing to pay for

FIGURE 3.1   From environmental analysis to industry analysis

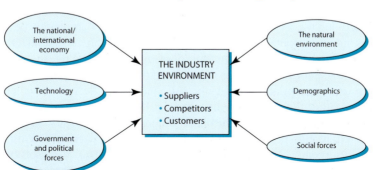

a product exceeds the costs incurred by the firm. But customer value does not translate directly into profit. The surplus of value over cost is distributed between customers and producers by the forces of competition. The stronger competition is among producers, the more of the surplus is received by customers as *consumer surplus* (the difference between the price they actually pay and the maximum price they would have been willing to pay) and the less is received by producers (as *producer surplus* or *economic rent*). A single supplier of umbrellas outside the Gare de Lyon on a wet Parisian morning can charge a price that fully exploits commuters' desire to keep dry. As more and more umbrella sellers arrive, so the price of umbrellas will be pushed closer to the wholesale cost.

However, the profit earned by Parisian umbrella sellers, or any other industry, does not just depend on the competition between them. It also depends upon their suppliers. If an industry has a powerful supplier—a single wholesaler of cheap, imported umbrellas—that supplier may be able to capture a major part of the value created in the local umbrella market.

Hence, the profits earned by the firms in an industry are determined by three factors:

- the value of the product to customers
- the intensity of competition
- the bargaining power of industry members relative to their suppliers and buyers.

Industry analysis brings all three factors into a single analytic framework.

Analyzing Industry Attractiveness

Table 3.1 shows the profitability of different US industries. Some industries consistently earn high rates of profit; others fail to cover their cost of capital. The basic premise that underlies industry analysis is that the level of industry profitability is neither random nor the result of entirely industry-specific influences: it is determined by the systematic influences of the industry's structure. The pharmaceutical industry and the automobile industry not only supply very different products but also have very different structures, which make one highly profitable and the other a nightmare of price competition and weak margins.

Small markets can offer particular profit opportunities if they can be dominated by a single firm. Strategy Capsule 3.1 gives examples of such niche markets.

The underlying theory of how industry structure drives competitive behavior and determines industry profitability is provided by industrial organization (IO) economics. The two reference points are the theory of monopoly and the theory of perfect competition; these form end points of the spectrum of industry structures. While a monopolist can appropriate in profit the full amount of the value it creates, under perfect competition the rate of profit falls to a level that just covers firms' cost of capital. These outcomes are the result of differences in industry structure (Table 3.2). In the real world, industries fall between these two extremes. During the 1990s (before the resurgence of the Apple Mac and entry of Linux), Microsoft held a near monopoly of the market for PC operating systems. Foreign exchange trading is close

TABLE 3.1 The profitability of US industries, 2000–2010

Industry[1]	Median ROE (%)[2]	Leading companies
Tobacco	33.5	Philip Morris Intl., Altria, Reynolds American
Household and Personal Products	27.8	Procter & Gamble, Kimberly-Clark, Colgate-Palmolive
Pharmaceuticals	20.5	Pfizer, Johnson & Johnson, Merck
Food Consumer Products	20.0	PepsiCo, Kraft Foods, General Mills
Food Services	19.9	McDonald's, Yum! Brands, Starbucks
Medical Products and Equipment	18.5	Medtronic, Baxter International, Boston Scientific
Petroleum Refining	17.6	ExxonMobil, Chevron, ConocoPhillips
Mining, Crude Oil Production	16.3	Occidental Petroleum, Devon Energy
Securities	15.9	KKR, BlackRock, Charles Schwab
Chemicals	15.7	Dow Chemical, DuPont, PPG Industries
Aerospace and Defense	15.7	Boeing, United Technologies, Lockheed Martin
Construction and Farm Equipment	14.5	Caterpillar, Deere, Illinois Tool Works
IT Services	14.1	IBM, Computer Sciences, SAIC
Specialty Retailers (non-apparel)	13.9	Home Depot, Costco, Lowe's
Communications Equipment	13.1	Cisco Systems, Motorola, Qualcomm
Healthcare Insurance and Managed Care	13.1	United Health Group, WellPoint, Aetna
Commercial Banks	12.4	Bank of America, JPMorgan Chase, Citigroup,
Engineering, Construction	12.3	Fluor, Jacobs Engineering, KBR
Computers, Office Equipment	12.1	Hewlett-Packard, Apple, Dell Computer
Diversified Financials	12.0	General Electric, Fannie Mae
General Merchandisers	11.6	Wal-Mart, Target, Sears Holdings
Energy	11.4	AES, AEP, Constellation Energy,
Pipelines	11.1	Plains All American Pipeline, Enterprise Products, ONEOK
Utilities: Gas and Electric	10.6	Execon, Southern, NextEra
Packaging and Containers	10.2	Ball, Crown Holdings, Owens-Illinois
Automotive Retailing and Services	9.8	AutoNation, Penske, Hertz
Food and Drug Stores	9.6	CVS, Kroger, Walgreens
Insurance: Property and Casualty	9.5	Berkshire Hathaway, AIG, Allstate
Insurance: Life and Health	8.7	MetLife, Prudential, Aflac
Hotels, Casinos, Resorts	8.5	Marriott International, Caesars, Las Vegas Sands
Metals	8.2	Alcoa, US Steel, Nucor
Semiconductors and Electronic Components	7.7	Intel, Texas Instruments, Jabil Circuit
Forest and Paper Products	7.3	International Paper, Weyerhaeuser, Domtar
Food Production	5.2	Archer Daniels Midland, Tyson Foods, Smithfield Foods
Telecommunications	5.8	Verizon, AT&T, Sprint Nextel
Motor Vehicles and Parts	4.4	GM, Ford, Johnson Controls
Entertainment	3.9	Time Warner, Walt Disney, News Corp.
Airlines	−11.3	AMR Corporation, United Airlines, Delta Air Lines

Notes:

[1]Industries with fewer than five firms were excluded (with the exception of tobacco). Also omitted were industries that were substantially redefined during the period.

[2]Median ROE for each industry averaged across the 11 years (2000–2010).

Source: Data from Fortune 500.

STRATEGY CAPSULE 3.1

Chewing Tobacco, Sausage Skins, and Slot Machines: The Joys of Niche Markets

UST is a subsidiary of Altria, the largest tobacco company in the US, which supplies "smokeless tobacco" (chewing tobacco and snuff) with brands such as Skoal, Copenhagen, and Red Seal. In 2010, Altria earned an operating margin of 52% on its sales of smokeless tobacco. Before it was acquired by Altria, UST was the most profitable company in the S&P 500, with an average ROCE (operating profit as percentage of capital employed) of 63% during 2003–2008. What's the secret of UST's profitability? It accounts for 55% of the US market for smokeless tobacco, and its long-established brands, its distribution through thousands of small retail outlets, and government restrictions on advertising tobacco products create formidable barriers to entry into this market.

Devro plc, based in the Scottish village of Moodiesburn, is the world's leading supplier of collagen sausage skins ("casings"). "From the British 'Banger' to the Chinese Lap Cheong, from the French Merguez

to the South American Chorizo, Devro has a casing to suit all product types." Its overall world market share is around 60%. During 2009–2010, its ROCE averaged 18.7%, significantly above the average for UK (FTSE 100) companies.

International Game Technology (IGT) based in Reno, Nevada is the world's dominant manufacturer of slot machines for casinos. IGT maintains its 70% US market share through close relations with casino operators and a continuous flow of new products. With heavy investment in R & D, new product saturation, tight control over distribution and servicing, and a policy of leasing rather than selling machines, IGT offers little opportunity to rivals. During 2007–2011, IGT earned an average ROE of 23.1% and ROCE of 19.0%, despite severe recession in the US casino industry.

Sources: www.altria.com, www.devro.com, and www.igt.com.

TABLE 3.2 The spectrum of industry structures

	Perfect Competition	Oligopoly	Duopoly	Monopoly
Concentration	Many firms	A few firms	Two firms	One firm
Entry and exit barriers	None	Significant		High
Product differentiation	Homogeneous product (commodity)	Potential for product differentiation		
Information availability	No impediments to information flow	Imperfect availability of information		

to being perfectly competitive, while most manufacturing and service industries are oligopolies: they are dominated by a small number of major companies.

Porter's Five Forces of Competition Framework

Table 3.2 identifies four structural variables influencing competition and profitability. In practice there are many features of an industry that determine the intensity of competition and the level of profitability. The most widely used framework for classifying

FIGURE 3.2   Porter's five forces of competition framework

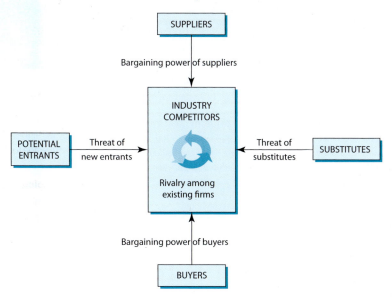

and analyzing these factors was developed by Michael Porter of Harvard Business School.[1] Porter's five forces of competition framework views the profitability of an industry (as indicated by its rate of return on capital relative to its cost of capital) as determined by five sources of competitive pressure. These five forces of competition include three sources of "horizontal" competition: competition from substitutes, competition from entrants, and competition from established rivals; and two sources of "vertical" competition: the power of suppliers and the power of buyers (Figure 3.2).

The strength of each of these competitive forces is determined by a number of key structural variables, as shown in Figure 3.3.

Competition from Substitutes

The price that customers are willing to pay for a product depends, in part, on the availability of substitute products. The absence of close substitutes for a product, as in the case of gasoline or cigarettes, means that consumers are comparatively insensitive to price (demand is inelastic with respect to price). The existence of close substitutes means that customers will switch to substitutes in response to price increases for the product (demand is elastic with respect to price). The internet has provided a new source of substitute competition that has proved devastating for a number of established industries. Travel agencies, newspapers, and telecommunication providers have all suffered severe competition from internet-based substitutes.

The extent to which substitutes depress prices and profits depends on the propensity of buyers to substitute between alternatives. This, in turn, depends on their price-performance characteristics. If city-center to city-center travel between Washington and New York is 50 minutes quicker by air than by train and the average traveler values time at $30 an hour, the implication is that the train will be competitive at fares of $25 below those charged by the airlines. The more complex the product and the more difficult it is to discern performance differences, the lower

FIGURE 3.3   The structural determinants of the five forces of competition

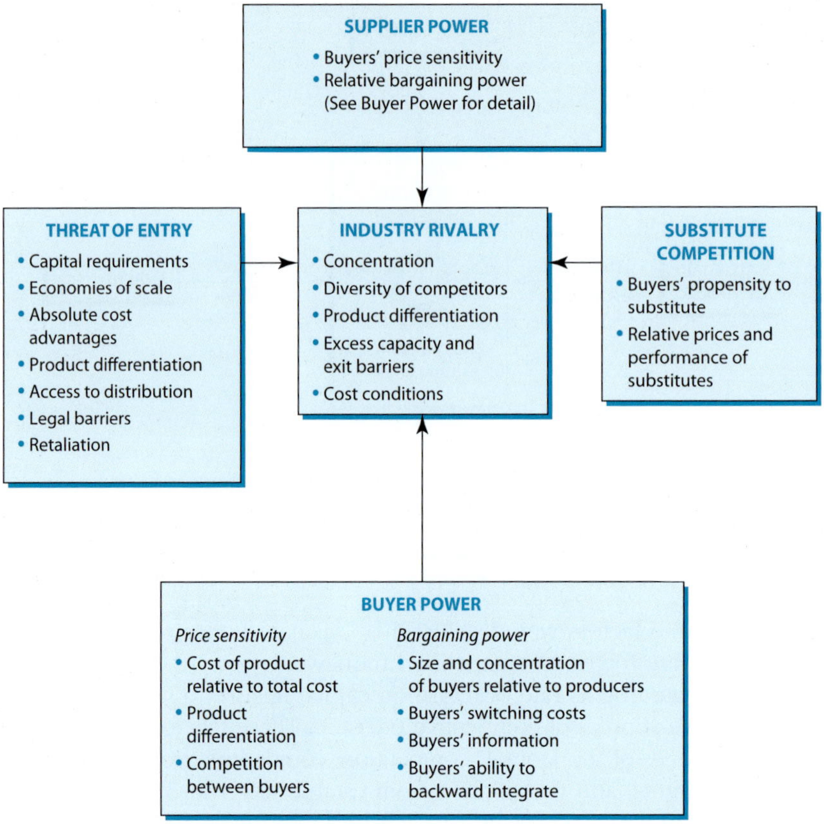

the extent of substitution by customers on the basis of price differences. The failure of low-priced imitations of leading perfumes to establish significant market share reflects consumers' difficulty in recognizing the performance characteristics of different fragrances.

Threat of Entry

If an industry earns a return on capital in excess of its cost of capital, it will act as a magnet to firms outside the industry. If the entry of new firms is unrestricted, the rate of profit will fall toward its competitive level. Increased health awareness in the US has encouraged increasing demand for fruit juice and smoothies. However, low entry barriers have resulted in about 4,000 new juice and smoothie bars being established since 2000 resulting in market saturation and a high rate of business failures.[2] Why is it that my wife, a psychotherapist, earns much less than our niece, a recently qualified medical doctor? Barriers to entry are one factor. In psychotherapy there are multiple accrediting bodies and limited state licensing, hence the entry barriers to psychotherapy are much lower than in medicine.

Threat of entry rather than actual entry may be sufficient to ensure that established firms constrain their prices to the competitive level. Only American Airlines offers a direct service between Dallas/Fort Worth and Santa Barbara, California, for example. Yet American may be unwilling to exploit its monopoly power to the full if Southwest or another airline can easily extend its routes to cover the same two cities. An industry where no barriers to entry or exit exist is contestable: prices and profits tend toward the competitive level, regardless of the number of firms within the industry.[3] Contestability depends on the absence of sunk costs—investments whose value cannot be recovered on exit. An absence of sunk costs makes an industry vulnerable to "hit and run" entry whenever established firms raise their prices above the competitive level.

In most industries, however, new entrants cannot enter on equal terms with those of established firms. A *barrier to entry* is any advantage that established firms have over entrants. The height of a barrier to entry is usually measured as the unit cost disadvantage faced by would-be entrants. The principal sources of barriers to entry are discussed below.

Capital Requirements   The capital costs of becoming established in an industry can be so large as to discourage all but the largest companies. The duopoly of Boeing and Airbus in large passenger jets is protected by the huge capital costs of establishing R & D, production, and service facilities for supplying these planes. Likewise with the business of launching commercial satellites: the costs of developing rockets and launch facilities make new entry highly unlikely. In other industries, entry costs can be modest. One reason why the e-commerce boom of the late 1990s ended in financial disaster for most participants is that the initial setup costs of new internet-based ventures were typically very low. Across the service sector more generally, start-up costs tend to be low. For example, start-up costs for a franchised pizza outlet begin at $150,000 for a Domino's and $638,000 for a Pizza Hut.[4]

Economies of Scale   The sources of high capital requirements for new entrants are also sources of scale economies. In industries that require large, indivisible investments in production facilities or technology or research or marketing, cost efficiency requires amortizing these indivisible costs over a large volume of output. The problem for new entrants is that they typically enter with a low market share and, hence, are forced to accept high unit costs. A major source of scale economies is new product development costs. Airbus's A380 superjumbo cost about $18 billion to develop and must sell about 400 planes to break even. Once Airbus had committed to the project, then Boeing was effectively excluded from the superjumbo segment of the market. In automobiles, scale economies in product development and purchasing mean that cost efficiency for a full-range automaker requires producing at least four million vehicles a year.

Absolute Cost Advantages   Established firms may have a unit cost advantage over entrants, irrespective of scale. Absolute cost advantages often result from the acquisition of low-cost sources of raw materials. Established oil and gas producers, such as Saudi Aramco and Gazprom, which have access to the world's biggest and most accessible reserves, have an unassailable cost advantage over more recent entrants such as Cairn Energy and BG Group. Absolute cost advantages may also result from economies of learning. Intel, AMD, and IBM's dominance of the market for advanced microprocessors for computers and video game consoles arises in part from the cost advantage they derive from their wealth of experience.

Product Differentiation   In an industry where products are differentiated, established firms possess the advantages of brand recognition and customer loyalty. The percentage of US consumers loyal to a single brand varies from under 30% in batteries, canned vegetables, and garbage bags, up to 61% in toothpaste, 65% in mayonnaise and 71% in cigarettes.[5] New entrants to such markets must spend disproportionately heavily on advertising and promotion to gain levels of brand awareness and brand goodwill similar to those of established companies. One study found that, compared to early entrants, late entrants into consumer goods markets incurred additional advertising and promotional costs amounting to 2.12% of sales revenue.[6]

Access to Channels of Distribution   For many new suppliers of consumer goods, the principal barrier to entry is likely to be gaining distribution. Limited capacity within distribution channels (e.g., shelf space), risk aversion by retailers, and the fixed costs associated with carrying an additional product result in retailers being reluctant to carry a new manufacturer's product. The battle for supermarket shelf space between the major food processors (typically involving "slotting fees" to reserve shelf space) further disadvantages new entrants. One of the most important competitive impacts of the internet has been allowing new businesses to circumvent barriers to distribution.

Governmental and Legal Barriers   Economists from the Chicago School claim that the only effective barriers to entry are those created by government. In taxicabs, banking, telecommunications, and broadcasting, entry usually requires a license from a public authority. From medieval times to the present day, companies and favored individuals have benefitted from governments granting them an exclusive right to ply a particular trade or offer a particular service. In knowledge-intensive industries, patents, copyrights, and other legally protected forms of intellectual property are major barriers to entry. In the pharmaceutical industry, the major players seek to delay entry by generic drug makers by extending their original patents through changes in dosage and delivery modes. Regulatory requirements and environmental and safety standards often put new entrants at a disadvantage in comparison with established firms because compliance costs tend to weigh more heavily on newcomers.

Retaliation   Barriers to entry also depend on the entrants' expectations as to possible retaliation by established firms. Retaliation against a new entrant may take the form of aggressive price-cutting, increased advertising, sales promotion, or litigation. The major airlines have a long history of retaliation against low-cost entrants. Southwest and other budget airlines have alleged that selective price cuts by American and other major airlines amounted to predatory pricing designed to prevent its entry into new routes.[7] To avoid retaliation by incumbents, new entrants may seek initial small-scale entry into less visible market segments. When Toyota, Nissan, and Honda first entered the US auto market, they targeted the small-car segments, partly because this was a segment that had been written off by the Detroit Big Three as inherently unprofitable.[8]

The Effectiveness of Barriers to Entry   Industries protected by high entry barriers tend to earn above-average rates of profit.[9] Capital requirements and advertising appear to be particularly effective impediments to entry.[10] The effectiveness of barriers to entry depends on the resources and capabilities that potential entrants possess. Barriers that are effective against new companies may be ineffective against established firms that are diversifying from other industries.[11] Google has used its massive web presence as a platform for entering a number of other markets, including Microsoft's seemingly impregnable position in browsers.

Rivalry between Established Competitors

In most industries, the major determinant of the overall state of competition and the general level of profitability is competition among the firms within the industry. In some industries, firms compete aggressively—sometimes to the extent that prices are pushed below the level of costs and industry-wide losses are incurred. In other industries, price competition is muted and rivalry focuses on advertising, innovation, and other non-price dimensions. The intensity of competition between established firms is the result of interactions between six factors. Let us look at each of them.

Concentration **Seller concentration** refers to the number and size distribution of firms competing within a market. It is most commonly measured by the *concentration ratio*: the combined market share of the leading producers. For example, the four-firm concentration ratio (CR4) is the market share of the four largest producers. In markets dominated by a single firm (for example P&G's Gillette in razor blades, Apple in MP3 players, or Altria in the US smokeless tobacco market), the dominant firm can exercise considerable discretion over the prices it charges. Where a market is dominated by a small group of leading companies (an oligopoly), price competition may also be restrained, either by outright collusion or, more commonly, by "parallelism" of pricing decisions.[12] Thus, in markets dominated by two companies, such as soft drinks (Coca-Cola and Pepsi), news weeklies (*Time* and *Newsweek*), and antivirus software (Symantec and McAfee), prices tend to be similar and competition focuses on advertising, promotion, and product development. As the number of firms supplying a market increases, coordination of prices becomes more difficult and the likelihood that one firm will initiate price-cutting increases. However, despite the frequent observation that the exit of a competitor reduces price competition, while the entry of a new competitor stimulates it, there is little systematic evidence that seller concentration increases profitability. Richard Schmalensee concludes that: "The relation, if any, between seller concentration and profitability is weak statistically and the estimated effect is usually small."[13]

Diversity of Competitors The extent to which a group of firms can avoid price competition in favor of collusive pricing practices depends on how similar they are in their origins, objectives, costs, and strategies. The cozy atmosphere of the US auto industry prior to the advent of import competition was greatly assisted by the similarities of the companies in terms of cost structures, strategies, and top management mindsets. The intense competition that affects the car markets of Europe and North America today is partly due to the different national origins, costs, strategies, and management styles of the competing firms. Similarly, the key challenge faced by OPEC is agreeing and enforcing output quotas among member countries that are sharply different in terms of objectives, production costs, politics, and religion.

Product Differentiation   The more similar the offerings among rival firms, the more willing are customers to switch between them and the greater is the inducement for firms to cut prices to boost sales. Where the products of rival firms are virtually indistinguishable, the product is a commodity and price is the sole basis for competition. Commodity industries such as agriculture, mining, and petrochemicals tend to be plagued by price wars and low profits. By contrast, in industries where products are highly differentiated (perfumes, pharmaceuticals, restaurants, management consulting services), price competition tends to be weak, even though there may be many firms competing.

Excess Capacity and Exit Barriers   Why does industry profitability tend to fall so drastically during periods of recession? The key is the balance between demand and capacity. Unused capacity encourages firms to offer price cuts to attract new business. Excess capacity may be cyclical (e.g., the boom–bust cycle in the semiconductor industry); it may also be part of a structural problem resulting from overinvestment and declining demand. In these latter situations, the key issue is whether excess capacity will leave the industry. **Barriers to exit** are costs associated with capacity leaving an industry. Where resources are durable and specialized, and where employees are entitled to job protection, barriers to exit may be substantial.[14] In the European and North American auto industry, excess capacity together with high exit barriers have devastated industry profitability. Conversely, rapid demand growth creates capacity shortages that boost margins. Expanding world trade, fueled by the growth of China, pushed up charter rates of large bulk carriers ("Capesizes") from under $18,000 a day at the beginning of 2003 to a peak of $233,988 per day on June 5, 2008. With the onset of global recession and fleet expansion by ship owners, rates declined precipitously to a mere $2,773 a day by November 26, 2008.[15] On average, companies in growing industries earn higher profits than companies in slow-growing or declining industries (Figure 3.4).

FIGURE 3.4   The impact of growth on profitability

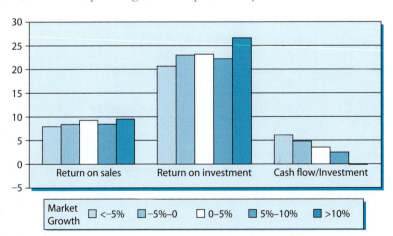

Source: R. D. Buzzell and B. T. Gale, *The PIMS Principles* (New York: Free Press, 1987): 56–7.

Cost Conditions: Scale Economies and the Ratio of Fixed to Variable Costs   When excess capacity causes price competition, how low will prices go? The key factor is cost structure. Where fixed costs are high relative to variable costs, firms will take on marginal business at any price that covers variable costs. The incredible volatility of bulk shipping rates reflects the fact that almost all the costs of operating bulk carriers are fixed. Similarly, in the airline industry the emergence of excess capacity almost invariably leads to price wars and industry-wide losses. The willingness of airlines to offer heavily discounted tickets on flights with low bookings reflects the very low variable costs of filling empty seats. "Cyclical" stocks are characterized not only by cyclical demand but also by a high ratio of fixed to variable costs, which means that fluctuations in revenues are amplified into much bigger fluctuations in profits.

Scale economies may also encourage companies to compete aggressively on price in order to gain the cost benefits of greater volume. If scale efficiency in the auto industry means producing four million cars a year, a level that is currently achieved by only five companies, the outcome is a battle for market share as each firm tries to achieve critical mass.

Bargaining Power of Buyers

The firms in an industry compete in two types of markets: in the markets for inputs and the markets for outputs. In input markets firms purchase raw materials, components, and financial and labor services. In the markets for outputs, firms sell their goods and services to customers (who may be distributors, consumers, or other manufacturers). In both markets the transactions create value for both buyers and sellers. How this value is shared between them in terms of profitability depends on their relative economic power. Let us deal first with output markets. The strength of buying power that firms face from their customers depends on two sets of factors: buyers' price sensitivity and relative bargaining power.

Buyers' Price Sensitivity   The extent to which buyers are sensitive to the prices charged by the firms in an industry depends on four main factors:

- The greater the importance of an item as a proportion of total cost, the more sensitive buyers will be about the price they pay. Beverage manufacturers are highly sensitive to the costs of aluminum cans because this is one of their largest single cost items. Conversely, most companies are not sensitive to the fees charged by their auditors, since auditing costs are a tiny fraction of total company expenses.
- The less differentiated the products of the supplying industry, the more willing the buyer is to switch suppliers on the basis of price. The manufacturers of T-shirts and light bulbs have much more to fear from Wal-Mart's buying power than have the suppliers of perfumes.
- The more intense the competition among buyers, the greater their eagerness for price reductions from their sellers. As competition in the world automobile industry has intensified, so component suppliers face greater pressures for lower prices.
- The more critical an industry's product to the quality of the buyer's product or service, the less sensitive are buyers to the prices they are charged. The

buying power of personal computer manufacturers relative to the manufacturers of microprocessors (Intel and AMD) is limited by the vital importance of these components to the functionality of PCs.

Relative Bargaining Power   Bargaining power rests, ultimately, on the refusal to deal with the other party. The balance of power between the two parties to a transaction depends on the credibility and effectiveness with which each makes this threat. The key issue is the relative cost that each party sustains as a result of the transaction not being consummated. A second issue is each party's expertise in managing its position. Several factors influence the bargaining power of buyers relative to that of sellers:

- Size and concentration of buyers relative to suppliers. The smaller the number of buyers and the bigger their purchases, the greater the cost of losing one. Because of their size, health maintenance organizations can purchase healthcare from hospitals and doctors at much lower costs than can individual patients. Empirical studies show that buyer concentration lowers prices and profits in the supplying industry.[16]
- Buyers' information. The better-informed buyers are about suppliers and their prices and costs, the better they are able to bargain. Doctors and lawyers do not normally display the prices they charge, nor do traders in the bazaars of Marrakesh or Chennai. Keeping customers ignorant of relative prices is an effective constraint on their buying power. But knowing prices is of little value if the quality of the product is unknown. In the markets for haircuts, interior design, and management consulting, the ability of buyers to bargain over price is limited by uncertainty over the precise attributes of the product they are buying.
- Ability to integrate vertically. In refusing to deal with the other party, the alternative to finding another supplier or buyer is to do it yourself. Large food-processing companies such as Heinz and Campbell Soup have reduced their dependence on the manufacturers of metal cans by manufacturing their own. The leading retail chains have increasingly displaced their suppliers' brands with their own-brand products. Backward integration need not necessarily occur—a credible threat may suffice.

Bargaining Power of Suppliers

Analysis of the determinants of relative power between the producers in an industry and their suppliers is precisely analogous to analysis of the relationship between producers and their buyers. The only difference is that it is now the firms in the industry that are the buyers and the producers of inputs that are the suppliers. The key issues are the ease with which the firms in the industry can switch between different input suppliers and the relative bargaining power of each party.

Because raw materials, semi-finished products, and components are often commodities supplied by small companies to large manufacturing companies, their suppliers usually lack bargaining power. Hence, commodity suppliers often seek to boost their bargaining power through cartelization (e.g., OPEC, the International Coffee Organization, and farmers' marketing cooperatives). Conversely, the suppliers of complex, technically sophisticated components may be able to exert considerable bargaining power. The dismal profitability of the personal computer industry may be attributed to the power exercised by the suppliers of key components (processors, disk drives, LCD screens) and the dominant supplier of operating systems (Microsoft).

Labor unions are important sources of supplier power. US industries where over 60% of employees are unionized earned a return on investment that was five percentage points lower than industries where less than 35% of employees were unionized. If its employees are unionized, as in airlines and automobiles, a business's profitability is reduced.[17]

Applying Industry Analysis to Forecasting Industry Profitability

Once we understand how industry structure drives competition, which, in turn, determines industry profitability, we can apply this analysis to forecast industry profitability in the future.

Identifying Industry Structure

The first stage of any industry analysis is to identify the key elements of the industry's structure. In principle, this is a simple task. It requires identifying who are the main players—the producers, the customers, the input suppliers, and the producers of substitute goods—then examining some of the key structural characteristics of each of these groups that will determine competition and bargaining power.

In most manufacturing industries identifying the main groups of players is straightforward; in other industries, particularly in service industries, mapping the industry can be more difficult. Consider the US television broadcasting industry. Where do we draw the industry boundaries? Is there a single TV distribution industry or do we identify separate industries for TV airwaves broadcasting, cable TV, and satellite TV? In terms of identifying buyers and sellers we see that there the industry has quite a complex value chain that includes the producers of TV shows, the networks, and cable channels that put together program schedules, and local TV stations and cable companies that undertake final distribution. The industry has two types of buyer: viewers and advertisers. Additional complexity is created by the fact that some companies are vertically integrated across several stages of the value chain—thus, network broadcasters such as Fox and NBC are backward integrated into TV production and forward integrated into final distribution through ownership of local TV stations. We shall return to issues of industry definition later in this chapter.

Forecasting Industry Profitability

We can use industry analysis to understand why profitability has been low in some industries and high in others but, ultimately, our interest is not to explain the past but to predict the future. Investment decisions made today will commit resources to an industry for years—often for a decade or more—hence, it is critical that we are able to predict what level of returns the industry is likely to offer in the future. Current profitability is a poor indicator of future profitability—industries such as newspapers, solar (photovoltaic) panels, and mobile phone handsets have suffered catastrophic declines in profitability. Conversely, several industries where returns were low—steel, metals mining, and several other "commodity industries"—have experienced remarkable revivals in profitability over the past decade. However, if an industry's profitability is determined by the structure of that industry then we can use observations of the structural trends in an industry to forecast the likely changes in competition and profitability. Changes in industry structure tend to be the result of fundamental shifts in customer buying behavior, technology, and firm strategies; these can often be anticipated well in advance of their impacts on competition and profitability.

To predict the future profitability of an industry, our analysis proceeds in three stages:

1 Examine how the industry's current and recent levels of competition and profitability are a consequence of its present structure.

2 Identify the trends that are changing the industry's structure. Is the industry consolidating? Are new players seeking to enter? Are the industry's products becoming more differentiated or more commoditized? Will additions to industry capacity outstrip growth of demand?

3 Identify how these structural changes will affect the five forces of competition and resulting profitability of the industry. Will the changes in industry structure cause competition to intensify or to weaken? Rarely do all the structural changes move competition in a consistent direction, typically some factors will cause competition to increase; others will cause competition to moderate. Hence, determining the overall impact on profitability tends to be a matter of judgment.

Strategy Capsule 3.2 discusses the outlook for profitability in the wireless handset industry.

Using Industry Analysis to Develop Strategy

Once we understand how industry structure influences competition, which in turn determines industry profitability, we can use this knowledge to develop firm strategies. First, we can develop strategies that influence industry structure in order to moderate competition; second, we can position the firm to shelter it from the ravages of competition.

Strategies to Alter Industry Structure

Understanding how the structural characteristics of an industry determine the intensity of competition and the level of profitability provides a basis for identifying opportunities for changing industry structure to alleviate competitive pressures. The first issue is to identify the key structural features of an industry that are responsible for depressing profitability. The second is to consider which of these structural features are amenable to change through appropriate strategic initiatives. For example:

● The remarkable profit revival in the world's steel industry during this century was mainly the result of rising demand from China; however, it was also

The Future of the Wireless Handset Industry

Wireless telephony has been one of the greatest growth industries of the past two decades—and almost as lucrative for the handset makers as for the service providers. During the 1990s, growth of handset sales in North America, Europe, and Japan averaged close to 50% each year and generated massive profits and shareholder value for the early leaders, Motorola and Nokia.

The current decade has witnessed a profound change in competition and margins. Despite continued demand growth (especially in emerging markets), profitability has fallen. During 2000–2005, the industry leaders—Nokia, Motorola, Sony-Ericsson, Samsung, LG, and Siemens—earned an average operating margin of 23% on their sales of mobile devices. By 2009, the top-seven suppliers (Nokia, Samsung, Apple, LG, RIM, Sony-Ericsson, and Motorola) were earning an average operating margin of 4% (although Apple was highly profitable, most of the others were loss making).

The structural changes undermining industry profitability included new entry—several Chinese and Taiwanese contact manufacturers—including HTC,

Huawei, ZTE, BenQ—introduced branded phones. As mature markets became saturated, so excess capacity emerged throughout the industry, which, in turn, reinforced the buying power of the major distributors of phones, the wireless service companies.

During 2012–2016, competition and profitability will be affected by several factors:

♦ New entry seems likely to continue. In the smartphone market, the availability of the Android platform will increase the number of firms competing in this segment.

♦ Most emerging markets, the BRIC countries in particular, are likely to become saturated.

♦ Commoditization is likely to threaten not just the low end of the market but also the smartphone market through the adoption of the Android platform.

♦ Mergers among telecom service providers will increase their buying power.

---

supported by the rapid consolidation of the industry, led by Mittal's merger with Arcelor, which was followed by the creation of Hebei Iron and Steel (China), Tata Steel-Corus (India/UK), and Nippon-Sumitomo (Japan).

● Excess capacity was a major problem in the European petrochemicals industry during the 1970s and 1980s. Through a series of bilateral plant exchanges, each company built a leading position within a particular product area.[18]

● In the US airline industry, the major airlines have struggled to change an unfavorable industry structure. In the absence of significant product differentiation, the airlines have used frequent-flyer schemes to build customer loyalty. Through hub-and-spoke route systems, the companies have achieved dominance of particular airports: American at Dallas/Fort Worth, US Airways at Charlotte NC, and Northwest at Detroit and Memphis. Mergers and alliances have reduced the numbers of competitors on many routes.[19]

● Building entry barriers is a vital strategy for preserving high profitability in the long run. A primary goal of the American Medical Association has been to maintain the incomes of its members by controlling the numbers of doctors trained in the US and imposing barriers to the entry of doctors from overseas.

The idea of firms reshaping their industries to their own advantage has been developed by Michael Jacobides. He begins with the premise that industries are in a state of continual evolution and that all firms, even quite small ones, have the potential to influence the development of industry structure to suit their own interests—thereby achieving what he calls *architectural advantage*.[20] Jacobides encourages firms to look broadly at their industry—to see their entire value chain and links with firms producing complementary goods and services. The key is then to identify "bottlenecks"—activities where scarcity and the potential for control offer superior opportunities for profit. Architectural advantages results from three sources:

- Creating one's own bottleneck: Apple's dominance of the music download market through iTunes is achieved through a digital rights management (DRM) strategy that effectively locks in consumers' through the incompatibility of its music files with other MP3 formats.
- Relieving bottlenecks in other parts of the value chain: Google developed Android to prevent other firms from gaining a bottleneck in operating systems for mobile devices which might have threatened Google's ability to transfer its dominance of search services from fixed to mobile devices.
- Redefining roles and responsibilities in the industries: IKEA's ability to become the world's biggest and most successful supplier of furniture was based upon a strategy which required a transfer of furniture assembly from furniture manufacturers to consumers.[21]

Positioning the Company

Recognizing and understanding the competitive forces that a firm faces within its industry allows managers to position the firm where competitive forces are weakest. The record industry, once reliant on sales of CDs, has been devastated by the substitute competition in the form of digital downloads, piracy, and file sharing. Yet not all segments of the recorded music business have been equally affected. The old are less inclined to turn to digital downloading than younger listeners are, with the result that classical music, country, and golden oldies have become comparatively more attractive than pop and hip hop genres.

Porter describes the success of US truck-maker Paccar in sheltering itself from the bargaining power of fleet buyers. By focusing on the preferences of independent owner-operators (e.g., by providing superior sleeping cabins, higher-specification seats, a roadside assistance program) Paccar has consistently been able to earn the higher rate of return in the industry.[22]

Effective positioning requires the firm to anticipate changes in the competitive forces likely to affect the industry. Traditional book retailing has been devastated by online retailers such as Amazon and e-books. The survivors are those that have positioned themselves to avoid these powerful competitive forces, for example by creating new revenue sources such as cafes and events for which admission is charged.

Defining Industries: Where to Draw the Boundaries

In our earlier discussion of the structure of the television broadcasting industry, I noted that a key challenge in industry analysis is defining the relevant industry. The Standard Industrial Classification (SIC) offers an official guide, but this provides limited practical assistance. Suppose Jaguar—the British-based luxury carmaker, now part of the Tata Group—is assessing its future prospects. In analyzing competition and forecasting industry profitability, should it consider itself part of the "motor vehicles and equipment" industry (SIC 371), the automobile industry (SIC 3712), or the luxury car industry? Should it view its industry as national (UK), regional (Europe), or global?

Industries and Markets

The first issue is clarifying what we mean by the term *industry*. Economists define an industry as a group of firms that supplies a market. Hence, a close correspondence exists between markets and industries. So, what's the difference between analyzing industry structure and analyzing market structure? The principal difference is that industry analysis, notably five forces analysis, looks at industry profitability being determined by competition in two markets: product markets and input markets.

Everyday usage makes a bigger distinction between industries and markets. Typically, *industries* are identified with relatively broad sectors, whereas *markets* are related to specific products. Thus, the firms within the packaging industry compete in many distinct product markets—glass containers, steel cans, aluminum cans, paper cartons, plastic containers, and so on.

Similar issues arise in relation to geographical boundaries. From an economist's viewpoint, the US automobile industry would denote all companies supplying the US auto market, irrespective of their location. In everyday usage, the term *US auto industry* typically refers to auto manufacturers located within the US (about 14 companies), and is often restricted to US-owned automakers (Ford and General Motors).

To identify and define an industry, it makes sense to start with the idea of a market: which firms compete to supply a particular product or service? At the outset, this approach may lead us to question conventional concepts of industry boundaries. For example, what is the industry commonly referred to as *banking*? Institutions called *banks* supply a number of different products and services each comprising different sets of competitors. The most basic distinction is between retail banking, corporate (and wholesale) banking, and investment banking. Each of these can be disaggregated into several different product markets. Retail banking comprises deposit taking, transaction services, credit cards, and mortgage lending. Investment banking includes corporate finance and underwriting, trading, and advisory services (such as mergers and acquisitions).

Defining Markets: Substitution in Demand and Supply

The central issue in defining industries is to establish who is competing with whom. To do this we need to draw upon the principle of *substitutability*. There are two dimensions to this: substitutability on the demand side and substitutability on the supply side.

Let us consider once more the market within which Jaguar competes. Starting with the demand side, are customers willing to substitute only between Jaguars and other luxury brands or are they willing to substitute between Jaguars and mass-market brands on the basis of price difference? If the former, Jaguar's relevant industry is the luxury car industry; if the latter, Jaguar is part of the auto industry. What about substitution between Jaguars and types of vehicle? If Jaguar customers are unwilling to substitute a Jaguar for a truck or a motorcycle on the basis of price, then Jaguar should not be viewed as part of the motor vehicles industry.

But this fails to take account of substitutability on the supply side. If manufacturers were able to switch their production from family sedans to luxury cars and if Jaguar could enter other parts of the automobile market, then, on the basis of supply-side substitutability, we could regard Jaguar as part of the broader automobile industry. The same logic can be used to define the major domestic appliances as an industry. Although consumers are unwilling to substitute between refrigerators and dishwashers, manufacturers can use the same manufacturing plants and distribution channels for different appliances.

The same considerations apply to geographical boundaries. Should Jaguar view itself as competing in a single global market or in a series of separate national or regional markets? The criterion here again is substitutability. If customers are willing and able to substitute cars available on different national markets, or if manufacturers are willing and able to divert their output among different countries to take account of differences in margins, then a market is global. The key test of the geographical boundaries of a market is price: if price differences for the same product between different locations tend to be eroded by demand-side and supply-side substitution, then these locations lie within a single market.

In practice, drawing the boundaries of markets and industries is a matter of judgment that depends on the purposes and context of the analysis. If Tata is considering the pricing and market positioning of its Jaguar cars, it must take a micro-level approach that defines markets in terms of individual models and individual countries. In considering decisions over investments in technology, component plants, and new products, Tata will view Jaguar as competing in the global automobile industry. The longer term are the decisions being considered, the more broadly should we define the relevant industry—substitutability is higher in the long run than in the short term.

Second, the boundaries of a market or industry are seldom clear-cut. The market in which an offering competes is a continuum rather than a bounded space. Thus, we may view the competitive market of Disneyland, Anaheim as a set of concentric circles. The closest competitor is Universal Studios Tour. Slightly more distant are Sea World and Six Flags. Further still might be a trip to Las Vegas, or a skiing weekend. Beyond these would be the broader leisure market that might include cinemas, beach vacations, and video games.

For the purposes of applying the five forces framework, industry definition is seldom critical. We define an industry "box" within which industry rivals compete, but because we include competitive forces outside the industry box, notably entrants and substitutes, the precise boundaries of the industry box are not greatly important. If we define Disneyland as competing within the broad entertainment industry, then beach and ski resorts are rivals; if we define Disneyland as competing in the theme park industry, then beach and ski resorts are substitutes.[23]

From Industry Attractiveness to Competitive Advantage: Identifying Key Success Factors

The five forces framework allows us to determine an industry's potential for profit. But how is industry profit shared between the different firms competing in that industry? Let us look explicitly at the sources of competitive advantage within an industry. In subsequent chapters I shall develop a more comprehensive analysis of competitive advantage. My goal in this chapter is to see how we can identify the factors within the industry environment that influence a firm's ability to outperform rivals—the industry's *key success factors*.[24] In Strategy Capsule 3.3, Kenichi Ohmae, former head of McKinsey's Tokyo office, discusses key success factors in forestry and their link with strategy.

Like Ohmae, our approach to identifying key success factors is straightforward and commonsense. To survive and prosper in an industry, a firm must meet two criteria: first, it must supply what customers want to buy; second, it must survive competition. Hence, we may start by asking two questions:

- What do our customers want?
- What does the firm need to do to survive competition?

To answer the first question we need to look more closely at customers of the industry and to view them not as a source of buying power and a threat to profitability but as the *raison d'être* of the industry and its underlying source of profit. This requires that we inquire: Who are our customers? What are their needs? How do they choose between competing offerings? Once we recognize the basis upon which customers' choose between rival offerings, we can identify the factors that confer success upon the individual firm. For example, if travelers choose airlines primarily on price, then cost efficiency is the primary basis for competitive advantage in the airline industry and the key success factors are the determinants of relative cost.

The second question requires that we examine the nature of competition in the industry. How intense is competition and what are its key dimensions? Thus, in airlines, it is not enough to offer low fares. To survive intense competition during recessionary periods an airline requires financial strength; it may also require good relations with regulators and government.

A basic framework for identifying key success factors is presented in Figure 3.5. Application of the framework to identify key success factors in three industries is outlined in Table 3.3.

Key success factors can also be identified through the direct modeling of profitability. In the same way that the five forces analysis models the determinants of industry-level profitability, we can also model firm-level profitability by identifying the drivers of a firm's relative profitability within an industry. Using the same approach as in Chapter 2 (Figures 2.1 and 2.3), we can disaggregate return on capital employed into component ratios, which then point to the main drivers of superior profitability. Figure 3.6 applies this analysis to identifying success factors in retailing.

In some industries, there are well-known formulae that link operating ratios to overall profitability. Strategy Capsule 3.4 uses such a formula used in the airline industry to identify key success factors.

STRATEGY CAPSULE 3.3
Probing for Key Success Factors

As a consultant faced with an unfamiliar business or industry, I make a point of first asking the specialists in the business, "What is the secret of success in this industry?" Needless to say, I seldom get an immediate answer and so I pursue the inquiry by asking other questions from a variety of angles in order to establish as quickly as possible some reasonable hypotheses as to key factors for success. In the course of these interviews it usually becomes quite obvious what analyses will be required in order to prove or disprove these hypotheses. By first identifying the probable key factors for success and then screening them by proof or disproof, it is often possible for the strategist to penetrate very quickly to the core of a problem.

Traveling in the US last year, I found myself on one occasion sitting in a plane next to a director of one of the biggest lumber companies in the country. Thinking I might learn something useful in the course of the five-hour flight, I asked him, "What are the key factors for success in the lumber industry?" To my surprise, his reply was immediate: "Owning large forests and maximizing the yield from them." The first of these key factors is a relatively simple matter: purchase of forestland. But his second point required further explanation. Accordingly, my next question was: "What variable or variables do you control in order to maximize the yield from a given tract?"

He replied: "The rate of tree growth is the key variable. As a rule, two factors promote growth: the amount of sunshine and the amount of water. Our company doesn't have many forests with enough of both. In Arizona and Utah, for example, we get more than enough sunshine but too little water and so tree growth is very low. Now, if we could give the trees in those states enough water, they'd be ready in less than 15 years instead of the 30 it takes now. The most important project we have in hand at the moment is aimed at finding out how to do this."

Impressed that this director knew how to work out a key factor strategy for his business, I offered my own contribution: "Then under the opposite conditions, where there is plenty of water but too little sunshine—for example, around the lower reaches of the Columbia River—the key factors should be fertilizers to speed up the growth and the choice of tree varieties that don't need so much sunshine."

Having established in a few minutes the general framework of what we were going to talk about, I spent the rest of the long flight very profitably hearing from him in detail how each of these factors was being applied.

Source: Kenichi Ohmae, *The Mind of the Strategist* (New York: McGraw-Hill, 1982): 85 © The McGraw-Hill Companies Inc., reproduced with permission.

In their battle for survival, the airlines have sought to optimize as many of these factors as possible in order to improve their profitability. To enhance revenue, several airlines have withdrawn from their most intensely competitive routes; others have sought to achieve a fare premium over the cut-price airlines through superior punctuality, convenience, comfort, and services. To improve load factors, companies have become more flexible in their pricing and in allocating different planes to different routes. Most notably, companies have sought to cut costs by increasing employee productivity, reducing overheads, sharing services with other airlines, and reducing salaries and benefits.

FIGURE 3.5   Identifying key success factors

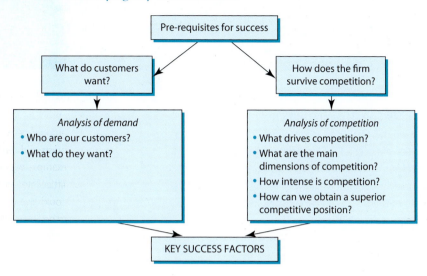

TABLE 3.3   Identifying key success factors: Steel, fashion clothing, and supermarkets

	What do customers want? (Analysis of demand)	**How do firms survive competition? (Analysis of competition)**	**Key success factors**
Steel	Low price Product consistency Reliability of supply Technical specifications (for special steels)	Commodity products, excess capacity, high fixed costs, excess capacity, exit barriers, and substitute competition mean intense price competition and cyclical profitability Cost efficiency and financial strength are essential	Cost efficiency requires: large-scale plants, low-cost location, rapid capacity adjustment Alternatively, high-technology, small-scale plants can achieve low costs through flexibility and high productivity Differentiation through technical specifications and service quality
Fashion clothing	Diversity of customer preferences Customers willing to pay premium for brand, style, exclusivity, and quality Mass market is highly price sensitive	Low barriers to entry and exit, low seller concentration, and buying power of retail chains imply intense competition Differentiation offers price premium, but imitation is rapid	Combining differentiation with low costs Differentiation based upon style, reputation, quality, and speed of response to changing fashions Cost efficiency requires manufacture in low-wage countries
Supermarkets	Low prices Convenient location Wide product range adapted to local preferences Fresh/quality produce, good service, ease of parking, pleasant ambience	Intensity competition depends on number and proximity of competitors Bargaining power a key determinant of cost of bought-in goods	Low costs require operational efficiency, large-scale purchases, low wages Differentiation requires large stores (to allow wide product range), convenient location, familiarity with local customer preferences

STRATEGY CAPSULE 3.4

Identifying Key Success Factors by Modeling Profitability: Airlines

Profitability, as measured by operating income per available seat-mile (ASM), is determined by three factors: yield, which is total operating revenues divided by the number of revenue passenger miles (RPMs); load factor, which is the ratio of RPMs to ASMs; and unit cost, which is total operating expenses divided by ASMs. Thus:

$$\frac{\text{Profit}}{\text{ASMs}} = \frac{\text{Revenue}}{\text{RPMs}} \times \frac{\text{RPMs}}{\text{ASMs}} - \frac{\text{Expenses}}{\text{ASMs}}$$

Some of the main determinants of each of these component ratios are the following:

◆ Revenue/RPMs

- intensity of competition on routes flown
- effective yield management to permit quick price adjustment to changing market conditions
- ability to attract business customers
- superior customer service.

◆ Load factor (RPMs/ASMs)

- competitiveness of prices
- efficiency of route planning (e.g., through hub-and-spoke systems)
- building customer loyalty through quality of service, frequent-flier programs
- matching airplane size to demand for individual flights.

◆ Expenses/ASMs

- wage rates and benefit levels
- fuel efficiency of aircraft
- productivity of employees (determined partly by their job flexibility)
- load factors
- level of administrative cost.

FIGURE 3.6 Identifying key success factors through analyzing profit drivers: The case of retailing

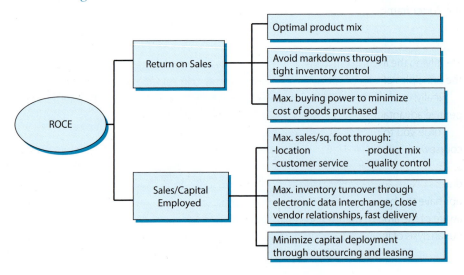

The usefulness of industry-level success factors in formulating strategy has been scorned by some strategy scholars. Pankaj Ghemawat observes that the "whole idea of identifying a success factor and then chasing it seems to have something in common with the ill-considered medieval hunt for the philosopher's stone, a substance that would transmute everything it touched into gold."[25] However, the existence of common success factors in an industry does not imply that firms should adopt similar strategies. In the fashion clothing business we identified a number of key success factors (Table 3.3), yet all the leading companies—Inditex (Zara), H&M, Diesel, and Mango—have adopted unique strategies to exploit these key success factors.

Summary

In Chapter 1 we established that a profound understanding of the competitive environment is a critical ingredient of a successful strategy. Despite the vast number of external influences that affect every business enterprise, our focus is the firm's industry environment which we analyze in order to evaluate the industry's profit potential and to identify the sources of competitive advantage.

The centerpiece of our approach is Porter's five forces of competition framework, which links the structure of an industry to the competitive intensity within it and to the profitability that it realizes. The Porter framework offers a simple yet powerful organizing framework for identifying the relevant features of an industry's structure and predicting their implications for competitive behavior.

The primary application for the Porter five forces framework is in predicting how changes in an industry's structure are likely to affect its profitability. Once we understand the drivers of industry profitability, we can identify strategies through which a firm can improve industry attractiveness and position itself in relation to these different competitive forces.

As with most of the tools for strategy analysis that we shall consider in this book, the Porter five forces framework is easy to comprehend. However, real learning about industry analysis and about the Porter framework in particular derives from its application. It is only when we apply the Porter framework to analyzing competition and diagnosing the causes of high or low profitability in an industry that we are forced to confront the complexities and subtleties of the model. A key issue is identifying the industry within which a firm competes and recognizing its boundaries. By employing the principles of substitutability and relevance, we can delineate meaningful industry boundaries.

Finally, our industry analysis allows us to make a first approach at identifying the sources of competitive advantage through recognizing key success factors in an industry.

I urge you to put the tools of industry analysis to work—not just in your strategic management coursework but also in interpreting everyday business events. The value of the Porter framework is as a practical tool—in helping us to understand the huge disparity in performance between the producers of airplanes and the airlines that fly them; in allowing us to predict which e-commerce start-ups have the best potential for making money. Through practical applications, you will also become aware of the limitations of the Porter framework. In the next chapter we will see how we can extend our analysis of industry and competition.

Quizzes and flashcards to test yourself further are available in your interactive e-book at **www.wileyopenpage.com**

Self-Study Questions

1. From Table 3.1, select a high-profit industry and a low-profit industry. From what you know of the structure of your selected industry, use the five forces framework to explain why profitability has been high in one industry and low in the other.

2. With reference to Strategy Capsule 3.1, use the five forces framework to explain why profitability has been so high in the US market for smokeless tobacco.

3. The major forces shaping the business environment of the fixed-line telecom industry are technology and government policy. The industry has been influenced by fiber optics (greatly increasing transmission capacity), new modes of telecommunication (wireless and internet telephony), deregulation, and privatization. Using the five forces of competition framework, show how each of these developments has influenced competition in the fixed-line telecom industry.

4. The leading companies in the online travel agency industry are Expedia, Travelocity (which owns Lastminute.com), Orbitz, Priceline, Cheaptickets and a host of others. The online agents compete both with traditional travel agents (American Express, Thomas Cook, Carlson) and direct online sales by airlines, cruise lines and car rental companies. Their biggest business is selling airline tickets, where they employ the services of computerized airline reservation systems such as Sabre, Amadeus, Worldspan and Galileo. Use Porter's five forces framework to predict the likely profitability of the online travel agency industry over the next ten years.

5. Wal-Mart (like Carrefour, Ahold, and Metro) competes in several countries of the world, yet most shoppers choose between retailers within a radius of a few miles. For the purposes of analyzing profitability and competitive strategy, should Wal-Mart consider the discount retailing industry to be global, national, or local?

6. What do you think are key success factors in:

   a. the pizza delivery industry?
   b. the credit card industry (where the world's biggest issuers are: Bank of America, JPMorgan Chase, Citigroup, American Express, Capital One, HSBC, and Discover)?

Notes

1. M. E. Porter, "The Five Competitive Forces that Shape Strategy," *Harvard Business Review* 57 (January 2008): 57–71.

2. "Drink Up," *Barron's* (July 23, 2012); Juice & Smoothie Bars in the US: Market Research Report (IBIS World, February 2012).

3. W. J. Baumol, J. C. Panzar, and R. D. Willig, *Contestable Markets and the Theory of Industry Structure* (New York: Harcourt Brace Jovanovich, 1982). See also M. Spence, "Contestable Markets and the Theory of Industry Structure: A Review Article," *Journal of Economic Literature* 21 (1983): 981–90.

4. "Annual Franchise 500," *Entrepreneur* (January 2009).

5. "Brand Loyalty is Rarely Blind Loyalty," *Wall Street Journal* (October 19, 1989): B1.

6. R. D. Buzzell and P. W. Farris, "Marketing Costs in Consumer Goods Industries," in H. Thorelli (ed.), *Strategy + Structure = Performance* (Bloomington, IN: Indiana University Press, 1977): 128–9.

7. In October 1999, the Department of Justice alleged that American Airlines was using unfair means in attempting to monopolize air traffic out of Dallas/Fort Worth, http://www.aeroworldnet.com/1tw05179.htm, accessed July 2, 2009.

8. M. Lieberman ("Excess Capacity as a Barrier to Entry," *Journal of Industrial Economics* 35, 1987: 607–27) argues that, to be credible, the threat of retaliation needs to be supported by incumbents investing in excess capacity so that they have the potential to flood the market.

9. See, for example, J. S. Bain, *Barriers to New Competition* (Cambridge, MA: Harvard University Press, 1956); and H. M. Mann, "Seller Concentration, Entry Barriers, and Rates of Return in Thirty Industries," *Review of Economics and Statistics* 48 (1966): 296–307.

10. J. L. Siegfried and L. B. Evans, "Empirical Studies of Entry and Exit: A Survey of the Evidence," *Review of Industrial Organization* 9 (1994): 121–55.

11. G. S. Yip, "Gateways to Entry," *Harvard Business Review* 60 (September/October1982): 85–93.

12. F. M. Scherer and D. R. Ross, *Industrial Market Structure and Economic Performance*, 3rd edn (Boston: Houghton Mifflin, 1990).

13. R. Schmalensee, "Inter-Industry Studies of Structure and Performance," in R. Schmalensee and R. D. Willig (eds), *Handbook of Industrial Organization*, 2nd edn (Amsterdam: North Holland, 1988): 976. See also M. A. Salinger, "The Concentration-Margins Relationship Reconsidered," *Brookings Papers: Microeconomics* (1990): 287–335.

14. C. Baden-Fuller (ed.), *Strategic Management of Excess Capacity* (Oxford: Basil Blackwell, 1990).

15. "Dry bulk shipping rates approach all-time low," *Financial Times* (November 27, 2008).

16. T. Kelly and M. L. Gosman, "Increased Buyer Concentration and its Effects on Profitability in the Manufacturing Sector," *Review of Industrial Organization* 17 (2000): 41–59.

17. R. D. Buzzell and B. T. Gale, *The PIMS Principles* (New York: Free Press, 1987): 67.

18. J. Bower, *When Markets Quake* (Boston: Harvard Business School Press, 1986).

19. M. Carnall, S. Berry, and P. Spiller, "Airline Hubbing, Costs and Demand," in D. Lee (ed.), *Advances in Airline Economics*, vol. 1 (Amsterdam: Elsevier, 2006).

20. M. G. Jacobides, "Creating and Capturing Value: From Innovation to Architectural Advantage,"*Business Insight* (London Business School, September 2008).

21. M. G. Jacobides, "Strategy Bottlenecks," *Capgemini Telecom and Media Insights* 63 (2010), www.capgemini.com/m/en/tl/Strategy_Bottlenecks.pdf, accessed December 17, 2011.

22. M. E. Porter, "The Five Competitive Forces that Shape Strategy," *Harvard Business Review* 57 (January 2008): 57–71.

23. For a concise discussion of market definition see Office of Fair Trading, *Market Definition* (London: December 2004), especially pp. 7–17.

24. The term was coined by Chuck Hofer and Dan Schendel (*Strategy Formulation: Analytical Concepts*, St Paul: West Publishing, 1977: 77). They define key success factors as "those variables that management can influence through its decisions and that can affect significantly the overall competitive positions of the firms in an industry."

25. P. Ghemawat, *Commitment: The Dynamic of Strategy* (New York: Free Press, 1991): 11.

4 Further Topics in Industry and Competitive Analysis

Economic progress, in capitalist society, means turmoil.

—JOSEPH A. SCHUMPETER, AUSTRIAN ECONOMIST, 1883–1950

OUTLINE

Introduction and Objectives

Last chapter was concerned with outlining Porter's five forces framework and showing how it can be applied to analyzing competition, predicting industry profitability, and developing strategy. The Porter framework is one of the most useful and widely applied tools of strategic analysis. It also has its limitations. In this chapter, we shall extend our analysis of industry and competition beyond the limits of the Porter framework.

By the time you have completed this chapter, you will be able to:

◆ recognize the limits of the Porter five forces framework, and extend the framework to include the role of complements as well as substitutes;

◆ recognize competition as a dynamic, even hypercompetitive, process, appreciate the insights that game theory offers into the dynamics of rivalry, and use competitor analysis to predict the competitive moves by rivals;

◆ segment an industry into its constituent markets, appraise the relative attractiveness of different segments and apply strategic group analysis to classify firms according to their strategic types.

Extending the Five Forces Framework

Does Industry Matter?

Porter's five forces of competition framework has been subject to two main attacks. Some have criticized its theoretical foundations, arguing that the "structure–conduct–performance" approach to industrial organization that underlies it lacks rigor (especially when compared with the logical robustness of game theory). Others have noted its empirical weaknesses. It appears that industry environment is a relatively minor determinant of a firm's profitability. Studies of the sources of interfirm differences in profitability have produced very different results (Table 4.1), but all acknowledge that industry factors account for a minor part (less than 20%) of variation in return on assets among firms.

Do these findings imply that industry doesn't matter and we relegate the analysis of industry and competition to a minor role in our strategic analysis? Let me offer a few thoughts.

We need to acknowledge that profitability differences within industries are greater than profitability differences between industries. In Table 3.1, the difference in return on equity (ROE) between the most and least profitable industries was 45 percentage points; yet, in computer and electronic equipment the spread in ROE between Apple and Hewlett-Packard was 131 percentage points, while in forest and paper products, the spread between Domtar and International Paper was 98 percentage points.[1]

TABLE 4.1   How much does industry matter?

	Percentage of variance in firms' return on assets explained by:		
	Industry effects (%)	**Firm effects (%)**	**Unexplained variance (%)**
Schmalensee (1985)	19.6	0.6	79.9
Rumelt (1991)	4.0	44.2	44.8
McGahan and Porter (1997)	18.7	31.7	48.4
Hawawini *et al.* (2003)	8.1	35.8	52.0
Roquebert *et al.* (1996)	10.2	55.0	32.0
Misangyi *et al.* (2006)	7.6	43.8	n.a.

Note: "Firm effects" combine business unit and corporate effects. The rows do not sum to 100% because other sources of variance are not reported.

Sources: R. Schmalensee, "Do markets differ much?" *American Economic Review* 75 (1985): 341–51; R. P. Rumelt, "How much does industry matter?" *Strategic Management Journal* 12 (1991): 167–85; A. M. McGahan and M. E. Porter, "How much does industry matter, really?" *Strategic Management Journal* 18 (1997): 15–30; G. Hawawini, V. Subramanian, and P. Verdin, "Is Performance Driven by Industry or Firm-Specific Factors? A New Look at the Evidence," *Strategic Management Journal* 24 (2003): 1–16; J. A. Roquebert, R. L. Phillips, and P. A. Westfall, "Markets vs. Management: What 'Drives' Profitability?" *Strategic Management Journal* 17 (1996): 653–64; V. F. Misangyi, H. Elms, T. Greckhamer, and J. A. Lepine, "A New Perspective on a Fundamental Debate: A Multilevel Approach to Industry, Corporate and Business Unit Effects," *Strategic Management Journal* 27 (2006): 571–90.

However, the usefulness of industry analysis is not conditional upon the relative importance of inter-industry and intra-industry profitability differences. Industry analysis is important because, without a deep understanding of their competitive environment, firms cannot make sound strategic decisions. Industry analysis is not relevant just to choosing which industries to locate within, as Michael Jacobides' concept of "architectural advantage" reveals, industry analysis is also important for establishing competitive advantage within an industry.

If our industry analysis is to fulfill this promise, it needs to go beyond the confines of the Porter five forces framework. We need to go further in understanding the determinants of competitive behavior between companies, in particular using more rigorous approaches to analyze the relationship between market structure and competition. We need to disaggregate broad industry sectors to examine competition within particular segments and among particular groups of firms. But let's begin by considering the potential to extend the Porter framework.

Complements: A Missing Force in the Porter Model?

The Porter framework identifies the suppliers of substitute goods and services as one of the forces of competition that reduces the profit available to firms within an industry. However, economic theory identifies two types of relationship between different products: *substitutes* and *complements*. While the presence of substitutes reduces the value of a product, complements increase its value: without ink cartridges my printer has very little value to me.

Given the importance of complements to most products—the value of my car depends on the availability of gasoline, insurance, and repair services; the value of

FIGURE 4.1 Five forces, or six?

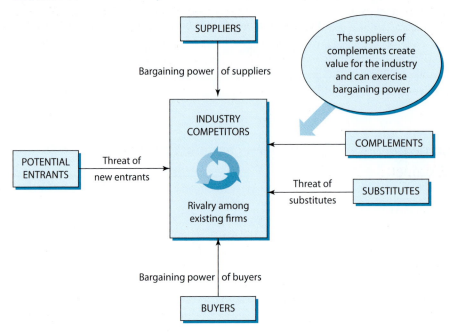

my razor depends upon the supply of blades and shaving foam—our analysis of the competitive environment needs to take them into account. The simplest way is to add a sixth force to Porter's framework (Figure 4.1).[2]

Complements have the opposite effect to substitutes. While substitutes reduce the value of an industry's product, complements increase it. Indeed, where products are close complements (as with my printer and ink cartridges), they have little or no value in isolation: customers value the whole system. But how is the value shared between the producers of the different complementary products? Bargaining power, and its deployment, is the key. During the early 1990s, Nintendo earned huge profits from its video game consoles. Although most of the revenue and consumer value was in the software, mostly supplied by independent developers, Nintendo was able to appropriate most of the profit potential of the entire system through establishing dominance over the games developers. Nintendo used its leadership in the console market and ownership of the console operating system to enforce restrictive developer licenses to software producers of games, and maintained tight control over the manufacture and distribution of games cartridges (from which Nintendo earned a hefty royalty).[3]

A similar hardware/software complementarity exists in personal computers—but here power has lain with the software suppliers—Microsoft in particular. IBM's adoption of open architecture meant that Microsoft Windows became a proprietary standard, while PCs were gradually reduced to commodity status. This is a very different situation from video games, where hardware suppliers keep proprietary control over their operating systems.

Where two products complement one another, profit will accrue to the supplier that builds the stronger market position and reduces the value contributed by the other. How is this done? The key is to achieve monopolization, differentiation, and shortage of supply in one's own product, while encouraging competition, commoditization, and excess capacity in the production of the complementary product. This is the same principle of creating a *bottleneck* that we discussed in the last chapter. In the PC sector, the hardware companies have sought to counteract the dominance of the software companies, especially Microsoft, by supporting the development of open-source software. IBM has been a major supporter of Linux;[4] Sun Microsystems is a key backer of Mozilla (which offers the Firefox browser).

Dynamic Competition: Hypercompetition, Game Theory, and Competitor Analysis

Hypercompetition

The Porter five forces framework is based upon the assumption that industry structure determines competitive behavior, which in turn determines industry profitability. But couldn't the relationships flow in the opposite direction: the quest for profit unleashes the competitive forces of innovation and entrepreneurship that transform industry structures? Joseph Schumpeter viewed competition as a "perennial gale of creative destruction" in which market-dominating incumbents are challenged, and often unseated, by rivals that deploy innovatory products and innovatory strategies.[5]

This view of Schumpeter (and the "Austrian school" of economics) that competition is a dynamic process in which industry structure is constantly changing raises the issue of whether competitive behavior should be seen as an outcome of industry structure or a determinant of industry structure.[6] The issue is the speed of structural change in the industry—if structural transformation is rapid, then the five forces framework does not offer a stable basis on which to predict competition and profitability.

In most industries, Schumpeter's process of "creative destruction" tends to be more of a breeze than a gale. In established industries entry occurs so slowly that profits are undermined only gradually,[7] while changes in industrial concentration tend to be slow.[8] One survey observed: "the picture of the competitive process . . . is, to say the least, sluggish in the extreme."[9] As a result, both at the firm and the industry level, profits tend to be highly persistent in the long run.[10]

But what about recent trends? Has accelerating technological change and intensifying international competition reinforced the processes of "creative destruction"? Rich D'Aveni argues that a general feature of industries today is **hypercompetition**: "intense and rapid competitive moves, in which competitors must move quickly to build [new] advantages and erode the advantages of their rivals."[11] If industries are hypercompetitive, their structures are likely to be less stable than in the past, superior profitability will tend to be transitory, and the only route to sustained superior performance is through continually recreating and renewing competitive advantage—we are experiencing an "age of temporary advantage."[12]

Despite the plausibility of this thesis and everyday observations that markets are becoming more volatile and market leadership more tenuous, systematic evidence of this trend is ambiguous. One large-scale statistical study concludes: "The heterogeneity and volatility of competitive advantage in US manufacturing industries has steadily and astonishingly increased since 1950. Industry structures are destabilizing.

These results suggest that a shift towards hypercompetition has indeed occurred."[13] Another study found that increased volatility was a feature not only of technology-intensive industries but also extended beyond manufacturing industries.[14] However, another study found a "lack of widespread evidence . . . that markets are more unstable now than in the recent past."[15]

The Contribution of Game Theory

Central to the criticisms of Porter's five forces as a static framework is its failure to take full account of competitive interactions among firms. In Chapter 1, we noted that the essence of strategic competition is the interaction among players, such that the decisions made by any one player are dependent on the actual and anticipated decisions of the other players. By relegating competition to a mediating variable that links industry structure with profitability, the five forces analysis offers little insight into competition as a process of interactive decision making by rival firms. Game theory allows us to model this competitive interaction. In particular, it offers two especially valuable contributions to strategic management:

- It permits the framing of strategic decisions. Apart from any theoretical value of the theory of games, game theory provides a structure, a set of concepts, and a terminology that allows us to describe and understand a competitive situation in terms of:
  - identity of the players;
  - specification of each player's options;
  - specification of the payoffs from every combination of options;
  - the sequencing of decisions using game trees.
- It can predict the outcome of competitive situations and identify optimal strategic choices. Through the insight that it offers into situations of competition and bargaining, game theory can predict the equilibrium outcomes of competitive situations and the consequences of strategic moves by any one player. Game theory provides penetrating insights into central issues of strategy that go well beyond pure intuition. Simple game models (e.g., the **prisoners' dilemma**) predict cooperative versus competitive outcomes, whereas more complex games permit analysis of the effects of reputation,[16] deterrence,[17] information,[18] and commitment,[19] especially within the context of multi-period games. Particularly important for practicing managers, game theory can indicate strategies for improving the structure and outcome of the game through manipulating the payoffs to the different players.[20]

Game theory offers illuminating insights into a wide variety of competitive situations. These include the Cuban missile crisis of 1962,[21] rivalry between Boeing and Airbus,[22] NASCAR race tactics,[23] auctions of airwave spectrum,[24] the 2008 financial crisis,[25] and the reasons why evolution has conferred such magnificent tails upon male peacocks.[26] In terms of applications to competition among business enterprises, game theory points to five aspects of strategic behavior through which a firm can improve its competitive outcomes: *cooperation, deterrence, commitment, changing the structure of the game being played*, and *signaling*.

Cooperation   One of the key merits of game theory is its ability to encompass both competition and cooperation. A key deficiency of the five forces framework is in viewing interfirm relations as exclusively competitive in nature. Central to Adam Brandenburger and Barry Nalebuff's concept of *co-opetition* is recognition of the competitive/cooperative duality of business relationships.[27] While some relationships are predominantly competitive (Coca-Cola and Pepsi) and others are predominantly cooperative (Intel and Microsoft), there is no simple dichotomy between competition and cooperation: all business relationships combine elements of both. For all their intense rivalry, Coca-Cola and Pepsi cooperate on multiple fronts, including common policies on sales of soda drinks within schools, environmental issues, and health concerns. They may also coordinate their pricing and product introductions.[28] Exxon and Shell have battled for over a century for leadership of the world's petroleum industry; at the same time they cooperate in a number of joint ventures. The desire of competitors to cluster together—antique dealers in London's Bermondsey Market or movie studios in Hollywood—points to the common interests of competing firms in growing the size of their market and developing its infrastructure.

In many business situations, competition results in inferior outcomes for participants than cooperation. The prisoners' dilemma game analyzes this predicament (Strategy Capsule 4.1).

Deterrence   As we saw in Strategy Capsule 4.1, one way of changing a game's equilibrium is through deterrence. The principle behind deterrence is to impose costs on the other players for actions deemed to be undesirable. By establishing the certainty that deserters would be shot, the British army provided a strong incentive to its troops to participate in advances on heavily fortified German trenches during the First World War.

The key to the effectiveness of any deterrent is that it must be credible. The problem here is that if administering the deterrent is costly or unpleasant for the threatening party, the deterrent is not credible. When King of Shaves (owned by KMI Ltd; annual sales $90 million) entered the UK razor market, Gillette might have threatened it with a price cut. But would such a threat have been credible? Once King of Shaves had entered, Gillette's dominant market share meant that a price cut would inflict more damage on itself than on its rivals.[29] Investing in excess capacity can be an effective means of discouraging entry. Prior to the expiration of its NutraSweet patents, Monsanto invested heavily in unneeded plant capacity to deter manufacturers of generic aspartame.[30] Conversely, in compact disks, the reluctance of the dominant firm (Philips) to invest heavily in new capacity to meet growing demand encouraged a wave of new entrants.[31]

Deterrence has provided a central theme in international relations. The nuclear arms race between the US and the then Soviet Union was based on the logic of "mutual assured destruction." However, the ability for deterrence to produce a stable, peaceful equilibrium depends on the willingness of the adversaries to be deterred. A central weakness of George W. Bush's "war on terror" was that ideologically motivated terrorists are not susceptible to deterrence.[32]

Commitment   For deterrence to be effective it must be credible, which means being backed by commitment. Commitment involves the elimination of strategic options: "binding an organization to a future course of action."[33] When Hernán Cortés destroyed his ships on arrival in Mexico in 1519, he communicated, both

STRATEGY CAPSULE 4.1

The Prisoners' Dilemma

The classic prisoners' dilemma game involves a pair of crime suspects who are arrested and interrogated separately. The dilemma is that each will rat on the other with the result that both end up in jail despite the fact that if both had remained silent they would have been released for lack of evidence.

The dilemma arises in almost all competitive situations—everyone could be better off with collusion. Consider competition between Coca-Cola and Pepsi in Ukraine, where each has the choice of spending big or small on advertising. Figure 4.2 shows the payoffs to each firm.

Clearly, the best solution for both firms is for them to each restrain their advertising expenditure (the upper left cell). However, in the absence of cooperation, the outcome for both firms is to adopt big budgets (the lower right cell)—the reason being that each will fear that any restraint will be countered by the rival seeking advantage by shifting to a big advertising budget. The resulting maxi-min choice of strategies (each company chooses the strategy that maximizes the minimum payoff) is a Nash equilibrium: no player can increase his/her payoff by a unilateral change in strategy. Even if collusion can be achieved, it will be unstable because of the incentives for cheating—a constant problem for OPEC, where the member countries agree quotas but then cheat on them.

How can a firm escape from such prisoners' dilemmas? One answer is to change a one-period game (single transaction) into a repeated game. In the above example of competition in advertising, a multi-period perspective allows the companies to recognize the futility of advertising campaigns that merely cancel one another out. In the case of supplier–buyer relations, where the typical equilibrium is a low-quality product at a low price, moving from a spot-transaction to a long-term vendor relationship gives the supplier the incentive to offer a better-quality product and the buyer to offer a price that reflects the preferred quality.

A second solution is to change the payoffs through deterrence. In the classic prisoners' dilemma, the Mafia shifts the equilibrium from the suspects both confessing to their both remaining silent by using draconian reprisals to enforce its "code of silence." Similarly, if both Coca-Cola and Pepsi were to threaten one another with aggressive price cuts should the other seek advantage through a big advertising budget, this could shift the equilibrium to the top-left cell.

FIGURE 4.2 Coca-Cola's and Pepsi's advertising budget: The prisoners' dilemma

COCA-COLA (Payoffs in $ millions)

		Small Advertising Budget	Big Advertising Budget
PEPSI	Small Advertising Budget	10 / 10	15 / −2
	Big Advertising Budget	−2 / 15	4 / 4

In each cell, the lower-left number is the payoff to Pepsi; the upper-right the payoff to Coke.

to Montezuma and his men, that there was no alternative to conquest of the Aztec empire. Once Airbus had decided to build its A380 superjumbo, it was critical to signal its commitment to the project. During 2000–2002, Airbus spent heavily on advertising the plane, even before completing the design phase, in order encourage airlines to place orders and discourage Boeing from developing a rival plane.

These commitments to aggressive competition can be described as *hard commitments*. A company may also make commitments that moderate competition; these are called *soft commitments*. For example, if a company commits to achieving certain target profit levels in the coming year, this would be a soft commitment: it would signal that, in the event of an aggressive initiative by a competitor, such as a price cut, the company would be more likely to accommodate that initiative rather than forego profitability by responding aggressively.

How different types of commitment affect a firm's profitability depend on the type of game being played. Where companies compete on price, game theory shows that they tend to match one another's price changes.[34] Hence, under price adjustments, hard commitments (such as a commitment to cut price) tend to have a negative profit impact and soft commitments (such as a commitment to raise prices) have a positive impact. Conversely, where companies compete on output, game theory shows that increases in output by one firm result in output reductions by the other.[35] Hence, under quantity adjustments, a hard commitment (e.g., a commitment to build new plants) will tend to have a positive effect on the committing firm's profitability because it will tend to be met by other firms reducing their output.[36]

Changing the Structure of the Game Creative strategies can change the structure of the competitive game. A company may seek to change the structure of the industry within which it is competing in order to increase the profit potential of the industry or to appropriate a greater share of the available profit. Thus, establishing alliances and agreements with competitors can increase the value of the game by increasing the size of the market and building joint strength against possible entrants. There may be many opportunities for converting win–lose (or even lose–lose) games into win–win games. A cooperative solution was found to the 1997 bidding war between Norfolk Southern and CSX for control of Conrail, for example. The bidding war was terminated when the two firms agreed to cooperate in acquiring and dismembering Conrail.[37]

In some cases, it may be advantageous for a firm to create competition for itself. By offering second-sourcing licenses to AMD, Intel gave up its potential monopoly over its x86 microprocessors. Although Intel was creating competition for itself, it also encouraged the adoption of the x86 chip by computer manufacturers (including IBM) who were concerned about overdependence on Intel. As we shall see in Chapter 9, standards battles often involve the deliberate sacrificing of potential monopoly positions by the main contestants.

Signaling Competitive reactions depend on how the competitor perceives its rival's initiative. The term *signaling* is used to describe the selective communication of information to competitors (or customers) designed to influence their perceptions and hence provoke or suppress certain types of reaction.[38] The use of misinformation is well developed in military intelligence. Ben McIntyre's book *Operation Mincemeat* describes how British Military Intelligence used a corpse dressed as a marine officer and carrying fake secret documents to convince German high command that the Allied landings would be in Greece, not Sicily.[39]

The credibility of threats is critically dependent on reputation.[40] Even though carrying out threats against rivals is costly and depresses short-term profitability, exercising such threats can build a reputation for aggressiveness that deters competitors in the future. The benefits of building a reputation for aggressiveness may be particularly great for diversified companies where reputation can be transferred from one market to another.[41] Hence, Procter & Gamble's protracted market share wars in disposable diapers and household detergents have established a reputation for toughness that protects it from competitive attacks in other markets.

Signaling may also be used to communicate a desire to cooperate. Price announcements can facilitate collusive pricing among firms.[42]

Is Game Theory Useful?

The value of game theory to strategic management has generated lively debate. For economists this seems paradoxical—to them game theory *is* the theory of strategy. The great virtue of game theory is its rigor. In microeconomics, the game theory revolution of the past 40 years has established the analysis of markets and firm behavior on a much more secure theoretical foundation.

However, the price of mathematical rigor has been limited applicability to real-world situations. Game theory provides clear predictions in highly stylized situations involving few external variables and restrictive assumptions. The result is a mathematically sophisticated body of theory that suffers from unrealistic assumptions, lack of generality, and an analysis of dynamic situations through a sequence of static equilibriums. When applied to more complex (and more realistic) situations, game theory frequently results in either no equilibrium or multiple equilibriums, and outcomes that are highly sensitive to small changes in initial assumptions. Overall, game theory has not developed to the point where it permits us to model real business situations in a level of detail that can generate precise predictions.[43]

In its empirical applications, game theory does a better job of explaining the past than of predicting the future. In diagnosing Nintendo's domination of the video games industry in the 1980s, Monsanto's efforts to prolong NutraSweet's market leadership beyond the expiration of its patents, or Airbus's wresting of market leadership from Boeing, game theory provides penetrating insight into the competitive situation and deep understanding of the rationale behind the strategies deployed. However, in predicting outcomes and designing strategies, game theory has been much less impressive—the use of game theory by US and European governments to design auctions for wireless spectrum has produced some undesirable and unforeseen results.[44]

So, where can game theory assist us in designing successful strategies? As with all our theories and frameworks, game theory is useful not because it gives us answers but because it can help us understand business situations. Game theory provides a set of tools that allows us to structure our view of competitive interaction. By identifying the players in a game, the decision choices available to each, and the implications of each combination of decisions, we have a systematic framework for exploring the dynamics of competition. Most importantly, by describing the structure of the game we are playing, we have a basis for suggesting ways of changing the game and thinking through the likely outcomes of such changes.

Game theory continues its rapid development and, although it is still a long way from providing the central theoretical foundation for strategic management, we draw upon it in several places in this book, especially in exploring competitive dynamics in highly concentrated markets. However, our emphasis in strategy formulation will be less on achieving advantage through influencing the behavior of competitors and much more on transforming competitive games through building positions of unilateral competitive advantage. The competitive market situations with which we shall be dealing will, for the most part, be different from those considered by game theory. Game theory typically deals with competitive situations with closely matched players where each has a similar range of strategic options (typically relating to price changes, advertising budgets, capacity decisions, and new product introductions). The outcome of these games is highly dependent on the order of moves, signals, bluffs, and threats. Our emphasis will be less on managing competitive interactions and more on establishing competitive advantage through exploiting uniqueness.

Competitor Analysis and Competitive Intelligence

In highly concentrated industries, the dominant feature of a company's competitive environment is likely to be the behavior of its closest rivals. In household detergents, Unilever's industry environment is dominated by the strategy of Procter & Gamble. The same is true in soft drinks (Coca-Cola and Pepsi), jet engines (GE, United Technologies, and Rolls-Royce), and financial information (Bloomberg and Reuters). Similar circumstances are common in local markets: the competitive environment of my local Costa coffee shop is dominated by the presence of Starbucks across the road. Game theory provides a theoretical apparatus for analyzing competitive inter-action between small numbers of rivals but, for everyday business situations, a less formal and more empirically based approach to predicting competitors' behavior may be more useful. Let us examine how information about competitors can help us to predict their behavior.

Competitive Intelligence   Competitive intelligence involves the systematic collection and analysis of information about rivals for informing decision making. It has three main purposes:

- to forecast competitors' future strategies and decisions;
- to predict competitors' likely reactions to a firm's strategic initiatives;
- to determine how competitors' behavior can be influenced to make it more favorable.

For all three purposes, the key requirement is to understand competitors in order to predict their responses to environmental changes and our own competitive moves. To understand competitors, it is important to be informed about them. Competitive intelligence is a growth field, with specialist consulting firms, professional associations,[45] and a flood of recent books.[46] About one-quarter of large US corporations have specialist competitive intelligence units.

The boundary between legitimate competitive intelligence and illegal industrial espionage is not always clear. The distinction between public and private information is uncertain and the law relating to trade secrets is much less precise than that which covers patents and copyrights. Well-publicized cases of information theft include the $100 million fine levied on the McLaren Mercedes Formula One team for possessing confidential technical information belonging to Ferrari and the theft by Kolon Industries of South Korea of trade secrets concerning the production of DuPont's Kevlar fiber.[47] More generally, the US National Counterintelligence Executive has alleged systematic industrial espionage by the China and Russia.[48]

A Framework for Predicting Competitor Behavior   Competitive intelligence is not simply about collecting information. The problem is likely to be too much rather than too little information. The key is a systematic approach that makes it clear what information is required and for what purposes it will be used. The objective is to understand one's rival. A characteristic of great generals from Hannibal to Patton has been their ability to go beyond military intelligence and to "get inside the heads" of their opposing commanders. Michael Porter proposes a four-part framework for predicting competitor behavior (Figure 4.3).

- *Competitor's current strategy*: To predict how a rival will behave in the future, we must understand how that rival is competing at present. As we noted in Chapter 1, identifying a firm's strategy requires looking at what the company says and what it does (see "Where Do We Find Strategy?" in Chapter 1). The key is to link the content of top management communication (with investors, the media, and financial analysts) with the evidence of strategic actions, particularly those that involve a commitment of resources. For both sources of information, company websites are invaluable.
- *Competitor's objectives*: To forecast how a competitor might change its strategy, we must identify its goals. A key issue is whether a company is driven by financial goals or market goals. A company whose primary goal is attaining

FIGURE 4.3   A framework for competitor analysis

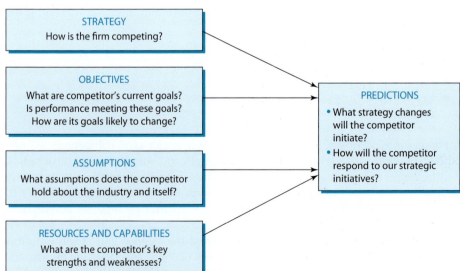

market share is likely to be much more aggressive a competitor than one that is mainly interested in profitability. The willingness of the US automobile and consumer electronics producers to cede market share to Japanese competitors was partly a result of their preoccupation with short-term profitability. By comparison, companies like Procter & Gamble and Coca-Cola are obsessed with market share and tend to react aggressively when rivals step on their turf. The most difficult competitors can be those that are not subject to profit disciplines at all—state-owned enterprises in particular. The level of current performance in relation to the competitor's objectives determines the likelihood of strategy change. The more a company is satisfied with present performance, the more likely it is to continue with its present strategy. But if performance is falling well short of target, radical strategic change, possibly accompanied by a change in top management, is likely.

- *Competitor's assumptions about the industry*: A competitor's strategic decisions are conditioned by its perceptions of itself and its environment. These perceptions are guided by the beliefs that senior managers hold about their industry and the success factors within it. Evidence suggests that not only do these systems of belief tend to be stable over time but they also tend to converge among the firms within an industry: what J.-C. Spender refers to as "industry recipes."[49] Industry recipes may engender "blindspots" that limit the capacity of a firm—even an entire industry—to respond to an external threat. During the 1960s, the Big Three US automobile manufacturers firmly believed that small cars were unprofitable. This belief was partly a product of their overhead allocation procedures. The result was a willingness to yield the fastest-growing segment of the US automobile market to imports. The complacency of British and US motorcycle manufacturers in the face of Japanese competition reflected similar beliefs (Strategy Capsule 4.2).

- *Competitor's resources and capabilities*: Evaluating the likelihood and seriousness of a competitor's potential challenge requires assessing the strength of that competitor's resources and capabilities. If our rival has a massive cash pile, it would be unwise for our company to unleash a price war by initiating price cuts. Conversely, if we direct our competitive initiative toward our rivals' weaknesses, it may be difficult for them to respond. Richard Branson's Virgin Group has launched a host of entrepreneurial new ventures, typically in markets dominated by a powerful incumbent—British Airways in airlines, EMI in music, Vodafone in wireless telecommunications. Branson's strategy has been to adopt innovative forms of differentiation that are difficult for established incumbents to respond to.

Segmentation and Strategic Groups

Segmentation Analysis[50]

In Chapter 3 we noted the difficulty of drawing industry boundaries and the need to define industries both broadly and narrowly according to the types of question we are seeking to answer. Initially, it may be convenient to define industries broadly, but for a more detailed analysis of competition we need to focus on markets that

STRATEGY CAPSULE 4.2
Motorcycle Myopia

During the 1960s, lightweight Japanese motorcycles began to flood Britain and North America. The chairman of BSA, Eric Turner, was dismissive of this competitive challenge to the dominant position of his Triumph and BSA brands:

> The success of Honda, Suzuki, and Yamaha has been jolly good for us. People start out by buying one of the low-priced Japanese jobs. They get to enjoy the fun and exhilaration of the open road and they frequently end up buying one of our more powerful and expensive machines.
>
> (*Advertising Age*, December 27, 1965)

Similar complacency was expressed by William Davidson, president of Harley-Davidson:

> Basically, we do not believe in the lightweight market. We believe that motorcycles are sports vehicles, not transportation vehicles. Even if a man says he bought a motorcycle for transportation, it's generally for leisure time use. The lightweight motorcycle is only supplemental. Back around World War I, a number of companies came out with lightweight bikes. We came out with one ourselves. We came out with another in 1947 and it just didn't go anywhere. We have seen what happens to these small sizes.
>
> (*American Motor Cycle*, September 15, 1966)

By 1980, BSA and Triumph had ceased production and Harley-Davidson was struggling for survival. The world motorcycle industry, including the heavyweight segment, was dominated by the Japanese.

are drawn more narrowly in terms of both products and geography. This process of disaggregating industries into specific markets we call **segmentation**.

Segmentation is particularly important if competition varies across the different submarkets within an industry such that some are more attractive than others. While Sony and Microsoft battled for dominance for leadership among so-called hard-core gamers with their technologically advanced PS3 and Xbox 360 consoles, Nintendo's Wii became a surprise market share leader by focusing on a large and underserved market segment: casual and older video game players. In the cutthroat tire industry, Pirelli has achieved superior margins by investing heavily in technology and focusing on high-performance tires for sports and luxury cars.[51]

The purpose of segmentation analysis is to identify attractive segments, to select strategies for different segments, and to determine how many segments to serve. The analysis proceeds in five stages (see Strategy Capsule 4.3 for an application; Strategy Capsule 4.4 looks at vertical segmentation).

1 *Identify key segmentation variables*: Our starting point is to determine the basis of segmentation. Segmentation decisions are essentially choices about which customers to serve and what to offer them: hence segmentation vari-ables relate to the characteristics of customers and the product (Figure 4.4). The most appropriate segmentation variables are those that partition the market most distinctly in terms of limits to substitution by customers (demand-side sub-stitutability) and by producers (supply-side substitutability). Price differentials are a good guide to market segments: distinct market segments tend to display sustained price differentials. Typically, segmentation analysis generates far too many segmentation variables and too many categories for each variable. For our analysis to be manageable and useful, we need to reduce these to two or three. To do this we need to (a) identify the most strategically significant segmentation variables and (b) combine segmentation variables that are closely correlated. For example, in the restaurant industry, price level, service level (waiter service/ self-service), cuisine (fast-food/full meals), and alcohol license (wine served/ soft drinks only) are likely to be closely related. We could use a single variable, restaurant type, with three categories—full-service restaurants, cafés, and fast-food outlets—as a proxy for all of these variables.

2 *Construct a Segmentation Matrix*: Once the segmentation variables have been selected and discrete categories determined for each, the individual segments may be identified using a two- or three-dimensional matrix. Strategy Capsule

FIGURE 4.4 The basis for segmentation: The characteristics of buyers and products

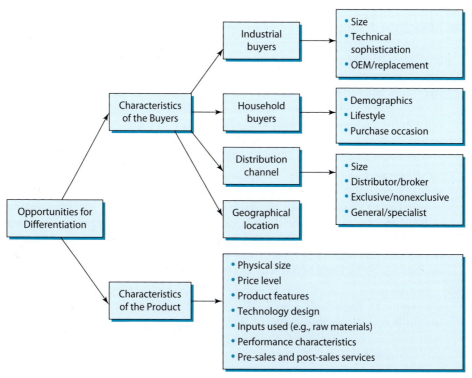

4.3 shows a two-dimensional segmentation matrix for the world automobile industry

3 *Analyze segment attractiveness*: Profitability within an industry segment is determined by the same structural forces that determine profitability within an industry as a whole. As a result, Porter's five forces of competition framework is equally effective in relation to a segment as to an entire industry. There are, however, a few differences. First, when analyzing the pressure of competition from substitute products, we are concerned not only with substitutes from other industries but also, more importantly, with substitutes from other segments within the same industry. Second, when considering entry into the segment, the main source of entrants is likely to be producers established in other segments within the same industry. The barriers that protect a segment from firms located in other segments are called *barriers to mobility* to distinguish them from the *barriers to entry*, which protect the industry as a whole.[52] When barriers to mobility are low, then the superior returns of high-profit segments tend to be quickly eroded. As Strategy Capsule 4.3 suggests, differences in competitive conditions between segments can make some much more profitable than others; however, these profit differentials are unlikely to be sustained over the long term.

Segmentation analysis can also be useful in identifying unexploited opportunities in an industry. Companies that have built successful strategies by concentrating on unoccupied segments include Wal-Mart (discount stores in small towns), Enterprise Rent-A-Car (suburban locations), and Edward Jones (full-service brokerage for small investors in smaller cities). This identification of unoccupied market segments is one dimension of what Kim and Mauborgne refer to as "blue ocean strategy": the quest for uncontested market space.[53]

4 *Identify the segment's key success factors (KSFs)*: Differences in competitive structure and in customer preferences between segments result in different KSFs. By analyzing buyers' purchasing criteria and the basis of competition within individual segments, we can identify KSFs for individual segments. For example, we can segment the US bicycle market into high-price enthusiasts' bikes sold through specialist bike stores and economy bikes sold through discount stores. KSFs in the enthusiast segment are technology, reputation, and dealer relations. In the economy segment, KSFs are low-cost manufacture (most likely in China) and a supply contract with a leading retail chain.

5 *Select segment scope*: Finally, a firm needs to decide whether it wishes to be a segment specialist or to compete across multiple segments. The advantages of a broad over a narrow segment focus depend on two main factors: similarity of KSFs and the presence of shared costs. If KSFs are different across segments, a firm will need to deploy distinct strategies which may require different capabilities for different segments. Harley-Davidson's attempt to compete in sports motorcycles through its Buell brand was a failure.

Where scale economies are important and costs can be shared across different segments, firms with a broad segment scope will tend to displace specialists. In automobiles, the ability of the large-scale automakers to use common platforms and components for specialist vehicles such as luxury cars and sports cars has resulted in the disappearance of most specialist automakers.

STRATEGY CAPSULE 4.3
Segmenting the World Automobile Industry

1   Identify key segmentation variables and categories. Possible segmentation variables include: price, size, engine power, body style, buyer type (retail versus fleet), and geographical market. We can reduce the number of segmentation variables—in particular, price, size, and engine power tend to be closely correlated. Other variables clearly define distinct markets (e.g., geographical regions and individual national markets).

2   Construct a segmentation matrix. The segmentation matrix in Figure 4.5 shows geographical regions (columns) and product types (rows). These product types combine multiple segmentation variables: price, size, design, and fuel type.

3   Analyze segment attractiveness. Applying five forces analysis to individual segments points to the attractiveness of the growth markets of Asia and Latin America (especially for luxury cars) as compared with the saturated, excess capacity laden markets of Europe and North America. In these mature markets, the hybrid and electric car segments may be attractive due to fewer competitors and lack of excess capacity.

4   Identify KSFs in each segment. In sports cars, technology and design aesthetics are likely to be key differentiators. In luxury cars, quality and interior design are likely to be essential. In family compact and mini-cars, low cost is the primary basis for competitive advantage.

5   Analyze attractions of broad versus narrow segment scope. Because of the potential to share technology, design, and components across models, all product segments are dominated by full-range mass-manufactures. In terms of geographical segments, only in the biggest markets (primarily China) have nationally focused producers survived.

FIGURE 4.5   A segmentation matrix of the World Automobile Market

PRODUCTS	North America	Western Europe	Eastern Europe	Asia	Latin America	Australia & NZ	Africa
Luxury cars							
Full-size cars							
Mid-size cars							
Small cars							
Station wagons							
Minivans							
Sports cars							
Sport utility							
Pickup trucks							
Hybrids							

REGIONS

Vertical Segmentation: Profit Pool Mapping

Segmentation is usually horizontal: markets are disaggregated according to products, geography, and customer groups. However, as we noted in the previous chapter when we discussed Michael Jacobides' approach to industry architecture, we can also segment an industry vertically by identifying different value chain activities. Bain & Company's profit pool analysis offers a way of mapping profitability differences between different vertical activities. Bain's *profit pool mapping* involves, first, estimating the industry's total profit by applying the average margin earned by a sample of companies in the industry to an estimate of the industry's total revenues and, second, estimating the profit at each stage of the value chain. This requires disaggregating profit data for *mixed players* (those engaged in multiple activities) and adding their segment profits to those earned by *pure players* (specialists in the single value chain activity). In the US automobile industry, downstream activities such as finance, leasing, insurance, and service and repair are much more profitable than manufacturing. In Figure 4.6 the area of each rectangle corresponds to the total profit for that activity.

FIGURE 4.6 The US auto industry profit pool

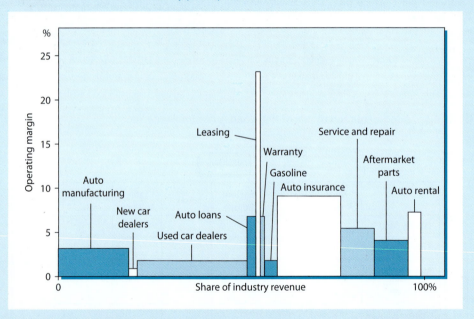

Source: Reprinted by permission of Harvard Business Review. From "Profit Pools: A Fresh Look at Strategy," O. Gadiesh and J. L. Gilbert, May/June 1998, p. 142, Copyright © 1998 by the Harvard Business School Publishing Corporation; all rights reserved.

Strategic Groups

Whereas segmentation analysis concentrates on the characteristics of markets as the basis for disaggregating industries, strategic group analysis segments an industry on the basis of the strategies of the member firms. A **strategic group** is "the group of firms in an industry following the same or a similar strategy along the strategic dimensions."[54] These strategic dimensions might include product range, geographical breadth, choice of distribution channels, level of product quality, degree of vertical integration, choice of technology, and so on. By selecting the most important strategic dimensions and locating each firm in the industry along them, it is possible to identify groups of companies that have adopted more or less similar approaches to competing within the industry. In some industries strategic groups are readily observable, for example airlines fall into two broad strategic groups: "legacy carriers" (such as United, JAL, and British Airways) and "low-cost carriers" (such as Southwest, Ryanair, and SpiceJet). Other industries are more complex: Figure 4.7 shows strategic groups within the world automobile industry; Figure 4.8 in the petroleum industry.[55]

Most of the empirical research into strategic groups has been concerned with competition and profitability between groups—the basic argument being that mobility barriers between strategic groups permit some groups of firms to be persistently more profitable than other groups.[56] In general, the proposition that profitability differences within strategic groups are less than differences between strategic groups has not received robust empirical support.[57] This may reflect the fact that the members of a strategic group, although pursuing similar strategies, are not necessarily in competition with one another. For example, within the European airline industry, budget airlines such as easyJet, airBaltic, SkyEurope, Volare, and Ryanair pursue similar strategies, but do not, for the most part, compete on the same routes. Hence, the main usefulness of strategic group analysis is in understanding strategic positioning, recognizing patterns of competition, and identifying strategic niches; it is less useful as a tool for analyzing interfirm profitability differences.[58]

FIGURE 4.7 Strategic groups within the world automobile industry

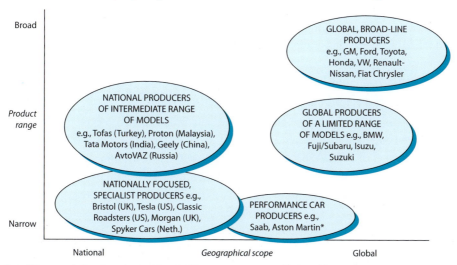

Note: *This group is almost empty: most firms in this group are now owned by broad-line producers

FIGURE 4.8   Strategic groups within the world petroleum industry

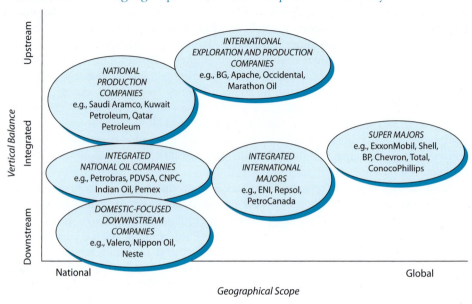

Summary

The purpose of this chapter has been to go beyond the basic analysis of industry structure, competition, and profitability presented in Chapter 3 to consider the dynamics of competitive rivalry and the internal complexities of industries.

In terms of industry and competitive analysis, we have extended our strategy toolkit in several directions:

◆ We have recognized the potential for complementary products to add value and noted the importance of strategies that can exploit this source of value.

◆ We have noted the importance of competitive interactions between close rivals and learned a structured approach to analyzing competitors and predicting their behavior. At a more sophisticated theoretical level, we have recognized how game theory offers insights into competition, bargaining, and the design of winning strategies.

◆ We examined the microstructure of industries and markets and the value of segmentation analysis and strategic group analysis in understanding industries at a more detailed level and in selecting an advantageous strategic position within an industry.

Quizzes and flashcards to test yourself further are available in your interactive e-book at **www.wileyopenpage.com**

Self-Study Questions

1. HP, Canon, Epson, and other manufacturers of inkjet printers make most of their profits from their ink cartridges. Why are cartridges more profitable than printers? Would the situation be different:

    a   if cartridges were manufactured by different firms from those which make printers?
    b   if cartridges were interchangeable between different printers?
    c   if patent and copyright restrictions did not prevent other firms from supplying ink cartridges that could be used in the leading brands of printer?

2. In November 2005, six of Paris's most luxurious hotels—including George V, Le Bristol, the Ritz, and Hotel de Crillon—were fined for colluding on room rates. Regular guests showed little concern—noting that, whatever the listed rack rate, it was always possible to negotiate substantial discounts. Using the prisoners' dilemma model, can you explain why the hotels were able to collude over their listed rates but not over discounts?

3. In August 2006, Rupert Murdoch's News International announced its intention of launching a free evening newspaper, *The London Paper*, to challenge Associated Newspapers' *London Evening Standard* (daily sales 390,000). Given that the *Evening Standard* was already believed to be loss making, the new competition could be fatal for the paper. What steps might Associated Newspapers take to deter News International from launching its new paper, and if it goes ahead with the launch, what would Associated Newspapers' best response be?

4. During 2007–2009, the Nintendo Wii established leadership over the Sony PS3 and Microsoft Xbox 360 in the market for video game consoles. Unlike Sony and Microsoft, Nintendo is completely dependent upon the video games industry for its revenues. How might Nintendo use the competitor analysis framework outlined in Figure 4.3 to predict the likely reactions of Sony and Microsoft to its market success?

5. How would you segment the restaurant market in your hometown? How would you advise someone thinking of starting a new restaurant which segments might be most attractive in terms of profit potential?

Notes

1. Data from http://money.cnn.com/magazines/fortune/fortune500/2011/industries/11/index.html.

2. A. Brandenburger and B. Nalebuff (*Co-opetition*, New York: Doubleday, 1996) propose an alternative framework, the *value net*, for analyzing the impact of complements.

3. See A. Brandenburger and B. Nalebuff, "The Right Game: Use Game Theory to Shape Strategy," *Harvard Business Review* (July/August 1995): 63–4; and A. Brandenburger, J. Kou, and M. Burnett, *Power Play (A): Nintendo in 8-bit Video Games* (Harvard Business School Case No. 9-795-103, 1995).

4. C. Baldwin, S. O'Mahony, and J. Quinn, *IBM and Linux (A)* (Harvard Business School Case No. 903-083, 2003).

5. J. A. Schumpeter, *The Theory of Economic Development* (Cambridge, MA: Harvard University Press, 1934).

6. See R. Jacobson, "The Austrian School of Strategy," *Academy of Management Review* 17 (1992): 782–807; and G. Young, K. Smith, and C. Grimm, "Austrian and Industrial Organization Perspectives on Firm-Level Competitive Activity and Performance," *Organization Science* 7 (May/June 1996): 243–54.

7. R. T. Masson and J. Shaanan, "Stochastic Dynamic Limit Pricing: An Empirical Test," *Review of Economics and Statistics* 64 (1982): 413–422; R. T. Masson and J. Shaanan, "Optimal Pricing and Threat of Entry: Canadian Evidence," *International Journal of Industrial Organization* 5 (1987): 520–535.

8. R. Caves and M. E. Porter, "The Dynamics of Changing Seller Concentration," *Journal of Industrial Economics* 19 (1980): 1–15; P. Hart and R. Clarke, *Concentration in British Industry* (Cambridge: Cambridge University Press, 1980).

9. P. A. Geroski and R. T. Masson, "Dynamic Market Models in Industrial Organization," *International Journal of Industrial Organization* 5 (1987): 1–13.

10. D. C. Mueller, *Profits in the Long Run* (Cambridge: Cambridge University Press, 1986).

11. R. D'Aveni, *Hypercompetition: Managing the Dynamics of Strategic Maneuvering* (New York: Free Press, 1994): 217–218.

12. R. A. D'Aveni, G. B. Dagnino, and K. G. Smith, "The Age of Temporary Advantage," *Strategic Management Journal* 31 (2010): 1371–85.

13. L. G. Thomas and R. D'Aveni, "The Rise of Hypercompetition in the US Manufacturing Sector, 1950–2002." Tuck School of Business, Dartmouth College, Working Paper No. 2004-11 (2004).

14. R. R. Wiggins and T. W. Ruefli, "Schumpeter's Ghost: Is Hypercompetition Making the Best of Times Shorter?" *Strategic Management Journal* 26 (2005): 887–911.

15. G. McNamara, P. M. Vaaler, and C. Devers, "Same As It Ever Was: The Search for Evidence of Increasing Hypercompetition," *Strategic Management Journal* 24 (2003): 261–78.

16. K. Weigelt and C. F. Camerer, "Reputation and Corporate Strategy: A Review of Recent Theory and Applications," *Strategic Management Journal* 9 (1988): 137–42.

17. A. K. Dixit, "The Role of Investment in Entry Deterrence," *Economic Journal* 90 (1980): 95–106; P. Milgrom and J. Roberts, "Informational Asymmetries, Strategic Behavior and Industrial Organization," *American Economic Review* 77, no. 2 (May 1987): 184–9.

18. P. Milgrom and J. Roberts, "Informational Asymmetries, Strategic Behavior and Industrial Organization," *American Economic Review* 77, no. 2 (May 1987): 184–9.

19. P. Ghemawat, *Commitment: The Dynamic of Strategy* (New York: Free Press, 1991).

20. See, for example: A. K. Dixit and B. J. Nalebuff, *Thinking Strategically: The Competitive Edge in Business, Politics, and Everyday Life* (New York: W. W. Norton, 1991); and J. McMillan, *Games, Strategies, and Managers* (New York: Oxford University Press, 1992).

21. G. T. Allison and P. Zelikow, *Essence of Decision: Explaining the Cuban Missile Crisis*, 2nd edn (Boston: Little, Brown and Company, 1999).

22. B. C. Esty and P. Ghemawat, "Airbus vs. Boeing in Superjumbos: A Case of Failed Preemption," Harvard Business School Working Paper No. 02-061 (2002).

23. D. Ronfelt, "Social Science at 190 mph on NASCAR's Biggest Superspeedways," *First Monday* 5 (February 7, 2000).

24. "Game Theory in Action: Designing the US Airwaves Auction," *Financial Times Mastering Strategy Supplement* (October 11, 1999): 4.

25. John Cassidy "Rational Irrationality," *New Yorker* (October 5, 2009).

26. J. Maynard Smith, "Sexual Selection and the Handicap Principle," *Journal of Theoretical Biology* 57 (1976): 239–42.

27. A. Brandenburger and B. Nalebuff, *Co-opetition* (New York: Doubleday, 1996).

28. T. Dhar, J.-P. Chatas, R. W. Collerill, and B. W. Gould, "Strategic Pricing between Coca-Cola Company and PepsiCo," *Journal of Economics and Management Strategy* 14 (2005): 905–31.

29. "A Sharp Act Gets an Edge," *Financial Times* (September 10, 2008).

30. *Bitter Competition: Holland Sweetener vs. NutraSweet (A)* (Harvard Business School Case No. 9-794-079, 1994).

31. A. M. McGahan, "The Incentive not to Invest: Capacity Commitments in the Compact Disk Introduction," in R. A. Burgelman and R. S. Rosenbloom (eds), *Research on Technological Innovation Management and Policy*, vol. 5 (Greenwich, CT: JAI Press, 1994).

32. D. K. Levine and R. A. Levine, "Deterrence in the Cold War and the War on Terror," UCLA Department of Economics Working Paper (2006).

33. D. N. Sull, "Managing by Commitments," *Harvard Business Review* (June 2003): 82–91.

34. Games where price is the primary decision variable are called *Bertrand models* after the 19th century French economist Joseph Bertrand.

35. Games where quantity is the primary decision variable are called *Cournot models* after the 19th century French economist Antoine Augustin Cournot.

36. F. Scott Morton, "Strategic Complements and Substitutes," *Financial Times Mastering Strategy Supplement* (November 8, 1999): 10–13.

37. R. Loving, *The Men who Loved Trains* (Bloomington, IA: Indiana University Press, 2006).

38. For a review of research on competitive signaling, see O. Heil and T. S. Robertson, "Toward a Theory of Competitive Market Signaling: A Research Agenda," *Strategic Management Journal* 12 (1991): 403–18.

39. B. Macintyre, *Operation Mincemeat: The True Spy Story that Changed the Course of World War II* (London: Bloomsbury, 2010).

40. For a survey of the strategic role of reputation, see K. Weigelt and C. Camerer, "Reputation and Corporate Strategy: A Review of Recent Theory and Applications," *Strategic Management Journal* 9 (1988): 443–54.

41. P. Milgrom and J. Roberts, "Predation, Reputation, and Entry Deterrence," *Journal of Economic Theory* 27 (1982): 280–312.

42. R. M. Grant, "Pricing Behavior in the UK Wholesale Market for Petrol," *Journal of Industrial Economics* 30 (1982): 271–92; L. Miller, "The Provocative Practice of Price Signaling: Collusion versus Cooperation," *Business Horizons* (July/August 1993).

43. On the ability of game theory to predict almost any equilibrium solution (the Pandora's Box Problem) see C. F. Camerer, "Does Strategy Research Need Game Theory?" *Strategic Management Journal*, Special Issue 12 (Winter 1991): 137–52; and F. M. Fisher, "The Games Economists Play: A Noncooperative View," *Rand Journal of Economics* 20 (Spring 1989): 113–124. Steve Postrel illustrates the point with a game theory model to explain the rationality of bank presidents setting fire to their trousers. See S. Postrel, "Burning Your Britches behind You: Can Policy Scholars Bank on Game Theory?" *Strategic Management Journal*, Special Issue 12 (Winter 1991): 153–5.

44. G. F. Rose and M. Lloyd, "The Failure of FCC Spectrum Auctions," (Washington DC: Center for American Progress, May 2006); P. Klemperer, "How not to Run Auctions: The European 3G Mobile Telecom Auctions. *European Economic Review* 46 (2002): 829–45.

45. Strategic and Competitive Intelligence Professionals; the Institute for Competitive Intelligence.

46. For example, S. Sharp, *Competitive Intelligence Advantage* (Hoboken, NJ: John Wiley & Sons, Inc., 2009); L. M. Fuld, *The Secret Language of Competitive Intelligence* (Indianapolis: Dog Ear Publishing, 2010).

47. "McLaren Docked F1 Points for Spying," *Financial Times* (September 14, 2007); "Kolon Loses $920 Million Verdict to DuPont in Trial Over Kevlar," *Washington Post* (September 15, 2011).

48. Office of the National Counterintelligence Executive, *Foreign Spies Stealing US Economic Secrets in Cyberspace: Report to Congress on Foreign Economic Collection and Industrial Espionage*, 2009–2011 (October 2011).

49. J.-C. Spender, *Industry Recipes: The Nature and Sources of Managerial Judgment* (Oxford: Blackwell, 1989). How social interaction promotes convergence of perceptions and beliefs is discussed by Anne Huff in "Industry Influences on Strategy Reformulation," *Strategic Management Journal* 3 (1982): 119–31.

50. This section draws heavily on M. E. Porter, *Competitive Advantage* (New York: Free Press, 1985): Chapter 7.

51. "Pirelli's Bet on High-performance Tires," *International Herald Tribune* (April 2, 2005).

52. R. E. Caves and M. E. Porter, "From Entry Barriers to Mobility Barriers: Conjectural Decisions and Contrived Deterrence to New Competition," *Quarterly Journal of Economics* 91 (1977): 241–62.

53. W. C. Kim and R. Mauborgne, "Blue Ocean Strategy: From Theory to Practice," *California Management Review* 47 (Spring 2005): 105–21.

54. M. E. Porter, *Competitive Strategy* (New York: Free Press, 1980): 129.

55. For more on strategic groups, see J. McGee and H. Thomas, "Strategic Groups: Theory, Research, and Taxonomy," *Strategic Management Journal* 7 (1986): 141–60.

56. A. Feigenbaum and H. Thomas, "Strategic Groups and Performance: The US Insurance Industry," *Strategic Management Journal* 11 (1990): 197–215.

57. K. Cool and I. Dierickx, "Rivalry, Strategic Groups, and Firm Profitability," *Strategic Management Journal* 14 (1993): 47–59.

58. K. Smith, C. Grimm, and S. Wally, "Strategic Groups and Rivalrous Firm Behavior: Toward a Reconciliation," *Strategic Management Journal* 18 (1997): 149–57.

5 Analyzing Resources and Capabilities

Analysts have tended to define assets too narrowly, identifying only those that can be measured, such as plant and equipment. Yet the intangible assets, such as a particular technology, accumulated consumer information, brand name, reputation, and corporate culture, are invaluable to the firm's competitive power. In fact, these invisible assets are often the only real source of competitive edge that can be sustained over time.

—HIROYUKI ITAMI, MOBILIZING INVISIBLE ASSETS

You've gotta do what you do well.

—LUCINO NOTO, FORMER VICE CHAIRMAN, EXXONMOBIL

OUTLINE

- ◆ **Introduction and Objectives**
- ◆ **The Role of Resources and Capabilities in Strategy Formulation**
  - Basing Strategy on Resources and Capabilities
  - Resources and Capabilities as Sources of Profit
- ◆ **Identifying Resources and Capabilities**
  - Identifying Resources
  - Identifying Organizational Capabilities
- ◆ **Appraising Resources and Capabilities**
  - Appraising the Strategic Importance of Resources and Capabilities

- Appraising the Relative Strength of a Firm's Resources and Capabilities
- ◆ **Developing Strategy Implications**
  - Exploiting Key Strengths
  - Managing Key Weaknesses
  - What about Superfluous Strengths?
  - Choosing the Industry Context
- ◆ **Summary**
- ◆ **Self-Study Questions**
- ◆ **Notes**

Introduction and Objectives

In Chapter 1, I noted that the focus of strategy thinking has been shifted from the external environment of the firm toward its internal environment. In this chapter, we will make the same transition. Looking within the firm, we will concentrate our attention on the resources and capabilities that firms possess. In doing so, we shall build the foundations for our analysis of competitive advantage (which began in Chapter 3 with the discussion of key success factors).

By the time you have completed this chapter, you will be able to:

♦ appreciate the role of a firm's resources and capabilities as a basis for formulating strategy;

♦ identify and appraise the resources and capabilities of a firm;

♦ evaluate the potential for a firm's resources and capabilities to confer sustainable competitive advantage;

♦ use the results of resource and capability analysis to formulate strategies that exploit internal strengths while defending against internal weaknesses.

We begin by explaining why a company's resources and capabilities are so important to its strategy.

The Role of Resources and Capabilities in Strategy Formulation

Strategy is concerned with matching a firm's resources and capabilities to the opportunities that arise in the external environment. So far, the emphasis of the book has been on the identification of profit opportunities in the external environment of the firm. In this chapter, our emphasis shifts from the interface between strategy and the external environment toward the interface between strategy and the internal environment of the firm—more specifically, with the resources and capabilities of the firm (Figure 5.1).

Increasing emphasis on the role of resources and capabilities as the basis for strategy is the result of two factors. First, as firms' industry environments have become more unstable, so internal resources and capabilities rather than external market focus have been viewed as comprising a more secure base for formulating strategy. Second, it has become increasingly apparent that competitive advantage rather than industry attractiveness is the primary source of superior profitability. Let us consider each of these factors.

Basing Strategy on Resources and Capabilities

During the 1990s, ideas concerning the role of resources and capabilities as the principal basis for firm strategy and the primary source of profitability coalesced into what has become known as the *resource-based view of the firm*.[1]

FIGURE 5.1 Analyzing resources and capabilities: The interface between strategy and the firm

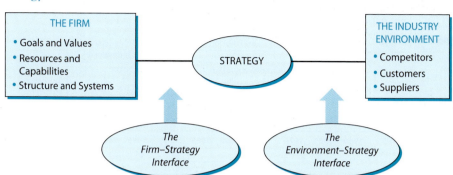

To understand why the resource-based view has had a major impact on strategy thinking, let us go back to the starting point for strategy formulation: the underlying purpose of the firm which can be answered by posing the question: "What is our business?" Conventionally, this question has been answered in terms of the market being served: "Who are our customers?" and "Which of their needs are we seeking to serve?"[2] However, in a world where customer preferences are volatile and the identity of customers and the technologies for serving them are changing, a market-focused strategy may not provide the stability and constancy of direction needed to guide strategy over the long term. When the external environment is in a state of flux, the firm itself, in terms of the bundle of resources and capabilities it possesses, may be a much more stable basis on which to define its identity.

This emphasis on resources and capabilities as the foundation of firm strategy was popularized by C. K. Prahalad and Gary Hamel in their 1990 landmark paper "The Core Competence of the Corporation."[3] The potential for capabilities to be the "roots of competitiveness," the sources of new products, and the foundation for strategy is exemplified by several companies, for example:

- Honda Motor Company is the world's biggest motorcycle producer and a leading supplier of automobiles but it has never defined itself either as a motorcycle company or a motor vehicle company. Since its founding in 1948, its strategy has been built around its expertise in the development and manufacture of engines; this capability has successfully carried it from motorcycles to a wide range of gasoline-engine products (Figure 5.2).
- Canon Inc. had its first success producing 35 mm cameras. Since then, it has gone on to develop fax machines, calculators, copy machines, printers, video cameras, camcorders, semiconductor manufacturing equipment, and many other products. Almost all of Canon's products involve the application of three areas of technological capability: precision mechanics, microelectronics, and fine optics.
- 3M Corporation expanded from sandpaper into adhesive tapes, audio and videotapes, road signs, floppy disks, and medical and household products. Its product list comprises over 30,000 separate items. Is it a conglomerate? Certainly not, claims 3M. Its vast product range rests on a foundation of core

FIGURE 5.2   Honda Motor Company: Product development milestones

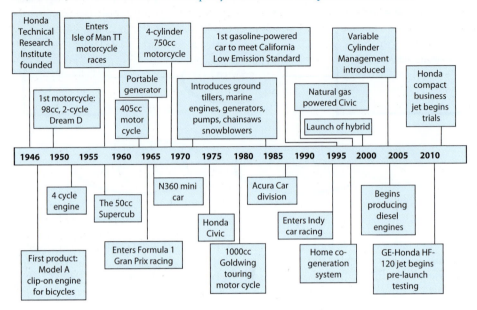

technological know-how relating to adhesives, thin-film coatings, and materials sciences supported by an outstanding ability to develop and launch new products.

In general, the greater the rate of change in a firm's external environment, the more likely it is that internal resources and capabilities rather than external market focus will provide a secure foundation for long-term strategy. In fast-moving, technology-based industries, basing strategy upon capabilities can help firms to outlive the life-cycles of their initial products. Microsoft's initial success was the result of its MS-DOS operating system for the IBM PC. However, by building outstanding capabilities in developing and launching complex software products and in managing an ecosystem of partner relationships, Microsoft extended its success to other operating systems (e.g., Windows), to applications software (e.g., Office), and to internet services (e.g., Xbox Live). Similarly, Apple's remarkable ability to combine technology, aesthetics, and ease of use has allowed it to expand beyond its initial focus on desktop and notebook computers into MP3 players (iPod), smartphones (iPhone), and tablet computers (iPad).

Conversely, those companies that when faced with radical technological change attempted to maintain their market focus have often experienced huge difficulties in building the new technological capabilities needed to serve their customers.

Eastman Kodak is a classic example. Its dominance of the world market for photographic products was threatened by digital imaging. Since 1990, Kodak invested billions of dollars developing digital technologies and digital imaging products. Yet, in January 2012, continuing losses on digital products and services forced Kodak into bankruptcy. Might Kodak have been better off by sticking with its chemical know-how, allowing its photographic business to decline while developing its interests in specialty chemicals, pharmaceuticals, and healthcare?[4]

Olivetti, the Italian manufacturer of typewriters and office equipment, offers a similar cautionary tale. Despite its early investments in electronic computing, Olivetti's attempt to recreate itself as a supplier of personal computers and printers was a failure. Might Olivetti have been better advised to deploy its existing expertise in electrical and precision engineering in other products?[5] This pattern of established firms failing to adjust to disruptive technological change within their own industries is well documented—in typesetting and in disk drive manufacturing, successive technological waves have caused market leaders to falter and have allowed new entrants to prosper.[6]

Resources and Capabilities as Sources of Profit

In Chapter 1, we identified two major sources of superior profitability: industry attractiveness and competitive advantage. Of these, competitive advantage is the more important. Internationalization and deregulation have increased competitive pressure within most sectors; as a result, few industries (or segments) offer cozy refuges from vigorous competition. As we observed in the previous chapter (Table 4.1), industry factors account for only a small proportion of interfirm profit differentials. Hence, establishing competitive advantage through the development and deployment of resources and capabilities, rather than seeking shelter from the storm of competition, has become the primary goal of strategy.

The distinction between industry attractiveness and competitive advantage (based on superior resources) as sources of a firm's profitability corresponds to economists' distinctions between different types of profit (or *rent*). The profits arising from market power are referred to as *monopoly rents*; those arising from superior resources are *Ricardian rents*, after the 19th century British economist David Ricardo. Ricardo showed that, in a competitive wheat market, when land at the margin of cultivation earned a negligible return fertile land would yield high returns. Ricardian rent is the return earned by a scarce resource over and above the cost of bringing it into production.[7] Most of the $5.8 billion of royalties earned by Dolby Laboratories from licensing its sound reduction technologies comprises Ricardian rents, as does most of the $238 million earned in 2011 by tennis player Rafael Nadal.

Distinguishing between profit arising from market power and profit arising from resource superiority is less clear in practice than in principle. A closer look at Porter's five forces framework suggests that industry attractiveness often derives from the ownership of strategic resources. Barriers to entry, for example, are typically the result of patents, brands, know-how, or distribution channels, learning, or some other resource possessed by incumbent firms. Monopoly is usually based on the ownership of a key resource such as a technical standard or government license.

The resource-based approach has profound implications for companies' strategy formulation. When the primary concern of strategy was industry selection and positioning, companies tended to adopt similar strategies. The resource-based view, by contrast, recognizes that each company possesses a unique collection of resources and capabilities; the implication is that the key to profitability is not doing the same as other firms but rather exploiting differences. Establishing competitive advantage involves formulating and implementing a strategy that exploits a firm's unique strengths.

The remainder of this chapter outlines a resource-based approach to strategy formulation. Fundamental to this approach is a thorough and profound understanding of the resources and capabilities of a firm. Such understanding provides a basis for selecting a strategy that exploits the key resource and capabilities of an organization.

The same approach is relevant to formulating our career strategies. A sound career strategy is one that recognizes one's strengths and weaknesses and effectively exploits strengths while minimizing vulnerability to weaknesses—see Strategy Capsule 5.1 for an example. The challenge for companies is the same. For both individuals and organizations the starting point is to identify the available resources and capabilities.

Identifying Resources and Capabilities

The first stage in the analysis of resources and capabilities is to identify the resources and capabilities of the firm—or, indeed, any organization since the analysis of resources and capabilities is as applicable to not-for-profit organizations as it is to business enterprises. It is important to distinguish between the **resources** and the **capabilities** of the firm: resources are the productive assets owned by the firm; capabilities are what the firm can do. Individual resources do not confer competitive advantage; they must work together to create organizational capability. Capability is the essence of superior performance. Figure 5.3 shows the relationships between resources, capabilities, and competitive advantage.

Our discussion of key success factors (KSFs)—the sources of competitive advantage within an industry—in Chapter 3 offers a starting point for our identification of

STRATEGY CAPSULE 5.1

Focusing Strategy around Core Capabilities: Lyor Cohen on Mariah Carey

The year 2001 was a disastrous one for Mariah Carey. Her first movie, *Glitter*, was a flop, the soundtrack was Carey's most poorly received album in a decade, her $80 million recording contract was dropped by EMI, and she suffered a nervous breakdown.

Lyor Cohen, the aggressive, workaholic chief executive of Island Def Jam records was quick to spot an opportunity: "I cold-called her on the day of her release from EMI and I said, I think you are an unbelievable artist and you should hold your head up high. What I said stuck on her and she ended up signing with us."

His strategic analysis of Carey's situation was concise: "I said to her, what's your competitive advantage? A great voice, of course. And what else? You write every one of your songs—you're a great writer. So why did

you stray from your competitive advantage? If you have this magnificent voice and you write such compelling songs, why are you dressing like that, why are you using all these collaborations [with other artists and other songwriters]? Why? It's like driving a Ferrari in first—you won't see what that Ferrari will do until you get into sixth gear."

Cohen signed Carey in May 2002. Under Universal Music's Island Def Jam Records, Carey returned to her core strengths: her versatile voice, song-writing talents, and ballad style. Her next album, *The Emancipation of Mimi*, was the biggest-selling album of 2005, and in 2006 she won a Grammy award.

Source: "Rap's Unlikely Mogul," *Financial Times* (August 5, 2002). © The Financial Times, reproduced with permission.

FIGURE 5.3   The links between resources, capabilities, and competitive advantage

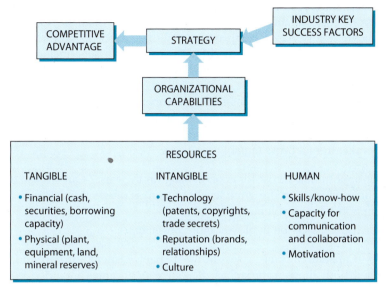

key resources and capabilities. Once we have identified the KSFs in an industry, it is a short step to identifying the resources and capabilities needed to deliver those success factors. For example:

- In budget airlines the KSF is low operating cost. This requires a standardized fleet of fuel-efficient planes; a young, motivated, non-unionized workforce; and a culture of frugality.
- In pharmaceuticals the KSF is the discovery and launch of new drugs. This requires high-quality researchers, drug-testing capability, and marketing and distribution capability.

However, as we shall see, identifying KSFs is only a starting point. To develop a comprehensive picture of an organization's resources and capabilities we need systematic frameworks for identifying and classifying different resources and capabilities.

Identifying Resources

Drawing up an inventory of a firm's resources can be surprisingly difficult. No such document exists within the accounting or management information systems of most corporations. The corporate balance sheet provides only a partial view of a firm's resources—it comprises mainly financial and physical resources. To broaden our view of a firm's resources, we can identify three main types of resource: tangible, intangible, and human resources.

Tangible Resources   Tangible resources are the easiest to identify and value: financial resources and physical assets are valued in the firm's balance sheet. Yet, balance sheets tend to obscure strategically relevant information and to distort asset values. Historic cost valuation can provide little indication of an asset's market value. Disney's movie library had a balance sheet value—based on production cost less amortization—of only $1.6 billion in 2011.[8] Its total land assets (including its 28,000 acres in Florida) were valued at a paltry $1.1 billion.

However, the primary goal of resource analysis is not to value a company's assets but to understand their potential for creating competitive advantage. This requires not just balance sheet valuation but information on the composition and characteristics of the resources. With that information we can explore two main routes to create additional value from a firm's tangible resources:

- What opportunities exist for economizing on their use? Can we use fewer resources to support the same level of business or use the existing resources to support a larger volume of business?
- Can existing assets be deployed more profitably?

Strategy Capsule 5.2 discusses how Michael Eisner's turnaround of Walt Disney used both these approaches. Resource economies included consolidating administrative activities into fewer headquarters buildings and spreading the costs of movie studios over a bigger volume; redeployment of resources included

---

STRATEGY CAPSULE 5.2
Resource Utilization: Revival at Walt Disney

In 1984, Michael Eisner became CEO of the Walt Disney Company. Between 1984 and 1988, Disney's sales' revenue increased from $1.66 billion to $3.75 billion, net income from $98 million to $570 million, and the stock market's valuation of the company from $1.8 billion to $10.3 billion.

The key to the Disney turnaround was the mobilization of Disney's considerable resource base. Prominent among Disney's underutilized resources were 28,000 acres of land in Florida. The acquisition of Arvida Corporation, a land development company, in 1984 assisted Disney in using its land holdings for hotels, convention facilities, residential housing, and a new theme park, the Disney-MGM Studio Tour.

To exploit its huge film library, Disney introduced videocassette sales of the Disney classics and began licensing packages of movies to TV networks. To put Disney's underutilized movie studios to work, Eisner doubled the number of movies in production while also making Disney a major producer of TV programs. Together with an expansion of animated movies, in 1988 Disney became America's leading studio in terms of box office receipts.

Above all, the new management team was exploiting Disney's most powerful and enduring asset: the affection of millions of people of different nations and different generations for the Disney name and the Disney characters. Recognition of the power of these resources allowed Disney to boost theme park admission charges, launch a chain of Disney Stores to push sales of Disney merchandise, and exploit overseas opportunities through Tokyo Disneyland and Disneyland Paris.

the exploitation of the Disney movie library releases on videocassette and then on DVD.

Intangible Resources   For most companies, intangible resources are more valuable than tangible resources. Yet, in companies' financial statements, intangible resources remain largely invisible—particularly in the US, where R & D is expensed.[9] The exclusion or undervaluation of intangible resources is a major reason for the large and growing divergence between companies' balance-sheet valuations (or book values) and their stock-market valuations (Table 5.1). Among the most important of these undervalued or unvalued intangible resources are brand names (Table 5.2). Interbrand values the Walt Disney brand at $29 billion; yet in Disney's balance sheet, the value of all its trademarks are a mere $1.2 billion. Brand names and other trademarks are a form of *reputational asset*: their value is in the confidence they instill in customers, suppliers, and business partners.

Like reputation, technology is an intangible asset whose value is not evident from most companies' balance sheets. Intellectual property in the form of patents, copyrights, trade secrets, and trademarks comprises technological and artistic resources where ownership is defined in law. However, some forms of technical know-how

TABLE 5.1   Large companies with the highest valuation ratios, March 2012

Company	Ratio	Country of listing
Hindustan Unilever	31.51	India
Colgate-Palmolive	19.25	USA
Yum! Brands	17.54	USA
Altria	16.76	USA
Boeing	15.4	USA
Priceline	13.36	USA
Coach	11.9	USA
Amazon	10.88	USA
BSky Broadcasting	10.83	UK
GlaxoSmithKline	9.02	UK
Tingyl	8.49	Hong Kong
Starbucks	8.42	USA
Intuitive Surgical	7.81	USA
British American Tobacco	7.71	UK
Diageo	7.37	UK
Medco Health Solutions	6.63	USA
Infosys	6.43	USA
Apple	6.22	USA
Celgene	5.99	USA
Shire	5.89	UK
Nike	5.25	USA
SAP	5.23	Germany
Coca-Cola	5.04	USA
PepsiCo	4.96	USA

Notes:
The table shows companies from among the world's top-500 companies by market capitalization with the highest ratios of market capitalization to balance-sheet net asset value.

Source: Yahoo! Finance, *Financial Times.*

TABLE 5.2   The world's most valuable brands, 2011

Rank	Brand	Value in 2011($ bn.)	Change from 2010
1	Coca-Cola	71.86	+2%
2	IBM	69.91	+8%
3	Microsoft	59.09	−3%
4	Google	55.32	+27%
5	General Electric	42.81	+0%
6	McDonald's	35.59	+6%
7	Intel	35.22	+10%
8	Apple	33.49	+58%
9	Disney	29.02	+1%
10	Hewlett-Packard	28.48	+6%
11	Toyota	27.76	+6%
12	Mercedes Benz	27.45	+9%
13	Cisco	25.31	+9%
14	Nokia	25.07	−15%
15	BMW	24.55	+10%
16	Gillette	23.99	+3%
17	Samsung	23.43	+20%
18	Louis Vuitton	23.17	+6%
19	Honda	19.43	+5%
20	Oracle	17.26	+16%

Note:
Brand values are calculated as the net present value of future earnings generated by the brand.
Source: Interbrand. Reproduced with permission from: http://www.interbrand.com/en/best-global-brands/best-global-brands-2008/best-global-brands-2011.aspx

may be valuable but property rights may be weak or non-existent. In recent years, companies have become more attentive to the value of their intellectual property. For IBM (with the world's biggest patent portfolio), Qualcomm (with its patents relating to CDMA digital wireless telephony), and ARM (with patents relating to RISC microprocessors), intellectual property is the most valuable resource that they own.

Exploiting the profit potential of intangible assets typically involves extending the range of products over which they are exploited. Nike has extended its brand from athletic shoes to a wide range of apparel and sports equipment; Dolby Laboratories has applied its sound reduction technology to a broad variety of audio products.

Human Resources   Human resources comprise the skills and productive effort offered by an organization's employees. Human resources do not appear on the firm's balance sheet—for the simple reason that the firm does not own its employees; it purchases their services under employment contacts. We view human resources as part of the resources of the firm because, typically, they are stable. Although employees are free to move from one firm to another (most employment contracts require no more than a month's notice on the part of the employee), in practice most employment relationships are long term. In the US the average length of time an employee stays with an employer is 4.0 years, in Europe it is longer—8.4 years in Great Britain and 11.7 in both France and Italy.[10]

Organizations devote considerable effort to appraising their human resources: both at the hiring stage and as part of performance reviews and career planning. Human resource appraisal has become far more systematic and sophisticated. Many organizations have established assessment centers specifically for the purpose of providing comprehensive, quantitative assessments of the skills and attributes of individual employees, and appraisal criteria are increasingly based upon empirical research into the components of superior job performance. *Competency modeling* involves identifying the set of skills, content knowledge, attitudes, and values associated with superior performers within a particular job category, then assessing each employee against that profile.[11] A key research finding is the critical role of psychological and social aptitudes in determining superior work—the interest in *emotional intelligence* reflects this.[12] These findings explain the growing trend among companies to "hire for attitude; train for skills."

The ability of employees to harmonize their efforts and integrate their separate skills depends not only on their interpersonal skills but also on the organizational context. This organizational context as it affects internal collaboration is determined by a key intangible resource: the culture of the organization. The term **organizational culture** is notoriously ill defined. Sebastian Green defines organizational (or corporate) culture as "an amalgam of shared beliefs, values, assumptions, significant meanings, myths, rituals, and symbols that are held to be distinctive." The observation that companies with sustained superior financial performance are frequently characterized by strong organizational cultures has led Jay Barney to view organizational culture as a firm resource of great strategic importance that is potentially very valuable.[13]

Identifying Organizational Capabilities

Resources are not productive on their own. A brain surgeon is close to useless without a radiologist, anesthetist, nurses, surgical instruments, imaging equipment, and a host of other resources. To perform a task, a team of resources must work together. An organizational capability is a "firm's capacity to deploy resources for a desired end result."[14] Just as an individual may be capable of playing the violin, ice-skating, and speaking Mandarin, so an organization may possess the capabilities needed to manufacture widgets, distribute them globally, and hedge the resulting foreign-exchange exposure. We use the terms *capability* and *competence* interchangeably.[15]

Our primary interest is in those capabilities that can provide a basis for competitive advantage—what have also been called *distinctive competences*.[16] Prahalad and Hamel introduced the term *core competences* to describe those capabilities fundamental to a firm's strategy and performance in that:

- they make a disproportionate contribution to ultimate customer value or to the efficiency with which that value is delivered
- they provide a basis for entering new markets.[17]

Prahalad and Hamel criticize US companies for emphasizing products over capabilities. Global leaders are those companies that develop core competences over the long term. Individual products may succeed or fail, the key is to learn from both success and failure in order to build capability.

Classifying Capabilities   Before deciding which organizational capabilities are "distinctive" or "core," the firms needs to take a comprehensive view of its full range of organizational capabilities. To identify a firm's organizational capabilities,

TABLE 5.3 A functional classification of organizational capabilities

Functional area	Capability	Exemplars
CORPORATE FUNCTIONS	Financial control	ExxonMobil, PepsiCo
	Management development	General Electric, Shell
	Strategic innovation	Google, Haier
	Multidivisional coordination	Unilever, Shell
	Acquisition management	Cisco Systems, Luxottica
	International management	Shell, Banco Santander
	Corporate social responsibility	Johnson & Johnson, Danone
MANAGEMENT INFORMATION	Integration of IT with managerial decision making	Wal-Mart, Capital One, Cemex
RESEARCH AND DEVELOPMENT	Research capability	IBM, Merck
	New product development	Apple, 3M
	Fast-cycle new product development	Canon, Inditex (Zara)
OPERATIONS	Operational efficiency	Briggs & Stratton, UPS
	Continuous improvement	Toyota, Harley-Davidson
	Flexibility and speed of response	Four Seasons Hotels
DESIGN	Product design capability	Apple, Alessi
MARKETING	Brand management	Procter & Gamble, LMVH
	Building reputation for quality	Johnson & Johnson
	Responding to consumer requirements	L'Oréal, Amazon
SALES AND DISTRIBUTION	Effective sales promotion and execution	PepsiCo, Pfizer
	Efficient, fast order processing	L.L.Bean, Dell Computer
	Speed of distribution	Amazon
SERVICE	Customer service	Singapore Airlines, Caterpillar

we need to have some basis for classifying and disaggregating the firm's activities. Two approaches are commonly used:

- A *functional analysis* identifies organizational capabilities within each of the firm's functional areas: Table 5.3 offers a framework for this.
- A *value chain analysis* identifies a sequential chain of the main activities that the firm undertakes. Michael Porter's generic **value chain** distinguishes between primary activities (those involved with the transformation of inputs and interface with the customer) and support activities (Figure 5.4). Porter's broadly defined value chain activities can be disaggregated to provide a more detailed identification of the firm's activities (and the capabilities that correspond to each activity). Thus, marketing might include market research, test marketing, advertising, promotion, pricing, and dealer relations.[18]

The Nature of Capability Drawing up an inventory of a firm's resources is fairly straightforward. Organizational capabilities are more elusive, partly because they are idiosyncratic—every organization has features of its capabilities that are unique and difficult to capture using simple functional and value chain classifications. Consider Apple's product design and product development capabilities. Apple has a remarkable ability to combine hardware technology, software engineering, aesthetics, ergonomics, and cognitive awareness to create products with a superior user interface and unrivalled market appeal. But identifying the components of

FIGURE 5.4   Porter's value chain

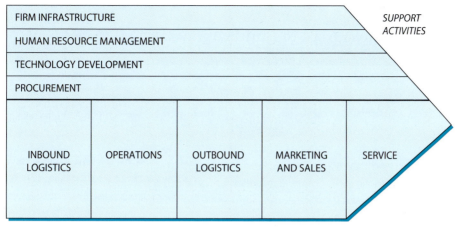

this product design/development capability and establishing where and with whom within Apple this capability is located is no simple task. Let us explore more closely the nature and the determinants of organizational capability.

From Resources to Capabilities: Routines and Integration   Capabilities are based upon routinized behavior. *Routinization* is an essential step in creating organizational capability—only when the activities of organizational members become routine can tasks be completed efficiently and reliably. In every McDonald's hamburger restaurant, operating manuals provide precise directions for a comprehensive range of tasks, from the placing of the pickle on the burger to the maintenance of the milkshake machine. In practice, personnel are routinized through continuous repetition, meaning operating manuals are seldom consulted.

These **organizational routines**—"regular and predictable behavioral patterns [comprising] repetitive patterns of activity"[19]—are viewed by evolutionary economists as the fundamental building blocks of what firms do and who they are. It is through the adaptation and replication of routines that firms develop. Like individual skills, organizational routines develop through learning by doing. Just as individual skills become rusty when not used, so it is difficult for organizations to retain coordinated responses to contingencies that arise only rarely. Hence, there tends to be a tradeoff between efficiency and flexibility. A limited repertoire of routines can be performed highly efficiently with near-perfect coordination. The same organization may find it extremely difficult to respond to novel situations.[20]

Creating organizational capability is not simply a matter of allowing routines to emerge. Combining resources to create capability requires conscious and systematic actions by management. These actions include: bringing the relevant resources together within an organizational unit, designing processes, creating motivation, and aligning the activity with the overall strategy of the organization. Strategy Capsule 5.3 discusses the integration of resources to establish capability.

The Hierarchy of Capabilities   Whether we start from a functional or value chain approach, the capabilities that we identify are likely to be broadly defined:

STRATEGY CAPSULE 5.3

Integrating Resources to Build Organizational Capability

Resources are combined to create organizational capabilities; however, an organization's capabilities are not simply an outcome of the resources upon which they are based.

In sport resource-rich teams are often outplayed by teams that create strong capabilities from modest resources. In European soccer, star-studded teams (e.g., Chelsea, Real Madrid, and Manchester United) are frequently humbled by those built from limited means (e.g., Borussia Dortmund, Arsenal, and Porto). In my former hometown, Washington DC, the Redskins (NFL), Wizards (NBA), and Capitals (NHL) were among the richest teams in their leagues but consistently disappointed their long-suffering fans. Similarly in international competition: having the world's fastest sprinters is of little use in relay races if they drop the baton.

In business too we see companies with modest resources outcompeting established giants. In vacuum cleaners, the tiny British start-up Dyson Ltd. took market share leadership from the domestic appliance giant Electrolux in both the UK and the US. Hyundai Motor assembled its first car, a Ford Cortina, in 1968; by 2012, it was the world's fourth-largest producer of automobiles; in telecom equipment it was the upstart Cisco rather than established incumbents Alcatel-Lucent, Ericsson, and Siemens that led the new era of package switching; in microprocessors for mobile devices, ARM rather than Intel or Texas Instruments is the market leader.

Several factors determine the effectiveness with which resources are combined to create capabilities (Figure 5.5):

◆ *Processes*: While the academic literature has emphasized the role of routines as the foundation of capability, for practical purposes it is easier to view capabilities as comprising processes: coordinated sequences of actions through which specific productive tasks are performed. These sequences can be mapped using a flowchart.[a] For example, the process of fixing bugs in a large program developed by a computer software company involved a process of 30 distinct activities that began with problem recognition and ended with changes in software documentation.[b]

◆ *Organization structure*: For effective coordination, the individuals performing an organizational capability need to be located within the same organizational unit. The product development performance of US and European automobile manufacturers was transformed when, following Japanese practice, they created cross-functional product development teams. Organizational units may be created for the explicit purpose of developing capabilities: *communities of practice* are informal networks of employees who share their knowledge of a particular activity. At Rio Tinto, some 90 communities of practice share know-how and best practices on

manufacturing capability, marketing capability, supply chain management capability. However, our recognition that capabilities are about processes and routines suggests that broadly defined capabilities can be disaggregated into more specialist capabilities. For example, human resource (HR) management capability can be disaggregated recruitment capability, HR appraisal capability, and career development capability—among others. At the same time even broadly defined functional capabilities integrate to form wider cross-functional capabilities: new product development,

FIGURE 5.5 Integrating resources into capabilities

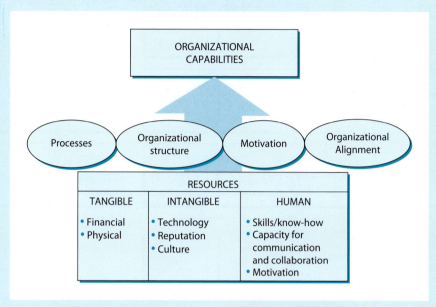

mining techniques, environmental issues, commercial activities, and more.

◆ *Motivation*: The effectiveness with which individuals combine their efforts to achieve organizational capabilities depends upon the extent to which they align their personal interests with those of the team and whether they are inspired to perform to the limit of their abilities. As we have already observed, and will continue to discover, leaders who can unify their organizational members around a clear strategic intent tend to be the most effective at combining resources with superior capabilities.

◆ *Organizational alignment*: As with so much of our strategic analysis, we come back to the issues of *fit*. The concept of organizational alignment has been applied to overall performance in relation to the consistency between environmental, strategic, and organizational factors.[c]

Notes:

[a]T. W. Malone, K. Crowston, J. Lee, and B. Pentland, "Tools for Inventing Organizations: Toward a Handbook of Organizational Processes," *Management Science* 45 (1999): 425–43.

[b]K. Crowston, "A Coordination Theory Approach to Organization Design," *Organization Science* 8 (1997): 157–75.

[c]T. C. Powell, "Organizational Alignment as Competitive Advantage," *Strategic Management Journal* 13 (1992): 119–134.

business development, the provision of customer solutions. What we observe therefore is a hierarchy of capabilities, for example:

● A hospital's ability to treat heart disease depends on its integration of capabilities relating to patient diagnosis, physical medicine, cardiovascular surgery, preoperative and postoperative care, as well as capabilities relating to training, information technology, and various administrative and support functions.

FIGURE 5.6   The hierarchy of organizational capabilities at a telecom equipment manufacturer

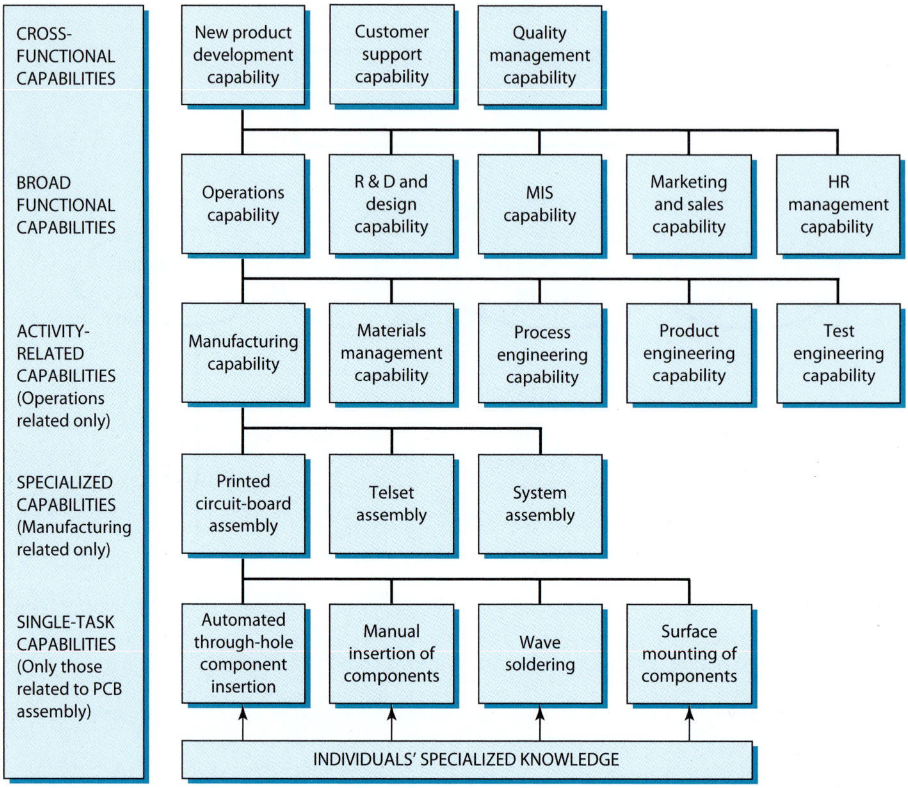

- Toyota's manufacturing ability—its system of *lean production*—integrates capabilities relating to the manufacture of components and subassemblies, supply-chain management, production scheduling, assembly, quality-control procedures, innovation management, and continuous improvement, inventory control, and various HR practices.

Figure 5.6 offers a partial view of the hierarchy of capabilities of a telecom equipment maker. As we ascend the hierarchy, capabilities become progressively more difficult to develop: higher-level capabilities require the broadest integration of know-how, typically across different functional departments. Hence, building new product development capabilities represents one of the greatest management challenges faced by many companies simply because of the vast array of technical and functional knowledge that must be integrated.[21]

Appraising Resources and Capabilities

Having identified the principle resources and capabilities of an organization, how do we appraise their potential for value creation? There are two fundamental issues:

FIGURE 5.7 Appraising the strategic importance of resources and capabilities

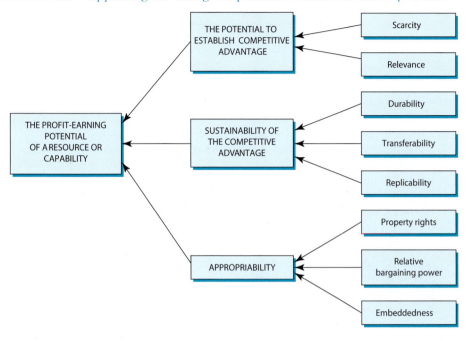

first, what is the strategic importance of different resources and capabilities and, second, what are the strengths of the focal firm in these resources and capabilities relative to competitors?

Appraising the Strategic Importance of Resources and Capabilities

Strategically important resources and capabilities are those with the potential to generate substantial streams of profit for the firm that owns them. This depends on three factors: establishing a competitive advantage, sustaining that competitive advantage, and appropriating the returns from the competitive advantage. Each of these is determined by a number of resource characteristics. Figure 5.7 shows the key relationships.

Establishing Competitive Advantage For a resource or capability to establish a competitive advantage, two conditions must be present:

- *Scarcity*: If a resource or capability is widely available within the industry, it may be necessary in order to compete but it will not be a sufficient basis for competitive advantage. In oil and gas exploration, technologies such as directional drilling and 3-D seismic analysis are widely available—hence they are "needed to play" but they are not "sufficient to win."
- *Relevance*: A resource or capability must be relevant to the KSFs in the market. British coal mines produced some wonderful brass bands, but these musical capabilities did little to assist the mines in meeting competition from

cheap imported coal and North Sea gas. As retail banking shifts toward automated teller machines and online transactions, so the retail branch networks
of the banks have become less relevant for customer service.

Sustaining Competitive Advantage Once established, competitive advantage
tends to erode; three characteristics of resources and capabilities determine the sustainability of the competitive advantage they offer:

- *Durability*: The more durable a resource, the greater its ability to support
  a competitive advantage over the long term. For most resources, including
  capital equipment and proprietary technology, the quickening pace of technological innovation is shortening their life spans. Brands, on the other hand,
  can show remarkable resilience to time. Heinz sauces, Kellogg's cereals,
  Guinness stout, Burberry raincoats, and Coca-Cola have been market leaders
  for over a century.
- *Transferability*: Competitive advantage is undermined by competitive imitation. If resources and capabilities are transferable—they can be bought
  and sold—then any competitive advantage that is based upon them will
  be eroded. Some resources, such as finance, raw materials, components,
  machines produced by equipment suppliers, and employees with generic
  skills are transferable and can be bought and sold with little difficulty.
  Other resources and most capabilities are not easily transferred—either
  they are entirely firm specific or their value depreciates on transfer. Some
  resources are immobile because they are specific to certain locations and
  cannot be relocated. A competitive advantage of the Laphroaig distillery
  and its 10-year-old, single malt whiskey is its water spring on the Isle of
  Islay, which supplies water flavored by peat and sea spray. Capabilities,
  because they combine multiple resources embedded in an organization's
  management systems, are also difficult to move from one firm to another.
  Another barrier to transferability is limited information regarding resource
  quality. In the case of human resources, hiring decisions are typically based
  on very little knowledge of how the new employee will perform. Sellers of
  resources have better information about the performance characteristics
  of resources than buyers do. This creates a problem of *adverse selection*
  for buyers.[22] Jay Barney has shown that different valuations of resources
  by firms can result in their being either underpriced or overpriced, giving
  rise to differences in profitability between firms.[23] Finally, resources are
  complementary: they are less productive when detached from their original
  home. Typically brands lose value when transferred between companies:
  the purchase of European brands by Chinese companies—Aquascutum
  by YGM, Cerruti by Trinity Ltd., Volvo by Geely—risks the diminution of
  brand equity.
- *Replicability*: If a firm cannot buy a resource or capability, it must build it.
  In financial services, most new product innovations can be imitated easily
  by competitors. In retailing, too, competitive advantages that derive from
  store layout, point-of-sale technology, and marketing methods are easy to
  observe and easy to replicate. Capabilities based on complex organizational
  routines are less easy to copy. Federal Express's national, next-day delivery

service and Singapore Airlines' superior inflight services are complex capabilities based on carefully honed processes, well-developed HR practices, and unique corporate cultures. Even when resources and capabilities can be copied, imitators are typically at a disadvantage to initiators.[24]

- *Appropriating the returns to competitive advantage*: Who gains the returns generated by superior resources and capabilities? Typically the owner of that resource or capability. But ownership may not be clear-cut. Are organizational capabilities owned by the employees who provide skills and effort or by the firm which provides the processes and culture? In human-capital-intensive firms, there is an ongoing struggle between employees and shareholders as to the division of the rents arising from superior capabilities. As Strategy Capsule 5.4 describes, bargaining between star employees and owners over the sharing of spoils is a characteristic feature of both investment banking and professional sports. This struggle is reminiscent of the conflict between labor and capital to capture surplus value described by Karl Marx. The prevalence of partnerships (rather than shareholder-owned companies) in law, accounting, and consulting firms is one solution to this conflict over rent appropriation. The less clear are property rights in resources and capabilities, the greater the importance of relative bargaining power in determining the division of returns between the firm and its members. The more deeply embedded are individual skills and knowledge within organizational routines, and the more they depend on corporate systems and reputation, the weaker the employee is relative to the firm.

Appraising the Relative Strength of a Firm's Resources and Capabilities

Having established which resources and capabilities are strategically most important, we need to assess how a firm measures up relative to its competitors. Making an objective appraisal of a company's resources and capabilities relative to its competitors' is difficult. Organizations frequently fall victim to past glories, hopes for the future, and their own wishful thinking. The tendency toward hubris among companies, and their senior managers, means that business success often sows the seeds of its own destruction.[25] Royal Bank of Scotland's acquisition-fuelled growth during 2000–2007 was based upon its perceived excellence in targeting and integrating acquisitions. This perception, rooted in the success of its first major acquisition, NatWest Bank, culminated in the disastrous takeovers of Citizens Bank of Ohio in 2004 and ABN Amro in 2007.[26]

Benchmarking is "the process of identifying, understanding, and adapting outstanding practices from organizations anywhere in the world to help your organization improve its performance."[27] Benchmarking offers a systematic framework and methodology for identifying particular functions and processes and then for comparing their performance with other companies'. By establishing performance metrics for different capabilities, an organization can rate its relative position. The results can be salutary: Xerox Corporation, a pioneer of benchmarking during the 1980s, observed the massive superiority of its Japanese competitors in cost efficiency, quality, and new-product development. More recent evidence shows wide gaps in most industries between average practices and best practices.[28]

STRATEGY CAPSULE 5.4

Appropriating Returns from Superior Capabilities: Employees vs. Owners

Investment banks offer an illuminating arena to view the conflict between employees and owners to appropriate the returns to organizational capability. Historically, Goldman Sachs was widely regarded as possessing outstanding capability in relation to merger and acquisition services, underwriting new issues, and proprietary trading. These capabilities combine several resources: a high level of employee skill, IT infrastructure, corporate reputation, and the company's processes and culture. All but the first of these are owned by the company. However, the division of returns between employees and owners suggests that the former has had the upper hand in appropriating rents (Table 5.4).

In professional sport, it would appear that star players are well positioned to exploit the full value of their contribution to their teams' performance. The $27.8 million salary paid to Kobe Bryant for the 2012/13 NBA season seems likely to fully exploit his value to the Los Angeles Lakers.

Similarly with CEOs. Disney's CEO, Robert Iger, was paid $31.4 million in 2011. But determining how much Iger contributed to Disney's 2011 net income of $5,260 million as compared with that of Disney's other 156,00 employees is unknown.

The more an organizational performance can be identified with the expertise of an individual employee, the more mobile is that employee, and the more likely that the employee's skills can be deployed with another firm, then the stronger is the bargaining position of that employee.

Hence, the emphasis that many investment banks, advertising agencies, and other professional service firms give to team-based rather than individual skills. "We believe our strength lies in . . . our unique team-based approach," declares audit firm Grant Thornton. However, employees can reassert their bargaining power through emphasizing team mobility: in September 2010, most of UBS's energy team moved to Citi.

TABLE 5.4   Profits, dividends, and employee compensation at Goldman Sachs

	2008	2009	2010	2011
Net profits	$4,440m	$13,390m	$8,354m	$4,442m
Dividends to ordinary shareholders	$638m	$579m	$819m	$780m
Total employee compensation	$20,237m	$16,190m	$15,380m	$12,200m
Compensation per employee	$344,900	$498,000	$430,000	$366,360

However, benchmarking carries risks. Dan Levinthal points to the danger of looking at specific practices without taking account of interdependencies with other processes and the organizational context more broadly: "Companies should be cautious about benchmarking or imitating certain policies and practices of other firms . . . the implicit assumption in this thinking is that the policy that is benchmarked and adopted is independent of what my firm is already doing. The best human resource management practice for Nordstrom may not be the best for McDonald's. It may actually be dysfunctional."[29]

My own experience with companies points to the need for benchmarking to be supplemented by more reflective approaches to recognizing strengths and weaknesses. I find it useful to get groups of managers together to ask them to identify things that the company has done well in recent years and things that it has done badly, then to ask whether any patterns emerge.

Developing Strategy Implications

Our analysis so far—identifying resources and capabilities and appraising them in terms of strategic importance and relative strength—can be summarized in the form of a simple display (Figure 5.8).

Our key focus is on the two right-hand quadrants of Figure 5.8. How do we exploit our key strengths most effectively? How can we address our key weaknesses in terms of both reducing our vulnerability to them and correcting them? Finally, what about our "inconsequential" strengths: are these really superfluous or are there ways in which we can deploy them to greater effect? Let me offer a few suggestions.

Exploiting Key Strengths

The foremost task is to ensure that the firm's critical strengths are deployed to the greatest effect:

- If some of Walt Disney's key strengths are the Disney brand, the worldwide affection that children and their parents have for Disney characters, and the company's capabilities in the design and operation of theme parks, the implication is that Disney should not limit its themes park activities to six locations (Anaheim, Orlando, Paris, Tokyo, Hong Kong, and Shanghai); it should open theme parks in other locations which have adequate market potential for year-round attendance.

FIGURE 5.8   The framework for appraising resources and capabilities

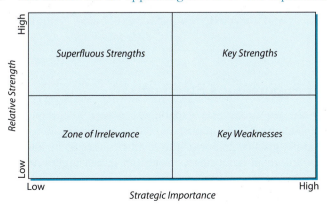

- If a core competence of quality newspapers such as the *New York Times*, the *Guardian* (UK), and *Le Monde* (France) is their ability to interpret events (especially in their home countries), can this capability be used as a basis for establishing new businesses such as customized business intelligence and other types of consulting in order to supplement their declining revenues from newspaper sales?

- If a company has few key strengths, this may suggest adopting a niche strategy. Harley-Davidson's key strength is its brand identity built on its 110-year heritage. Its strategy has been built around this single strength: a focus on super-heavyweight, traditionally styled, technologically backward motorcycles.

Managing Key Weaknesses

What does a company do about its key weaknesses? It is tempting to think of how companies can upgrade existing resources and capabilities to correct such weaknesses. However, converting weakness into strength is likely to be a long-term task for most companies. In the short to medium term, a company is likely to be stuck with the resources and capabilities that it has inherited.

The most decisive, and often most successful, solution to weaknesses in key functions is to *outsource*. Thus, in the automobile industry, companies have become increasingly selective in the activities they perform internally. During the 1930s, Ford was almost completely vertically integrated. At its massive River Rouge plant, which once employed over 100,000 people, coal and iron ore entered at one end, completed cars exited at the other. In 2004, Ford opened its Dearborn Truck Plant on the old River Rouge site. The new plant employed 3200 Ford workers and an equal number of suppliers' employees. Almost all component production was outsourced along with a major part of design, engineering, assembly, IT, and security. In athletic shoes and clothing, Nike undertakes product design, marketing, and overall "systems integration," but manufacturing, logistics, and many other functions are contracted out. We shall consider the vertical scope of the firm in greater depth in Chapter 11.

Clever strategy formulation can allow a firm to negate its vulnerability to key weaknesses. Consider once more Harley-Davidson. It cannot compete with Honda, Yamaha, and BMW on technology. The solution? It has made a virtue out of its outmoded technology and traditional designs. Harley-Davidson's old-fashioned, push-rod engines, and recycled designs have become central to its retro-look authenticity.

What about Superfluous Strengths?

What about those resources and capabilities where a company has particular strengths that don't appear to be important sources of sustainable competitive advantage? One response may be to lower the level of investment into these resources and capabilities. If a retail bank has a strong but increasingly underutilized branch network, it may be time to prune its real-estate assets and invest in web-based customer services.

However, in the same way that companies can turn apparent weaknesses into competitive strengths, so it is possible to develop innovative strategies that turn apparently inconsequential strengths into key strategy differentiators. Edward Jones' network of brokerage offices and 8000-strong sales force looked increasingly irrelevant in an era when brokerage transactions were going online. However, by emphasizing personal service, trustworthiness, and its traditional, conservative investment virtues, Edward Jones has built a successful contrarian strategy based on its network of local offices.[30]

In the fiercely competitive MBA market, business schools should also seek to differentiate on the basis of idiosyncratic resources and capabilities. Georgetown's Jesuit heritage is not an obvious source of competitive advantage for its MBA programs. Yet, the Jesuit approach to education is about developing the whole person; this fits well with an emphasis on developing the values, integrity, and emotional intelligence necessary to be a successful business leader. Similarly, Dartmouth College's location in the woods of New Hampshire far from any major business center is not an obvious benefit to its business programs. However, Dartmouth's Tuck Business School has used the isolation and natural beauty of its locale to create an MBA program that features unparalleled community and social involvement that fosters personal development and close network ties.

Choosing the Industry Context

In appraising resources and capabilities on the basis of strategic importance and relative strength we need to acknowledge that both these variables are context specific—both depend upon how we define the competitive environment of the focal firm. Consider the case of Harley-Davidson: if we view the relevant context as the world motorcycle industry, then technology is a critically important resource. If we view Harley as competing in the heavyweight-cruiser segment, then technology is less important. Similarly with the relative strength dimension—this depends critically upon which firms form our comparison set.

The choice of industry context is a matter of judgment. In general it is best to define industry context relatively broadly; otherwise, there is a risk that our resource/capability analysis becomes limited by the focal firm's existing strategy and we tend to exclude both threats from distant competitors and opportunities for radically new strategic departures.

More generally, however, we need to be alert to the limitations and weaknesses of our strategy frameworks. In the case of the Porter five forces of competition framework, the theoretical foundations of the model are largely obsolete and empirical support for the model is weak. Nevertheless, the five forces framework is a useful and revealing analytical tool. The key is to recognize that our analytical frameworks are not scientific theories: they are tools. In the case of the approach to analyzing resources and capabilities outlined here, our purpose is to make a start on identifying and understanding the resources and capabilities of organizations: the approach's value is in providing an overall picture of a firm's resource/capability profile within which more detailed analysis can then be pursued (Strategy Capsule 5.5).

STRATEGY CAPSULE 5.5

Resource and Capability Analysis in Action: Ducati Motor Holding S.p.A

TABLE 5.5 The resources and capabilities of Ducati (prior to the acquisition by Audi)

	Strategic importance (1 to 10)	Ducati's relative strength (1 to 10)
Resources		
Proprietary technology	Automotive technology is well-diffused throughout the industry (3)	A history of technical innovation, but few patents (6)
Location	Proximity to major markets, industry knowledge, and low cost inputs offer some advantages (4)	Italy is Europe's biggest motorcycle market and a center for engineering and design know-how (10)
Distribution	Critical to access the buyers and provide customer service (9)	Strong dealer network in Italy, weak in most other major markets (3)
Brand	Brand image important to buyers; scarce and costly to replicate (8)	Ducati an iconic brand with a long racing heritage (10)
Finance	Important for upgrading resources and capabilities (7)	Weak cash flow, parent company has limited financial resources (1)
Capabilities		
Manufacturing	Capabilities with regard to efficiency, quality, flexibility are critical to cost and user satisfaction (10)	Ducati high cost due to low output (about 32,000 bikes annually); history of quality problems (2)
Design	Good design essential, but designs easy to replicate (6)	History of appealing and innovative designs (10)
Engineering	Key input into successful new product development (8)	Strong in ingenuity and innovation (8)
New product development	Regular launch of new models critical to market presence (10)	Despite limited resources, strong record of successful new products (9)
Marketing	Media advertising, promotion, and community building important, but marketing capability not rare (6)	Effective in brand promotion and online presence (8)
Customer service	Essential for brand reputation and sales of accessories (7)	Weak, especially outside Italy (2)

Ducati combines sophisticated engineering with Italian design flair to produce a range of high-performance sports motorcycles. However, it inhabits an intensely competitive industry where it faces both large-scale manufacturers (Honda, Suzuki, Yamaha, BMW) and specialists (Harley-Davidson, Triumph, Piaggio, MV Agusta, and many more).

To identify resources and capabilities we can start with key success factors: what resources and capabilities are needed to compete effectively in the world motorcycle industry? We can supplement this list by considering the value chain of a typical motorcycle producer, then we can move on to appraising these resources and capabilities in terms of strategic importance and Ducati's relative strengths. Table 5.5 and Figure 5.9 show the results of this initial analysis.[31]

FIGURE 5.9   The resources and capabilities of Ducati Motor Holding S.p.A.

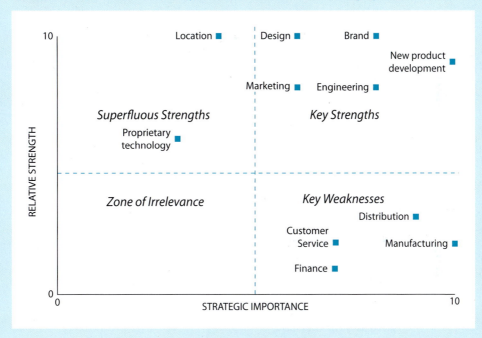

Summary

We have shifted the focus of our attention from the external environment of the firm to its internal environment. We have observed that internal resources and capabilities offer a sound basis for building strategy. Indeed, when a firm's external environment is in a state of flux, internal strengths are likely to provide the primary basis upon which it can define its identity and its strategy.

In this chapter we have followed a systematic approach to identifying the resources and capabilities that an organization has access to and then have appraised these resources and capabilities in terms of their potential to offer a sustainable competitive advantage and, ultimately, to generate profit.

Having built a picture of an organization's key resources and capabilities and having identified areas of strength and weakness, we can then devise strategies through which the organization can exploit its strengths and minimize its vulnerability to its weaknesses. Figure 5.10 summarizes the main stages of our analysis.

In the course of the chapter, we have encountered a number of theoretical concepts and relationships; however, the basic issues of resource and capability analysis are intensely practical. The management systems of most firms devote meticulous attention to some resources and capabilities, such as the physical and financial assets that are valued on their balance sheets, to brand awareness, and to the monitoring and appraisal of human resources, but comprehensive assessment is rare. Senior managers often refer to the "core competencies" and "distinctive capabilities" of their organizations, but identification of these strengths is typically subjective and impressionistic.

FIGURE 5.10   Summary: A framework for analyzing resources and capabilities

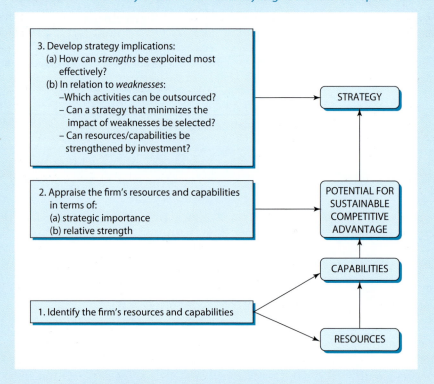

Because the resources and capabilities of the firm form the foundation for building competitive advantage, we shall return again and again to the concepts of this chapter. I shall also be extending the scope of our analysis. My emphasis has been on identifying, appraising, and deploying firms' existing resources and capabilities. A key challenge for companies is how they build capabilities to deal with the challenges of the future. We will address this issue in Chapter 8 when we discuss managing strategic change.

 Quizzes and flashcards to test yourself further are available in your interactive e-book at **www.wileyopenpage.com**

Self-Study Questions

1. Many bricks-and-mortar retailers have been devastated by competition from internet retailers—book retailers and travel agents in particular. Advise either a travel agent or a traditional book retailer how it might redeploy its existing resources and capabilities to build a viable business either by repositioning within its existing industry or moving into a new area of business.

2. Microsoft's main capabilities relate to the development and marketing of complex computer software. Its greatest resource is the huge installed base of its Windows operating system, which runs on 83% of the world's personal computers. Does Microsoft's entry into video game consoles indicate that its strategy is becoming divorced from its principal resources and capabilities?

3. I have argued that the part of discrepancy between firms' stock market value and their book value reflects the fact than intangible resources are typically undervalued or not valued at all in their balance sheets. For the companies listed in Table 5.1, which types of resource are likely to be absent or undervalued in the firms' balance sheets?

4. Many companies announce in their corporate communications: "Our people are our greatest resource." In terms of the criteria listed in Figure 5.7, can employees be considered of the utmost strategic importance?

5. The chapter argues that Apple's key capabilities are product design and product development which combine hardware technology, software engineering, aesthetics, ergonomics, and cognitive awareness to create products with a superior user interface and unrivalled market appeal. How easy would it be for Samsung to replicate these capabilities of Apple?

6. Given the profile of Ducati's resources and capabilities outlined in Table 5.5 and Figure 5.9, what strategy recommendations would you offer VW?

7. Apply resource and capability analysis to your own business school. Begin by identifying the resources and capabilities relevant to success in the market for business education, appraise the resources and capabilities of your school, and then make strategy recommendations regarding such matters as the programs to be offered and the overall positioning and differentiation of the school and its offerings.

Notes

1. The resource-based view is described in J. B.Barney, "Firm Resources and Sustained Competitive Advantage," *Journal of Management* 17 (1991): 99–120; J. Mahoney and J. R. Pandian, "The Resource-Based View within the Conversation of Strategic Management," *Strategic Management Journal* 13 (1992): 363–80; M. A. Peterlaf, "The Cornerstones of Competitive Advantage: A Resource-Based View," *Strategic Management Journal* 14 (1993): 179–92; and R. M. Grant, "The Resource-based Theory of Competitive Advantage," *California Management Review* 33 (1991): 114–35.

2. Ted Levitt ("Marketing Myopia," *Harvard Business Review*, July/August 1960: 24–47) recognized that a customer focus could result in firms defining their strategies too narrowly. Hence, he proposed that firms should define their strategies on the basis of the broad customer. For example, railroad companies should view themselves as being in the transportation business; oil companies should see themselves as energy companies. However, this fails to consider the resource implications of serving these broad customer needs. Can railroad companies enter the airline business or oil companies become successful electricity suppliers?

3. C. K. Prahalad and G. Hamel, "The Core Competence of the Corporation," *Harvard Business Review* (May/June1990): 79–91.

4. "Eastman Kodak: Failing to Meet the Digital Challenge," in R. M. Grant, *Cases to Accompany Contemporary Strategy Analysis* 8th edn (Oxford: Blackwell, 2013).

5. E. Danneels, B. Provera, and G. Verona, "Legitimizing Exploration: Olivetti's Transition from Mechanical to Electronic Technology," Management Department, Bocconi University, Milan, 2008.

6. M. Tripsas, "Unraveling the Process of Creative Destruction: Complementary Assets and Incumbent Survival in the Typesetter Industry," *Strategic Management Journal* 18, (Summer 1997): 119–42; J. Bower and C. M. Christensen, "Disruptive Technologies: Catching the Wave," *Harvard Business Review* (January/February 1995): 43–53.

7. A. Madhok and S. Li, "Ricardo Revisited: The Resource Based View, Comparative Advantage and Competitive Heterogeneity" (September 28, 2004). Available at SSRN: http://ssrn.com/abstract=611182, accessed 16 June, 2009.

8. Released theatrical productions less amortization, October 1, 2011 (Walt Disney Company, 10-K report).

9. "Why It Is So Hard to Value a Mystery?" *Financial Times* Special Report (January 7, 2008): 2.

10. *Economic Survey of the European Union*, 2007 (Paris: OECD, 2007).

11. E. Lawler, "From Job-Based to Competency-Based Organizations," *Journal of Organizational Behavior* 15 (1994): 3–15; L. Spencer and S. Spencer, *Competence at Work: Models for Superior Performance* (New York: John Wiley & Sons, Inc., 1993).

12. D. Goleman, *Emotional Intelligence* (New York: Bantam, 1995).

13. S. Green, "Understanding Corporate Culture and Its Relationship to Strategy," *International Studies of Management and Organization* 18 (Summer 1988) 6-28; J. Barney, "Organizational Culture: Can It Be a Source of Sustained Competitive Advantage?" *Academy of Management Review* 11 (1986): 656–65.

14. C. E. Helfat and M. Lieberman, "The Birth of Capabilities: Market Entry and the Importance of Prehistory," *Industrial and Corporate Change* 12 (2002) 725–60.

15. G. Hamel and C. K. Prahalad state: "the distinction between competencies and capabilities is purely semantic" (letter, *Harvard Business Review*, May/June1992: 164–5).

16. P. Selznick, *Leadership in Administration: A Sociological Interpretation* (New York: Harper & Row, 1957).

17. C. K. Prahalad and G. Hamel, "The Core Competence of the Corporation," *Harvard Business Review* (May/June1990): 79–91.

18. Porter's value chain provides the main framework of his book on *Competitive Advantage* (New York: Free Press, 1984). McKinsey & Company refers to the firm's value chain as its "business system." See C. F. Bates, P. Chatterjee, F. W. Gluck, D. Gogel, and A. Puri, "The Business System: A New Tool for Strategy Formulation and Cost Analysis," in *McKinsey on Strategy* (Boston: McKinsey & Company, 2000).

19. R. R. Nelson and S. G. Winter, *An Evolutionary Theory of Economic Change* (Cambridge, MA: Belknap, 1982).

20. As a result, specialists perform well in stable environments, while generalists do well in variable conditions: see J. Freeman and M. Hannan, "Niche Width and the Dynamics of Organizational Populations," *American Journal of Sociology* 88 (1984): 1116–45.

21. K. B. Clark and T. Fujimoto, *Product Development Performance* (New York: Free Press, 1991).

22. *Adverse selection* refers to the propensity for a market to be dominated by low-quality or risky offerings as a result of information asymmetry. This is also known as the *lemons problem*. See G. Akerlof, "The Market for Lemons: Qualitative Uncertainty and the Market Mechanism," *Quarterly Journal of Economics* 84 (1970): 488–500.

23. J. B. Barney, "Strategic Factor Markets: Expectations, Luck and Business Strategy," *Management Science* 32 (October 1986): 1231–41.

24. I. Dierickx and K. Cool ("Asset Stock Accumulation and Sustainability of Competitive Advantage," *Management Science* 35 (1989): 1504–13) point to two major disadvantages of imitation. They are subject to *asset mass*

efficiencies (the incumbent's strong initial resource position facilitates the subsequent accumulation of these resources) and *time compression diseconomies* (additional costs incurred by an imitator when seeking to rapidly accumulate a resource or capability e.g., "crash programs" of R & D and "blitz" advertising campaigns tend to be costly and unproductive).

25. D. Miller, *The Icarus Paradox: How Exceptional Companies Bring About Their Own Downfall* (New York: Harper-Business, 1990).

26. "Royal Bank of Scotland Investigation: the Full Story of How the 'World's Biggest Bank' Went Bust," *The Telegraph* (March 5, 2011), http://www.telegraph.co.uk/finance/newsbysector/banksandfinance/8363417/Royal-Bank-of-Scotland-investigation-the-full-story-of-how-the-worlds-biggest-bank-went-bust.html, accessed August 10, 2012.

27. "What is Benchmarking?" *Benchnet: The Benchmarking Exchange*, www.benchnet.com, accessed February 4, 2012.

28. "The Link between Management and Productivity," *McKinsey Quarterly* (February, 2006).

29. "A New Tool for Resurrecting an Old Theory of the Firm," Knowledge@Wharton, May 17, 2006 (http://knowledge.wharton.upenn.edu/article/1480.cfm, accessed February 4, 2012).

30. C. Markides, *All the Right Moves* (Boston: Harvard Business School Press, 1999).

31. This analysis of Ducati was undertaken prior to Ducati's acquisition by Audi, a subsidiary of Volkswagen AG. As part of the Volkswagen Group, Ducati's access to finance, engineering, design, technology, and several other resources and capabilities will be greatly enhanced.

6 Organization Structure and Management Systems: The Fundamentals of Strategy Implementation

> Ultimately, there may be no long-term sustainable advantage other than the ability to organize and manage.
>
> —JAY GALBRAITH AND ED LAWLER

> I'd rather have first-rate execution and second-rate strategy anytime than brilliant ideas and mediocre management.
>
> —JAMIE DIMON, CEO, JPMORGAN CHASE & CO.

> Many people regard execution as detail work that's beneath the dignity of a business leader. That's wrong. To the contrary, it's a leader's most important job.
>
> —LARRY BOSSIDY, FORMER CEO, HONEYWELL

OUTLINE

Introduction and Objectives

We spend a lot of our time strategizing: figuring out how we can best develop our careers; making plans for a summer vacation; thinking about how to improve our attractiveness to members of the opposite sex. Most of these strategies remain just wishful thinking: if strategy is to yield results, it must be backed by commitment and translated into action.

The challenges of strategy implementation are much greater for organizations than for individuals. Executing strategy requires the combined efforts of all the members of the organization. Many of those implementing strategy will have played no role in its formulation; others will find that the strategy conflicts with their own personal interests; some may not believe in the strategy. Even without these impediments, there is the simple truth that implementation tends to be neglected because it requires commitment, persistence, and hard work. "How many meetings have you attended where people left without firm conclusions about who would do what and when?" asks super-consultant, Ram Charan.[1]

We begin with the management systems through which strategy is linked to action and performance. As we shall see, formal strategic planning systems may not be particularly effective at formulating strategy; their primary value is in creating a mechanism for linking strategy to a system of implementation that involves operational planning, target setting, and resource allocation.

However, the challenge of strategy implementation goes beyond the tasks of operationalizing strategic decisions. The way in which a company organizes itself is fundamental to the effectiveness of its strategic management. Hence, a wider goal of this chapter is to introduce the concepts needed to understand the challenge of organizing and to provide a framework for designing organizational structure. Finally, we shall consider not just the role of organizational structure but also the informal aspects of an organization's social structure, namely its organizational culture.

The broad aim of this chapter is to introduce the reader to the fundamentals of strategy implementation: the basic aspects of organizational structure and systems that determine the effectiveness with which strategy is executed. In subsequent chapters we shall consider strategy implementation in particular business contexts. For example, Chapter 8 discusses the management of strategic change; Chapter 9 considers the organizational conditions conducive to innovation; Chapter 10 considers organizing to compete in mature industries; Chapter 12 examines the structure and systems of the multinational corporation; Chapter 14 deals with organizing the multibusiness company; Chapter 15 discusses the role of mergers, acquisitions, and alliances in strategy implementation.

By the time you have completed this chapter, you will be able to:

- understand how strategic planning links to operational planning, performance management, and resource allocation in implementing strategy;
- appreciate the basic principles that determine the structural characteristics of complex human organizations;
- select the organizational structure best suited to a particular business context;
- recognize how companies have been changing their organizational structures in recent years and the forces that have been driving these changes.

From Strategy to Execution

Strategic management has conventionally been viewed as a two-stage process: first, formulation, then implementation. As we observed in Chapter 1, the notion of strategic management as a top-down process in which top management formulates then the lower levels of the organization implement has been challenged by Henry Mintzberg. His strategy-as-process view recognized that in the process of implementation the *intended strategy* is reformulated and redirected by the *emergent strategy*.[2]

The notion that strategic management can be separated into self-contained formulation and implementation stages is wrong. The intended strategy of any organization is inevitably incomplete: it comprises goals, directions, and priorities, but it can never be a comprehensive plan. It is during the implementation phase that the gaps are filled in and, because circumstances change and unforeseen issues arise, inevitably the strategy changes. At the same time, strategy formulation must take account of the conditions of implementation. The observation "Great strategy; lousy implementation" is typically a misdiagnosis of strategic failure: a strategy which has been formulated without taking account of its ability to be implemented is a poorly formulated strategy. The conventional formulation–implementation sequence is summed up in the adage "Structure follows strategy." Yet, management guru Tom Peters argues the reverse: for Domino's Pizza, with its global network of 8000 franchised outlets, or Amway, with its pyramid of commission-based, independent distributors, the structure *is* the strategy.

Clearly, strategy formulation and implementation are interdependent. Nevertheless, the fact remains that purposeful behavior requires that action must be preceded by intention. Hence, a feature of all the strategic planning systems that I have encountered is recognition that a strategy cannot be implemented until it has been formulated. In these strategy processes, formulation is linked to implementation by systems of operational planning, performance management, and resource allocation.

The Strategic Planning System: Linking Strategy to Action

Small enterprises can operate successfully without an explicit strategy. If the business comprises a sole owner or a single family, the firm's strategy may exist only in the head of the owner-manager. Unless that owner-manager needs to write a business plan in order to attract outside financing, the strategy may never be articulated. There is no need to articulate the strategy because implementation is by the owner-manager, who knows what is in his/her own head.

Once the top management of a business comprises more than one person, strategy formulation has to become explicit. When they founded Apple Computer, Steve Jobs and Steve Wozniak each had ideas about what Apple II should be like and how it would be built and marketed. Agreeing a strategy required discussion between them. At many family firms, strategy is decided at the kitchen table.

As companies get larger, so the process of strategy making needs to be more formalized. Meetings must be held to allow managers to bring their different areas of knowledge, ideas, and perceptions together and to make decisions. Documents need to be created in order to communicate analysis and decisions from one part of the organization to another. A procedure needs to be established so that individuals and groups commit to the strategies that have been agreed.

The Annual Strategic Planning Cycle   Most large companies have a regular (normally annual, sometime bi-annual) strategic planning process that results in a document that is endorsed at the highest level of the company, normally the board of directors. The strategic planning process is a systematized approach that assembles information, shares perceptions, conducts analysis, reaches decisions, ensures consistency among those decisions, and commits managers to courses of action and performance targets.

Strategic planning processes vary between organizations. At some it is highly centralized. Even after the entrepreneurial start-up has grown into a large company, strategy making may remain the preserve of the chief executive. At MCI Communications, former CEO Orville Wright observed: "We do it strictly top-down at MCI."[3] At General Electric Company, Inc. and BP plc, the strategic planning process is more decentralized, driven primarily by bottom-up initiatives.

As companies mature, their strategic planning processes become more systematized and typically follow an annual cycle. Strategic plans tend to be for three to five years and combine top-down initiatives and directives and bottom-up strategy proposals. Figure 6.1 shows a typical strategic planning cycle. The principal stages are:

- The CEO typically initiates the process with some clear indications of strategic priorities—these will be influenced by the outcome of the previous performance reviews. In addition, the strategic planning unit may also offer input into the process in the form of assumptions or forecasts that provide a common basis for strategic planning by different units and levels within the organization. (Shell's 2011–2014 planning was undertaken as one of two alternative oil market scenarios: $60 a barrel and $80 a barrel.)
- On the basis of this framework of priorities and planning assumptions, the different organizational units—divisions and functional departments—create

FIGURE 6.1   The generic annual strategic planning cycle

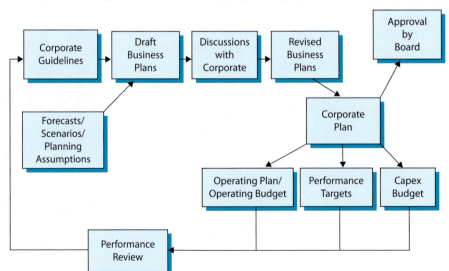

their strategic plans which are then presented at a series of review meetings (usually typically each involving a half-day or full day). On the basis of commentary from the CEO, CFO, and head of strategy (typically), the business plans are then revised.

Once agreed, the business plans are then integrated to create the corporate strategic plan that is then presented to the board for approval.

The Content of Strategic Plans   A strategic plan typically comprises the elements shown in Table 6.1.

Although strategic planning tends to emphasize the specific commitments and decisions that are documented in written strategic plans, the most important aspect of strategic planning is the strategy process: the dialog through which knowledge is shared and ideas communicated, and a consensus established. As General (later President) Dwight Eisenhower observed: "Plans are nothing; planning is everything." General von Moltke of Prussia made a similar point a century earlier: "No battle plan survives contact with the enemy."

Changes in strategic planning processes in recent decades have taken account of the need for flexibility and adaptation. Companies recognized the impossibility of forecasting the future and based their strategies less on medium- and long-term

TABLE 6.1   The contents of a strategic plan

Main components of a strategic plan	Illustration from Royal Dutch Shell strategic plan for 2011–2014
Corporate priorities: both strategic (e.g., gaining market leadership, portfolio rebalancing, competitive repositioning, new business development) and financial (e.g., sales growth, boosting profitability, debt reduction)	Goals: reinforce industry leadership, provide competitive shareholder return, help meet global energy demand in a responsible way
	Key differentiators: technology, project delivery capability, and operational excellence
	Medium-term focus: growth through upstream investment
Priorities of business strategies in terms of primary basis for competitive advantage (e.g., cost-reduction initiatives, innovation goals)	Upstream: focuses on exploration for new reserves with projects where technology and know-how add value, especially in Gulf of Mexico, North American tight gas, and Australian LNG. Also, selective acquisitions and exit from non-core petroleum assets
	Downstream: sustained cash generation by focusing on most profitable and growing businesses and exiting non-core refining capacity and selected retail positions
Strategic milestones: target dates for initiating or completing specific targets or for reaching certain performance goals	Project start-ups for 2012–13: Qatar gas-to-liquids plant, 2nd phase of BC-10 Brazilian oilfield, Gamusut-Kakap Malaysian oilfield
Resource commitments	Annual organic capital expenditure $25–$30 billion 2011–14; > 80% in upstream. Downstream investment to focus on marketing, especially in China, Brazil, and SE Asia
Performance targets and financial projections	Production: grow to 3.7m barrel/day by 2014
	Cash flow: $43 billion by 2012 (assuming $80/barrel oil)
	Safety: reduce injuries from 1.3 per million hours to zero

economic and market forecasts of the future and more on more general issues of strategic direction (in the form of vision, mission, and strategic intent) and alternative views of the future (e.g., using **scenario analysis**). Planning horizons have also shortened (two to five years is the typical planning period). The plans themselves have become less concerned with specific actions and more heavily oriented toward establishing overall performance goals.

In terms of process, strategic planning shifted from a control perspective, in which senior management used the strategic planning mechanisms as a means of controlling decisions and resource deployments by organizational units, toward a coordination perspective emphasizing dialogue, knowledge sharing, and consensus building. The result has been, first, that the strategic planning process has become increasingly informal with less emphasis on written documents and, second, that the role of strategic planning staff has diminished: responsibility for strategy making has been placed on the shoulders of line managers.[4]

The Link with Implementation   The strategy process achieves nothing unless the strategy is implemented. The key to strategy execution is achieved by linking the strategy process to action, through the operating plan; to motivation and accountability, through performance management; and to resource allocation, through capital budgeting. These implementation phases of the strategic planning process are shown in Figure 6.1; let us consider each of them.

Operating Plans

Implementing a strategy requires breaking down medium-term planning into a series of short-term plans that can be a focus for action and a basis for performance monitoring. At the basis of the annual operating plan are a set of performance targets that are derived from the series of annual plans. These performance targets are both financial (sales growth, margins, returns on capital) and operational (inventory turns, defect rates, number of new outlets opened). In the section on "Setting Performance Targets" in Chapter 2, I outlined the basic *cascading* logic for goal setting: beginning with overall goals of the organization as a whole, we can disaggregate these into more specific performance goals as we move down the organization. As Chapter 2 (pp. 45-47) shows, this can be based either on simple financial disaggregation or on using the balanced scorecard methodology. This approach to implementing strategy through establishing performance targets (not just for every organizational unit, but for every employee) has been widely used for over a half a century: *management by objectives* (the process of participative goal setting) was proposed by Peter Drucker in 1954.[5]

These performance targets become built into the annual operating budget. The operating budget is a pro forma profit-and-loss statement for the company as a whole and for individual divisions and business units for the upcoming year. It is usually divided into quarters and months to permit continual monitoring and the early identification of variances. The operating budget is part forecast and part target: it is set within the context of the performance targets established by the strategic plan. Each business typically prepares an operating budget for the following year that is then discussed with the top management committee and, if acceptable, approved. In some organizations the budgeting process is part of the strategic planning system: the operating budget is the first year of the strategic plans; in others, budgeting follows strategic planning.

Operational planning is more than setting performance targets and agreeing budgets; it also involves planning specific activities. As Bossidy and Charan explain: "An operating plan includes the programs your business is going to complete within one year . . . Among these programs are product launches; the marketing plan; a sales plan that takes advantage of market opportunities; a manufacturing plan that stipulates production outputs; and a productivity plan that improves efficiency."[6]

Allocating Resources: Capital Expenditure Budgeting

Capital expenditure budgets are established through both top-down and bottom-up processes. When organizational units prepare their business plans, they will indicate the major projects they plan to undertake during the strategic planning period and the capital expenditures involved. When top management aggregates business plans to create the corporate plan, it establishes capital expenditure budgets both for the company as a whole and for the individual business units.

It is then up to the individual units to submit capital expenditure requests for specific projects. Companies have standardized processes for evaluating and approving projects. Requests for funding are prepared according to a standardized methodology, typically based on a forecast of cash flows, which are then discounted at the company's cost of capital (adjusted to take account of the project's level of risk). The extent to which the project's returns are sensitive to key environmental uncertainties is also estimated. Capital expenditure approvals take place at different levels of a company according to their size. Projects up to $5 million might be approved by a business unit head; projects up to $25 million might be approved by divisional top management; larger projects might need to be approved by the top management committee, while the biggest projects require approval by the board of directors.

Organizational Design: The Fundamentals of Organizing

Implementing strategy is not just about strategic planning processes and linking them to goal setting, operational activities, and resource allocation. Strategy implementation encompasses the entire design of the organization. How a firm is organized determines its capacity for action. We saw in the previous chapter that the design of processes and structures are fundamental to organizational capabilities. The same is true in war: from the conquests of the Roman legions, to the one-sided outcome of the Franco-Prussian War and the Israeli victories in the Six-Day War (1967) and Yom Kippur War (1973), organizational superiority has played a critical role in military success.

Business enterprises come in many shapes and sizes. Samsung Corporation and Louie's Sandwich Bar on 32nd Street, New York share few organizational commonalities. When we include social enterprises, we expand the range of organizations even further. Yet, even giant corporations began as tiny start-ups. Strategy Capsule 6.1 summarizes some of the key developments in the development of the business corporation.

STRATEGY CAPSULE 6.1
The Emergence of the Modern Corporation

The large corporation, the dominant feature of the advanced capitalist economy, is of recent origin. At the beginning of the 19th century, most production, even in Britain, the most industrially advanced economy of the time, was undertaken by individuals and by families working in their own homes. In the US, the biggest business organizations in the mid-19th century were family-owned farms, especially some of the large plantations of the South.[a] The business corporation, one of the greatest innovations of modern society, resulted from two main sources: legal development and organizational innovation.

A corporation is an enterprise that has a legal identity: it can own property, enter into contracts, sue, and be sued. The first corporations were created by royal decree, notably the colonial trading companies: the British East India Company (1600), the Dutch East India Company (1602), and Hudson's Bay Company (1670). The introduction of limited liability, which protected shareholders from corporate debts, during the mid-19th century permitted large-scale equity financing.[b]

During the 19th century, most ideas about organization and management derived from the biggest organization of that time: the military. General von Moltke's organization of the Prussian army into divisions and general staff functions during the 1860s provided the basic model for large industrial corporations.[c] However, toward the end of the 19th century several organizational developments in the US formed the basis of "the second industrial revolution":

◆ *Line-and-Staff Structure*: Lack of transportation and communication meant that most companies operated in just one place. The railroad and the telegraph changed all that. In the US, the railroad companies were the first to create geographically separate operating units managed by an administrative headquarters. "Line" employees were engaged in operational tasks within operating units; "staff" comprised administrators and functional specialists located at head office. These simple line-and-staff structures developed into more complex functional structures; companies such as Sears Roebuck & Co. and Shell Transport and Trading managed numerous operating units with large functionally specialized headquarters.

◆ *The holding company* was a financial structure created by a parent company acquiring controlling equity stakes in a number of subsidiary companies. Its management structures were simple: the parent appointed the board of directors of the subsidiaries and received dividends, but otherwise there was little integration or overall managerial control. The holding company structure allows entrepreneurs such as Richard Branson and families such as the Tata family of India to control large business empires without the need for either the capital or the management structure required by an integrated corporation.

◆ *The multidivisional corporation:* During the 1920s, the multidivisional form began to replace both centralized, functional structures and loose-knit holding companies. At DuPont, increasing size and a widening product range strained the functional structure and overloaded top management. The solution devised by Pierre Du Pont was to decentralize: 10 product divisions were created, each with their own sales, R & D, and support activities. The corporate head office headed by an executive committee took responsibility for coordination, strategy, and resource allocation.[d] Soon after, General Motors, a loose holding company built by acquisition, adopted a similar structure to solve its problems of weak financial control and a confused product line. The new structure (shown in Figure 6.2) divided decision making between the division heads, each

FIGURE 6.2   General Motors Corporation: Organizational structure, 1921

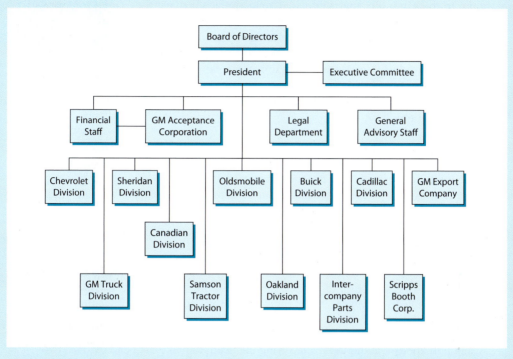

Source: A. P. Sloan, *My Years with General Motors* (Orbit Publishing, 1972): 57. © 1963 by Alfred P. Sloan. © renewed 1991, Alfred P. Sloan Foundation. Reproduced with Permission.

responsible for their division's operations and performance, and the president, as head of the general office and responsible for the corporation's development and control.[e] During the next 50 years, the multidivisional structure became the dominant organizational form for large corporations.

During recent decades, international expansion has been the dominant source of corporate growth. Industry after industry has been transformed by the emergence of global giants: Arcelor Mittal in steel, AB-Inbev in beer, Toyota in automobiles, McDonald's in fast food. Yet, despite the incredible success of the shareholder-owned corporations, other business forms continue to exist. Some sectors—agriculture, retailing, and many service industries—are dominated by family firms and individual proprietorships; partnerships predominate in professional service industries such as law; cooperatives are prominent in some sectors, especially agriculture; despite the privatization trend of the 1990s, state-owned enterprises are highly influential. Saudi Aramco, Indian Railways, China Mobile, China National Petroleum, and Royal Bank of Scotland are all industry leaders that are majority state-owned.

Notes:

[a] A. D. Chandler, *The Visible Hand: The Managerial Revolution in American Business* (Cambridge, MA: MIT Press, 1977): Chapter 2.

[b] J. Micklethwait and A. Wooldridge, *The Company: A Short History of a Revolutionary Idea* (New York: Modern Library, 2005).

[c] R. Stark, *Sociology*, 10th edn. (Belmont, CA: Wadsworth, 2006).

[d] A. D. Chandler, *Strategy and Structure* (Cambridge: MIT Press, 1962): 382–3.

[e] A. P. Sloan, *My Years with General Motors* (London: Sidgwick & Jackson, 1963): 42–56.

Despite their diversity, all business enterprises face the same challenge of designing structures and systems that match the particular circumstances of their own situation. In the same way that strategic management is a quest for unique solutions to the matching of internal resources and capabilities to external business opportunity, so organizational design is about selecting structures, systems, and management styles that can best implement such strategies. To establish principles, guidelines, and criteria for designing business organizations we need to consider the fundamental challenges of organizing.

To design a firm we must first recognize what it is supposed to do. According to Henry Mintzberg:

> Every organized human activity—from making pots to placing a man on the moon—gives rise to two fundamental and opposing requirements: the division of labor into various tasks, and the coordination of these tasks to accomplish the activity. The structure of the organization can be defined simply as the ways in which labor is divided into distinct tasks and coordination is achieved among these tasks.[7]

Specialization and Division of Labor

Firms exist because of their efficiency advantages in producing goods and services. The fundamental source of efficiency is *specialization* through the *division of labor* into separate tasks. Consider Adam Smith's description of pin manufacture:

> One man draws out the wire, another straightens it, a third cuts it, a fourth points it, a fifth grinds it at the top for receiving the head; to make the head requires two or three distinct operations; to put it on is a peculiar business, to whiten the pins is another; it is even a trade by itself to put them into the papers.[8]

Smith's pin makers produced about 4800 pins per person each day. "But if they had all wrought separately and independently, and without any of them having been educated to this peculiar business, they certainly could not each have made 20, perhaps not one pin, in a day." Henry Ford's assembly-line system introduced in 1913 was based on the same principle. Between the end of 1912 and early 1914 the time taken to assemble a Model T fell from 106 hours to six hours.

But specialization comes at a cost. The more a production process is divided between different specialists, the more complex is the challenge of integrating their separate efforts. The more volatile and unstable the external environment, the greater the number of decisions that need to be made and the greater are the coordination costs. Hence, the more stable the environment, the greater the optimal division of labor. This is true both for firms and for entire societies. Civilizations are built on increased divisions of labor, which is only possible through stability. As the recent histories of Somalia, Haiti, and the Congo have demonstrated so tragically, once chaos reigns, societies regress toward subsistence mode, where each family unit must be self-sufficient.

The Cooperation Problem

Integrating the efforts of specialist individuals involves two organizational problems: there is the cooperation problem—that of aligning the interests of individuals who have divergent goals—and the coordination problem—even in the absence of goal conflict, how do individuals harmonize their different activities?

The economics literature analyzes cooperation problems arising from goal misalignment as the **agency problem**.[9] An agency relationship exists when one party (the principal) contracts with another party (the agent) to act on behalf of the principal. The problem is ensuring that the agent acts in the principal's interest. Within the firm, the major agency problem is between owners (shareholders) and managers. The problem of ensuring that managers operate companies to maximize shareholder wealth is at the center of the corporate governance debate. During the 1990s, changes in top management remuneration—in particular the increasing use of stock options—were intended to align the interests of managers with those of shareholders.[10] However, it seems that bonus and stock option plans offer perverse incentives: encouraging either an emphasis on short-term over long-term profitability or even the manipulation of reported earnings (e.g., Enron, WorldCom).

Agency problems exist throughout the hierarchy. For individual employees, systems of incentives, monitoring, and appraisal encourage them to pursue organizational goals rather than doing their own thing or simply shirking. However, the organization structure itself may be part of the problem. Each department tends to create its own subgoals that conflict with those of other departments. The classic conflicts are between different functions: sales wishes to please customers, production wishes to maximize output, R & D wants to introduce mind-blowing new products, while finance worries about profit and loss.

Several mechanisms are available to management for achieving goal alignment within organizations:

- *Control mechanisms* typically operate through hierarchical supervision. Managers supervise the behavior and performance of subordinates who must seek approval for actions that lie outside their defined area of discretion. Control is enforced through positive and negative incentives: the primary positive incentive is the opportunity for promotion up the hierarchy; negative incentives are dismissal and demotion.

- *Performance incentives* link rewards to output: they include piece rates for production workers and profit bonuses for executives. Such performance-related incentives have two main benefits: first, they are high powered—they relate rewards directly to output—and, second, they economize on the need for costly monitoring and supervision of employees. Pay-for-performance becomes more difficult when employees work in teams or on activities where output is difficult to measure.

- *Shared values.* Some organizations are able to achieve high levels of cooperation and low levels of goal conflict without extensive control mechanisms or performance-related incentives. Churches, charities, clubs, and voluntary organizations typically display a commonality of values among members that supports common purpose. Among firms the presence of shared core values has long been recognized as an ingredient of sustained success.[11] Shared values encourage the perceptions and views of organizational members to converge, which facilitates consensus and avoids conflict. In doing so shared values can act as a control mechanism that is an alternative to bureaucratic control or financial incentives—Bill Ouchi refers to this as *clan control*.[12] An organization's values are one component of its culture. Strategy Capsule 6.2 discusses the role of organizational culture for aligning individual actions with company strategy.

STRATEGY CAPSULE 6.2
Organizational Culture as an Integrating Device

Corporate culture comprises the beliefs, values, and behavioral norms of the company, which influence how employees think and behave.[a] It is manifest in symbols, ceremonies, social practices, rites, vocabulary, and dress. While shared values are effective in aligning the goals of organizational members, culture as a whole exercises a wider influence on an organization's capacity for purposeful action. Organizational culture is a complex phenomenon. It is influenced by the external environment—in particular the national and ethnic cultures within which the firm is embedded. It may also be influenced by the social and professional cultures of organizational members. Most of all, it is a product of the organization's history: the founder's personality and beliefs tend to be especially influential. For example, the corporate culture of Walt Disney Company continues to reflect the values, aspirations, and personal style of Walt Disney. A corporate culture is seldom homogeneous: different cultures may be evident in the research lab, in sales, and within the accounting department.

Culture can facilitate both cooperation and coordination. In companies such as Starbucks, Shell, Nintendo, and Google, strong corporate cultures create a sense of identity among employees that supports communication and organizational routines. However, culture can also impede strategy implementation. Cultures can also be divisive and dysfunctional. At the British bank NatWest during the 1990s, John Weeks identified a "culture of complaining" which was a barrier to top-down strategy initiatives.[b] A culture is likely to support some types of corporate action but handicap others. Salomon Brothers (now part of Citigroup) was renowned for its individualistic, internally competitive culture that reinforced drive and individual effort but did little to support cooperation. The culture of the British Broadcasting Corporation reflects internal politicization, professional values, internal suspicion, and a dedication to the public good, but without a strong sense of customer focus.[c]

Cultures take a long time to develop and cannot easily be changed. As the external environment changes, a highly effective culture may become dysfunctional. The Los Angeles Police Department's culture of professionalism and militarism, which made it one of the most admired and effective police forces in America, later contributed to problems of isolation and unresponsiveness to community needs.[d]

While recognizing the importance of corporate culture—according to Merck's CEO, "Culture eats strategy for lunch!"[e] —it is far from being a flexible management tool at the disposal of chief executives. Culture is a property of the organization as a whole, which is not amenable to top management manipulation. CEOs inherit rather than create the culture of their organizations. The key issue is to recognize the culture of the organization and to ensure that structure and systems work with the culture and not against it. Where organizational culture supports strategy, it can be very valuable. First, it is cheap: as a control device it saves on the costs of monitoring and financial incentives; second, it permits flexibility: when individuals internalize the goals and principles of the organization, they can be allowed to use their initiative and creativity in their work.

Notes:

[a] E. H. Schein, "Organizational Culture," *American Psychologist* 45 (1990): 109–19.

[b] J. Weeks, *Unpopular Culture: The Ritual of Complaint in a British Bank* (Chicago: University of Chicago Press, 2004).

[c] T. Burns, *The BBC: Public Institution and Private World* (London: Macmillan, 1977).

[d] "LAPD: Storming the Rampart," *Economist* (December 2, 2000): 72.

[e] J. Weeks, "On Management: Culture Eats Strategy," *Management Today* (June 2006).

The Coordination Problem

The desire to cooperate is not enough to ensure that organizational members integrate their efforts—it is not a lack of a common goal that causes Olympic relay teams to drop the baton. Unless individuals can find ways of coordinating their efforts, production doesn't happen. As we have already seen in our discussion of organizational capabilities, the exceptional performance of Wal-Mart, the Cirque du Soleil, and the US Marine Corps Band derives less from the skills of the individual members as from superb coordination between them. Among the mechanism for coordination, the following can be found in all firms:

- *Rules and directives*: A basic feature of the firm is the existence of general employment contracts under which individuals agree to perform a range of duties as required by their employer. This allows managers to exercise authority by means of general rules ("Secret agents on overseas missions will have essential expenses reimbursed only on production of original receipts") and specific directives ("Miss Moneypenny, show Mr Bond his new cigarette case with 4G communication and a concealed death ray").
- *Routines*: Where activities are performed recurrently, coordination based on mutual adjustment and rules becomes institutionalized within organizational routines. As we noted in the previous chapter, these "regular and predictable sequences of coordinated actions by individuals" are the foundation of organizational capability. If organizations are to perform complex activities efficiently and reliably, rules, directives, and mutual adjustments are not enough—coordination must become embedded in routines.
- *Mutual adjustment*: The simplest form of coordination involves the mutual adjustment of individuals engaged in related tasks. In soccer or doubles tennis, players coordinate their actions spontaneously without direction or established routines. Such mutual adjustment occurs in leaderless teams and is especially suited to novel tasks where routinization is not feasible.

The relative roles of these different coordination devices depend on the types of activity being performed and the intensity of collaboration required. Rules are highly efficient for activities where standardized outcomes are required—most quality-control procedures involve the application of simple rules. Routines are essential for activities where close interdependence exists between individuals, be the activity a basic production task (supplying customers at Starbucks) or more complex (performing a heart bypass operation). Mutual adjustment works best for non-standardized tasks (such as problem solving) where those involved are well informed of the actions of their co-workers, either because they are in close visual contact (a chef de cuisine and his/her sous chefs) or because of information exchange (designers using interactive CAD software).

Hierarchy in Organizational Design

Hierarchy is the fundamental feature of organizational structure. It is the primary means by which companies achieve specialization, coordination, and cooperation. Despite the negative images that hierarchy often stimulates, it is a feature of all complex human organizations and is essential for efficiency and flexibility. The critical issue is not whether to organize by hierarchy—there is little alternative—but how the hierarchy should be structured and how the various parts should be linked.

Hierarchy as Control: Bureaucracy Hierarchy is an organizational form in which members of the organization are arranged in vertical layers; at intermediate layers each individual reports to a superior, and has subordinates to supervise and monitor. Hierarchy offers a solution to the problem of cooperation through the imposition of top-down control.

As an administrative mechanism for exercising centralized power, hierarchy was a feature of the government system of the Ch'in dynasty of China in the late third century BC and has been a feature of all large organizations in the fields of public administration, religion, and the military. For Max Weber, "the father of organizational theory," hierarchy was the central feature of his system of bureaucracy which involved: "each lower office under the control and supervision of a higher one"; a "systematic division of labor"; formalization in writing of "administrative acts, decisions, and rules"; and work governed by standardized rules and operating procedures, where authority is based on "belief in the legality of enacted rules and the right of those elevated to authority under such rules to issue commands."[13]

Weber's preference for rationality and efficiency over cronyism and personal use of hierarchical authority typical of his time encouraged organizational designs that sought safeguards against human traits such as emotion, creativity, fellowship, and idiosyncrasies of personality. As a result bureaucratic organizations have been referred to as *mechanistic*[14] or as *machine bureaucracies*.[15]

Hierarchy as Coordination: Modularity In a general sense, hierarchy is a feature of almost all complex systems:[16]

- The human body comprises subsystems such as the respiratory system, nervous system, and digestive system, each of which consists of organs, each of which is made up of individual cells.
- The physical universe is hierarchy with galaxies at the top, below them are solar systems and we can continue down all the way to atoms and further to of subatomic particles.
- Social systems comprise individuals, families, communities, and nations.
- A book consists of letters, words, sentences, paragraphs, and chapters.

Viewing organizations as natural hierarchies rather than as systems of vertical control points to the advantages of hierarchical structures in coordinating:

- *Economizing on coordination*: Suppose we launch a consulting firm with five partners. If we structure the firm as a "self-organized team" where coordination is by mutual adjustment (Figure 6.3a), 10 bilateral interactions must be managed. Alternatively, if we appoint the partner with the biggest feet as managing partner (Figure 6.3b), there are only four relationships to be managed. Of course, this says nothing about the quality of the coordination: for routine tasks such as assigning partners to projects, the hierarchical structure is clearly advantageous; for complex problem solving, the partners are better reverting to a self-organizing team to thrash out a solution. The larger the number of organizational members, the greater the efficiency benefits from

FIGURE 6.3   How hierarchy economizes on coordination

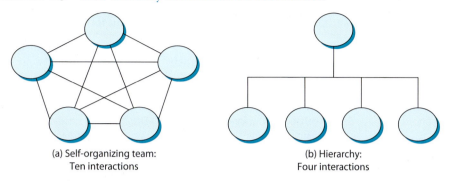

(a) Self-organizing team:
Ten interactions

(b) Hierarchy:
Four interactions

organizing hierarchically. Microsoft's Windows 8 development team involved about 3200 software development engineers, test engineers, and program managers. These were organized into 35 "feature teams," each of which was divided into a number of component teams. As a result, each engineer needed to coordinate only with the members of his or her immediate team. The modular structure of the Windows 8 development team mirrors the modular structure of the product.

- *Adaptability*: Hierarchical, modular systems can evolve more rapidly than unitary systems. This adaptability requires *decomposability*: the ability of each component subsystem to operate with some measure of independence from the other subsystems. Modular systems that allow significant independence for each module are referred to as *loosely coupled*.[17] The modular structure of Windows 8 allows a single feature team to introduce innovative product features and innovative software solutions without the need to coordinate with all 34 other teams. The key requirement is that the different modules must fit together—this requires a standardized interface. The multidivisional firm is a modular structure. At Procter & Gamble, decisions about developing new shampoos can be made by the Global Hair Care division without involving the Global Fabric Care, Global Health Care, or Duracell divisions. A divisional structure also makes it easier for P&G to add new businesses (Gillette, Wella) or to divest them (Folgers Coffee, Pringles).[18]

Contingency Approaches to Organization Design

Like strategy, organizational design has been afflicted by the desire to find the "best" way of organizing. During the first half of the 20th century, bureaucracy and scientific management were believed to be the best way of organizing. During the 1950s and 1960s, the human relations school recognized that cooperation and coordination within organizations was about social relationships, which bureaucracy stifled through inertia and alienation: Theory X had been challenged by Theory Y.

However, empirical studies pointed to different organizational characteristics being suited to different circumstances. Among Scottish engineering companies, Burns and Stalker found that firms in stable environments had *mechanistic forms*, characterized by bureaucracy; those in less stable markets had *organic forms* that were less formal and more flexible. Table 6.2 contrasts key characteristics of the two forms.

TABLE 6.2 Mechanistic versus organic organizational forms

Feature	Mechanistic forms	Organic forms
Task definition	Rigid and highly specialized	Flexible and broadly defined
Coordination and control	Rules and directives vertically imposed	Mutual adjustment, common culture
Communication	Vertical	Vertical and horizontal
Knowledge	Centralized	Dispersed
Commitment and loyalty	To immediate superior	To the organization and its goals
Environmental context	Stable with low technological uncertainty	Dynamic with significant technological uncertainty and ambiguity

Source: Adapted from Richard Butler, *Designing Organizations: A Decision-Making Perspective* (London: Routledge, 1991): 76, by permission of Cengage Learning.

By the 1970s, *contingency theory*—the idea there was no one best way to organize; it depended upon the strategy being pursued, the technology employed, and the surrounding environment—had become widely accepted.[19] Although Google and McDonald's are of similar sizes in terms of revenue, their structures and systems are very different. McDonald's is highly bureaucratized: high levels of job specialization, formal systems, and a strong emphasis on rules and procedures. Google emphasizes informality, low job specialization, horizontal communication, and the importance of principles over rules. These differences reflect differences in strategy, technology, human resources, and the dynamism of the business environments that each firm occupies. In general, the more standardized goods or services (beverage cans, blood tests, or haircuts for army inductees) are and the more stable the environment is, the greater are the efficiency advantages of the bureaucratic model with its standard operating procedures and high levels of specialization. Once markets become turbulent, or innovation becomes desirable, or buyers require customized products—then the bureaucratic model breaks down.

These contingency factors also cause functions within companies to be organized differently. Stable, standardized activities such as payroll, treasury, taxation, customer support, and purchasing activities tend to operate well when organized along bureaucratic principles; research, new product development, marketing, and strategic planning require more organic modes of organization.

As the business environment has become increasingly turbulent, the trend has been toward organic approaches to organizing, which have tended to displace more bureaucratic approaches. Since the mid-1980s, almost all large companies have made strenuous efforts to restructure and reorganize in order to achieve greater flexibility and responsiveness. Within their multidivisional structures, companies have decentralized decision making, reduced their number of hierarchical layers, shrunk headquarters staffs, emphasized horizontal rather than vertical communication, and shifted the emphasis of control from supervision to accountability.

However, the trend has not been one way. The financial crisis of 2008 and its aftermath have caused many companies to reimpose top-down control. Greater awareness of the need to manage financial, environmental, and political risks in sectors such as financial services, petroleum, and mining have also reinforced centralized control and reliance on rules. It is possible that the cycles of centralization and decentralization that many companies exhibit are a means by which they balance the tradeoff between integration and flexible responsiveness.[20]

Developments in ICT have worked in different directions. In some cases the automation of processes has permitted their centralization and bureaucratization (think of the customer service activities of your bank or telecom supplier). In other areas, ICT has encouraged informal approaches to coordination. The huge leaps in the availability of information available to organizational members and the ease with which they can communicate with one another has increased vastly the capacity for mutual adjustment without the need for intensive hierarchical guidance and leadership.

Organizational Design: Choosing the Right Structure

We have established that the basic feature of organizations is hierarchy. In order to undertake complex tasks, people need to be grouped into organizational units, and cooperation and coordination need to be established among these units. The key organizational questions are now:

- On what basis should specialized units be defined?
- How should decision-making authority be allocated?
- How should the different organizational units be assembled for the purposes of coordination and control?

In this section we will tackle two central issues in the design of organizations. First, on what basis should individuals be grouped into organizational units? Second, how should organizational units be configured into overall organizational structures?

Defining Organizational Units

In creating a hierarchical structure, on what basis are individuals assigned to organizational units within the firm? This issue is fundamental and complex. Multinational, multiproduct companies are continually grappling with the issue of whether they should be structured around product divisions, country subsidiaries, or functional departments, and periodically they undergo the disruption of changing from one to another. Employees can be grouped on the basis of:

- common tasks: cleaners will be assigned to maintenance services and teachers will assigned to a unit called a faculty;
- products: shelf fillers and customer services assistants will be assigned to one of the following departments: kitchen goods, tableware, bedding, or domestic appliances;
- location: the 141,000 associates that work in Starbucks stores are organized by location: each store employs an average of 16 people;
- process: in most production plants, employees are organized by process: assembly, quality control, warehousing, shipping. Processes tend to be grouped into functions.

How do we decide whether to use task, product, geography, or process to define organizational units? The fundamental issue is *intensity of coordination needs*: those individuals who need to interact most closely should be located within the same organizational unit. In the case of Starbucks, the individual stores are the natural units: the manager, the baristas, and the cleaners at a single location need to form a single organizational unit. British Airways needs to be organized by processes and functions: the employees engaged in particular processes—flying, in-flight services, baggage handling, aircraft maintenance, and accounts—need to be working in the same organizational units. These process units then can be combined into broader functional groupings: flight operations, engineering, marketing, sales, customer service, human resources, information, and finance.

This principle of grouping individuals according to the intensity of their coordination needs was developed by James Thompson in his analysis of interdependence within organizations. He distinguished three levels of interdependence: *pooled interdependence* (the loosest), where individuals operate independently but depend on one another's performance; *sequential interdependence*, where the output of one individual is the input of the other; and *reciprocal interdependence* (the most intense), where individuals are mutually dependent. At the first level of organization, priority should be given to creating organizational units for reciprocally interdependent employees (e.g., members of an oilfield drilling team or consultants working on a client assignment).[21]

In general, the priorities for the first level of organization tend to be clear: it is usually fairly obvious whether employees need to be organized by task, process, or location. How the lower-level organizational units should be grouped into broader organizational units tends to be less clear. In 1921 it was far from obvious as to whether DuPont would be better off with its functional structure or reorganized into product divisions. In taking over as Procter & Gamble's CEO in 2000, A. G. Lafley needed to decide whether to keep P&G's new-product divisional structure or revert to the previous structure in which the regional organizations were dominant.

In deciding how to organize the upper levels of firm structure the same principle applies. At Nestlé, it is more important for the managers of the chocolate plants to coordinate with the marketing and sales executives for chocolate than with the plant manager for Evian bottled water: Nestlé is better organized around product divisions than around functions. Hyundai Motor produces a number of different models of car and is present in many countries of the world; however, given its global strategy and the close linkages between its different models, Hyundai is better organized by function rather than by product or geography.

Over time, the relative importance of these different coordination needs changes, causing firms to change their structures. The process of globalization has involved easier trade and communication between countries and growing similarities in consumer preferences. As a result multinational corporations have shifted from geographically based structures to worldwide product divisions.

Alternative Structural Forms: Functional, Multidivisional, Matrix

On the basis of these alternative approaches to grouping tasks and activities we can identify three basic organizational forms for companies: the **functional structure**, the **multidivisional structure**, and the **matrix structure**.

The Functional Structure Single-business firms tend to be organized along functional lines. Grouping together functionally similar tasks is conducive to exploiting scale economies, promoting learning and capability building, and deploying standardized control systems. Since cross-functional integration occurs at the top of the organization, functional structures are conducive to a high degree of centralized control by the CEO and top management team.

However, even for single-product firms, functional structures are subject to the problems of cooperation and coordination. Different functional departments develop their own goals, values, vocabularies, and behavioral norms, which makes cross-functional integration difficult. As the size of the firm increases, the pressure on top management to achieve effective integration increases. Because the different functions of the firm tend to be tightly coupled rather than loosely coupled, there is limited scope for decentralization. In particular, it is very difficult to operate individual functions as semi-autonomous profit centers.

The real problems arise when the firm grows its range of products and businesses. As we noted with DuPont, during the early 20th century, once a functionally organized company expands its product range, coordination within each product area becomes difficult.

However, as companies and their industries mature, the need for efficiency, centralized control, and well-developed functional capabilities can cause companies to revert to functional structures. For example:

- When John Scully became CEO of Apple in 1984, the company was organized by product: Apple II, Apple III, Lisa, and Macintosh. Cross-functional coordination within each product was strong, but there was little integration across products: each had a different operating system, applications were incompatible, and scale economies in purchasing, manufacturing, and distributions could not be exploited. Scully's response was to reorganize Apple along functional lines to gain control, reduce costs, and achieve a more coherent product strategy.
- General Motors, pioneer of the multidivisional structure, has moved toward a more functional structure. As cost efficiency became its strategic priority, it maintained its brand names (Cadillac, Chevrolet, Buick) but merged these separate divisions into a more functionally based structure to exploit scale economies and faster technical transfer (compare Figure 6.4 with Figure 6.2).

The Multidivisional Structure   We have seen how the product-based, multidivisional structure emerged during the 20th century in response to the coordination problems caused by diversification. The key advantage of divisionalized structures (whether product based or geographically based) is the potential for decentralized decision making. The multidivisional structure is the classic example of a loose-coupled, modular organization where business-level strategies and operating decisions can be made at the divisional level, while the corporate headquarters concentrates on corporate planning, budgeting, and providing common services.

Central to the efficiency advantages of the multidivisional corporation is the ability to apply a common set of corporate management tools to a range of different businesses. At ITT, Harold Geneen's system of "managing by the numbers" allowed him to cope with over 50 divisional heads reporting directly to him. At BP, John Browne's system of "performance contracts" allowed direct reporting by over 20 "strategic performance units." Divisional autonomy also fosters the development of leadership capability among divisional heads—an important factor in grooming candidates for CEO succession.

FIGURE 6.4   General Motors Corporation: Organizational structure, 1997

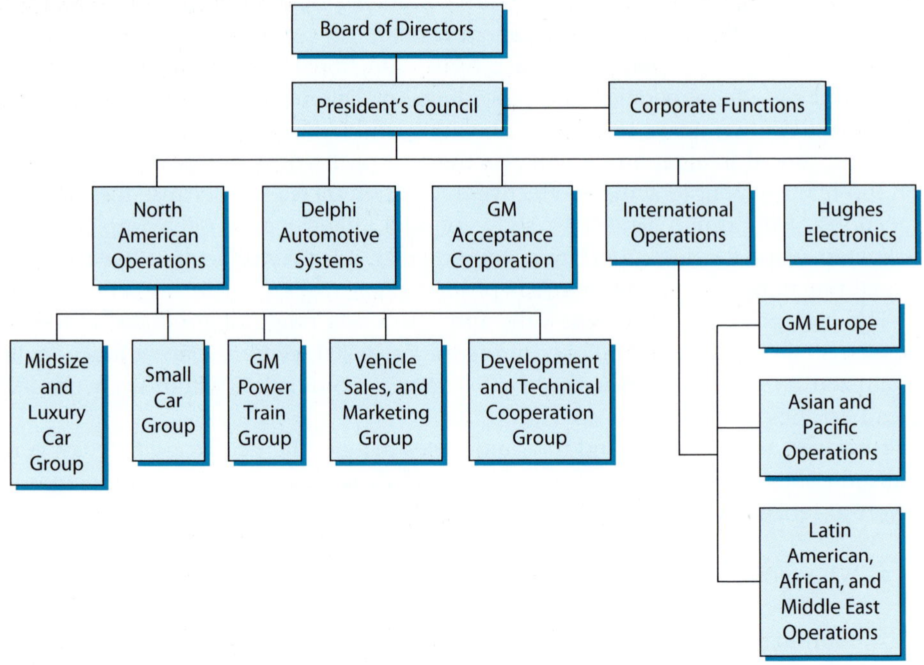

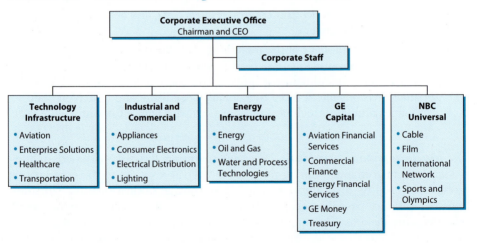

FIGURE 6.5   General Electric: Organizational structure, 2009

Source: Based on information in General Electric's Annual Report, 2008.

The large, divisionalized corporation is typically organized into three levels: the corporate center, the divisions, and the individual business units, each representing a distinct business for which financial accounts can be drawn up and strategies formulated. Figure 6.5 shows General Electric's organizational structure at the corporate and divisional levels.

In Chapter 14, we shall look in greater detail at the organization of the multibusiness corporation.

Matrix Structures   Whatever the primary basis for grouping, all companies that embrace multiple products, multiple functions, and multiple locations must coordinate across all three dimensions. Organizational structures that formalize coordination and control across multiple dimensions are called *matrix structures*.

Figure 6.6 shows the Shell management matrix (prior to reorganization in 1996). Within this structure, the general manager of Shell's Berre refinery in France reported to his country manager, the managing director of Shell France, but also to his business sector head, the coordinator of Shell's refining sector, as well as having a functional relationship with Shell's head of manufacturing.

Many diversified, multinational companies, including Philips, Nestlé, and Unilever, adopted matrix structures during the 1960s and 1970s, although in all cases one dimension of the matrix tended to be dominant in terms of authority. Thus, in the old Shell matrix the geographical dimension, as represented by country heads and regional coordinators, had primary responsibility for budgetary control, personnel appraisal, and strategy formulation.

FIGURE 6.6   Royal Dutch Shell Group: Pre-1996 matrix structure

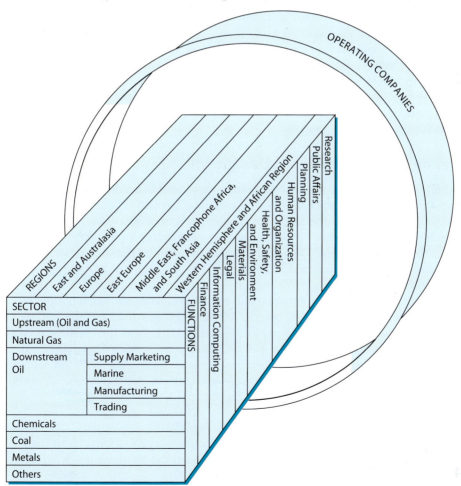

Since the 1980s, most large corporations have dismantled or reorganized their matrix structures. Shell abandoned its matrix during 1995–1996 in favor of a structure based on four business sectors: upstream, downstream, chemicals, and gas and power. During 2001–2002, the Swiss/Swedish engineering giant ABB abandoned its much-lauded matrix structure in the face of plunging profitability and mounting debt. In fast-moving business environments companies have found that the benefits from formally coordinating across multiple dimensions have been outweighed by excessive complexity, larger head-office staffs, slower decision making, and diffused authority. Bartlett and Ghoshal observe that matrix structures "led to conflict and confusion; the proliferation of channels created informational logjams as a proliferation of committees and reports bogged down the organization; and overlapping responsibilities produced turf battles and a loss of accountability."[22]

Yet, all complex organizations that comprise multiple products, multiple functions, and multiple geographical markets need to coordinate within each of these dimensions. The problem of the matrix organization is not attempting to coordinate across multiple dimensions—in complex organizations such coordination is essential. The problem is when this multidimensional coordination is over-formalized, resulting in a top-heavy corporate HQ and over-complex systems that slow decision making and dull entrepreneurial initiative. The trend has been for companies to focus formal systems of coordination and control on one dimension, then allowing the other dimensions of coordination to be mainly informal. Thus, while Shell is organized primarily around four business sectors and these sectors exercise financial and strategic control over the individual operating companies, Shell still has country heads, responsible for coordinating all Shell's activities in relation to legal, taxation, and government relations within each country, and functional heads, responsible for technical matters and best-practice transfer within their particular function, be it manufacturing, marketing, or HR.

Trends in Organizational Design

Consultants and management scholars have proclaimed the death of hierarchical structures and the emergence of new organizational forms. Two decades ago, two of America's most prominent scholars of organization identified a "new organizational revolution" featuring "flatter hierarchies, decentralized decision making, greater tolerance for ambiguity, permeable internal and external boundaries, empowerment of employees, capacity for renewal, self-organizing units, [and] self-integrating coordination mechanisms."[23]

In practice, there has been more organizational evolution than organizational revolution. Certainly major changes have occurred in the structural features and management systems of industrial enterprises, yet there is little that could be described as radical organizational innovation or discontinuities with the past. Hierarchy remains the basic structural form of almost all companies, and the familiar structural configurations—functional, divisional, and matrix—are still evident. Nevertheless, within these familiar structural features, change has occurred:

- *Delayering*: Companies have made their organizational hierarchies flatter. The motive has been to reduce costs and to increase organizational responsiveness. Wider spans of control have also changed the relationships between managers and their subordinates, resulting in less supervision and greater decentralization of initiative. At Tata Steel, the management hierarchy was reduced from 13 layers to five. In briefing the McKinsey lead consultant, the CEO, Dr Irani, observed: "We are over-staffed, no doubt, but more damaging is the lack of responsiveness to fleeting opportunities . . . Our decision making is not as fast as it should be with everyone looking over their shoulder for approval . . . The objective is to redesign job content more meaningfully. The purpose is to rejuvenate the organization by defining richer jobs with fewer hierarchical layers of reporting.[24]

- *Adhocracy and team-based organization*: Adhocracies, according to Henry Mintzberg, are organizations that feature shared values, high levels of participation, flexible communication, and spontaneous coordination. Hierarchy, authority, and control mechanisms are largely absent.[25] Adhocracies tend to exist where problem solving and other non-routine activities predominate and where expertise is prized. Individual teams involved in research, consulting, engineering, entertainment, and crisis response tend to be adhocracies. At a larger organizational scale, companies such as Google, W. L. Gore & Associates, and some advertising agencies have adopted team-based structures with many of the features of adhocracies.

- *Project-based organizations*: Closely related to team-based organizations are project-based organizations. A key feature of the project-based organization is recognition that work assignments are for a finite duration, hence the organization structure needs to be dynamically flexible. Project-based organizations are common in sectors such as construction, consulting, oil exploration, and engineering. Because every project is different and involves a sequence of phases, each project needs to be undertaken by a closely interacting team that is able to draw upon the know-how of previous and parallel project teams. As cycle times become compressed across more and more activities, companies are introducing project-based organization into their conventional divisional and functional structures—for example new product development, change management, knowledge management, and research are increasingly organized into projects.

- *Network structures*: A common feature of the many descriptions of new approaches to company organization is use of the term *network*. Bartlett and Ghoshal present the *transnational organization* as a multinational corporation organized as an integrated global network;[26] Goold and Campbell propose an organizational design that they call the *structured network*.[27] Viewing organizational structures in terms of networks derives from social network analysis where organizations (and other social institutions) are conceptualized in terms of the social relationships between the individuals and organizational units within them. This emphasis on patterns of communication and interaction rather than the formal relationships puts emphasis on the informal mechanisms through which coordination occurs and work gets done within organizations. Advances in information and communications technology have greatly increased the scope for coordination to occur outside of the formal structure, leading many observes to advocate the dismantling of much of the formal structures that firms have inherited.

- *Permeable organizational boundaries*: The benefits of specialization accrue to organizations as well as to individuals; at the same time, the complexity of most products has been increasing. As a result, firms have sought to narrow their corporate scope through outsourcing and refocusing upon core business activities, while relying on close relationships with partner firms to access a wider range of expertise. As we shall when we look more closely at strategic alliances (Chapter 15), localized networks of closely interdependent firms have been a feature of manufacturing for centuries. Such networks are a traditional feature of the industrial structure of much of northern Italy.[28] Hollywood and Silicon Valley also feature specialized firms that coordinate to design and produce complex products.[29]

These emerging organizational phenomena share several common characteristics:

- A focus on coordination rather than on control: In contrast to the command-and-control hierarchy, these structures focus almost wholly on achieving coordination. Financial incentives, culture, and social controls take the place of hierarchical control.
- Reliance on informal coordination where mutual adjustment replaces rules and directives: Central to all non-hierarchical structures is their dependence on voluntary coordination through bilateral and multilateral adjustment. The capacity for coordination through mutual adjustment has been greatly enhanced by information technology.
- Individuals in multiple organizational roles: Reconciling complex patterns of coordination with high levels of flexibility and responsiveness is difficult if job designs and organizational structures are rigidly defined. Increasingly, individual employees are required to occupy multiple roles simultaneously. For example, in addition to a primary role as a brand manager for a particular product category, a person might be a member of a committee that monitors community engagement activities, part of a task force to undertake a benchmarking study, and a member of a community of practice in web-based marketing.

Summary

Strategy formulation and strategy implementation are closely interdependent. The formulation of strategy needs to take account of an organization's capacity for implementation; at the same time, the implementation process inevitably involves creating strategy. If an organization's strategic management process is to be effective then its strategic planning system must be linked to actions, commitments and their monitoring, and the allocation of resources. Hence, operational plans and capital expenditure budgets are critical components of a firm's strategic management system.

Strategy implementation involves the entire design of the organization. By understanding the need to reconcile specialization with cooperation and coordination, we are able to appreciate the fundamental principles of organizational design.

Applying these principles, we can determine how best to allocate individuals to organizational units and how to combine these organizational units into broader groupings—in particular the choice between basic organizational forms such as functional, divisional, or matrix organizations.

We have also seen how company's organizational structures have been changing in recent years, influenced both by the demands of their external environments and the opportunities made available by advances in information and communication technologies.

The chapters that follow will have more to say on the organizational structures and management systems appropriate to different strategies and different business contexts. In the final chapter (Chapter 16) we shall explore some of the new trends and new ideas that are reshaping our thinking about organizational design.

 Quizzes and flashcards to test yourself further are available in your interactive e-book at **www.wileyopenpage.com**

Self-Study Questions

1. It has been argued that traditional approaches to strategic planning (as represented in Figure 6.1) are good systems for exercising control but are not much good for developing strategy, especially for organizations that are facing radical changes in their environment. What do you think some of the strengths and weaknesses of the traditional strategic planning system might be?

2. Referring to Strategy Capsule 6.1, as DuPont expanded its product range (from explosives into paints, dyes, plastics, and synthetic fibers) why do you think the functional structure (organized around manufacturing plants and other functions such as sales, finance, and R & D) became unwieldy? Why did the multidivisional structure based on product groups improve management effectiveness?

3. Within your own organization (whether a university, company, or not-for-profit organization), which departments or activities are organized mechanistically and which organically? To what extent does the mode of organization fit the different environmental contexts and technologies of the different departments or activities?

4. In 2008, Citigroup announced that its Consumer business would be split into Consumer Banking, which would continue to operate through individual national banks, and Global Cards, which would form a single global business (similar to Citi's Global Wealth Management division). On the basis of the arguments relating to the "Defining Organizational Units" section above, why should credit cards be organized as a global unit and all other consumer banking services as national units?

5. The examples of Apple Computer and General Motors (see "Functional Structure" section above) point to the evolution of organizational structures over the industry life-cycle. During the growth phase, many companies adopt multidivisional structures; during maturity and decline, many companies revert to functional structures. Why might this be? (Note: you may wish to refer to Chapter 8, which outlines the main features of the life-cycle model.)

6. Draw an organizational chart for a business school that you are familiar with. Does the school operate with a matrix structure (for instance, are there functional/discipline-based departments together with units managing individual programs)? Which dimension of the matrix is more powerful, and how effectively do the two dimensions coordinate? How would you reorganize the structure to make the school more efficient and effective?

Notes

1. L. Bossidy and R. Charan, *Execution: The Discipline of Getting Things Done* (New York: Random House, 2002): 71.

2. H. Mintzberg, "Patterns of Strategy Formulation," *Management Science* 24 (1978): 934–48; "Of Strategies: Deliberate and Emergent," *Strategic Management Journal* 6 (1985): 257–72.

3. *MCI Communications: Planning for the 1990s* (Harvard Business School Case No. 9-190-136, 1990): 1.

4. R. M. Grant, "Strategic Planning in a Turbulent Environment: Evidence from the Oil Majors," *Strategic Management Journal* 24 (2003): 491–518.

5. P. F. Drucker, *The Practice of Management* (New York: Harper, 1954).

6. L. Bossidy and R. Charan, *Execution: The Discipline of Getting Things Done* (New York: Random House, 2002): 227.

7. H. Mintzberg, *Structure in Fives: Designing Effective Organizations* (Englewood Cliffs, NJ: Prentice Hall, 1993): 2.

8. A. Smith, *The Wealth of Nations* (London: Dent, 1910): 5.

9. S. Ross, "The Economic Theory of Agency," *American Economic Review*, 63 (1973): 134–9; K. Eisenhardt, "Agency Theory: An Assessment and Reviews," *Academy of Management Review*, 14 (1989): 57–74.

10. I. T. Kay and S. Van Ritten, *Myths and Realities of Executive Pay* (Cambridge: Cambridge University Press, 2007): Chapter 6.

11. T. Peters and R. Waterman, *In Search of Excellence* (New York: Harper & Row, 1982).

12. W. G. Ouchi, *Theory Z* (Reading, MA: Addison-Wesley, 1981).

13. M. Weber, *Economy and Society: An Outline of Interpretive Sociology* (Berkeley, CA: University of California Press, 1968).

14. T. Burns and G. M. Stalker, *The Management of Innovation* (London: Tavistock Institute, 1961).

15. H. Mintzberg, *Structure in Fives: Designing Effective Organizations* (Englewood Cliffs: Prentice Hall, 1993): Chapter 9.

16. H. A. Simon, "The Architecture of Complexity," *Proceedings of the American Philosophical Society* 106 (1962): 467–82.

17. J. D. Orton and K. E. Weick, "Loosely Coupled Systems: A Reconceptualization," *Academy of Management Review* 15 (1990): 203–23.

18. On organizational modularity, see R. Sanchez and J. T. Mahoney, "Modularity, Flexibility, and Knowledge Management in Product and Organizational Design," *Strategic Management Journal* 17 (Winter 1996): 63–76; M. A. Schilling, "Toward a General Modular Systems Theory and its Application to Interfirm Product Modularity," *Academy of Management Review* 25 (2000): 312–334; and C. Baldwin and K. Clark, "Managing in an Age of Modularity," *Harvard Business Review* (September/October 1997): 84–93.

19. "The Contingency Theory of Organizational Design: Challenges and Opportunities," in R. M. Burton, B. Eriksen, D. D. Hakenssen, and C. C. Snow (eds), *Organization Design: The Evolving State of the Art* (New York: Springer-Verlag, 2006): 19–42.

20. J. Nickerson and T. Zenger refer to this as *structural modulation:* "Being Efficiently Fickle: A Dynamic Theory of Organizational Choice," *Organization Science* 13 (2002): 547–67.

21. J. D. Thompson, *Organizations in Action* (New York: McGraw-Hill, 1967). The nature of interdependence in organizational processes is revisited in T. W. Malone, K. Crowston, J. Lee, and B. Pentland, "Tools for Inventing Organizations: Toward a Handbook of Organizational Processes," *Management Science* 45 (March 1999): 489–504.

22. C. A. Bartlett and S. Ghoshal, "Matrix Management: Not a Structure, a Frame of Mind," *Harvard Business Review* (July/August 1990): 138–45.

23. R. Daft and A. Lewin, "Where are the theories for the new organizational forms?" *Organization Science* 3 (1993): 1–6.

24. R. Kumar, "De-Layering at Tata Steel," *Journal of Organizational Behavior Education* 1 (2006): 37–56.

25. H. Mintzberg, *Structure in Fives: Designing Effective Organizations* (Englewood Cliffs, NJ: Prentice Hall, 1993): Chapter 12.

26. C. Bartlett and S. Ghoshal, *Managing across Borders: The Transnational Solution*, 2nd edn (Boston, Harvard Business School, 1998).

27. M. Goold and A. Campbell, *Designing Effective Organizations* (San Francisco: Jossey-Bass, 2002).

28. M. H. Lazerson and G. Lorenzoni, "The Firms that Feed Industrial Districts: A Return to the Italian Source," *Industrial and Corporate Change* 8 (1999): 235–66; A. Grandori, *Interfirm Networks* (London: Routledge, 1999).

29. R. J. DeFilippi and M. B. Arthur, "Paradox in Project-based Enterprise: The Case of Film Making," *California Management Review* 42 (1998): 186–91.

III

BUSINESS STRATEGY AND THE QUEST FOR COMPETITIVE ADVANTAGE

7 The Sources and Dimensions of Competitive Advantage

SEARS MOTOR BUGGY: $395

For car complete with rubber tires, Timken roller bearing axles, top, storm front, three oil-burning lamps, horn, and one gallon of lubricating oil. Nothing to buy but gasoline.

. . . We found there was a maker of automobile frames that was making 75 percent of all the frames used in automobile construction in the United States. We found on account of the volume of business that this concern could make frames cheaper for automobile manufacturers than the manufacturers could make themselves. We went to this frame maker and asked him to make frames for the Sears Motor Buggy and then to name us prices for those frames in large quantities. And so on throughout the whole construction of the Sears Motor Buggy. You will find every piece and every part has been given the most careful study; you will find that the Sears Motor Buggy is made of the best possible material; it is constructed to take the place of the top buggy; it is built in our own factory, under the direct supervision of our own expert, a man who has had fifteen years of automobile experience, a man who has for the past three years worked with us to develop exactly the right car for the people at a price within the reach of all.

—EXTRACT FROM AN ADVERTISEMENT IN THE SEARS ROEBUCK & CO. CATALOG, 1909: 1150

If the three keys to selling real estate are location, location, location, then the three keys of selling consumer products are differentiation, differentiation, differentiation.

—ROBERT GOIZUETA, FORMER CHAIRMAN, COCA-COLA COMPANY

OUTLINE

Introduction and Objectives

In this chapter, we integrate and develop the elements of competitive advantage that we have analyzed in previous chapters. Chapter 1 noted that a firm can earn superior profitability either by locating in an attractive industry or by establishing a competitive advantage over its rivals. Of these two, competitive advantage is the more important. As competition has intensified across almost all industries, very few industry environments can guarantee secure returns; hence, the primary goal of a strategy is to establish a position of competitive advantage for the firm.

Chapters 3 and 5 provided the two primary components of our analysis of competitive advantage. The last part of Chapter 3 analyzed the external sources of competitive advantage: customer requirements and the nature of competition determine the key success factors within a market. Chapter 5 analyzed the internal sources of competitive advantage: the potential for the firm's resources and capabilities to establish and sustain competitive advantage.

This chapter looks more deeply at competitive advantage. We look first at the dynamics of competitive advantage, examining the processes through which competitive advantage is created and destroyed. This gives us insight into how competitive advantage can be attained and sustained. We then look at the two primary dimensions of competitive advantage: cost advantage and differentiation advantage and develop systematic approaches to their analysis.

By the time you have completed this chapter, you will be able to:

◆ identify the circumstances in which a firm can create and sustain competitive advantage over a rival and recognize how resource conditions create imperfections in the competitive process that offer opportunities for competitive advantage;

◆ distinguish the two primary types of competitive advantage: cost advantage and differentiation advantage;

◆ identify the sources of cost advantage in an industry, apply cost analysis to assess a firm's relative cost position, and recommend strategies to enhance cost competitiveness;

◆ appreciate the potential for differentiation to create competitive advantage, analyze the sources of differentiation, and formulate strategies that create differentiation advantage.

How Competitive Advantage Emerges and Is Sustained

To understand how **competitive advantage** emerges, we must first understand what competitive advantage is. Most of us can recognize competitive advantage when we see it: Wal-Mart in discount retailing, Singapore Airlines in long-haul air travel, Google in online search, Embraer in regional jets. Yet, defining competitive advantage is troublesome. At a basic level we can define it as follows: *When two or more* *firms compete within the same market, one firm possesses a competitive advantage over its rivals when it earns (or has the potential to earn) a persistently higher rate of profit.*

The problem here is that if we identify competitive advantage with superior profitability, why do we need the concept of competitive advantage at all? A key distinction is that competitive advantage may not be revealed in higher profitability—a firm may forgo current profit in favor of investing in market share, technology, customer loyalty, or executive perks.[1]

In viewing competitive advantage as the result of matching internal strengths to external success factors, I may have conveyed the notion of competitive advantage as something static and stable. In fact, as I acknowledged in Chapter 4 with the discussion of hypercompetition, competitive advantage is a disequilibrium phenomenon: it is created by change and, once established, it sets in motion the competitive process that leads to its destruction.

The Emergence of Competitive Advantage

The changes that generate competitive advantage can be either internal or external. Figure 7.1 depicts the basic relationships.

External Sources of Change For an external change to create competitive advantage, the change must have differential effects on companies because of their different resources and capabilities or strategic positioning. For example, in the six years prior to 2005, the average price of Brent crude was $22 a barrel. Between 2005 and 2011 it averaged $87 a barrel. The result was to shift the balance of competitive advantage in the European car industry. During 2005–2011, Fiat, Renault, and VW, all of which emphasized small, fuel-efficient cars, improved their profitability relative to that of Daimler and BMW, both of which emphasized larger cars.

The greater the magnitude of the external change and the greater the difference in the strategic positioning of firms, the greater the propensity for external change to generate competitive advantage, as indicated by the dispersion of profitability within

FIGURE 7.1 The emergence of competitive advantage

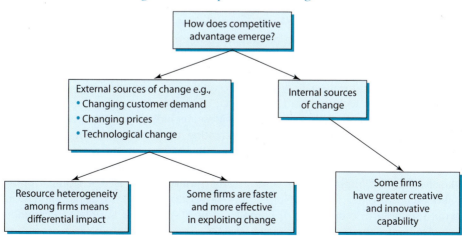

the industry. The world's tobacco industry has a relatively stable external environment and the leading firms pursue similar strategies with similar resources and capabilities. Competitive advantages, as reflected in interfirm profit differentials, tend to be small. The toy industry, on the other hand, comprises a heterogeneous group of firms that experience unpredictable shifts in consumer preferences and technology. As a result, profitability differences are wide and variable.

The competitive advantage that arises from external change also depends on firms' ability to respond to change. Any external change creates entrepreneurial opportunities that will accrue to the firms that exploit these opportunities most effectively. Entrepreneurial responsiveness involves one of two key capabilities:

- The ability to anticipate changes in the external environment. IBM has displayed a remarkable ability to renew its competitive advantage through anticipating, and then taking advantage of, most of the major shifts in the IT sector: the rise of personal computing, the advent of the internet, the shift in value from hardware to software, and the development of cloud computing.

- Speed. As markets become more turbulent and unpredictable, quick-response capability has become increasingly important as a source of competitive advantage. Quick responses require information. As conventional economic and market forecasting has become less effective, so companies rely increasingly on "early-warning systems" through direct relationships with customers, suppliers, and even competitors. Quick responses also require short cycle times so that information can be acted upon speedily. In fashion retailing, quick response to fashion trends is critical to success. Zara, the retail clothing chain owned by the Spanish company Inditex, has built a vertically integrated supply chain that cuts the time between a garment's design and retail delivery to under three weeks (against an industry norm of three to six months.[2] This emphasis on speed as a source of competitive advantage was popularized by the Boston Consulting Group's concept of *time-based competition*.[3] Advances in IT—the internet, real-time electronic data exchange, and wireless communication—have greatly enhanced response capabilities throughout the business sector.

Internal Sources of Change: Competitive Advantage from Innovation

Competitive advantage may also be generated internally through innovation which creates competitive advantage for the innovator while undermining the competitive advantages of incumbents—the process Schumpeter refers to as "creative destruction."[4] Although innovation is typically thought of as new products or processes that embody new technology, a key source of competitive advantage is *strategic innovation*—new approaches to doing business, including new business models.

Strategic innovation typically involves creating value for customers from novel products, experiences, or modes of product delivery. Thus, in the retail sector, competition is driven by a constant quest for new retail concepts and formats. This may take the form of big-box stores with greater variety (Toys "R" Us, Home Depot), augmented customer service (Nordstrom), novel approaches to display and store layout (Sephora in cosmetics), or completely new systems of supplying customers that reconfigure the entire value chain (IKEA).

In other sectors, too, competitive advantage typically goes to firms that have developed innovative strategies that have challenged conventional wisdom and conceptualized the way of doing business:

- Southwest Airlines' point-to-point, no-frills airline service using a single type of plane and flexible working methods has made it not only the only consistently profitable airline in North America but also a model for budget airlines throughout the world.
- Nike built its large and successful business on a business system that totally redesigned the shoe industry's traditional value chain—notably by outsourcing manufacturing and concentrating upon design and marketing, and orchestrating a vast global network of producers, logistics providers, and retailers.
- Metro International is a Swedish company that publishes *Metro* newspapers— free, daily newspapers distributed to commuters in major cities. By October 2009, there were 56 daily editions in 19 countries in 15 languages across Europe, North and South America, and Asia with 17 million daily readers.
- SixDegrees.com, launched in 1997, pioneered web-based social networking paving the way first for MySpace then Facebook.

Strategic innovations tend to involve pioneering along one or more dimensions of strategy:

- New industries: Some companies launch products which create a whole new market. Xerox created the plain-paper copier industry, Freddie Laker pioneered budget air travel, and Craig McCaw and McCaw Communications launched the mass market for wireless telephony. For Kim and Mauborgne, creating new markets is the purest form of **blue-ocean strategy**—the creation of "uncontested market space."[5]
- New customer segments: Creating new customer segments for existing product concepts can also open up vast new market spaces. Apple did not invent the personal computer, but it launched the home market for computers. So too with the videocassette recorder (VCR): it was developed by Ampex for use in television studios but introduced into the home by Sony and Matsushita. The success of the Nintendo Wii video games console was based upon extending video gaming into new customer segments.
- New sources of competitive advantage: Most successful blue-ocean strategies do not launch whole new industries—they introduce novel approaches to creating customer value. Dell created an integrated system for ordering, assembling, and distributing PCs, which permitted unprecedented customer choice and speed of fulfillment. Cirque de Soleil reinvented the circus as a multimedia entertainment spectacle. McKinsey & Company identify a key element of strategic innovation that it calls *new game strategy* as it involves reconfiguring the industry value chain in order to change the "rules of the game."[6] (Southwest Airlines and Nike, mentioned above, are examples.) In their study of rejuvenation among mature firms, Charles Baden-Fuller and John Stopford observe that strategic innovation often involves combining performance dimensions that were previously viewed as conflicting.

For example, Richardson, a UK kitchen knife producer, used an innovative design, process innovation, and a lean, entrepreneurial management to supply kitchen knives that combined price competitiveness, durability, sharpness, and responsive customer service.[7] However, Gary Hamel argues that firms need to go beyond strategic innovation: *management innovations* such as Procter & Gamble's brand management system and Toyota's lean production are likely to offer a more sustainable basis for competitive advantage.[8]

Sustaining Competitive Advantage

Once established, competitive advantage is eroded by competition. The speed with which competitive advantage is undermined depends on the ability of competitors to challenge either by imitation or innovation. Imitation is the most direct form of competition; thus, for competitive advantage to be sustained over time, *barriers to imitation* must exist. Rumelt uses the term **isolating mechanisms** to describe "barriers that limit the ex post equilibration of rents among individual firms."[9] The more effective these isolating mechanisms are, the longer competitive advantage can be sustained against the onslaught of rivals. In most industries, competitive advantage erodes slowly: interfirm profit differentials persist for a period of a decade or more.[10] However, as discussed in Chapter 4 (see the "Dynamic Competition" section), the advent of hypercompetition may have accelerated the process.

To identify the sources of isolating mechanisms, we need to examine the process of competitive imitation. For one firm to successfully imitate the strategy of another, it must meet four conditions: it must identify the competitive advantage of a rival, it must have an incentive to imitate, it must be able to diagnose the sources of the rival's competitive advantage, and it must be able to acquire the resources and capabilities necessary for imitation. At each stage the incumbent can create isolating mechanisms to impede the would-be imitator (Figure 7.2).

FIGURE 7.2   Sustaining competitive advantage: Types of isolating mechanism

REQUIREMENT FOR IMITATION	ISOLATING MECHANISM
Identification	—*Obscure* superior performance
Incentives for imitation	—*Deterrence*: signal aggressive intentions to imitators —*Preemption*: exploit all available investment opportunities
Diagnosis	—Rely on multiple sources of competitive advantage to create "*causal ambiguity*"
Resource acquisition	—Base competitive advantage on resources and capabilities that are *immobile* and *difficult to replicate*

Identification: Obscuring Superior Performance   A simple barrier to imitation is to obscure the firm's superior profitability. According to George Stalk of the Boston Consulting Group: "One way to throw competitors off balance is to mask high performance so rivals fail to see your success until it's too late."[11] In the 1948 movie classic *The Treasure of the Sierra Madre*, Humphrey Bogart and his partners went to great lengths to obscure their find from other gold prospectors.[12]

For firms that dominate a niche market, one of the attractions of remaining a private company is to avoid disclosing financial performance. Few food processors realized the profitability of canned cat and dog food until the UK Monopolies Commission revealed that the leading firm, Pedigree Petfoods (a subsidiary of Mars Inc.), earned a return on capital employed of 47%.[13]

The desire to avoid competition may be so strong as to cause companies to forgo short-run profits. The *theory of limit pricing*, in its simplest form, postulates that a firm in a strong market position sets prices at a level that just fails to attract entrants.[14]

Deterrence and Preemption   A firm may avoid competition by undermining the incentives for imitation. If a firm can persuade rivals that imitation will be unprofitable, it may be able to avoid competitive challenges. In Chapter 4 we discussed strategies of deterrence and the role of signaling and commitment in supporting them.[15] For deterrence to work, threats must be credible. Brandenburger and Nalebuff show how NutraSweet's aggressive price war against the Holland Sweetener Company gave it a reputation that deterred other would-be entrants into the aspartame market.[16]

A firm can also deter imitation by *preemption*—occupying existing and potential strategic niches to reduce the range of investment opportunities open to the challenger. Preemption can take many forms:

- Proliferation of product varieties by a market leader can leave new entrants and smaller rivals with few opportunities for establishing a market niche. Between 1950 and 1972, for example, the six leading suppliers of breakfast cereals introduced 80 new brands into the US market.[17]
- Large investments in production capacity ahead of the growth of market demand also preempt market opportunities for rivals. Monsanto's heavy investment in plants for producing NutraSweet ahead of its patent expiration was a clear threat to would-be producers of generic aspartame.
- Patent proliferation can protect technology-based advantage by limiting competitors' technical opportunities. In 1974, Xerox's dominant market position was protected by a wall of over 2000 patents, most of which were not used. When IBM introduced its first copier in 1970, Xerox sued it for infringing 22 of these patents.[18]

Diagnosing Competitive Advantage: Causal Ambiguity and Uncertain Imitability   If a firm is to imitate the competitive advantage of another, it must understand the basis of its rival's success. Consider Wal-Mart's success in discount retailing. For Wal-Mart's struggling competitor, Sears Holdings (owner of the Kmart chain of discount stores), it is easy to point to the differences between

Wal-Mart and itself. As one Wal-Mart executive commented: "Retailing is an open book. There are no secrets. Our competitors can walk into our stores and see what we sell, how we sell it, and for how much." The difficult task is to identify which differences are the critical determinants of superior profitability. Is it Wal-Mart's store locations (typically in small towns with little direct competition)? Its tightly integrated supply chain? Its unique management system? The information system that supports Wal-Mart's logistics and decision-making practices? Or is it a culture built on traditional rural American values of thrift and hard work? Similarly, problems face Sony or Nokia should they wish to imitate Apple's incredible success in smartphones and consumer electronics.

Lippman and Rumelt identify this problem as **causal ambiguity**: when a firm's competitive advantage is multidimensional and is based on complex bundles of resources and capabilities, it is difficult for rivals to diagnose the success of the leading firm. The outcome of causal ambiguity is *uncertain imitability*: if the causes of a firm's success cannot be known for sure, success is uncertain.[19]

Recent research suggests that the problems of strategy imitation may run even deeper. We observed in Chapter 5 that capabilities are the outcome of complex combinations of resources and that multiple capabilities interact to confer competitive advantage. Research into complementarity among an organization's activities suggests that these interactions extend across the whole range of management practices.[20] Strategy Capsule 7.1 describes Urban Outfitters as an example of a unique "activity system." Where activities are tightly linked, complexity theory—NK modeling in particular—predicts that, within a particular competitive environment, a number of *fitness peaks* will appear, each associated with a unique combination of strategic variables.[21] The implications for imitation is that to locate on the same fitness peak as another firm not only requires recreating a complex configuration of strategy, structure, management systems, leadership, and business processes but also means that getting it just a little bit wrong may result in the imitator missing the fitness peak and finding itself in an adjacent valley.[22]

One of the challenges for the would-be imitator is deciding which management practices are generic best practices and which are *contextual*—complementary with other management practices. For example, if we consider Sears Holdings' deliberation of which of Wal-Mart's management practices to imitate in its Kmart stores, some practices (e.g., employees required to smile at customers, point-of-sale data transferred direct to the corporate database) are likely to be generically beneficial. Others, such as Wal-Mart's "everyday low prices" pricing policy, low advertising sales ratio, and hub-and-spoke distribution are likely to be beneficial only when combined with other practices.

Acquiring Resources and Capabilities   Having diagnosed the sources of an incumbent's competitive advantage, the imitator's next challenge is to assemble the necessary resources and capabilities for imitation. As we saw in Chapter 5, a firm can acquire resources and capabilities in two ways: it can buy them or it can build them. The imitation barriers here are limits to the *transferability* and *replicability* of resources and capabilities. (See Chapter 5's "Sustaining Competitive Advantage" section for a discussion of these resource characteristics.) Strategy Capsule 7.2 looks at competitive advantage in different market settings.

STRATEGY CAPSULE 7.1
Urban Outfitters

During the three years to January 2009, Urban Outfitters Inc., which comprises 130 Urban Outfitters stores (together with Anthropologie and Free People chains), has grown at an average of 20% annually and earned a return on equity of 21%. The company describes itself as targeting well-educated, urban-minded, young adults aged 18 to 30 through its unique merchandise mix and compelling store environment: "We create a unified environment in our stores that establishes an emotional bond with the customer. Every element of the environment is tailored to the aesthetic preferences of our target customers. Through creative design, much of the existing retail space is modified to incorporate a mosaic of fixtures, finishes and revealed architectural details. In our stores, merchandise is integrated into a variety of creative vignettes and displays designed to offer our customers an entire look at a distinct lifestyle."

According to Michael Porter and Nicolaj Siggelkow, Urban Outfitters offers a set of management practices that is both distinctive and highly interdependent. The urban-bohemian-styled product mix, which includes clothing, furnishings, and gift items, is displayed within bazaar-like stores, each of which has a unique design. To encourage frequent customer visits, the layout of each store is changed every two weeks, creating a new shopping experience whenever customers return. Emphasizing community with its customers, it forgoes traditional forms of advertising in favor of blogs and word-of-mouth transmission. Each practice makes little sense on its own, but together they represent a distinctive, integrated strategy. Attempts to imitate Urban Outfitters' competitive advantage would most likely fail because of the difficulty of replicating every aspect of the strategy before integrating them in the right manner.

Source: Urban Outfitters Inc. 10-K Report to January 31, 2009 (Washington: Sec, 2008); M. E. Porter and N. Siggelkow, "Contextuality within Activity Systems and Sustainable Competitive Advantage," *Academy of Management Perspectives* 22 (May 2008): 34–56.

Types of Competitive Advantage: Cost and Differentiation

A firm can achieve a higher rate of profit (or potential profit) over a rival in one of two ways: either it can supply an identical product or service at a lower cost or it can supply a product or service that is differentiated in such a way that the customer is willing to pay a price premium that exceeds the additional cost of the differentiation. In the former case, the firm possesses a cost advantage; in the latter, a differentiation advantage. In pursuing cost advantage, the goal of the firm is to become the cost leader in its industry or industry segment. Cost leadership requires the firm to "find and exploit all sources of cost advantage [and] sell a standard, no-frills product."[23] Differentiation by a firm from its competitors is achieved "when it provides something unique that is valuable to buyers beyond simply offering a low price."[24] Figure 7.3 illustrates these two types of advantage. By combining the two types of competitive advantage with the firm's choice of scope—broad market versus narrow segment—Michael Porter has defined three generic strategies: cost leadership, differentiation, and focus (Figure 7.4).

STRATEGY CAPSULE 7.2
Competitive Advantage in Different Market Settings

The forces which create and destroy competitive advantage will operate differently in different types of market. Competitive advantage depends critically upon the existence of imperfections in the competitive process, which in turn are the result of the conditions under which the resources and capabilities needed to compete in the industry are supplied. The key distinction is between the two types of value-creating activity: *trading* and *production*. Trading involves arbitrage across space (trade) and time (speculation). Production involves the physical transformation of inputs into outputs.

In trading markets the limiting case is *efficient markets*, which correspond closely to perfectly competitive markets. The key condition is that prices reflect all available information (examples include the markets for securities, foreign exchange, and commodity futures). Because prices adjust instantaneously to newly available information, no market trader can expect to earn more than any other. Any differences in returns reflect either different levels of risk or random factors (luck). It is not possible to beat the market on any consistent basis—in other words competitive advantage is absent. This absence of competitive advantage reflects the conditions of resource. Both of the resources needed to compete—finance and information—are equally available to all traders. There is no basis for one to gain competitive advantage over another.

Competitive advantage in trading markets requires imperfections in the competitive process:

♦ Where there is an imperfect availability of information. Competitive advantage results from superior access to information—hence the criminal penalties for insider trading in most advanced economies.

♦ Where transaction costs are present, competitive advantage accrues to the traders with the lowest transaction costs. John Bogle has used this principle as the basis for creating his Vanguard mutual funds. The Vanguard S&P 500 Index fund with transaction and operating costs of 0.5% annually has outperformed 90% of US equity mutual funds.

♦ If markets are subject to systematic behavioral trends (e.g., the *small firm effect* or the *January effect*), competitive advantage accrues to traders who understand market psychology or utilize knowledge of systematic price patterns (chart analysis). Overshooting is a common aberration caused by imitative trading and converging expectations. This implies competitive advantage can be gained in the short term by following the herd (momentum trading) and longer term by recognizing the likelihood of correction (a contrarian strategy). Warren Buffett follows a highly successful contrarian strategy that is based upon being "fearful when others are greedy, and greedy when others are fearful."

In production markets the potential for competitive advantage is much greater because of the complex combinations of the resources and capabilities required, the highly differentiated nature of these resources and capabilities, and the imperfections in their supply. Within an industry, the more heterogeneous are firms' endowments of resources and capabilities, the greater the potential for competitive advantage. In the European electricity-generating industry, the growing diversity of players—utilities (EDF, ENEL), gas distributors (Gaz de France, Centrica), oil and gas majors (Shell, ENI), independent power producers (AES, E.ON), and wind generators—has expanded opportunities for competitive advantage and widened the profit differentials between them.

Differences in resource endowments also influence the erosion of competitive advantage. Where competitors possess similar bundles of resources and capabilities, imitation is easy. Where resource bundles are highly differentiated, competition is more likely to be through distinctive strategies.

FIGURE 7.3   Sources of competitive advantage

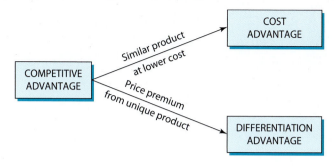

FIGURE 7.4   Porter's generic strategies

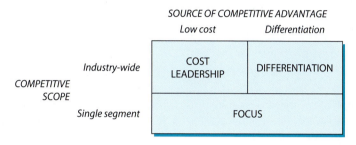

Cost Analysis

Historically, strategic management has emphasized cost advantage as the primary basis for competitive advantage in an industry. This focus on cost reflected the traditional emphasis by economists on price as the principal medium of competition. It also reflected the quest by large industrial corporations during the last century to exploit economies of scale and scope through investments in mass production and mass distribution. During the 1970s and 1980s, this preoccupation was reflected in the widespread interest in the experience curve as a tool of strategy analysis (Strategy Capsule 7.3).

In recent decades, companies have been forced to think more broadly and radically about cost efficiency. Growing competition from emerging market countries has created intense cost pressures for Western and Japanese firms, resulting in novel approaches to cost reduction, including outsourcing, offshoring, process re-engineering, lean production, and organizational delayering.

The Sources of Cost Advantage

There are seven principal determinants of a firm's unit costs (cost per unit of output) relative to its competitors; we refer to these as *cost drivers* (Figure 7.5).

The relative importance of these different cost drivers varies across industries, between firms within an industry, and across the different activities within a firm. By examining each of these different cost drivers in relation to a particular firm, we can analyze a firm's cost position relative to its competitors', diagnose the sources

STRATEGY CAPSULE 7.3
BCG and the Experience Curve

The experience curve has its basis in the systematic reduction in the time taken to build airplanes and Liberty ships during World War II.[25] In a series of studies, ranging from bottle caps and refrigerators to long-distance calls and insurance policies, the Boston Consulting Group (BCG) observed a remarkable regularity in the reductions in unit costs with increased cumulative output. Its *law of experience* states: the unit cost of value added to a standard product declines by a constant percentage (typically between 20 and 30%) each time cumulative output doubles (where "unit cost of value added" is the unit cost of production less the unit cost of bought-in components and materials).

The relationship between unit cost and production volume may be expressed as follows:

$$C_n = C_1 . n^{-a}$$

where C_1 is the cost of the first unit of production

C_n is the cost of the nth unit of production

n is the cumulative volume of production

a is the elasticity of cost with regard to output.

The experience curve has important implications for strategy. If a firm can expand its output faster than its competitors can, it can move down the experience curve more rapidly and open up a widening cost differential.[26] BCG concluded that a firm's primary strategic goal should be driving volume growth through maximizing market share. BCG identified Honda in motorcycles as an exemplar of this strategy.[27] The quest for market share was supported by numerous studies confirming a positive relationship between profitability and market share.[28] However, association does not imply causation—it seems likely that market share and profitability are both outcomes of some other source of competitive advantage—product innovation, or superior marketing.[29]

The weaknesses of the experience curve as a strategy tool are, first, it fails to distinguish several sources of cost reduction (learning, scale, process innovation); second, it presumes that cost reductions from experience are automatic—the reality is that they must be managed.

of inefficiency, and make recommendations as to how a firm can improve its cost efficiency.

Economies of Scale   The predominance of large corporations in most manufacturing and service industries is a consequence of economies of scale. Economies of scale exist wherever proportionate increases in the amounts of inputs employed in a production process result in lower unit costs. Economies of scale have been conventionally associated with manufacturing. Figure 7.6 shows a typical relationship between unit cost and plant capacity. The point at which most scale economies are exploited is the *minimum efficient plant size* (MEPS).

Scale economies arise from three principal sources:

● Technical input–output relationships: In many activities, increases in output do not require proportionate increases in input. A 10000-barrel oil storage tank does not cost five times as much as a 2000-barrel tank. Similar volume-related economies exist in ships, trucks, and steel and petrochemical plants.

FIGURE 7.5   The drivers of cost advantage

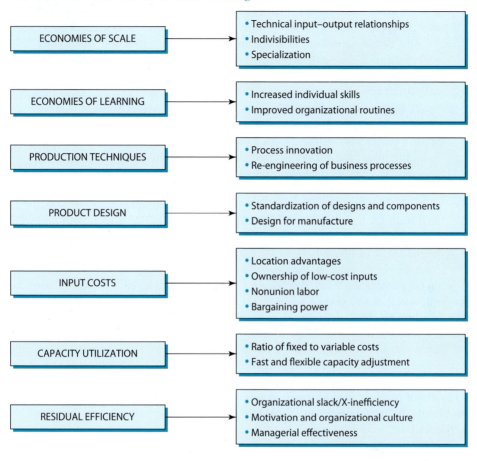

ECONOMIES OF SCALE
- Technical input–output relationships
- Indivisibilities
- Specialization

ECONOMIES OF LEARNING
- Increased individual skills
- Improved organizational routines

PRODUCTION TECHNIQUES
- Process innovation
- Re-engineering of business processes

PRODUCT DESIGN
- Standardization of designs and components
- Design for manufacture

INPUT COSTS
- Location advantages
- Ownership of low-cost inputs
- Nonunion labor
- Bargaining power

CAPACITY UTILIZATION
- Ratio of fixed to variable costs
- Fast and flexible capacity adjustment

RESIDUAL EFFICIENCY
- Organizational slack/X-inefficiency
- Motivation and organizational culture
- Managerial effectiveness

FIGURE 7.6   The long-run average cost curve for a plant

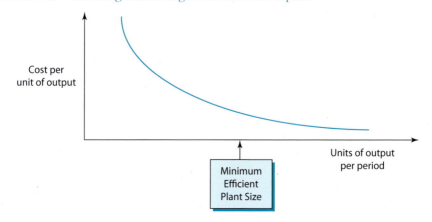

Cost per
unit of output

Units of output
per period

Minimum
Efficient
Plant Size

- Indivisibilities: Many resources and activities are "lumpy"—they are unavailable in small sizes. Hence, they offer economies of scale as firms are able to spread the costs of these items over larger volumes of output. A national TV advertising campaign or a research program into fuel cell technology will cost much the same whether it is being undertaken by Toyota or Mazda. However, the costs as a percentage of sales will be much lower for Toyota because it has almost eight times the sales of Mazda.

- Specialization: Increased scale permits greater task specialization that is manifest in greater division of labor. Mass production—whether in Adam Smith's pin factory or Henry Ford's auto plants (see Chapter 6)—involves breaking down the production process into separate tasks performed by specialized workers using specialized equipment. Specialization promotes learning, avoids time loss from switching activities, and assists mechanization and automation. Similar economies are important in knowledge-intensive industries such as investment banking, management consulting, and design engineering, where large firms are able to offer specialized expertise across a broad range of know-how.

Scale economies are a key determinant of an industry's level of concentration (the proportion of industry output accounted for by the largest firms). In many consumer goods industries, scale economies in marketing have driven industry consolidation. Figure 7.7 shows how soft drink brands with the greatest sales volume tend to have the lowest unit advertising costs for different brands. In other industries—especially aerospace, automobiles, software, and communication systems—the need to amortize the huge costs of new product development has forced consolidation (Table 7.1). Where product development is very costly, volume is essential to profitability: the Boeing 747 was hugely profitable because 1415 were built. Concorde, with only 20 planes built, was a financial disaster.

Despite the prevalence of scale economies, small and medium-sized companies continue to survive and prosper in competition with much bigger rivals. In automobiles, some medium-sized companies such as Peugeot, Renault, and BMW have been more profitable than industry leaders. In commercial banking, there is no

FIGURE 7.7   Economies of scale in advertising: US soft drinks

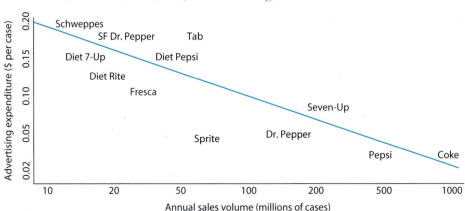

TABLE 7.1 Some of the world's most expensive new product development projects

Product	Lead company	Estimated development cost	Launch date
F-35 Lightning II joint strike fighter	Lockheed Martin	$240 billion[a]	2012[b]
B-2 Spirit "stealth bomber"	Northrup Grumman	$23 billion	December 1993[b]
A380 "super-jumbo"	Airbus Industrie	$19 billion	October 2007[b]
787 Dreamliner	Boeing	$16–$18 billion	3rd Quarter 2010[b]
Windows Vista	Microsoft	$7 billion	January 2007
PlayStation 3	Sony	$7 billion[c]	November 2006
Iridium wireless satellite communication system	Motorola/Iridium Satellite LLC	$6 billion	July 1999
Ford Contour/Mondeo	Ford Motor Company	$6 billion[d]	October 1992

Notes:
[a] Total program cost over 50 years estimated at $1.5 trillion.
[b] Date of entering service.
[c] Including development of Blu-ray DVD.
[d] Including costs of tooling.

evidence that big banks outperform smaller players either on profitability or costs.[30] How do small and medium-sized firms offset the disadvantages of small scale? First, by exploiting superior flexibility; second, by outsourcing activities where scale is critical to efficiency (e.g., specialist car makers typically license product designs and buy in engines); third, by avoiding the motivational and coordination problems that often afflict large organizations.[31]

Economies of Learning   The experience curve has its basis in learning-by-doing. Repetition develops both individual skills and organizational routines. In 1943, it took 40,000 labor-hours to build a B-24 Liberator bomber. By 1945, it took only 8000 hours.[32] The more complex a process or product, the greater the potential for learning. LCD flat screens are notoriously difficult to manufacture—a single defective chip may render an entire screen useless. The dominant position of Sharp and Samsung in flat screens is primarily a result of volume-based learning resulting in exceptionally high yields.[33] Learning occurs both at the individual level through improvements in dexterity and problem solving and at the group level through the development and refinement of organizational routines.[34]

Process Technology and Process Design   Superior process technologies can be a source of huge cost economies. Pilkington's float glass process gave it (and its licensees) an unassailable cost advantage in producing flat glass. Ford's moving assembly line reduced the time taken to assemble a Model T from 106 hours in 1912 to six hours in 1914. When process innovation is embodied in new capital equipment, diffusion is likely to be rapid. However, the full benefits of new process technologies typically require system-wide changes in job design, employee incentives, product design, organizational structure, and management controls. Between 1979 and 1986, General Motors spent $40 billion on new process technology with the goal of becoming the world's most efficient manufacturer of automobiles. Yet, in the absence of fundamental changes in organization and management, the productivity gains were meager. After a tour of Cadillac's state-of-the-art Hamtramck plant in Detroit, Toyota chairman Eiji Toyoda told a colleague, "It would have been embarrassing to comment on it."[35] By contrast, the system of lean production pioneered by Toyota involves an integrated combination of work practices including just-in-time scheduling, total quality management, continuous improvement (kaizen), teamwork, job flexibility, supplier partnerships, as well as improvement in capital equipment and IT.[36]

Business process re-engineering (BPR) is an approach to redesigning operational processes that gained massive popularity during the 1990s. "Re-engineering gurus" Michael Hammer and James Champy define BPR as: "the fundamental rethinking and radical redesign of business processes to achieve dramatic improvements in critical contemporary measures of performance, such as cost, quality, service, and speed."[37] BPR recognizes that operational and commercial processes evolve over time without consistent direction or systematic appraisal. Information technology typically automates existing processes—"paving over cowpaths."[38] BPR begins with the question: "If we were starting afresh, how would we design this process?" Hammer and Champy identify "commonalities, recurring themes, or characteristics" that can guide BPR:

- Combine several jobs into one.
- Allow workers to make decisions.
- Perform the steps of a process in a natural order.
- Recognize the need for variability in process to cope with different situations.
- Perform processes where it makes the most sense: if the accounting department needs pencils, don't insist on using the firm's purchasing department—allow purchases from the retail store down the street.
- Only require checks and controls where they are essential to efficiency.
- Minimize reconciliation.
- Appoint a case manager to provide a single point of contact at the interface between processes.
- Decentralized decisions: permit overall coordination simply through information sharing.

BPR has led to major gains in efficiency, quality, and speed (Strategy Capsule 7.4), but where business processes are complex and embedded in organizational routines (see "From Resources to Capabilities" section in Chapter 5), it is likely that no one in the organization fully understands the operation of existing processes. In such circumstances, Hammer and Champy's recommendation to "obliterate" existing processes and start with a "clean sheet of paper" runs the risk of destroying organizational capabilities that have been nurtured over a long period. While BPR had lost much of the popularity it had 20 years ago, firms continue to engage in *business process management*, where the emphasis has shifted from workflow management to the broader application of information technology (web-based applications in particular) to the redesign and enhancement of organizational processes.[39]

STRATEGY CAPSULE 7.4
Process Re-Engineering at IBM Credit

Michel Hammer and James Champy describe how business process re-engineering resulted in IBM reducing the time taken to approve requests by sales personnel for new customer credit approval from six days to four hours. Under the old system, five stages were involved:

1 an IBM salesperson telephoned a request for financing, which was logged on a piece of paper;

2 the request was sent to the credit department, which checked the customer's creditworthiness;

3 the request and credit check were sent to the business practices department where a loan covenant was drawn up;

4 the paperwork was passed to a pricer, who determined the interest rate;

5 the clerical group prepared a quote letter that was sent to the salesperson.

Frustrated by the delays and resulting lost sales, two managers undertook an experiment. They took a financing request and walked it through all five steps. They discovered that all five stages could be completed within 90 minutes!

The problem was that the process had been designed for the most complex credit requests that IBM received, whereas in the vast majority of cases no specialist judgment was called for: all that was needed was to check credit ratings and to plug numbers into standard algorithms. The credit approval process was redesigned by replacing the specialists (credit checkers, pricers, and so on) with generalists who undertook all five processes. Only where the request was non-standard or unusually complex were specialists called in. Not only was processing time reduced by 94%, but the number of employees involved was reduced and the total number of customer approvals greatly increased.

Source: Adapted from M. Hammer and J. Champy, *Re-engineering the Corporation: A Manifesto for Business Revolution* (New York: HarperBusiness, 1993): 36–9.

Product Design *Design-for-manufacture*—designing products for ease of production rather than simply for functionality and esthetics—can offer substantial cost savings, especially when linked to the introduction of new process technology.

- Volkswagen cut product development and component costs by redesigning its 30 different models around just four separate platforms. The VW Beetle, Audi TT, Golf, and Audi A3, together with several Seat and Skoda models, all share a single platform.
- The IBM "Proprinter," one of the most successful computer printers of the 1980s, owed its low costs (and reliability) to an innovative design that:
  - reduced the number of parts from 150, found in the typical PC printer, to 60;
  - designed the printer in layers so that robots could build it from the bottom up;
  - eliminated all screws, springs, and other fasteners that required human insertion and adjustment and replaced them with molded plastic components that clipped together.[40]

Service offerings, too, can be designed for ease and efficiency of production. Motel 6, cost leader in US budget motels, carefully designs its product to keep operating costs low. Its motels occupy low-cost, out-of-town locations; it uses standard motel designs; it avoids facilities such as pools and restaurants; and it designs rooms to facilitate easy cleaning and low maintenance. However, efficiency in service design is compromised by the tendency of customers to request deviations from standard offerings ("I'd like my hamburger with the bun toasted on one side only, please"). This requires a clear strategy to manage variability either through accommodation or restriction.[41]

Capacity Utilization Over the short and medium terms, plant capacity is more or less fixed and variations in output cause capacity utilization to rise or fall. Underutilization raises unit costs because fixed costs must be spread over fewer units of production; pushing output beyond normal full capacity also creates inefficiencies. Boeing's efforts to boost output during 2006–2011 resulted in increased unit costs due to overtime pay, premiums for night and weekend shifts, increased defects, and higher levels of maintenance. Hence, the ability to speedily adjust capacity to downturns in demand can be a major source of cost advantage. During the 2008–2009 recession, survival in hard-hit sectors such as house building, construction equipment, and retailing required moving early to cut capacity through shedding jobs and closing units. The key was to make adjustments in advance of downturns in demand: Caterpillar announced it was cutting 20,000 jobs on January 28, 2008, the same day it revealed that its sales in the previous quarter had increased from the previous year.[42]

Input Costs The firms in an industry do not necessarily pay the same price for identical inputs. There are several sources of lower input costs:

- Locational differences in input prices: The prices of inputs, and wage rates in particular, vary between locations. In the US, software engineers earned an average of $94,000 in 2011. In India, the average was $34,000. In less-skilled occupations, differentials are much wider: in auto assembly the hourly rate in Chinese plants was about $3 an hour in 2011 compared with $70 in the US (inclusive of benefits).[43]

- Ownership of low-cost sources of supply: In raw-material-intensive industries, ownership of low-cost sources of material can offer a massive cost advantage. In petroleum, lifting costs for the three "supermajors" (ExxonMobil, Royal Dutch Shell, and BP) were over $14 per barrel in 2007; for Saudi Aramco they were about $5.

- Non-union labor: Labor unions result in higher levels of pay and benefits and work restrictions that lower productivity. In the US airline industry, non-union AirTran had average salary and benefit cost per employee of $60,863 in 2007 compared with $87,245 for United (80% unionized).

- Bargaining power: The ability to negotiate preferential prices ad discounts can be a major source of cost advantage for industry leaders, especially in retailing.[44] Wal-Mart's UK entry (with its acquisition of Asda) was greeted with dismay by other British supermarket chains: they feared that Wal-Mart's massive bargaining power would allow Asda to gain preferential discounts from suppliers.

Residual Efficiency   Even after taking account of the basic cost drivers—scale, technology, product and process design, input costs, and capacity utilization—unexplained cost differences between firms typically remain. These residual efficiencies relate to the extent to which the firm approaches its efficiency frontier of optimal operation which depends on the firm's ability to eliminate "organizational slack"[45] or "X-inefficiency."[46] These surplus costs that keep the firm from maximum-efficiency operation are the inevitable result of employees—both in management and on the shop floor—maintaining some margin of slack in preference to the rigors of operating at maximum efficiency. Eliminating these excess costs often requires a threat to a company's survival, which then creates the impetus for rooting out institutionalized inefficiencies. When faced with bankruptcy or a precipitous fall in profitability, companies can demonstrate a remarkable capacity for paring costs—in his first year as CEO, Carlos Ghosn cut Nissan Motor's operating costs by 20%.[47] At firms such as Wal-Mart, Ryanair, and Air Asia, high levels of residual efficiency are the result of management systems and company values that are intolerant of unnecessary costs and glorify frugality.

Using the Value Chain to Analyze Costs

To analyze a firm's cost position, we need to look at individual activities. Chapter 5 introduced the *value chain* as a way of seeing the sequence of activities that a company or business unit performs. Each activity tends to be subject to a different set of cost drivers, which give it a distinct cost structure. A value chain analysis of a firm's costs seeks to identify:

1 the relative importance of each activity with respect to total cost;
2 the cost drivers for each activity and the comparative efficiency with which the firm performs each activity;
3 how costs in one activity influence costs in another;
4 which activities should be undertaken within the firm and which activities should be outsourced.

A value chain analysis of a firm's cost position comprises the following stages:

1 Disaggregate the firm into separate activities: Determining the appropriate value chain activities is a matter of judgment. It requires understanding the chain of processes involved in the transformation of inputs into output and its delivery to the customer. Very often, the firm's own divisional and departmental structure is a useful guide. Key considerations are:
   a the separateness of one activity from another;
   b the importance of an activity;
   c the dissimilarity of activities in terms of cost drivers;
   d the extent to which there are differences in the way competitors perform the particular activity.
2 Establish the relative importance of different activities in the total cost of the product: Our analysis needs to focus on the activities that are the major sources of cost. In disaggregating costs, Michael Porter suggests the detailed assignment

of operating costs and assets to each value activity. [48] Though the adoption of activity-based costing has made such cost data more available, detailed cost allocation can be a major exercise.[49] Even without such detailed cost break-down, it is usually possible to identify which activities are the principal sources of total cost and establish which activities are performed relatively efficiently or inefficiently.

3 Identify cost drivers: For each activity, what factors determine the level of cost relative to other firms? For some activities, cost drivers can be deduced simply from the nature of the activity and the types of cost incurred. For capital-intensive activities such as the operation of a body press in an auto plant, the principal factors are likely to be capital equipment costs, weekly production volume, and downtime between changes of dies. For labor-intensive assembly activities, criti-cal issues are wage rates, speed of work, and defect rates.

4 Identify linkages: The costs of one activity may be determined, in part, by the way in which other activities are performed. Xerox discovered that its high ser-vice costs relative to competitors' reflected the complexity of design of its copi-ers, which required 30 different interrelated adjustments.

5 Identify opportunities for reducing costs: By identifying areas of compara-tive inefficiency and the cost drivers for each, opportunities for cost reduc-tion become evident. If scale economies are a key cost driver, can volume be increased? If wage costs are excessive, will employees accept productivity-increasing measures; alternatively, can production be relocated? If an activity cannot be performed efficiently within the firm, can it be outsourced?

Figure 7.8 shows how the application of the value chain to automobile manufac-ture can yield suggestions for possible cost reductions.

Differentiation Analysis

A firm differentiates itself from its competitors "when it provides something unique that is valuable to buyers beyond simply offering a lower price."[50] Differentiation advantage occurs when a firm is able to obtain from its differentiation a price pre-mium in the market that exceeds the cost of providing the differentiation.

Every firm has opportunities for differentiating its offering to customers, although the range of differentiation opportunities depends on the characteristics of the product. An automobile or a restaurant offers greater potential for differentiation than cement, wheat, or memory chips. These latter products are called *commodities* precisely because they lack physical differentiation. Yet, according to Tom Peters, even commodities can be differentiated to create customer value: "Anything can be turned into a value-added product or service."[51] Consider the following:

- Cement is the ultimate commodity product, yet Cemex, based in Mexico, has become a worldwide supplier of cement and ready-mix concrete through emphasizing "building solutions"—one aspect of which is ensuring that 98% of its deliveries are on time (compared to 34% for the industry as a whole).[52]
- Online bookselling is inherently a commodity business—any online book-seller has access to the same titles and same modes of distribution. Yet

FIGURE 7.8   Using the value chain in cost analysis: An automobile manufacturer

SEQUENCE OF ANALYSIS	VALUE CHAIN	COST DRIVER
1. IDENTIFY ACTIVITIES Establish the basic framework of the value chain by identifying the principal activities of the firm.	PURCHASING COMPONENTS AND MATERIALS	Prices of bought-in components depend upon: • Order sizes • Average value of purchases per supplier • Location of suppliers
2. ALLOCATE TOTAL COSTS For a first-stage analysis, a rough estimate of the breakdown of total cost by activity is sufficient to indicate which activities offer the greatest scope for cost reductions.	R & D, DESIGN, AND ENGINEERING	Size of R & D commitment Productivity of R & D Number and frequency of new models Sales per model
3. IDENTIFY COST DRIVERS (See diagram.)	COMPONENT MANUFACTURE	Scale of plants Run length per component Capacity utilization Location of plants
4. IDENTIFY LINKAGES Examples include: 1. Consolidating purchase orders to increase discounts increases inventories. 2. High-quality parts and materials reduce costs of defects at later stages. 3. Reducing manufacturing defects cuts warranty costs. 4. Designing different models around common components and platforms reduces manufacturing costs.	ASSEMBLY	Scale of plants Number of models per plant Degree of automation Level of wages Location of plants
5. IDENTIFY OPPORTUNITIES COST REDUCTION For example: *Purchasing*: Concentrate purchases on fewer suppliers to maximize purchasing economies. Institute just-in-time component supply to reduce inventories.	TESTING AND QUALITY CONTROL	Level of quality targets Frequency of defects
R & D/Design/Engineering: Reduce frequency of model changes. Reduce number of different models (e.g., single range of global models). Design for commonality of components and platforms.	INVENTORIES OF FINISHED PRODUCTS	Predicatability of sales Flexibility of production Customers' willingness to wait
Component manufacture: Exploit economies of scale through concentrating production of each component on fewer plants. Outsource wherever scale of production or run lengths are suboptimal or where outside suppliers have technology advantages. For labor-intensive components (e.g., seats, dashboards, trim), relocate production in low-wage countries. Improve capacity utilization through plant rationalization or supplying components to other manufacturers.	SALES AND MARKETING	Size of advertising budget Strength of existing reputation Sales volume
	DISTRIBUTION AND DEALER SUPPORT	Number of dealers Sales per dealer Desired level of dealer support Frequency of defects requiring repair under warranty of recalls

Amazon has exploited the information generated by its business to offer a range of value-adding services: best-seller lists, reviews, and customized recommendations.

The lesson is this: differentiation is not simply about offering different product features; it is about identifying and understanding every possible interaction between the firm and its customers and asking how these interactions can be enhanced or changed in order to deliver additional value to the customer. This requires looking at both the firm (the supply side) and its customers (the demand side). While *supply-side analysis* identifies the firm's potential to create uniqueness, the critical issue is whether such differentiation creates value for customers and whether the value created exceeds the cost of the differentiation. Only by understanding what customers want, how they choose, and what motivates them can we identify opportunities for profitable differentiation.

Thus, differentiation strategies are not about pursuing uniqueness for the sake of being different. Differentiation is about understanding customers and how we can best meet their needs. To this extent, the quest for differentiation advantage takes us to the heart of business strategy. The fundamental issues of differentiation are also the fundamental issues of business strategy: Who are our customers? How do we create value for them? And how do we do it more effectively and efficiently than anyone else?

Because differentiation is about uniqueness, establishing differentiation advantage requires creativity: it cannot be achieved simply through applying standardized frameworks and techniques. This is not to say that differentiation advantage is not amenable to systematic analysis. As we have observed, there are two requirements for creating profitable differentiation. On the supply side, the firm must be aware of the resources and capabilities through which it can create uniqueness (and do it better than competitors). On the demand side, the key is insight into customers and their needs and preferences. These two sides form the major components of our analysis of differentiation.

The Nature and Significance of Differentiation

The potential for differentiating a product or service is partly determined by its physical characteristics. For products that are technically simple (a pair of socks, a brick), that satisfy uncomplicated needs (a corkscrew, a nail), or must meet rigorous technical standards (a spark plug, a thermometer), differentiation opportunities are constrained by technical and market factors. Products that are technically complex (an airplane), that satisfy complex needs (an automobile, a vacation), or that do not need to conform to particular technical standards (wine, toys) offer much greater scope for differentiation.

Beyond these constraints, the potential in any product or service for differentiation is limited only by the boundaries of the human imagination. For seemingly simple products such as shampoo, toilet paper, and bottled water, the proliferation of brands on any supermarket's shelves is testimony both to the ingenuity of firms and the complexity of customers' preferences. Differentiation extends beyond the physical characteristics of the product or service to encompass everything about the product or service that influences the value that customers derive from it. This means that differentiation includes every aspect of the way in which a company relates to its customers. Starbucks' ability to charge up to $5 for a cup of coffee (compared to a US average price of $1.38) rests not just on the characteristics of the coffee but also on the overall "Starbucks Experience" which encompasses the retail environment, the sense of community in which customers participate, and the values that Starbucks projects. Differentiation activities are not specific to particular functions such as design and marketing; they infuse all aspects of the relationship between an organization and its customers, including the identity and culture of a company.

Differentiation includes both tangible and intangible dimensions. *Tangible differentiation* is concerned with the observable characteristics of a product or service that are relevant to customers' preferences and choice processes, for example size, shape, color, weight, design, material, and performance attributes such as reliability, consistency, taste, speed, durability, and safety. Tangible differentiation also extends to products and services that complement the product in question: delivery, after-sales services, and accessories.

Opportunities for *intangible differentiation* arise because the value that customers perceive in a product is seldom determined solely by observable product features or objective performance criteria. Social, emotional, psychological, and esthetic considerations are present in most customer choices. For consumer goods and services the desire for status, exclusivity, individuality, security, and community are powerful motivational forces. Where a product or service is meeting complex customer needs, differentiation choices involve the overall image of the firm and its offering. Image differentiation is especially important for those products and services whose qualities and performance are difficult to ascertain at the time of purchase (so-called experience goods). These include cosmetics, medical services, and education.

Differentiation and Segmentation   Differentiation is different from segmentation. Differentiation is concerned with how a firm competes—the ways in which it can offer uniqueness to customers. Such uniqueness might relate to consistency (McDonald's), reliability (Federal Express), status (American Express), quality (BMW), and innovation (Apple). Segmentation is concerned with where a firm competes in terms of customer groups, localities, and product types.

Whereas segmentation is a feature of market structure, differentiation is a strategic choice made by a firm. Differentiation tends to lead to focusing upon particular market segments, but this is not necessarily so. Firms may locate within a segment without differentiating themselves from competitors within the same segment: Ameritrade, E-Trade, and Scottrade are all located within the online segment of the brokerage industry and yet are not significantly differentiated from one another. Conversely, IKEA, McDonald's, Honda, and Starbucks all pursue differentiation, but position themselves within the mass market spanning multiple demographic and socioeconomic segments.[53]

The Sustainability of Differentiation Advantage   Differentiation offers a more secure basis for competitive advantage than low cost does. A position of cost advantage is vulnerable to the emergence of new competitors from low-cost countries and to adverse movements in exchange rates. Cost advantage can also be overturned by innovation: discount brokerage firms were undercut by internet brokers, discount stores by online retailers. Differentiation advantage would appear to be more sustainable. Large companies that consistently earn above-average returns on capital—such as Colgate-Palmolive, Diageo, Johnson & Johnson, Kellogg's, Procter & Gamble, 3M, and Wyeth—tend to be those that have pursued differentiation through quality, branding, and innovation.

Analyzing Differentiation: The Demand Side

Analyzing customer demand enables us to determine which product characteristics have the potential to create value for customers, customers' willingness to pay for differentiation, and a company's optimal competitive positioning in terms of differentiation variables. Analyzing demand begins with understanding why customers buy a product or service. Market research systematically explores customer preferences and customer perceptions of existing products. However, the key to successful differentiation is to understand customers. To gain insight into customer requirements and preferences, simple, direct inquiry into the purpose of a product and the needs of its customers can often be far more illuminating than statistically validated market research (Strategy Capsule 7.5).

Virtually all products and services serve multiple customer needs. As a result, understanding customer needs requires the analysis of multiple attributes. Market research has developed several techniques for analyzing customer preferences in relation to product attributes which can guide decisions over product positioning and design:

- *Multidimensional scaling* (MDS) permits customers' perceptions of competing products to be represented graphically in terms of key product attributes.[54] For example, a survey of consumer ratings of competing pain relievers resulted in the mapping shown in Figure 7.9. Multidimensional scaling has also been used to classify 109 single-malt Scotch whiskies according to the characteristics of their color, nose, palate, body, and finish.[55]

- *Conjoint analysis* measures the strength of customer preferences for different product attributes. The technique requires, first, an identification of the underlying attributes of a product and, second, market research to rank hypothetical products that contain alternative bundles of attributes. The results can then be used to estimate the proportion of customers who would prefer a hypothetical new product to competing products already available in the market.[56] Conjoint analysis has been used to predict market shares of forthcoming new models of personal computer, to analyze windsurfer preferences, and to design new products—including Marriott's Courtyard hotel chain and nature tourism in the Amazon basin.

- *Hedonic price analysis* views products as bundles of underlying attributes.[57] Hedonic price analysis uses regression to estimate the implicit market price for each attribute. For example, price differences among European automatic washing machines can be related to differences in capacity, spin speed, energy consumption, number of programs, and reliability. A machine that spins at 1000 rpm sold at about a $200 price premium to one that spins at 800 rpm.[58] Similarly, price differences between models of personal computer reflect differences in processor speed, memory, and hard drive capacity.[59] The results of this analysis can then be used to make decisions as to what levels of each attribute to include within a new product and the price point for that product.

- *Value curve analysis* maps the performance characteristics of competing products, indicating the potential for new products that offer superior combinations of product characteristics. Kim and Mauborgne show how, in book retailing, applying value metrics—such as price, knowledge levels of staff, selection of books, store ambiance, store hours, and additional facilities to

STRATEGY CAPSULE 7.5

Understanding What a Product Is about

Getting back to strategy means getting back to a deep understanding of what a product is about. Some time ago, for example, a Japanese home appliance company was trying to develop a coffee percolator. Should it be a General Electric-type percolator, executives wondered? Should it be the same drip type that Philips makes? Larger? Smaller? I urged them to ask a different kind of question: Why do people drink coffee? What are they looking for when they do? If your objective is to serve the customer better, then shouldn't you understand why that customer drinks coffee in the first place? Then you would know what kind of percolator to make.

The answer came back: good taste. Then I asked the company's engineers what they were doing to help the consumer enjoy good taste in a cup of coffee. They said they were trying to design a good percolator. I asked them what influences the taste in a cup of coffee. No one knew. That became the next question we had to answer. It turns out that lots of things can affect taste—the beans, the temperature, the water. We did our homework and discovered all the things that affect taste . . .

Of all the factors, water quality, we learned, made the greatest difference. The percolator in design at the time, however, didn't take water quality into account

at all . . . We discovered next that grain distribution and the time between grinding the beans and pouring in the water were crucial. As a result we began to think about the product and its necessary features in a new way. It had to have a built-in dechlorinating function. It had to have a built-in grinder. All the customer should have to do is pour in water and beans . . .

To start you have to ask the right questions and set the right kinds of strategic goals. If your only concern is that General Electric has just brought out a percolator that brews coffee in 10 minutes, you will get your engineers to design one that brews it in seven minutes. And if you stick to that logic, market research will tell you that instant coffee is the way to go . . . Conventional marketing approaches won't solve the problem. If you ask people whether they want their coffee in 10 minutes or seven, they will say seven, of course. But it's still the wrong question. And you end up back where you started, trying to beat the competition at its own game. If your primary focus is on the competition, you will never step back and ask what the customers' inherent needs are, and what the product really is about.

position existing book stores—reveals opportunities for new approaches (such as that offered by Barnes & Noble).[60]

The Role of Social and Psychological Factors   Analyzing product differentiation in terms of measurable performance attributes tends to ignore customers' underlying motivations. Few goods or services only satisfy physical needs: most buying is influenced by social and psychological motivations, such as the desire to find community with others and to reinforce one's own identity. Psychologist Abraham Maslow proposed a hierarchy of human needs that progress from basic survival needs to security needs, to belonging needs, to esteem needs, up to the desire for self-actualization.[61] For most goods, brand equity has more to do with

FIGURE 7.9   Consumer perceptions of competing pain relievers: A multidimensional scaling mapping

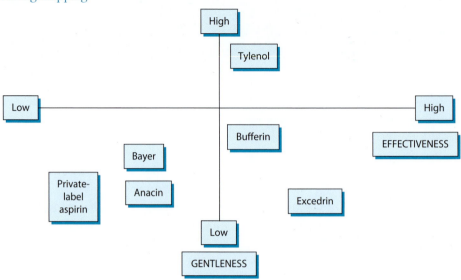

status and identity than with tangible product performance. The disastrous introduction of "New Coke" in 1985 was the result of Coca-Cola giving precedence to tangible differentiation (taste preferences) over intangible differentiation (authenticity).[62] Harley-Davidson harbors no such illusions: it recognizes quite clearly that it is in the business of selling lifestyle, not transportation.

If the dominant customer needs that a product satisfies are identity and social affiliation, the implications for differentiation are far reaching. In particular, to identify profitable differentiation opportunities requires that we analyze not only the product and its characteristics but also customers, their lifestyles and aspirations, and the relationship of the product to those lifestyles and aspirations. Market research that focuses upon traditional demographic and socioeconomic factors may be less useful than a deep understanding of consumers' relationships with a product. Tom Peters extols the merits of "naïve listening"[63] to customers. In practice a deeper understanding of consumers' lifestyles and perceptions may be necessary to interpret their words. Before opening its Fresh and Easy chain of food stores in California, British supermarket giant Tesco sent a team of executives to live with local families.[64] And going beyond functionality to explore the emotional and esthetic aspects of consumers' relationships with products has been central to Japanese approaches to marketing.[65]

Figure 7.10 summarizes the key points of this discussion by posing some basic questions that explore the potential for demand-side differentiation.

Analyzing Differentiation: The Supply Side

Demand analysis identifies customers' demands for differentiation and their willingness to pay for it, but creating differentiation advantage also depends on a firm's ability to offer differentiation. This in turn depends upon the activities that the firm performs and the resources it has access to.

FIGURE 7.10   Identifying differentiation potential: The demand side

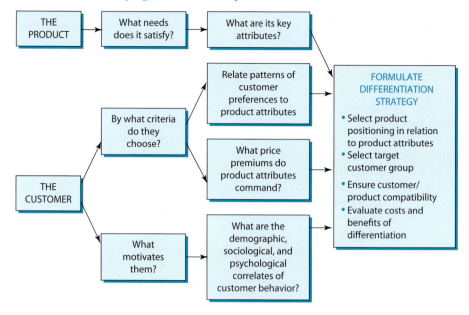

The Drivers of Uniqueness   Differentiation is concerned with the provision of uniqueness. A firm's opportunities for creating uniqueness in its offerings to customers are not located within a particular function or activity but can arise in virtually everything that it does. Michael Porter identifies several sources of uniqueness:

- product features and product performance;
- complementary services (such as credit, delivery, repair);
- intensity of marketing activities (such as rate of advertising spending);
- technology embodied in design and manufacture;
- quality of purchased inputs;
- procedures that influence the customer experience (such as the rigor of quality control, service procedures, frequency of sales visits);
- skill and experience of employees;
- location (such as with retail stores);
- degree of vertical integration (which influences a firm's ability to control inputs and intermediate processes).[66]

Differentiation can also occur through *bundling*—offering a combination of complementary products and services.[67] As markets mature, so products tend to go through phases of *unbundling*: products become commoditized while complementary services become provided by specialist suppliers. Electronic commerce has enabled customers to assemble their own bundles of goods and services with few transaction costs. The business of European tour operators has shrunk as most vacationers now use online travel and reservations systems to create their own customized vacations. The unbundling of products has encouraged the unbundling of companies.[68]

There are also trends in the opposite direction: the quest for new opportunities for differentiation has encouraged a *rebundling* of products and services into new systems. One of the major developments in business-to-business transactions in recent years has been the emphasis on "providing customer solutions"—producing a combination of goods and services that are tailored to the specific needs of the client. This involves a radical rethink of the business models in most companies.[69]

Product Integrity Differentiation decisions cannot be made on a piecemeal basis. Establishing a coherent and effective differentiation position requires the firm to assemble a complementary package of differentiation attributes. If Burberry, the British fashion house, wants to expand its range of clothing and accessories, it needs to ensure that every new product offering is consistent with its overall image as a quality-focused brand that combines traditional British style with contemporary edginess. *Product integrity* refers to the consistency of a firm's differentiation; it is the extent to which a product achieves:

> total balance of numerous product characteristics, including basic functions, esthetics, semantics, reliability, and economy . . . Product integrity has both internal and external dimensions. Internal integrity refers to consistency between the function and structure of the product—e.g., the parts fit well, components match and work well together, layout achieves maximum space efficiency. External integrity is a measure of how well a product's function, structure, and semantics fit the customer's objectives, values, production system, lifestyle, use pattern, and self-identity.[70]

Simultaneously achieving internal and external integrity is a complex organizational challenge: it requires a combination of close cross-functional collaboration and intimate customer contact.[71] This integration of internal and external product integrity is especially important to those supplying "lifestyle" products, where differentiation is based on customers' social and psychological needs. Here, the credibility of the image depends critically on the consistency of the image presented. One element of this integration is a linked identity between customer and company employees. For instance:

- Harley-Davidson's image of ruggedness, independence, individuality, and community is supported by a top management team that dons biking leathers and rides its "hogs" to owners' group rallies, and a management system that empowers shop-floor workers and fosters quality, initiative, and responsibility.
- MTV's capacity to stay at the leading edge of popular culture and still be cool after 30 years on the air owes much to a human resource strategy that involves recruiting and giving responsibility to young people.

This need for internal/external consistency explains why brand-conscious companies such as Nike, Levi-Strauss, and Apple have been so vigilant over issues of employee exploitation among their offshore suppliers.

Signaling and Reputation Differentiation is only effective if it is communicated to customers. But information about the qualities and characteristics of products is not always readily available to potential customers. The economics literature distinguishes between *search goods*, whose qualities and characteristics can be ascertained by inspection, and *experience goods*, whose qualities and characteristics are only recognized after consumption. This latter class of goods includes medical services, baldness treatments, frozen TV dinners, and wine. Even after purchase, performance attributes may be slow in revealing themselves. Bernie Madoff established Bernard L. Madoff Investment Securities LLC in 1960—it took almost half a century before the renowned investment house was revealed as a "giant Ponzi scheme."[72]

In the terminology of game theory (see Chapter 4), the market for experience goods corresponds to a classic prisoners' dilemma. A firm can offer a high-quality or a low-quality product. The customer can pay either a high or a low price. If quality cannot be detected, then equilibrium is established, with the customer offering a low price and the supplier offering a low-quality product, even though both would be better off with a high-quality product sold at a high price. The resolution of this dilemma is for producers to find some credible means of signaling quality to the customer. The most effective signals are those that change the payoffs in the prisoners' dilemma. Thus, an extended warranty is effective because providing such a warranty would be more expensive for a low-quality producer than a high-quality producer. Brand names, warranties, expensive packaging, money-back guarantees, sponsorship of sports and cultural events, and a carefully designed retail environment in which the product is sold are all signals of quality. Their effectiveness stems from the fact that they represent significant investments by the manufacturer that will be devalued if the product proves unsatisfactory to customers.

The more difficult it is to ascertain performance prior to purchase, the more important signaling is.

- A perfume can be sampled prior to purchase and its fragrance assessed, but its ability to augment the identity of the wearer and attract attention remains uncertain. Hence, the key role of branding, packaging, advertising, and lavish promotional events in establishing an identity for the perfume in terms of the implied personality, lifestyle, and aspirations of the user.
- In financial services, the customer cannot easily assess the honesty, financial security, or competence of the supplier. Hence, financial service companies emphasize symbols of security and stability: imposing head offices, conservative office decor, smartly dressed employees, and trademarks such as Prudential's rock and Travelers' red umbrella. Bernie Madoff's multibillion investment swindle was sustained by his close association with leading figures among New York's Jewish community, his prominent role in cultural and charitable organizations, and the aura of exclusivity around his investment club.

Brands Brands fulfill multiple roles. Most importantly, a brand provides a guarantee by the producer to the consumer of the quality of the product. It does so in several ways. At its most basic, a brand identifies the producer of a product. This ensures that the producer is legally accountable for the products supplied to market. Further, the brand represents an investment that provides an incentive to maintain quality and customer satisfaction. It is a credible signal of quality because of the disincentive of its owner to devalue it. As a result, a brand acts as a guarantee to the customer that reduces uncertainty and search costs. The more difficult it is to discern quality on inspection, and the greater the cost to the customer of purchasing a defective product, the greater the value of a brand: a trusted brand name is more important to us when we purchase mountaineering equipment than when we buy a pair of socks.

The traditional role of the brand as a guarantor of reliability is particularly significant in e-commerce. Internet transactions are characterized by the anonymity of buyers and sellers and lack of government regulation. As a result, well-established players in e-commerce—Amazon, Microsoft, eBay, and Yahoo!—can use their brand to reduce consumers' perceived risk.

By contrast, the value conferred by consumer brands such as Red Bull, Harley-Davidson, Mercedes-Benz, Gucci, Virgin, and American Express is less a guarantee of reliability and more an embodiment of identity and lifestyle. Traditionally, advertising has been the primary means of influencing and reinforcing customer perceptions. Increasingly, however, consumer goods companies are seeking new approaches to brand development that focus less on product characteristics and more on "brand experience," "tribal identity," "shared values," and "emotional dialogue." Traditional mass-market advertising is less effective for promoting this type of brand identity as word-of-mouth promotion deploying web-based social networks—what has been referred to as *viral marketing* or *stealth marketing*.[73]

The Costs of Differentiation   Differentiation adds cost. The direct costs of differentiation include higher-quality inputs, better-trained employees, higher advertising costs, and better after-sales service. The indirect costs of differentiation arise through the interaction of differentiation variables with cost variables. If differentiation narrows a firm's segment scope, it also limits the potential for exploiting scale economies. If differentiation requires continual product redesign, it hampers the exploitation of learning economies.

One means of reconciling differentiation with cost efficiency is to postpone differentiation to later stages of the firm's value chain. Economies of scale and the cost advantages of standardization are frequently greatest in the manufacturing of basic components. Modular design with common components permits scale economies while maintaining considerable product variety. All the major automakers have reduced the number of platforms and engine types and increased the commonality of components across their model ranges, while offering customers a greater variety of colors, trim, and accessory options.

New manufacturing technology and the internet have redefined traditional trade-offs between efficiency and variety. Flexible manufacturing systems and just-in-time scheduling have increased the versatility of many plants, made model changeovers less costly, and made the goal of an "economic order quantity of one" increasingly realistic. Automobile and domestic appliance plants increasingly produce multiple models on a single assembly line.[74] Internet communication allows consumers to design their own products and quickly communicate their requirements to manufacturers.

Bringing It All Together: The Value Chain in Differentiation Analysis

There is little point in identifying the product attributes that customers value most if the firm is incapable of supplying those attributes. Similarly, there is little purpose in identifying a firm's ability to supply certain elements of uniqueness if these are not valued by customers. The key to successful differentiation is matching the firm's capacity for creating differentiation to the attributes that customers value most. For this purpose, the value chain provides a particularly useful framework. Let's begin with the case of a producer good i.e., one that is supplied by one firm to another.

Value Chain Analysis of Producer Goods Using the value chain to identify opportunities for differentiation advantage involves three principal stages:

1 Construct a value chain for the firm and its customer. It may be useful to consider not just the immediate customer but also firms further downstream in the value chain. If the firm supplies different types of customers, it's useful to draw separate value chains for each major category of customer.

2 Identify the drivers of uniqueness in each activity of the firm's value chain. Figure 7.11 identifies some possible sources of differentiation within Porter's generic value chain.

3 Locate linkages between the value chain of the firm and that of the buyer. What can the firm do with its own value chain activities that can reduce the cost or enhance the differentiation potential of the customer's value chain activities? The amount of additional value that the firm creates for its customers through exploiting these linkages represents the potential price premium the firm can charge for its differentiation. Strategy Capsule 7.6 demonstrates the identification of differentiation opportunities by lining the value chains of a firm and its customers.

FIGURE 7.11 Using the value chain to identify differentiation potential on the supply side

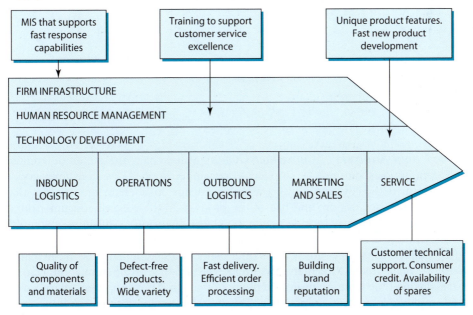

STRATEGY CAPSULE 7.6

Using the Value Chain to Identify Differentiation Opportunities for a Manufacturer of Metal Containers

The metal container industry is a highly competitive, low-growth, low-profit industry. Cans lack much potential for differentiation, and buyers (especially beverage and food canning companies) are very powerful. Cost efficiency is essential, but can we also identify opportunities for profitable differentiation? Following the procedure outlined above, we can construct a value chain for a firm and its customers, and then identify linkages between the two. Figure 7.12 identifies five such linkages:

1   Distinctive can designs (e.g., Sapporo's beer can) can support the customer's efforts to differentiate its product.

2   Manufacturing cans to high tolerances can minimize breakdowns on customers' canning lines.

3   Reliable, punctual can deliveries allow canners to economize on their can inventories.

4   An efficient order-processing system reduces canners' ordering costs.

5   Speedy, proficient technical support allows customers to operate their canning lines with high-capacity utilization.

FIGURE 7.12   Identifying differentiation opportunities by linking the firm's value chain to that of the customer

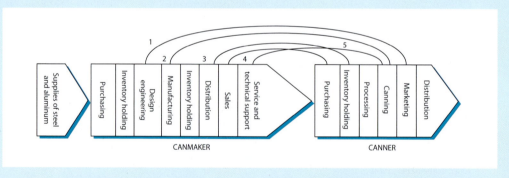

Value Chain Analysis of Consumer Goods   Value chain analysis of differentiation opportunities can also be applied to consumer goods. Few consumer goods are consumed directly: typically, consumers engage in a chain of activities that involve search, acquisition, and use of the product. In the case of consumer durables, the value chain may include search, purchase, financing, acquisition of complementary products and services, operation, service and repair, and eventual disposal. Such complex consumer value chains offer many potential linkages with the manufacturer's value chain, with rich opportunities for innovative differentiation. Harley-Davidson has built its strategy around the notion that it is not supplying motorcycles; it is supplying a customer experience. This has encouraged it to expand the scope of its contact with its customers to provide a wider range of services than any other motorcycle company. Even nondurables involve the consumer in a chain of activities. Consider a frozen TV dinner: it must be purchased, taken home, removed from the package, heated, and served before it is consumed. After eating, the consumer must clean any used dishes, cutlery, or other utensils. A value chain analysis by a frozen foods producer would identify ways in which the product could be formulated, packaged, and distributed to assist the consumer in performing this chain of activities.

Implementing Cost and Differentiation Strategies

The two primary sources of competitive advantage define two fundamentally different approaches to business strategy. A firm that is competing on low cost is distinguishable from a firm that competes through differentiation in terms of market positioning, resources and capabilities, and organizational characteristics. Table 7.2 outlines some of the principal features of cost and differentiation strategies.

Porter views cost leadership and differentiation as mutually exclusive strategies. A firm that attempts to pursue both is "stuck in the middle":

> The firm stuck in the middle is almost guaranteed low profitability. It either loses the high-volume customers who demand low prices or must bid away its profits to get this business from the low-cost firms. Yet it also loses high-margin business— the cream—to the firms who are focused on high-margin targets or have achieved differentiation overall. The firm that is stuck in the middle also probably suffers from a blurred corporate culture and a conflicting set of organizational arrangements and motivation system.[75]

TABLE 7.2 Features of cost leadership and differentiation strategies

Generic strategy	Key strategy elements	Resource and organizational requirements
Cost leadership	Scale-efficient plants	Access to capital
	Design for manufacture	Process engineering skills
	Control of overheads and R & D	Frequent reports
	Process innovation	Tight cost control
	Outsourcing (especially overseas)	Specialization of jobs and functions
	Avoidance of marginal customer	Incentives linked to quantitative target accounts
Differentiation	Emphasis on branding, advertising, design, service, quality, and new product development	Marketing abilities
		Product engineering skills
		Cross-functional coordination
		Creativity
		Research capability
		Incentives linked to qualitative performance targets

In practice, few firms are faced with such stark alternatives. Differentiation is not simply an issue of "to differentiate or not to differentiate." All firms must make decisions as to which customer requirements to focus on and where to position their product or service in the market. A cost leadership strategy typically implies limited-feature, standardized offerings, but this does not necessarily imply that the product or service is an undifferentiated commodity. Southwest Airlines and AirAsia are budget airlines with a no-frills offering yet have clear market positions with unique brand images. The VW Beetle shows that a utilitarian, mass-market product can achieve cult status.

In most industries, market leadership is held by a firm that maximizes customer appeal by reconciling effective differentiation with low cost—Toyota in cars, McDonald's in fast food, Nike in athletic shoes. The simultaneous pursuit of cost efficiency, quality, innovation, and brand building was a feature of Japanese suppliers of cars, motorcycles, consumer electronics, and musical instruments during the late 20th century. In many industries, the cost leader is not the market leader but a smaller competitor with minimal overheads, non-union labor and cheaply acquired assets. In oil refining, the cost leaders tend to be independent refining companies rather than integrated giants such as ExxonMobil or Shell. In car rental, the cost leader is more likely to be Rent-A-Wreck (a division of Bundy American Corporation) rather than Hertz or Avis. Reconciling cost efficiency with differentiation has been facilitated by management technique: total quality management has refuted the perceived tradeoff between quality and cost; flexible manufacturing systems have reconciled scale economies with variety.

Summary

Making money in business requires establishing and sustaining competitive advantage. Identifying opportunities for competitive advantage requires insight into the nature and process of competition within a market. Our analysis of the imperfections of the competitive process takes us back to the resources and capabilities needed to compete in a particular market and conditions under which these are available. Similarly, the isolating mechanisms that sustain competitive advantage are dependent primarily upon the ability of rivals to access the resources and capabilities needed for imitation.

Competitive advantage has two primary dimensions: cost advantage and differentiation advantage. The first of these, cost advantage, is the outcome of seven primary cost drivers. We showed that by applying these cost drivers and by disaggregating the form into a value chain of linked activities we can appraise a firm's cost position relative to competitors and identify opportunities for cost reduction. The principal message of this section is the need to look behind cost accounting data and beyond simplistic approaches to cost efficiency, and to analyze the factors that drive relative unit costs in each of the firm's activities in a systematic and comprehensive manner.

The appeal of differentiation is that it offers multiple opportunities for competitive advantage with a greater potential for sustainability than does cost advantage. The vast realm of differentiation opportunity extends beyond marketing and design to encompass all aspects of a firm's interactions with its customers. Achieving a differentiation advantage requires the firm to match its own capacity for creating uniqueness to the requirements and preferences of customers. The value chain offers firms a useful framework for identifying how they can create value for their customers by combining demand-side and supply-side sources of differentiation.

Finally, the basis of a firm's competitive advantage has important implications not just for the design of its strategy but for the design of its organizational structure and systems. Typically, companies that are focused on cost leadership design their organizations differently from those that pursue differentiation. However, the implications of competitive strategy for organizational design are complicated by the fact that, for most firms, cost efficiency and differentiation are not mutually exclusive—in today's intensely competitive markets, firms have little choice but to pursue both.

 Quizzes and flashcards to test yourself further are available in your interactive e-book at **www.wileyopenpage.com**

Self-Study Questions

1. Figure 7.1 implies that stable industries, where firms have similar resources and capabilities, offer less opportunity for competitive advantage than industries where change is rapid and firms are heterogeneous. Think of an example of each of these two types of industry. Is there any evidence that interfirm profit differences are wider in the more dynamic, heterogeneous industry than in the more stable, homogeneous industry?

2. Apple has successfully established itself as the market leader in smartphones with its iPhone. Can Apple sustain its leadership in this market? How?

3. Illy, the Italian-based supplier of quality coffee and coffee-making equipment, is launching an international chain of gourmet coffee shops. What advice would you offer Illy for how it can best build competitive advantage in the face of Starbucks' market leadership?

4. Which drivers of cost advantage (Figure 7.5) does Sears exploit in order to offer its Sears Motor Buggy "at a price within the reach of all"? (See quotation that opens this chapter.)

5. Target (the US discount retailer), H&M (the Swedish fashion clothing chain), and Primark (the UK discount clothing chain) have pioneered *cheap chic*—combining discount store prices with fashion appeal. What are the principal challenges of designing

and implementing a cheap chic strategy? Design a cheap chic strategy for a company entering another market e.g., restaurants, sports shoes, cosmetics, or office furniture.

6. To what extent are the seven cost drivers shown in Figure 7.5 relevant in analyzing the costs per student at your business school or educational institution? What recommendations would you make to your dean for improving the cost efficiency of your school?

7. Bottled water sells at least 200 times the price of tap water, with substantial price differentials between different brands. What are the key differentiation variables that determine the price premium that can be obtained for bottled water?

8. Advise a chain of movie theaters on a differentiation strategy to restore its flagging profitability. Use the value chain framework outlined in Strategy Capsule 7.6 to identify potential linkages between the company's value chain and that of its customers in order to identify differentiation opportunities.

Notes

1. Richard Rumelt argues that competitive advantage lacks a clear and consistent definition ("What in the World is Competitive Advantage?" Policy Working Paper 2003-105, Anderson School, UCLA, August, 2003).
2. K. Ferdows, M. A. Lewis, and J. Machuca, "Rapid-Fire Fulfillment," *Harvard Business Review* (November 2004): 104–10.
3. G. Stalk Jr., "Time: The Next Source of Competitive Advantage," *Harvard Business Review* (July/August, 1988): 41–51.
4. J. A. Schumpeter, *Capitalism, Socialism and Democracy* (London: Routledge, 1994, first published 1942): 82–3.
5. C. Kim and R. Mauborgne, "Blue Ocean Strategy," *Harvard Business Review* (October 2004).
6. R. Buaron, "New Game Strategies," *McKinsey Quarterly Anthology* (2000): 34–6.
7. C. Baden-Fuller and J. M. Stopford, *Rejuvenating the Mature Business* (London and New York: Routledge, 1992).
8. G. Hamel, "The Why, What, and How of Management Innovation," *Harvard Business Review* (February 2006).
9. R. P. Rumelt, "Toward a Strategic Theory of the Firm," in R. Lamb (ed.), *Competitive Strategic Management* (Englewood Cliffs, NJ: Prentice Hall, 1984): 556–70.
10. R. Jacobsen, "The Persistence of Abnormal Returns," *Strategic Management Journal* 9 (1988): 415–30; R. R. Wiggins and T. W. Ruefli, "Schumpeter's Ghost: Is Hypercompetition Making the Best of Times Shorter?" *Strategic Management Journal* 26 (2005): 887–911.
11. G. Stalk, "Curveball: Strategies to Fool the Competition," *Harvard Business Review* (September 2006): 114–22.
12. The film was based on the book by B. Traven, *The Treasure of the Sierra Madre* (New York: Knopf, 1947).
13. Monopolies and Mergers Commission, *Cat and Dog Foods* (London: Her Majesty's Stationery Office, 1977).
14. S. Martin, *Advanced Industrial Economics*, 2nd edn (Oxford: Blackwell Publishing, 2001): Chapter 8.
15. T. C. Schelling, *The Strategy of Conflict*, 2nd edn (Cambridge, MA: Harvard University Press, 1980): 35–41.
16. A. Brandenburger and B. Nalebuff, *Co-opetition* (New York: Doubleday, 1996): 72–80.
17. R. Schmalensee, "Entry Deterrence in the Ready-to-Eat Breakfast Cereal Industry," *Bell Journal of Economics* 9 (1978): 305–27.
18. Monopolies and Mergers Commission, *Indirect Electrostatic Reprographic Equipment* (London: Her Majesty's Stationery Office, 1976): 37, 56.
19. S. A. Lippman and R. P. Rumelt, "Uncertain Imitability: An Analysis of Interfirm Differences in Efficiency under Competition," *Bell Journal of Economics* 13 (1982): 418–38. See also: R. Reed and R. DeFillippi, "Causal Ambiguity, Barriers to Imitation, and Sustainable Competitive Advantage," *Academy of Management Review* 15 (1990): 88–102.
20. P. R. Milgrom and J. Roberts, "Complementarities and Fit: Strategy, Structure and Organizational Change in Manufacturing," *Journal of Accounting and Economics* 19 (1995): 179–208.
21. J. W. Rivkin, "Imitation of Complex Strategies," *Management Science* 46 (2000): 824–44.
22. M. E. Porter and N. Siggelkow, "Contextuality within Activity Systems and Sustainable Competitive Advantage," *Academy of Management Perspectives* 22 (May 2008): 34–56.
23. M. E. Porter, *Competitive Advantage* (New York: Free Press, 1985): 13.
24. M. E. Porter, *Competitive Advantage* (New York: Free Press, 1985): 120.

25. L. E. Yelle, "The Learning Curve: Historical Review and Comprehensive Survey," *Decision Sciences* 10 (1979): 302–28.

26. D. Ross, "Learning to Dominate," *Journal of Industrial Economics* 34 (1986): 337–53.

27. Boston Consulting Group, *Strategy Alternatives for the British Motorcycle Industry* (London: Her Majesty's Stationery Office, 1975).

28. R. Jacobsen and D. Aaker, "Is market share all that it's cracked up to be?" *Journal of Marketing* 49 (Fall 1985): 11–22.

29. R. Wensley, "PIMS and BCG: New Horizons or False Dawn?" *Strategic Management Journal* 3 (1982): 147–58.

30. M. Venzin, *Building an International Financial Services Firm: How Successful Firms Design and Execute Cross-border Strategies* (Oxford: Oxford University Press, 2009).

31. R. P. McAfee and J. McMillan, "Organizational Diseconomies of Scale," *Journal of Economics and Management Strategy* 4 (1996): 399–426.

32. L. Rapping, "Learning and World War II Production Functions," *Review of Economics and Statistics* (February 1965): 81–6.

33. G. Linden, J. Hart, S. A. Lenway, and T. P. Murtha, "Flying Geese as Moving Targets," *Industry and Innovation* 5 (June 1998): 11–34.

34. L. Argote, S. L. Beckman, and D. Epple, "The Persistence and Transfer of Learning in Industrial Settings,"*Management Science* 36 (1990): 140–54; M. Zollo and S. G. Winter, "Deliberate Learning and the Evolution of Dynamic Capabilities," *Organization Science* 13 (2002): 339–51.

35. M. Keller, *Collision* (New York: Doubleday, 1993): 169–71.

36. J. Womack and D. T. Jones, "From Lean Production to Lean Enterprise," *Harvard Business Review* (March/April 1994); J. Womack and D. T. Jones, "Beyond Toyota: How to Root Out Waste and Pursue Perfection," *Harvard Business Review* (September/October, 1996).

37. M. Hammer and J. Champy, *Re-engineering the Corporation: A Manifesto for Business Revolution* (New York: HarperBusiness, 1993): 32.

38. M. Hammer, "Re-engineering Work: Don't Automate, Obliterate," *Harvard Business Review* (July/August, 1990).

39. V. Glover and M. L. Marcus, "Business Process Transformation," *Advances in Management Information Systems* 9 (M. E. Sharpe, March 2008); R. Merrifield, J. Calhoun, and D. Stevens, "The Next Revolution in Productivity," *Harvard Business Review* (November 2006): 72–9.

40. R. E. Gomory, "From the Ladder of Science to the Product Development Cycle," *Harvard Business Review* (November/December 1989): 103.

41. F. X. Frei, "Breaking the Tradeoff between Efficiency and Service," *Harvard Business Review* (November 2006): 92–103.

42. "Caterpillar to Cut 20,000 Jobs as Downturn Worsens," *Wall Street Journal* (January 28, 2009).

43. J. W. Plunkett, *Plunkett's Automotive Almanac* 2011 (Houston, TX: Plunkett's Research).

44. "Buying Power of Multiproduct Retailers," *OECD Journal of Competition Law and Policy* 2 (March, 2000).

45. R. Cyert and J. March, *A Behavioral Theory of the Firm* (Englewood Cliffs, NJ: Prentice Hall, 1963).

46. H. Leibenstein, "Allocative Efficiency versus X-Efficiency," *American Economic Review* 54 (June 1966): 392–415.

47. K. Kase, F. J. Saez, and H. Riquelme, *The New Samurais of Japanese Industry* (Cheltenham: Edward Elgar, 2006).

48. M. E. Porter, *Competitive Advantage* (New York: Free Press, 1985): 87.

49. R. S. Kaplan and S. R. Anderson, "Time-Driven Activity-based Costing," *Harvard Business Review* (November 2004): 131–8; J. Billington, "The ABCs of ABC: Activity-based Costing and Management," *Harvard Management Update* (Boston: Harvard Business School Publishing, May 1999).

50. M. E. Porter, *Competitive Advantage* (New York: Free Press, 1985): 120.

51. T. Peters, *Thriving on Chaos* (New York: Knopf, 1987): 56.

52. "Cemex: Cementing a Global Strategy," Insead Case No. 307-233-1 (2007).

53. The distinction between segmentation and differentiation is discussed in P. R. Dickson and J. L. Ginter, "Market Segmentation, Product Differentiation and Marketing Strategy," *Journal of Marketing* 51 (April 1987): 1–10.

54. S. Schiffman, M. Reynolds, and F. Young, *Introduction to Multidimensional Scaling: Theory, Methods, and Applications* (Cambridge, MA: Academic Press, 1981).

55. F.-J. Lapointe and P. Legendre, "A Classification of Pure Malt Scotch Whiskies," *Applied Statistics* 43 (1994): 237–57. On the principles of MDS, see I. Borg and P. Groenen, *Modern Multidimensional Scaling: Theory and Application*(New York: Springer-Verlag, 1997).

56. P. Cattin and D. R. Wittink, "Commercial Use of Conjoint Analysis: A Survey," *Journal of Marketing* 46 (Summer 1982): 44–53.

57. K. Lancaster, *Consumer Demand: A New Approach* (New York: Columbia University Press, 1971).

58. P. Nicolaides and C. Baden-Fuller, *Price Discrimination and Product Differentiation in the European Domestic Appliance Market* (London: Center for Business Strategy, London Business School, 1987).

59. A. Pates, "A Reconsideration of Hedonic Price Indexes with an Application to PCs," *American Economic Review* 93 (2003): 1578–96.

60. C. Kim and R. Mauborgne, "Creating New Market Space," *Harvard Business Review* (January/February 1999): 83–93.

61. A. Maslow, "A Theory of Human Motivation," *Psychological Review* 50 (1943): 370–96.

62. "Coke Lore: The Real Story of New Coke," www.thecocacolacompany.com/heritage/cokelore_newcoke.html, accessed February 8, 2012.

63. T. Peters, *Thriving on Chaos* (New York: Knopf, 1987): 149.

64. "Fresh, but far from Easy," *Economist* (June 21, 2007).

65. J. K. Johansson and I. Nonaka, *Relentless: The Japanese Way of Marketing* (New York: HarperBusiness, 1996).

66. M. E. Porter, *Competitive Advantage* (New York: Free Press, 1985): 124–5.

67. S. Mathur, "Competitive Industrial Marketing Strategies," *Long Range Planning* 17, no. 4 (1984): 102–9.

68. J. Hagel and M. Singer, "Unbundling the Corporation," *McKinsey Quarterly* 3 (2000): 148–61.

69. K. R. Tuli, A. K. Kohli, and S. G. Bharadwaj, "Rethinking Customer Solutions: From Product Bundles to Relational Processes," *Journal of Marketing* 71, no. 3 (2007): 1–17.

70. K. Clark and T. Fujimoto, *Product Development Performance* (Boston: Harvard Business School Press, 1991): 29–30.

71. K. B. Clark and T. Fujimoto, "The Power of Product Integrity," *Harvard Business Review* (November/December, 1990): 107–18.

72. "The Madoff Affair: Going Down Quietly," *Economist* (March 14, 2009).

73. D. J. Watts and J. Peretti, "Viral Marketing for the Real World," *Harvard Business Review* (May 2007): 22–3.

74. J. Pine, B. Victor, and A. Boynton, "Making Mass-customization Work," *Harvard Business Review* (September/October 1993): 108–16.

75. M. E. Porter, *Competitive Strategy* (New York: Free Press, 1980): 42.

8 Industry Evolution and Strategic Change

> No company ever stops changing … Each new generation must meet changes—in the automotive market, in the general administration of the enterprise, and in the involvement of the corporation in a changing world. The work of creating goes on.
>
> —ALFRED P. SLOAN JR., PRESIDENT OF GENERAL MOTORS 1923–37, CHAIRMAN 1937–56

> It is not the strongest of the species that survive, nor the most intelligent, but the one that is most responsive to change.
>
> —CHARLES DARWIN

> You keep same-ing when you ought to be changing.
>
> —LEE HAZLEWOOD, THESE BOOTS ARE MADE FOR WALKING, RECORDED BY NANCY SINATRA, 1966

OUTLINE

Introduction and Objectives

Everything is in a state of constant change—the business environment especially. One of the greatest challenges of strategic management is to ensure that the firm keeps pace with changes occurring within its environment.

Change in the industry environment is driven by the forces of technology, consumer needs, politics, economic development, and a host of other influences. In some industries, these forces for change combine to create massive, unpredictable changes. For example, in telecommunications new digital and wireless technologies combined with regulatory changes have resulted in the telecom industry of 2012 being almost unrecognizable from that which existed 25 years ago. In other industries—food processing, aircraft production, and car rental—change is more gradual and more predictable. Change is not just the result of external forces. As we have seen, competition is a dynamic process in which firms vie for competitive advantage, only to see it eroded through imitation and innovation by rivals. The outcome is that industries are continually recreated by competition.

The purpose of this chapter is to help us to understand and manage change. To do this we shall explore the forces that drive change and look for patterns that can help us to predict how industries are likely to evolve over time. While recognizing that every industry follows a unique development path, there are common drivers of change that can help us to recognize similar patterns, thereby helping us to identify opportunities for competitive advantage.

Understanding, even predicting, change in an industry's environment is the easy part. By far the greatest challenge is ensuring the adaptation of the firm to that change. For individuals change is disruptive, costly, and uncomfortable. For organizations the forces of inertia are even stronger. As a result, the life cycles of firms tend to be much shorter than the life cycles of industries: changes at the industry level tend to occur through the death of existing firms and the birth of new firms rather than through continuous adaptation by a constant population of firms. We need to understand these sources of inertia in organizations to see how resistance to change can be overcome. Going beyond adaptation, some firms become initiators of change. What determines the ability of these firms to become game-changers in their industries?

Whether a firm is adapting to or initiating change, competing in a changing world requires the development of new capabilities that can help renew competitive advantage. How difficult can this be? The short answer is "Very." We will look not just at the difficulties of building new capabilities but also at the approaches that organizations can take to overcome these difficulties.

By the time you have completed this chapter, you will be able to:

♦ recognize the different stages of industry development and understand the factors that drive the process of industry evolution;

♦ identify the key success factors associated with industries at different stages of their development and recommend strategies, organizational structures, and management systems appropriate to these stages;

◆ appreciate the sources of organizational inertia, the challenges of managing strategic change, and be familiar with different approaches to strategic change—including the use of scenario analysis and the quest for ambidexterity;

◆ become familiar with the different approaches that firms have taken in developing organizational capabilities—and the merits and pitfalls of each;

◆ recognize the principal tools of knowledge management and the roles they can play in developing organizational capability.

The Industry Life Cycle

One of the best-known and most enduring marketing concepts is the *product life cycle*.[1] Products are born, their sales grow, they reach maturity, they go into decline, and they ultimately die. If products have life cycles, so the industries that produce them experience an **industry life cycle**. To the extent that an industry produces multiple generations of a product, the industry life cycle is likely to be of longer duration than that of a single product.

The life cycle comprises four phases: *introduction* (or *emergence*), *growth*, *maturity*, and *decline* (Figure 8.1). Let us first examine the forces that drive industry evolution, and then let us look at the features of each of these stages. Two factors are fundamental: demand growth and the production and diffusion of knowledge.

Demand Growth

The life cycle and the stages within it are defined primarily by changes in an industry's growth rate over time. The characteristic profile is an S-shaped growth curve.

- In the *introduction stage*, sales are small and the rate of market penetration is low because the industry's products are little known and customers are few. The novelty of the technology, small scale of production, and lack of experience mean high costs and low quality. Customers for new products tend to be affluent, innovation-oriented, and risk-tolerant.
- The *growth stage* is characterized by accelerating market penetration as technical improvements and increased efficiency open up the mass market.
- Increasing market saturation causes the onset of the *maturity stage*. Once saturation is reached, demand is wholly for replacement.
- Finally, as the industry becomes challenged by new industries that produce technologically superior substitute products, the industry enters its *decline stage*.

FIGURE 8.1 The industry life cycle

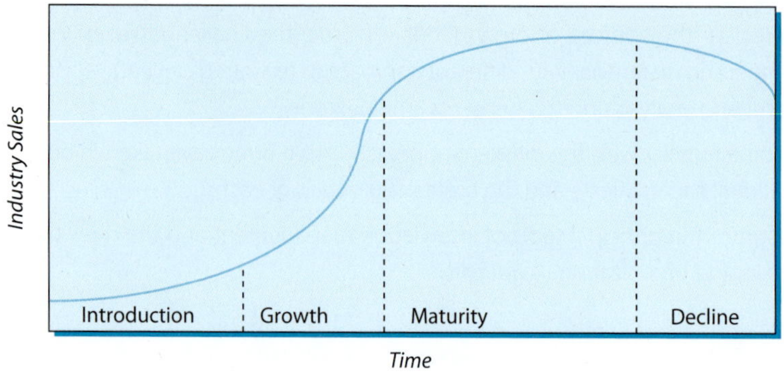

Creation and Diffusion of Knowledge

The second driver of the industry life cycle is knowledge. New knowledge in the form of product innovation is responsible for an industry's birth, and the dual processes of knowledge creation and knowledge diffusion exert a major influence on industry evolution.

In the introduction stage, product technology advances rapidly. There is no dominant product technology, and rival technologies compete for attention. Competition is primarily between alternative technologies and design configurations:

- The first 30 years of steam ships featured competition between paddles and propellers, wooden hulls and iron hulls, and, eventually, between coal and oil.
- The beginnings of the home computer industry during 1978–1982 saw competition between different data storage systems (audiotapes versus floppy disks), visual displays (TV receivers versus dedicated monitors), operating systems (CPM versus DOS versus Apple II), and microprocessors.

Dominant Designs and Technical Standards The outcome of competition between rival designs and technologies is usually convergence by the industry around a **dominant design**—a product architecture that defines the look, functionality, and production method for the product and becomes accepted by the industry as a whole. Dominant designs have included:

- The Underwood Model 5 introduced in 1899 established the basic architecture and main features of typewriters for the 20th century: a moving carriage, the ability to see the characters being typed, a shift function for upper-case characters, and a replaceable inked ribbon.[2]
- Leica's Ur-Leica camera developed by Oskar Barnack and launched in Germany in 1924 established key features of the 35 mm camera, though it was not until Canon began mass-producing cameras based on the Leica original that this design of 35 mm camera came to dominate still photography.
- When Ray Kroc opened his first McDonald's hamburger restaurant in Illinois in 1955, he established what would soon become a dominant design for the

FIGURE 8.2   Product and process innovation over time

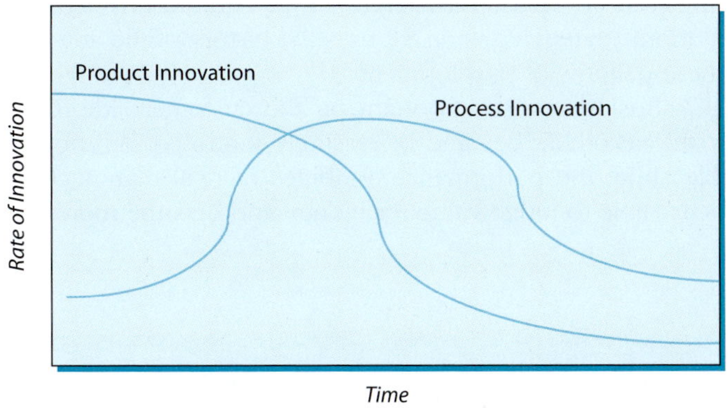

fast-food restaurant industry: a limited menu, no waiter service, eat-in and take-out options, roadside locations for motorized customers, and a franchising model of business system licensing.

The concepts of *dominant design* and **technical standard** are closely related. Dominant design refers to the overall configuration of a product or system. A technical standard is a technology or specification that is important for compatibility. A dominant design may or may not embody a technical standard. IBM's PC established the MS-DOS operating system and Intel x86 series of microprocessor as standards for personal computing that later evolved into the "Wintel" standard. Conversely, the Boeing 707 was a dominant design for large passenger jets but did not set industry standards in aerospace technology that would dominate subsequent generations of airplanes. Technical standards emerge where there are **network effects**—the need for users to connect in some way with one another. Network effects cause each customer to choose the same technology as everyone else to avoid being stranded. Unlike a proprietary technical standard, which is typically embodied in patents or copyrights, a firm that sets a dominant design does not normally own intellectual property in that design. Hence, except for some early-mover advantage, there is not necessarily any profit advantage from setting a dominant design.

Dominant designs also exist in processes. In the flat glass industry there has been a succession of dominant process designs from glass cylinder blowing to continuous ribbon drawing to float glass.[3] Dominant designs are present, too, in business models. In many new markets, competition is between rival *business models*. In home grocery delivery, dotcom start-ups such as Webvan and Peapod soon succumbed to competition from "bricks 'n' clicks" retailers such as Giant, and Wal-Mart (and Tesco in the UK).

From Product to Process Innovation   The emergence of a dominant design marks a critical juncture in an industry's evolution. Once the industry coalesces around a leading product design, there's a shift from radical to incremental product innovation. This transition may be necessary to inaugurate the industry's growth phase: greater standardization reduces risks to customers and encourages firms to invest in production capacity. The shift in emphasis from design to manufacture typically involves increased attention to process innovation as firms seek to reduce costs and increase product reliability through large-scale production methods (Figure 8.2). The combination of process improvements, design modifications, and scale economies results in falling costs and greater availability, which in turn drives rapidly increasing market penetration. Strategy Capsule 8.1 uses the history of the automobile industry to illustrate these patterns of development.

Knowledge diffusion is also important on the customer side. Over the course of the life cycle, customers become increasingly informed. As they become more knowledgeable about the performance attributes of rival manufacturers' products, so they are better able to judge value for money and become more price sensitive.

STRATEGY CAPSULE 8.1

Evolution of the Automobile Industry

The period 1890–1912 was one of rapid product innovation in the auto industry. After 1886, when Karl Benz received a patent on his three-wheel motor carriage, a flurry of technical advances occurred in Germany, France, the US, and the UK. Developments included:

- the first four-cylinder four-stroke engine (by Karl Benz in 1890);
- the honeycomb radiator (by Daimler in 1890);
- the speedometer (by Oldsmobile in 1901);
- automatic transmission (by Packard in 1904);
- electric headlamps (by General Motors in 1908);
- the all-steel body (adopted by General Motors in 1912).

Ford's Model T, introduced in 1908, with its front-mounted, water-cooled engine and transmission with a gearbox, wet clutch, and rear-wheel drive, acted as a dominant design for the industry. During the remainder of the 20th century, automotive technology and design converged. A key indicator of this was the gradual elimination of alternative technologies and designs. Volkswagen's Beetle was the last mass-produced car with a rear-mounted, air-cooled engine. Citroen abandoned its distinctive suspension and braking systems. Four-stroke engines with four or six inline cylinders became dominant. Distinctive national differences eroded as American cars became smaller and Japanese and Italian cars became bigger. The fall of the Iron Curtain extinguished the last outposts of nonconformity: by the mid-1990s, East German two-stroke Wartburgs and Trabants were collectors' items.

As product innovation slowed, so process innovation took off. In October 1913, Ford opened its Highland Park Assembly Plant, with its revolutionary production methods based on interchangeable parts and a moving assembly line. In the space of one year, chassis assembly time was cut from 12 hours and 8 minutes to 1 hour and 33 minutes. The price of the Model T fell from $628 in 1908 to $260 in 1924. Between 1908 and 1927, over 15 million Model T's had been produced.

The second revolutionary process innovation in automobile manufacturing was Toyota's system of *lean production*, involving a tightly integrated "pull" system of production embodying just-in-time scheduling, team-based production, flexible manufacturing, and total quality management. During the 1970s and 1980s, lean production diffused throughout the world's vehicle industry in the same way that Ford's mass-production system had transformed the industry half a century before.

Sources: www.ford.com; http://en.wikipedia.org/wiki/History_of_the_automobile.

How General Is the Life-Cycle Pattern?

To what extent do industries conform to this life-cycle pattern? To begin with, the duration of the life cycle varies greatly from industry to industry:

- The introduction phase of the US railroad industry extended from the building of the first railroad, the Baltimore and Ohio in 1827, to the growth phase of the 1870s. With the growth of road transport, the industry entered its decline phase during the late 1950s.
- The introduction stage of the US automobile industry lasted about 25 years, from the 1890s until growth took off in 1913–1915. Maturity set in during the mid-1950s, followed by decline during the past decade.
- In personal computers, the introduction phase lasted only about four years before growth took off in 1978. Between 1978 and 1983, a flood of new and established firms entered the industry. Toward the end of 1984, the first signs of maturity appeared: growth stalled, excess capacity emerged, and the industry began to consolidate around fewer companies; however, growth remained strong until the end of the 1990s.
- Digital audio players (MP3 players) were first introduced by Seehan Information Systems and Diamond Multimedia in 1997. With the launch of Apple's iPod in 2001, the industry entered its growth phase. By 2009, slackening growth indicated entry into the mature phase.

Over time, industry life cycles have become increasingly compressed. This is especially evident in e-commerce. Businesses such as online gambling, business-to-business online auctions, and online travel services went from initial introduction to maturity within a few years. Social networking was launched in 1997 by www.sixde grees.com. By 2005, a number of sites were rapidly building their networks, including MySpace, Orkut (Google), Badoo, and LinkedIn. However, it was Facebook that broke away from the pack, achieving 12 million users by the end of 2006, 100 million in August 2008, and 600 million at the beginning of 2011. Since then, monthly growth has slowed to a modest 3.5%. Cusumano and Yoffie argue that "competing on internet time" requires a radical rethink of strategies and management processes.[4]

Patterns of evolution also differ. Industries supplying basic necessities such as residential construction, food processing and clothing may never enter a decline phase because obsolescence is unlikely for such needs. Some industries may experience a rejuvenation of their life cycle. In the 1960s, the world motorcycle industry, in decline in the US and Europe, re-entered its growth phase as Japanese manufacturers pioneered the recreational use of motorcycles. The market for TV receivers has experienced multiple revivals: color TVs, computer monitors, flat-screen TVs, and, most recently, HDTVs. Similar waves of innovation have revitalized retailing (Figure 8.3). These rejuvenations of the product life cycle are not natural phenomena—they are typically the result of companies resisting the forces of maturity through breakthrough product innovations or developing new markets.

An industry is likely to be at different stages of its life cycle in different countries. Although the automobile markets of the EU, Japan, and the US have entered their decline phase, those of China, India, and Russia are in their growth phases. Multinational companies can exploit such differences: developing new products and

FIGURE 8.3   Innovation and renewal in the industry life cycle: Retailing

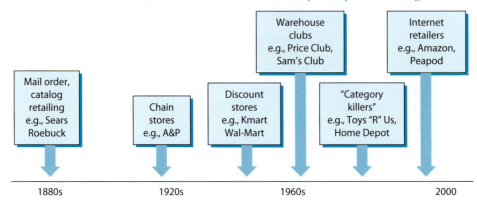

introducing them into the advanced industrial countries, then shifting attention to other growth markets once maturity sets in.

A further feature of industry evolution is shifting boundaries of industries—some industries converge (handheld consumer electronic devices such as wireless phones, portable game players, cameras, and calculators increasingly compete in a single market); other industries, such as computers and mortgage banking, tend to fragment. Jacobides argues that, to understand the dynamics of industry change, we need to look at broad sectors that comprise clusters of related industries.[5]

Implications of the Life Cycle for Competition and Strategy

Changes in demand growth and technology over the cycle have implications for industry structure, the population of firms, and competition. Table 8.1 summarizes the principal features of each stage of the industry life cycle.

Product Differentiation   The introduction stage typically features a wide variety of product types that reflect the diversity of technologies and designs—and the lack of consensus over customer requirements. Convergence around a dominant design is often followed by commoditization during the mature phase unless producers develop new dimensions for differentiation. Personal computers, credit cards, online financial services, wireless communication services, and internet access have all become commodity items which buyers select primarily on price. However, the trend toward commoditization also creates incentives for firms to create novel approaches to differentiation.

Organizational Demographics and Industry Structure   The number of firms in an industry changes substantially over the life cycle. The field of **organizational ecology**, founded by Michael Hannan, John Freeman, and Glen Carroll, analyzes the population of industries and the processes of founding and selection that determine entry and exit.[6] Some of the main findings of the organizational ecologists in relation to industry evolution are:

- The number of firms in an industry increases rapidly during the early stages of an industry's life. Initially, an industry may be pioneered by a few firms. However, as the industry gains legitimacy, failure rates decline and the rate

TABLE 8.1   The evolution of industry structure and competition over the life cycle

	Introduction	**Growth**	**Maturity**	**Decline**
Demand	Limited to early adopters: high-income, avant-garde	Rapidly increasing market penetration	Mass market, replacement/repeat buying. Customers knowledgeable and price sensitive	Obsolescence
Technology	Competing technologies, rapid product innovation	Standardization around dominant technology, rapid process innovation	Well-diffused technical know-how: quest for technological improvements.	Little product or process innovation
Products	Poor quality, wide variety of features and technologies, frequent design changes	Design and quality improve, emergence of dominant design	Trend to commoditization. Attempts to differentiate by branding, quality, and bundling	Commodities the norm: differentiation difficult and unprofitable
Manufacturing and distribution	Short production runs, high-skilled labor content, specialized distribution channels	Capacity shortages, mass production, competition for distribution	Emergence of overcapacity, deskilling of production, long production runs, distributors carry fewer lines	Chronic overcapacity, reemergence of specialty channels
Trade	Producers and consumers in advanced countries	Exports from advanced countries to rest of world	Production shifts to newly industrializing then developing countries	Exports from countries with lowest labor costs
Competition	Few companies	Entry, mergers, and exits	Shakeout, price competition increases	Price wars, exits
Key success factors	Product innovation, establishing credible image of firm and product	Design for manufacture, access to distribution, brand building, fast product development, process innovation	Cost efficiency through capital intensity, scale efficiency, and low input costs	Low overheads, buyer selection, signaling commitment, rationalizing capacity

of new firm foundings increases. The US automobile industry comprised 272 manufacturers in 1909,[7] while in TV receivers there were 92 companies in 1951.[8] New entrants have very different origins. Some are start-up companies (*de novo* entrants); others are established firms diversifying from related industries (*de alio* entrants).

- With the onset of maturity, the number of firms begins to fall. Very often, industries go through one or more *shakeout* phases during which the rate of firm failure increases sharply. After this point, rates of entry and exit decline and the survival rate for incumbents increases substantially.[9] The shakeout phase of intensive acquisition, merger, and exit occurs, on average, 29 years into the life cycle and results in the number of producers being halved.[10] In the US tire industry, the number of firms grew from one (Goodrich) in 1896 to 274 in 1922 before shakeout reduced the industry to 49 firms in 1936.[11]

- As industries become increasingly concentrated and the leading firms focus on the mass market, so a new phase of entry may take place as new firms create niche positions in the market. An example of this *resource partitioning* is the

US brewing industry: as the mass market became dominated by a handful of national brewers, so opportunities arose for new types of brewing companies—microbreweries and brew pubs—to establish themselves in specialist niches.[12]

However, in different industries structural change follows very different evolutionary paths. In most industries maturity is associated with increasing concentration, but in industries where scale economies are unimportant and entry barriers are low, maturity and commoditization may cause concentration to decline (as in credit cards, television broadcasting, and frozen foods). Some industries, especially where the first mover achieves substantial patent protection, may start out as near-monopolies, and then become increasingly competitive. Plain-paper copiers were initially monopolized by the Xerox Corporation and it was not until the early 1980s that the industry was transformed by a wave of new entry. Seemingly stable mature industries can be transformed within a few years by a wave of mergers. The world petroleum industry consolidated considerably during 1998–2001, as did the world steel industry during 2001–2007.

Location and International Trade   Industries migrate internationally during their life cycles as a result of shifts in demand and decreasing dependence on advanced knowledge. New industries begin in the advanced industrial countries because of the presence of affluent consumers and the availability of technical and scientific resources. As demand grows in other countries, they are serviced initially by exports, but a reduced need for sophisticated labor skills makes production attractive in newly industrialized countries. The advanced industrialized countries begin to import. With maturity, commoditization, and deskilling of production processes, production eventually shifts to developing countries where labor costs are lowest.

At the beginning of the 1990s, the production of wireless handsets was concentrated in the US, Japan, Finland, and Germany. By the end of the 1990s, South Korea had joined this leading group. Between 2005 and 2012, production in North America, Western Europe, and Japan was in rapid decline as manufacturing shifted to China, India, Brazil, Vietnam, Hungary, and Romania.

The Nature and Intensity of Competition   These changes in industry structure over the life cycle—commoditization, new entry, and international diffusion of production—have implications for competition: first, a shift from non-price competition to price competition; second, margins shrink as the intensity of competition grows.

During the introduction stage, the battle for technological leadership means that price competition may be weak, but heavy investments in innovation and market development depress profitability. The growth phase is more conducive to profitability as market demand outstrips industry capacity, especially if incumbents are protected by barriers to entry. With the onset of maturity, increased product standardization and excess capacity stimulate price competition, especially during shakeout. How intense this is depends a great deal on the balance between capacity and demand and the extent of international competition. In food retailing, airlines, motor vehicles, metals, and insurance, maturity was associated with strong price competition and slender profitability. In household detergents, breakfast cereals, cosmetics, and cigarettes, high seller concentration and strong brands have limited price rivalry and supported high margins. The decline phase is almost always associated with strong price competition (often degenerating into destructive price wars) and dismal profit performance.

Key Success Factors and Industry Evolution   These same changes in structure together with changes in demand and technology over the industry life cycle also have important implications for the sources of competitive advantage at each stage of industry evolution:

1 During the introductory stage, product innovation is the basis for initial entry and for subsequent success. Soon, however, other requirements for success emerge. In moving from the first generation of products to subsequent generations, investment requirements grow and financial resources become increasingly important. Capabilities in product development also need to be supported by capabilities in manufacturing, marketing, and distribution.

2 Once the growth stage is reached, the key challenge is scaling up. As the market expands, the firm needs to adapt its product design and its manufacturing capability to large-scale production. As Figure 8.4 shows, investment in R & D, plant and equipment, and sales tends to be high during the growth phase. To utilize increased manufacturing capability, access to distribution becomes critical. The transition to the growth stage of development imposes massive managerial and organizational challenges for young firms resulting from the need to develop new capabilities and establish more complex structures.

3 With the maturity stage, competitive advantage is increasingly a quest for efficiency, particularly in industries that tend toward commoditization. Cost efficiency through scale economies, low wages, and low overheads becomes the key success factor. Figure 8.4 shows that R & D, capital investment, and marketing are lower in maturity than during the growth phase.

4 The transition to decline intensifies pressures for cost cutting. It also requires maintaining stability by encouraging the orderly exit of industry capacity and capturing residual market demand. We consider the strategic issues presented by mature and declining industries more fully in Chapter 10.

Managing Organizational Adaptation and Strategic Change

We have established that industries change. But what about the companies within them? Let us turn our attention to business enterprises and consider both the impediments to change and the means by which change takes place.

Why is Change so Difficult? The Sources of Organizational Inertia

At the heart of all approaches to change management is the recognition that organizations find change difficult. Why is this so? Different theories of organizational and industrial change emphasize different barriers to change:

- *Organizational routines*: Evolutionary economists emphasize the fact that capabilities are based on organizational routines—patterns of coordinated interaction among organizational members that develop through continual repetition. The more highly developed are an organization's routines, the

FIGURE 8.4 Differences in strategy and performance between businesses at different stages of the industry life cycle

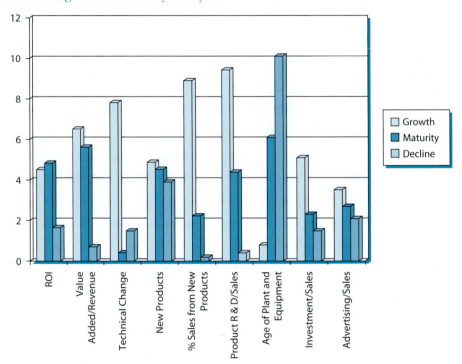

Note: The figure shows standardized means for each variable for businesses at each stage of the life cycle.
Source: C. Anderson and C. Zeithaml, "Stage of the Product Life Cycle, Business Strategy and Business Performance," *Academy of Management Journal* 27 (1984): 5–24.

more difficult it is to develop new routines. Hence, organizations get caught in **competency traps**[13] where "core capabilities become core rigidities."[14]

- *Social and political structures*: Organizations are both social systems and political systems. As social systems, organizations develop patterns of interaction that make organizational change stressful and disruptive.[15] As political systems, organizations develop stable distributions of power; change represents a threat to the power of those in positions of authority. Hence, both as social systems and political systems, organizations tend to resist change.

- *Conformity*: Institutional sociologists emphasize the propensity of firms to imitate one another in order to gain legitimacy. The process of **institutional isomorphism** locks organizations into common structures and strategies that make it difficult for them to adapt to change.[16] The pressures for conformity can be external—governments, investment analysts, banks, and other resource providers encourage the adoption of similar strategies and structures. Isomorphism also results from voluntary imitation— risk aversion encourages companies to adopt similar strategies and structures to their peers.[17]

- *Limited search*: The Carnegie School of organizational theory (associated with Herbert Simon, Jim March, and Richard Cyert) views *search* as the primary driver of organizational change. Organizations tend to limit search to areas close to their existing activities—they prefer *exploitation* of existing knowledge over *exploration* for new opportunities.[18] Limited search is reinforced, first, by **bounded rationality**—human beings have limited information processing capacity, which constrains the set of choices they can consider and, second, *satisficing*—the propensity for individuals (and organizations) to terminate the search for better solutions when they reach a satisfactory level of performance rather than to pursue optimal performance. The implication is that organizational change is triggered by declining performance.

● *Complementarities between strategy, structure, and systems*: Organizational economics,[19] sociotechnical systems,[20] and complexity theory[21] have all emphasized the importance of *fit* between an organization's strategy, structure, management systems, culture, employee skills—indeed, all the characteristics of an organization. Organizations struggle to establish complex, idiosyncratic combinations of multiple characteristics during their early phases of development in order to match the conditions of their business environment. However, once established, this complex configuration becomes a barrier to change. To respond to a change in its external environment, it is not enough to make incremental changes in few dimensions of strategy—it is likely that the firm will need to find a new configuration that involves a comprehensive set of changes (Strategy Capsule 8.2).[22] The implication is that organizations tend to evolve through a process of *punctuated equilibrium*, involving long periods of stability during which the widening misalignment between the organization and its environment ultimately forces radical and comprehensive change on the company.[23] Systematic changes that involve establishing a new configuration of activities that better matches the requirements of the external environment may require the appointment of a CEO from outside who is not wedded to the previous configuration.

Organizational Adaptation and Industry Evolution

Thinking about industrial and organizational change has been strongly influenced by ideas from evolutionary biology. Evolutionary change is viewed as an adaptive process that involves *variation*, *selection*, and *retention*.[24] The key issue is the level at which these evolutionary processes occur:

● *Organizational ecology* has been discussed in relation to changes in the number of firms in an industry over time. However, organizational ecology is a broader theory of economic change based on the assumption of organizational inertia. As a result, industry evolution occurs through changes in the population of firms rather than by adaptation of firms themselves. Industries develop and grow through new entry spurred by the imitation of initial successful entrants. The competitive process is a *selection mechanism*, in which organizations whose characteristics match the requirements of their environment can attract resources; those that do not are eliminated.[25]

● *Evolutionary economics* focuses upon individual organizations as the primary agents of change. The process of variation, selection, and retention takes place at the level of the *organizational routine*—unsuccessful routines are

STRATEGY CAPSULE 8.2

A Tight-Fitting Business System Makes Change Perilous: The Liz Claiborne Story

During the 1980s, Liz Claiborne became a highly successful designer, manufacturer, and retailer of clothes for professional women. Liz Claiborne's success was based upon a strategy that combined a number of closely linked choices concerning functions and activities.

◆ Design was based around a "color by the numbers" approach involving "concept groups" of different garments that could be mixed and matched.

◆ In department stores, Liz Claiborne encouraged the retailers to provide dedicated space to present Liz Claiborne's concept collections. Liz Claiborne also created a team of consultants whose jobs were to train retail staff at department stores and to ensure that the collections were being displayed correctly.

◆ Retailers could not purchase individual garment lines; they were required to purchase the entire concept group and had to submit a single order for each season—they could not reorder.

◆ Most manufacturing was contracted out to garment makers in SE Asia.

◆ To create close contact with customers, Liz Claiborne offered fashion shows at department stores, "breakfast clinics" where potential customers could see the latest collection, and introduced a point-of-sale data collection system to track customer preferences.

◆ Rather than the conventional four-season cycle of product introduction, Liz Claiborne operated a six-season cycle.

During the 1990s, Liz Claiborne performance went into a sharp decline. The key problem was the trend toward more casual clothes in the workplace. Moreover, financial pressures on department store chains made them less willing to buy complete collections. In response to retailer pressure, Liz Claiborne allowed reordering by retailers. However, once retailers could split orders into smaller, more frequent orders, the entire Liz Claiborne system began to break down since it could not adapt to the quick-response, fast-cycle model that was increasingly dominant within the garment trade. In 1994, Liz Claiborne appointed a new CEO who systematically rebuilt the business around a more casual look, with more flexibility within its collections (although still with a common "color card"), and around a shorter supply chain, with most production in North and Central America.

Source: N. Siggelkow, "Change in the Presence of Fit: The Rise, the Fall, and the Renaissance of Liz Claiborne," *Academy of Management Journal* 44 (2001): 838–57.

abandoned; successful routines are retained and replicated within the organization.[26] As we discussed in Chapter 5, these patterns of coordinated activity are the basis for organizational capability. While evolutionary theorists view firms as adapting to external change through the search for new routines, replication of successful routines, and abandonment of unsuccessful routines, such adaptation is neither fast nor costless.

Empirical evidence points to the importance of both processes. The ability of some companies to adapt is indicated by the fact that many have been leaders in

TABLE 8.2   World's biggest companies in terms of market capitalization, 1912 and 2012

1912	$billion	2012	$billion
US Steel	0.74	Apple	429
Standard Oil NJ (Exxon)	0.39	ExxonMobil	407
J&P Coates	0.29	Microsoft	254
Pullman	0.20	IBM	228
Royal Dutch Shell	0.19	Wal-Mart	212
Anaconda	0.18	Chevron	210
General Electric	0.17	China Mobile	204
Singer	0.17	General Electric	201
American Brands	0.17	China Construction Bank	198
Navistar	0.16	Google	194
British American Tobacco	0.16	Nestlé	191
De Beers	0.16	Johnson & Johnson	179

Sources: L. Hannah "Marshall's 'Trees' and the Global 'Forest': Were 'Giant Redwoods' Different?" in N. Lamoreaux, D. Raff, and P. Temin (eds), *Learning by Doing in Markets, Firms and Nations*, Chicago: University of Chicago Press, 1999: 253–94; *Financial Times* (February 6, 2012).

their industries for a century or more—BASF, the world's largest chemical company, has been a leader in chemicals since it was founded in 1865 as a producer of synthetic dyes. ExxonMobil and Royal Dutch Shell have led the world's petroleum industry for over a century.[27] Budweiser Budvar, the Czech beer company (that has a long-running trademark dispute with Anheuser-Busch) traces its origins to 1785. Mitsui Group, a Japanese conglomerate, is even older—its first business, a retail store, was established in 1673. GKN, the UK-based supplier of auto and aerospace components began as an ironworks in 1767.

Yet these companies are exceptions. Among the companies forming the original Dow Jones Industrial Average in 1896, only General Electric remains in the index today. Of the world's 12 biggest companies in 1912, just two were in the top 12 a century later (Table 8.2). And life spans are shortening: the average period in which companies remained in the S&P 500 was 90 years in 1935; by 2005 it was down to 15 years.

The changing identity of the world's biggest companies over the past century partly reflects the rise of new industries—notably the information and communications technology (ICT) sector, but also the failure of established firms to adapt successfully to the life cycles of their industries.

Even though the industry life cycle involves changes that are largely predictable, the changes in key success factors that we have already identified imply that the different stages of the life cycle require different resources and capabilities. Markides and Geroski show that the "innovators" that pioneer the creation of a new industry are typically different companies from the "consolidators" that develop it:

> The fact that the firms that create new product and service markets are rarely the ones that scale them into mass markets has serious implications for the modern corporation. Our research points to a simple reason for this phenomenon: the skills, mind-sets, and competences needed for discovery and invention are not

only different from those needed for commercialization; they conflict with the needed characteristics. This means that the firms good at invention are unlikely to be good at commercialization and vice versa.[28]

In plant biotechnology, the pioneers were research-based start-ups such as Calgene, Cetus Corporation, DNA Plant Technologies, and Mycogen. By 2012, the leading suppliers of genetically modified seeds were DuPont, Monsanto, Syngenta, and Dow Chemical—all long-established chemical firms. In US wireless telephony the pioneer was McCaw Communications; the current market leaders are AT&T and Verizon.

The typical pattern is that technology-based start-ups that pioneer new areas of business are acquired by companies that are well established in closely related industries, and these established incumbents offer the financial resources and functional capabilities needed to grow the start-up. Of course, some start-ups do survive both industry shakeouts and acquisition to become industry leaders: Google, Cisco Systems, and McDonald's are examples. Geoffrey Moore refers to this ability to make the transition from a start-up serving early adopters to an established business serving mainstream customers as "crossing the chasm."[29]

In most new industries we find a mixture of start-up companies (*de novo* entrants) and established companies that have diversified from other sectors (*de alio* entrants). Which firms are likely to be more successful? The basic issue is whether the flexibility and entrepreneurial advantages of start-ups outweigh the superior resources and capabilities of established firms. This further depends upon whether the resources and capabilities required in the new industry are similar to those present in an existing industry. Where these resource linkages are close, diversifying entrants are likely to have an advantage over new start-ups. Thus:

- In the US automobile industry, former bicycle, carriage, and engine manufacturers tended to be the best performers.[30]
- The US television manufacturing industry was dominated by former producers of radios.[31]

However, viewing this situation as competition between entrepreneurial, resource-poor start-ups and well-endowed established firms is over-simplistic. Start-up companies often possess some important resources. Many new firms are spinoffs from existing companies within the same industry—several studies show that a high proportion of new ventures are established by former employees of incumbent firms. In Silicon Valley most of the leading semiconductor firms, including Intel, trace their origins to Shockley Semiconductor Laboratories, the pioneer of integrated circuits.[32] A similar pattern is evident in the Akron tire industry.[33] These start-up entrepreneurs will carry with then know-how from their former employers.

Coping with Technological Change

Competition between new start-ups and established firms is not just a feature of the early phases of an industry's life cycle: it is ongoing. Any form of change in the external environment of an industry offers opportunities for newcomers to challenge incumbents. In vacuum cleaners, Dyson displaced established leaders Hoover and Electrolux in several countries' markets. In financial information services, Bloomberg took leadership from Reuters and Dow Jones. The major stumbling block for established firms is technological change. What does research tell us about why technological change is such a problem for established firms?

Competence enhancing and competence destroying technological change

Tushman and Anderson argue that some technological changes are "competence destroying"—they render obsolete the resources and capabilities of established firms. Other changes are "competence enhancing"—they preserve, even strengthen, the resources add capabilities of incumbent firms.[34] The quartz watch radically undermined the competence base of mechanical watchmakers, requiring transformation of the Swiss watch industry. Conversely, the turbofan, a major advance in jet engine technology, extended rather than weakened the capability base of existing aero engine manufacturers.

To determine the impact of a new technology on the competitive position of incumbent firms, it is necessary to look in detail at the implications of new technology for the individual resources and capabilities possessed by established firms. In the typesetting industry, the ability of incumbent firms to withstand the transition to radically new technologies rested upon their strengths in certain key resources that were not undermined by new technology: customer relationships, sales and service networks, and font libraries.[35]

Architectural and Component Innovation

A key factor determining the success of established firms in adapting to technological change is whether the technological innovation occurs at the *component* or the *architectural* level. Henderson and Clark argue that innovations which change the overall architecture of a product create great difficulties for established firms because an architectural innovation requires a major reconfiguration of a company's strategy and organizational structure.[36] In automobiles, the hybrid engine was an important innovation, but it did not require a major reconfiguration of car design and engineering. The battery-powered electric motor is an architectural innovation—it requires redesign of the entire car and involves carmakers in creating systems for recharging. In many sectors of e-commerce—online grocery purchases and online banking—the internet involved innovation at the component level (it provided a new channel of distribution for existing products). Hence, existing supermarket chains and established retail banks with their clicks 'n' bricks business models have dominated online groceries and online financial services. Similarly with the transistor radio: although a single component, it was an architectural innovation since it required established radio producers to radically change their approaches to product design, manufacturing, and marketing:

> In the mid-1950s engineers at RCA's corporate R & D center developed a prototype of a portable, transistorized radio receiver. The new product used technology in which RCA was accomplished (transistors, radio circuits, speakers, tuning devices), but RCA saw little reason to pursue such an apparently inferior technology. In contrast, Sony, a small, relatively new company, used the small transistorized radio to gain entry into the US market. Even after Sony's success was apparent, RCA remained a follower in the market as Sony introduced successive models with improved sound quality and FM capability. The irony of the situation was not lost on the R & D engineers: for many years Sony's radios were produced with technology licensed from RCA, yet RCA had great difficulty matching Sony's product in the marketplace.[37]

Disruptive Technologies   Clay Christiansen of Harvard Business School has also questioned why established firms find it so difficult to adapt to new technology. He distinguishes between new technology that is *sustaining*—it augments existing performance attributes—and new technology that is *disruptive*—it incorporates different performance attributes than the existing technology.[38]

In the disk-drive industry, some technological innovations—such as thin-film heads and more finely dispersed ferrous oxide disk coatings—have enhanced the dominant performance criterion: recording density. Such innovation has typically been led by established industry leaders. Other disk-drive technologies, notably new product generations with smaller diameters, were disruptive in their impact: established companies were, on average, two years behind newcomers in launching the new disk sizes and typically lost their industry leadership.[39] Incumbents' resistance to the new disk sizes reflected two factors: inferior initial performance and customer resistance. In 1987, Connor Peripherals began shipping a 3.5-inch disk drive. Industry leader Seagate had developed a 3.5-inch drive but halted its development for two reasons: first, it was inferior to the existing 5.25-inch disk in terms of capacity and cost per megabyte of memory; second, Seagate's main customers, the manufacturers of desktop PCs, showed no interest in the 3.5-inch disks. The 3.5-inch disks were adopted by Compaq and laptop makers. By 1990, the rapid development of the 3.5-inch disk had rendered the 5.25-disk obsolete.[40]

Similarly with other technologies. Steam-powered ships were initially slower, more expensive, and less reliable than sailing ships. The leading shipbuilders failed to make the transition to steam power because their leading customers, the transoceanic shipping companies, remained loyal to sail until after the turn of the 20th century. Steam power was used mainly for inland waters, which lacked constant winds. After several decades of gradual development for these niche markets, stream-powered ships were able to outperform sailing ships on ocean routes.

Managing Strategic Change

Given the many barriers to organizational change and the difficulties that companies experience in coping with disruptive technologies and architectural innovation, how can companies adapt to changes in their environment?

Just as the sources of organizational inertia are many, so too are the theories and methods of organizational change. Traditionally, the management of organizational change has been viewed as a distinct area of management. *Organizational development* (OD) comprises a set of methodologies through which an internal or external consultant acts as a catalyst for systemic change within a team or organizational unit.[41] Organizational development draws upon theories of psychology and sociology and is based upon a set of humanistic values. It emphasizes group processes (e.g., "T-groups") as vehicles for organizational change. The emphasis of organizational development is upon individual organizational units and bottom-up change in larger organizations. Because our emphasis is on strategic change—the redirection and adaptation of the whole organization—our emphasis will be on top-down change processes. Nevertheless, as the recent revolutions in Tunisia, Egypt, and Libya confirm, the power of bottom-up change should not be underestimated.

Dual Strategies and Organizational Ambidexterity

In Chapter 1 we learned that strategy has two major dimensions: positioning for the present and adapting to the future. As we observed then, reconciling the two is difficult. Derek Abell argues that "managing with dual strategies" is the most challenging dilemma that senior managers face:

> Running a successful business requires a clear strategy in terms of defining target markets and lavishing attention on those factors which are critical to success; changing a business in anticipation of the future requires a vision of how the future will look and a strategy for how the organization will have to adapt to meet future challenges.[42]

Abell argues that dual strategies require dual planning systems: short-term planning that focuses on strategic fit and performance over a one- or two-year period; and longer-term planning to develop vision, reshape the corporate portfolio, redefine and reposition individual businesses, develop new capabilities, and redesign organizational structures over periods of five years or more. Given the observation that companies are biased toward the exploitation of current resources and capabilities in relation to known opportunities, rather than exploration for new opportunities, most firms will emphasize short-term over long-term planning.

The challenges of reconciling "mastering the present" with "pre-empting the future" extend well beyond strategy formulation and the design of strategic planning systems. In recent years, Charles O'Reilly and Michael Tushman have stimulated interest in the **ambidextrous organization**, which is "capable of simultaneously exploiting existing competences and exploring new opportunities."[43] Two types of organizational ambidexterity have been identified:

- *Structural ambidexterity*: exploration and exploitation are undertaken in separate organizational units. It is usually easier to foster change initiatives in new organizational units rather than within the existing organization. For example, faced with the challenge of disruptive technologies, Christensen and Overdorf suggest that established companies develop products and businesses that embody the new technologies in organizationally separate units.[44] Such efforts show mixed results. IBM developed its PC in a separate unit in Florida—a thousand miles from IBM's corporate headquarters in New York. Its leader, Bill Lowe, claimed that this separation was critical to the team's creation of a product design and business system that was radically different from those of IBM's mainframes.[45] Xerox's Palo Alto Research Center (PARC) pioneered many of the technologies that formed the basis of the microcomputer revolution of the 1980s. However, few of these innovations were exploited by Xerox's New York-based establishment. Most flowed to nearby competitors Hewlett-Packard, Apple, Microsoft, and Sun Microsystems.[46] Similarly, GM's Saturn subsidiary set up in Tennessee to pioneer new approaches to manufacturing and marketing did little to revitalize the parent organization.[47] Attempts by Continental, United, British Airways, and several other legacy airlines to adapt to change by establishing budget airline subsidiaries were also costly failures.

● *Contextual ambidexterity* involves the same organizational units and the same organizational members pursuing both exploratory and exploitative activities. At Oticon, the Danish hearing aid company, employees were encouraged to sustain existing products while pursuing innovation and creativity.[48] Under the slogan "Innovation from Everyone, Everywhere" Whirlpool sought to embed innovation throughout its existing organization: "Innovation had been the responsibility of a couple of groups, engineering and marketing. Now, you have thousands of people involved."[49]

Tools of Strategic Change Management

If organizational change follows a process of punctuated equilibrium in which periods of stability are interspersed by periods of intense organizational upheaval, it follows that top management must play an active role in managing these interludes of strategic change. Most large companies exhibit periodic restructuring, involving simultaneous changes in strategy, structure, management systems, and top management personnel. Such restructuring typically follows declining performance caused either by a major external shock or by a growing misalignment between the firm and its external environment. For example, the oil and gas majors all underwent far-reaching restructuring during 1986–1992 following the oil price decline of 1986.[50] A challenge for top management is to undertake large-scale change before the company is pressured by declining performance.

Creating Perceptions of Crisis   Change initiatives frequently fail because they become overwhelmed by the forces of inertia. A crisis sets up the conditions for strategic change by loosening the organization's attachment to the status quo. The problem is that by the time the organization is engulfed in crisis it is already too late, hence the merits of the CEO creating the perception of impending crisis within the company so that necessary changes can be implemented well before the real crisis emerges. At General Electric, even when the company was reporting record profits, Jack Welch was able to convince employees of the need for change in order to defend against emerging threats. Andy Grove's effectiveness at communicating his dictum "Only the paranoid survive" helped Intel to maintain a continual striving for improvement and development despite its dominance of the market for PC microprocessors.

Establishing Stretch Targets   Another approach to weakening the powers of organizational inertia is to continually pressure the organizations by means of ambitious performance targets. The idea is that performance targets that are achievable but only with an extension of employee effort can motivate creativity and initiative while attacking complacency. Stretch targets are normally associated with short- and medium-term performance goals for individuals and organizational units. However, they also relate to long-term strategic goals. A key role of vision statements and ambitious strategic intent is to create a sustained sense of ambition and organizational purpose. These ideas are exemplified by Collins and Porras' notion of "Big Hairy Ambitious Goals" that I discussed in Chapter 1.

Creating Organizational Initiatives   Among the tools deployed by organizational leaders to influence their members, a potent one is an organization-wide initiative endorsed and communicated by the chief executive. Corporate initiatives sponsored by the CEO are effective for disseminating strategic changes, best practices, and management innovations. At General Electric Jack Welch was an especially effective exponent of using corporate initiatives to drive organizational change. These were built around communicable and compelling slogans such as "Be number 1 or number 2 in your industry," "GE's growth engine," "boundarylessness," "six-sigma quality," and "destroy-your-business-dot-com."

Reorganization and New Blood By reorganizing the company structure top management can create an opportunity for redistributing power, reshuffling top management, and introducing new blood. Periodic changes in organizational structure can stimulate decentralized search and local initiatives while encouraging more effective exploitation of the outcomes of such search.[51] A typical pattern is to oscillate from periods of decentralization to periods of centralization.[52]

Organizational change is also stimulated by recruiting new managers from outside the organization. Externally recruited CEOs result in more strategic change than those promoted from within.[53] In many cases, boards of directors seek out an external CEO for the explicit purpose of leading strategic change—e.g., George Fisher (from Motorola) and Antonio Perez (from HP) at Eastman Kodak, Lou Gerstner (from RJR Nabisco) at IBM, and Stephen Hester (from British Land) at Royal Bank of Scotland. Other members of the top management teams may also act as drivers of change: newcomers to top management hired outside the firms have been shown to be especially effective.[54]

Dynamic Capabilities

The ability of some firms—IBM, General Electric, 3M, Shell, and Toyota—to adapt to new circumstances while others ossify and fail implies differences in the capability base of different companies. David Teece and his colleagues introduced the term **dynamic capabilities** to refer to a "firm's ability to integrate, build, and reconfigure internal and external competences to address rapidly changing environments."[55]

The precise definition of a dynamic capability has proved contentious. Eisenhardt and Martin consider dynamic capabilities to be any capabilities that allow an organization to reconfigure its resources in order to adapt and change.[56] Winter and Zollo are more precise: a dynamic capability is a "higher level" process through which the firm modifies its operating routines.[57] These differences are important. If dynamic capabilities are simply those that allow change to occur they include product development capability, acquisition capability, research capability, and HR recruitment capabilities. But if dynamic capability is restricted to higher-level capabilities that manage change in lower-level capabilities, we are referring to capabilities that are more strategic and embedded in top management practices. Winter emphasizes that these higher-order change capabilities are not simply ad hoc problem solving: they are approaches to strategic change that are routine, highly patterned, and repetitious.[58]

IBM offers an example of these higher-level dynamic capabilities. Under the leadership of three CEOs—Lou Gerstner, Sam Palmisano, and Ginni Rometty—IBM has developed a system for managing strategic change that comprises its Business Leadership Model, strategy processes such as its "deep dive" and Emerging Business Opportunities methodologies, its Strategic Leadership Forum, and the Corporate Investment Fund (see Strategy Capsule 14.4 in Chapter 14 for additional information).[59]

Using Scenarios to Prepare for the Future   A company's ability to adapt to changes in its environment depends on its capacity to anticipate such changes. Yet predicting the future is hazardous, if not impossible. "Only a fool would make predictions . . . especially about the future," remarked movie mogul Samuel Goldwyn. But the inability to predict does not mean that it is not useful to think about what might happen in the future. *Scenario analysis* is a systematic way of thinking about how the future might unfold that builds on what we know about current trends and signals. Scenario analysis is not a forecasting technique, but a process for thinking and communicating about the future.

Herman Kahn, who pioneered their use first at the Rand Corporation and subsequently at the Hudson Institute, defined scenarios as "hypothetical sequences of events constructed for the purpose of focusing attention on causal process and decision points."[60] The multiple-scenario approach constructs several distinct, internally consistent views of how the future may look five to 25 years ahead (shorter in the case of fast-moving sectors). Its key value is in combining the interrelated impacts of a wide range of economic, technological, demographic, and political factors into a few distinct alternative stories of how the future might unfold. Scenario analysis can be either qualitative or quantitative or involve some combination of the two. Quantitative scenario analysis models events and runs simulations to identify likely outcomes. Qualitative scenarios typically take the form of narratives and can be particularly useful in engaging the insight and imagination of decision makers.

For the purposes of strategy making, scenario analysis is used to explore likely paths of industry evolution, to examine developments in particular country markets, to think about the impact of new technologies, and to analyze prospects for specific investment projects. Applied to industry evolution, scenarios can clarify and develop alternative views of how changing customer requirements, emerging technologies, government policies, and competitor strategies might have an impact on industry structure and what the implications for competition and competitive advantage might be.

However, as with most strategy techniques, the value of scenario analysis is not in the results but in the process. Scenario analysis is a powerful tool for bringing together different ideas and insights, for surfacing deeply held beliefs and assumptions, for identifying possible threats and opportunities, for generating and evaluating alternative strategies, for encouraging more flexible thinking by managers, and for building consensus. Evaluating the likely performance of different strategies under different scenarios can help identify which strategies are most robust and can assist in contingency planning by forcing managers to address "what if?" questions. Strategy Capsule 8.3 outlines the use of scenarios at Shell.

Shaping the Future   A succession of management gurus from Tom Peters to Gary Hamel have argued that the key to organizational change is not to adapt to external change but to create the future. Companies that adapt to change are doomed to playing catch-up; competitive advantages accrue to those companies that act as leaders and initiate change. Hamel and Prahalad's *new strategy paradigm* emphasizes the role of strategy as a systematic and concerted approach to redefining both the company and its industry environment in the future.[61]

According to Gary Hamel, in an age of revolution, "the company that is evolving slowly is already on its way to extinction."[62] The only option is to give up incremental improvement and adapt to a nonlinear world—revolution must be met by revolution. Achieving internal revolution requires changing the psychological and sociological norms of an organization that restricts innovation (Table 8.3).

STRATEGY CAPSULE 8.3
Multiple-Scenario Development at Shell

Royal Dutch Shell has pioneered the use of scenarios as a basis for long-term strategic planning in an industry where the life of investment projects (up to 50 years) far exceeds the time horizon for forecasting (two to three years). In 1967, a "Year 2000" study was inaugurated and scenario development soon became fundamental to Shell's planning process. Mike Pocock, Shell's former chairman, observed: "We believe in basing planning not on single forecasts, but on deep thought that identifies a coherent pattern of economic, political, and social development."

Shell views its scenarios as critical to its transition from planning toward strategic management, in which the role of the planning function is not so much to produce a plan but to manage a process, the outcome of which is improved decision making by managers. This involves continually challenging current thinking within the group, encouraging a wider look at external influences on the business, promoting learning, and forging coordination among Shell's 200-odd subsidiaries.

Shell's global scenarios are prepared about every four years by a team comprising corporate planning staff, executives, and outside experts. Economic, political, technological, and demographic trends are analyzed 20 years into the future. Shell's 2005–2025 scenarios were based on three sets of forces—market incentives, community, and coercion and regulation—and three objectives—efficiency, social cohesion, and security. Their interactions produced three scenarios, each embodying different social, political, and economic conditions:

◆ *Low Trust Globalization*: A legalistic world where emphasis is on security and efficiency at the expense of social cohesion.

◆ *Open Doors*: A pragmatic world emphasizing social cohesion and efficiency with the market providing built-in solutions to crises of security and trust.

◆ *Flags*: A dogmatic world where community and security values are emphasized at the expense of efficiency.

Once approved by top management, the scenarios are disseminated by reports, presentations, and workshops, where they form the basis for long-term strategy discussion by business sectors and operating companies.

Shell is adamant that its scenarios are not forecasts. They represent carefully thought-out stories of how the various forces shaping the global energy environment of the future might play out. Their value is in stimulating the social and cognitive processes through which managers envisage the future. Then CEO Jeroen van der Veer commented: "the imperative is to use this tool to gain deeper insights into our global business environment and to achieve the cultural change that is at the heart of our group strategy . . . I know that they broaden one's mindset and stimulate discussions."

Sources: P. Wack, "Scenarios: Uncharted Waters Ahead," *Harvard Business Review* (September/October, 1985): 72 and "Scenarios: Shooting the Rapids," *Harvard Business Review* (November/December 1985): 139; A. de Geus, "Planning as Learning," *Harvard Business Review* (March/April 1988): 70–4; P. Schoemacher, "Multiple Scenario Development: Its Conceptual and Behavioral Foundation," *Strategic Management Journal* 14 (1993): 193–214; *Shell Global Scenarios to 2025* (Shell International, 2005).

TABLE 8.3 Shaking the foundations

OLD BRICK	NEW BRICK
Top management is responsible for setting strategy	Everyone is responsible for setting strategy
Getting better, getting faster is the way to win	Rule-busting innovation is the way to win
IT creates competitive advantage	Unconventional business concepts create competitive advantage
Being revolutionary is high risk	More of the same is high risk
We can merge our way to competitiveness	There's no correlation between size and competitiveness
Innovation equals new products and new technology	Innovation equals entirely new business concepts
Strategy is the easy part; implementation the hard part	Strategy is the easy part only if you're content to be an imitator
Change starts at the top	Change starts with activists
Our real problem is execution	Our real problem is incrementalism
Big companies can't innovate	Big companies can become gray-haired revolutionaries

Source: Adapted by permission of Harvard Business School Press from *Leading the Revolution* by Gary Hamel. Boston, MA, 2000, pp. 280–1. Copyright © 2000 by the Harvard Business School Publishing Corporation; all rights reserved.

Hamel's challenge for managers to cast off their bureaucratic chains and become revolutionaries is invigorating and inspiring. But is revolutionary change among established companies either feasible or desirable? Some established companies have achieved radical change:

- Nokia underwent a metamorphosis from a manufacturer of paper and rubber goods to become a world leader in wireless handsets.
- BP transformed itself from a bureaucratic, state-owned UK-based oil company into a flexible, innovative (and accident-prone) global supermajor.
- Microsoft has successfully ridden a series of disruptive changes in the world's computer industry, including the transition, first, to object-oriented computing, then to internet-based networking, and currently to cloud computing.

However, for most established companies, efforts at radical change have resulted in disaster:

- Enron's transformation from a utility and pipeline company to a trader and market-maker in energy futures and derivatives ended in its demise in 2001;
- Vivendi's multimedia empire built on the base of a French water and waste utility fell apart in 2002;
- GEC's reincarnation as Marconi, a telecom equipment supplier, was swiftly followed by bankruptcy in 2002;
- RBS Group's transformation from a Scottish retail bank to the world's biggest commercial bank (as measured by total assets) through a series of cross-border acquisitions culminated in its rescue by the British government in 2008;

● Skandia's quest to become one of the world's most innovative insurance companies ended in a top management scandal and the sale of most of the company's businesses outside of Sweden.

The perils of radical strategic change are not difficult to understand. At their core is the difficulty that established companies experience in developing the new organizational capabilities needed by new circumstances or a new area of business. Let us turn to that issue now.

Developing New Capabilities

Ultimately, adapting to a changing world is about developing the necessary capabilities to renew competitive advantage. To get a glimpse into the challenges this presents, consider the distinctive capabilities (or core competences) of some of today's leading companies and ask, "Where did these capabilities come from?"

Early Experiences and Path Dependency   In many, many instances distinctive capabilities can be traced back to the circumstances which prevailed during the founding and early development of these companies. In other words, organizational capability is subject to **path dependency**—a company's capabilities today are the result of its history.[63] For example:

● How did Wal-Mart Inc., the world's biggest retailer, develop its outstanding capability in supply chain logistics? This superefficient system of warehousing, distribution, and vendor relationships was not the result of careful planning and design; it evolved from the circumstances that Wal-Mart faced during its early years of existence. Its small-town locations in Arkansas and Oklahoma resulted in unreliable delivery from its suppliers; consequently, Wal-Mart established its own distribution system. What about the other capabilities that contribute to Wal-Mart's remarkable cost efficiency? These too can be traced back to Wal-Mart's origins in rural Arkansas and the values of its founder, Sam Walton.

● Similarly with the world's leading oil and gas majors (Table 8.4). Despite long histories of competing together in the same markets, with near-identical products and similar strategies, the majors display very different capability profiles. Industry leaders ExxonMobil and Royal Dutch Shell exemplify these differences. ExxonMobil is known for its outstanding financial management capabilities exercised through rigorous investment controls and unrelenting cost efficiency. Royal Dutch Shell is known for its decentralized, international management capability, which allows it to adapt to different national environments and to become an "insider" wherever it does business. These differences can be traced back to the company's 19th-century origins. ExxonMobil (then Standard Oil New Jersey) acted as a holding company for Rockefeller's Standard Oil Trust, exercising responsibility for overall financial management. Shell was established to sell Russian oil in China and the Far East, while Royal Dutch was created to exploit Indonesian oil reserves. With head offices thousands of miles away in Europe, both parts of the group developed a decentralized, adaptable management style.

These observations are troubling for managers in established companies: if a firm's capabilities are determined during the early stages of its life, is it really possible to

TABLE 8.4   Distinctive capabilities as a consequence of childhood experiences: The oil majors

Company	Distinctive capability	Early history
ExxonMobil	Financial management	ExxonMobil's predecessor, Standard Oil (NJ), was the holding company for Rockefeller's Standard Oil Trust
Royal Dutch Shell	Coordinating a decentralized global network of 200 operating companies	Shell Transport & Trading headquartered in London and founded to sell Russian oil in China and the Far East Royal Dutch Petroleum headquartered in The Hague; founded to exploit Indonesian reserves
BP	Elephant hunting	Discovered huge Persian reserves, went on to find Forties field (North Sea) and Prudhoe Bay (Alaska)
ENI	Deal making in politicized environments	The Enrico Mattei legacy; the challenge of managing government relations in post-war Italy
Mobil	Lubricants	Vacuum Oil Co. founded in 1866 to supply patented petroleum lubricants

develop the new capabilities needed to adapt to current changes and the challenges of tomorrow? The presence of established capabilities and their embedding within organizational structure and culture present formidable barriers to building new capabilities. Indeed, the more highly developed a firm's organizational capabilities, the greater the barrier they create. Because Dell Computer's direct sales model was so highly developed, Dell found it difficult to adapt to selling through retail outlets as well. Hence the argument that core capabilities are simultaneously core rigidities.[64]

Integrating Resources to Create Capability   The encouraging fact is that companies do develop new capabilities—all companies that have survived over periods of multiple decades have done so by creating capabilities that they did not possess before. To appreciate how this is done let us look once more at the structure of organizational capability. In Chapter 5 (Strategy Capsule 5.3) we observed that organizational capability results from the combination of different resources, most importantly the skills of different organizational members. The effectiveness of this integration depends upon the presence of suitable processes, an appropriate organizational structure, motivation, and overall organizational alignment, especially with the organization's culture.

Using each of these components, organizations can put in place the building blocks for developing new capabilities:

- *Processes*: Without processes, organizational capability will be completely dependent on individual skills. With processes (or *organizational routines*) we can ensure that task performance is efficient, repeatable, and reliable. When Whirlpool launched its innovation drive, the emphasis was on creating processes: processes for training employees in the tools of innovation, processes for idea generation, and processes for idea selection and development.[65] Once processes are in place they are developed through routinization and learning—essential to capability development is the creation of mechanisms that facilitate learning-by-doing and ensure the retention and sharing of learning.

- *Structure*: The people and processes that contribute to an organizational capability need to be located within the same organizational unit if they are to achieve the coordination needed to ensure a high performance capability. When Royal Dutch Shell wanted to develop capability in breakthrough innovation, it created a new organizational unit: Gamechanger. When Ducati wanted to create the capabilities needed for a successful MotoGP racing team, it established Ducati Corse as a separate subsidiary. At several of the business schools I have worked, a common complaint among students has been the lack of integration across courses while a common aspiration of several MBA course directors has been to introduce multidisciplinary courses that involve students in cross-functional problem solving. However, little can be achieved if faculty members are located within specialist, discipline-defined departments and coordination across courses is limited to a single teachers' meeting held each semester.

- *Motivation*: Again we come back to the fundamental driver of performance in organizations: without motivation not only will individuals give less than their best but also, equally important, they will not set aside their personal preferences and prejudices to integrate as a team. At Honda Motor, the development of automotive capabilities, especially in engine design, was driven by the passion of its founder Soichiro Honda (Strategy Capsule 8.4)

- *Organizational alignment*: Finally, there is the issue of fit. Excellent capabilities require the components of capability to fit with one another and with the broader organizational context. Harley-Davidson's capabilities in delivering the "Harley Experience" are the result of a close fit between the human resources, the brand, the traditions, and the company's Milwaukie location. Imperfect alignment can stunt capability development: the failure of established airlines to launch low-cost subsidiaries (BA's Go, United's Ted, Continental's Continental Lite) reflects a misfit between the capabilities needed by a budget airline and the culture and management systems of legacy carriers. Corporate culture is a critical ingredient in this fit: in the privatized, competitive, deregulated telecom markets of the 21st century, former national monopolies such as British Telecom (BT), Deutsche Telecom, and Verizon have had difficulty developing the capabilities needed to compete successfully outside their home markets.

Developing Capabilities Sequentially   Developing new capabilities requires a systematic and long-term process of development that integrates the four components described above. For most organizations, the key challenge is not obtaining the underlying resources—indeed, many examples of outstanding capabilities have resulted from the pressures of resource shortage. Toyota's lean production capability was born during a period of acute resource shortage in Japan.

If integrating resources into capabilities requires establishing processes, developing these processes through routinization and learning, putting in place the right structure, motivating the people involved, and aligning the new capability with other aspects of the organization, the demands upon management are considerable. An organization must limit the number and scope of the capabilities that it is attempting

---

STRATEGY CAPSULE 8.4

Soichiro Honda and the Isle of Man TT

On March 20, 1954, when Honda Motor Company was still a tiny company of less than six years old, company president Soichiro Honda announced his intention to compete in the Isle of Man TT, which was then the world's premier motorcycle race:

Since I was a small child, one of my dreams has been to compete in motor vehicle races all over the world . . . I have reached the firm decision to enter the TT Races next year.

I will fabricate a 250 cc (medium class) racer for this race, and as the representative of our Honda Motor Co., I will send it out into the spotlight of the world. I am confident that this vehicle can reach speeds exceeding 180 km/h . . .

I address all employees! Let us bring together the full strength of Honda Motor Co. to win through to this glorious achievement. The future of Honda Motor Co. depends on this, and the burden rests on your shoulders. I want you to turn your surging enthusiasm to this task, endure every trial, and press through with all the minute demands of work and research, making this your own chosen path. The advances made by Honda Motor Co. are the growth you achieve as human beings, and your growth is what assures our Honda Motor Co. its future.

Honda's entry was delayed until 1958. In that year Honda won the manufacturer's prize.

---

to create at any point in time. One implication is that capabilities need to be developed sequentially rather than all at once.

The task of capability development is also complicated by the fact that we have limited knowledge about how to manage capability development. Hence, it may be helpful to focus not on the organizational capabilities themselves but on developing and supplying the products that use those capabilities. A trajectory through time of related, increasingly sophisticated products allows a firm to develop the "integrative knowledge" that is at the heart of organizational capability.[66] Panasonic utilized this approach in developing operational capabilities in countries when establishing manufacturing in new countries:

In every country batteries are a necessity, so they sell well. As long as we bring a few advanced automated pieces of equipment for the processes vital to final product quality, even unskilled labor can produce good products. As they work on this rather simple product, the workers get trained, and this increased skill level then permits us to gradually expand production to items with increasingly higher technology levels, first radios, then televisions.[67]

Where a company is developing an entirely new area of business, such a sequential approach can be effective. The key here is for each stage of development to be linked not just to a specific product (or part of a product) but also to a clearly defined set of capabilities. Strategy Capsule 8.5 looks at the sequential approach to capability development followed by Hyundai Motor.

STRATEGY CAPSULE 8.5

Hyundai Motor: Developing Capabilities through Product Sequencing

Hyundai's emergence as a world-class automobile pro-ducer is a remarkable example of capability develop-ment over a sequence of compressed phases (Figure 8.5). Each phase of the development process was charac-terized by a clear objective in terms of product outcome, a tight time deadline, an empowered development team, a clear recognition of the capabilities that needed to be developed in each phase, and an atmosphere of impending crisis should the project not succeed. The first phase was the construction of an assembly plant in the unprecedented time of 18 months in order to build Hyundai's first car—a Ford Cortina imported in semi-knocked down (SKD) form. Subsequent phases involved products of increasing sophistication and the develop-ment of more advanced capabilities.

FIGURE 8.5   Phased development at Hyundai Motor, 1968–1995

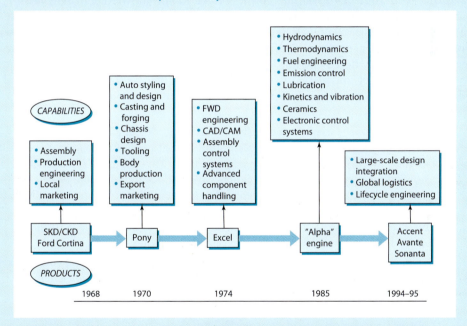

Source: L. Kim, "Crisis construction and organizational learning: Capability building and catching up at Hyundai Motor," *Organizational Science* 9 (1998): 506–21. © 1998 by the Institute for Operations Research and the Management Sciences. Reproduced with permission of the Institute for Operations Research and the Management Sciences via the Copyright Clearance Center.

The Contribution of Knowledge Management and the Knowledge-Based View

Since the early 1990s, our thinking about resources and capabilities and their man-agement has been extended greatly by a set of concepts and practices referred to as *knowledge management*. Knowledge management is an umbrella term that comprises a range of organizational processes and practices whose common feature is their concern with generating value from knowledge. The term is of recent vintage but much of its content is not: it includes many long-established organizational functions such as R & D, management information systems, employee training, and managing intellectual property; even strategic planning can be regarded as a knowledge management activity. Initially, knowledge management was primarily concerned with information technology, especially the use of databases, intranets, expert systems, and groupware for storing, analyzing, and disseminating information. Subsequent developments in knowledge management have been concerned less with data and more with *organizational learning*, especially the transfer of best practices and the derivation of "lessons learned" from ongoing activities. Knowledge management has attracted its share of skepticism and ridicule. Lucy Kellaway of the *Financial Times* observed that it has "attracted more needless obfuscation and wooly thinking by academics and consultants than any other [area]."[68]

Explicit and Tacit Knowledge   At the foundation of knowledge management is a set of concepts concerning the nature of knowledge and its role within the firm. These concepts have combined into what is known as the **knowledge-based view of the firm**—a conception of the firm as an assemblage of knowledge assets where value is created by deploying this knowledge.[69]

A key feature of knowledge that is critical to its role in creating organizational capability is the distinction between knowing *how* and knowing *about*:

- *Knowing about* is explicit: it comprises facts, theories, and sets of instructions. *Explicit knowledge* can be communicated at negligible marginal cost between individuals and across space and time. This ability to disseminate knowledge such that any one person's use does not limit anyone else's access to the same knowledge means that explicit knowledge has the characteristic of a public good: once created, it can be replicated among innumerable users at low cost. The digital revolution and the internet have further reduced the costs of disseminating explicit knowledge.

- *Know-how* is tacit in nature: it involves skills that are expressed through their performance (riding a bicycle, playing the piano). Such *tacit knowledge*, on the other hand, cannot be directly articulated or codified. It can only be observed through its application and acquired through practice. Hence, its transfer between people is slow, costly, and uncertain.

If explicit knowledge can be transferred so easily, it is seldom the foundation of sustainable competitive advantage. It is only secure from rivals when it is protected, either by intellectual property rights (patents, copyrights, trade secrets) or by secrecy ("The formula for Coca-Cola will be kept in a safe in the vault of our Atlanta headquarters guarded by heavily-armed Coca-Cola personnel."). The challenge of tacit knowledge is the opposite. If the culinary skills of award-winning chef Daniel Boulud have been acquired through intuition and learning-by-doing, how does he transfer this know-how to the chefs and managers of his six restaurants in New York, Las Vegas, and Palm Beach, Florida? To build organizational capability it is essential that the individual know-how can be shared within the organization. For consulting companies, the distinction between tacit (personalized) and explicit (systematized) knowledge defines their business model and is a central determinant of their strategy.[70]

The result is a "paradox of replication." In order to utilize knowledge to build organizational capability we need to replicate it; and replication is much easier if the knowledge is in explicit form. Yet, in doing so, we also make it easier for rivals to imitate our knowledge. Facilitating internal replication, while limiting external replication, is a key challenge for firms.[71]

Knowledge Management Activities that Contribute to Capability Development   Knowledge management can be represented as a series of activities that contribute to capability development by building, retaining, accessing, transferring, and integrating knowledge. Table 8.5 lists several knowledge-management practices.

TABLE 8.5   Knowledge-management practices

Knowledge process	Contributing activities	Explanation and examples
Knowledge identification	Intellectual property management	During recent decades companies have devoted much greater attention to identifying their intellectual property, and patents especially, with a view to better exploiting its value
	Corporate yellow pages	BP's Connect is a corporate yellow pages comprising personnel data that allows each employee to identify the skills and experience of other employees in the organization
Knowledge measurement	Intellectual capital accounting	The measurement and valuation of a firm's stock of knowledge was pioneered by Skandia, a Swedish insurance company, with its system of intellectual capital accounting. Dow Chemical uses intellectual capital metrics to link its intellectual property portfolio to shareholder value
Knowledge retention	Lessons learned	The US Army's Center for Lessons Learned distils the results of practice maneuvers, simulated battles, and actual operations into tactical guidelines and recommended procedures. All management consulting firms have post-project reviews to recognize and capture the knowledge produced in operational activities
Knowledge transfer and sharing	Databases	Project-based organizations typically store knowledge generated in client assignments in searchable databases. Accenture's Knowledge Xchange is an IT system that comprises a database, groupware, dedicated search engine, and an intranet that permits employees to input and access information
	Communities-of-practice	Communities of practice are informal, self-organizing networks for transferring experiential knowledge among employees engaged in the same occupation. These are increasingly being deliberately established and managed as a means of facilitating knowledge sharing and group learning
	Best practice transfer	Where operations are geographically dispersed, different units are likely to develop local innovations and improvements. Best practice methodology aims to identify then transfer superior practices

During its early development, knowledge management was heavily orientated toward information technology with the main emphasis on storing organizational knowledge within searchable databases. Growing recognition of the importance of tacit knowledge and the difficulties of articulating and codifying such experiential knowledge has shifted the focus more toward people-to-people modes of knowledge transfer.

STRATEGY CAPSULE 8.6
Knowledge Conversion and Knowledge Replication

Nonaka's theory of knowledge creation distinguishes between types of knowledge (tacit and explicit) and levels of knowledge (individual and organizational). Nonaka argues that knowledge conversion between tacit and explicit forms and between individual and organizational levels produces a "knowledge spiral" in which the organization's stock of knowledge broadens and deepens (Figure 8.6). For example, explicit knowledge is internalized into tacit knowledge in the form of intuition, know-how, and routines, while tacit knowledge is externalized into explicit knowledge through articulation and codification. Knowledge also moves

FIGURE 8.6 Knowledge conversion

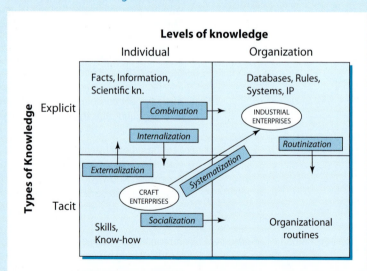

Source: Based upon I. Nonaka, "A Dynamic Theory of Organizational Knowledge Creation," *Organization Science* 5 (1994): 14–37.

However, the contribution of knowledge management to capability development in organizations may be less about specific techniques and more about the insight that the knowledge-based view has given to organizational performance and the role of management. For example, Ikujiro Nonaka's model of knowledge creation offers penetrating insights into the organizational processes through which knowledge is created and value is created from knowledge (Strategy Capsule 8.6)

between levels: individual knowledge is combined into organizational knowledge; individuals are socialized into organizational knowledge.

Nonaka's knowledge conversion framework can be used to illustrate the transformation of the *craft enterprise* based upon individual, tacit knowledge, to the *industrial enterprise* based upon explicit, organizational knowledge. This is a key stage in firm development that also marks the emergence of industrial society. This transition is depicted in Figure 8.6 and is illustrated by the following examples:

◆ Henry Ford's Model T was initially produced on a small scale by skilled workers, one car at a time. Ford's assembly line mass-production technology systematized that tacit knowledge and built it into machines and processes. The Ford industrial system was no longer dependent upon skilled craftsmen: the assembly lines could be operated by former farm workers and immigrants straight off the boat.

◆ When Ray Kroc discovered the McDonald brothers' hamburger stand in Riversdale, California, he quickly recognized the potential for systematizing and replicating their process. The result was a global fast-food empire in which the McDonald's business model was replicated through operating manuals and training programs, and now 400,000 employees serve 68 million customers daily. Most employees' culinary skills are rudimentary: the relevant knowledge is embedded within the McDonald's business system.

This systematization of knowledge offers massive potential for value creation. The craft enterprise is typically small scale, and skilled employees appropriate a major share of the value that is created. Systematization allows replication and deskilling. Ford and McDonald's were able to expand worldwide. The transformation of craft industries through systematization has been a key feature of the evolution of service industries led by Hilton in hotels, Hertz in car rental, Andersen Consulting (now Accenture) in IT consulting, and Starbucks in coffee shops.

This replication of knowledge is a powerful and lucrative source of scale economy. Its power is well recognized by venture capitalists: a key criterion for evaluating a new business proposal is: "Is it scalable?" Low-cost replication requires systematization: the translation of a business concept and operating system into a set of rules and procedures that provide programmed instructions for the creation of new business units. In some cases the knowledge embedded in a business system may be too complex to be fully articulated. In this case replication can still occur through imitation. In the case of microprocessors, fabrication processes are so complex and the know-how involved so deeply embedded that the only way that Intel can replicate its production capabilities is by replicating its lead plant in every detail—a process called *copy exactly*.[a]

Note:
[a]"Copy Exactly Factory Strategy" (www.intel.com/design/quality/mq_ce.htm). See also G. Szulanski and S. G. Winter, "Getting It Right the Second Time," *Harvard Business Review* (January 2002): 62–9.

Summary

A vital task of strategic management is to navigate the crosscurrents of change. But how can we manage change if we cannot predict it? Despite the failure of almost every forecasting method, help is available from two sources. First, some regularities are evident in the ways in which business environments evolve over time. Second, there is a large body of evidence that the difficulties firms experience in adapting to industrial and technological changes are the result of common factors. By understanding the sources of these barriers to adaptation, we can learn how to overcome them.

The life-cycle model allows us to understand some of the forces driving industry evolution and their impact on industry structure and the basis of competitive advantage. By identifying the stage of development of an industry, we can recognize the forces driving change and anticipate some of the likely directions of development.

Identifying regularities in the patterns of industry evolution is of little use if firms are unable to adapt to these changes. The challenge of adaptation is huge: the presence of organizational inertia means that industry evolution occurs more through the birth of new firms and the death of old ones rather than through adaptation by established firms. Established firms also experience problems in coping with new technologies—the technological changes that are especially devastating are those that are "competence destroying," "disruptive," or embody "architectural innovation."

A key challenge of managing change is the need for managers to operate in two time zones: they must optimize for today while preparing the organization for the future. The concept of the ambidextrous organization is an approach to resolving this dilemma. Other tools for managing strategic change include: creating perceptions of crisis, establishing stretch targets, corporate-wide initiatives, recruiting external managerial talent, dynamic capabilities, and scenario planning.

Whatever approach or tools are adopted to manage change, strategic change requires building new capabilities. To the extent that an organization's capabilities are a product of its entire history, building new capabilities is a formidable challenge. To understand how organizations build capability we need to understand how resources are integrated into capability—in particular, the role of processes, structure, motivation, and alignment. The complexities of capability development and our limited understanding of how capabilities are built point to the advantages of sequential approaches to developing capabilities.

Ultimately, capability building is about harnessing the knowledge which exists within the organization. For this purpose knowledge management offers considerable potential for increasing the effectiveness of capability development. In addition to specific techniques for identifying, retaining, sharing, and replicating knowledge, the knowledge-based view of the firm offers penetrating insights into the challenges of and potential for the creation and exploitation of knowledge by firms.

In the next two chapters, we discuss strategy formulation and strategy implementation in industries at different stages of their development: *emerging industries*, which are characterized by rapid change and technology-based competition, and *mature industries*.

Quizzes and flashcards to test yourself further are available in your interactive e-book at
www.wileyopenpage.com

Self-Study Questions

1. Consider the changes that have occurred in a comparatively new industry (e.g., wireless communication services, wireless handsets, video game consoles, online auctions, bottled water, online book retailing). To what extent has the evolution of the industry followed the pattern predicted by the industry life-cycle model? What particular features does the industry have that have influenced its pattern of evolution? At what stage of development is the industry today? How is the industry likely to evolve in the future?

2. Select a product that has become a *dominant design* for its industry (e.g., the IBM PC in personal computers, McDonald's in fast food, Harvard in MBA education, Southwest in budget airlines). What factors caused one firm's product architecture to become dominant? Why did other firms imitate this dominant design? To what extent has the dominant design evolved or been displaced?

3. The *resource partitioning* model argues that as industries become dominated by a few major companies whose strategies and products converge so opportunities open for new entrants to build specialist niches. Identify an opportunity for establishing a specialist new business in an industry dominated by mass-market giants.

4. Consider an industry facing fundamental technology change (e.g., the recorded music industry and digital technology, computer software and open-source, newspapers and the internet, automobiles and alternative fuels, corporate IT services and cloud computing). Develop two alternative scenarios for the future evolution of your chosen industry. In relation to one leading player in the industry, identify the problems posed by the new technology and develop a strategy for how the company might adapt to and exploit the changes you envisage.

5. Identify two sports teams: one that is rich in resources (such as talented players) but whose capabilities (as indicated by performance) have been poor; one that is resource-poor but has displayed strong team capabilities. What clues can you offer as to the determinants of capabilities among sports teams?

6. In 2006, Disney completed its acquisition of the film animation company Pixar for $7.4 billion. The high purchase price reflected Disney's eagerness to gain Pixar's animation capabilities, its talent (animators, technologists, and storytellers), and its culture of creativity. What risks does Disney face in achieving the goals of this acquisition?

7. The dean of your business school wishes to upgrade the effectiveness with which the school designs and delivers its educational programs and increase the effectiveness of its graduates in their subsequent careers. Advise your dean on what tools and systems of knowledge management might be deployed in order to support these goals.

Notes

1. T. Levitt, "Exploit the Product Life Cycle," *Harvard Business Review* (November/December 1965): 81–94; G. Day, "The Product Life Cycle: Analysis and Applications," *Journal of Marketing* 45 (Autumn 1981): 60–7.

2. J. M. Utterback and F. F. Suarez, "Patterns of Industrial Evolution, Dominant designs, and Firms' Survival," Sloan Working Paper no. 3600-93 (MIT, 1993).

3. P. Anderson and M. L. Tushman, "Technological Discontinuities and Dominant Designs," *Administrative Science Quarterly* 35 (1990): 604–33.

4. M. A. Cusumano and D. B. Yoffie, *Competing on Internet Time: Lessons from Netscape and Its Battle with Microsoft* (New York: Free Press, 1998).

5. M. G. Jacobides, "Industry Change through Vertical Disintegration: How and Why Markets Emerged in Mortgage Banking," *Academy of Management Journal* 48, no. 3 (2005): 465–98; M. G. Jacobides, C. Y. Baldwin, and R. Dizaji, "From the Structure of the Value Chain to the Strategic Dynamics of Industry Sectors," Academy of Management Presentation (Philadelphia, August 7, 2007).

6. G. Carroll and M. Hannan, *The Demography of Corporations and Industries* (Princeton, MA: Princeton University Press, 2000). For a survey see J. Baum, "Organizational Ecology," in S. R. Clegg, C. Hardy, and W. R. Nord (eds), *The SAGE Handbook of Organizational Studies* (Thousand Oaks, CA: SAGE Publications, 1996); and D. Barron, "Evolutionary Theory," in D. O. Faulkner and A. Campbell (eds), *The Oxford Handbook of Strategy* (Oxford: Oxford University Press, 2003), vol. 1: 74–97.

7. G. R. Carroll, L. S. Bigelow, M.-D. Seidel, and B. Tsai, "The Fates of de novo and de alio Producers in the American Automobile Industry, 1885–1981," *Strategic Management Journal* 17 (Summer 1996): 117–137.

8. S. Klepper and K. L. Simons, "Dominance by Birthright: Entry of Prior Radio Producers and Competitive Ramifications in the US Television Receiver Industry," *Strategic Management Journal* 21 (2000): 997–1016.

9. High rates of entry and exit may continue well into maturity. See T. Dunne, M. J. Roberts, and L. Samuelson, "Patterns of Firm Entry and Exit in US Manufacturing Industries," *Rand Journal of Economics* 19 (1988): 495–515.

10. S. Klepper and E. Grady, "The Evolution of New Industries and the Determinants of Industry Structure," *Rand Journal of Economics* 21 (1990): 27–44.

11. S. Klepper and K. Simons, "The Making of an Oligopoly: Firm Survival and Technological Change in the Evolution of the US Tire Industry," *Journal of Political Economy* 108 (2000): 728–60.

12. G. Carroll and A. Swaminathan, "Why the Microbrewery Movement? Organizational Dynamics of Resource Partitioning in the American Brewing Industry," *American Journal of Sociology* 106 (2000): 715–62.

13. B. Levitt and J. G. March, "Organizational Learning," *Annual Review of Sociology* 14 (1988): 319–40.

14. D. Leonard-Barton, "Core Capabilities and Core Rigidities: A Paradox in Managing New Product Development," *Strategic Management Journal* 13 (Summer 1992): 111–25.

15. M. T. Hannan, L. Polos, and G. R. Carroll, "Structural Inertia and Organizational Change Revisited III: The Evolution of Organizational Inertia," *Stanford GSB Research Paper* 1734 (April 2002).

16. P. J. DiMaggio and W. Powell, "The Iron Cage Revisited: Institutional Isomorphism and Collective Rationality in Organizational Fields," *American Sociological Review* 48 (1983): 147–60.

17. J.-C. Spender, *Industry Recipes* (Oxford: Blackwell Publishing, 1989).

18. J. G. March, "Exploration and Exploitation in Organizational Learning," *Organizational Science* 2 (1991): 71–87.

19. P. R. Milgrom and J. Roberts, "Complementarities and Fit: Strategy, Structure, and Organizational Change in Manufacturing," *Journal of Accounting and Economics* 19 (1995): 179–208; M. E. Porter and N. Siggelkow, "Contextual Interactions within Activity Systems," *Academy of Management Perspectives* 22 (May 2008): 34–56.

20. E. Trist, "The Sociotechnical Perspective," in A. H. Van de Ven and W. H. Joyce (eds), *Perspectives on Organization Design and Behavior* (New York: John Wiley & Sons, Inc., 1984).

21. J. W. Rivkin, "Imitation of Complex Strategies," *Management Science* 46 (2000): 824–44.

22. M. E. Porter and N. Siggelkow, "Contextual Interactions within Activity Systems," *Academy of Management Perspectives* 22 (May 2008): 34–56.

23. M. L. Tushman and E. Romanelli, "Organizational Evolution: A Metamorphosis Model of Convergence and Reorientation," in L. L. Cummins and B. M. Staw (eds), *Research in Organizational Behavior* 7 (1985): 171–222; E. Romanelli and M. L. Tushman, "Organizational Transformation as Punctuated Equilibrium: An Empirical Test," *Academy of Management Journal* 37 (1994): 1141–66.

24. H. E. Aldrich, *Organizations and Environments* (Stanford, CA: Stanford University Press, 2007).

25. For an introduction to organizational ecology, see M. T. Hannan and G. R. Carroll, "An introduction to organizational ecology," in G. R. Carroll and M. T. Hannan (eds), *Organizations in Industry* (Oxford: Oxford University Press, 1995): 17–31.

26. For a survey of evolutionary approaches, see R. R. Nelson, "Recent Evolutionary Theorizing about Economic Change," *Journal of Economic Literature* 33 (March 1995): 48–90.

27. ExxonMobil Corporation is a descendent of Standard Oil; Royal Dutch Shell was created in 1907 by Royal Dutch Petroleum Co. and Shell Transport and Trading Co.

28. C. Markides and P. Geroski, "Colonizers and Consolidators: The Two Cultures of Corporate Strategy," *Strategy and Business* 32 (Fall 2003).

29. G. A. Moore, *Crossing the Chasm* (New York: HarperCollins, 1991).

30. S. Klepper, "The Capabilities of New Firms and the Evolution of the US Automobile Industry," *Industrial and Corporate Change* 11 (2002): 645–66.

31. S. Klepper and K. L. Simons, "Dominance by Birthright: Entry of Prior Radio Producers and Competitive Ramifications in the US Television Receiver Industry," *Strategic Management Journal* 21 (2000): 997–1016.

32. D. A. Kaplan, *The Silicon Boys and Their Valley of Dreams* (New York: Morrow, 1999).

33. G. Buenstorf and S. Klepper, "Heritage and Agglomeration: The Akron Tyre Cluster Revisited," *Economic Journal* 119 (2009): 705–33.

34. M. L. Tushman and P. Anderson, "Technological Discontinuities and Organizational Environments," *Administrative Science Quarterly* 31 (1986): 439–65.

35. M. Tripsas, "Unravelling the Process of Creative Destruction: Complementary Assets and Incumbent Survival in the Typesetter Industry," *Strategic Management Journal* 18 (Summer 1997): 119–142.

36. R. M. Henderson and K. B. Clark, "Architectural Innovation: The Reconfiguration of Existing Systems and the Failure of Established Firms," *Administrative Science Quarterly* (1990): 9–30.

37. R. M. Henderson and K. B. Clark, "Architectural Innovation: The Reconfiguration of Existing Systems and the Failure of Established Firms," *Administrative Science Quarterly* (1990): 9–30.

38. J. Bower and C. M. Christensen, "Disruptive Technologies: Catching the Wave," *Harvard Business Review* (January/February 1995): 43–53.

39. C. M. Christensen, *The Innovator's Dilemma* (Boston: Harvard Business School Press, 1997).

40. C. M. Christensen, *The Innovator's Dilemma* (Boston: Harvard Business School Press, 1997).

41. T. G. Cummins and C. G. Worley, *Organization Development and Change*, 8th edn (Cincinnati, OH: Southwestern College Publishing: 2005).

42. D. F. Abell, *Managing with Dual Strategies* (New York: Free Press, 1993): 3.

43. C. A. O'Reilly and M. L. Tushman, "The Ambidextrous Organization," *Harvard Business Review* (April 2004): 74–81.

44. C. M. Christensen and M. Overdorf, "Meeting the Challenge of Disruptive Change," *Harvard Business Review* (March/April 2000): 66–76.

45. T. Elder, "Lessons from Xerox and IBM," *Harvard Business Review* (July/August 1989): 66–71.

46. "Xerox PARC: Innovation without Profit?" ICMR Case Study, 2004.

47. J. O'Toole, *Forming the Future: Lessons from the Saturn Corporation* (New York: Harper, 1996).

48. G. Verona and D. Ravasi, "Unbundling dynamic capabilities: An exploratory study of continuous product innovation," *Industrial and Corporate Change* 12 (2002): 577–606.

49. Interview with Nancy Snyder, Whirlpool's vice-president of leadership and strategic competency development, *Business Week* (March 6, 2006), http://www.businessweek.com/innovate/content/mar2006/id20060306_287425.htm?.

50. R. Cibin and R. M. Grant, "Restructuring among the World's Leading Oil Companies," *British Journal of Management* 7 (1996): 283–308.

51. N. Siggelkow and D. A. Levinthal, "Escaping Real (Non-benign) Competency Traps: Linking the Dynamics of Organizational Structure to the Dynamics of Search," *Strategic Organization* 3 (2005): 85–115.

52. J. Nickerson and T. Zenger, "Being Efficiently Fickle: A Dynamic Theory of Organizational Choice," *Organization Science* 13 (September/October 2002): 547–67.

53. M. F. Wiersema, "Strategic Consequences of Executive Succession within Diversified Firms," *Journal of Management Studies* 29 (1992): 73–94.

54. R. Agarwal, P.-L. Chen, and C. Williams, "Renewal through Rookies: The Growth Effects of Top Management Recruits from Different Levels, Organizations, and Industries," Working Paper, Bocconi University, Milan (2011).

55. D. J. Teece, G. Pisano, and A. Shuen, "Dynamic Capabilities and Strategic Management," *Strategic Management Journal* 18 (1997): 509–33.

56. K. M. Eisenhardt and J. A. Martin, "Dynamic Capabilities: What Are They?" *Strategic Management Journal* 21 (2000): 1105–21. See also H. Volberda, *Building the Flexible Firm* (Oxford: Oxford University Press, 1998).

57. M. Zollo and S. G. Winter, "Deliberate Learning and the Evolution of Dynamic Capabilities," *Organization Science* 13 (2002): *339–51;* S. G. Winter, "Understanding Dynamic Capabilities," *Strategic Management Journal* 24 (2003): 991–5.

58. S. G. Winter, "Understanding Dynamic Capabilities," *Strategic Management Journal* 24 (2003): 991–95.

59. J. B. Harreld, C. A. O'Reilly, and M. L. Tushman, "Dynamic Capabilities at IBM: Driving Strategy into Action," *California Management Review* 49, no. 4 (2007): 21–43.

60. H. Kahn, *The Next 200 Years: A Scenario for America and the World* (New York: William Morrow, 1976). For a guide to the use of scenarios in strategy making, see K. van der Heijden, *Scenarios: The Art of Strategic Conversation* (Chichester: John Wiley & Sons, Ltd, 2005).

61. G. Hamel and C. K. Prahalad, Competing for the Future (Boston: Harvard Business School Press, 1995).

62. G. Hamel, *Leading the Revolution* (Boston: Harvard Business School Press, 2000): 5.

63. B. Wernerfelt, "Why Do Firms Tend to Become Different?" in C. E. Helfat (ed.), *Handbook of Organizational Capabilities* (Oxford: Blackwell, 2006): 121–33.

64. D. Leonard-Barton, "Core Capabilities and Core Rigidities," *Strategic Management Journal* 13 (Summer 1992): 111–26.

65. N. T. Snyder and D. L. Duarte, *Unleashing Innovation: How Whirlpool Transformed an Industry* (San Francisco: Jossey-Bass, 2008).

66. C. E. Helfat and R. S. Raubitschek, "Product Sequencing: Co-evolution of Knowledge, Capabilities and Products," *Strategic Management Journal* 21 (2000): 961–79. The parallel development of capabilities and products has also been referred to as "dynamic resource fit." See: H. Itami, *Mobilizing Invisible Assets* (Boston: Harvard University Press, 1987): 125.

67. A. Takahashi, *What I Learned from Konosuke Matsushita* (Tokyo: Jitsugyo no Nihonsha, 1980); in Japanese, quoted by H. Itami, *Mobilizing Invisible Assets* (Boston: Harvard University Press, 1987): 25.

68. L. Kellaway, "Lucy Kellaway Column," *Financial Times* (June 23, 1999): 13.

69. R. M. Grant, "Toward a Knowledge-based Theory of the Firm," *Strategic Management Journal* 17 (Winter 1996): 109–22.

70. M. Hansen, N. Nohria, and T. Tierney, "What's Your Strategy for Managing Knowledge?" *Harvard Business Review* (March 1999): 106–16.

71. B. Kogut and U. Zander, "Knowledge of the Firm, Combinative Capabilities, and the Replication of Knowledge," *Organization Science* 3 (1992): 383–97; J. Rivkin, "Reproducing Knowledge: Replication without Imitation at Moderate Complexity," *Organization Science* 12 (2001): 274–93.

9 Technology-based Industries and the Management of Innovation

> Whereas a calculator on the ENIAC is equipped with 18000 vacuum tubes and weighs 30 tons, computers in the future may have only 1000 vacuum tubes and perhaps weigh only 1.5 tons.
>
> —POPULAR MECHANICS, MARCH 1949

> I can think of no conceivable reason why an individual should wish to have a computer in his own home.
>
> —KENNETH OLSEN, CHAIRMAN, DIGITAL EQUIPMENT CORPORATION, 1977

OUTLINE

Introduction and Objectives

In the previous chapter we saw that technology is the primary force that creates new industries and transforms existing ones. In the past four decades, new technologies have created many new industries: wireless telephony, biotechnology, photovoltaic power, fiber optics, robotics, and digital imaging. Other industries have been transformed by new technology: telecommunications equipment by internet protocols; the securities industry by online trading; the logistics industry by electronic data interchange (EDI), radio frequency identification (RFID), and global position systems (GPS). New technology is a source of opportunity, especially for new enterprises, but, as we saw in the previous chapter, adapting to new technologies presents major problems for many established companies.

Our focus in this chapter is on business environments where technology is a key driver of change and an important source of competitive advantage. These technology-intensive industries include both emerging industries (those in the introductory and growth phases of their life cycle) and established industries where technology continues to be the major driver of competition (such as pharmaceuticals, chemicals, telecommunications, and electronics). The issues we examine, however, are also relevant to a much broader range of industries where technology has the potential to create competitive advantage.

In the last chapter, we viewed technology as an external force that drove industrial change. In this chapter our primary concern will be the use of technology as a tool of competitive strategy. How can an enterprise best exploit the opportunities that technology offers in order to establish a competitive advantage?

By the time you have completed this chapter, you will be able to:

- analyze how technology is likely to affect industry structure and competition;
- identify the factors that determine the returns to innovation, and evaluate the potential for an innovation to establish competitive advantage;
- formulate strategies for exploiting innovation and managing technology, including:
  - assessing the relative advantages of being a leader or a follower in innovation
  - identifying and evaluating strategic options for exploiting innovation
  - designing strategies and tactics for winning standards wars
  - managing risk;
- design the organizational conditions needed to implement innovation and technology strategies.

This chapter is organized as follows. First, we examine the links between technology and competition in technology-intensive industries. Second, we explore the potential for innovation to establish sustainable competitive advantage. Third, we deal with key issues in designing technology strategies, including timing (to lead or to follow), alternative strategies for exploiting an innovation, setting industry standards, and managing risk. Finally, we examine the organizational conditions for the successful implementation of technology-based strategies.

Competitive Advantage in Technology-intensive Industries

Innovation forms the key link between technology and competitive advantage. It is the quest for competitive advantage that causes firms to invest in innovation; it is innovation that is responsible for new industries coming into being; and it is innovation that allows some firms to dominate their industries. Let us begin by exploring the conditions under which innovation generates profit.

The Innovation Process

Invention is the creation of new products and processes through the development of new knowledge or from new combinations of existing knowledge. Most inventions are the result of novel applications of existing knowledge. Samuel Morse's telegraph, patented in 1840, was based on several decades of research into electromagnetism from Ben Franklin to Ørsted, Ampère, and Sturgeon. The compact disk embodies knowledge about lasers developed several decades previously.

Innovation is the initial commercialization of invention by producing and marketing a new good or service or by using a new method of production. Once introduced, innovation diffuses: on the demand side, through customers purchasing the good or service; on the supply side, through imitation by competitors. An innovation may be the result of a single invention (most product innovations in chemicals and pharmaceuticals involve discoveries of new chemical compounds) or it may combine many inventions. The first automobile, introduced by Karl Benz in 1885, embodied a multitude of inventions, from the wheel, invented some 5000 years previously, to the internal combustion engine, invented nine years earlier. Not all invention progresses into innovation: among the patent portfolios of most technology-intensive firms are inventions that have yet to find a viable commercial application. Many innovations may involve little or no new technology: the personal computer was a new configuration of existing technologies; most new types of packaging, including the vast array of tamper-proof packages, involve novel designs but no new technology.

Figure 9.1 shows the pattern of development from knowledge creation to invention and innovation. Historically, the lags between knowledge creation and innovation have been long:

- Chester F. Carlson invented xerography in 1938 by combining established knowledge about electrostatics and printing. The first patents were awarded in 1940. Xerox purchased the patent rights and launched its first office copier in 1958. By 1974, the first competitive machines were introduced by IBM, Kodak, Ricoh, and Canon.
- The jet engine, employing Newtonian principles, was patented by Frank Whittle in 1930. The first commercial jet airliner, the De Havilland Comet, flew in 1957. Two years later, the Boeing 707 was introduced.

Recently, the innovation cycle has speeded up:

- The mathematics of *fuzzy logic* was developed by Lofti Zadeh at Berkeley during the 1960s. By the early 1980s, Dr Takeshi Yamakawa of the Kyushu Institute of Technology had patented integrated circuits embodying fuzzy

FIGURE 9.1 The development of technology: From knowledge creation to diffusion

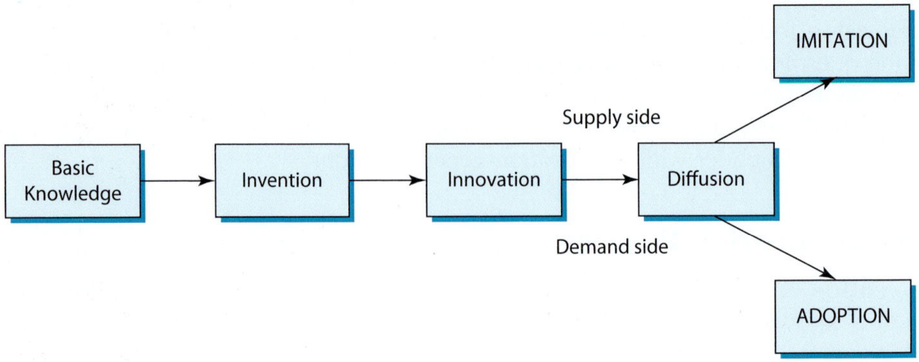

logic, and in 1987 Omron of Kyoto introduced fuzzy logic controllers for industrial machines. By 1991, the world market for fuzzy logic controllers was estimated at $2 billion.[1]

- The use of satellite radio signals for global positioning was developed by physicists at Johns Hopkins University in late 1950s. In 1978, the US Air Force launched its first experimental GPS satellite; the GPS system was fully operational by 1995. Commercial applications began in the early 1990s: Garmin launched its first GPS satellite navigation product in 1991. Car sat-nav systems were offered by Garmin in 1998 and TomTom in 2002.

- MP3, the audio file compression software, was developed at the Fraunhofer Institute in Germany in 1987; by the mid-1990s, the swapping of MP3 music files had taken off in US college campuses, and in 1998 the first MP3 player, Diamond Multimedia's *Rio*, was launched. Apple's iPod was introduced in 2001.

The Profitability of Innovation

"If a man can . . . make a better mousetrap than his neighbor, though he build his house in the woods, the world will make a beaten path to his door," claimed Emerson. Yet the inventors of new mousetraps, and other gadgets too, are more likely to be found at the bankruptcy courts than in the millionaires' playgrounds of the Caribbean. Certainly, innovation is no guarantor of fame and fortune, either for individuals or for companies. There is no consistent evidence that either R & D intensity or frequency of new-product introductions is positively associated with profitability.[2]

The profitability of an innovation to the innovator depends on the value created by the innovation and the share of that value that the innovator is able to appropriate. The value created by an innovation is distributed among a number of different parties. As Strategy Capsule 9.1 shows, different innovations result in very different distributions of value. In the case of aspartame, the innovator G. D. Searle with NutraSweet was the primary beneficiary. In the case of the personal computer, suppliers and consumers were the primary beneficiaries. In the case of smartphones, followers such as RIM, Apple, and Samsung have appropriated most of the value.

STRATEGY CAPSULE 9.1

How the Returns on Innovation Are Shared

The value created by an innovation is distributed among a number of different parties (Figure 9.2).

◆ *Aspartame*: Aspartame, the artificial sweetener, was discovered in 1965 by the drug company G. D. Searle & Co. In 1981, after FDA approval, it was launched as NutraSweet. NutraSweet was sold to soft drink producers and food processors at $200 a kilo: twenty times the price of saccharin and by 1986 was generating sales of $711 million. In 1985, Searle was acquired by Monsanto. In 1992, the main US patent on aspartame expired. Competition from rival producers began in Europe in 1986 and in the US in December 1992. In the first two decades of aspartame's market presence, the innovator, Searle/Monsanto, has appropriated a major part of the value created.

◆ *Personal computers*: The innovators—MITS, Tandy, Apple, and Xerox—earned modest profits from their innovation. The imitators—IBM, Dell, Compaq, Acer, Toshiba, and a host of other later entrants—did somewhat better, but their returns were overshadowed by the huge profits earned by the suppliers to the industry: Intel in microprocessors, Microsoft in operating systems, Seagate in disk drives, Sharp in flat-panel displays. However, because of strong competition in the industry, the greatest beneficiaries from the invention of the personal computer were consumers, who typically paid prices for their PCs that were far below the value that they derived.[3]

◆ *Smartphones*: These are wireless handsets with enhanced computing capability and internet access. The first were the IBM Simon (1993) and the Nokia 9000 series (1996). During 2000–2002, a host of followers entered the market, including Ericsson, Sony, Palm, and RIM. In 2007, the Apple iPhone was launched. While the pioneers all lost money, among the followers Apple and RIM (until recently) were highly profitable. Several suppliers have also been big winners, including ARM (microprocessors) and application suppliers such as Zynga.

FIGURE 9.2   Appropriation of value: Who gets the benefits from innovation?

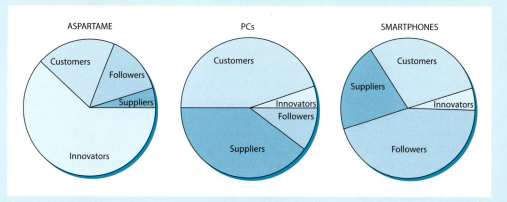

The term **regime of appropriability** is used to describe the conditions that influence the distribution of returns to innovation. In a strong regime of appropriability, the innovator is able to capture a substantial share of the value created: Pilkington's float glass process, Pfizer's Viagra, and Dyson's dual-cyclone vacuum cleaner—like Searle's NutraSweet—all generated huge profits for their owners. In a weak regime of appropriability, other parties derive most of the value. In e-book readers, the diversity of rivals, the prevalence of open standards, and competition from substitute products such as tablet computers suggest that no players are likely to earn massive profits.

The regime of appropriability comprises four key components which determine the innovator's ability to profit from innovation: property rights, the tacitness and complexity of the technology, lead time, and complementary resources.

Property Rights in Innovation   Appropriating the returns on innovation depends, to a great extent, on the ability to establish property rights in the innovation. It was the desire to protect the returns to inventors that prompted the English Parliament to pass the 1623 Statute of Monopolies, which established the basis of patent law. Since then, the law has been extended to several areas of **intellectual property**, including:

- *Patents*: Exclusive rights to a new and useful product, process, substance, or design. Obtaining a patent requires that the invention is novel, useful, and not excessively obvious. Patent law varies from country to country. In the US, a patent is valid for 17 years (14 for a design).
- *Copyrights*: Exclusive production, publication, or sales rights to the creators of artistic, literary, dramatic, or musical works. Examples include articles, books, drawings, maps, photographs, and musical compositions.
- *Trademarks*: Words, symbols, or other marks used to distinguish the goods or services supplied by a firm. In the US and the UK, they are registered with the Patent Office. Trademarks provide the basis for brand identification.
- *Trade secrets*: Offer a modest degree of legal protection for recipes, formulae, industrial processes, customer lists, and other knowledge acquired in the course of business.

The effectiveness of intellectual property law depends on the type of innovation being protected. For new chemical products (a new drug or plastic), patents can provide effective protection. For products that involve new configurations of existing components or new manufacturing processes, patents may fail to prevent rivals from innovating around them. The scope of the patent law has been extended to include life forms created by biotechnology, computer software, and business methods. Business method patents have generated considerable controversy, especially Amazon's patent on "one-click-to-buy" internet purchasing.[4] While patents and copyright establish property rights, their disadvantage (from the inventor's viewpoint) is that they make information public. Hence, companies often prefer secrecy to patenting as a means of protecting innovations.

In recent decades, companies have devoted increasing attention to protecting and exploiting the economic value of their intellectual property. When Texas Instruments began exploiting its patent portfolio as a revenue source during the 1980s, the technology sector as a whole woke up to the value of its knowledge assets. During the 1990s, TI's royalty income exceeded its operating income from other sources. One outcome has been an upsurge in patenting. An average of 231,000 patents were granted by the US Patent Office each year from 2009 to 2011; during 1980–1985 it was 67,000 annually.

Tacitness and Complexity of the Technology   In the absence of effective legal protection the extent to which an innovation can be imitated by a competitor depends on the ease with which the technology can be comprehended and replicated. This depends, first, on the extent to which the technical knowledge is codifiable. Codifiable knowledge, by definition, is that which can be written down. Hence, if it is not effectively protected by patents or copyright, diffusion is likely to be rapid and the competitive advantage not sustainable. Financial innovations such as mortgage-backed securities and credit default swaps embody readily codifiable knowledge that can be copied very quickly. Similarly, Coca-Cola's recipe is codifiable and, in the absence of trade-secret protection, is easily copied. Intel's designs for advanced microprocessors are codified and can be copied; however, the processes for manufacturing these integrated circuits are based on deeply tacit knowledge.

The second key factor is *complexity*. Every new fashion, from the Mary Quant miniskirt of 1962 to Jimmy Choo's wedge-heel espadrilles of 2012, involves simple, easy-to-copy ideas. Conversely, Airbus's A380 and Altera Corporation's Stratix V FPGA chip (possibly the world's most complex integrated circuit) present entirely different challenges for the would-be imitator.

Lead Time   Tacitness and complexity do not provide lasting barriers to imitation, but they do offer the innovator *time*. Innovation creates a temporary competitive advantage that offers a window of opportunity for the innovator to build on the initial advantage.

The innovator's *lead time* is the time it will take followers to catch up. The challenge for the innovator is to use initial lead-time advantages to build the capabilities and market position to entrench industry leadership. Microsoft, Intel, and Cisco Systems were brilliant at exploiting lead time to build advantages in efficient manufacture, quality, and market presence. Conversely, innovative British companies are notorious for having squandered their lead-time advantage in jet planes, radars, CT scanners, and genomics.

Lead time allows a firm to move down its learning curve ahead of followers. In new generations of microprocessors, Intel has traditionally been first to market, allowing it to move quickly down its experience curve, cut prices, and so pressure the profit margins of its rival, AMD.

Complementary Resources   Bringing new products and processes to market requires not just invention; it also requires the diverse resources and capabilities needed to finance, produce, and market the innovation. These are referred to as *complementary resources* (Figure 9.3). Chester Carlson invented xerography but was unable for many years to bring his product to market because he lacked the complementary resources needed to develop, manufacture, market, distribute, and service his invention. Conversely, Searle (and its later parent, Monsanto) was able to provide almost all the development, manufacturing, marketing, and distribution resources needed to exploit its NutraSweet innovation. As a result, Carlson was able

FIGURE 9.3   Complementary resources

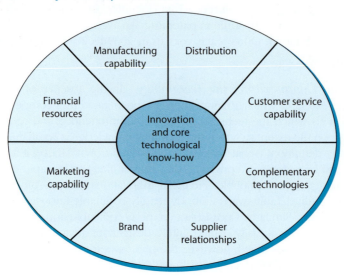

to appropriate only a tiny part of the value created by his invention of the plain-paper Xerox copier, whereas Searle/Monsanto was successful in appropriating a major part of the value created by its new artificial sweetener.

Complementary resources may be accessed through alliances with other firms, for example biotech firms ally with large pharmaceutical companies for clinical trials, manufacture, and marketing.[5] When an innovation and the complementary resources that support it are supplied by different firms, the division of value between them depends on their relative power. A key determinant of this is whether the complementary resources are *specialized* or *unspecialized*. Fuel cells may eventually displace internal combustion engines in many of the world's automobiles. However, the problem for the developers of fuel cells is that their success depends on automobile manufacturers making specialized investments in designing a whole new range of cars, service station owners providing specialized refueling facilities, and repair firms investing in training and new equipment. For fuel cells to be widely adopted will require that the benefits of the innovation are shared widely with the different providers of these complementary resources. Where complementary resources are generic, the innovator is in a much stronger position to capture value. Because Adobe Systems' Acrobat Portable Document Format (PDF) works with files created in almost any software application, Adobe is well positioned to capture most of the value created by its innovatory software product. However, one advantage of co-specialized complementary resources is that they raise barriers to imitation. Consider the threat that Linux presents to Microsoft Window's dominance of PC operating systems. Intel has adapted its microprocessors to the needs of Windows and most applications software is written to run on Windows, so the challenge for the Linux community is not just to develop a workable operating system but also to encourage the development of applications software and hardware that are compatible with the Linux operating system.

Which Mechanisms Are Effective at Protecting Innovation?

How effective are these different mechanisms in protecting innovations? Table 9.1 shows that, despite considerable variation across industries, patent protection is of limited effectiveness as compared with lead time, secrecy, and complementary manufacturing and sales/service resources. Indeed, since the late 1980s, the effectiveness of patents appeared to have declined despite the strengthening of patent law. Although patents are effective in increasing the lead time before competitors are able to bring imitative products to market, these gains tend to be small. The great majority of patented products and processes are duplicated within three years.[6]

Given the limited effectiveness of patents, why do firms continue to engage in patenting? Table 9.2 shows that, while protection from imitation is the principal motive, several others are also very important. In particular, much patenting activity appears to be strategic; it is directed toward blocking the innovation efforts of other companies and establishing property rights in technologies that can then be used in bargaining with other companies for access to their proprietary technologies. In semiconductors and electronics, cross-licensing arrangements— where one company gives access to its patents across a field of technology in exchange for access to another company's patents—are critical in permitting "freedom to design": the ability to design products that draw on technologies owned by different companies.[7]

TABLE 9.1   The effectiveness of different mechanisms for protecting innovation

	Secrecy (%)	Patents (%)	Lead-time (%)	Sales/service (%)	Manufacturing (%)
Product innovations					
Food	59	18	53	40	51
Drugs	54	50	50	33	49
Electronic components	34	21	46	50	51
Telecom equipment	47	26	66	42	41
Medical equipment	51	55	58	52	49
All industries	51	35	53	43	46
Process innovations					
Food	56	16	42	30	47
Drugs	68	36	36	25	44
Electronic components	47	15	43	42	56
Telecom equipment	35	15	43	34	41
Medical equipment	49	34	45	32	50
All industries	51	23	38	31	43

Note:
These data show the percentage of companies reporting that the particular mechanism, their sales and service, and their manufacturing capabilities were effective in protecting their innovations.
Source: W. M. Cohen, R. R. Nelson, and J. P. Walsh, "Protecting Their Intellectual Assets: Appropriability Conditions and Why US Manufacturing Firms Patent (Or Not)," NBER Working Paper No. W7552 (February 2000). © 2000. Reprinted by permission of the authors.

TABLE 9.2   Why do companies patent? (Responses by 674 US manufacturers)

	Product Innovations (%)	Process Innovations (%)
To prevent copying	95	77
For licensing revenue	28	23
To prevent law suits	59	47
To block others	82	64
For use in negotiations	47	43
To enhance reputation	48	34
To measure performance	6	5

Source: W. M. Cohen, R. R. Nelson, and J. P. Walsh, "Protecting Their Intellectual Assets: Appropriability Conditions and Why US Manufacturing Firms Patent (Or Not)," NBER Working Paper No. W7552 (February 2000). © 2000. Reprinted by permission of the authors.

Strategies to Exploit Innovation: How and When to Enter

Having established some of the key factors that determine the returns to innovation, let us consider some of the main questions concerning the formulation of strategies to manage technology and exploit innovation.

Alternative Strategies to Exploit Innovation

How should a firm maximize the returns to its innovation? A number of alternative strategies are available. Figure 9.4 orders them according to the size of the commitment of resources and capabilities that each requires. Thus, licensing requires little involvement by the innovator in subsequent commercialization, hence is a limited investment. Internal commercialization, possibly through creating a new enterprise or business unit, involves a much greater investment of resources and capabilities. In between there are various opportunities for collaboration with other companies. Joint ventures and strategic alliances typically involve substantial resource sharing between companies. On a more limited scale, specific activities may be outsourced to other companies.

Which mode of innovation is chosen by the firm depends on two sets of factors: the characteristics of the innovation and the resources and capabilities of the firm.

Characteristics of the Innovation   The extent to which a firm can establish clear property rights in an innovation is a critical determinant of its innovation strategy. Licensing is only viable where ownership in the innovation is protected by patent or copyrights. Thus, in pharmaceuticals, licensing is widespread because patents are clear and defensible. Many biotech companies engage only in R & D and license their drug discoveries to large pharmaceutical companies that possess the necessary complementary resources. Royalties from licensing its sound-reduction technologies accounted for 82% of Dolby Laboratories' 2011 revenues. Conversely, when Steve Jobs and Steve Wozniak developed their Apple I and Apple II computers, they had little option other than to go into business themselves: the absence of proprietary technology ruled out licensing as an option.

FIGURE 9.4   Alternative strategies for exploiting innovation

	Licensing	Outsourcing certain functions	Strategic alliance	Joint venture	Internal commercialization
Risk and return	Little investment risk but returns also limited. Risk that the licensee either lacks motivation or steals the innovation	Limits capital investment, but may create dependence on suppliers/partners	Benefits of flexibility. Risks of informal structure	Shares investment and risk. Risk of partner disagreement and culture clash	Biggest investment requirement and corresponding risks. Benefits of control
Resource requirements	Few	Permits external resources and capabilities to be accessed	Permits pooling of the resources and capabilities of more than one firm		Substantial requirements in terms of finance, production capability, marketing capability, distribution, etc.
Examples	Ericsson with its Bluetooth wireless technology; Dolby Labs with its sound reduction technology; Qualcomm and CDMA	Microsoft's XBox was largely designed by other companies and Flextronics does the manufacturing	Ballard's strategic alliance with DaimlerChrysler to develop fuel cells	Psion created Symbian as a joint venture with Ericsson, Nokia, and Motorola to develop the Symbian mobile phone operating system	Larry Page and Sergey Brin established Google Inc. to develop and market their internet search technology

The advantages of licensing are, first, that it relieves the company of the need to develop the full range of complementary resources and capabilities needed for commercialization and, second, that it can allow the innovation to be commercialized quickly. If the lead time offered by the innovation is short, multiple licensing can allow for a fast global rollout. The problem, however, is that the success of the innovation in the market is totally dependent on the commitment and effectiveness of the licensees. James Dyson, the British inventor of the bagless vacuum cleaner, created his own company to manufacture and market his "dual cyclone" vacuum cleaners after failing to interest any major appliance company in a licensing deal for his technology.

Resources and Capabilities of the Firm   As Figure 9.4 shows, different strategies require very different resources and capabilities. Hence, the choice of how to exploit an innovation depends critically upon the resources and capabilities that the innovator brings to the party. Start-up firms possess few of the complementary resources and capabilities needed to commercialize their innovations. Inevitably, they will be attracted to licensing or to accessing the resources of larger firms through outsourcing, alliances, or joint ventures. As we noted in the previous chapter, new industries often follow a two-stage evolution where "innovators" do the pioneering and "consolidators" with their complementary resources do the developing.

These established corporations with a wealth of resources and capabilities are better placed than start-ups for internal commercialization. Companies such as Sony, DuPont, Siemens, Hitachi, and IBM have strong traditions of pursuing basic research, then internally developing the innovations that arise.

However, even these companies have been forced into more technological collaborations with other companies. Ron Adner observes that innovation increasingly requires coordinated responses by multiple companies. Innovating firms need to identify and map their *innovation ecosystem*, then manage the interdependencies within it. The delayed introduction of HDTV can be attributed to inadequate coordination among TV manufacturers, production studios, and broadcasters.[8]

Timing Innovation: To Lead or to Follow?

To gain competitive advantage in emerging and technologically intensive industries, is it better to be a leader or a follower in innovation? As Table 9.3 shows, the evidence is mixed: in some products the leader has been the first to grab the prize; in others, the leader has succumbed to the risks and costs of pioneering. Optimal timing of entry into an emerging industry and the introduction of new technology are complex issues. The advantage of being an early mover depends on the following factors:

- *The extent to which innovation can be protected by property rights or lead-time advantages*: If an innovation is appropriable through a patent, copyright, or lead-time advantage, there is advantage in being an early mover. This is especially the case where patent protection is important, as in pharmaceuticals. Notable patent races include that between Alexander Bell and Elisha Gray to patent the telephone (Bell got to the Patent Office a few hours before Gray),[9] and between Celera Inc. and the National Institutes of Health to patent the sequence of the human genome.[10]

- *The importance of complementary resources*: The more important complementary resources are in exploiting an innovation, the greater the costs and risks of pioneering. Several firms—from Sir Clive Sinclair with a

TABLE 9.3 Leaders, followers, and success in emerging industries

Product	Innovator	Follower	The winner
Jet airliner	De Havilland (Comet)	Boeing (707)	Follower
Float glass	Pilkington	Corning	Leader
X-ray scanner	EMI	General Electric	Follower
Office PC	Xerox	IBM	Follower
VCRs	Ampex/Sony	Matsushita	Follower
Instant camera	Polaroid	Kodak	Leader
Microwave oven	Raytheon	Samsung	Follower
Video games player	Atari	Nintendo/Sony	Followers
Disposable diaper	Procter & Gamble	Kimberley-Clark	Leader
Compact disk	Sony/Philips	Matsushita, Pioneer	Leader
Web browser	Netscape	Microsoft	Follower
Web search engine	Lycos	Google	Follower
MP3 music players	Diamond Multimedia	Apple (iPod)	Follower
Operating systems for mobile phones	Symbian	Microsoft	Leader (until 2010)
Laser printer	Xerox, IBM	Canon	Follower
Flash memory	Toshiba	Samsung, Intel	Followers
E-book reader	Sony (Digital Reader)	Amazon (Kindle)	Follower
Social networking	SixDegrees.com	Facebook	Follower

Source: Based in part on D. Teece, *The Competitive Challenge: Strategies for Industrial Innovation and Renewal* (Cambridge: Ballinger, 1987): 186–8.

battery-driven car to General Motors with its fuel-cell car and Chevrolet Volt—failed commercially with their electric automobiles. The problem for the pioneer is that the development costs are huge because of the need to orchestrate multiple technologies and establish self-sufficiency across a range of business functions. Followers are also favored by the fact that, as an industry develops, specialist firms emerge as suppliers of complementary resources. Thus, in pioneering the development of the British frozen foods industry, Unilever's Bird's Eye subsidiary had to set up an entire chain of cold stores and frozen distribution facilities. Later entrants were able to rely on the services of public cold stores and refrigerated trucking companies.

- *The potential to establish a standard*: As we shall see later in this chapter, some markets converge toward a technical standard. The greater the importance of technical standards, the greater the advantages of being an early mover in order to influence those standards and gain the market momentum needed to establish leadership. Once a standard has been set, displacing it becomes exceptionally difficult. IBM had little success with its OS/2 operating system against the entrenched position of Microsoft Windows. Linux has succeeded in taking market share from Windows. However, the main reason for this is that Linux is free!

Optimal timing depends also on the resources and capabilities that the individual firm has at its disposal. Different companies have different *strategic windows*—periods in time when their resources and capabilities are aligned with the opportunities available in the market. A small, technology-based firm may have no choice but to pioneer innovation: its opportunity is to grab **first-mover advantage** and then develop the necessary complementary resources before more powerful rivals appear. For the large, established firm with financial resources and strong production, marketing, and distribution capabilities, the strategic window is likely to be both longer and later. The risks of pioneering are greater for an established firm with a reputation and brands to protect, while to exploit its complementary resources effectively typically requires a more developed market. Consider the following examples:

- In personal computers, Apple was a pioneer, IBM a follower. The timing of entry was probably optimal for each. Apple's resources were the vision of Steve Jobs and the technical genius of Steve Wozniak; only by pioneering could it hope to be successful. IBM had enormous strengths in manufacturing, distribution, and reputation. It could build competitive advantage even without a clear technological advantage. The key for IBM was to delay its entry until the time when the market had developed to the point where IBM's strengths could have their maximum impact.

- In the browser war between Netscape and Microsoft, Microsoft had the luxury of being able to follow the pioneer, Netscape. Microsoft's huge product development, marketing, and distribution capabilities, and, most important, its vast installed base of the Windows operating system allowed it to overhaul Netscape's initial lead.

- Although General Electric entered the market for CT scanners some four years after EMI, it was able to overtake EMI within a few years because of its ability to apply vast technological, manufacturing, sales, and customer service capabilities within the field of medical electronics.

The most effective follower strategies are those that initiate a new product's transition from niche market to mass market. According to Markides and Geroski, successful first movers pioneer new products that embody new technologies and new functionality.[11] The opportunity for the fast-second entrant is to grow the niche market into a mass market by lowering cost and increasing quality. Timing is critical. Don Sull argues that a successful follower strategy requires "active waiting": a company needs to monitor market developments and assemble resources and capabilities while it prepares for large-scale market entry.[12]

Managing Risks

Emerging industries are risky. There are two main sources of uncertainty:

- *Technological uncertainty* arises from the unpredictability of technological evolution and the complex dynamics through which technical standards and dominant designs are selected. Hindsight is always 20/20, but *ex ante* it is difficult to predict how technologies and the industries that deploy them will evolve.
- *Market uncertainty* relates to the size and growth rates of the markets for new products. When Xerox introduced its first plain-paper copier in 1959, Apple its first personal computer in 1977, or Sony its Walkman in 1979, none had any idea of the size of the potential market. Forecasting demand for new products is hazardous—most forecasting techniques are based on past data. Demand forecasts for new products tend to rely either on analogies[13] or expert opinion—e.g., combining expert insight and experience using the *Delphi technique*.[14]

If managers are unable to forecast technology and demand, then to manage risk they must be alert to emerging trends while limiting their exposure to risk through avoiding large-scale commitments. Useful strategies for limiting risk include:

- *Cooperating with lead users*: During the early phases of industry development, careful monitoring of and response to market trends and customer requirements is essential to avoid major errors in technology and design. Von Hippel argues that lead users provide a source of leading market indicators, can assist in developing new products and processes, and offer an early cash flow to fund development expenditures.[15] In computer software, *beta versions* are released to computer enthusiasts for testing. Nike has two sets of lead users: professional athletes who are trendsetters for athletic footwear and gang members and hip-hop artists who are at the leading edge of urban fashion trends. In communications and aerospace, government defense contracts play a crucial role in developing new technologies.[16]
- *Limiting risk exposure*: The financial risks of emerging industries can be mitigated by financial and operational practices that minimize a firm's exposure to adversity. By avoiding debt and keeping fixed costs low, a firm can lower its financial and operational gearing. Outsourcing and strategic alliance can also hold down capital investment and fixed costs.
- *Flexibility*: Uncertainty necessitates rapid responses to unpredicted events. Achieving such flexibility means keeping options open and delaying

commitment to a specific technology until its potential becomes clear. Large, well-resourced companies have the luxury of pursuing multiple strategic options (Strategy Capsule 9.2).

Competing for Standards

In the previous chapter, we noted that the establishment of standards is a key event in industry evolution. With the emergence of the digital, networked economy, more and more markets are affected by standards. For companies, the ability to influence or even own a standard is critical to establishing a competitive advantage. Indeed, ownership of an industry standard has the potential to offer returns that are unmatched by any other type of competitive advantage. Table 9.4 lists several companies which own key technical standards within a particular product category.

STRATEGY CAPSULE 9.2

Keeping Your Options Open: Microsoft in Operating Systems

♦ In 1988, as I wandered about the floor of Comdex, the computer industry's vast annual trade show, I could feel the anxiety among the participants. Since the birth of the IBM PC six years earlier, Microsoft's Disk Operating System (DOS) had been the de facto standard for PCs. But DOS was now starting to age. Everyone wanted to know what would replace it.

♦ Apple Computer, at the peak of its powers, had one of the largest booths showcasing the brilliantly graphical Macintosh operating system . . . Two different alliances of major companies, including AT&T, HP, and Sun Microsystems, offered graphical versions of Unix . . . And IBM was touting its new OS/2.

♦ Amid the uncertainty, there was something very curious about the Microsoft booth which resembled a Middle Eastern bazaar. In one corner, the company was previewing its highly criticized Windows system . . . In another, Microsoft touted its latest release of DOS. Elsewhere it was displaying OS/2, which it had developed with IBM. In addition, Microsoft was demonstrating new releases of Word and Excel that ran on Apple's Mac. Finally, in a distant corner, Microsoft displayed SCO Unix . . .

♦ "What am I supposed to make of this?" grumbled a corporate buyer standing next to me. Columnists wrote that Microsoft was adrift, that its chairman and COO, Bill Gates, had no strategy.

♦ Although the outcome of this story is now well known, to anyone standing on the Comdex floor in 1988 it wasn't obvious which operating system would win. In the face of this uncertainty, Microsoft followed the only robust strategy: betting on every horse.

Source: E. D. Beinhocker, "Robust Adaptive Strategies," *Sloan Management Review* (Spring 1999): 95–106. © 1999 from MIT Sloan Management Review/Massachusetts Institute of Technology. All rights reserved. Distributed by Tribune Media Services.

TABLE 9.4 Examples of companies that own de facto industry standards

Company	Product category	Standard
Microsoft	PC operating systems	Windows
Intel	PC microprocessors	x86 series
Sony/Philips	Compact disks	CD-ROM format
ARM (Holdings)	Microprocessors for mobile devices	ARM architecture
Oracle Corporation	Programming language for web apps	Java
Rockwell and 3Com	56K modems	V90
Qualcomm	Digital cellular wireless communication	CDMA
Adobe Systems	Common file format for creating and viewing documents	Acrobat Portable Document Format
Adobe Systems	Web page animation	Adobe Flash
Adobe Systems	Page description language for document printing	Post Script
Bosch	Antilock braking systems	ABS and TCS (Traction Control System)
IMAX Corporation	Motion picture filming and projection system	IMAX
Apple	Music downloading system	iTunes/iPod
Sony	High definition DVD	Blu-ray
NTT DOCOMO	Mobile phone payment system in Japan	Osaifu-Keitai

A characteristic of most of these companies is the fact that these standards have generated considerable profits and shareholder value.

Types of Standard

A *standard* is a format, an interface, or a system that allows interoperability. Adhering to standards allows us to browse millions of different web pages, ensures the light bulbs made by any manufacturer will fit any manufacturer's lamps, and keeps the traffic moving in Los Angeles (most of the time). Standards can be *public* or *private*.

- Public (or *open*) standards are those that are available to all either free or for a nominal charge. Typically, they do not involve any privately owned intellectual property, or the intellectual-property owners make access free (such as Linux). Public standards are set by public bodies and industry associations. Thus, the GSM mobile phone standard was set by the European Telecom Standards Institute. Internet protocols (standards governing internet addressing and routing) are mostly public. They are governed by several international bodies, including the Internet Engineering Task Force.
- Private (*proprietary*) standards are those where the technologies and designs are owned by companies or individuals. If I own the technology that becomes a standard, I can embody the technology in a product that others buy (Microsoft Windows) or license the technology to others who wish to use it (Qualcomm's CDMA).

Standards can also be classified according to who sets them. *Mandatory standards* are set by government and have the force of law behind them. They include standards relating to automobile safety and construction specifications and to TV broadcasting. *De facto standards* emerge through voluntary adoption by producers and users. Table 9.4 gives examples.

A problem with *de facto* standards is that they may take a long time to emerge, resulting in a duplication of investments and delaying the development of the market. It was 40 years before a standard railroad gauge was agreed in the US.[17] One reason for the slow transition of wireless telecoms in the US from analog to digital technology was continuing competition between TDMA and CDMA standards. By contrast, Europe officially adopted GSM (a close relative of TDMA) in 1992.[18] Delayed emergence of a standard may kill the technology altogether. The failure of quadraphonic sound to displace stereophonic sound during the 1970s resulted from incompatible technical standards, which inhibited audio manufacturers, record companies, and consumers from investing in the technology.[19]

Why Standards Appear: Network Externalities

Standards emerge in markets that are subject to **network externalities**. A network externality exists whenever the value of a product to an individual customer depends on the number of other users of that product. The classic example of network externality is the telephone. Since there is little satisfaction to be gained from talking to oneself on the telephone, the value of a telephone to each user depends on the number of other users connected to the same telephone system. This is different from most products. When I pour myself a glass of Glenlivet after a couple of exhausting MBA classes, my enjoyment is independent of how many other people in the world are also drinking Glenlivet. Indeed, some products may have *negative* network externalities—the value of the product is less if many other people purchase the same product. If I spend $3000 on an Armani silver lamé tuxedo and find that half my colleagues at the faculty Christmas party are wearing the same jacket, my satisfaction is lessened.

Network externalities do not require everyone to use the same product or even the same technology, but rather that the different products are *compatible* with one another through some form of common interface. In the case of wireless telephone service, it doesn't matter (as far as network access is concerned) whether I purchase service from AT&T, Nextel, or T-Mobile, because compatibility between each network allows connectivity. Similarly with railroads: if I am transporting coal from Wyoming to Boston, my choice of railroad company is not critical. Unlike in the 1870s, every railroad company now uses a standard gauge and is required to give "common carrier" access to other companies' rolling stock.

Network externalities arise from several sources:

- *Products where users are linked to a network*: Telephones, railroad systems, and email instant messaging groups are networks where users are linked together. Applications software, whether spreadsheet programs or video games, also links users—they can share files and play games interactively. User-level externalities may also arise through social identification. I watch *American Idol* and the Hollywood Oscar presentations on TV not because I enjoy them but so that I have something to talk to my colleagues about in the faculty common room.[20]

- *Availability of complementary products and services*: Where products are consumed as systems, the availability of complementary products and services depends on the number of customers for that system. Apple's key problem in the computer market is that, because the Macintosh accounts for only 9% of the installed base of personal computers, few leading software firms are writing Mac-based applications. I choose to drive a Ford Focus rather than a Ferrari Testarossa because I know that, should I break down 200 miles from Bismarck, North Dakota, spare parts and a repair service will be more readily available.

- *Economizing on switching costs*: By purchasing the product or system that is most widely used, there is less chance that I shall have to bear the costs of switching. By using Microsoft Office rather than Lotus SmartSuite, it is more likely that I will avoid the costs of retraining and file conversion when I become a visiting professor at another university.

The implication of network externalities is that they create *positive feedback*. Once a technology or system gains market leadership, it attracts a growing proportion of new buyers. Conversely, once market leadership is lost, a downward spiral is likely. This process is called *tipping*: once a certain threshold is reached, cumulative forces become unstoppable.[21] The result is a tendency toward a *winner-takes-all* market. Those markets subject to significant network externalities tend to be dominated by a single supplier (e.g., Microsoft in PC operating systems and office applications, eBay in internet auctions).

Once established, technical and design standards tend to be highly resilient. Standards are difficult to displace due to learning effects and collective lock-in. Learning effects cause the dominant technology and design to be continually improved and refined. Even where the existing standard is inherently inferior, switching to a superior technology may not occur because of collective lock in. The classic case is the QWERTY typewriter layout. Its 1873 design was based on the need to *slow* the speed of typing to prevent typewriter keys from jamming. Although the jamming problem was soon solved, the QWERTY layout has persisted, despite the patenting in 1932 of the more ergonomic Dvorak Simplified Keyboard (DSK).[22]

Winning Standards Wars

In markets subject to network externalities, control over standards is the primary basis for competitive advantage. Sony and Apple are unusual in that they lost their standards wars (in VCRs and personal computers, respectively) but returned as winners in other markets. Most losers in standards wars—Lotus in spreadsheet software, Netscape in browsers, WordPerfect in word processing software—become mere footnotes in the history of technology. What can we learn from these and other standards wars about designing a winning strategy in markets subject to network externalities?

The first key issue is to determine whether we are competing in a market that will converge around a single technical standard. This requires a careful analysis of the presence and sources of network externalities.

The second strategic issue in standards setting is recognizing the role of positive feedback: the technology that can establish early leadership will rapidly gain momentum. Building a "bigger bandwagon" according to Shapiro and Varian[23] requires the following:

- *Before you go to war, assemble allies*: You'll need the support of consumers, suppliers of complements, even your competitors. Not even the strongest companies can afford to go it alone in a standards war.
- *Preempt the market*: Enter early, achieve fast-cycle product development, make early deals with key customers, and adopt penetration pricing.
- *Manage expectations*: The key to managing positive feedback is to convince customers, suppliers, and the producers of complementary goods that you will emerge as the victor. These expectations become a self-fulfilling prophecy. The massive pre-launch promotion and publicity built up by Sony prior to the American and European launch of PlayStation 2 in October 2000 was an effort to convince consumers, retailers, and game developers that the product would be the blockbuster consumer electronics product of the new decade, thereby stymieing Sega's and Nintendo's efforts to establish their rival systems.

The lesson that has emerged from the classic standards battles of the past is that in order to create initial leadership and maximize positive feedback effects a company must share the value created by the technology with other parties (customers, competitors, complementors, and suppliers). If a company attempts to appropriate too great a share of the value created, it may well fail to build a big enough bandwagon to gain market leadership (Strategy Capsule 9.3). Thus, recent standards battles involve broad alliances, where the owner enlists the support of complementors and would-be competitors. In the 2006–2008 struggle between Sony (Blu-ray) and Toshiba (HD-DVD), each camp recruited movie studios, software firms, and producers of computers and consumer electronics using various inducements, including direct cash payments. The defection of Warner Brothers to the Sony camp was critical to the market tipping suddenly in Sony's favor. However, it appears that all the financial gains from owning the winning DVD standard were dissipated by the costs of the war.[24]

Achieving compatibility with existing products is a critical issue in standards battles. Advantage typically goes to the competitor that adopts an *evolutionary strategy* (i.e., offers backward compatibility) rather than one that adopts a *revolutionary strategy*.[25] A key advantage of the Sony PlayStation 2 over Microsoft Xbox and Nintendo Cube was its compatibility with the PlayStation 1. However, the limited compatibility of PlayStation 3 with PlayStation 2 was one of the many problems that limited the success of PlayStation 3.

What are the key resources needed to win a standards war? Shapiro and Varian emphasize the following:

- control over an installed base of customers;
- owning intellectual property rights in the new technology;
- the ability to innovate in order to extend and adapt the initial technological advance;
- first-mover advantage;
- strength in complements (e.g., Intel has preserved its standard in microprocessors by promoting standards in buses, chipsets, graphics controllers, and interfaces between motherboards and CPUs);
- reputation and brand name.[26]

STRATEGY CAPSULE 9.3

Building a Bandwagon by Sharing Value: Lessons from VCRs and PCs

Profiting from standards requires, first, setting the standard and, second, retaining a proprietary interest in the standard in order to appropriate part of its value. There is a tradeoff between the two—the more value a company tries to appropriate, the greater the difficulty in building early support for its technology. Consider the standards wars in VCRs and PCs:

In VCRs, Matsushita's VHS format won against Sony's Betamax format not because of the technical superiority of VHS but because—in contrast to Sony's tight proprietary control of Betamax—Matsushita licensed its VHS system to Sharp, Philips, GE, RCA, and others, allowing it to gain market leadership.

In personal computers, IBM was highly successful in setting the standard, partly because it did not restrict access to its technology. Its product specifications were openly available to "clone makers," and its suppliers (including Microsoft and Intel) were free to supply them with microprocessors and the MS-DOS operating system. IBM was remarkably successful at setting the standard, but failed to appropriate much value because it retained no significant proprietary interest in the standard—it was Intel and Microsoft that owned the key intellectual property. For Apple, the situation was the reverse. It kept tight control over its Macintosh operating system and product architecture, it earned high margins, but it forfeited the opportunity to set the industry standard.

The tradeoff between market acceptance of a technology and appropriating the returns to a technology is shown in Figure 9.5. Realizing the lessons of these two epic contests, the owners of technical standards have forfeited more and more value to complementors, competitors, and customers in order to establish market leadership. In the browser war of 1995–1998, both Netscape (Navigator) and Microsoft (Explorer) ended up giving away their products.

Companies are now seeking ways to reconcile market acceptance with value appropriation. Adobe gives away its Acrobat Reader to broaden the user base, but charges for the software needed to create PDF documents.

FIGURE 9.5 Standard wars of the 1970s and 1980s: Video cassette recorders and personal computers

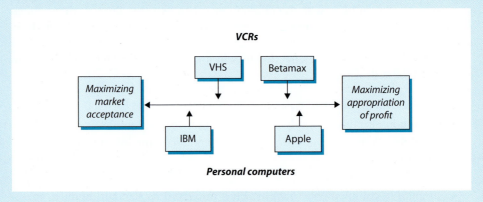

As companies become more familiar with the dynamics of standards competition, they are launching their strategic initiatives earlier, long before product release dates. As a result, standards wars are increasingly about the management of expectations. Companies are also more alert to the emergence of tipping points. As a result, standards wars are being resolved quicker: in high definition DVDs a mere 19 months elapsed between Toshiba's launch of its HD-DVD and its withdrawal from the market.

Implementing Technology Strategies: Creating the Conditions for Innovation

As we have noted previously, strategy formulation cannot be separated from its implementation. Nowhere is this more evident than in technology-intensive businesses.

Our analysis so far has taught us about the potential for generating competitive advantage from innovation and about the design of technology-based strategies but has said little about the conditions under which innovation is achieved. Incisive strategic analysis of how to make money out of innovation is of little use if we cannot generate innovation in the first place. We know that innovation requires certain resources—people, facilities, information, and time—but, like other capabilities, there is no predetermined relationship between R & D input and innovation output.[27] The productivity of R & D depends critically on the organizational conditions that foster innovation. What are these conditions and how do we create them?

Let's begin with the critical distinction between invention and innovation. While these activities are complementary, they require different resources and different organizational conditions. While invention depends on creativity, innovation requires collaboration and cross-functional integration.

Managing Creativity

The Conditions for Creativity   Invention is an act of creativity requiring knowledge and imagination. The creativity that drives invention is typically an individual act that establishes a meaningful relationship between concepts or objects that had not previously been related. This reconceptualization can be triggered by accidents: an apple falling on Isaac Newton's head or James Watt observing a kettle boiling. Creativity is associated with particular personality traits. Creative people tend to be curious, imaginative, adventurous, assertive, playful, self-confident, risk taking, reflective, and uninhibited.[28]

Individual creativity also depends on the organizational environment in which they work—this is as true for the researchers and engineers at Amgen and Google as it was for the painters and sculptors of the Florentine and Venetian schools. Few great works of art or outstanding inventions are the products of solitary geniuses. Creativity is stimulated by human interaction: the productivity of R & D laboratories depends critically on the communication networks that the engineers and scientists establish.[29] An important catalyst of interaction is *play*, which creates an environment of inquiry, liberates thought from conventional constraints, and provides the opportunity to establish new relationships by rearranging ideas and structures at a safe distance from reality. The essence of play is that it permits unconstrained forms of experimentation.[30] The potential for low-cost experimentation has expanded vastly thanks to advances in computer modeling and simulation that permit prototyping and market research to be undertaken speedily and virtually.[31]

Organizing for Creativity   Creativity requires management systems that are quite different from those that are appropriate for efficiency. In particular, creatively oriented people tend to be responsive to distinctive types of incentive. They desire to work in an egalitarian culture with enough space and resources to provide the opportunity to be spontaneous, experience freedom, and have fun in the performance of a task that, they feel, makes a difference to the strategic performance of the firm. Praise, recognition, and opportunities for education and professional growth are also more important than assuming managerial responsibilities.[32] Nurturing the drive to create may require a degree of freedom and flexibility that conflicts with conventional HR practices. At Google engineers have considerable discretion as to which project they join.

Organizational environments conducive to creativity tend to be both nurturing and competitive. Creativity requires a work context that is secure but not cozy. Dorothy Leonard points to the merits of *creative abrasion* within innovative teams— fostering innovation through the interaction of different personalities and perspectives. Managers must resist the temptation to clone in favor of embracing diversity of cognitive and behavioral characteristics within work groups—creating *whole brain teams*.[33] Exploiting diversity may require constructive conflict. Microsoft's development team meetings are renowned for open criticism and intense disagreement. Such conflict can spur progress toward better solutions.

Table 9.5 contrasts some characteristics of innovative organizations compared with those designed for operational efficiency.

From Invention to Innovation: The Challenge of Integration

Balancing Creativity and Commercial Direction   For creativity to create value, both for the company and for society, it must be directed and harnessed. Balancing creative freedom with discipline and integration is a key issue to companies such as Apple and Google, which position themselves on the leading edge of innovation. The problem is especially acute in media companies: "The two cultures—of the ponytail and the suit—are a world apart, and combustible together."[34] Many creative companies have been formed by frustrated innovators leaving established companies. Disney's 2006 acquisition of Pixar was motivated by its desire to reinvigorate its animated movies. Yet Pixar's John Lasseter, who was appointed creative head of Disney's animation studio had been fired from Disney 20 years earlier for his advocacy of computer animation![35] Conversely, HBO's remarkable run of successful TV series between 1999 and 2007 (*The Sopranos, Sex in the City, The Wire, Six Feet*

TABLE 9.5 The characteristics of "operating" and "innovating" organizations

	Operating organization	Innovating organization
Structure	Bureaucratic Specialization and division of labor Hierarchical control Defined organizational boundaries	Flat organization without hierarchical control Task-oriented project teams Fuzzy organizational boundaries
Processes	Emphasis on eliminating variation (e.g., six-sigma) Top-down control Tight financial controls	Emphasis on enhancing variation Loose controls to foster idea generation Flexible strategic planning and financial control
Reward systems	Financial compensation Promotion up the hierarchy Power and status symbols	Autonomy Recognition Equity participation in new ventures
People	Recruitment and selection based on the needs of the organization structure for specific skills: functional and staff specialists, general managers, and operatives	Key need is for idea generators who combine required technical knowledge with creative personality traits Managers must act as sponsors and orchestrators.

Source: Adapted from J. K. Galbraith and R. K. Kazanjian, *Strategy Implementation: Structure, Systems and Processes,* 2nd edn (St. Paul, MN: West, 1986).

Under, Empire Boardwalk—to mention just a few) reveals a remarkable ability to mesh creativity with commercial acuity.

Creative flair can lead to commercial success if it is focused upon *market need*. Few important inventions have been the result of spontaneous creation by technologists; almost all have resulted from grappling with practical problems. The invention of the Xerox copying process (xerography) by Chester Carlson, a patent attorney, was inspired by his frustration with the tedious task of making multiple copies of patent applications for submission to the US Patent Office. The old adage that "necessity is the mother of invention" explains why customers are such fertile sources of innovation—they are most acutely involved with matching existing products and services to their needs.[36] Involving customers in the innovation process is an initial stage in the move toward *open innovation* (which I will say more about below).

Organizational Approaches to the Management of Innovation   Reconciling creativity with commercial effectiveness is a major challenge for organizational design—as Table 9.5 shows, the organizational requirements of the two are very different. The organizational solution (as we explored in Chapter 6) comes from reconciling *differentiation* and *integration*. The creative and operational functions of the organization need different structures and systems. Yet, the key to successful innovation is in integrating creativity and technological expertise with capabilities in production, marketing, finance, distribution, and customer support. Achieving such integration is difficult. Tension between the operating and the innovating parts of organizations is inevitable. Innovation upsets established routines and threatens the status quo. The more stable the operating and administrative side of the organization, the greater the resistance to innovation. The opposition of the US naval establishment to continuous-aim firing, an innovation offering huge improvements in gunnery accuracy, illuminates this resistance to innovation.[37]

As innovation has become an increasing priority for established corporations, so chief executives have sought to emulate the flexibility, creativity, and entrepreneurial spirit of technology-based start-ups. Organizational initiatives aimed at stimulating new product development and the exploitation of new technologies include the following:

- *Cross-functional product development teams*: These have proven highly effective mechanisms for integrating creativity with functional effectiveness. Conventional approaches to new product development involved a sequential process that began in the corporate research lab then went "over the wall" to engineering, manufacturing, finance, and so on. Japanese companies pioneered autonomous product development teams staffed by specialists seconded from different departments with leadership from a "heavyweight" team manager who was able to protect the team from undue corporate influence.[38] Such teams have proven effective in deploying a broad range of specialist knowledge and, most importantly, integrating that knowledge flexibility and quickly, for example through rapid prototyping and concurrent engineering.[39]

- *Product champions*: These provide a means, first, for incorporating individual creativity within organizational processes and, second, for linking invention to subsequent commercialization. The key is to permit the individuals who are sources of creative ideas to lead the teams which develop those ideas—but also to allow this leadership to continue through into the commercialization phases. Companies that are consistently successful in innovation have the ability to design organizational processes that capture, direct, and exploit individuals' drive for achievement and success and their commitment to their innovations. The rationale for creating product champions is that these committed individuals can overcome resistance to change within the organization and generate the enthusiasm that attracts the involvement of others and forges cross-functional integration. Schön's study of 15 major innovations concludes that: "the new idea either finds a champion or dies."[40] A British study of 43 matched pairs of successful and unsuccessful innovations similarly concluded that a key factor distinguishing successful innovation was the presence of a "business innovator" to exert entrepreneurial leadership.[41] 3M Corporation has a long tradition of using product champions to develop new product ideas and grow them into new businesses (Strategy Capsule 9.4).

- *Buying innovation*: Recognition that small, technology-intensive start-ups have advantages in the early stages of the innovation process, while large corporations have superior capabilities, has encouraged large companies to enhance their technological performance by acquiring innovation from other firms. Such acquisition may involve licensing, outright purchase of patents, or acquiring the whole company. In biotechnology, pharmaceutical companies have pioneered this outsourcing of innovation. In addition to licensing drug patents, signing marketing agreements, and acquiring specialist biotech firms (these include Genentech by Roche in 2009, ICOS by Eli Lily in 2007, Chiron by Novartis in 2006, Scious by Johnson & Johnson in 2003), pharmaceutical companies have formed research alliances with biotech specialists.[42] In telecom equipment, Cisco Systems built its leading position in internet protocol switching technologies through acquiring small technology-intensive firms—55 of them between 1993 and 2000 alone.[43]

- *Open innovation*: The shift from vertically integrated systems of innovation, where companies develop their own technologies in-house and then exploit them internally, to more market-based systems, where companies buy in technology while also licensing out their own technologies, has given way to ideas of **open innovation**. As innovation increasingly requires the integration of multiple technologies often from traditionally separate scientific areas, so firms have been forced to look more widely in their sourcing technology and in sharing know-how. Evidence that external linkages promote innovation has reinforced firms' desire to seek technological knowledge from beyond their own borders.[44] Open innovation requires creating a network of collaborative relationships that comprises licensing deals, component outsourcing, joint research, collaborative product development, and informal problem solving and exchanges of ideas. Strategy Capsule 9.5 outlines Procter & Gamble's approach to open innovation.

- *Corporate incubators*: These are business developments established to fund and nurture new businesses based upon technologies that have been developed internally but have limited applications within a company's established businesses. Corporate incubators became very popular during the IT boom at the end of the 1990s, when companies saw the potential to generate substantial value from establishing then spinning off new tech-based ventures.[45] Despite a sound strategic and organizational logic, few major companies have achieved sustained success from the incubator units that they established and among the successful ones many have been sold to venture capital firms. A key problem, according to Hamel and Prahalad, is that: "Many corporate incubators became orphanages for unloved ideas that had no internal support or in-house sponsorship."[46] Despite their uneven track record, several leading companies have experienced considerable success in introducing company-wide processes for developing new businesses based upon internally generated innovations. Strategy Capsule 9.6 outlines the approaches of IBM and Cisco Systems.

STRATEGY CAPSULE 9.4
Innovation at 3M: The Role of the Product Champion

START LITTLE AND BUILD

We don't look to the president or the vice-president for R & D to say, all right, on Monday morning 3M is going to get into such-and-such a business. Rather, we prefer to see someone in one of our laboratories, or marketing, or manufacturing units bring forward a new idea that he's been thinking about. Then, when he can convince people around him, including his supervisor, that he's got something interesting, we'll make him what we call a "project manager" with a small budget of money and talent, and let him run with it. Throughout all our 60 years of history here, that has been the mark of success. Did you develop a new business? The incentive? Money, of course. But that's not the key. The key . . . is becoming the general manager of a new business . . . having such a hot project that management just has to become involved whether it wants to or not. (Bob Adams, Vice-President for R & D, 3M Corporation)

SCOTCHLITE

Someone asked the question, "Why didn't 3M make glass beads, because glass beads were going to find increasing use on the highways?" . . . I had done a little working in the mineral department on trying to color glass beads and had learned a little about their reflecting properties. And, as a little extra-curricular activity, I'd been trying to make luminous house numbers.

Well, this question and my free-time lab project combined to stimulate me to search out where glass beads were being used on the highway. We found a place where beads had been sprinkled on the highway and we saw that they did provide a more visible line at night . . . From there, it was only natural for us to conclude that, since we were a coating company, and probably knew more than anyone else about putting particles onto a web, we ought to be able to coat glass beads very accurately on a piece of paper.

So, that's what we did. The first reflective tape we made was simply a double-coated tape—glass beads sprinkled on one side and an adhesive on the other. We took some out here in St. Paul and, with the cooperation of the highway department, put some down. After the first frost came, and then a thaw, we found we didn't know as much about adhesives under all weather conditions as we thought . . .

We looked around inside the company for skills in related areas. We tapped knowledge that existed in our sandpaper business on how to make waterproof sandpaper. We drew on the expertise of our roofing people who knew something about exposure. We reached into our adhesive and tape division to see how we could make the tape stick to the highway better.

The resulting product became known as "Scotchlite." Its principal application was in reflective signs; only later did 3M develop the market for highway marking. The originator of the product, Harry Heltzer, interested the head of the New Products Division in the product, and he encouraged Heltzer to go out and sell it. Scotchlite was a success and Heltzer became the general manager of the division set up to produce and market it.

Source: "The Technical Strategy of 3M: Start More Little Businesses and More Little Businesses," *Innovation* 5 (1969).

STRATEGY CAPSULE 9.5
Procter & Gamble's Open Innovation Initiative

In 2000, it became clear that P&G's internally focused approach to innovation and new product development was incapable of delivering the growth targets that the company had set itself. Despite a research staff numbering 7500, P&G estimated that for every one of its own research scientists there were probably 200 outside the company with the potential to contribute to P&G's development efforts. When CEO A. G. Lafley challenged the company to obtain 50% of its innovations from outside the company, the quest for a new innovation model began.

P&G's *Connect and Develop* innovation model seeks to "identify promising ideas throughout the world and apply our own R & D, manufacturing, marketing and purchasing capabilities to them to create better and cheaper products, faster."

The starting point is to identify what P&G is looking for. The approach was to avoid "blue sky" innovation and seek ideas that had already been successfully embodied in a product, a prototype or a technology. To focus the search each business was asked to identify its top ten customer needs. These included: "reduce wrinkles, improve skin texture and tone. . .softer paper products with higher wet strength." These needs were then translated into specific technical requirements: for example biotechnology solutions that permit detergents to perform well at low temperatures. Priorities are then reordered by identifying initiatives which fit with existing areas of brand strength ("adjacencies") and those which have permitted strengthening of P&G's strategically important areas of technology ("technology game boards").

P&G's innovation network comprises a number of organizations:

♦ Within P&G, 70 *technology entrepreneurs* are responsible for developing external contacts and exploring

for innovation in particular localities and with a focus around particular product or technology areas.

♦ *Suppliers*. P&G has an IT platform that allows it to share technology briefs with its suppliers. This is complemented by regular meetings between senior P&G executives and senior executives at individual suppliers which explore mutual development opportunities.

♦ *Technology brokers*. P&G is a member (in some cases a founder member) of several prominent technology brokering networks. These include *NineSigma* which links companies with universities, private labs, government bodies, consultants and other potential solutions providers; *Innocentive*, which brokers solutions to science-based problems; *YourEncore*, a network of retired scientists and engineers; and Yet2.com, an online marketplace for intellectual capital.

These networks generate an enormous flow of suggestions and proposals that are initially screened and disseminated through P&G's *Eureka* online catalog. It is then up to executives within the business groups to identify interesting proposals, to pursue these with the external provider through P&G's External Business Development group, and to then move the initiative into their own product development process.

By 2005, 35% of P&G's new product launches had their origins outside the company. Some of P&G's most successful new products—including Swiffer cleaning cloths, Olay Regeneration, and Crest Spinbrush—had been initiated by outsiders.

Source: Reprinted by permission of Harvard Business Review. From "Connect and Develop: Inside Procter & Gamble's New Model for Innovation," L. Huston and N. Sakkab, March 2006, pp. 58–66, Copyright © 2006 by the Harvard Business School Publishing Corporation; all rights reserved.

STRATEGY CAPSULE 9.6
Incubating Innovation at IBM and Cisco Systems

IBM uses *Innovation Jam*—a massive online brainstorming process—to generate, select, and develop new business ideas. The 2006 Jam was based upon an initial identification of 25 technology clusters grouped into six broad categories. Web sites were built for each technology cluster and, for a 72-hour period, IBM employees, their families and friends, and suppliers and customers from all around the world were invited to contribute ideas for innovations based on these technologies. The 150,000 participants generated vast and diverse sets of suggestions that were subject to text mining software and review by 50 senior executives and technical specialists who worked in nine separate teams to identify promising ideas. The next phase of the Jam subjected the selected innovation ideas to comments and review by the online community. This was followed by a further review process in which the 10 best proposals were selected and a budget of $100 million was allocated to their development. The selected business ideas included a real-time foreign language translation service, smart healthcare payment systems, IT applications to environmental projects, and 3-D internet. The new businesses were begun as incubator projects and were then transferred to one or other of IBM's business groups. As well as divisional links, the new ventures were also subject to monthly review by IBM's corporate top management.

Cisco Systems created its *Emerging Technology Business Group* with the goal of creating 20 new ventures by 2012. Within 18 months, 400 ideas for new businesses had been posted on the Cisco wiki and the Emerging Technology Business Group had begun developing several of these suggestions, including *TelePresence*, a video surveillance security system and an IP interoperability and collaboration systems server for emergency services. By 2008, *TelePresence* was established as a regular business group. Like IBM's *Innovation Jam* a key feature of Cisco's incubator model is its close linkage with the rest of the company: the Emerging Technology Group is part of Cisco's R & D organization and is subject to close involvement by Cisco's senior management, including CEO John Chambers.

Sources: O. M. Bjelland and R. C. Wood, "An Inside View of IBM's Innovation Jam," *MIT Sloan Management Review* (Fall 2008): 32–43; T. Sanders, "Cisco Reinvents the Corporate Incubator," (July 27, 2007): http://www.vnunet.com/vnunet/news/2194961/cisco-reinvents-corporate, accessed 6 July, 2009.

Summary

In emerging and technology-based industries, nurturing and exploiting innovation is the fundamental source of competitive advantage and the focus of strategy formulation. Yet the basic tools of strategy analysis are the same as those that we have already encountered in this book. The fundamental strategic issues we are concerned with include the drivers of competition in these markets, the resources and capabilities through which a firm can establish competitive advantage, and the design of structures and systems to implement strategy.

Yet, the unpredictability and instability of these industries mean that strategic decisions in technology-driven industries have a very special character. The remarkable dynamics of these industries mean that difference between massive value creation and ignominious failure may be the result of small errors of timing or technological choices.

In technology-based industries, traditional approaches to strategy based upon forecasting and detailed planning are inadequate. The combination of speed and unpredictability of change means that effective strategies are those which combine clarity of vision with flexibility and responsiveness. The companies that have succeeded in emerging and technology-based industries are those that recognized most clearly the strategic characteristics of their industries and adapted most effectively to them. In industries that have been turned upside-down by technological change—whether telecommunications equipment, medical imaging, information storage, or sports equipment—it is companies that have understood the sources of competitive advantage and assembled the resources and capabilities needed to exploit them that have emerged as winners.

Our learning about how to compete in emerging and technology-based industries has included:

◆ understanding the innovation process, in particular the progression from knowledge creation to invention to innovation to diffusion, and some of the characteristics of these different stages;

◆ the determinants of the profitability of innovation, in particular the role of intellectual-property rights, the complexity and tacitness of the innovation, lead time, and complementary resources;

◆ the design of innovation strategies, including the choice between being an early mover or a follower; the relative merits of licensing, alliances, joint ventures, and internal development exploiting an innovation; and the management of risk;

◆ competing for standards requires recognizing the presence of network externalities and exploiting positive feedback mechanisms to gain market leadership; and the management of identifying the factors that determine the comparative advantages of being a leader or a follower in innovation.

Finally, we addressed strategy implementation in emerging and technology-based industries—creating the structure, management systems, and organizational climate conducive to innovation. Here we recognized some of the challenges of reconciling the conditions for creativity with those required for operational efficiency and commercial effectiveness.

Such dilemmas are central challenges for the managers of technology-intensive firms. A fundamental dilemma is that innovation is an unpredictable process requiring flexibility and market responsiveness, while strategy is about irreversible resource-allocation decisions involving long-term commitments. How can a company create the conditions for nurturing innovation while planning the course of its development? John Scully, a former CEO of Apple, observed: "Management and creativity might even be considered antithetical states. While management demands consensus, control, certainty, and the status quo, creativity thrives on the opposite: instinct, uncertainty, freedom, and iconoclasm."[47]

Fortunately, the experiences of companies such as Cisco Systems, 3M, Amgen, and IBM point to solutions to these dilemmas. The role of cross-functional development teams, product champions, and open innovation are examples of organizational initiatives that have assisted large, established firms in maintaining impressive records of innovation.

Quizzes and flashcards to test yourself further are available in your interactive e-book at **www.wileyopenpage.com**

Self-Study Questions

1. Trevor Baylis, a British inventor, submitted a patent application in November 1992 for a wind-up radio for use in Africa in areas where there was no electricity supply and people were too poor to afford batteries. He was excited by the prospects for radio broadcasts as a means of disseminating health education in areas of Africa devastated by AIDS. After appearances on British and South African TV, Baylis attracted a number of entrepreneurs and companies interested in manufacturing and marketing his clockwork radio. However, Baylis was concerned by the fact that his patent provided only limited protection for his invention: most of the main components—a clockwork generator and transistor radio— were long-established technologies. What advice would you offer Baylis as to how he can best protect and exploit his invention?

2. Table 9.1 shows that:

    a. patents have been more effective in protecting product innovations in drugs and medical equipment than in food or electronic components;

    b. patents are more effective in protecting product innovations than process innovations.

    Can you suggest reasons why?

3. Page 255 refers to James Dyson's difficulties in licensing his innovative vacuum cleaner (see http://www.cdf.org/issue_journal/dyson_fills_a_vacuum.html for further information). What lessons would you draw from Dyson's experience concerning the use of licensing by small firms to exploit innovation?

4. From the evidence presented in Table 9.3, what conclusions can you draw regarding the factors that determine whether leaders or followers win out in the markets for new products?

5. In the battle for dominance of the e-book reader market, Amazon with Kindle 2 was ahead of Sony with its Reader Digital Book. Kindle 2 had the biggest number of recent titles available, but thanks to a deal with Google, Sony had a huge number of out-of-copyright titles. What are the sources of network externalities in this market? Will e-book readers become a winner-takes-all market? Why has Amazon been able to gain a lead over Sony (and Samsung)? What can Sony do to fight back?

Notes

1. "The Logic that Dares Not Speak Its Name," *Economist* (April 16, 1994): 89–91.

2. In the US, the return on R & D spending was estimated at between 3.7% and 5.5%. See M. Warusawitharana, "Research and Development, Profits and Firm Value: A Structural Estimation," Discussion Paper (Washington, DC: Federal Reserve Board, September, 2008).

3. The excess of the benefit received by the consumer over the price they paid is called *consumer surplus*. See: D. Besanko, D. Dranove, and M. Shanley, *Economics*

of Strategy (New York: John Wiley & Sons, Inc., 1996): 442–3.

4. "Knowledge Monopolies: Patent Wars," *Economist* (April 8, 2000): 95–9; "Amazon Loses 1-Click Patent," *Forbes* (July 7, 2011).

5. F. T. Rothermael, "Incumbent Advantage through Exploiting Complementary Assets via Interfirm Cooperation," *Strategic Management Journal* 22 (2001): 687–99.

6. R. C. Levin, A. K. Klevorick, R. R. Nelson, and S. G. Winter, "Appropriating the Returns from Industrial Research and Development," *Brookings Papers on Economic Activity* 18, no. 3 (1987): 783–832.

7. P. Grindley and D. J. Teece, "Managing Intellectual Capital: Licensing and Cross-Licensing in Semiconductors and Electronics," *California Management Review* 39 (Winter 1997): 8–41.

8. R. Adner, "Match your Innovation Strategy to your Innovation Ecosystem," *Harvard Business Review* (April 2006): 17–37.

9. S. Shulman, *The Telephone Gambit* (New York: Norton, 2008).

10. "The Human Genome Race," *Scientific American* (April 24, 2000).

11. C. Markides and P. A. Geroski, *Fast Second* (San Francisco: Jossey-Bass, 2005).

12. D. Sull, "Strategy as Active Waiting," *Harvard Business Review* (September 2005): 120–129.

13. For example, data on penetration rates for electric toothbrushes and CD players were used to forecast the market demand for HDTVs in the United States (B. L. Bayus, "High-Definition Television: Assessing Demand Forecasts for the Next Generation Consumer Durable," *Management Science* 39 (1993): 1319–333).

14. See B. C. Twiss, *Managing Technological Innovation*, 2nd edn (New York: Longman, 1980).

15. E. Von Hippel, "Lead Users: A Source of Novel Product Concepts," *Management Science* 32 (July, 1986).

16. In electronic instruments, customers' ideas initiated most of the successful new products introduced by manufacturers. See E. Von Hippel, "Users as Innovators," *Technology Review* 5 (1976): 212–239.

17. A. Friedlander, *The Growth of Railroads* (Arlington, VA: CNRI, 1995).

18. C. Shapiro and H. R. Varian, *Information Rules: A Strategic Guide to the Network Economy* (Boston: Harvard Business School Press, 1999): 264–7.

19. S. Postrel, "Competing Networks and Proprietary Standards: The Case of Quadraphonic Sound," *Journal of Industrial Economics* 24 (December 1990): 169–86.

20. S. J. Liebowitz and S. E. Margolis ("Network Externality: An Uncommon Tragedy," *Journal of Economic Perspectives* 8 (Spring 1994): 133–50) refer to these user-to-user externalities as *direct externalities*.

21. M. Gladwell, *The Tipping Point* (Boston: Little, Brown and Company, 2000).

22. P. David, "Clio and the Economics of QWERTY," *American Economic Review* 75 (May 1985): 332–7; S. J. Gould, "The Panda's Thumb of Technology," *Natural History* 96, no. 1 (1986): 14–23. For an alternative view

see S. J. Liebowitz and S. Margolis, "The Fable of the Keys," *Journal of Law and Economics* 33 (1990): 1–26.

23. C. Shapiro and H. R. Varian, "The Art of Standards Wars," *California Management Review* 41 (Winter 1999): 8–32.

24. R. M. Grant "The DVD War of 2006–8: Blu-Ray vs. HD-DVD," *Cases to Accompany Contemporary Strategy Analysis*, 7th edn (Chichester: John Wiley & Sons, Ltd, 2010).

25. C. Shapiro and H. R. Varian, "The Art of Standards Wars," *California Management Review* 41 (Winter 1999): 15–16.

26. C. Shapiro and H. R. Varian, "The Art of Standards Wars," *California Management Review* 41 (Winter 1999): 16–18.

27. S. Ahn, "Firm Dynamics and Productivity Growth: A Review of Micro Evidence from OECD Countries," Economics Department Working Paper 297 (OECD, 2001).

28. J. M. George, "Creativity in Organizations," *Academy of Management Annals* 1 (2007): 439–77.

29. M. L. Tushman, "Managing Communication Networks in R & D Laboratories," *Sloan Management Review* 20 (Winter 1979): 37–49.

30. D. Dougherty and C. H. Takacs, "Team Play: Heedful Interrelating as the Boundary for Innovation," *Long Range Planning* 37 (December 2004): 569–90.

31. S. Thomke, "Enlightened Experimentation: The New Imperative for Innovation," *Harvard Business Review* (February 2001): 66–75. L. Grundy, J. Kickel, and C. Prather, "Building the Creative Organization," *Organizational Dynamics* (Spring 1994): 22–37.

32. R. Florida and J. Goodnight, "Managing for Creativity," *Harvard Business Review* (July/August 2005): 124–31.

33. D. Leonard and S. Straus, "Putting Your Company's Whole Brain to Work," *Harvard Business Review* (July/August 1997): 111–21; D. Leonard and P. Swap, *When Sparks Fly: Igniting Creativity in Groups* (Boston: Harvard Business School Press, 1999).

34. "How to Manage a Dream Factory," *Economist* (January 16, 2003).

35. "Lunch with the FT: John Lasseter," *Financial Times* (January 17, 2009).

36. E. Von Hippel (*The Sources of Innovation*, New York: Oxford University Press, 1988) provides strong evidence of the dominant role of users in the innovation process.

37. E. Morrison, "Gunfire at Sea: A Case Study of Innovation," in M. Tushman and W. L. Moore (eds), *Readings in the Management of Innovation* (Cambridge, MA: Ballinger, 1988): 165–78.

38. K. Clark and T. Fujimoto, *Product Development Performance: Strategy, Organization, and Management in the World Auto Industry* (Boston: Harvard Business School Press, 1991).

39. K. Imai, I. Nonaka, and H. Takeuchi, "Managing the New Product Development Process: How Japanese Companies Learn and Unlearn," in K. Clark, R. Hayes, and C. Lorenz (eds), *The Uneasy Alliance* (Boston: Harvard Business School Press, 1985).

40. D. A. Schön, "Champions for Radical New Inventions," *Harvard Business Review* (March/April, 1963): 84.

41. R. Rothwell, C. Freeman, A. Horlsey, V. T. Jervis, A. B. Robertson, and J. Townsend, "SAPPHO Updated: Project SAPPHO Phase II," *Research Policy* 3 (1974): 258–91.

42. G. P. Pisano, *Science Business: The Promise, the Reality, and the Future of Biotech* (Boston: Harvard Business School Press, 2006).

43. "Cisco's Chambers: The Route Ahead," ICFASI Case Study No. 306-172-1 (Chennai, 2006).

44. A. Arora, A. Fosfur, and A. Gambardella, *Markets for Technology* (Cambridge, MA: MIT Press, 2001); S. Breschi and F. Malerba, *Clusters, Networks and Innovation* (Oxford: Oxford University Press, 2005).

45. M. T. Hansen, H. W. Chesborough, N. Nohria and D. N. Sull, "Networked Incubators: Hothouse of the New Economy," *Harvard Business Review* (September/October 2000): 74–88; "How to Make the Most of a Brilliant Idea," *Financial Times* (December 6, 2000): 21.

46. G. Hamel and C. K. Prahalad, "Nurturing Creativity: Putting Passions to Work," *Shell World* (Royal Dutch Shell, September 14, 2007): 1–12.

47. J. Scully, *Odyssey* (Toronto: Fitzhenry and Whiteside, 1987): 18.

10 Competitive Advantage in Mature Industries

We are a true "penny profit" business. That means that it takes hard work and attention to detail to be financially successful—it is far from being a sure thing. Our store managers must do two things well: control costs and increase sales. Cost control cannot be done by compromising product quality, customer service, or restaurant cleanliness, but rather by consistent monitoring of the "vital signs" of the business through observation, reports, and analysis. Portion control is a critical part of our business. For example, each Filet-O-Fish sandwich receives 1 fluid ounce of tartar sauce and 0.5 ounces of cheese. Our raw materials are fabricated to exacting tolerances, and our managers check them on an ongoing basis. Our written specification for lettuce is over two typewritten pages long. Our French fries must meet standards for potato type, solid and moisture content, and distribution of strand lengths.

—EDWARD H. RENSI, PRESIDENT AND CHIEF OPERATING OFFICER, MCDONALD'S USA[1]

OUTLINE

- **Introduction and Objectives**
- **Competitive Advantage in Mature Industries**
  - Cost Advantage
  - Segment and Customer Selection
  - The Quest for Differentiation
  - Innovation
- **Strategy Implementation in Mature Industries: Structure, Systems, and Style**
  - Efficiency through Bureaucracy

- Trends in Strategy Implementation among Mature Businesses
- **Strategies for Declining Industries**
  - Adjusting Capacity to Declining Demand
  - Strategy Alternatives for Declining Industries
- **Summary**
- **Self-Study Questions**
- **Notes**

Introduction and Objectives

Despite the infatuation of both the media and the stock market with technology-based companies such as Google, Facebook, and Twitter, the fact remains that companies where most of us earn our living and spend most of our income are comparatively mature. The leading members of the Fortune Global 500 all belong to industries that have been with us for over a hundred years: petroleum, retailing, automobiles, financial services.

Despite their heterogeneity—they range from beauty parlors to steel production—mature industries present several similarities from a strategic perspective. The purpose of this chapter is to explore these characteristics of mature industries, identify strategies through which competitive advantage can be established within them, and recognize the implications of these strategies for structure, systems, and leadership style. As we shall see, maturity does not imply lack of opportunity. Companies such as H&M (fashion clothing), AirAsia (airlines), Starbucks (coffee shops), and Nucor (steel) have successfully deployed novel strategies in mature sectors. Mature sectors are typically inhabited by mature companies—Coca-Cola, ExxonMobil, and HSBC Holdings were founded in the 19th century, yet, over the past two decades, have achieved combinations of profitability and growth that would make most high-tech companies envious. Nor does maturity mean lack of innovation: as we shall see, many mature industries have been transformed by new technologies and new strategies.

By the time you have completed this chapter, you will be able to:

◆ recognize the principal strategic characteristics of mature industries;

◆ identify key success factors within mature industries and formulate strategies directed toward their exploitation;

◆ design organizational structures and management systems that can effectively implement such strategies;

◆ recognize the characteristics of declining industries, the opportunities for profit they may offer, and the strategy options available to firms.

Competitive Advantage in Mature Industries

Our analysis of the industry life cycle (Chapter 8) suggests that maturity has two principal implications for competitive advantage: first, it tends to reduce the number of opportunities for establishing competitive advantage; second, it shifts these opportunities from differentiation-based factors to cost-based factors.

Diminishing opportunities for sustainable competitive advantage in mature industries stem from:

● Less scope for differentiation advantage resulting from better informed buyers, product standardization, and lack of technological change.

- Diffusion of process technology means that cost advantages are difficult to obtain and sustain. Once a cost advantage is established, it is vulnerable to exchange rate movements and the emergence of low-cost overseas competitors.
- A highly developed industry infrastructure together with the presence of powerful distributors makes it easier for new entrants to attack established firms.

Warren Buffett, The Sage of Omaha, uses different words to convey a similar idea. He categorizes businesses into "franchises" and "businesses" and views the process of maturity as one of value destruction in which franchises degenerate into businesses:

> An economic franchise arises from a product or service that (1) is needed or desired; (2) is thought by customers to have no close substitute; and (3) is not subject to price regulation. Franchises earn high rates of return on capital . . . [and] can tolerate mismanagement . . . In contrast, "a business" earns exceptional profits only if it is a low-cost operator or if supply of its product or service is tight. And a business, unlike a franchise, can be killed by poor management.[2]

This trend toward deteriorating industry attractiveness is a constant threat in mature industries. The propensity toward overinvestment in capacity, internationalization, and commoditization exacerbates price competition and makes competitive advantage difficult to attain and even harder to sustain.

Cost Advantage

To the extent that differentiation advantages erode in many mature industries, cost emerges as the key success factor. What are the primary sources of low cost? Three cost drivers tend to be especially important:

- *Economies of scale*: In capital-intensive industries, or where advertising, distribution, or new product development is an important element of total cost, economies of scale are important sources of interfirm cost differences. The increased standardization that accompanies maturity greatly assists the exploitation of such scale economies. In automobiles, as with many other manufacturing industries, industry evolution has been driven by the quest for scale economies. The significance of scale economies in mature industries is indicated by the fact that the association between return on investment and market share is stronger in mature industries than in emerging industries.[3]
- *Low-cost inputs*: The quest for low-cost inputs explains the migration of maturing industries from the advanced to the newly industrializing countries of the world. But accessing low-cost inputs does not necessarily mean establishing operations in India or Vietnam. Established firms can become locked into high salaries and benefits, inefficient working practices, and bloated overheads inherited from more prosperous times. New entrants into mature industries may gain cost advantages by acquiring plant and equipment at bargain-basement levels and by cutting labor costs. Valero Energy Corporation

is the largest oil refiner in the US: it acquired loss-making refineries from the majors at below-book prices then operated them with rigorous cost efficiency. Convenience stores throughout North America and Western Europe are increasingly owned and operated by Asian immigrants. These businesses are typically operated by family members who are willing to work long hours without the usual employee fringe benefits and overtime pay.

- *Low overheads*: Some of the most profitable companies in mature industries are those able to slash overhead costs. In discount retailing, Wal-Mart is famous for its parsimonious approach to costs. Among the oil majors, Exxon is known for its rigorous control of overhead costs. Exxon's headquarters cost (relative to net worth) was estimated at less than one-quarter that of Mobil's.[4] When Exxon merged with Mobil, it was able to extract huge cost savings from Mobil. In newspaper and magazine publishing, newcomers such as EMAP in the UK and Media News Group in the US (run by "Lean" Dean Singleton) have deployed a strategy of acquiring titles then pruning overheads.

As cost inefficiencies tend to become institutionalized within mature enterprises, cost reduction may require drastic interventions. **Corporate restructuring**—intensive periods of structural and strategic change—typically involves cost reduction through outsourcing, headcount reduction, and downsizing, especially at corporate headquarters.[5] Successful turnaround strategies typically involve aggressive cost cutting. Empirical research among mature US businesses has identified three successful approaches:

- *Asset and cost surgery*: Aggressive cost reduction through reduction of excess capacity; halting of new investment in plant and equipment; and cutbacks in R & D, marketing expenditures, receivables, and inventories.
- *Selective product and market pruning*: Refocusing on segments that were most profitable or where the firm possessed distinctive strength.
- *Piecemeal productivity moves*: Adjustments to current market position rather than comprehensive refocusing or reorganizing, including reductions in marketing and R & D expenditures, higher capacity utilization, and increased employee productivity.[6]

Segment and Customer Selection

Sluggish demand growth, lack of product differentiation, and international competition tend to depress the profitability of mature industries. Yet, even unattractive industries may offer attractive niche markets with strong growth of demand, few competitors, and abundant potential for differentiation. As a result, segment selection can be a key determinant of differences in the performance of companies within the same industry. Wal-Mart's profitability was boosted by locating its stores in small and medium-sized towns where it faced little competition. In the auto industry, there is a constant quest to escape competition by creating new market segments with "crossover" vehicles that span existing segments. Opportunities for establishing new segments can arise from the strategies of market leaders. The more that incumbents focus on the mass market, the more likely it is that new entrants can carve out new market niches by supplying underserved customer needs—what Chapter 8 refers to as "resource partitioning."[7]

The logic of segment focus implies further disaggregation of markets—down to the level of the individual customer. Information technology permits new approaches to **customer relationship management** (CRM), making it possible to analyze individual characteristics and preferences, identify individual customers' profit contribution to the firm, and organize marketing around individualized, integrated approaches to customers. In the same way that Las Vegas casinos have long recognized that the major part of their profits derives from a tiny minority of customers—the "high rollers"—so banks, supermarkets, credit card companies, and hotels increasingly use transaction data to identify their most attractive customers, and those that are a drag on profitability.

The next stage in this process is to go beyond customer selection to actively target more attractive customers and transform less valuable customers into more valuable customers. For example, credit card issuer Capital One uses data warehousing, experimentation, simulation, and sophisticated statistical modeling to adjust the terms and features of its credit card offers to the preferences and characteristics of individual customers. Capital One estimates the lifetime profitability of each customer and analyzes the four key events in the credit card life cycle: acquiring the customer, stimulating the customer's card use, retaining the customer, and managing default.[8]

The Quest for Differentiation

Cost leadership, as we noted in Chapter 7, is difficult to sustain, particularly in the face of international competition. Hence, differentiating to attain some insulation from the rigors of price competition is particularly attractive in mature industries. The problem is that the trend toward commoditization narrows the scope for differentiation and reduces customer willingness to pay a premium for differentiation:

- In tires and domestic appliances, companies' investments in differentiation through product innovation, quality, and brand reputation have generated disappointing returns. Vigorous competition, price-sensitive customers, and strong, aggressive retailers have limited the price premium that differentiation will support.

- Attempts by airlines to gain competitive advantage through offering more legroom, providing superior in-flight entertainment, and achieving superior punctuality have met little market response from consumers. The only effective differentiators appear to be frequent-flier programs and services offered to first- and business-class travelers.

Standardization of the physical attributes of a product and convergence of consumer preferences constrains, but does not eliminate, opportunities for meaningful and profitable differentiation. Product standardization is frequently accompanied by increased differentiation of complementary services—financing terms, leasing arrangements, warranties, after-sales services and the like. In consumer goods, maturity often means a shift from physical differentiation to image differentiation. Entrenched consumer loyalties to specific brands of cola or cigarettes are a tribute to the capacity of brand promotion over long periods to create distinct images among near-identical products.

The intensely competitive retail sector produces particularly interesting examples of differentiation strategies. The dismal profitability earned by many retail chains (Toys "R" Us, Foot Locker, Rite Aid, and J.C. Penny in the US; Carrefour, Metro, and Royal Ahold in Europe) contrasts sharply with the sales growth and profitability of stores that have established clear differentiation through variety, style, and ambiance (Target, TJX, Limited Brands, and Costco in the US; Inditex from Spain; H&M and IKEA from Sweden). A further lesson from highly competitive mature sectors such as retailing is that competitive advantage is difficult to sustain. Most of the outstandingly successful retailers of the previous decade—Best Buy, Body Shop, and Marks & Spencer—have slipped into mediocrity.

Innovation

We have characterized mature industries as industries where the pace of technical change is low. In many mature industries—steel, textiles, food processing, insurance, and hotels—R & D expenditure is below 1% of sales revenue, while in US manufacturing as a whole just three sectors—computers and electronics, pharmaceuticals, and aerospace—account for 65% of R & D spending.[9] Nevertheless, measured by patenting activity, there is evidence that some mature industries are as innovative as emerging industries.[10] Even in mature low-tech products such as tires, brassieres, and fishing rods, continuing inventiveness is indicated by a steady flow of new patents (Strategy Capsule 10.1).

Despite an increased pace of technological change in many mature industries, the most opportunities for establishing competitive advantage are likely to arise from *strategic innovation*—including *new game strategies* and *blue-ocean strategies* that we discussed in Chapter 7. Indeed, as identified in Chapter 8, it may be that strategic innovation constitutes a third phase of innovation that becomes prominent once product and process innovation slacken. In addition to the *value chain reconfiguration* approach discussed in Chapter 7,[11] firms can seek strategic innovation by redefining markets and market segments. This may involve:

- *Embracing new customer groups*: Harley-Davidson has created a market for expensive motorcycles among the middle-aged, while in the maturing market for video game consoles Nintendo achieved remarkable success with its Wii by appealing to consumers outside the core market of young males. The most rapidly growing churches—for example Jehovah's Witnesses in Russia and Amway Christian Fellowship in America—tend to be those that recruit among non-church-going social and demographic groups.

- *Augmenting, bundling, and theming*: Some of the most successful approaches to differentiation in mature industries involve bundling additional products or services with the core offering. In book retailing, Barnes & Noble offers not only a wide range of titles but also Starbucks coffee shops within its stores. Neighborhood bookstores that have survived competition from the megastores and Amazon.com are often those that have added poetry readings, live music, and other recreational services. This augmenting and bundling of the product offering may extend to involve the customer

> ## STRATEGY CAPSULE 10.1
> # Innovation in Mature Industries: Brassiere Technology
>
> The first patent for a "breast-supporting device" was issued in the US in 1864. However, the first patent relating to an undergarment named "brassiere" was issued to Mary Phelps Jacob in 1913. By 1940, over 550 US patents for brassieres and related breast supporters had been issued.
>
> The technological quest for a better bra continued into the 21st century—between January 2000 and March 2012, the US Patent Office issued 727 patents relating to brassieres. Design innovations include:
>
> ◆ Wonderbra (owned by Sara Lee) introduced a "variable cleavage" bra equipped with a system of pulleys;
>
> ◆ the Airotic bra designed by Gossard (also owned by Sara Lee) features "twin air bags as standard"—these are inflatable by a "unique G-pump system";
>
> ◆ Charnos's Bioform bra replaces underwiring with soft molded polypropylene around a rigid ring—a design inspired by the Frisbee and engineered by Ove Arup, who also engineered London's Millennium Bridge (which had to be closed because of excessive wobbling);
>
> ◆ A team at University of Wollongong's Intelligent Polymer Research Institute is developing the world's first "smart-bra"—a sports bra that will adjust for breast movement during exercise.
>
> *Source:* "Bra Wars," *Economist* (December 2, 2000): 112; USTPO Patent Database; "The Physics of Bras," *Discover Magazine* (November 2005).

in an entire experience. Theming by retail stores (such as Disney Stores and American Girl) and restaurants (such as Hard Rock Café and Planet Hollywood) reflects the desire to involve customers in an experience that goes beyond the products being sold.[12]

● *Customer solutions*: Another approach to differentiation through bundling products and services is to offer *customer solutions*—an integrated bundle of products and support services that are offered as a customized package. For example, Alstom's rail transport division has transitioned from "being a supplier of goods to a system and service provider": rather than supplying locomotives, rolling stock, and signaling systems as standalone items, it offers "complete transport solutions for train availability during the life cycle of the product."[13] However, as a senior manager from the Italian engineering firm, Bonfiglioli, explained to me (interview, June 2008): "Supplying customer solutions is an appealing strategy, but execution is far from easy. Once we had sales representatives who visited customers carrying a product directory. Now the sales representative has to visit the customer with a team comprising product and maintenance engineers and a financial analyst."

● *Liberation from the maturity mindset*: The ability to create competitive advantage requires managers to free themselves from the cognitive limits associated with notions of maturity. Baden-Fuller and Stopford argue that maturity is a state of mind, not a state of the business—every enterprise has the potential for rejuvenation. The key to strategic innovation is for managers to prevent industry conventions from imprisoning their companies into conventional thinking about strategy. This means cultivating an entrepreneurial organization where middle managers are encouraged to experiment and learn.[14]

Costas Markides identifies several firms that have successfully broken away from conventional wisdom to establish a unique positioning within mature industries:

- Edward Jones, with 2000 offices, mostly in the US but also in Canada and the UK, has rejected the conventional wisdom that successful brokerage firms require scale economies, product diversification, e-commerce, and integration with investment banks. Each Edward Jones' office has just one investment adviser who is motivated to grow local business through face-to-face relationships; there are no proprietary investment products and no online investing.
- Enterprise Rent-A-Car has adopted a location strategy that is quite different from its major competitors, Hertz and Avis. Rather than concentrate on serving the business traveler through locating at airports and downtown, Enterprise concentrates on suburban locations, where it caters primarily to the consumer market.[15]

How do companies break away from the pack and achieve strategic innovation? The problem is that breaking with industry conventions requires confronting industry-wide systems of belief—what J.-C. Spender refers to as *industry recipes*."[16] This is likely to require that managers find ways of altering their *cognitive maps*— the mental frameworks through which they perceive and understand their industry environments.[17] This may explain why strategic innovation in mature industries is so often associated with firms that are either outsiders or peripheral players.

According to Gary Hamel, the role of strategy should be to foster revolution through reorganizing the strategy-making process. This means breaking top management's monopoly over strategy formulation, bringing in younger people from further down the organization, and gaining involvement from those on the periphery of the organization.[18] Ultimately, strategic innovation is likely to require a process of organization-wide change—a "journey of strategic renewal."[19]

Strategy Implementation in Mature Industries: Structure, Systems, and Style

Across most mature industries, the primary basis for competitive advantage is operational efficiency; however, as we have seen, cost efficiency must be reconciled with innovation and customer responsiveness. What kinds of organizational structures, management systems, and leadership styles do mature businesses need to adopt in order to achieve these multiple performance goals?

Efficiency through Bureaucracy

As we observed in Chapter 6, the conventional prescription for stable environments was *mechanistic* organizations characterized by centralization, precisely defined roles, and predominantly vertical communication.[20] Henry Mintzberg describes this formalized type of organization dedicated to the pursuit of efficiency as the *machine bureaucracy*.[21] Efficiency is achieved through standardized routines, division of labor, and close management control based on bureaucratic principles. Division of labor extends to management as well as operatives—high levels of vertical and horizontal specialization are typical among managers. Vertical specialization is evident in the concentration of strategy formulation at the apex of the hierarchy, while middle and junior management supervise and administer through the application of standardized rules and procedures. Horizontal specialization takes the form of functional structures.

The machine bureaucracy as described by Mintzberg is a caricature of actual organizations—probably the closest approximations are found in government departments performing highly routine administrative duties (e.g., the Internal Revenue Service or departments of motor vehicle licensing). However, in most mature industries, the features of mechanistic organizations are evident in highly routinized operations controlled by detailed rules and procedures. McDonald's is far from being a typical bureaucracy—in particular, the majority of outlets are franchises operated by independent companies—however, the cost efficiency and consistency that characterizes its performance is achieved through highly standardized and detailed operating procedures that govern virtually every aspect of how it does business (see the quotation that introduces this chapter). Similarly, in Marriott Hotels, HSBC, Toyota Motor Company, and Wal-Mart the ability of these huge organizations to achieve efficiency and consistent high quality is the result of management systems that draw heavily upon the principles of bureaucracy. The key features of these mature organizations are summarized in Table 10.1.

Trends in Strategy Implementation among Mature Businesses

When competitive advantage in mature industries was all about cost advantage through scale and division of labor, management practices based upon standardized processes, elaborately defined rules, hierarchical control, quantitative performance targets, and incentives closely linked to individual performance work well. However, as we have discussed, the requirements for success in mature industries and the strategies needed to achieve success given these requirements have become much more complex. In terms of cost efficiency, scale advantages have become less important than the flexibility to exploit low-cost inputs and to outsource to low-cost specialists, and creating an organizational environment that constantly strives to eliminate waste and discover new sources of efficiency.

The efficiency leaders in mature industries are not necessarily the biggest firms that are able to exploit scale benefits to the maximum: they are more likely to be companies that have dedicated themselves to efficiency through implementing performance-oriented management systems. Top-performing companies in mature businesses—UPS in delivery services, Wal-Mart in discount retailing, Nucor in steel, ExxonMobil in petroleum—are characterized by management systems that comprise integrated systems where performance goals are the centerpiece of strategy and

TABLE 10.1 Strategy implementation in mature industries: The conventional model

STRATEGY	The primary goal is cost advantage through economies of scale and capital-intensive production of standardized products/services
	Strategy formulation primarily the realm of top managers
	Middle managers responsible for strategy implementation
STRUCTURE	Functional departments (e.g., production, marketing, customer service, distribution)
	Distinction between line and staff
	Clearly defined job roles with strong vertical reporting/delegation relationships
CONTROLS	Performance targets are primarily quantitative and short term and are specified for all members of the organization
	Performance is closely monitored by well-established, centralized management information systems and formalized reporting requirements
	Financial controls through budgets and profit targets particularly important
INCENTIVES	Incentives are based on achievement of individual targets and take the form of financial rewards and promotion up the hierarchy
	Penalties exist for failure to attain quantitative targets, for failure to adhere to the rules, and for lack of conformity to company norms
COMMUNICATION	Primarily vertical for the purposes of delegation and reporting
	Lateral communication limited, often achieved through interdepartmental committees
LEADERSHIP	Primary functions of top management: control and strategic direction
	Typical CEO profiles include the *administrator*, who guides the organization through establishing and operating organizational systems and principles and building consensus (e.g., Alfred Sloan Jr. of General Motors); the *autocrat*, who uses top-down decision making and leads through centralization of power and force of personality (Lee Iacocca of Chrysler and Steve Jobs at Apple); and the *strategic leader*, who combines clear strategic direction with considerable decentralization of decision making (Sam Palmisano at IBM, Carlos Ghosn at Renault-Nissan, Jeff Immelt at GE).

these goals are implemented through financial controls, HR policies, and operating practices which are closely integrated with these goals.

Unifying an organization around the pursuit of efficiency requires management systems that allow disaggregation of company-wide goals into specific performance targets for departments and individuals—the *balanced scorecard* is one of the most widely used techniques for achieving this (see Chapter 2). Most important, however, is embedding performance goals within the company's organizational culture:

- Central to UPS's performance-driven management style is a corporate culture that simultaneously embraces high levels of employee autonomy and the company's "obsessive-compulsive personality."[22]
- Wal-Mart's culture of frugality reflects the values of founder Sam Walton. According to Wal-Mart executive Ron Loveless: "Sam valued every penny. People say that Wal-Mart is making $10 billion a year, or whatever. But that's

not how people within the company think of it. If you spent a dollar, the question was: 'How many dollars of merchandise would you need to sell to make that dollar?'"[23]

● Ryanair has mastered the art of managing for cost efficiency. From a simple strategic goal of being Europe's lowest-cost airline, Ryanair's route structure, choice of airports, fleet, ticketing system, and HR practices are meticulously aligned to cost minimization. Ryanair's obsession with cost cutting is reflected in the large proportion of employees that are on temporary contracts, the requirement that crews pay for their own uniforms and training, and a heavy emphasis on incentive pay (cabin crew receive a commission on inflight sales).[24]

Reconciling differentiation and innovation with a relentless drive for cost efficiency creates difficult challenges for designing management systems that promote these goals without blunting the imperatives for cost minimization. The conventional model for reconciling efficiency with innovation in mature companies is *internal differentiation*: innovation and entrepreneurship are the responsibility of specialist R & D, new product development, and business development units. However, some established companies in mature industries, including Toyota and Whirlpool, have embraced dispersed innovation, encouraging initiative and ideas from all employees.[25]

Strategies for Declining Industries

The transition from maturity to decline can be a result of technological substitution (typewriters, photographic film), changes in consumer preferences (canned food, men's suits), demographic shifts (children's toys in Europe), or foreign competition (textiles in the advanced industrialized countries). Shrinking market demand gives rise to acute strategic issues. Among the key features of declining industries are:

● excess capacity;
● lack of technical change (reflected in a lack of new product introduction and stability of process technology);
● a declining number of competitors, but some entry as new firms acquire the assets of exiting firms cheaply;
● high average age of both physical and human resources;
● aggressive price competition.

Despite the inhospitable environment offered by declining industries, research by Kathryn Harrigan has uncovered declining industries where at least some participants earned surprisingly high profits. These included electronic vacuum tubes, cigars, and leather tanning. However, elsewhere—notably in prepared baby foods, rayon, and meat processing—decline was accompanied by aggressive price competition, company failures, and instability.[26]

What determines whether or not a declining industry becomes a competitive bloodbath? Two factors are critical: the balance between capacity and output, and the nature of the demand for the product.

Adjusting Capacity to Declining Demand

The smooth adjustment of industry capacity to declining demand is the key to stability and profitability during the decline phase. In industries where capacity exits from the industry in an orderly fashion, decline can occur without trauma. Where substantial excess capacity persists, as has occurred among the oil refineries of America and Europe, in the bakery industry, in coal mining, and in long-haul bus transportation, the potential exists for destructive competition. The ease with which capacity adjusts to declining demand depends on the following factors:

- *The predictability of decline*: If decline can be forecast, it is more likely that firms can plan for it. The decline of traditional photography with the advent of digital imaging was anticipated and planned for. Conversely, the decline in sales of personal computers which began in 2011 was largely unexpected. The more cyclical and volatile the demand, the more difficult it is for firms to perceive the trend of demand, even after the onset of decline.
- *Barriers to exit*: Barriers to exit impede the exit of capacity from an industry. The major barriers are:
  - durable and specialized assets. Just as capital requirements impose a barrier to entry into an industry, those same investments also discourage exit. The longer they last and the fewer the opportunities for using those assets in another industry are, the more companies are tied to that particular industry.
  - costs incurred in plant closure. Apart from the accounting costs of writing off assets, substantial cash costs may be incurred in redundancy payments to employees, compensation for broken contacts with customers and suppliers, decommissioning the plant, and environmental cleanup.
  - managerial commitment. In addition to financial considerations, firms may be reluctant to close plants for a variety of emotional and moral reasons. Resistance to plant closure and divestment arises from pride in company traditions and reputation, managers' unwillingness to accept failure, and loyalties to employees and the local community.
- *The strategies of the surviving firms*: Smooth exit of capacity ultimately depends on the willingness of the industry players to close plants and divest assets. The sooner companies recognize and address the problem, the more likely it is that independent and collective action can achieve capacity reduction. In European gasoline retailing, for example, the problem of excess capacity was partially solved by bilateral exchanges of service stations among the major oil companies. Stronger firms in the industry can facilitate the exit of weaker firms by offering to acquire their plants and take over their after-sales service commitments. A key strategy among private equity firms has been initiating *roll-ups* in declining industries—consolidating multiple acquisitions. Between 1989 and 2010, KKR, a private equity firm, spent over $2 billion acquiring magazine titles and other print media businesses and created Primedia Inc. to manage them.[27]

Strategy Alternatives for Declining Industries

Conventional strategy recommendations for declining industries are either to divest or to harvest (i.e., to generate the maximum cash flow from existing investments without reinvesting). However, these strategies assume that declining industries are inherently unprofitable. If profit potential exists, then other strategies may be attractive. Harrigan and Porter identify four strategies that can profitably be pursued either individually or sequentially in declining industries:[28]

- *Leadership*: By gaining leadership, a firm is well placed to outstay competitors and play a dominant role in the final stages of an industry's life cycle. Once leadership is attained, the firm is in a good position to switch to a harvest strategy and enjoy a strong profit stream from its market position. Establishing leadership can be done by acquiring competitors, but a cheaper way is to encourage competitors to exit (and then acquire their plants). Inducements to competitors to exit may include showing commitment to the industry, helping to lower their exit costs, releasing pessimistic forecasts of the industry's future, and raising the stakes, for example by supporting more stringent environmental controls that make it costly for them to stay in business.

- *Niche*: Identify a segment that is likely to maintain a stable demand and that other firms are unlikely to invade, then pursue a leadership strategy to establish dominance within the segment. The most attractive niches are those that offer the greatest prospects for stability and where demand is most inelastic. In products facing technological obsolescence, established firms have often been successful in cultivating a lucrative high-price, high-quality segment. For example, Richemont has created a very profitable business based upon mechanical watches (Lange & Söhne, Baume et Mercier, Cartier, Piaget, Vacheron Constantin) and luxury fountain pens (Montblanc).

- *Harvest*: By harvesting, a firm maximizes its cash flow from existing assets, while avoiding further investment. A harvesting strategy seeks to boost margins wherever possible through raising prices and cutting costs by rationalizing the number of models, number of channels, and number of customers. Note, however, that a harvest strategy can be difficult to implement. In the face of strong competition, harvesting may accelerate decline, particularly if employee morale is adversely affected by a strategy that offers no long-term future for the business.

- *Divest*: If the future looks bleak, the best strategy may be to divest the business in the early stages of decline before a consensus has developed as to the inevitability of decline. Once industry decline is well established, it may be extremely difficult to find buyers.

Choosing the most appropriate strategy requires a careful assessment both of the profit potential of the industry and the competitive position of the firm. Harrigan and Porter pose four key questions:

- Can the structure of the industry support a hospitable, potentially profitable decline phase?

- What are the exit barriers that each significant competitor faces?
- Do your company strengths fit the remaining pockets of demand?
- What are your competitors' strengths in these pockets? How can their exit barriers be overcome?

Selecting an appropriate strategy requires matching the opportunities remaining in the industry to the company's competitive position. Figure 10.1 shows a simple framework for strategy choice.

FIGURE 10.1   Strategic alternatives for declining industries

		COMPANY'S COMPETITIVE POSITION	
		Strengths in remaining demand pockets	Lacks strength in remaining demand pockets
INDUSTRY STRUCTURE	Favorable to decline	LEADERSHIP or NICHE	HARVEST or DIVEST
	Unfavorable to decline	NICHE or HARVEST	DIVEST QUICKLY

Summary

Mature industries present challenging environments for the formulation and implementation of business strategies. Competition, and price competition in particular, is usually strong, and competitive advantage is often difficult to build and sustain: cost advantages are vulnerable to imitation; differentiation opportunities are limited by the trend to standardization.

Stable positions of competitive advantage in mature industries are traditionally associated with cost advantage from economies of scale or experience, with selecting the most attractive market segments and customers to serve, with creating differentiation advantage, and with pursuing technological and strategic innovation.

Implementing these strategies, especially those associated with rigorous cost efficiency, typically requires management systems based upon standardized processes and relentless performance management. However, as mature industries become increasingly complex and turbulent, so the pursuit of cost efficiency needs to be matched with flexibility, responsiveness, and innovation. Companies such as Wal-Mart, Coca-Cola, McDonald's, Banco Santander, and Toyota show remarkable capacity to reconcile vigorous cost efficiency with adaptability.

Declining industries present special challenges to companies: typically, they are associated with intense competition and low margins. However, such environments also present profitable opportunities for those firms that can orchestrate orderly decline from a position of leadership, establish a niche, or generate cash from harvesting assets.

Quizzes and flashcards to test yourself further are available in your interactive e-book at **www.wileyopenpage.com**

Self-Study Questions

1. Consider Table 3.1 in Chapter 3. Most of the least profitable US industries are mature industries. Yet at the top of the table are tobacco, personal and household products, and food consumer products, all mature industries. What is it about this latter group of industries that has allowed them to escape the intense price competition and low profitability often associated with mature sectors?

2. Established airlines are cutting costs to compete with the increasing number of budget airlines. Yet, it is unlikely that they will ever match the costs of Southwest, Ryanair, or AirAsia. Which, if any, of the strategies outlined in this chapter offers the best opportunity for the established airlines to improve their competitive position vis-à-vis the budget airlines?

3. Department stores (e.g., Federated Department Stores and Mays in the US, Selfridges and House of Fraser in the UK) face increasing competition from specialized chain retailers and discount stores. What innovative strategies might department stores adopt to revitalize their competitiveness?

4. Book retailing is in decline. From the strategy options identified in the section "Strategy Alternatives for Declining Industries," what recommendations would you offer to (a) Barnes & Noble and (b) an independent book retailer located in your vicinity?

Notes

1. E. H. Rensi, "Computers at McDonald's," in J. F. McLimore and L. Larwood (eds), *Strategies, Successes: Senior Executives Speak Out* (New York: Harper & Row, 1988): 159–60.
2. Letter to Shareholders, Annual Report of Berkshire Hathaway Inc., 1991.
3. R. D. Buzzell and B. T. Gale, *The PIMS Principles* (New York: Free Press, 1987): 279.
4. T. Copeland, T. Koller, and J. Murrin, *Valuation: Measuring and Managing the Value of Companies*, 3rd edn (New York: John Wiley & Sons, Inc., 2000): 305.
5. R. Cibin and R. M. Grant, "Restructuring among the World's Leading Oil Companies," *British Journal of Management* 7 (December 1996): 283–308.
6. D. C. Hambrick and S. M. Schecter, "Turnaround Strategies for Mature Industrial-Product Business Units," *Academy of Management Journal* 26, no. 2 (1983): 231–48.

7. G. R. Carroll and A. Swaminathan, "Why the Microbrewery Movement? Organizational Dynamics of Resource Partitioning in the American Brewing Industry," *American Journal of Sociology* 106 (2000): 715–762; C. Boone, G. R. Carroll, and A. van Witteloostuijn, "Resource Distributions and Market Partitioning: Dutch Daily Newspapers 1964–94," *American Sociological Review* 67 (2002): 408–31.
8. *Capital One Financial Corporation*, Harvard Business School Case No. 9-700-124 (2000).
9. National Science Foundation, *Research and Development in Industry*: 2002 (www.nsf.gov/statistics/industry).
10. A. M. McGahan and B. S. Silverman, "How Does Innovative Activity Change as Industries Mature?" *International Journal of Industrial Organization* 19, no. 7 (2001): 1141–60.
11. See section entitled: "Internal Sources of Change: Competitive Advantage from Innovation," Chapter 7.

12. B. J. Pine and J. Gilmore, "Welcome to the Experience Economy," *Harvard Business Review* (July/August 1998): 97–105.

13. A. Davies, T. Brady, and M. Hobday, "Organizing for Solutions: System Seller vs. System Integrator," *Industrial Marketing Management* 36 (2007): 183–93.

14. C. Baden-Fuller and J. Stopford, *Rejuvenating the Mature Business* (Boston: HBS Press, 1994): especially Chapters 3 and 4.

15. C. C. Markides, *All the Right Moves* (Boston: Harvard Business School Press, 1999).

16. J.-C. Spender, *Industry Recipes: The Nature and Sources of Managerial Judgment* (Oxford: Blackwell Publishing, 1989). On a similar theme, see also A. S. Huff, "Industry Influences on Strategy Reformulation," *Strategic Management Journal* 3 (1982): 119–131.

17. P. S. Barr, J. L. Stimpert, and A. S. Huff, "Cognitive Change, Strategic Action, and Organizational Renewal," *Strategic Management Journal* 13 (Summer 1992): 15–36.

18. G. Hamel, "Strategy as Revolution," *Harvard Business Review* 96 (July/August 1996): 69–82.

19. H. Volberda, C. Baden-Fuller, and F. van den Bosch, "Mastering Strategic Renewal," *Long Range Planning* 34 (April, 2001): 159–78.

20. T. Burns and G. M. Stalker, *The Management of Innovation* (London: Tavistock Institute, 1961).

21. H. Mintzberg, *Structure in Fives: Designing Effective Organizations* (Englewood Cliffs, NJ: Prentice Hall, 1983): Chapter 9.

22. G. Nieman, *Big Brown: The Untold Story of UPS* (Chichester: John Wiley & Sons, Ltd, 2007): 70.

23. C. Fishman, *The Wal-Mart Effect: The High Cost of Everyday Low Prices* (Harmondsworth: Penguin, 2006).

24. *Ryanair: Defying Gravity*, IMD Case No. 3-1633 (2007). Available from www.ecch.com.

25. "How Whirlpool Defines Innovation," *Business Week* (March 6, 2006).

26. K. R. Harrigan, *Strategies for Declining Businesses* (Lexington, MA: D. C. Heath, 1980).

27. "KKR and Primedia," *Adweek* (May 31, 2011).

28. K. R. Harrigan and M. E. Porter, "End-Game Strategies for Declining Industries," *Harvard Business Review* (July/August 1983): 111–120.

IV

CORPORATE STRATEGY

11 Vertical Integration and the Scope of the Firm

The idea of vertical integration is anathema to an increasing number of companies. Most of yesterday's highly integrated giants are working overtime at splitting into more manageable, more energetic units—i.e., de-integrating. Then they are turning around and re-integrating—not by acquisitions but via alliances with all sorts of partners of all shapes and sizes.

—TOM PETERS, LIBERATION MANAGEMENT

Bath Fitter has control of the product from raw material to installation. This control allows them to better guarantee the quality by knowing exactly how it is made, not outsourcing it to someone that could take shortcuts to manufacture the product without Bath Fitter knowing. Also, they control the measuring, installation, and customer facing representative. By doing this, Bath Fitter would be able to get accurate and fast feedback about how the product is being used, quality issues, or the ease of installation.

—"BATH FITTER HAS VERTICAL INTEGRATION," HTTP://BEYONDLEAN.WORDPRESS.COM/2011/08/29/

OUTLINE

Introduction and Objectives

Chapter 1 introduced the distinction between corporate strategy and business strategy. Corporate strategy is concerned primarily with the decisions over the scope of the firm's activities, including:

Product scope: How specialized should the firm be in terms of the range of products it supplies? Coca-Cola (soft drinks), SABMiller (beer), Gap (fashion retailing), and SAP (software) are specialized companies: each is engaged in a single industry sector. Sony Corporation, Berkshire Hathaway, and Tata Group are diversified companies—they span multiple industries.

Geographical scope: What is the optimal geographical spread of activities for the firm? In the restaurant business, Clyde's Restaurant Group owns 13 restaurants in the Washington DC area, Popeye's Chicken and Biscuits has outlets throughout the US, McDonald's Corporation operates in 121 different countries.

Vertical scope: What range of vertically linked activities should the firm encompass? Walt Disney is a vertically integrated company: it produces its own movies, distributes them to cinemas and through its own TV networks (ABC and Disney Channel), and uses the movies' characters in its retail stores and theme parks. Nike is much more vertically specialized: it designs and markets footwear and apparel but outsources most activities in its value chain, including manufacturing, distribution, and retailing.

The distinction between business and corporate strategy may be summarized as follows: *corporate strategy* is concerned with *where* a firm competes; *business strategy* is concerned with *how* a firm competes within a particular area of business.[1] So far, the primary focus of the book has been business strategy. In this final part, we shift our attention to corporate strategy: decisions that define the scope of the firm. I devote separate chapters to the different dimensions of scope—vertical scope (*vertical integration*), geographical scope (*multinationality*) and product scope (*diversification*). However, as we shall discover, the key underlying concepts for analyzing these different dimensions—economies of scope in resources and capabilities, transaction costs, and costs of corporate complexity—are common to all three.

In this chapter we begin by considering the overall scope of the firm. We then focus specifically on vertical integration. This takes us to the heart of the determinants of firm boundaries, in particular the role of *transaction costs*. As we shall discover, vertical integration has been a hot topic in corporate strategy. Opportunities for outsourcing, alliances, and electronic commerce have caused companies to rethink which of their activities should remain within their organizational boundaries.

By the time you have completed this chapter, you will be able to:

- recognize the role of firms and markets in organizing economic activity and apply the principles of *transaction cost economics* to explain why boundaries between firms and markets shift over time;

- understand the relative advantages of vertical integration and outsourcing in organizing vertically related activities, the factors that determine the relative efficiency of each, understand the circumstances that influence these relative advantages, and apply this understanding to decisions over whether a particular activity should be undertaken internally or outsourced;

◆ identify alternative ways of organizing vertical transactions—including spot market transactions, long-term contracts, franchise agreements, and alliances—and advise a firm on the most advantageous transaction mode given the characteristics and circumstances of the transaction.

Transaction Costs and the Scope of the Firm

In Chapter 6 (Strategy Capsule 6.1), we traced the development of the business corporation. Firms came into existence because of their efficiency advantages in organizing production. Let us explore this issue and consider the determinants of firm boundaries.

Firms, Markets, and Transaction Costs

Although the capitalist economy is frequently referred to as a "market economy," it actually comprises two forms of economic organization. One is the *market mechanism*, where individuals and firms, guided by market prices, make independent decisions to buy and sell goods and services. The other is the *administrative mechanism* of firms, where decisions concerning production and resource allocation are made by managers and imposed through hierarchies. The market mechanism was characterized by Adam Smith, the 18th century Scottish economist, as the "invisible hand" because its coordinating role does not require conscious planning. Alfred Chandler has referred to the administrative mechanism of firms as the "visible hand" because coordination involves active planning.[2]

Firms and markets may be viewed as alternative institutions for organizing production. Firms are distinguished by the fact that they comprise a number of individuals bound by employment contracts with a central contracting authority. But firms are not essential for organizing production. When I remodeled my basement, I contracted with a self-employed builder to undertake the work. He in turn subcontracted parts of the work to a plumber, an electrician, a joiner, a drywall installer, and a painter. Although the job involved the coordinated activity of several individuals, these self-employed specialists were not linked by employment relations but by market contracts ("$4,000 to install wiring, lights, and sockets").

Firms and markets coexist, but their relative roles vary. If we compare the supply of mainframe computers with that of the personal computer industry, the administrative mechanisms of firms predominate in the former, and markets are more important in the latter. Thus, in mainframes, IBM's System z computers comprise IBM's microprocessors, IBM's z/OS operating system, and IBM's applications software; IBM also undertakes distribution, marketing, and customer support. Personal computers, by contrast, involve a network of firms linked by market contracts: design and marketing is undertaken by firms such as HP, Acer, and Lenovo. Components are produced by firms such as Intel, Seagate, and Samsung. Assembly is outsourced to contract manufactures such as Asustek, Quanta Computer, and Foxconn. Customer support is also outsourced to specialist suppliers, often located in India or Eastern Europe.

What determines which activities are undertaken within a firm and which through the market? Ronald Coase's answer was *relative cost*.[3] Markets are not costless: making a purchase or sale involves search costs, the costs of negotiating and drawing up a contract, the costs of monitoring to ensure that the other party's side of the contract is being fulfilled, and the enforcement costs of arbitration or litigation should a dispute arise. All these costs are types of **transaction costs**.[4] If the transaction costs associated with organizing across markets are greater than the *administrative costs* of organizing within firms, we can expect the coordination of productive activity will be internalized within firms.

Consider the packaging business (Figure 11.1). With regard to vertical scope, which is more efficient: three independent companies—one producing raw materials (e.g., steel), the next producing semi-finished packaging materials (e.g., steel strip), and the third producing finished packaging (e.g., steel cans)—or having all three stages undertaken by a single company? In the case of product scope, should metal cans, plastic packaging, and domestic appliances be produced by three separate companies or are there efficiencies to be gained by merging all three into a single company? In the case of geographical scope, which is more efficient: three independent companies producing cans in the US, the UK, and Italy, or a single multinational company owning and operating the can-making plants in all three countries?

FIGURE 11.1   The scope of the firm: Specialization versus integration

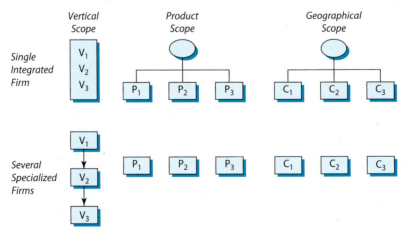

Note: In the integrated firm there is an administrative interface between the different vertical units (V), product units (P), and country units (C). Where there is specialization, each unit is a separate firm linked by market interfaces.

The Shifting Boundary between Firms and Markets

The answers to these questions have changed over time. During the 19th, and for most of the 20th century, companies grew in size and scope, absorbing transactions that had previously taken place across markets. Companies that were once small, specialized, and localized became large, integrated, diversified, and multinational. Applying Ronald Coase's principle, can we attribute this trend to a fall in the administrative costs of firms relative to the transaction costs of markets? Two factors have greatly increased the efficiency of firms in organizing economic activity:

- *Technology*: The telegraph, telephone, and computer have played an important role in facilitating communications within firms and expanding the decision-making capacity of managers.
- *Management techniques*: Developments in the principles and techniques of management have greatly expanded the organizational and decision-making effectiveness of managers. Beginning with the dissemination of double-entry bookkeeping in the 19th century,[5] and the introduction of scientific management in the early 20th century,[6] the past six decades have seen rapid advances in all areas of management theory and methods.

By the late 1960s, the growth in large corporations and the impressive achievements of the new tools of management science and corporate planning encouraged a widespread view that the *market economy* had been replaced by a *corporate economy*. The economist J. K. Galbraith predicted that the inherent advantages of firms over markets in deploying technology and planning production would result in capitalist economies becoming dominated by a small number of giant corporations.[7]

Yet, by the end of the 1990s, these predictions had been refuted by a sharp reversal of the trend toward increased corporate scope. Although large companies continued to expand internationally, the dominant trends of the past three decades have been "downsizing" and "refocusing," as large industrial companies reduced both their product scope through focusing on their core businesses and their vertical scope through outsourcing. As a result, the Forbes 500s share of total US private sector employment fell from 21.2% in 1980 to 14.9% in 1995.[8]

The contraction of corporate boundaries points to markets increasing their efficiency relative to firms' administrative processes. A key factor is greater turbulence of the business environment in recent decades. During periods of instability, the costs of administration within large, complex firms tend to rise as the need for flexibility and speed of response overwhelms traditional management systems. A second factor is the development of information and communications technology (ICT). The advent of computers reinforced the advantages of the giant corporation—only large organizations could afford them. But with the PC, internet, and mobile communication revolution, the benefits of leading-edge ICT have diffused to small firms and individuals, and the creation of virtual digital markets and electronic data interchange have revolutionized market transactions.

Let us focus now on just one dimension of corporate scope: vertical integration. The question we will consider is this: is it better to be vertically integrated or vertically specialized? With regard to a specific activity, the simple question for the firm is: *to make or to buy*? To answer this question, we shall draw in particular on Oliver

Williamson's analysis of transaction costs, which forms the basis for a theory of economic organization that is particularly useful in designing vertical relationships.[9]

The Benefits and Costs of Vertical Integration

Vertical integration refers to a firm's ownership of vertically related activities. The greater a firm's ownership extends over successive stages of the value chain for its product, the greater its degree of vertical integration. The extent of a firm's vertical integration is indicated by the ratio of its value added to its sales revenue: the more a firm makes rather than buys, the greater is its value added relative to its sales revenue.

Vertical integration can be either *backward* (or upstream) into its suppliers' activities or *forward* (or downstream) into its customers' activities. Vertical integration may also be *full* or *partial*. Some California wineries are fully integrated: they produce wine only from the grapes they grow, and sell it all through direct distribution. Most are partially integrated: their homegrown grapes are supplemented with purchased grapes; they sell some wine through their own tasting rooms, but most through independent distributors.

Strategies toward vertical integration have been subject to shifting fashions. For most of the 20th century the prevailing wisdom was that vertical integration was beneficial because it allowed superior coordination and reduced risk. During the past 25 years, there has been a profound change of opinion: outsourcing, it is claimed, enhances flexibility and allows firms to concentrate on those activities where they possess superior capabilities. Moreover, many of the coordination benefits associated with vertical integration can be achieved through collaboration between vertically related companies.

However, as in other areas of management, fashion is fickle. In the media sector, vertical integration between content and distribution has become viewed as a critical advantage in the face of rapid technological change. The resulting wave of mergers between content producers and distributors (TV broadcasters, cable companies, and internet portals) has transformed the industry (Strategy Capsule 11.1).

Our task is to go beyond fads and fashions to uncover the factors that determine whether vertical integration enhances or weakens performance.

The Benefits from Vertical Integration

Technical Economies from the Physical Integration of Processes   Proponents of vertical integration have often emphasized the *technical economies* it offers: cost savings that arise from the physical integration of processes. Thus, most steel sheet is produced by integrated producers in plants that first produce steel, then roll hot steel into sheet. Linking the two stages of production at a single location reduces transportation and energy costs. Similar technical economies arise in integrating pulp and paper production and from linking oil refining with petrochemical production.

However, although these considerations explain the need for the co-location of plants, they do not explain why vertical integration in terms of *common ownership* is necessary. Why can't steel and steel strip production or pulp and paper production be undertaken by separate firms that own facilities which are physically integrated

STRATEGY CAPSULE 11.1

Vertical Integration in the Media Sector: Value Creating or Value Destroying?

Considerable vertical integration has occurred between *content* producers (film studios, music publishing, newspapers) and distribution companies (TV broadcasters, cable, satellite TV, internet):

◆ News Corp. expanded from newspapers into movie production (Twentieth Century Fox), broadcast TV (Fox), satellite TV (Sky) and internet services (MySpace);

◆ Viacom owns cable TV channels (MTV, BET, Nickelodeon) and acquired studios (Paramount and DreamWorks).

◆ Time Warner is mainly involved in producing content (Warner Brothers studios, New Line Cinema, Time magazines, CNN news); its distribution mainly comprises cable channels (HBO, Turner Broadcasting, Cartoon Network). The merger of AOL and Time Warner, a vertically integrated content-internet distribution company was a disaster from the outset, and in 2009 AOL was spun off.

◆ Vivendi Universal was the result of the transformation of Compagnie Générale des Eaux, a water and waste management company, into a diversified, vertically integrated, media company led by Jean-Marie Messier which was subsequently broken up between 2002 and 2005 following massive losses.

◆ Disney's content production includes Walt Disney Studios, Pixar, Disney Theatrical Productions, Walt Disney Records, and Disney Publishing Worldwide. Distribution includes film distribution (Walt Disney Pictures, Disney Home Entertainment), broadcast TV (ABC), cable TV (ESPN, Disney Channel), radio (Radio Disney Network), and internet (Disney Online).

The question of whether vertical integration between media content and media distribution creates value was stimulated by the $54 billion hostile takeover bid made by Comcast, America's biggest cable operator, of Walt Disney in 2004. Here are two contrasting views.

STEVE ROSENBUSH

"Buying Disney shouldn't be a surprise. It's the logical next step," Comcast CEO Brian Roberts said at his February 11 press conference announcing his bid for the Mouse House.

It isn't enough to be just a media company, either. Most content providers benefit from having a certain amount of distribution, which helps lower their costs. That's why, in the future, media and communications will be dominated by hybrids such as News Corp. which recently acquired satellite-TV operator DirecTV.

Comcast's Roberts has embraced this future. The question now is whether Disney CEO Michael Eisner—who spurned an offer for a friendly deal—can accept the same future . . . Now that DirecTV is under Rupert Murdoch's control, it would be folly for Disney to pretend that it can still compete without a distribution partner of comparable stature. Comcast fits the bill. (*Business Week*, February 11, 2004).

JOHN KAY

Media content needs delivery, and vice versa . . . But this old idea is frequently rediscovered by visionary chief executives, excitable consultants, and greedy investment bankers: the people who proclaimed the AOL–Time Warner deal a marriage made in heaven. And it was revealed with Damascene force to Jean-Marie Messier, a humble French water carrier.

But activities can converge without requiring that the companies that undertake them converge. The erstwhile *maître du monde* might have drawn a useful lesson from his experience at Compagnie Générale des Eaux before his apotheosis as chief executive of Vivendi Universal: sewers and the stuff that goes down them do not need common ownership. (*Financial Times*, March 3, 2004) with one another? To answer this question, we must look beyond technical econo-mies and consider the implications of linked processes for *transaction costs*.

The Sources of Transaction Costs in Vertical Exchanges

Consider the value chain for steel cans, which extends from mining iron ore to the use of cans by food-processing companies (Figure 11.2). There is vertical integration between some stages; between others there is mostly market contracts between spe-cialist firms. In the final linkage—between can producing and canning—most cans are produced by specialist packaging companies (such as Crown Holdings and Ball Corporation); others are produced by food processors (such as Campbell's Soup and H.J. Heinz) that have backward integrated into can-making.[10]

The predominance of market contracts between steel strip production and can production is the result of low transaction costs in the market for steel strip: there are many buyers and sellers, information is readily available, and the switching costs for buyers and suppliers are low. The same is true for many other commodity products: few jewelry companies own gold mines; few flour-milling companies own wheat farms.

To understand why vertical integration predominates across steel production and steel strip production, let us see what would happen if the two stages were owned by separate companies. Because there are technical economies from hot-rolling steel as soon as it is poured from the furnace, steel makers and strip producers must invest in integrated facilities. A competitive market between the two stages is impos-sible; each steel strip producer is tied to its adjacent steel producer. In other words, the market becomes a series of *bilateral monopolies*.

Why are these relationships between steel producers and strip producers prob-lematic? To begin with, where a single supplier negotiates with a single buyer, there is no market price: it all depends on relative bargaining power. Such bargaining is likely to be costly: the mutual dependency of the two parties is likely to give rise to *opportunism* and *strategic misrepresentation* as each company seeks to enhance and exploit its bargaining power at the expense of the other. Hence, once we move from a competitive market situation to one where individual buyers and sellers are locked together in close bilateral relationships, the efficiencies of competitive markets are lost.

FIGURE 11.2   The value chain for steel cans

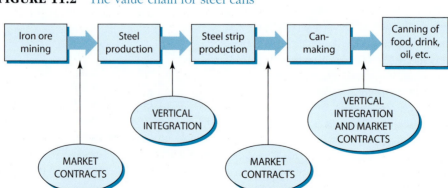

The culprits in this situation are *transaction-specific investments*. When a can-maker buys steel strip, neither the steel strip producer nor the can-maker needs to invest in equipment or technology that is specific to the needs of the other party. In the case of the steel producer and the steel roller, each company's plant is built to match the other party's plant. Once built, the plant's value depends upon the availability of the other party's complementary facilities—each seller is tied to a single buyer, which gives each the potential to *hold up* the other.

Thus, transaction-specific investments result in transaction costs arising from the difficulties of framing a comprehensive contract and the risks of disputes and opportunism that arise from contracts that do not cover every possible eventuality. Empirical research confirms the likelihood of vertical integration where transaction-specific investments are required:[11]

- Among automakers, specialized components are more likely to be manufactured in-house than commodity items such as tires and spark plugs.[12] Similarly, in aerospace, company-specific components are more likely to be produced in-house rather than purchased externally.[13]
- In the semiconductor industry, some companies specialize either in semiconductor design or in fabrication; others are vertically integrated across both stages (e.g., Intel, STMicroelectronics). The more technically complex the integrated circuit and, hence, the greater the need for the designer and fabricator to invest in close technical collaboration, the better the relative performance of integrated producers.[14]

The problem of hold-up could be eliminated by contracts that fully specify prices, quality, quantities, and other terms of supply under all possible circumstances over the entire life of the assets involved. But given uncertainty, it is impossible to anticipate every eventuality, and contracts are inevitably incomplete.

The Costs of Vertical Integration

The presence of transaction costs in intermediate markets does not mean that vertical integration is necessarily an efficient solution. Vertical integration avoids the costs of using the market, but internalizing a transaction imposes administrative cost. The size of this cost depends on several factors.

Differences in Optimal Scale between Different Stages of Production
Suppose that Federal Express requires delivery vans that are designed to meet its particular needs. To the extent that the van manufacturer must make transaction-specific investments, there is an incentive for Federal Express to avoid the ensuing transaction costs by building its own vehicles. Would this be an efficient solution? Almost certainly not: the transaction costs avoided by Federal Express are likely to be trivial compared with the inefficiencies incurred in manufacturing its own vans. Federal Express purchases about 40,000 trucks and vans each year, well below the 200,000 minimum efficient scale of an assembly plant.

The same logic explains why specialist brewers such as Anchor Brewing of San Francisco or Adnams of Suffolk, England are not backward integrated into cans like Anheuser-Busch InBev or SABMiller. Small brewers simply do not possess the scale needed for scale efficiency in can-making.

Developing Distinctive Capabilities   A key advantage of a company that is specialized in a few activities is its ability to develop distinctive capabilities in those activities. Even large, technology-based companies such as Xerox, Rolls-Royce, and Philips cannot maintain IT capabilities that match those of IT services specialists such as EDS, IBM, and Accenture. An important advantage of these IT specialists is the learning they gain from working with multiple clients. If General Motors' IT department only serves the in-house needs of GM, this limits the development of its IT capabilities.

However, this assumes that capabilities in different vertical activities are independent of one another and the required capabilities are generic rather than highly customized. Where one capability is closely integrated with capabilities in adjacent activities, vertical integration may help develop these integrated, system-wide capabilities. Thus, Wal-Mart keeps its IT in-house. The reason is that real-time information is central to Wal-Mart's supply chain management, in-store operations, and upper-level managerial decision making. Wal-Mart's need for tightly integrated information and communication services customized to meet its unique business systems inclines it toward in-sourcing.

Managing Strategically Different Businesses   These problems of differences in optimal scale and developing distinctive capabilities may be viewed as part of a wider set of problems—that of managing vertically related businesses that are strategically very different. A major disadvantage to FedEx of owning a truck-manufacturing company is that the management systems and organizational capabilities required for truck manufacturing are very different from those required for express delivery. These considerations may explain the lack of vertical integration between manufacturing and retailing. Firms that are integrated across design, manufacturing, and retailing, such as Zara and Gucci, are rare. Most of the world's leading retailers—Wal-Mart, Gap, Carrefour—do not manufacture. Similarly, few manufacturing companies retail their own products. Not only do manufacturing and retailing require very different organizational capabilities, they also require different strategic planning systems, different approaches to control and human resource management, and different top-management styles and skills.

These strategic dissimilarities are a key factor in the trend to vertically de-integrate. Marriott's split into two separate companies, Marriott International and Host Marriott, was influenced by the belief that *owning* hotels is a strategically different business from *operating* hotels. Similarly, the Coca-Cola Company spun off its bottling activities as Coca-Cola Enterprises Inc. partly because managing local bottling and distribution operations is very different from managing the global Coca-Cola brand and the production and distribution of concentrates.

Incentive Problems   Vertical integration changes the incentives between vertically related businesses. Where a market interface exists between a buyer and a seller, profit incentives ensure that the buyer is motivated to secure the best possible deal and the seller is motivated to pursue efficiency and service in order to attract and retain the buyer—these are termed *high-powered incentives*. With vertical integration, internal supplier–customer relationships are subject to *low-powered incentives*. When my office computer malfunctions, I call the university's IT department. The incentives for the in-house technicians to respond promptly to my email and voice messages are weak. If I were free to use an outside IT specialist, that specialist would only get the business if they were able to offer same-day service and would only get paid once the problem was resolved.

One approach to creating stronger performance incentives within vertically integrated companies is to open internal divisions to external competition. As we shall examine more fully in Chapter 14, many large corporations have created *shared service organizations*, where internal suppliers of corporate services—such as IT, training, and engineering—compete with external suppliers of the same services to serve internal operating divisions.

Competitive Effects of Vertical Integration   Vertical integration can be used to extend a monopoly position at one stage of an industry's value chain to adjacent stages: classic cases are Standard Oil and Alcoa. However, such cases are rare. Economists have shown that there is no additional monopoly profit to be extracted by extending a monopoly to adjacent stages of the value chain.[15]

A more likely risk is that, by vertically integrating, a company damages its competitive position in its original business because it now must compete with its customers or suppliers. When Disney forward integrated by acquiring the ABC TV network, this adversely affected Disney's relationships with other TV networks that were customers for Disney's TV productions, and made other studios (e.g., DreamWorks) more reluctant to collaborate with ABC in developing new TV productions.

Flexibility   Both vertical integration and market transactions can claim advantage with regard to different types of flexibility. Where the required flexibility is rapid responsiveness to uncertain demand, there may be advantages in market transactions. The lack of vertical integration in the construction industry reflects, in part, the need for flexibility in adjusting both to cyclical patterns of demand and to the different requirements of each project. Vertical integration may also be disadvantageous in responding quickly to new product development opportunities that require new combinations of technical capabilities. Some of the most successful new electronic products of recent years—Apple's iPod, Microsoft's Xbox, Dell's range of notebook computers—have been produced by contract manufacturers. Extensive outsourcing has been a key feature of fast-cycle product development throughout the electronics sector.

Yet, where system-wide flexibility is required, vertical integration may allow for speed and coordination in achieving simultaneous adjustment throughout the vertical chain. American Apparel is a rare example of a successful US *manufacturer* of apparel. Its tightly coordinated vertical integration from its Los Angeles design and manufacturing base to its 160 retail stores across 10 countries allows a super-fast design-to-distribution cycle. Vertical integration can also reinforce brand identity. Figure 11.3 shows an advertisement for American Apparel.

Compounding Risk   To the extent that it ties a company to its internal suppliers and internal customers, vertical integration represents a compounding of risk: problems at any one stage of production threaten production and profitability at all other stages. When union workers at a General Motors brake plant went on strike in 1998, GM's 24 US assembly plants were soon brought to a halt. If Disney animation studios fail to produce blockbuster animation movies that introduce new characters, then the knock-on effects are felt through plummeting DVD sales, lack of spin-off shows on the Disney Channel, reduction of merchandise sales in Disney Stores, and shortage of new attractions at Disney theme parks.

FIGURE 11.3   An American Apparel advertisement

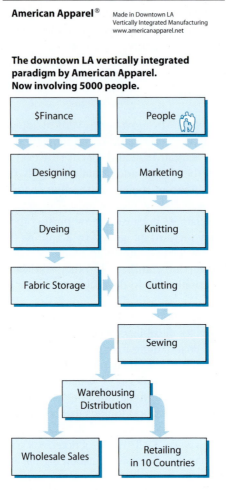

Source: American Apparel Inc.

Assessing the Pros and Cons of Vertical Integration

We have seen that vertical integration is neither good nor bad. As with most questions of strategy, it all depends upon the specific context. The value of our analysis is that we can identify the factors that determine the relative advantages of the market transactions *versus* internalization. Table 11.1 summarizes some of the key criteria. However, our analysis is not yet complete; we must consider some additional factors that influence the choice of vertical strategy, and in particular the fact that vertical relationships are not limited to the simple choice of make or buy.

Designing Vertical Relationships

Our discussion so far has compared vertical integration with arm's-length market contracts. In practice buyers and sellers can interact and coordinate their interests

TABLE 11.1   Vertical integration (VI) versus outsourcing: Some key considerations

Characteristics of the vertical relationship	Implication
How many firms are there in the vertically adjacent activity?	The fewer the number of firms, the greater the transaction costs and bigger the advantages of VI
Do transaction-specific investments need to be made by either party?	Transaction-specific investments are the primary source of transaction costs and increase the advantages of VI
How evenly distributed is information between the vertical stages?	The greater the information asymmetries, the more likely is opportunistic behavior and the greater the advantages of VI
How uncertain are the circumstances of the transactions over the period of the relationship?	The greater the uncertainties concerning costs, technologies, and demand, the greater the difficulty of writing contracts and the greater the advantages of VI
Are two stages similar in terms of the optimal scale of operation?	The greater the dissimilarity, the greater the advantages of market contracts as compared with VI
Are the two stages strategically similar (e.g., similar key success factors, common resources/capabilities)?	The greater the strategic similarity, the greater the advantages of VI over outsourcing
How great is the need for continual investment in upgrading and extending capabilities within individual activities?	The greater the need to invest in capability development, the greater the advantages of outsourcing over VI
How great is the need for entrepreneurial flexibility and drive in the separate vertical activities?	The greater the need for entrepreneurship and flexibility, the greater the advantages of high-powered incentives provided by market contracts and the greater the administrative disadvantages of VI
How uncertain is market demand?	The greater the unpredictability of demand, the greater the flexibility advantages of outsourcing
Does vertical integration compound risk, exposing the entire value chain risks affecting individual stages?	The heavier the investment requirements and the greater the independent risks at each stage, the more risky is VI

through a variety of relationships. Figure 11.4 shows a number of different types of relationship between buyers and sellers. These relationships may be classified in relation to two characteristics. First, the extent to which the buyer and seller commit resources to the relationship: arm's-length, spot contracts involve no resource commitment beyond the single deal; vertical integration typically involves a substantial investment. Second, the formality of the relationship: long-term contracts and franchises are formalized by the complex written agreements they entail; spot contracts typically involve little or no documentation and are governed by common law; collaborative agreements between buyers and sellers are usually informal—they are trust based; vertical integration allows management discretion to replace legal formality.

Different Types of Vertical Relationship

These different types of vertical relationship offer different combinations of advantages and disadvantages. For example:

- *Long-term contracts*: Market transactions can be either *spot contracts*—buying a cargo of crude oil on the Rotterdam petroleum market—or *long-term*

FIGURE 11.4 Different types of vertical relationship

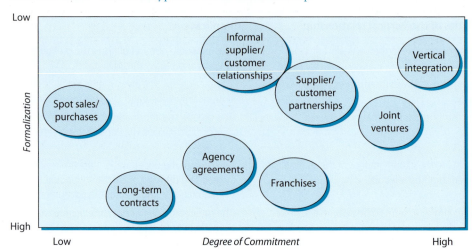

contracts—a series of transactions over a period of time that specify the terms of sales and the responsibilities of each party. Spot transactions work well under competitive conditions (many buyers and sellers and a standard product) where there is no need for transaction-specific investments by either party. Where closer supplier–customer ties are needed, particularly when one or both parties need to make transaction-specific investments, a longer-term contract can help avoid opportunism and provide the security needed to make the necessary investment. However, long-term contracts face the problem of anticipating the circumstances that may arise during the life of the contract: either they are too restrictive or so loose that they give rise to opportunism and conflicting interpretation. Long-term contracts often include provisions for the arbitration of contract disputes.

- *Vendor partnerships*: The greater the difficulties of specifying complete contracts for long-term supplier–customer deals, the greater the advantage of vertical relationships based on trust and mutual understanding. Such relationships can provide the security needed to support transaction-specific investments, the flexibility to meet changing circumstances, and the incentives to avoid opportunism. Such arrangements may be entirely *relational contracts*, with no written contract at all. The model for vendor partnerships has been the close collaborative relationships that many Japanese companies have with their suppliers. Japanese automakers have been much less backward integrated than their US or European counterparts but have also achieved close collaboration with component makers in technology, design, quality, and production scheduling.[16]

- *Franchising*: A franchise is a contractual agreement between the owner of a business system and trademark (the franchiser) that permits the franchisee to produce and market the franchiser's product or service in a specified area. Franchising brings together the brand, marketing capabilities, and business systems of the large corporation with the entrepreneurship and local knowledge of small firms. The franchising systems of companies such as

McDonald's, Century 21 Real Estate, Hilton Hotels, and 7-Eleven convenience stores facilitate the close coordination and investment in transaction-specific assets that vertical integration permits with the high-powered incentives, flexibility, and cooperation between strategically dissimilar businesses that market contracts make possible.

Choosing between Alternative Vertical Relationships

The criteria listed in Table 11.1 establish the basic features of the vertical relation that favor either market transactions or vertical integration. However, the availability of other types of vertical relationships, such as vendor partnerships and franchises, mean that vertical integration is not the sole solution to problems of transaction costs. Moreover, many of these relational contracts and hybrid arrangements have the capacity to combine the advantages of both vertical integration and market contracts.

Choosing the optimal vertical relationships needs to take account of additional factors to those listed in Table 11.1. In particular:

- *Resources, capabilities, and strategy*: Within the same industry, different companies will choose different vertical arrangements according to their reactive resource and capability strengths and the strategies they pursue. Thus, in fashion clothing, Zara's high level of vertical integration compared to H&M's or Gap's reflects strategy based upon fast-cycle new-product development and tight integration between its retail stores, designers, and manufacturers. While most fast-food chains have expanded through franchising, California-based In-N-Out Burger seeks to maintain its unique culture and distinctive business practices by directly owning and managing its restaurants. While most banks have been outsourcing IT to companies such as IBM and EDS, US credit card group Capital One sees IT as a key source of competitive advantage: "IT is our central nervous system . . . if we outsourced tomorrow we might save a dollar or two on each account, but we would lose flexibility and value and service levels."[17]

- *Allocation of risk*: Any arrangement beyond a spot contract must cope with uncertainties over the course of the contract. A key feature of any contract is that its terms allocate (often implicitly) risks between the parties. How risk is shared is dependent partly on bargaining power and partly on efficiency considerations. In franchise agreements, the franchisee (as the weaker partner) bears most of the risk—it is the franchisee's capital that is at risk and the franchisee pays the franchiser a flat royalty based on sale revenues. In oil exploration, outsourcing agreements between the oil majors (such as Chevron, ExxonMobil, and ENI) and drilling companies (such as Schlumberger or Halliburton) have moved from fixed-price contracts to risk-sharing agreements where the driller often takes an equity stake in the project.

- *Incentive structures*: Incentives are central to the design of vertical relationships. Incentives for opportunistic behavior are the bugbear of market contacts, while weak (low-powered) incentives for performance are the central problem of vertical integration. It seems possible that hybrid and intermediate governance modes offer the best solutions to the design of incentives. Toyota, Benetton, Boeing, and Marks & Spencer have relationships with their vendors that may involve formal contracts, but their essence is that they are long-term and trust based. The key to these relationships is that the promise of a long-term, mutually beneficial relationship trumps short-term opportunism.

Recent Trends

The main feature of recent years has been a growing diversity of hybrid vertical relationships that have attempted to combine the flexibility and incentives of market transactions with the close collaboration provided by vertical integration. Although collaborative vertical relationships are viewed as a recent phenomenon—associated with microelectronics, biotechnology, and other hi-tech sectors—local clusters of vertically collaborating firms are a long-time feature of the craft industries of Europe. This is especially true of northern Italy, both in traditional sectors such as textiles[18] and newer sectors such as packaging equipment[19] and motorcycles.[20]

The supplier networks of Japanese manufacturers with their knowledge sharing and collaborative new product development have become models for many large American and European companies.[21] There has been a massive shift from arm's-length supplier relationships to long-term collaboration with fewer suppliers. In many instances, competitive tendering and multiple sourcing have been replaced by single-supplier arrangements. These long-term vendor relationships often involve supplier certification, quality assurance programs, and technical collaboration.

The mutual dependence that results from close, long-term supplier–buyer relationships creates vulnerability for both parties. While trust may alleviate some of the risks of opportunism, companies can also reinforce their vertical relationships and discourage opportunism through equity stakes and profit sharing arrangements. For example: Commonwealth Bank of Australia took an equity stake in its IT supplier EDS Australia; pharmaceutical companies often acquire equity stakes in the biotech companies that undertake much of their R & D; and, as already noted, oilfield services companies are increasingly equity partners in upstream projects.

However, in this world of closer vertical relationships, some trends have been in the opposite direction. The internet has radically reduced the transaction costs of markets, particularly in pruning search costs and facilitating electronic payments. The result has been a revival in arm's-length competitive contracting through business-to-business e-commerce hubs such as Covisint (auto parts), Elemica (chemicals), and Rock & Dirt (construction equipment).[22] The incentives to disperse the value chain internationally, particularly to take advantage of low labor costs in emerging countries, has intensified and so has encouraged arm's-length outsourcing. In many sectors, manufacturing is outsourced to China and Southeast Asian countries; services (including call centers and software development) are outsourced to India. We shall return to these international dimensions of outsourcing in Chapter 12 (see "Location and the Value Chain").

The scope of outsourcing has extended from basic components to a wide range of business services, including payroll, IT, training, and customer service and support. Increasingly, outsourcing involves not just individual components and services but whole chunks of the value chain. In electronics, the design and manufacture of entire products are often outsourced to contract manufacturers such as Hon Hai Precision Industry Co., which makes Apple iPods, Nokia phones, and Sony's PlayStation.

Extreme levels of outsourcing have given rise to the concept of the *virtual corporation*: a firm whose primary function is to coordinate the activities of a network of suppliers and downstream partners.[23] In this organizational form the hub company has the role of *systems integrator*. The critical issue is whether a company that outsources most functions can retain the *architectural capabilities* needed to manage the *component capabilities* of the various partners and contractors. The risk is that the virtual corporation may degenerate into a "hollow corporation," where it loses the capability to evolve and adapt to changing circumstances.[24] If, as Prahalad and Hamel argue, core competences are embodied in "core products," then the more these core products are outsourced, the greater is the potential for the erosion of core competence.[25] Andrea Prencipe's research into aero engines points to the complementarity between architectural capabilities and component capabilities. Thus, even when the aero engine manufacturers outsource key components, they typically maintain R & D into those component technologies.[26] The problems experienced by Boeing in managing the outsourced network model it adopted for its 787 Dreamliner point to the complexity of the system integrator role.[27]

Summary

Our discussion of the shifting boundaries between markets and firms in the organization of economic activity introduced us to some of the important ideas concerning the relative efficiencies of markets and firms: the transaction cost of markets versus the administrative costs of firms. The tendency over the past 200 years for firms to grow in size and scope and to encompass more and more of the economic activity of society reflects the fall in the administrative costs of firms relative to the transactions costs of markets.

In relation to vertical integration decisions, transaction costs also play an important role. The presence of transaction-specific investments, small numbers of firms, and other sources of market inefficiency create important incentives for vertical integration.

However, transaction costs are only one factor to be taken into account when a firm decides which parts of its value chain to engage in. Among the other factors, the role of capabilities is critical: the most persuasive argument for vertical specialization is that firms need to focus on those activities they are best at. For most companies, their IT capabilities are inferior to those of IBM and their logistics capabilities inferior to those of Federal Express. Hence, it makes sense to outsource these activities. But this fails to take account of the linkages among capabilities in different value chain activities. If my product-development capabilities are dependent upon achieving real-time information on customer-buying patterns and my manufacturing capabilities require a highly flexible and responsive distribution capability, then I may need my IT services and logistics system to be tightly integrated with other functions and customized to their needs.

Moreover, vertical integration decisions are not simply make-or-buy choices: there is a wide variety of ways in which a company can structure vertical relationships. Vertical relationships between independent firms do not need to be arm's-length contracts: the recent growth in outsourcing has involved medium- and long-term relationships which are governed partly by contract, but also trust and mutual commitment. In a number of industries specialized types of vertical relationship have appeared such as franchising, dealership arrangements, and agency agreements. Such vertical forms can reconcile the coordination benefits of vertical integration with the capability advantages of vertical specialization. Similarly with internalization: vertical integration may involve a range of relationships between vertically related internal units, including quasi-market contracts.

Ultimately, vertical integration decisions revolve around two key questions. First, which activities will we undertake internally and which will we outsource? Second, how do we design our vertical arrangements with both external and internal suppliers and buyers?

 Quizzes and flashcards to test yourself further are available in your interactive e-book at **www.wileyopenpage.com**

Self-Study Questions

1. "The Shifting Boundary between Firms and Markets" section above argues that developments in information and communication technology (e.g., regarding telephones and computers) during most of the 20th century tended to lower the costs of administration within the firm relative to the costs of market transactions, thereby increasing the size and scope of firms. What about the internet? How has this influenced the efficiency of large integrated firms relative to small, specialized firms coordinated by markets?

2. "The Shifting Barrier between Firms and Markets" section notes that the large US companies account for a smaller percentage of total employment—a development that is attributed to a more turbulent business environment. Explain why external turbulence encourages outsourcing and increased focus on core business.

3. A large proportion of major corporations outsource their IT functions to specialist suppliers of IT services such as IBM, EDS (now owned by Hewlett-Packard), Accenture, and Capgemini. What transaction costs are incurred by these outsourcing arrangements and why do they arise? What are the offsetting benefits from IT outsourcing?

4. In Strategy Capsule 11.1, Steve Rosenbush argues that integration between media content and media distribution companies (and, specifically, between Disney and Comcast) is strategically advantageous. John Kay suggests that there is little need for common ownerships between distribution channels and the content they carry. Explain the arguments of each. Who do you agree with? As more content is being viewed via the internet and on mobile devices, how does this affect the arguments?

5. For its Zara brand, Inditex manufactures the majority of the garments it sells and undertakes all of its own distribution from manufacturing plants to its directly managed retail outlets. Benetton outsources most of its production, and most of its retail outlets are owned and operated by franchisees. Which is the superior system?

Notes

1. M. J. Piskorski ("A Note on Corporate Strategy," Harvard Business School 9-705-449, 2005) defines *corporate strategy* as: "a set of choices that a corporation makes to create value through configuration and coordination of its multimarket activities." In practice, determining the boundary between business strategy and corporate strategy depends on where we draw the boundaries of industries and markets.

2. A. Chandler Jr., *The Visible Hand: The Managerial Revolution in American Business* (Cambridge, MA: MIT Press, 1977).

3. R. H. Coase, "The Nature of the Firm," *Economica* 4 (1937): 386–405.

4. The term *interaction costs* has also been used to describe "the time and money expended whenever people and companies exchange goods, services or ideas." See J. Hagel and M. Singer, "Unbundling the Corporation," *Harvard Business Review* (March/April 1999): 133–44.

5. Double-entry bookkeeping has its origins in 14th-century Italy and was developed in Venice in the 16th century. See L. Zan, "Accounting and Management Discourse in Preindustrial Settings: The Venice Arsenal at the Turn of the Sixteenth Century," *Accounting and Business Research* 32 (2004): 145–75.

6. F. W. Taylor, *The Principles of Scientific Management* (New York: Bulletin of the Taylor Society, 1916).

7. J. K. Galbraith, *The New Industrial State* (Harmondsworth: Penguin, 1969).

8. L. J. White, "Trends in Aggregate Concentration in the United States," *Journal of Economic Perspectives* 16 (Fall 2002): 137–60.

9. O. E. Williamson, *Markets and Hierarchies: Analysis and Antitrust Implications* (New York: Free Press, 1975); O. E. Williamson, *The Economic Institutions of Capitalism: Firms, Markets and Relational Contracting* (New York: Free Press, 1985).

10. The situation is different in aluminum cans, where aluminum producers such as Alcoa and Pechiney are major producers of beverage cans.

11. For a review of empirical evidence on transaction costs and vertical integration see J. T. Macher and B. D. Richman, "Transaction Cost Economics: An Assessment of Empirical Research in the Social Sciences," *Business and Politics* 10 (2008): Article 1; and M. D, Whinston, "On the Transaction Cost Determinants of Vertical Integration," *Journal of Law Economics and Organization* 19 (2003): 1–23.

12. K. Monteverde and J. J. Teece, "Supplier Switching Costs and Vertical Integration in the Automobile Industry," *Bell Journal of Economics* 13 (Spring 1982): 206–13.

13. S. Masten, "The Organization of Production: Evidence from the Aerospace Industry," *Journal of Law and Economics* 27 (October 1984): 403–17.

14. J. T. Macher, "Technological Development and the Boundaries of the Firm: A Knowledge-based Examination in Semiconductor Manufacturing," *Management Science* 52 (2006): 826–43; K. Monteverde, "Technical Dialogue as an Incentive for Vertical Integration in the Semiconductor Industry," *Management Science* 41 (1995): 1624–38.

15. R. Rey and J. Tirole, "A Primer on Foreclosure," Chapter 33 in M. Armstrong and R. H. Porter (eds), *Handbook of Industrial Organization: Vol. 3* (Amsterdam: Elsevier, 2007).

16. J. H. Dyer, "Effective Interfirm Collaboration: How Firms Minimize Transaction Costs and Maximize Transaction Value," *Strategic Management Journal* 18 (1997): 535–56; J. H. Dyer, "Specialized Supplier Networks as a Source of Competitive Advantage: Evidence from the Auto Industry," *Strategic Management Journal* 17 (1996): 271–92.

17. L. Willcocks and C. Sauer, "High Risks and Hidden Costs in IT Outsourcing," *Financial Times* (May 23, 2000): 3.

18. N. Owen and A. C. Jones, *A Comparative Study of the British and Italian Textile and Clothing Industries,* Department of Trade and Industry (London: HMSO, 2003).

19. G. Lorenzoni and A. Lipparini, "The Leveraging of Interfirm Relationships as Distinctive Organizational Capabilities: A Longitudinal Study," *Strategic Management Journal* 20 (1999): 317–338.

20. G. Lorenzoni and A. Lipparini, "Organizing around Strategic Relationships: Networks of Suppliers in the Italian Motorcycle Industry," in K. O. Cool, J. E. Henderson, and R. Abate (eds), *Restructuring Strategy* (Oxford: Blackwell, 2005): 44–67.

21. J. H. Dyer and K. Nobeoka, "Creating and Managing a High-performance Knowledge-sharing Network: The Toyota Case," *Strategic Management Journal* 21 (2000): 345–68.

22. See www.covisint.com; www.elemica.com; www.rockanddirt.com.

23. "The Virtual Corporation," *Business Week* (February 8, 1993): 98–104; W. H. Davidow and M. S. Malone, *The Virtual Corporation* (New York: HarperCollins, 1992).

24. H. W. Chesborough and D. J. Teece, "When is Virtual Virtuous? Organizing for Innovation," *Harvard Business Review* (May/June 1996): 68–79.

25. C. K. Prahalad and G. Hamel, "The Core Competences of the Corporation," *Harvard Business Review* (May/June 1990): 79–91.

26. S. Brusoni, A. Prencipe, and K. Pavitt, "Knowledge Specialization, Organizational Coupling and the Boundaries of the Firm: Why Do Firms Know More Than They Make?" *Administrative Science Quarterly* 46 (2001): 597–621.

27. "Boeing's Dreamliner Delays Are a Nightmare," *Seeking Alpha*, http://seekingalpha.com/article/110735-boeing-s-dreamliner-delays-are-a-nightmare, accessed July 7, 2009.

12 Global Strategy and the Multinational Corporation

Soccer attracts limited interest in cricket-obsessed Pakistan. Yet, the Pakistan city of Sialkot produces the majority of the world's hand-sewn footballs. The world's leading supplier, Adidas, contracts with the major local producer, Forward Sports, which outsources to over 100 local stitching centers. Under pressure from new technology and activists opposing child labor, Sialkot's share of global football production has fallen from over 70% to under 25%. The Adidas' Tango 12 ball used in the Euro 2012 tournament is machine-made with no hand stitching. It is based on research done at Loughborough University in the UK, was lab tested in Germany, field tested in seven countries, and produced in China from materials sourced from China, Taiwan, and South Korea.

OUTLINE

Introduction and Objectives

There have been two primary forces driving change in business environment during the past half century. One is technology; the other is internationalization. Internationalization is a source of huge opportunity. In 1981, Infosys, with just six employees, was established in Pune, India. By supplying IT services to corporations throughout the world, Infosys had become the world's eighth-biggest IT services company (just behind its close neighbor, Wipro) with 145,000 employees. Internationalization is also a potent destroyer. For centuries, Sheffield, England was the world's leading center of cutlery manufacture. By 2012, only a few hundred people were employed making cutlery in Sheffield. The industry had been devastated by cheap imports first from South Korea and then from China. Nor is it just the industries in the mature industrial nations that have been ravaged by imports. Bulk imports of second-hand clothing from Europe and North America (much of it from charities and churches) has been ruinous for Kenya's textile and apparel sector.

Internationalization occurs through two mechanisms: trade and direct investment. The growth of world trade has consistently outstripped the growth of world output, increasing export/sales and import penetration ratios for all countries and all industries. For the OECD countries, total trade (imports and exports) rose from 11% of GDP in 1960 to 51% in 2010. Flows of foreign direct investment have risen even faster, reaching $1.5 trillion in 2011.[1]

The forces driving both trade and direct investment are, first, the quest to exploit market opportunities in other countries and, second, the desire to exploit resources and capabilities located in other countries. The resulting "**globalization** of business" has created vast flows of international transactions comprising payments for trade and services, flows of factor payments (interest, profits, and licensing fees), and flows of capital.

What does the internationalization of the world economy mean for our strategy analysis? As we have already noted, internationalization is both a threat and an opportunity. However, in terms of analysis, the primary implication of introducing the international dimension is that it adds considerable complexity to our strategy analysis—not just in broadening the scope of markets (and competition) but also in complicating the analysis of competitive advantage.

By the time you have completed this chapter, you will be able to:

- use the tools of industry analysis to examine the impact of internationalization on industry structure and competition;

- analyze the implications of a firm's national environment for its competitive advantage;

- formulate strategies for exploiting overseas business opportunities, including overseas market entry strategies and overseas production strategies;

- shape international strategies that achieve an optimal balance between global integration and national differentiation;

- design organizational structures and management systems appropriate to the pursuit of international strategies.

We begin by exploring the implications of international competition, first for industry analysis and then for the analysis of competitive advantage.

Implications of International Competition for Industry Analysis

Patterns of Internationalization

Internationalization occurs through *trade*—the sale and shipment of goods and services from one country to another—and *direct investment*—building or acquiring productive assets in another country. On this basis we can identify different types of industry according to the extent and mode of their internationalization (Figure 12.1):

- *Sheltered industries* are served exclusively by indigenous firms. They are sheltered from both imports and inward direct investment by regulation, trade barriers, or because of the localized nature of the goods and services they offer. The forces of internationalization have made this category progressively smaller over time. Sheltered industries are primarily fragmented service industries (dry cleaning, hairdressing, auto repair,), some small-scale production industries (handicrafts, residential construction), and industries producing products that are non-tradable because they are perishable (fresh milk, bread) or difficult to move (beds, garden sheds).

- *Trading industries* are those where internationalization occurs primarily through imports and exports. If a product is transportable, if it is not nationally differentiated, and if it is subject to substantial scale economies, exporting from a single location is the most efficient means to exploit overseas markets. This is the case with commercial aircraft, shipbuilding, and defense equipment. Trading industries also include products whose inputs are available only in a few locations: rare earths from China; caviar from Iran and Azerbaijan.

FIGURE 12.1   Patterns of industry internationalization

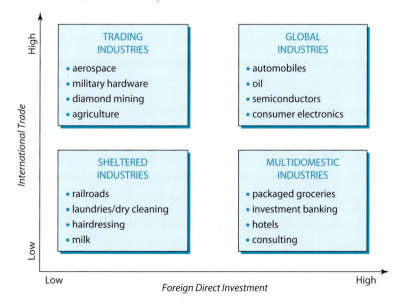

- *Multidomestic industries* are those that internationalize through direct investment—either because trade is not feasible (e.g., service industries such as banking, consulting, or hotels) or because products are nationally differentiated (e.g., frozen ready meals, book publishing).
- *Global industries* are those in which both trade and direct investment are important. These include most major manufacturing industries: automobiles, consumer electronics, semiconductors, pharmaceuticals, petroleum, and beer have high levels of both trade and direct investment.

By which route does internationalization typically occur? In the case of manufacturing companies, internationalization normally begins with exports, typically to countries with the least "psychic distance" from the home country. Later, a sales and distribution subsidiary is established in the overseas country. Eventually, the company develops a more integrated overseas subsidiary that undertakes manufacturing and product development as well.[2] In service industries, internationalization may involve replication (McKinsey & Co.), acquisition (HSBC), or franchising (McDonald's).[3]

Implications for Competition

Internationalization usually means more competition and lower industry profitability. In 1976, the US automobile market was dominated by GM, Ford, and Chrysler, with 84% of the market. By 2011, there were 14 companies with auto plants within the US; GM and Ford were the remaining indigenous producers accounting for just 35.7% of auto sales.

We can use Porter's five forces of competition framework to analyze the impact of internationalization on competition and industry profitability. If we define the industry in terms of the national market, internationalization directly influences three of the five forces of competition:

- *Competition from potential entrants*: Internationalization is a cause and a consequence of falling barriers to entry into most national markets. Tariff reductions, falling real costs of transportation, foreign-exchange convertibility, the removal of exchange controls, internationalization of standards, and convergence between customer preferences have made it much easier for producers in one country to supply customers in another. Entry barriers that are effective against domestic entrants may be ineffective against potential entrants that are established producers overseas.
- *Rivalry among existing firms*: Internationalization increases internal rivalry primarily because it increases the number of firms competing within each national market—it *lowers seller concentration*. The European market for motor scooters was once dominated by Piaggio (Vespa) and Innocenti (Lambretta). There are now over 25 suppliers of scooters to the European market, including BMW from Germany; Honda, Yamaha, and Suzuki from Japan; Kymco and Kwang Yang from Taiwan; BenZhou/Yiying, Baotian, Zhejiang, and Xingyue from China; Bajaj from India, and Baron and Vectrix from the US. Although internationalization has involved a massive wave of mergers and acquisitions, Ghemawat and Ghadar show that global concentration has declined as a result of national producers entering the global

market.[4] In addition internationalization stimulates competition by increasing investments in capacity and increasing the diversity of competitors.

● *Increasing the bargaining power of buyers*: The option of sourcing from overseas greatly enhances the power of industrial buyers. It also allows distributors to engage in international arbitrage: pharmaceutical distributors have become adept at searching the world for low-price pharmaceuticals then importing them for the domestic market.

Analyzing Competitive Advantage in an International Context

The growth of international competition over the past 20 years has been associated with some stunning reversals in the competitive positions of different companies. In 1989, US Steel was the world's biggest steel company; in 2012, ArcelorMittal based in Luxemburg and India was the new leader. In 1990, Motorola, Ericsson, and Siemens were the world leaders in wireless handsets. By 2012, Nokia, Samsung, and Apple were leaders.

To understand how internationalization has shifted the basis of competition, we need to extend our framework for analyzing competitive advantage to include the influence of firms' national environments. Competitive advantage, we have noted, is achieved when a firm matches its internal strengths in resources and capabilities to the key success factors of the industry. In international industries, competitive advantage depends not just on a firm's internal resources and capabilities but also on their national environments, in particular the availability of resources within the countries where they do business. Figure 12.2 summarizes the implications of

FIGURE 12.2 Competitive advantage in an international context

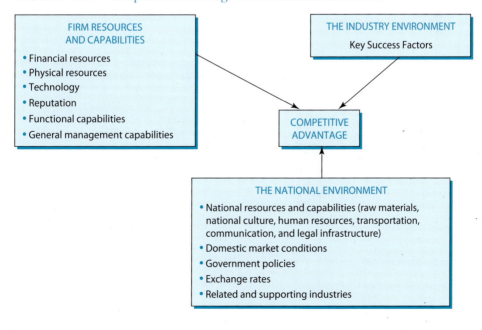

internationalization for our basic strategy model in terms of the impact both on industry conditions and firms' access to resources and capabilities.

National Influences on Competitiveness: Comparative Advantage

The effect of national resource availability on international competitiveness is the subject of the *theory of comparative advantage*. The theory states that a country has a comparative advantage in those products which make intensive use of those resources available in abundance within that country. Thus, Bangladesh has an abundant supply of unskilled labor. The US has an abundant supply of technological resources: trained scientists and engineers, research facilities, and universities. Bangladesh has a comparative advantage in products that make intensive use of unskilled labor, such as clothing, handicrafts, leather goods, and assembly of consumer electronic products. The US has a comparative advantage in technology-intensive products such as microprocessors, computer software, pharmaceuticals, medical diagnostic equipment, and management consulting services.

The term **comparative advantage** refers to the *relative* efficiencies of producing different products. So long as exchange rates are well behaved (do not deviate far from their purchasing power parity levels), then comparative advantage translates into competitive advantage. Comparative advantages are revealed in trade performance. Table 12.1 shows revealed comparative advantages for several product categories and several countries. Positive values show comparative advantage; negative values show comparative disadvantage.

Trade theory initially looked to natural resource endowments, labor supply, and capital stock as the main determinants of comparative advantage. Emphasis has shifted to the central role of knowledge (including technology, human skills, and management capability) and the resources needed to commercialize that knowledge (capital markets, communications facilities, and legal systems).[5] For industries where

TABLE 12.1   Indexes of revealed comparative advantage for certain broad product categories

	US	UK	Japan	Switzerland	Canada	Australia	Taiwan
Cereals	+0.83	−0.24	−0.99	−0.99	−0.80	+0.97	−0.78
Mineral fuels	−0.82	−0.11	−0.93	−0.50	+0.41	+0.26	−0.54
Pharmaceuticals	−0.25	+0.19	−0.51	+0.34	−0.32	−0.34	−0.78
Vehicles	−0.41	−0.25	+0.81	−0.68	+0.04	−0.69	+0.31
Aerospace	+0.58	−0.14	−0.44	−0.13	+0.26	−0.70	−0.50
Electrical and electronic equipment	−0.26	+0.08	+0.41	−0.02	−0.30	−0.74	+0.25
Optical, photo, medical, and scientific equipment	+0.09	−0.02	+0.21	+0.37	−0.36	−0.46	+0.20
Apparel (woven)	−0.92	−0.61	−0.96	−0.40	−0.59	−0.92	−0.29
Finance and insurance	−0.10	+0.56	+0.08	+0.69	−0.08	+0.05	−0.85

Note:
Revealed comparative advantage for each product group is measured as: (exports − imports)/(exports + imports).
Source: OECD.

scale economies are important, a large home market is an additional source of comparative advantage (e.g., the US in aerospace).[6]

Porter's National Diamond

Michael Porter has extended our understanding of international competitive advantage by emphasizing the dynamics through which resources and capabilities are developed.[7] Porter's *national diamond* framework identifies four key factors that determine a country's competitive advantage within a particular sector (Figure 12.3).[8]

1 *Factor conditions*: Whereas the conventional analysis of comparative advantage focuses on endowments of broad categories of resource, Porter emphasizes the role of highly specialized resources many of which are "home-grown" rather than "endowed." For example, in analyzing Hollywood's preeminence in film production, Porter points to the local concentration of highly skilled labor, including the roles of UCLA and USC schools of film. Also, resource constraints may encourage the development of substitute capabilities: in post-war Japan, raw material shortages spurred miniaturization and low-defect manufacturing; in Italy, restrictive labor laws have stimulated automation.

2 *Related and supporting industries*: One of Porter's most striking empirical findings is that national competitive strengths tend to be associated with "clusters" of industries. Silicon Valley's cluster comprises semiconductor, computer, software, and venture capital firms. For each industry, closely related industries are sources of critical resources and capabilities. Denmark's global leadership in wind power is based upon a cluster comprising wind turbine manufacturers, offshore wind farm developers and operators, and utilities.

3 *Demand conditions*: in the domestic market these provide the primary driver of innovation and quality improvement. For example:

   a Switzerland's preeminence in watches is supported by the obsessive punctuality of the Swiss.

   b Japanese dominant share of the world market for cameras by companies owes much to Japanese enthusiasm for amateur photography and customers' eager adoption of innovation in cameras.

FIGURE 12.3 Porter's national diamond framework

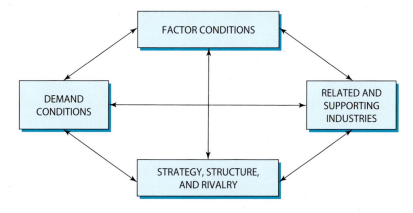

    c German dominance of the high-performance segment of the world automobile industry through Daimler, BMW, Porsche, and VW-Audi reflects German motorists' love of quality engineering and their irrepressible urge to drive on autobahns at terrifying speeds.

4 *Strategy, structure, and rivalry:* National competitive performance in particular sectors is inevitably related to the strategies and structures of firms in those industries. Porter puts particular emphasis on the role of intense domestic competition in driving innovation, efficiency, and the upgrading of competitive advantage. The international success of the Japanese in autos, cameras, consumer electronics, and office equipment is based upon domestic industries that feature at least six major producers, all strongly competitive with one another. Conversely, European failure in many hi-tech industries may be a result of European governments' propensity to kill domestic competition by creating *national champions.*

Consistency between Strategy and National Conditions

Establishing competitive advantage in global industries requires congruence between business strategy and the pattern of the country's comparative advantage. In wireless handsets, it is sensible for Chinese producers, such as ZTE and Huawei, to use their cost advantages to concentrate on the mass market and supply under distributors' brands; for Apple, Samsung, Sony, and RIM the emphasis needs to be differentiation through technology and design.

Achieving congruence between firm strategy and national conditions also extends to the embodiment of national culture within strategy and management systems. The success of US companies in many areas of high technology, including computer software and biotechnology, owes much to a business system of entrepreneurial capitalism which exploits a national culture that emphasizes individuality, opportunity, and wealth acquisition. The global success of Korean corporate giants such as Samsung and LG reflects organizational structures and management systems that embody Korean cultural characteristics such as loyalty, respect for authority, conformity to group norms, commitment to organizational goals, and work ethic—what Professor Young-Ryeol Park refers to as *dynamic collectivism.*[9]

Applying the Framework: International Location of Production

To examine how national resource conditions influence international strategies, we will look at two types of strategic decision in international business: first, where to locate production activities and, second, how to enter a foreign market. Let us begin with the first of these.

Firms move beyond their national borders not only to seek foreign markets but also to access the resources and capabilities available in other countries. Traditionally, multinationals established plants to serve local markets. Increasingly, decisions concerning where to produce are being separated from decisions over where to sell. For example, ST Microelectronics, the world leader in application-specific integrated circuits (ASICs), is headquartered in Switzerland; production is mainly in France, Italy, and Singapore; R & D is conducted mainly in France, Italy, and the US; and the biggest markets are the US, Japan, Netherlands, and Singapore.

Determinants of Geographical Location

The decision of where to manufacture requires consideration of three sets of factors:

- *National resource availability*: Firms should produce where they can benefit from favorable supplies of resources. For the petroleum industry this means exploring where the prospects of finding hydrocarbons are high. In assembly-based manufacturing it is a quest for low-cost labor. Table 12.2 shows differences in employment costs between countries. For the technology sector, access to specialist technical know-how is essential.
- *Firm-specific competitive advantages*: For firms whose competitive advantage is based on internal resources and capabilities, optimal location depends on where those resources and capabilities are situated and how mobile they are. Wal-Mart has experienced difficulty recreating its capabilities outside of the US. Conversely, Toyota and IKEA have successfully transferred their operational capabilities to their overseas subsidiaries.
- *Tradability*: The more difficult it is to transport a product and the more it is subject to trade barriers (such as tariffs and quotas), the more production will need to take place within the local market. Services—hairdressing, restaurant meals, banking, and the like—need to be produced in close proximity to where they are consumed.

Location and the Value Chain

The production of most goods and services comprises a vertical chain of activities where the input requirements of each stage vary considerably. Hence, different countries offer advantage at different stages of the value chain. Table 12.3 shows the pattern of international specialization within textiles and apparel. Similarly with consumer electronics: component production is research- and capital-intensive and is concentrated in the US, Japan, Korea, and Taiwan; assembly is labor-intensive and is concentrated in China, Thailand, and Latin America.

TABLE 12.2   Hourly compensation costs for production workers in manufacturing (US$)

	1975	2000	2010
Switzerland	6.09	21.24	53.20
Germany	6.31	24.42	43.76
Australia	5.62	14.47	40.60
France	4.52	15.70	40.55
US	6.36	19.76	34.74
Italy	4.67	14.01	33.41
Japan	3.00	22.27	31.99
UK	3.37	16.45	29.44
Spain	2.53	10.78	26.60
Korea	0.32	8.19	16.62
Taiwan	0.40	5.85	8.36
Mexico	1.47	2.08	6.23
Philippines	0.62	1.30	1.90

Source: US Department of Labor, Bureau of Labor Statistics. Reproduced with permission.

TABLE 12.3 Comparative advantages in textiles and clothing by vertical stage

	Fiber production	Spun yarn	Textiles	Apparel
Hong Kong	−0.96	−0.81	−0.41	+0.75
Italy	−0.54	+0.18	+0.14	+0.72
Japan	−0.36	+0.48	+0.78	−0.48
US	+0.96	+0.64	+0.22	−0.73

Note:
Fiber production includes both natural and synthetic fibers. Revealed comparative advantage is measured as (exports − imports)/(exports + imports).
Source: United Nations.

TABLE 12.4 Where does the iPhone4 come from?

Item	Supplier	Location
Design and operating system	Apple	US
Flash memory	Samsung Electronics	S. Korea
DRAM memory	Samsung Electronics	S. Korea
	Micron Technology	US
Application processor	Murata	Japan/Taiwan
Baseband	Infineon	Taiwan
	Skyworks	US
	TriQuint	
Power management	Dialog Semiconductor	Taiwan
Audio	Texas Instruments	US
Touchscreen control	Cirrus Logic	US
Accel and gyroscope	STMicroelectronics	Italy
E-compass	AKM Semiconductor	Japan
Assembly	Foxconn	China

Source: "Slicing an Apple," *Economist* (August 10, 2011), http://www.economist.com/node/21525685.

A key feature of recent internationalization has been the international fragmentation of value chains as firms seek to locate countries whose resource availability and cost best match each stage of the value chain.[10] Table 12.4 shows the international composition of Apple's iPhone; Figure 12.4 shows a similar breakdown of the Boeing 787 Dreamliner.

However, cost is just one factor in offshoring decisions. Cost advantages are vulnerable to exchange rate changes and inflationary pressures, so it is important to consider underlying issues concerning the availability and quality of resources and capabilities. Locational decisions are driven more by the potential for overall operational efficiency than by local wage rates.

As the examples of the iPhone and Boeing Dreamliner show, global sourcing is not only about cost efficiency: for technologically advanced products and services the location of sophisticated know-how is more important. Yet, even for knowledge-intensive goods and services, Western companies are finding that China, India, and other emerging market countries can offer world-class skills. For example, Jim Breyer, managing partner of Accel Partners, a Silicon Valley venture capitalist, observed: "Taiwan and China have some of the world's best designers of wireless chips and wireless software." In certain types of precision manufacturing, including

FIGURE 12.4   The globally dispersed production of the Boeing 787 Dreamliner

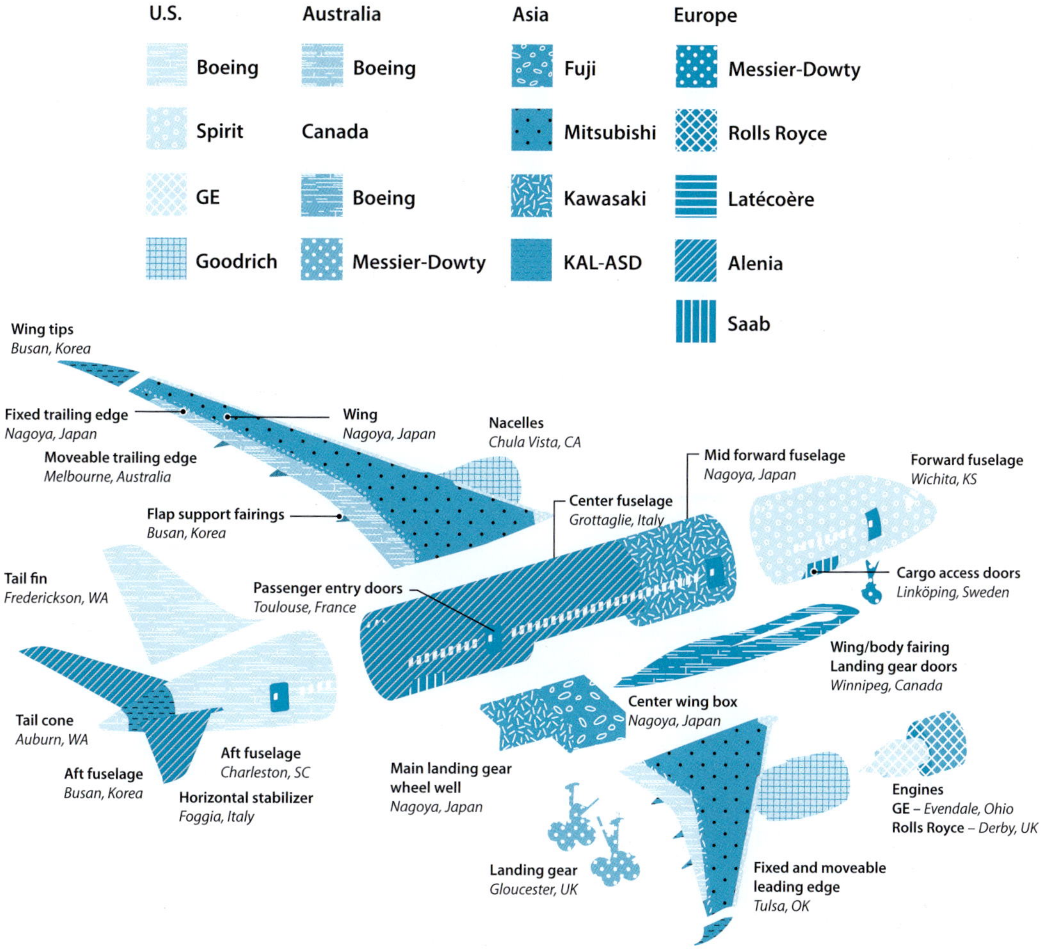

Source: Boeing Images, © 2010 Boeing Inc. Reprinted with permission.

the processes that produce magnesium alloy casing for notebook computers, companies such as Waffer in Taiwan offer some of the most sophisticated technology in the world. Most of the leading Indian IT outsourcing companies operate at level 5 (the highest level of expertise) of the Capability Maturity Model (CMM), an international measure of technical skill, while most internal IT departments in Western companies operate at level 2 or 3. Call centers, such as those operated by eTelecare, a Manila-based outsourcing provider, offer better average handling times and customer satisfaction relative to leading companies in the US.[11]

The benefits from fragmenting the value chain must be traded off against the added costs of coordinating globally dispersed activities. Apart from costs of transportation and higher inventories, a key cost of dispersed activities is time. Just-in-time scheduling often necessitates that production activities are carried out in close proximity to one another. Companies that compete on speed and reliability of delivery (e.g., Inditex and Dell) typically forsake the cost advantages of a globally dispersed value chain in favor of integrated operations with fast access to the final market.[12]

Figure 12.5 summarizes the relevant criteria in location decisions.

FIGURE 12.5 Determining the optimal location of value chain activities

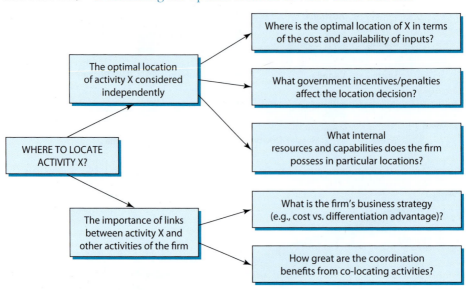

Applying the Framework: Foreign Entry Strategies

Firms enter foreign markets in pursuit of profitability. The profitability of entering a foreign market depends upon the attractiveness of that market and whether the firm can establish a competitive advantage within it. While market attractiveness can be a magnet for foreign multinationals—the size and growth of the Chinese economy has been irresistible to many Western companies—over the longer term, the key determinant of profitability is likely to be ability to establish competitive advantage vis-à-vis local firms and other multinationals.

A firm's potential for establishing competitive advantage has important implications for the means by which it enters a foreign market. The basic distinction is between market entry by means of *transactions* and market entry by means of *direct investment*. Figure 12.6 shows a spectrum of market entry options arranged according to the degree of resource commitment by the firm. Thus, at one extreme, there is exporting through individual spot-market transactions; at the other, there is the establishment of a wholly owned, fully integrated subsidiary.

How does a firm weigh the merits of different market entry modes? Five key factors are relevant:

1 *Is the firm's competitive advantage based on firm-specific or country-specific resources?* If the firm's competitive advantage is country-based, the firm must exploit an overseas market by exporting. Thus, to the extent that Shanghai Auto's competitive advantage in Western car markets is its low domestic cost base, it must produce in China and export to foreign markets. If Toyota's competitive advantage is its production and management capabilities, then as long as it can transfer these capabilities Toyota can exploit foreign markets either by exports or by direct investment.[13]

FIGURE 12.6   Alternative modes of overseas market entry

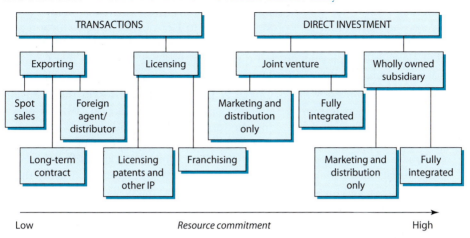

2 *Is the product tradable and what are the barriers to trade?* If the product is not tradable because of transportation constraints or import restrictions, then accessing that market requires entry either by investing in overseas production facilities or by licensing the use of key resources to local companies within the overseas market.

3 *Does the firm possess the full range of resources and capabilities for establishing a competitive advantage in the overseas market?* Competing in an overseas market is likely to require the firm to acquire additional resources and capabilities, particularly those related to marketing and distributing in an unfamiliar market. Accessing such country-specific resources is most easily achieved by collaborating with a firm in the overseas market. The form of the collaboration depends, in part, on the resources and capabilities required. If a firm needs marketing and distribution, it might appoint a distributor or agent with exclusive territorial rights. If a wide range of manufacturing and marketing capabilities is needed, the firm might license its product and/or its technology to a local manufacturer. In technology-based industries, licensing technology to local companies is common. In marketing-intensive industries, firms with strong brands can license their trademarks to local companies. Alternatively, a joint venture might be sought with a local manufacturing company. Danone, the French dairy products and drinks company, operates joint ventures in Russia, China, Indonesia, Iran, Mexico, Argentina, Saudi Arabia, and South Africa.

4 *Can the firm directly appropriate the returns to its resources?* Whether a firm licenses the use of its resources or chooses to exploit them directly (either through exporting or direct investment) depends partly on appropriability considerations. In chemicals and pharmaceuticals, the patents protecting product innovations tend to offer strong legal protection, in which case patent licenses to local producers can be an effective means of appropriating their returns. In computer software and computer equipment the protection offered by patents and copyrights is looser, which encourages exporting rather than licensing as a means of exploiting overseas markets. With all licensing arrangements, key considerations are the capabilities and reliability of the local licensee. This

is particularly important in licensing brand names, where the licenser must carefully protect the brand's reputation. Cadbury (now owned by Kraft Foods) licenses its trademarks and product recipes to Hershey for the production and sale of its Cadbury chocolate bars in the US. This arrangement reflects the fact that Hershey has production and distribution facilities in the US that Cadbury cannot match, and that Cadbury views Hershey as a reliable business partner.

5 *What transaction costs are involved?* A key issue that arises in the licensing of a firm's trademarks or technology concerns the transaction costs of negotiating, monitoring, and enforcing the terms of such agreements as compared with internationalization through a fully owned subsidiary. In overseas markets, Starbucks owns and operates its coffee shops, while McDonald's franchises its burger restaurants. McDonald's competitive advantage depends primarily upon the franchisee faithfully replicating the McDonald's system. This can be enforced effectively by means of franchise contracts. Starbucks believes that its success is achieved through creating the "Starbucks experience," which is as much about ambiance as it is about coffee. It is difficult to articulate the ingredients of this experience, let alone write it into a contract.

Issues of transaction costs are fundamental to the choices between alternative market entry modes. Barriers to exporting in the form of transport costs and tariffs are types of transaction costs; other costs include exchange rate risk and information costs. Transaction cost analysis has been central to theories of the existence of multinational corporations. In the absence of transaction costs in the markets either for goods or for resources, companies exploit overseas markets either by exporting their goods and services or by selling the use of their resources to local firms in overseas markets.[14] Thus, multinationals tend to predominate in industries where:

- firm-specific intangible resources such as brands and technology are important (transaction costs in licensing the use of these resources favor direct investment);
- exporting is subject to transaction costs (e.g., through tariffs or import restrictions);
- customer preferences are reasonably similar between countries.

Multinational Strategies: Global Integration versus National Differentiation

So far, we have viewed international expansion, whether by export or by direct investment, as a means by which a company can extend its competitive advantages from its home market into foreign markets. However, international scope may itself be a source of competitive advantage over geographically focused competitors. In this section, we explore whether, and under what conditions, firms that operate on an international basis are able to gain a competitive advantage over nationally focused firms. What is the potential for such "global strategies" to create competitive advantage? In what types of industry are they likely to be most effective? And how should they be designed and deployed in order to maximize their potential?

The Benefits of a Global Strategy[15]

A **global strategy** is one that views the world as a single, if segmented, market. There are five major sources of value from operating internationally.

Cost Benefits of Scale and Replication   Fifty years ago, Ted Levitt pointed out the advantage that companies that compete globally have over their local rivals.[16] Supplying the world market allows access to scale economies in product development, manufacturing, and marketing. (Ghemawat refers to these as benefits from *cross-border aggregation*.)[17] Exploiting these scale economies has been facilitated by the growing uniformity imposed by technology, communication, and travel: "Everywhere everything gets more and more like everything else as the world's preference structure is relentlessly homogenized," observed Levitt.[18] In many industries—commercial aircraft, semiconductors, consumer electronics, video games—firms have no choice: they must market globally to amortize the huge costs of product development. In service industries, the cost efficiencies from international operation derive primarily from economies in the replication of knowledge-based assets, including organizational capabilities.[19] Once a company has created a knowledge-based asset or product—whether a recipe, a piece of software, or an organizational system—it can be replicated in additional national markets at a fraction of the cost of creating the original. Disneyland theme parks in Tokyo, Paris, Hong Kong, and Shanghai replicate the rides and management systems that Disney develops for its parks in Anaheim and Orlando. This is the appeal of franchising: if you create a brilliantly innovative business offering dental care for dogs, why limit yourself to Santa Monica, California? Why not try to emulate McDonald's with its 67,000 outlets across 200 countries of the world?

Serving Global Customers   In several industries—for example investment banking, audit services, and advertising—the primary driver of globalization has been the need to service global customers.[20] Hence, auto-parts manufacturers have internationalized as they follow the major of the automobile producers. Law firms such as Baker & McKenzie, Clifford Chance, and Linklaters have internationalized mainly to better serve their multinational clients.

Exploiting National Resources: Arbitrage Benefits   As we have already seen, global strategy does not necessarily involve production in one location and then distributing globally. Global strategies also involve exploiting the efficiencies from locating different activities in different places. As we have seen, companies internationalize not just in search of market opportunities but also in search of resource opportunities. Traditionally, this has meant a quest for raw materials and low-cost labor. Increasingly, it means a quest for knowledge. For example, among semiconductor firms, a critical factor determining the location of overseas subsidiaries is the desire to access knowledge within the host country.[21] Ghemawat refers to this exploitation of differences between countries as *arbitrage*.[22] Arbitrage strategies are conventionally associated with exploiting wage differentials by offshoring production to low-wage locations; increasingly arbitrage is about exploiting the distinctive knowledge available in different locations.

Learning Benefits   The learning benefits of multinational operations go beyond *accessing* localized knowledge but extend to the *transfer* and *integration* of knowledge from different locations and the *creation* of new knowledge through interacting with different national environments. IKEA's expansion in Japan has required it to adjust to Japanese style and design preferences, Japanese modes of living, and the Japanese's fanatical quality-consciousness. As a result, IKEA has developed its capabilities with regard to both quality and design that it believes will enhance its competitiveness worldwide. According to the CEO of IKEA Japan, "One reason for us to enter the Japanese market, apart from hopefully doing very good business, is to expose ourselves to the toughest competition in the world. By doing so, we feel that we are expanding the quality issues for IKEA all over the world."[23]

Recent contributions to the international business literature suggest that this ability of multinational corporations (MNCs) to develop knowledge in multiple locations, to synthesize that knowledge, and to transfer it across national borders may be their greatest advantage over nationally focused companies.[24] The critical requirement for exploiting these learning benefits is that the company possesses some form of global infrastructure for managing knowledge that permits new experiences, new ideas, and new practices to be diffused and integrated.

Competing Strategically A major advantage of the Romans over the Gauls, Goths, and other barbarian tribes was their ability to draw upon the military and economic resources of the Roman Empire to fight local wars. Similarly, multinational companies possess a key strategic advantage over their nationally focused rivals when engaging in competitive battles in individual national markets: they can use resources from other national markets. At its most simple, this *cross-subsidization* of competitive initiatives in one market using profits from other markets involves *predatory pricing*—cutting prices to a level that drives competitors out of business. Such pricing practices are likely to contravene both the World Trade Organization's antidumping rules and national antitrust laws. More usually, cross-subsidization involves using cash flows from other markets to finance aggressive sales and marketing campaigns.[25] Evidence of firms charging lower prices in overseas than in domestic markets and lower export prices to overseas subsidiaries than those charged to third parties supports the argument that firms use domestic profits to subsidize price competition in overseas markets.[26]

Strategic competition between MNCs can result in complex patterns of attack, retaliation, and containment.[27] Fuji Film's sponsorship of the 1984 Olympic Games in Los Angeles was seen by Kodak as an aggressive incursion into its backyard; it responded by expanding its marketing efforts in Japan.[28]

The Need for National Differentiation

For all the advantages of global strategy, national market differences persist: with a few notable exceptions (Apple's iPod and iPad), most products designed to meet the needs of the "global customer" have lacked global appeal. Ford has struggled in its efforts to introduce a standardized global car: its Mondeo/Contour model was a disappointment; its 2012 Focus, produced at five plants throughout the world, is its latest attempt at a global car. The experience of most auto firms is that their global models become differentiated to meet the needs and preferences of different national markets.[29]

In some industries efforts toward globalization have met with little success. In washing machines, national preferences have shown remarkable resilience: French and US washing machines are primarily top loading, elsewhere in Europe they are mainly front loading; the Germans prefer higher spin speeds than the Italians do; US machines feature agitators rather than revolving drums; and Japanese machines are small. The pioneers of globalization in domestic appliances—Electrolux and Whirlpool—struggle to outperform national and regional specialists.[30] Similarly in retail banking, despite some examples of successful internationalization (Banco Santander, HSBC), most of the evidence points to few economies from cross-border integration and the critical need to adapt to local market conditions.[31]

Every nation represents a unique combination of a multitude of distinctive characteristics. How can we recognize and assess the extent of similarities and differences between countries for the purposes of international strategy formulation? Pankaj Ghemawat proposes four key components of distance between countries: *cultural, administrative and political, geographical*, and *economic*—his *CAGE* framework (Table 12.5).

Ghemawat's broad categories are only a starting point for exploring the national idiosyncrasies that make international expansion such a minefield. For consumer products firms, the structures of national distribution channels are critical. Procter & Gamble must adapt its marketing, promotion, and distribution of toiletries and household products to take account of the fact that, in the US, a few chains account for a major share of its US sales; in southern Europe, most sales are through small, independent retailers, while in Japan, P&G must sell through a multi-tiered hierarchy of distributors. The closer an industry to the final consumer, the more important cultural factors are likely to be. Strategy Capsule 12.1 considers some dimensions of national culture. It is notable that so few retailers have been successful outside their domestic markets. Wal-Mart, IKEA, H&M, and the Gap, are among the few retailers that are truly global. Even fewer have been as successful overseas as at home. For many, franchising has provided a lower-risk internationalization strategy.

TABLE 12.5   Ghemawat's CAGE framework for assessing country differences

	Cultural distance	Administrative and political distance	Geographical distance	Economic differences
Distance between two countries increases with	Different languages, ethnicities, religions, social norms Lack of connective ethnic or social networks	Absence of shared political or monetary association Political hostility Weak legal and financial institutions	Lack of common border, water-way access, adequate transportation or communication links Physical remoteness	Different consumer incomes Different costs and quality of natural, financial, and human resources Different information or knowledge
Industries most affected by source of distance	Industries with high linguistic content (TV, publishing) and cultural content (food, wine, music)	Industries viewed by government as strategically important (e.g., energy, defense, telecoms)	Products with low value-to-weight (cement), are fragile or perishable (glass, milk), or dependent upon communications (financial services)	Products whose demand is sensitive to consumer income levels (luxury goods) Labor-intensive products (clothing)

STRATEGY CAPSULE 12.1
How Do National Cultures Differ?

Do people differ between countries with regard to beliefs, norms, and value systems? The answer from a series of research studies is yes.

The best-known study of national cultural differences is by Geert Hofstede. The principal dimensions of national values he identified were:

♦ *Power distance*: The extent to which inequality, and decision-making power in particular, is accepted within organizations and within society. Power distance was high in Malaysia, and most Latin American and Arab countries; low in Austria and Scandinavia.

♦ *Uncertainty avoidance*: Preference for certainty and established norms was high in most southern European and Latin American countries; tolerance for uncertainty and ambiguity was high in Singapore, Sweden, the UK, the US, and India.

♦ *Individualism*: Concern for individual over group interests was highest in the US, the UK, Canada, and Australia. Identification with groups and the collective interest was strongest in Latin America and Asia (especially Indonesia, Pakistan, Taiwan, and South Korea).

♦ *Masculinity/femininity*: Hofstede identifies emphasis on work and material goals and demarcation of gender roles as *masculine*; emphasis on personal relationships rather than efficiency and belief in gender equality was viewed as *feminine*. Japan, Austria, Venezuela, and Italy scored high on masculinity; Scandinavia and the Netherlands scored very low.

Other studies have used different measures for characterizing national cultures. Other scholars emphasize different dimensions of national cultures. Fons Trompenaars (another Dutchman) identifies the US, Australia, Germany, Sweden and UK as *universalist societies*—relationships are governed by standard rules—Brazil, Italy, Japan, and Mexico are *particularist* societies—social relationships are strongly influenced by contextual and personal factors. In *affective* cultures, such as Mexico and the Netherlands, people display their emotions; in *neutral* cultures, such as Japan and the UK, people hide their emotions.

Sources: G. Hofstede, *Culture's Consequences: International Differences in Work-related Values* (Thousand Oaks, CA: SAGE Publications, 1984); F. Trompenaars, *Riding the Waves of Culture* (London: Economist Books, 1993).

Reconciling Global Integration with National Differentiation

Choices about internationalization strategy have been viewed as a tradeoff between the benefits of global integration and those of national adaptation (Figure 12.7).[32] Industries where scale economies are huge and customer preferences homogeneous call for a global strategy (e.g., jet engines). Industries where national preferences are pronounced and meeting them does not impose prohibitive costs favor multi-domestic strategies (e.g., retail banking). Indeed, in industries where there are few benefits from global integration, multinational firms may be absent (as in funeral services and laundries). Some industries may be low on both dimensions—car repair and office maintenance services are fairly homogeneous worldwide but lack significant

FIGURE 12.7 Benefits of global integration versus national differentiation

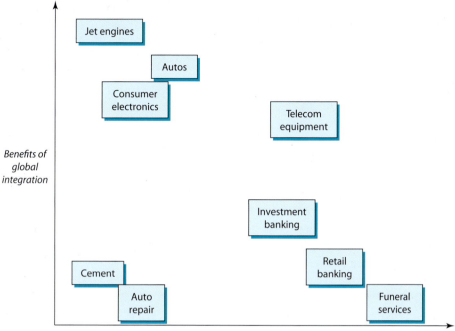

benefits from global integration. Conversely, other industries offer substantial benefits from operating on a global scale, but national preferences and standards may also necessitate considerable adaptation to the needs of specific national markets (telecommunications equipment, military hardware, cosmetics, and toiletries).

Reconciling conflicting forces for global efficiency and national differentiation represents one of the greatest strategic challenges facing MNCs. Achieving *global localization* involves standardizing product features and company activities where scale economies are substantial, and differentiating where national preferences are strongest and where achieving them is not over-costly. Thus, a global car such as the Honda Civic (introduced in 1972 and sold in 110 countries) now embodies considerable local adaptations, not just to meet national safety and environmental standards but also to meet local preferences for legroom, seat specifications, accessories, color, and trim. McDonald's, too, meshes global standardization with local adaptation (Strategy Capsule 12.2).

Reconciling global efficiency with national differentiation involves disaggregating the company by product and function. In retail banking, different products and services have different potential for globalization. Credit cards and basic savings products such as certificates of deposit tend to be globally standardized; checking accounts and mortgage lending are much more nationally differentiated. Similarly with business functions: R & D, purchasing, IT, and manufacturing have strong globalization potential; sales, marketing, customer service, and human resource management need to be much more nationally differentiated. These differences have important implications for how the MNC is organized.

STRATEGY CAPSULE 12.2
McDonald's Goes "Glocal"

For anti-globalization activists, McDonald's is a demon of globalization: it crushes national cuisines and independent, family-run restaurants with the juggernaut of US fast-food corporate imperialism. In reality, its global strategy is a careful blend of global standardization and local adaptation.

McDonald's menus include a number of globally standardized items—the Big Mac and potato fries are international features—however, in most countries McDonald's menus feature an increasing number of locally developed items. These include:

◆ Australia: A range of wraps including Seared Chicken, Tandoori Chicken, and Crispy Sweet Chili Chicken;

◆ France: Croque McDo (a toasted ham and cheese sandwich);

◆ Hong Kong: Grilled Pork Twisty Pasta and Fresh Corn Cup;

◆ India: Shahi Paneer McCurry Pan, McAloo Tikki, Veg Pizza McPuff;

◆ Saudi Arabia: McArabia Kofta, McArabia Chicken;

◆ Switzerland: Shrimp Cocktail, Chickenburger Curry;

◆ UK: A range of deli sandwiches including Spicy Veggie Deli (chickpea patty with coriander and cumin), and Sweet Chili Chicken Deli;

◆ US: Fruit & Maple Oatmeal, Frappes.

There are differences too in restaurant decor, service offerings (internet access in the UK; home delivery in India), and market positioning (outside the US McDonald's is more upmarket). In Israel, many McDonald's are kosher: they do not offer dairy products and are closed on Saturdays. In India, neither beef nor pork is served. In Germany, France, and Spain, McDonald's serves beer. A key reason that almost all of McDonald's non-US outlets are franchised is to

Strategy and Organization within the Multinational Corporation

These same factors—the benefits from global integration and need for national differentiation—that determine international strategies also have critical implications for the design of organizational structures and management systems to implement these strategies. As we shall see, one of the greatest challenges facing the senior managers of MNCs is aligning organizational structures and management systems to fit with the strategies being pursued.

The Evolution of Multinational Strategies and Structures

Over the past hundred years, the forces driving internationalization strategies have changed considerably. Yet, the structural configurations of MNCs have tended to persist. We discussed organizational inertia in Chapter 6; it seems likely that, because of their complexity, MNCs face particular difficulties in adapting their structures and systems to change. Chris Bartlett and Sumantra Ghoshal view MNCs as captives of facilitate adaptation to national environments and access to local know-how.

Yet, the principal features of the McDonald's business system are identical throughout the world. McDonald's values and business principles are seen as universal and invariant. Its emphasis on families and children is intended to identify McDonald's with fun and family life wherever it does business. Community involvement and the Ronald McDonald children's charity are also worldwide. Corporate trademarks and brands are mostly globally uniform, including the golden arches logo and "I'm lovin' it" tag line. The business system itself—the franchising, the training of managers and franchisees through Hamburger University, restaurant operations, and supplier relations—is also highly standardized.

McDonald's international strategy was about adapting its US model to local conditions. Now, as new menu items and business concepts are transferred between countries, it is using local differentiation to drive worldwide adaptation and innovation. For example, the McCafé gourmet coffeehouses within McDonald's restaurants were first developed in

Australia. By 2003, McCafés had become established in 30 countries. In responding to growing concern over nutrition and obesity McDonald's has drawn upon country initiatives with regard to ingredients, menus, and information labeling to support global learning.

Has McDonald's got the balance right between global standardization and local adaptation? Simon Anholt, a British marketing expert, argues: "By putting local food on the menu, all you are doing is removing the logic of the brand, because this is an American brand. If McDonald's serves what you think is a poor imitation of your local cuisine, it's going to be an insult." But according to McDonald's CEO Jim Skinner: "We don't run our business from Oak Brook. We are a local business with a local face in each country we operate in." His chief marketing manager, Mary Dillon, adds: "McDonald's is much more about local relevance than a global archetype. Globally we think of ourselves as the custodian of the brand, but it's all about local relevance."

Source: www.mcdonalds.com.

their history: their strategy-structure configurations today reflect choices they made at the time of their international expansion. Radical changes in strategy and structure are difficult: once an international distribution of functions, operations, and decision-making authority has been determined, reorganization is slow, difficult, and costly, particularly when host governments become involved. This *administrative heritage* of an MNC—its configuration of assets and capabilities, its distribution of managerial responsibilities, and its network of relationships—is a critical determinant of its current capabilities and a key constraint upon its ability to build new strategic capabilities.[33]

Bartlett and Ghoshal identify three eras in the development of the MNC (Figure 12.8):

- *The early 20th century* was the era of the European multinational. Companies such as Unilever, Shell, ICI, and Philips were pioneers of multinational expansion. Because of the conditions at the time of internationalization—poor transportation and communications, highly differentiated national markets—the companies created *multinational federations*: each national subsidiary was operationally autonomous and undertook the full range of functions, including product development, manufacturing, and marketing.

FIGURE 12.8   The development of the multinational corporation: Alternative parent–subsidiaries relations

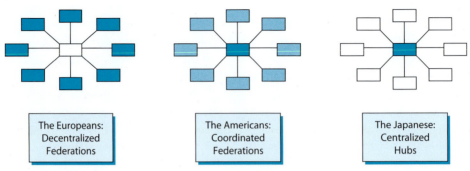

| The Europeans: Decentralized Federations | The Americans: Coordinated Federations | The Japanese: Centralized Hubs |

Note:
The density of shading indicates the concentration of decision making.
Source: C. A. Bartlett and S. Ghoshal, *Managing Across Borders: The Transnational Solution* (Boston: Harvard Business School Press, 1998). Copyright © 1989 by the Harvard Business School Publishing Corporation, all rights reserved.

- *After the Second World War* came the era of the American multinational. US dominance of the world economy was reflected in the pre-eminence of US multinationals such as GM, Ford, IBM, Coca-Cola, Caterpillar, and Procter & Gamble. While their overseas subsidiaries were allowed considerable autonomy, this was within the context of the dominant position of their US parent in terms of capital, new product and process technology, management capabilities, and management systems. Their US-based resources and capabilities provided the foundation for their international competitive advantages.

- *The 1970s and 1980s* saw the Japanese challenge. Honda, Toyota, Matsushita, NEC, and YKK pursued global strategies from centralized domestic bases. R & D and manufacturing were concentrated in Japan; overseas subsidiaries undertook sales and distribution. Globally standardized products manufactured in large-scale plants provided the basis for unrivalled cost and quality advantages. Over time, manufacturing and R & D were dispersed, initially because of trade protection by consumer countries and the rising value of the yen against other currencies.

The different administrative heritages of these different groups of MNCs continue to shape their strategies and organizational capabilities. The strength of European multinationals is adaptation to the conditions and requirements of individual national markets. The strength of the US multinationals is their ability to transfer technology and proven new products from their domestic strongholds to their national subsidiaries. Japanese MNCs are notable for the efficiency of global production and new product development. Yet, these core capabilities are also core rigidities. The challenge for European MNCs has been to achieve greater integration of their sprawling international empires; for Shell and Philips this has involved reorganizations over a period of more than two decades. For US MNCs such as Ford and Procter & Gamble it has involved nurturing the ability to tap their foreign subsidiaries for technology, design, and new product ideas. For Japanese MNCs such as Nomura, Hitachi, and

NEC the challenge is to become true insiders in the overseas countries where they do business.

Reconfiguring the MNC: The Transnational Corporation

Changing Organization Structure   For North American and European-based MNCs, the principal structural changes of recent decades have been a shift from organization around national subsidiaries and regional groupings to the creation of worldwide product divisions. For most MNCs, country and regional organizations are retained, but primarily for the purposes of national compliance and customer relationships. Thus, Hewlett-Packard, the world's biggest IT company, conducts its business through five global product groups: Enterprise Servers, Storage and Networking; Enterprise Services; Software; Personal Systems Group; and Imaging and Printing Group. Each of these product groups and each of HP's functions have activities in multiple countries. For example, HP Labs are in Palo Alto, California; Singapore; Bristol, UK; Haifa, Israel; St Petersburg, Russia; Bangalore, India; and Beijing, China. To assist geographical coordination, HP has regional headquarters for the Americas (in Houston), for Europe, the Middle East, and Africa (in Geneva), and for Asia Pacific (in Singapore). Because of the special importance of China and India, its head of the Personal Systems Group also has special responsibility for China and the head of the Imaging and Printing Group has special responsibility for India.

Reconciling Global Integration and National Differentiation: The Transnational   However, the formal changes in structure are less important than the changes in responsibilities, decision powers, and modes of coordination within these structures. The fundamental challenge for MNCs has been reconciling the advantages of global integration with those of national differentiation. Escalating costs of research and new product development have made global strategies with global product platforms essential. At the same time, meeting consumer needs in each national market and responding swiftly to changing local circumstances requires greater decentralization. Accelerating technological change further exacerbates these contradictory forces: despite the cost and "critical mass" benefits of centralizing research and new-product development, innovation occurs at multiple locations within the MNC and requires nurturing creativity and initiative throughout the organization. "It's the corporate equivalent of being able to walk, chew gum, and whistle at the same time," notes Chris Bartlett.

Bartlett argues that the simultaneous pursuit of responsiveness to national markets and global coordination requires "a very different kind of internal management process than existed in the relatively simple multinational or global organizations. This is the *transnational organization*."[34] The distinguishing characteristic of the transnational is that it becomes an integrated network of distributed and interdependent resources and capabilities (Figure 12.9). This necessitates that:

- Each national unit is a source of ideas, skills, and capabilities that can be harnessed for the benefit of the total organization.
- National units access global scale economies by designating them the company's world source for a particular product, component, or activity.

FIGURE 12.9 The transnational corporation

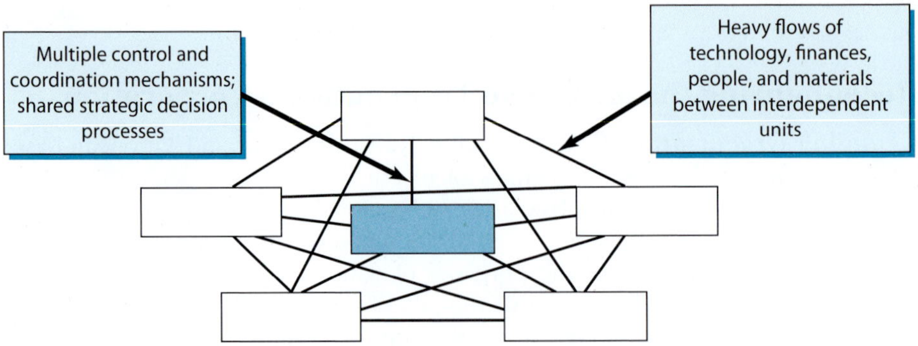

- The center must establish a new, highly complex managing role that coordinates relationships among units but in a highly flexible way. The key is to focus less on managing activities directly and more on creating an organizational context that is conducive to the coordination and resolution of differences. Creating the right organizational context involves "establishing clear corporate objectives, developing managers with broadly based perspectives and relationships, and fostering supportive organizational norms and values."[35]

Balancing global integration and national differentiation requires a company to adapt to the differential requirements of different products, different functions, and different countries. Procter & Gamble adopts global standardization for some of its products (e.g., Pringles potato chips and high-end perfumes); for others (e.g., hair care products and laundry detergent), it allows significant national differentiation. Across countries, P&G organizes global product divisions to serve most of the industrialized world because of the similarities between their markets, while for emerging market countries (such as China and India) it operates through country subsidiaries in order to adapt to the distinctive features of these markets. Among functions, R & D is globally integrated, while sales are organized by national units that are differentiated to meet local market characteristics.

The transnational firm is a concept and direction of development rather than a distinct organizational archetype. It involves convergence of the different strategy configurations of MNCs. Thus, companies such as Philips, Unilever, and Siemens have reassigned roles and responsibilities to achieve greater integration within their traditional "decentralized federations" of national subsidiaries. Japanese global corporations such as Toyota and Matsushita have drastically reduced the roles of their Japanese headquarters. American multinationals such as Citigroup and IBM are moving in two directions: reducing the role of their US bases while increasing integration among their different national subsidiaries.

Multinational corporations are increasingly locating management control of their global product divisions outside their home countries. When Philips adopted a product division structure, it located responsibility for medical electronics in its US subsidiary and leadership in consumer electronics in Japan. Nexans, the world's biggest manufacturer of electric cables, has moved the head office of five of its 20 product divisions outside of France. For example, the head of ships' cables is based in South Korea, the world leader in shipbuilding.[36] Aligning structure, strategy, and national resources may even require shifting the corporate headquarters—HSBC moved from Hong Kong to London; Tetra Pak from Lund, Sweden to Lausanne, Switzerland.[37]

A recent McKinsey study discovered that successful multinationals underperformed successful "national champions." The study identifies a "globalization penalty" reflecting the difficulties which MNCs experienced in:

- setting a shared vision and engaging employees around it;
- maintaining professional standards and encouraging innovation;
- building government and community relationships and business partnerships.

The interviews conducted for the study highlighted the challenges that MNCs faced in reconciling the challenges of local differentiation and global integration:

> Almost everyone we interviewed seemed to struggle with this tension, which often plays out in heated internal debates. Which organizational elements should be standardized? To what extent does managing high-potential emerging markets on a country-by-country basis make sense? When is it better, in those markets, to leverage scale and synergies across business units in managing governments, regulators, partners, and talent?[38]

Organizing R & D and New Product Development   Organizing for innovation represents one of the greatest challenges in reconciling local initiative with global integration. The traditional European decentralized model is conducive to local initiatives, but not to their global exploitation. Philips has an outstanding record of innovation in consumer electronics. In its TV business, its Canadian subsidiary developed its first color TV; its Australian subsidiary developed its first stereo sound TV and its British subsidiary developed teletext TVs. However, lack of global integration constrained its success on a worldwide scale. Conversely, many US multinationals have been effective at globally rolling out products and technologies developed at their US cores.

Transnational organizations assign national subsidiaries with global mandates that allow them to take advantage of local resources and capabilities while exploiting globally the results of their initiatives.[39] For example, P&G, recognizing Japanese obsessiveness over cleanliness, assigned increasing responsibility to its Japanese subsidiary for developing household cleaning products. Its Swiffer dust-collecting products were developed in Japan (using technology developed by other firms) then introduced into other markets. Where a local unit possesses unique capabilities, designating it a *center of excellence* can facilitate the dissemination of these capabilities throughout the multinational firm.[40]

Summary

Moving from a national to an international business environment represents a quantum leap in complexity. In an international environment, a firm's potential for competitive advantage is determined not just by its own resources and capabilities but also by the conditions of the national environment in which it operates, including input prices, exchange rates, and a host of other factors. The extent to which a firm is positioned across multiple national markets also influences its economic power.

Our approach in this chapter has been to simplify the complexities of international strategy by applying the same basic tools of strategy analysis that we developed in earlier chapters. For example, to determine whether a firm should enter an overseas market, our focus has been the profit implications of such an entry. This requires an analysis of (a) the attractiveness of the overseas market using the familiar tools of industry analysis and (b) the potential of the firm to establish competitive advantage in that overseas market, which depends on the firm's ability to transfer its resources and capabilities to the new location and their effectiveness in conferring competitive advantage.

However, establishing the potential for a firm to create value from internationalization is only a beginning. Subsequent analysis needs to design an international strategy: do we enter an overseas market by exporting, licensing, or direct investment? If the latter, should we set up a wholly owned subsidiary or a joint venture? Once the strategy has been established, a suitable organizational structure needs to be designed.

That so many companies that have been outstandingly successful in their home market have failed so miserably in their overseas expansion demonstrates the complexity of international management. In some cases, companies have failed to recognize that the resources and capabilities that underpinned their competitive advantage in their home market could not be readily transferred or replicated in overseas markets. In others, the problems were in designing the structures and systems that could effectively implement the international strategy.

As the lessons of success and failure from international business become recognized and distilled into better theories and analytical frameworks, so we advance our understanding of how to design and implement strategies for competing globally. We are at the stage where we recognize the issues and the key determinants of competitive advantage in an international environment. However, there is much that we do not fully understand. Designing strategies and organizational structures that can reconcile critical tradeoffs between global scale economies versus local differentiation, decentralized learning and innovation versus worldwide diffusion and replication, and localized flexibilities versus international standardization remains a key challenge for senior managers.

Quizzes and flashcards to test yourself further are available in your interactive e-book at **www.wileyopenpage.com**

Self-Study Questions

1. With reference to Figure 12.1, identify a *sheltered industry*—one that has been subject to little penetration either by imports or foreign direct investment. Explain why the industry has escaped internationalization. Explore whether there are opportunities for profitable internationalization within the industry and, if so, the strategy that would offer the best chance of success.

2. With reference to Table 12.1, what characteristics of national resources explain the different patterns of comparative advantage for the US and Japan?

3. According to Michael Porter's *Competitive Advantage of Nations*, some of the industries where British companies have an international advantage are: advertising, auctioneering of antiques and artwork, distilled alcoholic beverages, hand tools, and chemical preparations for gardening and horticulture. Some of the industries where US companies have an international competitive advantage are: photo film, aircraft and helicopters, computer hardware and software, oilfield services, management consulting, cinema films and TV programs, healthcare products and services, and financial services. For either the UK or the US, use Porter's national diamond framework (Figure 12.3) to explain the observed pattern of international competitive advantage.

4. When Porsche decided to enter the SUV market with its luxury Cayenne model, it surprised the auto industry by locating its new assembly plant in Leipzig in Eastern Germany. Many observers believed that Porsche should have located the plant either in Central or Eastern Europe where labor costs were very low or (like Mercedes and BMW) in the US where it would be close to its major market. Using the criteria outlined in Figure 12.5, can you explain Porsche's decision?

5. British expatriates living in the US frequently ask friends and relatives visiting from the UK to bring with them bars of Cadbury chocolate on the basis that the Cadbury chocolate available in the US (manufactured under license by Hershey's) is inferior to "the real thing." Should Kraft Foods continue Cadbury's licensing agreement with Hershey or should it seek to supply the US market itself, either by export from the UK or by establishing manufacturing facilities in the US?

6. Has McDonald's got the balance right between global standardization and national differentiation (Strategy Capsule 12.3)? Should it offer its franchisees in overseas countries greater initiative in introducing products that meet national preferences? Should it also allow greater flexibility for its overseas franchisees to adapt store layout, operating practices, and marketing? What aspects of the McDonald's system should McDonald's top management insist on keeping globally standardized?

Notes

1. Global Investment Trends (UNCTAD, 2011).

2. This process was proposed by J. Johanson and J.-E. Vahlne, "The Internationalization Process of the Firm," *Journal of International Business Studies* 8 (1977): 23–32.

3. S. L. Segal-Horn, "Globalization of service industries," in J. McGee (ed.), *The Blackwell Encyclopedia of Management: Strategic Management* (Oxford: Blackwell Publishing, 2005): 147–54.

4. P. Ghemawat and F. Ghadar, "Global Integration: Global Concentration," *Industrial and Corporate Change* 15 (2006): 595–624.

5. A key finding was that human capital (knowledge and skills) was more important than physical capital (plant and equipment) in explaining US comparative advantage. See W. W. Leontief, "Domestic Production and Foreign Trade," in R. E. Caves and H. Johnson (eds), *Readings in International Economics* (Homewood, IL: Irwin, 1968).

6. P. Krugman, "Increasing Returns, Monopolistic Competition, and International Trade," *Journal of International Economics* (November 1979): 469–79.

7. M. E. Porter, *The Competitive Advantage of Nations* (New York: Free Press, 1990).

8. For a review of the Porter analysis, see R. M. Grant, "Porter's Competitive Advantage of Nations: An Assessment," *Strategic Management Journal* 12 (1991): 535–48.

9. Y.-R. Park, "Korean Business Culture," Presentation, December 15, 2005, http://gc.sfc.keio.ac.jp/class/2005_14969/slides/10/, accessed July 7, 2009.

10. The linking of value-added chains to national comparative advantages is explained in B. Kogut, "Designing Global Strategies and Competitive Value-Added Chains," *Sloan Management Review* (Summer 1985): 15–38.

11. J. Hagel and J. S. Brown, "Thinking Global, Acting Local," *Financial Times* (August 9, 2005).

12. "Sum of the Parts," *Financial Times* (November 17, 2008).

13. The role of firm-specific assets in explaining the multinational expansion is analyzed in R. Caves, "International Corporations: The Industrial Economics of Foreign Investment," *Economica* 38 (1971): 127.

14. D. J. Teece, "Transactions Cost Economics and Multinational Enterprise," *Journal of Economic Behavior and Organization* 7 (1986): 21–45.

15. This section draws heavily upon G. S. Yip, *Total Global Strategy II* (Upper Saddle River, NJ: Prentice Hall, 2003).

16. T. Levitt, "The Globalization of Markets," *Harvard Business Review* (May/June 1983): 92–102.

17. P. Ghemawat, *Redefining Global Strategy: Crossing Borders in a World Where Differences Still Matter* (Boston: Harvard Business School, 2007).

18. T. Levitt, "The Globalization of Markets," *Harvard Business Review* (May/June 1983): 94.

19. S. G. Winter and G. Szulanski, "Replication as Strategy," *Organization Science* 12 (2001): 730–743.

20. D. B. Montgomery, G. S. Yip, and B. Villalonga, "Explaining Supplier Behavior on Global Account Management," Stanford Research Paper No. 1767 (November 2002). Abstract available at SSRN: http://ssrn.com/abstract=355240, accessed July 7, 2009.

21. P. Almeida, "Knowledge Sourcing by Foreign Multinationals: Patent Citation Analysis in the US Semiconductor Industry," *Strategic Management Journal* 17 (Winter 1996): 155–65.

22. P. Ghemawat, "The Forgotten Strategy," *Harvard Business Review* (November 2003): 76–84.

23. Comments by Tommy Kullberg (IKEA Japan) in "The Japan Paradox," conference organized by the European Commission, Director General for External Affairs (December 2003): 62–3, available at http://www.deljpn.ec.europa.eu/data/current/japan-paradox.pdf, accessed July 7, 2009.

24. A. K. Gupta and P. Govindarajan, "Knowledge Flows within Multinational Corporations," *Strategic Management Journal* 21 (April 2000): 473–96; P. Almeida, J. Song, and R. M. Grant, "Are Firms Superior to Alliances and Markets? An Empirical Test of Cross-Border Knowledge Building," *Organization Science* 13 (March/April 2002): 147–61.

25. G. Hamel and C. K. Prahalad, "Do You Really Have a Global Strategy?" *Harvard Business Review* (July/August 1985): 139–48.

26. B. Y. Aw, G. Batra, and M. J. Roberts, "Firm Heterogeneity and Export: Domestic Price Differentials: A Study of Taiwanese Electrical Products," *Journal of International Economics* 54 (2001): 149–69; A. Bernard, J. B. Jensen, and P. Schott, "Transfer Pricing by US Based Multinational Firms," Working Papers 08-29, Center for Economic Studies, US Census Bureau, 2008.

27. I. C. Macmillan, A. van Ritten, and R. G. McGrath, "Global Gamesmanship," *Harvard Business Review* (May 2003): 62–71.

28. R. C. Christopher, *Second to None: American Companies in Japan* (New York: Crown, 1986).

29. The Ford Mondeo/Contour is a classic example of a global product that failed to appeal strongly to any national market. See M. J. Moi, "Ford Mondeo: A Model T World Car?" Working Paper, Rotterdam School of Management, Erasmus University (2001); C. Chandler, "Globalization: The Automotive Industry's Quest for a World Car," *GlobalEdge Working Paper*, Michigan State University (1997).

30. C. Baden-Fuller and J. Stopford, "Globalization Frustrated," *Strategic Management Journal* 12 (1991): 493–507.

31. R. M. Grant and M. Venzin, "Strategic and Organizational Challenges of Internationalization in Financial Services," *Long Range Planning* 42 (October 2009).

32. P. Ghemawat (P. Ghemawat, *Redefining Global Strategy: Crossing Borders in a World Where Differences Still Matter*, Boston: Harvard Business School, 2007) proposes a three-way rather than a two-way analysis. In his Adaptation–Aggregation–Arbitrage (AAA) framework he divides integration into aggregation and arbitrage.

33. C. A. Bartlett and S. Ghoshal, *Managing across Borders: The Transnational Solution*, 2nd edn (Boston: Harvard Business School Press, 1998): 34.

34. C. Bartlett, "Building and Managing the Transnational: The New Organizational Challenge," in Michael E. Porter (ed.), *Competition in Global Industries* (Boston: Harvard Business School Press, 1986): 377.

35. C. Bartlett, "Building and Managing the Transnational: The New Organizational Challenge," in Michael E. Porter (ed.), *Competition in Global Industries* (Boston: Harvard Business School Press, 1986): 388.

36. "The Country Prince Comes of Age," *Financial Times* (August 9, 2005).

37. J. Birkinshaw, P. Braunerhjelm, U. Holm, and S. Terjesen, "Why Do Some Multinational Corporations Relocate Their Headquarters Overseas?" *Strategic Management Journal* 27 (2006): 681–700.

38. M. Dewhurst, J. Harris, and S. Heywood, "Understanding your globalization penalty," *McKinsey Quarterly* (June 2011).

39. J. Birkinshaw, N. Hood, and S. Jonsson, "Building Firm-specific Advantages in Multinational Corporations: The Role of Subsidiary Initiative," *Strategic Management Journal* 19 (1998): 221–42.

40. T. S. Frost, J. M. Birkinshaw, and P. C. Ensign, "Centers of Excellence in Multinational Corporations," *Strategic Management Journal* 23 (2002): 997–1018.

13 Diversification Strategy

> Telephones, hotels, insurance—it's all the same. If you know the numbers inside out, you know the company inside out.
>
> —HAROLD SYDNEY GENEEN, CHAIRMAN OF ITT, 1959–1978, AND
> INSTIGATOR OF 275 COMPANY TAKEOVERS

> Creating three independent, public companies is the next logical step for Tyco. . . the new standalone companies will have greater flexibility to pursue their own focused strategies for growth than they would under Tyco's current corporate structure. This will allow all three companies to create significant value for shareholders.
>
> —ED BREEN, CHAIRMAN AND CEO, TYCO INTERNATIONAL LTD, ANNOUNCING
> THE COMPANY'S BREAKUP, SEPTEMBER 19, 2011

OUTLINE

Introduction and Objectives

Answering the question "What business are we in?" is the starting point of strategy and the basis for defining the firm's identity. In their statements of vision and mission, some companies define their businesses broadly. Shell's objective is "to engage efficiently, responsibly, and profitably in oil, oil products, gas, chemicals, and other selected businesses." Other companies define their businesses more narrowly: McDonald's vision is "to be the world's best quick-service restaurant chain"; Caterpillar will "be the leader in providing the best value in machines, engines, and support services for companies dedicated to building the world's infrastructure and developing and transporting its resources."

The business scope of firms changes over time. The dominant trend of the past two decades has been "refocusing on core businesses." Philip Morris Companies, Inc. (now renamed Altria Group, Inc.) sold off 7-Up, Miller Brewing, and Kraft Foods and became a specialist tobacco company. Most widely diversified groups—US and European conglomerates such as ITT, Hanson, Gulf & Western, Cendant, Vivendi Universal, and Tyco—have broken up altogether.

Some companies have moved in the opposite direction. Microsoft, once a supplier of operating systems, expanded into application and networking software, information services, entertainment systems, and video games consoles. Google is no longer simply a search engine company; it supplies a wide array of information products, advertising management services, applications software, operating systems (including its Android mobile platform), and, most recently, wireless handsets.

Diversification is a conundrum. The quest to enter new fields of business has probably caused more value destruction than any other type of strategic decision. Yet, diversification also permits a firm to free itself of the restrictions of a single industry and access new growth opportunities.

Our goal in this chapter is to establish the basis on which companies can make corporate strategy decisions that create rather than destroy value. Is it better to be specialized or diversified? Is there an optimal degree of diversification? What types of diversification are most likely to create value?

In practice, we make these types of decision every day in our personal lives. If my car doesn't start in the morning, should I try to fix it myself or have it towed directly to the garage? There are two considerations. First, is repairing a car an attractive activity to undertake? If the garage charges $85 an hour but I can earn $600 an hour consulting, then car repair is not attractive to me. Second, am I any good at car repair? If I am likely to take twice as long as a skilled mechanic then I possess no competitive advantage in car repair.

Diversification decisions by firms involve the same two issues:

◆ How attractive is the industry to be entered?
◆ Can the firm establish a competitive advantage?

These are the very same factors we identified in Chapter 1 (Figure 1.5) as determining a firm's profit potential. Hence, no new analytic framework is needed for appraising diversification decisions: diversification may be justified either by the superior profit potential of the industry to be entered or by the ability of the firm to create competitive advantage in the new industry. The first issue draws on the industry analysis developed in Chapter 3; the second draws on the analysis of competitive advantage developed in Chapters 5 and 7.

Our primary focus will be the latter question: under what conditions does operating multiple businesses assist a firm in gaining a competitive advantage in each? This leads into exploring linkages between different businesses within the diversified firm—a phenomenon often referred to as *synergy*.

By the time you have completed this chapter, you will be able to:

◆ comprehend the factors causing the trends, first, toward diversification and, subsequently, toward refocusing;

◆ recognize the corporate goals that have motivated diversification and the tendency for growth and risk reduction to conflict with value creation;

◆ understand the conditions under which diversification creates value for shareholders, and assess the potential for value creation from economies of scope, internalizing transactions, and corporate parenting;

◆ appreciate the implications of different types of business relatedness for the success of diversification and the management of diversification.

Trends in Diversification over Time

As a background to our analysis of diversification decisions, let's begin by examining the factors that have influenced diversification strategies in the past.

The Urge to Diversify, 1950–1980

In Chapter 11, while discussing "The Shifting Boundary between Firms and Markets," I identified diversification as a major contributor to the widening scope of firms during the 20th century. Between 1950 and 1980, the expansion of companies into different product markets was a major source of corporate growth in all the advanced industrial nations.[1] The 1970s saw the peak of the diversification boom, with the emergence of a new corporate form—the *conglomerate*—represented in the US by ITT, Textron, and Allied Signal, and in the UK by Hanson, Slater-Walker, and BTR. These highly diversified enterprises were created from multiple, unrelated acquisitions. Their existence reflected the view that senior management no longer needed industry-specific experience; corporate management simply needed to deploy the new techniques of financial and strategic management.[2] Figure 13.1 shows changing patterns of diversification strategy during the latter part of the 20th century.

Refocusing, 1980–2009

After 1980, the diversification trend went into sharp reverse. Between 1980 and 1990, the average index of diversification for the Fortune 500 declined from 1.00 to

0.67.[3] Unprofitable "noncore" businesses were divested and many diversified companies fell prey to acquirers, who promptly restructured them.[4] Acquisition activity was extremely heavy during the 1980s—some $1.3 trillion in assets were acquired, including 113 members of the Fortune 500—but, unlike the previous decade, only 4.5% of acquisitions represented unrelated diversification.[5] Moreover, acquisitions by the Fortune 500 were outnumbered by dispositions. By the end of 2010 there were only 22 conglomerates left in the US of which three had announced their intention to split up.[6] The refocusing trend was strongest in the US, but was also evident in Canada and Europe and, to a lesser extent, in Japan.[7]

This trend toward specialization was the result of three principal factors.

Emphasis on Shareholder Value   The primary driver of refocusing was the reordering of corporate goals from growth to profitability. Sluggish growth and high interest rates during the early 1980s and from 1989 to 1990 exposed the inadequate profitability of many large, diversified corporations. Institutional shareholders, including pension funds such as California's Public Employees' Retirement system, became more active in pressuring top management for better shareholder returns—this led to increased CEO turnover.[8]

The surge in leveraged buyouts put further pressure on executives to boost shareholder returns. Kohlberg Kravis Roberts' $31 billion takeover of the tobacco and food giant RJR Nabisco in 1989 demonstrated that even the largest US companies were vulnerable to attack from corporate raiders.[9] The result was a rush by diversified giants to restructure before leveraged buyout specialists did it for them. Evidence of "conglomerate discounts"—that the stock market was valuing diversified companies at less than the sum of their parts—provided a further incentive for breakups.[10]

Turbulence and Transaction Costs   In Chapter 11, we observed that the relative costs of organizing transactions within firms and across markets depend on

FIGURE 13.1   Diversification strategies of large US and UK companies during the late 20th century

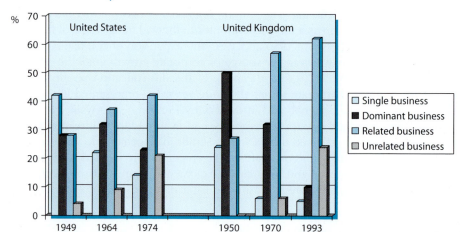

Sources: R. P. Rumelt, "Diversification Strategy and Profitability," *Strategic Management Journal* 3 (1982): 359–70; R. Whittington, M. Mayer, and F. Curto, "Chandlerism in Post-war Europe: Strategic and Structural Change in France, Germany and the UK: 1950–1993," *Industrial and Corporate Change* 8 (1999): 519–50; D. Channon, *The Strategy and Structure of British Enterprise* (Cambridge: Harvard University Press, 1973).

the conditions in the external environment. Administrative hierarchies are very efficient in processing routine transactions, but in turbulent conditions the pressure of decision making on top management results in stress, inefficiency, and delay. As the business environment has become more volatile, specialized companies are more agile than large diversified corporations where strategic decisions require approval at divisional and corporate levels. At the same time, external markets for resources, and capital markets especially, have become increasingly efficient. Many diversified companies have spun off their growth businesses because of the greater potential of external capital markets to fund their development.

Outside the mature industrialized countries, the situation is very different. Highly diversified business groups dominate the industrial sectors of many emerging countries: Tata Group and Reliance in India, Charoen Pokphand (CP) in Thailand, Astra International in Indonesia, Sime Darby in Malaysia, Grupo Alfa and Grupo Carso in Mexico. One reason for the continued dominance of large conglomerates in emerging market countries may be the higher transaction costs associated with their less sophisticated markets for finance, information, and labor that offer diversified companies advantages over their specialized competitors.[11]

Trends in Management Thinking   Optimism that new tools and systems of financial and strategic management would enable companies to span many different businesses has been replaced by recognition that competitive advantage requires focusing on key strengths in resources and capabilities. Deploying core resources and capabilities across different product markets can support profitable diversification. Hence, the focus of diversification analysis has been to identify the circumstances in which multibusiness activity can create value. Analysis of economies of scope, the transferability of resources and capabilities across industry boundaries,

FIGURE 13.2   The evolution of diversification strategies, 1960–2012

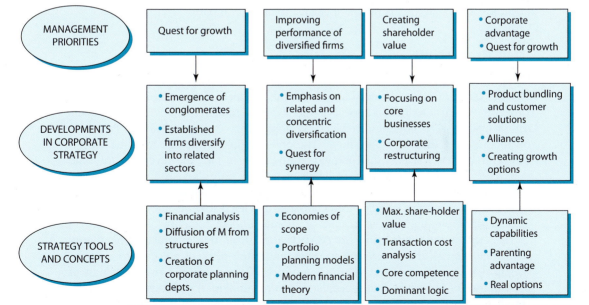

and the role of transaction costs have allowed us to be more precise about these circumstances. Mere linkages between businesses are not enough: the key to creating value is the ability of the diversified firm to share resources and transfer capabilities more efficiently than alternative institutional arrangements can. Moreover, it is essential that the benefits of these linkages are not outweighed by the additional management costs of exploiting them. Figure 13.2 summarizes some of the key developments in diversification strategy over the past 50 years.

Motives for Diversification

A critical development in the transition from diversification to refocusing was the reordering of corporate objectives. Corporate diversification for most of the 20th century was driven by two key objectives: *growth* and *risk reduction*. During the last two decades of the 20th century, decisions over firms' business portfolios were increasingly dominated by a third objective: *creating shareholder value*.

Growth

In the absence of diversification, firms are prisoners of their industry. For firms in stagnant or declining industries this is a daunting prospect, especially for top management. The urge to achieve corporate growth that outstrips that of a firm's primary industry is an appealing prospect for managers. Companies in low-growth, cash-flow-rich industries such as tobacco and oil have been especially susceptible to the temptations of diversification. During the 1980s, Exxon diversified into copper and coal mining, electric motors, and computers and office equipment; RJR Nabisco transformed itself from a tobacco company into a diversified consumer products company. In both cases diversification destroyed shareholder value. The leveraged buyout of RJR Nabisco by Kohlberg Kravis Roberts was followed by its breakup. Reynolds American, Inc. is now a specialist tobacco company.

Risk Reduction

If the cash flows of different businesses are imperfectly correlated, then bringing them together under common ownership reduces the variance of the combined cash flow. However, such risk reduction appeals to managers more than to owners. Shareholders can diversify risk by holding diversified portfolios. Hence, what advantage can there be in companies diversifying for them? The only possible advantage could be if firms can diversify at lower cost than individual investors. In fact, the reverse is true: the transaction costs to shareholders of diversifying their portfolios are far less than the transaction costs to firms diversifying through acquisition. Not only do acquiring firms incur the heavy costs of using investment banks and legal advisers, they must also pay an acquisition premium to gain control of an independent company.

The *capital asset pricing model* (CAPM) formalizes this argument. The theory states that the risk that is relevant to determining the price of a security is not the overall risk (variance) of the security's return but the *systematic risk*—that part of the variance of the return that is correlated with overall market returns. This is measured by the security's *beta coefficient*. Corporate diversification does not reduce systematic risk: if three separate companies are brought under common ownership, in the absence of any other changes, the beta coefficient of the combined company is simply the weighted average of the beta coefficients of the constituent companies. Hence, the simple act of bringing different businesses under common ownership does not create shareholder value through risk reduction.[12]

Empirical studies are generally supportive of the absence of shareholder benefit from diversification that simply combines independent businesses under a single corporate umbrella.[13] Unrelated diversification may even fail to lower unsystematic risk.[14]

Special issues arise once we consider the risk of bankruptcy. For a marginally profitable firm, diversification can help avoid cyclical fluctuations of profits that can push it into insolvency. However, diversification that reduces the risk of bankruptcy is beneficial to bondholders (and other creditors) rather than shareholders.[15]

Are there circumstances in which reductions in unsystematic risk can create shareholder value? If there are economies to the firm from financing investments internally rather than resorting to external capital markets, the stability in the firm's cash flow that results from diversification may reinforce independence from external capital markets. For ExxonMobil, BP, and the other major oil companies, one of the benefits of extending across upstream (exploration and production), downstream (refining and marketing), and chemicals is that the negative correlation of the returns from these businesses increases the overall stability of their cash flows. This in turn increases their capacity to undertake huge, risky investments in offshore oil production, transcontinental pipelines, and natural gas liquefaction. These benefits also explain why firms pursue hedging activities that only reduce unsystematic risk.[16]

The financial turmoil of 2008–2009 has created a new appreciation of the risk-spreading benefits of diversification. The seizing-up of credit markets toward the end of 2008 was less serious for large firms with diversified cash flows that were less dependent on banks providing working capital.

Value Creation: Porter's "Essential Tests"

If we return to the assumption that corporate strategy should be directed toward the interests of shareholders, what are the implications for diversification strategy? At the beginning of the chapter, we revisited our two sources of superior profitability: industry attractiveness and competitive advantage. In establishing the conditions for profitable diversification, Michael Porter refines these into "three essential tests" which determine whether diversification will truly create shareholder value:

- *The attractiveness test*: The industries chosen for diversification must be structurally attractive or capable of being made attractive.
- *The cost-of-entry test*: The cost of entry must not capitalize all the future profits.
- *The better-off test*: Either the new unit must gain competitive advantage from its link with the corporation or vice versa.[17]

The Attractiveness and Cost-of-Entry Tests   A critical realization in Porter's "essential tests" is that industry *attractiveness* is insufficient on its own. Although diversification allows a firm to access more attractive investment opportunities than are available in its own industry, it faces the challenge of entering a new industry. The second test, *cost of entry*, recognizes that for outsiders the cost of entry may counteract the attractiveness of the industry. Pharmaceuticals, corporate legal services, and defense contracting offer above-average profitability precisely because they are protected by barriers to entry. Firms seeking to enter these industries have a choice. They may acquire an established player, in which case the acquisition price will almost certainly fully capitalize the target firm's profit prospects (especially given the need to pay an acquisition premium over the market price of the target).[18] Alternatively, entry may occur through establishing a new corporate venture. In this case, the diversifying firm must directly confront the barriers to entry protecting that industry.[19]

Hewlett-Packard has diversified into IT services primarily because it views IT services as a more attractive industry than IT hardware. However, building an IT service business was expensive for HP: its $13.9 billion acquisition of EDS in 2008 was at a 30% premium over EDS's market value; its $10.3 billion acquisition of Autonomy in 2011 involved a 60% premium.

The Better-Off Test   Porter's third criterion for successful diversification—*the better-off test*—addresses the basic issue of competitive advantage: if two businesses producing different products are brought together under the ownership and control of a single enterprise, is there any reason why they should become any more profitable? Combining different, but related, businesses can enhance the competitive advantages of the original business, the new business, or both. For example:

- Procter & Gamble's 2005 acquisition of Gillette was intended to boost the competitive position of both companies through combining the two companies' global marketing and distribution networks, transferring Gillette's new product development capabilities to P&G, and increasing both companies' bargaining power relative to retail giants such as Wal-Mart.
- The spate of mergers between banks and insurance companies (Citigroup acquired Travelers, Allianz acquired Dresdner Bank, and Credit Suisse acquired Winterthur) was based upon the belief that cross-selling of banking and insurance products would benefit both sides of the new *bancassurance* companies.

Primacy of the Better-Off Test   In most normal circumstances it is only the better-off test that matters. In the first place, industry attractiveness is rarely a source of value from diversification—in most cases, cost-of-entry cancels out advantages of industry attractiveness.

The second reason why the better-off test normally dominates is that it can make sense for a company to enter an unattractive industry so long as the cost of entry is sufficiently discounted and the better-off test is met. When private equity firm Golden Gate Capital bought Eddie Bauer, Inc. in August 2009, the deal was motivated not by the attractiveness of the retail clothing sector but by Golden Gate's ability to buy the 400-store chain for a mere $286 million, then apply its financial and strategic management capabilities to revitalizing the sportswear chain. Sony Corporation's acquisition of CBS Records, Bertelsmann Music Group (BMG), and EMI Records, took Sony into the spectacularly unattractive music publishing industry. The attraction for Sony was building its integrated position in entertainment.

So, let us now further explore the ways in which diversification can make businesses "better off" through analyzing the relationship between diversification and competitive advantage.

Competitive Advantage from Diversification

If the primary source of value creation from diversification is exploiting linkages between different businesses, what are these linkages and how are they exploited? The critical linkages are those that arise through the sharing of resources and capabilities across different businesses.

Economies of Scope

The most general argument concerning the benefits of diversification focuses on the presence of **economies of scope** in common resources: "Economies of scope exist when using a resource across multiple activities uses less of that resource than when the activities are carried out independently."[20]

Economies of scope exist for similar reasons as economies of scale. The key difference is that economies of scale relate to cost economies from increasing output of a *single product*; economies of scope are cost economies from increasing the output of *multiple products*.[21] The nature of economies of scope varies between different types of resources and capabilities.

Tangible Resources   Tangible resources—such as distribution networks, information technology systems, sales forces, and research laboratories—offer economies of scope by eliminating duplication between businesses through creating a single shared facility. The greater the fixed costs of these items, the greater the associated economies of scope are likely to be. Entry by cable TV companies into telephone services and telephone companies into cable TV are motivated by the desire to spread the costs of networks and billing systems over as great a volume of business as possible. Common resources such as customer data bases, customer service centers, and billing systems have encouraged Centrica, Britain's biggest gas utility, to diversify into supplying electricity, fixed-line and mobile telephone services, broadband internet connections, home security systems, home insurance, and home-appliance repair.

Economies of scope also arise from the centralized provision of administrative and support services to the different businesses of the corporation. Within diversified companies, accounting, legal services, government relations, and information technology tend to be centralized, often through *shared service organizations* that supply common administrative and technical services to the operating businesses. Similar economies arise from centralizing research activities in a corporate research lab.

Intangible Resources   Intangible resources such as brands, corporate reputation, and technology offer economies of scope from the ability to extend them to additional businesses at low marginal cost.[22] Exploiting a strong brand across additional products is called *brand extension*. Starbucks has extended its brand to ice cream, packaged cold drinks, home espresso machines, audio CDs, and books.

Organizational Capabilities   Organizational capabilities can also be transferred within the diversified company. For example:

- LVMH is the world's biggest and most diversified supplier of branded luxury goods. Its distinctive capability is the management of luxury brands. This capability comprises market analysis, advertising, promotion, retail management, and quality assurance. These capabilities are deployed across Louis Vuitton (accessories and leather goods); Hennessey (cognac); Moët & Chandon, Dom Pérignon, Veuve Clicquot, and Krug (champagne); Céline, Givenchy, Kenzo, Christian Dior, Guerlain, and Donna Karan (fashion clothing and perfumes); TAG Heuer and Chaumet (watches); Sephora and La Samaritaine (retailing); Bulgari (jewelry); and some 25 other branded businesses.

- Sharp Corporation—originally established to manufacture metal products and the Ever Sharp Pencil—developed capabilities in the miniaturization of electronic products. It has introduced a stream of innovative products, beginning with the world's first transistor calculator (1964), the first LCD pocket calculator (1973), LCD color TVs, PDAs, internet viewcams, ultraportable notebook computers, mobile telephones, and photovoltaic cells.

Some of the most important capabilities in influencing the performance of diversified corporations are *general management capabilities*. General Electric possesses strong technological and operational capabilities at business level and it is good at sharing these capabilities between businesses (e.g., turbine know-how between jet engines and electrical generating equipment). However, its core capabilities are in general management and these reside primarily at the corporate level. They include its ability to motivate and develop its managers, its outstanding strategic and financial management that reconciles decentralized decision making with strong centralized control, and its international management capability. Similar observations could be made about 3M. While 3M's capabilities in technical know-how, new product development, and international marketing reside within the individual businesses, it is the corporate management capabilities and the systems through which they are exercised that maintain, nourish, coordinate, and upgrade these competitive advantages.[23]

Economies from Internalizing Transactions

Although economies of scope provide cost savings from sharing and transferring resources and capabilities, does a firm have to diversify across these different businesses to exploit those economies? The answer is no. Economies of scope in resources and capabilities can be exploited simply by selling or licensing the use of the resource or capability to another company. In Chapter 9, we observed that a firm can exploit proprietary technology by licensing it to other firms. In Chapter 12, we noted how technology and trademarks are licensed across national frontiers as an alternative to direct investment. Similarly across industries: Starbucks' extension of its brand to other products has been achieved primarily through licensing: Pepsi produces and distributes Starbucks Frappuccino; Unilever produces Tazo Tea beverages, Dreyer's produces Starbucks ice cream. Walt Disney exploits the enormous value of its trademarks, copyrights, and characters partly through diversification into theme parks, live theater, cruise ships, and hotels; but it also licenses the use of these assets to producers of clothing, toys, music, comics, food, and drinks, as well as to the franchisees of Disney's retail stores. Disney's income from licensing fees and royalties was over $2 billion in 2005.

Even tangible resources can be shared across different businesses through market transactions. Airport and railroad station operators exploit economies of scope in their facilities not by diversifying into catering and retailing but by leasing out space to specialist retailers and restaurants.

Are economies of scope better exploited internally within the firm through diversification or externally through market contracts with independent companies? The key issue is *relative efficiency*—what are the transaction costs of market contracts compared with the administrative costs of diversified activities? Transaction costs include the costs involved in drafting, negotiating, monitoring, and enforcing a contract, plus the costs of protecting against exploitation by the partner. The costs of internalization consist of the management costs of establishing and coordinating the diversified business.[24]

Consider the following:

- In the case of Walt Disney Company, it licenses Donald Duck trademarks to Florida's Natural Growers rather than setting up its own orange-juice company; it owns and operates Disneyland and Disney World theme parks but licenses its trademarks and technology to Oriental Land Company, the owner and operator of Tokyo Disneyland.
- Both Mars and Cadbury used their confectionary brands to enter the European ice cream market. Cadbury decided to license its brands to Nestlé. Mars entered the business itself by setting up production and distribution facilities, competing with Unilever and Nestlé. The result was that Cadbury made significant profits from its licenses whereas Mars experienced years of losses or low returns on its investment.

Finding the right answer is complex. It depends on the nature of the resource or capability that is generating the "better off" benefits. If the resource can be traded or licensed out for anything close to its real value, as in the case of the Donald Duck trademark or the confectionary brands, then it is not necessary to enter another business in order to capture the extra profitability. Cadbury captured more profitability by not entering the ice-cream business. If, on the other hand, the resource is one that cannot easily be traded, such as general management capabilities, then it will be necessary to enter the new business in order to create the extra profitability. There is little scope for 3M to deploy its new product development capabilities other than within its own business. Similarly, for Apple the only way for it to exploit its capabilities in user-friendly design was to diversify outside of its core computer business.

Virgin has a separate licensing company but it licenses its brand mainly to companies within the Virgin group. So why doesn't Virgin license its brand to companies it does not have an equity interest in? The answer presumably is that the brand is part of a package of benefits that Virgin offers, some of which could not be traded or licensed. For example, Virgin has developed special marketing skills around its brand, often using the brand and Richard Branson to gain press comment in place of expensive advertising.

Parenting Advantage

The recognition that it is only certain kinds of economies of scope that justify diversification led Goold, Campbell, and Alexander to propose the concept of *parenting value added* (an alternative to Porter's better-off test).[25] Parenting value comes from deploying the resources and general management skills possessed by the parent company. In Virgin's case they include the brand, Richard Branson's skill at attracting media coverage, and Virgin's business partnering capabilities. If these skills add value to a new business, then Virgin should think of entering that business. While Porter's better-off test focuses on the potential to share resources, Goold and his colleagues focus on the role of corporate managers in identifying and exploiting such linkages. Hence, they argue that parenting value added explains nearly all successful diversification because parenting is the central capability that is difficult to imitate and lies at the heart of the efficiency and effectiveness of the diversified corporation.

A further insight that arises from the parenting approach is that the criterion for diversification should not be the potential to add value from a diversification but whether the firm can *add more value than could any other parent*. General Electric's sale of NBC Universal to Comcast in 2011 reflected the fact that, irrespective of GE's capacity to add value to NBC Universal, Comcast (because of its other media interests) could add more value.

The Diversified Firm as an Internal Market

We see that economies of scope on their own do not provide an adequate rationale for diversification: they must be supported by potential to economize on transaction costs. In fact, the lower costs of managing transactions internally can offer "better off" efficiencies, even when no economies of scope are present.

Internal Capital Markets   Consider the case of financial capital. The diversified firm represents an internal capital market: the corporate allocating capital between the different businesses through the capital expenditure budget. Which is more efficient, the internal capital markets of diversified companies or the external capital market? Diversified companies have two key advantages:

- By maintaining a balanced portfolio of cash-generating and cash-using businesses, diversified firms can avoid the costs of using the external capital market, including the margin between borrowing and lending rates and the heavy costs of issuing new debt and equity.
- Diversified companies have better access to information on the financial prospects of their different businesses than that typically available to external financiers.[26]

Against these advantages is the critical disadvantage that investment allocation within the diversified company is a politicized process in which strategic and financial considerations are subordinated to turf battles and ego building. Evidence suggests that diversified firms' internal capital markets tend to cross-subsidize poorly performing divisions and are reluctant to transfer cash flows to the divisions with the best prospects.[27] However, the efficiency of capital allocation varies greatly across companies. Marakon Associates identified several conglomerates with exceptional performance in terms of ten-year shareholder returns. They included GE and Berkshire Hathaway of the US, Hutchison Whampoa of Hong Kong, Bouygues and Lagardère of France, Wesfarmers of Australia, ITC of India, and Grupo Carso of Mexico. These companies were characterized by: "Strict financial discipline, rigorous analysis and valuation, a refusal to overpay for acquisitions, and a willingness to close or sell existing businesses."[28]

Another form of organization that reduces the transaction costs of external capital markets is the *private equity firm*. These firms raise money creating a fund that is then used to buy businesses. Instead of raising money each time they want to buy a business, they do the money raising once. Moreover, they have developed ways of avoiding the agency problems of self-seeking managers. Each fund has to be closed and returned to investors within a set number of years, often 10–14 years. This encourages the managers in the private equity firm to take particular care when allocating money from the fund. They want to make sure that each allocation will produce a good return before the fund is closed. They also give equity stakes to the managers in charge of each business that will pay out when the business is sold. This reduces the motivation for playing politics. Finally, the managers leading the individual businesses do not participate in the management decisions of the private equity firm. Many corporations, in contrast, have the heads of the biggest divisions sitting on the corporate-level management committee (more on this in the next chapter).

Internal Labor Markets Efficiencies also arise from the ability of diversified companies to transfer employees, especially managers and technical specialists, between their divisions, and to rely less on hiring and firing. As companies develop and encounter new circumstances, so different management skills are required. The costs associated with hiring include advertising, time spent in interviewing and selection, and the costs of head-hunting agencies. The costs of dismissing employees can be very high where severance payments must be offered. A diversified corporation has a pool of employees and can respond to the specific needs of any one business through transfer from elsewhere within the corporation.

The broader set of career opportunities available in the diversified corporation may attract a higher caliber of employee. Graduating students compete intensely for entry-level positions with diversified corporations such as Canon, General Electric, Unilever, and Nestlé in the belief that these companies can offer richer career development than more specialized companies.

The informational advantages of diversified firms are especially important in relation to internal labor markets. A key problem of hiring from the external labor market is limited information. A résumé, references, and a day of interviews are poor indicators of how a new hire will perform in a particular job. The diversified firm that is engaged in transferring employees between different positions and different internal units can build detailed information on the competencies and characteristics of its employees. This informational advantage exists not only for individual employees but also for groups of individuals working together as teams. Hence, in exploiting a new business opportunity an established firm is at an advantage over the new firm, which must assemble its team from scratch.

Diversification and Performance

Where diversification exploits economies of scope in resources and capabilities in the presence of transaction costs, it has the potential to create value for shareholders. Diversification that seeks only growth or risk reduction is likely to destroy value. How do these predictions work in practice?

The Findings of Empirical Research

Empirical research into diversification has concentrated on two major issues: first, how do diversified firms perform relative to specialized firms and, second, does related diversification outperform unrelated diversification?

The Performance of Diversified and Specialized Firms Despite many empirical studies since the 1960s, consistent, systematic relationships between diversification and performance are lacking. Beyond a certain threshold, high levels of diversification appear to be associated with lower profitability, probably because of the organizational complexity that diversification creates. Among British companies, diversification was associated with increased profitability up to a point, after which further diversification was accompanied by declining profitability.[29] Several other studies have detected a similar curvilinear relationship between diversification and profitability.[30] McKinsey & Company points to the benefits of moderate diversification: "a strategic sweet spot between focus and broader diversification." Diversification, McKinsey argues, makes most sense when a company has exhausted growth opportunities in its existing markets and can match its existing capabilities to emerging external opportunities.[31] However, McKinsey also notes that "conglomerates have underperformed more focused companies . . . From 2002 to 2010, the revenues of conglomerates grew by 6.3% those of focused companies by 9.2%." Their return on capital and their total shareholder returns were also lower.

A key problem is distinguishing *association* from *causation*. If moderately diversified companies are generally more profitable than specialized firms, is it because diversification increases profitability or because profitable firms channel their cash flows into diversifying investments?

The performance effects of diversification depend on the mode of diversification. Mergers and acquisitions involving companies in different industries appear to perform especially poorly.[32]

More consistent evidence concerns the performance results of refocusing initiatives by North American and European companies: when companies divest diversified businesses and concentrate more on their core businesses, the result is, typically, increased profitability and higher stock-market valuation.[33] These findings may reflect a changing relationship between diversification and profitability over time: the growing turbulence of the business environment may have increased the costs of managing widely diversified corporations.

Related and Unrelated Diversification Given the importance of economies of scope in shared resources and capabilities, it seems likely that diversification into *related* industries should be more profitable than diversification into *unrelated* industries. Empirical research initially supported this prediction. Rumelt discovered that companies that diversified into businesses closely related to their core activities were significantly more profitable than those that pursued unrelated diversification.[34] By 1982, Tom Peters and Robert Waterman were able to conclude: "virtually every academic study has concluded that unchanneled diversification is a losing proposition."[35] This observation supported one of their "golden rules of excellence":

> *Stick to the Knitting*. Our principal finding is clear and simple. Organizations that do branch out but stick very close to their knitting outperform the others. The most successful are those diversified around a single skill, the coating and bonding technology at 3M for example. The second group in descending order, comprise those companies that branch out into related fields, the leap from electric power generation turbines to jet engines from GE for example. Least successful are those companies that diversify into a wide variety of fields. Acquisitions especially among this group tend to wither on the vine.[36]

Subsequent studies have clouded the picture: the superiority of related diversifiers may be the result of risk factors and industry influences;[37] unrelated may even outperform related diversification.[38] Several factors may be confusing the relationship. First, related diversification offers greater potential benefits than unrelated but the linkages it involves also create more difficult management problems. (I shall address this issue in the next chapter.) Second, the apparently poor results from unrelated diversification might be the result of poorly performing companies seeking to get far away from their existing businesses.[39] Finally, the distinction between "related" and "unrelated" diversification is not always clear: it may depend upon the strategy and characteristics of individual firms. Champagne and luggage are not obviously related products, but LVMH applies similar brand management capabilities to them both. Let us consider this issue further.

The Meaning of Relatedness in Diversification

If *relatedness* refers to the potential for sharing and transferring resources and capabilities between businesses, there are no unambiguous criteria to determine whether two industries are related; it all depends on the company undertaking the diversification. Empirical studies have defined relatedness in terms of similarities between industries in technologies and markets. These similarities emphasize relatedness at the *operational* level—in manufacturing, marketing, and distribution—typically activities where economies from resource sharing are small and achieving them is costly in management terms. Conversely, one of the most important sources of value creation within the diversified firm is the ability to apply common general management capabilities, strategic management systems, and resource allocation processes to different businesses. Such economies depend on the existence of *strategic* rather than *operational* commonalities among the different businesses within the diversified corporation.[40]

- Berkshire Hathaway is involved in insurance, candy stores, furniture, kitchen knives, jewelry, and footwear. Despite this diversity, all these businesses have been selected on the basis of their ability to benefit from the unique style of corporate management established by chairman Warren Buffett and CEO Charles Munger.

● Richard Branson's Virgin Group covers a huge array of businesses from airlines to health clubs. Yet they share certain strategic similarities: almost all are start-up companies that benefit from Branson's entrepreneurial zeal and expertise; almost all sell to final consumers and are in sectors that offer opportunities for innovative approaches to differentiation.

The essence of such strategic-level linkages is the ability to apply similar strategies, resource allocation procedures, and control systems across the different businesses within the corporate portfolio.[41] Table 13.1 lists some of the strategic factors that determine similarities among businesses in relation to corporate management activities.

Unlike operational relatedness, where the opportunities for exploiting economies of scope in joint inputs are comparatively easy to identify—even to quantify—strategic relatedness is more elusive. It necessitates an understanding of the overall strategic approach of the company and recognition of its corporate-level management capabilities.

Ultimately, the linkage between the different businesses within a company may depend upon the strategic rationale of the company. Prahalad and Bettis use the term *dominant logic* to refer to managers' cognition of the rationale that unifies the different parts of the company.[42] Such a common view of a company's identity and raison d'être is a critical precondition for effective integration across its different businesses. However, dominant logic needs to be underpinned by economic synergies. Otherwise, an appealing dominant logic—such as Allegis Corporation's desire to meet travelers' needs by combining airlines and hotels or General Mills meeting "the needs and wants of the homemaker" by diversifying into toys, fashion clothing, specialty retailing, and restaurants—will fail to translate into real value creation.

TABLE 13.1   The determinants of strategic relatedness between businesses

Corporate Management Tasks	Determinants of Strategic Similarity
Resource allocation	Similar sizes of capital investment projects
	Similar time spans of investment projects
	Similar sources of risk
	Similar general management skills required for business unit managers
Strategy formulation	Similar key success factors
	Similar stages of the industry life cycle
	Similar competitive positions occupied by each business within its industry
Performance management and control variables	Targets defined in terms of similar performance
	Similar time horizons for performance targets

Source: R. M. Grant, "On Dominant Logic, Relatedness, and the Link between Diversity and Performance," *Strategic Management Journal* 9 (1988): 641. Reused by permission of John Wiley & Sons, Ltd.

Summary

Diversification is like sex: its attractions are obvious, often irresistible, yet the experience is often disappointing. For top management it is a minefield. The diversification experiences of large corporations are littered with expensive mistakes: Exxon's attempt to build Exxon Office Systems as a rival to Xerox and IBM; Vivendi's diversification from water and environmental services into media, entertainment, and telecoms; Royal Bank of Scotland's quest to transform itself from a retail bank into a financial services giant. Despite so many costly failures, the urge to diversify continues to captivate senior managers. Part of the problem is the divergence between managerial and shareholder goals. While diversification has offered meager rewards to shareholders, it is the fastest route to building vast corporate empires. A further problem is hubris. A company's success in one line of business tends to result in the top management team becoming overconfident of its ability to achieve similar success in other businesses.

Nevertheless, for companies to survive and prosper over the long term they must change; inevitably, this involves redefining the businesses in which they operate. The world's two largest IT companies—IBM and Hewlett-Packard—are both over six decades old. Their longevity is based on their ability to adapt their product lines to changing market opportunities. Essentially, they have applied existing capabilities to developing new products, which have provided new growth trajectories. Similarly with most other long-established companies: for 3M, Canon, Samsung, and DuPont, diversification has been central to the process of evolution. In most cases, this diversification was not a major discontinuity, but an initial incremental step in which existing resources and capabilities were deployed to exploit a perceived opportunity.

If companies are to use diversification as part of their long-term adaptation and avoid the many errors that corporate executives have made in the past, then better strategic analysis of diversification decisions is essential. The objectives of diversification need to be clear and explicit. Shareholder value creation has provided a demanding and illuminating criterion with which to appraise investment in new business opportunities. Rigorous analysis also counters the tendency for diversification to be a diversion—corporate escapism resulting from the unwillingness of top management to come to terms with difficult conditions within the core business.

The analytic tools at our disposal for evaluating diversification decisions have developed greatly in recent years. In the late 1980s, diversification decisions were based on vague concepts of synergy that involved identifying linkages between different industries. We are now able to be much more precise about the need for economies of scope in resources and capabilities *and* the economies of internalization that are prerequisites for diversification to create shareholder value. Recognizing the role of these economies of internalization has directed attention to the role of top management capabilities and effective corporate management systems in determining the success of diversification.

Quizzes and flashcards to test yourself further are available in your interactive e-book at
www.wileyopenpage.com

Self-Study Questions

1. An ice-cream manufacturer is proposing to acquire a soup manufacturer on the basis that, first, its sales and profits will be more seasonally balanced and, second, from year to year, sales and profits will be less affected by variations in weather. Will this risk spreading create value for shareholders? Under what circumstances could this acquisition create value for shareholders?

2. Tata Group is one of India's largest companies, employing 424,000 people in many different industries, including steel, motor vehicles, watches and jewelry, telecommunications, financial services, management consulting, food products, tea, chemicals and fertilizers, satellite TV, hotels, motor vehicles, energy, IT, and construction. Such diversity far exceeds that of any North American or Western European company. What are the conditions in India that might make such broad-based diversification both feasible and profitable?

3. Giorgio Armani S.p.A. is an Italian private company owned mainly by the Armani family. Most of its clothing and accessories are produced and marketed by the company (some are manufactured by outside contractors). For other products, notably fragrances, cosmetics, and eyewear, Armani licenses its brand names to other companies. Armani is considering expanding into athletic clothing, hotels, and bridal shops. Advise Armani on whether these new businesses should be developed in-house, by joint ventures, or by licensing the Armani brands to specialist companies already within these fields.

4. General Electric, Berkshire Hathaway, and Richard Branson's Virgin Group each comprise a wide range of different businesses that appear to have few close technical or customer linkages. Are these examples of unrelated diversification and do the corporate and ownership links within each of the groups result in the creation of any value? If so, what are the sources of this value creation?

Notes

1. A. D. Chandler Jr., *Strategy and Structure: Chapters in the History of the Industrial Enterprise* (Cambridge, MA: MIT Press, 1962); R. P. Rumelt, *Strategy, Structure and Economic Performance* (Cambridge, MA: Harvard University Press, 1974); H. Itami, T. Kagono, H. Yoshihara, and S. Sakuma, "Diversification Strategies and Economic Performance," *Japanese Economic Studies* 11, no. 1 (1982): 78–110.

2. M. Goold and K. Luchs, "Why Diversify? Four Decades of Management Thinking," *Academy of Management Executive* 7, no. 3 (August 1993): 7–25.

3. G. F. Davis, K. A. Diekman, and C. F. Tinsley, "The Decline and Fall of the Conglomerate Firm in the 1980s: A Study in the De-Institutionalization of an Organizational Form," *American Sociological Review* 49 (1994): 547–70.

4. R. E. Hoskisson and M. A. Hitt, *Downscoping: How to Tame the Diversified Firm* (New York: Oxford University Press, 1994).

5. A. Shleifer and R. W. Vishny, "The Takeover Wave of the 1980s," *Science* 248 (July/September 1990): 747–9.

6. J. Cyriac, T. Koller, and J. Thomsen, "Testing the Limits of Diversification," *McKinsey Quarterly* (February 2012).

7. L. G. Franko, "The Death of Diversification: The Focusing of the World's Industrial Firms, 1980–2000," *Business Horizons* (July/August, 2004): 41–50.

8. During 2004–2006, CEO turnover reached an all-time high. See Booz Allen Hamilton, "CEO Succession 2006: The Era of the Inclusive Leader," *strategy+business* (Summer 2007), http://www.boozallen.com/media/file/Era_of_the_Inclusive_Leader_.pdf, accessed August 22, 2012.

9. B. Burrough, *Barbarians at the Gate: The Fall of RJR Nabisco* (New York: Harper & Row, 1990).

10. L. Laeven and R. Levine, "Is there a Diversification Discount in Financial Conglomerates?" *Journal of Financial Economics* 82 (2006): 331–67.

11. T. Khanna and K. Palepu, "Why Focused Strategies May Be Wrong for Emerging Markets," *Harvard Business Review* (July/August, 1997): 41–51; D. Kim, D. Kandemir, and S. T. Cavusgil, "The Role of Family Conglomerates in Emerging Markets," *Thunderbird International Business Review* 46 (January 2004): 7–20.

12. See any standard corporate finance text, for example R. A. Brealey, S. Myers, and F. Allen, *Principles of Corporate Finance*, 8th edn (New York: McGraw-Hill, 2006): Chapter 8.

13. See, for example, H. Levy and M. Sarnat, "Diversification, Portfolio Analysis and the Uneasy Case for Conglomerate Mergers," *Journal of Finance* 25 (1970): 795–802; R. H. Mason and M. B. Goudzwaard, "Performance of Conglomerate Firms: A Portfolio Approach," *Journal of Finance* 31 (1976): 39–48; J. F. Weston, K. V. Smith, and R. E. Shrieves, "Conglomerate Performance Using the Capital Asset Pricing Model," *Review of Economics and Statistics* 54 (1972): 357–63.

14. M. Lubatkin and S. Chetterjee, "Extending Modern Portfolio Theory into the Domain of Corporate Strategy: Does It Apply?" *Academy of Management Journal* 37 (1994): 109–36.

15. The reduction in risk that bondholders derive from diversification is termed the *coinsurance effect*. See L. W. Lee, "Coinsurance and the Conglomerate Merger," *Journal of Finance* 32 (1977): 1527–37.

16. S. M. Bartram, "Corporate Risk Management as a Lever for Shareholder Value Creation," *Financial Markets, Institutions and Instruments* 9 (2000): 279–324.

17. M. E. Porter, "From Competitive Advantage to Corporate Strategy," *Harvard Business Review* (May/June 1987): 46.

18. M. Hayward and D. C. Hambrick, "Explaining the Premiums Paid for Large Acquisitions," *Administrative Science Quarterly* 42 (1997): 103–27.

19. A study of 68 diversifying ventures by established companies found that, on average, breakeven was not attained until the seventh and eighth years of operation: R. Biggadike, "The Risky Business of Diversification," *Harvard Business Review* (May/June 1979): 103–111.

20. The formal definition of *economies of scope* is in terms of "subadditivity." Economies of scope exist in the production of goods $x_1, x_2, ..., xn$, if $C(X) < RiCi(xi)$ where: $X < Ri(xi)$

   $C(X)$ is the cost of producing all n goods within a single firm

   $RiCi(xi)$ is the cost of producing the goods in n specialized firms.

   See W. J. Baumol, J. C. Panzar, and R. D. Willig, *Contestable Markets and the Theory of Industry Structure* (New York: Harcourt Brace Jovanovich, 1982): 71–2.

21. Economies of scope can arise in consumption as well as in production: customers may prefer to buy different products from the same supplier. See T. Cottrell and B. R. Nault, "Product Variety and Firm Survival in Microcomputer Software," *Strategic Management Journal* 25 (2004): 1005–26.

22. There is some evidence to the contrary. See H. Park, T. A. Kruse, K. Suzuki, and K. Park, "Long-term Performance Following Mergers of Japanese Companies: The Effect of Diversification and Affiliation," *Pacific Basin Finance Journal* 14 (2006); and P. R. Nayyar, "Performance Effects of Information Asymmetry and Economies of Scope in Diversified Service Firms," *Academy of Management Journal* 36 (1993): 28–57.

23. The role of capabilities in diversification is discussed in C. C. Markides and P. J. Williamson, "Related Diversification, Core Competencies and Corporate Performance," *Strategic Management Journal* 15 (Special Issue, 1994): 149–65.

24. This issue is examined more fully in D. J. Teece, "Towards an Economic Theory of the Multiproduct Firm," *Journal of Economic Behavior and Organization* 3 (1982): 39–63.

25. M. Goold, A. Campbell, and M. Alexander, *Corporate-Level Strategy: Creating Value in the Multibusiness Company* (New York: John Wiley & Sons, Inc., 1994).

26. J. P. Liebeskind, "Internal Capital Markets: Benefits, Costs and Organizational Arrangements," *Organization Science* 11 (2000): 58–76.

27. D. Scharfstein and J. Stein, "The Dark Side of Internal Capital Markets: Divisional Rent Seeking and Inefficient Investment," *Journal of Finance* 55 (2000): 2537–64; V. Maksimovic and G. Phillips, "Do Conglomerate Firms Allocate Resources Inefficiently across Industries?" *Journal of Finance* 57 (2002): 721–67; R. Rajan, H. Servaes, and L. Zingales, "The Cost of Diversity: The Diversification Discount and Inefficient Investment," *Journal of Finance* 55 (2000): 35–84.

28. C. Kaye and J. Yuwono, "Conglomerate Discount or Premium? How Some Diversified Companies Create Exceptional Value," Marakon Associates (2003), http://www.nd.edu/~cba/cc/pdf/Doyle_Portfolio%20decision%20making.pdf, accessed August 22, 2012.

29. R. M. Grant, A. P. Jammine, and H. Thomas, "Diversity, Diversification and Performance in British Manufacturing Industry," *Academy of Management Journal* 31 (1988): 771–801.

30. L. E. Palich, L. B. Cardinal, and C. C. Miller, "Curvi-linearity in the Diversification–Performance Linkage:

An Examination of over Three Decades of Research," *Strategic Management Journal* 22 (2000): 155–74.

31. N. Harper and S. P. Viguerie, "Are You Too Focused?" *McKinsey Quarterly* (Special Edition, 2002): 29–37.

32. J. D. Martin and A. Sayrak, "Corporate Diversification and Shareholder Value: A Survey of Recent Literature," *Journal of Corporate Finance* 9 (2003): 37–57.

33. C. C. Markides, "Consequences of Corporate Refocusing: Ex Ante Evidence," *Academy of Management Journal* 35 (1992): 398–412; C. C. Markides, "Diversification, Restructuring and Economic Performance," *Strategic Management Journal* 16 (1995): 101–18.

34. R. P. Rumelt, *Strategy, Structure and Economic Performance* (Cambridge, MA: Harvard University Press, 1974).

35. T. Peters and R. Waterman, *In Search of Excellence* (New York: Harper & Row, 1982): 294.

36. T. Peters and R. Waterman, *In Search of Excellence* (New York: Harper & Row, 1982): 294.

37. H. K. Christensen and C. A. Montgomery, "Corporate Economic Performance: Diversification Strategy versus Market Structure," *Strategic Management Journal* 2 (1981): 327–43; R. A. Bettis, "Performance Differences in Related and Unrelated Diversified Firms," *Strategic Management Journal* 2 (1981): 379–83.

38. See, for example, A. Michel and I. Shaked, "Does Business Diversification Affect Performance?" *Financial Management* 13, no. 4 (1984): 18–24; G. A. Luffman and R. Reed, *The Strategy and Performance of British Industry: 1970–80* (London: Macmillan, 1984).

39. C. Park, "The Effects of Prior Performance on the Choice between Related and Unrelated Acquisitions," *Journal of Management Studies* 39 (2002): 1003–19.

40. For a discussion of relatedness in diversification, see J. Robins and M. F. Wiersema, "A Resource-Based Approach to the Multibusiness Firm: Empirical Analysis of Portfolio Interrelationships and Corporate Financial Performance," *Strategic Management Journal* 16 (1995): 277–300; J. Robins and M. F. Wiersema, "The Measurement of Corporate Portfolio Strategy: Analysis of the Content Validity of Related Diversification Indexes," *Strategic Management Journal* 24 (2002): 39–59.

41. R. M. Grant, "On Dominant Logic, Relatedness, and the Link between Diversity and Performance," *Strategic Management Journal* 9 (1988): 639–42.

42. C. K. Prahalad and R. A. Bettis, "The Dominant Logic: A New Linkage between Diversity and Performance," *Strategic Management Journal* 7 (1986): 485–502.

14 Implementing Corporate Strategy: Managing the Multibusiness Firm

Some have argued that single-product businesses have a focus that gives them an advantage over multibusiness companies like our own—and perhaps they would have, but only if we neglect our own overriding advantage: the ability to share the ideas that are the result of wide and rich input from a multitude of global sources. GE businesses share technology, design, compensation and personnel evaluation systems, manufacturing practices, and customer and country knowledge.

—JACK WELCH, CHAIRMAN, GENERAL ELECTRIC COMPANY, 1981–2001

OUTLINE

Introduction and Objectives

A multibusiness firm comprises a number of businesses—organized as business units, divisions, or subsidiaries—coordinated and controlled by a corporate headquarters. These businesses may be different product groups—as in the case of 3M or Samsung; they may be different regional and national businesses—as in the case of McDonald's and Banco Santander; or they may be vertically related businesses—as in the case of ExxonMobil or De Beers. The key feature of the multibusiness firm is that decision making is divided between the individual businesses, each of which is responsible for its own operational decisions, and the headquarters, which is responsible for corporate matters.

In the last chapter, I concluded that the case for diversification depends on whether the diversified company can create value by operating across multiple businesses. Chapters 11 and 12 arrived at the same conclusion in relation to vertical integration and multinational operations. Vertical integration, international expansion, or diversification may have the potential to create value, but value is only realized if these strategies are implemented effectively. This requires answering the following questions: How should the multibusiness corporation be structured? Through what systems and tools should management exercise control and coordination? What roles do the chief executive and top management team need to fulfill and what styles of leadership are likely to be most effective? Our quest to answer these questions requires us to look closely at the activities of the corporate head office and its relationships with the businesses.

The main focus of this chapter will be the mechanisms through which corporate management creates value, namely managing the business portfolio, managing individual businesses, managing linkages between businesses, and leading change. We then consider the problem of corporate governance in the large, multibusiness corporation.

By the time you have completed this chapter, you will be able to:

- recognize the principal organizational features of the multibusiness corporation;
- apply the techniques of portfolio analysis to corporate strategy decisions;
- understand how corporate headquarters manages its individual businesses through strategic planning and financial control and by managing linkages across businesses;
- analyze the fit between a firm's corporate strategy, organization structure, management systems, and leadership style;
- analyze the potential for value creation through restructuring a multibusiness corporation;
- appreciate the governance issues that impact the work of managers within the multibusiness corporation.

The Role of Corporate Management

For the multibusiness corporation to be viable, the benefits from bringing businesses under common ownership and control must exceed the costs of the corporate overlay. Goold, Campbell, and Alexander go further. They propose a tougher hurdle for multibusiness companies: for each and every business within the corporate portfolio not only must the additional profit from inclusion within the corporate fold exceed the cost of headquarters management but also the net gain should be bigger than that which any other potential corporate parent can offer.[1] (Otherwise, it would be profitable to sell the business.) This concept of *parenting advantage*—that a company must be able to add more value to a business than rivals could—directs our attention to the mechanisms through which multibusiness corporations create value for the businesses they own.

We shall focus on four activities through which corporate management adds value to its businesses:

- managing the overall corporate portfolio, including acquisitions, divestments, and resource allocation;
- managing each individual business;
- managing linkages among businesses;
- managing change.

In the four sections that follow we will consider each of these activities and establish the conditions under which they create value.

Managing the Corporate Portfolio

The basic questions of corporate strategy are "What businesses should we be in?" and "How should we manage those businesses in order to generate as much value from them as possible?" *Portfolio planning models* can assist help managers with both of these questions.

General Electric and the Development of Strategic Planning

Portfolio planning techniques were one outcome of the pioneering work in corporate strategy initiated by General Electric at the end of the 1960s.[2] GE comprised 46 divisions and over 190 businesses. To manage this sprawling industrial empire more effectively, GE launched a series of initiatives together with Boston Consulting Group, McKinsey & Company, Arthur D. Little, and Harvard Business School. The result was three key developments in strategic management at the corporate level. The first was the identification of *strategic business units (SBUs)*—businesses that were sufficiently self-contained to formulate a separate competitive strategy.[3] The other two were *portfolio planning models* and the *PIMS database*, which we will discuss below.

Portfolio Planning: The GE/McKinsey Matrix

The basic idea of a portfolio-planning model is to represent graphically the individual businesses of a multibusiness company in terms of key strategic variables that

FIGURE 14.1 The GE/McKinsey portfolio planning matrix

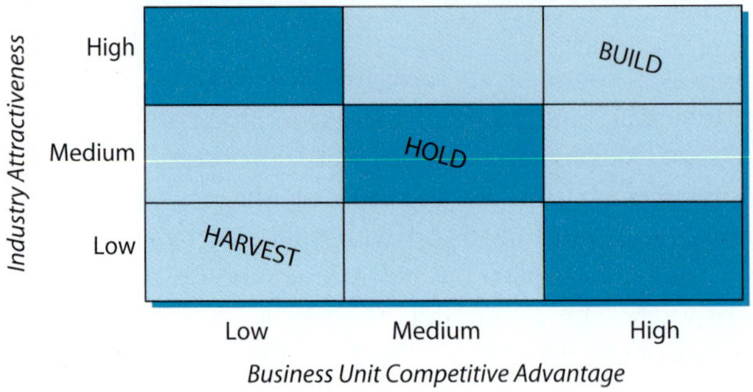

determine their potential for profit. These strategic variables typically relate to the attractiveness of their market and their competitive advantage within that market. This analysis can guide:

- allocating resources between the businesses on the basis of each business's market attractiveness and competitive position;
- formulating business unit strategy—by comparing the strategic positioning of each business, opportunities for repositioning (including divestment) can be identified;
- analyzing portfolio balance: a single display of all the company's businesses permits assessment of the overall balance of the portfolio in terms of *cash flow generation* and *growth prospects*;
- setting performance targets on the basis of each business's market attractiveness and its competitive position.

In the GE/McKinsey matrix (Figure 14.1) the industry attractiveness axis combines market size, market growth rate, market profitability (return on sales over three years), cyclicality, inflation recovery (potential to increase productivity and product prices), and international potential (ratio of foreign to domestic sales). Business unit competitive advantage combines market share, return on sales relative to competitors, and relative position with regard to quality, technology, manufacturing, distribution, marketing, and cost.[4] The strategy implications are shown by three regions of Figure 14.1.

Portfolio Planning: BCG's Growth–Share Matrix

The Boston Consulting Group's *growth–share matrix* also uses industry attractiveness and competitive position to compare the strategic positions of different businesses. However, it uses a single indicator as a proxy for each of these dimensions: industry attractiveness is measured by *rate of market growth* and competitive advantage by *relative market share* (the business unit's market share relative to that of its largest competitor). The four quadrants of the BCG matrix predict patterns of profits and cash flow and indicate strategies to be adopted (Figure 14.2).[5]

The simplicity of the BCG matrix is both its usefulness and its limitation. It can be prepared very easily and offers a clear picture of a firm's business portfolio in

FIGURE 14.2   The BCG growth–share matrix

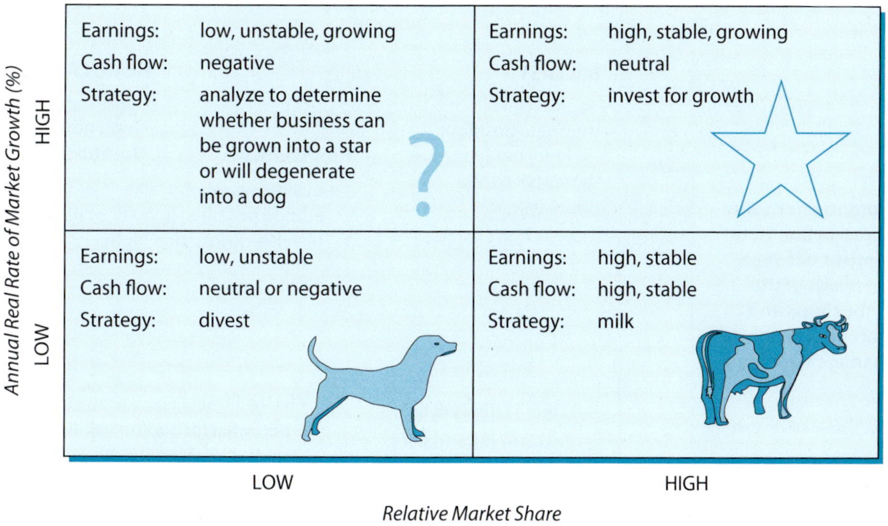

relation to some important strategic characteristics. Moreover, the analysis is versatile: it can be applied to business units and to the positioning of different products, brands, distribution channels, and customers. Though simplistic, it can be useful as a preliminary view before embarking upon a more detailed and rigorous analysis.

However, the simplistic approach of both the BCG and McKinsey business portfolio matrices has resulted in both losing their popularity as analytic tools. Apart from their naive approaches to the determinants of industry attractiveness and competitive advantage, there are problems relating to market definition. For example, in the BCG matrix, is BMW's auto business a dog because it holds less than 2% of the world auto market or a cash cow because it is market leader in the luxury car segment? An even greater problem is the implicit assumption that every business in the portfolio is independent—a direct denial of the basic rational for the multibusiness corporation: the synergistic linkages between businesses.[6]

Portfolio Planning: The Ashridge Portfolio Display

The Ashridge Portfolio Display is based upon Goold, Campbell and Alexander's concept of *parenting advantage*.[7] It takes account of the fact that the value-creating potential of a business within a company's business portfolio depends not just on the characteristics of the business (as assumed by the McKinsey and BCG matrices) but also on the characteristics of the parent. The focus, therefore, is on the *fit* between a business and its parent company. The positioning of a business along the horizontal axis of Figure 14.3 depends upon the parent's potential to create profit for the business by, for example, applying its corporate-level management capabilities, sharing resources and capabilities with other businesses, or economizing on transaction costs. The vertical axis measures the potential for value destruction by the parent. This can be caused by the costs of corporate overhead or the mismatch between the management needs of the business and the management systems and style of the parent (e.g., bureaucratic rigidity, incompatibility

FIGURE 14.3 Ashridge portfolio display: The potential for parenting advantage

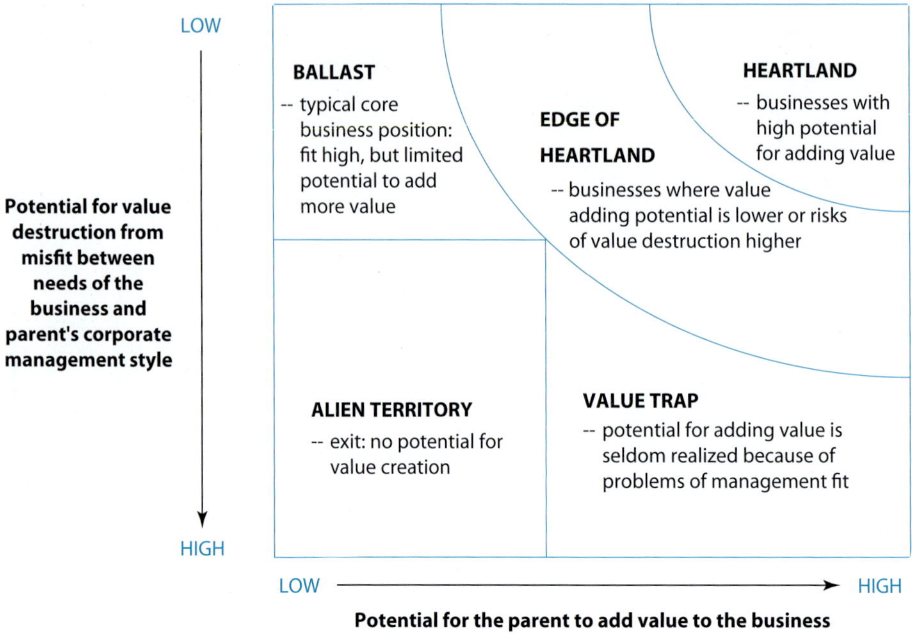

LOW

| | | |
| BALLAST | | HEARTLAND |

BALLAST
-- typical core business position: fit high, but limited potential to add more value

EDGE OF HEARTLAND
-- businesses where value adding potential is lower or risks of value destruction higher

HEARTLAND
-- businesses with high potential for adding value

Potential for value destruction from misfit between needs of the business and parent's corporate management style

ALIEN TERRITORY
-- exit: no potential for value creation

VALUE TRAP
-- potential for adding value is seldom realized because of problems of management fit

HIGH

LOW ⟶ HIGH

Potential for the parent to add value to the business

Source: Ashridge Strategic Management Centre.

with top management's mindset, politicization of decision making, and inappropriate strategic guidance).

In recognizing that businesses are not independent entities and introducing the role of strategic fit in influencing the potential for value creation and value destruction, the Ashridge matrix introduces the key issues of synergy that are ignored by other portfolio-planning matrices. The problem is complexity: both dimensions of the Ashridge matrix require difficult subjective evaluations that do not lend themselves to quantification.

Managing Individual Businesses

Some of the most important opportunities for corporate headquarters to create value arise from its ability to improve the strategic and operational management of its businesses, what Goold, Campbell, and Alexander call "standalone influence." This influence is exercised through the corporate parent's ability to:

> Appoint the general manager of each business and influence management development and succession planning within the businesses. It can approve or reject budgets, strategic plans, and capital expenditure proposals and it can influence the shape and implementation of these plans and proposals. It can provide advice and policy guidance to the businesses. The parent also influences the businesses by the hints and pressures passed on through both formal and informal line management meetings and contacts, and, more indirectly, through the corporate culture.[8]

The mechanisms through which the corporate headquarters exercises control over individual businesses can be divided into two types. Corporate management can control decisions, through requiring that certain decisions—typically those involving significant resource commitments—are referred upward for corporate approval. For example, the corporate HQ might require that capital expenditure requests that exceed $5 million are approved by the executive committee. Alternatively, corporate management can control businesses through setting and monitoring performance targets, backed by incentives and penalties to motivate their attainment. The distinction is between *input* and *output* control: the company can control the inputs into strategy (the decisions) or the output from strategy (the performance). Although most companies use a combination of input and output controls, there is an unavoidable tradeoff between the two: more of one implies less of the other. If the corporate HQ micromanages divisional decisions, it must accept the performance outcomes that will result from this. If the corporate HQ imposes rigorous performance targets, it must give divisional managers the freedom to make the decisions necessary to achieve those targets.

The Strategic Planning System

In Chapter 1, I stated that corporate strategy is set at the corporate level and business strategy is set at the business level. In reality, business strategies are formulated jointly by corporate and divisional managers. In most diversified, divisionalized companies, business strategies are initiated by divisional managers, and the role of corporate managers is to probe, appraise, amend, and approve divisional strategy proposals. The challenge for corporate management is to create a strategy-making process that reconciles the decentralized decision making essential to fostering flexibility, responsiveness, and a sense of ownership at the business level, with the ability of the corporate level to bring to bear its knowledge, perspective, and responsibility for the shareholder interest. Achieving an optimal blend of business-level initiative and corporate-level guidance and discipline is a difficult challenge for the multibusiness corporation. Common to the success of General Electric, ExxonMobil, Samsung, and Unilever is a system of strategic management that has managed this difficult tradeoff between business initiative and corporate control. Strategy Capsule 14.1 describes key elements of the strategic planning process at ExxonMobil.

Rethinking Strategic Planning   Since the early 1980s, the strategic planning systems of large firms have been bombarded by criticism from academics and consultants. Two features of corporate strategic planning systems have attracted particular scorn:

- *Strategic planning systems don't make strategy.* Ever since Henry Mintzberg attacked the "rational design" school of strategy (see Chapter 1), strategic planning systems have been castigated as ineffective for formulating strategy. In particular, formalized strategic planning has been viewed as the enemy of flexibility, creativity, and entrepreneurship. Marakon consultants Mankins and Steele observed that "strategic planning doesn't really influence most companies' strategy." The rigidities of formal planning cycles mean that "senior executives … make the decisions that really shape their companies'

STRATEGY CAPSULE 14.1
Strategic Planning at ExxonMobil

ExxonMobil is one of the world's biggest and most financially successful companies. Its strategic planning system reconciles long-term strategic planning with rigorous, short-term financial control; and centralized direction with flexible, responsive decision making among the divisions. ExxonMobil's strategic planning process follows an annual cycle that is similar to the generic strategic planning process outlined in Chapter 6 (Figure 6.1).

The principal stages of the planning cycle are as follows:

1   *Economic review and energy review* are forecasts of the economy and energy markets issued in February by the corporate planning department. They provide a basis for strategic planning.

2   *Business plans* are developed during spring and summer by individual businesses' units and are aggregated and refined by the global divisions into *divisional plans*. Their time horizon is ten years for the upstream divisions and five years for downstream divisions and chemicals. With input from the corporate planning department, the divisional plans are discussed, revised, and finally approved by the corporate management committee (during October).

3   *The corporate plan* aggregates the divisional plans. This is undertaken by the corporate-planning department then discussed and revised by the management committee, before submission to the board of directors for approval (during November).

4   *The financial forecast* comprises two-year forecasts of revenues, operating costs, capital expenditures, interest and other expenses, income, and cash flow for divisions and for the company as a whole. These provide the basis for *operating and capital budgets* for the upcoming year.

5   *The stewardship basis* comprises performance targets for the upcoming year. They include financial objectives, operating targets, safety and environmental objectives, and strategy mileposts.

6   *Stewardship reviews*: in February of each year, each division's performance for the previous year is evaluated against its stewardship objectives. These reviews involve presentations by the divisional top management to the management committee.

7   *Investment reappraisals* occur in August and September and involve the divisions reporting back on the outcomes of specific investment projects.

The annual strategic planning cycle is supplemented by *strategic studies*: ad hoc projects by the corporate-planning department that address specific strategic issues involving market, technological, and political changes.

Strategy making also involves informal communication and coordination between the different levels of the corporation. Communication between the management committee (comprising ExxonMobil's executive board members) and the divisional presidents and their management teams is supported by each member of the management committee acting as a contact director for two or three divisions. The dialog between the divisional presidents and members of the management committee is a mechanism for knowledge sharing and initiating strategic changes that adds flexibility to the formal strategic planning process. The result is a system of strategy formulation and performance management that is simultaneously top-down and bottom-up.

Fundamental to ExxonMobil's close integration of financial management with strategic planning is ExxonMobil's emphasis on *stewardship*—a doctrine of managerial accountability that makes each executive personally responsible to the corporation and its shareholders.

strategies … outside the planning process typically in an ad hoc fashion without rigorous analysis or productive debate." [9] They advocate "continuous, decision-oriented planning" of the kind they identify at Microsoft, Boeing, and Textron, where the top management team accepts responsibility for analyzing the critical issues that face the company and then takes strategic decisions.

- *Weak strategy execution*. Achieving more effective strategy execution means linking strategic planning to operational management. Larry Bossidy and Ram Charan argue that introducing *milestones*—specific actions or intermediate performance goals to be achieved at specified dates—can "bring reality to a strategic plan."[10] Thus, to keep Honeywell's strategy for cost cutting in its automotive business on track, managers developed a succession of milestones for shifting production overseas. As we noted in Chapter 2, the *balanced scorecard* offers another approach to cascading high-level strategic plans into specific functional and operational targets for different parts of the organization. Building on their balanced scorecard approach, Kaplan and Norton propose that *strategy maps* be used to plot the relationships between strategic actions and overall goals.[11] To link strategic planning more closely to its implementation, Kaplan and Norton recommend that companies upgrade their strategic planning units into *offices of strategy management*, which are responsible not just for managing the annual strategic planning cycle but also for overseeing the execution of strategic plans.[12]

Performance Management and Financial Control

Most multidivisional companies have a dual planning process: strategic planning concentrates on the medium and long term, financial planning controls short-term performance. Typically, the first year of the strategic plan includes the performance plan for the upcoming year in terms of an operating budget, a capital expenditure budget, strategy targets relating to market share, output, and employment levels, and specific strategic milestones. Annual performance plans are agreed between senior business-level managers and corporate-level managers. They are monitored on a monthly and quarterly basis. At the end of each financial year, they are probed and evaluated in performance review meetings between business and corporate management.

Performance targets emphasize financial indicators (return on invested capital, gross margin, growth of sales revenue) and include strategic goals (market share, new product introductions, market penetration, quality) and operational performance (output, productivity). Performance targets are usually specified in detail for the next year, with less detailed performance targets set for subsequent years. Monthly and quarterly monitoring focuses on the early detection of deviations from targets.

Performance targets are supported by management incentives and sanctions. Companies whose management systems are heavily orientated toward demanding profit targets typically use powerful individual incentives to create an intensely motivating environment for divisional managers. At ITT, Geneen's obsession with highly detailed performance monitoring, ruthless interrogation of divisional executives, and generous rewards for success developed an intensely competitive cadre of executives. They worked relentless, long hours and applied the same performance demands on their subordinates as Geneen did of them.[13] Creating a performance-driven culture requires unremitting focus on a few quantitative performance targets

STRATEGY CAPSULE 14.2
Performance Management at BP

BP's organizational philosophy, established by John Browne (CEO 1995–2007), emphasized three principles:

◆ BP operates in a decentralized manner, with individual business unit leaders (such as refinery managers) given broad latitude for running the business and direct responsibility for delivering performance.

◆ The corporate organization provides support and assistance to the business units through a variety of functions, networks, and peer groups.

◆ BP relies upon individual performance contracts to motivate people.

The group chief executive is responsible for presenting the five-year and annual group plans to the board for approval. The goals, metrics, and milestones in group plans are cascaded down in the plans for each of the segments, functions, and regions. Some of these same goals and metrics are reflected in individual performance contracts. A performance contract outlines the key results and milestones an employee is expected to achieve that year. Progress against targets and milestones in an employee's performance contract plays an integral part in annual bonus determinations. BP regards performance contracts as an essential component in delegating commitments for BP's annual plans to individual leaders. In performance contracts, BP attempts to set the goals high, but not so high that they cannot be reached. The performance contracts include financial, operational, strategic, and HSSE (health, safety, security, and environmental) objectives.

Source: Adapted from *The Report of the BP US Refineries Independent Safety Review Panel*, January 2007, with permission from BP International.

that can be monitored on a short-term basis. PepsiCo's obsession with monthly market share nourishes an intense, marketing-oriented culture. Chief executive Indra Nooyi observed: "We are a very objective-driven company. We spend a lot of time up front setting objectives and our guys rise to the challenge of meeting those objectives. When they don't meet the objectives, we don't have to flog them because they do it themselves."[14] One executive put it more bluntly: "The place is full of guys with sparks coming out of their asses."[15]

Even in businesses where interdependence is high and investment gestation periods are long, as in petroleum, short- and medium-term performance targets can be highly effective in driving efficiency and profitability. The performance management system of BP, the UK-based petroleum company, is described in Strategy Capsule 14.2. However, BP's performance-oriented culture has also been identified as a factor in several tragic accidents involving BP including explosions at its Texas City refinery (in 2005) and Deepwater Horizon drilling platform (in 2010).

Balancing Strategic Planning and Financial Control   One implication of the tradeoff between *input control* (controlling decisions) and *output control* (controlling performance) is that, in designing their corporate control systems, companies must emphasize either strategic planning or financial control. Michael Goold and

TABLE 14.1   Characteristics of different corporate management styles

	Strategic planning	**Financial control**
Business strategy formulation	Businesses and corporate HQ jointly formulate strategy The HQ coordinates strategies of businesses	Strategy formulated at business unit level Corporate HQ largely reactive, offering little coordination
Controlling performance	Primarily strategic goals with medium- to long-term horizon	Financial budgets set annual targets for ROI and other financial variables with monthly and quarterly monitoring
Advantages	Effective for exploiting (a) linkages among businesses, (b) innovation, (c) long-term competitive positioning	Business unit autonomy supports initiative, responsiveness, efficiency, and development of business leaders
Disadvantages	Loss of divisional autonomy and initiative Conducive to unitary strategic view Tendency to persist with failing strategies	Short-term focus discourages innovation and long-term development Limited sharing of resources and capabilities among businesses
Style suited to	Companies with few closely related businesses Works best in highly competitive, technology-intensive sectors where investment projects are large and long term	Highly diversified companies with low relatedness among businesses Works best in mature, low-tech sectors where investment projects are relatively small and short term

Source: Based on M. Goold and A. Campbell, *Strategies and Styles* (Oxford: Blackwell Publishing, 1987) with permission of John Wiley & Sons, Ltd.

Andrew Campbell found that the corporate management systems of British multibusiness companies emphasized one or the other.[16] The *strategic planning companies* emphasized the longer-term development of their businesses and had corporate HQs that were heavily involved in business-level planning. The *financial control companies* had corporate HQs that emphasized short-term budgetary control and rigorously monitored financial performance against ambitious targets, but had limited involvement in business strategy formulation—this was left to divisional and business unit managers. Table 14.1 summarizes key features of the two styles.

Over time, companies have made increasing use of financial control in managing their business units. This has occurred even in capital-intensive sectors with long time horizons, such as petroleum, where strategic planning has become increasingly oriented toward short- and medium-term financial targets.[17] However, one outcome of the financial crisis has been a discrediting of short-term shareholder value maximization and an increasing emphasis of strategic over financial management.

Managing Linkages across Businesses

As we saw in our chapters on vertical integration, international strategy, and diversification, the main opportunities for creating value in the multibusiness company arise from sharing resources and transferring capabilities among the different businesses within the company. This sharing occurs both through the centralization of common services at the corporate level and through direct linkages between the businesses.

Common Corporate Services

The simplest form of resource sharing in the multidivisional company is the centralized provision of common services and functions. These include corporate management functions such as strategic planning, financial control, treasury, risk management, internal audit, taxation, government relations, and shareholder relations. They also include business services that are more efficiently provided on a centralized basis, such as research, engineering, human resources management, legal services, management development, purchasing, and any other administrative services subject to economies of scale or learning.[18]

In practice, the benefits of the centralized provision of common services tend to be smaller than many corporate managers anticipate. Centralized provision can avoid costs of duplication but there can be little incentive among headquarters staff and specialized corporate units to meet the needs of their business-level customers. The experience of many companies is that corporate staffs tend to grow under their own momentum with few obvious economies from central provision and few benefits of superior services.

As a result, many companies separated their corporate headquarters into two groups: a *corporate management unit* responsible for supporting the corporate management team in core support activities such as strategic planning, finance, and legal, and a *shared services organization* responsible for supplying common services such as research, engineering, training, and information technology to the businesses. By 2000, shared corporate services accounted for 43% of headquarters staff among large UK corporations. To encourage efficiency and customer-orientation among these shared service organizations, some companies have operated them as profit centers supplying services on an arm's-length basis to internal operating units—sometimes in competition with external suppliers.

Procter & Gamble's Global Business Services organization employs 7,000 people in six "global hubs": Cincinnati (US), San Jose (Puerto Rico), Newcastle (UK), Brussels (Belgium), Singapore, and Manila (Philippines). It offers a wide range of business services, including IT, finance, facilities, purchasing, employee services, and business building solutions to P&G businesses in 170 countries. Through scale economies and standardizing systems, it has cut costs by over $800 million. Its innovations have included virtualization (e.g., replacing physical product mock-ups with virtual reality applications), accelerating internal collaboration (e.g., through video collaboration studios), providing decision support (e.g., its "Decision Cockpits"), and driving digital capabilities through creating a real-time environment.[19]

Deloitte's 2011 survey of global shared services found that:

- companies are structuring their shared service organizations around global hub-and-spoke configurations where the location of different services is determined primarily by labor factors, including cost, availability, language skills, and quality;
- as a result US- and European-based companies were increasingly locating service units in Asia and Latin America;
- as well as established transactional services such as IT, HR, and finance, shared service centers were increasingly being used for other functions, such as supply chain, marketing, real estate, and legal services;
- companies are increasingly blending shared services with the outsourcing of services;

- most companies realize considerable benefits form the shared services model, not only in cost but also in control, data visibility, and as a platform for growth.[20]

Business Linkages and Porter's Corporate Strategy Types

Exploiting economies of scope doesn't necessarily mean centralizing resources at the corporate level. Resources and capabilities can also be shared between the businesses. Michael Porter has argued that the way in which a company manages these linkages determines its potential to create value for shareholders.[21] He identifies four corporate strategy types:

- *Portfolio management*: The most limited form of resource sharing is where the parent company simply acquires a portfolio of attractive, soundly managed companies, allows them to operate autonomously, and links them through an efficient internal capital market.
- *Restructuring*: Conglomerates, such as Danaher and Textron in the US and Tomkins PLC and Invensys PLC in the UK, create value primarily by restructuring: acquiring poorly managed companies, then intervening to appoint new management, dispose of underperforming businesses, restructure balance sheets, and cut costs. As conglomerates have increasingly restructured themselves into oblivion (either transforming themselves into more focused industrial companies or breaking up entirely) private equity groups—such as Carlyle, KKR, Blackstone, and Texas Pacific in the US and Alchemy and Candover in the UK—have increasingly taken on the same restructuring role. These firms create investment funds organized as limited partnerships that make leveraged buyouts of private and public companies. The finding that, on average, the returns from private equity funds are lower than those on the stock market as a whole suggests that the value created by restructuring is limited.[22]
- *Transferring skills*: Organizational capabilities can be transferred between business units. LVMH transfers brand management and distribution capabilities among its different luxury-brand businesses. Sharp transfers its opto-electronics capabilities across a number of consumer, electronic, and office equipment products. Creating value by sharing skills requires that the same capabilities are applicable to the different businesses and that mechanisms are established to transfer these skills through personnel exchange and best practice transfer. As the opening quotation to this chapter indicates, sharing know-how and capabilities is at the heart of value creation at General Electric.
- *Sharing activities*: Porter argues that the most important source of value arises from exploiting economies of scope in common resources and activities. For these economies to be realized, corporate management must play a key coordinating role, including involvement in formulating business unit strategies and intervention in operational matters to ensure that opportunities for sharing R & D, advertising, distribution systems, and service networks are fully exploited. In some countries, Unilever has a single marketing and distribution organization that handles a wide range of different consumer

products.[23] The emergence of Samsung Electronics as a global leader in digital consumer products during the early part of the 21st century owed much to its development of advanced design capabilities. It's centers in London, Tokyo, San Francisco, and Seoul are shared across Samsung's different business units.[24]

The Role of the Corporate Headquarters in Managing Linkages

The closer the linkages among businesses, the greater the opportunities for creating value from sharing resources and transferring capabilities, and the greater the need for corporate headquarters to coordinate across businesses. We noted earlier that the *financial control* style of management occurs mainly in conglomerates where the independence of each business limits the coordinating role of the head office to manage the budgetary process and establish "framework conditions" for divisional planning.

In companies with more closely related businesses, such as the vertically integrated oil companies, or companies with close market or technological links (such as IBM, Procter & Gamble, American Express, and Alcoa), corporate management uses a *strategic planning* style, which is likely to involve not only coordination of strategies but also operational coordination to exploit the economies of scope and transferable skills discussed in Chapter 13. The extent of corporate involvement in interdivisional affairs is a key determinant of the size of the corporate headquarters. Berkshire Hathaway, which has almost no linkages among its businesses, has a corporate staff of about 50. Hewlett-Packard, with about the same sales but much closer linkages between its divisions, has close to 3000 employees at its Palo Alto head office. Where business units are linked through their sharing of a common resource or capability, the corporate headquarters is likely to be closely involved in the development and deployment of that resource or capability. For example, Pfizer and Corning Inc. have strong corporate R & D groups, Dow has a strong corporate manufacturing function, and Virgin's corporate team plays a key role in managing the Virgin brand.[25]

Developing and sharing resources and capabilities may require ad hoc organizational arrangements such as *cross-divisional task forces*. Such task forces might be formed for the introduction and dissemination of total quality management, to reengineer financial management practices, to promote fast-cycle new product development or to coordinate business development in China.

Sharing capabilities and know-how between businesses implies an important role for knowledge management in the multibusiness firm. In industries such as beer, cement, food processing, and telecommunication services international expansion offers few economies of scope in shared resources, the key to creating value from a global presence is through the transfer of innovation and sharing of know-how.

Exploiting linkages between businesses imposes costs. Though Porter may be right that the *potential* for value creation increases as a company moves from a loose, "portfolio management" strategy toward the more integrated "shared activity" strategy, this potential is not always realized. For example, most attempts at exploiting the potential for cross selling across different businesses have yielded disappointing results, especially in financial services.[26] Lorsch and Allen point to some of the management costs incurred in exploiting linkages between businesses. They compare three conglomerates with three vertically integrated paper companies.[27]

The coordination requirements of the paper companies resulted in greater involvement of head office staff in divisional operations, larger head office staffs, more complex planning and control devices, and a lower responsiveness to change in the external environment. By contrast, the conglomerates made little attempt to exploit linkages even if they were present:

> The conglomerate firms we had studied seemed to be achieving appreciable degrees of financial and managerial synergy but little or no operating synergy. Some of the firms saw little immediate payoff in this operating synergy; others met with little success in attempting to achieve it.[28]

The success with which the corporate headquarters manages linkages between businesses depends on top management's understanding of the commonalities among its different businesses. Ultimately, these commonalities have their basis in the underlying rationale for the corporation—what Prahalad and Bettis call *dominant logic*: "the way in which managers conceptualize the business and make critical resource allocation decisions."[29] The success of the multibusiness corporation depends upon strategic similarity among the different businesses that is consistent with an overall dominant logic.

Managing Change in the Multibusiness Corporation

Conceptions of the role of corporate management in the multibusiness company have shifted greatly over time. These shifting roles have been associated with different priorities with regard to value creation within the multibusiness corporation. During the 1970s and early 1980s, corporate management was concerned with the creation of large business empires. The motivation was partly growth but also the belief in the power of new tools of strategic and financial management to transcend industry boundaries. During the late 1980s, a profound shift in top management priorities occurred, and throughout the 1990s, the dominant theme was applying the logic and principles of shareholder value maximization to restructure diversified corporate empires. The principal sources of value were pruning business portfolios and exercising "standalone" influence to boost the performance of individual businesses. During the present century, the primary challenges have been, first, creating value through exploiting linkages between businesses and improving integration within the corporation and, second, increasing responsiveness to external change and accelerating the pace of organizational evolution. These shifts in strategic priorities have been associated with different leadership styles. Let me address each of these two major transitions.

Value Creation through Corporate Restructuring

During the late 1980s and 1990s, a large proportion of the largest corporations of North America and Europe underwent intense phases of corporate change typically triggered by declining financial performance or some external threat. Given the tendency for most multibusiness corporations to develop through a series of incremental strategy initiatives, periodic corporate restructuring based upon a comprehensive corporate review that appraises individual businesses and review of the overall business portfolio can be critical to revitalization.

McKinsey & Company's pentagon framework offers a systematic approach to analyzing the potential for increasing the market value of a multibusiness company through corporate restructuring.[30] The analysis comprises five stages—these correspond to the five nodes of Figure 14.4:

1 *The current market value of the company*: The starting point of the analysis is current enterprise value, which comprises the value of equity plus the value of debt. (As we know from Chapter 2, if securities markets are efficient, this equals the net present value of anticipated cash flow over the life of the company.)

2 *The value of the company as is*: Even without any changes to strategy or operations, it may be possible to value simply by managing external perceptions of a company's future prospects. Over the past two decades, companies have devoted increasing attention to managing investor expectations by increasing the quantity and quality of information flow to shareholders and investment analysts and establishing departments of investor relations for this purpose.

3 *The potential value of the company with internal improvements*: As we have seen, corporate management has opportunities for increasing the overall value of the company by making strategic and operational improvements to individual businesses that increase their cash flows. These might include exploiting global expansion opportunities, outsourcing certain activities, and cost-cutting opportunities.

4 *The potential value of the company with external improvements*: Having determined the potential value of its constituent businesses, corporate management needs to determine whether changes in the business portfolio can increase overall company value. The key is to apply the principle of parenting advantage: even after strategic and operating improvements have been made, can a business be sold for a price greater than its value to the company?

FIGURE 14.4   The McKinsey restructuring pentagon

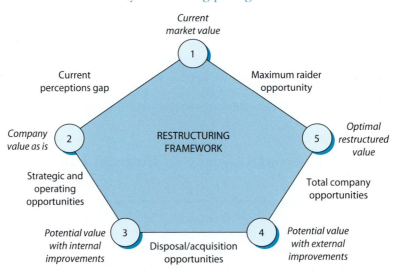

Source: T. E. Copeland, T. Koller, and J. Murrin, *Valuation* (New York: John Wiley & Sons, Inc. 1990).

5 *The optimum restructured value of the company*: The previous four steps establish maximum value potential of a company. Assuming that these changes could also be undertaken by an alternative owner of the company, the difference between the maximum restructured value and the current market value represents the profit potential available to a corporate raider.

   This type of analysis has been traditionally associated with leveraged buyout specialists and other corporate raiders. Faced with this threat, comprehensive corporate restructuring became widespread among large multibusiness companies (e.g., the restructuring wave by the oil majors during 1986–1992).[31]

   Leadership style associated with corporate restructuring is indicated by the nicknames given to some of the prominent exponents: "Chainsaw Al" Dunlap (at Scott Paper and Sunbeam), "Neutron Jack" Welch (at General Electric), and "Fred-the-Shred" Goodwin (at Royal Bank of Scotland). This points to an emphasis on cost cutting and asset divestment. The leadership mode associated with this approach is characterized by obsessive commitment to the maximization of shareholder value and the bottom-line results needed to achieve it, managing through performance targets and an emphasis on performance incentives (both compensation incentives and the threat of termination for underperformance).

Beyond Restructuring: How the Headquarters Can Drive Corporate Evolution

Disillusion with the shareholder value maximization model, diminishing returns to cost cutting, and the need to create new sources of corporate value have resulted in profound shifts in the corporate strategies of multibusiness companies. Increasingly, large multibusiness companies have sought to identify opportunities for innovation, for new product development, and for creating value from exploiting new and more sophisticated linkages between companies. Corporate headquarters are concerned less with the problem of control and more with the problem of identifying and implementing the means for creating value within and between their individual businesses. The use of the term *parenting* to describe the corporate role reflects this growing emphasis on corporate development. This emphasis has involved the corporate headquarters in a quest for new sources of value. To get a clearer idea of how this has happened let us look at three examples: GE under Jack Welch, Samsung Electronics, and IBM (see Strategy Capsules 14.3, 14.4, and 14.5). These examples point to three approaches to stimulating corporate adaptation:

- *Adaptive tension*: At General Electric, Jack Welch, CEO from 1981 until 2001, created a corporate management system that decentralized decision making to business-level managers but created a level of internal stress that counteracted complacency and fostered responsiveness to external change and a striving for constant performance improvement. While GE's "pressure cooker" atmosphere stimulated incremental change, Welch led systemic change through periodic corporate initiatives (such as his "boundarylessness," "six-sigma," and "be #1 or #2 in your industry" initiatives).
- *Institutionalizing strategic change*: As we have already noted, companies' strategic planning systems are seldom the sources of major strategic

STRATEGY CAPSULE 14.3
Jack Welch's Reinventing of Corporate Management

Jack Welch's 20-year tenure as chairman and CEO of General Electric began with an intensive period of restructuring, which transformed the business's portfolio and slashed costs. From 1984 onwards, however, Welch systematically rebuilt GE's management systems, redefining the role of the corporate headquarters and creating a decentralized system where the pressures of performance improvement and the drive to seize new opportunities fostered continual change. Welch's initiatives included:

◆ *Delayering*: Welch's fundamental criticism of GE's management was that it was slow and unresponsive. Welch eliminated GE's sector level of organization so that the 12 business heads reported directly to him. GE's layers of hierarchy were cut from nine or ten to four or five. The resulting broadening of spans of control meant that each executive was managing more direct reports, forcing executives to delegate decision making.

◆ *Changing the strategic planning system*: Welch replaced the staff-led, document-driven process with more personal, less formal, but very intensive face-to-face discussions. Data-heavy business plans were replaced by a slim "play-book" that summarized key strategic issues facing the business and proposed actions. Discussion of these issues and actions were the basis for a half-day review session where business heads and key executives met with Welch and his top-management team in an open dialogue.[a]

◆ *Redefining the role of headquarters*: The changes in the strategic planning system reflected broader changes in the role of the corporate headquarters. Welch viewed headquarters as interfering too much, generating too much paper, and failing to add value. His objective was to "turn their role 180 degrees from checker, inquisitor, and authority figure to facilitator, helper, and supporter ... Our job is to help, it's to assist, it's to make these businesses stronger, to help them grow and be more powerful."[b] The businesses were also expected to help one another: Welch's concept of the "boundaryless company" aimed at permeable internal boundaries allowing "integrated diversity"—the ability to transfer the ideas, business practices, and people freely and easily. "Boundaryless behavior combines 12 huge global businesses—each number one or number two in its markets—into a vast laboratory whose principal product is new ideas, coupled with a common commitment to spread them throughout the company."[c]

◆ *Work-out*: As well as being pressured from above by Welch and his management team, devisal managers were pressured from below. Work-out meetings were offsite meetings where the heads of a business or function were required to respond to criticisms and suggestions from subordinates.

Notes:

[a]*General Electric: Jack Welch's Second Wave (A)*, Case No. 9–391–248 (Boston: Harvard Business School, 1991).

[b]Jack Welch, "GE Growth Engine," speech to employees, 1988.

[c]"Letter to Share Owners," General Electric Company 1993 Annual Report (Fairfield, CT, 1994): 2.

STRATEGY CAPSULE 14.4
Reformulating Strategic Planning at IBM

IBM has a remarkable history of adapting to change. Its business has successfully transitioned from tabulating machines to mainframe computers, to personal computers, to networked information technology, to cloud computing. Within the space of 15 years it has also changed from a hardware into a software and services company. Under its past three CEOs, IBM's pace of evolution accelerated, assisted by IBM's processes for making and implementing strategy.

In 1999, CEO Lou Gerstner began a series of fundamental changes to IBM's strategic planning system which continued under his successor, Sam Palmisano. The outcome was the IBM Strategic Leadership Model, which linked processes for strategic insight with processes for strategy execution. Strategic insight involved several approaches to sensing new opportunities:

- The technology team meets monthly to assess emerging technologies and their market potential.

- The strategy team comprising a cross section of general managers, strategy executives, and functional managers meets monthly to review business unit strategies and recommend new initiatives.

- The integration and values team comprises 300 key leaders selected by the top management team responsible for integrating IBM through company-wide initiatives called "winning plays."

- A "deep dive" is a structured, analytical process conducted by an ad hoc team to explore a specific opportunity or strategic issue. It may result in a recommendation to enter a new area of business or to exit from a particular technology or product market.

The initiatives arising from these processes are then acted on by the three main executing vehicles:

- "Emerging business opportunities" is a business development process that recognizes that new business initiatives are likely to require management methods (and investment criteria) that are very different from established ones. Between 1999 and 2005, 18 EBOs were established, including Linux, autonomic computing, blade servers, digital media, network processing, and life sciences.

- "Strategic leadership forums" are three- to five-day workshops facilitated by IBM's Global Executive and Organizational Capability Group. Their purpose is to transform strategic initiatives into action plans and to address other pressing strategic issues, such as addressing poor performance in particular area of business. They are initiated by a senior manager and overseen by the strategy team.

- The Corporate Investment Fund finances new initiatives identified by the integration and values team or by EBOs. They are used to support winning play initiatives and other projects which aren't included in the annual budgeting process—possibly because that falls between businesses.

Source: J. B. Harreld, C. A. O'Reilly, and M. L. Tushman, "Dynamic Capabilities at IBM: Driving Strategy into Action," *California Management Review* 49 (Summer 2007): 21–43.

STRATEGY CAPSULE 14.5

Samsung Electronics: Top-Down Initiatives that Drive Corporate Development

Samsung is the biggest of South Korea's *chaelbols*—diversified groups of separate companies linked together by cross-shareholdings and controlled by the founding family. The Samsung group comprises 83 companies but has no legal identity; the closest to a parent company is Everland, in which the founding Lee family has a controlling 46% stake. The biggest company is Samsung Electronics, the world's largest electronics company in terms of sales. The head of the group, and chairman of Samsung Electronics, is Lee Kun-hee, son of the founder Lee Byung-chull and father of Jay Y. Lee, president of Samsung Electronics.

Samsung Electronics' rapid development has been the result of a series of large-scale corporate initiatives that are ambitious, focused, long-term, and driven by intense top-down commitment. In 1982, Samsung Electronics resolved to become world leader in memory devices—it achieved this in DRAM chips in 1992, then in 2004 began investing massively in flash memories. In 2000, it began producing batteries for mobile digital devices; by 2009, it was world leader, similarly with flat-panel televisions. These successes involved massive commitments of resources to technology (Samsung receives more US patents than any other company except IBM), manufacturing (for semiconductor production Samsung built the world's biggest fabrication complex), design (with the creation of design centers in five cities of the world), and the Samsung brand. The effectiveness of this resource mobilization has been supported by a culture and working practices that support high levels of coordination and commitment. Samsung's culture is built around many tales of outstanding endeavor, including constructing a four-kilometer paved road in a single day to ensure that Samsung's first integrated circuit plant could open on time.

In 2010–2011, based upon its analysis of long-term trends, Samsung established five new corporate initiatives, each of which would represent a major new business.

Samsung's new product development success has been supported by a knowledge management system which aims to exploit the expertise of the entire company. In April 2009, the Visual Display Division of Samsung Electronics' Digital Media Business had just completed work on a high-resolution LED TV when it was assigned a new project: it was required to roll out a high-definition, 3-D television within a year. To achieve this goal, the two task forces assigned to the project turned to Samsung Electronics' Test and Error Management System (TEMS), a knowledge management system containing a vast reservoir of information from every product development project undertaken at the company.

Source: "Samsung: The Next Big Bet," *Economist* (October 1, 2011); *Samsung Electronics*, HBS Case 9–705–508 (revised 2009); "Samsung Electronics' Knowledge Management System," *Korea Times* (Wednesday, October 6, 2010).

Sector	Investment ($billion)	Target sales, 2020 ($billion)	Target jobs, 2020
Solar panels	5.1	8.5	10,000
LED lighting	7.3	15.2	17,000
E-vehicle batteries	4.6	8.7	7,600
Biotech drugs	1.8	1.5	1,000
Medical devices	1.0	8.5	10,300

initiatives: the impetus for major strategy redirection usually comes from outside formal strategy processes. The IBM case example shows that strategic planning systems can be redesigned as systems for sensing external changes and responding to the opportunities these changes offer.

● *Top-down, large-scale development initiatives*: Throughout this book, we have pointed to the key role of *strategic intent*—top-down strategic goals—in unifying and motivating organizational members. In some companies, linking such strategic intent to specific projects and programs has been an especially powerful vehicle for corporate development. The rise of Samsung Electronics to become the world's largest electronics company has been on the basis of a small number of hugely ambitious development projects that have involved massive commitments of finance and human ingenuity and effort.

Adaptation to changing circumstances also requires timing. Intel's former CEO, Andy Grove emphasizes the importance of CEOs identifying *strategic inflection points*—instances where seismic shifts in a firm's competitive environment require a fundamental redirection of strategy.[32] Grove identifies three such key inflection points at Intel: the transition from DRAM chips to microprocessors as its core business, the choice of its x86 series of microprocessors in preference to a RISC architecture, and its decision to replace its faulty Pentium chips.[33]

Finally, managing change also requires creating the certainty that provides the security that allows people to leap into the unknown. Some of the companies that have been most effective in adapting to change—IBM, Philips, General Electric, Danone, and HSBC—have done so while emphasizing the continuity of their heritage and identity. Creating a sense of identity is more challenging for a company that spans several businesses than for one whose identity is determined by the products it offers (McDonald's or De Beers). It goes beyond "strategic relatedness" and "dominant logic" and embraces vision, mission, and culture. In the previous chapter, I observed that the luxury goods giant LVMH deploys its core brand management capabilities across several different businesses. Its success in doing so depends critically upon establishing a corporate identity that forms a cultural glue between these disparate businesses: "The common cultural trunk is based on the permanent search for quality of the products and the management, human relations based on responsibility and initiative, and rewarding competences and services."[34] It would appear that a stable, well-established organizational identity may support not only the management of diversity but also the management of change.[35]

Governance of Multibusiness Corporations

So far our discussion of the multibusiness corporation has focused on the means by which the corporate headquarters can create value. What we have not discussed is: value for whom? This takes us to the issue of **corporate governance**.

Corporate governance is the system by which companies are directed and controlled. Corporate governance centers on the role of boards of directors, which have primary responsibility for the governance of companies. The reason corporate governance is an important issue is because of the separation of ownership from control in large companies, especially public companies. Where ownership is highly dispersed, what is to prevent the management of a company from running the company for its own interests?

The challenges of corporate governance are not unique to multibusiness companies. Corporate governance presents problems to all companies where the owners are not directly engaged in managing the company. However, it is large corporations where the problems of separation of ownership and control are most acute, and large corporations also tend to be multibusiness corporations. Even a highly specialized company such as McDonald's is divided into regional groupings (US, Europe, Asia Pacific, and the Middle East), which are further divided into divisions (UK and Northern Europe, Russia and Eastern Europe, West USA, Central USA etc.). Moreover, the separation of decision authority between the corporate HQ and the individual businesses complicates corporate governance.

Let us begin by outlining the key issues of corporate governance in large companies, then deal specifically with the issues that arise in relation to the structures of multibusiness corporations.

The Challenge of Corporate Governance

Is Williamson right that the corporate head office can be relied upon to act as an "agent of the stockholders whose purpose is to monitor the operations of the constituent parts"? Among diversified firms, it seems that multidivisional structures are more conducive to profitability than alternative structural forms, yet it is also clear that multidivisional structures are no safeguard against agency problems. The most notorious examples of chief executives operating their companies as personal fiefdoms are found among divisionalized, multibusiness corporations—Howard Hughes at Hughes Corporation, Ken Lay at Enron, Dennis Kozlowski at Tyco, Jean-Marie Messier at Vivendi Universal, and Fred Goodwin at Royal Bank of Scotland. While the CEOs of diversified companies may avoid emotional commitment to particular businesses, this does not mean that they are more predisposed to shareholder return over the quest for Napoleonic personal grandeur.

Top management's pursuit of personal goals related to the aggrandizement of wealth, power, influence, and status in preference to owners' goals of value maximization are primarily a problem for public companies.[36] The critical problem is that the ability of shareholders to exercise effective control over management is limited by their large number. This creates, first, a coordination problem and, second, an incentive problem—if each shareholder owns only a small fraction of a company and if that company's shares only account for a small fraction of the shareholder's total wealth, then the costs of active engagement are high relative to the likely returns. Disgruntled shareholders typically sell their shares rather than oppose the incumbent management team.

Given widespread shareholder apathy, boards of directors tend to become tools of top management rather than agents of the shareholders.

Rights of Shareholders   Company law relating to the rights of shareholders typically covers shareholders' right to sell their shares, their right to company information (including access to audited financial statements), their right to elect and remove members of the board of directors, and their right to share in the profits of the company.

Although seemingly straightforward, these rights are often abrogated by companies. For example, managers are more likely than shareholders to oppose takeover by another company: while shareholders benefit financially, senior executives often lose their jobs. Hence, companies frequently create impediments to hostile takeover either in the form of special voting rights for certain classes of share or "poison pill" defenses. Yahoo! defended against a 2008 takeover bid from Microsoft through a provision that any hostile bid would trigger the creation of a rights issue to existing shareholders. To resist takeover by Mittal Steel, Arcelor attempted to make itself indigestible by arranging a merger with Russian steel giant Severstal.

In terms of rights to information: managers' desire to manipulate their companies' share prices has resulted in misreporting their financial results. Financial misreporting was at the center of the scandals that engulfed Enron and WorldCom in the US and Parmalat and Royal Ahold in Europe.[37] New standards of financial reporting include America's Sarbanes–Oxley Act.

Responsibilities of Boards of Directors The board of directors, according to *OECD Principles of Corporate Governance*, has the responsibility to "ensure the strategic guidance of the company, the effective monitoring of management by the board, and the board's accountability to the company and the shareholders."[38] This requires that:

- Board members act in good faith, with due diligence and care, in the best interest of the company and its shareholders.
- Board members review and guide corporate strategy, major plans of action, risk policy, annual budgets and business plans; set and monitor performance objectives; and oversee major capital expenditures; select, monitor, and compensate key executives; ensure the integrity of the corporation's accounting and financial reporting systems; and oversee the process of disclosure and communication.

The ability of the board to achieve these goals has been compromised by several impediments:

- The dominance of the board by executive directors: In both the US and UK and some other countries, the top management team (the CEO, CFO and other senior executives) are likely to be made up of board members.
- Combining the roles of board chair and CEO: This is common in the US, less so in most European companies. US opinion suggests that splitting board chair and CEO roles is neither an advantage nor disadvantage: it depends entirely upon the attributes of the person doing the job.[39] However, interlocking boards, where CEOs serve as independent members on one another's boards, does appear to be an unambiguous constraint on board independence.
- Boards have become increasingly preoccupied with compliance issues with the result that their role in guiding corporate strategy has shrunk.

Dominic Barton, global managing director of McKinsey & Company, argues that if boards are to become effective agents of long-term value creation they must devote much more time to their roles and need to have more relevant industry experience, and they need a small analytical staff to support their work.[40]

The harshest criticisms of board oversight have been in relation to management compensation. The escalation of CEO compensation among large public companies since the early 1990s has been little short of staggering. The paradox is that the massive payouts to CEOs have been the result of compensation systems designed to align management goals with those of shareholders, especially through the grant of stock options and emphasis on performance-related bonuses. Yet some of the biggest executive payouts have been by companies that have experienced shareholder returns that have ranged from indifferent to disastrous (Table 14.2). Performance bonuses and options packages have been extended down corporate hierarchies to include middle managers as well as the top management team. In the UK, salary comprised 54% of overall executive compensation as compared with bonuses 24%, and options and long-term incentive plans 22%.[41] Aspects of the poor alignment between executive compensation and shareholder value creation include linking bonuses to short-term performance, a failure to correct for overall stock market movements, and incentives for creating shareholder value not being matched by penalties for its destruction.[42]

The division of decision-making responsibilities between a corporate headquarters with responsibilities for the company as a whole and individual businesses has implications for corporate governance. This separation of powers may mitigate some of the problems of agency; there are also arguments that the multibusiness firm exacerbates agency problems.

TABLE 14.2   Highest-paid CEOs of US companies, 2011

Rank	CEO	Company	Total pay ($million)	Change on 2010 (%)
1	David Simon	Simon Property Group	137.2	+458
2	Leslie Moonves	CBS	68.4	+20
3	David Zaslav	Discovery Communications	52.4	+23
4	Sanjay K. Jha	Motorola Mobility	47.2	+262
5	Philippe P. Dauman	Viacom	43.1	−49
6	David M. Cote	Honeywell International	35.7	+135
7	Robert A. Iger	Walt Disney	31.4	+12
8	Clarence P. Cazalot Jr	Marathon Oil	29.9	+239
9	John P. Daane	Altera	29.6	+278
10	Alan Mulally	Ford Motor	29.5	+11
11	Gregory Q. Brown	Motorola Solutions	29.3	+113
12	Richard C. Adkerson	Freeport-McMoRan	28.4	−19
13	Ian M. Cumming	Leucadia National	28.2	+531
14	Brian L. Roberts	Comcast	26.9	−13
15	Jeffrey L. Bewkes	Time Warner	25.7	−2
16	Rex W. Tillerson	ExxonMobil	25.2	+17
17	Samuel J. Palmisano	IBM	24.2	−4
18	William C. Weldon	Johnson & Johnson	23.4	+1
19	James Dimon	JPMorgan Chase	23.1	+11
20	Louis R. Chenevert	United Technologies	22.2	+17

Source: "50 Highest-Paid CEOs of 2012: AP Pay Survey," www.therichest.org/business/50-highest-paid-ceos-2012/ (May 26, 2012).
Implications of the Multidivisional Form for Corporate Governance

The Theory of the M-form   While Alfred Chandler identified diffusion of the multidivisional form as a critical factor in the development of the multibusiness corporation,[43] Oliver Williamson provided its theoretical rationale.[44] Williamson argued that by distributing decision making between a corporate HQ and business divisions, the divisionalized firm (or in his terminology, the *M-form*) facilitated corporate governance in two ways:

- *Allocation of resources*: Resource allocation within any administrative structure is a political process in which power, status, and influence can triumph over purely commercial considerations.[45] To the extent that the multidivisional company can create a competitive internal capital market in which capital is allocated according to financial and strategic criteria, it can avoid much of the politicization inherent in purely hierarchical systems. The multidivisional company does this through operating an internal capital market where budgets are linked to past and projected divisional profitability, and individual projects are subject to a standardized appraisal process.

- *Agency problems*: The basic agency problem is that owners (shareholders) desire maximization of the value of the firm, while their agents (managers) are more interested in salaries, security, and power. Given the limited power of shareholders to discipline and replace managers and the weakness of boards to control management, the corporate head office of a multidivisional firm can act as an interface between shareholders and the divisional managers and enforce adherence to profit goals. With divisions designated as profit centers, financial performance can readily be monitored by the head office and divisional managers can be held responsible for performance failures. According to Williamson, multibusiness companies can be more effective profit maximizers than specialist companies can because of two critical advantages of the corporate head office over the board of directors of a single business company: first, the corporate head office has better access to information about the business and, second, it is easier for a corporate head office to replace business managers than it is for a board of directors.[46] At General Electric, ExxonMobil, and PepsiCo, this capacity for corporate headquarters to create strongly profit-oriented systems is particularly evident.

Problems of Divisionalized Firms   Rather than acting as an effective agent of shareholders and operating internal capital markets where resources are allocated to their most profitable uses, there is ample evidence that decision making in multibusiness firms tends to be highly politicized.[47] Moreover, rather than representing shareholders' interests, corporate headquarters are liable to become vehicles of CEO ambition that are divorced both from shareholders and from the realities of the businesses. Some of the most notorious examples of large-scale destruction of shareholder value—from Enron, WorldCom, and Parmalat through to Royal Bank of Scotland, Bank of America, and Kaupthing Bank of Iceland—involved empire-building CEOs of multibusiness companies.

In practice, multidivisional companies may lack the flexibility and responsiveness that their modular should, in principle, be capable of. Henry Mintzberg points to two key rigidities:[48]

- *Constraints on decentralization*: Individual divisions often feature highly centralized power that arises from divisional presidents' personal accountability to the head office. Moreover, the operational freedom of the divisional management exists only so long as the corporate head office is satisfied with divisional performance. Divisional underperformance typically leads to a curtailing of divisional autonomy as the corporate head office intervenes.

STRATEGY CAPSULE 14.6

Governance in Holding Companies

A holding company is a company that owns a controlling interest in a number of subsidiary companies. The term *holding company* is used to refer both to the parent company and to the group as a whole. Holding companies are common in Japan (notably the traditional *zaibatsu* such as Mitsubishi and Mitsui), in Korea (*chaelbols* such as LG, Hyundai, and SK) and the Hong Kong trading houses (Swire, Jardine Matheson, and Hutchison Whampoa). In the US, holding companies own the majority of US banking assets.

Within holding companies, the parent exercises control over the subsidiary through appointing its board of directors. The individual subsidiaries typically retain high levels of strategic and operational autonomy. Unlike the multidivisional corporation, the holding company lacks financial integration: there is no centralized treasury, profits accrue to the individual operating companies, and there is no centralized budgeting function—each subsidiary is a separate financial entity. The parent company provides equity and debt capital and receives dividends from the subsidiary.

Although the potential for exploiting synergies between businesses is more limited in the holding company than in the divisionalized corporation, the holding company structure has important advantages for large family-owned companies. The attractiveness of holding companies is that they allow family dynasties to retain ownership and control of business empires that diversify family wealth across multiple

sectors. At the same time their decentralization allows effective management of the group without the need for the parent company to develop a tremendous depth of management capability.

Thus, the Tata Group, India's biggest business concern with over $60 billion in revenue and 424,000 employees, is controlled by the Tata family through Tata Sons Ltd, parent company of the group. Among the many hundreds of subsidiaries, several are leading companies within their industries, including Tata Steel, Tata Motors (owner of Jaguar and Land Rover), Tata Tea (owner of the Tetley brand), and Tata Consulting Services. Twenty-seven Tata companies are publicly listed.

In contrast to the public corporations where the key governance problem is a tendency for salaried managers to operate the company in their own interests, the problems of holding companies relate to the rights of minority shareholders. At Fiat Group the Agnelli family exerts effective control with just 10% of the total equity. By acting in concert with banks and other leading families, a family can extend its influence with quite small ownership stakes: the Agnelli family was able to gain control of Telecom Italia despite owning a mere 0.6% of total equity.

Sources: M. Granovetter, "Business Groups and Social Organization," in N. J. Smelser and R. Swedberg, *Handbook of Economic Sociology* (Princeton, NJ: Princeton University Press, 2005): 429–50; F. Amatori and A. Colli, "Corporate Governance: The Italian Story," Bocconi University, Milan (December 2000).

- *Standardization of divisional management*: In principle, each division can adapt itself to the requirements of its business sector. In practice, there are powerful forces for standardizing control systems and management styles across the multidivisional corporation. The difficulties that many large, mature corporations experience with new business development often result from applying to new businesses the same management systems designed for existing businesses.[49]

However, we must recognize that, while the multidivisional corporation is the dominant organizational form for multibusiness firms in North America and much of Western Europe, it is not the only way to organize the multibusiness firm. Among family-owned companies and in much of Asia the holding-company structure is widespread. This creates rather different governance issues (Strategy Capsule 14.6).

Summary

In this chapter we have examined the role of the corporate headquarters in large, complex companies, namely those that manage multiple business units. Our focus has been on how corporate management creates value within these companies. We identified three principal types of value-creating activity:

- Managing the business portfolio: reallocating resources from unattractive to attractive industries. This requires the exercise of superior foresight by top management in order to anticipate industries with growing profit potential and exit from industries before the onset of decline.

- Managing individual businesses: increasing the performance of individual businesses by enhancing the quality of their decision making, installing better managers, and creating incentives that drive superior performance.

- Managing linkages among businesses: exploiting opportunities for sharing resources and transferring capabilities comprises multiple activities ranging from the centralized provision of functions to best practices transfer. The key is to ensure that the potential gains from exploiting such economies of scope are not outweighed by the costs of managing the added complexity.

In addition, the success of the multibusiness company is dependent upon two additional performance dimensions. The first is the capacity for change. While corporate restructuring is typically a periodic process of large-scale strategic and organizational change, typically in response to deteriorating financial performance, a bigger challenge is creating systems and attitudes that permit continuous strategic adaptation.

The second concerns corporate governance. Those who control large, complex companies are well positioned to appropriate the value that these companies create. In the case of public, multidivisional corporations, self-seeking senior managers are the primary culprits. In family-controlled holding companies it is the controlling family that tends to exploit its power at the expense of other owners.

Given multiple sources of value creation and value destruction, it is impossible to offer generic recommendations as to how a multibusiness company should implement its corporate strategy: each firm is unique in terms of its portfolio of products and markets, its resources and capabilities, its corporate culture, its administrative heritage, and the characteristics of its corporate managers. Highly diversified, divisionalized corporations can be superbly managed generators of value (General Electric and LVMH) or they can be vehicles for empire-building, egotistical executives (Vivendi Universal under Jean-Marie Messier and Tyco under Dennis Kozlowski). Family-controlled holding companies can be defensive institutions that pursue family interests at the expense of other shareholders (Parmalat) or creators of world-class businesses (Samsung). Given these factors, it is hardly surprising that empirical research offers limited guidance as to the correlates of superior performance among multibusiness firms. As with so many other aspects of strategic management, *fit* is the key—the consistency with which strategy, the characteristics of the external environment, resources, capabilities, structure, systems, leadership style, culture, and history interlink.

 Quizzes and flashcards to test yourself further are available in your interactive e-book at **www.wileyopenpage.com**

Self-Study Questions

1. You have been appointed CEO of Procter & Gamble, which owns many businesses ranging from laundry detergents to shaving products, skin care products, hair care products, dental products, and perfumes. Your VP of strategic planning has asked for your advice on which portfolio matrix—the McKinsey matrix, BCG matrix, or Ashridge matrix—she should use for analyzing P&G's portfolio of businesses. What advice would you offer her?

2. Apply the BCG matrix to the different programs that your institution offers. (You will need to make some informed guesses about market growth rates and relative market share.) Does this analysis offer useful strategy implications for the different programs?

3. The discussion of "performance management and financial control" identified two companies where the corporate HQ imposes a strong performance management system on its business units, PepsiCo and BP. For which company do you think a performance management system using financial targets is better suited?

4. Identify a poorly performing multibusiness company (examples might include Sony, Time Warner, Bombardier, Pearson, News International). Using the McKinsey pentagon framework, in which stage do you perceive the greatest opportunities for value creation through restructuring? (Use the company's web site or visit www.hoovers.com to access information on the company.)

5. Which do you think is a better organizational form for the diversified, multinational corporation: the divisionalized corporation (such as General Electric, Philips, and Sony) or the holding company (such as Tata Group, Samsung Group, and the Virgin Group)?

Notes

1. M. Goold, A. Campbell, and M. Alexander, *Corporate-Level Strategy: Creating Value in the Multibusiness Company* (New York: John Wiley & Sons, Inc., 1994).

2. *General Electric: Strategic Position: 1981*, Case No. 381-174 (Boston: Harvard Business School, 1981): 1.

3. McKinsey & Company has recently reconceptualized SBUs as *value cells*. See M. Giordano and F. Wenger, "Organizing for Value," *Perspectives on Finance and Strategy* 18 (2008).

4. For a fuller discussion of the GE/McKinsey matrix see "Enduring Ideas: The GE–McKinsey Nine-box Matrix," *McKinsey Quarterly* (September 2008).

5. For a fuller discussion of the BCG matrix see B. Henderson, *The Experience Curve Reviewed: IV: The Growth Share Matrix or Product Portfolio*, Boston: Boston Consulting Group (1973).

6. Booz Allen Hamilton claims that "dog" businesses can offer promising potential: H. Quarls, T. Pernsteiner, and K. Rangan, "Love Your Dogs," *strategy+business*, March 15, 2005, http://www.booz.com/media/file/Love_Your_Dogs.pdf, accessed August 23, 2012.

7. M. Goold, A. Campbell, and M. Alexander, *Corporate-Level Strategy: Creating Value in the Multibusiness Company* (New York: John Wiley & Sons, Inc., 1994).

8. M. Goold, A. Campbell, and M. Alexander, *Corporate-Level Strategy: Creating Value in the Multibusiness Company* (New York: John Wiley & Sons, Inc., 1994): 90.

9. M. C. Mankins and R. Steele, "Stop Making Plans; Start Making Decisions," *Harvard Business Review* (January 2006): 76–84.

10. L. Bossidy and R. Charan, *Execution: The Discipline of Getting Things Done* (New York: Crown Business, 2002): 197–201.

11. R. S. Kaplan and D. P. Norton, "Having Trouble with Your Strategy? Then Map It," *Harvard Business Review* (September/October 2000): 67–76.

12. R. S. Kaplan and D. P. Norton, "The Office of Strategy Management," *Harvard Business Review* (October 2005): 72–80.

13. Geneen's style of management is discussed in Chapter 3 of R. T. Pascale and A. G. Athos, *The Art of Japanese Management* (New York: Warner Books, 1982).

14. Tuck School of Business, CEO Speaker Series, September 23, 2002.

15. "Those Highflying PepsiCo Managers," *Fortune* (April 10, 1989): 79.

16. M. Goold and A. Campbell, *Strategies and Styles* (Oxford: Blackwell Publishing, 1987).

17. R. M. Grant, "Strategic Planning in a Turbulent Environment: Evidence from the Oil and Gas Majors," *Strategic Management Journal* 24 (2003): 491–518.

18. M. Goold, D. Pettifer, and D. Young, "Redesigning the Corporate Center," *European Management Review* 19, no. 1 (2001): 83–91.

19. P&G's Global Business Services: Transforming the way business is done, http://www.pg.com/en_US/downloads/company/PG_GBS_Factsheet.pdf, accessed September 7, 2012.

20. Deloitte Consulting LLP, *2011 Global Shared Services Survey Results: Executive Summary* (March 2011).

21. M. E. Porter, "From Competitive Advantage to Corporate Strategy," *Harvard Business Review* (May/June 1987): 46.

22. L. Phalippou and O. Gottschalg, "The Performance of Private Equity Funds," *Review of Financial Studies* 22 (2009): 1747–76; M. Humphery-Jenner, "Private Equity Fund Size, Investment Size, and Value Creation," *Review of Finance* (2011).

23. F. A. Maljers, "Corporate Strategy from a Unilever Perspective," in F. A. J. van den Bosch and A. P. de Man (eds), *Perspectives on Strategy: Contributions of Michael E. Porter* (Boston: Kluwer, 1997): 35–45.

24. "How Samsung Became a Global Champion," *Financial Times* (September 5, 2004).

25. M. Goold, D. Pettifer, and D. Young, "Redesigning the Corporate Center," *European Management Review* 19, no. 1 (2001): 83–91.

26. "Cross-selling's Elusive Charms," *Financial Times* (November 16, 1998): 21.

27. J. W. Lorsch and S. A. Allen III, *Managing Diversity and Interdependence: An Organizational Study of Multi-divisional Firms* (Boston: Harvard Business School Press, 1973).

28. J. W. Lorsch and S. A. Allen III, *Managing Diversity and Interdependence: An Organizational Study of Multi-divisional Firms* (Boston: Harvard Business School Press, 1973): 168.

29. C. K. Prahalad and R. Bettis, "The Dominant Logic: A New Linkage between Diversity and Performance," *Strategic Management Journal* 7 (1986): 485–502.

30. T. Copeland, T. Koller, and J. Murrin, *Valuation: Measuring and Managing the Value of Companies*, 3rd edn (New York: John Wiley & Sons, Inc., 2000).

31. R. Cibin and R. M. Grant, "Restructuring among the World's Largest Oil Companies," *British Journal of Management* 7 (December 1996): 411–28.

32. R. A. Burgelman and A. Grove, "Strategic Dissonance," *California Management Review* 38 (Winter 1996): 8–28.

33. A. Grove, *Only the Paranoid Survive* (New York: Bantam, 1999).

34. R. Calori, "How Successful Companies Manage Diverse Businesses," *Long Range Planning* 21 (June 1988): 85.

35. J. van Rekom, K. Corley, and D. Ravasi, "Extending and Advancing Theories of Organizational Identity," *Corporate Reputation Review* 11 (2008): 183–8.36.

36. Among private companies, the key governance problem is typically one set of owners (e.g., the founding family) enriching themselves at the expense of the other owners. See J. C. Coffee, "A Theory of Corporate Scandals:

Why the US and Europe Differ," Columbia Law School Working Paper No. 274 (March, 2005).

37. R. M. Grant and M. Visconti, "The Strategic Background to Corporate Accounting Scandals," *Long Range Planning* 39 (August 2006): 361–83.

38. *OECD Principles of Corporate Governance* (Paris: OECD, 2004).

39. "Splitting the Chairman and CEO Roles," *Business Week* (January 10, 2008): http://www.businessweek.com/managing/content/jan2008/ca2008018_642807.htm, accessed July 8, 2009.

40. D. Barton, "Capitalism for the Long Term," *Harvard Business Review* (March/April 2011): 84–92.

41. M. J. Conyon, S. I. Peck, L. E. Read, and G. V. Sadler, "The Structure of Executive Compensation Contracts: The UK Evidence," *Long Range Planning* 33 (August 2000): 478–503.

42. See, for example, P. Bolton, J. Scheinkman, and W. Xiong, "Pay for Short-term Performance: Executive Compensation in Speculative Markets," NBER Working Paper 12107 (March 2006); M. C. Jensen and K. J. Murphy, "Remuneration: Where We've Been, How We Got Here, What are the Problems," ECGI-Finance Working Paper 44 (2004).

43. A.D. Chandler, *Strategy and Structure* (Cambridge, MA: MIT Press, 1962).

44. O. E. Williamson, *Markets and Hierarchies: Analysis and Antitrust Implications* (New York: Free Press, 1975); and O. E. Williamson, "The Modern Corporation: Origins, Evolution, Attributes," *Journal of Economic Literature* 19 (1981): 1537–68.

45. J. L. Bower, *Managing the Resource Allocation Process* (Boston: Harvard Business School Press, 1986).

46. O. E. Williamson, "The Modern Corporation: Origins, Evolution, Attributes," *Journal of Economic Literature* 19 (1981): 1537–68.

47. T. R. Eisenmann and J. S. Bower, "The Entrepreneurial M-form: A Case Study of Strategic Integration in Global Media Companies," in J. L. Bower and C. G. Gilbert (eds), *From Resource Allocation to Strategy* (New York: Oxford University Press, 2005): 307–29.

48. H. Mintzberg, *Structure in Fives: Designing Effective Organizations* (Englewood Cliffs, NJ: Prentice Hall, 1983): Chapter 11.

49. J. Birkinshaw and A. Campbell, "Know the Limits of Corporate Venturing," FT Summer School, *Financial Times* (August 10, 2004).

15 External Growth Strategies: Mergers, Acquisitions, and Alliances

> When it comes to mergers, hope triumphs over experience.
>
> —IRWIN STELZER, US ECONOMIST AND COLUMNIST

OUTLINE

- ◆ **Introduction and Objectives**

- ◆ **Mergers and Acquisitions: Causes and Consequences**
  - The Motives for Mergers and Acquisitions
  - Empirical Evidence on Mergers and Acquisitions
  - Post-Merger Integration

- ◆ **Strategic Alliances**
  - Motives for Alliances

- ◆ **Summary**

- ◆ **Self-Study Questions**

- ◆ **Notes**

Introduction and Objectives

Mergers, acquisitions, and alliances are key instruments of corporate strategy as they are the principal means by which firms achieve major extensions in the scope of their activities. Mergers, acquisitions, and alliances are not strategies in themselves: they are tools of strategy—the means by which a firm pursues a particular strategic aim.

Mergers and acquisitions also represent one of the great paradoxes of strategic management. A slew of empirical studies have shown that mergers and acquisitions create little or no value overall. However, for *acquiring* firms, the evidence is clear: on average, acquisitions destroy shareholder value for the acquirer. The beneficiaries of mergers and acquisitions are the shareholders of the acquired firm together with the lawyers and investment bankers who arrange them. This being the case, why is acquisition the preferred means of corporate growth for so many companies?

Strategic alliances also raise interesting and important strategic issues. Increasingly firms are competing not independently but in collaboration with other firms. Indeed, some of these collaborators may include a firm's competitors. In exploring strategic alliances we extend our view of strategic management beyond the limits of the single firm.

Our goal is to look at the efficacy of mergers, acquisitions, and alliances as instruments of corporate strategy, the circumstances where they can be successful, and how they should be managed.

By the time you have completed this chapter, you will:

◆ be familiar with the factors that have motivated mergers and acquisitions;

◆ appreciate why so many mergers and acquisitions have generated disappointing results;

◆ be able to assess the potential for a merger or acquisition to create value for the forms involved;

◆ appreciate the challenges of post-merger integration;

◆ be familiar with the different types of strategic alliances and recognize the circumstances in which strategic alliances can create value for the partners.

Mergers and Acquisitions: Causes and Consequences

An **acquisition** (or takeover) is where one company purchases another. This involves the acquiring company (the acquirer) making an offer for the common stock of the other company (the acquiree) at a fixed price per share. Acquisitions can be "friendly," that is when they are supported by the board of the target company, or "unfriendly," when they are opposed by the target company's board—in the latter case they are known as *hostile takeovers*.

A **merger** is where two companies amalgamate to form a new company. This requires agreement by the shareholders of the two companies who then exchange their shares for shares in the new company. Mergers typically involve companies of similar size (Daimler and Chrysler; Exxon and Mobil), although, as in these two examples, one firm is usually the dominant partner. A higher market capitalization may allow a smaller company to merge with a much larger one (e.g., AOL and Time Warner). Where the companies involved are in different countries, a merger may be preferred to an acquisition for political reasons (e.g., Alcatel and Lucent, Daimler-Benz and Chrysler, Mittal Steel and Arcelor).

The term *merger* is sometimes used to denote both mergers and acquisitions—below I follow this popular convention. (Table 15.1 shows the biggest acquisitions of the current century.)

The Motives for Mergers and Acquisitions

At the beginning of this chapter I stated that mergers and acquisitions are not strategies in themselves but the tools of strategy. Can acquisition—essentially trading in companies—be a strategy in itself? For such an activity to qualify as a viable strategy, the essential condition is that the acquirer is better at valuing companies than the stock market is. This would allow the acquirer to identify undervalued companies, buy them, and then sell them once the market had corrected its valuation. Such a strategy can work for portfolio investment; for the acquisition of entire companies it does not work because of the costs involved. These comprise the acquisition premium that must be paid to take control of a company (typically 20–60%) and the transaction costs involved (legal and investment bank fees). Even for private equity

TABLE 15.1   Top-20 mergers and acquisitions of the 21st century

Year	Purchaser	Purchased	Value ($billion)
2000	Vodafone AirTouch PLC	Mannesmann	183
2000	AOL	Time Warner	165
2000	Pfizer	Warner-Lambert	90
2000	Exxon	Mobil	85
2007	Royal Bank of Scotland, Banco Santander, Fortis	ABN AMRO	79
2000	Glaxo Wellcome PLC	SmithKline Beecham PLC	76
2004	Royal Dutch Petroleum Co.	Shell Transport & Trading Co	75
2009	Gaz de France	Suez	75
2006	AT&T Inc.	BellSouth Corporation	73
2001	Comcast Corporation	AT&T Broadband	72
2002	Bell Atlantic	GTE	71
2000	SBC Communications	Ameritech	70
2009	Pfizer	Wyeth	68
2004	Sanofi-Synthélabo SA	Aventis SA	60
2002	Pfizer	Pharmacia Corporation	60
2007	Enel S.p.A.	Endesa SA	60
2004	JPMorgan Chase & Co	Banc One Corp	59
2007	Procter & Gamble	Gillette	57
2008	InBev	Anheuser-Busch	52
2008	Bank of America	Merrill Lynch	50

firms, which build investment funds comprising portfolios of acquired companies, the key to value creation is not simply buying and selling companies. They create value primarily through financial restructuring and strategic redirection. Hence, the starting point for any assessment of a merger or acquisition proposal has to be a clear recognition of its strategic objectives. These might include:

- acquiring strategically important resources and capabilities;
- seeking cost economies and market power;
- expanding into new geographical markets;
- diversifying into new industries.

Acquiring Resources or Capabilities   We discovered in Chapter 5 that the most valuable resources and capabilities are those that are not transferable and not easily replicated. Obtaining such resources and capabilities may require acquisition. The UK-based company Reckitt Benckiser was created by a merger in 1999; since then, it has used acquisition to build a large portfolio of brands that include Clearasil skin products, Dettol disinfectant, Durex contraceptives, Finish dishwashing products, Nurofen analgesics, Scholl footcare products, Woolite laundry products, and dozens more. US-based Fortune Brands has followed a similar strategy.

In technology-based industries, established companies regularly acquire small, start-up firms in order to acquire capabilities in emerging areas of technology. Between March 2005 and December 2011, Google acquired 95 mostly small technology-based companies which provided the basis for most of its new product launches. Over the same period, Microsoft made 71 acquisitions; these have provided Microsoft with the technical capabilities needed for it to build its position in video games, online advertising, internet telephony, and cloud computing. Each year, Microsoft hosts its VC Summit, where venture capitalists from all over the world are invited to market their companies. Walt Disney's 2006 acquisition of Pixar, the animated movie studio founded by John Lasseter and Steve Jobs, is a classic example of a large established company acquiring a small start-up in order to obtain technical and creative capabilities.

Acquisition can short circuit the tortuous process of developing internally a new organizational capability. However, using acquisitions to extend a company's capability base involves major risks. To begin with, acquisitions are expensive. In addition to the acquisition premium that must be paid, the targeted capability comes with a mass of additional resources and capabilities that are most likely surplus to requirements for the acquiring firm. Most importantly, once the acquisition has been made, the acquiring company must find a way to integrate the acquiree's capabilities with its own. All too often, culture clashes, personality clashes between senior managers, or incompatibilities of management systems can result in the degradation or destruction of the very capabilities that the acquiring company was seeking.

Cost Economies and Market Power from Horizontal Mergers   The most obvious benefits to acquisition are between companies in the same industry. The mergers between United and Continental Airlines which created the world's biggest airline and between Exxon and Mobil creating the world's biggest listed petroleum company both created massive cost economies by eliminating duplicate functions and exploiting scale economies, as well as increasing market power.

Geographical Extension   Acquisition is the most popular means of entry into foreign markets by larger companies. Acquisition allows firms to gain critical mass within an overseas market quickly and to overcome key "liabilities of foreignness"— notably lack of local knowledge, lack of local connections, and barriers to distribution. During the 21st century, geographical extension has been the most important motivation for mergers. Spurred by the trend toward globalization, cross-border mergers as a proportion of all mergers grew from 23% in 1998 to 45% in 2007.[1] In the process many industries have been transformed:

- In automobiles recent cross-border mergers have included Geely (China) and Volvo (Sweden), Tata Motors (India) and Jaguar and Land Rover (UK), Fiat (Italy) and Chrysler (US), GM (US) and Daewoo (South Korea), and Renault (France) and Nissan (Japan).
- Beer—an industry once populated by medium-sized, national companies— is now dominated by multinational giants such as Anheuser-Busch InBev, SABMiller, and Heineken. Each of these was created from scores of acquisitions: Heineken acquired 34 beer companies in 31 countries during 2002–2011.
- Luxottica has become the world's largest supplier of spectacles and sunglasses through a series of cross-border acquisitions, including LensCrafters, Ray-Ban, Sunglass Hut, Oakley, and Grupo Tecnol.

Diversification   Acquisition is the predominant mode of diversification for firms. The alternative—diversification by means of new business start-up—tends to be too slow for most companies. While a number of companies have formed internal "business incubators" for developing new business ventures, such start-ups seldom provide the basis for major diversifications (Samsung, 3M, and the Virgin Group are notable exceptions). By contrast, acquisition allows firms to quickly establish a major presence in a different sector. For example:

- IBM's transition from a hardware to a software and services company involved the acquisition of 115 companies between 2000 and 2011, including PwC Consulting, Rational Software Corp., Ascential Software Corp., Internet Security Systems, Cognos, SPSS Inc., and Netezza.
- Comcast, once a US provider of cable TV services, was transformed into a diversified telecommunication and entertainment company with the acquisition of AT&T Broadband, Adelphia Cable, and NBC Universal.

Diversification may also involve small acquisitions which provide a foundation for internal investment. For example, Microsoft's entry into video games with the launch of Xbox in November 2001 was preceded by the acquisition of several small companies, such as RenderMorphics (3-D graphics hardware), Exos (video game controllers), and a number of video game software developers (VGA-Animation Software, Electric Gravity, FASA Interactive, Bungie, and NetGames).

Empirical Evidence on Mergers and Acquisitions

As a means of strategy execution, the chief attraction of mergers and acquisitions (M&As) is the speed with which they can be put into effect. After spending a decade gradually expanding its range of corporate-banking activities into investment banking, Bank of America's 2009 acquisition of Merrill Lynch catapulted the firm into the ranks of the world's leading investment banks. The decision to acquire Merrill Lynch was made over a single weekend.

Yet these advantages of speed come at a cost. Empirical research into the performance consequences of mergers and acquisitions makes for depressing reading. The performance effects of mergers and acquisitions have been measured using both shareholder returns and accounting data on profitability. The only clear finding is that acquisitions benefit the shareholders of the acquired firms. For acquiring firms, studies show that the returns are, on average, either negative or insignificant from zero. Combining the effects on both acquirers and acquirees, the overall picture is one of small gains to mergers, typically around 2% of the combined market value of the companies involved.[2] Studies that use accounting data to compare post-merger profitability with pre-merger profitability show little consistency in their findings: "results from these accounting-based studies are all over the map."[3]

These findings are hardly surprising. The fact that the sole beneficiaries of M&A activity are the shareholders of the acquired companies is an inevitable result of the large acquisition premiums paid by acquirers. These acquisition premiums are also the main reason why the returns to acquirers are so poor. The inconsistency of findings reflects the heterogeneity of the phenomenon. Acquisitions are motivated by different strategic goals, and each involves a unique combination of circumstances. Even when mergers and acquisitions are grouped into different categories, the performance outcomes remain unclear. For example, one might expect that horizontal mergers (which increase market share and offer gains from scale economies) would be more successful than diversifying mergers; among diversifying mergers, it would be expected that the acquisition of firms in related businesses would outperform unrelated acquisitions. Yet both these highly plausible predictions fail to find robust empirical support.

When Do Mergers and Acquisitions Make Sense?   In the absence of strong general findings about the outcomes of mergers, we need to consider each proposed merger or acquisition on its own merits—which means subjecting it to systematic strategic appraisal. Let us start with the strategic goals of mergers and acquisitions.

The reason that shareholders should view acquisitions with extreme skepticism is that they are so appealing to top management, and CEOs in particular. Managerial incentives, both financial and psychic, tend to be associated more with a company's size than with its profitability. Acquisition is certainly the fastest way of growing. Even more dangerous is CEOs' quest for celebrity status; again, large-scale acquisitions are the surest way that a CEO can gain media coverage while projecting an image of power and influence. The combination of these two creates the phenomenon of *empire building*. The "titans of industry" that used multiple acquisitions to pursue ambitious growth—Jean-Marie Messier at Vivendi Universal, Fred Goodwin at Royal Bank of Scotland, Bernie Ebbers at WorldCom—appear to be victims of hubris (exaggerated self-confidence), leading to a distorted judgment and becoming increasingly divorced from reality.

The stock market may collude with such behavior. Michael Jensen suggests that CEOs of companies with overvalued equity will make equity-financed acquisitions to help support their share price.[4] AOL's merger with Time Warner may reflect this motive.

The further factor encouraging M&As that lack a convincing strategic rationale is the propensity for imitation. M&A activity is highly cyclical, with a heavy clustering in specific sectors during specific periods: the petroleum mergers of 1998–2002; the 1990s rush for banks and insurance companies to combine; the telecoms' urge to merge of 1998–2005; and the global consolidation of the beer, pharmaceuticals, and metals sectors during the past decade.[5] This sectoral clustering is associated with shocks affecting particular industries (e.g., deregulation in telecommunications or the repeal of the Glass–Stegall Act in banking). It is also reinforced by the propensity of firms to follow the leader: if firms resist the urge to merge, they risk being alone at the fringes of the dance floor with only unattractive dancing partners left.

The implications is that M&A decisions need to be based, first, upon a clear identification of what the acquirer's strategy is and how the proposed acquisition will contribute to that strategy and, second, upon a detailed and realistic assessment of what the outcome of the acquisition will be. This is easier with some acquisitions than it is with others. In the case of horizontal acquisitions, it is usually possible not just to identify the likely cost savings from integrating the two companies but also to come up with some realistic estimates of what those savings might be. Other sources of synergy are much more elusive. For example, estimates of the potential marketing benefits or the implications for innovation are likely to be much more speculative. Acquiring companies tend to overestimate the gains from mergers. Many diversifying mergers within financial services have been motivated by wildly optimistic forecasts of the potential for cross-selling and customers' desire for one-stop shopping. The risk is that acquirers fall victim to their own propaganda: in seeking to persuade the stock market about the benefits of an acquisition, they believe their own inflated estimates of potential synergies.

A realistic assessment of the potential gains from a merger or acquisition requires intimate knowledge of the target company. This is a bigger problem for hostile takeovers than for agreed acquisitions. However, even friendly takeovers are still prone to information asymmetry (the so-called *lemons problem*)—the seller knows much more about the acquisition target than the buyer, so the acquirer can be hoodwinked into overpaying. One year after its acquisition of Jaguar, a Ford executive commented: "If we had known what a terrible shape Jaguar was in, we would never had paid the price we did."

Post-Merger Integration

Case-study evidence shows that some of the most carefully planned mergers and acquisitions can end up as failures because of the problems of managing post-merger integration. The combination of Daimler-Benz and Chrysler was exemplary in its pre-merger planning; the outcome was disastrous. Not only did Chrysler's problems appear to be intractable but also Chrysler's demands on the group's top management negatively impacted the core Daimler-Benz business.[6]

Frequently, it appears that where the potential benefits of mergers and acquisitions are large the costs and risks of integrations are also large. Thus, Capron and Anand argue that cross-border acquisitions typically have the strongest strategic logic.[7] Yet, the evidence of DaimlerChrysler, BMW/Rover, and Alcatel-Lucent suggests that when differences in corporate culture are accentuated by differences in national culture the challenge of post-merger integration becomes immense.

A growing body of literature views acquisition as an organizational capability and points to the need for acquisition capabilities to be developed through explicit and experiential learning. Acquisition performance tends to increase with experience... although not at first. A learning threshold appears, after which subsequent acquisitions add value.[8] Explicit learning through the codification of acquisition processes also appears to be conducive to acquisition success.[9]

In common with my approach throughout this book, I consider that it is important to separate issues of pre-acquisition planning and post-acquisition management. In the long and rich history of acquisition disasters, poor post-acquisition management has been identified as the source of the problem. Yet, in many of these cases the integration problems could have been anticipated: the critical problem was going ahead with the acquisition without making an adequate assessment of post-merger management problems. Thus, in the case of Quaker Oats' acquisition of Snapple (universally known as "the billion-dollar blunder"), the critical problem—the impediments to integrating Snapple's distribution system with that of Quaker's Gatorade—were evident to the marketing managers and the franchised distributors of the two companies prior to the takeover.[10]

Conversely, Walt Disney's acquisition of Pixar was preceded by an anticipation of the problems that might arise and a careful and sensitive approach to planning, and then implementing, the integration of Pixar (Strategy Capsule 15.1).

Strategic Alliances

A **strategic alliance** is a collaborative arrangement between two or more firms to pursue agreed common goals. *Strategic alliances* take many different forms:

- A strategic alliance may or may not involve equity participation: the alliance between General Motors and Peugeot to develop cars together was reinforced by GM taking a 7% equity stake in Peugeot. Other alliances are agreements without any ownership stakes: the agreement between Nokia and Microsoft for Nokia to develop a range of new smartphones based upon the Windows phone-operating system involved no exchange of equity between the companies. A joint venture is a particular form of equity alliance where the partners form a new company that they jointly own: Dow Corning Inc. is a joint venture between Corning and Dow Chemical that produces silicon-based products. Volkswagen, China's leading automobile marque, operates through two main joint ventures, one with SAIC Motor and one with the FAW Group.
- Alliances are created to fulfill specific purposes:
  - Star Alliance is an agreement among 25 airlines (including United, Lufthansa, and Air Canada) to code share flights and link frequent-flier programs
  - Automobili Lamborghini and Callaway Golf Company formed an R & D alliance in 2010 to develop advanced composite materials
  - GlaxoSmithKline and Dr Reddy's Laboratories (a leading Indian pharma company) formed an alliance in 2009 to market Dr Reddy's products in emerging-market countries through GSK's sales and marketing network

---

STRATEGY CAPSULE 15.1

Walt Disney Company and Pixar

Most industry observers were pessimistic about Disney's $7.4-billion acquisition of rival animated movie producer Pixar in 2006. Most acquisitions of movie studios had experienced major difficulties: General Electric's NBC acquisition of Universal Studios and Viacom's of DreamWorks. The worries were that Disney's corporate systems would suppress Pixar's creativity and that Pixar's animators would leave. Although the two companies had allied for several years (Disney distributed Pixar movies), the relationship had not been smooth.

In fact, the acquisition appears to have been highly successful. Several Pixar movies have been massive box office successes—*Cars*, *WallE*, and *Toy Story 3*—and the "Disney machine" has generated massive revenues from DVDs, toys, and licensing. Disney's CEO, Bob Iger, claims that, compared with the earlier alliance between the two companies, ownership of Pixar has facilitated the closer coordination needed to exploit the synergies between the two companies.

Factors contributing to the success of the merger include:

◆ a high level of personal and professional respect among the key personnel at Pixar and Disney. In announcing the acquisition, CEO Iger commented: "We also fully recognize that Pixar's extraordinary record of achievement is in large measure due to its vibrant creative culture, which is something we respect and admire and are committed to supporting and fostering in every way possible";

◆ a rapid and honest communication to Pixar employees about the merger and its implications;

◆ prior to the acquisition, creating an explicit map of which elements of Pixar would remain unchanged and which would be adapted to and integrated with Walt Disney's existing activities and practices;

◆ Pixar's president Edwin Catmull was put in charge of Walt Disney Animation Studios;

◆ Bob Iger's ability to draw upon his personal experience of working for companies that had been acquired;

◆ an explicit list of guidelines to protect Pixar's creative culture: Pixar employees were able to keep their relatively generous health benefits and weren't forced to sign employment contracts;

◆ honoring commitments: according to Edwin Catmull: "Everything they've said they would do they have lived up to."

In one respect, the Disney–Pixar merger flouted conventional wisdom. According to Bob Iger: "There is an assumption in the corporate world that you need to integrate swiftly. My philosophy is exactly the opposite. You need to be respectful and patient."

Source: The Walt Disney Company Press Release, "Disney Completes Pixar Acquisition," Burbank, CA, May 5, 2006; "Disney: Magic restored," *The Economist*, April 17, 2008; "Disney and Pixar: The Power of the Prenup," www.nytimes.com/2008/06/01/business/media/01pixar.html?pagewanted=all.

○ The Rumaila Field Operating Organization is a joint venture among China National Petroleum Company, BP, and South Oil Company to operate Iraq's biggest oilfield;

● Alliances may be purely bilateral arrangements, or they may be a part of a network of interfirm relationships. One form of alliance network is the supplier network, exemplified by that of Toyota. Toyota's supplier network comprises first-level, second-level, and tertiary suppliers bound by long-term relationships with Toyota and supported by a set of routines that permit knowledge sharing and continuous improvement.[11] Clothing companies Inditex (Zara) and Benetton maintain similar networks. Another type of alliance network is the localized industry cluster that characterizes the industrial districts of Italy (e.g., Prato woolen knitwear cluster, Carrara stonecutting cluster, and Sassuolo ceramic tile cluster). The Hollywood film industry represents another such cluster. Relationships within these localized networks are based upon history and proximity and are informal rather than formal.[12]

Motives for Alliances

Alliances are motivated primarily by opportunities for exploiting complementarities between the resources and capabilities owned by different companies:

- Bulgari Hotels and Resorts is a joint venture that combines Bulgari's reputation for luxury and quality with Marriott International's capabilities in developing and operating hotels;
- Nike's alliance with Apple links Nike's capabilities with athletic shoes with Apple's microelectronics capabilities in order to offer real-time biometric data delivered to an iPod;
- Sasol Chevron Holdings is a 50/50 global joint venture that combines Sasol's gas-to-liquids technology with Chevron's reserves of natural gas and downstream distribution to build plants which convert natural gas into synthetic gasoline.

There has been a debate in the literature as to whether the primary aim of strategic alliances is to *access* the partner's resources and capabilities or to *acquire* them through learning.[13] The strategic alliance between Intel and DreamWorks Animation allows each company to access the other's capabilities in order to jointly develop next-generation 3-D films.[14] Conversely, General Motor's NUMMI joint venture with Toyota was motivated by GM's desire to learn about the Toyota Production System.[15]

In most instances alliances are about accessing rather than acquiring capabilities: for most firms the basic rationale of alliances is that they allow the firm to specialize in a limited range of capabilities while enabling the exploitation of specific opportunities that require a wider range of capabilities.[16] A key advantage of such alliances is the flexibility they offer: especially when making option-type investments.[17] IBM has several programs for funding collaborative research with universities throughout the world. The result is hundreds of projects where IBM commits relatively small amounts of funding to R & D projects with highly uncertain outcomes. Such projects give IBM the option, if successful, to first obtain intellectual property protection and then devote much larger resources to the commercial development of the innovation.[18]

Alliances also permit risk sharing. In petroleum, most upstream projects are joint ventures. Kazakhstan's Kashagan field, the biggest oilfield discovered in the last 30 years, is being developed by a consortium comprising ENI, Shell, Total,

ExxonMobil, KazMunayGas, ConocoPhillips, and Inpex. Most major defense contracts are undertaken by consortia: the F-35 jet fighter has a development cost of $235 billion. It is being built by Lockheed Martin and partners Northup Grumman and BAE Systems.

It is tempting to view a strategic alliance as a quick and low-cost means of extending the capabilities available to a firm. However, managing alliance relationships is itself a critically important organizational capability. *Relational capability* comprises building trust, developing interfirm knowledge sharing routines, and establishing mechanisms for coordination.[19] The more a company outsources its value chain activities to a network of alliance partners, the more it needs to develop the "systems integration capability" to coordinate and integrate the dispersed activities.[20] The delays that have plagued the Boeing 787 Dreamliner are one indicator of the challenges of managing a network of alliances in developing a complex, technologically advanced product.[21]

International Alliances Strategic alliances play a particularly important role in a firm's internationalization strategies. When entering an overseas market, the internationalizing firm will typically lack the local knowledge, political connections, and access to distribution channels that a local firm will possess. At the same time acquiring a local firm may not be an attractive option, either because local regulations or ownership patterns make acquisition difficult or because the internationalizing firm may be reluctant to make a large and irreversible financial commitment to the overseas market. In such circumstances, alliances—either with or without equity—can offer an attractive mode of foreign entry. By sharing resources and capabilities, alliances economize on the investment needed for major international initiatives. The FreeMove alliance formed by Telefónica Móviles (Spain), TIM (Italy), T-Mobile (Germany), and Orange (France) created a seamless third-generation, wireless communication network across Europe at a fraction of the cost incurred by Vodafone; it also allowed each firm access to the mobile network of the leading operator in at least five major European markets.[22]

Some firms have built their internationalization strategies almost entirely on cross-border alliances:

- Gazprom, the Russian gas giant, has alliances relating to pipeline projects with ENI (Italy), CNPC (China), EON (Germany), PDVSA (Venezuela), and MOL (Hungary); liquefied natural gas projects with Petro-Canada and Sonatrach (Algeria); and long-term supply arrangements with Gaz de France.
- General Motors has established a network of strategic alliances, most of them reinforced by equity participation, in order to build its presence in emerging markets and extend its range of small cars (Figure 15.1).

For the local partner, an alliance with a foreign firm can also be an attractive means of accessing resources and capabilities. In many emerging-market countries—notably China and India before their accession to the World Trade Organization—governments often oblige foreign companies to take a local partner in order to encourage the flow of technology and management capabilities to the host country. For example, China's automobile industry has been developed almost entirely through joint ventures with US, Japanese, and European automakers.

FIGURE 15.1 General Motors' network of international alliances with other automakers

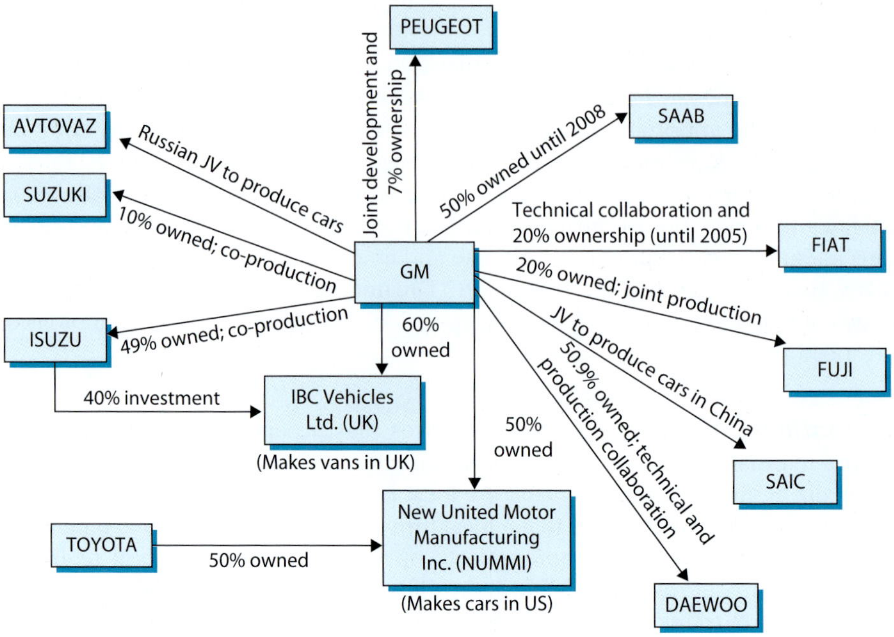

However, for all their attractions, international alliances are difficult to manage: the usual problems that alliances present—those of communication, agreement, and trust—are exacerbated by differences in language, culture, and greater geographical distance. Danone's joint venture with Wahaha created the largest drinks company in China; however, misunderstanding and misaligned incentives resulted in the joint venture collapsing in 2011.[23]

It is tempting to conclude that international alliances are most difficult where national cultural differences are wide (e.g., between Western and Asian companies). However, some alliances between Western and Asian companies have been highly successful (e.g., Fuji/Xerox and Renault/Nissan). Conversely, many alliances between Western companies have been failures: BT and AT&T's Concert alliance, the GM/Fiat alliance, and Swissair's network of airline alliances. Disagreements over the sharing of the contributions to and returns from an alliance are a frequent source of friction, particularly in alliances between firms that are also competitors. When each partner seeks to access the other's capabilities, "competition for competence" results.[24] During the 1980s, Western companies fretted about losing their technological know-how to Japanese alliance partners. In recent years, Western companies have been dismayed by the speed at which their Chinese partners have absorbed their technology and emerged as international competitors. In rail infrastructure, China's state-owned companies have used their partnerships with Germany's Siemens, France's Alstom, Japan's Kawasaki Heavy Industries, and Canada's Bombardier to build homegrown capabilities that are now being exported.[25] The complaints made by Western companies against their Chinese joint-venture partners in 2012 are almost identical to those made against Japanese joint-venture partners in the 1980s.[26]

Summary

Mergers and acquisitions can be useful tools of several types of strategy: for acquiring particular resources and capabilities, for reinforcing a firm's position within an industry, and for achieving diversification or horizontal expansion.

However, despite the plausibility of most of the stated goals that underlie mergers and acquisitions, most fail to achieve their stated goals. Empirical research shows that the gains flow primarily to the shareholders of the acquired companies.

These disappointing outcomes may reflect the tendency for mergers and acquisitions to be motivated by the desire for growth rather than for profitability. The pursuit of growth through merger is sometimes reinforced by CEO hubris, producing a succession of acquisitions that will ultimately lead to the company failing or restructuring.

A second factor in the poor performance consequences of many mergers are the unforeseen difficulties of post-merger integration. The diversity of mergers and their outcomes makes it very difficult to generalize about the types of merger or the approaches to integration that are associated with success.

Strategic alliances take many forms. In common is the desire to exploit complementarities between the resources and capabilities of different companies. Like mergers and acquisitions, and like relationships between individuals, they have varying degrees of success. Unlike mergers and acquisitions, the consequences of failure are usually less costly. As the business environment becomes more complex and more turbulent, the advantages of strategic alliances both in offering flexibility and in reconciling specialization with the ability to integrate a broad array of resources and capabilities become increasingly apparent.

Quizzes and flashcards to test yourself further are available in your interactive e-book at **www.wileyopenpage.com**

Self-Study Questions

1. Most of the mergers and acquisition in Table 15.1 are horizontal (i.e., they are between companies within the same sector). Some of these horizontal M&As are between companies in the same country; some cross national borders. Are there any reasons why horizontal M&A is likely to be more beneficial than other types of M&A (diversifying and vertical) and involve less risk? Among these horizontal M&As, which do you think will be more successful: those between companies in the same country or those that cross borders?

2. All of the CEOs associated with merger-intensive strategies (Jean-Marie Messier at Vivendi Universal, Fred Goodwin at Royal Bank of Scotland, Bernie Ebbers at WorldCom, Steve Case at AOL, Ed Whitacre at AT&T, Jeff Kindler at Pfizer, and Ivan Seidenberg at Verizon) have been male. Does this reflect the predominance of men among the ranks of CEOs, or is there something inherently masculine about the pursuit of growth through merger?

3. Commenting on the Pixar acquisition (Strategy Capsule 15.1), Disney's CEO stated: "You can accomplish a lot more as one company than you can as part of a joint venture." Do you agree? Illustrate your answer by referring to the some of the joint ventures (or alliances) referred to in this chapter. Would these have been more successful as mergers?

4. Different automobile companies have internationalized in different ways. Toyota has expanded organically, establishing subsidiaries in overseas markets. Ford went through a phase of acquisition (buying Volvo, Jaguar, Land Rover, and a major stake in Mazda). General Motors has favored strategic alliances (Figure 15.1). What do you see as the advantages and disadvantages of GM's alliance-based international strategy?

Notes

1. I. Erel, R. C. Liao, and M. S. Weisbach, *Determinants of Cross-Border Mergers and Acquisitions*, Fisher College of Business, Ohio State University (March 2011).

2. S. N. Kaplan, "Mergers and Acquisitions: A Financial Economics Perspective," University of Chicago, Graduate School of Business Working Paper (February, 2006); P. A. Pautler, *Evidence on Mergers and Acquisitions*, Bureau of Economics, Federal Trade Commission (September 25, 2001).

3. S. N. Kaplan, "Mergers and Acquisitions: A Financial Economics Perspective," University of Chicago, Graduate School of Business Working Paper (February, 2006): 8.

4. M. C. Jensen, "Agency Costs of Overvalued Equity," *Harvard Business School* (May 2004).

5. G. Andrade, M. Mitchell, and E. Stafford, "New Evidence and Perspectives on Mergers," *Journal of Economic Perspectives* 15 (Spring 2001): 103–20.

6. "DaimlerChrysler: Stalled," *Business Week* (September 10, 2003).

7. L. Capron and J. Anand, "Acquisition-based Dynamic Capabilities," in C. E. Helfat, S. Finkelstein, W. Mitchell, M. A. Peteraf, H. Singh, D. J. Teece, and S. G. Winter, *Dynamic Capabilities* (Malden, MA: Blackwell, 2007): 80–99.

8. S. Finkelstein and J. Haleblian, "Understanding Acquisition Performance: The Role of Transfer Effects," *Organization Science* 13 (2002): 36–47.

9. M. Zollo and H. Singh, "Deliberate Learning in Corporate Acquisitions: Post-acquisition Strategies and Integration Capabilities in US Bank Mergers," *Strategic Management Journal* 24 (2004): 1233–56.

10. C. E. Helfat, S. Finkelstein, W. Mitchell, M. A. Peteraf, H. Singh, D. J. Teece, and S. G. Winter, *Dynamic Capabilities* (Malden, MA: Blackwell, 2007): 57–62.

11. J. H. Dyer and K. Nobeoka, "Creating and Managing A High-Performance Knowledge-Sharing Network: The Toyota Case," *Strategic Management Journal* 21 (2000): 345–67.

12. "Local Partnership, Clusters and SME Globalization" Workshop Paper on Enhancing the Competitiveness of SMEs (OECD, June 2000).

13. D. C. Mowery, J. E. Oxley, and B. S. Silverman, "Strategic Alliances and Interfirm Knowledge Transfer," *Strategic Management Journal* 17 (Winter 1996): 77–93.

14. "Intel, DreamWorks Animation Form Strategic Alliance to Revolutionize 3-D Filmmaking Technology," (July 8, 2008), www.intel.com/pressroom/archive/releases/2008/20080708corp.htm, accessed April 2, 2012.

15. J. A. Badaracco, *The Knowledge Link: How Firms Compete through Strategic Alliances* (Boston: Harvard Business School Press, 1991).

16. R. M. Grant and C. Baden-Fuller, "A Knowledge Accessing Theory of Strategic Alliances," *Journal of Management Studies* 41 (2004): 61–84.

17. R. S. Vassolo, J. Anand, and T. B Folta, "Non-additivity in Portfolios of Exploration Activities: A Real Options-based Analysis of Equity Alliances in Biotechnology," *Strategic Management Journal* 25 (2004): 1045–61.

18. www.ibm.com/developerworks/university/collaborativeresearch/projects.html, accessed April 2, 2012.

19. P. Kale, J. H. Dyer, and H. Singh, "Alliance Capability, Stock Market Response and Long Term Alliance

Success," *Strategic Management Journal* 23 (2002): 747–67.

20. A. Prencipe, "Corporate Strategy and Systems Integration Capabilities," in A. Prencipe, A. Davies, and M. Hobday (eds), *The Business of Systems Integration* (Oxford: Oxford University Press, 2003): 114–132.

21. "Dreamliner Becomes a Nightmare for Boeing," *Der Spiegel* (March 3, 2011) http://www.spiegel.de/international/business/0,1518,753891,00.html, accessed March 10, 2011.

22. *Freemove: Creating Value through Strategic Alliance in the Mobile Telecommunications Industry*, IESE Case 0-305-013 (2004).

23. S. M. Dickinson, "Danone v. Wahaha: Lessons for Joint Ventures in China," www.chinalawblog.com/DanoneWahahaLessons.pdf, accessed April 5, 2012.

24. G. Hamel, "Competition for Competence and Inter-partner Learning within International Strategic Alliances," *Strategic Management Journal* 12 (1991): 83–103.

25. "China: A Future on Track," *Financial Times* (September 24, 2010).

26. See R. Reich and E. Mankin, "Joint Ventures with Japan Give Away Our Future," *Harvard Business Review* (March/April 1986).

16 Current Trends in Strategic Management

We live in a period of profound transition—and the changes are more radical perhaps than even those that ushered in the "Second Industrial Revolution" of the middle of the 19th century, or the structural changes triggered by the Great Depression and the Second World War.[1]

—PETER F. DRUCKER, MANAGEMENT THINKER AND WRITER, 1909–2005

We are at the very beginning of time for the human race. It is not unreasonable that we grapple with problems. But there are tens of thousands of years in the future. Our responsibility is to do what we can, learn what we can, improve the solutions, and pass them on.

—RICHARD FEYNMAN, 1918–1988; NOBEL PRIZE FOR PHYSICS, 1965

OUTLINE

- ◆ **Introduction**
- ◆ **The New Environment of Business**
  - Turbulence
  - Competition
  - Technology
  - Social Pressures and the Crisis of Capitalism
- ◆ **New Directions in Strategic Thinking**
  - Reorienting Corporate Objectives
  - Seeking More Complex Sources of Competitive Advantage

- Managing Options
- Understanding Strategic Fit
- ◆ **Redesigning Organizations**
  - Multi-Dimensional Structures
  - Coping with Complexity: Making Organizations Informal, Self-Organizing, and Permeable
- ◆ **The Changing Role of Managers**
- ◆ **Summary**
- ◆ **Notes**

Introduction

With the 21st century only in its second decade, it has become clear that the year 2000 marked a watershed, both in terms of the global economy and in terms of the development of business. Our challenge in this chapter is to assess what has changed in the business environment, whether the extreme turbulence that has characterized the century so far will continue, and, if so, what the implications for strategic management are.

We are in uncharted waters and, unlike the other chapters of this book, this chapter will not equip you with proven tools and frameworks that you can deploy directly in case analysis or in your own companies. Our approach is exploratory. We begin by reviewing the forces that are reshaping the environment of business. We will then draw upon concepts and ideas that are influencing current thinking about strategy and the lessons offered from leading-edge companies about strategies, organizational forms, and management styles that can help us to meet the challenges of this demanding era.

The New Environment of Business

The 21st century began with the bursting of the dot.com stock market bubble. March 2000 marked the beginning of the NASDAQ's decade-long bear market.[2] The following year saw the terrorist attacks of September 11, which triggered a train of events including the invasions of Afghanistan and Iraq. In November 2001, Enron, one of America's most successful and admired energy companies, entered bankruptcy—the first of a series of financial scandals that engulfed companies on both sides of the Atlantic. Unprecedented market turbulence was evident in commodities and foreign exchange: in one six-month period, NYMEX crude oscillated between $37 and $147 a barrel. The biggest financial trauma was the financial crisis that began with the fall of Lehman Brothers, in September 2008, followed by the collapse of the banking systems of Iceland and Ireland, and culminating in the Greek government's debt default of March 2012. Meanwhile, political turbulence reached new peaks with the overthrow of the Tunisian, Egyptian, and Libyan governments in the Arab Spring of 2011. Nor was instability restricted to the political and economic spheres. There were natural catastrophes, including the Indian Ocean tsunami of December 2004, Hurricane Katrina that devastated New Orleans in 2005, and major earthquakes affecting Iran (2003), Sichuan, China (2008), Haiti (2010), and Japan (2011).

The speed at which the Roaring Nineties (the last decade of the 20th century) turned into the Nightmare Noughties (the first decade of the 21st century) has been a profound shock to business leaders. To understand how companies are adjusting to the new conditions and the strategic options available to them, let us look more carefully at the major characteristics of today's business environment.

Turbulence

In reviewing the events of the 21st century, my focus was on the turbulence and unpredictability that has characterized the business environment. Almost all the events I listed—from the September 11 attacks of 2001 to the Arab Spring of 2011—were highly improbable and unpredicted, what have been called *black swan events* (Strategy Capsule 16.1).

A key issue is whether the black swan events we have witnessed between 2000 and 2011 simply reflect an unusual preponderance of extreme events or whether we are witnessing systematic changes that have made the business environment more crisis-prone. The latter seems likely. A feature of the global economy, and human society in general, is increasing interconnectedness through trade, financial flows, markets, and communication. Systems theory predicts that increasing levels of interconnectedness within a complex, nonlinear system increase the tendency for small initial movements to be amplified in unpredictable ways.

Shifts in the global balance of economic power will continue to undermine the ability of the leading industrial nations to control these disruptive forces. The rise of the BRIC countries is creating a multipolar world where the Old Order—the US, the EU, Japan, and the institutions they created (the World Bank, IMF, and OECD) are less able to offer global leadership. Looking ahead to 2025, the US National Intelligence Council predicts:

> The international system—as constructed following the Second World War—will be almost unrecognizable . . . owing to the rise of emerging powers, a globalizing economy, an historic transfer of relative wealth and economic power from west to east, and the growing influence of non-state actors.[3]

STRATEGY CAPSULE 16.1
Black Swan Events

The term *black swan*, a metaphor popularized by Nassim Taleb, refers to events that are extremely rare, have a major impact, and are unpredicted, despite the fact that they are rationalized retrospectively i.e., they *could* have been predicted. The term derives from the widespread belief that all swans were white until black swans were discovered in Western Australia at the end of the 17th century. Taleb argues that almost all significant events in human history are black swans: despite their rareness, the sources of black swan events are many, and their impact is amplified by the fact that they are not predicted.

Our vulnerability to black swan events is exacerbated by conventional approaches to risk management. These typically assume, first, that past events provide a basis for predicting future events and, second, that the probabilities of these events tend to be normally distributed. Extrapolating the past into the future makes strong assumptions about the stability of the underlying processes that generate uncertain events, while the very rareness of unusual events makes it very difficult to understand their causes. Growing awareness of *long tail* or *power law distributions* has brought into question conventional assumptions about the normal distribution of uncertain events.

Thus, Taleb's conclusion is that managing black swans is essentially about building robustness to reduce vulnerability to negative events and responsiveness to exploit positive ones.

Competition

Among the wide array of uncertainties that firms face when looking at the immediate future, there is one near certainty: that economic growth, especially in the advanced economies, will remain sluggish throughout the medium term. The aftermath of the consumer-led, debt-fuelled growth and the financial crisis has been the need for massive deleveraging by households, companies, and governments. The corporate sector is the least of the problems: debt/equity ratios are generally modest (indeed, a bigger problem is channeling firms' cash balances into productive investment). However, for the household and government sectors the problems are both serious and long-term. For the governments of the US, Europe, and Japan, expansive fiscal and monetary policies are making the problem increasingly intractable. With the economies of China, India, and Brazil also decelerating, the prospects for robust global growth seem remote.

In most sectors of the global economy, with a few notable exceptions, such as agriculture, excess capacity is the norm. Such conditions will fuel strong price competition and squeeze profit margins.

An additional source of competitive pressure is internationalization by companies from emerging-market countries. In China, India, and other countries, firms that were once contract manufacturers supplying OEM products for sale under their customers' brands are increasingly competing with those customers in final markets.[4] At the beginning of 2012 there were at least 30 Chinese and Indian firms supplying Android smartphones under their own brand names. The entrance of emerging-market firms onto the world stage has been marked by increasing numbers of cross-border acquisitions by companies from emerging countries (Table 16.1).

Technology

The potential for digital technologies to undermine established positions of competitive advantage and redraw industry barriers appears as great now as it was 20 years ago. Indeed, the pace of creative destruction is accelerating. Just as Netflix sealed the fate of Blockbuster, so Netflix may be a casualty of the displacement of DVDs by video streaming. Such uncertainties are part of a broader picture of disruption within what was once known as the "television industry" which now forms a part of

TABLE 16.1 Emerging-market corporations acquiring Western companies

Year	Acquirer	Country	Target	Country	Value ($million)
2011	HTC	Taiwan	S3 Graphics	US	300
2011	Geely	China	Volvo	Sweden	1,800
2008	Tata Motor	India	Jaguar Land Rover	UK	2,300
2007	CEMEX	Mexico	Rinker Group	US	14,200
2007	United Spirits Ltd	India	Whyte & Mackay Ltd	UK	1,176
2006	Mittal Steel	India	Arcelor	Lux/Fr.	32,800
2006	Tata Steel	India	Corus	UK/Neth.	7,800
2006	Tata Coffee Ltd	India	Eight O'Clock Coffee Co.	US	220
2006	China National Chemical Corp.	China	Adisseo	France	480

a much broader arena of ferment involving the producers of a wide array of digital content for distribution through multiple channels for viewing on a multitude of mobile and home-based digital devices. The impact of technology causing industries to converge then reconfigure is a pervasive feature of the digital landscape. In hand-held devices, Nokia cell phones, Apple iPods, Nintendo Gameboys, Palm PDAs, and RIM's BlackBerry smartphones once competed in different markets. Increasingly, mobile hand-held devices share functions and compete in a shared market space.

Social Pressures and the Crisis of Capitalism

For organizations to survive and prosper requires that they adapt to the values and expectations of society—what organizational sociologists refer to as *legitimacy*.[5] One fall-out from the 2008/9 financial crisis was the loss of legitimacy that many businesses suffered—financial service firms in particular. This negatively affected their reputations among consumers, the morale of their employees, the willingness of investors and financiers to provide funding, and the government policies toward them. As Chapter 2 (p. 51) has outlined, the loss of social legitimacy that affected many commercial and investment banks was a greater a threat to their survival than their weak balance sheets. Similar legitimacy challenges face Rupert Murdoch's News Corp. media empire following the "phone hacking" scandal at its British newspapers.[6]

The notion that the business enterprise is a social institution that must identify with the goals and aspirations of society has been endorsed by most leading management thinkers, including Peter Drucker, Charles Handy, and Sumantra Ghoshal.[7] The implication is that when the values and attitudes of society are changing so must the strategies and behaviors of companies. While anti-business sentiment has for the most part been restricted to the fringes of the political spectrum—neo-Marxists, environmentalists, and anti-globalization activists—the events of 2001 to 2012, including corporate scandals such as Enron and WorldCom and the financial crisis of 2008–2009, have moved disdain for business corporations and their leaders into the mainstream of public opinion.

A feature of growing disenchantment with market capitalism has been the undermining of the *Washington Consensus*—the widely held view that the competitive market economy based on private enterprise, deregulation, flexible labor markets, and liberal economic policies offers the best basis for stability and prosperity and, according to the World Bank and the IMF, the primary foundation for economic development.

Central to the fraying legitimacy of market capitalism has been widespread dismay over changes in the distribution of income and wealth. Figure 16.1 shows evidence of the growing income disparities that have been characteristic of increasing inequality in almost all countries of the world. One of the few unifying features of Occupy Wall Street—the diverse protest movement that has directed hostility toward financiers and the world's financial centers—is the protesters' identification with "we are the 99%": a reference to the 1% of the population that accounts for 42% of America's personal wealth.[8] The contrast between the massive compensation received by financial service executives and the destruction they have brought to employment and living standards for the mass of the population has undermined faith in market capitalism.

The relative economic decline of the US, Europe, and Japan relative to China and other emerging market countries has reinforced this waning confidence in free market capitalism. Between 2000 and 2011, the number of Global Fortune 500

FIGURE 16.1 Ratio of average CEO total direct compensation to average production worker compensation, 1965–2009

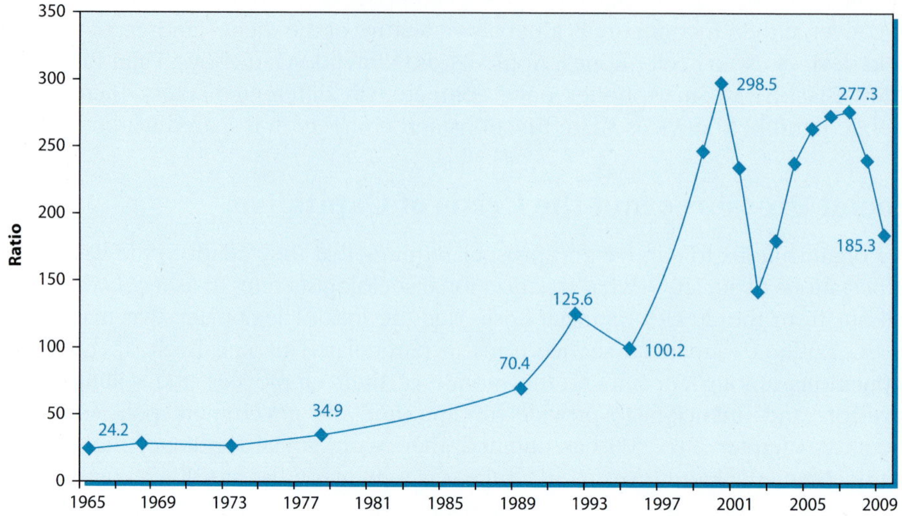

Sources: Economic Policy Institute based on data from *The Wall Street Journal*, Mercer, and Hay Group.

companies from the BRIC countries grew from 16 to 83. In 2010, China overtook Japan as the world's second-biggest economy. The growing prominence of Chinese state-owned multinationals in global markets has triggered debate over the merits of state-supported capitalism. As the *Economist* reports:

> the Chinese no longer see state-directed firms as a way-station on the road to liberal capitalism; rather, they see it as a sustainable model. They think they have redesigned capitalism to make it work better, and a growing number of emerging-world leaders agree with them. The Brazilian government, which embraced privatization in the 1990s, is now interfering with the likes of Vale and Petrobras, and compelling smaller companies to merge to form national champions.[9]

Recognition of the merits of **state capitalism** in combining the entrepreneurial drive of capitalism with the long-term orientation and coordinated resource deployment of government planning is one aspect of a growing interest in alternative forms of business enterprise. The United Nations' designation of 2012 as the "International Year of Cooperatives" did much to raise the profile of businesses that are mutually owned by consumers (e.g., credit unions), employees (e.g., the British retailing giant John Lewis Partnership), or by independent producers (e.g., agricultural marketing cooperatives). Cooperatives account for 21% of total production in Finland, 17.5% in New Zealand, and 16.4% in Switzerland. In Uganda and other African countries, cooperatives are the dominant organizational form in agriculture.[10]

Adapting to society's growing demands for fairness, ethics, and sustainability presents challenges for business leaders that extend beyond the problems of reconciling societal demands with shareholder interests. Should a company determine unilaterally the values that will govern its behavior, or does it seek to reflect those of the society in which it operates? Companies that embrace the values espoused by their founders are secure in their own sense of mission and can ensure a long-term consistency in their strategy and corporate identity (e.g., Walt Disney Company and Wal-Mart with respect to founders Walt Disney and Sam Walton). However, there is a risk that these values become out of step with those of society as a whole or with the requirements for business effectiveness. Thus, at British retailer Marks & Spencer and chocolate maker Cadbury, social responsibility and paternalism toward employees became a source of rigidity rather than a competitive advantage. Other companies have experienced the reverse: by taking account of the interests and needs of different stakeholders and of society at large, some companies report a greater responsiveness to their external environment, greater commitment from employees, and enhanced creativity.

New Directions in Strategic Thinking

The external pressures impacting firms is evident in the worldwide rise in company failures over the past decade. In the US, business bankruptcy filings grew from 19,695 in 2006 to a peak of 60,837 in 2009 before dropping to 47,806 in 2011. Major US bankruptcies of 2011–2012 have included AMR (the parent of American Airlines), Eastman Kodak, MF Global, Dynegy Holdings, Borders Group, and Blockbuster Entertainment. The pressures of a more demanding business environment are forcing companies to rethink their strategies.

Reorienting Corporate Objectives

The waning appeal of shareholder value maximization during the past decade culminated in the declaration by former GE chairman Jack Welch, a leading exponent of shareholder value maximization, that it was a "dumb idea." Yet adapting corporate goals to accommodate greater social and environmental responsibility restricts the ability of companies to survive increasingly intense competition. Recent efforts to reconcile a broader societal role with the need for profit maximization have emphasized either the need for companies to maintain social legitimacy or the potential for such a broadening of goals to open up new avenues for value creation—the central theme of Porter and Kramer's *shared value* concept.[11] The appeal of this broader concept of the role of the firm is that it maintains the fundamental orientation of the firm toward earning profit or, equivalently, value creation. (The value of the firm is the capitalized value of economic profit, or free cash flows, over its lifetime.)

The key reorientation of the doctrine of shareholder value creation is away from its 1990s preoccupation with stock market valuation towards a refocusing of top management priorities up on the fundamental drivers of enterprise value. This reflects a recognition that management cannot create stock market value: only the stock market can do that. What management can do is to generate the stream of profits that the stock market capitalizes into its valuation of the firm. Indeed, as I argued in Chapter 2, the critical focus of top management should not even be profits; it should be the strategic factors that drive profits: operational efficiency, customer satisfaction, innovation, and new product development.

The implication is not that business leaders abandon shareholder value maximization in favor of some woolly notion of pursuing stakeholder interests or to seek some new model of capitalism, but that they should focus more determinedly on identifying and managing the basic drivers of value creation.[12] Common to most of the corporate disasters of the 21st century from Enron and Parmalat to Royal Bank of Scotland and MF Global has been poor corporate strategies. Hence, to improve corporate performance, it is unlikely that a massive extension of government regulation, a new model of capitalism, or a re-engineering of human nature offer the best solutions. The most useful antidote to the threats of corporate empire building, CEO hubris, and blind faith in new business models is likely to be a stronger emphasis on the basic principles of strategy analysis. As Dick Rumelt has pointed out: "Bad strategy abounds!"[13]

Seeking More Complex Sources of Competitive Advantage

Focusing on strategy fundamentals does not necessarily lead to simple strategies. As we observed in Chapter 7, in today's dynamic business environment competitive advantages are difficult to sustain. As the rate of technology diffusion increases and new competitors with unassailable cost advantages emerge from newly industrializing countries, so established firms are under increasing pressure to access new sources of competitive advantage. A key feature of companies that have maintained both profitability and market share over many years—for example Toyota, Wal-Mart, 3M, Canon, Swatch, and Samsung—is their development of multiple layers of competitive advantage, including cost efficiency, differentiation, innovation, responsiveness, and global learning. As we shall see, reconciling the different requirements of different performance dimensions imposes highly complex organizational challenges that are pushing companies to fundamentally rethink their structures and management systems.

Thus, the ability of some companies to combine multiple capabilities recalls Isaiah Berlin's classification of intellectuals into foxes and hedgehogs: "The fox knows many things; the hedgehog knows one big thing."[14] Despite Jim Collins' praise for companies that have a single penetrating insight into the complexities of their business environments, it appears that companies that have built their strategy on such insight often have difficulty in adapting to subsequent changes in their markets: Toys "R" Us with big-box retailing, Dell with its direct sales model, General Motors with its multi-brand market segmentation strategy, AOL with dial-up internet access.[15]

Managing Options

As we observed in the last section of Chapter 2 ("Strategy as Options Management"), the value of the firm derives not only from the present value of its profit stream (cash flows) but also from the value of its options. During turbulent times, real options—growth options, abandonment options, and flexibility options—become increasingly important as sources of value. Taking account of options has typically involved adjustment of investment appraisal methodologies so that option values are incorporated into capital budgeting decisions. However, the implications of option thinking extend to the most fundamental aspects of a firm's strategy—and to the tool of strategy analysis that it employs. To take just one example of how a failure to take account of option value can lead to a misguided strategy, consider conventional approaches to corporate finance. The attraction of leveraged buyout has been to create shareholder value through substituting low-cost debt (the interest payments on which are tax deductible) for high-cost equity. Yet, such reductions in the cost of capital also destroy option value: highly leveraged firms have fewer opportunities to take advantage of unexpected investment opportunities (including acquisition) and have less flexibility in adjusting to an unexpected downturn.

Viewing strategy as the management of a portfolio of options shifts the emphasis of strategy formulation from making resource commitments to the creation of opportunities. Strategic alliances offer a particularly potent tool for creating growth options: they allow a firm to make limited investments in new technological and market opportunities that can be "exercised" through larger investments (possibly in the form of a joint venture or an outright acquisition) as more information emerges.

The adoption of options thinking also has far-reaching implications for our tools and frameworks of strategy analysis. For example:

- Industry analysis has taken the view that decisions about industry attractiveness depend on profit potential. However, if industry structure becomes so unstable that forecasting industry profitability is no longer viable, it is likely that industry attractiveness will depend much more on option value. From an options perspective, an attractive industry is one that is rich in options, for example an industry that produces a number of different products and comprises multiple segments, has many strategic groups, utilizes a diversity of alternative technologies and raw materials, and where internal mobility barriers tend to be low. Thus, consumer electronics, semiconductors, packaging, and investment banking would seem to be more attractive in terms of options than electricity or steel or car rental.

- An options approach also has major implications for the analysis of resources and capabilities. In terms of option value, an attractive resource is one that can be deployed in different businesses and support alternative strategies. A technological breakthrough in nanotechnology is likely to offer greater option value than a new process that increases the energy efficiency of blast furnaces will. A relationship with a rising politician is a resource that has more option value than a coalmine. Similarly with capabilities: a highly specialized capability, such as expertise in the design of petrochemical plants, offers fewer options than expertise in the marketing of fast-moving consumer goods. Dynamic capabilities are important because they generate new options: "Dynamic capabilities are the organizational and strategic routines by which firms achieve new resource combinations as markets emerge, collide, split, evolve, and die."[16]

Understanding Strategic Fit

Central to just about everything in this book is the notion of *strategic fit*. In Chapter 1, we looked at how strategy must *fit* with the business environment and with the firm's resources and capabilities; we viewed the firm as an *activity system* where all the activities of the firm fit together (Figure 1.3). In Chapter 6, we looked at *contingency approaches* to organizational design: the idea that the structure and management systems of the firm must fit with the firm's business environment.

In Chapter 8, we saw how complementarities between strategy, structure, and management systems can act as a barrier to change. In recent years our understanding of fit (or contingency) has progressed substantially as a result of two major concepts: complementarity and complexity. These concepts offer new insights into linkages within organizations.

Complementarity Research Complementarity research addresses the linkages among a firm's management practices. A key focus has been the transition from mass manufacturing to lean manufacturing where it has been observed that reorganizing production processes tends to be counterproductive without the simultaneous adaptation of a range of human resource practices.[17] Similarly, a six-sigma quality program needs to be accompanied by changes in incentives, recruitment policies, product strategy, and capital budgeting practices.[18]

At one extreme, recognition of complementarities in management practices makes it difficult to make generalizations about strategic management: every firm is unique and must create a unique configuration of strategic variables and management practices. In practice, strategic choices tend to converge on a limited number of *configurations*. Thus, successful adaptation among large European companies was associated with a small number of configurations of organizational structure, processes, and boundaries.[19]

Complexity Theory Organizations—like the weather, ant colonies, and flocks of birds, human crowds, and seismic activity—are *complex systems* whose behavior results from the interactions of a large number of independent agents. This behavior of complex systems has interesting features that have important implications for the management of organizations:

- *Unpredictability*: The behavior of complex adaptive systems cannot be predicted in any precise sense. There is no convergence on stable equilibria; cascades of change are constantly interacting to reshape competitive landscapes. As noted in Strategy Capsule 16.1, the outcomes tend to follow *power law distributions*: small changes typically have minor consequences but may also trigger major movements.[20]

- *Self-organization*: Complex biological and social systems have a capacity for **self-organization**. A bee colony or shoal of fish shows coordinated responses to external threats and opportunities without anyone giving orders. Groups of human beings also display coordinated behavior patterns e.g., when walking along crowded sidewalks. Quite sophisticated synchronized behavior can be achieved through adopting just a few simple rules. There are three main requirements for self-organization: *identity* that permits a common sense-making process within the organization, *information* that provides the possibility of synchronized behavior, and *relationships* that are the pathways through which information is transformed into intelligent, coordinated action.[21] I will discuss self-organization in the next section.

- *Inertia, chaos, and evolutionary adaptation*: Complex systems can stagnate into inertia (stasis) or become disorderly (chaos). In between is an intermediate region where the most rapid evolutionary adaptation occurs. Positioning at this *edge of chaos* results in both small, localized adaptations and occasional evolutionary leaps that allow the system to attain a higher *fitness peak*.[22] Kaufman's *NK model*, which allows the behavior of complex systems to be simulated, has been widely applied to the study of organizations.[23]

The Contextuality of Linkages within the Firm   Common to both the complementarity and complexity approaches to analyzing linkages among a firm's activities is the concept of *contextuality*—the extent to which the benefits from any particular activity depend upon which other activities are taking place.[24] Porter and Siggelkow identify two dimensions of this contextuality:

- *Contextuality of activities*: Some management activities are generic: their performance effects are independent of other activities—for example using computers for managing accounting systems is optimal for virtually all firms independently of what business the firm is in or how other activities are organized. The benefits from other activities are dependent upon what other activities are taking place. For example, payments linked to individual employee output only boost productivity if employees work independently.
- *Contextuality of interactions*: Do activities interact in similar ways across firms? Generic interactions are those which are the same for all firms. For example, the benefits from flexibility in manufacturing will always increase with increased product differentiation. Other interactions are context-specific. For example, in the case of Ryanair's activity system (Figure 1.3), the complementarity between a point-to-point route structure and 25-minute aircraft turnarounds in achieving high aircraft utilization is dependent upon the airline's policy of no through ticketing and no baggage transfers.[25]

Acknowledging the different ways in which a firm's activities interact offers insight into some of the complexities of strategic management. In particular, it helps us to understand why a strategy that has worked well for one company is a dismal failure when adopted by a competitor; it points to the risks in attempting to transfer "best practices" either from another firm or even from another part of the same firm; it allows us to see why piecemeal adaptations to external change often make the situation worse rather than better; and it reveals why post-merger integration is so treacherous.

Redesigning Organizations

A more complex, more competitive business environment requires that companies perform at higher levels with broader repertoires of capabilities. Building multiple capabilities and achieving excellence across multiple performance dimensions requires managing dilemmas. A company must produce at low cost while also innovating; it must deploy the massed resources of a large corporation while showing the entrepreneurial flair of a small start-up; it must achieve reliability and consistency while also making local adaptations to meet individual circumstances. We addressed one of these dilemmas: the challenge of *ambidexterity*—optimizing efficiency and effectiveness for today while adapting to the needs of tomorrow—in Chapter 8. In reality, the problem reconciling incompatible strategic goals is much broader: the challenge of today is reconciling *multiple* dilemmas—this requires *multi-dexterity*.

Implementing complex strategies with conflicting performance objectives takes us to the frontiers of management knowledge. We know how to devise structures and systems that drive cost efficiency; we know the organizational conditions conducive to innovation; we know a good deal about the characteristics of *high-reliability organizations*, we have insights into the sources of entrepreneurship. But how on earth do we achieve all of these simultaneously?

Multi-Dimensional Structures

Organizational capabilities, we have learned (Chapter 5), need to be embodied in processes and housed within organizational units that provide the basis for coordination between the individuals involved. The traditional matrix organization allows capabilities to be developed in relation to products, geographical markets, and functions. And the more capabilities an organization develops, the more complex its organizational structure becomes.

- The total quality movement of the 1980s resulted in companies creating organizational structures to implement quality management processes.
- The adoption of social and environmental responsibility by companies has resulted in the creation of structures devoted to these activities.
- The dissemination of knowledge management during the 1990s resulted in many companies setting up knowledge management structures and systems.
- The need to develop and exercise capabilities to meet the needs of large global customers has resulted in multi-national corporations establishing organizational units for managing key accounts.[26]
- The quest for innovation and organizational change has resulted in the establishment of organizational units that conduct "exploration" activities (see the discussion on ambidexterity in Chapter 8) these include project teams for developing new products and incubators for developing new businesses. They also include organizational change initiatives such as General Electric's "Work-Out" program and innovation structures such as IBM's online "Innovation Jam," a temporary organization that administers a biannual, 72-hour online session involving tens of thousands of contributors from inside and outside the company, then harvesting the results.[27] Such organizational structures that are outside companies' formal operating structures for the purposes of fostering *dynamic capabilities* have been described as *parallel learning structures*.[28]

Coping with Complexity: Making Organizations Informal, Self-Organizing, and Permeable

If firms expand their range of capabilities, the implications for organizational complexity are frightening. In Chapter 6, we observed that traditional matrix structures which combined product, geographical, and functional organizations proved unwieldy for many corporations. We are now introducing additional dimensions to the matrix!

Informal Organization   The solution to increased complexity is to rely upon informal rather than formal structures and systems. The organizational requirements for coordination are different from those required for compliance and control. Traditional hierarchies with bureaucratic systems are based upon the need for control. Coordination requires structures that support modularity, but within each module, team-based structures are often most effective in supporting organizational processes; and coordination between modules does not necessarily need to be managed in a directive sense—coordination can be achieved by means of standardized interfaces, mutual adjustment, and horizontal collaboration (see discussion of "The Coordination Problem" and "Hierarchy in Organizational Design" in Chapter 6.

The scope for team-based structures to reconcile complex patterns of coordination with flexibility and responsiveness is enhanced by the move toward project-based organizations. More companies are organizing their activities less around functions and continuous operations and more around time-designated projects where a team is assigned to a specific project with a clearly defined outcome and a specified completion date. While construction companies and consulting firms have always been structured around projects, a wide range of companies are finding that project-based structures featuring temporary cross-functional teams charged with clear objectives are more able to achieve innovation, adaptability, and rapid learning than more traditional structures. A key advantage of such temporary organizational forms is that they can avoid the ossification of structures and concentrations of power that more permanent structures encourage. W. L. Gore, the supplier of Gore-tex and other hi-tech fabric products, is an example of a team-based, project-focused structure that integrates a broad range of highly sophisticated capabilities despite an organizational structure that is almost wholly informal: there are no formal job titles and leaders are selected by peers. Employees ("associates") may apply to join particular teams, and it is up to the team members to choose new members. The teams are self-managed and team goals are not assigned from above but agreed through team commitments. Associates are encouraged to work with multiple teams.[29]

Reducing complexity at the formal level can foster greater variety and sophisticated coordination at the informal level. In general, the greater the potential for reordering existing resources and capabilities in complex new combinations, the greater the advantages of *consensus-based hierarchies*, which emphasize horizontal communication, over *authority-based hierarchies*, which emphasize vertical communication.[30]

Self-Organization   When discussing complexity theory, I identified three factors that are conducive to self-organization in complex systems: identity, information, and relationships. There is ample evidence of the role that these can play in substituting for traditional management practices.

- *Identity*: For coordination to be effective in the absence of top-down directives, it requires shared cognition of what the organization is and an emotional attachment toward what it represents. These form *organizational identity*—a collective understanding of what is presumed core, distinctive, and enduring about the character of an organization.[31]

   Organizations lose an enormous organizing advantage when they fail to create a clear and coherent identity. In a chaotic world, organizational identity needs to be the most stable aspect of the endeavor. Structures and programs come and go, but an organization with a coherent center is able to sustain itself through turbulence because of its clarity about who it is. Organizations that are coherent at their core move through the world with more confidence.[32]

A strong consensus around organizational identity provides a powerful basis for coordinated action that permits flexibility and responsiveness to be reconciled with continuity and stability. Of course, organizational identity, because it is permanent, can be an impediment to, rather than a facilitator of, change. The key challenge for organizational leaders is to reinterpret organizational identity in a way that can support and legitimate change. Michael Eisner at Disney, Lou Gerstner at IBM, and Franck Riboud at Danone all initiated major strategic changes, but within the constancy of their companies' identities. Organizational identity creates an important linkage between a firm's internal self-image and its market positioning. With the increase of symbolic influences on consumer choices, the linkage between product design, brand image, and organizational identity becomes increasingly important. For companies such as Apple, Alessi, and Bang & Olufsen, product design is an important vehicle for establishing and interpreting organizational identity.[33]

● *Information*: The information and communication revolution of the past two decades has transformed society's capacity for self-organization, as evident from the role of the BlackBerry Messenger in the London riots of 2011 and the role of Twitter in coordinating the anti-Putin protests in Moscow in 2011–2012. Within companies, information and communication networks support spontaneous patterns of complex coordination with little or no hierarchical direction. Indeed, real-time coordination is increasingly characterized by automated process where human intervention is absent (Strategy Capsule 16.2).

● *Relationships*: According to Wheatley and Kellner-Rogers, "Relationships are the pathways to the intelligence of the system. Through relationships, information is created and transformed, the organization's identity expands to include more stakeholders, and the enterprise becomes wiser. The more access people have to one another, the more possibilities there are. Without connections, nothing happens . . . In self-organizing systems, people need access to everyone; they need to be free to reach anywhere in the organization to accomplish work."[34] There is increasing evidence that a major part of the work of organizations is achieved through informal social networks.[35]

Breaking Down Corporate Boundaries   Even with informal coordination mechanisms, modular structures, and sophisticated knowledge management systems, there are limits to the range of capabilities that any company can develop internally. Hence, in order to expand the range of capabilities that they can deploy, firms collaborate in order to access the capabilities of other firms. This implies less distinction between what happens within the firm and what happens outside it. Strategic alliances, as we have already seen, permit stable yet flexible patterns for integrating the capabilities of different firms while also sharing risks. While localized networks of firms—such as those that characterize Italy's clothing, furniture, and industrial machinery industries—offer potential for building trust and interfirm routines, web-based technologies permit much wider networks of collaboration. The open innovation efforts described in this book—Procter & Gamble's "Connect & Develop" approach to new product development and IBM's "Innovation Jam"— both point to the power of ICT technologies to enable firms to draw upon ideas

STRATEGY CAPSULE 16.2
The Automated Economy

Management has always been closely identified with the management of people. This reflects the primary role of labor as a factor of production. Yet a growing feature of the modern economy is the replacement of people and human decision making by information technology. The economist Brian Arthur points to the emergence of a "second economy" where economic activity is coordinated entirely by machines. One example is the issuing of boarding cards by self-service machines at airports. On inserting a frequent-flier card or credit card, the machine issues a boarding pass, receipt, and luggage tag within the space of four or five seconds. Within these seconds, observes Arthur, a complex conversation takes place entirely among machines. With your identity established, your flight status is checked with the airline along with your past travel history. Your name is checked with the database of the Transportation Security Administration, and possibly with the National Security Agency. Your seat choice is confirmed, your frequent-flier status is checked, and mileage is credited. Your seat allocation takes account of the aircraft's loading system which ensures an even weight distribution of the fuselage. The disintermediation of human decision makers by intelligent systems that process information, optimize decisions, and coordinate subsequent activities is an increasingly common feature of distribution systems, financial services, even petroleum reservoir management. When you use a self-service checkout at a supermarket, an integrated information system links your purchases to shelf-filling activity within the store, deliveries from warehouse to store, and production planning and supply logistics by manufacturers.

Source: S. Hoover, "Digitized Decision Making and the Hidden Second Economy," Techonomy Conference, October 9, 2011; W. B. Arthur, "The Second Economy," *McKinsey Quarterly* (October 2011).

and expertise across the globe. The collaborative potential of the internet is most strongly revealed in open-source communities that build highly complex products, such as Linux and Wikipedia, through global networks of individual collaborators.[36]

The Changing Role of Managers

Changing external conditions, new strategic priorities, and different types of organization call for new approaches to management and leadership. The era of restructuring and shareholder focus was associated with *change masters*[37]—highly visible, individualistic, and often hard-driving management styles of CEOs such as Lee Iacocca at Chrysler, John Browne at BP, Michael Eisner at Disney, and Rupert Murdoch at News International. These leaders were, first and foremost, strategic decision makers, charting the direction and redirection of their companies, and making key decisions over acquisitions, divestments, new products, and cost cutting.

In the emerging 21st century organization, this "buck stops here" peak decision-making role may no longer be feasible, let alone desirable. As organizations and their environments become increasingly complex, the CEO is no longer able to access or synthesize the information necessary to be effective as a peak decision maker. Recent contributions to the literature on leadership have placed less emphasis on the role of executives as decision makers and more on their role in guiding organizational evolution. Gary Hamel is emphatic about the need to redefine the work of leadership:

> The notion of the leader as a heroic decision maker is untenable. Leaders must be recast as social-systems architects who enable innovation . . . In Management 2.0, leaders will no longer be seen as grand visionaries, all-wise decision makers, and ironfisted disciplinarians. Instead, they will need to become social architects, constitution writers, and entrepreneurs of meaning. In this new model, the leader's job is to create an environment where every employee has the chance to collaborate, innovate, and excel.[38]

Jim Collins and Jerry Porras also emphasize that leadership is less about decision making and more about cultivating identity and purpose:

> If strategy is founded in organizational identity and common purpose, and if organizational culture is the bedrock of capability, then a key role of top management is to clarify, nurture and communicate the company's purpose, heritage, personality, values, and norms. To unify and inspire the efforts of organizational members, leadership requires providing meaning to people's own aspirations. Ultimately this requires attention to the emotional climate of the organization.[39]

This changing role also implies that senior managers require different knowledge and skills. Research into the psychological and demographic characteristics of successful leaders has identified few consistent or robust relationships—successful leaders come in all shapes, sizes, and personality types. However, research using *competency modeling* methodology points to the key role of personality attributes that have been referred to by Daniel Goleman as *emotional intelligence*.[40] These attributes comprise: *self-awareness*, the ability to understand oneself and one's emotions; *self-management*, control, integrity, conscientiousness, and initiative; *social awareness*, particularly the capacity to sense others' emotions (empathy); and *social skills*, communication, collaboration, and relationship building. Personal qualities are also the focus of Jim Collins' concept of "Level 5 Leadership," which combines personal humility with an intense resolve.[41]

A similar transformation is likely to be required throughout the hierarchy. Informal structures and self-organization have also transformed the role of middle managers from being administrators and controllers into entrepreneurs, coaches, and team leaders.

The insights provided by complexity theory also offer more specific guidance to managers, in particular:

- *Rapid evolution requires a combination of both incremental and radical change*: While stretch targets and other performance management tools can produce pressure for incremental improvement, more decisive intervention may be needed to stimulate radical change. At IBM, Sam Palmisano's leadership between 2002 and 2012 refocused IBM upon research and innovation, expanded IBM's presence in emerging markets, and inaugurated a new era of social and environmental responsibility.[42]

- *Establishing simple rules*: If the coordinated behaviors of complex systems can be simulated with a few simple rules, it seems feasible that companies can be managed by a few simple rules with limited managerial direction. For instance, rather than plan strategy in any formal sense, rules of thumb in screening opportunities (*boundary rules*) can locate the company where the opportunities are richest. Thus, Cisco's acquisition strategy is guided by the rule that it will acquire companies with fewer than 75 employees of which 75% are engineers. Second, rules can designate a common approach to how the company will exploit opportunities (*how-to rules*). Thus, Yahoo! has a few rules regarding the look and functionality of new web pages, but then gives freedom to developers to design new additions.[43]
- *Managing adaptive tension*: If too little tension produces inertia and too much creates chaos, the challenge for top management is to create a level of adaptive tension that optimizes the pace of organizational change and innovation. This is typically achieved through imposing demanding performance targets, but ensuring that these targets are appropriate and achievable.

Summary

Since I began studying business strategy during the late 1970s, I have heard repeated calls for a revolution in the theory and practice of management. During the 1980s, Tom Peters invited managers to "thrive on chaos" and embrace "liberation management";[44] at the end of the 1990s, Peter Drucker observed that most of the assumptions underlying management had "outlived their usefulness" and needed reformulation;[45] most recently, Gary Hamel has established the Management Innovation Exchange "with the goal of making institutions of all kinds more adaptable, more innovative, more inspiring, and more socially accountable."[46]

The propensity for management theory and management practice to lag behind to reflect the priorities and thinking of an earlier era is a continuing dilemma for management scholars and practicing managers. Accelerating rates of change in the business environment have made this problem more acute. Our review of the changes that have taken place in the business environment since 2000 reveals the new challenges that face firms and their leaders, in particular the need to compete at a higher level along a broader front. A common feature of these challenges is that almost all of them present dilemmas: between competing for the present and adapting to the future, between efficiency and innovation, between centralized resource deployment and decentralized responsiveness, and so on.

In responding to these challenges, business leaders are supported by two developments. The first comprises emerging concepts and theories that offer both insight and the basis for new management tools. Key developments include complexity theory, the principles of self-organization, real option analysis, organizational identity, network analysis, and new concepts of innovation, knowledge management, and leadership.

A second area is the innovation and learning that results from adaptation and experimentation by companies. Long-established companies such as IBM and P&G have embraced open innovation;

technology-based companies such as Google, W. L. Gore, Microsoft, and Facebook have introduced radically new approaches to project management and human resource management, including allowing individuals to choose which projects to work on and giving them autonomy in innovation initiatives. In emerging-market countries we observe novel approaches to government involvement in business (China), new initiatives in managing integration in multibusiness corporations (Samsung), new approaches to managing ambidexterity (Infosys), and novel approaches to encouraging employee engagement (Haier).

At the same time, it is important not to overemphasize either the obsolescence of existing principles or methods of management. Many of the features of today's business environment are extensions of well-established trends rather than fundamental discontinuities. Indeed, it has typically been radically new management concepts and ideas that have been found wanting: the dawning of the "new economy," the new era of "virtual corporations," the revolutionary potential of "knowledge management," and the coordination benefits of the "networked organization" have all failed to convince. Certainly our strategy analysis will need to be adapted and augmented in order to take account of new circumstances; however, the basic tools of analysis—industry analysis, resource and capability analysis, the applications of economies of scope to corporate strategy decisions—remain relevant and robust. One of the most important lessons to draw from the major corporate failures that have scarred the 21st century—Enron, WorldCom, Lehman Brothers, and Royal Bank of Scotland—has been the realization that the rigorous application of the tools of strategy analysis outlined in this book might have helped these firms to avoid their misdirected odysseys.

Quizzes and flashcards to test yourself further are available in your interactive e-book at **www.wileyopenpage.com**

Notes

1. P. F. Drucker, *Management Challenges for the 21st Century* (New York: HarperCollins, 2001): ix–x.
2. The NASDAQ hit the all-time high of 5132 on March 10, 2000.
3. US National Intelligence Council, *Global Trends 2025: A Transformed World* (Washington DC, November 2008), www.dni.gov/nic/NIC_2025_project.html, accessed July 8, 2009.
4. J. Alceler and J. Oxley, "Learning by Supplying," Harvard Business School Discussion Paper (March 2012).
5. A. Y. Lewin, C. B. Weigelt, and J. D. Emery, "Adaptation and Selection in Strategy and Change," in M. S. Poole and A. H. van de Ven (eds), *Handbook of Organizational Change and Innovation* (New York: Oxford University Press, 2004): 108–60.
6. http://www.thedailybeast.com/articles/2012/03/28/murdoch-hacking-scandal-could-go-global-threaten-news-corp-core-tv-business.html, accessed April 14, 2012.
7. P. F. Drucker, *Managing in the Next Society* (London: St. Martin's Press, 2003); S. Ghoshal, C. A. Bartlett, and P. Moran, "A New Manifesto for Management," *Sloan Management Review* (Spring 1999): 9–20; C. Handy, *The Age of Paradox* (Boston: Harvard University Press, 1995).
8. *The One Percent* is a 2006 documentary produced by Jamie Johnson and Nick Kurzon and premiered on HBO in 2008.
9. "The Rise of State Capitalism," *Economist* (January 21, 2012).
10. http://www.worldwatch.org/membership-co-operative-businesses-reaches-1-billion, accessed April 14, 2012.
11. M. E. Porter and M. R. Kramer, "Creating Shared Value," *Harvard Business Review* (January 2011): 62–77 (see Chapter 2 for a discussion).
12. See, for example, P. Barnes, *Capitalism 3.0* (San Francisco: Berrett-Koehler, 2006); D. Rodrik, *The*

Globalization Paradox: Democracy and the Future of the World Economy (New York: W.W. Norton, 2011).

13. R. P. Rumelt, "The Perils of Bad Strategy," *McKinsey Quarterly* (June 2011).

14. I. Berlin, *The Hedgehog and the Fox* (New York: Simon & Schuster, 1953).

15. J. Collins, *Good to Great* (New York: HarperCollins, 2001).

16. K. M. Eisenhardt and J. A. Martin, "Dynamic Capabilities: What Are They?" *Strategic Management Journal* 21 (2000): 1105–21.

17. K. Laursen and N. J. Foss, "New Human Resource Management Practices, Complementarities and the Impact on Innovation Performance," *Cambridge Journal of Economics* 27 (2003): 243–63.

18. Six sigma is a quality management methodology first developed by Motorola in 1986 that aims to reduce defects among products and processes to less than 3.4 per million. See C. Gygi, N. DeCarlo, and B. Williams, *Six Sigma for Dummies* (Hoboken, NJ: John Wiley & Sons, Inc., 2005).

19. R. Whittington, A. Pettigrew, S. Peck, E. Fenton, and M. Conyon, "Change and Complementarities in the New Competitive Landscape," *Organization Science* 10 (1999): 583–600.

20. P. Bak, *How Nature Works: The Science of Self-organized Criticality* (New York: Copernicus, 1996).

21. M. J. Wheatley and M. Kellner Rogers, *A Simpler Way* (San Francisco: Berrett-Koehler, 1996).

22. P. Anderson, "Complexity Theory and Organizational Science," *Organization Science* 10 (1999): 216–232.

23. S. McGuire, B. McKelvey, L. Mirabeau, and N. Oztas, "Complexity Science and Organization Studies," in S. Clegg (ed.), *The SAGE Handbook of Organizational Studies* (Thousand Oaks, CA: SAGE Publications, 2006): 165–214.

24. M. E. Porter and N. Siggelkow, "Contextuality within Activity Systems and Sustainable Competitive Advantage," *Academy of Management Perspectives* 22 (May 2008): 34–56.

25. These issues are discussed in greater depth in M. E. Porter and N. Siggelkow, "Contextuality within Activity Systems and Sustainable Competitive Advantage," *Academy of Management Perspectives* 22 (May 2008): 34–56.

26. G. S. Yip and A. J. M. Bink, *Managing Global Customers: An Integrated Approach* (Oxford: Oxford University Press, 2007).

27. O. M. Bjelland and R. C. Wood, "An Inside View of IBM's 'Innovation Jam,'" *MIT Sloan Management Review* (Fall 2008): 32–40.

28. G. Bushe and A. B. Shani, *Parallel Learning Structures* (Reading, MA: Addison-Wesley, 1991).

29. G. Bushe and A. B. Shani, *Parallel Learning Structures* (Reading, MA: Addison-Wesley, 1991): Chapter 5.

30. J. A. Nickerson and T. R. Zenger, "The Knowledge-based Theory of the Firm: A Problem-solving Perspective," *Organization Science* 15 (2004): 617–632.

31. D. A. Gioia, M. Schultz, and K. G. Corley, "Organizational Identity, Image and Adaptive Instability," *Academy of Management Review* 25 (2000): 63–81.

32. M. J. Wheatley and M. Kellner-Rogers, "The Irresistible Future of Organizing," (July/August 1996), http://margaretwheatley.com/articles/irresistiblefuture.html, accessed August 27, 2012.

33. D. Ravasi and G. Lojacono, "Managing Design and Designers for Strategic Renewal," *Long Range Planning* 38, no. 1 (February 2005): 51–77.

34. M. J. Wheatley and M. Kellner-Rogers, "The Irresistible Future of Organizing," (July/August 1996), http://margaretwheatley.com/articles/irresistiblefuture.html, accessed August 27, 2012.

35. L. L. Bryan, E. Matson, and L. M. Weiss, "Harnessing the Power of Informal Employee Networks," *McKinsey Quarterly* (November 2007).

36. A. Wright, "The Next Paradigm Shift: Open Source Everything," http://www.brighthand.com/default.asp?newsID=14348, accessed July 8, 2009.

37. R. M. Kanter, *The Change Masters* (New York: Simon & Schuster, 1983).

38. G. Hamel, "Moon Shots for Management?" *Harvard Business Review* (February 2009): 91–8.

39. J. C. Collins and J. I. Porras, *Built to Last* (New York: Harper Business, 1996).

40. D. Goleman, "What Makes a Leader?" *Harvard Business Review* (November/December 1998): 93–102. See also J. C. Hayton and G. M. McEvoy, "Developing and Assessing Professional and Managerial Competence," *Human Resource Management* 45 (2006): 291–4.

41. J. Collins, "Level 5 Leadership: The Triumph of Humility and Fierce Resolve," *Harvard Business Review* (January 2001): 67–76.

42. "IBM's Sam Palmisano: A Super Second Act," *Fortune* (March 4, 2011).

43. For discussion of the role of rules in strategy making, see K. M. Eisenhardt and D. Sull, "Strategy as Simple Rules," *Harvard Business Review* (January/February 2001): 107–16.

44. T. Peters, *Thriving on Chaos* (New York: Knopf, 1987); T. Peters, *Liberation Management* (New York: Knopf, 1987).

45. P. F. Drucker, *Management Challenges for the 21st Century* (New York: HarperCollins, 2001): ix–x.

46. www.managementexchange.com.

CASES TO ACCOMPANY CONTEMPORARY STRATEGY ANALYSIS

EIGHTH EDITION

CASES

Kodak had staked its future on being a leader in digital imaging. Despite massive investment and a string of acquisitions and strategic alliances, Kodak's ability to establish competitive advantage within the digital imaging sector and to generate satisfactory returns from its investments remains in doubt. The case describes Kodak's digital imaging strategy, explores the reasons for the failure of Kodak's digital imaging strategy to generate profits, and looks at the options that remain for CEO Antonio Pérez.

logic of this motley crew of business ventures, to recognize the challenges Virgin faces, and to recommend what changes to strategy, structure, and management style are appropriate for the group. Should any of the businesses be divested? What criteria should be used to guide future diversification? Are changes needed in the financial and management structures of the group?

20 Google Inc.: What's the Corporate Strategy? 709

Google's core product is a highly successful web search engine. Yet, by 2012, Google has expanded into many areas of web services, computer software, and advertising management services. However, the acquisition of handset maker Motorola Mobility for $12.5 billion was a major leap into the unknown for Google. In addition to being Google's first entry into hardware, it added 20,000 new employees to its payroll. The challenge of the case is to identify the logic underlying Google's diversification beyond web search, to appreciate the strategic issues that arise from the complementarities between different products and services in the digital technology sector, and make recommendations for Google's future development.

21 Danone: Strategy Implementation in an International Food and Beverage Company 727

By 2012, Danone had grown to become one of the world's largest multinational food companies with four major business areas—fresh dairy products, water, baby nutrition, and medical nutrition—and a growing emphasis on emerging markets. Danone's growth had been achieved with a strategy and management system that was very different from its leading rivals'—Nestlé and Kraft Foods— or from other consumer product multinationals. Its strategy was entrepreneurial and decentralized: the heads of its country business units possessed substantial decision-making powers and local brands accounted for a high proportion of its total sales. Danone's business principles played a key role in its overall coordination, cohesiveness, and identity. The case seeks to comprehend the contribution of Danone's values and principles, and especially its commitments to social and environmental responsibility, to its competitive advantage and to the effectiveness of its strategy implementation, and to explore how Danone might improve its financial performance and shareholder returns in the future.

22 Jeff Immelt and the Reinventing of General Electric 746

Jeff Immelt's eleven years as CEO of GE were a period of unprecedented turmoil for the company. The case looks beyond GE's adjustments to meet the financial crisis of 2008/2009, to consider the corporate strategy and the organizational changes that Immelt put in place. To what extent was Immelt's emphasis on business development, innovation, and higher levels of organizational integration consistent with the trends in GE's business environment and with the company's resources and capabilities? Did GE possess the management systems and leadership capabilities needed to make Immelt's strategy work, or did the company need to look to more radical strategic solutions . . . including breakup?

23 Bank of America's Acquisition of Merrill Lynch 767

In December 2008, Bank of America's board had its final chance to withdraw from its acquisition of Merrill Lynch, one of the world's biggest investment banks. The acquisition offered Bank of America the chance to build America's biggest wealth-management company and to establish itself as a leading global corporate and investment bank. However, new evidence on Merrill Lynch's asset write-downs confirmed that Bank of America was overpaying for its acquisition. The case requires an assessment of the likely synergies from the merger, an evaluation of the "universal banking" model, and an appraisal of the challenges of integrating the two companies.

W. L. Gore, the manufacturer of Gore-Tex, has a unique organizational structure and management style built around its "lattice" principle. The result is a remarkable lack of hierarchy and exceptional decentralization of decision making, which is devolved to self-managing teams. The case offers the opportunity to consider the advantages and disadvantages of Gore's management structure, and the potential to apply it to other companies.

Case 1 Madonna: Sustaining Success in a Fast-moving Business

Although summer had barely begun, 2012 was proving to be an exceptionally busy year for Madonna Louise Ciccone. On February 3, her movie *WE*, based upon the love affair between King Edward VIII and Wallis Simpson, which she had written and directed, went on general release. Two days later, Madonna provided half-time entertainment at the NFL Super Bowl before 70,000 football fans and an estimated TV audience of 118 million. On March 26, *MDNA*, Madonna's 12th studio album and her first since *Hard Candy* in 2008, was released. *MDNA* went straight to the top of the *Billboard* album chart—although it stayed there for just one week.[1] On May 29 her concert tour would open in Tel Aviv; a further 76 performances would follow throughout the Middle East, Europe, and North America. Madonna would spend her 54th birthday on August 16 between concerts in Oslo and Zurich. The US leg of the tour would finish in Miami on November 20, to be followed by a continuation of the tour in South America and Australia. In addition, Madonna's commercial activities would include a major sponsorship deal with Smirnoff vodka, the launch of her Hard Candy health clubs, and her *Truth or Dare* brand, which would include fragrances and shoes.

Madonna's career achievements are summarized in her Wikipedia entry:

> Madonna has sold more than 300 million records worldwide and is recognized as the world's top-selling female recording artist of all time by the Guinness World Records. According to the Recording Industry Association of America (RIAA), she is the best-selling female rock artist of the 20th century and the second top-selling female artist in the United States, behind Barbra Streisand, with 64 million certified albums. In 2008, *Billboard* magazine ranked Madonna at number two, behind only The Beatles, on the *Billboard* Hot 100 All-Time Top Artists, making her the most successful solo artist in the history of the *Billboard* chart. She was also inducted into the Rock and Roll Hall of Fame in the same year. Considered to be one of the "25 Most Powerful Women of the Past Century" by *Time* for being an influential figure in contemporary music, Madonna is known for continuously reinventing both her music and image, and for retaining a standard of autonomy within the recording industry.[2]

Her success was also apparent in financial terms. *Forbes* magazine estimated her annual earnings as $58 million in 2010, $110 million in 2009, $40 million in 2008, and $72 million in 2007.[3] Over the past two decades the only female entertainer to come close to her in terms of income has been Oprah Winfrey.

This case was prepared by Robert M. Grant. ©2012 Robert M. Grant.

Beginnings

In July 1977, shortly before her nineteenth birthday, Madonna Louise Ciccone arrived in New York City with $35 in her pocket. She had left Ann Arbor, where she was majoring in dance at the University of Michigan. The third of eight children, she was raised in the suburbs of Detroit. Her mother had died when she was six years old. Her prospects in the world of show business looked poor. Apart from her training in dance, she had little musical background and no contacts.

Life in New York was a struggle. "I worked at Dunkin' Donuts, I worked at Burger King, I worked at Amy's. I had a lot of jobs that lasted one day. I always talked back to people and they'd fire me. I was a coat-check girl at the Russian Tea Room. I worked at a health club once a week."[4] While pursuing a series of dance engagements, she turned increasingly to music: the band Breakfast Club featured Madonna together with three male friends. Subsequently, she and a former Michigan boyfriend, Steve Bray, began working together on writing and performing songs in the dance music genre that was sweeping New York clubs at the beginning of the 1980s. Madonna also worked on her image—a form of glam-grunge that featured multilayered, multicolored combinations of thrift-store clothing together with scarves and junk jewelry. Her trademark look of messy, badly dyed hair, neon rubber brace-lets, black lace bras, white lace gloves, and chunky belt buckles would soon be copied by teenage girls throughout the world.

Madonna was quick to recognize the commercial implications of the new musical wave. The dance clubs were crucial and the DJs were the gatekeepers. Armed with her demo tapes, Madonna and her friends frequented the hottest dance clubs where they would make a splash with their flamboyant clothing and provocative dancing. At Danceteria, one of the staff referred to her as a "heat-seeking missile targeting the hottest DJs." DJ Mark Kamins introduced her to Mike Rosenblatt and Seymour Stein of Sire Records, a division of Warner Records. Her first 12-inch-single releases with Warner achieved local success, encouraged by New York's leading DJ, John "Jellybean" Benitez, who Madonna began dating in November 1982.

In July 1983, shortly before the release of her first album, she flew to Los Angeles to visit Freddie DeMann, manager of megastar Michael Jackson. DeMann remem-bers the meeting vividly: "I was knocked off my feet. I've never met a more physical human being in my life." DeMann agreed to become Madonna's manager.

By 1984, Madonna had become the hottest newcomer to US popular music. She made little secret of her ambition. At her national TV debut on *American Bandstand*, presenter Dick Clark asked her, "What do you really want to do when you grow up?" "Rule the world," she replied. While working on her second album, *Like a Virgin*, Madonna also entered the movie business, first, by playing a leading role in the movie *Desperately Seeking Susan* and, second, by marrying bad-boy actor Sean Penn.

Madonna on Top

Madonna's struggle for fame revealed a drive, determination, and appetite for hard work that would characterize her whole career. "I'm tough, I'm ambitious, and I know exactly what I want—and if that makes me a bitch, that's okay," she told the

London *News of the World* newspaper. On the set of *Desperately Seeking Susan* she maintained a blistering pace. "During the shoot we'd often get home at 11:00 or 12:00 at night and have to be back at 6:00 or 7:00 the next morning. Half the time the driver would pick up Madonna at her health club. She'd get up at 4:30 in the morning to work out first."[5]

While Madonna relied on some of the best minds and strongest companies in the entertainment business to manage and develop her career, there was little doubt as to who was calling the shots. Her swift exit from her marriage with Sean Penn further emphasized her unwillingness to allow messy personal relationships to compromise her career goals. For her third album, *True Blue*, released in June 1986, Madonna insisted on being co-producer.

The documentary of her 1990 "Blonde Ambition" tour, *Truth or Dare*, clearly revealed her hands-on management style. The tour established the pop concert as multimedia show embracing music, dance, and theater. Madonna was involved in every aspect of the show's design and planning, including auditioning dancers and musicians, planning, costume design, and choosing themes. Madonna worked closely with fashion designer Jean Paul Gaultier, whose metallic, cone-breasted costumes became one of the tour's most vivid images. On the tour itself, the *Truth or Dare* movie revealed Madonna as both creative director and chief operations officer. In addition to her obsessive attention to every detail of the show's production, she was the undisputed organizational leader responsible for building team spirit among the diverse group of dancers, musicians, choreographers, and technicians; motivating the troupe when times were tough; resolving disputes between her fractious male dancers; and enforcing the highest standards of commitment and effort.

The tour coincided with the summer 1990 release of *Dick Tracy*, the Disney movie that was a vehicle for Madonna and her high-profile lover Warren Beatty. Madonna's portrayal of Breathless Mahoney exuded her natural talents for style and seductiveness and did much to rectify the scathing reviews of her previous acting roles.

Sex, Religion, and Self-Promotion

In building her superstar image, Madonna began increasingly to court notoriety, and push up against the boundaries of acceptability. Her overt sexuality together with audacious, expletive-laced talk, and use of crucifixes as items of jewelry raised disquiet within conservative and religious circles. Madonna's explanation only added fuel to the fire: "Crucifixes are sexy because there's a naked man on them." Her efforts to enthrall and shock culminated in the music videos that accompanied her *Like a Prayer* album, released in 1989.

Piggybacking on Madonna-mania, PepsiCo paid Madonna $5 million for a commercial based on the album's title track *Like a Prayer*. But the day after the first broadcast of the Pepsi commercial, Madonna's own *Like a Prayer* music video appeared on MTV. The video was a stunning mixture of sex and religion that featured Madonna dancing in front of burning crosses, making love on an altar, and revealing stigmata on her hands. Threatened by boycotts from Christian groups and the American Family Association, PepsiCo pulled its Madonna commercial.

The explicit sexuality of Madonna's live and video performances resulted in her achieving new heights of controversy—and public awareness. The Blonde Ambition concerts were threatened with cancellation by Toronto city authorities and condemned as blasphemous by the Vatican. The *Justify My Love* video released in November 1990 set a new record for Madonna: it was banned by MTV for its portrayal of homosexuality, voyeurism, nudity, sado-masochism, and oral sex. Sex also provided the basis for Madonna's entry into book publishing. Her photographic "art" book *Sex* featured her in an array of sexual poses . . . it sold half a million copies in its first week.

Creating and Projecting Image

Madonna has been compared to previous superstars and goddesses of sex and glamor—Greta Garbo, Marilyn Monroe, Mae West, Brigitte Bardot—but she has gone further in creating a persona that transcends her work as an entertainer. Previous superstars had been defined by their movie roles, while the big names in popular music, from Lena Horne to Janet Jackson, have been famous primarily for their music. Madonna achieved a status that was no longer defined by her work. By the 1990s, she was no longer famous as a pop singer or an actress: she was famous for being Madonna. For the next decade she worked to reinforce this status. Strategically, superstar status has much to commend it. Joining the pantheon of superstars acts as insulation from comparison with lesser mortals. As her website proclaimed: "Madonna is icon, artist, provocateur, diva, and mogul."

In her acting roles the key was to take roles that were primarily vehicles for Madonna to be Madonna. Her successes in *Desperately Seeking Susan* and *Dick Tracy* were the result of roles where Madonna could be herself. However, both these roles were to be eclipsed by Madonna's portrayal of Eva Perón in the movie version of the Andrew Lloyd Webber musical *Evita*. While in previous roles Madonna had been able to use her talents as a singer, a poser, a sharp talker, and a seductress, in *Evita* Madonna found a role that paralleled her own rags-to-riches story. Like Madonna, Evita had working-class origins, a burning ambition, and had used sex and shrewd judgment to become a legend in her time. The film, released in December 1996, was a huge commercial and critical success. As *Q* magazine's Paul Du Noyer remarked, "If ever there was an ideal vehicle for Madonna's dream of transcendent stardom, this must be it."[6]

The images through which Madonna projected herself to her audience were subject to periodic, radical transformations. The street-kid look of the early 1980s was replaced by the darker more intense sexuality of the late 1980s involving themes of sado-masochism and bisexuality. During the early 1990s, she increasingly invoked the imagery of past stars, most notably Marilyn Monroe. Like all successful fantasies, these images were near flawless in their comprehensiveness, integration, and attention to detail. They comprised a combination of dress, makeup, language, and social behavior, and they were closely linked to Madonna's style of music at the time.

Probably the most radical of these image changes occurred in the late 1990s, following the birth of her first child, Lourdes, on October 14 1996. Motherhood was accompanied by a host of lifestyle and image changes for Madonna. She substituted yoga for pumping iron; she began to study Kabbalah (a "mystical interpretation of the Old Testament," she explained); she developed a close circle of women friends and became less available to the media. Her interviews were amazingly devoid of sex, expletives, and shock value. "I think [motherhood] made me face up to my more feminine side . . . What I missed and longed for was that unconditional love that a mother gives you. And so, having my daughter is the same kind of thing. It's like that first, true, pure, unconditional love."[7]

Lifestyle changes were reflected in her music: Madonna's new album, *Ray of Light*, incorporated a host of new influences: electronic music, traditional Indian music, Madonna's social and philosophical musings, and reflections on her own unhappy childhood. Her TV and video performances revealed a series of entirely new looks. Yet despite her downplaying of aggressiveness and sexuality in favor of a softer, more feminine image, the critical acclaim and commercial success of *Ray of Light* pointed to Madonna's remarkable capacity to adapt to maturity and renew her popularity.

Following the birth of her second child, Rocco, in August 2000, and subsequent marriage to British actor/director Guy Ritchie, Madonna became increasingly involved in social and philanthropic activities. She was a major donor of the Raising Malawi foundation, which provided support for orphaned children in Malawi. Inevitably, these charitable activities became vehicles for publicity as well as sources of controversy for Madonna. In October 2006, her adoption of a 13-month-old Malawian, David Banda, created a furor that involved developing-world politicians, anti-globalization activists, religious leaders, and assorted intellectuals. Madonna became immersed in a global debate over "cash for babies" and "one law for the rich; another for the poor." Her adoption of a second Malawian child in 2009 was eventually permitted after being initially blocked by the courts in Malawi.

Madonna as Mogul

Madonna's preoccupation with her "art" and her "freedom of artistic expression" extended to an acute interest in her intellectual property rights. While her early hits had been written by professional songwriters who pocketed royalties from their copyrights, since 1986 Madonna's was always the first name to appear on her song credits and she co-produced most of her recordings.

Not only did Madonna maintain control over her own content, she increasingly wanted a cut in distribution. In April 1992, she signed a $60 million deal with Time Warner, Inc. This created Maverick Records, a music production company (together with TV, video, and music publishing wings) as a joint venture between Madonna and Time Warner, with Warner Records providing distribution. Although Madonna remained contracted to Warner Records for her own recordings, Maverick offered an avenue for her to develop and promote other singers and musicians.

Madonna was quick to recognize the impact of digital technology and the internet on the traditional business model of the pop music industry. In the pre-digital world, live performances were primarily vehicles to publicize new album releases. By 2000, file sharing and illegal downloading were killing the revenues of the record companies. Seeing the emergence of concert tours as the dominant revenue stream,

Madonna returned to concert touring in 2001. The "Drowned World" tour was followed by the "Re-invention" tour of 2004 and the "Confessions" tour of 2006.

When Maverick began losing money (along with most other record companies), Madonna appreciated the need to reorganize her own commercial arrangements. Her exit was credited by industry observers as strategic brilliance. Maverick sued Warner Music for "improper accounting." Afraid of bad publicity and long-running litigation, Warner resolved the matter by buying out Madonna's share of Maverick for $10 million in 2004.

Free of contractual commitments, Madonna was able to court a new business partner. In 2007, she signed a $120 million, 10-year contract with Live Nation, the world's largest concert promotion company. "The business paradigm has shifted," she said upon signing. "As a creative artist and a businesswoman I have to acknowledge that." Most observers believed that Madonna had gained the better part of the deal—and with no music distribution capability, it seemed likely that Live Nation would license Madonna's next album back to her old record company, Warner. However, her "Sticky and Sweet" tour restored faith in Madonna as a money machine. The tour set new standards in global scope, longevity, and revenue generation: the $408 million it generated made it the highest-grossing concert tour by a solo artist. With 85 sell-out concerts between August 2008 and September 2009 spanning every continent of the world, Madonna confirmed her ability to recruit a whole new generation of fans, many of whom had not been born when she recorded her debut album.

Notes

1. The record's debut was boosted by packaging the album with ticket sales for the upcoming Madonna concert tour. See www.huffingtonpost.com/2012/04/10/madonnas-mdna-fail-album-sales_n_1416094.html, accessed August 30, 2012.
2. "Madonna (entertainer)," http://en.wikipedia.org/wiki/Madonna_(entertainer), accessed August 23, 2011.
3. "Madonna," (October 2010), http://www.forbes.com/profile/madonna/, accessed November 2 2011.
4. M. Bego, *Madonna: Blonde Ambition* (New York: Cooper Square, 2000): p. 46.
5. C. Arrington, "Madonna," *People*, March 11, 1985.
6. "Commanding" (Review of *Evita*), *Q* (December 1996), www.pauldunoyer.com/pages/journalism/journalism_item.asp?journalismID=250, accessed October 29, 2009.
7. M. Murphy, "Madonna Confidential," *TV Guide* (April 11–17, 1998).

A video clip relating to this case is available in your interactive e-book at **www.wileyopenpage.com**

Case 2 Starbucks Corporation, April 2012

If the rise of Starbucks from a single Seattle coffee store to the world's biggest supplier of coffee drinks is now part of the mythology of American entrepreneurial capitalism, the story of its guiding genius, Howard Schultz, fits a much older folklore, that of "the hero's return." After lifting Starbucks from obscurity to become one of the world's most successful service corporations, Schultz stepped down from the CEO position in 2000. By 2007, Starbucks' performance was flagging: margins and same-store sales were both in decline. Amidst fears of market saturation, increasing competition, and depressed consumer expenditure, Starbucks' share price fell dramatically. At the board's request, Schultz returned as CEO in January 2008. After two years of turnaround and revitalization, Starbucks' fortunes were restored. Growth had been rekindled, operating profits and margins hit new records (Table 1), and on April 13, 2012, Starbuck's shares closed at an all-time high of $62, up from $10 in March 2009 (Figure 1).

For many observers, including the owners of the Milanese cafes that had provided the inspiration for Starbucks, the Starbucks story is little short of miraculous. America's first coffeehouse had opened in Boston in 1676: how could brewing a better cup of coffee in the 1980s produce a company with a market value of $45 billion? Given the ubiquity of good coffee, could Starbucks possibly sustain its success?

The Starbucks Story

The rise of Starbucks from a single store in Seattle's Pike Place Market to a Fortune 500 company (number 229 on Fortune's 2012 listing) is an exemplary tale of American entrepreneurship.

Starbucks Coffee, Tea and Spice had been founded by college buddies Gerald Baldwin and Gordon Bowker. In 1981, Howard Schultz visited their store. It was a revelation. "I realized the coffee I had been drinking was swill." Captivated by the business potential that Starbucks offered, Schultz encouraged the founders to hire him as head of marketing. Shortly afterwards, Schultz experienced a second revelation. On a trip to Milan, he discovered that drinking coffee was more than experiencing the taste of good coffee: it was the ambiance of the coffee bar, the social

This case was prepared by Robert M. Grant. ©2012 Robert M. Grant.

TABLE 1 Starbucks Corporation: Financial and operating performance, 2005–2011

12 months to end-Sept. ($m)	2011	2010	2009	2008	2007	2006	2005
RESULTS OF OPERATIONS							
Net revenues							
Company-operated retail	9,632.4	8,963.5	8,180.1	8,771.9	7,998.3	6,583.1	5,391.9
Specialty	2,068.0	1,743.9	1,594.5	1,611.1	1,413.2	1,203.8	977.4
Total net revenues	11,700.4	10,707.4	9,774.6	10,383.0	9,411.5	7,786.9	6,369.3
Cost of sales	4,949.3	4,458.6	4,324.9	4,645.3	3,999.1	3,178.8	n.a.
Store operating expenses	3,665.1	3,551.4	3,425.1	3,745.1	3,215.9	2,687.8	n.a.
Other operating expenses	402.0	293.2	264.4	330.1	294.2	253.7	n.a.
Depreciation and amortization	523.3	510.4	534.7	549.3	467.2	387.2	n.a.
General and administrative expenses	636.1	569.5	453.0	456.0	489.2	479.4	n.a.
Restructuring charges	—	53.0	3,324.0	266.9	—	—	n.a.
Total operating expenses	10,175.8	9,436.1	9,334.5	9,992.7	8,465.6	6,986.9	n.a.
Operating income	1,728.5	1,419.4	562.0	503.9	1,053.9	894.0	780.5
Net earnings	1,245.7	945.6	390.8	315.5	672.6	564.3	494.4
Net cash from operations	1,612.4	1,704.9	1,389.0	1,258.7	1,331.2	1,131.6	922.9
Capital expenditures (net)	531.9	440.7	445.6	984.5	1,080.3	771.2	643.3
BALANCE SHEET							
Working capital (deficit)	1,719.1	977.3	454.8	(441.7)	(459.1)	(405.8)	(17.7)
Total assets	7,360.4	6,385.9	5,576.8	5,672.6	5,343.9	4,428.9	3,513.7
Short-term borrowings	—	—	—	713.0	710.3	700.0	277.0
Long-term debt	549.5	549.4	549.3	550.3	550.9	2.7	3.6
Shareholders' equity	4,384.9	3,674.7	3,045.7	2,490.9	2,284.1	2,228.5	2,090.3
STORE INFORMATION							
Percentage change in same store sales							
United States (%)	8	7	(6)	(5)	4	7	9
International (%)	5	6	(2)	2	7	8	6
Consolidated (%)	8	7	(6)	(3)	5	7	8
Stores opened during the year (net of closures)							
United States							
Company-operated stores	(2)	(57)	(474)	445	1065	810	580
Licensed stores	(342)	60	35	438	723	733	596
International							
Company-operated stores	144	(16)	105	236	286	240	177
Licensed stores	345	236	289	550	497	416	319
Total	145	223	(45)	1,669	2,571	2,199	1672
Number of stores							
United States							
Company-operated stores	6,705	6,707	6,764	7,238	6,793	5,728	4,918
Licensed stores	4,082	4,424	4,364	4,329	3,891	3,168	2,435
International							
Company-operated stores	2,326	2,182	2,198	2,093	1,831	1,457	1,217
Licensed stores	3,890	3,545	3,309	3,020	2,496	2,087	1,671
Total	17,003	16,858	16,635	16,680	15,011	12,440	10,241

Note:
Figures in parentheses denote a loss.

FIGURE 1 Starbucks' share price ($), May 2004–May 2012

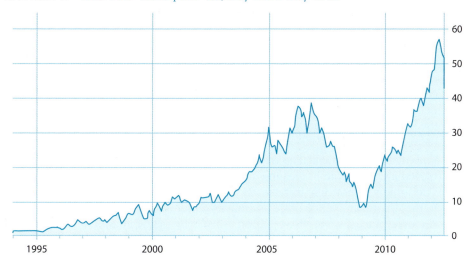

interactions it housed, and the art of the barista in preparing the coffee. His ideas for recreating Starbucks to be a place where people would come to share the experience of drinking great coffee rather than to buy coffee beans failed to persuade the founders. Schultz left to open his own Italian-styled coffee bar, Il Giornale. In 1987, he acquired the Starbucks chain of six stores, merged it with his three Il Giornale bars, and adopted the Starbucks name for the enlarged company.

Schultz's original idea of replicating Italian coffee bars (where customers mostly stand to drink coffee) was adapted to "the American equivalent of the English pub, the German beer garden and the French café."[1] With the addition of Wi-Fi, Starbucks stores became a place to work as well as to socialize. By 1992, Starbucks had grown to 165 outlets and, having gone public, Schultz was able to accelerate that growth using the $27 million from the stock offering. Expansion followed a cluster pattern: opening multiple stores in a single metro area. The idea was to increase Starbucks' local brand awareness and facilitate customers' ability to find a Starbucks close to their home and work. International expansion began with Japan in 1996 and the UK in 1998. Starbucks relied mainly on organic growth, but occasionally Schultz made acquisitions: the UK-based Seattle Coffee Company in 1998, Seattle's Best Coffee and Torrefazione Italia in 2003, and Diedrich Coffee in 2006.

Starbucks' Strategy

Starbucks' strategy was grounded in its mission "to inspire and nurture the human spirit—one person, one cup and one neighborhood at a time." To put this mission into practice required Starbucks to not just serve excellent coffee but also engage its customers at an emotional level. As Schultz explained: "We're not in the coffee business serving people, we are in the people business serving coffee."

Central to the Starbucks' strategy was Schultz's concept of the "Starbucks Experience," which centered on the creation of a "third place"—somewhere other than home and work where people could engage socially while enjoying the shared experience of drinking good coffee. The Starbucks Experience combined several elements:

- Coffee beans of a high, consistent quality and the careful management of a chain of activities that resulted in their transformation into the best possible espresso coffee: "We're passionate about ethically sourcing the finest coffee beans, roasting them with great care, and improving the lives of the people who grow them." The appendix at the end of this case explains the arrangements under which Starbucks sourced its coffee beans (see "Product Supply").

- Employee involvement. The counter staff at Starbucks stores—the baristas— played a central role in creating and sustaining the Starbucks Experience. Their role was not only to brew and serve coffee but to engage customers in the unique ambiance of the Starbucks coffee shop. Starbucks' human resource practices were based upon a distinctive view about the company's relationship with its employees. If Starbucks was to engage customers in an experience which extended beyond the provision of good coffee, then it was going to have to employ the right store employees who would be the critical providers of this experience. This required employees who were committed and enthusiastic communicators of the principles and values of Starbucks. This in turn required the company to regard its employees as business partners. Starbucks' human resource practices were tailored, first, to attracting and recruiting people whose attitudes and personalities were consistent with the culture of the company and, second, to foster trust, loyalty, and a sense of belonging, which would, in turn, facilitate their engagement with the Starbucks' experience. Starbucks selected employees with care and rigor, placing a heavy emphasis on adaptability, dependability, capacity for teamwork, and willingness to further Starbucks' principles and mission. Its training program extended beyond basic operational and customer-service skills and placed particular emphasis on educating employees about coffee. Unique among catering chains, Starbucks provided health insurance for almost all regular employees, including part-timers.

- Community relations and social purpose. Schultz viewed Starbucks as part of a broader vision of common humanity: "I wanted to build the kind of company my father never had the chance to work for, where you would be valued and respected wherever you came from, whatever the color of your skin, whatever your level of education. Offering healthcare was a transforming event in the equity of the Starbucks brand that created unbelievable trust among our people. We wanted to build a company that linked shareholder value to the cultural values that we want to create with our people."[2] Schulz's vision was of a company that would earn good profits but would also do good in the world. This began at the local level: "Every store is part of a community, and we take our responsibility to be good neighbors seriously. We want to be invited in wherever we do business. We can be a force for positive action—bringing together our partners, customers, and the community to contribute every day." It extended to Starbuck's global role: "we have the opportunity to be a different type of global company. One that makes a profit but at the same time demonstrates a social conscience."

- The layout and design of Starbucks stores were seen as critical elements of the experience. Starbucks has a store design group that is responsible for the design of the furniture, fittings, and layout of Starbucks' retail outlets. Like everything else at Starbucks, store design is subject to meticulous analysis and planning, following Schultz's dictum that "retail is detail." While every Starbucks store is adapted to reflect its unique neighborhood, "there is a sub-liminal unifying theme to all the stores that ties into the company's history and mission—'back to nature' without the laid-back attitude; community-minded without stapled manifestos on the walls. The design of a Starbucks store is intended to provide both unhurried sociability and efficiency on-the-run, an appreciation for the natural goodness of coffee and the artistry that grabs you even before the aroma. This approach is reflected in the designers' generous employment of natural woods and richly layered, earthy colors along with judicious high-tech accessorizing . . . No matter how individual the store, over-all store design seems to correspond closely to the company's first and evolv-ing influences: the clean, unadulterated crispness of the Pacific Northwest combined with the urban suavity of an espresso bar in Milan."[3]

- Starbucks' location strategy—its clustering of 20 or more stores in each urban hub—was viewed as enhancing the experience both in creating a local "Starbucks buzz" and in facilitating loyalty by Starbucks' customers. Starbucks' analysis of sales by individual store found little evidence that closely located Starbucks stores cannibalized one another's sales. To expand sales of coffee-to-go, Starbucks began adding drive-through windows to some of its stores and building new stores adjacent to major highways.

Diversification

Broadening Starbucks' product range was partly about responding to customer demand (for example requests for iced coffee eventually led to Frappuccino) and partly about building the Starbucks Experience. "The overall strategy is to build Starbucks into a destination," explained Kenneth Lombard, then head of Starbucks Entertainment. This involved adding food, music, books, and videos. As a music publisher and retailer of CDs, Starbucks was hugely successful, particularly its "Artists Choice" series where well-known musicians chose their favorite tracks. "I had to get talked into this one," says Schultz. "But then I began to understand that our customers looked to Starbucks as a kind of editor. It was like, 'We trust you. Help us choose.'"

Increasingly, Starbucks diversified its business model to include other ownership and management formats, additional products, and different channels of distribu-tion. These included:

- Licensed coffee shops and kiosks. The desire to reach customers in a variety of locations eventually caused Starbucks to abandon its policy of only sell-ing through company-owned outlets. Its first licensing deal was with Host Marriot, which owned food and beverage concessions in several US airports. This was followed by licensing arrangements with Safeway and Barnes & Noble for opening Starbucks coffee shops in their stores. Overseas, Starbucks increasingly relied upon licensing arrangements with local companies.

- Distribution of Starbucks retail packs of Starbucks coffee through supermar-kets and other retail food stores.

- Licensing of Starbucks brands to PepsiCo and Unilever for the supply of Starbucks bottled drinks (such as Frappuccino and Tazo teas).
- Starbucks' involvement in financial services began with its Starbucks prepaid store card, which was later combined with a Visa credit card (the Starbucks/Bank One Duetto card). The Starbucks card allowed entry to the Starbucks reward program, which offered free drinks and other benefits to regular customers.

Reformulating the Strategy, 2008–2012

After 20 years of continuous expansion accompanied by rising profits and a soaring stock price, Starbucks' downturn was unexpected and rapid. Starbucks' stock-market valuation was the leading indicator of the problems to come. After reaching a peak of $40 in October 2006, the share price declined by more than 75% over the next two years (Figure 1). During 2007, growth of same-store sales and operating profits slowed. Amidst increasing concern over Starbucks' current strategy and future prospects and convinced that the source of Starbucks' woes was the compromising of Starbucks' core values that had resulted from the company's growth spurt, chairman and founder Howard Schultz returned as CEO at the beginning of 2008. Starbucks' financial results for 2008 and 2009 revealed how Starbucks' performance had deteriorated (Table 1).

Getting Starbucks Back on Track

Schultz based his turnaround strategy on two major thrusts. First was retrenchment. Soon after his reappointment as CEO, Schultz announced a sharp cutback in planned US new store openings and revised operational practices to improve cost efficiency. In the summer of 2008, Schultz announced the closure of 600 US stores and the majority of its stores in Australia. The store closures resulted in almost 6,000 job losses; in addition, 700 positions were cut in corporate and support positions. The cost cutting extended to the office of the CEO: Schultz cut his own salary from $1.2 million to $10,000 and put two of Starbucks' three corporate jets up for sale. This reduced operating costs by $500 million in 2009.[4]

The second thrust was the reaffirmation of Starbucks' values and business principles, including revitalization of the "Starbucks Experience" and reconnection with its customers. Reinvigorating Starbucks' social commitment played a central role in the rediscovery process. During 2008, a company-wide reconsideration of Starbucks' purpose and principles resulted in a revised mission statement and a stronger commitment to corporate social responsibility. Starbucks' 2008 annual leadership meeting was held in New Orleans where 10,000 Starbucks employees participated in a variety of community projects for cleanup and restoration in the aftermath of Hurricane Katrina. Other initiatives included the launch of Starbucks Shared Planet: an environmental sustainability and community service program.

Schultz reviewed operating practices to examine their consistency with the Starbucks Experience and Starbucks' image. One key change was a return to "handmade" coffee. To speed up coffee making, Starbucks had replaced its La Marzocco espresso machines, which required baristas to grind coffee for each cup, with automatic Verismo machines, which merely required baristas to press a button. During 2008, Starbucks spent millions installing new coffee machines where cups of coffee were made individually from freshly ground beans. Schultz pushed for a review and revision of Starbucks' food menu. A key change was withdrawing toasted breakfast sandwiches whose aromas masked that of the coffee: "The breakfast sandwiches drive revenue and profit but they are in conflict with everything we stand for in terms of the coffee and the romance of the coffee."[5]

Reconnecting with customers involved extensive use of social media: Starbucks was a pioneer in using Facebook for promotional and loyalty-building purposes. In collaboration with Square Inc., it pioneered the use of mobile payments through its Starbucks card. Using the Starbucks card apps (for Android and iPhone), Starbucks cardholders could use their cell phones to pay at Starbucks stores and to automatically recharge their cards.

Most of all, Schultz traveled Starbuck's far-flung empire to meet with employees ("partners") to reinforce Starbucks' values, and to reignite their drive and enthusiasm. At a series of meetings held in concert halls and other venues, Schultz recounted inspiring tales that exemplified the "humanity of Starbucks" and the role that managers played in creating an experience that "values and respects" customers. At the same time Schultz challenged his store managers with the severity of the current situation, with the need to return to the values and practices that had made Starbucks a special place, and the efforts that would be required to lift Starbucks' performance.[6]

By re-emphasizing Starbucks' core values, reversing store expansion, eliminating non-core products, and returning to the quality of the coffee and customer service, Schultz viewed his role as putting Starbucks back on the right road after a period in which growth had become "carcinogenic":

> When you look at growth as a strategy, it becomes somewhat seductive, addictive. But growth should not be—and is not—a strategy; it's a tactic. The primary lesson I've learned over the years is that growth and success can cover up a lot of mistakes . . . When we reviewed some of the underperforming stores, I was horrified to learn that the stores that we ultimately had to close had been open less than 18 months. When you look at that—the money invested and the money that we had to write off—those decisions were made with a lack of discipline. Also, I think there were times, during that period when we were chasing growth, when we were making decisions that were kind of complicit with the stock price. That's a very, very dangerous road to go down.[7]

Return to Growth

With operational efficiency and customer connections restored, Starbucks' food offerings revamped, and commitment to the company's values and principles reinvigorated, Starbucks' increasingly shifted its emphasis to growth opportunities. The difference, according to Schultz, was that growth would be "disciplined." Revenue growth was sought in two main areas: the grocery trade and international markets.

New Products and Alternative Distribution Channels A key thrust was to grow Starbuck's brand and product positioning within the grocery sector. The most significant move on this front was the introduction of Via, a new type of instant coffee, launched in February 2009 at $2.95 for a pack of three individual servings and $9.95 for 12 servings. Via used a patented process which allowed the company to "absolutely replicate the taste of Starbucks coffee." In less than two years, Via's sales reached $200 million. Other products for making coffee at home included single-serving K-Cups (for use with Green Mountain's Keurig coffee makers and Starbucks' own Verismo coffee pod espresso system. Starbucks also sought to expand sales under its Seattle's Best Coffee brand. In November 2011, Starbucks acquired premium juice maker Evolution Fresh Inc. with a view to expanding retail distribution of fruit juices and to open its own juice bars.

Under Schultz's leadership Starbucks' Consumer Products Group became the fastest-growing part of the company. A key feature of its strategy was exploiting complementarities between Starbucks' coffeehouses and the retail trade. Schultz explained the business model:

> Starbucks can seed and introduce new products and new brands inside our stores. We introduced Via instant coffee in our stores. Instant coffee is a $24 billion global category that has not had any innovation in over 50 years. And no growth. If we took Via and we put it into grocery stores and it sat on a shelf, it would have died. But we can integrate Via into the emotional connection we have with our customers in our stores. We did that for six to eight months and succeeded well beyond expectations in our stores. And as a result of that, we had a very easy time convincing the trade, because they wanted it so badly.[8]

This integration of the use of Starbucks' stores to lead sales through traditional grocery channels is outlined in Figure 2.

An indication of increased strategic focus on the grocery trade was Starbucks' decision to withdraw from its agreement with Kraft Foods for the distribution of its packaged coffees, in order for Starbucks to undertake its own distribution.

International Expansion   Schultz viewed emerging markets, China in particular, as a huge opportunity for Starbucks:

> The big opportunity, in terms of total stores, is what's happening in China; we've got 800 stores in greater China, 400 in the mainland. When all is said and done, we'll have thousands. We're highly profitable there. We've been there 12 years, and I would say that the hard work—in terms of building the foundation to get access to real estate, design stores, and operate them—is well in place.[9]

India was next: in January 2012, Starbucks announced the formation of a 50/50 joint venture with Tata Global Beverages to establish a chain of Starbucks coffeehouses in India.

FIGURE 2   Starbucks' "Blueprint for Profitable Growth"

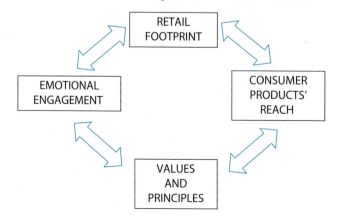

"Blueprint for Profitable Growth"   By early 2011, Starbucks was able to articulate its strategy for expansion as its "Blueprint for Profitable Growth." At the base of the model were Starbucks' values and business principles. According to Schultz: "Over our 40-year history, we have built the Starbucks brand with a goal of staying true to our values and our guiding principles with a deep sense of humanity. Going forward, we will continue to focus on what made us a different kind of company, one that balances profitability and social conscience while providing exceptional shareholder value."[10] This in turn provided the basis for Starbucks' emotional engagement with its customers. In addition to the face-to-face engagement cultivated through Starbucks' in-store experience, Starbucks' increasingly sought to use social networking and other digital media in order to extend and deepen its relationships with customers. Simultaneously, Starbucks would expand the scope of its customer engagement through growing its network of stores both through geographical expansion and seeking new opportunities through licensing. For example, through its alliance with Autogrill's HMSHost, Starbucks would expand beyond the 360 Starbucks locations currently operated by HMSHost in airports, on motorways, and in railway stations in North America and Europe. To exploit its growing brand strength, customer awareness, and loyalty, Starbucks would then expand its offerings of consumer products in the grocery trade and other distribution channels.

The Market for Coffee

Table 2 shows the world's leading importers of coffee and indicates per capita consumptions of coffee (the table omits coffee-producing countries with high per capita consumption such as Brazil, Costa Rica, and Vietnam).

TABLE 2   The world's leading coffee importing countries, 2006

Country	Imports (million kg)	Imports per head (kg)
United States	1,428.30	4.78
Germany	1,126.14	13.66
Japan	475.80	3.72
Italy	456.00	7.73
France	367.74	6.01
Belgium/Luxembourg	275.82	25.10
Spain	271.50	6.00
Canada	256.26	7.86
United Kingdom	241.98	4.00
Netherlands	195.48	11.92
Russia	188.22	1.33
Poland	167.52	4.40
Sweden	121.74	13.37
Austria	115.50	13.92
Algeria	109.26	3.26
Korea, Republic of	100.02	2.06
Switzerland	92.34	12.31
Australia	79.80	3.87

The US is the world's biggest market for coffee. Expenditure on coffee (for consumption at home, at work, and at catering establishments) was estimated at $47.5 billion in 2011. The market was split roughly equally between sales for the home-brewed coffee and sales of ready-brewed coffee. The market for the former was declining, while the latter was growing.

The US market could also be segmented between "ordinary" coffee and "specialty" coffee (also known as "premium" or "gourmet" coffee). Also, specialty coffee-houses had been a feature of US cities, especially those of the east and west coasts, for many decades. Starbucks' achievement had been to bring quality coffee to the mass market. Sales of premium brewed coffee were estimated to have grown from about $3.5 billion in 2000 to about $12 billion in 2011, with the number of coffee shops roughly doubling over the same period to reach 28,000.

Although Starbucks had been the primary driver of this growth, its success had spawned many imitators. These included both independent coffeehouses and chains, most of which were local or regional, although some aspired to grow into national chains. Table 3 identifies some of the leading chains.

In addition to specialty coffeehouses, most catering establishments in the US, whether restaurants or fast-food chains, served coffee as part of a broader menu of food and beverages. Increasingly, these outlets were seeking to compete more directly with Starbucks by adding premium coffee drinks to their menus. McDonald's had introduced a premium coffee (which consumer reports rated more highly than Starbucks' coffee) and had added its McCafés to a growing proportion of its burger restaurants both in North America and Europe. Burger King and Dunkin' Donuts had also moved upmarket in their coffee offerings. McDonald's and Dunkin' Donuts both targeted Starbucks in their advertising. The McDonald's web site Unsnobbycoffee.com implicitly identified Starbucks as overpriced and "snobbish."

Outside of the US, Starbucks faced different competitive situations country by country. In most of them, competition was even more intense than in the US. Starbucks' withdrawal from Australia was a consequence of a highly sophisticated coffee market developed and educated by Italian, southern European, and the Middle Eastern immigrants. Throughout continental Europe Starbucks had to deal with well-developed markets with high standards of coffee preparation and strong local preferences.

TABLE 3 Leading chains of coffee shops in the US, 2011

Company	US outlets, 2011	Headquarters
Starbucks	10,789	Seattle, WA
Tim Hortons	714	Oakville, Ontario
Caribou Coffee	415	Brooklyn Center, MN
Coffee Bean and Tea Leaf	296	Los Angeles, CA
Peet's Coffee	193	Emeryville, CA
Tully's Coffee	180	Seattle
Coffee Beanery	131	Flushing, MI
It's A Grind Coffeehouse	105	Long Beach, CA
Dunn Bros	85	St Paul, MN
PJ's Coffee	50	New Orleans, LA
Port City Java	32	Wilmington, NC

As well as competition from the bottom (McDonald's, Dunkin' Donuts), Starbucks faced competition from the top. The upmarket Italian coffee roaster illycaffè S.p.A was expanding in the US through franchise arrangements with independent coffee-houses. One scenario for the US gourmet coffee market was that once Starbucks had educated North Americans about the joy of good coffee these new coffee connoisseurs would go on to seek superior alternatives to Starbucks.

The specialty coffee market was also seeing a revolution in home-brewed coffee. Sales of Italian-style espresso coffee makers (which used highly pressurized hot water to make coffee) had grown rapidly since 2000. A particular growth area had been single-serve coffee pod systems pioneered by Nestlé's Nespresso subsidiary. Other entrants into this market had been Keurig with its K-Cup system, the Senseo system launched by Philips and Sara Lee, and Kraft's Tassimo system. In 2010, Lavazza S.p.A and Green Mountain Coffee Roasters Inc. created an alliance to develop a new range of single-serve espresso coffee makers. In March 2012, Starbucks joined the fray by launching its own single serve, home coffee makers under its Verismo brand.

Looking Ahead

The release of Starbucks quarterly financial results on April 26, 2012 offered further confirmation of the strength of Starbucks' recovery under Schultz's leadership and reinforced the view that the downturn of 2007/2008 had been an aberration resulting from Starbuck's overeager pursuit of growth (Table 4).

Yet amidst the acclaim for Schultz's remarkable success in returning Starbucks to profitability and growth, many of the concerns that had worried investment analysts in 2008 had not disappeared: the US recovery and the world economy remained

TABLE 4 Starbucks Corporation: Results for three quarters ending July 1, 2012

	9 months ending July 1, 2012	9 months ending July 3, 2011	Change
TOTAL COMPANY			
Net new stores	648	160	+488
Revenues ($m)	9,935	8,669	+15%
Of which: Company-owned stores ($m)	7,869	7,162	+10%
—Licensed stores ($m)	905	741	+22%
—CPG, foodservice, and other ($m)	1,162	766	+52%
Operating income ($m)	1,478	1,280	+15%
Operating margin	14.9%	14.8%	+0.1%
REVENUES BY REGION			
Americas	7,424	6,769	+10%
Europe, Middle East, Africa	858	757	+13%
China, Asia-Pacific	523	391	+34%
Channel Development[a]	974	618	+58%

Note:
[a] Comprises Consumer Products Group and Foodservice.
Source: US Securities and Exchange Commission, Starbucks Corporation, Form 10-Q, Quarterly Period Ended July 1, 2012, File Number: 0-20322, Washington, DC 20549.

fragile and the competitive forces that had threatened Starbucks in 2008 appeared even stronger in 2012. Some had doubts about the consistency and coherence of Starbucks' strategy. After refocusing Starbucks on its core values and core identity, might Schultz's multiple initiatives be a distraction for the company? For those who had perceived an uneasy relationship between Starbucks' claim to be providing authentic, gourmet coffee and its offerings of syrup-flavored coffees, the introduction of instant coffee was viewed as brand-threatening. Starbuck's push into the grocery trade was taking the company into an intensely competitive field where it would need to develop new capabilities. Barclays Capital analyst Jeff Bernstein commented: "They're starting a new chapter from scratch. While viewed favorably by most, the question has to be: Do you realize the magnitude of the task you're taking on?"[11]

Appendix: Extracts from Starbucks Corporation 10-K Report for Fiscal Year 2011

The Business

General   Starbucks is the premier roaster, marketer and retailer of specialty coffee in the world, operating in more than 50 countries. Formed in 1985, Starbucks Corporation's common stock trades on the NASDAQ Global Select Market ("NASDAQ") under the symbol "SBUX." We purchase and roast high-quality whole bean coffees that we sell, along with handcrafted coffee and tea beverages and a variety of fresh food items, through company-operated stores. We also sell a variety of coffee and tea products and license our trademarks through other channels such as licensed stores, grocery and national foodservice accounts. In addition to our flagship Starbucks brand, our portfolio also includes Tazo® Tea, Seattle's Best Coffee®, and Starbucks VIA® Ready Brew.

Our objective is to maintain Starbucks standing as one of the most recognized and respected brands in the world. To achieve this goal, we are continuing the disciplined expansion of our store base, primarily focused on growth in countries outside of the US. In addition, by leveraging the experience gained through our traditional store model, we continue to offer consumers new coffee products in multiple forms, across new categories, and through diverse channels. Starbucks Global Responsibility strategy and commitments related to coffee and the communities we do business in, as well as our focus on being an employer of choice, are also key complements to our business strategies.

Company-operated Stores   Revenue from company-operated stores accounted for 82% of total net revenues during fiscal 2011. Our retail objective is to be the leading retailer and brand of coffee in each of our target markets by selling the finest quality coffee and related products, and by providing each customer a unique *Starbucks Experience*. The *Starbucks Experience* is built upon superior customer service as well as clean and well-maintained company-operated stores that reflect the personalities of the communities in which they operate, thereby building a high degree of customer loyalty.

Our strategy for expanding our global retail business is to increase our market share in a disciplined manner, by selectively opening additional stores in new and existing markets, as well as increasing sales in existing stores, to support our long-term strategic objective to maintain Starbucks standing as one of the most recognized and respected brands in the world. Store growth in specific existing markets will vary due to many factors, including the maturity of the market.

A summary of total company-operated store data for the periods indicated

	Net stores opened year ending		Stores open as of	
	Oct. 2, 2011	Oct. 3, 2010	Oct. 2, 2011	Oct. 3, 2010
United States	(2)	(57)	6,705	6,707
Canada	37	24	836	799
United Kingdom	6	(65)	607	601
China	58	29	278	220
Germany	8	(2)	150	142
Thailand	8	2	141	133
Other	27	(3)	314	287
Total International	144	(15)	2,326	2,182
Total Company-operated	142	72	9,031	8,889

Starbucks retail stores are typically located in high-traffic, high-visibility locations. Our ability to vary the size and format of our stores allows us to locate them in or near a variety of settings, including downtown and suburban retail centers, office buildings, university campuses, and in select rural and off-highway locations. To provide a greater degree of access and convenience for non-pedestrian customers, we continue to selectively expand development of drive-thru retail stores.

Starbucks stores offer a choice of regular and decaffeinated coffee beverages, a broad selection of Italian-style espresso beverages, cold blended beverages, iced shaken refreshment beverages, a selection of premium teas, distinctively packaged roasted whole bean coffees, and a variety of Starbucks VIA® Ready Brew soluble coffees. Starbucks stores also offer a variety of fresh food items, including selections focusing on high-quality ingredients, nutritional value and great flavor. Food items include pastries, prepared breakfast and lunch sandwiches, oatmeal and salads, as well as juices and bottled water. In addition to being offered in our US and Canada stores, during fiscal 2011, we expanded our food warming program into our stores in China, with over 90% of the stores in these markets providing warm food items as of the end of fiscal 2011. A focused selection of beverage-making equipment and accessories are also sold in the stores. Each Starbucks store varies its product mix depending upon the size of the store and its location. To complement the in-store experience, in company-operated Starbucks stores in the US, we also provide customers free access to wireless internet.

Retail sales mix by product type for company-operated stores

Fiscal year ended	Oct. 2, 2011	Oct. 3, 2010	Sep. 27, 2009
Beverages (%)	75	75	76
Food (%)	19	19	18
Coffee-making equipment & other merchandise (%)	4	4	3
Whole bean coffees (%)	2	2	3
Total (%)	100	100	100

Licensed Stores   Product sales to and royalty and license fee revenues from US and International licensed stores accounted for 9% of total revenues in fiscal 2011. In our licensed store operations, we leverage the expertise of our local partners and share our operating and store development experience. Licensees provide improved, and at times the only, access to desirable retail space. Most licensees are prominent retailers with in-depth market knowledge and access. As part of these arrangements, we receive royalties and license fees and sell coffee, tea and related products for resale in licensed locations. Employees working in licensed retail locations are required to follow our detailed store operating procedures and attend training classes similar to those given to employees in company-operated stores. For our Seattle's Best Coffee brand, we use various forms of licensing, including traditional franchising.

Starbucks total licensed stores by region and country as of October 2, 2011

Asia Pacific		Europe/Middle East/Africa		Americas	
Japan	935	Turkey	153	United States	4,082[a]
South Korea	367	UK	128	Mexico	318
Taiwan	221	United Arab Emirates	94	Canada	284
China	218	Spain	75	Other	92
Philippines	183	Kuwait	67		
Malaysia	121	Saudi Arabia	65		
Hong Kong	117	Greece	59		
Indonesia	109	Russia	52		
New Zealand	35	Other	169		
Total	2334	Total	862	Total	4,776

Note:

[a]Includes closure of 475 Seattle's Best Coffee locations in Borders Bookstores.

Consumer Packaged Goods   Consumer packaged goods includes both domestic and international sales of packaged coffee and tea to grocery and warehouse club stores. It also includes revenues from product sales to and licensing revenues from manufacturers that produce and market Starbucks and Seattle's Best Coffee branded products through licensing agreements. Revenues from sales of packaged coffee and tea comprised 4% of total net revenues in fiscal 2011. In prior years through the first several months of fiscal 2011, we sold a selection of Starbucks and Seattle's Best Coffee branded packaged coffees and Tazo® teas in grocery and warehouse club stores throughout the US and to grocery stores in Canada, the UK and other European countries through a distribution arrangement with Kraft Foods Global, Inc. Kraft managed the distribution, marketing, advertising and promotion of these products as a part of that arrangement. During fiscal 2011, we successfully transitioned these businesses, including the marketing, advertising, and promotion of these products, from our previous distribution arrangement with Kraft and began selling these products directly to the grocery and warehouse club stores. We also sell packaged coffee and tea directly to warehouse club stores in international markets.

Revenues from licensing our branded products accounted for 1% of total net revenues in fiscal 2011. We license the rights to produce and market Starbucks and Seattle's Best Coffee branded products through several partnerships both domestically and internationally. We also sell ingredients to these licensees to manufacturer our branded products. Significant licensing agreements include:

- The North American Coffee Partnership, a joint venture with the Pepsi-Cola Company in which Starbucks is a 50% equity investor, manufactures and markets ready-to-drink beverages, including bottled Frappuccino® beverages and Starbucks DoubleShot® espresso drink and Seattle's Best Coffee® ready-to-drink espresso beverages in the US and Canada;
- licensing agreements with Arla, Suntory, and Dong Suh Foods for the manufacturing, marketing and distribution of Starbucks Discoveries®, a ready-to-drink chilled cup coffee beverage, in Europe, Japan and South Korea, respectively;
- a licensing agreement with a partnership formed by Unilever and Pepsi-Cola Company for the manufacturing, marketing and distribution of Starbucks super-premium Tazo® Tea beverages in the US; and
- a licensing agreement with Unilever for the manufacturing, marketing and distribution of Starbucks® super-premium ice cream products in the US.

Foodservice Revenues from foodservice accounts comprised 4% of total net revenues in fiscal 2011. We sell Starbucks® and Seattle's Best Coffee® whole bean and ground coffees, a selection of premium Tazo® teas, Starbucks VIA® Ready Brew, and other related products to institutional foodservice companies that service business and industry, education, healthcare, office coffee distributors, hotels, restaurants, airlines and other retailers. We also sell our Seattle's Best Coffee® through arrangements with national accounts. The majority of the sales in this channel come through national broadline distribution networks with SYSCO Corporation, US Foodservice™, and other distributors.

Product Supply Starbucks is committed to selling only the finest whole bean coffees and coffee beverages. To ensure compliance with our rigorous coffee standards, we control coffee purchasing, roasting and packaging, and the global distribution of coffee used in our operations. We purchase green coffee beans from multiple coffee-producing regions around the world and custom roast them to our exacting standards, for our many blends and single origin coffees. We buy coffee using fixed-price and price-to-be-fixed purchase commitments, depending on market conditions, to secure an adequate supply of quality green coffee . . .

We depend upon our relationships with coffee producers, outside trading companies and exporters for our supply of green coffee. We believe, based on relationships established with our suppliers, the risk of non-delivery on such purchase commitments is remote.

To help ensure sustainability and future supply of high-quality green coffees and to reinforce our leadership role in the coffee industry, Starbucks operates Farmer Support Centers in Costa Rica and Rwanda, among other locations. The Farmer Support Centers are staffed with agronomists and sustainability experts who work with coffee farming communities to promote best practices in coffee production designed to improve both coffee quality and yields.

Global Responsibility We are committed to being a deeply responsible company in the communities where we do business around the world. Our focus is on ethically sourcing high-quality coffee, reducing our environmental impacts and contributing positively to communities. Starbucks Global Responsibility strategy and commitments are integral to our overall business strategy. As a result, we believe we deliver benefits to our stakeholders, including employees, business partners, customers, suppliers, shareholders, community members and others. For an overview of Starbucks Global Responsibility strategy and commitments, please visit www.starbucks.com.

Operating Segments

The following tables summarize our results of operations by segment for fiscal 2011 and 2010.

United States

Fiscal year ended	Oct. 2011 ($million)	Oct. 2010 ($million)	Oct. 2011 (as % of total net revenues)	Oct. 2010 (as % of total net revenues)
Total net revenues	8,038.0	7,560.4	100.0	100.0
Cost of sales incl. occupancy costs	3,093.9	2,906.1	38.5	38.4
Store operating expenses	2,891.3	2,831.9	36.0	37.5
Other operating expenses	62.7	204.8	0.8	0.7
Depreciation and amortization	343.8	350.7	4.3	4.6
General & administrative expenses	83.7	85.9	1.0	1.3
Restructuring charges	—	27.2	—	0.4
Total operating expenses	6,475.4	6,279.3	80.6	82.9
Operating income	1,562.6	1291.1	19.4	17.1

International

Fiscal year ended	Oct. 2011 ($million)	Oct. 2010 ($million)	Oct. 2011(as % of total net revenues)	Oct. 2010(as % of total net revenues)
Total net revenues	2,626.1	2,288.8	100.0	100.0
Cost of sales incl. occupancy costs	1,259.8	1,078.2	48.0	47.1
Store operating expenses	773.8	719.5	29.5	31.4
Other operating expenses	91.9	85.7	3.5	3.4
Depreciation & amortization	118.5	108.6	4.5	4.7
General & administrative expenses	132.9	126.6	5.1	5.5
Restructuring charges	—	25.8	—	1.1
Total operating expenses	2,376.9	2,144.4	90.5	93.7
Income from equity investees	100.5	80.8	3.8	3.5
Operating income	349.7	225.2	13.3	9.8

Global Consumer Products Group

Fiscal year ended	Oct. 2011 ($million)	Oct. 2010 ($million)	Oct. 2011 (as % of total net revenues)	Oct. 2010 (as % of total net revenues)
Total net revenues	860.5	707.4	100.0	100.0
Cost of sales incl. occupancy costs	492.5	384.9	57.2	54.4
Other operating expenses	153.9	117.0	17.9	16.5
Depreciation & amortization	2.4	3.7	0.3	0.5
General & administrative expenses	14.3	11.0	1.7	1.6
Total operating expenses	663.1	516.6	77.1	73.0
Income from Equity Investees	75.6	70.6	8.8	10.0
Operating income	273.0	261.4	31.7	37.0

Other[a]

Fiscal year ended	Oct 2, 2011 ($m)	Oct 3, 2010 ($m)	Change %
Total net revenues	175.8	150.8	16.6
Cost of sales	103.1	89.4	15.3
Other operating expenses	93.5	34.9	167.9
Depreciation & amortization	58.6	47.4	23.6
General & administrative expenses	405.2	334.1	21.3
Total operating expenses	660.4	505.8	30.6
Gain on sale of properties	30.2	0.0	n.m.
Loss from equity investee	(2.4)	(3.3)	(27.3)
Operating loss	(456.8)	(358.3)	27.5

Note:
[a]*Other* comprises the Seattle's Best Coffee operating segment, the Digital Ventures business, and expenses pertaining to certain corporate administrative functions. Revenues are mainly from Seattle's Best Coffee.

Notes

1. J. Wiggins "When the Coffee Goes Cold," *Financial Times* (December 13, 2008).
2. Quoted in: *Howard Schultz: Building the Starbucks Community* (Harvard Business School Case No. 9-406-127, 2006).
3. "Starbucks: A Visual Cup o' Joe, "Contemporary Design Foundation," www.cdf.org/issue_journal/starbucks_a_visual_cup_o_joe.html, accessed May 15, 2009.
4. Starbucks Corporation, press release, Starbucks Reports First Quarter Fiscal 2009 Results (January 28, 2009).
5. M. Allison, "Schultz Concerned about Consumers, Not Competitors," *Seattle Times* (January 31, 2008), http://seattletimes.com/html/businesstechnology/2004155269_starbucksadd31.html, accessed August 30, 2012.
6. A meeting at London's Barbican Center is described in J. Wiggins "When the Coffee Goes Cold," *Financial Times* (December 13, 2008).
7. "Starbucks' Quest for Healthy Growth: An Interview with Howard Schultz," *McKinsey Quarterly* (March 2011).
8. "Starbucks' Quest for Healthy Growth: An Interview with Howard Schultz," *McKinsey Quarterly* (March 2011).
9. "Starbucks' Quest for Healthy Growth: An Interview with Howard Schultz," *McKinsey Quarterly* (March 2011).
10. "Starbucks Outlines Blueprint for Profitable Growth at Annual Shareholders Meeting," Starbucks Corporation press release (March 23, 2011).
11. "Latest Starbucks Concoction: Juice," *Wall Street Journal* (November 11, 2011).

A video clip relating to this case is available in your interactive e-book at
www.wileyopenpage.com

Case 3 Valuing Facebook

The initial public offering of 15% of the equity of Facebook, Inc. on May 18 was one of the few events that pierced the overall gloom of the financial markets during the spring of 2012. With over 900 million members at the time of its IPO, Facebook was the most successful of the Web 2.0 start-ups.[1] It was widely recognized for having pioneered a social revolution. It was also seen to offer one of the greatest business opportunities of the 21st century as it sought to monetize its vast treasure trove of information on its huge base of users and their social interactions.

The lead up to Facebook's IPO was accompanied by a fervent debate as to what Facebook was worth. In its revised prospectus, Facebook indicated that its "initial public offering price will be between $28 and $35 per share." On May 15, just three days before trading in Facebook shares was to begin on the NASDAQ, the issuing price for the shares was raised to between $34 and $38. Was Facebook a "once in a lifetime opportunity"[2] or was it "muppet bait"?[3]

Valuation Methodologies

Attempts to value Facebook followed one of two major approaches: the use of comparables and discounted cash flow (DCF) estimates. Facebook used both these approaches in assessing the value of its shares.

Valuations Based on Comparables

The simplest and most widely used means of valuing the equity of an unlisted company is to use "comparables." This involves, first, identifying publicly traded companies that are similar to the unlisted company; second, calculating valuation ratios for these public companies; and, third, applying these valuation ratios to the earnings, revenues, or net assets of the unlisted company. Facebook described this approach as the "Guideline Public Company Method," or "GPCM."

> GPCM assumes that businesses operating in the same industry will share similar characteristics and that the subject business's value will correlate to those characteristics. Therefore, a comparison of the subject business to similar businesses whose financial information and public market value are available may provide a reasonable basis to estimate the subject business's value. The GPCM provides an estimate of value using multiples derived from the stock prices of publicly traded companies. In selecting guideline public companies for this analysis, we focused primarily on

This case was prepared by Robert M. Grant. ©2012 Robert M. Grant.

FIGURE 1   Facebook's quarterly revenues and growth rate of revenues

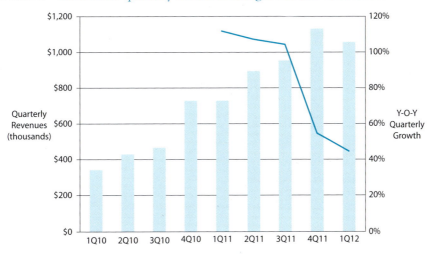

Source: Derived from Facebook, Inc. Amendment No. 5 to Form S1 Registration Statement, US Securities and Exchange Commission, Washington, D.C. 20549, May 3, 2012

quantitative considerations, such as financial performance and other quantifiable data, as well as qualitative considerations, such as industry and economic drivers.[4]

Most estimates of Facebook's market value were based upon applying to Facebook's projected earnings the same price earnings (P/E) ratios that the stock market use to value other rapidly growing technology and e-commerce companies. Henry Blodget of the online magazine *Business Insider* compared Facebook with tech giants Google and Apple on the basis of price/earnings ratios. On projected 2013 earnings per share for Facebook, which ranged from $0.40 to $1, a launch price of $38 would imply a P/E ratio of between 38 and 95; by comparison, Google's 2013 P/E ratio was 12 and Apple's 10.

So, what factors might justify a higher P/E for Facebook than for Google or Apple? The obvious one was superior earnings growth. The key problem here, noted Blodget, was that Facebook's revenue growth was slowing (Figure 1). The effect on Facebook's earnings would be reinforced by the difficulty in maintaining its 50% operating margin: "Facebook's next 2 billion users will be a lot less valuable monetarily than the first 1 billion. The world's richest people are already on Facebook. And those are the people advertisers want to reach," noted Blodget. Taking these factors into account and assuming 2013 earnings per share of $0.80, Blodget suggested that "a fair price for Facebook might be between $16-$24."[5]

SeekingAlpha also compared P/E ratios and growth rates of earnings per share. The results are shown in Table 1.

Looking ahead to 2013, SeekingAlpha came up with almost identical forward-looking P/E ratios as Henry Blodget. The difference was the inclusion of LinkedIn: it had a P/E ratio (based on estimated 2013 earnings) of 83—a significant premium over Facebook.

SeekingAlpha also compared the companies' cash per share (from the pro forma balance sheet) and operating cash flow per share (Table 2).

SeekingAlpha concluded by noting: "Facebook is much cheaper than LinkedIn, its closest peer, and yet its growth, both historical and projected, is slower than that of LinkedIn. The company is more expensive than either Apple or Google, yet went

TABLE 1 Facebook and its peers: Earnings per share

Company	Trailing P/E ratio	Earnings per share					
		2011	2010	2009	2008	2007	CAGR[a] (%)
Facebook	89[b]	$0.46	$0.28	$0.10	($0.06)	($0.16)	66.31[c]
LinkedIn	660	$0.11	$0.07	($0.10)	($0.11)	$0.00	105.13[d]
Google	18	$29.76	$26.31	$20.41	$13.31	$13.29	17.50
Apple	16	$27.68	$15.15	$9.08	$6.78	$3.93	47.76

Notes:
[a] Cumulative average annual growth rate.
[b] Assuming an IPO price of $38.
[c] Three-year only (CAGR not calculable where earnings negative).
[d] Based on growth in net income, not earnings per share.
Source: http://seekingalpha.com/article/603341-valuing-facebook-against-its-peers-can-a-case-be-made-for-the-stock.

TABLE 2 Facebook and its peers: Cash and cash flow per share

	Facebook	**LinkedIn**	**Google**	**Apple**
Cash per Share	$4.85	$5.57	$94.99	$116.60
Price/Cash Ratio	7.88	17.78	6.32	4.55
Operating Cash Flow Per Share	$0.76	$1.52	$45.69	$56.16
Price/Operating Cash Flow	50.30	65.15	13.14	9.44

Note:
The price/cash and price/operating cash flow ratios for Facebook assume an IPO price of $38.
Source: http://seekingalpha.com/article/603341-valuing-facebook-against-its-peers-can-a-case-be-made-for-the-stock.

public at a lower P/E ratio than both Apple and Google. . . Would we recommend Facebook shares to readers? The answer is a very qualified yes."

DCF Valuation

The Facebook prospectus describes the "Discounted Cash Flow Method," or "DCFM," as follows:

> DCFM involves estimating the future cash flows of a business for a certain discrete period and discounting such cash flows to present value. If the cash flows are expected to continue beyond the discrete time period, then a terminal value of the business is estimated and discounted to present value. The discount rate reflects the risks inherent in the cash flows and the market rates of return available from alternative investments of similar type and quality as of the valuation date.[6]

This approach was used by the *Financial Times'* Lex column. Its valuation model estimated Facebook's free cash flows to 2018, then calculated the company's "terminal value" at the end of 2018.

Free cash flow estimation followed these steps:

1. Estimate revenues for 2012–2018 by making assumptions about Facebook's annual rate of revenue growth in each year. (Lex's assumption was that revenue growth would decelerate during 2012–2018.)

2. Estimate operating cash flow. EBITDA (earnings before interest, tax, depreciation, and amortization) can be used as a proxy for operating cash flow. This can be derived from sales revenue by assuming an EBITDA/sales ratio for each year. (Lex's assumption was that Facebook's EBITDA/sales ratio would continue at its 2011 level of 50%.)

3. Estimate capital expenditure (capex) by assuming a capex/sales ratio for each year between 2012 and 2018. (Lex assumed that Facebook's capex/sales ratio would remain high during 2012 before declining sharply.)

4. Free cash flow is roughly equal to EBITDA minus capex.

5. After 2018, Facebook's free cash flows can be assumed to grow at a constant rate into perpetuity (on the assumption that social networking continues as a viable business or that Facebook is capable of evolving its business into something different).

To value Facebook, free cash flows need to be discounted at the cost of equity capital, which it estimated using the capital asset pricing model (CAPM) formula:

$$\text{Cost of equity capital} = R_F + \beta (E_{RP})$$

where

R_F is the risk free rate of interest
β is the security's beta coefficient (a measure of systematic risk)
E_{RP} is the equity risk premium (the rate of return in excess of the risk-free rate that investors require in order to hold the market portfolio of equities).

Calculating DCF value then used the following formula:

$$DCF = \frac{C_{12}}{(1+r)} + \frac{C_{13}}{(1+r)^2} + \frac{C_{14}}{(1+r)^3} + \frac{C_{15}}{(1+r)^4} + \frac{C_{16}}{(1+r)^5} + \frac{C_{17}}{(1+r)^6} + \frac{C_{18}}{(1+r)^7} + \frac{H}{(1+r)^7}$$

where C_{12} to C_{18} is the free cash flow in each year from 2012 to 2018, and r is the cost of equity capital.

The horizon value at the end of 2018 was calculated by assuming that Facebook's free cash flow continues to grow at a constant rate, in which case the 2018 horizon value is given by the following formula:

$$H = \frac{C_{18}}{(r-g)}$$

where C_{18} is the cash flow in 2018, r is the cost of equity capital, and g is the terminal growth rate.

TABLE 3   Estimating Facebook's DCF value

	2011	2012	2013	2014	2015	2016	2017	2018
Sales growth (%)	88	70	60	50	40	30	20	10
EBITDA ratio (%)	50	50	50	50	50	50	50	50
Capex/sales ratio	30	30	20	10	5	5	5	5
Cost of equity (%)[a]	9.5	9.5	9.5	9.5	9.5	9.5	9.5	9.5
Terminal growth rate (%)	—	—	—	—	—	—	—	3

Note:

[a]Assumes a 10-year Treasury rate of 2% (the risk-free rate of interest), a 5% equity risk premium, and a Facebook beta coefficient of 1.5.
Source: Lex in depth: Facebook, May 2, 2012. http://www.ft.com/cms/s/2/8a21debe-944e-11e1-bb47-00144feab49a. html#ixzz1wqhsO4Uw. Reproduced by permission of *The Financial Times*.

Lex then asked, "What kind of assumptions would be required to reach a $100 billion-plus valuation?" Table 3 shows the projections of sales, EBITDA and capex that Lex hypothesized.

Plugging in these numbers gave a company valuation of $109 billion and a value per share of $43.59. The unanswered question was: How realistic were these projections?

What Will Determine Facebook's Future Profits?

Whichever valuation method was adopted, the critical issue was forecasting Facebook's future profits. In the case of the comparables approach, the key to deciding what P/E ratio to apply to Facebook's earnings per share was the likely growth of earnings per share into the future. In the case of DCF valuation, while reasonable predictions could be made concerning Facebook's cost of equity capital and its capex requirements, the greatest uncertainties concerned its ability to generate strong profit growth over the medium and long term.

Facebook's long-term profit performance would depend upon its ability to compete in two markets. First, its continuing ability to dominate the market for social networking and to ensure that its platform would remain a leading portal for access to a range of online experiences for users. Second, its ability to compete with a wide range of other media providers to obtain a growing share of advertising revenues.

Facebook and the Social Networking Business

Facebook's website went live on February 4, 2004 as a directory for undergraduate students at Harvard University and quickly extended, first to other colleges and then more widely. It was not the first social networking website. Early entrants were SixDegrees.com in 1997, Makeoutclub and Friends Reunited in 2000, and Hub Culture and Friendster in 2002. In May 2003, LinkedIn was launched, followed by MySpace (August 2003) and Orkut (launched by Google in January 2004). During 2007, Facebook overtook MySpace (acquired by News Corp. in 2005) as the world's leading social networking site in terms of number of members and number of visits.

Once it had established market leadership, Facebook's subsequent growth was propelled by two factors. First, network effects: users were drawn to the site where most of their friends were already members. Second, Facebook's rapid addition of new services, such as instant messaging, "Virtual Gifts," "Social Bookmarketing," and "Facebook Connect." In May 2007, Facebook launched F8, a platform for developers to build applications to run on the Facebook site. The result was a massive expansion of Facebook applications.

Looking ahead, Facebook's dominant position in social networking (except in a few countries) offers it tremendous resilience against newcomers. However, as it expands its range of services it increasingly comes into competition with other suppliers of online services such as Google, Apple, and Twitter. As a platform it also benefits from network effects: developers will target their best applications at the biggest platforms.

But will Facebook retain, let alone increase, its appeal to users? The *Financial Times* pointed to some key risks:

Many of the connections users have formed could cease to be of interest. The network starts to carry more noise than information. People look for something more interesting. Social networks have inherent stabilizers as they grow but may also have a big destabilizer: boredom.

This problem is compounded, it seems likely, by the ever-increasing probability that your mother (or father or teacher) is on Facebook. That is, as user numbers increase, it becomes less cool. The company would argue it does not need to be cool. Once its user base reaches a certain size, it becomes irreplaceable. Should Facebook attain a stable monopoly on social networking, it would be easy to dream of a time when searching for information, reading news, watching television, writing a document or talking on the telephone are activities conducted on the Facebook platform or given a social dimension imported from and controlled by Facebook. It is this picture that makes some analysts think the company could be worth $100bn or more. Certainly, the potential revenue pool is enormous.

But users may not stay loyal for ever. True, all the data that make up a user's identity – comments, pictures, likes, connections with friends – are in effect owned by, and trapped on, Facebook. The company has carefully made it costly to leave. The question is whether the costs are high enough to prevent flitting among the networks and tools that have not been invented yet. It is hard to quit using Microsoft's software or Google's search engine, not just because of network effects but also because almost everyone needs to do things those tools make possible. Competitors are more expensive or not as good. Facebook simply is not essential to life or work in the same way.[7]

Facebook's Advertising Pull

To generate revenue, Facebook must convert its 900-million user base and huge volume of daily visits into a vehicle for advertising. In competing for online advertising revenues, Facebook competes with almost every other website that offers free online services to drive advertising revenues. However, Facebook's competitive advantage in attracting advertising is not only that it is one of the world's two-most-visited websites (along with Google): it is the potential it offers advertisers to target their advertising according to user interests and needs.

Facebook pointed to four unique advantages it was able to offer advertisers. The first was *reach*—the huge audience that accessed Facebook:

> For example, a movie studio seeking to increase awareness of an upcoming film release can reach a broad audience of Facebook users on the day or week before the film's opening. By advertising the release of *Transformers: Dark of the Moon* on Facebook, Paramount Studios reached 65 million users in the United States in a single day.[8]

The second was *relevance*—the ability to target a relevant and appropriate audience for an ad:

> CM Photographics, a wedding photography business based in Minneapolis, Minnesota, used Facebook ads to reach the users it cared most about: women aged 24 to 30 living near Minneapolis who shared their relationship status on Facebook as "engaged." In 2011, CM Photographics generated a significant increase in revenue after spending $1,544 to purchase advertising on Facebook.[9]

The third was *social context*—the highlighting of a friend's connections with a particular brand. An example is Facebook's "Sponsored Stories" product:

> When a user posts on Facebook that he or she has "checked in" to a Starbucks store, this checkin creates a story that can be shown in the friends' News Feeds. Although all of a user's friends may be eligible to view this checkin story, only a fraction of the user's friends will typically see it (based on factors such as when the user's friends check their News Feeds and our ranking of all the content that is available to show to each of the user's friends). Starbucks can purchase sponsored stories to significantly increase the reach, frequency of distribution, and prominence of this story to the user's friends.[10]

Finally, Facebook offered a superior medium for advertisings to *engage* with potential customers:

> Many of our ad products offer new and innovative ways for our advertisers to interact with our users, such as ads that include polls, encourage comments, or invite users to an event. Additionally, any brand or business can have a presence on Facebook by creating a Facebook Page. Through Pages, we give brands the opportunity to form direct and ongoing relationships with their customers, with the potential to turn them into valuable advocates.[11]

Such targeting of advertising opened Facebook to two threats. One was the risk of alienating users, particularly if they increasingly viewed Facebook more as a device for commercial exploitation than as a facilitator for their social relationships; the other was the threat of regulation either on the basis of privacy concerns or antitrust legislation.

Finally, the growing shift of internet access to mobile devices was unfavorable to the display of advertisements because of the small screen size of most mobile devices.

The *Financial Times*' Lex reporters recommended paying particular attention to Facebook's growth in revenue per user: "The numbers do not look good. There is still double-digit growth but there is a clear pattern of deceleration. Revenue growth is coming more from adding users than from making ads work better."[12]

EXHIBIT 1

Facebook: An Overview

Our mission is to make the world more open and connected. Facebook enables you to express yourself and connect with the world around you instantly and freely.

We build products that support our mission by creating utility for users, developers, and advertisers:

Users. We enable people who use Facebook to stay connected with their friends and family, to discover what is going on in the world around them, and to share and express what matters to them to the people they care about.

Developers. We enable developers to use the Facebook Platform to build applications (apps) and websites that integrate with Facebook to reach our global network of users and to build products that are more personalized, social, and engaging.

Advertisers. We enable advertisers to engage with more than 900 million monthly active users (MAUs) on Facebook or subsets of our users based on information they have chosen to share with us such as their age, location, gender, or interests. We offer advertisers a unique combination of reach, relevance, social context, and engagement to enhance the value of their ads.

We generate substantially all of our revenue from advertising and from fees associated with our Payments infrastructure that enables users to purchase virtual and digital goods from our Platform developers. In 2011, we recorded revenue of $3,711 million, operating income of $1,756 million, and net income of $1,000 million. In the first quarter of 2012, we recorded revenue of $1,058 million, operating income of $381 million, and net income of $205 million. We were incorporated in July 2004 and are headquartered in Menlo Park, California.

$(million)	2007	2008	2009	2010	2011	Q1, 2011	Q1, 2012
Operations data							
Revenue	153	272	777	1,974	3,711	731	1,058
Cost of revenue	41	124	223	493	860	167	277
Marketing and sales cost	32	76	115	184	427	68	159
R & D cost	81	47	87	144	388	57	153
General and administrative cost	123	80	90	121	280	51	88
Total costs	277	327	515	942	1,955	343	677
Income (loss) from operations	(124)	(55)	262	1,032	1,756	388	381

Interest and other income (expense), net	(11)	(1)	(8)	(24)	(61)	10	1
Income (loss) before income taxes	(135)	(56)	254	1,008	1,695	398	382
Provision for income taxes	3	—	25	402	695	165	177
Net income (loss)	(138)	(56)	229	606	1,000	233	205
Calculation of free cash flow							
Net cash from operating activities	11	8	155	698	1,549	345	441
Purchases of property and equipment	(55)	(70)	(33)	(293)	(606)	(153)	(453)
Property and equipment acquired under capital leases	(11)	(26)	(56)	(217)	(473)	(211)	(38)
Free cash flow	(55)	(88)	66	188	470	(19)	(50)
Balance sheet items							
Cash and marketable securities	305	297	633	1,785	3,908	—	3,910
Working capital	250	279	703	1,857	3,705	—	3,655
Property and equipment	82	131	148	574	1,475	—	1,855
Total assets	448	505	1,109	2,990	6,331	—	6,859
Total liabilities	174	170	241	828	1,432	—	1,587
Stockholders' equity	273	335	868	2,162	4,899	—	5,272

Note:
Figures In parentheses denote a loss.
Source: Facebook, Inc. Amendment No. 5 to Form S1 Registration Statement, US Securities and Exchange Commission, Washington, D.C. 20549, May 3, 2012, p. 43.

Notes

1. Web 2.0 refers to the development of the World Wide Web as an interactive, collaborative medium.
2. "The High Cost of Lost Opportunity," http://maximizesocialmedia.com/social-media-agency-the-high-cost-of-lost-opportunity, accessed June 5, 2012.
3. Henry Blodget, "Facebook is 'Muppet Bait,'" http://articles.businessinsider.com/2012-05-10/news/31648770_1_mark-zuckerberg-facebook-cnbc, accessed September 4, 2012.
4. Facebook, Inc. Amendment No. 5 to Form S1 Registration Statement, US Securities and Exchange Commission, Washington, DC 20549, May 3, 2012, p. 76.
5. Henry Blodget, "Well, Now That Everyone Has Sobered Up, Let's Figure Out What Facebook Is Actually Worth. . ." Business Insider, May 21, 2012, http://www.businessinsider.com/what-is-facebook-worth-2012-5, accessed September 4, 2012.
6. Facebook, Inc. Amendment No. 5 to Form S1 Registration Statement, US Securities and Exchange Commission, Washington, DC 20549, May 3, 2012, p. 76.
7. "Lex in depth: Facebook," May 2, 2012, http://www.ft.com/cms/s/2/8a21debe-944e-11e1-bb47-00144feab49a.html#ixzz1wqhsO4Uw, accessed September 11, 2012.
8. Facebook, Inc. Amendment No. 5 to Form S1 Registration Statement, US Securities and Exchange Commission, Washington, DC 20549, May 3, 2012, p. 88.
9. Facebook, Inc. Amendment No. 5 to Form S1 Registration Statement, US Securities and Exchange Commission, Washington, DC 20549, May 3, 2012, p. 89.
10. Facebook, Inc. Amendment No. 5 to Form S1 Registration Statement, US Securities and Exchange Commission, Washington, DC 20549, May 3, 2012, p. 90.
11. Facebook, Inc. Amendment No. 5 to Form S1 Registration Statement, US Securities and Exchange Commission, Washington, DC 20549, May 3, 2012, p. 90.
12. "Lex in depth: Facebook," May 2, 2012, http://www.ft.com/cms/s/2/8a21debe-944e-11e1-bb47-00144feab49a.html#ixzz1wqhsO4Uw, accessed September 11, 2012.

A video clip relating to this case is available in your interactive e-book at **www.wileyopenpage.com**

Case 4   The US Airline Industry in 2012

The year 2011 was another dismal one for US airlines in terms of financial performance. Despite an increase in both passenger numbers and revenues for the year, profits were down on 2010. In total, US airlines earned net profits of about $0.4 billion, representing a net margin of less than 1%. The dire financial state of the industry was underlined by AMR (the parent of American Airlines) entering Chapter 11 bankruptcy in November 2011. This ended AMR's distinguished record of being the only one of the major legacy airlines to have avoided bankruptcy. In 2005, Delta, United, Northwest, and US Airways had all filed for bankruptcy protection.

The early months of 2012 offered little hope of improvement. Airline revenues were up by 8.2% during the first quarter of 2012 compared to the same quarter of 2011. However, as a result of higher costs, net income was down by 73.6%: net margins had deteriorated from −3.2% to −5.2%.[1]

The woes of the US airline industry during the 21st century were typically attributed to the triple-whammy of the September 11, 2001 terrorist attacks, the high price of crude oil, and the 2008 financial crash. Certainly, each of these was a powerful force in boosting costs and depressing demand. Yet, the financial problems of the US airline industry predated these events. Even during the generally prosperous 1990s, the US airline industry had been barely profitable. Outside the US, the state of the airline business was little better. The IATA, the worldwide association of airlines, showed that the global airline industry had consistently failed to earn returns that covered its cost of capital (Figure 1; see also Table 1).

However, amidst the gloom, several airline executives expressed optimism about the future. At a Merrill Lynch conference on May 17, 2012, the CFO of United Continental Holdings Inc., John Rainey, observed that, compared to the past, the airline companies had become more disciplined and financially oriented. Instead of competing for market share through capacity growth, the major airlines were cutting capacity. Between the fourth quarter of 2006 and the first quarter of 2012, the major airlines would each cut capacity by between 3% and 10%. Southwest was the exception—its capacity would increase by 15%.[2] In addition, the consolidation of the industry would reduce the number of competitors which would help support fares. Revenue generation would also be assisted by the unbundling of fares: the growing practice of charging separately for seat reservations, baggage services, and onboard refreshments. According to US Bureau of Transportation Statistics, airline yields (revenue per occupied seat per mile) increased from 14.4 cents in the fourth quarter of 2010 to 16.8 cents a year later.[3]

The airlines had also made progress in cost reduction. Competition from low-cost carriers (LCCs) such as Southwest and JetBlue, had forced the "legacy carriers" into an endless quest for cost efficiencies and a reexamination of their business models. In particular, they had confronted the labor unions and gained substantial

This case was prepared by Robert M. Grant. ©2012 Robert M. Grant.

concessions on pay, benefits, and working practices. Chapter 11 bankruptcy had given the airlines a new flexibility in addressing some of the rigidities of their legacy systems—in particular pruning employee and retiree benefits and introducing more flexible working practices.

FIGURE 1   Return on capital and cost of capital for the world airline industry, 1993–2010

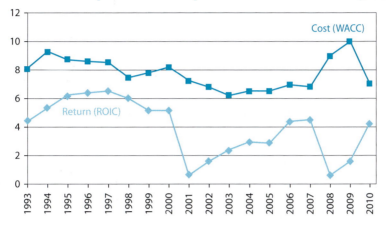

Source: Airlines for America, based on data from IATA and Deutsche Bank.

TABLE 1   Revenues, profits, and employment of the five largest US airlines

	United	Delta	American	Southwest	US Airways
Revenues ($ billion)					
2007	19.1	19.2	22.9	9.9	11.7
2008	19.3	22.7	23.8	11.0	12.1
2009	16.3	28.1	19.9	10.4	10.5
2010	23.3	31.8	22.2	15.6	11.9
2011	37.1	35.1	24.0	12.1	13.1
Net margin (%)					
2007	2.0	8.4	2.3	6.5	6.1
2008	(27.1)	(12.2)	(9.3)	1.6	(26.4)
2009	(4.0)	(4.4)	(7.4)	1.0	(2.0)
2010	1.1	1.9	(2.1)	3.8	4.2
2011	2.7	2.4	(8.2)	1.1	0.5
ROA (%)[a]					
2007	2.6	0.3	2.5	7.0	6.1
2008	(24.2)	(10.0)	(9.7)	3.8	(26.4)
2009	(3.5)	(2.8)	(5.8)	0.7	(2.8)
2010	0.6	1.4	(2.1)	3.0	0.9
2011	2.2	2.0	(8.3)	1.0	6.4
Employees					
2002	72,000	76,100	109,500	33,700	46,600
2008	53,000	83,822	84,100	35,512	32,691
2011	87,000	78,400	66,533	45,392	31,500

Note:

[a] ROA: Return on assets = net income/total assets.

Source: 10-K reports of companies.

Orders for new aircraft from the US airlines also pointed toward confidence in the future. In July 2011, AMR had placed an order for 460 planes—the largest in its history—with Boeing and Airbus. In May 2012, it made a progress payment of $162 million to the plane-makers, despite its bankruptcy filing. During the early part of 2012, United Continental was negotiating with Boeing and Airbus for 180 new planes, an order worth up to $15 billion.

Was it possible that the new climate of realism and financial prudence in the industry and the willingness of the airlines to reduce capacity when demand was weak would usher in a new era of prosperity for the industry? For many airline executives, consolidation supported by steadily growing demand for airline travel could offer a way out of the fierce price competition, low margins, poor labor relations, and frequent encounters with bankruptcy that had characterized the industry.

Others were less optimistic. The problems of the airline industry could not be attributed to the specific circumstances of the time: international terrorism, high fuel prices, or the financial crisis and its aftermath. Dismal profitability had been a near constant feature of the US airline industry since deregulation. And the situation was little different in other countries: almost all European airlines were losing money. Nor could poor industry performance be attributed to inept management. Despite criticism of the managerial effectiveness of the legacy carriers, the LCCs were also weak financial performers. Even the much-lauded Southwest Airlines had failed to cover its cost of capital during 2008–2011. "We've been here before, many times," observed one industry veteran. "Just when the industry seems to be climbing out of the mire, the industry's dire economics reassert themselves."

From Regulation to Competition

The history of the US airline industry comprises two eras: the period of regulation up until 1978 and the period of deregulation thereafter.

The Airlines under Regulation (Pre-1978)

The first scheduled airline services began in the 1920s: mail rather than passengers was the primary business. In the early 1930s, a transcontinental route structure was built around United Airlines in the north, American Airlines in the south, and TWA through the middle. To counter the threat of instability from growing competition (notably from Delta and Continental), in 1938 Congress established the Civil Aeronautics Board (CAB) with the authority to administer the structure of the industry and competition within it. The CAB awarded interstate routes to the existing 23 airlines; established safety guidelines; approved mergers, acquisitions, and interfirm agreements; and set fares and airmail rates (on the basis of cost plus a reasonable rate of return). Industry structure ossified: despite more than 80 applications, not a single new carrier was approved between 1938 and 1978.

During the 1970s, the impetus grew for less government regulation and greater reliance on market forces. Political arguments for deregulation were supported by new developments in economics. The case for regulation had been based traditionally on arguments about *natural monopoly*—competitive markets were impossible in industries where scale economies and network effects were important. During the early 1970s, the *theory of contestable markets* was developed. The main argument was that industries did not need to be competitively structured in order to result in competitive outcomes. So long as barriers to entry and exit were low then the potential for hit-and-run entry would cause established firms to charge competitive prices and earn competitive rates of return. The outcome was the Airline Deregulation Act, which, in October 1978, abolished the CAB and inaugurated a new era of competition in the airline industry.[4]

The Impact of Deregulation

The abolition of controls over entry, route allocations, and fares resulted in a wave of new entrants and an upsurge in price competition. By 1980, 20 new carriers— including People Express, Air Florida, and Midway—had set up.

Deregulation was also accompanied by increased turbulence in the industry: the oil shock of 1979, recession, and the air-traffic controllers' strike of 1981. During 1979–1983, the industry incurred widespread losses that triggered bankruptcies (between 1978 and 1984 over 100 carriers went bust) and a wave of mergers and acquisitions. Despite strong expansion from 1982 onward, the industry experienced a profit slump in 1990–1994. Figure 2 shows industry profitability since deregulation. Profitability is acutely sensitive to the balance between demand and capacity: losses result from industry load factors falling below the breakeven level (Figure 3). The role of competition in driving efficiency is evident from the near-continuous decline in real prices over the period (Figure 4).

FIGURE 2   Profitability of the US airline industry, 1978–2008

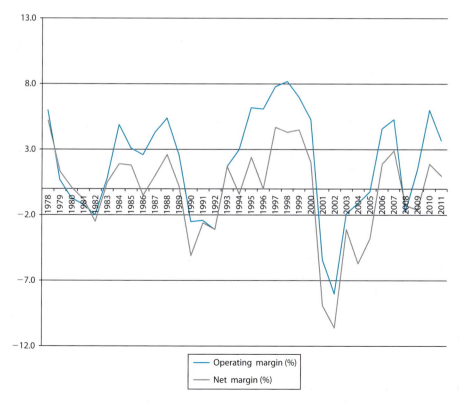

Source: Bureau of Transportation Statistics.

FIGURE 3 Load factor in the US airline industry, 1978–2007

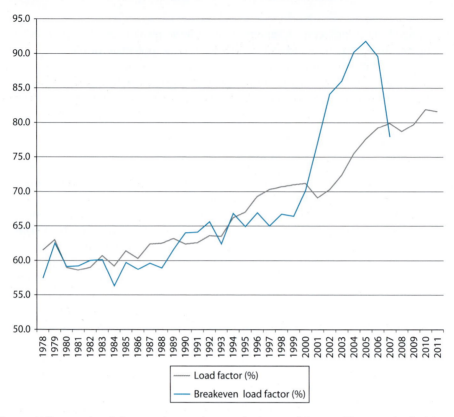

Source: Air Transport Association, annual economic reports (various years); Bureau of Transportation Statistics.

FIGURE 4 Average fares in the US airline industry, 1995–2011

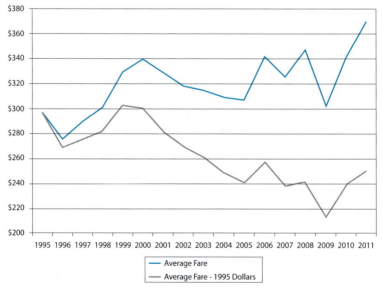

Source: Bureau of Transportation Statistics.

Firm Strategy and Industry Evolution

Changes in the structure of the airline industry during the 1980s and 1990s were primarily a result of the strategies of the airlines as they sought to adjust to the new conditions of competition in the industry and to gain competitive advantage.

Route Strategies: The Hub-and-Spoke System

During the l980s, the major airlines reorganized their route maps. A system of predominantly point-to-point routes was replaced by one where each airline concentrated its routes on a few major airports linked by frequent services using large aircraft, with smaller, nearby airports connected to these hubs by shorter routes using smaller aircraft. This hub-and-spoke system offered two major benefits:

- It allowed greater efficiency through reducing the total number of routes needed to link a finite number of cities within a network and concentrating traveler and maintenance facilities in fewer locations. It permitted the use of larger, more cost-efficient aircraft for inter-hub travel. The efficiency benefits of the hub-and-spoke system were reinforced by scheduling flights so that incoming short-haul arrivals were concentrated at particular times to allow passengers to be pooled for the longer-haul flights on large aircraft.
- It allowed major carriers to establish dominance in regional markets and on particular routes. Table 2 shows cities where a single airline held a dominant local market share. The hub-and-spoke system also created a barrier to the entry of new carriers, who often found it difficult to obtain gates and landing slots at the major hubs.

TABLE 2 Local market share of largest airline for selected US cities (by passenger numbers), 2011

City	Airline	Share of passengers (%)
Dallas/Fort Worth	American	71.83
Miami	American	69.56
Atlanta	Delta	63.74
Baltimore	Southwest	57.57
Charlotte	US Airways	56.75
Houston	Continental	55.06
Minneapolis–St. Paul	Delta	50.00
Newark	Continental	45.88
Detroit	Delta	44.17
Cincinnati	Delta	37.74
San Francisco	United	33.18
Denver	United	23.93

Source: Bureau of Transportation Statistics.

TABLE 3 Concentration in the US airline industry

Year	CR4 (%)	Year	CR4 (%)
1935	88	1987	64.8
1939	82	1990	61.5
1949	70	1999	66.4
1954	71	2002	71.0
1977	56.2	2005	55.4
1982	54.2	2011	54.3

Note:
The four-firm concentration ratio (CR4) measures the share of the industry's passenger miles accounted for by the four largest companies. During 1935–1954, the four biggest companies were United, American, TWA, and Eastern. During 1982–2005, the four biggest companies were American, United, Delta, and Northwest. The 2011 data relate to American, United, Delta, and Southwest.
Source: US Department of Transportation.

The hub-and-spoke networks of the major airlines were reinforced by alliances with local commuter airlines. Thus American Eagle, United Express, and Delta Shuttle were franchise systems established by AMR, United Airlines, and Delta, respectively, whereby regional airlines used the reservation and ticketing systems of the major airlines and coordinated their operations and marketing policies with those of their bigger partners.

Mergers

New entry during the period of deregulation had reduced seller concentration in the industry (Table 3). However, the desire of the leading companies to build national (and international) route networks encouraged a wave of mergers and acquisitions in the industry, some triggered by the financial troubles that beset several leading airlines. Had it not been for government intervention on antitrust grounds, consolidation would have gone further; however, Department of Justice approval of the Delta–Northwest and United–Continental mergers during 2009–2010 suggested a more lenient approach to airline mergers. Figure 5 shows some of the main mergers and acquisitions. During 2002–2011, despite several major mergers, concentration declined as a result of capacity reduction by the biggest airlines and market share gains by LCCs.

Prices and Costs

Intensification of competition following deregulation was most evident in the pricing of air tickets. Price cutting was typically led either by established airlines suffering from weak revenues and excess capacity or by LCCs. The new, low-cost entrants played a critical role in stimulating the price wars that came to characterize competition after deregulation. People Express, Braniff, New York Air, and Southwest all sought aggressive expansion through rock-bottom fares made possible by highly efficient cost structures and a bare-bones service (the LCCs economized on in-flight meals, entertainment, and baggage handling). Although most of the low-cost

FIGURE 5 Mergers and acquisitions among major US passenger airlines, 1981–2012

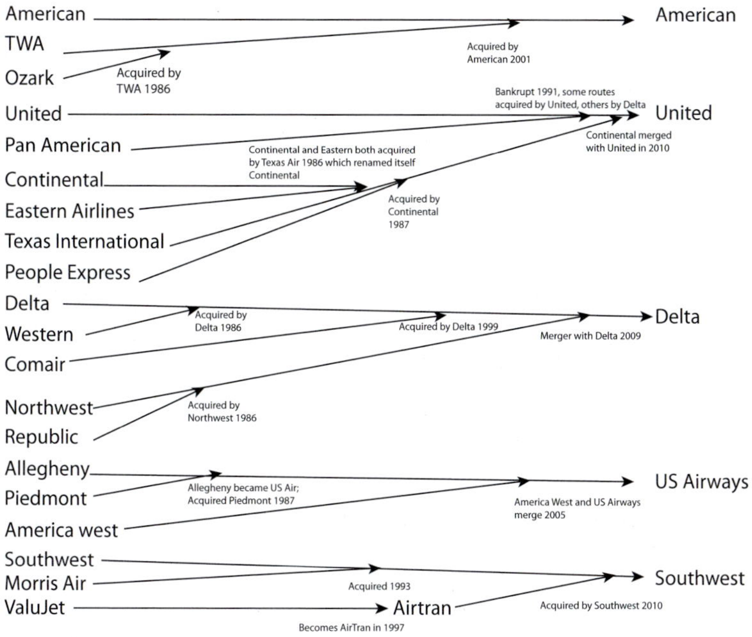

Source: Updated from S. Borenstein, "The Evolution of U.S. Airline Competition," *Journal of Economic Perspectives* 6(2), 1992, p. 48.

newcomers failed during the early years of airline deregulation, they were soon replaced by new entrepreneurs eager to start up their own airlines.

Price cutting by the major carriers was highly selective. Fare structures became increasingly complex as airlines sought to separate price-sensitive leisure customers from price-inelastic business travelers. As a result, fare bands widened: advanced-purchased economy fares with Saturday night stays were as little as one-tenth of the first-class fare for the same journey.

Price cuts were also selective by route. Typically, the major airlines offered low prices on those routes where they faced competition from low-cost rivals. Southwest, the biggest and most successful of the LCCs, complained continually of predatory price cuts by its larger rivals. However, the ability of the major airlines to compete against the budget airlines was limited by the majors' cost structures, including infrastructure, restrictive labor agreements, old airplanes, and commitments to extensive route networks. To meet the competition of low-cost newcomers, several of the majors set up new subsidiaries to replicate the strategies and cost structures of the budget airlines. These included Continental's Continental Lite (1994), UAL's Shuttle by United (1995), Delta's Song (1993), and United's Ted (1994) and were all expensive failures.

The legacy airlines were more successful in cutting their own costs: during 2001–2011, union contracts were renegotiated, inefficient working practices terminated, unprofitable routes abandoned, and staffing reduced. However, higher fuel prices hit the major airlines more heavily than they did the LCCs. Not only did the LCCs have newer, more fuel-efficient planes but their stronger financial positions allowed them to hedge through forward contracts.

The Quest for Differentiation

Under regulation, price controls resulted in airline competition shifting to non-price dimensions: customer service and in-flight food and entertainment. Deregulation brutally exposed the myth of customer loyalty: most travelers found little discernible difference among the offerings of different major airlines and were becoming more indifferent as to which airline they used on a particular route. As airlines increasingly cut back on customer amenities, efforts at differentiation became primarily focused upon business and first-class travelers. The high margins on first- and business-class tickets provided a strong incentive to attract these customers by means of spacious seats and intensive in-flight pampering. For leisure travelers it was unclear whether their choice of carrier was responsive to anything other than price, and the low margins on these tickets limited the willingness of the airlines to increase costs by providing additional services.

The most widespread and successful initiative to build customer loyalty was the introduction of frequent-flyer schemes. American's frequent-flyer program was launched in 1981 and was soon followed by all the other major airlines. By offering free tickets and upgrades on the basis of miles flown, and setting threshold levels for rewards, the airlines encouraged customers to concentrate their air travel on a single airline. By the end of 2006, airlines' unredeemed frequent-flyer distance had surged to over 10 trillion miles. By involving other companies as partners—car-rental companies, hotel chains, credit card issuers—frequent-flyer programs became an important source of additional revenue for the airlines, being worth over $10 billion annually.

The Industry in 2012

The Airlines

At the beginning of 2012, the US airline industry (including air cargo firms) comprised 151 companies, many of them local operators. Table 4 lists those with annual revenues exceeding $100 million. The industry was dominated by five major passenger airlines: United, American, Delta, US Airways, and Southwest. The importance of the leading group was enhanced by its networks of alliances with smaller airlines. In addition, domestic alliances with regional airlines, the Big 3, were also core members of international alliances: United with Star Alliance, American with the oneworld alliance, and Delta with SkyTeam.

Market for Air Travel

Airlines were the dominant mode of long-distance travel in the US. For shorter journeys, cars provided the major alternative. Alternative forms of public transportation— bus and rail—accounted for a small proportion of journeys in excess of a hundred miles. Only on a few routes (notably Washington–New York–Boston) did trains provide a viable alternative to air.

Most forecasts pointed to continued growth in the demand for air travel, but at a much slower rate than in earlier decades. During the 1980s and 1990s, passenger miles flown grew at a rate of 5% per annum and then slowed during the next decade. Boeing predicted that annual growth in air travel (in terms of revenue passenger

TABLE 4   The US airline companies in 2011[a]

Airline	Employees	Airline	Employees
Major Carriers			
AirTran	7,704	Hawaiian	4,438
Alaska	9,635	JetBlue	14,362
American	69,810	Kalitta Air	1,174
American Eagle	10,887	SkyWest	10,378
Atlas Air	1,529	Southwest	38,945
Delta	82,181	US Airways	32,257
Federal Express	151,308	United	87,440
Frontier	5,073	United Parcel Service	5,592[b]
National Carriers			
ABX Air	480	Miami Air International	380
Air Transport Intl	409	North American	638
Air Wisconsin	2,814	Omni Air Express	830
Allegiant Air	1,760	PSA Airlines	1,057
Amerijet Intl	608	Pinnacle	5,492
ASTAR USA	269	Polar Air Cargo	145
Centurion Cargo	226	Republic	2,011
Colgan Air	1,826	Ryan International	465
Comair	1,709	Shuttle America	1,844
Compass	1,076	Southern Air	713
Evergreen International	378	Spirit	2,850
Executive	2,014	Sun Country Airlines	968
ExpressJet	9,699	USA Jet	306
GoJet Airlines	769	Virgin America	2,421
Horizon Air	3,062	Vision	444
Mesa Airlines	1,820	World	888
Large Regional Carriers			
Aerodynamics Inc.	195	Kalitta Charters II	84
Aloha Air Cargo	347	Lynden Air Cargo	171
Asia Pacific	42	National Air Cargo Group	219
Avjet	161	Northern Air Cargo	230
Capital Cargo Intl	178	Tatonduk Outfitters Ltd	299
Florida West	90	Tradewinds	154
Gulf and Caribbean Cargo	94		
Medium Regional Carriers			
Ameristar Air Cargo	47	KaiserAir	144
Caribbean Sun Airlines	81	Prescott Support Company	46
Dynamic	49	Sierra Pacific	28
Falcon Air Express	162	Swift Air	105

Note:
[a] The list includes both passenger and freight-carrying airlines.
[b] UPS Airlines only.
Source: Bureau of Transportation Statistics.

miles) would grow by an average annual rate of 2.9% during 2010–30, the slowest of any of the world's major markets.[5] Some observers thought this overoptimistic, citing not just depressed consumer spending but also the upsurge in video conferencing that suggested that the long-anticipated shift from face-to-face to virtual business meetings had finally arrived.

Changes were occurring within the structure of demand. Of particular concern to the airlines was evidence that the segmentation between business and leisure customers was breaking down. Conventional wisdom dictated that the demand for air tickets among leisure travelers was fairly price elastic; that of business travelers was highly inelastic. Hence, the primary source of airline profit was high-margin business fares. During 2008–2009, increasing numbers of companies changed their travel policies to limit or eliminate employee access to premium-class air travel.[6]

Changes in the distribution of airline tickets contributed to increased price competition. The advent of the internet had decimated traditional travel agencies—retailers that specialized in the sale of travel tickets, hotel reservations, and vacation packages. Airline tickets were increasingly sold by online travel agents such as Expedia and Travelocity, or through airlines' own websites. However, the airlines were slower than e-commerce start-ups in exploiting the opportunities of the internet. A key impact of the internet was providing consumers with unparalleled price transparency, permitting the lowest price deals to be quickly spotted.

The decline of the traditional travel-agent sector was hastened by the elimination of commissions paid to travel agents. By 2008, commissions paid by airline companies to resellers fell to 1% of operating expenses (Table 5), down from 6.2% in 1991. By 2012, the traditional travel agency industry was dominated by a few global leaders such as American Express and Thomas Cook.

TABLE 5   Operating costs in the US airline industry, 2006 and 2008

Cost item	Increase in cost (%) 2000–2011	Percentage of total operating expenses 2006	2008	2011[j]
Labor	39[a]	23.8	24.4	22.1
Fuel	268[b]	25.5	35.9	30.7
Professional services	17[c]	7.8	8.1	7.3
Food and beverage	(38)[d]	1.5	1.3	1.5
Landing fees	70[e]	2	1.9	2.0
Maintenance material	(9)[f]	1.4	2.3	1.7
Insurance	62[g]	0.1	0.5	0.4
Passenger commissions	(73)[h]	1.3	1.0	1.1
Communication	(19)[i]	0.9	1.0	0.9
Advertising and promotion	(45)[j]	0.8	0.6	0.6
Transport-related and other operating expenses	346	22.3	23.1	21.6

Notes:
[a]Compensation per employee;
[b]cost per gallon;
[c]per available seat mile;
[d]per revenue seat mile;
[e]per ton landed;
[f]per aircraft block hour;
[g]aircraft and non-aircraft;
[h]as % of passenger revenue;
[i]per enplanement;
[j]to 3rd quarter.
Source: Airlines for America, Cost Index for US Passenger Airlines.

Airline Cost Conditions

Labor and fuel costs were by far the biggest individual cost items (Table 5). A key feature of the industry's cost structure was the very high proportion of fixed costs. For example, because of union contracts, it was difficult to reduce employment and hours worked during downturns. The majors' need to maintain their route networks and flight schedules meant that planes flew even when occupancy was very low. The desire to retain the integrity of the entire network made the airlines reluctant to shed unprofitable routes during downturns. An important implication of the industry's cost structure was that, at times of excess capacity, the marginal costs of filling empty seats on scheduled flights was extremely low.

Labor   The industry's labor costs were boosted by high levels of employee remuneration: average pay in the scheduled airline sector was $55,640 in 2011 (a slight decline since 2007). In private sector employment as a whole, average remuneration was $38,300). Pilots, co-pilots, and flight engineers earned an average of $119,180; flight attendants $41,640.[7] Labor costs for the major network airlines were boosted by low labor productivity resulting from rigid working practices that were part of the employment contracts agreed with unions. Their employees belonged to one of a dozen major unions: the Association of Flight Attendants, the Air Line Pilots Association, and the International Association of Machinists and Aerospace Workers being the most important. Despite these unions' tradition of militancy and past success in negotiating pay increases well above the rate of inflation, since 2001 the precarious financial state of the airlines and the flexibility offered by Chapter 11 bankruptcy had enabled the airlines to impose pay restrictions and more flexible working practices.

Fuel   How much a carrier spent on fuel was dependent on the age of its aircraft and its average flight length. Newer planes and longer flights led to higher fuel efficiency. Fuel-efficiency considerations had encouraged plane manufacturers to develop long-distance, wide-body planes with two rather than four engines. Fuel represented the most volatile and unpredictable cost item for the airlines due to fluctuations in the price of crude oil. Between January 2002 and June 2008, New York spot crude prices rose from $19 to $140 a barrel before falling to $40 in December 2008. Oil prices were on a rising trend during 2009 and 2010, then during 2011 and the first five months of 2012 traded in a range between $80 and $110.

An airline's fuel costs also depended upon two other factors: the changing relationship between crude prices and jet fuel prices and the airlines' procurement strategies:

- During 2010 to 2012, the effects of high crude oil prices were exacerbated by a widening margin between the price of jet fuel and the price of crude. Historically, jet fuel had sold at a 15–20% premium over crude oil. During 2012, the margin widened to 33%.[8]
- High, volatile fuel prices encouraged the airlines to hedge using options and futures contracts and make forward contacts. The extent of hedging varied between airlines according to their expectations about the future direction of prices and whether they had the financial resources for hedging. In March 2012, hedging of 2012 fuel requirements varied from almost 100% (Southwest) to 0% (US Airways); United was at 32% JetBlue 27%.[9]

Delta Airlines took its fuel hedging one step further by becoming an active trader of jet fuel and crude oil. In 2011, it moved its jet fuel procurement unit into its treasury services department and hired oil traders from Wall Street, including Jon Ruggles from Merrill Lynch. However, its most audacious move was buying the 185,000 barrel/day Trainer oil refinery in Pennsylvania from ConocoPhillips for $180 million. Delta estimated that the purchase would allow it to cut $300 million annually from its $12 billion jet fuel bill. The refinery would be supplied with crude by BP, which would also exchange refined products from the refinery for jet fuel. As a result, the refinery would provide 80% of Delta's US fuel needs. In addition, it believed that its fuel-trading activities would benefit from having a physical product to trade and access to detailed information on production costs.[10]

Equipment Aircraft were the biggest capital expenditure item for the airlines. In 2012, with list prices for commercial jetliners ranging from $75 million for a Boeing 737 to $390 million for an Airbus A380, the purchase of new planes represented a major source of financial strain for the airlines. While Boeing and Airbus competed fiercely for new business (especially when their order book was low, as in 2002–2004), aggressive discounts and generous financing terms for the purchase of new planes disguised the fact that a major source of profits for the aircraft manufacturers was aftermarket sales. Over the past 20 years, the number of manufacturers of large jets declined from four to two. Lockheed ceased civilian jet manufacture in 1984; McDonnell Douglas was acquired by Boeing in 1997. The leading suppliers of regional jets were Bombardier of Canada and Embraer of Brazil. During 2005–2011, Boeing's return on equity averaged 36%.

Increasingly, airlines were leasing rather than purchasing planes. The world's two biggest aircraft owners were both leasing companies: GECAS (a subsidiary of General Electric) with 1,732 planes and ILFC (a subsidiary of AIG) with 1,031. The attraction of leasing was that, first, many US airlines lacked the financial resources to purchase planes and, second, their borrowing costs were higher than those of leasing from companies.[11]

Airport Facilities Airports play a critical role in the US aviation industry. They are hugely complex, expensive facilities and few in number. Only the largest cities are served by more than one airport. Despite the rapid, sustained growth in air transport since deregulation, Denver International Airport is the only major new airport to have been built since 1978. Most airports are owned by municipalities; they typically generate substantial revenue flows for the cities. Landing fees are set by contracts between the airport and the airlines and are typically based on aircraft weight. New York's La Guardia airport has the highest landing fees in the US, charging over $6,000 for a Boeing 747 to land. In 2011, the airlines paid over $2 billion to US airports in landing fees and a further $3 billion in passenger facility charges.

Four US airports—JFK and La Guardia in New York, Newark, and Washington's Reagan National—are officially "congested" and takeoffs and landings there are regulated by the government. At these airports, slots were allocated to individual airlines, who subsequently assumed de facto ownership and engaged in trading them. According to Jeff Breen of Cambridge Aviation Research, "Slots are a lot like baseball franchises. Once you have one, you have it for life."[12]

Cost Differences between Airlines One of the arguments for deregulation had been that there were few major economies of scale in air transport; hence large and small airlines could coexist. Subsequently, little evidence has emerged of large airlines gaining systematic cost advantages over their smaller rivals. However, there are economies associated with network density: the greater the number of routes within a region, the easier it is for an airline to gain economies of utilization of aircraft, crews, and passenger and maintenance facilities. In practice, cost differences between airlines are due more to managerial, institutional, and historical factors than to the influence of economies of scale, scope, or density. The industry's cost leader, Southwest, built its strategy and management systems around the goal of low costs. By offering services from minor airports, with limited customer service, a single type of airplane, job-sharing among employees, and salary levels substantially less than those paid by other major carriers, Southwest, Jet Blue, and other LCCs had the industry's lowest operating costs per available seat mile (ASM), despite flying relatively short routes. However, the gap has narrowed: in 2006, US Airways (traditionally the highest-cost airline) had cost per ASM that was double that of JetBlue; in 2011, the difference was tiny (Table 6).

Capacity utilization (load factor) is a key determinant of operating cost per ASM. Profitability depends on achieving breakeven levels of capacity operation. Operating below breakeven capacity means not only that fixed costs are spread over a smaller number of passengers but also that there are big incentives to cut prices in order to attract additional business. The industry's periodic price wars tended to occur during periods of slack demand and on routes where there were several competitors and considerable excess capacity. The industry's rising average load factor during 2011 and early 2012 was taken as a favorable indicator of moderating competitive pressures.

Achieving high load factors while avoiding ruinously low prices was a major preoccupation for the airlines. All the major airlines adopted *yield-management systems*—highly sophisticated computer models that combine capacity, purchasing data, and forecasts to continually adjust pricing. The goal is to maximize revenue for each flight.

Entry and Exit

Hopes by the deregulators that the US airline business would be a case study of competition in a "contestable market" were thwarted by two factors: significant barriers to both entry and exit and evidence that potential competition ("contestability") was no substitute for the real thing.[13] The capital requirements for setting up an airline can be low (a single leased plane will suffice), but offering a scheduled airline service requires setting up a whole system comprising gates, airline, and aircraft certification, takeoff and landing slots, baggage handling services, and the marketing and distribution of tickets. At several airports, the dominance of gates and landing slots by a few major carriers made entry into particular routes difficult and forced start-up airlines to use secondary airports. Despite the challenges of entry barriers and the dismal financial performance of the industry, airlines seemed to offer a strange attraction to entrepreneurs. The most recent major entrant was Richard Branson's Virgin America, which began service in August 2007. International airlines were also potential entrants into the US domestic market. The second stage of the US–EU Open Skies agreement lifted the 25% ownership limit on US airlines and offered greater potential for European airlines to offer services between US cities.

TABLE 6   Operating data for the larger airlines, 2006, 2008, and 2011

Airline	ASMs (billions)			Load factor (%)			Operating revenue per ASM (cents)			Operating expense per ASM (cents)		
	2006	2008	2011	2006	2008	2011	2006	2008	2011	2006	2008	2011
American	175.9	150.4	154.4	82.0	82.2	82.0	12.5	14.5	11.6	12.5	15.7	14.3
United[a]	139.8	123.2	219.4	82.1	81.3	82.8	13.1	14.9	11.8	13.1	16.2	13.2
Delta[b]	133.5	117.3	234.6	77.8	82.3	82.1	13.0	16.3	12.9	13.6	16.3	14.1
Southwest[c]	85.2	94.9	120.5	73.0	71.2	80.9	9.5	10.7	13.0	8.5	10.3	12.4
US Airways	83.9	68.3	72.6	77.6	81.8	83.7	15.7	16.8	11.7	15.2	19.2	13.1
JetBlue	23.8	29.7	8.5	82.5	80.5	81.4	7.6	10.5	10.6	7.5	10.2	11.7
Alaska	23.2	22.3	29.6	76.4	77.3	84.5	11.3	13.3	13.4	11.5	13.4	13.1

Notes:
[a]Merged with Continental in 2010.
[b]Merged with Northwest in 2010.
[c]Merged with AirTran in 2010.
Source: Bureau of Transportation Statistics; 10-K reports of companies.

A key factor intensifying competition in the industry has been the barriers to exit that prevent the orderly exit of companies and capacity from the industry. The tendency for loss-making airlines to continue in the industry for long periods can be attributed to two key exit barriers: first, contracts (especially with employees) give rise to large closure costs; second, Chapter 11 of the bankruptcy code allows insolvent companies to seek protection from their creditors (and from their existing contracts) and to continue to operate under supervision of the courts. A critical problem for otherwise financially healthy airlines was meeting competition from bankrupt airlines, which had the benefit of artificially lowered costs.

Looking to the Future

At the end of May 2012, the US airline industry presented a mixed picture. The financial picture remained dire—the total market capitalization of all quoted US airline companies was $30.1 billion—less than the market value of Starbucks, less than one-third of the market value of Facebook on the day of its initial public offering, and about one-half of that of the industry's major supplier, Boeing. The credit position was no better: with the sole exception of Southwest, all the US airlines had a "speculative" credit rating. Nor was there any clear sign of relief from crippling fuel prices.

Yet there were positives. As a result of consolidation and the efforts to remove excess capacity, the industry appeared to be on a better structural footing than it had been for decades. These improvements were reflected in the escalation of fares in recent years. In addition, the major network airlines had been successful in reducing their cost base through productivity improvements and reductions in compensation and benefits. As a result, the LCCs no longer had a substantial cost advantage. However, a key issue for the airlines was whether the beneficiaries from improvements in cost efficiency were the airlines' shareholders (through higher profits) or their customers (through lower fares).

The evidence of previous revivals in the industry suggested that they came to an end either as a result of external events or by the industry's own propensity to over-invest. In the case of the two previous upturns (1996–1999 and 2006–2008) external events were the critical factors (the September 11 terrorist attacks and the financial crisis of 2008). The eagerness of the airlines to order new planes suggested that the newfound financial prudence and capacity discipline might evaporate once the industry's fortunes improved.

Notes

1. Airlines for America, *Toward Global Competitiveness, Economic Empowerment and Sustained Profitability*, May 18, 2012, http://www.slideshare.net/a4amediarelations/a4-a-indy-review-12884873, accessed September 12, 2012.
2. John Rainey, Presentation to Bank of America Merrill Lynch Global Transportation Conference, May 17, 2012.
3. US Department of Transportation, Bureau of Transportation Statistics, 4th Quarter 2011 Airline Financial Data, May 17, 2012.
4. Abolition of the CAB meant that the primary responsibility for airline regulation was with the Federal Aviation Administration, which was responsible for airline safety.
5. Boeing Current Market Outlook, "Long-Term Market," http://active.boeing.com/commercial/forecast_data/index.cfm, accessed September 27, 2012.
6. "Business Travel Blues," *Washington Post*, March 17, 2009, http://www.washingtonpost.com/wp-dyn/content/article/2009/03/17/AR2009031701280.html, accessed October 20, 2009.
7. US Bureau of Labor Statistics, National Industry-Specific Occupational Employment and Wage Estimates for NAICS 481000, Air Transportation.
8. Airlines for America, *Toward Global Competitiveness, Economic Empowerment and Sustained Profitability*, May 18, 2012, http://www.slideshare.net/a4amediarelations/a4-a-indy-review-12884873, accessed September 12, 2012.
9. Bloomberg, "Jet Fuel Hedging Positions for U.S., Canadian Airlines," March 26, 2012. http://www.bloomberg.com/news/2012-03-26/jet-fuel-hedging-positions-for-u-s-canadian-airlines-table-.html, accessed September 12, 2012.
10. Reuters, "Delta buys refinery, becoming first airline to make own fuel," April 30, 2012, http://www.reuters.com/article/2012/05/01/delta-idUSL1E8FUED720120501, accessed September 12, 2012; "Delta ups the ante in war against Wall Street," *Fortune*, April 12, 2012.
11. "Aircraft leasing: Buy or rent?" *Economist*, January 21, 2012.
12. "Should Airlines Be Allowed to Trade Airport Slots?" *Tribune Media Services*, October 18, 2010, http://www.frommers.com/articles/7023.html, accessed September 11, 2012.
13. On the principles of contestability and its application to the US airline industry, see S. Martin, "The Theory of Contestable Markets," discussion paper, Department of Economics, Purdue University, July 2000.

Case 5   Ford and the World Automobile Industry in 2012

On April 1, 2012, Bob Shanks, Ford Motor Company's controller, was promoted to chief financial officer. One of Shanks' first tasks was to review the financial forecasts for 2012–2016 prepared by his predecessor, Lewis Booth.

Ford's turnaround since the crisis of 2007–2008 had been remarkable. After a loss of $14.7 billion in 2008, Ford earned net profits of $20.2 billion in 2011. The recovery had been much more rapid than anticipated: Ford's business plan of December 2008 projected breakeven in 2011.[1] Shanks attributed the turnaround to three factors: first, government measures in North America and Europe to stimulate demand through incentives for scrapping old cars and subsidies for purchasing new, fuel-efficient models; second, the recovery of demand in several major markets, including China, India, Brazil, and the US; third, Ford's own restructuring. The "One Ford" transformation plan introduced in 2006 had closed plants; cut employment from 295,000 to 164,000; divested Jaguar, Land Rover, and Volvo; cut ownership of Mazda from 33% to 3% integrated Ford's global activities; and accelerated product development—with an emphasis on small, fuel-efficient cars.

Despite these successes, Shanks was worried about Ford's ability to sustain its profitability. Shanks was convinced of the soundness of the One Ford strategy and the company's capacity to implement it. His concerns related primarily to the overall health of the global automobile industry.

The collapse in industry profitability in 2007–2009 and the bankruptcies of General Motors and Chrysler were not simply consequences of the financial crisis. They also reflected the massive structural problems of the industry—most notably, too many firms with too much capacity chasing too little demand. The catastrophic decline in industry revenues and profits in 2008 promised a major industry restructuring. Daimler's CEO had predicted that 2009 would be a "Darwinian year" for the auto industry. Yet, the industry's pre-crisis structure survived almost intact. The *Financial Times* commented:

> Instead of natural selection, something else happened: governments around the world, from Canada and Brazil to Russia and South Korea, stepped in with prodigious amounts of cash to keep car plants open and assembly lines running. All told, automakers have benefited from well in excess of $100 billion of direct bail-out funds or indirect state aid . . . the biggest ever short-term intervention in manufacturing . . . The money has prevented a necessary shake-out in an industry

This case was prepared by Robert M. Grant. ©2012 Robert M. Grant.

that has long had too many producers. Consultants at PwC estimate the industry has the capacity to build 86 million units this year, almost a record—and 31 million more than the 55 million vehicles that it will sell.[2]

Even before the financial crisis hit, the financial performance of the industry was dire: between 1990 and 2008 the world's five biggest automakers (GM, Toyota, Ford, Daimler-Chrysler, and Volkswagen) had earned on average a net margin of 1.1%, their return on invested capital had failed to cover their cost of capital, and together they had destroyed billions of dollars in shareholder value. However, despite the lack of exit or consolidation by the leading automakers, it was clear that the structure of the industry was far from remaining static. The shift of demand from the mature industrial nations to the growing markets of Asia, Eastern Europe, and Latin America was accompanied by the emergence of new competitors from these same regions. Meanwhile, new technologies and environmental concerns, including the growing use of all-electric vehicles, were redirecting the industry's development path. Understanding how these different forces would impact the overall profit potential of the world automobile industry would be a key determinant of Ford's financial performance in the coming years.

Development of the World Automobile Industry[3]

The Growth of Demand and Production

Vehicles powered by internal combustion appeared in Europe during the 1880s. Gottlieb Daimler and Karl Benz were among the first to build them. By the end of the 19th century, hundreds of small companies were producing automobiles both in Europe and in America.

During the 20th century, the industry followed different development paths in different parts of the world. The US auto industry grew rapidly during 1910–1928 and 1946–1965 before reaching market saturation (Figure 1 and Table 1). The automobile industries of Western Europe and Japan also experienced a maturing of their markets, with production peaking in 1989–1990. In all the advanced industrial countries, the increased longevity of cars dampened market demand (Figure 2).

FIGURE 1   US motor vehicle production, 1900–2011

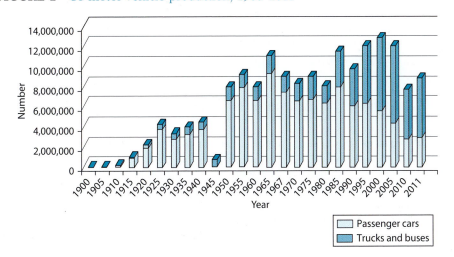

TABLE 1   World motor vehicle production by countries and regions (% of world total)[a]

	1960	1989	1994	2000	2005	2008	2010	2011
US	52.0	23.8	24.5	22.2	20.0	18.6	12.9	10.8
Western Europe	38.0	31.7	31.2	29.9	28.4	20.7	14.6	14.4
Central and E. Europe	2.0	4.8	4.3	4.6	5.4	9.5	7.7	8.0
Japan	1.0	18.2	21.2	17.7	17.0	16.7	12.6	10.5
Korea	n.a.	1.8	4.6	5.0	5.3	5.5	5.6	5.8
China	n.a.	n.a.	2.7	3.5	5.7	13.3	23.6	23.2
World total (millions)	12.8	49.5	50.0	57.4	66.8	69.4	76.1	80.1

Note:
[a] Motor vehicles include automobiles, trucks, and buses.
Source: Reproduced from *Ward's Automotive Yearbook, 2011*, edited by A. K. Binder with permission from Ward's Automotive Group.

FIGURE 2   Median age of passenger cars in the US

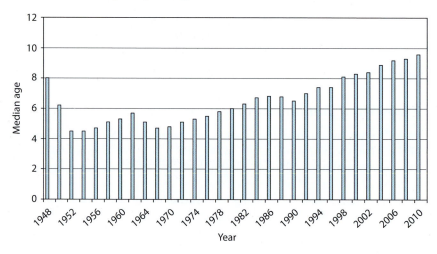

Source: R. L. Polk & Co.

Despite declining output in the advanced industrialized countries, the world automobile industry has continued to grow (Figure 3). This growth has been the result of growing output from the newly industrializing countries, notably Korea, China, Brazil, and India (see Table 1). As a result, the proportion of world output contributed by the traditional production centers—the US, Western Europe, and Japan—fell from 77% in 1994 to 40% in 2010 (Table 2).

The Evolution of the Automobile

The early years of the industry were characterized by considerable uncertainty over the design and technology of the motorcar. The first "horseless carriages" were precisely that: they followed design features of existing horse-drawn carriages and buggies. Soon, a bewildering variety of technologies were competing. The internal-combustion engine vied with steam-propulsion and electric motors. Transmission

FIGURE 3   World motor vehicle production (cars and trucks), 1985–2011

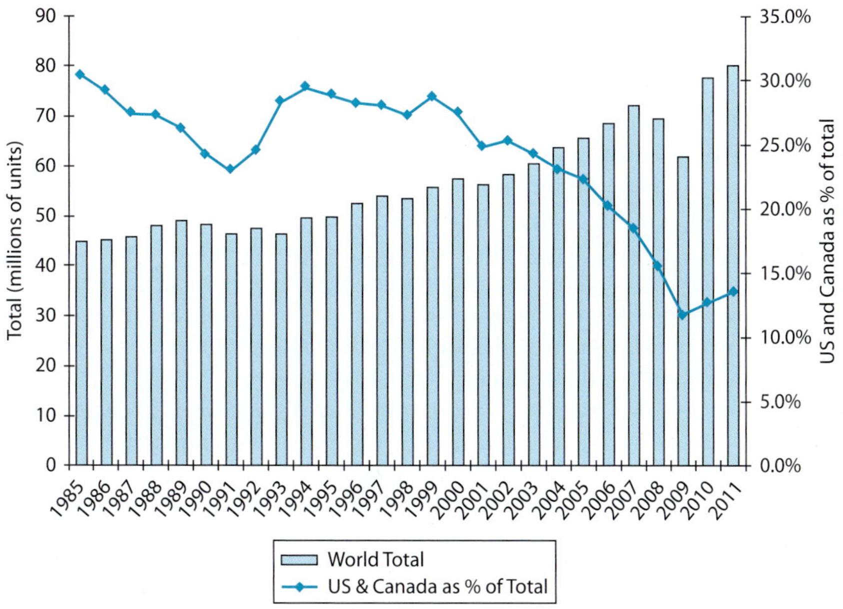

TABLE 2   Leading automobile-producing countries (thousands of cars; excludes trucks)

	1987	1990	1995	2000	2005	2010	2011
China	n.a.	n.a.	356	620	3,118	13,897	14,485
Japan	7,891	9,948	7,664	8,363	9,017	8,310	7,159
Germany	4,604	4,805	4,360	5,132	5,350	5,552	5,872
S. Korea	793	987	1,893	1,881	2,195	3,866	4,222
India	n.a.	n.a.	394	541	999	2,832	3,054
US[a]	7,099	6,077	6,338	5,542	4,321	2,731	2,966
Brazil	789	663	1,312	1,348	2,009	2,585	2,535
France	3,052	3,295	3,051	2,883	3,113	1,924	1,931
Spain	1,403	1,679	1,959	2,445	2,098	1,914	1,819
Russia[b]	1,329	1,260	834	967	1,288	1,208	1,738
Mexico	266	346	710	1,130	846	1,386	1,657
UK	1,143	1,296	1,532	1,641	1,596	1,270	1,344
Czech Rep.	n.a.	n.a.	193	428	599	1,070	1,192
Canada	810	1,072	1,339	1,551	1,356	967	990
Poland	301	256	260	533	527	785	740
Italy	1,701	1,874	1,422	1,442	726	573	486

Notes:

n.a.: not available.

[a]The production data for the US do not include the large volumes of pick-up trucks and SUVs produced by the automobile companies classed as trucks.

[b]USSR in 1987 and 1990.

Source: Reproduced from *Ward's Automotive Yearbook, 2011*, edited by A. K. Binder with permission from Ward's Automotive Group.

systems, steering systems, and brakes all displayed a remarkable range of technologies and designs.

Over the years, technologies and designs converged. The Ford Model T with its front-mounted, water-cooled, four-cylinder engine represented the first dominant design in automobiles. Convergence continued throughout the 20th century with the elimination of the most distinctively different technologies and designs. Air-cooled engines, such as those of the VW Beetle, disappeared along with Citroen's distinctive suspension systems. Power trains standardized around four cylinders, in-line engines, with V-6 and V-8 configurations for larger cars. Front-wheel drive became standard on smaller cars; suspension, steering, braking systems, and body shapes became more similar. Technological progress was incremental, comprising new materials, new safety features, multi-valve cylinders, and applications of electronics such as traction control systems, electronic fuel injection, variable suspension, satellite navigation systems, and intelligent monitoring systems.

Convergence also occurred across countries. The distinctive differences that once distinguished American, French, and Japanese cars largely disappeared, partly due to the manufacturers' promotion of global models. The same market segments are present in different countries, though the sizes of these segments vary greatly across countries. In the US, mid-size family sedans, SUVs, and pick-up trucks are the largest segments; in Europe and Asia, small family cars (subcompacts) form the largest market segment.

This trend toward design convergence and piecemeal innovation was interrupted by the introduction of electric cars. This was hardly a disruptive technology: the first electrically powered cars and buses were in use at the beginning of the 20th century. In 1900, 28% of all automobiles produced in the US were all electric. Their reintroduction was incremental: in 1997 both Toyota and Audi introduced mass-produced hybrid cars, 100 years after Ferdinand Porsche had developed the first hybrid car in which an internal combustion engine powered an electric motor. The launch of highway-capable, mass-produced, all-electric cars was much anticipated but long delayed, despite the well established markets for neighborhood electric vehicles (NEVs): golf carts, maintenance vehicles, and site-transport vehicles. At the beginning of 2012, all the leading vehicle manufacturers had all-electric models in development, but the only mass-marketed, all-electric, plug-in cars were the Nissan Leaf and the Mitsubishi i-MiEV.

Changes in Manufacturing Technology

At the beginning of the 20th century, car manufacture, like carriage-making, was a craft industry. Few companies produced more than a 1,000 automobiles annually. When Henry Ford began production in 1903, he used a similar approach. His vision of an affordable, mass-produced automobile required the development of more precise machine tools that would permit interchangeable parts. In 1913, he instituted his new system of production. Components were produced either in batches or continuously and were then assembled on moving assembly lines by semi-skilled workers. The productivity gains were enormous. In 1912, it took 23 hours to assemble a Model T; 14 months later, it took just four.

Toyota's *lean production* was the second major revolution in process technology. Toyota developed its system in postwar Japan, where shortages of key materials encouraged extreme parsimony and avoidance of inventories and waste. Lean production combined statistical process control, just-in-time scheduling, quality circles, teamwork, and flexible production (multiple models were manufactured on a single production line). During the 1980s and 1990s, all the world's car manufacturers redesigned their manufacturing processes to incorporate aspects of Toyota's lean production.

Flexible, lean plants reduced the importance of scale economies in assembly. Minimum efficient scale once required plants to produce at least 400,000 units a year After 1990, most new assembly plants had capacities of between 150,000 and 300,000 units per annum. However, scale economies remained important in components and subassemblies: the minimum efficient scale for an engine plant was around 1 million units annually.

New Product Development

The increasing complexity of new cars in terms of electronics, and new safety and environmental standards, caused the cost of developing new models to rise steeply. Taking an entirely new mass-production model from drawing board to production line typically costs between $2 billion and $6 billion. Ford's 2012 Focus marked a new step in the firm's globalization: a near identical global model would be produced at plants in the US, Germany, Thailand, and China. Small automakers had the choice of merging or forming alliances with bigger rivals, or seeking niche positions. Geographically focused manufacturers such as Tofas of Turkey and Proton of Malaysia licensed designs from the global automakers. The tiny Morgan Company survived by making the same handcrafted sports car that it had designed in the late 1930s. The quest to economize on new product development costs also encouraged a variety of strategic alliances and joint ventures among the automakers.

To economize on new product development costs, a major trend in the industry was to use a single *platform* for multiple models. A platform comprised a vehicle's architecture, including its floor pan, suspension system, and layout of engine, gearbox, and major components. While the major carmakers widened their model ranges, they increasingly based these around a few platforms, typically between four and six. Similarly with major components: in engines, Ford moved to three engine families: the V-8/V-10, the V-6, and the I-4 (four in-line cylinders). The I-4 engine had over 100 variations, an annual volume of 1.5 million, and was built at three different plants—one in North America, one in Europe, and one in Japan.

The World Auto Industry in 2012

The Manufacturers

The ranks of the leading producers were dominated by US, Japanese, and Western European companies, plus Hyundai of Korea (Table 3). All were multinational: Toyota, GM, and Ford each produced more vehicles outside their home countries than within. Relative to comparable industries—aircraft, motorcycles, or construction equipment—the auto industry remained fragmented. In 2011, there were 18 manufacturers with annual output exceeding one million vehicles and the three-firm concentration ratio (measured by units of production) was 31.5%. Despite many

TABLE 3 The world's leading auto producers (thousands of units)[a]

		1992	1996	2002	2005	2007	2010	2011
GM	US	6,764	8,176	8,326	9,200	9,350	8,476	9,026
Volkswagen	Germany	3,286	3,977	5,017	5,243	6,268	7,341	8,160
Toyota	Japan	4,249	4,794	6,626	7,974	8,534	8,557	7,900
Hyundai[b]	S. Korea	874	1,402	2,642	2,534	3,987	5,765	6,530
Ford	US	5,742	6,611	6,729	6,818	6,248	5,524	5,695
Nissan	Japan	2,963	2,712	2,719	3,569	3,770	4,214	4,834
SAIC Motor Group[c]	China	n.a.	n.a.	n.a.	n.a.	n.a.	3,580	3,641
Peugeot	France	2,437	1,975	3,262	3,375	3,457	3,603	3,549
Honda	Japan	1,762	2,021	2,988	3,391	3,912	3,643	3,137
Dongfeng Motor[c]	China	n.a.	n.a.	n.a.	—	—	2,615	n.a.
FAW[c]	China	n.a.	n.a.	n.a.	1,047	1,436	2,558	n.a.
Suzuki	Japan	888	1,387	1,704	2,630	2,596	2,893	2,802
Renault[d]	France	1,929	1,755	2,329	2,533	2,669	2,627	2,722
Daimler	Germany	605	993	4,456	4,829	4,635	1,940	2,111
Chrysler	US	2,476	2,958				1,578	1,855
Changan Auto[c]	China	n.a.	n.a.	n.a.	n.a.	n.a.	1,900	n.a.
Fiat	Italy	1,800	2,545	2,191	1,708	2,679	2,081	2,033
BMW	Germany	598	641	1,091	1,328	1,542	1,481	1,669
Mitsubishi	Japan	1,599	1,452	1,821	1,381	1,412	1,174	1,129
Mazda	Japan	1,248	984	1,044	1,149	1,287	1,100	1,016
Tata Motors	India	n.a.	n.a.	n.a.	n.a.	588	836	910
AvtoVAZ[c]	Russia	674	562	703	732	736	650	805
Fuji Heavy Industries	Japan	648	525	542	571	585	622	639
Daihatsu	Japan	610	691	n.a.	909	856	—[e]	—[e]

Notes:

n.a.: not available.

[a]For some companies the figures show total units produced; for others it shows total units sold.

[b]Includes Kia.

[c]Includes the entire output of the joint ventures in which the company is a partner.

[d]Includes Dacia and Samsung Motors.

[e]Included in Toyota.

Source: Company websites.

mergers and acquisitions (Table 4), the industry's consolidation was limited by the emergence of new competitors (from China and India especially). The crisis of 2008–2009 resulted in several divestments, but only one major merger: of Fiat and Chrysler.

Outsourcing and the Role of Suppliers

Henry Ford's system of mass production was supported by intensive backward integration. At Ford's giant River Rouge plant, iron ore entered at one end and Model Ts emerged at the other. Ford even owned rubber plantations in the Amazon basin. Since 1980, the quest for lower costs and increased flexibility has resulted in a massive outsourcing of materials, components, and services. At the end of the 1990s, GM and

TABLE 4   Mergers and acquisitions among automobile manufacturers, 1986–2011

Year	Acquirer	Target	Notes
2010	Geely (China)	Volvo (Sweden)	Sold by Ford for $1.3bn
	Spyker Cars (Netherlands)	Saab Auto (Sweden)	Sold by GM for $1bn
2009	Volkswagen (Germany)	Suzuki (Japan)	Acquires 20% stake
	Fiat (Italy)	Chrysler (US)	Acquires 35% stake, later increased to 58%
	Volkswagen	Porsche (Germany)	Acquires 49%
	Beijing Auto (China)	Fujian Motor; Changfeng Motor (China)	
2008	Tata (India)	Jaguar Cars, Land Rover (UK)	Sold by Ford
	SAIC Motor Group (China)	Nanjing Automobile (China)	SAIC combines MG and Rover brands
2005	Nanjing Automobile	Rover (UK)	
	Toyota (Japan)	Fuji Heavy Industries (Japan)	Acquired 8.7% stake from GM
2002	GM (US)	Daewoo (S. Korea)	42% of equity acquired
2000	Renault (France)	Samsung Motors (S. Korea)	70% of equity acquired
	GM	Fiat	20% of equity acquired
	DaimlerChrysler (Germany)	Hyundai (S. Korea)	10% of equity acquired
	DaimlerChrysler	Mitsubishi Motors (Japan)	34% of equity acquired
1999	Renault (France)	Nissan (Japan)	38.6% of equity acquired
	Ford (US)	Volvo	Acquires car business only
	Ford	Land Rover	Acquired from BMW
	Toyota	Daihatsu	51% stake acquired
1998	Daimler-Benz (Germany)	Chrysler	Biggest auto merger ever
	VW (Germany)	Rolls Royce Motors (UK)	Acquired from Vickers PLC
	Hyundai (S. Korea)	Kia (S. Korea)	
	Daewoo (S. Korea)	Ssangyong Motor (S. Korea)	
	Daewoo (S. Korea)	Samsung Motor (S. Korea)	
1997	Proton (Malaysia)	Lotus (UK)	
	BMW (Germany)	Rover (UK)	
1996	Daewoo (S. Korea)	FSO (Poland)	
	Daewoo (S. Korea)	FS Lublin (Poland)	
	Ford (US)	Mazda (Japan)	Increases stake from 25% to 33%
1995	Fiat (Italy)	FSM (Poland)	
1994	Daewoo (S. Korea)	Oltcit/Rodae (Romania)	
1991	Volkswagen	Skoda (Czech Rep.)	31% stake later increased to 100%
1990	GM	Saab-Scandia (Sweden)	50% of equity acquired
	Ford	Jaguar	
1987	Ford	Aston Martin (UK)	
	Chrysler	Lamborghini (Italy)	
1986	Volkswagen	Seat (Spain)	

Ford both spun off their component businesses as separate companies: Delphi and Visteon, respectively. Relationships with suppliers also changed. The Japanese model of close, collaborative, long-term relationships with their first-tier suppliers has displaced the US model of contract-based, arm's-length relationships. The new system has resulted in the component companies gaining increased responsibility for technological development, especially for sophisticated subassemblies such as transmissions, braking systems, and electrical and electronic equipment. The component producers have also grown in size and global reach. Bosch, Denso, Johnson Controls, and Delphi are as big as some of the larger automobile companies (Table 5).

TABLE 5 Revenues and profitability of the biggest automotive component suppliers

	Revenues ($billion)				ROA (%)	ROE (%)
	1994	**2000**	**2008**	**2011**	**2010–2011**	**2010–2011**
Robert Bosch (Germany)	19.6	29.1	58.5	67.3	5.2	8.8
DENSO Corp. (Japan)	11	18.2	40.3	37.7	4.4	5.0
Johnson Controls (US)	7.1	17.2	35.9	41.7	5.0	16.8
Aisin Seiki (Japan)	7.3	8.9	27.2	26.4	3.3	8.0
Magna International (Canada)	n.a.	10.5	28.2	24.1	5.4	14.2
TRW Automotive Holdings (US)	n.a.	n.a.	n.a.	16.2	10.2	37.0
Delphi Automotive (UK)	n.a.	29.1	18.1	13.8	8.9	21.6
Eaton (US)	4.4	8.3	15.4	13.7	6.6	15.3
Valeo (France)	3.8	8.9	11.4	14.1	4.9	25.5
Lear Corp (US)	3.1	14.1	13.6	14.2	6.6	17.8

Notes:
n.a.: not available.
ROA: Return on assets = net income/total assets.
ROE: Return on equity = net income/shareholders' equity.
Sources: *Financial Times, Fortune, Forbes* magazine.

The Quest for Cost Reduction

Strong competition pressured companies to seek cost reduction through several sources:

- *Economies of scale* were critically important in research, component production, and product development. According to Sergio Marchionne, the CEO of Fiat and Chrysler, efficiency for a global auto producer required producing at least five million cars a year: companies producing less would struggle to survive.[4]

- *Economies of scope*: Many cost economies could be exploited across different models. Investments in technology, dealerships, and marketing could be applied across all models. Indeed, the use of common components and platforms meant that economies of scope were often converted into economies of scale. By 2012, all the leading automakers had model ranges that covered almost every product segment from luxury cars to mini-cars, including SUVs. However, Ford had narrowed its product range by selling its Jaguar, Land Rover, and Volvo subsidiaries.

- *Worldwide outsourcing* has grown from individual components to major subassemblies (such as engines and steering systems), even to complete cars (including design and engineering). An important source of cost saving from outsourcing derives from component suppliers' lower wages and benefits compared to the auto assemblers.

- *Just-in-time scheduling*, a key element of lean production, permitted radical reductions in inventories and work-in-progress.

- *Off-shoring*: Geographical shifts in production were partly the result of automakers seeking lower-cost manufacturing locations. Toyota moved production from Japan to lower-cost locations in Southeast Asia; Volkswagen from Germany to central and eastern Europe.

- *Collaboration*: Collaborative arrangements included joint-venture plants, technology alliances, component supply agreements, and joint marketing agreements. In emerging-market countries, most new auto plants were joint ventures between local and overseas companies. These arrangements economized on the costs of developing new technologies and new products, and accessing overseas markets. Peugeot's alliance with GM, announced in February 2012, was indicative of the financial pressures being faced by medium-sized producers. The alliance would involve pooling R & D and purchasing, sharing vehicle platforms, and GM acquiring a 7% stake in Peugeot.

Despite constant cost cutting, the major automakers were unable to rival low-cost producers in China, India, and elsewhere. Tata Motors' 2009 launch of its Nano model—four-seater, 623cc city car, with fuel consumption of 70 miles per gallon and priced at a mere $2,200—was a major shock to the multinational automakers. However, the subsequent difficulties that the Nano encountered in terms of production, safety, and market acceptance point to the sheer complexity of bringing an innovative new model to market and the challenges facing emerging market automakers in rivaling the experience and expertise of the established giants.[5]

Excess Capacity

The greatest structural problem of the industry was excess capacity. Ever since the early 1980s, the growth of production capacity had outstripped the growth in the demand for cars. Import restrictions had exacerbated the problem. During the 1980s and early 1990s, North American production capacity grew substantially as a result of Japanese companies building greenfield "transplants." Further big additions to world production capacity resulted from the expansion of the Korean car industry during 1992–1997. Since 2000, the main additions to capacity were in Eastern Europe, Asia, and Latin America, where all the world's leading automakers rushed to build new plants to serve growing demand. The biggest overhangs of excess capacity were in North America and Europe (Table 6), but even in China, where demand grew by almost 50% annually between 2002 and 2011, growth of capacity outstripped growth of demand. Looking ahead,

TABLE 6   Automobile production capacity utilization

	2008	2009	2010	2011
North America	79%	44%	65%	69%
South America	82%	62%	76%	75%
Europe	82%	61%	70%	78%
Japan and Korea	86%	72%	78%	81%
Southern Asia	89%	83%	81%	82%

the prospects reducing excess capacity were limited by, first, the resistance of national governments to plant closures and, second, continuing investment in new plants in emerging-market countries: in China capacity utilization was forecast to fall to 66% by 2016 as new plants continued to be built despite slowing domestic demand. In 2012, VW announced it would build its seventh plant in China, while Ford announced its fifth.

Internationalization

International expansion was driven primarily by the automakers' desire to gain access to growing markets; to exploit scale economies in purchasing, technology, and new product development; and to seek low-cost manufacturing locations (Table 7). Although Ford and General Motors began their international expansion back in the 1920s, until the 1970s the world auto industry was made up of separate national markets where each national market was dominated by indigenous producers. The global strategies of the Japanese automakers changed all that. After 1980, the main strategic priority of all the world's major auto companies was to build global presence through acquisition, alliance, and joint venture. As a result of internationalization, the dominance of national champions was undermined (Table 8).

Outlook for the Future

As he reviewed the forces likely to impact the world automobile industry during the next five years, Shanks struggled to assess what the overall outcome of so many conflicting forces would be for industry profitability.

On the demand side, the outlook was quite favorable: most forecasts of worldwide automobile sales pointed to an annual growth of around 5% between 2012 and 2016, the only depressed market being Europe.

The key problems were on the supply side. Market growth would not translate into adequate profit margins if the chronic overhang of excess capacity remained.

TABLE 7   Hourly compensation for motor vehicle workers (US$/hour, including benefits)

	1975	1984	1994	2004	2006	2010[a]
Germany	7.9	11.9	34.7	44.0	45.9	43.8
US	9.6	19.0	27.0	33.9	35.1	34.7
UK	4.1	7.4	16.0	29.4	30.0	29.4
France	5.1	8.2	18.8	26.3	29.4	40.6
Japan	3.6	7.9	25.9	27.4	27.8	32.0
Spain	3.7	5.3	15.4	21.5	24.2	26.6
S. Korea	0.5	1.7	7.8	15.8	19.0	16.6
Italy	5.2	8.0	16.3	21.7	18.6	33.4
Mexico	2.9	2.6	3.0	3.5	3.7	6.2

Note:
[a]The 2010 data relate to all manufacturing industry; the data for earlier years refer to motor vehicle manufacture only.
Source: US Department of Labor, Bureau of Labor Statistics.

TABLE 8 Automobile market shares in individual countries (%)

	1988	2006	2010
US[a]			
GM	36.3	23.5	19.1
Ford	21.7	16.7	16.5
Chrysler	11.3	8.8	9.3
Toyota	6.9	13.9	15.3
Honda	6.2	8.8	10.7
FRANCE			
Renault	29.1	24.8	22.1
Peugeot	34.2	28.2	32.4
VW	9.2	11.6	11.0
Ford	7.1	6.0	5.1
ITALY			
Fiat	59.9	28.5	30.1
VW/Audi	11.7	10.8	11.6
Ford	3.7	7.8	9.1
Peugeot	n.a.	9.6	10.3
Renault	7.1	6.4	5.2
GERMANY			
VW/Audi	28.3	27.8	n.a.
GM (Opel)	16.1	9.7	n.a.
Ford	10.1	8.0	n.a.
Daimler	9.2	11.3	n.a.
UK			
Ford	26.3	18.5	15.8
GM (Vauxhall)	13.7	12.7	12.8
Peugeot	8.7	10.0	8.8
VW/Audi	5.9	12.9	16.0
BMW (and Rover)	15.0	4.6	6.9
JAPAN			
Toyota	43.9	40.4	34.4
Nissan	23.2	14.0	12.8
Honda	10.8	12.2	14.2
Suzuki	n.a.	12.1	11.4
KOREA			
Hyundai	55.9	50.0	37.6
Kia	25.0	23.3	28.2
Daewoo	19.1	10.0	22.7
CHINA			
Shanghai GM	n.a.	n.a.	10.4
Shanghai VW	n.a.	n.a.	9.7
FAW Volkswagen	n.a.	n.a.	8.9
Beijing Hyundai	n.a.	n.a.	6.1
Dongfeng PSA	n.a.	n.a.	6.0
BYD	n.a.	n.a.	5.5
Chery	n.a.	n.a.	5.1

Notes:
[a]The market share data are for passenger cars only with the exception of the US, which is for cars and light trucks.
n.a.: not available.
Sources: Japan Automobile Manufacturers Association; Korean Automobile Manufacturers Association; A. K. Binder (ed.), *Ward's Automotive Yearbook*, Wards Communications, Southfield, MI, various years.

In the mature markets, there seemed little prospect that plant closures would eliminate the overhang of excess capacity. In the newly industrializing countries, especially Asia and Latin America where Ford had pinned most of its hopes, the indications were that capacity expansion would outstrip sales growth.

Not only had the financial crisis of 2008–2009 failed to result in the wave of mergers and acquisitions among automakers that many had predicted, but also a host of new players was appearing on the global stage. It was clear that the ambitions of Chinese and Indian auto manufacturers extended well beyond their national borders.

Looking further ahead, Shanks saw the possibility for technological and environmental factors to force a major upheaval in the auto industry's development path. The introduction of all-electric cars, while offering the prospects for new demand, might also be an opportunity for newcomers to muscle in on the market domains of the major automakers. Despite the tiny market share of hybrid and all-electric vehicles, environmental concerns, environmental regulation, and depleting oil reserves point to their potential to displace conventional automobiles. Despite heavy investments by most of the leading car makers in both hybrid and all-electric autos, leaders in electrical vehicles include Magna International (the Canadian auto parts producer), Tesla (a Californian producer of luxury electrical cars), Smiths Electrical (a leader in electrically powered trucks), BYD Auto (the leading Chinese producer of hybrid and electric cars), and Think Global (a Norwegian producer of electric cars owned by the Russian firm Electric Mobility Solutions).

Amidst the various factors which promised increased competition and intensified price-cutting, there were also some rays of light. Historically, small cars had been loss-making for the major manufacturers. That seemed to be changing: the success of the BMW Mini and the Fiat Cinquecento pointed to the willingness of consumers to pay premium prices for small cars that combined fuel economy, safety, and attractive design. Ford's Focus model embodied a stronger orientation to design features . . . and a higher price. Mass customization to make cars reflect the preferences and personalities of their owners offered a further route to increased product differentiation.

Appendix: Company Sales and Profitability, 1980–2011

COMPANY SALES ($billion)

	1980–1984[a]	1985–1989[a]	1990–1994[a]	1995–1999[a]	2000–2004[a]	2005–2009[a]	2010	2011
Toyota	18	42	82	107	125	205	229	205[c]
VW	16	28	48	64	96	143	168	214
GM	68	110	128	169	186	167	135	150
Ford	42	77	96	149	166	155	129	136
Daimler[b]	12	34	59	71	166	153	129	143
Honda	8	18	35	50	62	94	104	108
Nissan	16	26	51	57	58	90	102	106
Hyundai Motor	n.a.	n.a.	n.a.	18	38	70	97	68
BMW	5	10	21	34	45	70	80	92
Peugeot	13	19	28	35	58	73	74	78
Mitsubishi	12	14	25	32	27	43	61	23
Renault	15	31	31	37	44	52	52	57
Fiat	18	27	42	50	59	72	47	48
Mazda	n.a.	12	21	18	19	27	27	28

Notes:
[a]Annual average.
[b]Daimler-Chrysler 2000–2006.
[c]Estimated.
n.a.: not available.
Source: Companies' financial statements; Hoovers.

COMPANY PROFITABILITY (Return on Equity, %)

	1980–1984[a]	1985–1989[a]	1990–1994[a]	1995–1999[a]	2000–2004[a]	2005–2009[a]	2010	2011
Toyota	12.6	10.6	6.1	6.8	10.1	7.0	4.8	2.7
VW	1.6	6.3	(0.4)	11.1	6.8	5.5	25.0	26.8
GM[b]	11.4	11.8	3.2	27.5	11.7	(10.5)	17.1	24.1
Ford	0.4	21.8	5.9	35.4	(7.7)	(10.4)	122.6[c]	819.9[c]
Daimler	24.3	18.3	6.9	22.1	7.7	4.8	14.9	14.3
Honda	18.1	11.8	5.3	15.1	13.2	8.0	6.6	4.5
Nissan	10.3	4.7	3.6	(0.1)	29.3	7.4	10.3	10.8
Hyundai Motor	n.a.	n.a.	n.a.	4.4	10.6	12.0	20.0	18.2
BMW	14.8	10.4	9.7	(4.0)	15.4	10.8	22.1	18.1
Peugeot	(15.2)	36.7	12.5	3.0	13.4	(1.4)	9.1	4.1
Mitsubishi	10.0	7.9	4.8	(5.3)	(113.3)	(12.7)	6.5	9.0
Renault	(152.4)	51.1	9.1	11.0	14.7	14.4	18.3	8.7
Fiat	10.9	18.7	6.8	7.6	(24.2)	9.9	15.2	4.5
Mazda	n.a.	4.8	5.0	6.3	(34.2)	9.6	(18.4)	(13.9)

Notes:
[a]Annual average.
[b]GM made a net loss of $2 billion in 2006, $39 billion in 2007, and $31 billion in 2008.
[c]Ford's ROE is inflated in 2010 and 2011 by its very small equity base: in 2011, equity represent 4% of capital employed.
n.a.: not available.
Figures in parentheses denote a loss.
Source: Companies' financial statements; Hoovers.

Notes

1. Ford Motor Company, business plan submitted to the Senate Banking Committee, December 2, 2008.
2. "U.S. Car Industry: Back on the Road," *Financial Times*, June 17, 2009.
3. Automobiles (passenger motor cars) that are used to transport people are normally distinguished from commercial vehicles (trucks), which are used to transport goods. However, in the US, sport-utility vehicles (SUVs) and pick-up trucks (classed as light trucks) are used primarily for personal transportation. Ideally, we would like to define the automobile industry as comprising automobiles and light trucks (small vans, pick-up trucks, SUVs, passenger vans), but excluding heavy trucks and large buses. However, most of the statistics we use say that "automobiles" exclude light trucks while "motor vehicles" comprise automobiles and all trucks and buses.
4. "Fiat's Marchionne sees auto-industry consolidation," *MarketWatch*, September 9, 2011, http://www.market watch.com/story/fiats-marchionne-sees-auto-industry-consolidation-2011-09-09, accessed September 12, 2012.
5. "Tata's Nano: Stuck in low gear," *Economist*, August 20, 2011.

A video clip relating to this case is available in your interactive e-book at **www.wileyopenpage.com**

Case 6 Wal-Mart Stores Inc., June 2012

If you don't want to work weekends, you shouldn't be in retail.

—SAM WALTON (EXPLAINING THE SATURDAY CORPORATE MEETING)

Wal-Mart's shareholders' meeting on Friday June 1, 2012 was to have been the culmination of the company's 50th anniversary celebrations—50 years previously, founder Sam Walton had opened his first store in Rogers, Arkansas. About 6,000 shareholders and employees (including 2,000 from Wal-Mart's international operations) gathered at the University of Arkansas's Bud Walton Arena to be hosted by Chairman Rob Walton (son of the founder) and entertained by Justin Timberlake, Lionel Ritchie, Juanes, and Celine Dion.

Despite the massive build-up to the meeting, *Forbes* described it as "a gloomy affair."[1] The "one big happy family" festive atmosphere typical of Wal-Mart events had been overshadowed by disquiet over the Mexican bribery scandal that had erupted in April 2012 concerning payments by Wal-Mart Mexico to local officials to facilitate the issue of building permits for new Wal-Mart stores, Wal-Mart's initial attempt to cover-up the incident only exacerbated the problem.

Yet, despite the mood of disappointment and suspicion that had affected Wal-Mart's relations with employees and investors alike, the business was in rude health. On May 17, Wal-Mart had reported results for the first quarter of its financial year. Sales were up 8.6% on the previous year, operating income was up 8.3%, and return on equity for the 12-month period was 18.1%. The day before the shareholders' meeting, Wal-Mart's stock hit an all-time high.

For all of Wal-Mart's huge size—with 2.2 million employees, it was the world's biggest private-sector employer and was second only to ExxonMobil in terms of sales—a constant theme of the chairman, Rob Walton, and the CEO, Mike Duke, was Wal-Mart's continuity with its roots: continuity as a family-owned company, continuity of its low-price strategy, and continuity of its small-town values. Yet, for all this emphasis on Wal-Mart's timeless character, it was clear to Duke that times were changing for Wal-Mart.

As Wal-Mart continually expanded its range of goods and services—into groceries, fashion clothing, music downloads, online prescription drugs, financial services, and health clinics—so it was forced to compete on a broader front. While Wal-Mart

This case was prepared by Robert M. Grant. ©2012 Robert M. Grant.

could seldom be beaten on price, it faced competitors that were more stylish (T. J. Maxx), more quality-focused (Whole Foods), more service-oriented (Lowe's, Best Buy), and more focused in terms of product range. In its traditional area of discount retailing, Target was proving an increasingly formidable competitor. In warehouse clubs, its Sam's Clubs ran a poor second to Costco.

Increasing size boosted Wal-Mart's buying power but it also brought problems. Wal-Mart's success had rested heavily upon its ability to combine huge size with remarkable speed and responsiveness. Critical to this was its short chain of command and close relationship between the top management team and individual store managers. A key component in this linkage had been Wal-Mart's Saturday-morning meeting at its Bentonville HQ. In January 2008, the growing size of the meeting and increasing difficulty of getting all Wal-Mart executives back to Bentonville resulted in the company changing these meetings, which the company had described as "the pulse of our culture," from weekly to monthly.[2]

Increased size also made Wal-Mart a bigger target for opponents. For years Wal-Mart had been under attack by organized labor seeking to unionize Wal-Mart's two million employees. More recently, "The Beast of Bentonville" had attracted the ire of environmentalists, anti-globalization activists, women's and children's rights advocates, small-business representatives, and a growing number of legislators of varying political hues. In response, Wal-Mart had become increasingly image-conscious and was a late but enthusiastic convert to social and environmental responsibility. The result was a series of senior appointments to new executive positions—a head of global ethics and a new executive vice president of government relations—plus more top management time spent in Washington and with the media.

Wal-Mart's growing geographical scope also raised complex strategic and organizational issues. Unlike other successful global retailers (such as IKEA), Wal-Mart did not have a consistent approach to different national markets: It had different strategies and operated under different names in different countries. Moreover, its success varied greatly from country to country. While most of Wal-Mart's growth was outside of the US, its international business was significantly less profitable than that of the US. Wal-Mart's transformation into a multinational corporation presented a challenge for its identity and culture, both of which were firmly rooted in its southwestern US, small-town heartland.

In his address to the 2012 shareholders' meeting, Mike Duke focused almost exclusively on Wal-Mart's culture and values:

> If we look back on our success over the past 50 years and ask the simple question: "Why Wal-Mart and not another retailer?" I believe there's a simple answer. It's the culture, it's the beliefs, and it's the enduring values that live within us and are expressed through our actions every day. No matter who we are or where we come from, our values pull us together and keep us together. They constantly push us forward to become a better and stronger company. This is my message to you today: The values that built Wal-Mart, defined Wal-Mart, and sustained Wal-Mart for the past 50 years will drive our success and make us proud for the next 50 years . . .
>
> But we cannot slow down. We have to accelerate — pushing, leading, experimenting, innovating. It's not enough just to keep up. We have to stay out in front. And as we do that, we must continue to hold tight to the values that have always made us special. I believe what we believe will only become more important in the complex and rapidly changing world ahead.

We all know our three basic beliefs: respect for the individual, service to our customers, striving for excellence. These are the pillars of our culture. But there's a foundation on which they stand. It's made up of enduring values that we all share, that truly make us special, that connect us all at a human level.[3]

Duke went on to articulate five core values which he identified as the bedrock of Wal-Mart's success:

- *Integrity:* the basis of trust and exemplified by Sam Walton;
- *Opportunity:* "If you work hard, develop your skills, and do a good job, you can advance at Wal-Mart . . . nearly 75% of the store management team started as hourly associates."
- *Family and community:* "We aren't just associates and customers in our stores. We're people who grew up together, worship together, and live on the same streets. We're friends and neighbors. At Wal-Mart, we are family and community."
- *Work with a purpose:* "Our purpose is helping our customers save money so they can live better . . . At Wal-Mart, you better believe our work adds up to better lives and a better world."
- *Responsibility:* "When you're given so much, you have a responsibility to give back and do good. Wal-Mart is making food healthier, our planet greener, and the communities we work in and live in stronger. We're making a difference—a big, big difference."

These values would provide the basis for Wal-Mart's future success:

We can't possibly envision what the world, what retailing, what Wal-Mart will look like in another 50 years. But if we stay true to the foundation that Sam Walton built, we'll continue to be a better company, a stronger company and a prouder company. And over the next 50 years, there will be no limit to the good we can do around the world. We'll help millions more customers do what they aspire to do for themselves and their families—to save money and live better.[4]

History of Wal-Mart

Between 1945 and 1961, Sam Walton and his brother, Bud, developed a chain of 15 Ben Franklin franchised variety stores across rural Arkansas. At this time, the first discount retailers (large-format stores offering a broad range of products) were appearing in large towns (it was believed that a population of 100,000 was necessary to support a discount store). Sam Walton believed that, if the prices were right, discount stores could be viable in smaller communities: "Our strategy was to put good-sized stores into little one-horse towns that everyone else was ignoring."[5] The first Wal-Mart opened in 1962; by 1970 there were 30 Wal-Mart stores in small and medium-sized towns in Arkansas, Oklahoma, and Missouri.

Distribution was a problem for Wal-Mart:

Here we were in the boondocks, so we didn't have distributors falling over themselves to serve us like our competitors in larger towns. Our only alternative was to build our own distribution centers so that we could buy in volume at attractive prices and store the merchandise.[6]

In 1970, Walton built his first distribution center, and in the same year took the company public in order to finance the heavy investment incurred. Replicating this structure of large distribution hubs serving up to 100 discount stores formed the basis of Wal-Mart's expansion strategy. By 1980, Wal-Mart had 330 stores across the South and into the Midwest. By 1995, Wal-Mart was in all 50 states. Geographical expansion was incremental. In developing a new area, Wal-Mart built a few stores that were served initially by extending distribution from a nearby cluster. When a critical mass of stores had been established, Wal-Mart would build a new distribution center. As Wal-Mart became a national retail chain, so it entered more developed retailing areas, including larger cities, where it met stronger competition from other discount chains. In its early days, the local Wal-Mart was the only discount store in town—by 1993, 55% of Wal-Mart stores faced direct competition from Kmart and 23% from Target.[7]

Different Store Formats

Wal-Mart experimented continually with alternative retail formats. Some, like Helen's Arts and Crafts and Dot Deep Discount Drugstores, were unsuccessful. Others—Sam's warehouse clubs, Supercenters, and Neighborhood Markets—grew rapidly:

- Sam's warehouse clubs were not retail outlets: they required membership and were not open to the public. They carried a limited range of products with most items offered in multipacks and catering-size packs, and customer service was minimal. The business model was to maximize economies in purchasing, minimize operating costs, and offer members very low prices. Supercenters were Wal-Mart's large-format stores (averaging a floor space of 187,000 square feet, compared with 102,000 square feet for a Wal-Mart discount store and 129,000 square feet for a Sam's Club).
- Supercenters were modeled on the European concept of the hypermarket that had been pioneered by the French retailer Carrefour. A Supercenter combined a discount store with a grocery supermarket: in addition, a Supercenter incorporated specialty units such as an eyeglass store, hair salon, dry cleaners, and photo lab. They were open 24 hours a day, seven days a week.
- Neighborhood Markets were supermarkets with an average floor space of 42,000 square feet.
- Wal-Mart also built a substantial online business through its websites www.walmart.com and www.samsclub.com. Its online presence was extended through its online pharmacy and music download service.

International Expansion

Wal-Mart's international expansion abroad began in 1992 when it established a joint venture with Mexico's largest retailer, Cifra SA and opened discount stores and Sam's Clubs in several Mexican cities. By 1998, Wal-Mart had entered Europe, Asia, and South America. Table 1 summarizes Wal-Mart's international development.

TABLE 1   Wal-Mart stores by country, January 2012

Country	Stores	Notes
US	4,479	Included 3,029 Supercenters, 629 discount stores, 611 Sam's Clubs, 196 Supermarkets, and 14 small formats
Mexico	2,088	In 1991 formed JV with Cifra. Chains include Wal-Mart, Bodegas, Suburbia, VIPS, and Mercamas. In 2000, Wal-Mart acquired 51% of Cifra and took control of the joint venture. By 2003, Wal-Mart Mexico was the country's biggest retailer.
Canada	333	Entered in 1994 by acquiring 120 Woolco stores from Woolworth and converting them to Wal-Mart discount stores.
Argentina	88	Entered 1995: greenfield venture
Brazil	512	Entered 1995: JV with Lojas Americana. Includes Todo Dia, Bompreço, and Sonae stores
China	377	In 1996 built a Wal-Mart Supercenter and Sam's Club in Shenzen. Continued to grow organically, then in 2006 acquired Trust-Mart with its 102 stores
UK	541	Entered 1999 by acquiring Asda. Operates Wal-Mart superstores, and Asda supermarkets and discount stores
Japan	419	Entered 2002: acquired 38% of Seiyu; 2008 Seiyu became a wholly owned subsidiary of Wal-Mart. Mainly small stores but some superstores
Costa Rica	200	Acquired 30% of CARHCO, a subsidiary of Royal Ahold in 2005. Shareholding later increased to 51%.
El Salvador	79	
Guatemala	200	
Honduras	70	
Nicaragua	73	
Chile	316	Entered January 2009 by acquiring Distribución y Servicio SA
India	15	Entered May 2009; JV with Bharti Enterprises
Africa	347	Entered 2011 by acquiring 51% of Massmart Holdings Ltd; 305 stores in South Africa, also stores in Botswana, Ghana, Lesotho, Malawi, Mozambique, Namibia, Nigeria, Swaziland, Tanzania, Uganda, and Zambia
Total	10,130	

Source: www.walmartstores.com.

Wal-Mart's overseas expansion followed no standard pattern: sometimes it entered through greenfield entry, sometimes through joint venture, in some countries it acquired an existing retailer. Its most successful overseas operations were in the adjacent countries of Mexico and Canada. The UK and China were also major markets for Wal-Mart. In several countries Wal-Mart had struggled to establish itself. In Germany, Wal-Mart sold its 85 stores to Metro after eight years of losses. Wal-Mart withdrew from South Korea in 2006. In Japan, its Seiyu chain has been a consistent loss maker.[8]

Faced with market saturation in the US, China's vast market potential became increasingly attractive to Wal-Mart's top management. Yet, growing its presence in such a complex and highly politicized market presented major challenges for Wal-Mart. In 2011, Wal-Mart became a target for the now-deposed, populist party leader Bo Xilai. In Mr Bo's regional stronghold, Chongqing, 13 Wal-Mart stores were closed for two months after mislabeling ordinary pork as organic. In 2012, Wal-Mart was forced to slow its pace of expansion in China because of the difficulty of finding suitable sites for its big-box, single-floor stores.[9]

The biggest challenge for Wal-Mart's international expansion was the need to adapt its retailing system to the specific circumstances of each country it entered. Each country was distinguished by differences in consumer habits and preferences, infrastructure, the competitive situation, and the political and regulatory environment. One indicator of the diversity of Wal-Mart's retail environments was the great variety in its store formats outside the US—ranging from 5,000 sq. ft. Mexican *bodegas* to the 31,000,000 sq. ft. Sam's Club in Shanghai.

The most striking feature of Wal-Mart's performance in overseas markets was its inconsistency: from outstanding success (Mexico) to dismal failure (Germany). Its strongest performance was in adjacent countries (Mexico and Canada).

Sam Walton

Wal-Mart's strategy and management style was inseparable from the philosophy and values of its founder. Until his death in 1992, Sam Walton was the embodiment of Wal-Mart's unique approach to retailing. After his death, Sam Walton's beliefs and business principles continued to be the beacon that guided Wal-Mart's identity and its development.

For Sam Walton, thrift and value for money were a religion. Undercutting competitors' prices was an obsession that drove his unending quest for cost economies. Walton established a culture in which every item of expenditure was questioned. Was it necessary? Could it be done cheaper? He set an example that few of his senior colleagues could match: he walked rather than took taxis, shared rooms at budget motels while on business trips, and avoided any corporate trappings or manifestations of opulence or success. For Walton, wealth was a threat and an embarrassment rather than a reward and a privilege. His own lifestyle gave little indication that he was America's richest person (before being eclipsed by Bill Gates). He was equally disdainful of the display of wealth by colleagues: "We've had lots of millionaires in our ranks. And it drives me crazy when they flaunt it. Every now and then somebody will do something especially showy, and I don't hesitate to rant and rave about it at the Saturday morning meeting. I don't think that big mansions and flashy cars is what the Wal-Mart culture is supposed to be about."[10]

His attention to detail was legendary. As chairman and chief executive, he was quite clear that his priorities lay with his employees ("associates"), customers, and the operational details through which the former created value for the latter. He shunned offices in favor of spending time in his stores. Most of his life was spent on the road (or in the air, piloting his own plane) making impromptu visits to stores and distribution centers. He collected information on which products were selling well in Tuscaloosa; why margins were down in Santa Maria; how a new display system for children's clothing in Carbondale had boosted sales by 15%. His passion for detail extended to competitors' stores as well as his own: as well as visiting their stores, he was known to count cars in their parking lots.

Central to his leadership role at Wal-Mart was his relationship with his employees, the Wal-Mart associates. In an industry known for low pay and hard working conditions, Walton created a unique spirit of motivation and involvement. He believed fervently in giving people responsibility, trusting them, but also continually monitoring their performance.

After his death in 1992, Sam Walton's habits and utterances became enshrined in operating principles. For example, Wal-Mart's "10-foot attitude" pledge is based on Sam Walton's request to a store employee that: "I want you to promise that whenever you come within 10 feet of a customer, you will look him in the eye, greet him and ask if you can help him."[11] The "Sundown Rule"—that every request, no matter how big or small, gets same-day service—has become the basis for Wal-Mart's fast-response management system. "Three Basic Beliefs" became the foundation for Wal-Mart's corporate culture. These beliefs comprised:

- *Service to our customers*: "Every associate—from our CEO to our hourly associates in local stores—is reminded daily that our customers are why we're here. We do our best every day to provide the greatest possible level of service to everyone we come in contact with."
- *Respect for the individual*: associates, customers, and members of the community involved valuing and recognizing the contributions of colleagues, owning "what we do with a sense of urgency" and empowering "each other to do the same," and communicating by "listening to all associates and sharing ideas and information."
- *Striving for excellence*: this comprised innovating by continuous improvement and trying new ways of doing things, pursuing high expectations, and working as a team by "helping each other and asking for help."[12]

Sam Walton's ability to attract the affection and loyalty of both employees and customers owed much to his ability to generate excitement within the otherwise sterile world of discount retailing. He engendered a positive attitude among Wal-Mart employees and he reveled in his role as company cheerleader. Wal-Mart's replacement of its mission slogan, "Everyday Low Prices" by "Save Money, Live Better" was intended to reflect Walton's insistence that Wal-Mart played a vital role in the happiness and well-being of ordinary people.

Wal-Mart in 2012

The Business

Wal-Mart describes its business as follows:

> Wal-Mart Stores, Inc. operates retail stores in various formats around the world and is committed to saving people money so they can live better. We earn the trust of our customers every day by providing a broad assortment of quality merchandise and services at everyday low prices ("EDLP") while fostering a culture that rewards and embraces mutual respect, integrity and diversity. EDLP is our pricing philosophy under which we price items at a low price everyday so our customers trust that our prices will not change under frequent promotional activity . . . During the fiscal year ended January 31, 2012, we generated net sales of approximately $443.9 billion.
>
> Currently, our operations comprise three reportable business segments: the Walmart US segment; the Walmart International segment; and the Sam's Club segment.
>
> - Our Walmart US segment is the largest segment of our business, accounting for approximately 60% of our fiscal 2012 net sales and operates retail stores in various formats in all 50 states in the US and Puerto Rico, as well as Walmart's online retail operations, walmart.com.

TABLE 2 Wal-Mart: Performance by segment (year ending January 31)

	2002	2003	2004	2005	2006	2007	2008	2009	2010	2011	2012
Sales ($billion)											
Wal-Mart Stores	139.1	157.1	174.2	191.8	209.9	226.3	239.5	255.7	259.9	260.3	264.2
Sam's Clubs	29.4	31.7	34.5	37.1	39.8	41.6	44.4	46.9	47.8	49.4	53.7
International	35.5	40.8	47.6	56.3	62.7	77.1	90.6	98.6	97.4	109.2	125.9
Sales increase (%)											
Wal-Mart Stores	14.1	12.9	10.9	10.1	9.4	7.8	5.8	6.8	1.6	0.1	1.5
Sam's Clubs	9.7	7.8	8.8	7.5	7.3	4.5	6.7	5.6	1.9	3.5	8.8
International	10.6	14.9	16.7	18.3	11.4	30.2	17.5	9.1	(1.2)	12.1	15.2
Operating income ($billion)											
Wal-Mart Stores	10.3	11.8	12.9	14.2	15.3	16.6	17.5	18.8	19.3	19.9	20.3
Sam's Clubs	1.0	1.0	1.1	1.3	1.4	1.5	1.6	1.6	1.5	1.7	1.8
International	1.5	2.0	2.4	3.0	3.3	4.3	4.8	4.9	4.9	5.6	6.2
Operating income/sales (%)											
Wal-Mart Stores	7.4	7.5	7.4	7.4	7.3	7.3	7.3	7.3	7.4	7.6	7.7
Sam's Clubs	3.5	3.2	3.3	3.5	3.5	3.6	3.6	3.4	3.1	3.4	3.4
International	4.1	4.9	5.0	5.3	5.3	5.5	5.2	5.0	4.5	5.1	4.9

Source: Wal-Mart Stores, Inc., 10-K reports.

- Our Walmart International segment consists of retail operations in 26 countries. This segment generated approximately 28% of our fiscal 2012 net sales. The Walmart International segment includes numerous formats of retail stores, restaurants, Sam's Clubs and online retail operations that operate outside the US.
- Our Sam's Club segment consists of membership warehouse clubs operated in 47 states in the US and Puerto Rico, as well as the segment's online retail operations, samsclub.com. Sam's Club accounted for approximately 12% of our fiscal 2012 net sales.[13]

Table 2 shows sales and profits for these three business segments.

Performance

Table 3 summarizes some key financial data for Wal-Mart during the period 1994 to 2006. Table 4 shows Wal-Mart's recent performance compared with other discount retailers.

Wal-Mart Stores' Operations and Activities

Purchasing and Vendor Relationships

The size of Wal-Mart's purchases and its negotiating ability mean that Wal-Mart is both desired and feared by manufacturers. As a Wal-Mart vendor, a manufacturer gains unparalleled access to the US retail market. At the same time, Wal-Mart's

TABLE 3 Wal-Mart Stores, Inc.: Financial summary 1998–2012 (year ended January 31)

	2000	2001	2002	2003	2004	2005	2006	2007	2008	2009	2010	2011	2012
Net sales	165	191	218	230	256	285	312	345	375	401	405	419	444
Net sales increase (%)	19.6	15.8	14.1	5.5	12.0	11.3	9.5	11.7	8.6	7.2	1.0	4.4	5.9
US same-store sales increase, (%)	8.2	5.0	5.9	6.0	4.0	3.3	3.4	2.0	1.6	3.5	(0.8)	(0.6)	1.6
Gross margin (%)	21.2	21.5	21.1	22.6	22.3	22.8	23.1	23.5	24.1	24.3	24.9	24.8	24.5
SG&A[a] expense as % of sales	16.4	16.5	16.6	17.4	17.5	18.0	18.2	18.5	19.1	19.4	19.7	19.4	19.2
Interest expense	0.8	1.1	1.1	0.8	0.7	0.9	1.2	1.6	1.8	1.9	1.9	2.0	2.1
Income taxes	3.3	3.7	3.9	4.4	5.1	5.6	5.8	6.2	6.9	7.1	7.4	7.5	7.9
Operating income	9.1	11.4	12.1	13.3	15.2	17.3	18.7	20.5	22.0	22.8	24.0	25.5	26.5
Net income	5.4	6.3	6.7	8.0	9.1	10.3	11.2	11.3	12.7	13.4	14.4	16.9	16.3
Current assets	24.4	26.6	28.2	30.7	34.5	38.9	43.8	47.6	47.6	48.8	48.8	52.0	54.9
Inventories	20.2	21.6	22.7	24.4	26.6	29.8	32.2	33.7	35.2	34.5	32.7	36.4	40.7
Fixed assets	36.0	40.9	45.8	51.4	58.5	68.1	79.3	88.4	97.0	95.7	102.3	105.0	110.0
Total assets	70.3	78.1	83.5	94.8	104.9	120.2	138.2	151.8	163.5	163.2	170.4	180.8	193
Current liabilities	25.8	28.9	27.3	32.5	37.4	43.2	48.8	52.2	58.5	55.3	56.8	58.6	62.3
Long-term debt[b]	16.7	15.7	18.7	19.6	20.1	23.3	30.1	30.7	33.4	34.5	39.5	43.7	47.0
Shareholders' equity	25.8	31.3	35.1	39.5	43.6	49.4	53.2	61.6	64.6	65.3	70.5	68.5	71.3
Current ratio	0.9	0.9	1.0	0.9	0.9	0.9	0.9	0.9	0.8	0.9	0.8	0.9	0.9
Return on assets[c] (%)	9.5	8.7	8.5	9.0	9.0	9.3	8.9	8.8	8.5	8.4	8.7	9.3	8.4
Return on equity[d] (%)	22.9	22.0	20.1	21.0	21.0	22.6	22.5	22.0	21.0	21.2	21.2	24.6	22.8
Other data (units)													
US discount stores	1,801	1,736	1,647	1,568	1,478	1,353	1,209	1,075	971	891	898	706	629
US Supercenters	721	888	1,066	1,258	1,471	1,713	1,980	2,256	2,447	2,612	2,620	2,913	3,022
US Sam's Clubs	463	475	500	525	538	551	567	579	591	602	611	609	611
US Neighborhood Markets[e]	7	19	31	49	64	85	100	112	132	153	185	190	196
International units	1,004	1,071	1,170	1,272	1,355	1,587	2,285	2,757	3,121	3,615	4,099	4,587	5,651
Employees (thousand)	1,140	1,244	1,383	1,400	1,400	1,600	1,800	2,100	1,900	2,100	2,100	2,100	2,200

Notes:

Figures in parentheses denote a loss.

[a]SG&A: sales, general, and administration (cost of doing business).

[b]Including long-term lease obligations.

[c](Net income before minority interest, equity in unconsolidated subsidiaries, and cumulative effect of accounting change)/Average assets.

[d]Net income/Average shareholders' equity.

[e]And other small-format stores.

Source: Wal-Mart Stores Inc., 10-K reports.

TABLE 4 Wal-Mart and its competitors: Performance comparisons ($billions except where noted)

	Wal-Mart		Target		Dollar General		Costco[a]	
	2010	2011	2010	2011	2010	2011	2010	2011
Sales revenue	418.90	443.80	65.70	68.40	13.04	14.81	76.26	87.05
Operating Income	25.50	26.50	5.20	5.30	1.27	1.49	2.08	2.44
Total net income	16.90	16.30	2.90	2.90	0.63	0.77	1.32	1.54
Inventories	36.44	40.71	7.50	7.90	1.77	2.01	5.64	6.64
Total current assets	52.01	54.98	17.20	16.40	2.37	2.28	11.71	13.71
Total assets	180.78	193.41	43.70	46.60	9.55	9.69	23.82	26.76
Total current liabilities	58.60	62.30	10.00	14.20	1.37	1.51	10.06	12.05
Long-term debt	40.69	44.07	18.10	16.50	3.29	2.62	2.14	1.25
Total liabilities	99.30	106.37	28.10	30.70	6.86	6.53	12.89	14.19
Shareholder's equity	71.25	75.76	15.40	15.80	4.05	4.67	10.83	12.00
Financial ratios								
Gross profit margin (%)	24.91	24.80	30.44	30.12	32.04	31.73	10.83	10.69
Operating margin (%)	6.09	5.97	7.91	7.75	9.77	10.07	2.72	2.80
Net profit margin (%)	4.03	3.67	4.41	4.24	4.82	5.18	1.73	1.77
SG&A[b] expense/sales (%)	19.67	19.41	20.40	20.61	22.24	21.67	10.28	9.97
Depreciation and amortization/sales (%)	1.81	1.83	3.04	3.07	1.32	1.76	1.04	0.98
Total asset turnover	2.32	2.29	1.50	1.47	1.37	1.53	3.20	3.25
Inventory turnover	11.50	10.90	6.09	6.05	5.02	5.03	12.06	11.71
Long term debt/equity	0.57	0.58	1.18	1.04	0.81	0.56	0.20	0.10
Current ratio	0.89	0.88	1.72	1.15	1.73	1.51	1.16	1.14
Operating income/assets (%)	14.10	13.72	11.90	11.37	13.30	7.91	5.56	5.76
Return on equity (%)	23.72	21.52	18.83	18.35	15.49	16.42	12.22	12.85

Notes:
[a]FY ends in August.
[b]SG&A: sales, general, and administration (cost of doing business).

buying power and ferocious cost cutting results in most suppliers having their margins squeezed until they are razor-thin. Purchasing is centralized. All dealing with US suppliers takes place at Wal-Mart's Bentonville headquarters. Would-be suppliers are escorted to one of the cubicles on "Vendor Row." Furnishings comprise just a table and folding chairs . . . sometimes not even chairs. Suppliers regard the experience of selling to Wal-Mart as intimidating and grueling: "Once you are ushered into one of the Spartan little buyers' rooms, expect a steely eye across the table and be prepared to cut your price."[14] Another vendor commented: "All normal mating rituals are verboten. Their highest priority is making sure everybody at all times in all cases knows who's in charge . . . They talk softly, but they have piranha hearts, and if you aren't totally prepared when you go in there, you're in deep trouble."[15] To avoid dependence on any one supplier, Wal-Mart limits the total purchases it obtains from any one supplier. The result is an asymmetry of bargaining power: Wal-Mart's biggest supplier, Procter & Gamble, accounts for about 3% of Wal-Mart's sales, but this represents 18% of P&G's revenues.

The requirements that Wal-Mart imposes on its suppliers extends well beyond low prices. Increasingly, Wal-Mart involves itself in its suppliers' employment and environmental policies, imposing requirements which it monitors through third-party audits. On October 22, 2008, Wal-Mart's then-CEO, Lee Scott, addressed the CEOs and factory managers of over 1,000 Wal-Mart suppliers in Beijing's Shangri-La Hotel:

> A year from now, each and every one of you who chooses to make a commitment will be a more socially and environmentally responsible company. And that will make a difference. It will make a difference for you, for Walmart, for China, for our customers, and yes, for the planet . . . We need to ask ourselves: Is a product made in a factory that is a responsible steward of the environment and our natural resources? . . . I firmly believe that a company that cheats on overtime and on the age of its labor, that dumps its scraps and its chemicals in our rivers, that does not pay its taxes or honor its contracts, will ultimately cheat on the quality of its products . . . If a factory does not meet these requirements, they will be expected to put forth a plan to fix any problems. If they still do not improve, they will be banned from making products for Walmart.[16]

By 2012, Wal-Mart's *Standards for Suppliers Manual* ran to 46 pages.

Wal-Mart combines ruthless bargaining with close collaboration with its bigger suppliers. Wal-Mart's cooperation with Procter & Gamble provides a model for these relationships. The companies began electronic data interchange (EDI) at the beginning of the 1990s. By 1993, there were 70 P&G employees working at Bentonville to manage sales and deliveries to Wal-Mart.[17] EDI was extended to almost all Wal-Mart's US vendors. Through Wal-Mart's "Retail Link" system of supply-chain management, data interchange included point-of-sale data, levels of inventory, Wal-Mart's sales forecasts, vendors' production and delivery schedules, and electronic funds transfer. Suppliers could log on to the Wal-Mart database for real-time store-by-store information on sales and inventory for their products. This collaboration gave Wal-Mart faster replenishment, lower inventory, and a product mix tuned to local customer needs; it allowed suppliers to plan their production and deliveries.

Warehousing and Distribution

Wal-Mart is a world leader in distribution logistics. While most discount retailers rely heavily on their suppliers and third-party distributors for distribution to their individual stores, 82% of Wal-Mart's purchases are shipped to Wal-Mart's own distribution centers from where they are distributed in Wal-Mart trucks. The efficiency of the system rests on Wal-Mart's hub-and-spoke configuration. Distribution centers (hubs) span over a million square feet, operate 24 hours a day, and serve between 75 and 110 stores within a 200-mile radius. Deliveries into distribution centers are either in suppliers' trucks or Wal-Mart trucks, then deliveries are made to Wal-Mart stores. The grouping of Wal-Mart stores allows trucks to deliver partial loads to several Wal-Mart stores on a single trip. On backhauls, Wal-Mart trucks bring returned merchandise from stores and pick up from local vendors, allowing trucks to be over 60% full on backhauls.

Wal-Mart continually seeks ways to make its logistics system cheaper, faster, and more reliable:

- Its cross-docking system allows goods arriving on inbound trucks to be unloaded and reloaded on outbound trucks without entering warehouse inventory.

- Its "Remix" adds a new tier to its distribution system: third-party logistic companies are responsible for making smaller, more frequent pick-ups from suppliers, establishing "consolidation centers" throughout the US, then making frequent deliveries to Wal-Mart's distribution centers, allowing a five-day rather than four-week ordering cycle from suppliers.

- The international extension of Wal-Mart's procurement system involves it purchasing directly from overseas suppliers, rather than through importers, and therefore taking control of import logistics. In 2002, it established a global purchasing center in Shenzen and another in Shanghai. In Baytown, Texas it created a four-million sq. ft. import distribution center.[18]

- Wal-Mart was a pioneer of radio frequency identification (RDFI) for logistics management and inventory control.

Wal-Mart continually seeks incremental improvements to its logistics systems. In the year ended January 2009, it reported higher inventory turnover and lower distribution costs as a result of packing its trucks more tightly.

In-Store Operations

Wal-Mart's management of its retail stores is based upon its objective of creating customer satisfaction by combining low prices, a wide range of quality products carefully tailored to customer needs, and a pleasing shopping experience. Wal-Mart's management of its retail stores is distinguished by the following characteristics:

- *Merchandising*: Wal-Mart stores offered a wide range of nationally branded products. Between 2006 and 2009, it had expanded its range of brands, focusing in particular on upscale brands. Traditionally, Wal-Mart had placed less emphasis on own-brand products than other mass retailers; however, during 2008–2010, Wal-Mart made major investments in its range of "Great Value" private-label products. Under its "Store of the Community" philosophy, Wal-Mart has long sought to tailor its range of merchandise to local market needs on a store-by-store basis. Greater sophistication in analyzing point-of-sale data for individual stores facilitated Wal-Mart's responsiveness to local needs (see below).

- *Decentralization of store management*: Individual store managers were given considerable decision-making authority in relation to product range, product positioning within stores, and pricing. This differed from most other discount chains, where decisions over pricing and merchandising were made either at head office or at regional offices. Decentralized decision-making power was also apparent within stores, where the managers of individual departments (e.g., toys, health and beauty, consumer electronics) were expected to develop and implement their own ideas for increasing sales and reducing costs.

- *Customer service*: Discount stores were open from 9 a.m. to 9 p.m. weekdays, with shorter hours on weekends. Supercenters were open continuously. Despite the fanatical emphasis on cost efficiency, Wal-Mart went to great lengths to engage with its customers at a personal level. Stores employed "greeters"—often retired individuals—who would welcome customers and hand out shopping baskets. Within the store, all employees were expected to look customers in the eye, smile at them, and offer a verbal greeting. Wal-Mart's "Satisfaction Guaranteed" program assured customers that Wal-Mart would accept returned merchandise on a no-questions-asked basis.

Marketing

At the core of Wal-Mart's strategy was Sam Walton's credo that "There is only one boss: the customer" and the belief that value for customers equated to low prices. Hence, Wal-Mart's marketing strategy was built upon its slogan "Everyday Low Prices." In contrast to other discount chains, Wal-Mart did not engage in promotional price-cutting.

If "Everyday Low Prices" was the foundation of Wal-Mart's relationship with its customers, then it would mean that it was to spend less on advertising and other forms of promotion than its rivals. Its advertising/sales ratio in 2012 was 0.55%—most of its rivals had advertising/sales ratios of between 1.5% and 3.0% (Target's was 2.0%). Nevertheless, with an advertising budget of over $2 billion, Wal-Mart was among the world's biggest advertisers in 2012.

Wal-Mart went to considerable efforts to communicate an identity based upon traditional American virtues of hard work, thrift, individualism, opportunity, and community. This identification with core American values was buttressed by a strong emphasis on patriotism and national causes.

However, as Wal-Mart increasingly became a target for pressure from politicians, NGOs, and labor unions, it was increasingly forced to adapt its image and business practices. In 2005, Mike Duke's predecessor, Lee Scott, committed Wal-Mart to a program of environmental sustainability and set ambitious targets for renewable energy, the elimination of waste, and a shift in product mix toward environmentally friendly products.[19] Two years later, Wal-Mart published the first of its annual sustainability reports.

Commitment to social and environmental responsibility was part of a wider effort by Wal-Mart to broaden its consumer appeal and counter the attempts by activist groups to characterize Wal-Mart as a heartless corporate giant whose success was built upon exploitation and oppression. The desire to reposition and renew Wal-Mart's relationship with its customers and with society culminated in a 2008 company-wide image makeover that included a new corporate logo. The new logo coincided with a program of store redesign that included wider aisles, improved lighting, and lower shelves.[20]

Information Technology

Wal-Mart was a pioneer in applying information and communications technology to support decision making and promote efficiency and customer responsiveness. Wal-Mart was among the first retailers to use computers for inventory control, to initiate EDI with its vendors, and to introduce bar code scanning for point-of-sale and inventory control. To link stores and cash register sales with supply chain management and inventory control, Wal-Mart invested $24 million in its own satellite in 1984.

By 1990, Wal-Mart's satellite system was the largest two-way, fully integrated private satellite network in the world, providing two-way interactive voice and video capability, data transmission for inventory control, credit card authorization, and enhanced EDI. During the 1990s, Wal-Mart pioneered the use of data-mining for retail merchandising:

> At Wal-Mart, information technology gives us that knowledge in the most direct way: by collecting and analyzing our own internal information on exactly what any given shopping cart contains. The popular term is "data-mining," and Wal-Mart has been doing it since about 1990. The result, by now, is an enormous database of purchasing information that enables us to place the right item in the right store at the right price. Our computer system receives 8.4 million updates every minute on the items that customers take home—and the relationship between the items in each basket.
>
> Data analysis allows Wal-Mart to forecast, replenish, and merchandise on a product-by-product, store-by-store level. For example, with years of sales data and information on weather, school schedules and other pertinent variables, Wal-Mart can predict daily sales of Gatorade at a specific store and automatically adjust store deliveries accordingly.[21]

Point-of-sale data analysis also assisted in planning store layout:

> There are some obvious purchasing patterns among the register receipts of families with infants and small children. Well-thought-out product placement not only simplifies the shopping trip for these customers—with baby aisles that include infant clothes and children's medicine alongside diapers, baby food and formula—but at the same time places higher-margin products among the staples . . . The common thread is simple: We are here to serve the customer; and customers tend to buy from us when we make it easy for them. That sounds like a simple idea. But first you must understand the customer's needs. And that's where information comes in.[22]

The central role of IT was in integrating Wal-Mart's entire value chain. Point-of-sale data from store checkouts was the basis for inventory replenishment, deliveries from suppliers, and top management decision making:

> Combine these information systems with our logistics—our hub-and-spoke system in which distribution centers are placed within a day's truck run of the stores—and all the pieces fall into place for the ability to respond to the needs of our customers, before they are even in the store. In today's retailing world, speed is a crucial competitive advantage. And when it comes to turning information into improved merchandising and service to the customer, Wal-Mart is out in front.[23]

Human Resource Management

Wal-Mart's human-resource practices were based upon Sam Walton's beliefs about relations between the company and its employees and between employees and customers. All employees, from executive-level personnel to checkout clerks, are known as "associates." Wal-Mart claims that its relations with its associates are based on respect, high expectations, close communication, and clear incentives.

Wal-Mart's employees receive relatively low pay (most hourly paid retail workers received between $6.50 and $14 in 2012). However, these rates are, on average, slightly above those paid at other discount chains. Employee benefits include a company health plan that covers 94% of Wal-Mart's employees and a retirement scheme that covers all employees with a year or more of service.

Wal-Mart's compensation system includes profit incentives, which extended to hourly employees. A stock purchase plan is also available to employees.

Despite strenuous efforts by unions to recruit Wal-Mart employees, union penetration remains low. Wal-Mart resisted the unionization of its employees in the belief that union membership created a barrier between the management and the employees in furthering the success of the company and its members. At many of its overseas subsidiaries, however, Wal-Mart works closely with local unions.[24]

Associates are encouraged to use their initiative and to be flexible, especially in relation to serving customers and identifying opportunities for cost saving. They receive continual communication about their company's performance and about store operations. Close collaboration between managers and front-line employees is a feature of every aspect of Wal-Mart's operations. Performance incentives include sharing with employees savings from reductions in "shrinkage" (theft). Wal-Mart's shrinkage rate is about half the industry average.

Orchestrating employee enthusiasm and involvement is a central feature of Wal-Mart's management style. Meetings from corporate to store level feature the "Wal-Mart Cheer"—devised by Sam Walton after a visit to Korea. The call and response ritual ("Give me a W!" "Give me an A!", etc.) includes the "Wal-Mart squiggly" in which employees shake their backsides in unison.

Wal-Mart's human resource practices are an ongoing paradox. The enthusiasm it generates among employees helps to generate a level of involvement and empowerment that is unusual among large retail chains. At the same time, the intense pressure for cost reduction and sales growth frequently results in cases of employee abuse. In several adverse court decisions, Wal-Mart has been forced to compensate current and former employees for unpaid overtime work and for failure to ensure that workers received legally mandated rest breaks. However, a class action suit that alleged that Wal-Mart had systematically discriminated against female employees was rejected by the Supreme Court in 2011.

Organization and Management Style

Wal-Mart's management structure and management style is also a product of Sam Walton's principles and values. As Wal-Mart grew in size and geographical scope, Walton was determined that corporate executives should keep closely in touch with customers and store operations. The result was a structure in which communication between individual stores and the Bentonville headquarters was, and remains, both close and personal. Wal-Mart's regional vice presidents are each responsible for supervising between 10 and 15 district managers (who, in turn, are in charge of eight to 12 stores). The key to Wal-Mart's fast-response management system is linkage between the stores and headquarters. This was designed for speed of communication and decision making between the corporate headquarters and the operational units: stores and warehouses. The critical links in this system were the regional vice presidents. Most large retailers had regional offices; Wal-Mart's regional VPs had no offices. There time was spent visiting stores and warehouses in their regions Monday to Thursday, then returning to Bentonville on Thursday night for Friday and Saturday meetings. At the Friday meetings information from the field would be presented and shared, first thing Saturday the weekly sales statistics would be available, by Saturday morning actions would be agreed and the regional VPs would be contacting their district managers about actions for the coming week. According to former CEO, David Glass: "By noon on Saturday we had all our corrections in place. Our competitors, for the most part, got their sales results on Monday for the week prior. Now, they're already ten days behind, and we've already made the corrections."

The Saturday morning meeting was preceded by three other key corporate meetings:

- On Thursday afternoons, the operations meeting reviewed non-merchandising matters, including inventory management, supply-chain efficiencies, and new store development. Senior executives attended together with logistics, planning, and information managers. The meetings were held standing up to encourage brevity.

- Fridays began with the 7 a.m. management meeting, which involved Wal-Mart's 200-odd senior managers, including the regional vice presidents, who returned from their territories on Thursday evenings.

- This was followed by the merchandising meeting, which involved corporate executives, regional VPs, and buyers. The meeting provided buyers with direct insights into what was selling and what was not, gave regional VPs a means to instantly solve merchandising problems in their stores, and, lastly, included reports on what the competition was doing. The meeting dealt with stockouts, excess inventory, new product ideas, and a variety of merchandising errors. By early afternoon, the regional VPs and merchandisers were emailed a "priority note" of specific actions that they should take action on by the end of the day.

The two-and-a-half-hour Saturday morning meetings beginning at 7 a.m. most clearly represented Wal-Mart's unique management style. The Saturday meetings involved information sharing, education, motivation, and fun. They began with a review of the week's performance data and then involved question-and-answer sessions targeting examples of good and bad performance. They also included presentations that focused on merchandising best practices or new product lines. The highlights were the guest appearances, which in the past have included CEOs such as Carlos Ghosn, Steve Jobs, or Jack Welch, celebrity entertainers, or sports stars. The meetings closed with a talk from the CEO. After a guest appearance at the meeting, Microsoft's CEO, Steve Ballmer commented: "I think they've got a tool that's amazing . . . The Saturday meeting is all about sharing best practices and about being accountable. It's about a culture of performance, and it's about reminding people that business has got to be executed every day. Those are disciplines every company needs."[25]

By 2008, it became apparent that Wal-Mart's increasing size was making these meetings increasingly cumbersome—not to mention the fact that Wal-Mart's largest auditorium could no longer accommodate the participants. In January 2008, Wal-Mart announced that its legendary Saturday meeting would occur monthly and would be held at nearby Bentonville High School. The Saturday meetings were relayed to Wal-Mart stores, warehouses, and offices in all the countries that Wal-Mart did business.

Some managers saw the downgrading of the Saturday-morning meeting as a long-overdue recognition that one of the world's biggest corporations could no longer be run with the same personalized, Arkansas-focused management style put in place by Sam Walton. Others interpreted it differently: Wal-Mart was losing the unique spirit and driving force that had been the basis of its success for four decades.

Notes

1. L. Hetter, "Walmart's Annual Party A Gloomy Affair," *Forbes*, June 1, 2012. http://www.forbes.com/sites/lauraheller/2012/06/01/walmarts-annual-party-a-gloomy-affair/.
2. "Wal-Mart Alters Regular Saturday Meeting," *Morning News*, January 14, 2008, www.nwaonline.net/articles/2008/01/14/business/011508bizsatmeetings.txt, accessed October 16, 2009.
3. M. Duke, "Walmart's Enduring Values," 2012 shareholders' meeting, June 1, 2012.
4. M. Duke, "Walmart's Enduring Values," 2012 shareholders' meeting, June 1, 2012.
5. S. Walton, *Sam Walton: Made in America* (New York: Bantam Books, 1992).
6. *Forbes*, August 16, 1982, p. 43.
7. "Wal-Mart Stores, Inc.," Harvard Business School Case No. 9–974–024, 1994.
8. "Why Wal-Mart Can't Find Happiness in Japan," *Fortune*, July 27, 2007.
9. "Walmart in China: It's the Boxes, Stupid," *Financial Times*, June 1, 2012.
10. S. Walton, *Sam Walton: Made in America* (New York: Bantam Books, 1992).
11. "Sam's Way," *Wal-Mart*, 2012, www.walmart.com/cservice/aw_samsway.gsp, accessed September 13, 2012.
12. "Culture," http://corporate.walmart.com/our-story/working-at-walmart/culture, accessed September 20, 2012.
13. Wal-Mart Inc., 2009 10-K report.
14. Bill Saporito, "A Week Aboard the Wal-Mart Express," *Fortune*, August 24, 1992, p. 79.
15. Bill Saporito, "A Week Aboard the Wal-Mart Express," *Fortune*, August 24, 1992, p. 79.
16. Orville Schell, "How Walmart Is Changing China," *Atlantic Magazine*, December 2011.
17. "Lou Pritchett: Negotiating the P&G Relationship with Wal-Mart," Harvard Business School Case No. 9-907-011, 2007.
18. "Inside the World's Biggest Store," *Time Europe*, January 20, 2003.
19. "The Green Machine," *Fortune*, July 31, 2006.
20. "Wal-Mart Moves Upmarket," *Business Week*, June 3, 2009.
21. Wal-Mart Stores, Annual Report, 1999, p. 9.
22. Wal-Mart Stores, Annual Report, 1999, p. 9.
23. Wal-Mart Stores, Annual Report, 1999, p. 11.
24. "Wal-Mart Works with Unions Abroad, but not at Home," *Washington Post*, June 7, 2011.
25. J. Prevor, "Wal-Mart Sheds Another Tradition: Saturday Morning Meetings Cancelled," *Perishable Pundit*, January 23, 2008, http://www.perishablepundit.com/index.php?date=01/23/08&pundit=2, accessed September 13, 2012.

A video clip relating to this case is available in your interactive e-book at **www.wileyopenpage.com**

Case 7 Harley-Davidson, Inc., May 2012

You've shown us how to be the best. You've been leaders in new technology. You've stuck by the basic American values of hard work and fair play . . . Most of all, you've worked smarter, you've worked better, and you've worked together . . . as you've shown again, America is someplace special. We're on the road to unprecedented prosperity . . . and we'll get there on a Harley.

—PRESIDENT RONALD REAGAN, HARLEY-DAVIDSON PLANT, YORK, PA, MAY 6, 1987

The recovery of this company since the 1980s has been truly remarkable. When you were down in the dumps, people were saying American industry was finished, that we couldn't compete in the global economy, that the next century would belong to other countries and other places. Today, you're not just surviving—you're flourishing, with record sales and earnings; and one of the best-managed companies in America.

—PRESIDENT BILL CLINTON, HARLEY-DAVIDSON PLANT, YORK, PA, NOVEMBER 10, 1999

I've been impressed by Harley-Davidsons. It's one of America's finest products. And today I add to my impressions about the product, the impressions of the workforce . . . I'm impressed by the esprit de corps, I'm impressed by the fact that these people really enjoy what they're doing, I'm impressed by the fact that they're impressed by the product they make.

—PRESIDENT GEORGE W. BUSH, HARLEY-DAVIDSON PLANT, YORK, PA, AUGUST 16, 2006

When Keith Wandell took over as CEO of Harley-Davidson, Inc. on May 1, 2009, he was the first outsider to be appointed to the top job since Harley-Davidson's management buyout in 1981. He was also the first CEO of Harley since that date to have presided over a period of declining output and sales.

From 1984 to 2008, Harley's output and revenue had grown in every single year. The financial crisis of 2008 put an abrupt end to Harley's growth trend (Figure 1). After decades of customer waiting lists and shortage of production capacity, Wandell was thrust into a situation of plummeting orders, excess inventory, and a growing mountain of bad debt as customers defaulted on their loan payments.

This case was prepared by Robert M. Grant. ©2012 Robert M. Grant.

FIGURE 1   Annual shipments of motorcycles by Harley-Davidson

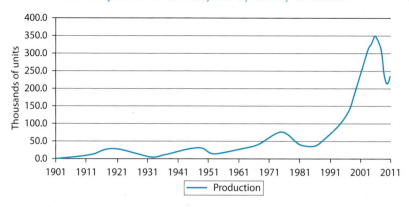

Wandell's initial actions included restoring funding for Harley's consumer lending activity, cutting back production, laying off employees, discontinuing the Buell brand and closing its plant, and putting recently acquired MV Agusta up for sale. As a result of a sharp drop in sales revenue and one-off restructuring costs, Harley posted a net loss in 2009, its first in 25 years. (Appendix 1 provides details of Harley-Davidson's financial performance.)

Stabilizing the business was Wandell's immediate priority, but even more important was establishing "a bold, clear strategic direction that would maximize our opportunities going forward and restore the Company as a strong business that could consistently grow over the long haul."[1] During 2010 and 2011, Wandell led a comprehensive transformation strategy which included a rethinking and restructuring of Harley's manufacturing operations, the transformation of its product development system, and a drive to build distribution and grow sales in the emerging markets of Asia and Latin America.

Yet, despite the early successes of Wandell's turnaround strategy, there was still the worry that Harley's best days might be behind it.

Harley's long-term profit growth depended on its ability to keep expanding the sales of its high-priced, heavyweight motorcycles. With North America and Europe accounting for 88% of Harley's revenues and with both regions mired in debt, unemployment, and depressed consumer spending, it seemed likely that the demand for luxury leisure products costing between $8,000 and $28,000 would continue to be subdued.

If the world economy was unlikely to offer much tailwind, to grow sales Harley would need to grow its market share at the expanse of rivals'—but here Harley was constrained by the fact that it already accounted for more than 55% of the US heavyweight motorcycle market.

Indeed, Harley's own market position might be vulnerable to competition. While no other company could replicate the emotional attachment of riders to the "Harley Experience," there was always the risk that motorcycle riders might seek a different type of experience and become more attracted to the highly engineered sports models produced by European and Japanese manufacturers. Such concerns were fueled by demographic trends. Harley's core market was the baby-boomer generation—and this cohort was moving more toward retirement homes than outdoor sports. Would the next cohorts—Generation X and Generation Y—have the same affinity for noisy, heavyweight motorcycles and the cultural values that Harley-Davidson represented?

The History of Harley-Davidson

From Birth to Maturity, 1903–1981

Harley-Davidson, Inc. was founded in 1903 by William Harley and brothers William Davidson, Arthur Davidson, and Walter Davidson. Their first model had a three-horsepower engine and was made in the Davidson's family shed. In 1909, Harley introduced its two-cylinder, V-twin engine with its deep, rumbling sound: this engine type would be the characteristic feature of Harley-Davidson motorcycles for the next hundred years. With the closure of the Indian Motorcycle factory in Springfield, Massachusetts in 1953, Harley-Davidson became the sole survivor of the 150 US motorcycle producers that had existed in 1910.

The postwar era saw new challenges for Harley-Davidson. Increasing affluence and the rise of youth culture created a growing demand for motorcycles. However, this was satisfied primarily by imports: first the British (by 1959, BSA, Triumph, and Norton took 49% of the US market), then the Japanese. Initially, Harley benefitted from the rebirth of motorcycling as a leisure activity, but soon it was facing direct competition: in 1969, Honda introduced its four-cylinder CB750, a huge technical advance on anything produced by Harley or the British. Harley's acquisition by AMF compounded the problems: expansion of production capacity to 75,000 units a year led to horrendous product quality problems followed by financial losses and a declining market share.

Rebirth, 1981–2008

In 1981, Vaughn Beals and a group of Harley's senior managers led a leveraged buyout of Harley. Harley-Davidson emerged as an independent, privately owned company, heavily laden with debt. The buyout coincided with a severe recession and soaring interest rates. Harley's sales fell and during 1981 and 1982 it lost a total of $60 million. Only by drastically cutting costs and gaining temporary protection from Japanese imports did Harley survive.

The management team devoted itself to rebuilding production methods and working practices. Managers visited several Japanese automobile plants and carefully studied Toyota's just-in-time (JIT) system. Less than four months after the buyout, Harley management began a pilot JIT inventory and production-scheduling program called "MAN" (Materials-As-Needed) in its Milwaukee engine plant. Within a year, all of Harley's manufacturing operations were being converted to JIT: components and sub-assemblies were "pulled" through the production system in response to final demand, and management and labor collaborated in introducing quality management.

Increasing sales and a return to profitability allowed Harley to go public in 1986. The new funding supported investment in new models, in plants, and in dealerships. Harley's share of the super-heavyweight market (over 850cc) grew from about 30% in 1986 to over 60% in 1990. Growth continued throughout the 1990s, both in the heavyweight motorcycle market and in Harley's share of that market. Throughout the 1990s, Harley's biggest challenge was satisfying the surging demand for its products. In 1996, Harley announced its Plan 2003 to dramatically increase production capacity in the period preceding its 100th anniversary in 2003. New production plants in Kansas City and York, Pennsylvania, the launch of new models, and international expansion resulted in sales exceeding 300,000 in 2004, a tenfold increase on 1983.

The Heavyweight Motorcycle Market

Until the financial crisis of 2008–2009, the heavyweight segment (over 650cc) had been the most rapidly growing part of the world motorcycle, with the US accounting for a major portion of this growth. Sales of heavyweight motorcycles in the major markets of the world almost trebled between 1990 and 2008.

In North America, Harley was the leader in heavyweight bikes with over half the market (Table 1). Overseas, Harley had been unable to replicate this market dominance, despite strong sales in a few markets. Harley achieved the remarkable feat of becoming heavyweight market leader in Japan, pushing Honda into second place. The European market was more fragmented, with Harley being among a leading group that included Honda, BMW, Suzuki, Yamaha, Kawasaki, and Triumph, each with market shares in the 8–15% range (Table 2).

The heavyweight motorcycle market comprised three segments:

- *Cruiser motorcycles*: These were "big, noisy, low riding, unapologetically macho cycles,"[2] typically with V-twin, large displacement engines and an upright riding position. Their design reflected the dominance of styling over either comfort or speed. For the urban males (and some females) in congested cities such as Los Angeles, New York, Paris, and Tokyo, the cruiser motorcycle, while a practical mode of transportation, was primarily a statement of style. The cruiser segment was practically created by Harley and represented over half of the heavyweight market in the US. Most of Harley's competitors in this segment had imitated the main features of the traditional Harley design.
- *Touring motorcycles*: These included cruisers specially equipped for longer-distance riding and bikes especially designed for comfort over long distances

TABLE 1   Retail sales of heavyweight motorcycles (651+ cc), 2003–2011 (thousands of units)

	2003	2004	2005	2006	2007	2008	2009	2010	2011
North America (total)	495	531	554	579	555	477	304	260	271
Harley-Davidson	238	256	265	282	267	235	174	154	162[a]
Market share (%)	48.1	48.2	47.8	48.6	48.7	49.3	53.2	54.9	55.7
Europe (total)	323	336	351	377	372	384	314	301	293
Harley-Davidson[b]	26	25	30	34	42	45	40	41	44
Market share (%)	8.1	7.3	8.5	9.1	11.3	11.7	12	12.7	13.7
Asia-Pacific									
Harley-Davidson	15	10	11	13	23	25	23	21	21[c]
Latin America									
Harley Davidson	n.a.	n.a.	n.a.	n.a.	3	8	6	6	7

Notes:
[a]Of which, US 151,683; Canada 10,502.
[b]Includes Middle East and Africa.
[c]Of which Japan 11,015.
Source: Harley-Davidson 10-K reports.

TABLE 2 Market shares in heavyweight motorcycles (651 + cc), 2005–2007 (%)

	North America			Europe		
	2005	2006	2007	2005	2006	2007
Harley-Davidson	47.8	48.6	48.7	8.9	9.1	9.6
Honda	16.6	15.1	14.3	13.0	14.6	12.3
Kawasaki	6.9	7.1	7.5	12.6	10.7	11.3
Suzuki	12.6	13.1	12.7	13.3	14.8	16.5
Yamaha	9.3	8.8	9.2	15.8	15.5	13.6
BMW	3.3	—	—	17.7	16.5	15.1
Ducati	—	—	—	5.2	5.2	5.9
Triumph	—	—	—	5.0	5.1	6.5
Other	4.5	7.3	8.3	8.5	8.5	9.2

Source: Harley-Davidson, annual reports, 2005, 2007.

(including the Honda Goldwing and the bigger BMWs). These tourers featured luxuries such as audio systems, two-way intercoms, and heaters. While Harley led this segment on the basis of style and image, Honda and BMW had engineered their motorcycles for greater smoothness and comfort over long distances through the use of multi-cylinder, shaft-drive engines and advanced suspension systems.

- *Performance motorcycles*: These were based on racing bikes, with high-technology, high-revving engines offering speed, acceleration, race-track styling, and minimal concessions to rider comfort. The segment was the most important in the European and Asia-Pacific markets, representing 62% and 65% of total heavyweight bike sales respectively. The segment was dominated by Japanese motorcycle companies, with a strong representation of European specialists such as Ducati and Triumph. Harley had competed in this segment during 1993–2010 with its offshoot, Buell Motorcycles.

Unlike its Japanese competitors, Harley was highly market focused. Harley's models were all concentrated on the narrow super-heavyweight segment (over 850cc).

Harley-Davidson in 2012

The Brand

Harley's top management team considered the Harley-Davidson image and the loyalty it engendered among its customers its greatest assets. Harley-Davidson was an archetype of American style. The famed spread eagle signified not just the brand of one of the world's oldest motorcycle companies but also an entire lifestyle with which it was associated. Harley has been described as "the ultimate biker status symbol . . . a quasi religion, an institution, a way of life."[3] Together with a few other companies, possibly Walt Disney and Levi Strauss, Harley had a unique relationship with American culture. The values that Harley represented—individuality, freedom, and adventure—could be traced back to the cowboy and frontiersman of yesteryear, and before that to the quest that brought people to America in the first place. As the sole surviving American motorcycle company from the pioneering days of the industry, Harley-Davidson represented a tradition of US engineering and manufacturing.

This appeal of the Harley brand was central not just to the company's marketing but also to its strategy as a whole. The central thrust of the strategy was reinforcing and extending the relationship between the company and its consumers. Harley-Davidson had long recognized that it was not selling motorcycles: it was selling the Harley Experience. Harley-Davidson made relentless efforts in all its communications— whether to customers, dealers, investors, or suppliers—to convey this experience:

> A chill sweeps through your body, created by a spontaneous outburst of pure, unadulterated joy. You are surrounded by people from all walks of life and every corner of the globe. They are complete strangers, but you know them like your own family. They were drawn to this place by the same passion—the same dream. And they came here on the same machine. This is one place you can truly be yourself. Because you don't just fit in. You belong.[4]

Customers and Customer Relations

If the appeal of the Harley motorcycle was the image it conveyed and the lifestyle it represented, then the company had to ensure that the experience matched the image. To increase Harley's involvement in its consumers' riding experience, it formed the Harley Owners' Group (HOG) in 1983. Through HOG, the company became involved in organizing social and charity events. Employees, from the CEO down, were encouraged to take an active role in HOG activities. Each year, senior managers typically attended a total of more than 150 shows, rallies, and rides. The bond between the company and its customers was captured by its chief designer, Willie G. Davidson: "We ride with you." The HOG provided the organizational link for this sense of community: "the feeling of being out there on a Harley-Davidson motorcycle links us like no other experience can. It's made HOG like no other organization in the world . . . The atmosphere is more family reunion than organized meeting."[5] The loyalty of Harley owners was reflected in their continuing reinvestment in Harley products: purchasing Harley-branded accessories and apparel, customizing and upgrading their bikes, and eventually trading them in for a new (typically more expensive) model. Almost half of all sales were to repeat customers.

Harley's success had been built upon a massive market repositioning. Traditionally, Harley owners had been blue-collar youngsters; during the 1980s and 1990s Harley owners became increasingly middle-aged and upper-income:

> The average US retail purchaser of a new Harley-Davidson motorcycle is a married male in his mid to late forties (nearly two-thirds of US retail purchasers of new Harley-Davidson motorcycles are between the ages of 35 and 54) with a median household income of approximately $87,000. Nearly three-quarters of the US retail sales of new Harley-Davidson motorcycles are to buyers with at least one year of education beyond high school and 32% of the buyers have college/graduate degrees. Approximately 12% of US retail motorcycle sales of new Harley-Davidson motorcycles are to female buyers.[6]

The Products

Broadening Harley's market appeal had major implications for product policy and design. Ever since its disastrous foray into small bikes during the AMF years, Harley had recognized that its competitive advantage lay with super-heavyweight bikes. Here it stuck resolutely to the classic styling that had characterized Harleys since its early years. At the heart of the Harley motorcycle was the air-cooled V-twin engine that had been Harley's distinctive feature since 1909. Harley's frames, handlebars, fuel tanks, and seats also reflected traditional designs.

Harley's commitment to traditional design features may be seen as making a virtue out of necessity. Its smaller corporate size and inability to share R & D across cars and bikes (unlike Honda and BMW) limited its ability to invest in technology and new products. As a result, Harley lagged far behind its competitors in the application of automotive technologies: its motorcycles not only looked old-style, much of the technology was old-style. When Harley introduced its new Twin Cam 88 engine in 1998, *Motorcycle* magazine reported:

> Honda comes out with an average of two new (or reworked) motors every year. The other Japanese manufacturers are good for about one. Count on Ducati and BMW to do something every few years. That leaves only Moto Guzzi and Harley . . . The Twin Cam 88 is Harley's first new engine since the Evolution Sportster motor of 1986, and their first new Big Twin motor since the original Evolution, released in 1984.[7]

Harley's engines most clearly represented its commitment to tradition in the face of technological change. Long after Honda had moved to multiple valves per cylinder, overhead camshafts, liquid cooling, and electronic ignition, Harley continued to rely on air-cooled push-rod engines. In suspension systems, braking systems, and transmissions, Harley lagged far behind Honda, Yamaha, and BMW.

Nevertheless, Harley was engaged in constant upgrading—principally incremental refinements to its engines, frames, and gearboxes—aimed at improving power delivery and reliability, increasing braking power, and reducing vibration. Harley also accessed automotive technology through alliances with other companies, including Porsche AG, Ford, and Gemini Racing Technologies.

Despite being a technological laggard, Harley was very active in new product development and the launching of new models. By 2012, Harley offered 34 different models. Harley's product development efforts had been assisted by doubling the size of its Product Development Center in 2004 and the creation of a Prototyping Lab. Most of Harley's product development efforts were limited to style changes, new paint designs, and engineering improvements. However, after 2000, Harley had accelerated technological progress and had introduced more-radical new-product developments. Its V-Rod model introduced in October 2001 featured innovative styling and an all-new liquid-cooled engine. The Buell range had also allowed greater scope for Harley's engineers, particularly in engines and frame designs. In 2006, Harley introduced another new engine, the Twin Cam 96, which featured electronic ignition and was teamed with a new six-speed gearbox.

It is notable that between January 2000 and April 2012, Harley was awarded 188 US patents, many of these related to peripheral items: saddlebag mounting systems, footpegs, seats, backrests, electrical assemblies, and motorcycle music systems.

Over the same period Honda was awarded 10,982 US patents, Suzuki 625, and Kawasaki 2,002.

Central to Harley's product strategy was the idea that every Harley rider would own a unique, personalized motorcycle as a result of the company offering a wide range of customization opportunities. New bikes allowed multiple options for seats, bars, pegs, controls, and paint jobs, with the potential for augmentation through a range of 7,000 accessories and special services such as "Chrome Consulting."

Reconciling product differentiation with scale economies was a continuing challenge for Harley. The solution was to offer a wide range of customization options while standardizing on key components. Thus, Harley's broad model range involved "permutations of four": four engine types, four basic frames, four styles of gas tank, and so on.

The Harley product line also covered a wide price range. The Sportster model was positioned as an entry-level bike, beginning at $7,999, less than one-third of the price of the Electra Glide Ultra Limited, with "custom color" at $25,014. Top of the price range was the three-wheeler Tri-Glide at $31,824 (with two-tone paint).

The Buell Exit

Founded by ex-Harley engineer Erik Buell, Buell Motor Company developed bikes that used Harley engines and other components but mounted them on a lighter, stiffer frame. Harley acquired complete ownership of Buell in 1998. Buell offered Harley the opportunity to broaden its appeal to younger riders and those more interested in speed and maneuverability. The lighter weight and superior handling were also seen as especially appealing to European customers. In the US, the typical Buell customer was seven years younger than the average Harley buyer; the price range of Buell bikes was also lower. The Buell Blast, with its 490cc single-cylinder engine and a price tag of $4,595, was a major departure for Harley: its first entry into middleweight motorcycles since the 1970s. Yet, despite heavy investments in developing and launching new models, Buell's sales were disappointing (Table 3). Four months after his arrival at Harley-Davidson, Wandell announced the discontinuation of Buell and the closure of its plant.

Distribution

Upgrading Harley's distribution network was central to its resurgence during the 1980s and 1990s. At the time of the buyout, many of Harley's 620 US dealerships were operated by enthusiasts, with erratic opening hours, a poor stock of bikes and spares and indifferent customer service. If Harley was in the business of selling a lifestyle and an experience, then dealers played a pivotal role in delivering that experience. Moreover, if Harley's target market had shifted toward mature, upper-income individuals, Harley needed to provide a retail experience commensurate with the expectations of this group.

Harley's dealer development program increased support for dealers while imposing higher standards of pre- and after-sales service, and requiring better dealer facilities. The dealers were obliged to carry a full line of Harley replacement parts and accessories and to offer an expanding range of services: in addition to traditional services such as service and repair and financing, dealers offered test ride facilities,

TABLE 3 Harley-Davidson shipments 2001–2011 (thousands of units)

	2001	2002	2003	2004	2005	2006	2007	2008	2009	2010	2011
H-D motorcycles											
US	186.9	212.8	237.7	260.6	266.5	273.2	241.5	206.3	144.4	131.6	152.2
Export	47.5	50.8	53.5	56.7	62.5	76.0	89.1	97.2	78.5	78.8	80.9
Motorcycle product mix (%)											
Sportster	21.6	19.4	19.7	22.0	21.3	18.5	21.8	20.0	21.4	19.5	21.3
Custom	50.4	53.7	52.0	48.6	45.2	46.2	43.7	46.4	40.9	41.4	39.2
Touring	28.0	26.8	28.4	29.4	33.5	35.4	34.5	33.6	37.7	39.0	39.5
Buell motorcycles	9.9	10.9	10.0	9.9	11.2	12.5	11.5	13.1	9.5	2.6	0.2
Company total	244.3	274.5	301.2	327.2	340.2	361.6	342.1	316.4	232.4	213.0	233.2

Source: Harley-Davidson 10-K reports, various years.

rider instruction classes, motorcycle rental, consulting services for customizing bikes through dealer-based design centers and chrome consultants, and insurance services. Over 90% of Harley dealerships in the US were exclusive: most other motorcycle manufacturers sold through multi-brand dealerships.

Dealer relations were a continuing strategic priority for Harley. Its Retail Environments Group established a meticulous set of performance standards and guidelines for dealers that covered every aspect of managing the showroom and interacting with actual and potential customers. Harley-Davidson University was established to "enhance dealer competencies in every area, from customer satisfaction to inventory management, service proficiency, and front-line sales."[8]

Other Products

Sales of parts, accessories, and "general merchandise" (clothing and collectibles) represented 14.8% of total revenue in 2011 (Table 4), much higher than for most other motorcycle companies. Clothing sales included not just traditional riding apparel but also a wide range of men's, women's, and children's leisure apparel.

Only a small proportion of the clothing, collectibles, and other products bearing the Harley-Davidson trademark were sold through the Harley dealership network. Most of the "general merchandising" business represented licensing of the Harley-Davidson name and trademarks to third-party manufacturers of clothing, giftware, jewelry, toys, and other products. L'Oréal offered a line of Harley-Davidson cologne. To expand sales of licensed products, Harley dealers opened a number of secondary retail location and alternative retail outlets, which sold clothing, accessories, and giftware but not motorcycles.

Harley-Davidson Financial Services (HDFS) is Harley's financial services arm supplying credit, insurance, and extended warranties to Harley dealers and customers. Between 2000 and 2007, it was Harley's most rapidly growing source of profit, contributing almost 12% of operating profit in 2007. However, the credit crunch hit the business hard. Unable to securitize its customer loans, Harley was forced to retain these loans on its own books, causing a large increase in its current assets.

TABLE 4 Harley-Davidson's non-motorcycle sales, 2003–2011 ($ million)

	2003	2004	2005	2006	2007	2008	2009	2010	2011
Parts and accessories	712.8	781.6	815.7	862.3	868.3	858.7	767.2	749.2	816.5
General merchandise	211.4	223.7	247.9	277.5	305.4	313.8	282.2	259.1	274.1
Financial services	279.5	305.3	331.6	384.9	416.2	377.0	494.7	682.7	649.4

Source: Harley Davidson 10-K reports.

During 2010–2011, HDFS was placed on a firmer financial footing and its revenue and profit grew strongly with half of all US retail sales of motorcycles financed by HDFS. By 2011, HDFS contributed almost one-third of Harley's operating income.

International Expansion

A key part of Harley-Davidson's growth strategy was expanding sales outside of the US. A critical issue was the extent to which Harley needed to adapt its products, image, and customer approach to conditions in overseas markets. Harley's image was rooted in American culture: to what extent was Harley's appeal to European and Asian customers rooted in its status as an American icon? "The US and Harley are tied together," observed Hugo Wilson of Britain's *Bike* magazine, "the guy who's into Harleys here is also the guy who owns cowboy boots. You get a Harley and you're buying into the US mystique."[9] At the same time, the composition of demand and customer profiles was different in overseas markets.

Europe was the focal point of Harley's overseas ambitions, simply because it was the second-largest heavyweight motorcycle market in the world. Europe was also a huge challenge for Harley. It had never had a major position in Europe. Also, the European motorcycle market was very different from the American market: 70% of the heavyweight motorcycle market was for performance bikes, while touring and cruiser bikes accounted for just 30%. European buyers were knowledgeable and style-conscious, but their style preferences were different from those of US riders. European roads and riding styles were also different from the US. As a result, Harley modified some of its models for the European market. The Sportster, for example, was given straight handlebars instead of curled buckhorns and a new suspension system to improve cornering. Its name was changed to the "Custom 53." As in the US, HOG played a critical role in building brand image and customer loyalty.

In July 2008, Harley extended its European presence with the $105 million acquisition of MV Agusta, an Italian manufacturer of premium, high-performance sport motorcycles—including the F4-R with a 1078cc, four-cylinder, liquid-cooled engine, producing 190hp. Whatever plans Harley had to revitalize MV Agusta, to expand Harley's European dealership network, or to build a stronger presence among younger riders, they were not implemented. On August 6, 2010, Harley sold MV Agusta back to its previous owner for €3 ($3.9).

With Europe mired in recession during 2009–2012, Harley's international strategy turned increasingly to the growth markets of Asia and Latin America. Harley established an Asia-Pacific regional headquarters in Singapore, which distributed to Harley dealers in Australia, China, India, and Japan; and Latin America headquarters based in Miami. In 2011, Harley opened an assembly plant in India. (This was

TABLE 5 Harley-Davidson's dealership network

	US		Canada		Europe		Asia Pacific		Latin America	
	2008	**2011**	**2008**	**2011**	**2008**	**2011**	**2008**	**2011**	**2008**	**2011**
Full-service dealerships	686	635	71	69	383	369	201	230	32	44

TABLE 6 Harley-Davidson's main facilities, 2011

Location	Function	Square Feet
Menomonee Falls, WI	Motorcycle powertrain production	881,600
Milwaukee, WI	Corporate office	515,000
Milwaukee, WI	Museum	130,000
Tomahawk, WI	Fiberglass/plastic parts production and painting	226,000
Wauwatosa, WI	Plant closed in 2010; production moved to Menomonee Falls, WI	430,000
Wauwatosa, WI	Product development center	409,000
Franklin, WI	Distribution center	255,000
York, PA	Motorcycle parts fabrication, painting, assembling Softail models	582,400
Kansas City, MO	Motorcycle parts fabrication and painting and Dyna, Sportster	450,000
Carson City, NV	Financial services	100,000
Naples, FL	Motorcycle testing	820,000
Yucca, AZ	Motorcycle testing	79,000
Bawal, India	Assembly of bikes for Indian market	68,200
Manaus, Brazil	Assembly of bikes for Brazilian market	100,000
Adelaide, Australia	Motorcycle wheels; to be fully outsourced by 2013	485,000

Source: Harley-Davidson 10-K report, 2011.

its second overseas assembly plant; the first was in Brazil in 1999.) Table 1 shows Harley's overseas sales.

Establishing dealerships was the key to penetrating international markets. Table 5 shows Harley's dealership network.

Manufacturing

As already noted, Harley-Davidson's development during the 1980s and 1990s focused heavily on upgrading its manufacturing operations: capacity expansion permitted investment in new plant and equipment and the introduction of more advanced process technologies. Particular emphasis was placed on developing manufacturing capabilities through total quality management, JIT scheduling, CAD/CAM, and the devolution of responsibility and decision making to the shop floor. Table 6 shows Harley's main manufacturing and development facilities.

Despite the constant development of its manufacturing facilities and operational capabilities, Harley's low production volumes relative to Honda and the other Japanese manufacturers imposed significant cost disadvantages, especially in the purchase of components. Despite this lack of bargaining muscle, Harley sought close, collaborative relations with key suppliers. Its supplier advisory council (SAC) served "not only to improve purchasing efficiency, but also to provide a forum to share information, ideas, and strategy."[10]

Harley's capacity for efficiency was also limited by its dispersed manufacturing operations: engine manufacture in Milwaukee, Wisconsin and assembly in York, Pennsylvania and Kansas City, Missouri. To cut costs, Harley initiated a program of plant consolidation. The two Milwaukee-area powertrain plants would be combined into a single facility and the separate paint and frame operations at York, Pennsylvania would be merged into a single plant. New agreements negotiated with unions allowed for more flexible employment arrangements and working practices, which supported the introduction of a new enterprise resource planning (ERP) system at the York plant. The new system would mean that manufacturing would be driven by customer demand, every production line would have the flexibility to build every model, and inventories would be reduced.

People and Management

Central to Harley-Davidson's renaissance during the 1980s and 1990s was the creation of a new relationship between management and employees. After the 1981 management buyout, Harley's new management team systematically rethought management–employee relationships and implemented a new approach built on involvement, self-management, open communication, and team-based organizations. At the Kansas plant, production was performed by 8- to 15-member *natural work groups*; representatives from these teams formed four *process operating groups* for fabrication, engine production, assembly, and painting; overall plant management was performed by a 14-member *plant leadership group*.[11] Team-based structures extended up to top management level, where three functional teams—the Create Demand Circle (CDC), the Produce Product Circle, and the Provide Support—were coordinated by the Strategic Leadership Council.[12]

Despite Harley's commitment to employee participation and development, the production cut-backs and cost cutting pressures during 2009–2012 created tensions between the company and its employees. On April 1, 2012, a new labor agreement went into effect whereby Harley's unions agreed to headcount reductions and more flexible working practices.[13]

Competition

Despite Harley's insistence that it was supplying a unique Harley experience rather than competing with other motorcycle manufacturers, the more it took market share from other manufacturers and expanded its product range and geographical scope, the more it came into direct competition with other producers. The clearest indication of direct competition was imitation: Honda, Suzuki, Yamaha, and Kawasaki had long been offering V-twin cruisers styled closely along the lines of the classic Harleys, but at lower prices and with more advanced technologies. In competing against Harley, the Japanese manufacturers' key advantage was the scale advantages deriving from vastly greater volume. However, despite their large price premium,

Harley-Davidson motorcycles benefitted from a much smaller rate of depreciation than other brands.

Almost all of Harley's competitors were, compared to Harley, highly diversified. Honda, BMW, and Suzuki were important producers of automobiles, and more than one-third of Yamaha's turnover came from boats and snowmobiles. These companies could benefit from sharing technology, engineering capabilities, and marketing and distribution across their different vehicle divisions—and their size conferred purchasing power.

Harley's success attracted imitators. These included not only the Japanese big four which introduced retro-styled, V-twin cruisers but also new domestic competitors— including Excelsior, Polaris (Victory), and a resuscitated Indian—had all entered the super-heavyweight market with cruiser bikes selling at prices exceeding those of Harley (the Indian Vintage Chief cost $35,499).

Figure 2 shows competitive product offerings, while Table 7 shows price comparisons. Appendix 2 gives profiles of several leading competitors.

Meeting the Challenges of Tomorrow

By May 2012, Keith Wandell's confidence that Harley could adapt to the difficult economic circumstances that had proceeded the 2008–2009 financial crisis seemed justified. The first-quarter financial results for 2012 showed a year-on-year revenue growth of 16.7% and a net income growth of 44.3%. Increases in manufacturing

TABLE 7   Price comparison of V-twin, cruiser motorcycles, 2009

Manufacturer/model	Engine	Retail price ($)
Harley-Davidson		
Sportster 883 Low	V-twin, air-cooled, 883cc	6,999
Fat Boy	V-twin, air-cooled, 1540cc	15,999
VRSC V-Rod Muscle	V-twin, liquid-cooled, 1131cc	17,199
Heritage Softail Classic	V-twin, air-cooled, 1450cc	17,999
Honda		
Shadow Spirit 750	V-twin, liquid-cooled, OHC, 745cc	7,699
VTX1300C	V-twin, liquid-cooled, OHC, 1312cc	10,299
VTX1800N	V-twin, liquid-cooled, OHC, 1800cc	13,699
Suzuki		
Boulevard S50	V-twin, liquid-cooled, OHC, 805cc	7,199
Boulevard C90	V-twin, air-cooled, OHC, 1475cc	11,299
Boulevard M109R	V-twin, liquid-cooled, 1783cc	13,799
Kawasaki		
Vulcan 900 Classic	V-twin, 8-valve, OHC	7,499
Vulcan 1600 Mean Streak	V-twin, air-cooled, 1552cc	11,099
Yamaha		
V-Star Custom Road Star	V-twin, OHC, air-cooled, push-rod, 649cc	6,290
Polaris		
Victory Kingpin	V-twin, 4-valve per cylinder, 1634cc	16,399

Source: Websites of different motorcycle manufacturers.

FIGURE 2 Cruiser motorcycles

Harley-Davidson Fat Boy

Honda Shadow Spirit 750

Yamaha Roadstar

Suzuki Boulevard C50

Kawasaki Vulcan 900

Polaris Victory Kingpin

efficiency had contributed a large proportion of the improvements in profitability. Looking to 2013, Wandell anticipated that Harley's restructuring program would generate cost savings of around $310 million over the year.

Yet, despite the vast improvement as compared with the dark days of 2009, Harley was a long way from returning to its traditional growth trajectory. Wendell estimated that Harley's total sales in 2012 would be between 245,000 and 250,000 bikes, a long way short of the 361,600 bikes it shipped in 2006.

Morningstar's Jamie Katz emphasized the demographic factors which would hold back Harley's market potential within the US:

We estimate the median age of a Harley buyer to be just younger than 50 . . . and according to the US Census the [40- to 49-year-old group] is set to decline 2.5% between 2010 and 2015 . . . With a shrinking core customer base and an increasing proportion of baby boomers moving out of this age segment, we believe more conservative behavior on the part of this older group could act as a drag on sales growth.[14]

A major thrust of Harley's marketing had been to broaden its demographic base with programs targeting women riders, "Harlistas" (Latino riders), "Iron Elite" (African American riders), and "Harley's Heroes" (military and veteran riders. However, the big challenge was appealing to the upcoming generations. As the *New York Times* noted, "As Harley keeps most of its focus on its aging consumers, rivals like BMW, Honda and Yamaha are attracting younger customers who seem less interested in cruising on what their old man rides."[15]

The very success of Harley in expanding its output and market share may have contributed to its declining desirability. "Traditionally, Harley-Davidson had a very loyal consumer," commented Anthony Gikas, senior research analyst at Piper Jaffray. "But those riders lost interest in the brand because everyone has a Harley bike. It's not a club anymore."[16]

One Milwaukee blogger summarized Harley's dilemma:

So what does Harley do? One tack would be to stay focused on what it does best: big bikes. While that strategy may make sense on some fronts (focus on what you know, stay loyal to the brand identity, etc.), that approach will mean greatly reduced growth prospects and could doom it if the current consumer spending environment holds out long term. And meanwhile its core audience just gets older.

Or it could do what people have been saying what it should do for years (and what Harley itself has suggested, intermittently, it may do): Make smaller, more affordable bikes. That's harder than it sounds, as it would force Harley to compete against the Japanese manufacturers on their own turf. But if the market is moving away from Harley, does it have a choice?[17]

Appendix 1: Selected Items from Harley-Davidson Financial Statements, 2003–2011 ($million)

	2003	2004	2005	2006	2007	2008	2009	2010	2011
Income statement									
Net sales	4,624	5,015	5,342	5,801	5,727	5,594	4,781	4,859	5,311
Gross profit	1,666	1,900	2,040	2,233	2,114	1,931	1,386	1,427	1,555
R & D	150	171	179	177.7	186	164	143	136	145
Selling, administrative and engineering expense	684	727	762	846	901	985	979	1020	1061
Operating income, of which:	1,149	1,361	1,470	1,603	1,426	1,029	197	559	829
–Financial services	168	189	192	211	212	83	(117)	181	268
Interest income/(expense)	23	23	23	27	22	9	(22)	(90)	(45)
Other income/(expense)	26	25	25	25	0	5	74	47	50
Income before taxes	1,166	1,379	1,488	1,624	1,448	1,034	178	390	792
Income taxes	405	490	528	581	514	379	108	130	244
Net income	761	890	960	1,043	934	655	(55)	146	599
Balance sheet									
Assets									
Cash	329	275	141	238	403	594	1,630	1,021	1,526
Finance receivables held for investment	1,391	1,656	1,943	2,101	1,575	1,378	1,436	1,080	1,168
Accounts receivable, net	112	121	122	143	181	296	269	262	219
Inventories	208	227	221	288	350	401	323	326	418
Total current assets	2,729	3,683	3,145	3,551	3,467	5,378	4,341	4,066	4,542
Property, plant and equipment, net	1,046	1,025	1,012	1,024	1,061	1,094	906	815	809
Total assets	4,923	5,483	5,255	5,532	5,657	7,829	9,155	9,430	9,674
Current liabilities									
Current portion of long-term debt	324	495	205	832	398	0	1,332	0	399
Accounts payable	224	244	271	763	300	324	162	225	255
Total current liabilities	956	1,173	873	1,596	1,905	2,604	2,268	2,013	2,698
Non-current liabilities									
Long-term debt	670	800	1,000	870	980	2,176	4,144	2,516	2,396
Other long-term liabilities	86	91	82	109	152	175	155	152	140
Post-retirement healthcare benefits	127	150	61	201	193	274	264	254	268
Stockholders' equity	2,958	3,218	3,084	2,757	2,375	2,116	2,108	2,207	2,420
Total liabilities and equity	4,923	5,483	5,255	5,532	6,796	6,786	9,155	9,430	9,674
Cash flows									
Operating activities	597	832	961	762	798	2,685	609	1,163	885
Capital expenditures	(2227)	(2214)	(2198)	(2220)	(2242)	(2232)	(116)	(170)	(189)
Total investing activities	(2540)	(2570)	(177)	(235)	(391)	(2393)	(863)	145	(63)
Financing activities	81	2,316	21,272	2,637	21,038	1,293	1,381	(1856)	(309)
Net increase in cash	137	254	2,134	97	164	191	1,134	(542)	(505)

Note:
Figures in parentheses denote a loss.
Source: Harley-Davidson 10-K reports, various years (www.harleydavidson.com).

Appendix 2: Comparative Financial Data for Honda, Yamaha, and Harley-Davidson ($million, unless otherwise indicated)

	Honda Motor			Yamaha Motor			Harley-Davidson		
	2009	2010	2011	2009	2010	2011	2009	2010	2011
Revenue	101,916	92,210	107,479	4,676	4,458	4,496	4,781	4,859	5,311
Gross margin (%)	26	25	27	37	35	37	39	43	42
SGA expense	18,720	14,374	16,629	1,579	1,500	1,484	702	756	788
Operating income	1,931	3,910	9,852	141	73	158	197	559	829
Net income after tax	1395	3038	6777	(210)	(53)	61	(55)	146	599
Net margin	1.37	3.29	6.31	(4.49)	(1.19)	1.36	3.05	12.33	(1.04)
Op. income/assets (%)	1.60	3.13	7.08	3.39	1.70	3.37	2.15	5.93	8.57
Total assets	120,319	124,990	139,157	4,163	4,322	4,701	9,155	9,430	9,674
Cost of goods sold	75,532	68,946	78,134	2,956	2,885	2,854	2,900	2,749	3,106
Inventory turnover	5.96	6.86	7.22	3.60	3.86	3.31	8.98	8.43	7.43
Inventories	12,664	10,056	10,822	821	747	862	323	326	418
Total equity	40,795	46,525	53,517	2,497	2,538	2,824	2,108	2,207	2,420
Return on equity (%)	3	7	13	(8)	(2)	2	(3)	7	25
Operating cash flow	3,906	16,597	12,878	(22.75)	428.53	272.35	609	1,163	885
Cash flow from investing activities	(11,538)	(6,403)	(8,796)	(265)	(137)	(117)	(863)	145	(63)
R & D expenditure	5,733	4,980	5,864	236	234	270	143	136	145
Advertising expenditure	n.a.	n.a.	n.a.	233	195	193	80	75	82
Motorcycles shipped (thousands of units)	10,114	9,639	11,445	n.a.	n.a.	n.a.	232	213	233.2
Employees	181,876	176,815	179,060	26,803	25,658	26,816	6,900	6,900	6,600

Note:
Figures in parentheses denote a loss.
Source: Harley-Davidson financial reports.

Notes

1. "Letter to Shareholders," Harley-Davidson, Inc., annual report, 2009.
2. G. Strauss, "Born to be Bikers," *USA Today*, November 5, 1997.
3. M. Ballon, "Born to be Wild," *Inc.*, November, 1997, p. 42.
4. Harley-Davidson, Inc., annual report, 2000.
5. See *Geelong Harley-Davidson*, http://www.geelongharley-davidson.com.au/hog.asp, accessed September 14, 2012.
6. Harley-Davidson, Inc. 10-K report for 2008, p. 8.
7. *Motorcycle*, February 1998.
8. "Knowledge is Horespower," Harley-Davidson, Inc., annual report, 2003, http://www.harley-davidson.com/company/investor/ar/2003/g_dealer01.htm, accessed September 14, 2012.
9. Quoted in "Motorcycle Maker Caters to the Continent," *USA Today*, April 22, 1998.
10. K. R. Fitzgerald, "Harley's Supplier Council Helps Deliver Full Value," *Purchasing*, September 5, 1996.
11. S. Roth, "Harley's Goal: Unify Union and Management," *Kansas City Business Journal*, May 16, 1997.
12. C. Fessler, "Rotating Leadership at Harley-Davidson: From Hierarchy to Interdependence," *Strategy and Leadership*, July 17, 1997.
13. "Harley-Davidson workers brace for big change," *Business Journal*, Milwaukee, April 27, 2012.
14. J. M. Katz, "Operational Changes Set the Stage for Harley's Growth but Shrinking Core Demographic is a Reality," *Morningstar*, May 29, 2012.
15. "Harley, You're Not Getting Any Younger," *New York Times*, March 21, 2009.
16. "Harley, You're Not Getting Any Younger," *New York Times*, March 21, 2009.
17. See "Screw it, let's ride is not a strategy," City Brawler, January 23, 2009, http://brewcitybrawler.typepad.com/brew_city_brawler/2009/01/screw-it-lets-ride-is-not-a-strategy.html, accessed September 14 2012.

A video clip relating to this case is available in your interactive e-book at
www.wileyopenpage.com

Case 8 Manchester United: Preparing for Life without Ferguson

The last week of July 2012 was a hectic time for Manchester United's CEO, David Gill. On July 22, the team had arrived in Shanghai, a part of the team's 22,000-mile summer tour involving matches in South Africa, China, Norway, Germany, and Sweden. Ostensibly, the summer tour was for training purposes before the English Premier League season began on August 15. In reality, the summer tour was primarily for commercial purposes. Manchester United (ManU) had the most international fan base of any sports team in the world, a critical asset for ManU's sponsorship and licensing arrangements. On the plane carrying the team, players would be outnumbered by ManU's commercial staff, who would be engaged with meeting existing sponsors and negotiating new licensing and sponsorship deals.

The Shanghai leg of the tour was particularly significant. More than half of ManU's 350 million fans were based in Asia, where their massive following in Asia translated into substantial revenues. In addition to merchandise sales and broadcasting deals, ManU's portfolio of Asian sponsors included telecom, financial services, and drinks companies.

However, David Gill's main focus was on two key initiatives that would have major implications for ManU's finances over the coming years. The first was a new sponsorship deal with General Motors. By the beginning of August, Gill was hoping to announce a seven-year contract with GM under which ManU would receive $559 million (almost $80 million a year) for displaying GM's Chevrolet brand on the team's shirts. This would be more than double the amount paid by insurance company Aon, its current shirt sponsor, and would set a new record for a football club sponsorship contract. According to GM's director of global marketing strategy, the key attraction was ManU's global fan base:

> When Manchester United played against Manchester City, that audience around the world scaled to 600 million people. Compare that to the Super Bowl here in the States, which is roughly 110 million, and you're talking five times that audience watching one regular-season game. It's significant.[1]

The second initiative was ManU's initial public offering on the New York Stock Exchange set for August 10. During the next week, roadshow presentations would be made to potential investors in Singapore, Kuala Lumpur, London, and New York. The much-delayed public offering of 10% of the ManU's equity (currently owned by the US-based Glazer family) would help to reduce the club's massive debt burden.

This case was written by Robert M. Grant with assistance from Simon I. Peck, Christopher Carr, and Timothy Smith. Copyright © 2012 Robert M. Grant.

By strengthening its balance sheet, ManU would be better placed to finance new player acquisitions—a major priority following its loss of the English Premier League championship to big-spending, cross-town rival Manchester City and its disappointing performance against Europe's leading teams in the UEFA Champions League during the previous season. After acquiring Japanese midfielder Shinji Kagawa, from Borussia Dortmund for £12 million ($19 million), ManU was close to agreeing the transfer of Arsenal striker Robin van Persie, for £24 million ($38).

While all these issues were important priorities for David Gill to resolve before the English Premier League season kicked off on August 18, they paled into insignificance compared to a much bigger issue that clouded ManU's future: the likely retirement of veteran team manager, Sir Alex Ferguson. On December 31 2012, Ferguson would celebrate his 71st birthday. During his 26 years as team manager, he had been the architect of ManU's two-decade dominance of the English league. Despite expressing no intention of retiring ("Retirement is for young people," he had announced),[2] Gill believed that Ferguson was unlikely to stay beyond two more seasons.

The implications of Ferguson's departure were far-reaching. Ferguson had built an entire infrastructure of scouting, training, team discipline, and team tactics and strategy. The transition to a post-Ferguson era was not simply a question of finding an outstanding soccer coach: it would require a transformation of the club. Gill realized that planning the Ferguson succession would require him and the ManU board to ponder the fundamental issues of what determined success in English and European soccer and how success could be sustained beyond the tenure of a single coach.

The Competitive Environment

The English League

The top league in English professional football is the Premier League, comprising the top 20 teams. Each team plays every other team twice, once at home and once away, with teams receiving three points for a win, one for a tie, and zero for a loss. At the end of every season, the three teams at the bottom of the Premier League are replaced by the top three in the league below. The Premier League team that accumulates the most points throughout the season wins the Championship. The other main domestic honor is the FA (Football Association) Cup, in which teams from all the English leagues compete in an elimination tournament. Table 1 shows the top-performing teams in the English league between 1990 and 2012.

The European League

The Champions League is composed of the 32 top teams in European football. Teams qualify by finishing at or near the top of their respective national leagues. In England, the top four teams qualify. The latter phase of the Champions League season is a knockout competition that results in one team winning the Champions League. Qualifying for the Champions League is a critical objective for the top European teams because of the prestige and substantial TV and gate revenues that

TABLE 1 The top-performing clubs in English football, 1990–2012

Season ending	League champion	Second place	Third place	FA Cup winner
2012	Man. City	Man. United	Arsenal	Chelsea
2011	Man. United	Chelsea	Man. City	Man. City
2010	Chelsea	Man. United	Arsenal	Chelsea
2009	Man. United	Liverpool	Chelsea	Chelsea
2008	Man. United	Chelsea	Arsenal	Portsmouth
2007	Man. United	Chelsea	Liverpool	Chelsea
2006	Chelsea	Man. United	Liverpool	Liverpool
2005	Chelsea	Arsenal	Man. United	Arsenal
2004	Arsenal	Chelsea	Man. United	Man. United
2003	Man. United	Arsenal	Newcastle United	Arsenal
2002	Arsenal	Liverpool	Man. United	Arsenal
2001	Man. United	Arsenal	Liverpool	Liverpool
2000	Man. United	Arsenal	Leeds United	Chelsea
1999	Man. United	Arsenal	Chelsea	Man. United
1998	Arsenal	Man. United	Liverpool	Arsenal
1997	Man. United	Newcastle United	Arsenal	Chelsea
1996	Man. United	Newcastle United	Liverpool	Man. United
1995	Blackburn Rovers	Man. United	Nottingham Forest	Everton
1994	Man. United	Blackburn Rovers	Newcastle United	Man. United
1993	Man. United	Aston Villa	Norwich City	Arsenal
1992	Leeds United	Man. United	Sheffield Wednesday	Liverpool
1991	Arsenal	Liverpool	Crystal Palace	Tottenham Hotspur
1990	Liverpool	Aston Villa	Tottenham Hotspur	Man. United

Note:
Man.: Manchester.
Source: www.european-football-statistics.co.uk.

it offers. The revenues associated with the Champions League have created a major gulf between the "big five teams"—ManU, Chelsea, Liverpool, Arsenal, and Manchester City—and the rest.

Table 2 shows the top teams in Europe based on performance in both national and European competitions.

The Players

The critical determinant of team performance in professional soccer is the quality of the players that make up the team. The world's leading players in the twelve-month period April 2011–April 2012 are shown in Table 3.

Competition for superstar players has been a key aspect of the intensifying rivalry among Europe's top clubs. The growing global market for football and football merchandise has greatly increased the value of top-class players in terms of their contribution to team performance and their individual market pull. The second factor has been an influx of new finance into football—especially into the acquisition of English Premier League clubs by US, Middle East and Russian investors. As a result, despite the global recession, transfer fees hit new highs during the summer of 2009. Table 4 shows some of the biggest transfer deals.

TABLE 2   The top 25 European football clubs, 2000–2012

Club (country)	Total points 2000–2012	Club	Total points 2000–2011
Barcelona (Spain)	1,984	Olympiakos SF Piraeus (Greece)	1,372
Man. United (England)	1,841	Sporting CP (Portugal)	1,292
Real Madrid (Spain)	1,818	FK Shakhtar Donetsk (Ukraine)	1,247
Bayern Munich (Germany)	1,752	AFC Ajax (Netherlands)	1,237
Chelsea (England)	1,686	FK Dynamo Kyiv (Ukraine)	1,235
Arsenal (England)	1,651	Benfica (Portugal)	1,181
FC Porto (Spain)	1,577	Juventus (Italy)	1,154
Inter Milan (Italy)	1,573	Panathinaikos FC (Greece)	1,136
AC Milan (Italy)	1,503	SV Werder Bremen (Germany)	1,116
PSV Eindhoven (Netherlands)	1,502	FC Schalke 04 (Germany)	1,103
Liverpool (England)	1,464	Celtic FC (Scotland)	1,097
Valencia (Spain)	1,450	Sevilla FC (Spain)	1,090
AS Roma (Italy)	1,433	Bayer Leverkusen (Germany)	1,047
Olympique Lyonnais (France)	1,379	Rangers FC (Scotland)	1,009

Note:
Points are based upon club performance in national leagues, national cup competitions, and Champions League and the UEFA Europa League. National performance is adjusted according to the standard of competition in the national leagues.
Source: www.european-fooball-statistics.co.uk.

Football Finances

If the critical resource determining a team's performance is the quality of its players, then the ability to acquire quality players depends on a club's financial resources. There are two major sources of a club's financial resources: its cash flows from its commercial activities and its financing by investors and lenders.

Revenues

Football club revenues derive from three main sources:

- *Match-day revenues*: Revenues from ticket sales depend upon the number of home games played, attendance, and seat prices. Attendance depends primarily upon stadium capacity. Match-day revenues have increased substantially for most clubs driven by increases in stadium capacity and rising prices, especially from the sale of corporate boxes and VIP hospitality packages.
- *Broadcasting revenues*: Football is the world's most popular televised sport. In England, broadcasting rights are negotiated between the Premier League and the TV networks. At the time of writing (2012), TV rights to Premier League games were held by Sky TV and ESPN with the BBC owning the rights to replaying excerpts of games. Broadcasting revenues are distributed among the clubs with each receiving an average of over £50 million annually.
- *Sponsorship and commercial revenues* comprise payments from companies for advertising rights at stadiums and on club websites, sponsorship

TABLE 3   The world's top-performing footballers, April 2012

Rank	Player	Team	Rank	Player	Team
1	L. Messi	Barcelona	26	R. Lewandowski	Bor. Dortmund
2	M. Gómez	Bayern Munich	27	A. Iniesta	Barcelona
3	A. Robben	Bayern Munich	28	W. Rooney	Man. United
4	R. van Persie	Arsenal	29	C. Fàbregas	Barcelona
5	K. Benzema	Real Madrid	30	M. Götze	Bor. Dortmund
6	C. Ronaldo	Real Madrid	31	E. Abidal	Barcelona
7	G. Higuaín	Real Madrid	32	N. Subotić	Bor. Dortmund
8	E. Džeko	Man. City	33	G. Bale	Tottenham
9	G. Piqué	Barcelona	34	F. Malouda	Chelsea
10	Falcao	Atlético Madrid	35	L. Piszczek	Bor. Dortmund
11	L. Suarez	Liverpool	36	M. Hummels	Bor. Dortmund
12	K. Huntelaar	FC Schalke 04	37	T. Müller	Bayern Munich
13	T. Vermaelen	Arsenal	38	Pepe	Real Madrid
14	F. Ribéry	Bayern Munich	38	H. Badstuber	Bayern Munich
15	S. Ramos	Real Madrid	38	J. Lescott	Man. City
16	R. Soldado	Valencia	41	M. Reus	Mönchengladbach
17	E. Adebayor	Tottenham	42	L. Remy	Marseille
18	D. Alves	Barcelona	43	Marcelo	Real Madrid
19	D. Van Buyten	Bayern Munich	44	Y. Touré	Man. City
20	D. Villa	Barcelona	45	S. Agüero	Man. City
21	Michu	Rayo Vallecano	46	J. Boateng	Bayern Munich
22	Xavi	Barcelona	47	C. Pizarro	Werder Bremen
23	S. Kagawa	Bor. Dortmund	48	M. Vorm	Swansea City
24	C. Puyol	Barcelona	49	J. Terry	Chelsea
25	D. Sturridge	Chelsea	50	D. Welbeck	Man. United

Note:
The rankings are based upon detailed analysis of the performance of players in the major European leagues during the previous 12 months.Bor.: Borussia.
Source: www.castrolfootball.com/rankings/rankings/.

agreements, and licenses to reproduce clubs' trademarks on official club merchandise (replica shirts, scarves, games, drinking mugs, toys, and other products). Most clubs have two leading sponsors: the supplier of team kit (e.g., Nike, Adidas, or Puma) and the company whose corporate logo appears on the team's shirts. Major sponsorship deals include Barcelona and Qatar Foundation (£25 million a year), Bayern Munich and Deutsche Telecom (£24 million a year), Manchester United and Aon (£20 million a year), and Liverpool and Standard Chartered Bank (£20 million a year). Sponsorship and licensing revenues are concentrated on a few leading clubs: Real Madrid and Barcelona receive about 65% of the La Liga's commercial revenue. Individual players can have a major impact on a club's sponsorship and licensing revenues. Real Madrid's position as the world's biggest-earning club owes much to its star-studded team. ManU's huge popularity in South Korea was influenced by the presence of Park Ji-Sung in the team.

Table 5 shows financial data for Europe's leading clubs.

TABLE 4 Biggest player transfer fees in European football (to April 2012)

Rank	Player	From	To	Transfer Fee (€m)	Year
1	Cristiano Ronaldo	Man. United	Real Madrid	94	2009
2	Zinedine Zidane	Juventus	Real Madrid	86	2001
3	Zlatan Ibrahimović	Inter Milan	Barcelona	72	2009
4	Kaká	AC Milan	Real Madrid	68	2009
5	Luís Figo	Barcelona	Real Madrid	60	2000
6	Fernando Torres	Liverpool	Chelsea	58	2011
7	Gianluigi Buffon	Parma	Juventus	57	2001
8	Andriy Shevchenko	AC Milan	Chelsea	52	2006
9	Hernán Crespo	Parma	Lazio	48	2000
10	Christian Vieri	Lazio	Inter Milan	47	1999
11	Juan Verón	Lazio	Man. United	46	2001
12	Rui Costa	Fiorentina	AC Milan	45	2001
13	Sergio Agüero	Atlético Madrid	Man. City	45	2012
14	Rio Ferdinand	Leeds	Man. United	45	2002
15	Javier Pastore	Palermo	Paris St. Germain	42	2011
=16	Andy Carroll	Newcastle United	Liverpool	40	2011
=16	Sergio Agüero	Atlético Madrid	Man. City	40	2011
=16	Radamel Falcao	FC Porto	Atlético Madrid	40	2011
=16	Cesc Fàbregas	Arsenal	FC Barcelona	40	2011
17	Robinho	Real Madrid	Man. City	38	2008

Source: Adapted from http://en.wikipedia.org/wiki/Transfer_(association_football)#Highest_fees.

Costs

Wages and salaries, most of which are accounted for by players' salaries, are the biggest cost item for European clubs. Wages as a percentage of revenues were lowest in the Bundesliga (54%) and highest in Serie A (77%).[3] In the English Premier League, Chelsea and Manchester City were the leaders in offering the most lucrative player contracts: in 2010, Manchester City offered £11 million a year to Yaya Touré.

The other major cost items for the leading soccer clubs are player transfer fees. Players are transferred between clubs both on terms agreed between the two clubs and with the player concerned. Players are signed to clubs on contracts of up to five years. At the end of their contracts, they become free agents. The rise in transfer fees over the past ten years was driven by three big-spending clubs: Real Madrid, Chelsea, and Manchester City.

Sources of Finance

Only a few European football clubs are publicly listed companies (these include Ajax, Celtic, and Lazio); most are privately owned. Traditionally, football club owners were rich, local businessmen, for example Juventus is owned by the Agnelli family (Fiat), AC Milan by Silvio Berlusconi, Inter Milan by Massimo Moratti, and Olympique de Marseille by Robert Louis-Dreyfus. Recently, European football has attracted international equity. English clubs owned by foreign-born billionaires include Chelsea (Roman Abramovich), Manchester City (Sheikh Mansour bin Zayed Al Nahyan), Queens Park Rangers (Lakshmi Mittal of AlcelorMittal Steel), and

TABLE 5 Financial data from the leading European football clubs, 2010–2011

		Revenue[a] (€m)	Match day[a] (%)	Broadcasting[a] (%)	Commercial[a] (%)	Operating[b] profit (€m)	Club Value[c] (€m)
1	Real Madrid	479.5	26	36	38	155.1	1,360
2	FC Barcelona	450.7	25	41	34	69.6	947
3	Man. United	367.0	33	36	31	129.0	1,620
4	Bayern Munich	321.4	22	22	56	65.2	895
5	Arsenal	251.1	41	39	20	71.0	936
6	Chelsea	249.8	30	45	25	55.1	551
7	AC Milan	235.1	15	36	49	21.0	717
8	Inter Milan	211.4	16	58	26	(60.9)	355
9	Liverpool	203.3	22	36	42	32.6	449
10	FC Schalke 04	202.4	18	37	45	73.2	425
11	Tottenham Hotspur	181.0	26	51	23	43.5	409
12	Man. City	169.6	17	35	48	(89.1)	321
13	Juventus	153.9	8	57	35	(27.5)	428
14	Olympique de Marseille	150.4	17	52	31	3.9	349
15	AS Roma	143.5	12	64	24	1.6	354
16	Bor. Dortmund	138.5	20	23	57	23.9	394
17	Olympique Lyonnais	132.8	15	52	33	(2.2)	385
18	Hamburger SV	128.8	32	21	47	12.3	355
19	Valencia	116.8	23	57	20	16.7	288
20	Napoli	114.9	19	58	30	42.0	283

Notes:

Figures in parentheses denote a loss.

[a] These data are from Deloitte Sports Group, "Football Money League, 2012, Deloitte LLP".

[b] Operating profit excludes the amortization of players. Data from "The world's most valuable soccer teams, 2012," *Forbes*.

[c] Team values are based on estimate future club revenues. Data from "The world's most valuable soccer teams, 2012," *Forbes*.

Fulham (Mohammed Al-Fayed of Harrods). ManU and Liverpool are both owned by US investors (the Glazer family and New England Sports Ventures, respectively). In Spain and Germany most of the leading clubs are owned by their fans.

Profitability

Despite large and growing revenues, European professional football is unprofitable. Deloitte estimated the operating margin of the Bundesliga at 8.1% in 2009–2010 compared to 4.0% for the English Premier League (Table 6), and losses for both the Serie A and La Liga.[4] Lack of profitability reflects the fact that most clubs are run for sporting rather than financial success.

Changes agreed by football's European governing body, UEFA, will fundamentally change the financial dynamics of the sport. The "financial fair play" rules require that from 2012 onwards clubs competing in European must break even.

Teams and Team Building

There were two routes to acquiring world-class players: to buy them or to develop them. The extent to which a club is reliant upon buying players is indicated by its expenditure on transfer fees. Table 7 shows that Real Madrid, Chelsea, and Manchester City are distinguished by their massive expenditures on star players. Other top-performing teams—notably Bayern Munich, Barcelona, Arsenal, and Valencia—emphasize developing their own players through their youth academies.

Coaching

The fact that great players are not enough to create outstanding team performance points to the key role played by coaches. The sustained success of a team is typically associated with the leadership role of a single coach: Ancelotti at AC Milan, Guardiola at Barcelona, van Gaal at Ajax, and, most notably, Ferguson at ManU. As the developer of talent, team architect, motivator, and source of strategy and tactics,

TABLE 6 Financial results for the top six English football clubs, 2011

Team	Revenue (£million)	Wages as percentage of operating revenues[a]	Net debt, (£million)	Interest payable, (£million)	Pre-tax profit (£million)
Arsenal[b]	227	55	98	19.0	13
Chelsea	226	75	734	0.8	(71)
Liverpool	184	70	65	18.0	(53)
Man. City	153	114	34	4.0	(197)
Man. United	331	46	308	34.0	34
Tottenham	164	56	125	12.0	2

Notes:
Figures in parentheses denote a loss.
[a] Operating revenues are the sum of revenues from match days, TV and broadcasting, and commercial.
[b] Includes revenue from sale of former stadium.
Source: Guardian Datablog, http://www.guardian.co.uk/news/datablog/2011/may/19/football-club-accounts-debt.

TABLE 7 Investment in players by leading European football clubs

Club	Performance points 2000–2012	Gross transfer fees, 2003–2012 (£million)[a]	Net transfer fees, 2003–2012 (£million)[a]	Size of squad, April 2012	Average age of squad, April 2012	Market value of squad (£million)
Barcelona	1,984	577	352	22	27.2	520
Man. United	1,841	424	77	28	26.7	370
Real Madrid	1,818	987	714	23	26.4	475
Bayern Munich	1,752	317	210	25	26.1	315
Chelsea	1,686	816	638	25	27.6	335
Arsenal	1,651	259	(11)	26	26.2	265
FC Porto	1,577	234	(211)	24	25.1	185
Inter Milan	1,573	458	105	27	28.9	210
AC Milan	1,503	237	(2)	34	29.0	240
PSV Eindhoven	1,502	115	(2)	28	24.4	78
Liverpool	1,464	485	192	25	27.0	205
Valencia	1,450	222	35	26	26.4	160
AS Roma	1,433	226	109	27	27.3	145
Olympique Lyonnais	1,379	228	44	31	24.9	135
Juventus	1,154	420	196	24	27.0	215
Man. City	786	622	453	24	27.0	410

Note:

Figures in parentheses denote a loss.

[a] Covers transfers from the beginning of the 2003–2004 season to the end of April 2012.

Sources: www.european-fooball-statistics.co.uk; www.transfermarkt.co.uk.

the coach is the individual most responsible for team success. Yet, what determines a great coach is hard to judge. As Table 8 shows, successful coaches do not conform to any single leadership style or personality type. Different coaching styles fit different teams and different circumstances: coaches that achieve outstanding success with one team can be dismal failures with another.

However, some common factors are apparent. An eye for talent is critical, in particular the ability to recognize outstanding potential before it is developed. Second, the ability to develop talent within a team context. Third, the ability to mix and balance individual players into effective team combinations. Fourth, the ability to adapt tactics and playing styles to suit different opponents and different circumstances. Finally, all great coaches are able to motivate their players and inspire respect and loyalty from them.

Management and Organization

Running a professional football club involves two distinct areas of management: managing the team for on-the-pitch performance and managing commercial activities to generate revenue and profit. Most English and Scottish clubs are organized

TABLE 8   The world's top football coaches, 2011

Coach[a]	Teams coached
Alex Ferguson	St. Mirren 1974–8; Aberdeen 1978–86; Manchester United 1986–
Guus Hiddink	PSV Eindhoven 1987–90, 2002–6; Valencia 1991–4; Netherlands 1995–8; Real Madrid 1998–9; Real Betis 1999–2000; S. Korea 2000–2; Australia 2005–6; Chelsea 2009; Russia 2006–10, Turkey 2010–
José Mourinho	UD Leiria 2001–2; FC Porto 2002–4; Chelsea 2004–7; Inter Milan 2008–10; Real Madrid 2010–
Marcello Lippi	Cesena 1989–91; Lucchese 1991–2; Atalanta 1992 –3; Napoli 1993–4; Juventus 1994–9, 2001–4, Inter Milan 1999–2000; Italy 2004–6, 2008–
Fabio Capello	AC Milan 1991–6, 1997–8; Real Madrid 1996–7, 2006–7; AS Roma 1999–2004; Juventus 2004–6; England 2008–12
Roberto Mancini	Fiorentina 2001–2; Lazio 2002-4; Inter Milan 2004–8; Man. City 2009–
Arsene Wenger	Nancy 1984–7; Monaco 1987–94; Arsenal 1994–
Giovanni Trapattoni	Milan 1974–6; Juventus 1976–88, 1991–4; Inter Milan 1986–91; Bayern Munich 1994–5, 1996–8; Fiorentina 1998–2000; Italy 2000–4; Benfica 2004–5; Salzburg 2006–8; Ireland 2008–
Carlo Ancelotti	Parma 1996–9; Juventus 1999–2001; AC Milan 2001–9; Chelsea 2009–11
Frank Rijkaard	Netherlands 1998–2000; Sparta Rotterdam 2001–2; Barcelona 2003–8; Galatasaray 2009–10; Saudi Arabia 2011–
Louis van Gaal	Ajax 1991–7; Barcelona 1997–2000, 2002–3; Netherlands 2000–2; AZ 2005–9; Bayern Munich 2009–11
Ottmar Hitzfeld	Aarau 1984–88; Grasshopper Club Zürich 1988–91; Bor. Dortmund 1991–7; Bayern Munich 1998–2004, 2007–8; Switzerland 2008–
Pep Guardiola	Barcelona 2008
Vicente del Bosque	Real Madrid 1994, 1996, 1999–2003; Beşiktaş 2004–5; Spain 2008–

Note:
[a] Includes coaches active as of October 2011 and is in no particular order.
Sources: "World Best Soccer Coaches," http://shareranks.faqs.org/7026,World-best-soccer-coaches; "World Football: 11 Best Currently Active Managers"; http://bleacherreport.com/articles/448586/world-football-11-best-currently-active-managers; "Top 50 Managers of All Time," *Times on Line*, September 12, 2007.

to achieve a clear separation between these two. Club owners appoint a board of directors, which typically select a CEO to take charge of administrative and commercial matters, and a team manager, who is responsible for coaching, team selection, and player acquisition (subject to budgets determined by the board).

Not all English clubs achieve a clear separation between commercial and team matters. Typically, this is because of the desire of owners to involve themselves in managing the team. At Chelsea, Roman Abramovich has conflicted with his managers over player acquisition, team selection, and playing style.

Blurring of responsibilities is also a feature of many continental European clubs. Barcelona and Real Madrid are both owned by their local supporters, who elect the club president. These presidents oversee both commercial and team management. Real Madrid's president, Florentino Pérez, is heavily involved in team selection and player acquisition. Meanwhile, the tenure of coaches is short. Real Madrid hired and fired 11 head coaches between 2003 and July 2010. At Inter Milan, club president and owner Massimo Moretti is heavily involved in team management. Between the 2007/8 season and the beginning of the 2011/12 season, Inter had five different coaches.

Many continental European clubs also feature a division of decision-making responsibility between the coach and a "director of football" (or "sporting director" or "technical director"). This arrangement is intended to allow the coach to focus his efforts on the first team, while the director of football handles the management of reserve and youth teams, scouting for new players, and is an interface between the coach and club's owner or chairman.

Different coaches are associated with different strategies: Barcelona's Giardiola and Arsenal's Wenger favor attacking football based upon fast, accurate passing and dominance of the midfield; Manchester City's Mancini and Real Madrid's Mourinho are committed to solid defenses. Some clubs (e.g., Arsenal) favor youth; others (Real Madrid, Manchester City, and AC Milan) favor proven experience.

One key resource of the club is not amenable to management: the fans. Not only are fans the primary source of club revenue; they are the custodians of a club's culture and heritage. Where a club's fans identify with the club's coach and endorse the style of football being played—as at Barcelona under Guardiola and Liverpool under Dalglish—their support can have a major impact on team performance. At the same time their disaffection can be a critical source of demotivation and dissention.

The one thing that was abundantly clear to any observer of the "beautiful game" was that there was no simple recipe for success. Individual resources, whether money, players, or outstanding coach, were all key ingredients, but on their own were insufficient to guarantee success. To understand success it was necessary to look at the full range of resources—of which fans were certainly a key component.

Manchester United: The Club and the Company

Manchester United Football Club was founded in 1878. Old Trafford, ManU's stadium, saw its first game in 1910. During the 1950s and 1960s, ManU rose to prominence under the leadership of its legendary team manager: Matt Busby. However, in 1958, on a return flight from a European game, a plane crash killed eight of the "Busby Babes." After a decade of rebuilding by Busby, ManU became the first English team to win the European Cup, in 1968. Between Busby's retirement in 1969 and Alex Ferguson's arrival in 1986, ManU did not win a single league championship and Liverpool became England's pre-eminent club.

The Ferguson Era

Ferguson was recruited by ManU because of his remarkable success at Aberdeen, where he had broken the historical dominance of Scottish football by Rangers and Celtic and had taken Aberdeen all the way to the European Cup.

Ferguson was born into a working-class family in Govan, a tough, shipbuilding community close to Glasgow, a city famous for the passion and loyalty of its football fans. After a playing career in the Scottish league, Ferguson began coaching, first with East Stirlingshire then with St. Mirren before joining Aberdeen.

During his first six years at ManU, Ferguson systematically rebuilt the team. He culled the existing squad and acquired talented new players such as Mark Hughes, Paul Ince, Eric Cantona, and Roy Keane. However, success came slowly. In 1990, ManU achieved its first major trophy: the FA Cup, but not until 1993 did ManU win the league championship.

While recreating ManU's first team, Ferguson expanded the scouting staff in order to widen the quest to sign talented young players. In 1990, ManU won the English League youth championship with a team that included Ryan Giggs, David Beckham, Nicky Butt, Gary and Phil Neville, and Paul Scholes. Between 1994 and 2003, these homegrown young players formed the nucleus of a ManU team that dominated English football. The pinnacle of this golden era came when ManU achieved a triumph unprecedented in English football history: the team won the English league championship, the FA Cup, the Champions League, and the Intercontinental Cup when they defeated the South American champions, Palmeiras.

Between 2003 and 2008, Ferguson rebuilt the ManU team again. Key members of the trophy-winning team of 1999, including David Beckham, Roy Keane, Peter Schmeichel, Andy Cole, and Jaap Stam were sold. The new team—which included talents such as Rio Ferdinand, Cristiano Ronaldo, Wayne Rooney, Louis Saha, Edwin van der Sar, Patrice Evra, Nemanja Vidić, Anderson, Park Ji-Sung, Michael Carrick, Nani, and Carlos Tevez—demonstrated its effectiveness by winning the Champions League in 2008.

Between 2009 and 2012, Ferguson engaged in a renewed phase of team rebuilding which involved the sale or retirement of key players, such as Ronaldo, van der Saar, Tevez, and Saha, and the acquisition of Javier Hernández, Antonio Valencia, David de Gea, Ashley Young, and Phil Jones.

Ownership and Structure

Between 1991 and 2003, Manchester United PLC was a public company, listed on the London Stock Exchange. In 2005, the company was acquired by the American businessman Malcolm Glazer, owner of the Tampa Bay Buccaneers—a National Football League franchise. The deal created outrage among ManU fans; not only was Glazer "a yank who knows nothing about football" but his purchase was financed mainly by debt. Under Glazer's ownership, the board of Manchester United Ltd comprises Glazer's six children with Joel Glazer as chairman.

The hands-off approach of the Glazer family to team management is reinforced by the legal separation between the parent company, Manchester United Ltd, and its subsidiary, Manchester United Football Club Ltd (MUFC), which owns and operates the club. The MUFC board includes former player Sir Bobby Charlton and CEO David Gill; none of the Glazers are on the MUFC board. However, the issue of ManU's debt and its implications for expenditure on new players continued to be a source of friction between fans and the Glazers. Figure 1 shows ManU's organizational structure.

Ferguson's Management Style

In a business where the performance expectations of owners and fans are focused on the short term, Ferguson's emphasis has been on success over the long term:

> My aim in management has always been to lay foundations that will make a club successful for years, or even decades . . . When I joined United on 6 November 1986, they had gone 19 years without a title. No-one had to tell me that if I did not end that drought I would be a failure. Putting them in a position to challenge consistently would, I knew, be a long haul. I would have to build from the bottom up, rectifying the flaws I had recognized and spreading my influence and self-belief through every layer of the organization. I wanted to form a personal link with everyone around the place—not just the players, the coaches and the backroom staff but the office workers, the cooks and servers in the canteen and the laundry ladies. All had to believe that they were part of the club and that a resurgence was coming.[5]

The starting point was training and team discipline. Ferguson declared war on alcohol—a problem endemic to British professional soccer and an indulgence

FIGURE 1 Manchester United's governance structure

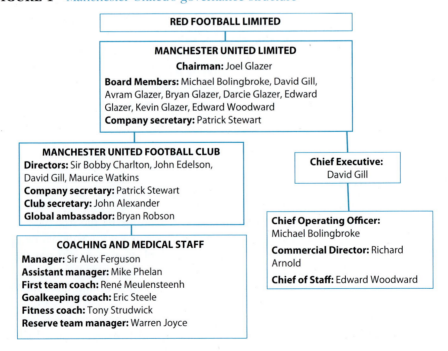

that Ferguson viewed as incompatible with professional sport. The new, rigorous training regime included meticulous attention to attendance, punctuality, and effort. His training sessions built individual and team skills through continuous repetition: "refining technique to the point where difficult skills become a matter of habit."

Developing the team for the long term focused heavily on identifying and developing new talent: "From the moment I became manager of United, I was committed to the creation of a youth policy that would be the envy of every other club in Britain. The first imperative was to find the raw talent."[6]

One of Ferguson first initiatives at ManU was to expand the scouting staff from five to over 20 and instruct them to seek only the most outstanding talent. Manchester United's Youth Academy was built into what Ferguson declared was the finest youth coaching program in the country. Increasingly, ManU's scouts scoured the world for new players. By 2008, ManU's worldwide scouting network included two full-time scouts in Brazil.[7]

For Ferguson, acquiring talented players was merely the starting point: the essence of developing players lay in developing skills within the context of team coordination:

> The best teams stand out because they are teams; because the individual members have been so truly integrated that the team functions with a single spirit. There is a constant flow of mutual support among the players, enabling them to feed off strengths and compensate for weaknesses. They depend on one another, trust in one another. A manager should engender that sense of unity. He should create a bond among his players and between him and them that raises performance to heights that were unimaginable when they started out as disparate individuals.[8]

Ferguson's approach to motivating his players involved a combination of loyal support and, where he identified unnecessary mistakes or lack of effort, withering criticism. Ferguson's resolute support for his players allowed him to induce exquisite performances from volatile and difficult-to-manage players such as Eric Cantona, Roy Keane, and Wayne Rooney. At the same time, Ferguson was ruthless whenever he perceived lack of total commitment by players. He was renowned for his temper and for ferocious verbal tirades delivered at such close range that they became known as "Ferguson's hairdryer." Ferguson's half-time talks to his team could have a powerful re-energizing effect. At the European Cup Final in 1999, ManU was losing 1–0 at the end of the first half. He told his team: "At the end of this game, the European Cup will be only six feet away from you and you'll not even be able to touch it if we lose. And for many of you that will be the closest you will ever get. Don't you dare come back in here without giving your all."

Central to Ferguson's management style was his insistence that no player was bigger than the club. The result of this has been well-publicized clashes with some of his leading players, typically resulting in them being demoted to the substitutes' bench or being sold to other clubs. Ferguson's belief that total player commitment was the essence of outstanding team performance meant that character was an essential ingredient in the players he sought and retained. Players like Rooney, Park, Scholes, and Giggs were renowned for their unflagging effort and work ethic.

In terms of team strategy and match tactics, Ferguson was committed to control over the midfield. This required "controlled, sustained possession that calls for players adept at holding the ball and spreading calculated and accurate passes . . . A high standard of passing in central midfield was the core of United's football."[9] In the effort to emulate the style of possession football interspersed with lightning attacks pioneered by the top Italian teams, Ferguson's team design was based on a closely coordinated midfield group built around players such as Keane, Scholes, Beckham, and Giggs supporting creative strikers such as Cantona, van Nistelrooy, Ronaldo, and Rooney.

In terms of team configuration, Ferguson favored a combination of youth and experience. The championship winning team of 2010/11 featured a quartet of players—Giggs, Neville, Scholes, and van der Saar whose average age exceeded 37 years together with under-21s such as John O'Shea, Federico Macheda, and the Da Silva twins. Ferguson's emphasis on nurturing young talent is reinforced by his willingness to sell top players that are highly valued by big spending teams. Star players David Beckham, van Nistelrooy, and Cristiano Ronaldo were each sold to Real Madrid (Ronaldo for a world record transfer fee of £80 million). As a result, ManU's net expenditure on player transfers has been modest relative to other leading European clubs.

Ferguson is also a leading exponent of "squad rotation"—reconfiguring a team in order to rest key players and to adapt tactics in order to exploit opponents' vulnerabilities. During consecutive games, ManU's starting team can vary substantially; while in the course of a game, Ferguson makes extensive use of substitutes. This team flexibility requires that players develop broad repertoires of coordination—playing in different combinations and adapting their style of play according to the different talents of different teammates.[10]

Commercial and Financial Performance

ManU and Real Madrid are regarded as the most commercially focused clubs in European football. In building a global fan base then converting that support into revenues, the two are models for other European clubs. According to former commercial director Andy Anson: "We're not just a sports club, we are an international brand."

In July 2012, ManU's official sponsors included:

- AON: the US-based insurance company and ManU's principal sponsor
- Nike: ManU's kit sponsor
- 23 other "official partners," including: DHL, Budweiser, Audi, Betfair, Hublot (watches), Singha Beer, Smirnoff (vodka), Turkish Airlines, Thomas Cook (travel), Saudi Telecom, Mister Potato, Epson, Concha y Toro (wine), Bharti Airtel, PCCW (Hong Kong telecom), Telekom Malaysia, Viva (telecom in Bahrain and Kuwait), Airtel Africa, MTN (telecom, southern Africa), Tri Indonesia (telecom), Türk Telekom, and Globacom (telecom, west Africa).

Commercial initiatives have included:

- MU Finance offering credit cards, mortgages, and retirement planning products.
- MU Mobile offering SMS and video streaming services to ManU fans.

- MUTV, which shows ManU games on webTV.
- Manchester United Soccer Schools located in the UK, US, Canada, Switzerland, Singapore, Malaysia, and at Disneyland in Paris and Hong Kong.
- The Manchester United Superstore offers a wide range of ManU licensed products both through the Old Trafford retail store and online through http://store.manutd.com.

ManU's Old Trafford stadium hosts a wide variety of events. In addition to the ManU museum and stadium tours, its suites, bars, and ballroom are used for conferences, receptions, parties, and weddings. Expansion of the stadium in 2006 gave a substantial boost to ManU's revenues, primarily from the 7,500 additional seats.

Details of ManU's financial performance are provided in Appendix 1; its business strategy is outlined in Appendix 2.

Looking to the Future

As CEO David Gill concluded a conference call with the two separate management teams responsible for ManU's roadshow presentations (one covering the US; the other covering Europe and Asia), he realized the interdependency of the factors influencing ManU's future success. Future profitability depended upon the club's ability to grow its commercial and broadcasting revenues. But this would only be possible if ManU could retain its preeminence in the English league and position among the top five clubs of Europe. But this would require strengthening the team, which in turn would require a successful IPO giving ManU the financial strength to compete for the world's top footballing talent.

Yet, top-class players were only one component contributing to outstanding team performance. Even more important was a team manager who could construct the team and sustain a network of processes for identifying, attracting, developing, and integrating these players.

With Alex Ferguson's retirement fast approaching, the issue for ManU was not simply finding a top-class coach who could replace Ferguson, but how the club's entire system could develop to reach higher standards of performance. Several outstanding successful football coaches had already expressed their interest in succeeding Ferguson—most notably Jose Mourinho, who many saw as the only candidate with the authority, personality, and track record to step into Ferguson's shoes. However, the problem for Mourinho or any other newcomer would be the disruption caused by the inevitable rebuilding of the systems, philosophy, and style established during Ferguson's 26-year tenure. Gill wondered whether a smoother transition might be achieved if one of Ferguson's current or former assistants was appointed as successor. The assistant manager at the time was Mike Phelan and the head of the youth academy was Brian McClair; previous assistants included Carlos Queiroz, Steve McCLaren, Walter Smith, and Ole Gunnar Solskjær. Another route to continuity would be to appoint a former ManU player such as Gary Neville (who was an assistant coach to the England national team)—or, even a current player such as Ryan Giggs or Paul Scholes.

Appendix 1: Manchester United: Selected Financial Data, 2000–2011 (£million)

	2011[a]	2010[a]	2009[a]	2008[a]	2007[a]	2006[a]	2005[a]	2004[b]	2003[b]	2002[b]	2001[b]	2000[b]
Turnover	331.4	286.4	278.5	257.1	212.2	167.8	157.2	169.1	173.0	146.1	129.6	116.0
Group operating profit before depreciation and amortization	111.3	99.8	92.8	86.1	79.8	46.3	46.1	58.3	57.3	41.4	38.2	35.1
Depreciation	(5.5)	(7.1)	(7.4)	(7.3)	(7.6)	(5.1)	(6.1)	(6.6)	(7.3)	(6.9)	(6.5)	(5.1)
Amortization of players	(39.2)	(40.1)	(37.6)	(35.5)	(24.3)	(23.4)	(24.2)	(21.8)	(21.0)	(17.6)	(10.2)	(13.1)
Exceptional costs	(4.7)	—	—	—	—	—	(7.3)	—	(2.2)	(1.4)	(2.1)	(1.3)
(Loss)/profit on disposal of players	4.5	12.7	80.7	21.8	11.8	12.5	(0.6)	(3.1)	12.9	17.4	2.2	1.6
Net interest receivable/ (payable)	(34.0)	(39.4)	(0.2)	0.5	0.3	0.7	2.5	1.1	(0.3)	0.0	0.7	0.5
Pre-tax profit on ordinary activities	34.0	25,3	127.6	66.4	59.6	30.1	10.8	27.9	39.3	32.3	21.8	16.8
Taxation	(23.6)	(8.3)	(34.8)	(19.9)	(17.3)	(9.2)	(4.2)	(8.5)	(9.6)	(7.3)	(7.4)	(4.8)
Net profit	10.4	16.8	93.0	46.8	42.3	21.6	6.5	19.4	29.8	25.0	14.8	12.0
Fixed assets	308.0	258.5	281.4	267.5	283.0	229.0	202.8	204.5	n.a.	n.a.	n.a.	n.a.
Current assets[c]	595.1	669.8	337.6	179.2	115.3	71.8	83.5	24.3	n.a.	n.a.	n.a.	n.a.
Total liabilities[c]	(760.8)	(798.6)	(238.4)	(155.6)	(82.5)	(31.4)	50.3	53.4	n.a.	n.a.	n.a.	n.a.
Total equity	142.2	134.0	381.9	294.0	245.3	202.7	180.8	173.4	156.4	137.4	120.5	115.0

Notes:

The data relate to Manchester United PLC for 2000–2005 and Manchester United Ltd for 2006–2011. Due to accounting changes, the data for 2000–2004 are not comparable to those for 2005–2010.

Figures in parentheses denote a loss.

n.a.: not applicable.

[a] Year to June 30.

[b] Year to July 31.

[c] In 2010, £509 million of new debt was issued. The proceeds were transferred to the parent company, Red Football Ltd, to pay off the debts incurred by the Glazer family in acquiring ManU.

Source: Manchester United annual reports.

Appendix 2: Manchester United: Extracts from Offer Prospectus

Our Competitive Strengths

We believe our key competitive strengths are:

- *One of the most successful sports teams in the world*: Founded in 1878, Manchester United is one of the most successful sports teams in the world — playing one of the world's most popular spectator sports. We have won 60 trophies in nine different leagues, competitions and cups since 1908. Our on-going success is supported by our highly developed football infrastructure and global scouting network.

- *A globally recognized brand with a large, worldwide following*: Our 134-year history, our success and the global popularity of our sport have enabled us to become what we believe to be one of the world's most recognizable brands. We enjoy the support of our global community of 659 million followers. The composition of our follower base is far-reaching and diverse, transcending cultures, geographies, languages and socio-demographic groups, and we believe the strength of our brand goes beyond the world of sports.

- *Ability to successfully monetize our brand*: The popularity and quality of our globally recognized brand make us an attractive marketing partner for companies around the world. We have built a diversified portfolio of sponsorships with leading brands such as Nike, Aon, DHL, Epson, Turkish Airlines and Singha. Our community of followers is strong in emerging markets, particularly in certain regions of Asia, which enables us to deliver media exposure and growth to our partners in these markets.

- *Sought-after content capitalizing on the proliferation of digital and social media*: We produce content that is followed year-round by our global community of followers. Our content distribution channels are international and diverse, and we actively adopt new media channels to enhance the accessibility and reach of our content. We believe our ability to generate proprietary content, which we distribute on our own global platforms as well as via popular third party social media platforms such as Facebook, constitutes an on-going growth opportunity.

- *Well established global media and marketing infrastructure driving commercial revenue growth*: We have a large global team dedicated to the development and monetization of our brand and to the sourcing of new revenue opportunities. The team has considerable experience and expertise in sponsorship sales, customer relationship management, marketing execution, advertising support and brand development. This experience and infrastructure enables us to deliver an effective set of marketing capabilities to our partners on a global basis. Our team is dedicated to the development and monetization of our brand and to the sourcing of new revenue opportunities.

- *Seasoned management team and committed ownership*: Our senior management has considerable experience and expertise in the football, commercial, media and finance industries.

Our Strategy

We aim to increase our revenue and profitability by expanding our high growth businesses that leverage our brand, global community and marketing infrastructure. The key elements of our strategy are:

- *Expand our portfolio of global and regional sponsors*: We are well positioned to continue to secure sponsorships with leading brands. Over the last few years, we have implemented a proactive approach to identifying, securing and supporting sponsors. This has resulted in a 21.5% compound annual growth rate in our sponsorship revenue from fiscal year 2009 through fiscal year 2011 (the growth rate from fiscal year 2009 to fiscal year 2010 was 10.0% and from fiscal year 2010 to fiscal year 2011 was 34.2%). Our historical growth rates do not guarantee that we will achieve comparable rates in the future. In addition to developing our global sponsorship portfolio, we are focused on expanding a regional sponsorship model, segmenting new opportunities by product category and territory. As part of this strategy, we have opened an office in Asia and are in the process of opening an office in North America. These are in addition to our London and Manchester offices.

- *Further develop our retail, merchandising, apparel & product licensing business*: We will focus on growing this business on a global basis by increasing our product range and improving distribution through further development of our wholesale, retail and e-commerce channels. Manchester United branded retail locations have opened in Singapore, Macau, India and Thailand, and we plan to expand our global retail footprint over the next several years. In addition, we will also invest to expand our portfolio of product licensees to enhance the range of product offerings available to our followers.

- *Exploit new media & mobile opportunities*: The rapid shift of media consumption towards internet, mobile and social media platforms presents us with multiple growth opportunities and new revenue streams. Our digital media platforms, such as mobile sites, applications and social media, are expected to become one of the primary methods by which we engage and transact with our followers around the world.

- In addition to developing our own digital properties, we intend to leverage third party media platforms and other social media as a means of further engaging with our followers and creating a source of traffic for our digital media assets. Our new media & mobile offerings are in the early stages of development and present opportunities for future growth.

- *Enhance the reach and distribution of our broadcasting rights*: The value of live sports programming has grown dramatically in recent years due to changes in how television content is distributed and consumed. Specifically, television consumption has become more fragmented and audiences for traditional scheduled television programming have declined as consumer choice increased with the emergence of multi-channel television, the development of technologies such as the digital video recorder and the emergence of digital viewing on the internet and mobile devices. The unpredictable outcomes of live sports ensures that individuals consume sports programming in real time and in full, resulting in higher audiences and increased interest from television broadcasters and advertisers. We are well positioned to benefit from the increased value and the growth in distribution associated with the Premier League, the Champions League and other competitions. Furthermore, MUTV, our global broadcasting platform, delivers Manchester United programming to 54 countries around the world. We plan to expand the distribution of MUTV by improving the quality of its content and its production capabilities.

- *Diversify revenue and improve margins*: We aim to increase the revenue and operating margins of our business as we further expand our high growth commercial businesses, including sponsorship, retail, merchandising, licensing and new media & mobile. By increasing the emphasis on our commercial businesses, we will further diversify our revenue, enabling us to generate improved profitability.

Source: Securities and Exchange Commission, Manchester United Ltd Form F-1 Registration Statement, Washington, DC, July 3, 2012.

Notes

1. "Manchester United's global appeal goes from strength to strength," *Daily Telegraph* (July 16, 2009). Reproduced with permission.
2. "Q&A with Manchester United's Alex Ferguson," *New York Times*, January 21, 2012.
3. "European football market grows to €16.3 billion," Deloitte press release June 9, 2011, http://www.deloitte.com/view/en_GX/global/press/global-press-releases-en/8a17eba725990310VgnVCM2000001b56f00aRCRD.htm, accessed September 16, 2011.
4. "European football market grows to €16.3 billion," Deloitte press release June 9, 2011. http://www.deloitte.com/view/en_GX/global/press/global-press-releases-en/8a17eba725990310VgnVCM2000001b56f00aRCRD.htm, accessed September 16, 2011.
5. Alex Ferguson, *Managing My Life*, Hodder & Stoughton, London, 1999, p. 242.
6. Alex Ferguson, *Managing My Life*, Hodder & Stoughton, London, 1999, p. 242.
7. "Manchester United Invest in Brazilian Talent," *Independent*, October 17, 2008.
8. Alex Ferguson, *Managing My Life*, Hodder & Stoughton, London, 1999, p. 274.
9. Alex Ferguson, *Managing My Life*, Hodder & Stoughton, London, 1999, p. 437.
10. "Sir Alex Ferguson Proves Mastery at Manchester United with Rotation System," *The Times*, May 11, 2009.

A video clip relating to this case is available in your interactive e-book at **www.wileyopenpage.com**

Case 9　AirAsia: The World's Lowest-cost Airline

By 2009, AirAsia had established itself as Asia's most successful low-cost airline. Between January 2002 and March 2009, AirAsia had expanded from two aircraft and 200,000 passenger journeys to 79 aircraft and 11.8 million passenger journeys. Its route network had grown beyond Malaysia to cover 10 Southeast Asian countries. In addition to its hub in Kuala Lumpur (KL), Malaysia, it had replicated its system by establishing associated airlines in Thailand and Indonesia.

By 2007, UBS research showed that AirAsia was the world's lowest-cost airline with costs per available seat kilometer (ASK) significantly below those of Southwest, Jet Blue, Ryanair, or Virgin Blue (Figure 1). It was also one of the world's most profitable airlines. In 2008, when very few of the world's airlines made any profit at all, AirAsia earned a return on assets of 4%.[1] In 2009, it won the Skytrax Award as "The World's Best Low Cost Airline."

AirAsia had built its business on the low-cost carrier (LCC) model created by Southwest Airlines in the US and replicated throughout the world by a host of imitators. AirAsia had adapted the basic LCC model to the market, geographical, and institutional features of Southeast Asia while preserving the principal operational

FIGURE 1　Costs in US cents per available seat kilometer for different low-cost airlines

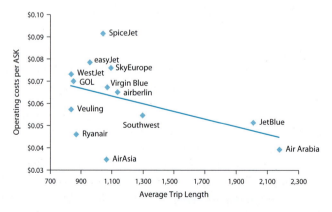

Source: AirAsia Presentation, CLSA Forum, Hong Kong, September 2007.

Written by Robert M. Grant. The case draws upon a report written by Sara Buchholz, Nadia Fabio, Andrés Ileyassoff, Laurent Mang, and Daniele Visentin: *AirAsia: Tales from a Long-haul Low Cost Carrier*, Bocconi University (2009), and from an earlier case by Thomas Lawton and Jonathan Doh: *The Ascendance of AirAsia: Building a Successful Budget Airline in Asia* (Ivey School of Business, Case No. 9B08M054 2008). Used by permission of the authors. © 2012, Robert M. Grant.

features of the strategy. However, in 2007, AirAsia embarked upon a major departure from the LCC model: expansion into long-haul flights by inaugurating routes to Australia and China and then, in 2009, to India and the UK. The conventional wisdom was that the efficiency of the LCC model was dependent upon short and medium-distance flights with a single type of aircraft and minimal customer amenities—intercontinental flights required contravening these basic conditions. Very few LCCs had ventured into long-haul; even fewer had made a success of it.

To evaluate AirAsia's potential to expand from being a regional carrier to an international airline would require a careful analysis of the basis of its existing cost advantage and an evaluation of the transferability of these cost advantages to the long-haul market.

The History of AirAsia

The growth of AirAsia is closely associated with the entrepreneurial effort of Tony Fernandes. Son of a Malaysian doctor, Fernandes was sent to boarding school in Britain with a view to following his father's footsteps into the medical profession. Tony had other ideas and, after an accounting degree at the London School of Economics, he went into music publishing, first with Virgin, then Time Warner. He describes his decision to start an airline as follows:

> I was watching the telly in a pub and I saw Stelios [Haji-Ioannou] on air talking about easyJet and running down the national carrier, British Airways. (Sound familiar? Hahaha.) I was intrigued as I didn't know what a low cost carrier was but I always wanted to start an airline that flew long haul with low fares.
>
> So I went to Luton and spent a whole day there. I was amazed how people were flying to Barcelona and Paris for less than 10 pounds. Everything was organized and everyone had a positive attitude. It was then at that point in Luton airport that I decided to start a low cost airline.[2]

He subsequently met with Conor McCarthy, former operations director of Ryanair. The two developed a plan to form a budget airline serving the Southeast Asia market.

Seeking the support of the Malaysian government, Fernandes was encouraged by Prime Minister Mahathir Mohammad to acquire a struggling government-owned airline, AirAsia. With their own capital and support from a group of investors, they acquired AirAsia for one Malaysian ringgit (RM)—and assumed debts of RM40 million (about $11 million). In January 2002, AirAsia was relaunched with just three planes and a business model that McCarthy described as: "a Ryanair operational strategy, a Southwest people strategy, and an easyJet branding strategy."[3]

Fueled by rising prosperity in Malaysia and its large potential market for leisure and business travelers seeking inexpensive domestic transportation, AirAsia's domestic business expanded rapidly. In January 2004, AirAsia began its first international service from KL to Phuket in Thailand; in February 2004, it sought to tap the Singapore market by offering flights from Johor Bahru, just across the border from Singapore, and in 2005 it began flights to Indonesia.

International expansion was financed by its initial public offering (IPO) in October 2004, which raised RM717 million. Airline deregulation across Southeast Asia greatly facilitated international expansion. To exploit the market for budget travel in Thailand and Indonesia, AirAsia adopted the novel strategy of establishing joint-venture companies in Thailand (Thai AirAsia) and Indonesia (Indonesia AirAsia) to create new hubs in Bangkok and Jakarta. In both cases, the operations of these companies were contracted out to AirAsia, which received a monthly fee from these associate companies.

From the beginning, Fernandes had set his sights on long-haul travel, guided by the example of his hero, Freddie Laker, the pioneer of low-cost transatlantic air travel. However, this risked his good relations with the Malaysian government because it put AirAsia into direct competition with the national airline, Malaysia Airlines. Hence, Fernandes established a separate company, AirAsia X to develop its long-haul business. AirAsia X is owned 16% by AirAsia (with an option to increase to 30%), 48% by Aero Ventures (co-founded by Tony Fernandes), 16% by Richard Branson's Virgin Group, with the remaining 20% owned by Bahrain-based Manara Consortium and Japan-based Orix Corporation. Operationally, AirAsia and AirAsia X are closely linked.

In 2007, flights began to Australia, followed by China. By July 2009, AirAsia X had flights from KL to the Gold Coast, Melbourne, and Perth in Australia; Tianjin and Hangzhou in China; and Taipei and London using five Airbus A340s, with three more to be delivered by year-end. Planned future routes included Abu Dhabi (October 2009), India (2010), and later Sydney, Seoul, and New York. At Abu Dhabi, AirAsia X planned to have a hub that would serve Frankfurt, Cairo, and possibly East Africa too: "You just can't get to East Africa from Asia," observed Fernandes.[4] To support its expansion, AirAsia X ordered 10 Airbus A350s for delivery in 2016.

AirAsia's Strategy and Culture

Strategy

AirAsia described its strategy as follows:

- Safety first: partnering with the world's most renowned maintenance providers and complying with world airline regulations.
- High aircraft utilization: implementing the region's fastest turnaround time at only 25 minutes, assuring lower costs and higher productivity.
- Low fare, no frills: providing guests with the choice of customizing services without compromising on quality and services.
- Streamline operations: making sure that processes are as simple as possible.
- Lean distribution system: offering a wide and innovative range of distribution channels to make booking and traveling easier.
- Point-to-point network: applying the point-to-point network keeps operations simple and costs low.[5]

Prior to its expansion into long-haul, AirAsia identified its geographical coverage as encompassing three-and-a-half hours' flying time from its hubs. Fernandes' confidence in his growth strategy rested on the fact that "This area encompasses a population of about 500 million people. Only a small proportion of this market regularly travels by air. AirAsia believes that certain segments of this market have been under-served historically and that the Group's low fares stimulate travel within these market segments."[6] Its slogan "Now Everyone Can Fly!" encapsulated AirAsia's goal of expanding the market for air travel in Southeast Asia.

To penetrate its target market, AirAsia placed a big emphasis on marketing and brand development. "The brand is positioned to project an image of a safe, reliable low-cost airline that places a high emphasis on customer service while providing an enjoyable flying experience." For an LCC, AirAsia had comparatively large expenditures on TV, print, and internet advertising. AirAsia used its advertising expenditures counter-cyclically: during the SARS outbreak and after the Bali bombings, AirAsia boosted its spending on advertising and marketing. In addition, it sought to maximize the amount of press coverage that it received. AirAsia also built its image through co-branding and sponsorship relationships. A sponsorship deal with the AT&T Williams Formula 1 race car team resulted in AirAsia painting one of its A320s in the livery of a Williams race car. Its sponsorship of Manchester United encouraged it to paint its planes with the portraits of Manchester United players. It also sponsored referees in the English Premier League. A cooperative advertising deal with *Time* magazine resulted in an AirAsia plane being painted with the *Time* logo.

Its internet advertising included banner ads on the Yahoo mobile homepage and a Facebook application for the Citibank–AirAsia credit card. The overall goals were increasing visibility, encouraging interaction, and allowing users to immerse themselves in the AirAsia brand.

This heavy emphasis on brand building provided AirAsia with a platform for offering services that met a range of traveler needs. AirAsia offered an AA express shuttle bus connecting airports to city centers with seats bookable simultaneously with online booking of plane tickets. Fernandes also founded Tune Hotels, a chain of no-frills hotels co-branded with AirAsia. Tune Money offered online financial services—again co-branded with AirAsia.

Culture and Management Style

AirAsia's corporate culture and management style reflected Tony Fernandes' own personality: informal, friendly, and cheerful. In the same way that culture and brand identity of Southwest Airlines and the Virgin airlines (Virgin Atlantic, Virgin Blue, and Virgin America) reflect the personalities of founders Herb Kelleher and Richard Branson, respectively, Fernandes has used his personality and personal style to create a distinct identity for AirAsia. His usual dress of jeans, open-neck shirt, and baseball cap provide a clear communication of AirAsia's unstuffy, open culture. Its team spirit, commitment to job flexibility, and lack of hierarchy were reinforced from the top: Fernandes worked one day a month as a baggage handler, one day every two months as cabin crew, and one day every three months as a check-in clerk.

The share offer prospectus described AirAsia's culture as follows:

> The Group prides itself on building a strong, team-orientated corporate culture. The Group's employees understand and subscribe to the Group's core strategy and actively focus on maintaining low costs and high productivity. AirAsia motivates its employees by awarding bonuses based upon each employee's contribution to AirAsia's productivity, and expects to increase loyalty through its ESOS [employee share ownership scheme] which will be available to all employees. The Group's

management encourages open communication which creates a dynamic working environment, and meets all its employees on a quarterly basis to review AirAsia's results and generate new ways to lower costs and increase productivity. Employees . . . frequently communicate directly with AirAsia's senior management and offer suggestions on how AirAsia can increase its efficiency or productivity . . .

In addition to the above, AirAsia:

- inculcates enthusiasm and commitment among staff by sponsoring numerous social events and providing a vibrant and friendly working environment
- strives to be honest and transparent in its relations with third parties . . .
- fosters a non-discriminatory, meritocratic environment where employees are offered opportunities for advancement, regardless of their education, race, gender, religion, nationality or age, and
- emphasizes maintaining a constant quality of service throughout all of AirAsia's operation through bringing together to work on a regular basis employees based in different locations.[7]

AirAsia's Operations

AirAsia's operations strategy comprised the following elements:

- *Aircraft*: In common with other LCCs, AirAsia operated a single type of aircraft, the Airbus A320. (It switched from Boeing 737s in 2005.) A single aircraft type offered economies in purchasing, maintenance, pilot training, and aircraft utilization.
- *No-frills flights*: AirAsia offered a single class, which allowed more seats per plane. For example, when it was operating its Boeing 737s, these were equipped with 148 seats, compared to 132 for a typical two-class configuration. Customer services were minimal: complimentary meals and drinks were not served on board—but snacks and beverages could be purchased, passengers paid for baggage beyond a low threshold, and there was no baggage transfer between flights. AirAsia did not use aerobridges for boarding and disembarking passengers, which was another cost-saving measure. Flights were ticketless and there was no assigned seating. Such simplicity allowed quick turnaround of planes, which permitted better utilization of planes and crews.
- *Sales and marketing*: AirAsia engaged in direct sales through its website and call center. As a result, it avoided paying commission to travel agents.
- *Outsourcing*: AirAsia achieved simplicity and cost economies by outsourcing those activities that could be undertaken more effectively and efficiently by third parties. Thus, most aircraft maintenance was outsourced to third parties, contracts being awarded on the basis of competitive bidding. Most of AirAsia's information technology requirements were also outsourced.

TABLE 1 Comparing operational and financial performance between AirAsia and Malaysia Airlines, 2008

	AirAsia	Malaysia Airlines
Operating data		
Passengers carried (millions)	11.81	13.76
Available seat kilometers (billions)	18.72	53.38
Revenue passenger kilometers (billions)	13.49	36.18
Seat load factor (%)	75.0	67.8
Cost per available seat kilometers (sen[a])	11.66	22.80
Revenue per available seat kilometers (sen)	14.11	20.60
Number of aircraft in fleet December 31, 2008	78.0	109.0
Number of employees	3,799	19,094
Aircraft utilization (hours per day)	11.8	11.1
Financial data (RM, millions)[a]		
Revenue	2,635	15,035
Other operating income	301.8	466.0
Total operating expense	2,966.0	15,198.3
of which:		
—Staff costs	236.8	2,179.9
—Depreciation	347.0	327.9
—Fuel costs	1,389.8	6,531.6
—Maintenance and overall	345.1	1,146.4
—Loss on unwinding derivatives	830.2	—
—Other operating expenses[b]	139.2	5,020.0
Operating profit	(351.7)	305.5
Finance cost (net)	517.5	60.8
Pre-tax profit	(869.2)	264.7
After-tax profit	(496.6)	245.6
Total assets	9,520.0	10,071.6
of which:		
—Aircraft, property, plant and equipment	6,594.3	2,464.8
—Inventories	20.7	379.7
—Cash	153.8	3,571.7
—Receivables	694.4	2,020.1
Debt	6,690.8	433.4
Shareholders' equity	1,605.5	4,197.0

Notes:

Figures in parentheses denote a loss.

[a]RM: Malaysian ringgit; 1 ringgit: 100 sen (cents). During 2008/9 the average exchange rate was US$1 = RM3.43.

[b]For AirAsia the main components were aircraft lease expenses and loss on foreign exchange. For Malaysia Airlines the main components were hire of aircraft, sales commissions, landing fees, and rent of buildings.

- *Information technology*: AirAsia used Navitair's Open Skies computer reservations system (CRS), which linked Web-based sales and inventory system, which also linked with AirAsia's call center. The CRS was integrated with AirAsia's yield management system (YMS) that priced seats on every flight according to demand. The CRS also allowed passengers to print their own boarding passes. In 2006, AirAsia implemented a wireless delivery system which enabled customers to book seats, check flight schedules, and obtain real-time updates on AirAsia's promotions via their mobile phones—an important facility in the Asia-Pacific region because of the extensive use of mobile phones. The YMS helped AirAsia to maximize revenue by providing trend analysis and optimize pricing; it also gave information on future passenger numbers that was used by AirAsia's Advanced Planning and Scheduling (APS) system to minimize operational costs by optimizing supply chain and facilities management. These two IT systems allowed AirAsia to reduce costs in logistics and inbound activities. During 2005, AirAsia adopted an ERP (enterprise resource planning) system to support its processes, facilitate month-end financial closing, and speed up reporting and data retrieval.[8] This was superseded by an advanced planning and scheduling system, which optimized AirAsia's supply chain management and forecasted future resource requirements.

● *Human resource management*: Human resource management had been a priority for AirAsia since its relaunch under Tony Fernandes. A heavy emphasis was given to selecting applicants on the basis of their aptitudes, then creating an environment and a system which developed employees and retained them. AirAsia's retention rates were exceptionally high, which it regarded, first, as an indicator of motivation and job satisfaction and as a cost-saving measure—because employees were multi-skilled, AirAsia's training costs per employee tended to be high. Job flexibility at all levels of the company, including administration, was a major source of productivity for AirAsia.

AirAsia: Cost Information

To offer a comparative view of AirAsia's operational efficiency and cost position, Table 1 provides operating and financial information on Malaysia's two leading airlines: Malaysia Airlines and AirAsia. Although Malaysia Airlines' route network was very different from that of AirAsia's (Malaysia Airlines had a larger proportion of long-haul routes), it was subject to similar cost conditions as AirAsia.

For the first time since its relaunch in 2002, AirAsia made a loss in 2008. This was the result of Fernandes' decision to unwind AirAsia's futures contracts for jet fuel purchased. When crude oil prices started to tumble during the latter half of 2008, Fernandes believed that AirAsia would be better off taking a loss on its existing contracts in order to benefit from lower fuel prices.

Going Long-haul

Fernandes was aware that expanding from short-haul flights in Southeast Asia to flights of more than four hours to China, Australia, Europe, and the Middle East required major changes in operating practices and major new investments, primarily in bigger planes. The creation of AirAsia X was intended to facilitate a measure of operational independence for the long-haul flights while also spreading the risks of this venture among several investors. The investors in AirAsia X also contributed valuable expertise: Virgin Group had experience in establishing and operating four airlines (Virgin Atlantic, Virgin Express, Virgin Blue, and Virgin

USA), and the chairman of Air Ventures was Robert Milton, the former CEO of Air Canada.

Table 2 shows the principal differences in AirAsia and AirAsia X's operations and services.

Kuala Lumpur to London: Price and Cost Comparisons

A comparison of prices and costs allows a clearer picture of AirAsia's ability to compete in the long-haul market—a market in which AirAsia had to establish itself against some of the world's major airlines. Between KL and London, AirAsia was in competition with at least six international airlines, the closest of which were Malaysia Airlines, Emirates, and British Airways.

A comparison of economy, round-trip airfares between the two cities is shown in Table 3. As Table 4 shows, these fare differentials reflected differences in cost between AirAsia and its long-haul competitors. These cost differences do not take account of differences in load factors, which can have a major effect on the average cost per passenger. AirAsia reported that its KL–London flights had a load factor in excess of 90%. For the airlines as a whole, Table 5 shows load factors.

TABLE 2 Comparing AirAsia and AirAsia X

	AirAsia	**AirAsia X**
Concept	Low cost short-haul, no-frills	Low cost long-haul, no frills
Flying range	Within four hours' flying time from departing city	More than four hours' flying time from departing city
Aircraft	Airbus A320 with 180 seats	Airbus A330 with more than 330 seats
Cabin configuration	Single class	Economy and Premium (previously known as XL)
Seat option	Unassigned seating, plus Xpress Boarding option	Assigned seating with seat request option
In-flight dining	Range of light meals and snacks available for purchase onboard	Pre-ordered full meals available including Asian, Western, vegetarian, and kids' meal; light snacks also available for purchase onboard

TABLE 3 Fare comparisons: AirAsia and its competitors between Kuala Lumpur and London

	AirAsia X[a] (US$)	**Cheapest other airline[b] (US$)**	**AirAsia price advantage (%)**	**Cheapest other airlines**
KL–London round trip	433.96[c]	683.68	36.5	1. Gulf Air 2. Qatar Air 3. Emirates
London–KL round trip	433.96[c]	530.35	18.2	1. Emirates 2. Etihad 3. Gulf Air

Notes:
[a]Average fare between September 1 and October 1, 2009.
[b]Average of lowest airline fare on each day between September 1 and October 1, 2009.
[c]Average outbound fare: $187.87; average inbound fare: $209.48; meals and baggage charges: $36.61.

TABLE 4 Flight operating cost comparison: Kuala Lumpur to London (in US$)

	AirAsia	British Airways	Malaysia Airlines	Emirates	
Aircraft type	Airbus 340-300	Boeing 747-400	Boeing 747-400	Boeing 777-300	
Route[a]	KUL–STN	KUL–LHR	KUL–LHR	KUL–DXB–LHR	
Maximum passenger capacity	286	337	359	360	
				KUL–DXB	DXB–LHR
Flight fuel cost	79,299	159,522	159,522	77,525	80,822
Leasing costs	5,952	0	0	0	0
En route navigation charges	7,949	12,294	12,294	1,435	6,613
Terminal navigation arrival charges	419	645	645	0	645
Landing/parking	1,100	2,200	2,200	2,200	2,200
Departure handling	6,000	12,000	12,000	12,000	12,000
Arrival handling	6,000	12,000	12,000	12,000	12,000
Segment totals				105,160	114,280
Total cost per flight[b]	106,719	198,661	198,661	219,440	
Average cost per passenger[b]	373.14	589.50	553.37	609.56	

Notes:
[a]KUL = Kuala Lumpur, STN = London Stansted, LHR = London Heathrow, DXB = Dubai.
[b]Excluding maintenance, depreciation, meal services, and crew salaries.
Source: S. Buchholz, N. Fabio, A. Ileyassoff, L. Mang, and D. Visentin, *AirAsia: Tales from a Long-haul Low Cost Carrier* (Bocconi University, 2009). Data based on NewPacs Aviation Tool Software. Used by permission of the authors.

TABLE 5 Difference between airlines in load factors (%)

	2004	2005	2006	2007	2008
AirAsia	77.0	75.0	78.0	80.0	75.5
Emirates	73.4	74.6	75.9	76.2	79.8
British Airways	67.6	69.7	70.0	70.4	71.2
Malaysia Airlines	69.0	71.5	69.8	71.4	67.8

Source: S. Buchholz, N. Fabio, A. Ileyassoff, L. Mang, and D. Visentin, "AirAsia: Tales from a Long-haul Low Cost Carrier," (case report, Bocconi University, 2009). Used by permission of the authors.

The Outlook for Long-haul

There can be little doubt that AirAsia had been remarkably successful in building a budget airline in Southeast Asia. Its cost efficiency, growth rate, brand awareness, and awards for customer service, airline management, and entrepreneurship all pointed to outstanding achievement, not simply in replicating the LCC business model pioneered by Southwest Airlines but in adapting that model and augmenting it with innovation, dynamism, and marketing flair that derived from Tony Fernandes' personality and leadership style.

However, its AirAsia X venture presented a whole set of new challenges. AirAsia had successfully transferred several of its competitive advantages from AirAsia to AirAsia X. The low costs associated with fuel-efficient new planes, secondary airports, and human resources practices had allowed AirAsia X to become the low-cost operator on most of its routes. The AirAsia brand and corporate reputation provided AirAsia X with credibility on each new route it inaugurated. By sharing web-based and telephone flight booking systems along with administrative and operational services between the two airlines, AirAsia X was able to secure cost efficiencies that would not be possible for an independent start-up.

Nevertheless, doubts remained over AirAsia X's ability to compete with established international airlines. Unlike AirAsia, which was attracting a whole new market for domestic and regional air travel, AirAsia X would have to take business away from the established international airlines whose business models offered some key competitive advantages over that of long-haul LCCs. In particular, the dense domestic and regional route networks of the established carriers offered feeds for their intercontinental flights. These complementarities were supported by through-ticketing, baggage transfer, and frequent-flyer schemes. Their sources of profit were very different from the LCCs: most of their profit was earned from first- and business-class travelers, which permitted subsidization of economy-class fares.

These challenges pointed to the advantages of closer integration of AirAsia X with AirAsia. AirAsia X's CEO, Azran Osman-Rani, had argued for the operational and financial rationale of merging AirAsia X into AirAsia: "It would be difficult for AirAsia in the future if it did not have trunk routes as [this] is where the traffic volumes come from, so AirAsia needs growth from AirAsia X and the merger allows it to tap growth opportunities in the long-haul markets." Responding to allegations that the real rationale for the merger was to allow AirAsia to finance AirAsia X's losses, Azran said: "Rubbish, we can clearly dispute that. For the first quarter ended March 31, 2009 our net profit was RM 18 million and we are net cash flow positive. We even had a little cash at RM 3 million. We are in a very good position and on a much firmer footing and now is an interesting time to talk about a merger."[9]

Notes

1. Operating profit before depreciation, amortization, and interest as a percentage of average total assets.
2. See www.tonyfernandesblog.com, accessed June 3, 2009.
3. Quoted by T. Lawton and J. Doh, *The Ascendance of AirAsia: Building a Successful Budget Airline in Asia* (Ivey School of Business, Case No. 9B08M054, 2008).
4. "AirAsia X to Hub in Abu Dhabi: AirAsia CEO," *Khaleej Times*, August 5, 2009.
5. "Corporate Profile," http://www.airasia.com/ot/en/corporate/corporateprofile.page?, asccessed September 27, 2012.
6. "AirAsia Berhad," *Offering Circular*, October 29, 2004, p. 3.
7. "AirAsia Berhad," *Offering Circular*, October 29, 2004, p. 5.
8. C. Cho, S. Hoffman Arian, C. Tjitrahardja, and R. Narayanaswamy, *AirAsia: Strategic IT Initiative* (student report, Faculty of Economics and Commerce, University of Melbourne, 2005).
9. "AirAsia X CEO backs Merger with AirAsia Bhd," *The Star Online*, July 23, 2009, http://biz.thestar.com.my/news/story.asp?file=/2009/7/23/business/4369512&sec=business.

 A video clip relating to this case is available in your interactive e-book at **www.wileyopenpage.com**

Case 10 Eastman Kodak's Quest for a Digital Future

When Eastman Kodak Company declared bankruptcy ("voluntary Chapter 11 business reorganization") on January 19, 2012, CEO Antonio Perez was emphatic that this was not the end of the road for Kodak:

> Kodak is taking a significant step toward enabling our enterprise to complete its transformation. At the same time as we have created our digital business, we have also already effectively exited certain traditional operations, closing 13 manufacturing plants and 130 processing labs, and reducing our workforce by 47,000 since 2003. Now we must complete the transformation by further addressing our cost structure and effectively monetizing non-core IP assets. We look forward to working with our stakeholders to emerge a lean, world-class, digital imaging and materials science company.[1]

Yet, for all Perez's emphasis on continuing development and prospects for the future, the fact remained that after billions of dollars of investment in new technologies and new products, Kodak had failed to build a viable digital imaging business. Kodak's strategy of transitioning from traditional photography into digital imaging had been in place for over two decades. In 1990, Kodak had launched its Photo CD system for storing photographic images; in 1991, it had introduced its first digital camera and, in 1994, its new CEO, George Fisher, had declared: "We are not in the photographic business . . . we are in the picture business."

With leadership from senior executives recruited from Motorola, Apple, General Electric, Silicon Graphics, and Hewlett-Packard, Kodak's digital imaging efforts had established some notable successes. In digital cameras, Kodak was US market leader for most of 2004–10; globally, it ranked third after Canon and Sony. It was a technological leader in megapixel image sensors. It was global leader in retail printing kiosks and digital minilabs.

Financial performance was a different story. In 1991, Eastman Kodak was America's 18th-biggest company by revenues; by 2011, it had fallen to 334th: over the same period its employment had shrunk from 133,200 to 17,100. During the first decade of this century, its operating losses totaled $3.8 billion.

As Antonio Perez prepared for his weekly meeting with Kodak's chief restructuring officer, James Mesterharm, he reflected on Kodak's two decades of decline. How

---

This case was prepared by Robert M. Grant. ©2012 Robert M. Grant.

could a company that had been a pioneer of digital imaging and had invested so heavily in building digital capabilities and launching new digital imaging products have failed so miserably to generate income from its efforts? And what did the future hold for Kodak?

Kodak's History, 1901–1993

George Eastman transformed photography from a professional, studio-based activity into an everyday consumer hobby. His key innovations were silver halide roll film and the first fully portable camera. The Eastman Kodak Company established in Rochester, New York in 1901 offered a full range of products and services for the amateur photographer: "You push the button, we do the rest" was its first advertising slogan. By the time George Eastman died in 1932, Eastman Kodak was one of the world's leading multinational corporations with production, distribution, and processing facilities throughout the world and with one of the world's most recognizable brand names.

After the Second World War, Kodak entered a new growth phase with an expanding core business and diversification into chemicals (its subsidiary, Eastman Chemical, exploited its polymer technology) and healthcare (Eastman Pharmaceutical was established in 1986). Kodak also faced major competitive challenges. In cameras, Kodak's leadership was undermined by the rise of the Japanese camera industry; in film, Fuji Photo Film Company embarked on a strategy of aggressive international expansion. In addition, new imaging technologies were emerging: Polaroid pioneered instant photography; Xerox led the new field of electrostatic plain-paper copying; while the advent of the personal computer ushered in a variety of new printing technologies.

Early Moves into Electronics

Kodak's top management was well aware of technological developments in imaging during the 1980s. The R & D initiatives launched resulted in products that embodied several new electronic technologies:

- The world's first megapixel electronic image sensor (1986), followed by a number of new products for scanning and electronic image capture.
- Computer-assisted image storage and retrieval systems for storing, retrieving, and editing graphical and microfilm images.
- Data storage products included floppy disks (Verbatim was acquired in 1985) and 14-inch optical disks (1986).
- Plain-paper office copiers (Kodak acquired IBM's copier business in 1988).
- The Photo CD system (1990) allowed digitized photographic images to be stored on a compact disk, which could then be viewed and manipulated on a personal computer.
- Kodak's first digital camera, the 1.3 megapixel DCS-100, priced at $13,000 launched in 1991.

Committing to a Digital Future

Kodak's commitment to a digital imaging strategy was sealed with the appointment of George Fisher as CEO. Fisher had a doctorate in applied mathematics, ten years of R & D experience at Bell Labs, and had led strategic transformation at Motorola. To focus Kodak's efforts on the digital challenge, Fisher's first moves were to divest Eastman Chemical Company and most of Kodak's healthcare businesses (other than medical imaging) and to create a single digital imaging division headed by newly hired Carl Gustin (previously with Apple and Digital Equipment).

Kodak's Digital Strategy

Under three successive CEOs—George Fisher (1993–1999), Dan Carp (2000–2005), and Antonio Perez (2005–2012)—Kodak developed a digital strategy intended to transform Kodak from a traditional photographic company to a leader in the emerging field of digital imaging. The scale and scope of this transformation was clearly recognized by all three CEOs. In 2005, Antonio Perez summarized the "fundamental challenges" that Kodak was engaged in (Figure 1).

During 1993–2011, Kodak's strategy embodied four major themes:

- an incremental approach to managing the transition to digital imaging;
- different strategies for the consumer market and for the professional and commercial markets;
- external sourcing of knowledge through hiring, alliances, and acquisitions;
- an emphasis on printed images;
- harvesting the traditional photography business.

FIGURE 1   Eastman Kodak's "Fundamental Challenges"

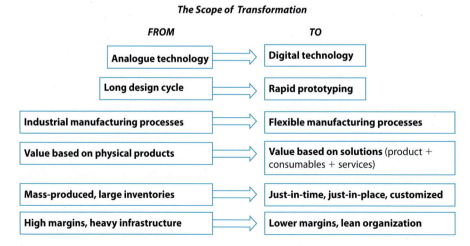

Source: A. Perez, "Creating the New Kodak," J. P. Morgan Technology Conference, May 2005.

An Incremental Approach

"The future is not some harebrained scheme of the digital information highway or something. It is a step-by-step progression of enhancing photography using digital technology," declared Fisher in 1995.[2] This recognition that digital imaging was an evolutionary rather than a revolutionary change would be the key to Kodak's ability to build a strong position in digital technology. If photography was to switch rapidly from the traditional chemical-based technology to a wholly digital technology where customers took digital pictures, downloaded them onto their computers, edited them, and transmitted them through the internet to be viewed electronically, Kodak would face an extremely difficult time. Not only would the new digital value chain make redundant most of Kodak's core competitive advantages (its silver halide technology and its global network of retail outlets and processing facilities): most of this digital value chain was already in the hands of computer hardware and software companies.

Fortunately for Kodak, during the 1990s digital technology made only selective incursions into traditional photographic imaging. As late as 2000, digital cameras had achieved limited market penetration; the vast majority of photographic images were still captured on traditional film.

Hence, central to Kodak's strategy, was a hybrid approach where Kodak introduced those aspects of digital imaging that could offer truly enhanced functionality for users. Thus, in the consumer market, Kodak recognized that image capture would continue to be dominated by traditional film for some time (digital cameras offered inferior resolution compared with conventional photography). However, digital imaging offered immediate potential for image manipulation and transmission.

If consumers continued to use conventional film while seeking the advantages of digitization for editing and emailing their pictures, this offered a valuable opportunity for Kodak's vast retail network. Kodak had installed its first self-service facility for digitizing, editing, and printing images from conventional photographs in 1988. In 1994, Kodak launched its Picture Maker, a self-service kiosk located in retail stores where customers could edit and print digital images from a variety of digital inputs, or from digital scans of conventional photo prints. Picture Maker allowed customers to edit their images (zoom, crop, eliminate red-eye, and add text) and print them in a variety of formats. George Fisher emphasized the central role of retail kiosks in Kodak's digital strategy:

> Four years ago, when we talked about the possibilities of digital photography, people laughed. Today, the high-tech world is stampeding to get a piece of the action, calling digital imaging perhaps the greatest growth opportunity in the computer world. And it may be. We surely see it as the greatest future enabler for people to truly "Take Pictures. Further." We start at retail, our distribution stronghold . . . We believe the widespread photo-retailing infrastructure will continue to be the principal avenue by which people obtain their pictures. Our strategy is to build on and extend this existing market strength which is available to us, and at the same time be prepared to serve the rapidly growing, but relatively small, pure digital market that is developing. Kodak will network its rapidly expanding installed base of Image Magic stations and kiosks, essentially turning these into nodes on a massive, global network. The company will allow retailers to use these workstations to bring digital capability to the average snapshooter, extending the value of these

images for the consumers and retailers alike, while creating a lucrative consumable business for Kodak.[3]

Despite growing ownership of inkjet printers, a very large proportion of consumers continued to use photo-print facilities in retail stores. By the beginning of 2004, Kodak was the clear leader in self-service digital printing kiosks, with 24,000 installed Kodak Picture Makers in the US and over 55,000 worldwide.

Kodak also used digital technology to enhance the services offered by photofinishers. Thus, the Kodak I.Lab system offered a digital infrastructure to photofinishers that digitized every film negative and offered better pictures by fixing common problems in consumer photographs.

Despite the inferior resolution of digital cameras, Fisher recognized their potential and pushed Kodak to establish itself in this highly competitive market. In addition to high-priced digital single reflex lens cameras for professional use, Kodak developed the QuickTake camera for Apple: at $75 it was the cheapest digital camera available in 1994. In March 1995, Kodak introduced the first full-featured digital camera priced at under $1,000.

The Consumer Market: Emphasizing Simplicity and Ease of Use

Kodak pursued different approaches to consumer and professional/commercial markets. While the commercial and professional market offered the test-bed for Kodak's advanced digital technologies, the emphasis in the consumer segment was to maintain Kodak's position as mass-market leader by providing simplicity, quality, and value. Kodak's incremental strategy was most evident in the consumer market, providing an easy pathway for customers to transition to digital photography while exploiting Kodak's core brand and distribution strengths. This transition path was guided by Kodak's original vision of "You push the button, we do the rest." Kodak envisages itself as the mass-market leader in digital imaging, providing security, reliability, and simplicity for customers bewildered by the pace of technological change. Thus, Kodak would offer an array of services that would allow consumers to digitize conventional photographs, edit digitized images, and obtain printed photographs in a variety of formats.

Simplicity and mass-market leadership also implied that Kodak provided the fully integrated set of products and services needed for digital photography. "For Kodak, digital photography is all about ease of use and helping people get prints—in other words, getting the same experience they're used to from their film cameras," noted Martin Coyne, head of Kodak's Photographic Group.[4] A systems approach rather than a product approach recognized that most consumers had neither the time nor the patience to read instructions and to integrate different devices and software. Kodak believed that its integrated system approach would have particular appeal to women, who made up the major part of the consumer market.

The result was Kodak's EasyShare system, launched in 2001. According to Willy Shih, head of digital and applied imaging, EasyShare's intention was to:

> provide consumers with the first easy-to-use digital photography experience . . . Digital photography is more than just about digital cameras. This is just the first step . . . People need to get their pictures to their PCs and then want to share by

printing or e-mail. So we developed a system that made the full experience as easy as possible.[5]

The result would be a comprehensive digital system within which consumers could take digital pictures on digital cameras or phone-cameras (or have conventional photographs digitized), view their images on a variety of devices, and print their digital images at home, at retail kiosks, or through Kodak's online processing service. Figure 2 shows Kodak's conceptualization of its EasyShare system.

By 2005, most of the main elements of the EasyShare system were in place:

- Kodak's range of EasyShare digital cameras had carved out a strong position in a crowded market (by 2005 some 40 companies were offering digital cameras).

- EasyShare software allowed the downloading, organization, editing, and emailing of images and the ordering of online prints. EasyShare software was bundled with Kodak's cameras as well as being available for downloading for free from Kodak's website.

- The EasyShare printer dock introduced in 2003 was the first printer which incorporated a camera dock allowing the "one touch simple" thermal-dye printing direct from a camera. Antonio Perez's arrival in 2003 reinforced Kodak's push into printers: "If a company wants to be a leader in digital imaging, it necessarily has to participate in digital output."[6]

- Online digital imaging services: Kodak had been quick to recognize the potential of the internet for allowing consumers to transmit and store their photographs and order prints. Kodak's Picture Network was launched in 1997. Consumers could have their conventional photographs digitized by a retail photo store, then uploaded to a personal internet account on Kodak's Picture Network. The following year Kodak launched its online printing service, *PhotoNet*, enabling consumers to upload their digital photo files and

FIGURE 2   Kodak's EasyShare Network: "Your Pictures—Anytime, Anywhere"

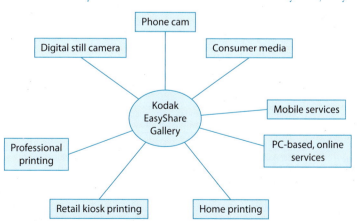

Source: Based upon Bob Brust, "Completing the Kodak Transformation," Presentation, Eastman Kodak Company, September 2005. Reproduced by permission of Eastman Kodak Company.

order prints of them. Kodak also partnered with AOL to offer *You've Got Pictures*. By acquiring Ofoto in 2001, Kodak became the leader in online photofinishing and online image storage. In January 2005, Kodak renamed Ofoto "Kodak EasyShare Gallery."

By 2005, therefore, Kodak was present across the entire digital value chain—this integrated presence was underpinned by technological strengths at each of these stages (Figure 3).

Kodak's technological capabilities meant that it was positioned at each of the principal stages in the digital imaging value chain even though, at most of these stages, it lacked market leadership (Figure 3).

Professional, Commercial, and Healthcare Markets

The commercial and professional markets were important to Kodak for two reasons. First, they were lead customers for many of Kodak's cutting-edge digital technologies: news photographers were early adopters of digital cameras; the US Department of Defense pioneered digital imaging for satellite imaging, weather forecasting, and surveillance activities; NASA used Kodak cameras and imaging equipment for its space missions, including the Mars probe and the IKONOS Earth-orbiting satellite. For many commercial applications ranging from real estate brokerage to security systems, digital imaging offered huge advantages because of its ability to transmit images (especially through the internet) and link with sophisticated IT management systems for image storage and retrieval. The huge price premium of commercial consumer products (up to 100 times that of a basic consumer version) made it attractive to focus R & D on these leading-edge users in the anticipation of trickle-down to the consumer market.

In commercial printing and publishing (which became the Graphic Communications Group in 2005), Kodak assembled a strong position in commercial

FIGURE 3   Kodak's technological position within the digital imaging chain

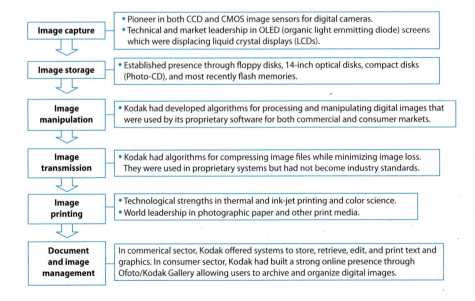

scanning, formatting, and printing systems for the publishing, packaging, and data processing industries. Kodak's opportunity was to exploit the transition from traditional offset printing to digital, full-color, variable printing. This opportunity built on two key strengths: first, Kodak's proprietary inkjet technology (including its technically superior inks) and, second, its leadership in variable-data printing—printing that permitted individually customized output (as in personalized sales catalogues or bills). Kodak built its commercial printing business on both internally developed technologies and acquisitions—notably Heidelberg's Nexpress and Digimaster businesses, and Scitex, supplier of Versamark high-speed inkjet printers. Kodak also built a presence in pre-press and workflow systems used by commercial printers.

In medical imaging, Kodak also faced the decline of its sales of X-ray film and in related chemicals and accessories. Through a series of acquisitions and internal developments, Kodak established a portfolio of products for digital X-rays, laser imaging, picture archiving and communications systems—including systems for digitizing and storing conventional X-rays. Kodak also built up a strong position in dental imaging systems comprising hardware, software, and consumables. Kodak sold its Health Group to Onex Healthcare Holdings in 2007 for $2.55 billion.

Kodak's capability in creating integrated imaging and information solutions was of particular value in certain public sector projects. Kodak's digital scanning and document management systems were used in national censuses in the US, the UK, France, Australia, and Brazil. At the German post office, a Kodak team achieved a world record, creating digitized copies of 1.7 million documents in 24 hours.

Hiring, Alliances, and Acquisitions

Kodak's business system had been based upon vertical integration and self-sufficiency: at its Rochester base, Kodak developed its own technology, produced its own products, and supplied them worldwide through its vast global network. In digital imaging, not only did Kodak lack much of the expertise needed to build a digital imaging business but also the pace of technological change was too rapid to rely on in-house development. Hence, as Kodak transformed its capability base from chemical to digital imaging, it looked outside for the knowledge it required.

Kodak had traditionally been a lifetime-employment company that grew its own senior executives. The arrival of George Fisher from Motorola changed all that. Under Fisher's leadership Kodak launched a major hiring campaign to put in place the executives and technical specialists it needed for its new digital strategy. Key executives who relocated from Silicon Valley to Rochester included Kodak's first head of its digital imaging division, Willy Shih, whose prior experience included Silicon Graphics and IBM. Kodak also brought in senior hires from Xerox, Hewlett-Packard, Lexmark, Apple, GE Medical Electronics, Olympus Optical, and Lockheed Martin. Table 1 shows the backgrounds of Kodak's top management team.

Kodak acknowledged that the digital imaging chain already included companies that were well established, sometimes dominant, in particular activities. For example, Adobe Systems dominated image-formatting software; Hewlett-Packard, Epson, and Canon were leaders in inkjet printers for home use; and Microsoft dominated PC operating systems. Willy Shih, head of Kodak's digital imaging products from 1997 to 2003, observed: "We have to pick where we add value and commoditize where we can't."[7] The challenge was to identify activities and products where Kodak could add value.

TABLE 1   Eastman Kodak's senior management team, April 2012

Name	Position	Joined Kodak	Prior company experience
Robert L. Berman	Senior Vice President	1982	Kodak veteran
Philip J. Faraci	President and COO	2004	Phogenix Imaging, Gemplus
Stephen Green	Director, Business Development, Asia-Pacific	2005	Creo Inc.
Pradeep Jotwani	President, Consumer Business	2010	Hewlett-Packard
Brad W. Kruchten	President Film and Photofinishing Systems Group	1982	Kodak veteran
Antoinette McCorvey	CFO and Senior Vice President	1999	Monsanto/Solutia
Gustavo Oviedo	Chief Customer Officer	2006	Schneider Electric
Antonio M. Perez	Chairman and CEO	2003	Hewlett-Packard
Laura G. Quatela	General Counsel and Chief Intellectual Property Officer	1999	Clover Capital Management, Inc., SASIB Railway GRS, and Bausch & Lomb Inc.
Isidre Rosello	General Manager, Digital Printing Solutions	2005	Hewlett-Packard
Eric H. Samuels	Chief Accounting Officer and Corporate Controller	2004	KPMG, Ernst & Young
Patrick M. Sheller	Chief Administrative Officer, General Counsel and Secretary	1993	McKenna, Long & Aldridge, Federal Trade Commission
Terry R. Taber	Vice President	1980	Kodak veteran

Note:
Includes corporate officers, senior vice presidents, and division heads.
Source: www.kodak.com. Reproduced by permission of Eastman Kodak Company.

In many cases this meant partnering with companies that were already leaders in digital technologies and hardware and software products. Kodak forged a web of joint ventures and strategic alliances with Canon (for developing and manufacturing digital, SLR cameras), AOL (You've Got Pictures service for uploading, storing, and sharing digital photographs), Intel (development of digital image storage media and ASP system for archiving and downloading medical images), Hewlett-Packard (technology exchange; Phogenix Imaging joint venture to develop inkjet solutions for Kodak photo-finishing labs), Olympus (sharing digital camera technology), Sanyo Electric Co. (joint development of OLED displays), and IBM (manufacturing alliance to produce CMOS imaging sensors).

Kodak made acquisitions where it believed that a strong proprietary position was essential to its strategy and in technologies where it needed to complement its own expertise. Although Kodak's profits were under pressure for most of the period, its size and balance-sheet strength meant that it was still one of the financially strongest firms in the industry. The bursting of the stock-market bubble in technology stocks in 2000 allowed Kodak to make a number of key acquisitions for modest outlays. Its major acquisitions over the period are shown in Table 2.

Emphasis on Printed Images

A consistent feature of Kodak's digital strategy from 1993 to 2012 was the belief that digital technology would not eliminate printed images. Kodak's emphasis on printed images was reinforced by its own capabilities: the printing of photographic

TABLE 2   Kodak's major acquisitions, 1994–2011

Date	Company	Description
1994	Qualex, Inc.	Provider of photo-finishing services; acquired to complement Kodak's online photofinishing service
1997	Wang Laboratories	Acquisition of Wang's software unit
1997	Chinon Industries	Japanese camera producer; majority stake acquired; outstanding shares purchased in 2004
1998	PictureVision, Inc.	Provider of PhotoNet online digital imaging services and retail solutions; complement to Kodak's Picture Network business
1998	Shantou Era Photo Material, Xiamen Fuda Photographic Materials	Strengthened Kodak's position in photographic film in China
1999	Imation	Supplier of medical imaging products and services
2000	Lumisys, Inc.	Provider of desktop computed radiography systems and X-ray film digitizers
2001	Bell & Howell	Imaging businesses only acquired
2001	Ofoto, Inc.	Leading US online photofinisher
2001	Encad, Inc.	Wide-format commercial inkjet printers
2003	PracticeWorks	Digital dental imaging and dental practice management software
2003	Algotec Systems Ltd.	Developer of picture archiving systems
2003	Lucky Film Co., Ltd.	Acquisition of 20% of China's leading photographic film supplier
2003	LaserPacific Media Corporation	Provider of post-production services for filmmakers
2004	NexPress	Acquired Heidelberg's 50% of this joint venture, which supplied high-end, on-demand color printing systems and black-and-white variable-data printing systems
2004	Scitex Digital Printing	A leader in high-speed variable data inkjet printing (renamed Kodak Versamark, Inc.)
2004	National Semiconductor	Acquisition of National's imaging sensor business
2005	Kodak Polychrome Graphics LLC	Kodak acquires Sun Chemical's 50% stake in the joint venture, which is a leader in graphic communication
2005	Creo Inc.	Leading supplier of pre-press and workflow systems used by commercial printers
2008	Design2Launch	Developer of collaborative end-to-end digital workflow solutions for transactional printing
2008	Intermate A/S	Danish supplier of Intelligent Print Data Stream software for managing high speed printers
2009	Böwe Bell & Howell	Acquisition of document scanner division
2011	Tokyo Ohka Kogyo Co., Ltd.	Acquisition of TOK's relief printing plates business

Source: Eastman Kodak 10-K reports, various years.

and other images onto paper and other media lay at the heart of Kodak's traditional chemical and chromatic know-how. Throughout the Fisher/Carp/Perez era, Kodak continued to invest heavily in its printing know-how and in printers: both commercial and consumer. Under Perez, the impetus behind photographic printers for the consumer market intensified, reflecting Perez's own background as former head of Hewlett-Packard's printer division.

Perez's decision to make a major investment to build Kodak's presence in the market for consumer inkjet printers has been the most widely criticized of all Kodak's digital imaging initiatives. Even with Kodak's "treasure trove" of inkjet technologies and its tweaking of the traditional "razors-and-blades" model by charging low prices for ink and higher prices for printers, establishing Kodak in such a mature, intensely

EXHIBIT 1
Eastman Kodak's business segments

CONSUMER DIGITAL IMAGING GROUP ("CDG") SEGMENT

CDG's mission is to enhance people's lives and social interactions through the capabilities of digital imaging and printing technology. CDG's strategy is to drive profitable revenue growth by leveraging a powerful brand, a deep knowledge of the consumer, and extensive digital imaging and materials science intellectual property.

◆ **Digital Capture and Devices** includes digital still and pocket video cameras, digital picture frames, accessories, and branded licensed products. These products are sold directly to retailers or distributors, and are also available to customers through the Internet ... As announced on February 9, 2012, the Company plans to phase out its dedicated capture devices business...

◆ **Retail Systems Solutions'** product and service offerings to retailers include kiosks and consumables, Adaptive Picture Exchange ("APEX") drylab

systems and consumables, and after sale service and support ... Kodak has the largest installed base of retail photo kiosks in the world.

◆ **Consumer Inkjet Systems** encompasses Kodak All-in-One desktop inkjet printers, ink cartridges, and media ...

◆ **Consumer Imaging Services**: Kodak Gallery is a leading online merchandise and photo sharing service ...

GRAPHIC COMMUNICATIONS GROUP ("GCG") SEGMENT

GCG's strategy is to transform large graphics markets with revolutionary technologies and customized services that grow our customers' businesses and Kodak's business with them.

◆ **Prepress Solutions** is comprised of digital and traditional consumables, including plates, chemistry, and media, prepress output device equipment and

competitive market would be a struggle. By 2011, Kodak held only 6% of the US market, compared to 60% for Hewlett-Packard.

Harvesting the Traditional Photography Business

On the basis that the transition to digital photography would be gradual, Kodak believed that the transition period would give it the opportunity to generate cash flows from its legacy film business while investing in digital imaging technologies and products. Kodak's prediction of a gradual transition from film to digital imaging was largely correct. Through the 1990s, film sales continued to grow in the US, reaching a peak of 800 million rolls in 1999. However, the decline that began in 2000 accelerated during the first decade of the 21st century. By 2004, sales had halved to under 400 million. By 2011, sales had fallen to below 100,000.

Kodak's forecasts proved wrong in relation to emerging market demand. Kodak's acquisitions of Chinese photographic film producers were based on the assumption related services, and proofing solutions. Prepress solutions also include flexographic packaging solutions, which is one of Kodak's four digital growth initiative businesses.

◆ **Digital Printing Solutions** includes high-speed, high-volume commercial inkjet printing equipment, consumables, and related services, as well as color and black-and-white electrophotographic printing equipment . . .

◆ **The Business Services and Solutions** group's product and service offerings are composed of high-speed production and workgroup document scanners, related services, and digital controllers for driving digital output devices, and workflow software and solutions. Workflow software and solutions, which includes consulting and professional business process services, can enable new opportunities for our customers to transform from a print service provider to a marketing service provider . . .

FILM, PHOTOFINISHING AND ENTERTAINMENT GROUP ("FPEG") SEGMENT

FPEG provides consumers, professionals, and the entertainment industry with film and paper for imaging and photography. Although the markets . . . are in decline . . . due to digital substitution, FPEG maintains leading market positions for these products. The strategy of FPEG is to provide sustainable cash generation by extending our materials science assets in traditional and new markets.

◆ **Entertaining Imaging** includes origination, intermediate, and color print motion picture films, special effects services, and other digital products and services for the entertainment industry.

◆ **Traditional Photofinishing** includes color negative photographic paper, photochemicals, professional output systems, and event imaging services.

◆ **Industrial Materials** encompasses aerial and industrial film products, film for the production of printed circuit boards, and specialty chemicals, and represents a key component of FPEG's strategy of extending and repurposing our materials science assets.

◆ **Film Capture** includes consumer and professional photographic film and one-time-use cameras.

Source: Eastman Kodak 10-K report, 2011: pp. 5–8. Reproduced by permission of Eastman Kodak Company.

that sales of roll film would continue to increase into the 21st century. In reality, the transition to digital imaging occurred at much the same pace in emerging markets as in the mature industrialized countries.

Under Perez, Kodak accelerated its withdrawal from film. During 2011 and 2012, it withdrew several film products, including film for slides. It also withdrew from other unprofitable markets (including cameras) and divested other businesses, including its Kodak EasyShare Gallery to rival Shutterfly. Retrenchment was accompanied by accelerated job cutting.

Eastman Kodak in 2012

Eastman Kodak's business was organized around three business segments. Exhibit 1 describes each of these segments.

Competition

In most of the markets where it competed, Kodak was subject to intense competition: as with most forms of digital hardware, the dominant forces were many players, low entry barriers, falling real prices, and commoditization. In the case of digital cameras, phones incorporating cameras had decimated all but the quality segment of the market. Online photographic services were also ferociously competitive: Kodak's Gallery was the market leader, but it competed with a host of other online competitors, including: Shutterfly, Snapfish, Walmart.com's Photo Center, Fujifilmnet.com, Yahoo Photos, and Sears.com.

Kodak's highest margins were earned on consumables, notably photographic paper. However, Kodak faced strong competition, mainly from Xerox, Hewlett-Packard, 3M, and Oji, as well as from many minor brands. In supplying photo-finishers and commercial printers, Kodak was able to benefit from its leadership in retail kiosks and labs. To fight commoditization in printing paper, Kodak pioneered a number of technical advances, particularly in inkjet printing paper, including its Colorlast technology, designed to preserve the fidelity and vibrancy of photographic prints. However, across all markets, Kodak was suffering from the growing trend for consumers to view their photographs on screens rather than in printed form.

In commercial markets, competitive price pressures were less severe than in the consumer sector, in particular the opportunity for Kodak to differentiate its offering through packaging hardware, software, and services into customized "user solutions."

Kodak's Resources and Capabilities

Digital imaging was a classic "disruptive technology."[8] For traditional photographic companies it was "competence destroying"[9]—the new technological regime meant that many of their resources and capabilities became close to useless. For the camera companies—Nikon, Canon, Olympus, and Pentax, for example—digital imaging was not such a threat: digital backs could be added to standard camera architectures; optical capabilities remained important. For the film companies—Kodak, Fujifilm, and Agfa—digital imaging rendered chemical capabilities obsolete. This is why the transition period between traditional and digital imaging was so important for Kodak. During the transition period, Kodak could exploit its brand loyalty and vast distribution system to offer hybrid solutions, while building the resources and capabilities required for digital imaging. The problem for Kodak was that it was now competing with companies that had well-developed microelectronics and software engineering capabilities: Canon, Hewlett-Packard, Sony, Adobe Systems, to mention just a few.

By the time it had entered bankruptcy in January 2012, Kodak was clearly in a weakened state; nevertheless, it had maintained, and accumulated, potentially valuable resources and capabilities.

- *Brand*: Kodak's traditional resource strengths had been its brand and its global distribution presence. Two decades of decline and wrenching technological changes had weakened both. Yet, as late as 2011, MPP Consulting had ranked Kodak the 77th most valuable US brand. Yet, for all Kodak's brand recognition, the key issue was the extent to which it added value and market appeal to Kodak's consumer and commercial products.

- *Distribution*: Kodak's distribution presence was still unrivalled in the industry. However, as demand for printed photographs declined, so this too was a depreciating asset.

- *Technology*: For two decades Kodak had maintained one of the world's biggest research efforts in imaging. During 2000–2005, its research labs in the US, the U.K., France, Japan, China, and Australia had employed more than 5000 engineers and scientists, including more than 600 PhDs. Between 1975 and 2011, Kodak had been issued 16,760 patents. During 2011–2012, it sought to sell its patents in order to raise capital. Table 3 identifies some of Kodak's principal areas of technological strength.

TABLE 3   Kodak's technical capabilities

Area of technology	Kodak capabilities
Color science	Kodak is a leader in the production, control, measurement, specification, and visual perception of color, essential to predicting the performance of image-capture devices and imaging systems. Kodak has pioneered *colorimetry*—measuring and quantifying visual response to a stimulus of light.
Image processing	Includes technologies to control image sharpness, noise, and color reproduction. It is used to maximize the information content of images and to compress data for economical storage and rapid transmission. Kodak is a leader in image processing algorithms for automatic color balancing, object and text recognition, and image enhancement and manipulation. These are especially important in digital photo-finishing for image enhancement, including adjustments for scene reflectance, lighting conditions, sharpness, and a host of other conditions.
Imaging systems analysis	Provides techniques to measure the characteristics of imaging systems and components. Predictive system modeling is especially important in Kodak's new product development, where it can predict the impact of individual components on the performance of the entire system.
Sensors	A world leader in image sensor technology, with 30 years' experience in the design and manufacture of both CCD and CMOS electronic image sensors used in cameras, machine vision products, and satellite and medical imaging.
Ink technology	A world leader in dyes and pigments for color printing. Pioneer of micro-milling technology (originally invented for drug delivery systems). It has advanced knowledge of humectants (which keep print-head nozzles from clogging), and surface tension and viscosity modifiers (which control ink flows).

(continued)

TABLE 3 Kodak's technical capabilities (*Continued*)

Area of technology	Kodak capabilities
Inkjet technology	Innovations in the electronic and thermal control of inkjet heads coupled with innovation in inks have given Kodak technological advantages in ink-jet printing. In commercial printing, Kodak's continuous inkjet technology has permitted the flexibility of inkjet printing to be matched with substantial improvements in resolution and color fidelity.
Microfluidics	Microfluidics, the study of miniature devices that handle very small quantities of liquids, is relevant to film coating, fluid mixing, chemical sensing, and liquid inkjet printing.
Print media	A leader in applying polymer science and chemical engineering to ink-receiving materials. Expertise in specially constructed inkjet media in which layers of organic/inorganic polymers are coated onto paper or clear film and multi-layer coated structures of hydrogels and inorganic oxides.
Electronic display technology	Through its joint venture with Sanyo, Kodak pioneered organic light-emitting diode (OLED) technology for self-luminous flat panel displays. Kodak's OLED display panels extended from small-screen devices to larger displays.
Software	EasyShare software focused on ease of image manipulation, printing, and storage (even without a computer). Commercial software leads in workflow solutions (Kodak EMS Business Software), scanning software (Perfect Page), and printing software (Kodak Professional Digital Print Production Software); strengths in control software and printing algorithms that overcome technical limitations of inkjet printing and optimize color and tone reproduction (e.g. the Kodak One Touch Printing System).

Source: www.kodak.com.

- *New Product Development*: Despite Kodak's strengths in basic and applied research and its long history of successful new product launches, the company had struggled to move away from its traditional long and meticulous product development process to embrace the fast-cycle world of electronics.

- *Financial Resources*: Chapter 11 had given Kodak freedom from its creditors and allowed it to cut retiree health benefits. However, it offered little escape from its pension obligations. While its US pension scheme was judged fully funded, its UK pension fund required an additional $800 million top-up. By the end of the first quarter of 2012, Kodak's financial position was showing some improvements: with selling, general and administrative expenses down by $84 million and investment in unprofitable businesses cut, Kodak's cash balance was $1.4 billion, up $500 million from the end of 2011. However, under Chapter 11 protection, Kodak would not be able to seek new sources of financing and would be tightly constrained as to any strategic initiatives that required significant capital expenditure.

Table 4 shows financial data for Eastman Kodak, while Table 5 shows data for its business segments.

TABLE 4   Eastman Kodak: Selected financial data, 2006–2011 ($million)

	2011	2010	2009	2008	2007	2006
From income statement						
Sales	6,022	7,167	7,609	9,416	10,301	10,568
Cost of goods sold	5,135	5,221	5,850	7,247	7,757	8,159
Selling, general, and admin.	1,159	1,275	1,298	1,606	1,802	1,950
R & D costs	274	318	351	478	525	578
Operating earnings	(600)	(336)	(28)	(821)	(230)	(476)
Interest expense	156	149	119	108	113	172
Other income (charges)	(2)	26	30	55	86	65
Restructuring costs	121	70	226	140	543	416
Income taxes	9	114	115	(147)	(51)	221
Net earnings	(764)	(687)	(210)	(442)	676	(601)
From balance sheet						
Total current assets	2,703	3,786	4,303	5,004	6,053	5,557
Including:						
Cash	861	1,624	2,024	2,154	2,947	1,496
Receivables	1,103	1,196	1,395	1,716	1,939	2,072
Inventories	607	746	679	948	943	1,001
Property, plant, and equipment	895	1,037	1,254	1,551	1,811	2,602
Other long-term assets	803	1,109	1,227	1,728	4,138	3,509
Total assets	4,678	6,226	7,691	9,179	13,659	14,320
Total current liabilities	2,150	2,820	2896	3,438	4,446	4,554
Including:						
Payables	706	959	2,811	3,267	3,794	3,712
Short-term borrowings	152	50	62	51	308	64
Other liabilities:						
Long-term borrowings	1,363	1,195	1,129	1,252	1,289	2,714
Post-employment liabilities	3,053	2,661	2,694	2,382	3,444	3,934
Other long-term liabilities	462	625	1,005	1,119	1,451	1,690
Total liabilities	7,028	7,301	7,724	8,191	10,630	12,932
Shareholders' equity	(2350)	(1075)	(33)	988	,3029	1,388
Total liabilities (and equity)	4,678	6,226	7,691	9,179	13,659	14,320
From cash flow statement						
Cash flows from operating activities:						
Net earnings	(764)	(687)	(209)	(442)	676	(601)
Non-cash restructuring and rationalization costs, asset impairments, and other charges	17	635	28	801	336	138
Net cash from operating activities	(998)	(219)	(136)	168	328	956
Cash flows from investing activities:						
Additions to properties	(128)	(149)	(152)	(254)	(259)	(335)
Proceeds businesses/assets sales	153	32	156	92	227	178
Acquisitions, net of cash acquired	(27)	—	(17)	(38)	(2)	(3)
Net cash used in investing activities	(25)	(112)	(22)	(188)	2408	(225)
Net cash flows from financing activities	246	(74)	33	(746)	(1294)	(947)
Number of employees	17,100	18,800	20,250	24,400	26,900	40,900

Note:
Figures in parentheses denote a loss.
Source: Eastman Kodak annual reports.

TABLE 5 Eastman Kodak: Results by business segments, 2007–2011 ($million)

	2011	2010	2009	2008	2007
Net sales from continuing operations					
Consumer Digital Imaging Group	1,739	2,731	2,626	3,088	3,247
Film, Photofinishing, and Entertainment Group	1,547	1,762	2,262	2,987	3,632
Graphic Communications Group	2,736	2,674	2,718	3,334	3,413
All other	—	—	3	7	9
Consolidated total	6,022	7,167	7,609	9,416	10,301
Earnings (losses) from continuing operations					
before interest and taxes					
Consumer Digital Imaging Group	(349)	278	(10)	(177)	(17)
Graphic Communications Group	(191)	(95)	(107)	31	104
Film, Photofinishing, and Entertainment Group	34	91	187	196	281
All other	—	(1)	(16)	(17)	(25)
Total of segments	(506)	273	54	33	343
Segment total assets:					
Consumer Digital Imaging Group	929	1,126	1,198	1,647	2,442
Graphic Communications Group	1,459	1,566	1,734	2,190	3,723
Film, Photofinishing, and Entertainment Group	913	1,090	1,991	2,563	3,778
All other	—	1	—	8	17
Total of segments	3,301	3,782	4,923	6,408	9,960

Note:
Figures in parentheses denote a loss.

Reflections

As Perez reflected upon Kodak's two decades of digital transformation, he was struck by the paradox of Kodak's progress. In terms of adapting to a highly disruptive technological revolution, Kodak had been surprisingly successful. For a company that had dominated its traditional market for so long and so thoroughly as Kodak had, to survive the annihilation of its core technology, and to build the capabilities needed to become a significant player in a radically different area of technology was unusual. Yet, in terms of financial performance, Kodak had failed: for all of Kodak's technical and market achievements, Perez and his two predecessors, Dan Carp and George Fisher, had been unable to build a financially viable digital imaging business. Where had they gone wrong?

- It was difficult to argue that Kodak had been too slow or that it had failed to recognize the digital threat—as early as 1979 Kodak produced a remarkably accurate forecast of the evolution of digital imaging and it had been a pioneer of digital cameras.[10]
- It was also difficult to argue that Kodak had failed in implementing its digital strategy in terms of being a laggard in developing the capabilities needed to compete in digital imaging. Kodak's market leadership in digital cameras pointed to its ability to build technological know-how, apply that know-how to develop attractive new products, and market those products in fiercely competitive digital markets.

EXHIBIT 2

Fujifilm Holdings Corporation

	1992			2011		
	Sales ($million)	Net income ($million)	Employees	Sales ($million)	Net income ($million)	Employees
Fujifilm Holdings[a]	9,126	593	24,868	27,440	1,412	35,274
Eastman Kodak[b]	20,577	1,146	132,600	6,022	(764)	17,100

Notes:

Figures in parentheses denote a loss.

[a] 2011 data are for financial year to March 31, 2012.

[b] 2011 data are for year ended December 31, 2011.

Despite the strong similarities between Fujifilm and Kodak—both companies were heavily dependent on film during the early 1990s and both had diversified into other imaging technologies (Fujifilm had a major position in plain-paper copiers through its Fuji/Xerox joint venture)—the two companies responded to the digital revolution with different strategies which led to very different financial results.

Like Kodak, Fujifilm recognized the implications of digital imaging for its core business and struggled to adapt its strategy. However, a key difference was Fuji's recognition that digital imaging alone would be unlikely to support the business of a large company, hence its emphasis on diversification. Under its chief executive, Shigetaka Komori, Fujifilm underwent a major restructuring between 2000 and 2010 (especially during 2005/6 and 2009/10) involving business closures, employee layoffs, and financial write-downs.

Comparing Fujifilm and Kodak in 2012, the most obvious difference is Fujifilm's business diversity. Its three business segments comprise a variety of different businesses:

Imaging solutions (14.8% of total sales) included traditional photo imaging products (photographic paper, film, and supplies) and electronic imaging (mainly digital cameras).

Information solutions (40.5% of total sales) included medical systems, pharmaceuticals, cosmetics, flat panel display materials, graphic arts materials, data storage tapes, industrial X-rays, and optical devices.

Document solutions (44.8% of total sales) comprised office supplies, office printers, and document product services.

Fujifilm's diversification has combined selective acquisitions (since 2000, $9 billion has been spent on 40 acquisitions) and internal development based upon Fujifilm's existing technical capabilities. In particular, it has built upon its chemical and coatings expertise to diversify into cosmetics, pharmaceuticals (especially drug delivery systems), components for LCD panels, and a variety of plastics products. The quest to exploit technical capabilities in "functional compound molecular design, chemical reaction control, and organic synthesis technologies" resulted in several discoveries. For example, human skin was observed to be similar to photographic film: it contained collagen and was about the same thickness. Fujifilm discovered that many of the antioxidants used to preserve photographic film could be used for skin care products.

Sources: www.fujifilm.com; "The last Kodak moment?" *Economist*, January 14, 2012; Stefan Kohn, "Disruptive innovations applied: A review of the imaging industry," http://www.iande.info/wp-content/uploads/2011/03/StefanKohnDisruptiveInnovationsFujifilm.pdf, accessed September 20, 2012.

- Perhaps Kodak's emphasis had been on the wrong markets and wrong products? Kodak's biggest losses had been in the consumer market, Kodak's traditional stronghold. Was this market simply too unattractive because of intense competition? Had Perez's emphasis on printing been misplaced? Might Kodak's scarce resources been better spent on other parts of the digital value chain (such as image capture through cameras and sensors and displays)?

- A further possibility was that Kodak's vision of establishing itself as a leader in digital imaging was misconceived. In 2000, Kodak had announced its intention to be at the center of the $225 billion "infoimaging" industry. But did this "infoimaging" industry really exist? While some products were specific to digital imaging—editing software such as Adobe's Photoshop, sensors for image scanning, online imaging archive—for the most part, digital imaging was part of the overall computing and communication sector. It comprised smartphones and tablet computers, broadband services, data storage devices, printers, and social networking services.

Finally, Perez wondered as to what lessons could be drawn from the comparative success of Fujifilm. For all of Fuji's similarities to Kodak, its performance had been radically different: its revenues had grown (in terms of US dollars), and it had been consistently profitable (Exhibit 2).

Perez's reflections on Kodak's past were cut short by the arrival of James Mesterharm, from turnaround consultants AlixPartners, who had been appointed Kodak's chief restructuring officer. Together Perez and Merterham would discuss the implications of Chapter 11 bankruptcy for Kodak's corporate strategy for 2012 and beyond.

Notes

1. "Eastman Kodak Company and its U.S. Subsidiaries Commence Voluntary Chapter 11 Business Reorganization," Press Release, January 19, 2012.
2. "Kodak's New Focus," *Business Week*, January 30, 1995, pp. 62–8.
3. Eastman Kodak Company, "Kodak Leaders Outline Road Ahead to get Kodak 'Back on Track'," press release, November 11, 1997.
4. Eastman Kodak Company, "The Big Picture: Kodak and Digital Photography," www.Kodak.com/US/en/corp/presscenter/presentations/020520mediaforum3.shtml.
5. See www.Kodak.com/US/en/corp/presscenter/presentations/020520mediaforum3.shtml, accessed October 29, 2009.
6. Interview with Antonio Perez, President and COO, Kodak, *PMA Magazine*, February 2004.
7. "Why Kodak Still Isn't Fixed," *Fortune*, May 11, 1998.
8. J. L. Bower and C. M. Christensen, "Disruptive Technologies: Catching the Wave," *Harvard Business Review* (January/February 1995).
9. M. Tushman, and P. Anderson, "Technological Discontinuities and Organizational Environments," *Administrative Science Quarterly* 31 (1986): 439–65.
10. Andrew Hill of the *Financial Times* observed: "In 1979, the company put together a graphic timeline laying out roughly when Kodak's customers would make the transition to digital imaging, starting with government clients, moving through graphic businesses and ending, in about 2010, with retail consumers. In 1991, the group drew up a digital strategy . . . Even the potential threat from camera-enabled mobile phones was 'war-gamed' by Kodak executives in the early 2000s." ("A Victim of Its Own Success," *Financial Times*, April 2, 2012.)

A video clip relating to this case is available in your interactive e-book at **www.wileyopenpage.com**

Case 11 Raisio Group and the Benecol Launch [A]

During 1996, Raisio Group, a 57-year-old grain-milling company based in Raisio in southwest Finland, emerged from obscurity to become the second-most-valuable public company in Finland (after Nokia) and the focus of worldwide attention. The launch of Benecol, its cholesterol-lowering margarine, at the end of 1995 had attracted the interest of food processors and supermarket groups throughout the world and fueled a surge of investor interest. Demand for the product had out-stripped Raisio's capability to produce the active ingredient in Benecol, stanol ester. On the Helsinki stock market, foreign demand pushed Raisio's share price from FIM61 at the beginning of the year to FIM288 at the end (after touching FIM322 during the summer).[1] CEO Matti Salminen commented:

> 1996 will go down in the Raisio Group's history as the "Benecol year"—such was the role of this new cholesterol-reducing margarine in increasing the Group's visibility and raising its profile in all our sectors of operations. Although we have not been able to meet even the domestic demand for Benecol margarine so far, the product is already known worldwide and great expectations are attached to it. The Benecol phenomenon quintupled the value of our shares, increasing the Group's capitalization by billions of Finnish marks.[2]

It was the international prospects for Benecol margarine (and potentially other food products incorporating stanol ester) that had drawn a bevy of stock analysts and portfolio managers to Raisio's headquarters. Not only was the potential market for Benecol considered huge—the US alone was seen as having a multi-billion-dollar market potential—but also the profit opportunities also appeared excellent. In Finland, Benecol was selling at about six times the price of regular margarine. In addition to being first to market, Raisio had the ability to sustain its market leadership through its patents relating to the production and use of the active ingredient, stanol ester, and recognition of its Benecol brand name.

However, within Raisio a vigorous debate had broken out as to the best strategy for exploiting the vast commercial potential that Raisio's innovation offered. This debate focused on two issues. The first was whether Raisio's emphasis should be on supplying its Benecol margarine or its active ingredient, stanol ester. Despite the phenomenal success of Benecol margarine in Finland, margarine was only one of a number of potential food and drink products to which stanol ester could be added.

The B part of this case is available from the publisher. This case draws upon an earlier case by Michael H. Moffett and Stacey Wolff Howard, *Benecol: Raisio's Global Nutriceutical* (Thunderbird, The American Graduate School of International Management, Case No. A06-99-0004, 1999). I am grateful to Ayan Bhattacharya for assistance in preparing this case. Copyright © 2012 Robert M. Grant.

Several Raisio managers argued that the company could exploit its innovation more widely if it supplied stanol ester to a number of food and drink companies. A second issue concerned the means by which Raisio would exploit the international potential of its innovation. Although Raisio was a significant margarine manufacturer in Finland, it possessed few facilities and limited experience outside its home market. A number of multinational food companies and leading food retailers had approached Raisio expressing interest in licensing agreements, joint ventures, and supply agreements—for Benecol margarine, for stanol ester, and for both. Should Raisio license its intellectual property to other firms, create joint ventures with foreign companies, or keep its technology in-house and use it to build a multinational presence for itself?

History of Raisio

The Raisio Group began life in 1939 as Vehnä Oy, a grain-milling company located in the town of Raisio. In 1950, a vegetable oil factory called Oy Kasviöljy-Växtolje Ab was founded next to the milling plant. The two companies cooperated in introducing rapeseed cultivation to Finland. They eventually merged in 1987 to form Raisio Tehtaat Oy Ab.[3] From cereals and vegetable oil, the company expanded into animal feeds, malt production, potato starch, and margarine. In the 1960s, production of starch provided the basis for the supply of a number of chemical products, mainly to the paper industry.

During this period Raisio developed a substantial export business. This began with malt exports to Sweden, followed by exports of margarine, pasta and other food products to the Soviet Union and subsequently to Poland. In the St. Petersburg area of Russia and in Estonia, Raisio's Melia-branded products were market leaders in flour, pasta, and muesli. Finland's accession to the European Union in 1995 allowed Raisio to expand its sales to other European countries. By 1996, 39% of Raisio's sales were outside of Finland. Raisio's increased international presence included margarine plants in Sweden and Poland and joint-venture plants supplying starch and other products for the paper industry in Sweden, the US, France, Germany, and Indonesia.

From its earliest days, Raisio had shown considerable entrepreneurial initiative and technical ingenuity. Its first oil-milling plant was constructed by its own employees using spare parts, scrap metal, and innovative improvisation. Raisio's first margarine plant was built partly to stimulate demand for its rapeseed oil, which was not widely used in margarine production at that time. Raisio also maintained an active program of R & D. Benecol was the result of Raisio's research into plant sterols. Raisio's annual report tells the story:

> The cholesterol-reducing effects of plant sterols were known as early as the 1950s and ever since that time, scientists all over the world have been studying plant sterols and their properties.
>
> In 1972, a project led by Professor Pekka Puska was launched in North Karelia. The purpose of the project, which enjoyed international prestige, was to reduce the high cardiovascular rates in the region.
>
> In 1988, the Department of Pharmacy at the University of Helsinki started cooperation with the Helsinki and Turku Central Hospitals and the Raisio Group aimed at studying the effect of rapeseed oil on blood cholesterol levels. Professor Tatu

Miettinen, who had already done extensive research on fat metabolism, suggested research on plant sterols to the Raisio Group.

The following year, R & D Manager Ingmar Wester (of Raisio's Margarine Sub-division) and his research team found a way of turning plant sterol into fat-soluble stanol ester suitable for food production. A patent application was filed in 1991. This started a period of intense research aimed at producing indisputable evidence of the cholesterol-reducing effect of stanol ester. In 1993, the North Karelia project launched a long-range stanol ester study as part of its other clinical research.

The digestive tract receives cholesterol from two sources i.e., food and the human body itself. Normally, some 50% of the cholesterol that enters the digestive tract is disposed of and the rest is absorbed by the body. Fat-soluble plant stanol was shown as efficiently preventing the absorption of cholesterol. In a diet containing stanol ester, 80% of the cholesterol entering the digestive tract is disposed of and only 20% is absorbed by the body. The plant stanol itself is not absorbed, but disposed of naturally.

The findings of the North Karelia study were published in the New England Journal of Medicine in November 1995. (The article reported that, after a 14-month trial, a daily intake of 25 grams reduces total cholesterol in the bloodstream by 10% and the level of more harmful LDL cholesterol by 14%.) At the same time the first patents were issued for the production and use of stanol ester.

The first stanol ester product, Benecol margarine, was introduced on the Finnish market. The interest it aroused soon exceeded all expectations both in Finland and internationally. The registered name, Benecol, has since been confirmed as the common name for all products containing stanol ester.

Production of stanol ester began with experimental equipment, which limited the supply. The availability of plant sterol, the raw material, was another limiting factor. All plants contain small amounts of plant sterol, but it can be recovered economically only from plants processed in very large quantities. Since there had been no demand for plant sterols, no investments had been made in separation facilities.[4]

Exhibit 1 describes the cholesterol-reducing properties of sterols and stanols. The Appendix gives information on Raisio's main patents relating to stanol ester.

Raisio in 1997

At the beginning of 1997, the Raisio Group had annual sales of $866 million and 2594 employees. The group comprised three divisions:

- foodstuffs (47% of total sales), including the subdivisions: margarine (39% of sales), Melia Ltd (flour, pasta, breakfast cereal, muesli), oil milling, potato processing (mainly frozen French fries), malting, and Foodie Oy (rye products, pea soup, frozen pastry dough, salad dressings)
- chemicals (34% of sales)
- animal feeds (19% of sales).

Outside of Finland, Raisio had subsidiaries in Sweden, Estonia, Latvia, the UK, France, Spain, Germany, Belgium, Poland, Canada, the US, and Indonesia. Raisio

Sterols play a critical role in maintaining cell membranes in both plants and animals. Plant sterols (phytosterols) can reduce the low-density lipoprotein (LDL) in human blood, therefore reducing the risk of coronary heart disease. In plants, more than 40 sterols have been identified, of which sitosterol, stigmasterol, and campesterol are the most abundant.

Plant stanols (phytostanols) are similar to sterols and are found naturally in plants—though in much smaller quantities than sterols.

The effect of plant sterols in lowering human cholesterol levels has been known since the 1950s. Sitosterol has been used as a supplement and as a drug (Cytellin, marketed by Eli Lilly) to lower serum cholesterol levels. However, the use of plant sterols was limited by problems of poor solubility.

An important breakthrough was made by Finnish chemist Ingvar Wester, who hydrogenated plant sterols (derived from tall oil, a byproduct of pinewood pulp) to produce stanol, and then esterified the stanol to produce stanol ester, which is fat-soluble. Unlike sterol ester, stanol ester is not absorbed by the body. Clinical trials in Finland showed that stanol ester reduced total blood serum cholesterol in humans by up to 15%.

Plant sterols can also be produced as a byproduct of vegetable oil processing. One of the final stages of the processing of vegetable oil is deodorization—high-temperature distillation that removes free fatty acids. Sterols can be recovered from the resulting distillate.

Plant sterols themselves have a waxy consistency and a high melting point, creating solubility issues for the food processor. While they are oil-dispersible to some extent in their raw form, the amount required to produce an efficacious effect in a finished product can cause granulation. The answer to this problem is esterification: to make stanols and sterols fat-soluble. During 1996, Unilever was working on the esterification of plant sterols. Meanwhile, Archer Daniels Midland was believed to be developing processes that would allow the introduction of sterols into nonfat systems, thus creating entirely new product lines (e.g., adding sterols to beverages).

also had joint ventures in Mexico (49% ownership) and Chile (50%). Figure 1 shows Raisio's share price. Table 1 shows Raisio's financial performance.

The Benecol Launch

Raisio launched Benecol margarine with a retail price of around FIM25 ($4.50) for a 250g tub—this compared with FIM4 for regular margarine. Despite the high price, the product flew off the shelves as quickly as it appeared and Raisio was forced to institute a system of rationing supplies to distributors. During 1996, Raisio estimated that it was only able to satisfy about two-thirds of domestic demand.

To facilitate the speedy development of the Benecol business, in March 1996 Benecol margarine was transferred from the margarine subdivision to a separate Benecol unit. The unit was headed by Jukka Kaitaranta, who reported to the deputy chief executive and head of the Food Division, Jukka Maki. It was intended

FIGURE 1   Raisio's share price (unrestricted shares, Helsinki Stock Exchange)

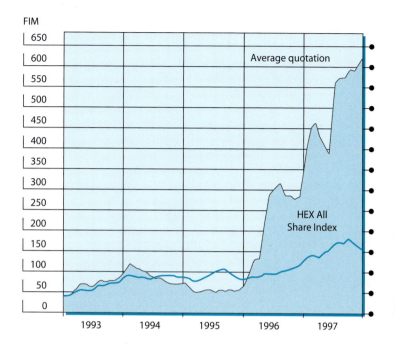

TABLE 1   Raisio's financial performance, 1987–1996

	1987	1988	1989	1990	1991	1992	1993	1994	1995	1996
Sales[a]	2,011	2,184	2,487	2,557	2,315	3,070	3,549	3,518	3,224	3,928
Change (%)	+9	+9	+14	+3	−9	+33	+16	−1	−8	+22
Exports from Finland[a]	126	106	110	136	172	241	389	358	519	735
International sales[a]	288	16	189	217	279	405	561	568	886	1,541
Operating margin[a]	214	247	232	213	316	431	492	428	383	420
Operating margin/ sales (%)	10.6	11.3	9.3	8.3	13.6	14.0	13.9	12.2	11.9	10.7
Profit after depreciation[a]	147	167	120	90	185	252	294	230	183	196
Percentage of turnover	7.3	7.6	4.8	3.5	8.0	8.2	8.3	6.5	5.7	5.0
Pre-tax profit[a,b]	97	98	91	64	63	114	185	35	140	162
Pretax profit/ Sales (%)	4.8	4.5	3.7	2.5	2.7	3.7	5.2	1.0	4.3	4.1
Return on equity (%)	15.5	15.3	5.4	0.1	6.9	10.3	10.3	9.4	6.8	5.8
Return on investment (%)	12.6	13.1	9.0	5.8	10.7	13.7	12.4	10.3	8.5	8.5
Shareholders' equity[a]	670	994	1,123	1,224	1,246	1,246	1,517	1,564	1,648	1,973

(*continued*)

TABLE 1   Raisio's financial performance, 1987–1996 (*Continued*)

	1987	1988	1989	1990	1991	1992	1993	1994	1995	1996
Balance sheet total[a]	1,831	2,257	2,493	2,872	2,702	3,268	3,302	3,071	3,175	3,678
Equity ratio (%)	36.0	44.3	46.0	46.7	47.3	44.3	46.5	51.4	52.1	54.0
Quick ratio	0.8	1.0	0.8	0.8	0.9	0.8	1.0	1.1	0.9	1.1
Current ratio	1.6	1.7	1.6	1.5	1.6	1.5	1.6	1.6	1.6	1.8
Gross investment[a]	101	329	269	462	197	293	174	188	380	387
Gross investment/ Sales (%)	5.0	15.1	10.8	18.1	8.5	9.5	4.9	5.3	11.8	9.9
R & D expenditure[a]	16	28	31	52	31	35	40	54	54	87
R & D expenditure/ Sales (%)	0.8	1.3	1.2	2.0	1.3	1.1	1.1	1.5	1.7	2.2
Direct taxes[a]	5	10	27	25	20	20	47	21	32	64
No. of employees	1,538	1,581	1,877	1,987	803	1,985	2,106	1,958	2,054	2,365

Notes:
[a] In FIM million.
[b] Before appropriations, taxes, and minority interest.
Source: Raisio Group annual reports.

that, during 1997, Benecol would become a separate division within Raisio. The Benecol Unit was responsible for developing all aspects of the business. It was responsible for acquiring plant sterol, producing stanol ester, managing international publicity for the project, and conducting research.

The key problem was the limited supplies of the active ingredient, stanol ester. While plant sterols, the raw material from which stanol ester is produced, are a common byproduct of industries that mass-process vegetable matter, almost no one had the systems in place to collect them. Raisio's primary source of supply of plant stanols was UPM-Kymmene, Europe's biggest pulp and paper company. During 1996, it negotiated increased supplies from UPM-Kymmene and sought access to sterols from vegetable oil processors. Also in 1996, the Group built its first stanol ester plant, which was located in Raisio, and announced plans for a second plant to bring total stanol ester capacity up to 2000 tonnes a year by January 1998. Mr Kari Jokinen, chief executive of Raisio's margarine division, estimated that this production of stanol ester would allow the production of 25 million kg of margarine, which could supply a total market of 60 million people.[5] The Benecol Unit also began work on a new 1500 m² R & D laboratory at Raisio's main industrial site.

During 1996, Raisio began planning for the international launch of Benecol. Its first overseas market was to be Sweden. The Swedish launch would be facilitated by Raisio's acquisition of a 77.5% stake in Carlshamm Mejeri AB, one of Sweden's main margarine producers, for $44.4 million. However, Raisio's horizons were not limited to Scandinavia, or even Europe. Benecol margarine was seen as having a huge international potential. Sales to the US market could be massive, given that Americans spent some $33 billion a year on health foods and slimming products. Some estimates suggested that sales of Benecol margarine could reach $3 billion.

By January 1997, Raisio was being bombarded with requests and proposals from all over the world. Sainsbury's, at the time Britain's leading supermarket chain, requested an own-label version of Benecol margarine.[6] Other food processing companies were interested in purchasing licenses either for Benecol margarine or for Raisio's stanol ester technology, or for both.

Raisio's senior executives recognized that product formulation, marketing strategy, and distribution policies would need to be adapted to the requirements of different national markets. Moreover, there were complex national regulations relating to the marketing of food products, especially those that included additives claiming to have health benefits. The Raisio executives were especially interested in an approach from McNeil Consumer Products, a division of the US-based pharmaceutical and consumer products company Johnson & Johnson. McNeil was the world's biggest supplier of over-the-counter medicines and was known by its leading brand-name products such as Tylenol, Imodium, and Motrin. McNeil was headquartered in Fort Washington, Pennsylvania and was able to field a range of relevant resources, not least Johnson & Johnson's worldwide marketing and distribution system.

Competition

In formulating a strategy for the global exploitation of Benecol, Raisio faced a number of uncertainties. One issue that especially concerned Raisio executives was the potential for Benecol to encounter competition. In 1991, Raisio had filed its first patent relating to its process for the production of stanol ester from plant sterols and for its use in reducing cholesterol as an additive to human foods. In 1996, its first US patent relating to stanol ester was issued. In the same year, Raisio filed a broader patent relating to the processing and use of stanol ester (see the Appendix). However, a number of competing products were available for reducing cholesterol. In particular, the cholesterol-reducing properties of naturally available plant sterols were well known. While Raisio believed it owned the only effective means for converting plant sterols into a fat-soluble form, it thought it likely that other processes might offer alternative approaches to the use of plant sterols as a food additive. Tor Bergman, head of chemicals (and soon to be appointed head of the Benecol Division as well) reckoned that Raisio had an 18- to 24-month lead over competitors.

Apart from plant sterols and stanols, a growing array of cholesterol-reducing drugs was available on the market. The major category was statins, which included lovastatin (brand name Mevacor), simvastatin (brand name Zocor), pravastatin (brand name Pravachol), fluvastatin (brand name Lescol), and atorvastatin (brand name Lipitor). Statins worked through slowing down the production of cholesterol by the body and by increasing the liver's ability to remove the LDL-cholesterol already in the blood.

In addition, there are a number of natural food products that have the effect of reducing cholesterol within the blood. These include fish oil, garlic, flax seed, dietary fiber, policosanol (fatty alcohols derived from waxes of sugar cane), and guggulipid (an ancient herb from India).

Regulation

Benecol margarine falls into a wide category of products generally referred to as "nutraceuticals" or "functional foods." These are food products or supplements that

EXHIBIT 2
Country Regulations Relating to "Functional Foods"

UNITED STATES

Under the 1990 Nutrition Labeling and Education Act (NLEA), the US Food and Drug Administration allowed health claims in the case of certain well-documented relationships, for example between calcium and osteoporosis and sodium and hypertension.

The 1997 Food and Drug Administration Modernization Act (FDAMA) allowed for two types of health claim:

◆ Authoritative statement health claims (e.g., relating to wholegrain foods and risk of heart disease and certain cancers, and potassium and risk of high blood pressure and stroke).

◆ Qualified claims restricted to dietary supplements—typically in the form of pills, capsules, tablets, or liquids, labeled as dietary supplements and not represented or marketed for consumption as a conventional food or sole item of a meal. Such claims could be based on a preponderance of scientific evidence.

In practice, this meant three possible paths for gaining approval of a food product offering stated health benefits:

◆ As a dietary supplement: This was the simplest path. The applicant had to file notification to the FDA 60 days prior to commercial rollout together with supporting evidence.

◆ As a food additive: This was a more time-consuming process involving much stronger evidence and a determination by an independent panel of experts assembled by the applicant and reporting to the FDA.

◆ As a pharmaceutical: Finally, a new food product could be approved as a drug. This process typically required several years.

CANADA

The Canadian Food and Drug Act stipulated that all products represented for the cure, treatment, mitigation, prevention, risk reduction, and correction or modification of body structure and function be regulated as a "drug" regardless of the available scientific evidence.

EUROPEAN UNION

During the 1990s, the EU was in the process of harmonizing legislation among its individual member countries regarding health claims for food products. Regulation No. 258/97 concerning novel foods and novel food ingredients applied to new foods or ingredients that were primary molecular structures,

may have a functional or physiological effect that is beneficial. Nutraceuticals have traditionally included food supplements such as vitamin pills, herbal products, and more recently food products with additives that offer particular nutritional benefits: energy-enhancing drinks, vitamin-enriched cereals, and the like. Nutraceuticals occupy a middle ground between food and medicines. The regulations relating to them also fall between food regulations and drug regulations. They also vary greatly between countries. Japan was one of the few countries that recognized functional foods as a distinct category and, since 1991, has had a well-developed administrative micro-organisms, or were isolated from plants or isolated from animals (but this was not applicable to food additives). Such novel foods were to be assessed by the government of a Member State, which would make an initial assessment to determine whether the product met EU standards of safety and accurate labeling and whether an additional assessment was needed.

If neither the Commission nor the Member States raise an objection, and if no additional assessment is required, the Member State informs the applicant that he or she may place the product on the market . . . Any decision or provision concerning a novel food or food ingredient which is likely to have an effect on public health must be referred to the Scientific Committee for Food.

Fast-track approval was possible for products that were essentially similar to products already on the market but entirely new products required a full assessment by the Scientific Committee for Food. It would appear that Benecol was a new food product (given its first-time use of stanol ester). However, the fact that it had already been marketed in Finland before the EU's regulation had taken effect might provide it with a loophole to avoid full-assessment approval.

JAPAN

In 1991, Japan became the first global jurisdiction to implement a regulatory system for functional foods. Under the Japanese system, "foods for specific health use" (FOSHU) had a specific regulatory

approval process separate from foods fortified with vitamins and minerals and dietary supplements not carrying FOSHU claims. "Foods for specific health use" are defined as "foods in the case of which specified effects contributing to maintain health can be expected based on the available data concerning the relationship between the foods'/food's contents and health, as well as foods with permitted labeling which indicates the consumer can expect certain health effects upon intake of these particular foods." Approved FOSHU bear a seal of approval from the Japanese Ministry of Health, Labor and Welfare (MHLW) identifying their role in disease prevention and health promotion. To achieve FOSHU status and an approved health claim, companies submit a scientific dossier to MHLW, which includes scientific documentation demonstrating the medical and nutritional basis for the health claim, including the recommended dose of the functional ingredient. The MHLW has established a detailed approval process, which typically takes about one year to complete. Japan was estimated to have the world's second-largest functional food market behind the US.

Sources: Michael H. Moffett and Stacey Wolff Howard, *Benecol: Raisio's Global Nutraceutical,* (Thunderbird, The American Graduate School of International Management, 1999); Sean A. MacDonald, "A Comparative Analysis of the Regulatory Framework Affecting Functional Food and Functional Food Ingredient Development and Commercialization in Canada, the United States (US), the European Union (EU), Japan and Australia/New Zealand," Agriculture and Agri-Food Canada, (August 2004).

system for vetting and approving health claims relating to food. Canada, on the other hand, made no distinction between functional foods and drugs in relation to health claims—inevitably, this resulted in a highly restrictive regulatory climate for functional foods. Typically, regulations required that claims regarding the beneficial effects of food products could only be health claims (improved health) and not medicinal claims (claims relating to the prevention or cure of a disease). The most important markets for Benecol would be the US and European Union. Here the regulations were far from clear-cut (Exhibit 2).

The Emerging Strategy

Up until 1997, Raisio had pursued a largely self-sufficient strategy for the exploitation of its stanol ester technology. It had fabricated stanol ester itself in its own plant using its own technology. Rather than selling the stanol ester to other food manufacturers for incorporation into their own products, it had followed a strategy of vertical integration. Its stanol ester was used only in its own branded margarine, Benecol, which was produced in its own factories and marketed and distributed through its own sales and distribution system.

If it was to exploit the full potential of its innovation, Raisio would need to draw upon the resources of other companies. Clearly the market for cholesterol-reducing foods was worldwide. Moreover, the potential for using stanol ester in foods was not restricted to margarine. Raisio envisaged its use in a variety of health-food products, including salad dressings, dairy products, and snack bars. If Raisio's stanol ester technology was to be exploited effectively throughout the EU, in North America, the Far East, and Australasia, then this would require food-processing facilities, market knowledge, regulatory know-how, and distribution facilities, the provision of which was quite beyond Raisio's ability. Time was a critical issue. Raisio patents related to its own process of producing stanol ester and incorporating it within food products. While Raisio's technology and the patent protection it had received bought it a few years' lead-time, it was likely that other companies would find alternative approaches to the use of plant sterols as a cholesterol-reducing food additive.

In Johnson & Johnson, Raisio had a potential partner that had the capabilities needed to introduce Benecol margarine, and other Benecol products, to the world market. Johnson & Johnson possessed global manufacturing, marketing, and distribution capabilities, together with extensive experience in the food and drug approval procedures of the US, Europe, and most other countries. It was widely considered one of the most effective health-product marketing companies in the world, with an outstanding reputation for quality and social responsibility, a global sales and distribution reach, and vast experience in guiding products through government regulations relating to foods and drugs. It viewed nutraceuticals as an important strand of its growth strategy. Its first nutraceutical was Lactaid for people unable to digest lactose. Lactaid was sold in caplets and as lactose-reduced milk and lactose-free foods. It also supplied sucralose, a low-calorie sweetener that had been approved by the US Food and Drug Administration and was sold in nearly 30 countries.

At the same time, there were voices within Raisio that saw risks in an exclusive relationship with Johnson & Johnson. If stanol ester were a potential additive to a wide range of products, would it make sense for Raisio to become identified with a single product—margarine—and would it be desirable for Raisio to link its fortunes with a single partner? An alternative approach for Raisio would be to focus on the supply of its key ingredient, stanol ester. At one meeting of Raisio's executive committee, the case of Monsanto and NutraSweet was discussed. It was noted that, following the development of NutraSweet (the branded name for aspartame), Monsanto did not forward integrate into the production of diet foods and beverages but became a supplier of NutraSweet to a wide range of different beverage suppliers and food processors.

In relation to the production and supply of stanol ester, Raisio also faced some critical strategic choices. The crucial problem in 1996 appeared to be limited capacity for producing stanol ester. Even with a new plant planned for 1997, Raisio would still be unable to supply the potential market for Benecol margarine in Finland and nearby markets. If, as anticipated, the demand for Benecol products was to be worldwide, it would need to produce stanol ester in all regions where Benecol products were manufactured and marketed. Thus, even if Raisio agreed a licensing agreement with Johnson & Johnson to produce and market Benecol products, Raisio would need to specify the terms under which stanol ester would be supplied. All Raisio's sterol requirements were supplied by UPM-Kymmene, the pulp and paper group. Raisio had cooperated closely with UPM-Kymmene in developing the technology for separating plant sterols during wood pulp processing. To ensure access to adequate supplies of plant sterols for its stanol ester production, Raisio would need to collaborate closely with the processors of forest and agricultural products. Raisio was considering forming a joint venture with UPM-Kymmene specifically for the extraction and supply of plant sterols. Irrespective of whether the global licensing deal with Johnson & Johnson for the production and distribution of Benecol products went ahead, Raisio faced critical decisions with regard to the production of stanol ester and the supply of plant sterols. Should it keep its production of stanol ester in-house or should it license this technology also?

Appendix
Raisio's Principal Patents Relating to Stanol Ester

US Patent No. 5,502,045 "Use of a Stanol Fatty Acid Ester for Reducing Serum Cholesterol Level"

Inventors: Tatu Miettinen, Hannu Vanhanen, Ingmar Wester.

Assignee: Raision Tehtaat Oy AB

Filed: November 22, 1993

Awarded: March 26, 1996

Abstract   The invention relates to a substance which lowers cholesterol levels in serum and which is a.beta.-sitostanol fatty acid ester or fatty acid ester mixture, and to a method for preparing the same. The substance can be used as such or added to a food.

Claims   We claim:

1. The method of reducing the absorption of cholesterol into the bloodstream comprising orally introducing into the body an effective amount of a substance containing a.beta.-sitostanol fatty acid ester prepared by the interesterification of .beta.-sitostanol with a fatty acid ester containing between 2 and 22 carbon atoms in the presence of an interesterification catalyst.

2. The method according to claim 1, wherein the interesterification of .beta.-sitostanol is carried out in a solvent free food grade process.

3. The method according to claim 2, wherein the interesterification occurs at a temperature of approximately 90 degree-120 degree C and a vacuum of approximately 5–15 mmHg.

4. The method according to claim 3, wherein the catalyst is sodium ethylate.

5. The method of claim 1, wherein the fatty acid ester comprises a mixture of fatty acid esters.

6. The method according to claim 1, wherein the .beta.-sitostanol is prepared by hydrogenation of a commercial .beta.-sitosterol mixture.

7. The method according to claim 1, wherein the interesterification is carried out in the presence of a stoichiometric excess of the fatty acid ester.

8. The method according to claim 1, wherein an effective amount of the substance is between about 0.2 and about 20 grams per day.

Extract from "Description" Section

The present invention relates to the use of a sterol of an entirely different type for lowering the cholesterol level in serum. What is involved is fatty acid esters of alpha-saturated sterols, especially sitostanol fatty acid esters (sitostanol = 24-ethyl-5. alpha. -cholestane-3.beta.-ol), which have been observed to lower cholesterol levels in serum with particular efficacy. The said esters can be prepared or used as such, or they can be added to foods, especially to the fatty part of a food. The sitostanol fatty acid ester mixture is prepared by hardening a commercial .beta.-sitosterol mixture (sitosterol = 24-ethyl-5-cholestene-3.beta.-ol) .beta.-sitostanol can be prepared by a prior-known cholesterol hardening technique by hardening .beta.-sitosterol by means of a Pd/C catalyst in an organic solvent . . . This mixture has the approval of the FDA (Cytellin, Eli Lilly). A hardening degree of over 99% is achieved in the reaction. The catalyst used in the hardening is removed by means of a membrane filter, and the obtained sitostanol is crystallized, washed and dried. In accordance with the invention, the .beta.-sitostanol mixture, which contains campestanol approx. 6%, is esterified with different fatty acid ester mixtures by a commonly known chemical interesterification technique . . . A methyl ester mixture of the fatty acids of any vegetable oil can be used in the reaction. One example is a mixture of rapeseed oil and methyl ester, but any fatty acids which contain approx. 2 to 22 carbon atoms are usable. The method according to the invention for the preparation of stanol fatty acid esters deviates advantageously from the previously patented methods in that no substances other than free stanol, a fatty acid ester or a fatty acid ester mixture, and a catalyst are used in the esterification reaction. The catalyst used may be any known interesterification catalyst, such as Na-ethylate.

US Patent No. 5,958,913 "Substance for Lowering High Cholesterol Level in Serum and Methods for Preparing and Using the Same"

Inventors: Tatu Miettinen, Hannu Vanhanen, Ingmar Wester.

Assignee: Raisio Benecol Ltd.

Filed: November 5, 1996

Awarded: September 28, 1999

Abstract The invention relates to a substance which lowers LDL cholesterol levels in serum and which is fat soluble .beta.-sitostanol fatty acid ester, and to a method for preparing and using the same. The substance can be taken orally as a food additive, food substitute or supplement. A daily consumption of the .beta.-sitostanol ester in an amount between about 0.2 and about 20 grams per day has been shown to reduce the absorption of biliary and endogenic cholesterol.

Claims What is claimed is:

1. A food composition suitable for reducing blood serum cholesterol levels or reducing absorption of cholesterol from the intestines into the bloodstream, the food composition comprising a nutritional substance and a blood serum cholesterol level reducing or cholesterol absorption reducing effective amount of a sterol component comprising at least one 5.alpha.-saturated sterol fatty acid ester.

2. The food composition as claimed in claim 1, wherein the sterol component comprises .beta.-sitostanol fatty acid ester.

3. The food composition as claimed in claim 1, wherein the fatty acid contains about 2 to 22 carbon atoms.

4. The food composition as claimed in claim 2, wherein the fatty acid contains about 2 to 22 carbon atoms.

5. The food composition as claimed in claim 1, wherein the 5.alpha.-saturated sterol fatty acid ester is produced by esterifying the alpha-saturated sterol and a fatty acid ester in a solvent-free food grade process.

6. The food composition as claimed in claim 2, wherein the .beta.-sitostanol fatty acid ester is produced by esterifying .beta.-sitostanol and a fatty acid ester in a solvent-free food grade process.

7. The food composition as claimed in claim 5, wherein the esterifying step is conducted in the presence of an esterification catalyst.

8. The food composition as claimed in claim 6, wherein the esterifying step is conducted in the presence of an esterification catalyst.

9. The food composition as claimed in claim 7, wherein the esterification catalyst comprises sodium ethylate.

10. The food composition as claimed in claim 8, wherein the esterification catalyst comprises sodium ethylate.

11. The food composition as claimed in claim 5, wherein the esterifying step is conducted at a temperature of about 90–120 degree C under a vacuum of about 5–15 mmHg.

12. The food composition as claimed in claim 6, wherein the esterifying step is conducted at a temperature of about 90–120 degree C under a vacuum of about 5–15 mmHg.

13. The food composition as claimed in claim 5, wherein the esterifying step is conducted without the presence of additional interesterifiable lipids.

14. The food composition as claimed in claim 6, wherein the esterifying step is conducted without the presence of additional interesterifiable lipids.

15. The food composition as claimed in claim 1, wherein the nutritional substance comprises a member selected from the group consisting of cooking oil, margarine, butter, mayonnaise, salad dressing and shortening.

16. The food composition as claimed in claim 2, wherein the nutritional substance comprises a member selected from the group consisting of cooking oil, margarine, butter, mayonnaise, salad dressing and shortening.

17. A method for reducing the cholesterol level in blood serum of a subject in need thereof, comprising orally administering to the subject the food composition as claimed in claim 1, wherein the sterol component is present in a blood serum cholesterol level reducing effective amount.

18. A method for reducing the cholesterol level in blood serum of a subject in need thereof, comprising orally administering to the subject the food composition as claimed in claim 2, wherein the sterol component is present in a blood serum cholesterol level reducing effective amount.

19. The method as claimed in claim 17, wherein about 0.2 to 20 grams per day of the sterol component are orally administered.

20. The method as claimed in claim 18, wherein about 0.2 to 20 grams per day of the sterol component are orally administered.

21. A method for reducing the absorption of cholesterol from the intestines into the bloodstream of a subject in need thereof, comprising orally administering to the subject the food composition as claimed in claim 1, wherein the sterol component is present in a cholesterol absorption reducing effective amount.

22. A method for reducing the absorption of cholesterol from the intestines into the bloodstream of a subject in need thereof, comprising orally administering to the subject the food composition as claimed in claim 2, wherein the sterol component is present in a cholesterol absorption reducing effective amount.

23. The method as claimed in claim 21, wherein about 0.2 to 20 grams per day of the sterol component are orally administered.

24. The method as claimed in claim 22, wherein about 0.2 to 20 grams per day of the sterol component are orally administered.

Brief Description of the Invention   The present invention relates to a sterol of an entirely different type for lowering the cholesterol levels in blood serum. The substance comprises a fatty acid ester of alpha saturated sterols, especially sitostanol fatty acid esters, which have been observed to lower cholesterol levels in serum with particular efficacy.

The present invention includes a method of reducing the absorption of cholesterol into the bloodstream from the digestive tract by orally introducing into the body an effective amount of a fatty acid ester of a beta-sitostanol. More preferably, the invention further includes orally introducing between about 0.2 and about 20 grams per day of beta-sitostanol fatty acid ester into the body. The ester is introduced either as a food additive, a food substitute or a food supplement. When used as a food additive, the fatty acid ester of the beta-sitostanol may be added to food products such as cooking oils, margarines, butter, mayonnaise, salad dressings, shortenings, and other foods having an essential fat component.

Notes

1. FIM = Finnish currency, the markka. The average exchange rate during 1996 was US$1 = FIM4.54.
2. Raisio Group, "Chief Executive's Review," Annual Report, 1996, p. 3.
3. The company was renamed Raisio Group PLC in September 1997. Throughout this case we shall refer to the company as "Raisio."
4. Raisio Group, Annual Report, 1997, p. 38.
5. "Market Split over 'Miracle' Margarine," *Financial Times*, October 25, 1996, p. 26.
6. "Wonder spread from Finland," *The Grocer*, May 18, 1996, p. 9.

A video clip relating to this case is available in your interactive e-book at **www.wileyopenpage.com**

Case 12 Video Game Console Industry in 2012: The Next Round

At the beginning of 2012, the three remaining suppliers of video game consoles were facing an uncertain future. A new generation of video game consoles was dawning—the eighth since the beginnings of the industry in 1972—but only Nintendo had announced a new model: the Wii U would be launched late in 2012. Sony and Microsoft were known to be developing new models which would be launched late in 2013; however, neither had provided any details.

The reluctance of either Sony or Microsoft to make announcements concerning their next generation of consoles reflected their uncertainty over the evolution of the console market. Both companies had been shocked by the outcome of the most recent round of competition. The remarkable success of Nintendo's Wii, which had outsold the more sophisticated and powerful consoles of Sony and Microsoft, had overturned much of the conventional wisdom concerning key success factors in the industry. Both Sony and Microsoft had based their strategies on the assumptions that, first, consoles were increasingly becoming multifunctional home entertainment platforms and, second, that their primary target markets were "hardcore" gamers (primarily males aged between 13 and 30). The Nintendo Wii had shown that an easy-to-use, dedicated console targeted at the casual user could out-sell the more technologically advanced machines from Sony and Microsoft. Was Wii an aberration or did it point to a new evolutionary path for the video console market?

Nintendo's eagerness to take the lead in the new generation of consoles was a consequence of the rapid decline in the sales of its Wii model. Conversely, Sony and Microsoft sought to extend the lives of their PS3 and Xbox 360 models (Sony had committed to a 10-year life cycle for PS3); however, neither company wished to leave the field clear for Nintendo. There was also a risk that, unless the console market could sustain the interest of users, the video game market might be lost to other hardware devices, notably mobile devices such as smartphones and tablet computers. All three companies kept a wary eye on Apple. After dominating the music business with iPod and iTunes, video games seemed a natural extension to Apple's ambitions in home entertainment. Already its iPad was being positioned as a game-playing device.

Increasing competition between different types of hardware—video game consoles, PCs, portable game players (such as the Nintendo DS and the PlayStation Portable), mobile phones, and tablet computers—had implications for the console makers' market positioning. The success of the Wii was primarily due to its appeal

This case was prepared by Robert M. Grant. ©2012 Robert M. Grant.

among causal video game players. However, these casual players were increasingly playing video games on multifunctional devices such as PCs, smartphones, and tablet computers than on dedicated video game consoles.[1] If consoles were to lose casual game players to other hardware devices, the console makers might be inclined to return to their traditional focus: the hard-core gamer for whom the video games console offered unparalleled speed and graphical realism.

History of the Video Game Industry, 1972–2012

The history of the video game console comprises a series of product generations, each defined by the power of the microprocessors used in the consoles and each lasting about five years (Table 1).

The First and Second Generations, 1972–1985: The Atari Era

The home video games market emerged during the 1970s as an extension of arcade video games. The first generation of home video consoles were dedicated machines that embodied a single game. One of the first was *Pong*, created by Nolan Bushnell in 1972. He formed Atari to market this game player. The second generation of players featured 4-bit processors and interchangeable cartridges. The Atari 2600 unleashed a craze for video games driven by *Space Invaders* (released in 1979) and *Pac-Man* (1981). Atari was unable to prevent independent software developers from marketing games for the Atari 2600. During 1982, 20 new suppliers of Atari-compatible consoles entered the market and 350 new game titles were released in

TABLE 1 Worldwide unit sales of video game consoles by product generation

Generation	Second, 1978–1985[a]	Third, 1985–1990	Fourth, 1991–1995	Fifth, 1995–1998	Sixth, 1999–2005	Seventh, 2006–2012[b]
Leader	Atari 2600: 30m	Nintendo NES: 60m	Nintendo Super NES: 49m	Sony PS: 102m	Sony PS2: 150m	Nintendo Wii: 96m
#2	Others: 12m	Sega Master System: 13m	Sega Genesis: 40m	Nintendo 64: 33m	MS Xbox: 24m	MS Xbox 360: 67m
#3	—	Others: 8m	Others: 16m	Sega Saturn: 9m	GameCube: 22m	Sony PS3: 64m
Others	—	—	—	Others: 3m	Dreamcast: 11m	—
Global sales	42m	81m	105m	147m	207m	227m

Notes:
[a] The product generations overlapped one another by much more than is indicated by the table. For example, sixth-generation consoles (especially the PS2) continued to sell strongly in 2006 and 2007, long after the launch of seventh-generation consoles. The sales data relate to the sales of each console over its entire life, not just to the years indicated for each generation.
[b] The sales data are up to end-March 2012.
Source: Wikipedia.

that year. With declining sales of consoles and oversupply of games, Atari's parent, Warner, incurred massive losses.

The Third Generation, 1985–1990: The Nintendo Era

In 1983, Nintendo, the leading Japanese supplier of arcade video games, released its 8-bit Famicom home video system. In 1985, the Famicom—renamed the Nintendo Entertainment System (NES)—was launched in the US. By 1988, Nintendo held 80% of the $2.3 billion US video games industry—chiefly as a result of the hugely popular games created by Nintendo's legendary games developer, Sigeru Miyamota: *Donkey Kong*, *Legend of Zelda*, and *Super Mario Brothers*.

Nintendo's market dominance and huge profits rested upon its careful management of the relationship between hardware and software. Nintendo kept tight control of the supply of games, managing their quality and releases. Developers were required to follow strict rules for the creation and release of games for the NES console. Cartridges incorporated a "security chip" that ensured that only cartridges manufactured by Nintendo could run on the NES. Nintendo charged games publishers a 20% royalty and a manufacturing fee of $14 per cartridge (the manufacturing cost was $7). The minimum order—10,000 cartridges for the Japanese market and 50,000 for the US market—had to be paid in advance. Any game developed for the NES could not be released on a competing system for two years.

By 1991, Nintendo's sales exceeded $4.4 billion, its stock market value exceeded that of Sony, and about one-third of US and Japanese households owned an NES.

The Fourth Generation, 1991–1995: Sega vs. Nintendo

Sega, like Atari and Nintendo, began in arcade games. In October 1988, it launched its 16-bit Genesis home video system in Japan, and in the US in September 1989. With the introduction of *Sonic the Hedgehog* in June 1991 and with strong support from independent games developers, sales of the Genesis took off.

Nintendo launched its 16-bit Super-NES, in September 1991. Its huge strength in its home market allowed it to maintain its leadership in Japan, but in the US and Europe, Sega's bigger library of 16-bit titles (by January 1993 it offered 320 games, compared to 130 for Nintendo) allowed it to rival Nintendo for market leadership.

The Fifth Generation, 1995–1998: Sony PlayStation

With the launch of its 32-bit Saturn console in November 1994, Sega sought to build on the success of its Genesis console. However, a month later Sony introduced its PlayStation console, the result of a six-year development effort led by Ken Kutaragi, Sony's video games guru. Both PlayStation and Saturn used CD-ROMs rather than cartridges. However, PlayStation was launched with an impressive number of new game titles: the result of courting top games developers, financing game development, and providing comprehensive software development tools. Sony also entered with a powerful array of resources: a strong brand reputation, global distribution capability, and content from its movie division. Compared to Sega's ill-coordinated Saturn launch (few game titles and haphazard distribution), the launch of PlayStation was well orchestrated and supported by massive advertising, including cryptic prelaunch advertisements that fueled a buzz of anticipation within the gamer community. Meanwhile, Nintendo attempted to recapture market leadership by leap-frogging Sony in technology. Its 64-bit N-64 console was released in June 1996 at a low price ($199 compared to $299 for PlayStation), but retaining its cartridge system, which involved higher manufacturing costs and less flexibility in meeting unexpected demand for hit games. The lower fixed costs of producing and distributing CDs allowed Sony to compete by offering a much bigger library of games than Nintendo could, many of which targeted niche markets and minority interests.[2] By 1998, PlayStation was leader in most of the world's major markets.

The Sixth Generation, 1999–2005: Sony vs. Microsoft

With the launch of its Dreamcast console in November 1998, Sega once again led the new generation of video game consoles. Fifteen months later, Sony launched PlayStation 2 (PS2). Kutaragi's brief had been to design a games machine with performance that exceeded any PC and with graphics processing power ten times that of the original PlayStation. With cinematic-style graphics, a DVD player, and the potential for internet connectivity, PS2 aspired to be a multifunctional entertainment device. However, the technical complexity of PS2 created problems both for the supply of key components and the availability of new games, resulting in a hesitant launch.

In 2001, the industry's competitive landscape was transformed by the exit of Sega, which announced its intention to focus exclusively on games software, and the entry of Microsoft. Despite just 19 games and a poor reception in Japan, Xbox combined three key strengths: its technological advances (an internal hard disk, a 733MHz processor, 64MB of memory, a DVD player, and an ethernet port), the hit game *Halo*, and Microsoft's online capabilities. In November 2002, Microsoft launched its Xbox Live, which allowed online interactive gaming and the direct downloading of games.

Nintendo, with its GameCube console, was the last to join the new generation of video game consoles.

By 2004, Sony had emerged as the clear market leader, with Microsoft a strong second in the US and Europe, and Nintendo a strong second in Japan.

The Seventh Generation, 2006–2012: Nintendo's Renaissance

Microsoft Xbox 360 Building on the momentum from its successful launch of Xbox, Microsoft led the new generation of consoles with its Xbox 360 released on November 25, 2005, the first ever console with a near-simultaneous global launch as opposed to a phased rollout. Xbox 360 represented a shift in market positioning by Microsoft. While the original Xbox emphasized processing power and focused on hardcore gamers, Xbox 360 emphasized versatility, design, and coolness with a particular focus on its multiplicity of entertainment and online capabilities, including viewing high-definition TV shows.

Sony PS3 PS3 was launched on November 11, 2006 after many months of delay, caused by Sony's technological ambitiousness—notably its decision to make PS3 the flagship for the Blu-ray DVD drive and its adoption of an advanced multicore-cell processor developed jointly with IBM and Toshiba.PS3 imposed large losses on

Sony: in addition to massive development and launch costs, the component cost of each PS3 exceeded $800, while its retail price was $499.[3] In addition, the complexity and high cost of developing games for the PS3 meant that there were few games that fully exploited its technical capabilities; Sony was obliged to cut its royalty rate to encourage developers to write for PS3. After a slow start PS3 sales gained momentum during 2008–2010.

Nintendo Wii Nintendo's launch of its Wii console in November 2006 was overshadowed by attention given to the PS3. Nintendo had been largely written off by most industry observers: it had neither the financial nor the technological resources to match those of Sony and Microsoft. Yet, the Wii proved to be a sensation. Technologically, the Wii was backward—compared to the PS3 and Xbox 360, it was seriously underpowered in terms of both speed and graphics, and it lacked a hard drive, DVD player, and ethernet port. Its innovative feature was its remote wand-like controller that was sensitive to a range of hand movements. This allowed Wii to be used for a variety of new sport and exercise applications—*Wii Fit* was one of the biggest selling titles of 2008–2010. Wii was also more accessible and easy to use than other consoles. This attribute was exploited by a marketing strategy that targeted a very broad demographic, including older people. During 2007–2008, Wii established a clear market lead over the PS3 and Xbox 360, which it maintained during 2009 and 2010—though only in unit sales—in terms of revenue it was overtaken by both Sony and Microsoft.

The success of the Wii challenged the conventional wisdom of the industry that the primary market was males aged between 13 and 30 and that the key to accessing this demographic group was to court hardcore gamers when developing and launching new models. This required a combination of hardware with immense processing power and brilliant graphics and games with cinematic quality, graphic realism, strong characters, and complex storylines.

The Video Games Industry in 2012

The Market for Video Games

At the beginning of 2012, video games continued to be a growth industry. Worldwide sales of video game software and dedicated hardware (both consoles and handheld game players) was estimated by DFC Intelligence at $66 billion worldwide in 2010 and expected to grow to $81 billion by 2016.[4] Most of this growth would be outside the mature markets of North America, Europe, and Japan; indeed, US consumer expenditures on video games had been in decline for several years (Figure 1).

Nevertheless, even within the US, games playing remained a major leisure pursuit. Over 40% of households owned video game consoles and 67% of households played video games. Worldwide, the user base of video game players was broadening. Once the preserve of teenage boys, by 2011 the majority of the age group 18–44 played video games, and even among 55- to 64-year-olds 26% played video games. Female participation had also increased strongly. However, in terms of intensity of game playing, teenage boys remained clear leaders: US males between 12 and 17 with a video game console in their home spent an average of 14 hours a week playing video games.

FIGURE 1   US consumer expenditure on video games and consoles, 1990–2011 ($billion)

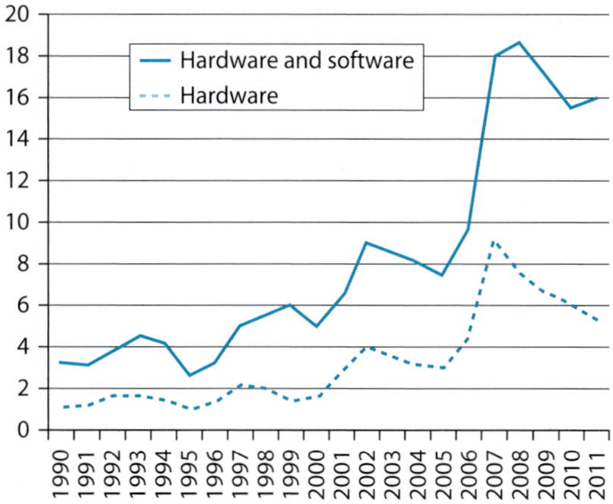

The composition of the market was changing rapidly in terms of both hardware and software. Video games were shifting from home-based devices such as consoles and PCs to mobile devices, while the distribution of games was shifting from packaged software sold by retail stores to direct downloads, subscriptions, and cloud access.

Software

Each video game console supplier ("platform provider") licensed third-party software companies to develop and distribute games for its system. Two types of company were involved in video games software: video game publishers, which were responsible for financing, manufacturing, marketing, and distributing video games; and video game developers, which developed the software. Publishing was increasingly dominated by a few large companies (Table 2). Typically, the software publisher submitted a proposal or a prototype to the console maker for evaluation and approval. The licensing agreement between the software company and the hardware provider gave the console maker the right to approve game content and control over release timing, and provided for a royalty payment from the software company. Game developers were paid a royalty, typically between 5 and 15%, based on the publisher's revenues from the game. The console makers were also major developers and publishers responsible for some of the most popular video games (Table 3).

Escalating game development costs were a result of the demand for multifeatured, 3-D, cinematic-quality games that could utilize the potential of increasingly powerful consoles. Atari's *Pac-Man* released in 1982 was created by a single developer and cost about $100,000. Activision's *Call of Duty: Black Ops* involved over 100 software engineers, about three years' development, about $28 million in development cost, and about the same in launch promotion. Released in November 2010, it generated $650 million of sales in its first five days. Its sequel, *Call of Duty: Modern Warfare 3*, which was released a year later, realized revenues of $775 million within five days.

TABLE 2 Leading publishers of video games, 2011

Publisher	Ranking[a]	Total games published[b]	Total games developed[b]
Nintendo	1	960	225
Electronic Arts	2	864	150
Activision Blizzard	3	544	135
Ubisoft	4	636	81
Take Two	5	93	7
Sony	6	375	38
ZeniMax Media	7	78	68
THQ	8	476	36
Square Enix	9	206	96
Microsoft	10	414	66
Konami	11	880	430
Sega	12	1,080	333
Capcom	13	460	317
Nexon	14	10	6
Namco Bandai Games	15	382	153

Notes:

[a] The rankings are by *Game Developer* magazine. They are based on multiple criteria which include quality as well as size.

[b] Data from Giant Bomb; they show games published and developed over the life of the company, http://www.giantbomb.com/company.

TABLE 3 Top-12 console games in the US (units sold January–October 2011)

Title/platform	Publisher	Units sold
Call of Duty: Black Ops (PS3 and X360)	Activision	4.6m
FIFA Soccer 12 (PS3 and X360)	ElectronicArts	4.5m
Wii Sports Resort (Wii)	Nintendo	4.3m
Wii Sports (Wii)	Nintendo	4.3m
Gears of War 3 (X360)	Microsoft	4.2m
L.A. Noire (PS3 and X360)	TakeTwo	3.7m
Just Dance 2 (Wii)	Ubisoft	3.5m
Kinect Adventures! (X360)	Microsoft	3.4m
Mario Kart Wii (Wii)	Nintendo	2.8m
Zumba Fitness (Wii)	Majesco	2.7m
Wii Fit Plus (Wii)	Nintendo	2.7m
Mortal Kombat (PS3 and X360)	WarnerBros.	2.3m

Source: VGChartz Worldwide Yearly Chart, http://www.vgchartz.com/yearly.php. Reproduced with permission from VGChartz Ltd.

In terms of cost and revenue patterns, video games closely resembled movies: they incurred substantial upfront costs and a mere few became money-spinning blockbusters. Most successful new releases were sequels to earlier games—this created valuable brand franchises (such as *Super Mario Brothers*, *Grand Theft Auto*, *Call of Duty*, and *Halo*).

The past generation of consoles had seen a major shift in the balance of power between console makers and the games publishers. In earlier generations, the console makers were dominant, enforcing exclusivity and imposing heavy royalty payments on the publishers. Consolidation among publishers (caused by rising development costs) and increased competition from different types of hardware platform had changed all that. Exclusivity ties had disappeared from most licensing contracts; most leading games titles were cross-platform. The only popular games exclusive to a single platform were typically those developed in-house by the console makers.

At the same time, the games publishers were also facing new pressures. The licensing fees paid by software publishers for exclusive rights to the intellectual property of media companies and sports organizations grew substantially between 1998 and 2002. The rights to a game based on a hit movie (e.g., *Harry Potter*) could cost several million dollars. For sports games, the major leagues (NFL, NHL, MLB, NBA, and FIFA) required an upfront payment, plus a royalty of 5 to 15% of the publisher's revenue from the game. They were also facing increased competitive pressure from software companies offering free games over the internet. Bigpoint, with some 150 million subscribers, offers games free but earns about $20 monthly per subscriber from the sale of add-ons and special features.

Not only did software sales exceed hardware sales; software was responsible for virtually all of the industry's profit. The console makers followed a "razors and blades" business model: the consoles were sold at a loss; profits were recouped on software sales (both games developed internally and royalties received from third-party games publishers). The result was strongly cyclical earnings for the platform providers: the launch of a new console would result in massive cash outflows; only with a substantial installed base would the platform provider begin to recoup the investment made.

The Console Makers

For the console suppliers, the period 2006–2011 had been a difficult one. Sony's experience with its PS3 demonstrated how the deteriorating economics of the console business meant that it was increasingly difficult to recoup the massive expenditures needed to launch a technologically ambitious new model. While Sony's original PlayStation and its PS2 had been highly profitable, since the launch of PS3, Sony's video games business had incurred substantial losses. While Microsoft had the satisfaction of achieving its goal of establishing itself as a major force within the video games business, the costs were high: it had incurred substantial losses since entering the video games business in 2001. As for Nintendo, despite winning the current round of competition in terms of unit sales, it had failed to achieve either the market dominance or the financial returns that market leaders had achieved during earlier generations.

Reluctance to incur the costs of developing new models was the major motivation behind Sony and Microsoft's desire to extend the lives of their current models. In 2011, both followed Nintendo in releasing motion-sensitive controllers for their consoles. The release of Microsoft's Kinect and Sony's Move coincided with a steep decline in Wii sales.

One bright spot was the growth in online, interactive game playing, which offered an additional revenue source for the console makers. Microsoft's Xbox Live and Sony's PlayStation Network earned revenues from subscriptions and third-party royalties. However, the risks in this business became apparent when Sony was forced to shut down its PlayStation Network during April 2011 following a cyber-attack in which the credit card details of subscribers were stolen.

Looking to the Future

As the three leading console providers planned for the next generation of consoles, they realized that their strategies needed to take careful account of the changing dynamics of competition in the industry. The weakening of the console makers relative to the games publishers, in particular their inability to force exclusivity upon the publishers, implied that video games would no longer be a winner-take-all industry as they had been in the 1980s and 1990s. Moreover, the expanding number and variety of video game players suggested that the market was segmenting, for example the Wii appealed to different users than the Xbox and PlayStation.

The future role of the games console as a home entertainment device was also unclear. Sony and Microsoft had envisaged their video game consoles as multifunctional home entertainment devices. The willingness of Sony and Microsoft to devote so many resources to their video games businesses was because they viewed the video game console not just as an important product in its own right but also as a basis for building their strategic positions within the home entertainment market. Yet, the Wii was essentially a dedicated games console. To what extent would video consoles become devices for playing movies, downloading and storing entertainment content, and interacting remotely as opposed to specialized gaming machines?

Appendix
Financial Data for the Leading Console Makers

NINTENDO (YEAR ENDING MARCH 31) IN BILLIONS OF YEN

	2001	2002	2003	2004	2005	2006	2007	2008	2009	2010	2011	2012
Total sales	463	554	504	514	515	509	966	1,672	1,838	1,434	1,014	648
Operating income	85	119	100	110	113	91	226	487	555	357	171	(37)
Net income	97	106	67	33	87	98	174	257	279	229	78	(43)
Op. income/ Av. total assets (%)	9.7	9.5	8.9	10.5	9.7	7.9	19.5	27.0	31.7	21.0	10.1	(2.4)
Return on av. equity (%)	12.2	12.0	7.4	3.7	9.6	10.4	16.8	11.0	19.9	16.8	5.7	(4.2)

Note:
Figures in parentheses denote a loss.

SONY (YEAR ENDING MARCH 31) IN BILLIONS OF YEN

	2001	2002	2003	2004	2005	2006	2007	2008	2009	2010	2011	2012
Sales	7,315	7,578	7,474	7,496	7,160	7,475	8,296	8,871	7,729	7,214	7,181	6,403
Of which:												
Games	661	1,004	936	754	703	918	974	1,219	1,685[a]	1,512[a]	1,493[a]	3,137[b]
Operating income	225	135	185	99	114	191	150	475	(227)	32	200	(67)
Of which:												
Games	(51)	84	113	68	43	9	(232)	(124)	(87)[a]	(83)[a]	36[a]	(230)[b]
Net income (loss)	17	15	116	89	164	124	126	369	(98)	(41)	(259)	(457)
Op. income/ Av. total assets (%)	3.1	1.7	2.2	1.1	1.2	1.9	0.6	2.9	(1.8)	0.3	1.6	(0.5)
ROE (%)	0.1	0.1	4.8	3.6	6.3	4.1	3.9	10.8	(3.1)	(1.4)	(9.4)	(15.6)

Notes:
Figures in parentheses denote a loss.
[a]For 2009–2011, the segment data for Sony are for "Networked Products and Services." This includes both games consoles and PCs.
[b]For 2012, Games are included within the Consumer Products and Services segment.

MICROSOFT (YEAR ENDING JUNE 3) IN $MILLION

	2002	2003	2004	2005	2006	2007	2008	2009	2010	2011	2012
Sales	28,365	32,187	36,835	39,788	44,282	51,122	60,420	58,437	62,484	69,943	75,000[e]
Of which: Entertainment and devices	2,453	2,748	2,731	3,110	4,292	6,069	8,140	6,416	6,224	8,716	9,200[e]
Operating income	11,910	13,217	9,034	14,561	16,472	18,524	22,492	20,363	24,098	27,161	28,000[e]
Of which: Entertainment and devices	(847)	(924)	(1,011)	(451)	(1,283)	426	(1,969)	288	573	1,135	600[e]
Net income	7,829	9,993	8,168	12,254	12,599	14,065	17,681	14,569	18,760	23,150	23,000[e]
ROA (%)	18.8	17.9	10.3	17.6	23.6	29.3	30.9	27.2	27.8	27.9	26.0[e]
ROE (%)	15.7	17.6	11.7	19.9	28.6	16.45	42.47	38.5	43.7	44.8	40.0[e]

Notes:
Figures in parentheses denote a loss.
[e] Estimated.

Notes

1. The success of *Angry Birds*, a video game played primarily on mobile phones, was especially salutary to the console makers. Launched in 2009 for the Apple iPhone, 300 million copies of *Angry Birds* had been downloaded by the end of 2011.
2. In 1997, the average PlayStation game sold 69,000 copies; the average N-64 title sold over 400,000 copies.
3. "Delays likely for Sony's PlayStation 3," *Financial Times*, February 20, 2006.
4. "With online sales growing, video game market to hit $81B by 2016 (exclusive)," VentureBeat, September 7, 2011, http://venturebeat.com/2011/09/07/with-online-sales-growing-video-game-market-to-hit-81b-by-2016-exclusive/, accessed September 21, 2012.

A video clip relating to this case is available in your interactive e-book at **www.wileyopenpage.com**

Case 13 The DVD War of 2005–2008: Blu-Ray vs. HD-DVD

On Tuesday, February 19, 2008, Toshiba announced that it would stop manufacturing HD-DVD discs and players. The announcement marked the end of the battle between Toshiba and Sony to establish the format standard for the next generation of digital versatile discs (DVDs).[1]

In the history of standards wars, the war between the rival DVD formats was surprisingly short. The coalescing of technological development of next-generation DVDs around two competing formats only began in 2002 and open warfare did not break out until summer 2005, when attempts to reach agreement on a single standard finally broke down. Products featuring the new technologies did not appear until April 2006 in the case of HD-DVD and June 2006 in the case of Blu-ray. Products based upon one or other of the two formats competed for market supremacy for a mere 18 months. Then, it was all over. During the first six weeks of 2008 Toshiba's position crumbled and Sony emerged victorious.

The Technology

The optical disc was invented in 1958 by David Paul Gregg, whose patent was registered in 1961. The first commercial product using the technology was the laserdisc system launched by Philips and MCA in 1978. However, optical discs failed to displace video cassettes as a video storage medium.

The breakthrough for optical discs was Philips and Sony Corporation's development of the compact disc in 1983, which became the dominant medium for audio recordings. The CD was followed by the DVD, which was introduced to Japan in 1996, the US in 1997, and Europe in 1998. The successful launch of the DVD was the result of an industry-wide forum that forced the proponents of different formats to agree a common technological standard. This industry group became the DVD Forum.

The impetus for developing a high-definition DVD came from the emergence of high-definition television (HDTV) during the 1990s. With HDTV seen as the next wave in consumer electronics, there came the need for a storage medium capable of holding high-definition images. The distinctive feature of both HD-DVD and Blu-ray formats was the use of short-wavelength blue-laser technology instead of the red lasers used in earlier generations. Blue lasers allowed a vast increase in the amount of data that could be stored on a standard 12-centimeter disc.

The key difference between HD-DVD and Blu-ray was in the thickness of the DVD's protective plastic layer: the HD-DVD retained the 0.6 mm thickness common

This case was prepared by Robert M. Grant. ©2012 Robert M. Grant.

to conventional DVDs; Blu-ray featured a 0.1 mm coating. The result was that a dual-layer Blu-ray DVD could hold 50 GB (gigabytes) of data, compared to 30 GB for a dual-layer HD-DVD. This compared to 8.5 GB for a conventional DVD.

For content owners—film studios in particular—Blu-ray had an additional advantage. While both formats incorporated the new AACS (Advanced Access Content System) anti-piracy device, Blu-ray included an additional layer of protection. However, Microsoft was concerned that the additional protection provided by Blu-ray restricted the ability of PC users to integrate video images with other computer functions. In July 2005, Bill Gates argued that the Blu-ray standard had to change to "work more smoothly with personal computers."

Blu-ray's technical refinements came at some cost. HD-DVDs could be manufactured by modifying the production line used for making ordinary DVDs: "It is a simple and low-cost step to go from manufacturing standard DVDs to producing HD-DVDs," said Mark Knox, a Toshiba spokesman. "The changes [for a factory] cost less than $150,000."[2] Blu-ray discs required major changes in manufacturing processes and manufacturing equipment. The implication was that, for content owners and consumers, Blu-ray discs would be more costly.

Neither format could be played on existing DVD players. Moreover, HD-DVD players could not play Blu-ray discs, and vice versa. Hence, movie studios and video games publishers faced the prospect of having to stock media in three formats: HD-DVD, Blu-ray, and conventional DVDs. Both HD-DVD and Blu-ray players were "backward compatible," that is they could play conventional DVDs.

As far as economizing on the number of formats that content producers needed to manufacture and distributors needed to stock, one of the advantages envisaged by the HD-DVD camp was the ability to produce an HD-DVD disc of a game or movie that also included a standard DVD version of the content. In September 2006, Toshiba announced: "Toshiba, in collaboration with disc manufacturer Memory Tech Japan, has successfully combined an HD-DVD and DVD to a single 3-layer, twin-format disc. The resulting disc conforms to DVD standards so it can be played on DVD players, and also on HD-DVD players."[3]

Moreover, the benefits of Blu-ray's greater storage capacity were not readily apparent at the time. Existing high-definition formats for full-length movies could be easily accommodated on both types of disc. Blu-ray's ability to "to fit an entire season of a television series" on a single disc, and "offer multiple versions of the same film" seemed marginal benefits to most consumers. The case for Blu-ray over HD-DVD seemed to rest primarily on its potential for accommodating future developments in video entertainment: "You open up a whole new spectrum of creative possibilities," said Tim Baxter, senior vice-president of strategic marketing at Sony Corp. of America. "This format is about gearing up for this holiday season and the next 10 years."[4]

Battle Commences

During the buildup to the product launches, both sides worked hard to enlist allies. The Blu-ray Disc Association formed in February 2002; it included Hitachi, Panasonic, Pioneer, Philips, Samsung, Sharp, Sony, and Thomson as founder members, and was later joined by Dell Computer, Mitsubishi, and TDK. The HD-DVD Promotion Group comprised Toshiba, NEC, Sanyo, Microsoft, Kenwood, Intel, Venturer Electronics, and

Memory-Tech Corporation. Some companies were members of both groups. These included Hewlett-Packard, LG, Acer, Asus, Lite-On, Onkyo, Meridian, and Alpine.

Blu-ray was the favorite among the leading film studios: Disney, Fox, Lions Gate, MGM, and of course Sony Pictures had aligned with Blu-ray, while Universal was the only major studio to join the HD-DVD camp. Paramount (including subsidiaries Nickelodeon Movies, MTV Films, DreamWorks Pictures, and DreamWorks Animation) and Warner Brothers supported both standards.

Even while both camps were developing products incorporating the two incompatible standards, attempts to avoid a costly format war continued. However, on August 22, 2005, the Blu-ray Disc Association and DVD Forum announced that the negotiations to unify their standards had failed. From then on the race was on to bring discs and hardware to market as quickly as possible in order to build market share leadership.

HD-DVD was first to market with the Toshiba HD-A1 launched in the US on April 18, 2006 at a retail price of $499. The Samsung BD-P1000 was the first Blu-ray disc player. It was launched at the end of June 2006 at a retail price of $999.

In April 2006, Universal and Warner Brothers both began releasing HD-DVDs of existing movies at prices of between $29 and $35. Sony Pictures was first to release movies on Blu-ray, with an initial release of eight movies at $28.95 to coincide with the launch of the Samsung BD-P1000. However, the early Blu-ray movies suffered from major quality problems. Several movies suffered from poor film-to-disc transfers and until October 2006 only single-layer recording was possible on Blu-ray discs which limited their capacity to 25 GB.[5]

The other two major product categories incorporating the new-generation DVD drives were personal computers and video game consoles. Both Toshiba and Sony were major players in personal computers. Toshiba released an HD-DVD-compatible notebook, the Qosmio G35-AV650. In May 2006, Sony launched a Vaio notebook with a Blu-ray drive. By the end of 2006, NEC and Hewlett-Packard had introduced notebooks with HD-DVDs, while Dell joined Sony in adding Blu-ray to one of its notebook models.

In video game consoles, the market leaders were Sony with its PlayStation and Microsoft with its Xbox. The battle for the next generation of consoles began with Microsoft's launch of its Xbox 360 in November 2005. The Xbox 360 came with a standard DVD drive. In November 2006, Microsoft launched an HD-DVD drive as a separate plug-in unit for its Xbox 360 priced at $200 in the US and £130 in the UK. Microsoft's reluctance to include a built-in HD-DVD player was a result of, first, the lack of games developed to exploit HD-DVD capabilities and, second, its belief that online access to games would displace DVD distributed games within a few years.

For Sony, its new PS3 video game console formed a central component of its Blu-ray strategy. Sony's decision to launch its PS3 with a Blu-ray disc player was widely viewed as a strategic blunder. It delayed the launch of the PS3, giving Microsoft lead-time of over a year in the new generation of consoles. It also greatly increased the cost of PS3. The cost and complexity of developing games that utilized the technical potential of Blu-ray meant that very few new high-definition games were available at launch. Launched at a price of $499 in the US, the PS3 was seen as something of a desperate gamble by Sony, faced with the market momentum of Xbox 360 and the low-cost challenge of the Nintendo Wii. At $499 it was estimated that Sony would lose over $200 on every unit sold.

Video games developers and publishers were slower than the movie studios to sign up for one or other of the rival formats. However, on January 7, 2007, Sony received a major boost when Electronic Arts (the world's biggest games software company) and Vivendi Universal Games (owner of Activision Blizzard) joined the Blu-ray association.

Distributors bore considerable cost burdens because of the standards war. The leading retailers (including Wal-Mart, Target, and Best Buy) and movie distributors such as Blockbuster and Netflix felt obliged to carry both formats.

Tipping Point

The central battle was for the support of the movie studios. Despite the initial preference of the majority of the major studios for Blu-ray, financial and other incentives resulted in several defections. Early in 2005, Warner Brothers and Paramount had backed HD-DVD, but in October 2005 both announced support for both formats. However, in August 2007, Paramount and DreamWorks Animation SKG dropped Blu-ray and announced that their high-definition movies would be released exclusively on HD-DVD. The studios mentioned cost and technical advantages but most observers believed that the offer from Toshiba of $150 million in cash and promotional guarantees was a bigger factor. Sony's influence with the movie studios was reinforced by two factors: first, its ownership of Sony Pictures; second, the strong Hollywood connections of Sony's CEO, Sir Howard Stringer.

Growing frustration with dual formats resulted in several distributors abandoning HD-DVD. In June 2007, Blockbuster, the largest US movie rental company, adopted Blu-ray exclusively after test marketing both formats and finding that over 70% of high-definition rentals were Blu-ray discs. In July 2007, Target Corporation began carrying only Blu-ray standalone players in its stores.

During 2007, sales of Blu-ray decisively overtook sales of HD-DVD in both hardware and software, with PS3 providing a particularly strong boost for Blu-ray. Home Media Research estimated that, for 2007 as a whole, Blu-ray outsold HD-DVD players by three to one in the US, 10 to one in Europe, and 100 to one in Japan.

A critical event in the battle was Warner Brothers' announcement on January 4, 2008 that it would drop support for HD-DVD from June 2008. The significance of Warner's move was that it was the biggest player in DVD movies. Toshiba responded by cutting the price of its HD-DVD players by up to 50%; however, there was little it could do to prevent the chain reaction that followed the Warner announcement. In January 2008, UK retailer Woolworths said it would stock only Blu-ray discs from March 2008. On February 11, 2008, Best Buy began recommending Blu-ray as the customer's digital format choice. Then, on February 15, 2008, Wal-Mart, the largest DVD retailer in the US, announced that it would discontinue HD-DVD products from June 2008. Also in February, Netflix, the largest online video rental service, began phasing out its HD-DVD inventory.

On February 19, 2008, Universal Studios—the only studio to have consistently supported HD-DVD from the outset—defected to Blu-ray. On the same day, Toshiba announced it would cease developing, manufacturing, and marketing HD-DVD players and recorders. The next day Paramount, the remaining movie studio supporter of HD-DVD, announced its move to Blu-Ray.

Even before Toshiba's announcement the fate of HD-DVD was clear. On February 16, 2008, the *New York Times* published its obituary:

HD-DVD, the beloved format of Toshiba and three Hollywood studios, died Friday after a brief illness. The cause of death was determined to be the decision by

Wal-Mart to stock only high-definition DVDs and players using the Blu-ray format. There are no funeral plans . . .[6]

Costs and Benefits

No reliable data are available concerning the costs and benefits of the DVD war to the main participants. Clearly Toshiba was the chief loser in financial terms. The Nikkei business daily reported that for its financial year ending March 31, 2008 Toshiba was likely to book a 100 billion yen loss ($986 million) relating to the termination of its HD-DVD project.[7] However, most observers believed that the full cost, including R & D expenditures, incentive payments to partners, forced price reductions on hardware, and inventory write-offs, would be much greater.

To what extent was Sony a winner? Its costs included not only the massive R & D expenditures on Blu-ray but also the costs of supporting its alliance partners, price cuts in hardware and software, and the significant costs of delaying the launch of PS3 until Blu-ray was ready. Moreover, the revenues generated by Sony's Blu-ray technology would be limited, first, by Sony's offer of highly favorable licensing terms in order to attract supporters to the Blu-ray camp and, second, by the likelihood that the commercial life of Blu-ray would be short. Professor Pai-Ling Yin of MIT's Sloan School of Management stated:

> Technology markets are characterized by waves of innovation, where the latest and greatest of last year is replaced by the latest and greatest of next year. Joseph Schumpeter described this pattern as "the perennial gale of creative destruction." Blu-ray and HD-DVD are simply the next generation of discs, replacing the standard DVD of the last generation. Thus, there is but a limited amount of time (until the appearance of the next generation technology) for the firms and the technology of this generation to reap the rewards of being the shiny new item on the block.[8]

By failing to agree on a common standard, the time available to exploit the current generation of media storage technology before it was rendered obsolete was greatly reduced: "The reality is that relative to the sales that could have been garnered from faster and higher volumes of DVD players had Sony and Toshiba been able to come to some agreement, both firms have lost."[9]

Notes

1. The correct interpretation of the DVD acronym is a matter of dispute. The two most common are "digital versatile disc" and "digital video disc."
2. "Format Wars: Everyone Could End Up Losing," *Financial Times*, April 3, 2006.
3. See "Three-Layer Disc Combines DVD, HD DVD," September 11, 2006, http://www.digitaltrends.com/home-theater/three-layer-disc-combines-dvd-hd-dvd/, accessed October 17, 2009.
4. "Format Wars: Everyone Could End Up Losing," *Financial Times*, April 3, 2006.

5. "Two years of battle between HD-DVD and Blu-ray: A retrospective," http://www.engadgethd.com/2008/02/20/two-years-of-battle-between-hd-dvd-and-blu-ray-a-retrospective/, accessed November 12, 2008.
6. "Taps for HD-DVD as Wal-Mart Backs Blu-ray," *New York Times*, February 16, 2008.
7. "The Fall of HD-DVD Will Cost Toshiba $986 Million," March 17, 2008, http://www.dailytech.com/article.aspx?newsid=11069, accessed October 17, 2009.

8. "What Are the Lessons of the Blu-ray/HD-DVD Battle?" *A Freakonomics Quorum*, March 4, 2008, http://www .freakonomics.blogs.nytimes.com/2008/03/04/what-are-the-lessons-of-the-blu-rayhd-dvd-battle-a-freakonomics-quorum/, accessed November 12, 2008. Quoted with permission from Pai-Ling Yin.

9. "What Are the Lessons of the Blu-ray/HD-DVD Battle?" *A Freakonomics Quorum*, March 4, 2008, http://www .freakonomics.blogs.nytimes.com/2008/03/04/what-are-the-lessons-of-the-blu-rayhd-dvd-battle-a-freakonomics-quorum/, accessed November 12, 2008. Quoted with permission from Pai-Ling Yin.

 A video clip relating to this case is available in your interactive e-book at **www.wileyopenpage.com**

Case 14 *New York Times*: Seeking Salvation within a Declining Industry

The announcement by the New York Times Company (NYT) of its annual financial results on February 2, 2012 did little to quell concerns over the future of the publisher of the *New York Times*, *Boston Globe*, and *International Herald Tribune*.

On February 4th, Henry Blogett of *Business Insider* blog published "The Incredible Shrinking New York Times," in which he acknowledged NYT's successful cost cutting and debt restructuring, but pointed to the long-run deterioration of the business and the fact that, even if the NYT website could be turned into a solid money maker, these revenues would not substitute for the declining print sales.[1]

Eric Jackson of Ironfire Capital LLC was even more pessimistic. His presentation "The End Game of the New York Times" made the following observations:

- Advertising revenue is evaporating and will continue to decline.
- Cost reduction has hit a plateau.
- Pension costs are rising at 2.7% annually.
- Operating cash flow is likely to be negative in 2012.
- Cash at the end of 2011 was $280m, down from $400m 12 months before.

On the basis of these trends, Jackson predicted that, by 2015, NYT would be unable to continue as a standalone business.[2]

Despite the difficult financial situation, NYT senior executives reaffirmed their faith in the company's capacity for reinvention and in the resilience of demand for its high-quality journalism. In an interview with Evan Smith, CEO of the *Texas Tribune*, Executive Editor of *The Times* Jill Abramson pointed to the growing global audience for its news reporting, news analysis, and opinion pieces, which *The Times* was offering across a growing range of different media platforms.[3] At NYT's annual shareholder meeting, Arthur Sulzberger Jr, board chairman, reaffirmed the company's commitment to its long-term strategy:

> As we all know, all of us in the news and information business are undergoing profound transformation and facing the great challenges that come with such a moment. We must re-imagine the manner in which we deliver the news and do so while maintaining critical journalistic standards.
>
> Our company is in just such a place – with all the hardship and promise this entails. That is why it is critical that we work to define our future.

This case was prepared by Robert M. Grant. ©2012 Robert M. Grant.

There's a trend in media today that the pace of change and financial pressures make creating lower quality news acceptable, if not inevitable. We fundamentally disagree. Too many news organizations have retreated from the hard, expensive business of on-the-ground reporting. We have not.

At *The New York Times* and the *International Herald Tribune* our readers rely on us for our ability to deliver both the news and the in-depth analysis that provides context for that reporting.

We have learned that, rather than choosing to consume that content on one platform over another, our readers access *The Times* on multiple platforms throughout the day – in print, online, via mobile or smart phone and through their tablets.

That means our challenge is to find new and better ways to create, deliver, and monetize our products so that the varying interests, and the unique experiences offered by each different type of device, are considered together.

We know that *The Times* has the ability to target our incredibly respected and coveted content to its audiences, both online and in print.

For example, Business Day addresses the most urgent topics in the business world; Technology provides robust and original content with both analysis and up-to-the-minute news. *The New York Times Magazine* continues to be a Sunday ritual for people across the country; and it has become a sought-after destination for readers who want to know about fashion, travel, design and entertainment.

Our audience is both strong and loyal. More than 845,000 print subscribers have been with *The Times* for two years or more. NYTimes.com has maintained its strong reach, with 33 million average monthly unique users in the US and 48 million globally in 2011.

We must continue to explore where media consumption is growing and moving, and be prepared to capitalize on these changes in consumption.

Sulzberger's commitment to quality journalism and to offering it across multiple media had formed the cornerstones of NYT's strategy for over a decade. As early as 1999, he had outlined the company's strategic direction in a staff presentation:

At the heart of this presentation are plans for ensuring that, a decade from now and a century from now, *The New York Times* will still be the leader in its field of quality journalism, regardless of how it is distributed. These plans entail our moving from a strategy focused on the specific products we produce to one built around our audience—*a quality audience strategy*. Our goal is to know our audience better than anyone else; to meet their informational and transactional needs—by ourselves where we can; in partnership with others when necessary; and to serve them in print and digitally, continuously and on-demand.[4]

At NYT's 2009 Annual Stockholders' Meeting, Sulzberger recognized the inevitable decline in print revenues and outlined the company's initiatives for building its online revenues:

How can we enhance our digital revenue sufficiently so that we have the financial foundation necessary to support our news gathering operations, be they at *The New York Times*, the *Boston Globe* or any of our regional news outlets?

At The New York Times Company, we are focusing on three key levers to achieve this essential goal: attracting more users, deepening their engagement and then earning revenue from their usage. To do all this effectively has and will continue to require our making bets on how this new medium will evolve and then making investments in that vision. This is certainly not an easy task, but our insights into human behavior and digital evolution are helping to guide us.

Throughout 2008 and the first months of 2009, we have continued to create a new form of web journalism that is both informative and compelling. Our goal is to respond to our audiences' demand for interactivity, community and multimedia, as well as news and information on an increasingly wide range of topics. We are aggressively responding to our readers' desire to do something with our content. Our readers want to share it, or blog it, or comment on it. They want to use our journalism as raw material for what they make . . .

Our strategy is rooted in the fundamental premise that we must be OF the internet, not ON it, requiring all of us to move from merely publishing our content on the web to becoming full web publishers . . .

Specifically we are in the process of rethinking the value of what we are offering. As you will hear in the months ahead, we will be:

- Engaging in a thoughtful analysis of brand loyalty and circulation revenue.
- Exploring a new online financial strategy.
- Leveraging the added value we bring to advertisers in terms of brand, technology and thought leadership.[5]

By 2012, Sulzberger was able to report progress on several of these fronts:

The Times has 4.8 million Twitter followers on its main page which, as MediaBistro recently reported, makes *The New York Times* the 7th most popular brand on Twitter. And more than 400 individual *Times* journalists are active on Twitter . . .

We also have more than 2.5 million fans across our *Times* Facebook pages.

Some additional social facts: The 3,900 videos in *The Times's* YouTube channel have been viewed almost 45 million times; NYTimes.com had more than 2 million user comments in 2011.

We are experimenting with how Google+, Pinterest and other communities can provide different ways to complement our reporting and enhance our storytelling capabilities to include video.

And by our own internal data, *The Times* is the most blogged-from source on the Internet.

And our digital efforts are being recognized. Last month at the 2012 National Magazine Awards for Digital Media, the award for outstanding use of video by magazines was presented to *The New York Times Magazine*, and just this month The Times received nominations for eight Webby Awards – which honor the best of the Web – for our online content and mobile applications.

When we think of international, we know that 33% of *The Times's* traffic and 10% of our digital subscribers are from outside the US . . . In September The Times launched India Ink, an English-language blog offering news and analysis about Indian politics, culture, business, sports and lifestyle. The blog provides a distinct perspective on the news and events that matter most to Indians and those who follow news about India, both on the subcontinent and abroad. We are looking closely at other strategic international opportunities and ways to extend the global reach of The Times, including potential collaborations for new products and services that will make our content more broadly available to our international audiences. We are focused particularly on countries where there are growing economies, and we are exploring, among other things, native language Web sites and mobile and tablet apps.

And as this is both a presidential election year and an Olympic year, we are even more excited to show our wares, including our Election 2012 app for iPhone and Android, an essential destination and comprehensive resource for those following the presidential campaign.

As we head into an Olympic summer, we have entered into an interesting collaboration with Reuters to launch an exclusive product available to online publishers for coverage of the London Olympic Games. This new publishing platform, which we developed, delivers: high quality coverage through images, text and video with technology, tools and data displays which can be easily embedded ready to publish results pages and more. Additionally, real-time data results power widgets and pages that display live results including medal counts and standings, athlete statistics and event schedules. Media companies that use this exclusive product will be able to integrate Olympics content and data into their Web sites.[6]

The challenge was monetizing this growing online presence. During 2009–2011, company revenues were stagnant (Table 1). The NYT's share price failed to reflect the chairman's optimism. On the day of the Annual Stockholders' Meeting, NYT's

TABLE 1   New York Times Company, Inc.: Selected financial data ($million, except where indicated)

	2011	2010	2009	2008	2007	2006
Revenues	2,323	2,393	2,440	2,948	3,195	3,290
Operating costs	2,093	2,137	2,308	2,792	2,928	2,996
Impairment of assets	164	16	4	198	11	814
Gain on sale of assets	—	—	5	—	(28)	—
Operating (loss)/profit	56.7	23.4	74.1	(40.6)	227.4	(520.6)
Interest expense, net	85.2	85.1	81.7	47.8	39.8	50.7
Income from continuing operations	(40.2)	108.7	1.6	(66.1)	(108.9)	(568.2)
Discontinued operations	—	—	(1.2)	8.3	99.8	24.7
Net income	(40.2)	108.7	19.9	(57.8)	208.7	(543.4)
Property, plant and equipment	1,085	1,157	1,250	1,354	1,468	1,375
Total assets	2,883	3,286	3,089	3,402	3,473	3,856
Long-term debt and lease obligations	698	996	769	1,059	1,035	1,446
Total liabilities	2,374	2,622	1,986	n.a.	n.a.	n.a.
Stockholders' equity	506	656	604	504	978	820
ROE (%)	(7)	17	4	(8)	23	(48)
Total debt to total capitalization (%)	60	60	56	68	51	64
Operating margin (%)	2	10	3	(1)	7	(16)
Current assets to current liabilities	1.46	1.7	1.00	0.60	0.68	0.91
Employees (full-time equivalent)	7,273	7,414	7,665	9,346	10,231	11,585

Notes:
Figures in parentheses denote a loss.
ROE: Return on equity.
Source: New York Times Company, Inc., 10-K report, 2011.

FIGURE 1   New York Times Company share price ($), 2007–2012

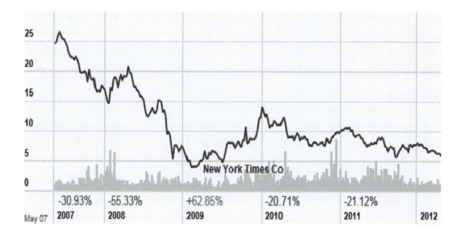

shares closed at $6.32: 21% down on the year and 74% down on the level five years earlier (Figure 1). Shareholders had been further jolted by the abrupt departure of NYT's CEO, Janet Robinson, in December 2011 and dismayed by the failure to find a replacement.

The New York Times Company in 2012

The Business

In 2012, NYT comprised two business segments:

- The News Media Group, which consisted of:
  - the New York Times Media Group, which included *The Times*, NYTimes.com, the *International Herald Tribune*, and a New York City radio station, WQXR-FM;
  - the New England Media Group, which included the *Boston Globe* (the *Globe*), Boston.com, and the *Worcester Telegram and Gazette*;
- the About Group, which consisted of the websites of About.com, ConsumerSearch.com, UCompareHealthCare.com, and Caloriecount.about.com.

Most of the NYT's other business interests had been sold in order to provide financial support for its core news businesses. In particular, its Regional Media Group of sixteen daily newspapers in six different states had been sold in January 2012 for $143 million. Other divestments included its equity interest in Fenway Sports Group (owner of the Boston Red Sox and Liverpool Football Club) had been reduced to less than 5%. It still held equity interests in a Canadian newsprint company, Metro Boston (a free daily newspaper), Fenway Park stadium, New England Sports Network (a regional cable sports network), and Roush Fenway Racing (a NASCAR team).

TABLE 2   New York Times Company: Segment results ($million)

	2011	2010	2009
Revenues			
News Media Group	2,212.6	2,257.4	2,319.4
About Group	110.8	136.1	121.1
Total	2,323.4	2,393.5	2,440.4
Operating profit			
News Media Group	60.9	219.2	21.2
About Group	40.7	62.0	50.9
Corporate	(44.8)	(47.1)	2.0
Total	56.7	234.1	74.1
Gain on sale of investment	71.2	9.1	—
Net income/(loss) from joint ventures	0.0	19.0	20.7
Premium on debt redemptions	46.4	—	9.3
Net interest expense	85.2	85.1	81.7
(Loss)/income from continuing operations before income taxes	(3.7)	177.2	37.8

Note:
Figures in parentheses denote a loss.
Source: New York Times Company, Inc. 10-K report, 2011.

TABLE 3   Average daily circulation of New York Times Company newspapers (thousands of copies)

	2011[a]	2009	2007
New York Times (Monday–Friday)	1,317.1	959.2	1,066.6
New York Times (Sunday)	1,781.1	1,405.2	1,529.7
International Herald Tribune	226.2	219.2	241.6
Boston Globe (Monday–Friday)	206.9	264.5	364.6
Boston Globe (Sunday)	354.8	419.1	544.1

Note:
[a] Includes (for the first time) online subscriptions
Source: New York Times Company, Inc., 10-K reports for 2011 and 2008; data from Audit Bureau of Circulations.

As Table 2 shows, the News Media Group accounted for most of NYT's revenue; however, shrinking advertising revenues and falling circulation (resulting from increasing competition from free newspapers and nonprint sources of news) had placed major pressures on margins. Table 3 shows circulation for NYT's three major newspaper titles.

Within the News Media Group, *The Times* is the company's jewel. It is the only general daily newspaper to be distributed in all 50 states of the US. In terms of journalistic reputation it is unsurpassed: the newspaper and its journalists have earned more than double the number of Pulitzer prizes than any other newspaper. Its columnists include Nicholas Krista, Thomas Friedman, and Nobel Prize-winning economist Paul Krugman. The company has attributed its ability to raise the cover price of *The Times* (up from $1 to $2.50 between July 2007 and January 2012) to the appeal of its quality journalism.

NYT had struggled for years to define an online business model. Even though NYTimes.com website was attracting 19.5 million monthly visitors by 2008 and

TABLE 4 New York Times Company: Principal revenue and cost components ($million)

	2011	2010	2009	2008
Total revenues	2,323.4	2,393.5	2,440.4	2,948.9
of which:				
—Advertising	1,221.5	1,300.4	1,336.3	1,779.7
—Circulation	941.5	931.5	936.5	910.2
—Other	160.4	161.6	167.7	259.0
Total production costs	957.5	961.8	1,021.2	1,315
of which:				
—Raw materials	161.7	160.4	166.4	250.8
—Wages and benefits	495.6	498.3	524.8	622.7
—Other	300.2	303.1	330.1	441.6
Selling, general and administrative costs	1,019.6	1,054.2	1,152.9	1,332.1
Depreciation and amortization	116.5	121.0	133.7	144.4
Total operating costs	2,093.5	2,136.9	2,307.8	2,791.6

Source: New York Times Company, Inc., 10-K report, 2011.

33 million by 2011, the advertising revenues generated by the website were disappointing. As a result, the company introduced an online subscription in March 2011. By the end of the year there were 390,000 paid subscribers to digital subscription packages, e-readers, and replica editions of *The Times* and the *International Herald Tribune*. However, the biggest source of concern for NYT's management was the decline in print advertising revenues. In 2007, advertising had provided two-thirds of the company's revenues; by 2011 it was barely one-half (Table 4).

Cost Cutting

The principal response by NYT's management to shrinking revenues had been to cut costs. Between 2008 and 2012, the major sources of cost economies were:

- Consolidation of operations: *The Times* had consolidated two of its New York printing plants into a single facility, saving $30 million annually; the *Globe* had done the same with its two plants, saving about $18 million annually.
- Loss-making businesses were closed: in 2009, NYT closed City & Suburban, its retail and news-stand distribution business in the New York area.
- Outsourcing: functions such as advertising service, circulation telemarketing, customer service, and financial back-office functions were outsourced together with printing for smaller newspapers.
- Newsprint and production costs were reduced: by eliminating some newspaper sections (e.g., magazines and TV guides) and reducing the page size of *The Times*.
- Workforce reduction: Positions were eliminated both in production activities and in administrative and marketing activities. However, a high level of unionization (over one-half of employees) and complex union agreements

(with ten different unions) limited the scope for cutting employment. Pension costs and retiree benefits were also major expenses that were not amenable to cost cutting. Bloomberg estimated that "about 70 percent of its estimated $237 million operating profit went to pension contributions and interest costs, compared with 19 percent in 2007."[7] Negotiations with unions over pay, benefits, and severance payments were made more difficult when it was revealed that departing CEO Janet Robison had received a payout of $21 million.

The US Newspaper Industry

The Pew Research Center's report on the "State of News Media 2012" made depressing reading for NYT's top management. During 2011, the report noted:

- Advertising revenues were $23.9 billion; despite gains in online revenue of 6.8%, total ad revenues were down 7.3%. In 2000, they were $48.7 billion. Revenue is predicted to fall again in 2012. Circulation revenues added about $10 billion resulting in total revenues of $34 billion, down from $59.2 billion in 2000 (Figures 2 and 3).
- Most newspapers are profitable on an operating basis, many with margins in the mid-teens. But net margins—after interest, taxes, and special charges—are razor-thin. Most papers achieved profitability largely through cutting.
- Audiences continue to hold up much better than revenues; although print circulation continued to decline in 2011, audiences on various digital platforms grew.
- Sunday print editions did relatively well in 2011. Sunday advertising accounts for 35–50% of the total for most papers. Some newspapers were planning to

FIGURE 2   Ad revenue drops while circulation revenue remains stable

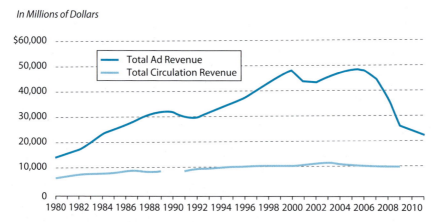

In Millions of Dollars

Note:
Numbers are rounded. There are no circulation revenue figures for 1990. Figures from 2003 onward for total ad expenditures includes online.
Source: Newspaper Association of America — Pew Research Center's Project for Excellence in Journalism, published March 19, 2012; http://stateofthemedia.org/?src=prc-headline.

FIGURE 3 Print advertising revenue falls, online grows

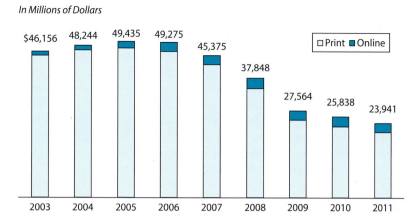

In Millions of Dollars

Note:
Numbers are rounded.
Source: Newspaper Association of America — Pew Research Center's Project for Excellence in Journalism
Published March 19, 2012; http://stateofthemedia.org/?src=prc-headline.

print only a Sunday edition; their weekly editions would be either digital editions or free tabloid versions.

- Charging for online access became a major trend in the industry. The dominant approach was the "metered model": allowing free views of a limited number of articles, so a site retains its traffic from search, links, and social media recommendations, but charging for unlimited access. The model also allows organizations to sell "bundled subscriptions" comprising print newspapers, website access, and often mobile and tablet editions too. Despite notable holdouts (e.g., *Washington Post, USA Today*), large numbers of papers plan to introduce charging during 2012.

- In January 2012, the industry launched NewsRight, seeking to collect royalties for the newspapers and news wire services from content originators from aggregators who redistribute and resell their content. Licensing offers a potentially large source of additional revenues to newspapers.[8]

In Search of Online Business Model

The struggles of NYT with charging for NYTimes.com is indicative of the difficulty that all newspapers have experienced in establishing a viable business model for their online editions and creating synergies between their web and print editions. In the case of NYTimes.com, fees were initially collected from international users but then subsequently dropped in an effort to increase the online audience. In 2005, it introduced TimesSelect, which charged an annual $49.95 fee for premium content and access to *The Times'* online archives. It generated only $10 million a year and was discontinued in 2007 in the belief that the increased advertising revenues from free access would outweigh the loss of subscription revenue. Disappointing advertising revenues and belief in the superiority of the "metered access" model resulted in the reintroduction of a digital subscription service in March 2011.

However, some industry observers believed that the hybrid model—print and digital editions—was doomed to failure. Rick Wartzman, Director of the Drucker Institute, argued: "Dead-tree editions must immediately yield to all-internet operations. The presses need to stop forever, with the delivery trucks shunted off to the scrapyard." He proposed the *Huffington Post* (recently acquired by AOL) as the model for an online newspaper and suggested that if the *Los Angeles Times* went online only it could operate with a staff of 275 and earn a net margin of 10%.[9] Eric Schmidt, CEO of Google, also argued for the free content with revenues derived from advertising. Only where content is unique, he argued, will users be willing to pay. For most news, there is no alternative to providing it free because it is available from so many online sources. The opportunity for online newspapers was to offer targeted advertising linked to customized content—that's where he saw Google as being an essential partner for the newspaper companies.[10]

The Pew Report was optimistic about the readership potential of mobile devices (smartphones and tablets) but pessimistic about revenue generation. Newspaper readership on mobile devices had risen by 65% in the year to September 2011 to September 2010 with most readers using news organizations' apps (rather than accessing content through a browser). However, the potential for newspapers to access mobile advertising revenues seemed limited. Similarly with social media and e-readers: "Newspaper organizations have cranked up their Twitter and Facebook efforts, finding social media both a means to drive traffic to their stories and a reporting resource to find sources quickly during breaking news events . . . As yet, though, neither social media nor e-readers are a revenue difference-maker. And Facebook is already booking 14% of all internet display ads."[11]

Video advertising offered another revenue source (worth about $300 million in 2011); however, "the field was dominated by digital-only enterprises, such as YouTube, and by "pure play" advertorials or targeted electronic classifieds for jobs or cars."[12]

Looking to the Future

In deciding on its next CEO, a critical issue for NYT's board was whether the new CEO would be expected to continue the company's current strategy, which focused upon sustaining its investment in quality journalism, developing digital revenue sources, while relying on cost cutting and asset sales to plug the financial shortfall, or seek someone who would pioneer a new strategy.

In his presentation on NYT's deteriorating prospects, Eric Parker of Ironside Capital suggested that the only ways for the company to avoid the coming financial crunch were: to keep selling on-core assets, to seek additional finance (as in 2009 when it had borrowed $250 million from Mexican billionaire Carlos Slim), to find a buyer, to find a rich benefactor, or to seek Chapter 11 bankruptcy protection (which would allow it to renegotiate union agreements and retiree benefits). Parker saw no future for advertising-supported print newspapers and believed that the only viable business models for news organizations were:

- financial data and news subscription services (e.g., Bloomberg and Thompson/Reuters)
- cable subscription (e.g., Comcast, Disney, CBS)

- digital news provided by larger internet companies (e.g., Yahoo!)
- Copycat blogging supported by banner ads (e.g., *Huffington Post*).

The emphasis by Sulzberger on the critical social role of quality journalism raised the issue of whether the public corporation was the best ownership model for the NYT. Among newspaper proprietors throughout the world, profit typically took second place behind individual ego and political influence. Like professional sports franchises, rich individuals were attracted to newspaper ownership, even if it meant losing money.

Another possibility was that NYT could become a social enterprise. Newspapers had long been viewed as a critical component of democracy: informing public opinion and exposing the wrongdoings of politicians and government officials. Penelope Muse Abernathy of the University of North Carolina proposed four options for newspaper funding: establishing an endowment that funds a paper's news department; charitable support for some aspects of the paper's coverage, such as foreign or cultural coverage; purchase of the paper by a university or other educational institution; and sale to an angel investor who would run the paper as a "low-profit limited liability corporation."[13]

The announcement on August 14, 2012 that Mark Thompson, the Director-General of the British Broadcasting Corporation, had been appointed CEO of the NYT did little to answer any of these questions. The decision to appoint someone with no experience in newpapers, but who was recognized as an innovator in digital media clearly indicated the priorities of the NYT board. However, the only certainty about the new management era was that it would be chairman Arthur Sulzberger rather than CEO Mark Thompson who would have the final say over the future direction of the NYT.

Notes

1. Henry Blodget and Kamelia Angelova, "The Incredible Shrinking New York Times," *Business Insider*, February 4, 2012.
2. Eric Jackson, "End Game of the New York Times," Ironfire Capital LLC, April 5, 2012.
3. "The future of the *New York Times*," Evan Smith interviews Jill Abramson (March 12, 2012), http://schedule.sxsw.com/2012/events/event_IAP100249, accessed September 22, 2012.
4. Repeated at the New York Times Company's 2009 annual meeting of stockholders, April 23, 2009.
5. Repeated at the New York Times Company's 2009 annual meeting of stockholders, April 23, 2009.
6. Repeated at the New York Times Company's 2009 annual meeting of stockholders, April 23, 2009.
7. "New York Times Co. Faces Leadership Vacuum after Robinson Ouster," (January 27, 2012), http://www.bloomberg.com/news/2012-01-27/new-york-times-co-faces-leadership-vacuum.html, accessed September 22, 2012.
8. "The State of the News Media 2012," Pew Research Center's Project for Excellence in Journalism, 2012.
9. "Out with the Dead Wood for Newspapers," *Business Week*, March 10, 2009.
10. "View from the Top: Eric Schmidt of Google," *Financial Times*, May 21, 2009.
11. "The State of the News Media 2012," Pew Research Center's Project for Excellence in Journalism, 2012.
12. "The State of the News Media 2012," Pew Research Center's Project for Excellence in Journalism, 2012.
13. P. M. Abernathy, "A Nonprofit Model for the New York Times?" Duke Conference on Nonprofit Media, May 4–5, 2009.

A video clip relating to this case is available in your interactive e-book at **www.wileyopenpage.com**

Case 15

Eni SpA: The Corporate Strategy of an International Energy Major

By May 2012, Paolo Scaroni had been CEO of the Italian energy giant Eni for seven years. His strategy had deviated little from that of his predecessor, Vittorio Mincato (CEO from 1998 to 2005). It comprised two major thrusts:

- a commitment to organic growth strategy with a particular emphasis on oil and gas exploration and production (E&P);
- a vertically integrated approach to Eni's natural gas business through linking Eni's gas fields in north and west Africa and gas supplied from its alliance partner, Gazprom, to its downstream gas business in Europe by pipelines (and, more recently, liquefied natural gas).

The strategy had achieved some notable successes. Since 2000, Eni had grown its petroleum output and reserves by more than most of the other majors, revenues had increased almost fourfold, return on capital employed had averaged 14.8% over the period, and in terms of market capitalization Eni was Europe's tenth-most-valuable company.

In his strategy presentation on March 15, 2012, Scaroni committed Eni to a continuation of this strategy:

- During 2012–2015, capital investment would rise to €15 billion annually, of which 75% would go to E&P. The target was for petroleum production to grow by more than 3% each year during 2012–2015.
- Eni would continue to grow its natural gas business. The majority of Eni's increased petroleum output would be natural gas; downstream, Eni would grow its sales of gas to European business and retail customers by 18% and 28% respectively; Eni would continue to invest in pipelines, including the proposed South Stream pipeline (a joint venture with Gazprom, EDF, and Wintershall) from Russia to Austria and Italy.

However, in pursuing this strategy, Scaroni recognized that Eni would face some strong headwinds. Expanding upstream production was becoming increasingly challenging: exploration was moving to technically challenging frontier regions such as the

---

This case was prepared by Robert M. Grant. ©2012 Robert M. Grant.

Arctic and ocean floors, resource nationalism and political instability was a constant threat in producer countries, and competition in the upstream sector continued to grow.

Eni's vertically integrated gas strategy faced more immediate threats. Pipelines played a critical role in linking gas production to consumers. Eni's ownership of domestic gas transportation had long been under attack from the European Commission. In 2012, the new Italian government under Mario Monti made it clear that Eni would have to relinquish its 52% ownership of Snam Rete Gas, the gas network owner. The European Commission had also pressured Eni to sell its ownership stakes in several international pipelines on the basis that it had limited competition in the Italian gas market by restricting third-party access.

Eni's strategy of vertical integration in gas was also threatened by shareholder activism. Eni's share price had long been at a discount to its peers' (as measured by most valuation ratios). Knight Vinke, who owned 1% of Eni's equity, valued Eni's shares at €21 (they had traded in a range of €11.83 to €18.72 in the 12 months to May 2012) and believed that the best way for Eni to release value would be to spin off its downstream gas business entirely.

Other investors considered that Eni's refining and marketing, and chemicals businesses were better candidates for divestment. Both were declining businesses that were only marginally profitable.

Finally, Eni's strategy attracted the ire of environmental groups disappointed by the company's lack of investment in renewable energy sources and concerned over the environmental consequences of individual projects—most notably Eni's tar sands project in Congo.

The History of Eni

Mattei and the Creation of Eni, 1926–1962[1]

In 1926, Italian Prime Minister Benito Mussolini established Agip (Azienda Generali Italiana Petroli) as a state-owned oil company.[2] At the end of the Second World War, Enrico Mattei, a former partisan, was appointed head of Agip and instructed to dismantle this relic of fascist economic intervention. Contrary to instructions, Mattei renewed Agip's exploration efforts and, in 1948, discovered a substantial gas field in northern Italy's Po Valley. In 1949, Mattei also took over the management of SNAM, the Italian gas distribution company. On February 10, 1953, the government merged Agip, SNAM, and other state-owned energy activities to form Ente Nazionale Idrocarburi (Eni) with the task of "promoting and undertaking initiatives of national interest in the fields of hydrocarbons and natural gases." Mattei was appointed its first chairman and chief executive. Eni's 36 subsidiaries extended well beyond oil and gas to include engineering services, chemicals, soap, and real estate.

Mattei's vision was for Eni to become an integrated, international oil and gas company that would ensure the independence of Italy's energy supplies and make a substantial contribution to Italy's postwar regeneration. In doing so he became a national hero: "He embodied great visions for postwar Italy—antifascism, the resurrection and rebuilding of the nation, and the emergence of the 'new man' who had made it himself, without the old boy network."[3]

Eni's international growth reflected Mattei's daring and resourcefulness. The international oil majors, which Mattei referred to as the "Seven Sisters" because of their collusive tendencies, had tied up most of the world's known sources of oil in the Middle East and Latin America. The production-sharing agreement that Mattei signed with the Shah of Iran in 1957 marked the beginning of a fundamental shift of power from the oil majors to producer governments and established Eni as the *enfant terrible* of the oil business. The Iranian agreement was revolutionary. It created a jointly owned exploration and production company headed by an Iranian chairman and with the proceeds shared between Eni and the Iranian National Oil Company. This "Mattei formula" was replicated in Libya, Egypt, Tunisia, and Algeria during 1958–1960. Mattei also concluded a barter deal for crude oil from the Soviet Union: by 1960, Italy was the biggest customer for Soviet oil after China.

All the time Mattei was building political support within Italy. To meet the political needs of government and individual politicians, Eni became involved in acquiring struggling companies. By 1962, Eni was "engaged in industries as various as motels, highways, chemicals, soap, fertilizers, synthetic rubber, machinery, instruments, textiles, electrical generation and distribution, contract research, engineering and construction, publishing, nuclear power, steel pipe, cement, investment banking, and even education, to mention only a few."[4]

Eni under State Control, 1962–1992[5]

Mattei died in a plane crash on October 27, 1962 at the age of 56. He left a sprawling corporate empire whose strategy had been Mattei's own vision and whose integrating force had been Mattei's charisma and personal authority. Mattei had been president not just of Eni but also of its main operating companies.[6] Without his leadership, power shifted to the politicians and Eni became an instrument of government economic, industrial, and employment policies.[7] After 1975, the chairman of Eni lost direct control of its operating companies: their chief executives were appointed by government on the basis of political considerations. Nevertheless, Eni continued to expand its oil and gas interests. Major initiatives included the 1969 agreement to purchase natural gas from the Soviet Union (which involved Eni building a pipeline from the Austrian/Czechoslovak border to Italy), the Trans-Med Pipeline from Algeria and Tunisia to Italy, and offshore projects in West Africa. Financial performance remained weak: Eni earned significant profits only during 1988–1990 (Figure 1).

The Bernabè Era: Privatization and Transformation, 1992–1998

Pressured by the European Commission and the new European Monetary Union to cut the public-sector deficit and reduce state intervention in industry, in June 1992, reformist Prime Minister Giuliano Amato announced the first steps in granting Eni greater autonomy. Eni became a joint-stock company and its relations with government were transferred to the Treasury. At the same time, Franco Bernabè, a 44-year-old economist with almost no line-management experience, was appointed CEO.

Bernabè possessed a clear vision of Eni's future as a privatized, integrated energy company, shorn of its various diversified businesses.[8] The corruption scandal that swept Italy in 1993 gave Bernabè the opportunity to launch a radical transformation of Eni. During March 1993, Eni's chairman, Gabriele Cagliari, and several senior Eni board members and executives were arrested on corruption charges.[9] By the summer of 1993, Bernabè had comprehensively restructured the management of Eni and its subsidiaries with the replacement of some 250 board members.[10]

Bernabè's corporate strategy was "to reduce Eni from being a loose conglomerate to concentrate on its core activity of energy."[11] The sale of Nuovo Pignone (a turbine manufacturer) was followed by halving capacity at EniChem, Eni's troubled chemicals business. During 1993, Bernabè's first whole year as chief executive, 73 Eni businesses were closed or sold and employment was cut by 15,000. Cost savings and asset sales resulted in a profit of almost $2 billion in 1994.[12]

Following Eni's initial public offering, its shares commenced trading in Milan, London, and New York on November 21, 1995. After more than 40 years of looking to politicians in Rome for guidance, Eni's top management had to adjust to a new set of masters: the global investment community.

The new creed of shareholder value creation encouraged further refocusing: "Eni's strategy is to focus on businesses and geographical areas where, through size, technology, or cost structure, it has a leading market position. To this end, Eni intends to implement dynamic management of its portfolio through acquisitions, joint ventures, and divestments. Eni also intends to outsource non-strategic activities."[13] Capital investment became increasingly concentrated upon upstream activities. In refining and marketing, and petrochemicals, costs were reduced and assets sold.

The results were striking (see Figure 1). Between 1992 and 1998, Eni halved its debt, turned a loss into a substantial profit, and reduced employment by 46,000. In 1998, Bernabè was appointed to lead another newly privatized giant: Telecom Italia.

FIGURE 1 The Development of Eni, 1985–2011

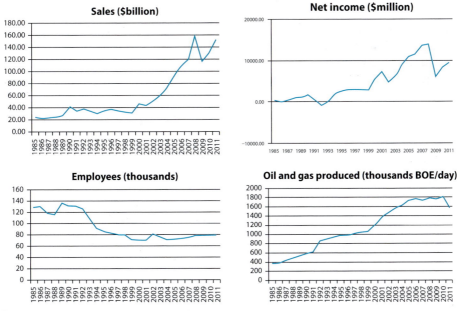

Note:

BOE: barrels of oil-equivalent.

Source: Eni annual reports for various years.

The Mincato Era: 1998–2005: "Disciplined Growth"

Vittorio Mincato was a veteran line manager whose 42 years at Eni had included 15 years as chairman of EniChem, where he had led comprehensive turnaround and restructuring. In the 1999 annual report, Mincato outlined the strategy he intended to pursue:

> The four-year plan approved at the end of 1999 derives from a new strategic vision that features, on one side, an aggressive growth option in upstream activities and, on the other, a customer-oriented approach in the energy markets.
>
> For the upstream sector we devised a plan calling for 50% growth in hydrocarbon production by 2003. Such an objective will be made up of two components. The first is represented by ordinary growth . . . the second component of growth is related to mergers and acquisitions. . .
>
> In the natural gas sector, Eni has been active at three levels. First, it followed an internationalization strategy in downstream activities with the aim of selling at least 10 billion cubic meters of natural gas per year by 2003 in foreign growth markets. . . Second, with the creation of EniPower, Eni started to restructure its activities in the electricity sector, an area which represents a necessary step to strengthen its position in the gas chain, in view of the fact that most of the growth in demand for natural gas in Europe will come from the expansion of combined cycle electricity production.
>
> To support the opening up of the natural gas market in Italy, we started to restructure our activities at Snam, separating . . . transport activities from supply and sale.
>
> The scope of the changes affecting our industry will require on our part the achievement of strong efficiency improvements. For this reason, plans to cut costs have been revised, raising to €1 billion (an increase of €250 million) the amount of savings that Eni plans to achieve through cost cutting by 2003 . . . while costs will be cut across all sectors, strong measures will be taken in the Petrochemical sector—whose weight in terms of net capital will decline to 7% by 2003.[14]

By the time he retired in 2005, Mincato had won plaudits from investors and industry leaders both for the clarity of Eni's strategy and the effectiveness of its execution. Upstream, Eni extended its exploration activities in Kazakhstan (where Eni took over operatorship of the huge Kashagan oilfield), West Africa, Iran, and the Gulf of Mexico. While the other oil majors were engaged in mega-mergers, Eni limited itself to medium-sized acquisitions: British Borneo in May 2000 (€1.3 billion), LASMO in December 2000 (€4.1 billion), and Fortum's Norwegian oil and gas assets in November 2002 ($1.1 billion).

Major pipeline projects included the Blue Stream pipeline to move gas from Russia to Turkey under the Black Sea and the Greenstream pipeline from Libya to Italy. Both were built by Eni's affiliate Saipem.

Eni extended its downstream gas business by acquiring 50% of Spain's Union Fenosa Gas, 50% of GVS in Germany, and 33% of Galp Energia in Portugal. Eni also entered the gas markets of Hungary, Greece, and Croatia. Within Italy, Eni began investing heavily in power generation.

In refining and marketing and in chemicals, Eni pursued rationalization and cost reduction. Eni's chemical business was consolidated into a separate company, Polimeri Europa.

Internally, Mincato sought to make Eni a more integrated corporation. Between 2000 and 2004, Mincato transformed Eni from a holding company into a multidivisional corporation. The main subsidiary companies, which had operated with their own boards of directors and chief executives, were reorganized into three divisions: exploration and production, gas and power, and refining and marketing. A key aspect of integration was a company-wide human resources strategy that emphasized training, appraisal, and career planning over traditional "personnel" activities.

To forge a clearer identity and image for Eni, the slogan "Eni's Way" was adopted as the company's tag line in advertising and corporate communication. The key themes that "Eni's Way" embraced were technological strength, originality, spirit of adventure, and social and environmental responsibility.

Strategy under Scaroni, 2005–2012

Prior to his appointment as CEO of Eni, Paolo Scaroni had been CEO of Enel, Italy's largest electricity supplier, and CEO of Pilkington, the British glass company. He was a graduate of Bocconi University and held an MBA from Columbia University. His appointment was greeted with dismay by *The Economist*:

> Corporate governance [in Italy] continues to suffer big reverses, none bigger than the ousting last week by the government of Vittorio Mincato, the boss of Eni, the world's sixth-largest oil and gas company. Not only was this talented and apolitical manager replaced by somebody who knows nothing of the industry (Paolo Scaroni, boss of Enel, Italy's electrical utility); but also that ignorance is now shared by Eni's entire board.[15]

Early skepticism was allayed by Scaroni's effectiveness as a communicator, especially with the investment community, and as an international dealmaker. From the outset, Scaroni made it clear that he would not deviate substantially from Mincato's "disciplined growth" strategy. In an interview with the *Financial Times*, he committed Eni to a ten-year strategy of turning Eni into one of the world's oil and gas majors: "We will use our unique features to build a long-term growth strategy . . . We want to use the dimensions of our company and the dimensions of our country as a positive." Like Mincato, he emphasized organic growth: "I do not see a climate for acquisitions today . . . In the game of cash, we are not the richest."[16]

Upstream Growth

Under Scaroni, Eni's capital expenditure more than doubled with about 70% going into E&P. Major upstream initiatives included:

- Kazakhstan: Eni's giant Kashagan oilfield with upward of 15 billion barrels of oil was the world's biggest oil find in 30 years. Eni held a 16.81% stake and was the field's operator. It was Eni's biggest upstream project and Scaroni's biggest headache. The project suffered from recurrent cost overruns (the estimated development cost rose from an initial $57 billion to $156 billion), delays (start-up was pushed back from 2005 to end-2012), and accusations of environmental violations from the Kazak government. The Kazak government blamed Eni's mismanagement of the project; Eni pointed to the technical, geological, and logistical complexities of the project and the world shortage of engineers, geologists, and technicians. In January 2009, a joint operating company replaced Eni as the developer of the field.

- In Russia, Eni built upon its historical relationship as one of the biggest customers of Soviet gas, to broaden its relationship with Gazprom. This involved Eni acquiring equity stakes in four Russian oil companies, a joint venture with Gazprom to build South Stream, a contract signed in 2012 to import gas from Gazprom, and E&P projects in the Samburgskoye and Urengoskoye fields.

- In Congo, Eni negotiated an agreement with the Republic of Congo that some observers hailed as a model for future oil company relations with host governments. The May 2008 agreement involved Eni investing $3 billion in a variety of projects. In addition to onshore and offshore E&P projects, Eni would build two power plants that would use associated gas from Eni's M'Boundi oilfield. The project included distribution infrastructure and would provide 80% of Congo's electricity needs. In addition, Eni would develop a palm oil plantation to produce biofuels. The Eni Foundation planned to fund local health clinics and a program of vaccination of children.

- In Libya, Eni built on its status as Libya's longest partner in oil production and biggest buyer of Libyan oil by extending its concession for a further 25 years and agreeing with the Libyan government to sell it a 10% equity stake in Eni.[17] By May 2012, Libyan production was getting back to normal following the overthrow of the Gaddafi regime.

- Eni extended its E&P activities into new areas. In some cases these were the result of acquisitions. These included: Maurel and Prom's assets in Congo for $1.4 billion (February 2007), a Gulf of Mexico oilfield from Dominion Resources for $4.8 billion (April 2007), Burren Energy PLC with its gas fields in Turkmenistan and India for €2.36 billion (January 2008), and First Calgary Petroleum Ltd with upstream assets in Algeria for €0.7 billion (November 2008). Australia, East Timor, Indonesia, and Pakistan were also growth areas for Eni. However, these developments paled into insignificance when compared to Eni's discoveries of two major gas fields off Mozambique. The size of these fields was estimated at between 47 and 52 trillion cubic feet of gas (equivalent to 8.1 to 9.0 billion barrels of oil).

- As Eni's gas fields extended well beyond its core Mediterranean region, so it looked increasingly to LNG as a means of monetizing these reserves. LNG allowed Eni to extend geographically both its production and marketing of gas: downstream it planned to expand sales of gas both to Asia and the US. By 2012, Eni held equity interests in LNG trains in Egypt, Libya, Nigeria, Angola, Oman, Trinidad, Indonesia, and Australia; and in regasification plants in Italy, Spain, Portugal, and the US. It was planning an LNG plant in Mozambique to exploit its newly discovered gas fields there.

Tables 1 and 2 show Eni's geographical distribution of production and reserves. Eni's geographical distribution of its upstream activities contrasted sharply with that of most other petroleum majors'. Their major sources of hydrocarbons were North America and the Middle East. Eni's focus on Africa and the former Soviet

TABLE 1   Eni's hydrocarbon production and reserves by region

	Italy	North Sea	North Africa	West Africa	Rest of world	World
Production (thousands of BOE/day)						
2011	186	216	438	370	371	1,581
2010	183	222	602	400	408	1,815
2009	169	247	573	360	420	1,769
2008	199	237	645	335	381	1,797
2007	212	261	594	327	342	1,736
2006	238	282	555	372	323	1,770
2005	261	283	480	343	370	1,737
2004	271	308	380	316	349	1,624
2003	300	345	351	260	306	1,562
2002	316	308	354	238	256	1,472
2001	308	288	317	233	223	1,369
2000	333	168	306	225	155	1,187
Reserves (millions of BOE)						
2011	703	590	1,922	1,141	1,853	6,209

Note:
BOE: barrels of oil-equivalent.

Source: Eni annual reports for various years.

TABLE 2   Eni's major hydrocarbon producing
countries 2011 and 2000 (thousands of BOE/day)

	2011	2000
Egypt	236	180
Italy	186	308
Nigeria	160	98
Norway	131	84
Libya	112	87
Congo	108	69
Kazakhstan	106	42
Angola	98	64
US	98	46
UK	80	202
Algeria	72	35
Pakistan	58	4

Note:
BOE: barrels of oil equivalent.

Union reflected, first, its comparative youth and, second, its capacity to build cordial relations in countries that were conventionally viewed as difficult places to do business. According to Steve LeVine: "Italy's Eni continues to pioneer a successful path to survival in Big Oil's treacherous new world—get in bed, don't compete with the world's state-owned oil companies . . . Where its brethren bicker with Hugo Chavez and Vladimir Putin, Eni has found a comfortable embrace."[18]

Doing business with the autocratic and unrepresentative governments of Libya, Algeria, Nigeria, Angola, Kazakhstan, and Russia resulted in Eni being accused of being opportunistic and unprincipled. Scaroni's response was matter-of-fact: "We deal with countries that have gas. If Switzerland had gas, we would deal with Switzerland." At the root of Eni's flexible, innovative approach to relationships with producer countries was acceptance of the fact that the balance of power has shifted in favor of the producer countries: "The fact is, the oil is theirs . . . If you are looked at as a partner, you are allowed to exploit their oil; if not, you are pushed aside."[19]

Downstream: Building the European Gas Business

In possessing a large downstream gas business, Eni was unique among the majors. While all the majors were vertically integrated in oil, gas distribution had historically been in the hands of specialist companies: state-owned monopolies such as British Gas and Gaz de France in Europe or regulated local utilities in the US.

Scaroni was keen to maintain Eni's strong position in the European gas market, where he believed that Eni's vertical integration offered it a key competitive advantage:

> Eni has a very distinctive way of dealing with the gas in Europe. We are both upstream with our E&P division, and downstream in distribution, transport and sales. Just to give you an idea of how integrated these two divisions are, 35% of our equity gas is sold through our Gas & Power division, so we are already where most of our competitors in the midstream and downstream business of gas would like to be: integrated upstream, and generating our sales from our own equity gas . . . Then of course we have a wide portfolio of sourcing of gas, which goes from Algeria to Libya, Poland, Norway, and of course, Russia . . . There is no other player that has such a privileged position in the European market—I hope we will demonstrate to you that for each segment of our business—and we have exciting opportunities for growth.[20]

Marco Alvera, in charge of gas supplies, listed these advantages:

> Our gas, be it equity or contracted, comes from ten different countries. This gives us considerable diversity and security of supply. Second, we can leverage on a growing integrated LNG business. Third, we have attractive contractual structures and terms. Fourth, we have access to a very large set of transportation and storage assets across Europe from north to south and east to west. Finally, we have significant commercial flexibility that allows us to vary, on a daily basis, the amounts of gas produced or drawn from each of our contracts.[21]

As a result of the pipeline and storage system through which Eni brought gas to Italy from the North Sea, from Russia and from North Africa, it could easily supply other countries of Europe. Moreover, its long history had given it profound knowledge of the industry and a set of relationships which, in the case of Gazprom, has existed for almost half a century. "Summing up," said Alvera, "I would say that no other operator in the European gas market can claim to have the same scale and asset backed flexibility as Eni's Gas and Power division. Enhancing our optimization capabilities, as we continue our transition from former state monopoly in Italy to a true European leader in the gas market, will push us even further into a league of our own."

FIGURE 2   Eni's vertical chains in oil and gas

OIL (millions of tonnes)

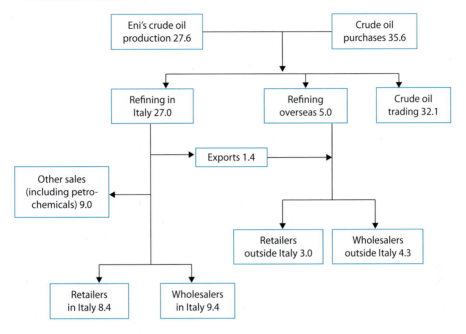

NATURAL GAS (billion cubic meters)

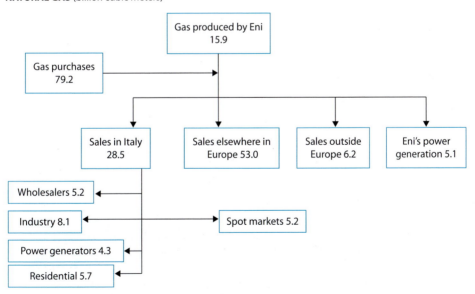

The European Commission had other ideas. European directives on competition in natural gas required Eni to limit its share of the Italian downstream gas market to 50% and vest its gas storage and gas transportation assets into separate, regulated companies. Eni had transferred its Italian gas transportation network to a separate company, Snam Rete Gas, which it listed on the Milan stock exchange in December 2001. In 2008, Eni sold its gas storage company, Stogit and its gas distribution company, Italgas, to Snam Rete Gas for a total of €4.8 billion. However, Eni still retained 52% ownership in Snam; in 2012, the Italian government decreed that Eni should sell its stake by September 2013. Eni was also required to sell ownership stakes in several international pipelines.

Downstream oil was a different story. Unlike most other oil and gas majors, the refining and marketing of oil products was a comparatively minor part of Eni's downstream business, accounting for a mere 6.4% of Eni's fixed assets. Refining and marketing were heavily focused on Italy, where Eni held 31% of the market for fuels. Under Scaroni, Eni continued to shrink its refining capacity, reduce its number of retail outlets, and narrow its geographical scope (it sold its downstream businesses in Spain and Portugal). Despite cost cutting and technical upgrading, the depressed state of the downstream market meant that Eni's refining and marketing sector lost money in 2009, 2010, and 2011.

Eni's vertical chains for oil and gas are shown in Figure 2. Note that, despite Eni's commitment to international expansion in both upstream and downstream gas, Italy still accounted for almost one-third of Eni's total revenues in 2011 (Figure 3).

FIGURE 3 Eni's sales by geographic area ($million)

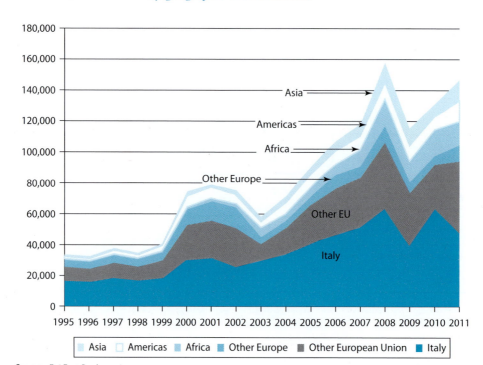

Source: *Eni Fact Books*, various years.

The Petroleum Sector in 2012

The petroleum sector comprises two major segments: upstream and downstream. Upstream is concerned with the exploration and production of oil and gas; in the downstream segment, gas and oil have separate value chains. In oil the primary activities are refining and marketing (where marketing includes both wholesale and retail distribution of fuels). In gas the primary downstream activities are distribution and marketing. Linking upstream and downstream are mid-stream activities comprising the transportation of oil and gas (pipeline and marine) and trading.

The Companies

The petroleum sector featured three main types of company:

- The *oil and gas majors* were characterized by their age, size, international scope, and vertical integration. They were among the oldest and largest companies in the industry. Between 1998 and 2002, a wave of mergers and acquisitions resulted in the emergence of an elite group of "super majors" comprising ExxonMobil, BP, Royal Dutch Shell, ChevronTexaco, ConocoPhillips, and Total (Table 3). The extent of economic benefits from

TABLE 3   Major mergers and acquisitions among the petroleum majors[a]

Major oil companies, 1995	Revenues, 1995 ($billion)	Date merged	Major oil companies, 2011	Revenues, 2011 ($billion)
Exxon	124	1999	Exxon Mobil Corp.	433.5
Mobil	75			
Royal Dutch Petroleum	110	2004	Royal Dutch Shell	470.2
Shell Transport & Trading				
Enterprise Oil	1	2002		
British Petroleum	56		BP	375.5
Amoco	28	1998		
Arco	16	2000		
Chevron	31	2001	Chevron	236.6
Texaco	36			
Total	28		Total	216.2
PetroFina	n.a.	1999		
Elf Aquitaine	n.a.	2000		
Conoco	15	2002	ConocoPhillips	230.7
Philips Petroleum	13			
Tosco	n.a.	2001		
Eni	36		Eni	143.2
Repsol	21		Repsol YPF	72.8
YPF	5	1999		

Note:
[a]Only includes acquisitions of companies with revenues exceeding $1 billion.

662 CASES TO ACCOMPANY CONTEMPORARY STRATEGY ANALYSIS

these mergers and acquisitions remains disputed. The costs of developing oil and gas fields and building LNG (liquefied natural gas) facilities were huge, but typically these were undertaken as joint ventures, not by single firms. A large portfolio of upstream projects allowed the cost of infrastructure to be spread and risks to be pooled. However, there was little evidence that scale economies offered significant advantages to "super majors" over mere "majors." The majors differed in their chemical activities. Some of the majors were major petrochemical producers (e.g., ExxonMobil, Royal Dutch Shell, and Total). Others had divested most of their chemical activities (e.g., BP and Chevron).

- The *national oil companies (NOCs)* were the state-owned enterprises (mostly monopolies) created by producer governments to manage their countries' petroleum reserves. In terms of production and reserves, the NOCs dominated the ranks of the leading petroleum companies in 2012 (Table 4). Most were created

TABLE 4 The world's top-30 petroleum companies by size of reserves

Company	State ownership	Reserves (million BOE)
National Iranian Oil Company (Iran)	100%	315,757
Saudi Arabian Oil Company (Saudi Arabia)	100%	307,143
Petróleos de Venezuela SA (Venezuela)	100%	241,744
Qatar General Petroleum Corporation (Qatar)	100%	178,508
Iraq National Oil Company (Iraq)	100%	135,503
Abu Dhabi National Oil Company (UAE)	100%	128,439
Kuwait Petroleum Corporation (Kuwait)	100%	112,269
Nigerian National Petroleum Corporation (Nigeria)	100%	69,145
National Oil Company (Libya)	100%	55,767
Sonatrach (Algeria)	100%	39,379
OAO Gazprom (Russia)	50%	29,261
OAO Rosneft (Russia)	75%	22,885
PetroChina Co. Ltd. (China)	87%	22,475
BP Corporation (United Kingdom)	0%	17,829
Egyptian General Petroleum Corporation (Egypt)	100%	17,597
Exxon Mobil Corporation (United States)	0%	17,420
Petróleos Mexicanos (Mexico)	100%	13,319
OAO Lukoil (Russia)	0%	13,029
Royal Dutch/Shell (Netherlands)	0%	12,585
Petróleo Brasileiro SA (Brazil)	37%	12,531
Sonangol (Angola)	100%	11,370
Chevron Corporation (United States)	0%	10,648
Petroleum Development Oman LLC (Oman)	100%	10,628
Total (France)	5%	10,395
ConocoPhillips (United States)	0%	6,733
Eni (Italy)	30%	6,680
Petróleos de Ecuador (Ecuador)	90%	6,558
Petronas (Malaysia)	100%	5,986
Statoil (Norway)	67%	5,195
Suncor Energy Inc. (Canada)	0%	4,920

Note:
BOE: barrels of oil equivalent.
Source: "OGJ 200/100," *Oil & Gas Journal*, October 1, 2011.

between the mid-1960s and the early 1980s by nationalizing the oil assets of the majors. During 2000–2012, the relationship between the majors and the NOCs shifted substantially. Rising crude prices and growing nationalism among oil producing countries resulted in the increasing desire of the NOCs for greater control over their countries' hydrocarbon resources and bigger shares of production and revenues. In Venezuela, Bolivia, and Russia, foreign oil companies were forced to transfer upstream assets to the national government or to local companies. Elsewhere higher taxes were imposed and participation agreements renegotiated. Increasingly, the NOCs have become direct competitors of the majors. Some, such as Petrobras and CNOOC, became important international players. Others, such as Saudi Aramco, Kuwait Petroleum, and PDVSA, established large downstream (and petrochemical) businesses, which depressed margins in refining and bulk chemicals. With the help of oil service companies, such as Halliburton and Schlumberger, the NOCs had access to modern technologies and became less dependent upon the majors.

- *Independents*: At all vertical levels, specialist companies played an important role. In exploration and production, companies such as Devon Energy, Anadarko, Cairn Resources, and Woodside Petroleum were important players, especially in exploring frontier regions. Their operational and financial success contradicted the arguments of the majors that huge size was an essential requirement in the petroleum industry. In refining, independent refiners such as Valero in the US grew as the majors sold off downstream assets. (Appendix 3 lists the world's largest oil and gas companies with publicly traded shares.)

Vertical Integration Strategies

A key feature of the strategies of majors had been vertical integration throughout the value chain from exploration through to retailing gasoline and other refined products. The rationale for vertical integration had been the need for security of supply and of market outlets. However, in the case of oil, the development of a global infrastructure of transportation and storage, competitive markets for both crude and refined products, and the presence of specialist companies at every stage of the value chain had reduced (if not eliminated) the advantages of vertical integration. While most majors remained vertically integrated, few had close operational linkages between their oilfields and refineries, and all had withdrawn from some stages of the value chain, for example outsourcing oilfield services and marine transportation. ConocoPhillips went further: in 2011, it spun off its downstream businesses into a separate company, Phillips 66 Company:

> We have recognized that it is no longer a strategic advantage to have a complex, integrated business model. Two independent businesses, focused on specific portions of the energy industry, have greater potential to outperform competition and create differentiated value.[22]

In gas the situation was different. The physical difficulties of transporting and storing gas meant that monetizing gas reserves required dedicated investments in transportation, liquefaction, and storage to link production to consumption. The lack of an integrated global market in gas was indicated by the geographical price differences that were much wider than in oil. In oil, the London trader Brent and New York trader Texas West Intermediate tended to be within 10% of one another. In May 2012, US gas prices had fallen to $2 for one million BTUs (British thermal unit), the comparable price in Europe was $6 to $8, and in Asia up to $16.[23] Forward integration by the petroleum majors into downstream gas was mainly through directly supplying large industrial customers or through alliances and long-term contracts with gas marketing companies. Vertical integration along the gas chain had also encouraged most of the majors to invest in electricity generation.

For all the majors, gas had emerged as a key strategic priority. Once regarded as a worthless impediment that was flared, the world demand for gas was growing twice as fast as the demand for oil. In 2011, gas consumption (in terms of oil equivalency) was 85% that of oil. While the 20th century was the "age of oil," the first half of the twenty-first century was predicted to be the "era of gas" by some petroleum industry experts.

Technology and Knowledge Management

The quest for reserves had taken the petroleum majors to the Arctic and the depths of the ocean. It had encouraged companies to develop enhanced recovery techniques in order to extend the lives of mature fields. It resulted in the production of synthetic crudes from sulfur-heavy petroleum, from coal, and from tar sands and oil shale. Gas-to-liquids technologies were being deployed to produce gasoline from natural gas.

The result was increased dependence upon technology. Nevertheless, investments in R & D by the majors were modest (less than 0.3% of revenues in recent years). Increasingly, the majors outsourced technology-intensive activities to other companies. Upstream, the technological leaders in directional drilling, 4-D seismic modeling, and "intelligent oilfield" management were the oil service companies, Schlumberger in particular.

However, the knowledge requirements of the petroleum business extended beyond technology. The technical, logistical, political, and financial complexities of the business meant that a critical driver of competitive advantage was the ability to learn from experience and transfer that learning throughout the company. By the early years of the new century, all the leading oil and gas companies had adopted some form of knowledge management to increase the efficiency of their knowledge capture, storage, and utilization. Many of the new knowledge management systems relied heavily on web-based technology, distributed computing, and digital wireless communication to enhance the speed and quality of decision making.

Exploration and Production The oil price rise of 2002–2012 (from $22 in 2002 to over $100 during the early part of 2012) had reinforced the industry's conventional wisdom that upstream provides the primary source of profit for the energy industry. For all the petroleum majors, their upstream divisions were their most profitable businesses: during 2006-2011, ExxonMobil, Royal Dutch Shell, BP, Chevron, Total, and Eni each earned a rate of return on capital in E&P that was at least double what they earned in refining and marketing. Although upstream activities accounted for only one-fifth of their revenues, they contributed about three-quarters of overall profits during 2004–2011. Table 5 shows rates of return by business for US petroleum companies.

TABLE 5   US petroleum companies return on investment by line of business, 1980–2009 (%)

	1980–1984	1985–1989	1990–1994	1995–1999	2000–2003	2004–2007	2008–2009
US oil and gas production	15.4	4.0	5.8	10.1	14.4	19.00	7.1
US refining and marketing	5.1	8.0	2.7	5.7	7.9	22.3	(2.1)
Foreign oil and gas production	19.3	12.2	9.1	12.4	12.9	21.5	13.7
Foreign refining and marketing	10.4	6.8	10.1	7.0	6.2	19.7	9.3
Downstream gas	n.a.	n.a.	n.a.	n.a.	7.3	8.2	7.4

Note:
n.a.: not available.
Figures in parentheses denote a loss.
Source: Energy Information Administration, performance profiles of major energy producers, US Department of Energy (various years).

The profitability of E&P depends critically upon the price of oil, which is determined primarily by the relationship between demand and production capacity. During 2000–2012, increasing demand from India and China was the major impetus behind rising oil prices (Figure 4). At the same time, output was constrained by political factors. Economic sanctions on Iran, internal disruption in Libya, Egypt, Iraq, and Nigeria, resource nationalism, and underinvestment in Venezuela, Russia,

FIGURE 4   Oil prices: West Texas intermediate crude per barrel, 1982–2012 ($)

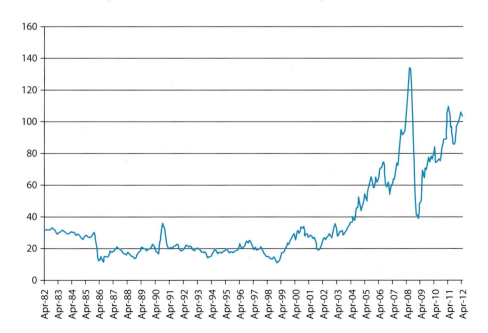

TABLE 6 Oil and gas production and reserves by country

	Oil production (thousand barrels/day)			Gas production (billion m³/day)			Oil reserves (bn barrels)	Gas reserves (tn m³)
	2010	2007	1991	2010	2007	1991	2010	2010
Saudi Arabia	10,007	10,413	8,820	83.9	75.9	35	264.5	8.0
Russia	10,270	9,978	9,326	588.9	607.4	600	77.4	44.8
US	7,513	6,879	9,076	611.0	545.9	510	30.9	7.7
Iran	4,245	4,404	3,500	138.5	111.9	26	137.0	29.6
China	4,071	3,743	2,828	96.8	69.3	15	14.8	2.8
Canada	3,336	3,309	1,980	159.8	183.7	105	32.1	1.7
Mexico	2,958	3,477	3,126	55.3	46.2	28	11.4	0.5
UAE	2,849	2,915	2,639	51.0	49.2	24	97.8	6.0
Kuwait	2,508	2,626	185	11.6	12.6	1	101.5	1.8
Venezuela	2,471	2,613	2,501	28.5	28.5	22	211.2	5.5
Iraq	2,460	2,145	279	1.3	1.5	n.a.	115	3.2
Nigeria	2,402	2,356	1,890	33.6	28.4	4	37.2	5.3
Norway	2,137	2,556	1,923	106.4	89.7	27	6.7	2.0
Algeria	1,809	2,000	1,351	80.4	83.2	53	12.2	4.5
UK	1,339	1,636	1,919	57.1	72.4	51	2.8	0.3

Notes:
Bn: billion.
tn: trillion.
Source: BP Statistical Review of World Energy, 2008 and 2011. Reproduced by permission of BP p.l.c.

and Mexico all limited the flow of oil to world markets. When increased supply or lack of demand causes the oil market to soften, prices are supported by production quotas imposed by the Organization of Petroleum Exporting Countries (OPEC) and by Saudi Arabia, which acts as a "swing producer"—adjusting its output to stabilize world prices. The tendency for petroleum rich countries to have autocratic, often oppressive, regimes created the potential for political instability (Table 6).

High oil prices combined with restricted access to existing reserves caused the companies to move increasingly to deep-water exploration and nonconventional oils (tar sands, oil shale) causing finding costs to escalate (Figure 5).

The desire to control rising upstream costs encouraged the oil and gas companies to outsource more and more of their E&P activities. Drilling, seismic surveys, rig design, platform construction, and oilfield maintenance were increasingly undertaken by oilfield service companies. As these oilfield service companies developed their expertise and their proprietary technologies, and grew through mergers and acquisitions, so sector leaders such as Schlumberger, Baker Hughes, Halliburton, and Diamond Offshore Drilling emerged as powerful players within the petroleum industry.

The attractive rates of return earned in the upstream sector meant that capital investment by the integrated majors became increasingly focused upon the upstream sector. Between 2000 and 2008, the leading majors invested between three and four times as much upstream as downstream (Table 7). During previous decades, capital investment was split more evenly between upstream and downstream.

FIGURE 5   US petroleum companies' finding costs per barrel of oil equivalent

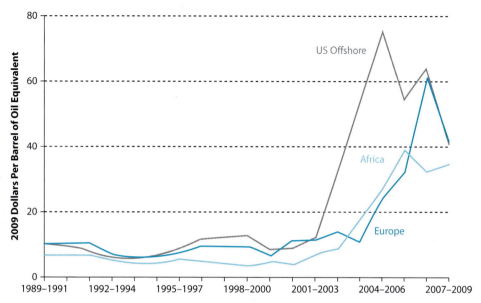

Notes:
Costs are a quotient of costs and reserve additions for each three-year period.
BOE: Barrels of oil equivalent.
Source: US Energy Information Administration, Form EIA-28 (Financial Reporting System).

TABLE 7   Capital expenditures among the majors, 2003–2011

	Average annual capital expenditure ($billion)		Capital expenditure on E&P as % of the total	
	2003–2007	2008–2011	2003–2007	2008–2011
ExxonMobil	17.0	30.5	78.2	82.6
Royal Dutch/Shell	16.4	26.6	68.0	78.2
BP	17.9	24.9	69.3	79.1
Total	12.2	23.9	72.3	65.2
Chevron	10.8	21.9	77.0	90.2
Conoco Phillips	11.4	11.3	57.9	86.7
Eni	9.6	16.1	65.7	69.8

Source: Company annual reports.

Refining and Marketing   In oil, downstream businesses included refining and the wholesale and retail marketing and distribution of refined oil products. The main refined products in order of importance were: gasoline, diesel fuel, aviation fuel, heating oil, liquefied petroleum gas (LPG), and petrochemical feedstocks (e.g., naphtha). As already noted, downstream has been less profitable than upstream: in their refining and marketing businesses, the majors typically earned rates of return that barely covered their costs of capital. As a result, all the majors divested refining and marketing assets and concentrated their capital expenditures on their upstream businesses (Table 7).

The main problem in refining was excess capacity. Demand for refined products was declining in Europe and North America and new refining capacity was coming on stream in the Middle East and Asia as a result of downstream investments by NOCs. In retailing, profitability was also dismal due to excess capacity and new entry by supermarket chains into gasoline distribution (especially in France and the UK).

Downstream Gas and Power   Among the petroleum majors, Eni was unusual in being established on natural gas rather than oil. For most of the majors, oil had been their dominant interest and, as a result, few had pursued the same strategy of vertical integration that they had in oil. In most countries, gas distribution had been undertaken by state-owned or state-regulated utilities. The rising demand for natural gas caused all the majors to reorient their upstream activities toward gas, while privatization and deregulation of downstream gas gave them the opportunity to increase their presence in gas marketing and distribution. Similarly with the deregulation of electricity markets: the petroleum majors could enter power generation directly or supply natural gas to independent power producers.

However, the downstream markets for gas and power did not offer the petroleum rates of return comparable with their upstream businesses.

Chemicals   The petrochemical sector displayed many of the same structural features as oil refining: capital-intensive processes producing commodity products, many competitors, and a continual tendency for excess capacity (much of it resulting from new investment by Asian and Middle Eastern producers) to drive down prices and margins. Competitive advantage in chemicals depended upon scale economies, technological advantages (such as patented products and processes), and low costs of feedstock. Among the oil and gas majors there were two distinct views about chemicals. Some, like Eni, saw chemicals as a fundamentally unattractive industry and believed that chemical plants were better run by chemical companies. Others (including ExxonMobil, Shell, and Total) viewed chemicals as part of their core business and believed that integration between refining and petrochemicals offered them a cost advantage.

The Outlook for Eni in 2012

Two decades of steady development under three CEOs—Bernabè, Mincato, and Scaroni—had transformed Eni from an inefficient, state-owned conglomerate into a highly profitable, international energy company with a strong identity and clear strategic direction.

At the heart of Eni's strategy was its commitment to steady organic growth of its upstream business. The restoration of Eni's production in Libya and its huge gas discoveries off Mozambique, underpinned Scaroni's confidence in this strategy. The cornerstones of Eni's upstream strategy would be its commitment to close, collaborative relationships with the governments and NOCs of producer countries and its own technical excellence. With regard to the latter, Eni's close relationship with the oilfield services company Saipem (in which it held a 42% equity stake) provided it with in-house technical capabilities that other oil majors could not match. Eni had continued to develop its technical and operating capabilities because of its preference for operating its joint venture oil and gas fields. To the extent that producer governments were interested in the transfer of technical expertise to their own national oil companies, Eni believed that its technical strengths would make it a preferred partner for producer countries. Technical strengths also allowed Eni to increasingly focus its attention on large (and typically technically complex) oil and gas fields

Saipem's technical capabilities were also a key element in Eni's vertically integrated gas strategy. Eni's trans-Mediterranean pipelines had been critical in allowing Eni to develop its gas resources in North Africa and maintain its dominance of the Italian gas market. As it was increasingly forced to look elsewhere to expand its gas sales, pipelines would continue to play a role. As a result of the Blue Stream pipeline, Turkey had become a major gas market for Eni.

Downstream oil and chemicals represented challenges for Eni. Both were low-profit industries. However, in refining and marketing, Eni held a strong strategic position: with over 30% of the Italian market Eni was well positioned to exploit economies of scale and economies of distributing density.

The situation in chemicals was more difficult. Not only was the petrochemical sector an intensely competitive, low-margin business but also Eni lacked scale and distinctive technological advantages. Chemicals had been a loss maker for Eni for many years. However, at his March 2012 strategy presentation, Scaroni announced a change of strategy. After trying, unsuccessfully, to sell the business, Scaroni announced a turnaround strategy based upon "Regaining competitiveness within the chemicals business" through "refocusing the chemicals portfolio on added-value products," expansion outside of Europe through licensing, alliances, and joint ventures, and efficiency improvements to reduce costs. One element of the new strategy was an agreement with Novamont SpA to convert Eni's Porto Torres chemical plant into a bio-based chemical complex to produce bio-plastics, bio-lubricants, and bio-additives from vegetable raw materials.

Over time, Eni had become more explicit in articulating its strategy—especially in explaining how it was positioning itself within its markets to build competitive advantage based upon its distinctive assets and capabilities. In 2012, it presented an integrated view of its strategy, corporate governance, and business principles which it described as "Eni's Business Model" (Figure 6).[24] Key components of this model were:

- major elements of Eni's strategy in its different business areas e.g., its emphasis on "diversified supply portfolio" and "integrated midstream infrastructure" in its gas business;
- the "drivers" of its competitive advantage, including its emphasis on "profitable growth," "strategic partnerships with NOCs," and seeking "operatorship";
- the "pillars" which define its approach to doing business, such as "integration," "inclusiveness," and "innovation."

However, the successful implementation of this strategy would depend on several factors. The disruption that the Arab Spring had created for Eni was a clear indicator

FIGURE 6 Eni's business model

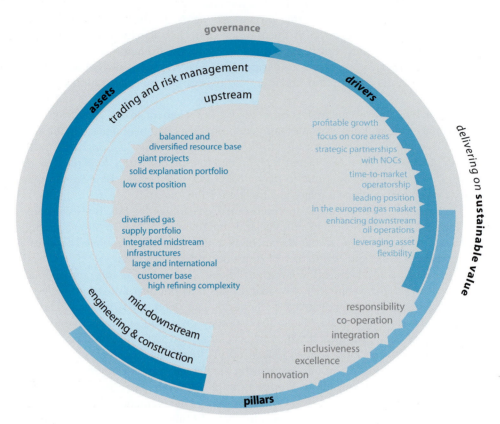

Source: Eni Fact Book, 2011, p. 11.

of the oil majors' vulnerability to political turmoil. Would Eni's efforts to build collaboration with the governments and petroleum companies of Russia and Venezuela fall victim to political uncertainties in these countries? Would the growing role of NOCs in the world petroleum industry mean that Eni, along with the other Western majors, would be reduced to an increasingly marginal role?

And would Eni be successful in persuading the investment community of the wisdom of its strategy? Despite its huge discoveries off Mozambique, Eni's market valuation still lagged several of its peers on the basis of conventional valuation rations (Table 8).

Finally, fulfilling Eni's potential would require developing the coordination and responsiveness that it often talked about, but probably had yet to fully achieve. Despite Eni's transformation from a loose-knit holding company to a more tightly integrated divisional corporation, it still faced internal challenges to the successful execution of its strategy. Many insiders doubted whether Eni had yet established the degree of close, flexible coordination across organizational boundaries that would be needed for its strategic partnerships with governments and NOCs, its time-to-market capabilities, and asset flexibility to really work.

TABLE 8 Valuation multiples for petroleum majors, May 2011

	Price/earnings ratio	Price/book ratio	Price/sales ratio	Price/cash flow
Exxon Mobil Corp.	10.10	2.48	0.91	7.1
British Petroleum PLC	5.16	1.07	0.33	3.6
ChevronTexaco Corp.	7.48	1.59	0.79	5.1
Total SA	6.82	2.26	0.32	4.0
Royal Dutch Shell PLC	6.90	1.22	0.43	4.9
Eni SpA	7.56	1.14	0.52	4.0
Repsol YPF SA	7.30	0.68	0.26	5.2
ConocoPhillips	5.90	1.02	0.31	3.4

Sources: Hoover's Online; *Financial Times.*

A final internal challenge was internationalization. For all Eni's emphasis on international growth, it remained a very Italian company. Its board of directors and its 13-person top management team were both comprised exclusively of Italians.

Appendix 1: Eni SpA: Financial Highlights, 2006–2011

($billion except where indicated)	2008	2009	2010	2011
Exchange rate ($/€)	1.473	1.394	1.326	1.393
Net sales from operations	159.3	116.0	130.6	152.7
Operating profit	27.5	16.8	21.4	24.3
Adjusted operating profit	32.1	18.3	22.9	25.0
Net profit	13.0	6.1	8.4	9.6
Adjusted net profit	15.0	7.3	9.1	9.7
Net cash from operating activities	32.1	15.5	19.5	20.0
Capital expenditures	21.4	19.1	18.4	18.7
Investments	6.3	3.2	0.5	0.5
Cash dividends	7.2	5.8	4.8	5.1
R & D expenditures	0.32	0.29	0.29	0.27
Total assets at year-end	171.7	168.8	174.8	199.1
Shareholders' equity (including minority interests)	71.5	69.8	73.9	84.1
Net borrowings	27.1	32.1	34.6	39.0
Net capital employed	98.5	101.9	108.5	123.2
Share price at year end	24.66	24.8	21,6	22,3
Market capitalization ($billion)	89.26	89.9	78.5	80.8
ROACE	15.7%	9.2%	10,7%	9.9%

Appendix 2: Eni's Operating Performance, 2004–2011

	2004	2005	2006	2007	2008	2009	2010	2011
Proved hydrocarbon reserves (m BOE)	7218	6837	6436	6370	6600	6571	6843	7086
Reserve life index (years)	12.1	10.8	10.0	10.0	10.0	10.2	10.3	12.3
Hydrocarbon production (k BOE/day)	1624	1737	1770	1736	1797	1769	1815	1581
Worldwide gas sales (bn m^3)	87.03	94.21	98.10	98.96	104.23	103.72	97.06	96.76
Electricity sold (TWH)	16.95	27.56	31.03	33.19	29.93	33.96	39.54	40.28
Refinery throughput (m tonnes)	37.69	38.79	38.04	37.15	35.84	34.55	34.8	31.96
Refinery capacity (k barrels/day)	504	524	534	544	544	747	757	767
Sales of refined products (m tonnes)	53.54	51.63	51.13	50.14	50.68			
Retail sales (m tonnes)	14.40	13.72	12.48	12.65	12.67	12.02	11.73	11.37
Number of service stations	9140	6282	6294	6441	5956	5986	6167	6287
Av. service station throughput (k liters/year)	1970	1926	2470	2486	2502	2477	2353	2206
Engineering and services: orders acquired (€m)	5784	8395	11172	11845	13860	9917	12935	12505
Order backlog (€m)	8521	10122	13191	15390	19105	18730	20505	20417

Notes:
BOE: barrels of oil equivalent.
m: million.
k: thousand.
bn: billion.
TWH: terawatt-hour.
bn m^3: billion cubic meters.

Appendix 3: Top-40 Oil and Gas Companies among the Forbes Global 2000, April 2011

Forbes' Rank	Company	Country	Sales ($billion)	Profits ($billion)	Assets ($billion)	Market value ($billion)
1	ExxonMobil	US	433.5	41.1	331.1	407.4
4	Royal Dutch Shell	Netherlands	470.2	30.9	340.5	227.6
7	PetroChina	China	310.1	20.6	304.7	294.7
10	Petrobras	Brazil	145.9	20.1	319.4	180.0
11	BP	UK	375.5	25.7	292.5	147.4
12	Chevron	US	236.6	26.9	209.5	218.0
15	Gazprom	Russia	117.6	31.7	302.6	159.8
18	Total	France	216.2	15.9	213.0	132.4
24	Sinopec-China Petroleum	China	391.4	11.6	179.8	104.2
27	ConocoPhillips	US	230.9	12.4	153.2	98.8
29	Eni	Italy	143.2	8.9	178.7	97.6
41	Statoil	Norway	111.6	13.1	127.8	89.0
47	GDF Suez	France	117.5	5.2	275.2	58.3
68	Lukoil	Russia	111.4	10.4	90.6	55.3
71	Rosneft	Russia	59.2	11.3	106.0	79.6
73	EDF	France	84.6	3.9	297.5	45.7
124	Reliance Industries	India	59.5	4.3	69.0	50.4
126	China Shenhua Energy	China	33.1	7.3	63.6	84.2
128	Schlumberger	Netherlands	39.5	5.0	55.2	102.4
134	Suncor Energy Inc.	Canada	39.1	4.2	73.4	51.8
137	Ecopetrol	Colombia	35.6	8.4	47.6	119.7
140	Repsol YPF	Spain	72.8	2.8	88.8	30.1
145	Occidental Petroleum	US	24.1	6.8	60.0	81.6
146	Conic	Hong Kong	27.1	8.0	49.7	96.3
149	TNK-BP Holding	Russia	60.2	9.0	37.1	51.6
166	BG Group	UK	20.3	4.1	60.8	83.2
167	PTT PCL	Thailand	76.9	3.3	43.8	32.9
171	Oil & Natural Gas	India	26.3	5.0	51.0	46.6
176	JX Holdings	US	115.9	3.8	74.1	15.8
198	Apache	US	16.9	4.6	52.1	41.9
200	Surgutneftegas	Russia	20.3	4.3	46.6	39.9
237	Valero Energy	US	126	2.1	42.8	15.5
268	Hess	US	37.9	1.7	39.1	21.3
271	Canadian Natural Resources	Canada	13.5	2.6	46.4	38.8
273	Gas Natural Group	Spain	27.3	1.7	59.1	16.5
275	NextEra Energy	US	15.3	1.9	57.2	25.0
276	Duke Energy	US	14.5	1.7	62.5	28.1
279	Husky Energy	Canada	22.9	2.2	31.8	25.1
283	Sasol	South Africa	21.0	2.9	26.1	32.2
285	Indian Oil	India	63.7	1.8	43.4	13.2

Notes

1. We refer throughout the case to "Eni." For most of its history, the company's full name was Ente Nazionale Idrocarburi but it was known by the acronym ENI. In August 1992, the company's name was changed to Eni SpA.

2. Recognizing the strategic importance of oil, other European governments created national oil companies: the British government had purchased a controlling interest in BP in 1914; France established the Compagnie Française des Pétroles (Total) in 1924.

3. D. Yergin, *The Prize*, Simon & Shuster, New York, 1992, p. 23.

4. D. Yergin, *The Prize*, Simon & Shuster, New York, 1992, p. 23.

5. Section sourced from company report, "L'Eni di Fronte a un Bivio," Eni SpA, 2002.

6. D. Votaw, *The Six-Legged Dog: Mattei and ENI: A Study in Power* (University of California Press, Berkeley, CA, 1964), p. 71.

7. "L'Eni di Fronte a un Bivio," Eni SpA, 2002, p. 5.

8. *Franco Bernabè at Eni* (Harvard Business School Case 9-498-034, April 7, 1998).

9. Chairman Gabriele Cagliari later committed suicide in prison.

10. "L'Eni di Fronte a un Bivio," Eni SpA, 2002, p. 11.

11. "Eni Savors the Taste of Freedom," *Financial Times*, June 9, 1994.

12. ENI SpA, Securities and Exchange Commission, Form 20F, 1996.

13. Securities and Exchange Commission, *ENI SpA, 20-F for 1996*, p. 3.

14. "Letter to Shareholders," Eni, Annual Report, 1999, pp. 4–5.

15. "Italy: The Real Sick Man of Europe," *Economist*, May 19, 2005.

16. "Eni's New Chief Intends to Become a Big Player," *Financial Times*, September 22, 2005.

17. "Rome's Colonial Past Key to Libya's Eni Stake," *Financial Times*, December 9, 2008.

18. See http://oilandglory.com/labels/ENI.html, accessed October 19, 2009.

19. "How Italy's ENI Vastly Boosted Oil Output," *Business Week*, April 20, 2009.

20. Eni SpA Gas seminar conference call, December 1, 2006.

21. Eni SpA Gas seminar conference call, December 1, 2006.

22. ConocoPhillips, "Repositioning," 2011, http://www.conocophillips.com/EN/newsroom/Pages/RepositioningFAQs.aspx, accessed September 24, 2012.

23. "Europe's Failed Natural Gas Strategy," *Der Spiegel*, May 18, 2012.

24. *Eni Fact Book, 2011*, p. 11.

A video clip relating to this case is available in your interactive e-book at **www.wileyopenpage.com**

Case 16 American Apparel: Vertically Integrated in Downtown LA

American Apparel's reversal of fortunes in mid-2010 was sudden and sharp. Since its first retail store in 2003, American Apparel had been one of America's fastest-growing clothing companies with one of the hottest fashion brands. Its retail presence had expanded from the US and Canada to 18 other countries. In 2008, it was placed second (after Nike) in the *Cassandra Report*'s listing of "Top Trendsetter Brands" (beating Apple into third place) and CEO Dov Charney was named "Retailer of the Year" in the Annual Michael Awards. The problems began in July 2010 when the company's auditor, Deloitte & Touche, resigned after discovering "material weaknesses" in the company's financial controls. Amidst warnings of declining sales and an operating loss, American Apparel's share price hit a low of 66 cents in September 2010—down from a high of $16.80 in December 2007. Mounting losses during 2010 resulted in American Apparel breaching the terms of covenants on its $80 million loan from Lion Capital, forcing American Apparel to issue a bankruptcy warning.

American Apparel's strategic priorities shifted 180 degrees. In 2009, it had targeted annual growth rates of 20% in sales growth and 20–25% in earnings per share over the next few years.[1] Between 2010 and 2012, its emphasis was cost cutting, cash conservation, and financial restructuring. During the latter part of 2010, new, experienced senior managers were brought in, turnaround specialist FTI Consulting hired, and new sources of finance sought.

However, the task of putting American Apparel back on its feet was compromised by disagreements over the sources of American Apparel's problems. While CEO Dov Charney firmly believed that the answer to his company's woes lay in operational improvements to cut costs and boost efficiency, other observers expressed doubts about the viability of American Apparel's strategy. The company had defied the conventional wisdom of the rag trade: instead of outsourcing production to contract manufacturers in low-wage countries, American Apparel had followed a vertically integrated strategy with production concentrated in Los Angeles. Charney believed that the higher costs of manufacturing in the US could be offset by the price premium from superior quality, styling, and image, and by the advantages of speed to market. Critical to these advantages was American Apparel's tight linkage between design, manufacture, marketing, and retailing.

Others saw the CEO's personality and lifestyle as the source of American Apparel's woes. Dov Charney was a self-proclaimed hustler whose workplace behavior and

This case was written by Robert M. Grant with assistance from Ellen A. Drost and Stephen J. J. McGuire. © 2012 Robert M. Grant.

frank opinions about and attitudes toward progressive social issues and sex generated controversy, and considerable media attention. Britain's *Guardian* newspaper
described Charney as: "this maverick Canadian entrepreneur, who apparently rel-
ishes his reputation as a pervert and a libertine."[2] His portrayal as an exhibitionist
and sexual predator was reinforced by five sexual harassment suits brought by former employees against American Apparel and its CEO.

The T-Shirt Business

T-shirts, like denim jeans, are quintessentially American clothing products. About
1.4 billion cotton T-shirts are sold in North America annually with a retail value of
about $20 billion. Originally underwear garments, T-shirts are the most common
summer outerwear garment for weekend Americans. The designs and words they
carry are important statements of personal identity, indicating affiliation with a
sports team, college, political movement, religion, charity, or specific social event.
Yet despite the T-shirt's place in American culture, the vast majority are imported
(Table 1). Several US manufacturers, such as Gildan Activewear, Hanesbrands, and
Delta Apparel own plants in Central America and the Caribbean. A high proportion of imported T-shirts are made from cotton grown in the US, the world's largest
exporter of cotton fiber.[3] The average import price of a T-shirt in 2010 was $2.60.[4]
The US garment industry as a whole had shrunk dramatically. When the quota system known as the Multifiber Agreement was created in 1974, 1.4 million Americans
worked in the garment industry. By the time it was abolished in 2006, only 270,000
remained.

The US T-shirt market features a wide variety of suppliers. At the wholesale
level, blank T-shirts are sold by major suppliers (such as Gildan Activewear,
Hanesbrands, Russell Athletic, and Fruit of the Loom) to screen printers that add

TABLE 1 Imports of knitted cotton shirts into the
United States, 2010

Source country	Value of imports, trade categories 338 and 339 ($ billion)
China	3.54
Vietnam	1.54
Indonesia	1.17
India	0.82
Honduras	0.81
Guatemala	0.64
Cambodia	0.64
Pakistan	0.60
El Salvador	0.53
Mexico	0.51
Total from all countries	13.85

Source: US trade statistics.

TABLE 2   Sales and profits of leading fashion apparel companies, 2011

	Sales ($billion)	Net income ($billion)	Return on assets (%)
Gap (US)	14.55	0.83	10.97
Inditex (Spain)	13.80	1.90	15.17
H&M (Sweden)	16.40	2.36	27.46
VF (US)	9.46	0.88	11.27
Next (UK)	5.47	0.64	23.81
Ross Stores (US)	8.61	0.66	20.85
Esprit Holdings (China)	4.35	0.01	(5.66)
Hanesbrands (US)	4.64	0.27	6.58
Abercrombie & Fitch (US)	4.16	0.13	4.29
J. Crew (US)	1.72	0.12	19.10
Gildan Activewear (US)	1.73	0.16	9.43
American Apparel (US)	0.55	(0.04)	(11.97)

Note:
Figures in parentheses denote a loss.
Source: www.hoovers.com; companies' annual reports.

their own designs or corporate and club logos. At the retail level, many different types of retailer compete: independent specialty stores, department stores, and chains such as Gap, Urban Outfitters, H&M, American Eagle, and Forever 21. The price dispersion is wide: at Sears, a basic T-shirt retails at $6.99, while at Nordstrom, a Versace limited-edition T-shirt costs $225. Table 2 shows some leading suppliers of casual clothing.

Dov Charney and the Development of American Apparel

Dov Charney has been described as a "brilliant entrepreneur," "an exhibitionist," a "champion of social liberation," and a "sleaze-ball." In some respects he was a traditionalist: emphasizing his Jewish roots, his affection for the *shmata* business, and his desire to recreate America as a manufacturing nation.

Charney's entrepreneurial interest in the garment business was first demonstrated at age 16, when he purchased American-made T-shirts from K-Mart in the US and then drove them to Canada in a U-Haul truck. He sold them outside the old Montreal Forum at concerts.[5] He dropped out of Tufts University during his senior year, borrowed $10,000 from his father, and moved to South Carolina, where he started his T-shirt business: "Heavy, The American Apparel Company," which went bust when its contract manufacturer closed down production.[6]

Charney moved to California, where in 1998 he met Sam Lim, an owner of a cutting-and-sewing facility located under a freeway in Los Angeles.[7] Together with an associate of Lim's, the pair formed a company named "Two Koreans and a Jew," which eventually developed into American Apparel.[8]

Building American Apparel

Under Charney's leadership, American Apparel developed as a vertically integrated T-shirt manufacturer whose activities extended from knitting cotton yarn, through cutting and sewing, to dyeing and finishing. The main customers were screen printers who printed their own designs and logos and retailed the products. American Apparel's main competitors were the blank T-shirt giants Hanes and Fruit of the Loom. American Apparel differentiated itself by focusing on quality and design. In contrast to the standard loose-fitting, heavy-knit T-shirts, American Apparel offered tightly fitting women's and men's T-shirts with finer thread and a closer knit.

In October 2003, American Apparel opened its first retail store. Charney viewed the Los Angeles store more as an experiment than as a new business: "It's supposed to be a place for some of the intellectuals of the company and customers to hang out . . . It's not a money-maker—let's put it that way."[9] The Los Angeles store was quickly followed by others in New York and Montreal. By the end of 2004, American Apparel operated 34 stores in North America and three in the UK. Charney was totally committed to developing the business. As late as 2005, as CEO of American Apparel, he drew a salary of less than $100,000: his priority was the long-term development of the company. "We need to dig in deeper, to penetrate the market we're in right now . . . We're building our foundation right now. We want to be the best at what we do, and once we are . . . once we're strong, then we can take on the world."[10] By 2005, American Apparel was the largest garment manufacturer in the US.

In December 2007, American Apparel was listed on the New York Stock Exchange. Fueled by the injection of equity capital, American Apparel embarked upon a new phase of expansion, opening 80 stores in 2008 and entering five new countries (Austria, Belgium, Spain, Brazil, and Australia).

The Controversial Mr Charney

Dov Charney's key fashion innovation was in turning T-shirts into garments that enhanced the sexual attractiveness of the wearer. However, sexuality played a wider role in the success of American Apparel. In addition to its sexually provocative advertising, the company had a culture that acknowledged the sexual drives of its customers and its employees and embraced sexual conduct and sexual content as part of openness and creativity. If American Apparel's key product differentiation was the sex appeal of its fashion garments, then sexual openness within the company might enhance its ability to design and market these products.

Charney's own contribution to this culture included his wearing American Apparel underwear (and nothing else) while in the office and sexual relationships with his employees. "I'm not saying I want to screw all the girls at work," stated Charney, "but if I fall in love at work it's going to be beautiful and sexual."[11] Between 2005 and 2007, American Apparel faced four sexual harassment lawsuits, three of which were dropped after confidential settlements were reached. The fourth resulted in a wider investigation by the Los Angeles office of the Equal Employment Opportunity Commission into sexual harassment at American Apparel.[12] Charney attributed the lawsuits to disgruntled employees seeking personal gain by exploiting California's litigious culture.[13]

As a result of the lawsuits, American Apparel required employees to sign a document that declared:

> American Apparel is in the business of designing and manufacturing sexually charged T-shirts and intimate apparel, and uses sexually charged visual and oral communications in its marketing and sales activities. Employees working in the design, sales, marketing and other creative areas of the company will come into contact with sexually charged language and visual images. This is a part of the job for employees working in these areas.[14]

Charney's overt sexuality was not the only source of American Apparel's legal difficulties. In 2009, American Apparel was found to be employing illegal immigrants and was forced to dismiss 1,500 workers. In 2010, its failure to provide accurate financial information to its auditors resulted in a class action from some of its shareholders.

American Apparel's Strategy and Operations

By the beginning of 2012, American Apparel was one of the leading suppliers of T-shirts to the US market, both blank T-shirts sold to screen printers and final products supplied under its own brand through its retail stores. Its Los Angeles manufacturing plant was by far the biggest garment-manufacturing facility in the US. This reflected the dominance of imported garments in the US market: most fashion clothing companies concentrated on design, marketing, and distribution, with manufacturing outsourced and offshored.

The distinctive feature of American Apparel was its high level of vertical integration: not only did it undertake most stages of production at its Los Angeles headquarters but also it performed its own design, marketing, and advertising, and owned and operated all its retail stores, even its overseas stores. As a result, American Apparel's business system achieved remarkable speed and flexibility:

> Our vertically integrated business model, with manufacturing and various other elements of our business processes centered in downtown Los Angeles, allows us to play a role in originating and defining new and innovative trends in fashion, while enabling us to quickly respond to market and customer demand for classic styles and new products. For our wholesale operations, being able to fulfill large orders with quick turn-around allows American Apparel to capture business. The ability to swiftly respond to the market means that our retail operations can deliver on-trend apparel in a timely manner and maximize sales of popular styles by replenishing product that would have otherwise sold out.[15]

From design concept to the American Apparel store rack, a garment took as little as two weeks. Within a day, a designer could come up with an idea, design a garment, create a pattern, cut it, and have it sewn together. By the evening, the garment could be photographed on a model and emailed for Charney's immediate opinion. If the garment was approved by Charney, it would be prepared for testing in a few American Apparel retail stores. Customer purchases were tracked and analyzed, and if the product were successful, it would be put into full production for shipping to the rest of American Apparel's retail locations.

Table 3 shows financial information for the company.

TABLE 3 American Apparel: Selected financial data, 2005–2011 ($million)

	2011	2010	2009	2008	2007	2006	2005
Operating statement items							
Net sales	547.3	533.0	558.8	545.1	387.0	264.7	188.1
Cost of sales	252.4	253.1	238.9	245.9	171.6	138.4	101.0
Gross profit	294.9	279.9	319.9	299.2	215.5	126.3	87.1
Total operating expenses	318.2	330.0	295.5	263.1	184.4	135.1	76.8
of which:							
Selling costs	209.8	218.2	198.5	168.5	115.6	84.0	45.8
Retail store impairment costs	4.3	8.6	3.3	15.6	10.7	6.7	4.2
General and administrative	104.1	103.2	93.6	78.9	58.1	36.8	26.9
Income from operations	(23.3)	(50.1)	24.4	36.1	31.1	9.3	10.2
Interest expense	33.2	23.8	22.6	13.9	17.5	10.8	6.3
Income before income taxes	(37.6)	(74.2)	4.9	21.4	15.3	(0.3)	4.0
Income tax provision	1.7	12.2	3.8	7.3	(0.2)	1.3	0.4
Net income	(39.3)	(86.3)	1.1	14.1	15.5	(1.6)	3.6
Balance sheet items							
Current assets	230.7	216.5	186.3	187.0	152.8	97.0	85.8
of which:							
Inventories	185.8	178.1	141.2	148.2	106.4	76.5	67.5
Total assets	324.7	328.0	327.6	333.0	233.4	163.1	124.2
Current liabilities	143.4	213.2	64.9	74.3	150.7	59.8	44.9
of which:							
Overdraft and current bank debt	52.3	141.8	3.7	3.8	102.8	6.2	9.3
Accounts payable	33.9	31.5	19.7	26.3	21.9	30.1	18.3
Long-term debt	98.9	5.6	71.4	100.0	0.6	52.7	43.0
Total liabilities	276.6	252.9	170.2	196.6	171.5	136.5	110.3
Stockholders' equity	48.1	75.0	157.3	136.4	171.5	11.7	13.9
Cash flows							
Net cash from operations	2.0	(32.0)	45.0	21.2	(5.4)	7.7	(1.1)
Net cash used in investing activities	(10.8)	(15.7)	(20.9)	(72.2)	(23.8)	(16.9)	(15.9)
Net cash provided by financing activities	12.6	48.2	(25.5)	41.2	44.5	10.6	17.4

Note:
Figures in parentheses denote a loss.
Source: American Apparel, 10-K reports, various years.

Product Development and Design

Recreating the T-shirt as a fashion garment was at the heart of American Apparel's business proposition. Design required careful attention to fit, texture, shape-retention, and color. "We've fashionized and brought fashion to the commodity setting," Charney explained, arguing that his main achievement was "feminizing the blank T-shirt industry."[16] Previously, T-shirts were "bulky, one-size-fits-all" garments that were not gender specific. The company explained that:

> We employ an in-house staff of designers and creative professionals to develop updated versions of timeless, iconic styles. Led by our chief executive officer, Dov Charney, this team takes its inspiration from classic styles of the past, as well as the latest emerging fashion trends. Our design team will often continue to update or renew a style long after its launch.[17]

American Apparel employed an in-house team of designers at its Los Angeles headquarters. The team didn't read fashion magazines and paid little attention to catwalk fashion trends. It developed "updated versions of timeless, iconic styles" and took "inspiration from classic styles of the past, as well as the latest emerging fashion trends." [18] The clothing represented a retro urban-chic style with a 1970s flavor. Designers often went to vintage clothing stores to find inspirations for new designs. The team was led by Dov Charney, who hired each member of the product development department, searching for designers he felt had the "eye for what's next."[19] He personally approved all new garment designs. The team took its inspiration from classic styles of the past, as well as from emerging style trends among young adults living in metropolitan cities such as Los Angeles, London, and New York.

By 2009, the company had expanded its product range well beyond the T-shirt. It offered over 20,000 stock keeping units (SKUs), including fabric shirts, dresses, denim jeans, sweaters, jackets, swimwear, babywear, and a variety of accessories, such as bags, hats, scarves, and sunglasses—even sweaters for dogs. American Apparel intended to continue to introduce new merchandise to complement its existing products and draw new customers.

Manufacturing

American Apparel's headquarters and main manufacturing facility were housed at the former Southern Pacific Railroad depot in downtown Los Angeles comprising 800,000 square feet of floor space. Dyeing and finishing were at a separate facility in California. Capacity shortage at its Los Angeles facility resulted in American Apparel expanding production to nearby plants in Hawthorne, South Gate, and Garden Grove. The company described its production operations as follows:

> Purchased yarn is sent to knitters to be knit into "greige" fabric, which is fabric that is not dyed or processed . . . As of December 31, 2011, our knitting facilities knit approximately 85% of the total fabric used in our garments and had approximately 80 employees.
>
> Knitted greige fabric . . . is batched for bleaching and dyeing and transported to our dyeing and finishing facilities, or other commissioned dye houses . . . As of December 31, 2011, our dyeing and finishing facilities in the Los Angeles metropolitan area dye approximately 99% of the total fabric used in our garments and had approximately 200 employees.
>
> Most fabric is shipped to our primary manufacturing facility in downtown Los Angeles, where it is inspected and then cut on manual and automated cutting tables, and subsequently sewn into finished garments . . . Garments are sewn by

teams of sewing operators typically ranging from five to fifteen operators, depending on the complexity of a particular garment. Each sewing operator performs a different sewing operation on a garment before passing it to the next operator. Sewing operators are compensated on a modified piece-rate basis. Quality control personnel inspect finished garments for defects and reject any defective product . . . As of December 31, 2011, approximately 3,000 employees were directly involved in the cutting, sewing, and hosiery operations at the downtown Los Angeles facility.[20]

An employee's occupation was indicated by attire. Piece workers wore casual clothes of jeans and T-shirts. Supervisors, mechanics, cleaners, and cutters wore T-shirts of a particular color with their position labeled in both English and Spanish on the front. Quality-control supervisors wore purple shirts, line supervisors blue shirts, and mechanics red shirts.

Retail and Wholesale Distribution

At the beginning of 2012, American Apparel owned and operated 249 retail stores in 20 countries (Table 4). The company described its retail operations as follows:

> Our retail operations principally target young adults aged 20 to 32 via our unique assortment of fashionable clothing, accessories and compelling in-store experience. We have established a reputation with our customers who are culturally sophisticated, creative, and independent minded. Our product offerings include basic apparel and accessories for men and women, as well as apparel for children. Stores average approximately 2,500–3,000 square feet of selling space. Our stores are located in large metropolitan areas, emerging neighborhoods, and select university communities. We strive to instill enthusiasm and dedication in our store managers and sales associates through regular communication with the stores.[21]

American Apparel favored locations away from traditional high streets using non-traditional retail buildings with unique environments. Store selection and design were undertaken by Jordan Parnass, a lifelong friend of Dov Charney, and his firm JPDA. Location scouts searched cities for areas that were populated by artists and

TABLE 4   American Apparel's retail outlets

No. of retail stores, Dec. 31	2011	2010	2009	2008	2007	2006
US	143	157	160	147	105	93
Canada	37	40	40	37	30	26
International	69	76	81	75	47	30

Source: American Apparel, 10-K report for 2008.

musicians and for the hangouts of young adults. Once an ideal location for a store was spotted, designers from JPDA researched the "regional flavor" and developed design concepts that incorporated this flavor together with the characteristics of the building's structure.[22] Stores included a converted movie theater and a former auto-garage.[23]

American Apparel's wholesale business sold to about a dozen authorized distributors and over 10,000 screen printers. The latter printed blank products with corporate logos, brands, and other images. Wholesale customers were served by a call center at its Los Angeles headquarters. The company prided itself on the fast turnaround of orders: orders received before 6:30 p.m. were shipped the same day.

American Apparel offered online retail sales through its www.americanapparel. com website. There were localized websites for the US, Canada, the UK, Europe, Switzerland, Japan, South Korea, Australia, Mexico, and Brazil.

Tables 5 and 6 show American Apparel's sales, profits, and assets by segment and by country.

TABLE 5 American Apparel's financial results by business segment ($million)

	2011	2010	2009	2008	2007	2006
US wholesale						
Sales	156.5	149.0	141.5	162.7	144.5	127.8
Gross profit	42.6	32.0	36.2	46.9	40.1	31.7
Operating income[a]	22.4	11.2	15.5	21.0	19.7	14.2
Identifiable assets	141.7	130.0	153.7	178.1	125.4	n.a.
Capital expenditure	3.6	4.7	4.6	7.1	5.3	4.3
US retail						
Sales	174.8	177.6	191.3	168.7	115.6	80.2
Gross profit	117.2	117.5	136.4	127.9	88.8	63.0
Operating income[a]	(4.7)	(18.5)	17.3	33.5	24.8	11.5
Identifiable assets	84.8	92.9	119.4	98.9	60.0	n.a.
Capital expenditure	4.9	7.6	11.2	30.9	9.3	8.6
Canada						
Sales	61.9	65.6	69.0	67.3	42.4	30.6
Gross profit	35.8	43.3	43.2	40.1	27.1	19.2
Operating income[a]	(3.7)	5.1	14.0	10.8	1.5	3.5
Identifiable assets	30.1	32.9	17.5	17.1	16.5	n.a.
Capital expenditure	0.4	1.5	1.4	4.7	2.0	1.7
International						
Sales	154.2	140.7	156.9	146.4	84.5	46.4
Gross profit	99.3	87.1	104.0	84.2	59.4	31.7
Operating income[a]	8.4	(5.1)	15.3	8.0	14.8	4.7
Identifiable assets	68.0	72.2	37.0	38.9	31.5	n.a.
Capital expenditure	2.1	2.0	3.8	18.3	7.1	2.4

Notes:
Figures in parentheses denote a loss.
n.a.: not applicable.
[a] Before corporate expense, interest, other income, and foreign currency adjustment.
Source: American Apparel, 10-K report for 2008.

TABLE 6 Geographical distribution of sales and fixed assets, 2009–2011 ($million)

	2011	2010	2009
Net sales by location of customer			
United States	331,290	326,607	332,846
Canada	61,866	65,638	69,983
Europe (excluding UK)	68,130	68,958	81,252
United Kingdom	40,039	32,535	34,214
Japan	14,176	10,716	14,122
Korea	9,749	9,547	9,443
Australia	11,557	9,474	9,105
Other foreign countries	10,529	9,514	8,810
Total consolidated net sales	547,336	532,989	558,775
Property and equipment, at December 31			
United States	49,906	61,754	71,451
Canada	5,041	7,063	8,767
Europe (excluding UK)	4,134	6,257	9,987
United Kingdom	5,091	5,784	6,292
Japan	1,141	1,290	2,827
Korea	308	394	632
Australia	1,146	1,311	1,299
Other foreign countries	671	1,547	2,055
Total consolidated	67,438	85,400	103,310
Total property and equipment	67,438	85,400	103,310

Source: American Apparel, 10-K report for 2008.

Employee Relations: A "Sweat-Shop" Free Environment

American Apparel summarized its approach to human resource management as follows:

> We view our employees as long-term investments and adhere to a philosophy of providing employees with decent working conditions in a technology driven environment which allows us to attain improved efficiency, while promoting employee loyalty.[24]

Rates of pay exceeded the going rates for the job: even the lowest-paid workers earned around double the minimum wage. Workers were offered subsidized healthcare for themselves and their families, subsidized lunches, free parking, bus passes, and low-cost auto insurance. There were on-site massage therapists who provided regular services for all employees. Yoga classes were also available, along with a health-and-wellness specialist who provided counseling. Workers could take bathroom breaks at any time and use their cell phones for quick personal calls during working hours. Workers received training to improve their job and management skills as well as English and math classes. The human resources department also assisted employees in completing their tax returns and in opening bank accounts.

Marketing and Social Responsibility

American Apparel's approach to marketing was radically different from that of most fashion clothing companies. It developed all of its marketing and advertising in-house. Its advertisements were striking. The photographs used in advertising and promotion were often taken by Charney and other amateur photographers. Models were all amateurs—employees, customers, and friends—who posed without makeup or fancy hair-dos. They did not conform to conventional notions of style and beauty: they often featured skin blemishes and asymmetrical features. Not only are the models natural and ordinary, so too are the poses and locations: American Apparel ads depict young men and women sitting on the floor, lying on beds, or lounging on a sofa. As the *New York Times* observed: the advertisements have a "flashbulb-lighted, lo-fi sultriness to them" looking more like photos on Facebook than ads on a billboard or glossy magazine.[25]

They were also sexually suggestive. In April 2012, Britain's Advertising Standards Authority banned eight images on American Apparel's website it found objectionable. Its objection referred explicitly to the "voyeuristic and amateurish quality to the images which served to heighten the impression that the ads were exploitative of women and inappropriately sexualized young women."

American Apparel also avoided mainstream media. Its advertising was directed mainly to online sites and alternative newspapers such as *The Village Voice*, *LA Weekly*, and *The Onion*, and online publications such as *Purple Fashion* and *Fantastic Man*.

American Apparel was active in social and political causes. It hired employees from Homeboy Industries, an organization that assisted at-risk youths and former gang members. It was prominent in supporting free trade and immigrant rights. It used its "Made in USA" and "Sweatshop Free" credentials as part of its advertising messages. It also pioneered environmentally friendly clothing, including its *Sustainable Edition* organic cotton line.

Managing Turnaround, 2010–2012

Measures to stabilize American Apparel's financial position included the following:

- *New senior management appointments* included Marty Staff (previously of Ralph Lauren and Calvin Klein) as head of business development, Thomas Casey (previously Blockbuster's CFO) as company president, and John Lutterell (previously with Gap) as CFO. Following disagreements with CEO Charney, Marty Staff left American Apparel in October 2011. He commented on leaving: "Dov is a one-man band and I don't think I realized how singular that vision is. When I joined, I don't think I realized how actively Dov manages every part of the company—from design to IT to marketing to finance. All roads lead through Dov."[26] Tom Casey left the following month.
- *Store closures*: A review of the performance and prospects for each retail outlet resulted in a number of store closures. During 2010 and 2011, the number of American Apparel stores worldwide was cut from 281 to 249.

- *Refinancing*: Restoring American Apparel's liquidity position involved rene-gotiating its loan agreement with Lion Capital, borrowing $80 million from Crystal Financial LLC at 9% above LIBOR, and raising $21.7 million from issu-ing common stock.

- *Cost-cutting measures* included cost efficiencies in raw material purchases, streamlining logistics operations, reducing corporate expenses, improving merchandizing, and rationalizing staffing levels.

- *Increasing sales*: A major initiative by Marty Staff was to expand American Apparel's wholesale business by exploiting its fast-turnaround capability and to grow sales in other retailers' stores. During 2011, American Apparel expanded its sales through London's Selfridges and Paris's Galeries Lafayette. American Apparel also sought to boost retail sales by means of promo-tional offers, especially through Groupon. Through improving the American Apparel website and the fulfillment process, the company increased online sales: during 2011, online consumer net sales increased by 14.5% to $24.3 million (US online sales were included in the sales figures for the US whole-sale segment).

Looking to the Future

By spring 2012, American Apparel's financial situation was looking much more sta-ble. Sales for the first quarter of 2012 were 14% above the previous year and Dov Charney expressed optimism over the company's ability to refinance its borrowings at lower rates of interest.

However, no fundamental redirection of American Apparel's strategy had taken place. The company's reports and press releases affirmed its commitment to vertical integration, to continuing to expand its "retail footprint," and to broaden its product range.

American Apparel had demonstrated the market potential for premium-priced, casual knitwear that embodied "urban cool." But was this business model, which rested upon American Apparel's LA-based production facilities, globally scalable? International expansion meant longer supply chains, increased logistical complexity, and increased diversity of customers. The broadening product range added fur-ther complexity to purchasing, manufacturing, and distribution. Overall, American Apparel's tightly coordinated, vertically integrated business model was being stretched in multiple directions.

Even if this strategy were sound, American Apparel's capacity to implement it effectively was open to doubt. As several of the new senior management hires had discovered, American Apparel was still Dov Charney's baby and, despite its size and geographical spread, he remained the critical link that held everything together. The enforced pause in American Apparel's expansion had allowed the company to develop its financial, operational, and logistical systems, but did it possess the mana-gerial capacity to cope with a new round of expansion?

Notes

1. American Apparel, Investor Presentation June 2009, Piper Jaffray Consumer Conference, June 9, 2009, http://investors.americanapparel.net/events.cfm, accessed October 29, 2009.

2. "The rise and fall of American Apparel," *Guardian*, Wednesday 25 August 2010, http://www.guardian.co.uk/business/2010/aug/25/rise-fall-american-apparel?INTCMP=SRCH, accessed September 23, 2012.

3. P. Rivoli, *The Travels of a T-Shirt in the Global Economy: An Economist Examines the Markets, Power, and Politics of World Trade*, 2nd edn (John Wiley & Sons, Ltd, Chichester, 2009).

4. "Textiles and Apparel Market Prices," http://www.emergingtextiles.com/?q=art&s=110501-us-cotton-knot-shirt-import&r=free, accessed April 30, 2012.

5. D. Charney, interview, "The New Rich," *20/20*, ABC, 2006; M. Mendelssohn, "Sweatshop-Free Zone," *The Gazette*, May 23, 2004.

6. D. Charney, interview, "The New Rich," *20/20*, ABC (2006); M. Silcott, "Dov Charney, 32, Senior Partner, American Apparel," *The Counselor*, April, 2001.

7. J. Elwain, "American Apparel Takes on the T-Shirt," *Bobbin Magazine*, May, 2001.

8. A. A. Nieder, "The Branding of Blank Tees," http://americanapparel.net/presscenter/articles/20000818caapparelnews.html, accessed August 18, 2008.

9. C. M. Chensvold, "American Apparel Opens Three Retail Stores," *California Apparel News*, October 31, 2003.

10. J. Elwain, "American Apparel Takes on the T-Shirt," *Bobbin Magazine*, May, 2001.

11. J. Mankiewicz "Sexy Marketing or Sexual Harassment?" NBC Dateline, http://www.msnbc.msn.com/id/14082498/, accessed July 28, 2006.

12. American Apparel, 10-K report for 2008, 2009, p. 31.

13. "Living on the Edge at American Apparel," *Business Week*, July 27, 2007.

14. J. Wolf, "And You Thought Abercrombie & Fitch Was Pushing It?" *New York Times Magazine*, April 23, 2006.

15. American Apparel, 10-K report for 2011, p. 7.

16. D. Charney, Interview, "Worldwide," Chicago Public Radio, November 13, 2003.

17. American Apparel, 10-K report for 2011, p. 10.

18. American Apparel, 10-K report for 2011, p. 7.

19. D. Charney, interview, "Charlie Rose," KQED9 (TV broadcasting station), July 2006.

20. American Apparel, 10-K report for 2011, pp. 8–9.

21. American Apparel, 10-K report for 2011, p. 9.

22. A. DiNardo, "The Anti-Brand," *Visual Store*, December 4, 2006.

23. A. DiNardo, "The Anti-Brand," *Visual Store*, December 4, 2006.

24. American Apparel, 10-K report for 2011, p. 11.

25. J. Wolf, "And You Thought Abercrombie & Fitch Was Pushing It?" *New York Times Magazine*, April 23, 2006.

26. "Marty Staff explains he left American Apparel because of Dov Charney," *Fashionably Just*, October 29, 2011.

 A video clip relating to this case is available in your interactive e-book at **www.wileyopenpage.com**

Case 17 Outback Steakhouse: Going International

By 1995, Outback Steakhouse was one of the fastest-growing and most acclaimed restaurant chains in North America. Astute positioning within the intensely competitive US restaurant business, the high quality of its food and service, and a relaxed ambiance that echoed its Australian theme had propelled the chain's spectacular growth (Table 1).

Chairman and co-founder Chris Sullivan believed that at the current rate of growth (around 70 new restaurants each year) Outback would be facing market saturation within five years. Outback's growth opportunities were either to diversify into alternative restaurant concepts (it had already started its Carrabba's Italian Grill restaurants) or to expand internationally.

> We can do 500–600 [Outback] restaurants, and possibly more over the next five years . . . [however] the world is becoming one big market, and we want to be in place so we don't miss that opportunity. There are some problems, some challenges with it, but at this point there have been some casual restaurant chains that have gone [outside the US] and their average unit sales are way, way above the sales level they enjoyed in the United States. So the potential is there. Obviously,

TABLE 1 Outback Steakhouse, Inc.: Growth and profitability, 1990–1995

	Revenue ($million)	Net income ($million)	Return on average equity (%)	Company-owned restaurants	Franchised and JV restaurants	Total restaurants
1990	34	2.3	41.2	23	0	23
1991	91	6.1	34.4	49	0	49
1992	189	14.8	23.6	81	4	85
1993	310	25.2	22.2	124	24	148
1994	516	43.4	27.4	164	50	214
1995	734	61.3	27.0	262	58	320[a]

Note:

[a]Of these, 297 were Outback Steakhouses and 23 were Carrabba's Italian Grills.

By Marilyn L. Taylor and Robert M. Grant. This case is an abridged version of an earlier case "Outback Steakhouse Goes International" by Marilyn L. Taylor, George M. Puia, Krishnan Ramaya, and Madelyn Gengelbach (used by permission of the authors). It has been augmented with material from company reports and from "A Stake in the Business," by Chris T. Sullivan, *Harvard Business Review*, September 2005, pp. 57–64. Copyright © 2012 Marilyn L. Taylor and Robert M. Grant.

there are some distribution issues to work out, things like that, but we are real excited about the future internationally. That will give us some potential outside the United States to continue to grow as well.[1]

In late 1994, Hugh Connerty was appointed the president of Outback International to lead the company's overseas expansion. Connerty had considerable experience in the restaurant business and had been Outback's most successful franchisee, developing a number of Outback restaurants in northern Florida and southern Georgia. Connerty grasped the opportunity enthusiastically:

> We have had hundreds of franchise requests from all over the world. [So] it took about two seconds for me to make that decision [to become president of Outback International] . . . I've met with and talked to other executives who have international divisions. All of them have the same story. At some point in time a light goes on and they say, "Gee we have a great product. Where do we start?" I have traveled quite a bit on holiday. The world is not as big as you think it is. Most companies who have gone global have not used any set strategy.[2]

Connerty's challenges were to decide in which countries to locate; whether to franchise, directly manage, or joint venture; how the Outback restaurant concept should be adapted to overseas markets; and what pace of expansion to target.

Outback's Strategy

Outback was founded by Chris Sullivan, Bob Basham, and Tim Gannon, who had met as management trainees at the Steak and Ale restaurant chain. They noted that while red meat consumption was declining, steakhouses remained extremely popular. They saw an untapped opportunity for serving quality steaks at an affordable price, filling the gap between high-priced and budget steakhouses. They believed an Australian theme would associate the restaurants with adventure, the outdoors, and a friendly, casual atmosphere. Outback would differentiate itself by the excellence of its food and by offering a dining experience that would be cheerful, fun, and comfortable:

The company believed that it differentiated its Outback Steakhouse restaurants by:

- emphasizing consistently high-quality ingredients and preparation of a limited number of menu items that appeal to a broad array of tastes;
- featuring generous portions at moderate prices;
- attracting a diverse mix of customers through a casual dining atmosphere emphasizing highly attentive service;
- hiring and retaining experienced restaurant management by providing general managers the opportunity to purchase a 10% interest in the restaurants they manage;
- limiting service to dinner (generally from 4:30 p.m. to 11:00 p.m.), which reduces the hours of restaurant management and employees.[3]

Quality of food was paramount. This began with the raw materials. Outback viewed suppliers as partners and was committed to work with them to ensure quality and to develop long-term relationships. Outback's food costs were among the highest in the industry, not just in terms of ingredients but also in preparation, with most items prepared from scratch within each restaurant. For example, Outback's croutons were made daily on site with 17 different seasonings and cut into irregular shapes to indicate that they were handmade.

The emphasis on quality extended to service. Among Outback's "principles and beliefs" was "No rules, just right": employees would do whatever was needed to meet the needs and preferences of customers.

Quality and service were achieved through a management model which contrasted sharply with that of most other restaurant chains. CEO Chris Sullivan explained Outback's approach:

> There are three kinds of turnover in the restaurant business—customer, employee and table. Most restaurant chains worry about the first, resign themselves to the second, and encourage the third. At Outback it's not as straightforward as that; we believe that all three are integrally related. Specifically, our management model and approach reflect the importance we place on fighting employee turnover. One of our catchphrases is "fully staffed, fully trained." You can't be either of those things if a restaurant is a revolving door. Besides, customers like to see a familiar face.
>
> Restaurant work can be stressful. The better the staffers, the more intent they will be on doing things right—and the more frustrated they will become with the facilities and tools they've been given if they get in the way, whether the problem is dull knives or not enough burners . . . Bob Basham insisted on making all of our kitchens at least 2500 square feet and keeping lots of cool air flowing through them. The kitchens occupy half of the typical Outback restaurant's floor plan space that other restaurants allocate to revenue-producing tables. But we wanted to offer a bigger menu than the typical casual restaurant, so we knew we would have to give the cooks and prep people the space to pull it off.
>
> Likewise, we never assign our servers to cover more than three tables; the industry standard is five or six . . . A wide range of customers choose to dine with us on a variety of occasions . . . It has to be the customer who sets the pace for the meal, not the server or the kitchen staff. But for that to happen our servers need time to figure out the mood and expectations of a given table on a given evening, and the kitchen has to be well enough staffed and equipped to turn around orders without delay. . .
>
> We think that employees who are not overstressed stay in their jobs longer than those who are; that employees who stay have time to master their jobs, become familiar with their regular customers' preferences, and learn to operate as teams; that the combination of mastery, memory, and calm is more likely to afford customers themselves a relaxing, enjoyable experience; and that diners who are not hustled through their meals are more likely to come back. In short, low employee turnover leads to well-paced table turnover, which ultimately leads to low customer turnover.[4]

Outback's strategy was distinctive in other respects too. First, Outback served only dinner. According to Sullivan, the conventional wisdom that restaurants needed to be open for lunch and dinner in order to make efficient use of capital ignored the hidden costs of longer hours of opening: the costs of extra staff and employee turnover, the disruptive effects of shift changes, and the fact that employees who worked lunchtime would be tired in the evening, the time when they needed to be at their freshest. Similarly for the food: food prepared in the morning would lose its freshness by evening.

Second, Outback located in residential areas rather than downtown. This reinforced the merits of evening-only opening, kept rents low, and encouraged customer and employee loyalty. As Sullivan explained: "The suburbs are our outback."

Third, Outback's management and ownership structure was unusual. Each of Outback's directly owned restaurants was a separate partnership where Outback Steakhouse, Inc. was the general partner owning between 71% and 90%. Each restaurant was headed by a "managing partner," while between 10 and 20 restaurants within an area were overseen by a regional manager, who was called a "joint venture partner," or "JVP." Sullivan explained the relationship as follows:

> The terms "managing partner" and "joint venture partner" aren't symptoms of title inflation. They straightforwardly describe people's roles and relationships to the organization. All managing partners, most of whom start as hourly employees, must invest $25 000 of their own money—not because Outback needs the capital, but because their financial contributions make them committed investors in the business they'll be running. They must also sign a five-year contract, and they are granted roughly 1000 shares of restricted stock, which vest only at the end of their contracts. In return, managing partners can keep 10% of the cash flow their restaurants generate each year. The idea is to ensure that at the end of five years each of them will have stock worth around $100 000 . . . At the end of five years, successful managers are encouraged to sign up with the same restaurant or to manage a different one. . .
>
> Outback's JVPs, who number around 60, must invest $50000, which entitles them to 10% of cash flow of all the restaurants they oversee after the partners have received their 10%. Whereas the managing partners focus on operations and community relations, the Japes focus on monitoring performance, finding and developing new locations, and identifying and developing new managers, managing partners, and Japes like themselves. The Japes are the only management layer between the six operations executives at headquarters and the managing partners at the individual restaurants.[5]

Initially, all Outback restaurants were directly owned and managed. However, in 1990, Outback began selective franchising, but only to franchisees who were fully committed to Outback's principles and beliefs.

Human resource management was also distinctly different from most restaurant chains'. One executive described Outback's approach as: "Tough on results, but kind with people." Employee selection was rigorous and included aptitude tests, psychological profiles, and interviews with at least two managers. The goal was to create an entrepreneurial climate that emphasized learning and personal growth. All employees were eligible for health insurance and the company's stock ownership plan. All employees were expected to contribute to continuous innovation and improvement:

> Almost all our innovations bubble up from the individual restaurant, often originating with our servers or kitchen staffers. They'll suggest an idea to the restaurant manager who will try it on an experimental basis. If the recommended menu or process change clicks, the managing partner communicates the idea to his or her JVP . . . If the suggested change meets company standards, videos and other materials showing how to implement it are distributed to other JVPs. Each is free to take it or not.[6]

During 1993, Outback formed a joint venture with Houston-based Carrabba's Italian Grill and, in 1995, acquired the rights to develop Carrabba's nationally. Carrabba's Italian Grills were run with an ownership structure and operating and management practices that were similar to Outback Steakhouse's.

Preparing for International Expansion

Hugh Connerty, president of Outback International, outlined his approach to international expansion as follows:

> We have built Outback one restaurant at a time . . . There are some principles and beliefs we live by. It almost sounds cultish. We want International to be an opportunity for our suppliers. We feel strongly about the relationships with our suppliers. We have never changed suppliers. We have an undying commitment to them and in exchange we want them to have an undying commitment to us. They have to prove they can build plants [abroad].
>
> I think it would be foolish of us to think that we are going to go around the world buying property and understanding the laws in every country, the culture in every single country. So the approach that we are going to take is that we will franchise the international operation with company-owned stores here and franchises there so that will allow us to focus on what I believe is our pure strength, a support operation.[7]

Connerty believed that his experience in developing Outback franchises in the US would provide the guidelines for overseas expansion:

> Every one of the franchisees lives in their areas. I lived in the area I franchised. I had relationships that helped with getting permits. That isn't any different than the rest of the world. The loyalties of individuals that live in their respective areas [will be important]. We will do the franchises one by one. The biggest decision we have to make is how we pick that franchise partner. That is what we will concentrate on. We are going to select a person who has synergy with us, who thinks like us, who believes in the principles and beliefs.
>
> Trust is foremost and sacred. The trust between [Outback] and the individual franchisees is not to be violated. The company grants franchises one at a time. It takes a lot of trust to invest millions of dollars without any assurance that you will be able to build another one.[8]

As for the geographical pattern of expansion, Connerty's initial thoughts were to begin close to home before going on to tackle Latin America and the Far East:

> The first year will be Canada. Then we'll go to Hawaii. Then we'll go to South America and then develop our relationships in the Far East, Korea, Japan . . . the Orient. The second year we'll begin a relationship in Great Britain and from there a natural progression throughout Europe. But we view it as a very long-term project. I have learned that people [in other countries] think very different than Americans.[9]

Overseas Expansion by US Restaurant Chains

The international market offered substantial growth opportunities for US restaurant chains. For fast-food franchise chains—notably McDonald's, Burger King, and Kentucky Fried Chicken (KFC)—international sales accounted for up to one-half of total sales, although for many "international" was limited to Canada and Puerto Rico. Among "casual dining" chains—such as Denny's, Applebee's, T.G.I. Friday's, and Tony Roma's—relatively few had ventured beyond North America. Table 2 shows the international presence of leading US restaurant franchise chains.

The attraction of overseas markets was that their restaurants markets were typically less saturated than those of the US and most of the local competition was made up of independent, family-owned restaurants rather than large chains. In overseas markets it was anticipated that market trends would follow those of the US, in particular that greater affluence and a declining role of family life would result in increased eating away from home.

It was notable that, in overseas markets, not only had success been achieved principally by fast-food chains but also most of the leaders were subsidiaries of large multinationals with many decades of international experience. For example, KFC, Taco Bell, and Pizza Hut were subsidiaries of PepsiCo, while Burger King was a subsidiary of British conglomerate Grand Metropolitan.

A key impetus to overseas expansion was the maturing of the US market. By 1994, there were over 3,000 franchisers in the US operating close to 600,000 franchised outlets. Not only was competition intense but also growth was slowing. Sales per store were growing at 3% during the early 1990s.

However, overseas markets also represented a substantial management challenge. Among the problems that other restaurant chains had encountered were the following:

- *Market demand*: The extent to which market demand existed for a particular type of restaurant depended on levels of disposable income, urbanization,

TABLE 2   The ten largest US restaurant franchise chains, 1994

	Total sales ($million)	International sales ($million)	Total outlets	International outlets
McDonald's	25,986	11,046	15,205	5,461
Burger King	7,500	1,400	7,684	1,357
KFC	7,100	3,600	9,407	4,258
Taco Bell	4,290	130	5,614	162
Wendy's	4,277	390	4,411	413
Hardee's	3,491	63	3,516	72
Dairy Queen	3,170	300	3,516	628
Domino's	2,500	415	5,079	840
Subway	2,500	265	179	8,450
Little Caesars	2,000	70	4,855	155

Source: "Top 50 Franchises," *Restaurant Business*, November 1, 1995, pp. 35–41.

demographics, and a host of other social, economic, and lifestyle factors. Most critical to a specific company were national preferences with regard to cuisine and dining conventions. Even McDonald's, whose name had become synonymous with global standardization, adapted substantially to local differences: "Croque McDos" in France, rice burgers in Hong Kong, "McArabia Koftas" in Saudi Arabia, kosher outlets in Israel, no beef or pork products in India.

● *Cultural and social factors* are critical influences on customer preferences with regard to menus, restaurant facilities, and overall ambiance; they are also important with regard to employee management practices and entrepreneurial potential.

● *Infrastructure*: Transportation and communication, basic utilities such as power and water, and locally available supplies were important elements in the decision to introduce a particular restaurant concept. A restaurant must have the ability to get resources to its location. Easy access to the raw materials for food preparation, equipment for manufacture of food served, and mobility for employees and customers were essential.

● *Raw material supplies*: Overseas restaurant chains needed local supplies of food and drink. The US International Trade Commission noted that: "International franchisers frequently encounter problems finding supplies in sufficient quantity, of consistent quality, and at stable prices. Physical distance also can adversely affect a franchise concept and arrangement. Long distances create communication and transportation problems, which may complicate the process of sourcing supplies, overseeing operations, or providing quality management services to franchisees."[10] While a franchise chain could develop its own supply chain e.g., McDonald's when it entered the Soviet Union, the investment of management time and money could be substantial.

● *Regulations and trade restrictions*: Import restrictions are relatively unimportant in the restaurant business given that most food products are locally sourced. However, some countries have made the import of restaurant equipment difficult and expensive. Restrictions on foreign direct investment are of major significance only in emerging market countries. Far more challenging are national regulations relating to food standards, business licensing, and business contracts. Establishing new businesses in most countries involves far more regulation than within the US. Franchise agreements are an especially difficult area because they involve complex contractual agreements between franchisor and franchisee regarding trademark licensing, royalty payments, and requirements for quality control and quality monitoring. Despite the provisions of the Uruguay Round's General Agreement on Trade in Services, most countries failed to make public their restrictions on franchising. In some countries some usual terms of franchise agreements have been viewed as restraints on commerce. Employment law was also important, particularly with regard to restrictions on employers' ability to dismiss or lay off employees and requirements for union recognition and national collective bargaining arrangements over wages and working conditions.

Notes

1. M. L. Taylor, G. M. Puia, K. Ramaya, and M. Gengelback, "Outback Steakhouse Goes International," in A. A. Thompson and A. J. Strickland, *Strategic Management: Concepts and Cases*, 11th edn, McGraw-Hill, New York, 1999, pp. C296–7. Reproduced by kind permission of the authors and NACRA.

2. M. L. Taylor, G. M. Puia, K. Ramaya, and M. Gengelback, "Outback Steakhouse Goes International," in A. A. Thompson and A. J. Strickland, *Strategic Management: Concepts and Cases*, 11th edn, McGraw-Hill, New York, 1999, p. C291.

3. Outback Steakhouse, Inc., 10K report, 1996.

4. Reprinted by permission of Harvard Business Review. From "A Stake in the Business" by Chris T. Sullivan, pp. 57–64, September 2005. Copyright © 2005 by the Harvard Business School Publishing Corporation; all rights reserved.

5. Reprinted by permission of Harvard Business Review. From "A Stake in the Business" by Chris T. Sullivan, pp. 57–64, September 2005. Copyright © 2005 by the Harvard Business School Publishing Corporation; all rights reserved.

6. Reprinted by permission of Harvard Business Review. From "A Stake in the Business" by Chris T. Sullivan, pp. 57–64, September 2005. Copyright © 2005 by the Harvard Business School Publishing Corporation; all rights reserved.

7. M. L. Taylor, G. M. Puia, K. Ramaya, and M. Gengelback, "Outback Steakhouse Goes International," in A. A. Thompson and A. J. Strickland, *Strategic Management: Concepts and Cases*, 11th edn, McGraw-Hill, New York, 1999, p. C297. Reproduced by kind permission of the authors and NACRA.

8. M. L. Taylor, G. M. Puia, K. Ramaya, and M. Gengelback, "Outback Steakhouse Goes International," in A. A. Thompson and A. J. Strickland, *Strategic Management: Concepts and Cases*, 11th edn, McGraw-Hill, New York, 1999, p. C297. Reproduced by kind permission of the authors and NACRA.

9. M. L. Taylor, G. M. Puia, K. Ramaya, and M. Gengelback, "Outback Steakhouse Goes International," in A. A. Thompson and A. J. Strickland, *Strategic Management: Concepts and Cases*, 11th edn, McGraw-Hill, New York, 1999, p. C299. Reproduced by kind permission of the authors and NACRA.

10. US International Trade Commission, *Industry and Trade Summary: Franchising* (Washington, DC, 1995, pp. 15–16).

A video clip relating to this case is available in your interactive e-book at **www.wileyopenpage.com**

Case 18 Vodafone in 2012: Rethinking International Strategy

In May 2012, Vittorio Colao was approaching the fourth anniversary of his appointment as CEO of Vodafone PLC. His four years of leadership had been a relatively quiet time for Vodafone's 84,000 employees. Each of Colao's predecessors has been associated with ambitious development plans and major strategic changes at the company. Vodafone's first CEO, Sir Gerald Whent (1988–1996), had built Vodafone into Britain's leading provider of mobile telecommunications. His successor, Sir Christopher Gent (1997–2003), had led hectic international expansion that had turned Vodafone into the world's biggest telecom operator. Arun Sarin (2003–2008) pushed the integration of Vodafone's sprawling empire.

By contrast, Colao had not unveiled a new strategic vision for Vodafone; from the moment he took up the CEO's job, he made clear that his stewardship would be devoted to improving Vodafone's anemic profitability. In his first strategy announcement in November 2008, and in subsequent presentations over the next three years, he outlined the initiatives Vodafone would take to boost its bottom-line performance:

- Improving operational performance through including both cost reduction and enhanced customer service.
- Pursuing growth opportunities in three main areas: emerging markets, mobile data services, and comprehensive telecom solutions for business customers ("enterprise partners").
- Driving shareholder returns through a disciplined approach to capital investment and making selective divestment in situations where assets were worth more to a potential buyer than they were to Vodafone.

By the time Vodafone announced its annual results for the financial year to March 31st, 2012, it was clear that the strategy was bearing fruit, despite the difficult economic conditions that Vodafone was facing in its core European markets (Table 1 details Vodafone's financial performance). For Vodafone's long-suffering shareholders, the new strategic direction was particularly welcome. "After years of acquisition-fuelled growth, a focus on the more mundane matter of efficiency is just what the world's biggest mobile operator needs," proclaimed the *Financial*

This case was prepared by Robert M. Grant. ©2012 Robert M. Grant.

TABLE 1   Vodafone Group PLC: Financial highlights, 2005–2011 (£million, except where indicated)

(Year ended 31 March)	2012	2011	2010	2009	2008	2007	2006	2005
Income statement								
Revenue	46,417	45,884	44,472	41,017	35,478	31,104	29,350	26,678
Operating (loss)/profit	11,187	5,596	9,480	5,857	10,047	(1,564)	(14,084)	7,878
Adjusted operating profit[a]	11,532	11,800	11,456	11,757	10,075	9,531	9,399	8,353
(Loss)/profit before taxation	9,549	9,498	8,674	4,189	9,001	(2,383)	(14,853)	7,285
Net (loss)/profit for the financial year	7,003	7,870	8,618	3,080	6,756	(5,297)	(21,821)	6,518
Cash flows								
Net cash flows from operating activities	14,824	15,392	13,064	12,213	10,474	10,328	10,190	9,240
Net cash flows from investing activities	(6,307)	(5,658)	(7,437)	(6,834)	(8,544)	3,865	(6,654)	(4,122)
Free cash flow[b]	8,518	7,049	7,244	4,987	5,540	6,127	6,418	6,592
Balance sheet data								
Total assets	139,576	151,220	156,985	152,699	127,270	109,617	126,738	147,197
Shareholders' equity	78,202	87,555	90,381	86,162	78,043	67,067	85,425	113,800
Long-term debt	28,362	28,375	28,632	22,662	17,798	16,750	14,898	12,246
Profit ratios								
Operating profit/total assets (%)	8.0	3.7	6.0	3.8	`8.0	(1.4)	(11.1)	5.4
Return on equity[c] (%)	9.0	9.0	9.5	3.6	8.7	(7.8)	(23.6)	5.9

Notes:
[a]Excludes non-operating income of associates, impairment losses, and other income and expense.
[b]Free cash flow measures cash available for reinvestment, shareholder returns, or debt reduction. It is calculated by subtracting net expenditures on fixed assets from operating cash flow.
[c]After tax (loss)/profit as a percentage of shareholders' equity.

Times' Lex column.[1] During 2011, Vodafone was able to launch a £4 billion share buy-back program (financed by the sale of its 44% stake in the French mobile phone business SFR) and offer a £4.5 billion special dividend to shareholders (financed by a $10 billion payout by its US joint venture, Verizon Wireless). Under Colao's tenure, Vodafone's shares had increased by 17% (Figure 1), a sharp contrast to its European peers (over the same period, July 1, 2008 to May 7, 2012, Deutsche Telekom was down 5%, Telefónica had declined by 34%, and France Telecom by 45%).

However, despite winning support for his leadership both within Vodafone and among investors, Colao realized that, while cost cutting, asset pruning, and portfolio adjustments were essential to putting Vodafone on a more secure financial footing, they did not address the big question marks that clouded Vodafone's future.

Foremost among these was Vodafone's international strategy. The most distinctive feature of Vodafone's competitive positioning within wireless communication services was its international spread: with 302 million mobile customers and a presence

FIGURE 1 Vodafone shareprice, 2007–2012 (pence)

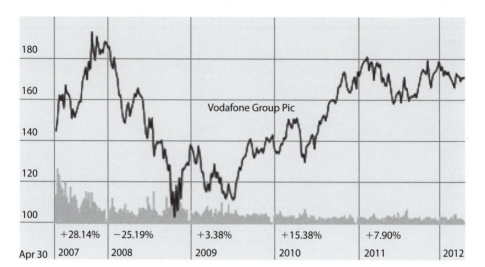

in 52 countries of the world, Vodafone offered a global presence that was unmatched in the industry (Table 2). But how far could this broad international scope be translated into a competitive advantage for Vodafone? Vodafone had been created as a portfolio of largely independent national operators sharing a common brand and a common approach to business. A critical issue for Colao was how far Vodafone could better exploit its global presence through closer cross-border integration of its functions and operations. Despite the efforts of Colao's predecessor, Arun Saran, to create a single global presence through his "One Vodafone" strategy, the potential for integration had been constrained by Vodafone's lack of control over some of its businesses. Some of Colao's most significant strategic decisions had been the divestment of Vodafone's minority investments, most notably in Japan, China, and France (Table 2). Still unresolved was the future of Vodafone's biggest minority holding: its 45% ownership of Verizon Wireless.

Vodafone's ability to leverage its international presence was especially important given the major changes taking place in the telecommunications sector. Technological changes, notably the introduction of third generation (3G) and now fourth generation (4G), had spurred the development of mobile internet access and the introduction of a wide range of hand-held mobile devices, most notably smartphones and tablet computers. These technological developments had been exploited by enterprising companies such as Apple and Google to establish themselves as leading players within the mobile communication sector. Vodafone was investing heavily to ensure that it was a leader in providing mobile broadband connectivity. However, the problem was that control over value-adding applications was increasingly being lost to the owners of handset platforms (Apple, Google, and RIM) with the risk that Vodafone and other wireless service companies became providers of commoditized connection services. If the service providers were to regain strategic leadership within the sector, Vodafone, because of its size and global scope, was best positioned to lead the initiative.

TABLE 2   Vodafone's global reach, March 2011 (including customer numbers, in millions)

Customers of controlled businesses				Partner markets	
	2011	2008	2005	Country	Operator
Germany	36.7	35.5	29.2	Afghanistan	Roshan
Italy	23.4	22.9	18.2	Armenia	MTS
Spain	17.3	16.9	12.9	Austria	A1
UK	19.1	18.7	16.3	Bahrain	Zain
Albania	1.6	1.4	0.7	Belgium	Proximus
Greece	3.9	5.9	4.4	Bulgaria	Mobiltel
Ireland	2.2	2.2	2.0	Caribbean	Digicel
Malta	0.2	0.2	0.2	Chile	Entel
Netherlands	5.0	4.6	4.0	Croatia	VIPnet
Portugal	6.5	5.6	4.1	Cyprus	Cytamobile-Vodafone
Czech Rep.	3.2	2.9	2.1	Denmark	TDC
Romania	9.2	9.6	6.1	Estonia	Elisa
Hungary	2.7	2.6	2.0	Faroe Islands	Vodafone Faroe Islands
Turkey	16.8	15.5	—	Finland	Elisa
Poland	3.4	3.6	1.8	Guernsey	Airtel-vodafone
Egypt	31.8	10.4	6.1	Honduras	Digicel
S. Africa[a]	26.5	16.5	7.5	Hong Kong	SmarTone-Vodafone
Tanzania[a]	8.9	—	—	Iceland	Vodafone Iceland
Congo[a]	4.2	—	—	Japan	SoftBank
Mozambique	3.1	—	—	Jersey	Airtel-vodafone
Lesotho	0.8	—	—	Latvia	BITÉ
Kenya[b]	6.9	5.3	1.4	Lithuania	BITÉ
Qatar	0.8	—	—	Luxembourg	Tango
India	134.6	46.1	1.6	Macedonia	VIP operator
Australia	3.6	4.0	3.1	Malaysia	Celcom
New Zealand	2.5	2.5	2.0	Norway	TDC
Fiji	0.3	0.3	0.1	Panama	Digicel
Group	367.5	327.2	127.7	Russia	MTS
Non-controlled businesses				Serbia	VIP mobile
Company	*Country*	*Ownership*		Singapore	M1
Verizon Wireless	US	45%		Slovenia	Si.mobile-Vodafone
Polkomtel	Poland	24.4%		Sri Lanka	Dialog
Bharti Airtel	India	4.4%		Sweden	TDC
SFR	France	sold		Switzerland	Swisscom
China Mobile	China	sold		Thailand	DTAC
SoftBank	Japan	Sold		Turkmenistan	MTS
				Ukraine	MTS
				UAE	Du
				Uzbekistan	MTS

Notes:

[a] Through Vodafone subsidiary, Vadocom.

[b] Through Vodafone's 40% ownership of Safaricom.

Source: Vodafone Group PLC, annual report 2011.

Vodafone's International Expansion, 1984–2012

Vodafone was formed in 1984 as a subsidiary of Racal Electronics PLC, a British-based defense and electronics company. It was established to exploit the opportunities made available by the new cellular technology for wireless communication. After its initial public offering in 1988, Vodafone began its international expansion, initially by acquiring minority stakes in other wireless telecom companies and by establishing joint ventures to bid for licenses in countries launching cellular systems. With the appointment of Chris Gent as CEO in 1997, Vodafone embarked upon a succession of overseas acquisitions (Table 3).

TABLE 3 Vodafone's acquisitions and divestments, 1989–2012

Year	Company	Country	Notes
1989	Telecel	Malta	JV with TeleMalta; Vodafone owns 80%
1990	SFR	France	4% equity acquired by Vodafone
1991	AB Nordic Tel	Sweden, Denmark	10% equity acquired by Vodafone
1991	Pacific Link Communication Ltd	Hong Kong	30% equity acquired by Vodafone
1993	Vodacom	S. Africa	JV with Vodafone owning 35%
1993	Panafon	Greece	JV with Vodafone owning 45%
1996	Talkland	UK	Vodafone acquires remaining 2/3 of equity for £30.6 million
1996	Peoples Phone	UK	Reseller with 181 stores acquired for £77 million
1996	Astec Communications	UK	Service provider with 21 stores acquired for £77 million
1998	Misrfone	Egypt	Vodafone owns 30% of the JV. Wins license to build Egypt's 2nd mobile network
1998	BellSouth New Zealand Ltd	New Zealand	Acquired; renamed Vodafone New Zealand
1999	AirTouch Communications, Inc.	US	$62 billion merger creates Vodafone Airtouch. Includes 3.2 million US subscribers, and 1.1 million in Germany, Italy (Omnitel), Poland, Japan, and India
2000	Verizon Wireless	US	Merges US wireless assets of Vodafone and Bell Atlantic
2000	Mannesmann	Germany	Acquired for £112 billion; adds 9.5 million subscribers
2001	Eircell	Ireland	Acquired for €5 million; rebranded Vodafone Ireland; adds 1.2 million subscribers
2001	TDC	Denmark	First "Partner Networks" agreement for co-branded services to Denmark
2001	China Mobile (Hong Kong)	Hong Kong	Strategic alliance agreed
2001	Swisscom	Switzerland	25% of equity acquired
2001	Airtel Movil SA	Spain	Equity interest increased to 91.6%
2001	Japan Telecom and J-Phone	Japan	Acquired 69.7% of J-Phone, Japan's third-largest mobile operator with 11 million subscribers, and 66.7% of Japan Telecom, its parent
2002	Radiolinja	Finland and Estonia	Partner Network Agreements signed

(Continued)

TABLE 3   Vodafone's acquisitions and divestments, 1989–2012 (*Continued*)

Year	Company	Country	Notes
2002	Vizzavi	France/UK	Vodafone buys out Vivendi's 50% share of the Vizzavi mobile internet portal for €142.7 million
2003	Mobilcom; BITÉ	Austria; Lithuania	Partner Network Agreements signed
2004	Cytamobile	Cyprus	Partner Network Agreements signed
2004	AT&T Wireless	US	$38 billion offer fails; Cingular bids higher
2005	Connex	Romania	Equity stake raised to 99% also buys Czech mobile operator
2005	Oskar	Czech Republic	Acquired
2006	Vodafone Sweden	Sweden	Sold for €970 million (£660 million)
2006	Vodafone Japan	Japan	97.7% stake sold to Softbank £6.9 billion
2006	Belgacom Mobile SA; Swisscom Mobile AG	Belgium; Switzerland	25% interests in the two companies sold for a total of £3.1 billion
2007	Hutchison Essar	India	Acquired 52% of India's fourth-biggest wireless operator with 22.9 million subscribers for $10.9 billion
2007	Bharti Airtel	India	Sold Group's 5.60% direct shareholding in Bharti Airtel for $1.6 billion
2007	Tele2	Italy and Spain	Acquired for €775 million
2007	Qatar Foundation	Qatar	Vodafone allies with Qatar Foundation to build 2nd mobile network in Qatar
2008	Arcor	Germany	Acquires remaining 26.4% of Arcor for €460 million
2008	Ghana Telecom.	Ghana	Acquired 70% of equity for £486 million
2008	BroadNet Czech AS	Czech Republic	Acquired by Vodafone Czech Republic
2008	Crazy John's	Australia	Vodafone acquires 83% of the Australian retailer and Mobile Virtual Network Operator
2009	Alltel Wireless	US	Acquired by Verizon Wireless for $5.9 billion
2009	Hutchison Telecom (Australia)	Australia	The Australian businesses of Vodafone and Hutchison merge to create Vodafone Hutchison Australia
2009	Vodacom S. Africa	S. Africa	Additional 15% of equity acquired for £1.6 billion
2009	Central Telecom	UK	Acquired UK-based systems integrator
2010	China Mobile	China	3.2% equity stake sold for £4.3 billion
2010	SoftBank	Japan	Investments in Softbank sold for £0.5 billion
2011	Essar	India	Acquires Essar's 33% stake in Vodafone-Essar for $5.46 billion; Vodafone-Essar has 134 million subscribers
2011	SFR	France	Vodafone sells 44% stake in SFR to Vivendi for €7.95 billion
2012	Cable & Wireless Worldwide	UK	Acquires C&WW, a supplier of (mainly fixed-line) telecom services to corporate customers, for £1 billion

Source: Vodafone annual reports, various years.

The strategic rationale behind Vodafone's international expansion was explained by Alan Harper, a former group strategy director:

> We have always been mobile focused . . . Our vision has been to leverage scale and scope benefits, reduce response time and ensure effective delivery to customers. This we have achieved by collecting or acquiring national operating companies and giving them a mission of a challenger company . . . For example, Vodafone with SFR is a challenger to France Telecom in France, Vodafone UK is a challenger to British Telecom in the UK, Vodafone Germany is a challenger to Deutsch Telecom in Germany. With this challenger mindset we nurture and instill an entrepreneurial spirit among Vodafone companies and in this respect we do not behave as a traditional telephone company . . . The cultural alignment of people within Vodafone is a key issue in sustaining this challenger and entrepreneurial mindset. To focus on this cultural alignment we give autonomy to the local entity and reiterate that the local entity did not join a global company like IBM or HP. The local entity has to work within a matrix structure and keep alive the "challenger mindset" on fixed line telephony and other incumbents, challenge the status quo every day, and evolve by being local entrepreneurs."[2]

This emphasis on local autonomy meant that Vodafone did not integrate its international acquisitions in any systematic way. Some subsidiaries were migrated immediately to the Vodafone brand; but, if the existing local brand was strong, it might be retained for many years. Vodafone transferred its operating and marketing practices and pricing structure where appropriate, but otherwise its main influence on its acquired companies was to transfer its culture of entrepreneurship and competitive spirit. It also transferred its strategic priorities, notably its desire to be number one or number two in market share in every country it operated (this was seen as critical to spreading the fixed costs of infrastructure, technology, and marketing). In addition, Vodafone placed a major emphasis on gaining market share through differentiation and premium services rather than price-cutting.

Sarin and the Quest for Integration

The 21st century brought difficult times for Vodafone. The first major problem was overpaying at government auctions for licenses for 3G wireless communication. Between 2000 and 2001, Vodafone paid over $30 billion for the new licenses (including $9.5 billion for a single 3G license in the UK). Like many of its competitors, Vodafone had greatly overestimated the commercial potential of 3G wireless communication. Amortization of 3G license costs and write-offs of goodwill from acquisitions resulted in Vodafone reporting net losses of £45 billion ($72 billion) between 2001 and 2004.

The second hit was the bursting of the TMT (technology, media, and telecommunications) stock-market bubble. After hitting an all-time peak early in 2001, Vodafone's share price declined by 72% over the next 30 months.

The response of the new CEO, Arun Sarin, was the launch of the One Vodafone project in 2003. *The Economist* described some key features of the initiative:

> Sir Chris [Gent] collected the pieces: Mr. Sarin's mission was to fit them together to achieve economies of scale and so to justify Vodafone's bigger-is-better strategy. For the past 15 months, Mr. Sarin has been doing just that, though mostly behind

the scenes. Only now is the curtain finally being raised, with the launch this month of "third-generation" (3G) mobile services in 12 European countries and a relaunch in Japan. The roll-out of 3G, Mr. Sarin agrees, will provide litmus tests of both his own leadership and Vodafone's ability to function as a unified entity.

Redrawing organization charts, rationalising back-room systems and cutting costs are hardly the sorts of activities that generate headlines, so Vodafone seems a less dynamic firm than it was under Sir Chris. But this dull-but-necessary work is what Mr. Sarin is good at, and what Vodafone needs to bring its sprawling divisions together. His "One Vodafone" project has sorted out the behind-the-scenes spaghetti at Vodafone's national affiliates, so that they are now all using the same technology. This cuts costs by making it possible to develop a new service once, and then introduce it in many markets simultaneously.

Mr. Sarin has also restructured Vodafone's management. The bosses of its large regional operations now report directly to him. The head of marketing at each national operator now reports to the group head of marketing, rather than simply to his local boss, and so on. The aim is to bind the national operators together and give Mr. Sarin more direct control of his firm. Aligning structure with strategy in this way will, he hopes, enable the firm to "execute flawlessly."

This is not rocket science. Simplifying Vodafone's structure, he believes, is the foundation for making 3G a success, for it enables Vodafone to reap the benefits of its global scale. A single technology platform allows it to test handsets or services in one market and then deploy them everywhere. It ensures seamless international roaming, even for video calling. And it has allowed Vodafone to use its Japanese operation as a test-bed for 3G.

By far the greatest benefit of Vodafone's scale is its resulting clout with handset-makers. It has set strict standards for its 3G handsets, and even the biggest handset-makers have no choice but to comply with them if they want Vodafone's business. Using the same technology in both Japan and Europe means that Vodafone can offer Japanese handset-makers access to European markets and Western firms access to the Japanese market, while playing them off against each other.[3]

The new structure introduced at the beginning of 2005 included:

- Six geographically defined businesses that would report directly to the CEO. These comprised the UK, Germany, Italy, Asia-Pacific, other EMEA[4] and affiliate companies.

- Stronger global functions, each of which would report directly to the CEO. Marketing would include a new multinational corporate unit serving global corporate customers and would be responsible for global handset procurement. Technology would be responsible for standardizing network design and IT shared services. Business Development was a new function responsible for driving Vodafone's product and services portfolio into affiliates and "Partner Networks."

- Two top-management committees to oversee the execution of the strategy set by the main board. The Executive Committee would focus on strategy, financial structure, and organizational development. The Integration and Operations Committee would be responsible for operational and budgetary planning, and product and service development. Both committees were chaired by Arun Sarin.

Alan Harper, head of strategy, explained:

> With acquisitions all over the world, one of our challenges is to integrate seamlessly not only technology (which, by the way, is more or less similar across the world) but also people . . . The challenge of this restructuring program is to balance the need for coordination and synergies with local initiatives . . . We are trying to integrate national operating units . . . and trying to leverage scale and scope while trying to retain the local autonomy and responsiveness of our challenger national units.[5]

The One Vodafone program involved business integration across a range of activities including billing (in 2005, Vodafone operated eight different billing systems), network design, procurement, IT (including back office, ERP/HR, and data center processes), service-center platforms, roaming, customer services, and retail operations. According to Harper:

> What One Vodafone tries to achieve is to simplify the integration issues in terms of brand strength and integrating local culture and processes. We centralize all our marketing efforts, branding and product development. Technology is standardized. Network design is coordinated. Best practices are benchmarked by Advance Services. Knowledge is shared . . . We keep and encourage local initiatives such as customer services, and sales. . .[6]

The limits of the One Vodafone program were immediately apparent in three key markets: Japan, the US, and France. Japan and the US used cellular wireless technologies that differed from the GSM European standard used by Vodafone across its other markets. (Verizon Wireless used CDMA, which was incompatible with GSM.) Vodafone's inability to exploit any significant economies between its US interests and its presence elsewhere was further exacerbated by Verizon Wireless operating under the Verizon Wireless rather than the Vodafone brand.

International integration was also constrained by other distinctive features of national markets, notably differences in consumer preferences and different levels of technological development. Japan (along with Korea) was regarded as the world's most advanced wireless market, adopting new wireless technologies at least two years earlier than Europe. Vodafone's introduction of its global range of handsets in Japan led to an exodus of Japanese subscribers: the phones were seen as technologically backward. The US, by contrast, had been a laggard in the adoption of 3G wireless technologies, mainly because of its multiple, incompatible, wireless standards.

France was the third problem country in terms of integrating into Vodafone's global network. As with Verizon Wireless, Vodafone possessed a minority share of SFR (44%) and SFR had not adopted the Vodafone brand. Moreover, SFR supplied mobile, fixed-line, and internet communication services, while Vodafone was exclusively a wireless company.

These problems together with strong competitive and regulatory pressures in the mature markets encouraged a major reconfiguration in Vodafone's international portfolio, in particular a growing emphasis on emerging markets and divestment in several mature markets. Between 2005 and 2008, Vodafone made acquisitions in Eastern Europe, Africa, and Asia, while divesting in Japan, Sweden, the Netherlands, Belgium, and Switzerland.

Vodafone also shifted its emphasis from equity to non-equity modes of internationalization. Historically, Vodafone's partnering agreements with overseas operators related only to roaming services. Beginning with Iceland in 2006, partner agreements became more like franchise agreements where the partner used Vodafone's services and content for its own customers and sometimes adopted the Vodafone brand.

Vodafone's International Strategy under Colao, 2008–2011

Since taking over as CEO in July 2008, a key priority in Vittorio Colao's quest for increasing profitability and shareholder value was to exploit Vodafone's international presence more effectively. This involved several changes to the international integration strategy initiated by Sarin.

Organizational Structure

In October 2010, Vodafone reformulated its organizational structure in order to "simplify the organisation; enhance our focus on key commercial and financial priorities; and increase the speed we can bring new services to market and respond to industry changes."[7] The regional structure was consolidated into just two regions: Europe and AMAP (Africa, the Middle East, and Asia-Pacific). Responsibility for minority businesses, notably the US and France, was taken away from the regions and placed directly with the CEO, CFO, and head of strategy and business development. Two new functional units were created: Commercial—which comprised Marketing, Vodafone Business Services, Vodafone Global Enterprise, Partner Markets, and other commercial units—and Group Technology—which brought together all technology functions in Vodafone. Figure 2 shows the new structure.

FIGURE 2 Vodafone's organizational structure, October 2011

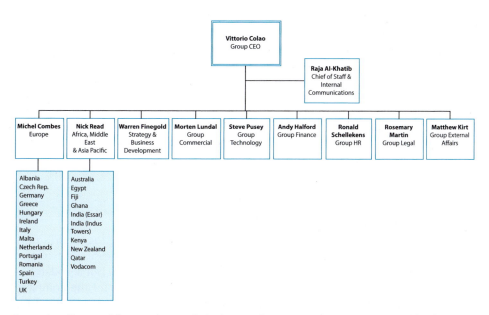

Source: http://www.vodafone.com/content/index/investors/management/organisation_structure.html.

Portfolio Changes

As already noted, Colao initiated some significant changes in Vodafone's international portfolio. In particular, the sale of businesses where Vodafone lacked a controlling stake, notably Vodafone's businesses in Japan, China, and France. Colao also sustained Sarin's strategy of growing in emerging markets, albeit at a much slower pace. Colao made acquisitions in South Africa, India, and Ghana. Looking ahead, Vodafone predicted that a combination of increasing market penetration of mobile phones and comparatively rapid economic growth would mean that the demand for mobile telephony would continue to grow much faster in emerging markets than in mature markets. However, as the Appendix shows, the higher growth rate in emerging markets did not always result in higher profit margins.

Building Corporate Business

A major Vodafone imitative under Colao was building Vodafone's presence in the corporate market. Vodafone Global Enterprise had been established in 2007 to manage relationships with Vodafone's 270 largest multinational corporate customers. Under Colao, it became a major plank of Vodafone's growth strategy through offering an integrated range of fixed, mobile, and broadband services for multinational corporations seeking a single worldwide supplier. Services included central ordering, customer self-serve web portals, telecommunications expense management tools, device management, and guaranteed service levels.[8]

Growing Mobile Data

The market for telephony services was changing rapidly. It was expected that between 2010 and 2014 revenue from fixed-line communication would decline by $70 billion, revenue from mobile voice would increase by $24 billion, fixed-line data by $49 billion, and mobile data by $138 billion.[9] Exploiting the growing demand for mobile internet connectivity was central to Vodafone's strategy. Heavy investment in 3G network coverage in Europe (and elsewhere) meant that Vodafone was able to offer data download speeds that, on average, were 40% faster than the fastest competitor's. Vodafone was also pioneering 4G/LTE (long-term evolution) networks in Germany and the US prior to rollout elsewhere.

Vodafone believed that its international scope offered it important advantages in introducing new mobile technologies in terms of its relations with equipment suppliers, economies in purchasing equipment and developing software, and the ability to exploit learning and knowledge transfer.

The Future of Vodafone

Under Colao's leadership, Vodafone has reinforced its position as the world's most international telecommunications provider, while divesting businesses that offered limited prospects for integrating within Vodafone's global network. But if Vodafone's international scope was to be a source of competitive advantage for the company, it was clear to Colao that Vodafone needed to find additional sources of value from international integration.

Economies from International Scope

For the industry as a whole, it was not obvious that the benefits of international scope exceeded the costs of coordinating global networks of subsidiaries and joint ventures. Certainly, the telecom service industry was very different from telecommunications equipment or software, where a global presence was essential to viability. Among the companies listed in Table 4, some—such as Deutsche Telekom, Vodafone, Telefónica Móviles, Hutchison Whampoa, and América Móvil—were internationally diversified; others—such as AT&T, Verizon Communications, China Mobile, and Telecom Italia—were nationally focused.

Indeed, in common with other service industries such as airlines and retail banking, the international experiences of many telecom companies had been disappointing. Reflecting on the disastrous overseas acquisitions spree of NTT DoCoMo in telecoms and Swissair in airlines, the *Wall Street Journal* observed:

> In the mobile industry, the significant fixed-cost components of the business (networks, product development, and brand advertising and promotion) provide unit cost advantages to the national market leader compared with its followers. . .
>
> Despite regulatory changes, the economics of the mobile industry remain primarily national in nature. That is, it is clearly better to be a market leader in one country than a follower in two countries. . .

TABLE 4 World's largest telecommunication service companies

	Revenue 2010 ($billion)	Revenue 2008 ($billion)	ROA 2010 (%)
AT&T	124.6	124.0	7.4
Nippon Telegraph and Telephone	120.3	103.7	2.5
Verizon Communications	106.6	97.4	1.1
Deutsche Telekom	82.7	90.3	1.3
Telefónica Móviles	80.4	84.8	7.8
China Mobile	76.7	65.0	6.0
Vodafone	71.3	69.0	5.1
France Télécom	62.0	78.3	5.2
América Móvil	48.1	31.0	10.1
KDDI Corporation	40.1	34.8	6.6
China Telecom	38.5	31.8	0.5
Vivendi	38.2	37.2	3.7
Comcast	37.9	34.3	3.0
Telecom Italia	36.9	45.1	3.4
SoftBank	35.1	26.6	3.9
Sprint Nextel	32.6	35.6	(6.7)
BT Group	31.8	36.6	6.3
Hutchison Whampoa	26.9	n.a.	2.8
Telstra	22.1	22.4	10.2

Notes:
Figures in parentheses denote a loss.
ROA: Return on assets.
n.a.: not applicable.
Source: Fortune Global 500 (2011).

When both NTT DoCoMo and Swissair convinced themselves they needed to expand beyond domestic boundaries to survive, the race to fulfill their global aspirations seems to have resulted in a set of investments more focused on the number of flags on a boardroom map rather than on these basic economics driving superior profitability in their industries. The risks of these two aggressive expansion strategies were further compounded by not having control over most of their international investments . . . In short order DoCoMo accumulated direct or indirect stakes in nine mobile operators—most for cash, at the peak of the telecom bubble. But this acquisition spree resulted in equity stakes in only two market leaders and these were in relatively minor geographic markets . . . Worse still, all these investments were minority stakes and so would appear to give DoCoMo limited ability to exert control over critical strategic and operational issues at these operators.[10]

The economies from cross-border integration were in four main areas:

- Procurement: notably in network equipment, handsets and software. These benefits of global purchasing depended, of course, on common technologies across national subsidiaries. Vodafone's global purchasing organization is based in Luxemburg.
- Global developing technology and new products and services.
- Marketing and brand development.
- Common service functions such as IT, billing, HR, and finance. As part of the One Vodafone project, Booz & Company had developed a three-stage integration process that involved building the business case for integration, designing common standards and a common service platform, and, finally, implementing.

However, having subsidiaries in different national markets was neither a necessary nor sufficient condition for exploiting these scale economies. As Vodafone's disastrous experience in Japan had shown, the world telecom market was fragmented not just by technology and regulation but also by customer preferences. Vittorio Colao observed: "Culture influences the lifestyle, and the lifestyle influences the way we communicate. If you don't leave your phone on in a meeting in Italy, you are likely to miss the next one." Conversely, in Japan using mobile phones in public places is frowned upon, if not prohibited, one reason why the Japanese have been leading consumers of mobile data services. Cultural factors also influence intensity of usage: Germans spend on average just 89 minutes each month on mobile calls, for Americans it is 788 minutes, while Puerto Ricans top the table with 1,875 minutes.[11]

Some economies can be exploited without investing in overseas markets. Through its partner agreements, Vodafone was able to exploit its brand and deploy its products and services without even partial ownership of a local operator.

Learning and Innovation Benefits of International Scope   In addition to the cost economies from international scope, there were also user benefits, in effect a differentiation advantage. This was certainly the case in serving multinational corporations where integrated international communication was a critical requirement. For individual users, the advantages of an international service provider were less clear since international roaming could be offered through access agreements with domestic providers in each country. The key roaming benefits of having subsidiaries in different countries was the ability to offer *seamless roaming services*—identical services in each country. It also allowed the flexibility to offer promotional deals, for example in the summer of 2009 Vodafone offered: "No Roaming Charge in Over 35 Countries This Summer!"

Some of the most promising opportunities for Vodafone to create value from its global network involved exploiting the potential for learning and cross-border transfer of knowledge and innovation. Through Vodafone's globally integrated functions, it should be possible to exploit globally ideas, innovations, and know-how that arose in particular locations. For example, in Germany Vodafone had pioneered the introduction of 4GLTE telephony through which it offered high-speed mobile internet access and intended to develop a stream of new services, including video-on-demand. The experience gained and products developed in Germany would then be rolled out elsewhere. The exemplar for international transfer of local innovation was Vodafone's M-Pesa system (Exhibit 1).

Colao believed that advancing technology and opportunities for developing new products and services would greatly increase the potential for Vodafone to leverage its international scope. In terms of products these related primarily to the potential for 3G and 4G communications to support a wide range of mobile internet applications. In terms of the customer experience, Vodafone was an industry leader in developing online billing, online customer support, and mobile click-to-pay systems that could enhance Vodafone's potential to be a provider of mobile internet applications. Future growth areas identified by Vodafone included:

- machine-to-machine (M2M) mobile communication allowing fleets of vehicles, vending machines, and ATMs to be in constant communication with corporate IT systems;
- third-party billing allowing subscribers to charge their purchases directly to their Vodafone account;

EXHIBIT 1
M-Pesa

M-Pesa (M for "mobile"; *pesa* is Swahili for "money") is a mobile-phone-based money transfer service developed by Vodafone's Kenyan affiliate, Safaricom. Initially intended as a service through which microfinance borrowers could receive and repay loans using the retail outlets of Safaricom resellers, the service became a national system for making all sorts of payments and transfers. Two years after its launch in March 2007, it had captured 6.5 million subscribers in Kenya with two million daily transactions. Vodafone partners with IBM Global Services for operational support of M-Pesa.

In 2008, M-Pesa (under the name M-Paisa) was launched in Afghanistan, initially for the purpose of paying police salaries. It was subsequently launched in Tanzania and South Africa by Vodacom. Further developments include introduction into Egypt and India, and the extension of the service to international as well as domestic payments.

Source: http://en.wikipedia.org/wiki/M-Pesa.

- near-field communication allowing point-of-sale purchases to be made by swiping a mobile phone;
- mobile advertising.[12]

Vodafone's Strategic Positioning in Relation to Industry Evolution

Vodafone's ability to use its global position to exploit the rapid growth in mobile internet usage would depend very much on its power and influence within the broad ICT sector.

At a very basic level, Vodafone was disadvantaged by its mobile-only focus. A key market trend was the integration of fixed and mobile communication through bundled offerings to customers. Some domestically focused operators offered "quadruple play" bundles, comprising fixed and mobile telephony, broadband internet access, and television services. Vodafone had been slow in responding to this trend: "Vodafone management has no strategy for convergence," observed one analyst in 2006.[13]

A key component of Colao's strategy was a "total communications" initiative. For the Global Enterprise program, "total communications" meant Vodafone being a single source for all a multinational corporation's communication needs. For smaller businesses there was Vodafone One Net: mobile and fixed-line communication with a single number and single billing. For the consumer market it meant providing broadband through a DSL router, but allowing the customer immediate mobile broadband access while waiting for the fixed-line service to be connected.

This total communications approach required Vodafone to lease fixed-line capacity from other telecom providers, for example BT in Great Britain and Telecom Italia in Italy. Vodafone also acquired some of its own fixed-line capacity, Tele2's fixed-line and broadband services in Italy and Spain.

The trend toward bundling fixed and mobile communication was one that Vodafone was able to respond to fairly easily. Other changes in the industry were more problematic.

During the first two generations of wireless communication, the service providers were the dominant players in the industry. In addition to providing mobile connectivity, they were also the biggest retailers of handsets. However, with 3G communication and the introduction of smartphones, the balance of power in the industry had shifted considerably. By 2011, the key drivers of industry evolution and the creators of consumer value were the companies that were the handset makers, notably RIM (Blackberry) and Apple (iPhone, iPad). It was these companies rather than the service providers that were the primary sources of user applications. Their power lay in software rather than hardware, notably in their proprietary operating systems. This key role of operating systems for mobile devices meant that the other key players in wireless communication were also software companies that owned operating systems: Google with its Android platform and Microsoft with Windows Mobile.

The remarkable success of Apple's iPhone was salutary for Vodafone. The iPhone had positioned Apple as a key gateway into mobile internet services through Apple's applications store, which offered support for third-party developers who created content for the iPhone. Moreover, because of Apple's exclusive deal with O2 (owned by Telefónica), Vodafone had been unable to distribute iPhones or act as a service provider for iPhone users until 2008.[14] In response, Vodafone launched its own software applications store—the Joint Innovation Lab—in May 2009. Verizon Wireless,

China Mobile, and SoftBank partnered in the venture, whose aim was to produce a single platform for developers to create mobile widgets and applications on multiple operating systems and to access the partners' combined 1.1 billion-customer base.[15]

Threatened by the growing dominance of Apple and Google in the smartphone market, in 2011 Nokia formed an alliance with Microsoft to create a Windows-based mobile telephony platform. Colao's hope was that a four-way battle for mobile device platforms between Apple, RIM, Google's Android, and Microsoft/Nokia might offer some respite to the wireless service provides. A key fear of Colao had been that, if Apple's iPhone and iPad were to dominate the mobile internet access, Apple would also become the dominant supplier of wireless applications, and Vodafone and its competitors would increasingly become suppliers of commoditized connection services. Not only would this trend mean that Apple and its allies would increase their share of the profit pool at the expense of the service providers, it would also limit the potential for Vodafone to create value from exploiting cross-border synergies through offering new services and an enhanced user experience.

Appendix: Vodafone Performance by Country and Region, 2011 and 2012

	Revenue (£million)		EBITDA[a] (£million)		Av. operating margin[b] (%)	Capital expenditure (£million)	
	2012	2011	2012	2011	2011/2	2012	2011
Germany	8,233	7,900	2,965	2,952	18.9	880	824
Italy	5,658	5,722	2,514	2,643	32.0	621	590
Spain	4,763	5,133	1,193	1,562	15.0	429	517
UK	5,397	5,271	1,294	1,233	7.0	575	516
Other Europe							
Greece	875	927	202	233	4.6	78	108
Netherlands	1,775	1,672	600	568	19.8	243	173
Portugal	1,065	1,101	446	455	25.3	151	150
Romania	701	710	262	259	10.8	80	98
Turkey	1,704	1,566	265	189	n.a.	266	435
Other	2,232	2,277	704	729	15.2	274	266
Europe	**32,181**	**32,015**	**10,445**	**10,823**	**17.1**	**3,597**	**3,677**
India	4,265	3,855	1,122	985	0.9	805	870
Vodacom	5,638	5,479	1,930	1,844	17.2	723	572
Egypt	1,262	1,329	552	607	26.2	210	292
Other	2,703	2,642	511	563	1.5	583	462
Africa, Middle East and Asia-Pacific	**13,868**	**13,304**	**4,115**	**3,999**	**10.1**	**2,321**	**2,196**
Group[c]	**46,417**	**45,884**	**14,475**	**14,670**	**25.3**	**6,365**	**6,219**

Notes:
[a]EBITDA: Earnings before interest, tax, depreciation, and amortization.
[b]Adjusted operating profit/revenue.
[c]Group operating profit includes earnings from non-controlled businesses.
Source: Vodafone PLC, preliminary results year-ended March 31, 2012.

Notes

1. "Vodafone," Lex column, *Financial Times*, May 19, 2009.
2. Quoted in "Vodafone: Out of Many, One," (ESSEC Business School Case Study, 2005): 9.
3. "Foundation and Empire," *Economist*, November 25, 2004.
4. "EMEA" stands for Europe, Middle East, and Africa.
5. Quoted in "Vodafone: Out of Many, One," (ESSEC Business School Case Study, 2005): 9.
6. Quoted in "Vodafone: Out of Many, One," (ESSEC Business School Case Study, 2005): 9.
7. D. Pittman, "Vodafone streamlines group structure," *Mobile News*, 9 September 2010. http://www.mobile newscwp.co.uk/2010/09/vodafone-streamlines-organisa tional-structure/, accessed September 25, 2012.
8. Vodafone Group PLC, annual report, 2009, p. 20.
9. Vodafone Group PLC, annual report, 2011, p. 15.
10. "When Global Strategies Go Wrong," *Asian Wall Street Journal*, April 4, 2002. Reproduced with permission from Bain & Company.
11. "Mobile-phone culture: The Apparatgeist calls," *Economist*, December 30, 2009.
12. "Focus in key areas of growth potential: New services," Vodafone annual report, 2011.
13. "Vodafone: Calling for a Rethink," *Economist*, January 26, 2006.
14. "Vodafone in Consolidation Call," *Financial Times*, July 24, 2009.
15. See www.jil.org, accessed May 28, 2009.

A video clip relating to this case is available in your interactive e-book at
www.wileyopenpage.com

Case 19 The Virgin Group in 2012

At the beginning of 2012, Richard Branson was 61 years old and his Virgin group of companies had been in business for 43 years. Yet neither Branson nor his business activities showed much sign of lacking entrepreneurial vigor. In financial services, Virgin Money was in the process of a major expansion of its UK retail presence through acquiring the government-owned Northern Rock with its 75 branches, 2,100 employees, and one million account holders. In health clubs, Virgin Active, boosted by its acquisition of rival Esporta, was expanding into new markets in Asia and Latin America. In healthcare, Virgin was using its acquisition of Assura to establish itself in primary healthcare services in the UK. In communications Virgin's initiatives included the launch of Virgin Mobile in Chile, Colombia, Brazil, Poland, and Oman and cloud computing services for corporate customers in the UK. It was also rumored that Virgin was planning to enter concert promotion and that its first event would be a series of concerts by the Rolling Stones. Meanwhile, in the travel business, Virgin continued to be a pioneer: the Virgin Galactic spaceship service was undergoing test flights and selling seats at $200,000 each.

Yet despite Branson prominence as Britain's best-known entrepreneur and one of its richest individuals,[1] his Virgin group of companies remained a mystery to most observers (and to many insiders as well). At the beginning of 2012, there were 228 Virgin companies registered at Britain's Companies House (68 of which were identified as "removed" or "recently dissolved"). In addition, there were Virgin companies registered in some 25 other countries. These companies were linked through a complex network of parent–subsidiary relations involving a number of companies identified as "holding companies." For most of the Virgin companies the ultimate parent was identified as Virgin Group Holdings Ltd, which was registered in the British Virgin Islands.

The complexity of Virgin's legal and ownership structure meant that its financial condition was opaque. Doubts had frequently been expressed about the overall financial health of the group.[2] Branson was dismissive of such speculation, claiming that analysts and journalists misunderstood his business empire. Each Virgin company, he argued, was financed on a stand-alone basis and attempts to consolidate the income and assets of the companies were irrelevant and misleading. Branson emphasized that the financial performance goals of a private company were different from a public corporation. Public companies needed to demonstrate strong short-term earnings performance. For private companies it was better to avoid short-term profits in order to limit tax liabilities; long-term growth in the value of the business was the key goal of the Virgin companies. When building long-term value, it was quite normal for a business to incur losses for many years. Cash flow and capital value rather than accounting profits were Branson's preferred performance indicators.[3]

This case was prepared by Robert M. Grant. ©2012 Robert M. Grant.

Underlying questions about financial performance were concerns over the strategic rationale and the manageability of the Virgin group. The group comprised around 300 separate companies (in addition to over 160 UK-registered companies there were many Virgin companies registered in overseas countries), these companies covered a wide range of businesses. In an era of corporate refocusing, when most conglomerate companies had either divested their diversified businesses or broken up altogether, the Virgin group was an anomaly. A major concern was the need to maintain coordination, accountability, and strategic control of this dispersed business empire. A key vulnerability was the Virgin brand: with such broad business coverage it risked becoming overextended and its integrity damaged.

Despite a new management structure involving the appointment of co-CEOs in July 2011, Branson remained the inspiration and unifying force within the group. As he became less involved in Virgin's business activities and more involved in Virgin's environmental and charity activities, would Virgin need to replace its informal, free-wheeling management style with a more formalized control structure? Or should it even consider break-up with the sale or floatation of its individual businesses?

Development of the Virgin Group, 1968–2012

Richard Branson's business career began while he was a student at Stowe, a private boarding school. His startup magazine, *Student*, was first published on January 26, 1968. The magazine displayed features that would characterize many of Branson's subsequent entrepreneurial initiatives. It targeted the baby-boomer generation, appealing to its optimism, irreverence, and anti-authoritarianism, and its interests in fashion, popular music, and avant-garde culture. And it filled a "gaping hole in the market." The early success of the magazine encouraged Branson to leave school at the age of 17, before taking final exams.

Virgin Records

Branson's next venture was mail-order records. With almost no fixed investment and little working capital, Branson could easily undercut the established retail chains. The name "Virgin" was suggested by one of his associates who saw the name as proclaiming their commercial innocence. In 1971, Virgin Records opened its first retail store, on London's busy Oxford Street.

Entry into record publishing resulted from a meeting with an unknown musician, Mike Oldfield. Branson installed a recording studio in his Oxfordshire home and the resulting album, *Tubular Bells*, released in 1973, was an instant hit, eventually selling over five million copies worldwide. The Virgin record label then went on to sign up bands, several of whom, such as the Sex Pistols, had been shunned by the major record companies. During the 1980s Virgin Records grew rapidly, with the signing of Phil Collins, Human League, Simple Minds, and Boy George's Culture Club.

Virgin Atlantic Airways

Virgin Atlantic began with a phone call from Randolph Fields, a Californian lawyer who proposed founding a transatlantic, cut-price airline. To the horror of his colleagues at Virgin Records, Branson was enthralled with the idea. On June 24, 1984,

Branson appeared in a First World War flying outfit to celebrate the inaugural flight of Virgin Atlantic in a second-hand 747 bought from Aereolíneas Argentinas. Unlike Branson's other businesses, the airline business was highly capital-intensive and heavily regulated; it also required a completely new set of business skills, such as the need to collaborate with governments, banks, and aircraft manufacturers.

Virgin Atlantic's huge financing needs encouraged Branson to seek an initial public offering for most of Virgin's businesses other than Virgin Atlantic. In 1985, 35% of Virgin Group PLC was listed on the London and NASDAQ stock markets.

Branson's experience as chairman of a public corporation was frustrating: the financial community's expectations of the role and responsibilities of a chairman of a public corporation were incompatible with his personality and lifestyle. Following the October 1987 stock market crash, Branson took the opportunity to raise £200 million to buy out external shareholders.

Virgin Everywhere!

As a private company, Virgin continued to expand, using both internal cash flows, mainly from Virgin Atlantic Airways, and external financing. Between 1988 and 2011, Virgin launched a near-continuous stream of new businesses (see the timeline in the Appendix). These new businesses were concentrated around a few main areas of opportunity:

- *Travel*: The success of Virgin Atlantic, which extended its route network and won many customer service awards, encouraged Branson to launch other airlines. These followed the business model of the low-cost carriers, but with the addition of Virgin's distinctive approach to differentiating its in-flight experience. New airlines included the Brussels-based Virgin Express (later merged into Brussels Airlines), Vintage Air Tours flying restored DC-3s between Orlando and Key West, Virgin Blue in Australia, Virgin America in the US, Pacific Blue in New Zealand, and V Australia with services between Sydney and Los Angeles.[4] Other aviation ventures included Virgin Lightships, offering airship advertising; Virgin Galactic; and Virgin Balloons.

- *Holidays*: Linked to Virgin's airline interests were investments in hotels and vacation services, including a lodge and wildlife park in South Africa.

- *Retailing*: Virgin's record stores provided a platform for internationally expanding retail interests. The Our Price chain of UK record stores was a joint venture between Virgin and WHSmith. Virgin Megastores pioneered "experience-based retailing" not just in the UK but also in Japan, the US, Australia, and Europe. Virgin Bride was a UK chain of bridal stores.

- *Information and communication technology*: The developments in digital technologies created a new field of opportunity for Branson. The advent of the internet allowed Virgin to expand its retail interests into the online retailing of a number of products, including automobiles, wine, and music downloads. The most successful of these was Virgin Direct (later renamed Virgin Money), a joint venture with Norwich Union, offering credit cards and other personal financial products. The start of cellular communication encouraged the launch of Virgin Mobile, a joint venture with Deutsche Telekom, which pioneered the "virtual network operator" model of wireless service (Virgin Mobile purchased network access from other providers). The Virgin Mobile strategy was then replicated in the US, Australia, South Africa, and South East Asia. Virgin.net, an internet service provider, was a joint venture with cable operator NTL. NTL subsequently acquired both Virgin.net and Virgin Mobile UK to create Virgin Media Inc., the UK's first "quadruple play" provider offering TV, broadband internet, mobile, and fixed-line phone services. Virgin Group held a 10.6% shareholding in Virgin Media and licensed the Virgin brand to it.

- *Deregulation and privatization*: Virgin's cell phone business was only possible because of the deregulation of telecommunications in Britain and other countries. The wave of privatization and deregulation of the 1980s and 1990s offered other entrepreneurial opportunities for Branson to exploit the Virgin brand and its flair for innovative customer service. Virgin acquired two passenger rail franchises that were combined to form Virgin Rail, a joint venture with Stagecoach, a transportation specialist. Deregulation in Australia permitted the launch of Virgin Blue. Virgin also bid, unsuccessfully, to operate the British National Lottery.

- *International expansion*: During 1998–2011, much of Virgin's growth was outside the UK. This involved replicating successful Virgin ventures overseas, such as Virgin Mobile, Virgin Active, Virgin Money, and Virgin's airline interests. Virgin's international expansion concentrated on North America, Australia, and South Africa.

Other new ventures launched by Virgin defied categorization; they were the result of opportunism and Branson's whims. These included health clubs (Virgin Active), biofuels (Virgin Fuels, Virgin Bioverda), video games (Virgin Interactive), drinks (Virgin Drinks, Virgin Cola), clothing and cosmetics (Victory Corporation), and Virgin Health Bank, where parents could store the blood stem cells from their newly born babies.

Focusing the Group, 2005–2011

Throughout its history, Virgin has divested some of its ventures either wholly or partially. Some of these divestments were to tap sources of investment funding (e.g., the sale of 49% of Virgin Atlantic to Singapore Airlines in 1999 and the floating of Virgin Blue). In other cases it was because Branson wished to release equity to fund more attractive businesses (e.g., the sales of Virgin Records, Virgin Megastores, and Virgin Mobile UK). During recent years, the pace of divestment by Virgin increased as it sought to eliminate financially unsuccessful businesses. These included, among others, Virgin Vie, Virgin Cosmetics, Virgin Cars, Virgin Bikes, Virgin Brides, Virgin Drinks, Virgin Mobile Singapore, and Virgin Money USA.

The Virgin Group of Companies in 2012

On its corporate website, Virgin describes itself as follows:

Virgin is a leading branded venture capital organisation and is one of the world's most recognised and respected brands. Conceived in 1970 by Sir Richard Branson,

FIGURE 1   Virgin's business portfolio

Travel	Lifestyle	Media and Mobile	People and Planet
V Australia	Virgin Active UK	Virgin Mobile Australia	Virgin Earth
Virgin Atlantic Airways	Virgin Active Australia	Virgin Mobile Canada	Virgin Green Fund
Virgin Australia	Virgin Active Italia	Virgin Mobile France	Virgin Unite
Virgin America	Virgin Active Portugal	Virgin Mobile India	
Virgin Holidays	Virgin Active South Africa	Virgin Mobile South Africa	**Money**
Virgin Holidays + Hip Hotels	Virgin Active Spain	Virgin Mobile UK	Virgin Money UK
Virgin Holiday Cruises	Virgin Experience Days	Virgin Mobile USA	Virgin Money Australia
Virgin Limited Edition	Virgin Racing	Virgin Media	Virgin Money South Africa
Virgin Vacations	Virgin Balloon Flights	Virgin Produced	Virgin Money Giving
Virgin Trains	The Virgin Voucher		

Other Virgin Businesses

Virgin Books	Virgin Connect	Virgin Digital Help	Virgin Galactic
Virgin Games	Virgin Gaming	Virgin Health Bank	Virgin HealthMiles
Virgin Life Care	Virgin Limobike	Virgin Wines Australia	Virgin Wines UK
Virgin Wines US			

Music

Virgin Megastore

Virgin Radio International

Virgin Festivals

Entrepreneur

Note:

Includes *only* those companies listed on the Virgin website.

Source: http://www.virgin.com/companies. Reproduced with permission.

the Virgin Group has gone on to grow very successful businesses in sectors ranging from mobile telephony to transportation, travel, financial services, media, music
and fitness.

Virgin has created more than 300 branded companies worldwide, employing
approximately 50,000 people, in 30 countries. Global branded revenues in 2009
exceeded £11.5 billion (approx. US$18 billion).

We believe in making a difference. Virgin stands for value for money, quality,
innovation, fun and a sense of competitive challenge. We deliver a quality service
by empowering our employees and we facilitate and monitor customer feedback
to continually improve the customer's experience through innovation.[5]

Most of the business activities of the Virgin Group are conducted through the 49
companies listed on the Virgin website. These companies are grouped into six
categories plus Virgin Entrepreneur, Virgin's business start-up function (Figure 1).

The Virgin Brand

The Virgin brand was the group's greatest single asset. It was unusual in terms of
the range of products it encompassed. Could a brand that extended from rail travel
to recorded music have any meaningful identity? The Virgin website offers the following explanation:

All the markets in which Virgin operates tend to have features in common: they are
typically markets where the customer has been ripped off or under-served, where
there is confusion and/or where the competition is complacent. In these markets,

Virgin is able to break into the market and shake it up. Our role is to be the consumer champion, and we do this by delivering to our brand values, which are:

- Value for Money: Simple, honest and transparent pricing—not necessarily the cheapest on the market.
- Good Quality: High standards, attention to detail, being honest and delivering on promises.
- Brilliant Customer Service: Friendly, human and relaxed; professional but not corporate.
- Innovative: Challenging convention with big and little product/service ideas; innovative, modern and stylish design.
- Competitively Challenging: Sticking two fingers up to the establishment and fighting the big boys—usually with a bit of humor.
- Fun: Every company in the world takes itself seriously so we think it's important that we provide the public and our customers with a bit of entertainment—as well as making Virgin a nice place for our people to work.[6]

These attributes were conveyed to customers through Virgin's approach to differentiating its offerings. Virgin Atlantic pioneered a range of innovative customer services (principally for its business class passengers). These included inflight massages, hair stylists, aroma therapists, and limousine and motorcycle airport transportation services. In 1998, it introduced a speedboat service along the Thames from Heathrow to the City of London, allowing financiers to dodge London traffic jams. British Airways—huge, stodgy, and bureaucratic—provided the ideal adversary against which Virgin Atlantic could position itself. When British Airways was experiencing problems erecting its giant Ferris wheel, the London Eye, Virgin positioned a blimp above the site bearing the message "BA Can't Get It Up!"

Some of Branson's ventures seemed to be inspired more by a sense of fun and eagerness to "stick it to the big boys" than by commercial logic. When Virgin Cola was introduced in 1994 (packaged in a "Pammy" bottle modeled on the body of *Baywatch* star Pamela Anderson), the goal, according to Branson, was to "drive Coke out of the States."[7] By 1997, Virgin Cola was losing £5 million on revenues of £30 million.

Virgin's ability to extend its brand so widely pointed to the broad appeal of Virgin's values and business principles. Much of this appeal was linked with Richard Branson's persona and style. The values and characteristics that the Virgin brand communicated are inseparable from Richard Branson as entrepreneur, joker, and "acceptable face of capitalism."

By identifying with Branson's personality and values, the Virgin brand allowed Virgin companies to position themselves as distinctive alternatives to established market leaders. Thus, the difference between Virgin Atlantic and BA, between Virgin Cola and Coca Cola, and between Virgin Money and the major banks was not primarily about products; it was more about the companies' identity and how they related to their customers.

The affection of the British public for Branson, and the appeal of the Virgin brand, reflected the alignment between Branson's values and sense of fair play with some of the traditional values that defined the British character. In battling huge, anonymous corporations, Branson recalled the heroes of yesteryear who fought against tyranny and evil: King Arthur, Robin Hood, and St. George. His willingness to appear in outlandish attire reflected a British propensity for eccentric dressing-up, whether for fancy-dress parties, Morris dancing, or the House of Lords. But this distinctiveness also raised questions as to the appeal of the Virgin brand outside of Britain. It was unclear whether Branson and the Virgin brand could achieve the same rapport with consumers in other countries as they did in Britain.

A key risk was overextension of the Virgin brand. The head of brand identity at Landor Associates commented: "He's still way too unfocused. He should get out of businesses that don't fit the Virgin/Branson personality, such as beverages, cosmetics, certainly financial services, or come up with another brand name for them."[8] If one Virgin business underperformed, it might contaminate the entire brand. One source of risk was Virgin Rail: the structural problems of Britain's congested rail infrastructure made it difficult to provide a reliable, punctual service.

Despite his renown, Branson, too, might be waning in market appeal. Was there a risk that, having seen Branson as flight attendant, Branson in a wedding dress, Branson with different world leaders, and Branson's hot-air ballooning stunts, the public might tire of his exploits?

Richard Branson and the Virgin Business Development Model

Almost all of the Virgin businesses were new start-ups. From the founding of *Student* magazine through to the formation of Virgin Galactic, Branson's strength as a businessman was in conceiving and implementing new business ideas, not that Branson was the source of all of Virgin's new business ideas: he acted as a magnet for would-be entrepreneurs from both inside and outside the Virgin group. The idea for Virgin Bride had originated with a Virgin Atlantic employee dismayed by the products and services offered by existing UK bridal stores. Virgin Active South Africa resulted from Nelson Mandela's request that Branson acquire a South African health club chain that had gone bankrupt putting thousands of jobs at risk. Virgin encouraged the submission of new business ideas to its corporate development offices in London, Sydney, and New York.

Virgin's approach to business start-ups reflected Branson's values of innocence, innovation, and irreverence for authority. His business ventures, just like his sporting exploits, reflected a "just live life" attitude and a "bigger the challenge, greater the fun" belief. He was particularly drawn to markets where conservatism and lack of imagination by incumbent firms resulted in underserved customers. Here Virgin's "new" and "anti-establishment attitude" could offer customers a better alternative. Financial services were one sector where Branson hoped to bring a breath of fresh air.

However, by 2012, Virgin's business development initiatives were more about systems than about Branson's entrepreneurial intuition:

> When we start a new venture, we base it on hard research and analysis. Typically, we review the industry and put ourselves in the customer's shoes to see what could make it better. We ask fundamental questions: Is the customer confused or badly served? Is this an opportunity for restructuring a market and creating competitive advantage? What are the competitors doing? Is this an opportunity for building the Virgin brand? Can we add value? Will it interact with our other businesses? Is there an appropriate trade-off between risk and reward?

We are also able to draw on talented people from throughout the Group. New ventures are often steered by people seconded from other parts of Virgin, who bring with them the trademark management style, skills and experience. We frequently create partnerships with others to combine industry specific skills, knowledge, and operational expertise.

Contrary to what some people may think, our constantly expanding and eclectic empire is neither random nor reckless. Each successive venture demonstrates our devotion to picking the right market and the right opportunity.

Once a Virgin company is up and running, several factors contribute to making it a success. The power of the Virgin Brand; Richard Branson's personal reputation; our unrivalled network of friends, contacts and partners; the Virgin management style; the way talent is empowered to flourish within the group. To some traditionalists, these may not seem hard headed enough. To them, the fact that Virgin has minimal management layers, no bureaucracy, a tiny board and no massive global HQ is an anathema. But it works for us! The proof of our success is real and tangible.

Our companies are part of a family rather than a hierarchy. They are empowered to run their own affairs, yet the companies help one another, and solutions to problems often come from within the Group somewhere. In a sense we are a commonwealth, with shared ideas, values, interests and goals.[9]

The Virgin Group's Management Structure and Style

As already noted, the legal and ownership structure of the Virgin group was, and still is, highly complex. A number of holding companies own, either wholly or partially, the equity of Virgin's many operating companies. For example:

- Virgin Money Ltd was the main UK operating company of Virgin Money; however, its activities were contracted out to Virgin Money Management Services Ltd. It was a subsidiary of Virgin Money Holdings (UK) Ltd, which was a subsidiary of Virgin Financial Services UK Holdings Ltd.
- West Coast Trains Ltd, Virgin's main UK rail franchise, was owned by Virgin Rail Group, which was owned by Virgin Rail Group Holdings Ltd, the majority of which was owned by Virgin Holdings Ltd, which was a subsidiary of Virgin Wings Ltd.

These holding companies were, for the most part, ultimately owned by Virgin Group Holdings Limited, a private company registered in the British Virgin Islands and owned by Richard Branson and a series of family trusts.

This financial and legal structure reflected Branson's wariness of the financial community and his unconventional ideas about business. Virgin's intricate structure involving offshore private companies and holding companies which disguised the identity of minority shareholders through the use of bearer shares cloaked the Virgin empire in a thick veil of secrecy.[10] However, it also allowed Virgin to retain the entrepreneurial dynamism of a collection of mostly medium-sized companies which were able to draw upon the enthusiasm and commitment of their employees.

Branson's approach to management reflected his values and personality. Informality and disrespect for convention were central to Branson's way of business. His dislike of office buildings and the usual symbols of corporate success was reflected in the absence of a corporate head office and his willingness to do business from his family homes, whether a houseboat in Maida Vale or his Necker Island Caribbean retreat. This lack of separation between work, family, and leisure—indicated by the involvement of cousins, aunts, childhood friends, and dinner-party acquaintances in business relationships—reflected a view of business as part of life which, like life, should involve excitement, creativity, and fun. His hands-off approach to his business empire was based upon giving autonomy and incentives to talented managers that he trusted. Once a new Virgin business was up and running, it was handed over to a trusted managing director and financial controller. The top management team were provided with equity stakes or options and expected to develop the company. A large number of Virgin managers have become millionaires.

Branson's management approach also reflected the social changes during his formative years. To many of his generation he embodied the spirit of "New Britain." In a country where business leaders were members of the establishment and identified with the existing social structure, Branson was seen as a revolutionary. Despite a privileged family background, Branson had the ability to transcend the social classes that traditionally divided British society and segmented consumer markets. As such, he was part of a movement that sought to escape the Old Britain of fading empire, class antagonism, Victorian values, and stiff-upper-lip hypocrisy.

Branson's antipathy toward authority and convention was reflected in his disrespect for conventional business principles. He argued that Virgin's network of small companies combined "small is beautiful" with "strength through unity." In a speech to the Institute of Directors in 1993, he explained the business maxims that he believed to be necessary for success: "Staff first, then customers and shareholders" should be the chairman's priority if the goal is better performance. Other guiding principles included: "Shape the business around the people"; "Build don't buy"; "Be best, not biggest"; "Pioneer, don't follow the leader"; "Capture every fleeting idea"; and "Drive for change."

Since the beginning of the 21st century, the management of the Virgin group has become more formalized. In particular:

- Virgin Management Ltd is the source of management leadership to the group. As the website explains:

  At the centre, Virgin Management Ltd (VML) provides advisory and managerial support to all of the different Virgin companies and our specialist Sector teams around the world. Our people in London, New York and Sydney offer regional support and between us and the Sector teams we manage Virgin's interests across the whole of the Virgin Group.

  VML's fastidious number-crunchers get to manage Virgin's financial assets in the group, our witty marketeers and intelligent communicators get to protect and maximise the value of the Virgin brand and our touchy-feely people teams ensure Virgin is an employer of choice.[11]

- Sector teams, each headed by a managing partner, provide oversight to companies within a particular area of business: "These bigwigs look after interests in aviation, media & telecom, financial services, health & wellness, leisure, and Green (clean technology) investments. The specialists keep our companies on their toes and ensure we keep developing better experiences and world beating products."[12]

- Virgin Enterprises Ltd owns and manages the Virgin brand. Neil Hobbs, intellectual property lawyer for Virgin Enterprises, explained: "Our role is both to optimize and enhance the value of the brand and to protect that by ensuring that that value is not diminished through infringement by third parties. Virgin Enterprises licenses companies both within and outside the Virgin Group to use the Virgin brand."[13] During the year to end-March 2011, royalties from licensing the Virgin brand to members of the group and to other companies amounted to just under £35 million.

In July 2011, Virgin underwent a significant management reorganization with the appointment of two co-chief executives to head Virgin Group Holdings Ltd: David Baxby, head of both Virgin Asia-Pacific and the aviation business, and Josh Bayliss, general counsel.

The company described the move as part of a long-term plan devised by Peter Norris, chairman, and Mr Murphy. "The aim now is to stick our heads above the parapet and look at the Far East, look at South America, look more at North America. We look to establish bridgeheads into new markets and then bring in partners," said spokesman Nick Fox.

Mr Baxby, 37, a former Goldman Sachs banker, and Mr Bayliss, 38, would be based in London and Geneva, as part of a small senior team of managers. Virgin's chief financial officer, Mark Poole—who spent 20 years at the company—would also step down, to be replaced by an internal candidate. The new co-chiefs would oversee all the company's investments, which included operations in telecoms and media, banking, rail, aerospace, health and renewable energy.

Nevertheless, formal structures and process formed a minor part of the Virgin management system. At the heart were two critical components of the system: culture and personal relations.

The Virgin culture was the organizational embodiment of Branson's eccentricity, sense of fun, disrespect for hierarchy, informality, commitment to employees and consumers, and belief in hard work and individual responsibility. While the working environment was informal, anti-corporate, and defined by the popular culture of its era, expectations were high in terms of commitment, acceptance of personal responsibility, long hours of work when needed, and striving to meet performance goals.

In terms of personal relationships, Virgin's ability to launch so many new businesses and prevent its business empire falling into chaos depended critically upon Branson and his core of long-term associates who formed the senior management team of the Virgin Group and occupied key executive positions within individual operating companies.

Key executives at Virgin Group during the first decade of this century included:

- Will Whitehorn was Branson's right-hand man for two decades. In 2011, he retired as CEO of Virgin Galactic.

- Gordon McCallum joined Virgin in 1997 as group strategy director from McKinsey & Company. He pioneered Virgin's entry into telecom and since September 2005 was CEO of Virgin Management Ltd.
- Stephen Murphy had a career in finance with Mars, Unilever, and Quaker Oats. At Virgin he headed Virgin's airline businesses before becoming CEO of Virgin Group Holdings Ltd, a position he relinquished at the end of 2011.
- David Baxby was head of Virgin Asia-Pacific and the aviation business; from January 2012 he took over as co-CEO of Virgin Group Holdings.
- Josh Bayliss was Virgin's general counsel before being appointed co-CEO of Virgin Group Holdings together with David Baxby.
- Patrick McCall was formerly an investment banker at UBS Warburg before becoming a member of the top management team at Virgin Management Ltd and a board member of several Virgin companies.
- Rowan Gormley led several Virgin start-ups, including Virgin Money and Virgin Wine, before leaving Virgin in 2008.
- Frances Farrow joined Virgin Atlantic from the law firm Binder Hamlyn and became CEO of Virgin USA, Inc.
- Peter Norris was head of Barings Bank; after several years as strategy adviser to Virgin, he became chairman of Virgin Group Holdings Ltd.
- Carla Stent was COO of Virgin Management Ltd. She previously held senior positions at Barclays Bank and Thomas Cook.

Source: Virgin press releases (www.virgin.com) and various web sources.

Virgin's Financial Performance

Financial reporting by the Virgin companies was fragmented, hard to locate, and difficult to interpret. No consolidated accounts existed for the group as a whole. In addition to the many operating companies, ownership of these companies lay with a number of holding companies and intermediate holding companies. Tracking financial results over time was difficult because investments in Virgin operating companies were frequently transferred between group companies. UK-registered Virgin companies submitted audited financial statements to Companies House (a government agency). Table 1 shows financial results for some of the Virgin's major subsidiaries.

Virgin's financial management emphasized maximizing the returns to Virgin Group equity through high financial leverage and the use of equity partners to finance Virgin's business ventures. Typically, Virgin was able to use the Virgin brand and Branson's celebrity status to obtain 51% or more of the equity of new ventures while contributing a minority of the equity capital. For example, Virgin's stake in Virgin Direct required an initial outlay of only £15 million; its partner, AMP, put £450 million into the joint venture. Branson put only £2,000 into Virgin Clothing and Virgin Vie; equal partner, Victory Corporation, invested £20 million. At Virgin Blue, Branson's initial investment was a mere A$12 million. Virgin's joint-venture partners included Singapore Airlines (owned 49% of Virgin Atlantic), Stagecoach PLC

TABLE 1 Financial results for selected Virgin companies, 2010–2011

Company	Revenue (£million)	Net profit (£million)	ROE (%)	Employees	Year ending	Comments
Virgin Wings Ltd	3,339.1	(57.3)	n.a.[a]	12,744	31/03/10	Virgin's main parent company for its UK businesses. Main subsidiary is Virgin Holdings Ltd
Virgin Holdings Ltd	3,175.6	(29.0)	(1.6)	12,744	31/03/10	Investment holding company for Virgin's UK-based travel, telecom, and other businesses
Virgin Enterprises Ltd	35.1	41.7	40.1	n.a.	31/03/11	Owns and licenses Virgin brand
Virgin Management Ltd	5.6	(33.2)	(15.6)	111	31/03/10	Manages Virgin group companies
Virgin Active Group Ltd	445.2	(8.5)	n.a.[a]	8,971	31/12/10	Operates chain of health clubs
Virgin Atlantic Airways Ltd	2,263.5	11.2	6.4	7,546	28/02/11	Airline
Virgin Money Ltd	73.9	31.3	85.3	n.a.	31/12/10	Owns Virgin's credit card business
Virgin Financial Services UK Holdings Ltd	n.a.	76.8	63.0	281	31/12/10	Owns Virgin's UK financial services businesses
Virgin Rail Group Ltd	n.a.	29.8	125.2	4,456	05/03/11	Owns West Coast Trains Ltd
Virgin Rail Group Holdings Ltd	797.8	37.9	53.5	2,912	05/03/11	Owns Virgin Rail Group
Virgin Media Inc.	3,875.8	(141.4)	(11.1)	12,400	31/12/10	Offers "quad play" telecom services in UK. Virgin Group owns 10.7%

Notes:
Figures in parentheses denote a loss.
n.a.: not available.
ROE: Return on equity.
[a] = ROE cannot be calculated because of negative shareholders' equity.

Source: Various annual reports submitted to Companies House.

(49% owner of Virgin Rail), Citicorp (co-owner of Virgin Money Australia), and Tata Group (co-owner of Virgin Mobile India).

Looking to the Future

The management changes of 2010–2011—and notably the appointment of co-CEOs and the creation of a sector management structure to achieve coordination among Virgin companies within related businesses—suggested a move toward greater centralization in the management of Virgin's sprawling empire. These management changes reflected changes in Virgin's strategy. The rate at which Virgin was launching new businesses was much lower during 2000–2011 than during the previous two decades. Virgin was showing a greater willingness to divest businesses where there were eager acquirers and close businesses that lacked profitability or growth potential. Virgin was even willing to enter new businesses by acquisition rather than start-up.

But establishing a strategic direction for Virgin was confounded by the different views within the group as to the nature of Virgin's business model. The preponderance of finance experts and former investment bankers among its senior management encouraged many to think of Virgin as a private equity fund. Yet, private equity companies (such as Blackstone, Carlyle, and Kohlberg Kravis Roberts) were engaged in the acquisition (and subsequent divestment) of established businesses, not in creating them from scratch. Others viewed Virgin as a conglomerate; yet, although highly diversified, conglomerates too were in the business of acquiring established businesses. Branson had likened Virgin to a Japanese *keiretsu*: there were clear parallels in terms of equity linkages, interlocking directorships, collaboration between member companies, and a focus on long-term development. The Virgin website referred to Virgin as a "branded venture capital organization"; however, venture capital firms were engaged in financing other people's start-ups: Virgin created its own businesses, typically using other people's money.

Clearly, the strategy and structure of the Virgin group did not fit within any existing category of business enterprise. A more relevant question for Virgin was what should its business model be? If Virgin's core resource was its brand, did it need to own the businesses that bore its name: could it simply operate as a brand franchising organization licensing its brand to other companies (as it did with Virgin Records and Virgin Media)? If the core of its business was creating new businesses, then perhaps it should organize itself as an incubator of new start-ups. This would also imply divesting businesses once they were up and running.

Whichever strategic model Virgin followed, it seemed likely that it would need to continue to make changes to its structure and management system. The informal, collaborative approach that had allowed the Virgin group to survive and develop despite a turbulent economic environment had depended greatly upon Richard Branson and his personal leadership. Inevitably, his role within the group would diminish over time.

Appendix: The History of Virgin

1968	First issue of *Student* magazine, January 26.
1970	Start of Virgin mail-order operation.
1971	First Virgin record shop opens in Oxford Street, London.
1972	Virgin recording studio opens at The Manor near Oxford, England.
1977	Virgin record label launched with Mike Oldfield's *Tubular Bells*.
	Virgin Records signs the Sex Pistols.
1978	Virgin opens The Venue nightclub in London.
1983	Virgin Vision formed to enter broadcasting and produce and distribute films and videos. Vanson Developments formed as real-estate development company.
	Virgin Games (computer games software publishing) launched.
1984	Virgin Atlantic Airways and Virgin Cargo launched.
	First hotel investment (Denya, Mallorca). Virgin Vision launches The Music Channel, a 24-hour satellite-delivered music station and releases its first feature film, *1984*, with Richard Burton and John Hurt.
1985	Virgin Holidays formed.
1986	Virgin Group PLC, comprising the music, retail and property, and communications divisions, floated on London Stock Exchange. Placement of 35% of equity raises $56 million. Virgin's aviation, clubs, and vacation businesses remain part of the privately owned Voyager Group.
1987	Virgin Records forms subsidiaries in the US and Japan.
	British Satellite Broadcasting (in which Virgin has minority interest) awarded satellite broadcasting license. (Virgin sells its shareholding in 1988.)
	Virgin acquires Mastertronics Group, distributor of Sega video games in Europe.
	Virgin Airship & Balloon Company launched to provide aerial marketing services.
1988	Virgin Broadcasting formed to further develop Virgin's radio and TV interests.
	Virgin Hotels formed.
	Virgin Megastores opened in Sydney, Paris, and Glasgow.
	Branson takes Virgin private with £248 million bid for outstanding shares.
1989	Virgin Music Group sells 25% stake to Fujisankei Communications for $150 million.
	Virgin Vision (video distribution) sold to MCEG of Los Angeles for $83 million.
1990	Virgin Retail Group and Marui form joint venture company to operate Megastores in Japan.
	Virgin Lightships formed to develop helium airships for advertising.
1991	W. H. Allen PLC acquired. Merged with Virgin Books to form Virgin Publishing.
	Sale of Virgin Mastertronic to Sega. Remaining part of the business becomes
	Virgin Games. Virgin Retail Group forms 50:50 joint venture with WHSmith to develop UK retail business.
1992	Sale of Virgin Music Group to Thorn EMI PLC.
	Joint venture with Blockbuster to develop Megastores in Europe, Australia, and the US.
	Virgin Communications launches Virgin Radio, Britain's first national commercial rock station.
	Vintage Air Tours established to fly Orlando–Florida Keys in vintage DC-3s.
1993	Virgin Games floated as Virgin Interactive Entertainment PLC, with Hasbro and Blockbuster taking minority equity stakes.
	Virgin Euromagnetics launches a range of personal computers.

1994	Virgin Cola Company formed as joint venture with Cott Corp.
	Agreement with W. Grant to launch Virgin Vodka.
	Virgin acquires WHSmith's 75% stake in Our Price retail music stores.
	Virgin Retail Group forms joint ventures to develop Megastores in Hong Kong and South Korea.
	Virgin City Jet service launched between Dublin and London City Airport.
1995	Virgin Direct Personal Financial Service is launched as a joint venture with Norwich Union (its equity later acquired by Australian Mutual Provident).
	MGM Cinemas acquired to create Virgin Cinemas.
1996	Virgin Travel Group acquires Euro-Belgian Airlines to form Virgin Express.
	V2 record label and music publishing company launched.
	London & Continental Railways (Virgin a minority shareholder) wins £3-billion contract to build the Channel Tunnel Rail Link and operate Eurostar rail services.
1997	Virgin Rail awarded franchise to operate the West Coast train services.
	Virgin.net, an internet service provider, formed with NTL.
	Victory Corporation, a joint venture with Rory McCarthy, launches the Virgin Clothing and Virgin Vie toiletry products.
	Majority share in Virgin Radio sold to Chris Evans's Ginger Media Group.
	Virgin Bride retail chain formed.
	Virgin One telephone bank account and "one-stop integrated financial service" launched in collaboration with Royal Bank of Scotland.
1998	Virgin Entertainment acquires WHSmith's 75% stake in Virgin/Our Price.
1999	Virgin sells its UK cinema chain to UGC for £215 million.
	Virgin launches mobile phone service in joint venture with Deutsche Telekom's One-to-One (November).
	Forty-nine percent of Virgin Atlantic sold to Singapore Airlines for £600 million.
2000	Virgin Mobile launches US wireless phone service in joint venture with Sprint.
	Virgin Mobile Australia (a joint venture with Cable & Wireless) launched.
	Virgin announces the closing of its clothing company.
	Virgin Cars launched to sell new cars online.
	Virgin and Bear Stearns form Lynx New Media, a $130-million venture capital fund.
	Inaugural flight of Virgin Blue, Virgin's low-cost Australian airline.
	Branson knighted by the Queen: becomes Sir Richard Branson.
	Virgin fails to win franchise to run Britain's government-owned National Lottery.
2001	Fifty percent of Virgin Blue sold to Patrick Corporation for A$138 million.
	Virgin expands into Singapore and South East Asia with joint ventures with local companies in radio stations, cosmetic retailing, and wireless phone services.
	Virgin.net merges its ISP and portal businesses.
	Sixteen French Virgin Megastores sold to Lagardère Media for €150 million.
2002	Virgin Bikes (UK) begins direct sale of new motorcycles at discount prices.
	Virgin Mobile offers wireless telecom services in the US.
2003	Virgin Blue initial public offering; Virgin retains 25% of equity.
2004	Fifty percent stake of Virgin Money repurchased from AMP for £90 million.
	Virgin Digital launched. Offers online music store and digital music download capabilities.
	Virgin Cars and Virgin Bikes sold to MotorSolutions Ltd.
2005	Virgin Mobile launched in Canada.
	Virgin Active UK acquires rival health club chain, Holmes Place.

2006	NTL acquires Virgin Mobile to offer broadband, mobile telephone, and TV services; rebranded as Virgin Media in 2007.
	Virgin Mobile and Virgin Money launched in South Africa.
	Virgin Fuel established to produce a clean fuel.
	Virgin Mobile Australia acquired by Optus, a joint-venture partner.
	Virgin Cars closed.
2007	Virgin Health Bank launched.
	Virgin America, a San Francisco-based airline, begins operations.
	Virgin Megastores UK sold.
2008	Virgin Blue Holdings launches Virgin Australia International Airlines offering trans-Pacific flights.
	Virgin Mobile India, a joint venture with Tata Teleservices, launched.
2009	Virgin Green Fund established to acquire equity in renewable energy ventures.
	Virgin Vie closed.
	Sprint Nextel acquires Virgin Mobile USA.
2010	Healthcare provider Assura Medical Ltd. Acquired by Virgin Healthcare Holdings.
	Virgin Money UK acquires Church House Trust to obtain a banking license.
	Virgin Racing, a Formula One team, launched.
	Virgin Gaming offers interactive playing of popular video games.
	Launch of Virgin Produced, a film and television production company based in Los Angeles, California.
	Virgin Cosmetics and Virgin Money USA are closed.
2011	Virgin Active acquires rival Esporta for £80 million.
	Virgin Active acquires UK rival, Esporta. CVC Capital Partners acquire 51% of Virgin Active.
	Virgin Unite, Virgin's charitable foundation, launches Branson Centre of Entrepreneurship to encourage job creation in the Caribbean.

Source: www.virgin.com.

Notes

1. Forbes estimated Branson's net worth at $2.4 billion, making him Britain's fifth-richest individual.
2. "Behind Branson," *Economist*, February 21, 1998, pp. 63–6; "The Future for Virgin," *Financial Times*, August 13, 1998, pp. 24–5.
3. Richard Branson, letter to *Economist*, March 7, 1998, p. 6.
4. In 2011, Virgin Blue, Pacific Blue, and V Australia merged to form Virgin Australia.
5. "The Virgin Brand," http://www.virgin.com/about-us, accessed September 27, 2012. Reproduced with permission.
6. "The Virgin Brand," http://www.virgin.com/about-us, accessed September 27, 2012. Reproduced with permission.
7. P. Robison, "Briton Hopes Beverage Will Conquer Coke's Monopoly," *Bloomberg News*, December 14, 1997.
8. M. Wells, "Red Baron," *Fortune magazine*, July 3, 2000.
9. "The Virgin Brand," http://www.virgin.com/about-us, accessed September 27, 2012. Reproduced with permission.
10. By registering in the British Virgin Islands, Virgin Group Holdings Ltd is not liable to local taxes and is allowed "maximum confidentiality and anonymity"; see http://www.offshorecorporation.com/bvi-company.
11. "The Virgin Brand," http://www.virgin.com/about-us, accessed September 27, 2012. Reproduced with permission.
12. "The Virgin Brand," http://www.virgin.com/about-us, accessed September 27, 2012. Reproduced with permission.
13. "Consolidating and Protecting the Licensed Virgin Brand," http://www.cscorporatedomains.com/downloads/IPScan_issue10_virgin.pdf, accessed March 3, 2007.

A video clip relating to this case is available in your interactive e-book at **www.wileyopenpage.com**

Case 20 Google Inc.: What's the Corporate Strategy?

June 2012

The launch of Google's email system, Gmail, in April 2004 marked the beginning of a host of new product launches and new business initiatives at Google. With $1.67 billion from its initial public offering (IPO), Google expanded rapidly. Between its August 2004 IPO and the end of 2011, Google acquired 99 different companies.[1]

Initially, new products extended the scope of Google's information search and its ability to exploit the advertising potential of its search engine. However, with the acquisition of YouTube, the video-sharing website, for $1.65 billion in 2006, the launch of the Android operating system for mobile devices in 2007, and the introduction of the Chrome web browser in September 2008, which was followed by the announcement that Chrome would be extended into an open-source computer operating system, several observers were baffled as to the direction and rationale of Google's corporate strategy. A key concern was that Google's many ambitious initiatives were adding cost and distracting management at a time when advertising revenues were being squeezed by the economic downturn. Chris O'Brien of the *San Jose Mercury* summed up the feelings of many in a blog entitled "Google's growing identity crisis":

> There are a handful of reasons people generally cite for Google's success. The power of its search engine algorithm. The elegance of a business model that matches text ads to searches. A restless, innovative culture continually striving to improve and evolve its products.
>
> Here's what always struck me about Google: its simplicity. At the start, Google did one thing phenomenally well. Its search engine was so superior that the company's name became synonymous with search itself. And its home page was, and remains, a visual model of simplicity: a sea of white space, the Google logo, a search box, a couple of links—and no ads.
>
> The homepage aside, though, Google increasingly feels like a company running in a thousand directions at once. Over the past year, it has released a steady stream of high-profile products that seem to have little or no relation to the core identity expressed on its corporate homepage: "Google's mission is to organize the world's information and make it universally accessible and useful." The problem is that in expanding into so many different areas—productivity applications, mobile operating system, a Web browser—that the identity of Google itself has become

---

This case was prepared by Robert M. Grant. ©2012 Robert M. Grant.

muddled. No doubt, this all follows some clear logic from inside the Googleplex. But from the outside, it's getting harder every day to articulate what Google is. Is it a Web company? A software company? Something else entirely?[2]

The replacement of CEO Eric Schmidt by co-founder Larry Page on April 4, 2011 was viewed as the end of "adult supervision" for Google's youthful founders. Schmidt, a Silicon Valley veteran, had been installed as CEO by Page and Brin in 2001. After Page's first year at the helm, *Wired* magazine's discerned a new era of focus in Google's strategy:

> Page's reign has been characterized by focus. Focus on product. Focus on the threat from a social networking movement embodied by Facebook. A focusing of Google itself, from a collection of disparate services to a single one with intermeshed components. And a more focused leadership structure where every employee can cite a single name when asked who is in charge. Google is Larry's company now.[3]

However, concerns about Google's propensity for reckless expansion resurfaced with its acquisition of Motorola Mobility, the wireless handset maker, for $12.5 billion—Google's first multi-billion-dollar acquisition. Whereas all Google's prior acquisitions had been of software companies, with Motorola Google had now become a hardware producer as well.

The concern of many stock analysts was that most of Google's diversifying initiatives had done little to boost revenue, let alone generate profit. The *Financial Times'* Lex column had dubbed Google a "one-trick pony": "Google has what amounts to a license to print money. By inserting itself between the shops and shoppers of the world, the search provider takes a small commission every time it connects the two." Beyond its core search business, Google's activities added cost, but little revenue: "Just look at YouTube . . . running costs will be between $500m and $1bn this year, while revenues will only be in the region of $240m . . . the economics appear unsustainable.[4] The Motorola acquisition reinforced these fears:

> Even in the best of scenarios, digesting Motorola will be a challenge. The company, with 20,000 employees, lost 20 percent of its market share in 2011 . . . Motorola will likely drag down Google's earnings for years to come. Barclays' analyst Anthony Di Clemente assumes that the combined company will deliver profit margins of 41 percent in 2012, vs. 55 percent if Google remains separate from Motorola.
>
> Google's dive into hardware could also alienate device makers like Samsung and HTC, which rely on the Android operating system for almost all their phones. If Google prioritizes Motorola over its competitors—say, giving it earlier access to Android upgrades—they might rely more on other operating systems, such as Microsoft's soon-to-be-released Windows 8. "They need to be very careful that they don't damage the ecosystem they've so carefully built," says Bill Whyman, an analyst with International Strategy & Investment Group. Otherwise, he warns, the results could be "disastrous."[5]

Independent investment analysis Henry Blodget was even more skeptical: "Google is taking on the extraordinary challenge of buying a dying smartphone manufacturing elephant—Motorola—and going into the hardware manufacturing game. This is a huge, risky, and distracting move for Google, and the odds are that it will fail spectacularly."[6] Table 1 lists Google's key financial data.

TABLE 1 Google Inc.: Key financial data, 2004–2011 ($million)

	2004	2005	2006	2007	2008	2009	2010	2011
Income data								
Revenues	3,189	6,139	10,605	16,594	21,796	23,651	29,321	37,905
Costs and expenses								
Cost of revenues	1,469	2,577	4,225	6,649	8,622	8,844	10,417	13,188
R & D	395	600	1,229	2,120	2,793	2,843	3,762	5,162
Sales and marketing	296	468	850	1,461	1,946	1,984	2,799	4,589
General and administrative	188	387	752	1,279	1,803	1,668	1,962	2,724
Total costs and expenses	2,549	4,121	7,055	11,510	15,164	15,339	18,940	26,163
Income from operations	640	2,017	3,550	5,084	6,632	8,312	10,381	11,742
Net interest income	10	124	461	590	316	69	415	584
Income before income taxes	650	2,142	4,011	5,674	5,854	8,381	10,796	12,326
Net income	399	1,465	3,077	4,204	4,227	6,520	8,505	9,737
Balance sheet data								
Cash and marketable securities	2,132	8,034	11,243	14,218	15,845	24,485	34,975	44,626
Long-term liabilities	43	107	128	611	1,226	1,746	1,614	5,516
Total stockholders' equity	2,929	9,418	17,039	22,689	28,238	36,004	46,241	58,145

Source: Google, 10-K report, 2008.

The History of Google, 1996–2012

The Google Search Engine

Larry Page and Sergey Brin were PhD students at Stanford University. In January 1996, Page's search for a dissertation topic led him to examine the linkage structure of the World Wide Web. Page and Brin developed a page-ranking algorithm that used backlink data (references by a web page to other web pages) to measure the importance of any web page. Although several rudimentary web search engines were in existence, most selected web pages on the basis of the frequency with which a particular search word appeared. They called their search engine "Google" and on September 15, 1997 registered the domain name "google.com." They incorporated Google Inc., on September 7, 1998 in Menlo Park, California. Google's "PageRank" algorithm was granted a patent on September 4, 2001.

Search engines met the need of the rapidly growing number of people who were turning to the World Wide Web for information and commercial transactions. As the number of websites grew exponentially, locating relevant web content became a critical need. Page and Brin were not alone. Among the early crawler-based web search engines were WebCrawler, Lycos, Excite, Infoseek, Inktomi, Northern Light, and AltaVista. Several of these search engines became popular *portal sites*—websites that offered users their first port of entry to the web. Other portal sites soon recognized the need to offer a search facility. Yahoo! licensed AltaVista's search engine, then in 1998 replaced AltaVista with Inktomi.

The Google search engine attracted a rapidly growing following because of its superior page ranking and its simple design—it did not compromise its search functionality by attempting to become a portal. In 2000, Google began selling advertisements—paid web links associated with search keywords. These "sponsored links" were brief, plain text ads with a click-on URL, which appeared alongside with web search results for specific keywords. Advertisers bid for keywords; it was these "cost-per-click" bids weighted by an ad's click-through rate (CTR) that determined the order in which a sponsored link would appear. In offering a web-based advertising system linking third-party advertisers to a search engine of informational website, Google's system copied many of the features of the then market leader, Overture. After 2000, Google experienced explosive growth and was boosted in May 2002 by AOL's decision to adopt Google's search engine and its paid listings service.

After two rounds of venture capital funding, Google became a public company on August 19, 2004 when an IPO of about 7% of Google's shares raised $1.67 billion, giving Google a market capitalization of $23 billion.

Organizing the World's Information

The financial boost provided by Google's IPO fueled even more rapid development of its business. In its core web search business, Google was continually seeking to improve users' search experiences while finding ways to better monetize its dominance of web search through advertising. However, the most striking feature of Google's development was its determination to grow beyond its core web search business. This expansionist urge reflected the company's raison d'être: it had never seen itself just as an internet search engine. Its declared mission was "to organize the world's information and make it universally accessible and useful." Google's IPO prospectus had elaborated this intent:

> We serve our users by developing products that enable people to more quickly and easily find, create and organize information. We place a premium on products that matter to many people and have the potential to improve their lives, especially in areas in which our expertise enables us to excel.
>
> Search is one such area. People use search frequently and the results are often of great importance to them. For example, people search for information on medical conditions, purchase decisions, technical questions, long-lost friends and other topics about which they care a great deal. Delivering quality search results requires significant computing power, advanced software and complex processes—areas in which we have expertise and a high level of focus.[7]

Google's quest to meet the information needs of society caused it to continually seek opportunities for accessing new information and provide it through additional media channels. As Exhibit 1 shows, Google's quest to provide accessibility to the world's information had taken it into new communication media (notably wireless telephony, but also radio, TV, and video games) and sources of information beyond third-party websites.[8] These new sources of information included images (Google Image Search), maps (Google Maps), academic articles (Google Scholar), books (Google Book Search), satellite imagery (Google Earth), news (Google News), patents (Google Patent Search), video (Google Video; YouTube), finance (Google Finance), and web logs (Google Blog Search).

However, Google's entrepreneurial and technological dynamism also resulted in initiatives that extended beyond the accessing and organizing of information. Since the introduction of Gmail in 2004, Google offered a widening array of software and services for communicating, creating, and manipulating 2D and 3D images, producing documents, creating web pages, managing time, and social networking. For example, Google Docs is a suite of office productivity software for creating, storing, and sharing text documents, spreadsheets, and presentations; Blogger is software that allows individuals to create their own web logs; Google Groups allows individuals to establish and support communication within a group formed around a particular interest or identity; Orkut and Google+ are social networking services; and Picasa is downloadable software for organizing, editing, and sharing photographs. Appendix 1 provides a timeline of Google's development.

Most of these additional products and services offered no new revenue opportunities for Google. However, Google was also expanding its advertising-based revenue model. Google's primary source of advertising revenue was AdWords, which was launched in 2000. Advertisers specify the words that should trigger their ads and the maximum amount they are willing to pay per click. When a user searches google.com, short text advertisements appear as "sponsored links" on the right side of the screen.

AdSense uses an advertisement placement technology developed by Applied Semantics (acquired in 2003). It allows Google to place ads on third-party websites. In 2011, 28% of Google's advertising revenue was derived from partners' websites, and 72% from its own websites (Table 2). Appendix 2 explains AdWords and AdSense in greater detail.

TABLE 2 Google's revenues, 2006–2011 ($million)

	2006	2007	2008	2009	2010	2011
Advertising revenues of which:						
—Google websites	6,332.8	10,624.7	14,413.8	15,723.0	19,444.0	26,145.0
—Google Network websites	4,159.8	5,787.9	6,714.7	7,166.0	8,792.0	10,396.0
—Total advertising revenues	10,492.6	16,412.6	21,128.5	22,889	28,236	36,531
Licensing and other revenues	112.3	181.4	6,67.1	762.0	1,085.0	1,374.0
Total revenues	10,604.9	16,594.0	21,795.6	23,651.0	29,321.0	37,905.0

Source: Google Inc., 10-K report, 2008.

In 2007 and 2008, Google's diversification efforts took a dramatic new turn with Google's entry into mobile telephony and web browsers.

Android and Mobile Telephony

Google acquired Android Inc. in 2005 and accelerated the development of its Linux-based operating system for mobile devices. In 2007, it formed the Open Handset Alliance, in which 86 hardware, software, and telecommunication companies devoted themselves to advancing open standards for mobile devices. In November 2007, it launched the Android wireless communication software platform. *PC Advisor* commented:

> Google's announcement of the Android mobile development platform . . . is yet another example of the lengths the company will go to keep its advertising business growing at a jaw-dropping rate. It is also another awe-inspiring—or terrifying, depending on one's perspective—display of the engineering and business resources Google can unleash and of the power it has to influence, disrupt and rearrange markets . . . In a nutshell, Google announced a free, open-source application development platform called Android for mobile devices with the intention of eclipsing existing operating systems from Microsoft, Symbian, Palm and others . . . Android will have a complete set of components, including a Linux-based operating system, middleware stack, customizable user interface and applications. Google envisions that with Android, developers will flood the mobile market with new applications and online services that can be written once and deployed in many phones, something that, as Google sees it, the current mobile technical fragmentation prevents . . . Ultimately, what is propelling Google in this effort is its core advertising business, which the company recognizes it must extend to the mobile market.[9]

The following month (December 2007), Google entered the Federal Communication Commission's auction of 700MHz wireless spectrum. Interestingly, Google had no desire to win the auction. Its intention was to force the major telecom service providers into the auction so that a new section of the wireless spectrum would be developed for the wireless internet service. Google's lobbying had already ensured that whoever developed this portion of spectrum would be required to allow users to download any software application they wanted on their mobile device and to use any mobile devices they liked on that wireless network. The auction was won by AT&T and Verizon (who bid a total of $16 billion). Some thought the real winner was Google: while AT&T and Verizon would bear the costs of developing the 700MHz waveband, Google would be able to offer its Android system and mobile internet services without the need for any upfront investment.[10]

By May 2012, it was clear that Android was a spectacular success not only in preventing the domination of the smartphone and tablet market by Apple but also in establishing market leadership (Table 3). Android's success can be attributed to two main factors. First, its adoption by a large number of handset manufacturers of which by far the most important had been Samsung with 45% of the Android phones shipped in the first three months of 2012. Second, the ability of Android to attract large numbers of application developers. By May 25, 2012, there were an estimated 450,000 applications for Android.

TABLE 3   Shipments of smartphones, classified by operating system, 2011–2012

Mobile operating system	Unit shipments		Market share	
	2012 Q1 (million)	2011 Q1 (million)	2012 Q1 (%)	2011 Q1 (%)
Android (Google)	89.9	36.7	59.0	36.1
iOS (Apple)	35.1	18.6	23.0	18.3
Symbian (Nokia)	10.4	26.4	6.8	26.0
Blackberry OS (RIM)	9.7	13.8	6.4	13.6
Linux	3.5	3.2	2.3	3.1
Windows Phone 7, Windows Mobile (Microsoft)	3.3	2.6	2.2	2.6
Other	0.4	0.3	0.3	0.3
TOTAL	152.3	101.6	100.0	100.0

Source: IDC Worldwide Mobile Phone Tracker, May 24, 2012. Reproduced with permission of IDC.

Chrome

Google's announcement of its Chrome web browser on September 2, 2008 generated huge publicity, but little surprise. It was widely known that founders Brin and Page had wanted to launch a web browser since Google's early days. For several years Google had been a major source of technical and financial support for Mozilla's Firefox browser. According to Google's head of product development, Sundar Pichai: "Google's entire business is people using a browser to access us and the web." Google's explanation of its decision to launch its own browser emphasized the improved functionality for users: "Google Chrome is a browser that combines a minimal design with sophisticated technology to make the web faster, safer, and easier," claimed Google's website. Microsoft's Internet Explorer (IE), by contrast, was limited by the legacy of its 15-year history.

However, most observers believed that Google's strategic intention was not simply a superior user experience. Google also saw a threat from the new version of Microsoft's IE. Version 8 of IE, launched in beta mode in August 2008, allowed an "InPrivate" protection mode that would delete cookies and make it more difficult to track users' browsing habits. The result would be to limit Google's ability to use such information for targeted advertising.

Others believed that Google's primary intention was not so much to protect itself against Microsoft as to launch a direct attack upon Microsoft's dominance of personal computing and to speed the transition of computing to a new online environment:

> [Google Chrome] is an explicit attempt to accelerate the movement of computing off the desktop and into the cloud—where Google holds advantage. And it's an aggressive move destined to put the company even more squarely in the crosshairs of its rival Microsoft.[11]

The announcement ten months later that Google would add an operating system to its Chrome browser was seen as confirmation that the primary motivation of Chrome was to strike against the core of Microsoft's market strength.

The Motorola Acquisition

Google's own explanation for its acquisition of Motorola placed considerable weight on Motorola's rich portfolio of patents relating to wireless communication. Since July 2011, when a consortium of technology companies led by Apple and Microsoft purchased more than 6,000 mobile-device-related patents from Nortel Networks for about $4.5 billion, Google's Android was vulnerable. Motorola's patents would give Google a bigger bargaining chip and make it stronger for countering legal threats from competitors armed with their own patents, and Apple in particular.

Other commentators emphasized a different aspect of the acquisition: Google's potential to integrate more closely hardware and software development in the smartphone and tablet market. According to Phil McKinney of HP: "Everyone is figuring out that if you want to survive, you really want to control the experience end to end. The ability to control both the hardware platform and OS is absolutely critical."

The Motorola acquisition might also support Google's efforts to build its presence in mobile internet use. Motorola's Motoblur, a user interface that pulled together Twitter, Facebook, and other social sites, into a single stream of data, was viewed as having considerable potential for Google, especially if integrated with Google+. Larry Page also saw value in Motorola's expertise with other web-connected devices found around the home, including TV set-top boxes: "I think there's an opportunity to accelerate innovation in the home business by working together with the cable and telco industry as we go through a transition to internet protocol."[12] Motorola Mobility's CEO, agreed: "Our home business is uniquely positioned to capitalize on the convergence of mobile and home environments in partnership with our key customer."[13]

The unanswered question was the implications of Google having an in-house smartphone producer for its relations with Samsung, HTC, and other Android partners.

Google+

Google's first foray into social networking was the launch of Orkut in January 2004, the result of a project by a Google software engineer, Orkut Büyükköktenas. Orkut became successful in certain countries, most notably Brazil, India, and Estonia, but in most of the world was eclipsed by Facebook. Google's subsequent attempts to establish itself in social networking included Google Friend Connect (launched 2008, retired in March 2012) and Google Buzz (launched 2010, retired in 2011).

By 2011, Google executives began to view Facebook as Google's most dangerous competitor. The initial warning came in March 2010 when Facebook overtook Google as the most visited website within the US. The battle to capture internet users was one arena of competition; however, of greater financial significance to Google was competition for advertising:

> If you were an advertiser, who would you rather place your ads with? On the one hand, you have a company that will attempt to gear ads to things like the search history of its users. On the other hand, you have a company that knows where its users went to college, where they work, who they are friends with, what they're reading and sharing, and their favorite bands, books, foods, and colors. Advertisers want to target their ads to the people most likely to be receptive to them, and information is the key to targeting. The more information available, the better the targeting.[14]

There was also the threat that Facebook might compete directly with Google's core search business. In 2011, Facebook received a patent for a search algorithm— "Visual tags for search results generated from social network information"—which generated search results and ranked them according to popularity within a person's group of Facebook friends. *Business Insider*'s Pascal-Emmanuel Gobry commented: "It's at least conceivable that with enough tweaking Bing and Facebook could combine in some way into serious competition for Google."[15]

Google's Management and Capabilities

Google's phenomenal growth and capacity for innovation rested upon a management system that was unique, even by the unorthodox standards of Silicon Valley. Management scholar Gary Hamel identified several key features of this system:

- *Hiring policy*: Google's hiring was highly selective: "Google's leaders believe that one exceptional technologist is many times more valuable than one average engineer; hence they insist on hiring only the brightest of the bright— folks out on the right-hand end of the bell-shaped curve. They also believe that if you let one 'bozo' in, more will surely follow. Their logic is simple: A-level people want to work with A-level people."[16] This also meant that Google was a target for other software companies: Facebook's employees included large numbers of Google alumni.
- A *"dramatically flat, radically decentralized" organization*: According to Hamel: "In many ways, Google is organized like the internet itself: it's highly democratic, tightly connected, and flat. Like so much of Google's culture, the source of the company's radical decentralization can be traced back to Brin and Page, both of whom attended Montessori schools and credit much of their intellectual independence to that experience. Says Mayer: 'They don't like authority and they don't like being told what to do.' Brin and Page understand that breakthroughs come from questioning assumptions and smashing paradigms."[17]
- *Small, self-managing teams*: "Roughly half of Google's 10000 employees—all those involved in product development—work in small teams, with an average of three engineers per team. Even a large project such as Gmail, which might occupy 30 people, is broken into teams of three or four, each of which works on a specific service enhancement, such as building spam filters or improving the forwarding feature."[18] Teams appoint their own leaders, and engineers can switch teams without the need for permission from the HR department.
- *Rapid, low-cost experimentation*: "Evolutionary adaptation isn't the product of a grand plan, but of relentless experimentation . . . Google's 'just-try-it' philosophy is applied to even the company's most daunting projects, like digitizing the world's libraries . . . Google Book Search began with a makeshift experiment aimed at answering a critical question; in this case: how long does it take to digitize a book? To find out, Page and Mayer rigged up a piece of plywood with a couple of clamps and proceeded to photograph each page of a 300-page book, using a metronome to keep pace. With Mayer flipping

pages, and one half of Google's founding team taking digital snapshots, it took 40 minutes to turn the ink into pixels. An optical character recognition program soon turned the digital photos into digital text, and within five days the pair had ginned up a piece of software that could search the book. That kind of step-wise, learn-as-you-go approach has repeatedly helped Google to test critical assumptions and avoid making bet-the-farm mistakes."[19]

The result was a constant impetus towards creativity, innovation, and entrepreneurial initiative. Indeed, given the caliber and characteristics of Google's employees, it was difficult to see how Google could not be a hotbed for innovation:

> Our employees, who have named themselves Googlers, are everything. Google is organized around the ability to attract and leverage the talent of exceptional technologists and business people. We have been lucky to recruit many creative, principled and hard working stars. We hope to recruit many more in the future. We will reward and treat them well . . . Because of our employee talent, Google is doing exciting work in nearly every area of computer science . . . Talented people are attracted to Google because we empower them to change the world; Google has large computational resources and distribution that enables individuals to make a difference. Our main benefit is a workplace with important projects, where employees can contribute and grow.[20]

The culture of creativity and innovation was institutionalized through Google's "70-20-10" rule, which stipulated that Google would devote 70% of its engineering resources to developing the core business, 20% to extend that core into related areas, and 10% allocated to fringe ideas. As a result, Google employees are able to spend a significant amount of their time working on pet projects of their own choosing.

Underlying Google's capacity for innovation and the effective implementation of new initiatives was a set of resources that few other technology-based companies could match. With an operating cash flow of $7.9 billion in 2008 and a cash pile of $15.8 billion, Google was a financial powerhouse matched only by Microsoft, IBM, HP, and Apple. This financial strength allowed Google to buy its way through acquisition into almost any market or area of technology. Most of the time Google did not need to buy its way into a new market: it was ranked as the world's second-most-valuable brand (after Apple), with a value of $111 billion in 2011.[21] Most important was a user base unmatched by any other IT company. With 776 million unique visitors to its website every day, it reached an estimated 77% of the world's internet audience daily.

Future Challenges

Google's first-quarter results announced on April 12, 2012 allayed fears that it might be losing its market dominance in online advertising. Its gross revenues for the quarter were up 24%, to $10.65 billion year-on-year; earnings were up 60% to $2.89 billion. Ninety-six percent of revenues came from advertising, compared to 97% the previous year. The US accounted for 46% of revenues. Cost-per-click was down 12% year-on-year, but this was the result of the shift of Google's business toward mobile internet access.

In terms of immediate threats, Google biggest concerns arose less from the market and more from the government and judicial arenas. These threats fell into three main areas:

- *Privacy*: The US Federal Trade Commission's privacy framework had tried to ensure that Google could not link its tracking data to identifiable individuals. European regulators were particularly concerned about the privacy policy that Google put into effect on March 1, 2012. Google did away with privacy rules for individual products and instead put in an umbrella policy that covered all 60 or so of Google web services. However, this aggregation of data into large single-user profiles was believed by the EU to contravene its data protection guidelines. In addition, Google's Street View aroused intense concern over invasion of individual privacy.
- *Antitrust*: Google's dominant share of internet search meant that it was a monopoly in terms of the competition laws of many countries of the world. In May 2012, its main threats were from the EU. The EU's competition commissioner had notified Google of four concerns it had of Google's business practices, which the Commission believed might constitute an abuse of market dominance: Google's promotion of its own products over rivals' in searches for items such as shopping; its copying and re-display of content from restaurant sites; its restrictions on competitors' ads appearing alongside its own; and the portability of advertising campaigns from Google's AdWords system.
- *Patent infringement claims*: Google had attracted a number of claims of patent infringement. One of the biggest, Oracle's claim that Android infringed its Java patents, was dismissed in May 2012.

However, when asked at a Google customer conference about the threats the company faced, CEO Larry Page did not hesitate: "Google," he responded. "There are basically no companies that have good slow decisions. There are only companies that have good fast decisions. As companies get bigger, they slow down decision making, and that's a big problem."

The speed with which Apple and Facebook had replaced Microsoft as Google's primary threats pointed to Google's need for vigilance and responsiveness. Page's concern about the impact of Google's expansion was echoed in its annual report for 2012:

We have experienced rapid growth in our headcount and operations, which has placed, and will continue to place, significant demands on our management, operational, and financial infrastructure. If we do not effectively manage our growth, the quality of our products and services could suffer, which could negatively affect our brand and operating results. Our expansion and growth in international markets heighten these risks as a result of the particular challenges of supporting a rapidly growing business in an environment of multiple languages, cultures, customs, legal systems, alternative dispute resolution systems, regulatory systems, and commercial infrastructures. To effectively manage this growth, we will need to continue to improve our operational, financial and management controls, and our reporting systems and compliance procedures. These systems enhancements and improvements will require significant capital expenditures and management resources. Failure to implement these improvements could hurt our ability to manage our growth and our consolidated financial position.[22]

These risks were amplified by the strains of integrating Google's many acquisitions. These included: "Diversion of management time and focus from operating our business to acquisition integration challenges; implementation or remediation of controls, procedures, and policies at the acquired company; integration of the acquired company's accounting, human resource, and other administrative systems, and coordination of product, engineering, and sales and marketing functions."[23]

Given the breadth of the challenges that Google faced, had the time come for Google's leading trio—Page, Brin, and Schmidt—to scale back Google's ambitions and draw boundaries around Google's corporate strategy?

Appendix 1: Google Timeline

January 1996	Larry Page and Sergey Brin begin collaborating on a search engine called BackRub.
September 1998	Google Inc. incorporated in Menlo Park, California; hires its first employee.
June 1999	Google obtains $25 million in venture capital funding. Moves to new Googleplex HQ in Mountain View, California.
September 1999	Google.com officially launched.
January – December 2000	Continued enhancements to Google. First ten non-English language versions. Google becomes the world's most widely used search engine. Introduction of AdWords. Google Toolbar allows users to perform a Google search without visiting Google homepage.
February 2001	Acquires the assets of Deja.com, organizes its Usenet archive into a searchable format.
August 2001	Dr Eric Schmidt, former CEO of Novell and CTO of Sun Microsystems, appointed CEO.
September 2001	Google becomes profitable.
December 2001	Launch of Google Image Search and Google Catalog Search (for searching mail-order catalogues).
February 2002	Google Search Appliance introduced: allows search to be extended beyond firewalls to company intranets, e-commerce sites, and university networks. Google Compute allows available processing on users' computers to solve computation-intensive scientific problems.
May 2002	AOL selects Google to provide search and advertising to its 34 million members.
September 2002	Google News launched: access to 4500 leading news sources worldwide.
December 2002	Froogle, a product search service, launched.
April 2003	Acquisition of Applied Semantics. Launch of Google AdSense allows highly targeted ads to be placed adjacent to their content.
January 2004	Local Search allows geographically focused web search and personalized search on Google Labs, enabling users to specify their interests and customize their search results.
April 2004	Launch of Gmail, a web-based mail service. Gmail also delivers relevant ads adjacent to mail messages.
July 2004	Acquires Picasa Inc., helps users to organize, manage, and share their digital photos.
August 2004	IPO of GOOG on NASDAQ through a Dutch auction process.
October 2004	Release of Google Desktop Search. Also Google SMS launched. Acquisition of Keyhole Corp., a digital and satellite image mapping company.
November 2004	Google index of web pages exceeds eight billion.
December 2004	Launch of Google Groups: allows users to create and manage their own email groups and discussion lists. Google Book Search begins scanning of books from the world's leading libraries.

January 2005	Launch of Google Maps: provides map views and satellite views.
June 2005	Google Labs offers Personalized Homepages. Launch of Google Earth.
August 2005	Launch of Google Talk: free internet telephony.
September 2005	Release of Google Blog Search.
October 2005	Launch of Google Reader combines blog, web page, and news sources onto a single screen.
November 2005	Launch of Google Base for uploading of content in a structured, searchable format. Google Analytics replaces Urchin as an online advertising management tool.
January 2006	Google Video Store offers range of content using a new Google Video Player. Google domain in China announced.
February 2006	Google Chat: integrates email and instant messaging within a web browser. Updated version of Google Desktop released. Google Page Creator facilitates creation of web pages.
March 2006	Debut of Google Finance: financial and business information.
April 2006	Release of Google Calendar for easy accessing and sharing of personal calendars.
June 2006	AdWords launches click-to-play Video Ads. Google Checkout launched: provides faster, more convenient online shopping. Google Maps available to businesses for embedding in their own websites.
August 2006	SketchUp acquired. Google partners with EarthLink to offer free Wi-Fi for the city of San Francisco.
November 2006	Google Apps for Education offers Google services to teachers and students. Google for Educators offers elementary teachers Google Certification through the Google Teacher Academy.
October 2006	Acquisition of YouTube. Release Web-based applications Docs and Spreadsheets. Acquisition of Jobspot, a collaborative wiki platform, which later becomes Google Sites.
December 2006	Release of Patent Search indexing more than seven million US patents.
January 2007	Partnership with China Mobile announced.
February 2007	Acquisition of Adscape, producer of in-game advertising producer.
April 2007	Acquisition of DoubleClick. Froogle changed to Google Product Search. Acquisition of Zenter, software to create and share online presentations. Acquisition of TiSP, a home broadband service.
June 2007	Acquisition of FeedBurner, provider of tools for site feed management and analysis.
September 2007	AdSense for Mobile introduced.
November 2007	Android, an open-source platform for mobile devices, announced. Program to invest in low-cost electricity from renewable sources announced.
January 2008	Google bids for license in the 700MHz spectrum auction.
February 2008	Launch of Google Sites (following acquisition of JotSpot), allows creation of collaborative websites with embedded videos, documents, and calendars.
May 2008	Release of Google Health for the online collection, storage, and management of individuals' medical records and health information.
June 2008	Google Finance offers real-time stock quotes. Launch of Google Site Search: site owners can enable Google-powered searches on their own websites.
September 2008	Announcement of Chrome web browser. T-Mobile announces the G1, the first phone built on the Android operating system.
February 2009	Google Latitude for mobile devices allows sharing your location.
March 2009	Launch of Google Ventures to invest in innovation and new technology.
June 2009	Launch of Google Squared allows complex search queries, and the collection and organization of facts from the web. All for Good, a search interface for volunteer activities. Release of beta version of AdSense for Mobile Applications.
July 2009	Google Chrome OS announced.
August 2009	Acquisition of On2 Technologies, a video compression technology company.
September 2009	Introduction of DoubleClick Ad Exchange, a real-time marketplace for online publishers and ad networks/agency networks to buy and sell display advertising space.
October 2009	Introduction of Google Maps Navigation, a GPS navigation system that includes 3D views and voice guidance.

(Continued)

January 2010	New China policy: Google will no longer censor search results on Google.cn.
February 2010	Google to build and test ultra-high-speed broadband networks in US cities.
May 2010	Acquires AdMob, a mobile display advertising company. Google invests in a utility-scale renewable energy project.
August 2010	Acquires Slide, a social technology company that builds new ways for people to connect online across numerous platforms.
October 2010	Place Search allows search organized around specific locations.
December 2010	Google eBookstore allows browsing and search through more than three million e-books.
April 2011	Invests $168 million in Californian solar energy power plant and $100 million in wind farm in Oklahoma.
June 2011	Launch of Google+. Google's electric vehicle charging infrastructure is the largest in the country. Google invests $280 million in solar installations for homeowners.
August 2011	Acquisition of Motorola Mobility agreed.
September 2011	Acquisition of Zagat: to be a cornerstone of Google's local offerings. After its 90-day field trial, Google+ moves to open signups.
November 2011	Google Music launched: users can buy, play, and share music, and store it in the cloud.
January 2012	Launch of "Search, plus Your World": when a user performs a signed-in search on Google, the results page may include Google+ content from Google+ contacts together with relevant Google+ profiles and Google+ pages.

Source: Google Inc., "Our history in depth," http://www.google.com/about/company/history. Reproduced with permission from Google Inc.

Appendix 2: Extract from Google, 10-K Report for 2011, Item 1: The Business

Overview

Google is a global technology leader focused on improving the ways people connect with information. We aspire to build products that improve the lives of billions of people globally. Our mission is to organize the world's information and make it universally accessible and useful. Our innovations in web search and advertising have made our website a top internet property and our brand one of the most recognized in the world.

We generate revenue primarily by delivering relevant, cost-effective online advertising. Businesses use our AdWords program to promote their products and services with targeted advertising. In addition, the third parties that comprise the Google Network use our AdSense program to deliver relevant ads that generate revenue and enhance the user experience . . .

Our business is primarily focused around the following key areas: search, advertising, operating systems and platforms, and enterprise.

Search

We maintain a vast index of websites and other online content, and make it available through our search engine to anyone with an internet connection. Our search technologies sort through an ever-growing amount of information to deliver relevant and useful search results in response to user queries. We integrate innovative features into our search service and offer specialized search services to help users tailor their search. In addition, we are constantly improving and adding to our products and services, to provide users with more relevant results so that users find what they are looking for faster.

Advertising

Google Search   With AdWords, advertisers create simple text-based ads that then appear beside related search results or web content on our websites and on thousands of partner websites in our Google Network, which is the network of third parties that use our advertising programs to deliver relevant ads with their search results and content. Most of our AdWords customers pay us on a cost-per-click basis . . . We also offer AdWords on a cost-per-impression basis that enables advertisers to pay us based on the number of times their ads appear on our websites and our Google Network Members' websites as specified by the advertiser.

Our AdSense program enables websites that are part of the Google Network to deliver ads from our AdWords advertisers that are relevant to the search results or content on their websites. We share the majority of the revenues generated from these ads with the Google Network Members that display the ads.

Google Display   Display advertising comprises the videos, text, images, and other interactive ads that run across the web on computers and mobile devices, including smart phones and handheld computers such as netbooks and tablets. The Google Display Network provides advertisers services related to the delivery of display advertising across publishers participating in our AdSense program, publishers participating in the DoubleClick Ad Exchange, and Google-owned sites such as YouTube and Google Finance.

Through our DoubleClick advertising technology, we provide to publishers, agencies, and advertisers the ad serving technology, which is the infrastructure that enables billions of ads to be served each day across the web. Our DoubleClick Ad Exchange creates a real-time auction marketplace for the trading of display ad space.

In addition, YouTube provides a range of video, interactive, and other ad formats for advertisers to reach their intended audience . . . YouTube also offers analytic tools to help advertisers understand their audience and derive general business intelligence.

Google Mobile   Mobile advertising is still in relative infancy, though the mobile device is quickly becoming the world's newest gateway to information . . . Google Mobile extends our products and services by providing mobile-specific features to mobile device users. Our mobile-specific search technologies include search by voice, search by sight, and search by location. Google Mobile also optimizes a large number of Google's applications for mobile devices in both browser and downloadable form. In addition, we offer advertisers the ability to run search ad campaigns on mobile devices with popular mobile-specific ad formats, such as click-to-call ads in which advertisers can include a phone number within ad text.

Google Local   Google is committed to providing users with relevant local information. We've organized information around more than 50 million places globally from various sources across the web. Users can find addresses, phone numbers, hours of operation, directions and more for millions of local queries like shops, restaurants, parks and landmarks right on Google.com, on Google Maps and on Google Maps for mobile. They can also discover more places that are right for them by rating the places they've been, and getting customized recommendations based on their tastes and those of their friends directly within Google Maps. Our products and services also help local business owners manage their online presence and connect with potential customers. Millions of business owners have verified their free business listings via Google Places to ensure that users have up-to-date information about their establishments, and to contribute additional details such as photos and products/services offered. Google Offers brings people daily deals from local and national businesses, redeemable for discounted goods or services. From restaurants to spa treatments to outdoor adventures, Google has deals from the best businesses a city has to offer as well as popular national brands.

Operating Systems and Platforms

Android   Working closely with the Open Handset Alliance, a business alliance of more than 75 technology and mobile companies, we developed Android, a free, fully open source mobile software platform that any developer can use to create applications for mobile devices and any handset manufacturer can install on a device . . .

Google Chrome OS and Google Chrome   Google Chrome OS is an open source operating system with the Google Chrome web browser as its foundation. Both the Google Chrome OS and the Google Chrome browser are built around the core tenets of speed, simplicity, and security. Designed for people who spend most of their time on the web, the Google Chrome OS is a new approach to operating systems. We are working with several original equipment manufacturers to bring computers running Google Chrome OS to users and businesses. The Chrome browser runs on Windows, Mac, and Linux computers.

Google+   In June 2011, we launched Google+, a new way to share online just like users do in the real world, sharing different things with different people. Google+ has added new users every week since its launch. As of January 2012, over 90 million people have joined Google+.

Google TV   Google TV is a platform that gives consumers the power to experience television and the internet on a single screen, with the ability to search and find the content they want to watch. The Google TV platform is based on the Android operating system and runs the Google Chrome browser.

Google Books   The Google Books platform (including reading applications, an electronic bookstore (eBookstore), book search, and personal library management) is designed to help people discover, search, and consume content from printed books online. Through the Google eBookstore, we make available for sale popular books in electronic book format to complement our large collection of free public domain books.

Enterprise

Google's enterprise products provide familiar, easy-to-use Google technology for business settings. Through Google Apps, which includes Gmail, Google Docs, Google Calendar, and Google Sites, among other features, we provide hosted, web-based applications that people can use on any device with a browser and an internet connection. In addition, we provide our search technology for use within enterprises through the Google Search Appliance (real-time search of business applications, intranet applications, and public websites), on their public-facing sites with Google Site Search (custom search engine), and Google Commerce Search (for online retail enterprises). We also provide versions of our Google Maps Application Programming Interface (API) for businesses (including fully interactive Google Maps for public and internal websites), as well as Google Earth Enterprise (a behind-the-company-firewall software solution for imagery and data visualization). Our enterprise solutions have been adopted by a variety of businesses, governments, schools, and non-profit organizations. Google Apps is the first cloud computing suite of message and collaboration tools to receive US government security certification.

Competition

Our business is characterized by rapid change and converging, as well as new and disruptive, technologies. We face formidable competition in every aspect of our business, particularly from companies that seek to connect people with information on the web and provide them with relevant advertising. We face competition from:

- General purpose search engines, such as Yahoo and Microsoft's Bing.
- Vertical search engines and e-commerce websites, such as Kayak (travel queries), Monster.com (job queries), WebMD (for health queries), and Amazon.com and eBay (e-commerce). Some users will navigate directly to such websites rather than go through Google.
- Social networks, such as Facebook and Twitter. Some users are relying more on social networks for product or service referrals, rather than seeking information through general purpose search engines.
- Other forms of advertising, such as television, radio, newspapers, magazines, billboards, and yellow pages, for ad dollars. Our advertisers typically advertise in multiple media, both online and offline.
- Mobile applications on iPhone and Android devices, which allow users to access information directly from a publisher without using search engines.
- Providers of online products and services. A number of our online products and services, including Gmail, YouTube, and Google Docs, compete directly with new and established companies, which offer communication, information, and entertainment services integrated into their products or media properties.

Source: Google, 10-K Report for 2011, Item 1: The Business. Reproduced with permission from Google Inc.

Notes

1. "List of mergers and acquisitions by Google," *Wikipedia*, http://en.wikipedia.org/wiki/List_of_acquisitions_by_Google, accessed May 25, 2012.

2. "Google's Growing Identity Crisis," Chris O'Brien's blog, July 19, 2009, http://www.mercurynews.com/ci_12853656?IADID, accessed July 20, 2009.

3. S. Levy, "Larry Page's First Year as Google CEO: Impatience Is a Virtue," *Wired*, April 4, 2012. http://www.wired.com/epicenter/2012/04/opinion-levy-page-first-year/all/1, accessed May 24, 2012.

4. "Lex: Google the One-trick Pony," *Financial Times*, April 17, 2009.

5. "Google's Bid to Be Everything to Everyone," *Business Week*, May 24, 2012. http://mobile.businessweek.com/magazine/googles-bid-to-be-everything-to-every-one-02162012.html, accessed May 24, 2012.

6. H. Blodget, "Apple's iPhone has staged a monster comeback, Android is now dead in the water," *Business Insider*, March 30, 2012, http://articles.businessinsider.com/2012-03-30/tech/31258390_1_tablet-market-smart-phone-market-iphone, accessed September 27, 2012.

7. Google Inc. SEC form 424B3, filed November 23, 2004.

8. At the March 2008 Federal Communications Commission's auctioning of licenses to "C-block" spectrum, Google was one of the bidders. Google was delighted to lose out to winning bids from AT&T and Verizon that together amounted to over $18 billion because the FCC had decreed that the new spectrum owners would be required to open their networks to third-party providers. Hence, Google would be free to offer its wireless service without the need to invest in infrastructure. See: "An Auction that Google was Content to Lose," *New York Times*, April 4, 2008, www.nytimes.com/2008/04/04/technology/04auction.html?_r51&oref5slogin, accessed October 23, 2009.

9. "Analysis: Google's Android Mobile Strategy Explained," *PC Advisor*, November 6, 2007, http://www.pcadvisor.co.uk/news/index.cfm?newsid511248, accessed July 21, 2009.

10. "Wireless Auction: Google Likely Out, and Happy," *Forbes*, February 6, 2008.

11. "Inside Chrome: The Secret Project to Crush IE and Remake the Web," *Wired*, October 16, 2008.

12. "Why Google Wants Motorola," *MIT Technology Review*, August 15, 2011, http://www.technologyreview.com/printer_friendly_article.aspx?id=38320, accessed September 27, 2012.

13. "Why Google Wants Motorola," *MIT Technology Review*, August 15, 2011, http://www.technologyreview.com/printer_friendly_article.aspx?id=38320, accessed September 27, 2012.

14. J. Carney, "Why Facebook is a Threat to Google's Earnings," April 12, 2012, http://www.cnbc.com/id/47030496/Why_Facebook_Is_a_Threat_to_Google_s_Earnings, accessed May 26, 2012.

15. A. Chansanchai, "Future Facebook Searches a Threat to Google?" http://www.technolog.msnbc.msn.com/technology/technolog/future-facebook-searches-threat-google-124436, accessed May 26, 2012.

16. G. Hamel, *The Future of Management* (Harvard Business School Press, Boston, 2007).

17. G. Hamel, *The Future of Management* (Harvard Business School Press, Boston, 2007).

18. G. Hamel, *The Future of Management* (Harvard Business School Press, Boston, 2007).

19. G. Hamel, *The Future of Management* (Harvard Business School Press, Boston, 2007).

20. Letter from the Founders, "An Owner's Manual," for Google's Shareholders, http://investor.google.com/ipo_letter.html, accessed 30 March, 2008. Reproduced with permission from Google Inc.

21. "Brandz Top 100 Ranking," *Financial Times*, May 9, 2012.

22. Google Inc., 10-K report to the SEC for 2011, p. 16. Reproduced with permission from Google Inc.

23. Google Inc., 10-K report to the SEC for 2011, pp. 11–12.

A video clip relating to this case is available in your interactive e-book at **www.wileyopenpage.com**

Case 21　Danone: Strategy Implementation in an International Food and Beverage Company

At the beginning of 2012, Franck Riboud was beginning his sixteenth year as chairman and CEO of Danone, the French-based food and beverage multinational. During this period, Riboud had transformed Danone from a diversified food, beverage, and glass container company selling mainly in France, Spain, and Italy, into an international supplier of dairy products, bottled water, baby foods, and health foods.

During the next three years, Danone would continue to emphasize international expansion with a particular focus on large markets which offered the potential for double-digit growth rates—in particular: Mexico, Indonesia, China, Russia, the US, and Brazil. Riboud believed that the growing demand in emerging market countries for improved nutrition—dairy products in particular—and a growing trend among consumers in the advanced countries toward healthier eating would underpin Danone's revenue and earnings growth, despite the challenges of global economic uncertainty and rising world food prices.

At the same time, Riboud was concerned over Danone's ability to manage its increasingly disparate business empire. Under the father-and-son team of Antoine and Franck Riboud, Danone had developed a distinctive management style that combined strong values with a decentralized, entrepreneurial approach to business development.

As a result, Danone's approach to international expansion had been opportunistic and fragmented. In some countries, it had grown by acquisition; in others, by joint venture or organic growth. Some businesses were built around global brands, for example Evian water and Danone yogurt; other products and brands were specific to individual countries.

Danone's entrepreneurial approach to developing international business had yielded major successes in penetrating new markets, most notably Russia, which had become Danone's biggest national market. At the same time, Danone had experienced some painful reversals; most notably in China, when in September 2009, after ten years of dispute and acrimony, Danone sold its 51% interest in its drinks joint ventures to its partner, Wahaha.[1]

Written by Robert M. Grant and Angela Amodio. The case draws upon an earlier case: "Danone: The Corporate Strategy of a Food and Beverage Giant," by A. Amodio and R. M. Grant, Copyright © 2010 SDA Bocconi, Milano. © 2012, Robert M. Grant and Angela Amodio.

For all Danone's success in becoming the world's biggest dairy products company, its financial performance lagged behind that of other leading food and beverage multinationals such as Nestlé, Unilever, PepsiCo, and Kraft Foods. These companies managed through closely integrated, centralized global business divisions; a more consistent approach to market development; and with stronger headquarters control over national business units.

Danone's distinctive management style had been molded by the idiosyncratic approach of its CEO. "I was never made for this," Franck Riboud told the *Financial Times*. "I preferred surfing. I never planned a career path. I came into Danone by accident."[2] The same article described Riboud as "rumpled, tieless, favouring zip-up jumpers and colourful language" and seeking inspiration from people and travel rather than from management books. There was no doubt that Danone's unusual leadership style and freewheeling approach to business development had encouraged initiative, adaptation, and growth. But would the next phase of Danone's business development require a more disciplined and systematic management style?

Danone's Development, 1973–2011

Groupe Danone was created by the 1973 merger between the French glassmaker BSN built by Franck Riboud's father, Antoine, and Gervais Danone, a French/Spanish dairy products company famous for its Gervais fresh cheese and Danone yogurt. Under Riboud Senior, Danone diversified into beer (Kronenbourg), water (Evian), Italian cheese (Galbani), biscuits (Lu, Nabisco), sauces (HP), and baby food (Blédina).

In 1996, Franck Riboud replaced his father as chairman and CEO. The younger Riboud redirected Danone's development: divesting the glass, beer, sauces, Italian cheese, and biscuits business and refocusing around four major divisions: dairy products, water, baby foods, and medical nutrition,[3] and shifting Danone's toward international expansion, especially into emerging market countries.

During his 15 years as Danone's CEO, Franck Riboud imposed a consistent strategic direction on the group, even before taking over as CEO he outlined the criteria guiding Danone's strategy:

> Our priorities for international growth are the businesses where our know-how equals or betters that of the world leaders. Which of course means fresh dairy products, biscuits and water. But we do not rule out any of our businesses on principle, provided we can rapidly win strategic weight in the region concerned. As for these regions themselves, what counts for us is the size of the population and the outlook for rapidly rising standards of living. Countries in Eastern Europe meet the criteria, as do those in the Asia-Pacific area, in particular India, Indonesia, Malaysia and China. The same goes for Latin America, especially Mexico, Brazil and Argentina.[4]

Franck Riboud's rebuilding of Danone's business portfolio involved a multiplicity of acquisitions, piece-by-piece process of divestments, and creation of joint ventures and non-equity alliances. Only rarely did Danone enter a country through greenfield start-up.

- *Acquisitions*: Between 2000 and November 2010, Danone acquired 37 companies (including YoCream in the US and Numico in the Netherlands). In addition, it acquired minority stakes in 26 companies. It divested 34 companies, including its entire biscuit division.

● *Joint ventures*: Danone has made extensive used of joint ventures to enter new markets and develop new areas of business. These have allowed it to access local knowledge and distribution capability, economize on its limited managerial resources, and achieve rapid market penetration. By 2009, joint ventures accounted for almost 30% of its sales. Partners have included Chiquita Brands in the US, Al Safi in Saudi Arabia, Yakult and Avesthagen in India, Alquería in Colombia, and Grameen in Bangladesh, as well as Mengniu, Bright Foods, Weight Watchers, and the Wahaha Group in China. In 2010, Danone created its biggest joint venture when it announced the merger of its Russian and CIS dairy business with that of Unimilk to create the region's largest supplier of fresh dairy products. Several of these joint ventures have involved Danone in conflicts with its partners: its troubled Chinese joint venture with Wahaha being the most contentious. In some cases, Riboud first built a global business, and then sold it off: in 2007, Danone sold its biscuits (cookies and crackers) division to Kraft Foods and invested the proceeds in acquiring the Dutch-based Numico, thereby creating Danone's medical nutrition division.

Figures 1 and 2 show the transformation of Danone's business and geographical scope under Franck Riboud's leadership.

FIGURE 1   Danone's sales by business lines, 1996–2011

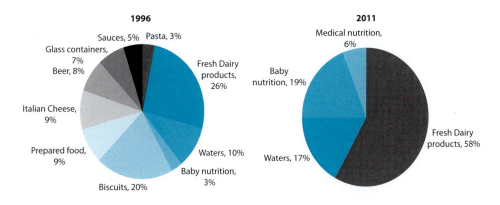

FIGURE 2   Danone's sales by geographical area, 1996–2011

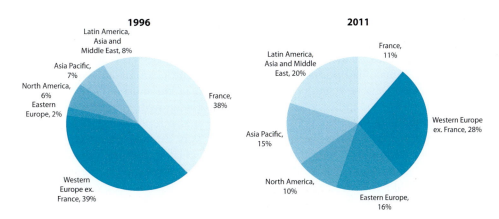

Danone in 2012

The Businesses

Danone was organized into four business areas:

- *Fresh Dairy Products* accounted for almost 60% of total sales, giving Danone a global market share of about 27%. Danone's dairy products comprised a number of yogurt and fromage frais products sold under the brand names Danone (Dannon in the USA) and Gervais. Recent growth had come from several new product lines: probiotic products sold under the Actimel and Activia brands (Bio in certain countries), low-fat products (Taillefine, Vitalinea, and Ser), and products formulated specially for children under the Danonino, Danimals, and Petit Gervais brands. Fresh dairy products were formulated to meet the nutritional needs and preferences of individual national markets. In China, Bio (sold as Activia in most other countries) established market leadership in the "digestive comfort" category. In South Africa, Nutriday, a yogurt product, has been Danone's lead dairy product. In Indonesia, Danone's chocolate milk drink Milkuat Pouch was relaunched as a frozen yogurt. In countries lacking refrigerated distribution networks, Danone relied on localized micro-plants and designed its products for longer shelf-life at room temperature.

- *Water*. Danone was the world's second-largest supplier of bottled water (after Nestlé). It combined global brands Evian and Volvic with a number of strong local brands—Aqua in Indonesia, Mizone in China, and Bonafont in Brazil and Mexico. Emerging markets (particularly in Asia and Latin America) were especially attractive, because of the health advantages of bottled water over both sweetened soft drinks and alternative sources of drinking water.

- *Baby Nutrition*: Infant formula, to complement breast-feeding, comprised three-quarters of the sales of the Baby Nutrition division. The remaining quarter was made up of sales of cereal-based and other solid foods for infants and toddlers. Sales were mostly under local brands, with products formulated to meet local needs. Western Europe, especially France and the UK, was the biggest market for Baby Nutrition, but the most rapidly growing markets were in Asia, especially China and Indonesia. In Indonesia, Danone's SGM and Gizikita brands emphasized affordability.

- *Medical Nutrition* comprised a range of products designed to meet the nutritional needs of people with specific nutritional needs as a result of old age, illness, or medical treatment and convalescence. The 2007 acquisition of Numico had positioned Danone as the European market leader in this sector. Danone regarded medical nutrition as "the most attractive segment in the food industry today" as a result of its growth, potential for innovation, and lack of cyclical vulnerability. It also represented a challenging market for Danone since it required "very extensive research, unremitting communication with healthcare and regulatory authorities and a special distribution system." Danone aimed at developing global brands for its medical nutrition products, including Nutricia, Neocate, Fortimel, and

Respifor. Danone's entry into medical nutrition represented a return to its origins: Danone was initially founded in 1919 by Dr Isaac Carasso, who had produced yogurt that was sold through pharmacies to counter a variety of ailments.

Tables 1, 2, and 3 show the breakdown of Danone's sales and profits by business and by region.

During 2011, Russia displaced France as Danone's largest market in terms of sales. This resulted from the Unimilk merger. In terms of percentage share of total

TABLE 1   Net sales by business lines, 2006–2011 (€million)

	2011	%	2010	%	2009	%	2008	%	2007	%	2006	%
Fresh Dairy Products	11,235	58.2	9,732	57.2	8,555	57.1	8,697	57.1	8,299	65.0	7,933	65.7
Waters	3,229	16.7	2,868	16.9	2,578	17.2	2,874	18.9	3,535[a]	27.7	3,942	32.7
Baby Nutrition	3,673	19.0	3,355	19.7	2,924	19.5	2,795	18.4	809[b], [c]	6.3	n.a.	—
Medical Nutrition	1,181	6.1	1,055	6.2	925	6.2	854	5.6	133[c]	1.0	n.a.	—
Total	19,318	100.0	17,010	100.0	14,982	100.0	15,220	100.0	12,776	100.0	12,068[d]	100.0

Notes:
[a] Water sold in China under the Wahaha brand was not consolidated after July 1, 2007.
[b] Blédina's sales and trading operating income, previously included in Fresh Dairy Products figures, were integrated into Baby Nutrition from 2007.
[c] The 2007 data for Baby Nutrition and Medical Nutrition relate to just two months of activity (Numico was acquired on October 31, 2007).
[d] Includes sales of the Biscuit and Cereal Products business line that were not sold to Kraft.
n.a.: not available.
Source: Danone annual reports, various years.

TABLE 2   Trading operating income by business segment, 2006–2011 (€million)

	2011	%	2010	%	2009	%	2008	%	2007	%	2006	%
Fresh Dairy Products	1,475	51.9	1,365	52.9	1,244	54.2	1,224	53.9	1,133	66.8	1,089	68.2
Waters	424	14.9	371	14.4	324	14.1	368	16.2	480	28.3	494	30.9
Baby Nutrition	798	24.9	635	24.6	536	23.4	489	21.5	74[a], [b]	4.4	n.a.	—
Medical Nutrition	236	8.3	207	8.0	190	8.3	189	8.3	7[b]	0.4	n.a.	—
Total	2,843	100.0	2,578	100.0	2,294	100.0	2,270	100.0	1,696	100.0	1,597	100.0

Notes:
[a] Blédina's sales and trading operating income, previously included in Fresh Dairy Products figures, were integrated into Baby Nutrition from 2007.
[b] The 2007 data for Baby Nutrition and Medical Nutrition relate to just two months of activity (Numico was acquired on October 31, 2007).
n.a.: not available.
Source: Danone annual reports, various years.

TABLE 3 Net sales and operating income by region, 2006-2011 (€ millions)

	2011	%	2010	%	2009	%	2008	%	2007	%	2006	%
Net Sales												
Europe	10,809	56.0	9,449	55.8	8,960	59.8	9,524	62.6	7,670	60.0	6,814	56.5
Asia	2,862	14.8	2,386	14.0	1,877	12.5	1,854	12.2	1,643	12.9	2,206	18.3
Rest of the world	5,647	29.2	5,175	30.2	4,145	27.7	3,842	25.2	3,463	27.1	3,048	25.3
Total	19,318	100.0	17,010	100.0	14,982	100.0	15,220	100.0	12,776	100.0	12,068	100.0
Trading operating income												
Europe	1,509	53.1	1,483	57.5	1,437	62.6	1,496	65.9	1,107	65.3	1,024	64.1
Asia	580	20.4	445	17.3	333	14.5	313	13.8	177	10.4	206	12.9
Rest of the world	754	26.5	649	25.2	524	22.8	461	20.3	412	24.3	367	23.0
Total	2,843	100.0	2,578	100.0	2,294	100.0	2,270	100.0	1,696	100.0	1,597	100.0

Note:
Europe includes Western, Central, and Eastern Europe; Asia includes the Pacific region, Australia, and New Zealand; and the Rest of the world includes North and South America, Africa, and the Middle East.
Source: Danone annual reports, various years.

sales, Danone's top-ten markets were: Russia (11%), France (11%), Spain (7%), the US (7%), Indonesia (6%), Mexico (5%), China (5%), Argentina (5%), Germany (5%), and the UK (5%).

Organizational Structure

Groupe Danone is governed by a board of directors which at the beginning of 2012 comprised:

- Franck Riboud, Chairman and Chief Executive Officer of Danone
- Emmanuel Faber, Co-Chief Operating Officer
- Bernard Hours, Co-Chief Operating Officer of Danone
- Bruno Bonnel, Chairman, Sorobot SAS
- Richard Goblet d'Alviella, Vice-Chairman, Sofina SA
- Yoshihiro Kawabata, Managing Director, Yakult Honsha Co., Ltd
- Christian Laubie, Collège du Haut Conseil du Commissariat aux Comptes
- Jean Laurent, Chairman, Foncière des Régions
- Hakan Mogren, Company Director
- Benoît Potier, Chairman and CEO, L'Air Liquide SA
- Guylaine Saucier, Company Director
- Jacques Vincent, Chairman, CompassionArt
- Isabelle Seillier, Chairman, JPMorgan, France
- Jean-Michel Severino, Head of Research, FERDI.

FIGURE 3 The organizational structure of Groupe Danone

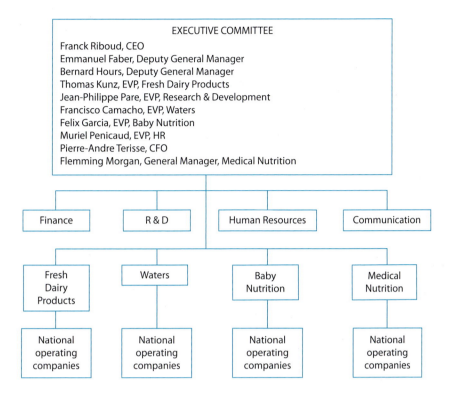

The top management team of the Danone is the executive committee, the members of which are shown in Figure 3. Operational management is undertaken by the four business divisions, each of which coordinates a number of national operating companies. These are listed in Appendix 1.

When companies are acquired, they are integrated within Danone's existing business sectors, often being renamed: Olait, acquired in 2006, became Danone Dairy Egypt; when Danone took 100% ownership of its Japanese joint venture, Calpis Ajinomoto Danone, it was renamed Danone Japan. To accommodate larger acquisitions, Danone may reorganize its corporate structure. On acquiring Numico, Danone created two new business divisions, Baby Nutrition and Medical Nutrition, to which Numico's different products and brands were allocated together with existing Danone products and products (e.g., Danone transferred its Blédina products from Fresh Dairy Products to Baby Nutrition).

Management Systems and Style

Among large multinational corporations, Danone is distinguished by its exceptional level of decentralization. According to Franck Mougin, a former head of HR:

> Our President reiterates his commitment to decentralisation and his desire to remain in touch with the markets. In the group, a managing director who is in

charge of an activity in a country is the decision-maker even if he operates in a cultural environment which helps integration. Headquarters can merely suggest options to him, but cannot impose conditions. We think that there are more disadvantages than advantages in looking for synergies and the success of our decentralised management can be seen in our local brands in China and Indonesia, for example. The desire to preserve our autonomy, while at the same time integrating entities into organisational and cultural plans, led us to develop what we call the networking attitude.[5]

Franck Riboud viewed decentralization as a key attribute in pursuing Danone's strategy of growth:

Now is the time to widen our lead on competitors and I'm convinced that Danone is well equipped to do that. We have the right culture for it, and our lean, decentralized organization gives the managers of our subsidiaries full responsibility—the most effective motivation. That agility, that freedom from unnecessary constraints, is an even more decisive competitive strength in our current environment.[6]

Decentralization allowed Danone to align its brands and products to the characteristics of local markets. Danone both retained and continued to introduce local brands when most other consumer goods multinationals were migrating consumers from national to global brands. Decentralization also meant that Danone could be quicker than competitors in planning and launching new products: Danone's front-line managers could execute new initiatives without the need for extensive consultation or approvals from above. Such flexibility and speed were central to Danone's goal of quickly establishing itself as a leading player in markets which were developing rapidly. Thus, in Asia where the demand for dairy products was growing rapidly, Danone sought to move quickly in creating products with high customer acceptability and sought to ensure extensive distribution.

However, for Danone to add value to its individual business units, it needed to coordinate across its national subsidiaries in order to realize the benefits from global brands, centralized R & D, global products, and the sharing of know-how and best practices. As a result, Danone had put in place a number of systems in place to facilitate communication and coordination and create what Franck Mougin referred to as its "networking approach." At the basis of this coordination is an ERP system implemented by Accenture in 2000. This provides Danone with the information platform and standardized processes that facilitate communication, coordination, control and the exchange of good practices throughout the company.

Reconciling coordination with decentralization was reinforced by cultivating and diffusing a common approach to management. Danone's leadership development program aimed to develop team leaders "in a distinctive leadership culture inspired by our Danone Values and leveraging the strengths of the Danone Leadership CODE (Committed, Open, Doer, Empowered). Leadership development involved one-week residential programs at the Danone campus for groups of between 100 and 300 managers and Danone Learning Solutions—training programs that could be used by managers in any location. One feature of Danone's management development was an emphasis on team learning, including its "High Performing Teams Accelerator Workshop" and "Innovation Labs" methodology to develop collaborative approaches to breakthrough solutions.[7]

Knowledge Management

Danone's knowledge management provided the organizational mechanisms for solving problems and sharing know-how. According to Benedikt Benenati, former Director of Communication and Development, the key feature of Danone's knowledge management system was its simplicity. In preference to formal knowledge sharing devices such as databases and PowerPoint presentations, Danone encapsulated ideas and experiences in pictures, videos, and stories. Communication mechanisms included peer-to-peer problem resolution in which a manager with a problem became a "taker," a manager with a possible solution a "giver," and exchange was mediated by a "facilitator." Once a problem was resolved it became a "nice story." For broad-based sets of problems where a wider exchange of know-how was needed, Danone established a "Market Place." The first of these was for R&D managers. To brief participants to Market Place sessions, Danone produces a "Little Book of Practices" in which "good" (not necessarily "best") practices were listed. The various devices used to simplify knowledge sharing, includes "Message in a Bottle," in which a participant is allowed just two minutes to outline a problem and request assistance, and where knowledge can be physically shared.

Because of Danone's geographical spread, most knowledge sharing and problem solving must occur through virtual mechanisms using the group's intranet. Here the key tool is Danone's "Who's Who" directory that allows each manager to identify colleagues with relevant expertise.[8]

Danone's informal system of knowledge management was viewed by Mr Riboud as entirely consist with its management system: it allowed a high level of decentralization of initiatives and problem solving and used lateral rather than vertical communication. Also, the process lent itself to be applied within the different local contexts according to the different working cultures and attitudes. It has been likened to a neural system in which Danone's individual subsidiaries were linked with regional knowledge hubs located in Paris, Barcelona, Amsterdam, Moscow, New York, Buenos Aires, Shanghai, and Singapore, and these hubs are linked with one another. The system allowed adaptability to local conditions, a multiplicity of stimuli, and a linking of stimuli to responses in the form of actions.[9]

As a central strategic thrust for the whole company, research and development played a key role in linking the Danone global network in its mission to "bring health through food to as many people as possible." Danone Research employed 1,200 technical personnel in 15 different countries developing expertise in:

- microbiology, yogurt starters, and probiotics
- clinical research and epidemiology
- human nutrition and physiology
- immunology
- neurosciences
- metabolic programming
- water sciences
- food design, food preservation, and packaging.

Danone operated two major research centers, the Daniel Carasso Centre outside Paris and the Centre for Specialized Nutrition in the Netherlands. These centers were involved with over 200 scientific partnerships throughout the world. The research efforts of the two corporate research centers were closely linked with R & D activities conducted by four business groups.

Principles and Values

At the core of Danone's management system was a set of principles and values that were first enunciated by Antoine Riboud in 1972. Underlying them was the belief that there could be no sustainable business development without human development.

In 1996, Danone established a working group to identify the central values which Danone represented and aspired to. Three values were identified: Openness, Enthusiasm, and Humanism, to which a fourth, Proximity, was added in 2004. Danone's commitment to these values guided its relationships with its employees, its customers, the communities within which it operated, and the natural environment. In 2008, Franck Riboud reiterated Danone's commitment to social responsibility:

> An enterprise exists and lasts only because it creates value for society as a whole . . . The raison d'être of the enterprise lies in its social usefulness. It is to serve society and mankind, in the everyday lives of men and women, through the products, services, employment or even the dividends it provides". In today's economic context, this commitment is more relevant than ever in helping to realise the Danone mission: to bring health through food to as many people as possible.[10]

Danone's human resource policies were articulated in a document first published in 1974 and now in its fourth edition. Every Danone business was required to uphold International Labor Organization conventions as well as committing to the development of skills and talents among all employees and to innovation through diversity.

In relation to environmental sustainability, Danone's programs included:

- climate change; in 2009, Danone committed to reducing its output of CO_2 per kilogram of product by 30% by 2012, and its energy consumption by 20%;
- biodiversity: Danone established targets for protecting and restoring biodiversity through its production and sourcing policies.
- protection of water sources;
- redesigning packaging to minimize its environmental impact;
- supporting eco-friendly agriculture.

In 2009, Danone created the Danone Ecosystem Fund with a budget of €100 million to support projects that created sustainable jobs in activities directly related to Danone's activities, particularly in agriculture and distribution. Projects included Proxicity, a new distribution service for independent local retailers, and the creation of cooperatives of small milk producers in Ukraine.

Danone's pursuit of social and environment responsibility was not driven only by altruism: Riboud believed that the pursuit of broad social and environmental goals also created revenues and profits for the company. Danone's values were seen as integral to its whole approach to business: "the group has developed a uniquely distinctive corporate culture emphasizing responsiveness, adaptability and the ability to accelerate innovation through networking. Operational responsibilities are broadly decentralised."[11] This culture and the commitment to social goals that it reflected were seen as central to Danone's business model:

> The group's management believes that this business model constitutes a key competitive advantage. It is primarily a factor in collective efficiency and internal motivation. It is also a factor that is strongly appealing, given the increasing sensitivity of employees to the notion of the enterprise being competitive and socially responsible. Finally, it is a powerful lever for developing a relationship of trust between the company and its partners.[12]

The integration of business performance with the creation of social and environmental value took the form of a three-year strategy launched by Danone's executive committee in 2009. The strategy involved four strategic priorities:

- *Health*: Strengthening of the group's ability to deliver relevant benefits that address issues of nutrition and health.
- *For All*: New business and economic models to provide quality nutritional solutions to people with low purchasing power in a growing number of countries around the world.
- *Nature*: Accelerating the momentum to take into consideration environmental impacts through the reduction of water and carbon footprint.
- *People*: The company evolving as a venue for development for all employees and encouraging their involvement in social programs.

Emerging Market Strategy

The close linkage between Danone's strategy, its values, and its management systems and style were particularly evident in its approach to emerging markets. Danone was attracted to emerging countries primarily because of the growth opportunities that they offered: between 1996 and 2011, the proportion of Danone's sales from outside Western Europe had grown from 21 to 62%. At the heart of Danone's strategy for 2012–2014 was growth in the "MICRUB" countries—Danone's acronym for Mexico, Indonesia, China, Russia, the US, and Brazil.[13] At the same time, Danone's more mature European market would play a key role in generating the financial resources needed to fund expansion in these emerging markets and providing the expertise and products to fuel international growth: some of Danone's greatest successes in Asia-Pacific were with dairy and baby products first developed in Europe.

Danone's country business units in emerging markets were expected to be innovative and responsive in adapting to local needs and local opportunities. At the same time they were encouraged to build upon Danone's existing brands, existing product platforms, the expertise of other country units, and its wealth of research-based nutritional knowledge. For example, Danone's efforts to combat nutritional deficiencies deployed its flagship brand for children, Danonino. This provided a product platform that could be adapted to the nutritional requirements of children in the fourteen countries where it was distributed. In Brazil, for example, it was enriched with calcium, iron, zinc, and vitamins E and D; in Mexico, the main additive was iron to counter anemia; in Japan, with vitamins A and D; in Spain, with calcium; in France, with vitamin D; and in Russia, with iodine and vitamin D.

As part of Danone's "For All" theme, the company linked social development projects with the goal of affordability. In 2005, Danone collaborated with Muhammad Yunus of the Grameen Group to establish the Danone Communities Fund to support businesses that furthered economic and social development within low-income communities. Supported projects included:

- Grameen Danone Foods, which provided micronutrient fortified yogurt to children in Bangladesh for 6 cents a carton. The plant, about 200 km north of Dacca, was a mere one-hundredth the size of most of Danone's yogurt plants. It used milk bought from famers in local villages, and was distributed by a network of local women who sold it door-to-door.
- La Laiterie du Berger (The Shepherd's Dairy) collected and processed milk from local cattle herders in Senegal.
- 1001 Fontaines pour Demain (1001 Fountains for Tomorrow) distributed drinking water in rural Cambodia.

By 2009, these initiatives to support nutrition and development among communities of poor people were broadened into Danone's Base of the Pyramid (BOP) program. BOP operated as a business unit within the Fresh Dairy Products group, where it coordinated initiatives involving smaller, more flexible plants; new product formulations and packaging; and new distribution channels.

Future Challenges

For all of Franck Riboud's success at transforming Danone and setting it upon a sustainable growth path, Danone's financial results were far from spectacular. For the period 2000 to 2009, Danone's sales showed little overall growth (Appendix 2), while profitability had been below that of its two major competitors, Nestlé and Kraft Foods (Appendix 3).

Given the trend in the food and beverage industry toward consolidation (Table 4), Danone remained vulnerable. In 2005, Danone was rescued from a takeover bid by PepsiCo only by the intervention of the French government.

Riboud was convinced that Danone's strategy was pointing the company in the right direction. With the sale of the biscuits division, the acquisition of Numico, and its emphasis on expansion in emerging markets, Riboud believed that Danone's strategy was now well aligned with its mission statement of "bringing health through food to as many people as possible."

Some uncertainties as to Danone's business portfolio still remained. In particular, should Danone continue to hold onto its water business, or should it sell it to one of the eager potential buyers (most likely one of Japan's leading drinks companies: Suntory, Kirin, or Asahi).[14] Of greater concern to Riboud was the need for Danone to strengthen its competitive position relative to rivals. With consolidation in the

TABLE 4 Mergers and acquisitions in the food and beverage sector, 2010–2011

Acquired	Acquirer	Amount ($billion)
Cadbury PLC (UK; chocolate)	Kraft Foods (US)	153
Danisco (Denmark; food additives, biofuel	DuPont (US)	65
Del Monte Foods (US; fruit, juices)	KKR and other private equity groups	53
Winn-Bill-Dan Foods (Russia; dairy products, juices)	PepsiCo (US)	54
P&G's Pringles business (US; snack foods)	Diamond Foods (US)	24
Yoplait (France; yogurt and dairy products)	General Foods (US)	12
Prometheus Labs (US; nutritional solutions to gastrointestinal ailments)	Nestlé (Switzerland)	11
Hansa-Milch (Germany; dairy products) and Allgäuland-Käsereien (Germany; dairy products)	Arlan Foods (Sweden/Denmark)	Not disclosed

Note:
KKR: Kohlberg Kravis Roberts.

industry—especially in dairy products, and with so many companies investing in the field of medical nutrition, and with constant pressure from the bargaining power of giant retailers such as Wal-Mart, Carrefour, and Tesco—Danone was likely to face increasing competitive pressures. As a result, attaining competitive advantage was critical to achieving satisfactory levels of profitability and growth. Riboud and his executive team were convinced that the group's emphasis upon quality, affordability, and innovation directed toward health benefits was consistent both with market opportunities and with Danone's capabilities. However, a key issue was whether Danone's efforts were too fragmented and whether it was gaining sufficient benefit from cross-border linkages. For all of Danone's commitment to decentralization and local autonomy, Riboud was well aware of the advantages of global integration in purchasing, brands, and new product development.

In 2009, Riboud called for increased efforts to exploit cross-border synergies:

Ties and communication among the units within each business line are now functioning well, but there is room for improvement in relations between business lines and between our operations in Europe and those in other parts of the world. Cross-company operation is perhaps partly a question of structure, but it is above all a matter of attitude. We want the people in the group to learn to work together, whatever the product lines they are concerned with. We need a real cultural revolution in this area. Which does not mean any dilution of the principle of decentralized operation: operational management remains the responsibility of business units, which are now larger and have more resources. Our aim is not centralization, but greater collective efficiency.

To achieve that, we are making some changes in the role of management at Group level. In the past, the Group supported its business units from behind the scenes, but it now needs to take center stage. Instead of confining itself to finance and human resources management, it has extended its reach by stages to areas such as research and purchasing over the past few years and, more recently, to the use of the Danone signature and certain aspects of relationships with retailers.[15]

Despite progress in strengthening Danone's corporate functions—notably IT, HR, and research—Danone was still unique among its peers in terms of the extent of its decentralization and the scope of decision making authority that was given to the heads of its country business units. Riboud was convinced that Danone's collaborative culture was superior to conventional, authority-based management systems in terms of fostering flexibility and initiative. But how could this be adapted to become more effective in ensuring more effective cross-border integration of purchasing, marketing, and new product rollouts and stronger unity around the values and strategic priorities of Danone?

Appendix 1: Danone's Operating Subsidiaries (fully consolidated companies)

FRESH DAIRY PRODUCTS

Algeria	Danone Djurdjura Algerie	Italy	Danone Spa
Argentina	Danone Argentina (99%)	Japan	Danone Japan
Austria	Danone Gesmbh	Kazakhstan	Danone Berkut Llp (46%); Danone (51%)
Belgium	N.V Danone SA	Mexico	Danone De Mexico; Derivados Lacteos (60%)
Belarus	Danonebel (51%)	Netherlands	Danone Nederland BV; Danone Cis Holdings BV (88%)
Brazil	Danone Ltda	Poland	Danone Sp Z.O.O
Bulgaria	Danone Serdika	Portugal	Danone Portugal SA (56%)
Canada	Danone Canada Delisle	Romania	Danone SRL
Chile	Danone Chile	Russia	Danone Industria (51%); Danone Volga (46%); Unimilk (50%)
China	Danone China	Ukraine	Unimilk Ukraine (50%); Danone Ukraine (51%); Danone Dnipro (51%)
Colombia	Danone Alqueria (93%)	Saudi Arabia	Alsafi Danone Co. (50%)
Croatia	Danone	Serbia	Danone Adriatic
Cyprus	Dairy Jv Holdings Ltd (51%)	Slovakia	Danone Spol
Czech Republic	Danone AS	Slovenia	Danone Slovenia
Egypt	Danone Dairy Egypt; Danone Dairy Farm	South Africa	Danone Southern Africa Ltd; Mayo (70%)
Finland	Danone Finland	S. Korea	Danone Korea
France	Danone Produits Frais; Dansource; Stonyfield France; Danone Chiquita Fruits (51%)	Spain	Danone SA (58%); Danone Canaries (48%)
Germany	Danone Gmbh	Sweden	Danone AB; Proviva AB (51%); Lunnarps AB (51%)
Greece	Danone Greece	Switzerland	Danone Switzerland
Guatemala	Danone Guatemala	Thailand	Danone Dairy Thailand
Hungary	Danone Kft	Turkey	Danone Tikvesli
India	Danone India	UK	Danone Ltd
Indonesia	Pt Danone Dairy Indonesia	Uruguay	Danone (Fort Massis)
Iran	Danone Sahar (70%)	US	Dannon Company; Stonyfield Farm (85%); Swirl Co.; Yocream
Ireland	Danone Ltd		

WATERS

Algeria	Danone Tessala Boissons	Iran	Damavand (70%)
Argentina	Aguas Danone	Mexico	Bonafont; CGA; Aga Pureza (50%)
Belgium	Danone Water Benelux	Poland	Womir Spa; Zywiec Zdroj
Brazil	Danone Water Bresil	Spain	Aguas Font Vella Y Lanjaron (79%)
China	Danone Premium Brands; Robust Drinking Water (92%); Shenzhen Health Drinks	Switzerland	Évian Volvic Suisse
Denmark	Aqua D'or (90%)	Turkey	Danone Hayat
France	Évian; Volvic; Seat	UK	Danone Waters (UK and Ireland
Germany	Danone Waters Deutschland	Uruguay	Salus (94%)
India	Danone Narang Beverages (51%)	US	Danone Waters of America
Indonesia	Aqua (Pt Tirta Investama) (74%)		

BABY NUTRITION

Argentina	Kasdorf SA; Nutricia Bago SA (51%)	Latvia	Nutritia Latvia
Australia	Nutricia Australia Pty Ltd	Lithuania	Uab Nutricia Baltics
Austria	Milupa Gmbh	Malaysia	Dumex (Malaysia) Sdn. Bhd.
Belgium	NV Nutricia België	Mexico	Danone Baby Nutrition Mexico, SA
Brazil	Support Produtos Nutricionais Ltda	Netherlands	Nutricia Nederland BV; Nutricia Cuijk BV; Nutricia Export BV; Danone Trading BV; Danone Research BV
China	International Nutrition Co. Ltd	New Zealand	Nutricia Ltd (NZ)
Colombia	Danone Baby Nutrition Colombia	Poland	Nutricia Polska (50%); Nutricia Zaklady Produkcyne (50%)
Czech Republic	Nutricia A.S.; Nutricia Deva AS	Portugal	Milupa Comercial SA
Finland	Nutricia Baby Oy Ltd	Romania	Milupa SRL
France	Blédina; Danone Baby Nutrition Africa & Overseas	Russia	Ojsc Istra Nutricia Baby Food; LLC Nutricia
Germany	Milupa Gmbh; Central Laboratories Friedrichsdorf Gmbh	Slovakia	Nutricia Slovakia SRO
Greece	Numil Hellas SA	Spain	Numil Nutrición SRL
Hong Kong	Danone Baby Food Co. (HK) Ltd	Switzerland	Milupa SA; Danone Financial Services SA
Hungary	Numil Hungary Kft.	Thailand	Dumex Ltd Thailand (99%)
Indonesia	Pt Nutricia Indonesia Sejahtera; Pt Sari Husada; Pt Sugizindo	Turkey	Numil Turkey Try
Iran	Mashhad Milk Powder Industries Co. (60%)	Ukraine	Nutricia Ukraine LLC
Ireland	Nutricia Ireland Ltd	UK	Nutricia Ltd
Italy	Mellin Spa	Vietnam	Danone Vietnam Company Ltd
Kazakhstan	Nutricia Kazakhstan LLP		

MEDICAL NUTRITION

Argentina	Advanced Medical Nutrition	Indonesia	Pt Nutricia Medical Nutrition
Austria	Nutricia Nahrungsmittel Gmbh	Italy	Nutricia Italia Spa
Canada	Nutricia Canada	Mexico	Danone Medical Nutrition Mexico SA
China	Nutricia Pharmaceutical Co. Wuxi	Netherlands	NV Nutricia; Gordia N
Colombia	Nutricia Colombia Ltda	Norway	Nutricia Norge AS
Denmark	Nutricia A/S	Spain	Nutricia SRL
Finland	Nutricia Clinical Oy Ltd	Sweden	Nutricia Nordica AB
France	Nutricia Nutrition Clinique SAS	Switzerland	Nutricia SA
Germany	Pfrimmer Nutricia Gmbh	UK	Complan Foods Ltd; Scientific Hospital Supplies International Ltd
Hong Kong	Nutricia Clinical Ltd; Nutricia Clinical Export Ltd	US	Nutricia North America Inc.

Note:

For those subsidiaries that are not 100% owned, the equity share is shown in parentheses.

Appendix 2: Selected Financial Information for Danone, 2000–2011 (values in €million)

	2011	2010	2009	2008	2007	2006	2005	2004	2003	2002	2001
Consolidated income statement data											
Net sales	19,318	17,010	14,982	15,220	12,776	12,068	13,024	12,273	13,131	13,555	14,470
Net sales increase (%)	13.57	13.54	(1.56)	19.13	5.87	(7.34)	6.12	(6.53)	(3.13)	(6.32)	1.28
Trading operating income	2,943	2,578	2,294	2,270	1,696	1,597	1,738	1,608	1,604	1,590	1,609
Operating income	2,729	2,498	2,511	2,187	1,546	1,560	1,706	1,559	1,604	1,590	1,609
Income before tax	2,435	2,489	2,022	1,603	1,369	1,530	1,596	1,569	1,474	1,938	672
Net income attributable to the group	2,040	2,043	1,361	1,313	4,180	1,353	1,464	449	839	1,283	132
Consolidated balance sheet data											
Current assets	6,112	5,895	4,407	4,888	4,394	6,154	6,118	5,427	6,537	9,053	5,036
Non-current assets	22,314	22,204	22,466	21,982	23,182	10,702	10,607	10,652	4,171	4,092	5,425
Total assets	28,426	28,099	26,873	26,865	27,576	16,856	16,725	16,079	14,305	15,275	16,900
Net debt	9,031	6,946	6,562	11,055	11,261	2,902	3,572	4,538	2,692	2,269	4,827
Shareholders' equity	12,196	11,987	13,225	8,644	9,018	5,823	5,280	4,256	4,824	5,807	5,947
Current liabilities	6,962	7,203	5,856	4,898	6,813	4,248	4,560	3,781	n.a.	n.a.	n.a.
Consolidated cash flow data											
Cash flow from operating activities	2,605	2,476	2,000	1,754	1,611	1,930	1,847	1,694	1,653	1,641	2,240
Cash flow from investing activities	(767)	(552)	214	(569)	(8,098)	(263)	312	214	n.a.	n.a.	n.a.
Ratios											
Operating margin (%)	14.13	14.68	16.76	14.91	13.27	13.23	13.34	13.10	12.22	11.73	11.12
Current ratio	0.88	0.82	0.75	1.00	0.64	1.45	1.34	1.44	—	—	—
ROA (%)	8.57	8.86	7.52	5.97	4.96	9.08	9.54	9.76	10.30	12.69	3.98
ROE (%)	16.73	17.14	10.29	15.19	46.35	23.24	27.73	10.55	17.39	22.09	2.22

Notes:
Figures in parentheses denote a loss.
ROA: Return on a sets (income before tax/total assets).
ROE: Return on equity.
n.a.: not available.
Sources: Danone annual reports; French GAAP from 2001 to 2003; IFRS from 2004 to 2011.

Appendix 3: Performance Comparisons for Danone's Main Competitors, 2011

	Danone	Nestlé SA	Friesland Campina NV[a]	Kraft Foods	Parmalat SpA	Tingyi Holding Corp.
Revenues (€m)	19.3	68.7	9.6	42.1	4.5	6.9
Net income (€m)	2.04	8.06	0.22	2.75	0.17	0.4
Total assets (€bn)	28.4	93.8	5.7	72.7	2.7	3.4
Debt (€m)	9.0	18.3	0.7	20.9	0.1	0.5
Employees	101,886[b]	328,000	19,036	126,000	13,932	64,309
Market capitalization (7 May 2012, €bn)	34.5	151.7	n.a.	41.0	3.0	11.5
Ratios						
Operating margin (%)	14.1	15.0	4.2.	12.2	4.4	8.4
Net margin (%)	9.1	11.3	2.2	6.5	3.8	6.4
Revenue growth, 2009–2011 (%)	+28.7	−5.6	+17.6	+44.7	+2.6	+66.7
ROE (%)	10.3	13.8	10.1	10.0	4.8	18.6
Asset turnover (Revenues/assets)	0.56	0.73	1.68	0.58	1.63	1.79
Revenue per employee (€k)	185	209	507	334	324	73
Operating profit per employee (€k)	31	31	21	40	14	9
Five-year total return to shareholders, to May 2012 (%)	+16	+58	n.a.	+62	−27	+235

Notes:
ROE: Return on equity.
[a]Friesland Campina data is for 2008.
[b]Including Unimilk.
n.a.: not available.
Sources: Amadeus; companies' annual reports.

Notes

1. Although Danone owned 51% of the joint venture compared to Wahaha's 49%, the management of the joint venture was entirely in the hands of Wahaha's chairman, Mr Zong, and the drinks produced by the joint venture were sold under Wahaha's brand names. The dispute concerned a series of companies set up by Mr Zong to produce and sell drinks that were identical to those of the joint venture and sold under the same Wahaha brand. See: Steven M. Dickinson, "Danone v. Wahaha: Lessons for Joint Ventures in China," http://www.chinalawblog.com/DanoneWahahaLessons.pdf, accessed September 28, 2012.
2. S. Daneshkhu, "The off-the-wall executive," *Financial Times*, November 20, 2010.
3. The last of these businesses, medical nutrition, was added in 2007 with the acquisition of Royal Numico NV (usually known simply as Numico) and followed the sale of Danone's biscuits division of Kraft Foods.
4. Speech to the meeting of heads of group business units, Evian, October 12–13, 1995.
5. F. Mougin and B. Benenati, *Story-Telling at Danone: A Latin Approach to Knowledge Management*, Seminar presentation, Les Amis de l'Ecole de Paris, April 1, 2005.
6. Interview – April 2009 from www.danone.com.
7. F. Mougin and B. Benenati, *Story-Telling at Danone: A Latin Approach to Knowledge Management*, Seminar presentation, Les Amis de l'Ecole de Paris, April 1, 2005.
8. "Learning by Danone: Programs 2010," http://www.danone.com/images/pdf/learning-by-danone.pdf.
9. Presentation by B. Hours "Strategic Business Overview," Danone Investor Seminar, Amsterdam, November 17–18, 2009.
10. Danone, Danone Sustainability Report 2009, (Paris, 20120, p. 9).
11. Danone, Danone Sustainability Report 2009, (Paris, 20120, p. 9).
12. Danone, Danone Sustainability Report 2009, (Paris, 20120, p. 10).
13. Interestingly, Danone viewed the US as an emerging market based upon the growth potential which Danone perceived for its products.
14. In October 2011, Suntory denied that it was negotiating with Danone to buy its water business, and Danone's CFO stated that water was "still strategic" to Danone, http://www.reuters.com/article/2011/10/18/us-danone-suntory-idUSTRE79H3R020111018, accessed September 28, 2012.
15. "Building Danone," Danone Panorama: Special Issue.

A video clip relating to this case is available in your interactive e-book at **www.wileyopenpage.com**

Case 22 Jeff Immelt and the Reinventing of General Electric

On April 25, 2012 Jeff Immelt, chairman and CEO of the General Electric Company (GE), presided over the company's annual shareholders' meeting in Detroit, Michigan. As representatives of the "99 Percent Movement" protesting GE's low rate of corporate tax were ushered from the hall, and GE's board members and corporate officers took their seats, Immelt had a few minutes to reflect upon his eleven years as head of GE.

Immelt knew that taking over from Jack Welch—"living legend" and "best manager of the 20th century"—would be a difficult challenge. Little did he know just how tough his job would be.

Four days after Immelt took over the chairman's suite, two hijacked airliners crashed into New York's World Trade Center, setting off a train of events that would profoundly affect GE's business environment. A month later, Enron's collapse precipitated a crisis of confidence over corporate governance, financial reporting, and business ethics. The mounting controversy over financial statement manipulation and executive compensation soon engulfed GE, which was forced to restate earnings and reveal the details of Welch's staggeringly generous retirement package. Then came the financial crisis of 2008–2009: a major blow to GE since its financial services arm, GE Capital, was one of America's biggest financial services businesses and for two decades had been GE's primary growth engine. It was now seen as a ticking time bomb of bad debts requiring asset write-downs. In 2008, GE downgraded its earnings forecasts, cut its dividend, suspended its share buyback program, and sought a $3-billion equity injection from Warren Buffett. In the following March, S&P cut GE's credit rating from AAA to AA+.

Yet, throughout this eleven-year period of turbulence, Immelt had systematically put in place a long-term transformation strategy for GE. This strategy had involved reconfiguring GE's business portfolio around two core businesses (infrastructure and specialty financial services), reorienting GE's performance goals toward revenue growth, refocusing GE's competitive advantage around technological innovation and customer service, and adjusting GE's structure, management processes, and corporate culture.

By the time of the 2012 shareholders' meeting, the results of the strategy were becoming apparent:

> GE today is the world's biggest infrastructure company, and we have a great midmarket lending company in GE Capital. Really, two main core businesses, and our goal is really to expand our infrastructure footprint. We're more than $100 billion globally today and continue to build a valuable specialty finance business.

This case was prepared by Robert M. Grant. ©2012 Robert M. Grant.

The things we work on are superior technology, leadership in growth regions, services and customer relationships, margin expansion and smart capital allocation. At our core we're a technology company. Keith said we invest about 6% of our revenue back into R & D. It's about $6 billion. We'll launch more than 880 new products next year . . .

Services are important for the Company. It's about 70% of our industrial earnings, about $45 billion in revenue. Here we're just really trying to help our customers make more money. We continue to invest in technology that upgrades our customers' performance.

GE is a very global company. As Keith said, about 60% of our revenue is outside the United States. Industrial growth regions, these are really the emerging markets like Asia, the Middle East, places like that. We have a lot of leadership there. Our businesses are growing there substantially. In resource rich regions we're growing in excess of 20%. And rising Asia, like China and India, are growing 10% to 15%.

Lastly, we fly under the banner of GE Works. We're really focused on being mission based, moving, curing and powering the world, believing in continuous improvement. Really a relentless drive to solve customer problems, to create a world that works better. But very much based on our terms and our people and we think that's what makes GE great.[1]

The changing shape of GE's overall business makeup is shown in Figure 1. However, for all of Immelt's success in transforming GE's business model and guiding GE through the challenges of the 21st century, financial performance had lagged. During 2002–2003, Immelt had established ambitious performance targets for GE: sales growth at 2–3 times that of global GDP, 10% plus earnings growth and 20% plus return on total capital.[2] GE's performance had fallen well short of these targets (Table 1). GE's share price told the story: when Immelt's appointment had been announced late in 2000, GE's stock was trading at $53. For most of 2001–2008, GE's

FIGURE 1   General Electric strategic overview: A stronger portfolio

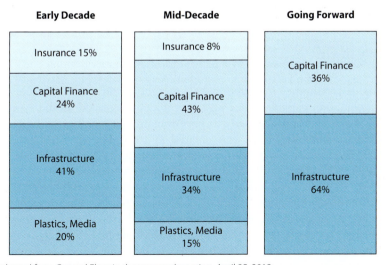

Source: Adapted from General Electric shareowners' meeting, April 25, 2012.

TABLE 1 General Electric: Performance indicators, 2001 and 2011

Year	Sales ($billion)	Net income ($billion)	Return on equity (%)	Return on invested capital (%)	Market capitalization, 31st Dec. ($billion)	Employees (thousand)	Non-US employees (%)
2001	125.9	13.7	26.0	27.0	397.9	310	49.0
2011	147.3	14.2	11.9	11.6	187.8	301	56.5

shares fluctuated between $20 and $40, but in the midst of the financial crisis GE's stock fell below $6 (March 5, 2009); by April 26, 2012 it had climbed to $19.81.

Immelt had been widely applauded for deft leadership of GE in guiding it, more or less unscathed, through the financial crisis and taking steps to rebalance GE away from financial services toward technology-based, industrial businesses. Moreover, Immelt had sustained GE's emphasis on long-term development built upon investment in technology, developing new businesses, international expansion, and upgrading GE's manufacturing base. Yet without a sustained improvement in GE's financial performance, the doubts about GE remained.

For all Immelt's reframing of GE as an "infrastructure company with two core businesses," GE remained a widely diversified enterprise. Although Immelt forcefully argued that GE was not a conglomerate, most investment analysts regarded it as such and, as a result, there was always the possibility that it could create shareholder value by being broken up (as had happened to most other conglomerates, including ITT, Tyco International, General Mills, Fortune Brands, and Vivendi Universal). The case against highly diversified companies was reinforced by the growing recognition of the need for in-depth domain expertise for senior managers. Andrew Hill of the *Financial Times* raised the question: "If the demand is now for depth over breadth, will there be enough 'serial masters' capable of understanding, let alone running, companies of the scale and scope of General Electric? And if not, at what point will the market judge that such companies are simply too big to manage?"[3]

Table 2 summarizes GE's financial performance during 2006–2011.

A History of GE

The GE that Jeffrey Immelt inherited in 2001 was the world's most valuable company (in terms of market capitalization) and was widely regarded as the world's most successful. It was the only company to have remained a member of the Dow Jones industrial index since the index was created in 1896. The key to its success had been to combine massive size with constant adaptation. Over the decades GE had adapted both its business portfolio and its management systems to the demands and opportunities of a changing world.

GE was founded in 1892 from the merger of Thomas Edison's Electric Light Company with the Thomas Houston Company. Its business was based upon exploiting Edison's patents relating to electricity generation and distribution, light bulbs, and electric motors. Throughout the twentieth century GE was not only one of the world's biggest industrial corporations but also "a model of management—a laboratory studied by

TABLE 2 General Electric: Selected financial data, 2006–20011 ($billion)

	2011	2010	2009	2008	2007	2006
GE Consolidated						
Revenues	147.3	150.2	156.8	182.5	172.5	151.6
Net earnings	14.2	11.6	11.0	17.4	22.2	20.7
Cash from operating activities	33.4	36.1	24.6	48.6	43.3	31.5
Cash used for investing activities	19.9	32.4	43.0	(35.4)	(69.5)	(52.6)
Return on average equity (%)	11.9	12.1	11.6	15.9	20.4	19.8
Stock price range ($)	21.65–14.02	19.70–13.75	17.52–5.87	38.52–12.58	42.15–33.90	38.49–32.06
Year-end closing stock price ($)	17.91	18.29	15.13	16.20	37.07	37.21
Total assets	717.2	747.8	781.8	797.8	795.7	697.3
Long-term borrowings	243.5	293.3	336.2	330.1	319.0	260.7
Total employees	301,000	287,000	304,000	323,000	327,000	319,000
—US	131,000	133,000	134,000	152,000	155,000	155,000
—Other countries	170,000	154,000	170,000	171,000	172,000	164,000
GE data (industrial businesses)						
Short-term borrowings	2.2	0.5	0.5	2.4	4.1	2.1
Long-term borrowings	9.4	9.6	11.7	9.8	11.7	9.0
Shareowners' equity	116.4	118.9	117.3	104.7	115.6	111.5
Total capital invested	129.0	133.1	135.3	123.5	137.8	128.2
Return on average capital invested (%)	11.6	11.8	10.6	14.8	18.9	18.5
Borrowings as % of capital invested	9.0	7.6	9.0	9.9	11.4	8.7
Working capital	(0.0)	(1.6)	(1.6)	3.9	6.4	7.5
GECS[a] data (financial services)						
Revenues	49.1	49.91	51.8	71.3	71.9	61.4
Net earnings	6.5	2.2	1.4	7.1	10.3	10.7
Shareowner's equity	77.1	69.0	70.8	53.3	57.7	54.1
Total borrowings	443.1	470.5	493.3	514.6	500.9	426.3
Ratio of debt to equity at GECS	5.75:1	6.82:1	6.96:1	8.76:1	8.10:1	7.52:1
Total assets	584.5	605.3	650.4	660.9	646.5	565.3

Notes:
Figures in parentheses denote a loss.
[a]GECS: General Electric Capital Services, which owns GE Capital.
Source: General Electric, 10-K reports, various years.

business schools and raided by other companies seeking skilled executives."[4] Under the leadership of Charles Coffin, between 1892 and 1922, GE successfully married Edison's industrial R & D laboratory to a business system capable of turning scientific discovery into marketable products. After the Second World War, Chairman Ralph Cordiner, assisted by Peter Drucker, pioneered new approaches to the systematization of corporate management. Under Fred Borch (CEO 1963–1972), GE's corporate management system based on strategic business units and portfolio analysis became a model for most diversified corporations. Reg Jones, GE's chairman from 1972 to 1981, linked GE's techniques of strategic planning to its systems of financial management.

During his two decades at GE's helm, Jack Welch had led the most comprehensive strategic and organizational upheavals in GE's long history. Welch reformulated GE's business portfolio through exiting low-growth extractive and manufacturing businesses and expanding services—financial services in particular. By the time he retired, GE Capital represented almost half of GE's revenues and the majority of its assets. At the heart of Welch's remaking of GE was the creation of a performance culture supported by comprehensive systems for setting and monitoring performance targets and providing powerful incentives for their achievement:

> Changing the culture—opening it up to the quantum change—means constantly asking not how fast am I going, how well am I doing versus how well I did a year or two before, but rather, how fast and how well am I doing versus the world outside. Are we moving faster, are we doing better against that external standard?
>
>   Stretch means using dreams to set business targets—with no real idea of how to get there . . . We certainly didn't have a clue how we were going to get to 10 inventory turns [a year] when we set that target. But we're getting there, and as soon as we become sure we can do it—it's time for another stretch.[5]

Welch declared war on GE's elaborate bureaucracy and stripped out layers of hierarchy. His management style was direct, personal, and often confrontational: managers were encouraged to commit to ambitious performance targets, after which they and their subordinates were under intense pressure to deliver. Every aspect of GE's management systems was redesigned from the ground up, from strategic planning to human resources. Welch also introduced periodic challenges for the whole organization. These included: "Be #1 or #2 in your global industry"; "Work-out," a process for company meetings that allowed grassroots ideas about organizational change to be implemented; "Six Sigma," a program of company-wide initiatives to improve quality and reliability; and "Destroy your business dot.com," an initiative to drive adoption of internet technologies.

The outcome was two decades of outstanding corporate performance. Between 1981 and 2001, revenues grew from $30 billion to $126 billion, net income from under $2 billion to $14 billion, and stock market capitalization from $14 billion to $510 billion: an average annual return to stockholders of 24%.

Jeff Immelt

Jeffrey R. Immelt was appointed CEO of GE at the age of 44. He had previously been head of GE's Plastics business and, most recently, head of Medical Systems. He had an economics and applied math degree from Dartmouth and an MBA from Harvard. He claimed that his own experience of GE extended beyond his two decades with the firm: his father spent his entire career at GE. On being recruited from Harvard by GE in 1982, Immelt was identified as a "young high potential," which meant that his progress would be carefully tracked by top management at GE. In 1987, Immelt attended the executive development course at Crotonville, GE's management development center. This course was considered the gateway to the executive ranks of GE. At GE Appliances, GE Plastics, and GE Medical Systems, Immelt acquired a reputation for turning around troubled units, driving customer service and exploiting new technologies. He also demonstrated the ability to motivate others, an aptitude that he had revealed as an offensive tackler for Dartmouth's football team in the 1970s.[6]

In December 1994, the GE board began to consider possible candidates to replace Jack Welch. Immelt was one among a list of some 20 GE executives submitted by Welch for board consideration. After five years of careful monitoring and assessment the list had shrunk to three: Jim McNerney, Bob Nardelli, and Immelt.

Immelt's emergence as frontrunner owed much to his outstanding success at GE Medical Systems, which he led from 1997 to 2001. He demonstrated strong leadership capabilities in energizing and motivating others: "He brought the life and energy that drives major growth," commented GE's head of HR.

His personality and leadership style contrasted sharply with those of Welch. "Where Welch ruled through intimidation and thrived as something of a cult figure, Immelt opts for the friendlier, regular-guy approach. He prefers to tease where Welch would taunt. Immelt likes to cheer people on rather than chew them out. That style has given him a very different aura within GE. He may not be a demigod, but it's his man-of-the-people nature that draws praise from the top ranks to the factory floor."[7] This different style of leadership had implications for the organizational and management changes that Immelt would introduce; however, it was radical changes in GE's business environment that would be the dominant drivers of GE's strategic and organizational development.

GE's Business Environment, 2001–2012

The remarkable growth in profits and stock market valuation that Welch had achieved was against a backdrop of an economy effused with optimism, confidence, and growth. The new century presented a whole new set of challenges. In his first letter to shareholders, Immelt observed: "The exuberance of the late 1990s and the inevitable downturn have created difficult times. Entire industries have collapsed, poor business models have been exposed, large companies have filed for bankruptcy and corporate credibility has been called into question."[8]

In this world of turbulence, Immelt initially believed that GE's diversified portfolio of businesses would provide GE with the stability to weather business cycles. Yet, the experience of the 21st century was that the returns to different businesses tended to become increasingly correlated. Indeed, during the financial crisis, contagion became the norm; problems in any one business would tend to infect other businesses.

A further key change in the business environment was the discrediting of the 1990s' obsession with shareholder value maximization. From the outset, Immelt was anxious to disassociate himself from cruder versions of shareholder value maximization. In all his communications to shareholders, Immelt was emphatic that the job of the CEO was not to manage the stock price but to manage the company for the long-term earnings growth that would drive the stock price: "We all want the stock to go up. But to do that we have to manage the company. In fact, the only way you can run GE is to believe that performance will ultimately drive the stock."[9]

The critical challenge of the business environment of the 21st century, believed Immelt, was identify the potential sources of profit for GE. Under Welch, GE had created value cost reduction, eliminating underperforming assets, and exploiting the opportunities offered by financial services. By the time Immelt took over, these sources of value had been mined out: GE would need to look into new areas. Top-line growth, he reasoned, would have to be the driver of bottom-line returns. Yet, given the generally poor outlook for growth in the world economy, growth opportunities were likely to be meager: "I looked at the world post-9/11 and realized that over the next 10 or 20 years, there was not going to be much tailwind."

In identifying opportunities for profitable organic growth, Immelt sought to identify key global trends that would offer business opportunities for GE. Four external trends emerged as paramount:

- *Demography*: The aging of the world's population would create opportunities for goods and services required by older people, in particular healthcare services. Population growth in the developing world would also offer expanding demand for many of GE's other businesses, including entertainment.
- *Infrastructure*: GE predicted massive investments in infrastructure. GE's positioning in infrastructure products, services, and financing offered it opportunities in energy, aviation, rail transportation, water, and oil and gas production.
- *Emerging markets*: China, India, Eastern Europe, Russia, the Middle East, Africa, Latin America, and South East Asia would offer rates of GDP growth around three times that of the world as a whole. These countries would be key centers of business opportunity for GE.
- *Environment*: The challenges of global warming, water scarcity, and conservation would become increasingly pressing, creating the need for technologies and innovatory responses to alleviate these problems.

GE's Growth Strategy

Growth, organic growth in particular, became the central theme of Immelt's strategy for GE. In 2002, he committed GE to an organic growth rate of 8% per annum (under Welch organic growth had averaged 5% a year) and to "double digit" earnings growth. This 8% revenue growth was based upon the idea that GE should be able to grow at between two and three times that of world GDP. Profits would grow faster than revenues, explained Immelt, because of reductions in general and administrative expenses as a percentage of sales and higher margins resulting from new products and services. Between 2002 and 2007, GE comfortably met these targets: revenues grew at 13% each year; operating earnings at 14%. However, in the wake of the financial crisis, both revenues and profits went into a sharp decline.

Reshaping the Business Portfolio

To position GE for stronger growth, the company would need to exit slow-growth businesses, reallocate resources to businesses where growth prospects were strong, and enter new businesses. A key theme in Immelt's reshaping of GE's business portfolio toward higher growth was the creation of new "growth platforms." Growth platforms could be extensions of existing businesses or they could be entirely new areas of business. Identifying new growth platforms became a central strategic challenge for GE's businesses.

In several cases, GE's growth platforms involved existing businesses where there was potential to greatly expand the company's market presence. For example:

- *Healthcare*: GE was the world leader in diagnostic imaging: X-ray equipment, CT scanners, and MRI scanners. Under Immelt it became a major area of growth for GE, expanding its range of products and services and its geographical presence. Key acquisitions included: Amersham (a UK-based diagnostics and medical equipment company), HPSC (financial services for medical and dental practices), and Abbott Diagnostics (the world's leading provider of in vitro diagnostics).

- *Energy*: Power generation was GE's oldest business; in addition it had developed a promising business supplying equipment to the oil and gas sector. Immelt viewed energy as a particularly attractive growth platform for GE. One major growth area was alternative energy. Here, key acquisitions included Enron's wind energy business, BHA Group, which supplied emission-reduction equipment, ChevronTexaco's coal gasification business, and AstroPower, which supplied solar energy products. Another was oil and gas, where GE diversified its offerings of products and services through acquiring Vetco Gray (subsea platforms) and Hydril Pressure Control (petroleum drilling equipment).

- *Broadcasting and entertainment*: During 2001–2007, GE's expanded its entertainment activities beyond its NBC broadcasting and cable TV businesses. Key acquisitions were Telemundo, which took GE into the fast-growing market for Spanish-language broadcasting and Vivendi Universal's entertainment business, which took GE into film studios and theme parks. However, by 2009, it was increasingly evident that NBC Universal did not fit with Immelt's identification of GE as a technology-based industrial company. As a result, NBC Universal was merged with Comcast's cable TV channels, with the new company 49% owned by GE and 51% by Comcast (GE received $6.2 billion from Comcast).

- *Technology infrastructure*: Infrastructure provided a valuable umbrella for a number of Immelt's growth initiatives. In 2003, he announced: "We are taking the company to a place where few can follow: big, fundamental, high technology infrastructure industries in which GE can have enormous competitive advantage."[10] Growth platforms included: security systems, where GE's acquisitions included InVision Technologies (explosive detection systems), Edwards Systems Technology (fire detection), and Interlogix (security systems); water treatment, where GE acquired Ionics and BetzDearborn; and aerospace, where GE built upon its strong position in jet engines to diversify into avionics (Smiths Aerospace was a major acquisition).

Developing growth platforms involved the analysis and segmentation of markets (see the Appendix) to identify high-growth segments that offered the potential for attractive returns, building upon GE's existing businesses, and using acquisitions to help deploy GE's financial, technical, and managerial resources to build a leading position. Immelt explained the approach:

We did a lot of heavy lifting in our portfolio because we didn't have enough juice. We saw where we needed to go and we found that we wouldn't get there with our existing businesses. So, we bought homeland security, biotech, water—businesses that would give us a stronger foundation for innovation.[11]

In addition to the sale of a majority share in NBC Universal, GE also exited other businesses, most notably plastics, where it believed that high petroleum prices would limit growth opportunities. However, by far its greatest divestment challenge was its financial services business, GE Capital. For all Immelt's emphasis on GE as a technology-based, industrial company, GE Capital continued to grow over most of his tenure. For 2006 and 2007, GE Capital accounted for 49% of GE's total net profit (up from 25% in 2001). GE Capital's growth during 2001–2007 had been reinforced by acquisitions in equipment leasing, commercial finance, credit cards, and consumer finance. However, even before the financial crisis, Immelt was committed to pruning GE Capital. During 2004 and 2005, GE sold most of its insurance businesses. The financial crisis created urgent pressures to shrink GE Capital's assets (i.e., reducing its loan exposure), increase its liquidity, improve its risk profile, and redefine its role within GE. Increasingly, GE Capital was reconceived as a supplier of specialist financial service with a particular emphasis on "mid-market lending and leasing, financing in GE domains and a few other specialty finance segments."[12] Table 3 lists GE's principal acquisitions and disposals.

TABLE 3   General Electric's principal acquisitions and disposals, 2001–2012

2001	NBC acquires Telemundo, a leading Spanish language television network.
2003	GE Healthcare acquires Instrumentarium.
2003	GE Capital acquires Transamerica Finance from AEGON.
2004	NBC acquires the entertainment assets of Vivendi Universal, to form NBC Universal (80% owned by GE).
2004	GE Healthcare acquires Amersham PLC for $9.5 billion.
2004	GE Capital acquires Dillard's credit card unit for $1.25 billion.
2004	GE sells 60% of GE Capital International Services (GECIS) to private equity companies, Oak Hill Capital Partners and General Atlantic, for $500 million.
2004	GE's life and mortgage insurance businesses spun off as Genworth Financial.
2004	GE Security acquires InVision Technologies, a leading manufacturer of airport security equipment.
2005	GE Commercial Finance acquires the financial assets of Bombardier, a Canadian aircraft manufacturer for $1.4 billion.
2006	GE Healthcare acquires IDX Systems, a medical software firm, for $1.2 billion.
2006	GE Advanced Materials division is sold to Apollo Management for $3.8 billion.
2006	GE Water & Process Technologies acquires Zenon Environmental Systems for $758 million.
2006	Sale of GE Insurance Solutions and GE Life to Swiss Re for $6.5 bn.
2007	GE Aviation acquires Smiths Aerospace for $4.6 billion.
2007	GE Oil and Gas acquires VetcoGray for $1.4 billion.
2007	GE Plastics is sold to Saudi Arabia Basic Industries Corp. for $11.7 billion.
2007	GE NBC Universal acquires Oxygen Media (cable TV channel).
2008	GE Co. acquires Vital Signs Inc. for $860 million.
2008	GE Energy Infrastructure acquires Hydril Pressure Control (oilfield equipment).
2008	GE Capital finance acquires Merrill Lynch Capital, CitiCapital, and Bank BPH.
2009	GE increases its ownership in BAC to 75%.
2010	GE Healthcare acquires Clarient, Inc.
2010	GE Capital deconsolidates Regency Energy Partners LP and sells its general partnership interest in Regency.
2011	GE Energy Infrastructure acquires Converteam, Dresser, Inc., the Well Support division of John Wood Group PLC, Wellstream PLC, and Lineage Power Holdings, Inc.

GE's Competitive Advantage

A major theme in all Immelt's speeches and strategy presentations as chairman and CEO was emphasis of the competitive advantages that GE shared across its different businesses. Immelt placed a particular emphasis on three sources of competitive advantage: technology and innovation, customer focus and integrated solutions, and global presence.

Technology and Innovation   Immelt identified technology as a major driver of GE's future growth and emphasized the need to speed up the diffusion of new technologies within GE and turn the corporate R & D center into an intellectual hothouse. His commitment to technology was signaled by expanding GE's R & D budgets. This began with a $100-million upgrade to GE's corporate R & D center in Niskayuna, New York and was followed by the construction of new Global Research Centers in Shanghai, Munich, and Rio de Janeiro. In 2012, GE claimed to have 37,000 technologists working in its businesses and in its research centers.

Immelt's emphasis on technology reflected his belief that the primary driver of sales was great products: "You can be six sigma, you can do great delivery, you can be great in China, you can do everything else well—but if you don't have a good product, you're not going to sell much."[13] Increasing product quality and product innovation became a critical performance indicator for all of GE's businesses.

Under Immelt, GE focused its research upon fewer, bigger, longer-term programs. This emphasis was reflected in GE's Advanced Technology Programs in molecular imaging and diagnostics, nanotechnology, energy conversion, advanced propulsion, and sustainable energy.

Immelt was particularly interested in identifying and supporting projects that offered large-scale market potential. "Imagination Breakthroughs" were promising projects with the potential to create $100 million in sales over a three-year period. By mid-2006, some 100 Imagination Breakthroughs had been identified and individually approved by Immelt. Imagination Breakthroughs included:

- *Evolution hybrid locomotive*: An energy-saving locomotive that would use energy lost in braking to be stored in batteries.
- *Smart Grid*: A marriage of IT with electrical infrastructure to support twenty-first-century energy needs.
- *Sodium batteries*: A novel, patented battery technology for large-scale electricity storage.

GE's "Ecomagination" was a program of product and business development launched in 2005 as "GE's commitment to address challenges such as the need for cleaner, more efficient sources of energy, reduced emissions, and abundant sources of clean water."[14] The Ecomagination program provided funding and coordination for developing environmentally friendly products and business solutions across GE's different business divisions. In 2011, it was credited with generating $21 billion of clean energy revenue.

Customer Focus and Integrated Solutions   Throughout his career at GE, Immelt emphasized customer orientation and the value of spending time with customers, building relationships with them, and working on their problems. Soon after taking over as CEO, Immelt emphasized the primacy of customer focus:

We're dramatically changing our resource base from providing support to creating value. Every business has functions that add high value by driving growth. These are the functions that deal with the customer, create new products, sell, manufacture, manage the money and drive controllership. Call that the front room. Every business has backroom support functions that sometimes are so large and bureaucratic they create a drain on the system and keep us from meeting our customers' needs and keep us from growing. So we're going to take more of the back-room resources and put them in the front room—more sales people, more engineers, more product designers. We're changing the shape of this company and we're doing it during a recession."[15]

The increased customer focus involved increased investment in GE's marketing function, including hiring talented marketing executives and developing processes for identifying new product and service offerings and unmet customer needs.

A major avenue for translating enhanced customer focus into value creation for GE was through bundling products with support services to offer customized "customer solutions." Expanding the range of customer service offerings to include technical services, financial services, training, and other forms of customer support. Creating customer solutions required coordination across GE's businesses. For example, in the case of a new hospital development, there might be opportunities not just for medical equipment but also for lighting, turbines, and other GE businesses as well. To exploit new opportunities that cut across GE's existing divisional structure, GE began to create cross-business, high-visibility marketing campaigns.

As we shall see, increasing GE's capacity to serve customers better with integrated solutions was a key consideration in Immelt's reorganization of GE's structure, which combined and reorganized GE's divisional structure (see below).

Global Presence   Immelt believed that some of the biggest payoffs from greater customer orientation would come from GE's increased success in international markets. Positioning GE to compete in growing emerging markets was a central strategic priority for GE. In 2011, Immelt appointed vice chairman John Rice to lead its international growth efforts, with particular emphasis on high-growth markets such as China, India, the Middle East, and Brazil. Maximizing GE's potential in these markets required a coordinated approach across GE's businesses: "A great example is our spectacular success with the Beijing 2008 Olympic Games. This event produced $2 billion of revenues across multiple GE platforms, while building our relationships in China. In 2008, we announced a multifaceted partnership with Mubadala, the commercial investing arm of Abu Dhabi, which includes a commercial finance joint venture, projects in renewable energy, and a training center in Abu Dhabi. Mubadala will also become a 'Top 10' GE investor."[16] In 2009, GE announced its "Company-to-Country" strategy where GE worked directly with government in order to meet local needs across a range of infrastructure investments. China, India, and Brazil were the focal points for GE's top-down business initiatives. In 2012, GE announced that, in "Nigeria, we are building out a comprehensive 'Company-to-Country' approach to address infrastructure challenges; Nigeria should be our next billion-dollar country."[17]

Internationalization involved a fundamental rethink of GE's approach to product development and a thorough overhaul of products and services to meet local market needs. GE's traditional approach had been to develop products for the US market, then to offer simpler, less costly "de-featured" versions to emerging markets. Combining GE's international emphasis with its increasing customer focus reoriented GE toward a "customer-optimization" approach to product development where local teams were given greater freedom in adapting and innovating products for their own markets. The outcome was "reverse innovation": many of the product concepts developed to meet the needs of emerging-market customers could be subsequently applied to GE's clients of the advanced industrialized nations. For example, a low-cost, portable, battery-operated ultrasound machine designed to meet the needs of physicians in India and China became a commercial success in the US.[18]

Exploiting global opportunities also involved globalizing GE's organization and its talent base. For example, the headquarters of GE Healthcare was moved to the UK, while in 2011 it announced the transfer of its X-ray business from Wisconsin to Beijing, China. Internationalization of the workforce included core corporate functions: by 2006, of 400 younger members of GE's audit staff, about 60 were Indian.

Changing the GE Management Model

The management system that Immelt inherited had been reformulated by his predecessor and mentor, Jack Welch, but was also a product of 120 years of continuous development. Immelt respected GE's management systems and processes, and recognized that many of them were so deeply embedded within GE's culture that they were integral to GE's identity and the way it viewed the world. At the core of GE's management system was its management development—its so-called "talent machine"—and its system of performance management.

Leadership Development and Performance Management

From the early days, GE was committed to internally developed leadership: all of its CEOs were promoted from within the company. GE's meritocratic system of development and promotion was put in place by Charles Coffin, the CEO who succeeded Edison in 1892. Since then, GE had been a "CEO factory" producing top management talent not only for GE but also for corporations worldwide. Its management development system rested on two key pillars: its corporate university at Crotonville, New York and its "Session C" system for tracking managers' performance, planning their careers, and formulating succession plans for every management position at GE from department heads upwards. Under Welch the Session C reviews became all-day events at each of GE's businesses where Welch and the division CEO reviewed the performance and potential of every manager.

GE's management appraisal and development processes together with its financial and strategic planning systems formed the core of GE's performance management system. Under Jack Welch, GE's system of performance management became increasingly based upon quantitative targets that allowed focus and accountability. Immelt was equally committed to GE's metrics-driven approach to performance management: "Nothing happens in this company without an output metric," observed Immelt. All of Immelt's strategic initiatives—from earnings and organic growth targets to productivity improvements, reductions in overhead costs and six sigma quality—were linked to precise quantitative targets. In 2005, GE standardized its customer satisfaction metrics, focusing on "net promoter scores" (the percentage of customers who would recommend GE to a friend, minus the percentage who wouldn't).

Immelt's strategic initiatives represented a challenge to GE's metrics-based performance management system. Goals such as innovation, enterprise selling, and environmental sustainability tended to be less amenable to quantification and objective measurement than goals of cost efficiency, productivity, and profitability.

The shifting of strategic priorities also had implications for GE's management development system. As with Jack Welch, Immelt saw his most important task as helping to develop GE's managerial talent. Implementing GE's growth strategy required that GE's employees internalized growth as part of their personal mission. This required inculcating among GE's managers the necessary skills and aptitudes to become "growth leaders." A benchmarking exercise investigating the management characteristics of fifteen companies with outstanding records of revenue growth resulting in the identification of five "growth traits." These included: external focus, imagination and creativity, decisiveness and clear thinking ability, inclusiveness, and deep "domain expertise" (knowledge of the particular business).

These growth traits became part of GE's annual HR review, with each of GE's top 5,000 people rated on each of the five traits and the results of the assessment built into their subsequent development plans. Career planning also changed: because of the importance of domain expertise, managers were required to stay longer in each job.

Changing Organizational Structure

The most visible of the management changes introduced by Immelt concerned the overall structure of the organization. Between 2002 and 2008, Immelt reversed several of the major structural changes that Welch had introduced during the 1980s. As part of "delayering" and his effort to create a more responsive company, Welch had broken up GE's major industrial sectors into smaller divisions. In order to facilitate greater cross-business integration, the bundling of products and services into "systems," and the creation of new "growth platforms," Immelt progressively reorganized GE's divisions into a smaller number of broad-based sectors. Reorganizations in 2002, 2005, and 2008 reduced the number of business sectors reporting to Immelt from twelve to five; before a further reorganization in 2010 increased them to seven (Figures 2 and 3).

Innovation and New Business Development

A key challenge was to reconcile GE's famous obsession with profitability and cost control with nurturing the innovation needed to drive growth. Innovation, especially when it included big, long-term projects, involved substantial risk. The danger was that GE's obsession with performance metrics might discourage business unit heads from making big bets on promising new opportunities. Furthermore, given the fact that many of the biggest opportunities were likely to require cooperation

FIGURE 2 General Electric's organizational structure, 2001

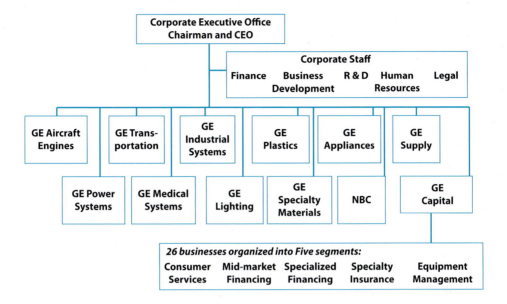

FIGURE 3 General Electric's organizational structure, 2012

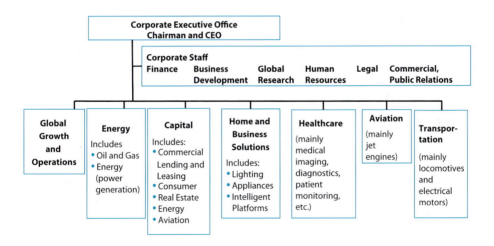

across divisions further increased the likelihood that they would fail to get the support they needed. The Imagination Breakthroughs initiative (referred to above) was designed to ensure that major innovatory projects would receive the investment and attention needed to exploit their potential. To ensure the rapid development of promising projects, funding decisions were placed, not with the business sectors, but with Immelt and the top management team. Once approved, these projects were protected from normal budget pressures. About half involved new products and the other half involved changing commercial structure. Immelt saw these Innovation

Breakthroughs as a means of focusing attention on the goal of business creation and development. Given that some of these projects involved substantial levels of investment (GE's hybrid locomotive, for example, would require tens of millions of dollars), by lifting these projects from the business level to the corporate level, it took pressure off the business heads. One problem, observed Immelt, was that GE did not possess sufficient product managers and systems engineers to put in charge of high-visibility programs that were characterized by high risk and the potential for substantial returns.

Marketing and Sales

Realizing Immelt's goal of a customer-driven company required revitalization of GE's marketing function: "Marketing was the place where washed-up salespeople went," observed Immelt.[19] Upgrading GE's marketing was achieved through creating the new senior position of Chief Marketing Officer, the recreation of GE's Advanced Marketing Seminar, developing an Experienced Commercial Leadership Program, and requiring that every business appoint a VP-level head of marketing. Most important was the creation of GE's Commercial Council, which brought together GE's leading sales and marketing leaders to develop new business ideas, to transfer best practices, and instill a commercial culture within GE. A key initiative was "At the Customer, For the Customer," a program that deployed six sigma in marketing, sales, and customer relations activities, applied GE's six sigma methodologies to customers' own businesses, and used new metrics to track customer satisfaction and customer attitudes.

As with all aspects of GE's approach to management, marketing was subject to the same systematized, metrics-driven analysis as all other functions were within the firm, often with some startling revelations:

> We're getting the sales force better trained and equipped with better tools and metrics. A good example is what we're doing to create discipline around pricing. Not long ago, a guy here named Dave McCalpin did an analysis of our pricing in appliances and found out that about $5 billion of it is discretionary. Given all the decisions that sales reps can make on their own, that's how much is in play. It was the most astounding number I'd ever heard—and that's just in appliances. Extrapolating across our businesses, there may be $50 billion that few people are tracking or accountable for. We would never allow something like that on the cost side. When it comes to the prices we pay, we study them, we map them, we work them. But with the prices we charge, we're too sloppy.[20]

The GE Growth Process

Very soon after his appointment as GE's chairman and CEO in 2001, Immelt had articulated his strategic vision of GE as a technology-based, customer-focused, growth-orientated industrial powerhouse. Implementing this vision was a longer-term project. Immelt's changes in GE's organizational structure, its management development and appraisal system, and its marketing and technology functions were all efforts to align GE's structure, systems, and processes with the intended strategy. By 2006, these various initiatives had coalesced in Immelt's mind around an integrated system that he referred to as the "GE Growth Process." As Immelt explained:

> If you run a big multibusiness company like GE and you're trying to lead trans-
> formative change, that objective has to be linked to hitting levers across all of the
> businesses—and it must keep that up over time. So you've got to have a process.
> That's true from an internal standpoint, but it's also the only way you get paid in
> the marketplace. Investors have to see that it's repeatable.
>
> I knew if I could define a process and set the right metrics, this company could go
> 100 miles an hour in the right direction. It took time, though, to understand growth
> as a process. If I had worked out that wheel-shaped diagram in 2001, I would have
> started with it. But in reality, you get these things by wallowing in them awhile. We had
> a few steps worked out in 2003, but it took another two years to fill in the process.[21]

During 2006, Immelt's view of GE's growth engine as an integrated, six-part process was disseminated throughout the organization and became a key part of Immelt's communication to GE's external constituencies (Figure 4).

The Challenge of Integration and Complexity

Common to most of the organizational changes initiated by Immelt was the desire to create value through the many parts of GE working together more closely and more

FIGURE 4   General Electric's six-part growth process

Source: General Electric, annual report, 2005, p. 8.

effectively. "Working at GE is the art of thinking and playing big; our managers have to work cross-function, cross-region, cross-company. And we have to be about big purposes," observed Immelt.[22]

However, greater integration across GE's different businesses created complex coordination problems. Consider GE initiatives relating to product bundling and customer solutions through its "Enterprise Selling" and "Company-to-Country" initiatives. At one level these strategies are intuitive and straightforward:

> If somebody's building a hospital, that might represent a total package of $1 billion, of which the GE market potential might be $100 million. We're probably already talking to the C-suite because we sell the medical equipment. What we need to do is set things up so that the medical rep can bring in the lighting rep, the turbine rep, and so on.

Similarly with whole countries:

> In Qatar, the emir wants to know everybody doing business in his country. In a dinner set up to talk about oil and gas bids, he might say, "Jeff, I'm going to put $10 billion into a hospital," or he might mention that they're going to buy GE engines for Qatar Airways.[23]

However, the organizational ramifications were complex. Sales and marketing staff becoming less focused upon their particular business and more oriented toward the opportunities provided from across the company as a whole. In practice, this created complex problems of organization, expertise, and incentives. Exhibit 1 describes the difficulties encountered in the apparently simple bundling of medical diagnostic equipment with consulting services.

As Immelt recognized, organizing to meet customer needs implied a different type of organizational structure from organizing for operational efficiency. Similar challenges existed in relation to GE's efforts to develop large-scale innovations that cut across its existing business-based structure. Reconciling these different coordination needs posed organizational challenges that even GE had not fully resolved:

> I've found that few companies are actually structured to deliver products and services in a synchronized way that's attractive from a customer's perspective. Individual units are historically focused on perfecting their products and processes, and give little thought to how their offerings might be even more valuable to the end user when paired with those of another unit. It's not just that the status quo doesn't reward collaborative behavior—although the right incentives are also critical. It's that the connections literally aren't in place.
>
> One way to forge those connections is to do away with traditional silos altogether and create new ones organized by customer segments or needs. Many companies, however, are understandably reluctant to let go of the economies of scale and depth of knowledge and expertise associated with non-customer-focused silos. A company organized around geographies can customize offerings to suit local preferences, for instance, while a technology-centric firm can be quick to market with technical innovations. In many cases, functional and geographic silos were created precisely to help companies coordinate such activities as designing

innovative products or gaining geographic focus. A customer focus requires them to emphasize a different set of activities and coordinate them in a different way.

In their initial attempts to offer customer solutions, companies are likely to create structures and processes that transcend rather than obliterate silos. Such boundary-spanning efforts may be highly informal—even as simple as hoping for or encouraging serendipity and impromptu conversations that lead to unplanned cross-unit solutions. But the casual exchange of information and ideas is generally most effective among senior executives, who have a better understanding than their subordinates of corporate goals and easier access to other leaders in the organization.[24]

Establishing informal collaboration across divisional boundaries was the way in which companies such as Samsung, IBM, and 3M had responded to the conflicting requirements for responsiveness and integration. For GE, however, flexible boundary spanning risked conflicting both with GE's metrics-based system of performance management and with its culture of internal competition. Internal competition—between divisions and business units for resources and between individuals for performance bonuses and promotion—was a fundamental feature of its management systems and organizational culture.

Immelt's efforts to create a more integrated GE had also changed the relationship between GE's corporate headquarters and the businesses. Under Welch, there was a clear division of roles and responsibilities between the business divisions and that of the corporate HQ. The business divisions with their individual CEOs were

---

EXHIBIT 1

General Electric Medical Systems Customer Solutions Initiative

One of the earliest initiatives to exploit opportunities for bundling products and services was to combine the sale of medical imaging equipment with consulting services. In 2001, GE Medical Systems (soon to become GE Healthcare) created a new unit, Performance Solutions, to provide an integrated approach to hospital diagnostic imaging departments by combining equipment with technical support and patient-management systems. A lead customer was Stanford University Medical Center, which transitioned to all-digital imaging for its hospital and outpatient unit.

After a promising start, by 2005 Performance Solutions was in trouble. The medical equipment sales people had limited understanding of the consulting services being offered by the Performance Solutions unit and provided few sales leads for the new integrated offering. They were also reluctant to share their customers with sales personnel from Performance Solutions. Meanwhile, the sales personnel from Performance Solutions considered themselves "solution providers" and felt constrained by having to limit their solutions exclusively to GE offerings.

Source: Based upon R. Gulati, "Silo Busting: How to Execute on the Promise of Customer Focus," *Harvard Business Review* (May 2007).

responsible for running their own businesses both operationally and strategically. The role of the corporate headquarters was both to support the businesses through various centralized services and to drive business performance by putting divisional top management under intense pressure to deliver.

As headquarters became increasingly involved in promoting and supporting developmental initiatives (e.g., Imagination Breakthroughs and Enterprise Selling), so the corporate HQ became more of a partner with the business divisions rather than an overseer of divisional performance and interrogator of business strategies.

As a result, much of the simplicity and directness associated with Welch's management style had been supplanted by an emphasis on managing integration, which inevitably involved more intricate and sophisticated approaches to strategy execution. Developing new products, businesses, and customer solutions required new and more complex cross-business and cross-functional coordination within GE. The new performance requirements were being built on top of GE's existing commitments to efficiency, quality, and financial performance. Could this added complexity be borne by a company that was steadily growing larger and encompassing a widening portfolio of businesses and products? Most US companies that had achieved outstanding performance by successfully combining innovation with efficiency in fast-moving business environments were fairly specialized. Certainly the great majority of companies on *Fortune*'s list of "most admired companies" were strongly based on a single core business. To find examples of highly diversified, multinational corporations that were also outstandingly successful, Immelt had to look far beyond US shores to Samsung and the Tata Group. As Immelt reminded his top managers, GE was entering uncharted waters: "The business book that can help you hasn't been written yet."

Appendix: General Electric Segment Performance

REVENUE AND PROFIT, 2007–2011 ($MILLION)

	2011	2010	2009	2008	2007
Revenues					
Energy Infrastructure	43,694	37,514	40,648	43,046	34,880
Aviation	18,859	17,619	18,728	19,239	16,819
Healthcare	18,083	16,897	16,015	17,392	16,997
Transportation	4,885	3,370	3,827	5,016	4,523
Home and Business Solutions	8,465	8,648	8,443	10,117	11,026
Total industrial revenues	93,986	84,048	87,661	94,810	84,245
GE Capital	45,730	46,422	48,906	65,900	65,625
Segment profit					
Energy Infrastructure	6,650	7,271	7,105	6,497	5,238
Aviation	3,512	3,304	3,923	3,684	3,222
Healthcare	2,803	2,741	2,420	2,851	3,056
Transportation	757	315	473	962	936
Home and Business Solutions	300	457	370	365	983
Total industrial profit	14,022	14,088	14,291	14,359	13,435
GE Capital	6,549	3,158	1,325	7,841	12,179

ASSETS AND INVESTMENT IN PROPERTY, PLANT AND EQUIPMENT ($MILLION)

	Assets			Property, plant and equipment additions		
	2011	2010	2009	2011	2010	2009
Energy Infrastructure	54,389	38,606	36,663	2,078	954	1,012
Aviation	23,567	21,175	20,377	699	471	442
Healthcare	27,981	27,784	27,163	378	249	302
Transportation	2,633	2,515	2,714	193	69	68
Home and Business Solutions	4,645	4,280	4,955	278	229	201
GE Capital	552,514	565,337	597,877	9,882	7,674	6,442
Total	717,242	747,793	781,949	13,564	9,821	8,670

Source: General Electric Company, 10-K report, 2011

GE CAPITAL: FINANCIAL DATA BY BUSINESS SEGMENT ($MILLION)

	2011	2010	2009	2008	2007	2006
Revenues						
Commercial Lending and Leasing	18,178	18,447	20,762	26,742	27,267	25,833
GE Money	n.a.	n.a.	n.a.	25,012	24,769	19,508
Consumer	16,781	17,204	16,794	n.a.	n.a.	n.a.
Real Estate	3,712	3,744	4,009	6,646	7,021	5,020
Energy Financial Services	1,223	1,957	2,117	3,707	2,405	1,664
GE Commercial Aviation Services	5,262	5,127	4,594	4,901	4,839	4,353
Profit						
Commercial Lending and Leasing	2,720	1,554	963	1,805	3,801	3,503
GE Money	n.a.	n.a.	n.a.	3,664	4,269	3,231
Consumer	3,551	2,523	1,282	n.a.	n.a.	n.a.
Real Estate	(928)	(1,741)	(1,541)	1,144	2,285	1,841
Energy Financial Services	440	367	212	825	677	648
GE Commercial Aviation Services	1,150	1,195	1,016	1,194	1,211	1,174
Total assets						
Commercial Lending and Leasing	193,869	202,650	205,827	232,486	229,608	n.a.
GE Money	n.a.	n.a.	n.a.	183617	209178	n.a.
Consumer	139,000	147,327	176,046	n.a.	n.a.	n.a.
Real Estate	60,873	72,630	81,505	85,266	79,285	n.a.
Energy Financial Services	18,357	19,549	22,616	22,079	18,705	n.a.
GE Commercial Aviation Services	48,821	49,106	51,066	49,455	47,189	n.a.

Notes:
n.a.: not available.
Figures in parentheses denote loss.
Source: General Electric, 10-K report, 2011.

Notes

1. Transcript, General Electric Company Annual Shareholder Meeting, April 25, 2012.
2. "Letter to Stakeholders," General Electric, annual report, 2002, p. 3.
3. "Can a Specialist Run General Electric?" March 7, 2012, http://blogs.ft.com/businessblog/2012/can-a-specialist-run-general-electric/#axzz1tv41XKUt.
4. "What Makes GE Great?" *Fortune*, March 6, 2006, pp. 90–96.
5. General Electric, annual report, 1993, p. 5.
6. "Running the house that Jack built," *Business Week*, October 2, 2000.
7. "The Days of Welch and Roses," *Business Week*, April 29, 2002.
8. General Electric, annual report, 2002.
9. Address to shareholders, Annual Shareowners' Meeting, Philadelphia, April 26, 2006.
10. Letter to stakeholders," General Electric, annual report, 2002, p. 9.
11. Reprinted by permission of *Harvard Business Review*. From "Growth as a Process: An Interview with Jeff Immelt," June 2006. Copyright © 2006 by the Harvard Business School Publishing Corporation; all rights reserved.
12. "Letter to shareowners," General Electric, annual report, 2011, p. 5.
13. Reprinted by permission of *Harvard Business Review*. From "Growth as a Process: An Interview with Jeff Immelt," June 2006. Copyright © 2006 by the Harvard Business School Publishing Corporation; all rights reserved.
14. "GE Launches Ecomagination," General Electric press release, May 9, 2005.
15. "GE Launches Ecomagination," General Electric press release, May 9, 2005.
16. General Electric, annual report 2008, pp. 6–7.
17. "Letter to shareowners," General Electric annual report, 2011: pp. 6.
18. J. R. Immelt, V. Govindarajan, and C. Trimble, "How GE is Disrupting Itself," *Harvard Business Review*, October 2009: pp. 56–65.
19. Reprinted by permission of *Harvard Business Review*. From "Growth as a Process: An Interview with Jeff Immelt," June 2006. Copyright © 2006 by the Harvard Business School Publishing Corporation; all rights reserved.
20. Reprinted by permission of *Harvard Business Review*. From "Growth as a Process: An Interview with Jeff Immelt," June 2006. Copyright © 2006 by the Harvard Business School Publishing Corporation; all rights reserved.
21. Reprinted by permission of *Harvard Business Review*. From "Growth as a Process: An Interview with Jeff Immelt," June 2006. Copyright © 2006 by the Harvard Business School Publishing Corporation; all rights reserved.
22. Reprinted by permission of *Harvard Business Review*. From "Growth as a Process: An Interview with Jeff Immelt," June 2006. Copyright © 2006 by the Harvard Business School Publishing Corporation; all rights reserved.
23. Reprinted by permission of *Harvard Business Review*. From "Growth as a Process: An Interview with Jeff Immelt," June 2006. Copyright © 2006 by the Harvard Business School Publishing Corporation; all rights reserved.
24. Reprinted by permission of *Harvard Business Review*. From "Growth as a Process: An Interview with Jeff Immelt," June 2006. Copyright © 2006 by the Harvard Business School Publishing Corporation; all rights reserved.

A video clip relating to this case is available in your interactive e-book at **www.wileyopenpage.com**

Case 23 Bank of America's Acquisition of Merrill Lynch

December 2008

On the afternoon of Monday, December 22, 2008, Ken Lewis, chairman and CEO of Bank of America Corporation, was preparing for a special meeting of Bank of America's board of directors, which would be held by telephone at 4 p.m.

The meeting was critical to the future of Bank of America and to the future careers of Lewis and his top management team. The meeting offered the board its final opportunity to pull the plug on its acquisition of Merrill Lynch & Company, which was to be consummated in ten days' time (January 1, 2009).

The acquisition, announced on September 15, 2008 (see Exhibit 1 for the press release), would create America's biggest financial services company in terms of total assets. It was the culmination of a succession of acquisitions by Bank of America, which had taken it far from its home base in Charlotte, North Carolina. Under Hugh McColl, its CEO from 1983 to 2001, North Carolina National Bank first became NationsBank, then, after its 1998 acquisition of San Francisco-based BankAmerica, it changed its name to Bank of America Corporation. Table 1 shows Bank of America's principal acquisitions.

TABLE 1   Bank of America's growth by acquisition

Year	Company acquired	Notes
1960	Security National Back of Greensboro merges with American Commercial Bank of Charlotte	Merged bank named North Caroline National Bank (NCNB)
1982	First National Bank of Lake City (Florida)	First out-of-state acquisition by NCNB
1991	C&S/Sovren of Atlanta	NCNB changes its name to NationsBank
1993	MNC Financial of Maryland	
1998	BankAmerica Corporation of San Francisco	NationsBank renamed Bank of America
2004	Fleet Boston Financial Corporation	Expands into Northeast
2006	MBNA	Bank of America becomes largest US credit-card issuer
2007	US Trust	Bank of America becomes leading US private bank for wealthy individuals
2007	ABN AMRO North America	Major subsidiary: La Salle Bank Corp.
2008	Countrywide Financial	Bank of America becomes US's largest mortgage lender
2008	Merrill Lynch & Company, Inc.	September 15 bid to take effect January 1, 2009

This case was prepared by Robert M. Grant. ©2012 Robert M. Grant.

EXHIBIT 1

Press Release: Bank of America Buys Merrill Lynch Creating Unique Financial Services Firm

CHARLOTTE (September 15, 2008)—Bank of America Corporation today announced it has agreed to acquire Merrill Lynch & Co., Inc. in a $50 billion all-stock transaction that creates a company unrivalled in its breadth of financial services and global reach. "Acquiring one of the premier wealth management, capital markets, and advisory companies is a great opportunity for our shareholders," Bank of America Chairman and Chief Executive Officer Ken Lewis said. "Together, our companies are more valuable because of the synergies in our businesses." "Merrill Lynch is a great global franchise and I look forward to working with Ken Lewis and our senior management teams to create what will be the leading financial institution in the world with the combination of these two firms," said John Thain, chairman and CEO of Merrill Lynch.

Under the terms of the transaction, Bank of America would exchange 0.8595 shares of Bank of America common stock for each Merrill Lynch common share. The price is 1.8 times the stated tangible book value. Bank of America expects to achieve $7 billion in pretax expense savings, fully realized by 2012. The acquisition is expected to be accretive to earnings by 2010. The transaction is expected to close in the first quarter of 2009. It has been approved by directors of both companies and is subject to shareholder votes at both companies and standard regulatory approvals. Under the agreement, three directors of Merrill Lynch will join the Bank of America Board of Directors.

The combined company would have leadership positions in retail brokerage and wealth management. By adding Merrill Lynch's more than 16,000 financial advisers, Bank of America would have the largest brokerage in the world with more than 20,000 advisers and $2.5 trillion in client assets.

The combination brings global scale in investment management, including an approximately 50% ownership in BlackRock, which has $1.4 trillion in assets under management. Bank of America has $589 billion in assets under management. Adding Merrill Lynch both enhances current strengths at Bank of America and creates new ones, particularly outside of the United States. Merrill Lynch adds strengths in global debt underwriting, global equities and global merger and acquisition advice. After the acquisition, Bank of America would be the number one underwriter of global high yield debt, the third largest underwriter of global equity and the ninth largest adviser on global mergers and acquisitions based on pro forma first half of 2008 results.

Source: http://newsroom.bankofamerica.com/press-release/corporate-and-financial-news/bank-america-buys-merrill-lynch-creating-unique-financial, accessed October 1, 2012. Reproduced with permission.

Despite the size of the acquisition, it was not the result of careful strategic planning. The merger announcement came the same day that Lehman Brothers filed for Chapter 11 bankruptcy protection amidst growing fears that the global financial system was going into meltdown. Anticipating that Merrill Lynch might be the next major financial institution to fail, the acquisition was hastily brokered by the chairman of the Federal Reserve Board, Ben Bernanke, and the US Treasury Secretary, Hank Paulson. Announcing the merger, Bank of America's chairman and CEO, Ken Lewis, stated: "The fact that we could put this transaction together in less than 48 hours is a great statement on the strength of both our teams, but also on the great strategic fit which, from the instant that we talked about it, became clear that this transaction would make a lot of sense."

Others were less convinced that the transaction made sense. The biggest concern was that Bank of America was overpaying. The *Financial Times*' Lex column commented:

Even if Merrill is being taken out at a third of its 52-week high, it is, in the circumstances, hardly a steal at 1.8 times tangible book value and 12 times 2009 earnings. Mr. Thain's willingness to accept market realities has enabled Merrill shareholders to escape a total wipe-out. As Jamie Dimon noted after acquiring Bear Stearns, there is a difference between buying a house and buying a house that's on fire. While flames are licking at Merrill's outhouses, Mr. Thain has persuaded BofA's Ken Lewis there is still plenty of time to douse them. But until Mr. Lewis can prove that Merrill has suffered only cosmetic damage, he will struggle to get investors excited about promised savings worth $7bn or 10% of the cost base. BofA's shares fell 15%, destroying $23bn of value.

If the deal proceeds to plan, BofA would secure the Merrill brand and the largest retail broker network in the US, with a 17,000-strong herd of financial advisers as well as a leading investment bank and wealth management franchise. There are, though, two big dangers. First, much of the risk Merrill has "offloaded" in its vendor-financed sale of toxic securities could come back to haunt its new owner. Second, a culture war between two workforces remunerated according to different pay systems seems unavoidable.[1]

During the final quarter of 2008, pessimism about the merger continued to grow. Bank of America's share price declined from $29.55 on September 16, 2008 to $13.53 on December 22. The main concern was Merrill's balance sheet. On October 16, Merrill reported a third-quarter loss of $5.1 billion resulting mostly from a write-down in the value of its CDOs (collateralized debt obligations) and other real-estate related assets.

By mid-December it was becoming clear that Merrill's fourth-quarter results would be even worse than the dreadful third-quarter figures. On December 14, 2008, Bank of America's chief financial officer, Joe Price, advised Ken Lewis that Merrill Lynch's financial condition was deteriorating. During the previous week, Merrill Lynch's projected fourth-quarter losses had risen from $9 billion to $12 billion.

These revelations about the full horrors of Merrill's financial position removed any lingering doubts over whether Bank of America had overpaid for Merrill: current losses and future write-downs probably meant that Merrill Lynch was worth absolutely nothing. The issue for Lewis and the board was whether to invoke the "MAC clause" in the merger agreement, which allowed the merger to be called off in the event of a "materially adverse event" occurring.

There followed a flurry of communications between Lewis, Bernanke, Paulson, and officials at the US Treasury. After informing them of Bank of America's desire to exit the merger, Lewis became a target of sustained pressure from the Department of the Treasury in particular.

Paulson reminded Lewis of the risks to the entire US financial system that would result from Bank of America's rescinding of the merger agreement, risks that would inevitably have a major impact upon Bank of America itself. Paulson also indicated that, should Bank of America invoke the MAC clause, the US government would seek the removal of Bank of America's board and top management team. However, if Bank of America went ahead with the merger, the Treasury and Federal

Reserve System would provide whatever assistance was needed by Bank of America to restore its capital and to protect it against the adverse impact of "toxic" Merrill Lynch assets.[2]

As Lewis got ready to speak to his fellow board members, he realized that he was faced with the most difficult decision of his entire career. If Bank of America went ahead with the merger, Merrill's appalling financial situation would be a major drag on Bank of America's performance, would depress its share price, and would undoubtedly anger shareholders. However, beyond the short term, probably the next two to three years, he believed that shareholders would reap considerable long-run benefit from the strategic advantages of the new global colossus. And yet, rescinding the deal would free Bank of America from Merrill Lynch's acute financial problems, but the implications were troubling. Rescinding would postpone, possibly forever, Lewis's desire to create the world's pre-eminent universal bank. Even more serious, it might be the trigger for the financial calamity that President Bush had forewarned in his recognition that: "This sucker might go down!"[3] The implications for Bank of America, especially if Paulson made good on his threat to remove Bank of America's board, were hardly appealing.

The potential conflict between Lewis's moral obligations to his shareholders and to his country was further complicated by his legal duties. As chairman and CEO, Lewis was required to inform shareholders of company matters relevant to their interests. Although shareholders had on December 5 approved the acquisition of Merrill Lynch, this was without the new projections of Merrill's fourth-quarter losses. When Lewis had raised issues of disclosure with Bernanke and Paulson, he had been given the opinion that such disclosure would not be conducive to the stability of the US financial system.[4]

The Strategic Issues Arising from the Merger

The strategic arguments in favor of the merger were outlined in a joint press conference by the two CEOs (Ken Lewis and John Thain) made on September 15, 2008. Lewis saw Merrill Lynch as adding critical strengths to Bank of America in relation to both individual financial services and corporate financial services. Figure 1 shows two slides from their presentation.

In terms of individual financial services, Merrill Lynch's US-wide network of local offices and its army of financial advisers would represent a massive extension of Bank of America's existing brokerage and wealth-management services. In addition, Bank of America anticipated that the combination of the largest US wealth-management organization with one of America's biggest retail banks with presence in 31 states would offer considerable opportunity for offering a wider range of financial services to the clients of each.

Merrill Lynch's much bigger presence outside of the US would also offer Bank of America the opportunity to build a truly international wealth-management business.

In terms of Bank of America's corporate and investment banking, the merger would transform Bank of America from a provider of corporate banking services with comparatively small-scale investment banking activities into one of the world's leading investment banks. Not only was Merrill strongly positioned in all the world's major financial centers; it had also established a strong position in the emerging markets of Asia, Eastern Europe, Latin America, Africa, and the Middle East, most

FIGURE 1 Extract from merger presentation by Ken Lewis and John Thain

Creating the Premier Financial Services Company in the World

Ken Lewis	John Thain
Bank of America	Merrill Lynch
Chairman and CEO	Chairman and CEO

Strategic Rationale

• *Diversify business mix*

• *Significant enhancement to our investment banking capabilities*

    —*Creates leading positions in*

        • *Global Debt Underwriting*
        • *Global Equities*
        • *Global M&A Advisory*

• *Leadership position in retail brokerage and wealth management*

    — *20,000 financial advisors (16,690 Merrill Lynch advisors)*
    — *$2.5 trillion in client assets*

• *Brings global scale in investment management*

    —*50% ownership stake in BlackRock with $1.4 trillion in AUMs*
    — *Columbia funds have $425 billion in AUMs (total BAC AUMs $589 billion)*

(AUM = Assets Under Management)

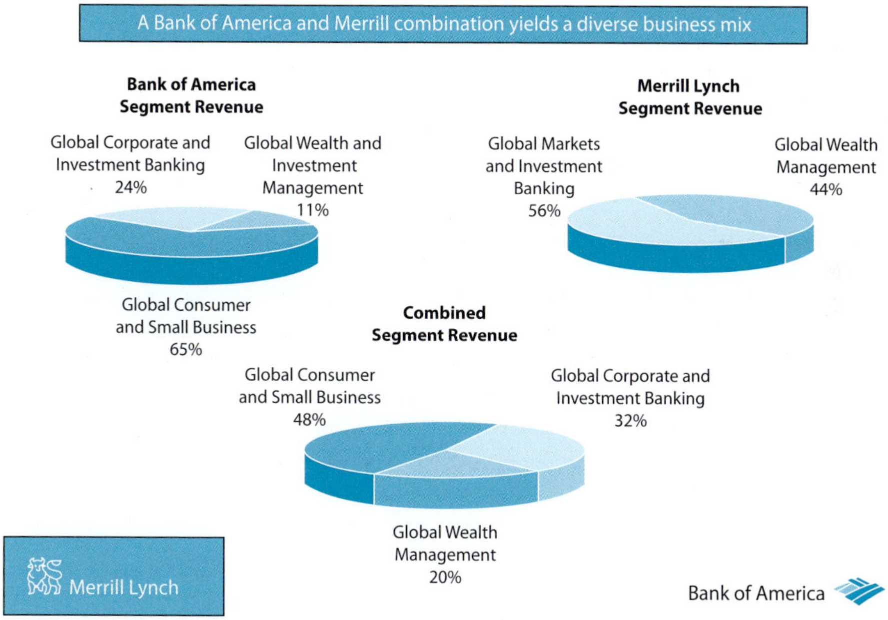

A Bank of America and Merrill combination yields a diverse business mix

Bank of America Segment Revenue

Global Corporate and Investment Banking 24%
Global Wealth and Investment Management 11%
Global Consumer and Small Business 65%

Merrill Lynch Segment Revenue

Global Markets and Investment Banking 56%
Global Wealth Management 44%

Combined Segment Revenue

Global Consumer and Small Business 48%
Global Corporate and Investment Banking 32%
Global Wealth Management 20%

Merrill Lynch

Bank of America

notably in the BRIC countries. Appendices 1 and 2 provide information on the businesses and performance of the two companies.

Some of the contentious aspects of the merger extended beyond the specifics of the Merrill Lynch acquisition to the overall strategy of Bank of America. Bank of America was one of a small number of US banks—the others were Citigroup and

JPMorgan Chase—that had taken advantage of the repeal of the Glass–Stegall Act to combine commercial and investment banking. This so-called universal banking model was common in Europe, where UBS, Deutsche Bank, Credit Suisse, BNP-Paribas, Barclays, Royal Bank of Scotland, and Unicredit had long combined conventional banking services with capital market activities, corporate advisory services, market making, and proprietary trading.

The financial crisis of 2008–2009 had confirmed the robustness of the universal banking model. Among the major US investment banks, only Goldman Sachs and Morgan Stanley had survived. The universal banks were able to pick up the pieces: in addition to Bank of America's acquisition of Merrill Lynch, JPMorgan Chase acquired Bear Stearns. The universal banks had demonstrated the advantages of risk spreading as a result of diversification, plus the stability advantages of financing through retail bank deposits rather than relying on wholesale money markets. In addition, there were the strategic advantages that had traditionally been argued for the universal banks. First, the "one stop shopping" benefits in relation to both individual and corporate/institutional customers of offering a comprehensive range of products and services. Second, the vertical integration benefits of having a retail distribution network to support investment banking activities such as underwriting and securitization.

There were others who believed that the benefits of combining investment and commercial banking were small, while the costs were potentially great. These critics pointed to the fact that few financial institutions had been able to make "cross-selling" financial products work well, while the organizational and management difficulties of administering diversified, multinational financial service companies were huge. Citigroup was often quoted as an example of a financial service company whose size and complexity had made it unmanageable. Part of the problem was in designing management systems that exploited the synergies between commercial and investment banking while avoiding the inherent conflict of interests that multiple relationships with the same client posed (Exhibit 2).

EXHIBIT 2

Universal Banks Need Careful Monitoring

The recent failure of Bear Stearns, Lehman Brothers and Merrill Lynch as independent banks has raised questions about the future of investment banking. The transformation of Goldman Sachs and Morgan Stanley into banking holdings is the last nail in the coffin for investment banks as we knew them for a century. At the same time, the growth of new giants such as JPMorgan Chase, Bank of America, Wells Fargo and Barclays looks like the triumph of the universal banking model over specialized banks.

As the US Treasury and regulators attempt to stop the financial meltdown, they are also redefining the banking model in unintended ways that may sow the seeds of financial turbulence in the future. By encouraging or allowing banks such as JPMorgan, Bank of America and Barclays to rescue weaker banks, useful as it is in the short term, they are also nurturing bigger universal banks. Their sheer size will not only strengthen the unwritten TBTF principle ("too big to fail"). The emerging banking model, based on financial conglomerates with a high degree of diversification, also creates problems for banking stability.

Financial history tells us conglomerates are complex to manage. They usually run profitable businesses whose margins fund other underperforming units, which is one of the reasons why investors put a discount on their share price. But financial conglomerates also involve additional problems related to risk management, conflicts of interest and capital allocation, which create huge challenges for regulators and banking stability as a whole.

The first basic problem that universal banks face is risk management. On the one hand, these banks offer low-risk, traditional banking services—such as deposit-taking and commercial lending—with guaranteed deposits and an insurance mechanism set up by governments. Yet they also run trading units, lend money for mergers and acquisition, manage individuals' portfolios, invest their savings in exotic products and design complex structured loans. These banks look more stable because they are more diversified, but in this diversification lies the problem.

There are a few universal banks in the US, such as Bank of America and JPMorgan, which have weathered the storm so far reasonably well. It is also true that European banks such as Santander or BBVA have been successful with a universal model, although they are strong retail banks and not as diversified as their US competitors. If one leaves these exceptions aside, managing the traditional banking business together with risky financial operations not only makes the basic banking function riskier, but also puts pressure on the whole bank. This is one of the reasons for the huge problems at the heart of the financial woes of Merrill Lynch, UBS, Fortis and Wachovia.

In universal banks, conflicts of interest are ubiquitous. This is an old story that often comes back. It happened during the internet bubble, when some banks played different roles for different parties: advising on M&A, lending to fund some acquisitions, leading initial public offerings or managing portfolios. Chinese walls were torn down and some bankers unethically exploited those conflicts of interest. Public uproar and some regulatory changes calmed the storm but did not eradicate the intrinsic problem.

Disclosure and shareholders' protection is another important issue. By definition, capital allocation in conglomerates is complex to make and complex to discern. Unless banks make a huge effort to explain it in a clear way, neither investors nor regulators really understand where their risk lies, as the recent crisis has shown.

The conflicts of interest inherent in universal banks are not enough to forbid their existence or to go back to the US Glass–Steagall Act. But regulators should monitor them more closely and ask them to separate legally and operationally the basic banking intermediary function from other financial services. Banks should fully disclose their capital allocation and risk in a clearer way, both for shareholders and investors.

Auditors can also help here. Just have a look at the annual reports of some of the failed banks over the past three years and one gets the feeling, most of the time, that they were almost immune to risk.

A dynamic economy needs well-functioning banks. But the universal model needs a clear separation of regulated and unregulated activities and better transparency and disclosure. Unless we address this challenge, we may end up not only with larger banks but with a weaker financial system in the future.

Source: J. Canals, Universal banks need careful monitoring, *Financial Times*, October 19, 2008. Reproduced by permission of Prof. Jordi Canals, IESE Business School, University of Navara.

Appendix 1: Bank of America Corporation: Business Activities and Performance (extracts from 10-K report for 2007)

General

Bank of America Corporation ("Bank of America" or the "Corporation") is a Delaware corporation, a bank holding company and a financial holding company under the Gramm-Leach-Bliley Act. Our principal executive offices are located in the Bank of America Corporate Center, Charlotte, North Carolina 28255.

Through our banking subsidiaries (the "Banks") and various nonbanking subsidiaries throughout the US and in selected international markets, we provide a diversified range of banking and nonbanking financial services and products through three business segments: Global Consumer and Small Business Banking, Global Corporate and Investment Banking and Global Wealth and Investment Management. We currently operate in 32 states, the District of Columbia and more than 30 foreign countries. The Bank of America footprint covers more than 82% of the US population and 44% of the country's wealthy households. In the US we serve approximately 59 million consumer and small business relationships with more than 6,100 retail banking offices, more than 18,500 ATMs and approximately 24 million active online users. We have banking centers in 13 of the 15 fastest growing states and hold the top market share in six of those states . . .

As of December 31, 2007, there were approximately 210,000 full-time equivalent employees within Bank of America and our subsidiaries. Of these employees, 116,000 were employed within Global Consumer and Small Business Banking, 21,000 were employed within Global Corporate and Investment Banking and 14,000 were employed within Global Wealth and Investment Management . . .

($billion, except where indicated)	2007	2006	2005	2004	2003
Income statement					
Net interest income	34.4	34.6	30.7	28.0	20.5
Noninterest income	31.9	38.0	26.4	22.7	18.3
Total revenue, net of interest expense	66.3	72.6	57.2	50.7	38.8
Provision for credit losses	8.4	5.0	4.0	2.8	2.8
Noninterest expense, before merger and restructuring charges	36.6	34.8	28.3	26.4	20.2
Merger and restructuring charges	0.4	0.8	0.4	0.6	—
Income before income taxes	20.9	32.0	24.5	20.9	15.8
Income tax expense	5.9	10.8	8.0	7.0	5.0
Net income	15.0	21.1	16.5	13.9	10.8

($billion, except where indicated)	2007	2006	2005	2004	2003
Performance ratios (%)					
Return on average assets	0.94	1.44	1.30	1.34	1.44
Return on average common shareholders' equity	11.08	16.27	16.51	16.47	21.50
Return on average tangible shareholders' equity	22.25	32.80	30.19	28.93	27.84
Total ending equity to total ending assets	8.56	9.27	7.86	9.03	6.76
Total average equity to total average assets	8.53	8.90	7.86	8.12	6.69
Dividend payout	72.26	45.66	46.61	46.31	39.76
Market price per share of common stock					
Closing ($)	41.26	53.39	46.15	46.99	40.22
High closing ($)	54.05	54.90	47.08	47.44	41.77
Low closing ($)	41.10	43.09	41.57	38.96	32.82
Market capitalization	183.1	238.0	184.6	190.1	115.9
Average balance sheet					
Total loans and leases	776.2	652.4	537.2	472.6	356.2
Total assets	1,602.1	1,466.7	1,269.9	1,044.6	749.1
Total deposits	717.2	673.0	632.4	551.6	406.2
Long-term debt	169.9	130.1	97.7	92.3	67.1
Total shareholders' equity	136.7	130.5	99.9	84.8	50.1
Asset quality					
Allowance for credit losses	12.1	9.4	8.4	9.0	6.6
Nonperforming assets measured at historical cost	5.9	1.9	1.6	2.5	3.0
Allowance for loan and lease losses as % of total loans and leases	1.33	1.28	1.40	1.65	1.66
Net charge-offs	6.5	4.5	4.6	3.1	3.1
Net charge-offs as % of average loans and leases	0.84	0.70	0.85	0.66	0.87
Nonperforming loans and leases as % of total loans and leases	0.64	0.25	0.26	0.42	0.77
Nonperforming assets as % of total loans, leases and foreclosed properties	0.68	0.26	0.28	0.47	0.81
Ratio of the allowance for loan and lease losses at December 31 to net charge-offs	1.79	1.99	1.76	2.77	1.98
Capital ratios (period end)					
Risk-based capital:					
Tier 1	6.87	8.64	8.25	8.20	8.02
Total	11.02	11.88	11.08	11.73	12.05
Tier 1 Leverage	5.04	6.36	5.91	5.89	5.86

GLOBAL CORPORATE AND INVESTMENT BANKING

2007 ($billion)	Total	Deposits	Card services	Consumer real estate	ALM[a] and other
Net interest income	28.8	9.4	16.6	2.3	0.5
Non-interest income:					
—Card income	10.2	2.1	8.0	0.0	—
—Service charges	6.0	6.0	—	0.0	—
—Mortgage banking income	1.3	—	—	1.3	—
—All other income	1.3	(0.0)	0.9	0.1	0.4
—Total non-interest income	18.9	8.2	9.0	1.4	0.4
Total revenue, net of interest expense	47.7	17.6	25.5	3.7	0.9
Provision for credit losses	12.9	0.3	11.3	1.0	0.3
Noninterest expense	20.1	9.1	8.3	2.0	0.6
Income (loss) before income taxes	14.7	8.2	5.9	0.6	(0.1)
Income tax expense	5.3	3.08	2.2	0.2	(0.2)
Net income	9.4	5.2	3.7	0.4	0.1
Net interest yield[b] (%)	8.15	2.97	7.87	2.04	n.m.
Return on average equity	14.94	33.61	8.43	9.00	n.m.
Efficiency ratio[b]	42.07	51.81	32.49	55.24	n.m.
Period end—total assets	443.0	358.6	257.0	133.3	n.m.

Notes

Figures in parentheses denote a loss.

n.m.: not meaningful.

[a]Asset and liability management.

[b]The efficiency ratio measures the costs expended to generate a dollar of revenue; net interest yield evaluates how many basis points we are earning over the cost of funds.

The strategy for GCSBB is to attract, retain and deepen customer relationships. We achieve this strategy through our ability to offer a wide range of products and services through a franchise that stretches coast to coast through 32 states and the District of Columbia. We also provide credit-card products to customers in Canada, Ireland, Spain and the United Kingdom. In the US we serve approximately 59 million consumer and small-business relationships utilizing our network of 6149 banking centers, 18753 domestic branded ATMs, and telephone and internet channels. Within GCSBB there are three primary businesses:

- *Deposits* provides a comprehensive range of products to consumers and small businesses. Our products include traditional savings accounts, money market savings accounts, CDs and IRAs, and noninterest and interest-bearing checking accounts. Debit card results are also included in Deposits.
- *Card Services* provides a broad offering of products, including US Consumer and Business Card, Unsecured Lending, and International Card. We offer a variety of cobranded and affinity credit-card products and have become the leading issuer of credit cards through endorsed marketing in the US and

Europe. During 2007, Merchant Services was transferred to Treasury Services within GCIB.

- *Consumer Real Estate* generates revenue by providing an extensive line of consumer real estate products and services to customers nationwide. Consumer Real Estate products are available to our customers through a retail network of personal bankers located in 6149 banking centers, mortgage loan officers in nearly 200 locations and through a sales force offering our customers direct telephone and online access to our products. Consumer Real Estate products include fixed and adjustable rate loans for home purchase and refinancing needs, reverse mortgages, lines of credit and home equity loans. Mortgage products are either sold into the secondary mortgage market to investors while retaining the Bank of America customer relationships or are held on our balance sheet for ALM purposes . . . The Consumer Real Estate business includes the origination, fulfillment, sale and servicing of first mortgage loan products, reverse mortgage products and home equity products.

GLOBAL CORPORATE AND INVESTMENT BANKING

2007 ($billion)	Total	Business lending	Capital market and advisory	Treasury services
Net interest income	11.2	5.0	2.8	3.8
Noninterest income:				
—Service charges	2.8	0.5	0.1	2.1
—Investment and brokerage services	0.9	0.0	0.9	0.1
—Investment banking income	2.5	—	2.5	—
—Trading account profits (loss)	(5.2)	(0.2)	(5.1)	0.1
—All other income	1.1	0.8	(1.0)	1.1
—Total noninterest income	2.2	1.2	(2.5)	3.3
Total revenue, net of interest expense	13.4	6.2	0.3	7.1
Provision for credit losses	0.7	0.6	—	0.0
Noninterest expense	11.9	2.2	5.6	3.9
Income (loss) before income taxes	0.8	3.4	(5.3)	3.3
Income tax expense	0.3	1.2	(2.0)	1.2
Net income (loss)	0.5	2.1	(3.4)	2.1
Net interest yield (%)	1.66	2.00	n.m.	2.79
Return on average equity (%)	1.19	13.12	(25.41)	26.31
Efficiency ratio	88.88	34.98	n.m.	54.02
Period end—total assets	776.1	305.5	413.1	180.4

Notes:
Figures in parentheses denote a loss.
n.m.: not meaningful.

Global Corporate and Investment Banking provides a wide range of financial services both to our issuer and investor clients, who range from business banking clients to large international corporate and institutional investor clients, using a strategy to deliver value-added financial products and advisory solutions. Global Corporate and Investment Banking's products and services are delivered from three primary businesses: Business Lending, CMAS and Treasury Services are provided to our clients through a global team of client relationship managers and product partners. In addition, ALM/Other includes the results of ALM activities and other GCIB activities (such as commercial insurance business, which was sold in the fourth quarter of 2007). Our clients are supported through offices in 22 countries, which are divided into four distinct geographic regions: US and Canada; Asia; Europe, Middle East and Africa; and Latin America.

- *Business Lending* provides a wide range of lending-related products and services to our clients . . . Products include commercial and corporate bank loans and commitment facilities, which cover our business banking clients, middle market commercial clients and our large multinational corporate clients. Real-estate lending products are issued primarily to public and private developers, homebuilders and commercial real-estate firms. Leasing and asset-based lending products offer our clients innovative financing solutions. Products also include indirect consumer loans, which allow us to offer financing through automotive, marine, motorcycle and recreational vehicle dealerships. Business Lending also contains the results for the economic hedging of our risk to certain credit counterparties utilizing various risk mitigation tools.

- *Capital Markets and Advisory Services* provides financial products, advisory services and financing globally to our institutional investor clients in support of their investing and trading activities. We also work with our commercial and corporate issuer clients to provide debt and equity underwriting and distribution capabilities, merger-related advisory services and risk management solutions using interest rate, equity, credit, currency and commodity derivatives, foreign exchange, fixed income and mortgage-related products. The business may take positions in these products and participate in market-making activities dealing in government securities, equity and equity-linked securities, high-grade and high-yield corporate debt securities, commercial paper, mortgage-backed securities and ABS. Underwriting debt and equity, securities research and certain market-based activities are executed through Banc of America Securities, LLC, which is a primary dealer in the US.

- *Treasury Services* provides integrated working capital management and treasury solutions to clients worldwide through our network of proprietary offices and special clearing arrangements. Our clients include multinationals, middle-market companies, correspondent banks, commercial real estate firms and governments. Our products and services include treasury management, trade finance, foreign exchange, short-term credit facilities and short-term investing options. Net interest income is derived from interest-bearing and noninterest-bearing deposits, sweep investments, and other liability management products. Deposit products provide a relatively stable source of funding and liquidity. We earn net interest spread revenues from investing this liquidity in earning assets through client-facing lending activity and our ALM activities.

GLOBAL WEALTH AND INVESTMENT MANAGEMENT

2007 ($billion)	Total	US Trust	Columbia Management	Premier Banking and Investments
Net interest income	3.9	1.0	0.0	2.7
Noninterest income:				
—Investment and brokerage services	4.2	1.2	1.9	1.0
—All other income	(0.1)	0.1	(0.4)	0.1
—Total noninterest income	4.1	1.3	1.5	1.1
Total revenue, net of interest expense	7.9	2.3	1.5	3.8
Provision for credit losses	14	14	—	27
Noninterest expense	4.6	1.6	1.2	1.7
Income before income taxes	3.3	0.7	0.3	2.0
Income tax expense	1.2	0.3	0.1	0.7
Net income	2.1	0.5	0.2	1.3
Net interest yield (%)	3.06	2.69	n.m.	2.70
Return on average equity (%)	18.87	17.25	11.29	72.44
Efficiency ratio (%)	58.50	68.67	79.39	45.31
Period end—total assets	157.2	51.0	2.6	113.3

Notes:

Figures in parentheses denote a loss.

n.m.: not meaningful.

Global Wealth and Investment Management provides a wide offering of customized banking, investment and brokerage services tailored to meet the changing wealth management goals of our individual and institutional customer base. Our clients have access to a range of services offered through three primary businesses:

- *US Trust, Bank of America Private Wealth Management.* In July 2007, we completed the acquisition of US Trust Corporation for $3.3 billion in cash combining it with The Private Bank and its ultra-wealthy extension, Family Wealth Advisors, to form US Trust. The results of the combined business were reported for periods beginning on July 1, 2007. Prior to July 1, 2007, the results solely reflect that of the former Private Bank. US Trust provides comprehensive wealth management solutions to wealthy and ultra-wealthy clients with investable assets of more than $3 million. In addition, US Trust provides resources and customized solutions to meet clients' wealth structuring, investment management, trust and banking services as well as specialty asset management services (oil and gas, real estate, farm and ranch, timberland, private businesses and tax advisory). Clients also benefit from access to resources available through the Corporation including capital markets products, large and complex financing solutions and its extensive banking platform.

- *Columbia Management.* Columbia is an asset-management business serving the needs of institutional clients and individual customers. Columbia provides asset management products and services, including mutual funds and separate accounts. Columbia mutual fund offerings provide a broad array of investment strategies and products including equity, fixed income (taxable and nontaxable) and money market (taxable and nontaxable) funds. Columbia distributes its products and services directly to institutional clients and distributes to individuals through US Trust, PB&I and nonproprietary channels including other brokerage firms.

- *Premier Banking and Investments.* Premier Banking and Investments includes Banc of America Investments, our full-service retail brokerage business and our Premier Banking channel. Premier Banking and Investments brings personalized banking and investment expertise through priority service with client-dedicated teams. It provides a high-touch client experience through a network of approximately 5,600 client-facing associates to our affluent customers with a personal wealth profile that includes investable assets plus a mortgage that exceeds $500,000 or at least $100,000 of investable assets.

Source: 10-K report for 2007. Reproduced with permission.

Appendix 2: Merrill Lynch & Co., Inc.: Business Activities and Performance (extracts from 10-K report for 2007)

The Business

Merrill Lynch was formed in 1914 and became a publicly traded company on June 23, 1971. In 1973, we created the holding company, ML & Co., a Delaware corporation that, through its subsidiaries, is one of the world's leading capital markets, advisory and wealth management companies with offices in 40 countries and territories. In our Global Wealth Management ("GWM") business, we had total client assets in GWM accounts of approximately $1.2 trillion at December 26, 2008. As an investment bank, we are a leading global trader and underwriter of securities and derivatives across a broad range of asset classes and we serve as a strategic advisor to corporations, governments, institutions and individuals worldwide. In addition, as of December 26, 2008, we owned approximately half of the economic interest of BlackRock, Inc. ("BlackRock"), one of the world's largest publicly traded investment management companies with approximately $1.3 trillion in assets under management at the end of 2008 . . .

Our activities are conducted through two business segments: Global Markets and Investment Banking ("GMI") and GWM. In addition, we provide a variety of research services on a global basis.

Global Markets and Investment Banking

The Global Markets division consists of the Fixed Income, Currencies and Commodities ("FICC") and Equity Markets sales and trading activities for investor clients and on a proprietary basis, while the Investment Banking division provides a wide range of origination and strategic advisory services for issuer clients. Global Markets makes a market in securities, derivatives, currencies, and other financial instruments to satisfy client demands. In addition, Global Markets engages in certain proprietary trading activities. Global Markets is a leader in the global distribution of fixed income, currency and energy commodity products and derivatives. Global Markets also has one of the largest equity-trading operations in the world and is a leader in the origination and distribution of equity and equity-related products. Further, Global Markets provides clients with financing, securities clearing, settlement and custody services and also engages in principal investing in a variety of asset classes and private equity investing. The Investment Banking division raises capital for its clients through underwritings and private placements of equity, debt and related securities and loan syndications. Investment Banking also offers advisory services to clients on strategic issues, valuation, mergers, acquisitions and restructurings.

Global Wealth Management

Global Wealth Management, our full-service retail wealth management segment, provides brokerage, investment advisory and financial planning services, offering a broad range of both proprietary and third-party wealth management products and services globally to individuals, small- to mid-size businesses and employee benefit plans. Global Wealth Management comprises Global Private Client ("GPC") and Global Investment Management ("GIM").

Global Private Client provides a full range of wealth management products and services to assist clients in managing all aspects of their financial profile through the Total MerrillSM platform. Total MerrillSM is the platform for GPC's core strategy offering investment choices, brokerage, advice, planning and/or performance analysis to its clients. Global Private Client's offerings include commission and fee-based investment accounts, banking, cash management and credit services, including consumer and small business lending and Visa® cards; trust and generational planning; retirement services and insurance products.

Global Private Client services individuals and small- and middle-market corporations and institutions through approximately 16,090 financial advisors as of December 26, 2008.

Global Investment Management includes our interests in creating and managing wealth management products, including alternative investment products for clients. GIM also includes our share of net earnings from our ownership positions in other investment management companies, including BlackRock.

	GMI	GWM
Clients	Corporations, financial institutions, institutional investors, and governments	Individuals, small- to mid-size businesses, and employee benefit plans
Products and businesses	**Global Markets** (comprising Fixed Income, Currencies and Commodities ("FICC") and Equity Markets) Facilitates client transactions and makes markets in securities, derivatives, currencies, commodities and other financial instruments to satisfy client demands Provides clients with financing, securities clearing, settlement, and custody services. Engages in principal and private equity investing, including managing investment funds, and certain proprietary trading activities **Investment Banking** Provides a wide range of securities origination services for issuer clients, including underwriting and placement of public and private equity, debt and related securities, as well as lending and other financing activities for clients globally Advises clients on strategic issues, valuation, mergers, acquisitions and restructurings	**Global Private Client ("GPC")** Delivers products and services primarily through our Financial Advisors ("FAs") Commission fee-based investment accounts Banking, cash management, and credit services, including consumer and small business lending and Visa cards. Trust and generational planning. Retirement services. Insurance products **Global Investment Management ("GIM")** Creates and manages hedge funds and other alternative investment products for GPC clients Includes net earnings from our ownership positions in other investment management companies, including our investment in BlackRock

RESULTS BY GEOGRAPHICAL AREA, 2008

($billion)	2008	2007	2006
Net revenues			
Europe, Middle East and Africa	(2.39)	5.97	6.90
Pacific Rim	0.07	5.07	3.70
Latin America	1.24	1.40	1.01
Canada	0.16	0.43	0.39
Total non-US	(0.92)	12.87	11.99
United States	(11.67)	(1.62)	21.79
Total net revenues	(12.59)	11.25	33.78
Pretax earnings from continuing operations			
Europe, Middle East, and Africa	(6.74)	1.211	2.09
Pacific Rim	(2.56)	2.40	1.20
Latin America	0.34	0.63	0.36
Canada	0.0	0.24	0.18
Total non-US	(8.95)	4.48	3.83
United States	(32.88)	(17.31)	5.98
Total pretax earnings from continuing operations	(41.83)	(12.83)	9.810

Note:

Figures in parentheses denote a loss.

RESULTS BY BUSINESS SEGMENT

($million)	GMI	GWM	MLIM	Corporate	Total
2008					
Noninterest revenues	(25.42)	10.46	—	(1.68)	(16.63)
Net revenues	(26.46)	12.78	—	1.09	(12.59)
Noninterest expenses	15.08	10.43	—	3.72	29.24
Pretax (loss)/earnings from continuing operations	(41.54)	2.35	—	(2.63)	(41.83)
Year-end total assets	568.87	97.85	—	0.83	667.54
2007					
Noninterest revenues	(4.95)	11.72	—	(1.07)	5.701
Net revenues	(2.67)	14.02	—	(0.10)	11.25
Noninterest expenses	13.68	10.39	—	0.01	24.08
Pretax (loss)/earnings from continuing operations	(16.35)	3.63	—	(0.12)	(12.83)
Year-end total assets	920.39	99.20	—	0.47	1,020.05

Note:

Figures in parentheses denote a loss.

Source: 10-K report for 2007. Reproduced with permission.

Notes

1. "BofA/Merrill Lynch," *Financial Times*, September 16, 2008. http://www.ft.com/cms/s/2/d285ebc8-82ff-11dd-907e-000077b07658.html#axzz1yzXSaW3l. Reproduced by permission of the *Financial Times*.

2. See letter from Andrew M. Cuomo (State of New York Attorney General) to Christopher Dodd (Chair, Senate Banking Committee), Barney Frank (Chair, House Financial Services Committee), Mary Schapiro (Chair, SEC), and Elizabeth Warren (Chair, Congressional Oversight Panel), April 23, 2009, concerning "Bank of America -Merrill Lynch Merger Investigation," http://online.wsj .com/public/resources/documents/BofAmergLetter-Cuomo4232009.pdf, accessed May 10, 2012.

3. As discussion of the $700 billion bailout package "dissolved into a verbal brawl in the Cabinet Room of the White House," President Bush warned: "If money isn't loosened up, this sucker could go down," *New York Times*, September 26, 2008.

4. The facts regarding conversations between Lewis and US government officials are disputed. See: "Paulson Threatened Lewis," *Forbes*, July 15, 2009, http://www .forbes.com/2009/07/15/paulson-lewis-fed-markets-equity-bank-america-bernanke.html, accessed May 10, 2012.

A video clip relating to this case is available in your interactive e-book at **www.wileyopenpage.com**

Case 24 W. L. Gore & Associates: Rethinking Management?

> If a man could flow with the stream, grow with the way of nature, he'd accomplish more and he'd be happier doing it than bucking the flow of the water.
>
> —W. L. GORE

Malcolm Gladwell (author of *The Tipping Point* and *Outliers*) described his visit to W. L. Gore & Associates (Gore) as follows:

> When I visited a Gore associate named Bob Hen, at one of the company's plants in Delaware, I tried, unsuccessfully, to get him to tell me what his position was. I suspected, from the fact that he had been recommended to me, that he was one of the top executives. But his office wasn't any bigger than anyone else's. His card just called him an "associate." He didn't seem to have a secretary, one that I could see anyway. He wasn't dressed any differently from anyone else, and when I kept asking the question again and again, all he finally said, with a big grin, was, "I'm a meddler."[1]

The absence of job titles and the lack of the normal symbols of hierarchy are not the only things that are different about Gore. Since its founding in 1958, Gore has deliberately adopted a system of management that contrasts sharply with that of other established corporations. While the styles of management of all start-up companies reflect the personality and values of their founders, the remarkable thing about Gore is that, as a $2.5-billion company with 8,500 employees ("associates") in facilities located in 24 countries of the world, its organizational structure and management systems continue to defy the principles under which corporations of similar size and complexity are managed.

The Founding of Gore

Wilbert L. (Bill) Gore left DuPont in 1958 after 17 years as a research scientist. At DuPont, Gore had been working on a new synthetic material called

This case was prepared by Robert M. Grant. ©2012 Robert M. Grant.

polytetrafluoroethylene (PTFE), which it had branded "Teflon." Gore was convinced that DuPont's commitment to a business model based on large industrial markets for basic chemical products had caused it to overlook a whole range of innovative applications for PTFE. In forming a business together with his wife, Vieve, Gore was also motivated by the desire to create the energy and passion that he had experienced when working in small research teams at DuPont on those occasions when they were given the freedom to pursue innovation.

Working out of their own home in Newark, Delaware, and with the help of their son, Bob, the Gore, first product was Teflon-insulated cable (which was used for the Apollo space program among other applications).

The company's biggest breakthrough was the result of Bob Gore's discovery of the potential of Teflon to be stretched and laced with microscopic holes. The resulting fabric had several desirable properties; in particular, it shed water droplets but was also breathable. Gore-Tex received a US patent in 1976. Not only did it have a wide range of applications for outdoor clothing, the fact that Gore-Tex was chemically inert and resistant to infection made it an excellent material for medical applications such as artificial arteries and intravenous bags. The potential to vary the size of the microscopic holes in Gore-Tex made it ideal for a wide range of filtration applications.

Origins of the Gore Management Philosophy

FundingUniverse.com describes the development of Bill Gore's management ideas as follows:

> From their basement office, the Gores expanded into a separate production facility in their hometown of Newark, Delaware. Sales were brisk after initial product introductions. By 1965, just seven years after the business had started, Gore & Associates was employing about 200 people. It was about that time that Gore began to develop and implement the unique management system and philosophy for which his company would become recognized. Gore noticed that as his company had grown, efficiency and productivity had started to decline. He needed a new management structure, but he feared that the popular pyramid management structure that was in vogue at the time suppressed the creativity and innovation that he valued so greatly. Instead of adopting the pyramid structure, Gore decided to create his own system.
>
> During World War II, while on a task force at DuPont, Gore had learned of another type of organizational structure called the lattice system, which was developed to enhance the ingenuity and overall performance of a group working toward a goal. It emphasized communication and cooperation rather than hierarchy of authority. Under the system that Gore developed, any person was allowed to make a decision as long as it was fair, encouraged others, and made a commitment to the company. Consultation was required only for decisions that could potentially cause serious damage to the enterprise. Furthermore, new associates joined the company on the same effective authority level as all the other workers, including Bill and Vieve. There were no titles or bosses, with only a few exceptions, and commands were replaced by personal commitments.

New employees started out working in an area best suited to their talents, under the guidance of a sponsor. As the employee progressed there came more responsibility, and workers were paid according to their individual contribution. "Team members know who is producing," Bill explained in a February 1986 issue of the *Phoenix Business Journal*. "They won't put up with poor performance. There is tremendous peer pressure. You promote yourself by gaining knowledge and working hard, every day. There is no competition, except with yourself." The effect of the system was to encourage workers to be creative, take risks, and perform at their highest level.[2]

Bill Gore's ideas about management were influenced by Douglas McGregor's *The Human Side of Enterprise*, which was published as Gore's own company was in its start-up phase. In it, McGregor identifies two models of management: the conventional model of management, rooted in Taylor's scientific management, and Weber's principles of bureaucracy, which he terms "Theory X." At its core is the assumption that work is unpleasant, that employees are motivated only by money, and that management's principal role is to prevent shirking. "Theory Y" is rooted in the work of the human relations school of management, which assumes that individuals are self-motivated, anxious to solve problems, and capable of working harmoniously on joint tasks.

A key element in Bill Gore's management thinking related to the limits of organizational size. He believed that the need for interpersonal trust would result in organizations declining in effectiveness once they reached about 200 members. Hence, in 1967, rather than expand their Delaware facility, Bill and Vieve decided to build a second manufacturing facility in Flagstaff, Arizona. From then on, Gore built a new facility each time an existing unit reached 200 associates.

According to Malcolm Gladwell, Gore's insistence upon small organizational units is an application of a principle developed by anthropologist Robin Dunbar. According to Dunbar, social groups are limited by individuals' capacity to manage complex social relationships. Among primates, the size of the typical social group for a species is correlated with the size of the neocortex of that species' brain. For humans, Dunbar estimates that 148 is the maximum number of individuals that a person can comfortably have social relations with. Across a range of different societies, Dunbar found that 150 was the typical maximum size of tribes, religious groups, and army units.[3]

Organization Structure and Management Principles

The Gore organization does include elements of hierarchy. For example, as a corporation, it is legally required to have a board of directors—this is chaired by Bob Gore. There is also a CEO, Terri Kelly. The company is organized into four divisions (fabrics, medical, industrial, and electronic products) each with a recognized "leader." Within these divisions there are specific business units, each based upon a group of products. There are also specialized, company-wide functions such as human resources and information technology.

What is lacking is a codified set of ranks and positions. Gore associates are expected to adapt their roles to match their skills and aptitudes. The basic organizational units are small, self-managing teams.

Relationships within teams and between teams are based upon the concept of a lattice rather than a conventional hierarchy. The idea of a lattice is that every organizational member is connected to every other organizational member within the particular facility. In the lattice, communication is peer to peer, not superior to subordinate. For Bill Gore, this was a more natural way to organize. He observed that in most formal organizations it was through informal connections that things actually got done: "Most of us delight in going around the formal procedures and doing things the straightforward and easy way."[4]

Leadership is important at Gore, but the basic principle is that of natural leadership: "If you call a meeting and people show up—you're a leader."[5] Teams can appoint team leaders; they can also replace their team leaders. As a result, every team leader's accountability is to the team. "Someone who is accustomed to snapping their fingers and having people respond will be frustrated," says John McMillan, a Gore associate. "I snap my fingers and nobody will do anything. My job is to acquire followership, articulate a goal and get there . . . and hope the rest of the people think that makes sense."[6]

New associates are assigned to a "sponsor" whose job is to introduce the new hire to the company and guide him or her through the lattice. The new hire is likely to spend time with several teams during the first few months of employment. It is up to the new associate and a team to find a good match. An associate is free to find a new sponsor if desired. Typically, each associate works on two or three different project teams.

Annual reviews are peer based. Information is collected from at least 20 other associates. Each associate is then ranked against every other associate within the unit in terms of overall contribution. This ranking determines compensation.

The company's beliefs, management principles, and work culture are articulated on its website (Exhibit 1).

Innovation

The success of Gore's unusual management system is its capacity for innovation. Between 1976 and the end of May 2012, Gore received 1,026 US patents. Even more remarkable has been its ability to extend its existing technological breakthroughs to a wide variety of new applications. Central to Gore's ability to innovate is its willingness to allow individuals the freedom to pursue their own projects: each associate is allowed a half day each week of "dabble time." The company's website gives examples of the results of these initiatives (Exhibit 2).

Gary Hamel closes his discussion of Gore with the following challenge:

Bill Gore was a 40-something chemical engineer when he laid the foundations for his innovation democracy. I don't know about you, but a middle-aged polytetra-fluoroethylene-loving chemist isn't my mental image of a wild-eyed management innovator. Yet think about how radical Gore's vision must have seemed back in 1958. Fifty years later, postmodern management hipsters throw around terms like complex adaptive systems and self-organizing teams. Well, they're only a half century behind the curve. So ask yourself, am I dreaming big enough yet? Would my management innovation agenda make Bill Gore proud?[7]

EXHIBIT 1
What We Believe

Founder Bill Gore built the company on a set of beliefs and principles that guide us in the decisions we make, in the work we do, and in our behavior toward others. What we believe is the basis for our strong culture, which connects Gore associates worldwide in a common bond.

FUNDAMENTAL BELIEFS

Belief in the individual: If you trust individuals and believe in them, they will be motivated to do what's right for the company.

Power of small teams: Our lattice organization harnesses the fast decision-making, diverse perspectives, and collaboration of small teams.

All in the same boat: All Gore associates are part owners of the company through the associate stock plan. Not only does this allow us to share in the risks and rewards of the company; it gives us an added incentive to stay committed to its long-term success. As a result, we feel we are all in this effort together, and believe we should always consider what's best for the company as a whole when making decisions.

Long-term view: Our investment decisions are based on long-term payoff and our fundamental beliefs are not sacrificed for short-term gain.

Guiding Principles

◆ *Freedom*: the company was designed to be an organization in which associates can achieve their own goals best by directing their efforts toward the success of the corporation; action is prized; ideas are encouraged; and making mistakes is viewed as part of the creative process. We define freedom as being empowered to encourage each other to grow in knowledge, skill, scope of responsibility, and range of activities. We believe that associates will exceed expectations when given the freedom to do so.

◆ *Fairness*: everyone at Gore sincerely tries to be fair with each other, our suppliers, our customers and anyone else with whom we do business.

◆ *Commitment*: we are not assigned tasks; rather, we each make our own commitments and keep them.

◆ *Waterline*: everyone at Gore consults with other associates before taking actions that might be "below the waterline"—causing serious damage to the company.

Working in Our Unique Culture

Our founder Bill Gore once said, "The objective of the Enterprise is to make money and have fun doing so." And we still believe that, more than 50 years later.

Because we are all part owners of the company through the associate stock plan, Gore associates expect a lot from each other. Innovation and creativity; high ethics and integrity; making commitments and standing behind them. We work hard at living up to these expectations as we strive for business success.

But we also trust and respect each other and believe it's important to celebrate success.

Gore is much less formal than most workplaces. Our relationships with other associates are open and informal and we strive to treat everyone respectfully and fairly. This type of environment naturally promotes social interaction and many associates have made lifelong friends with those they met working at Gore.

Do Something You're Passionate About

At Gore, we believe it's important to have passion for what you do. If you're passionate about your work, you are naturally going to be highly self-motivated and focused. If you feel pride and ownership, you will want to do whatever it takes to be successful and have an impact. So when you apply for an opportunity at Gore, be sure you're going to be passionate about the work you'll be doing.

The Lattice Structure and Individual Accountability

Gore's unique "lattice" management structure, which illustrates a nonhierarchical system based on interconnection among associates, is free from traditional bosses and managers. There is no assigned authority, and we become leaders based on our ability to gain the respect of our peers and to attract followers.

You will be responsible for managing your own workload and will be accountable to others on your team. More importantly, only you can make a commitment to do something (for example, a task, a project, or a new role)—but once you make a commitment, you will be expected to meet it. A "core commitment" is your primary area of concentration. You may take on additional commitments depending on your interests, the company's needs, and your availability.

Relationships and Direct Communication

Relationships are everything at Gore—relationships with each other, with customers, with vendors and suppliers and with our surrounding communities. We encourage people to build and maintain long-term relationships by communicating directly. Of course we all use e-mail, but we find that face-to-face meetings and phone calls work best when collaborating with others.

Sponsors

Everyone at Gore has a sponsor, who is committed to helping you succeed. Sponsors are responsible for supporting your growth, for providing good feedback on your strengths and areas that offer opportunities for development and for helping you connect with others in the organization.

Source: www.gore.com/en_xx/careers/whoweare/about-gore.html, W. L. Gore & Associates: Beliefs, Principles and Culture. Reproduced by permission of W. L. Gore & Associates.

EXHIBIT 2
Examples of innovation at W. L. Gore & Associates

CHANGE MUSIC

How did the creators of GORE-TEX® products—worn by outdoor enthusiasts and people with active lifestyles all over the world—invent a new kind of guitar string?

Although manufacturers have coated their guitar strings for many years to make them last longer by protecting them from perspiration, oil, and dirt the coating severely compromised the quality of the sound.

Gore had no presence in the music industry until one associate envisioned a completely new type of guitar string that would prevent string contamination, last longer, and be more comfortable for musicians to play. Relying on the company's unique culture and mentoring system to support his efforts, he formed a cross-functional team—including Michael and John—to make it happen.

Each member of the Gore team had the knowledge and know-how needed to develop this exciting new product. With the entrepreneurial spirit characteristic of Gore, they took this innovative concept to the marketplace in less than two years.

But the team's commitment to integrity didn't stop in the lab. They asked 15,000 musicians to test the new strings for sound quality before the product was introduced. Since then, revolutionary ELIXIR® Strings have inspired a generation of musicians all over the world to pick up their guitars and play. And their ELIXIR® Strings experience and the challenges they overcame have changed their lives too.

Change Lives

How did the creators of GORE-TEX® products—worn by outdoor enthusiasts and people with active lifestyles all over the world—invent material to patch human hearts?

For people with a serious heart problem known as an atrial septal defect, or "hole in the heart," open heart surgery was once the only treatment. The surgeon makes an incision in the chest to expose the heart; a heart-lung bypass machine pumps blood while the heart is stopped and the defect is patched. Many patients with this condition are infants and small children, for whom this surgery poses an even greater risk.

A dedicated team of Gore associates—including Hannah, Nitin, and Sarah—developed a minimally invasive device that physicians implant through a cardiac catheter to permanently close the hole without major surgery. Driven by Gore's core values of integrity, innovation, and quality, the team spent years perfecting the device before taking it to market. Patients treated this way experience much less pain, recover much more easily and quickly, and have less scarring.

Since then, the GORE HELEX septal occluder has changed the way doctors treat patients with this heart defect and has helped thousands of patients throughout the world—more than half of them infants and children—lead normal, healthy lives. And the team's experience with the septal occluder product changed their lives, too.

Change Industries

How did the creators of GORE-TEX® products—worn by outdoor enthusiasts and people with active lifestyles all over the world—invent material that protects firefighters from heat, flames, and hazardous chemicals?

Gore makes a line of protective fabrics based on its patented membrane technologies. These fabrics are used by Gore's customers—garment manufacturers—as one layer of protective clothing for military and law enforcement uniforms, medical protective wear, workwear, and turnout gear for fire and safety personnel.

Firefighters rely on protective gear—including boots, pants, jackets, gloves, and headgear—to keep them safe. While already incorporating waterproof and breathable GORE-TEX® fabric to improve the comfort and quality of their gear, the firefighting industry identified a need for barrier fabrics that also protected firefighters against bloodborne pathogens and common fire ground chemicals. Dave, Henri, and Ron were part of a cross-functional team that set out to engineer high-performance CROSSTECH® protective barrier fabric to meet this need.

By building relationships with firefighters, suppliers, and industry experts, the global Gore team came to understand the extreme conditions that firefighters are exposed to. Harnessing deep knowledge of Gore's membrane technologies and their passion for making a difference, they developed Gore protective barrier fabrics that change the way firefighters respond to emergencies. And their fire service experience and the challenges they overcame have changed their lives, too.

Source: "Associates Stories," http://www.gore.com/en_xx/careers/associatestories/1234722965408.html, accessed October 1, 2012. Reproduced by permission of W. L. Gore & Associates.

Notes

1. M. Gladwell, *The Tipping Point* (Little, Brown & Co., London, 2000).
2. "W. L. Gore & Associates, Inc. History," http://www.fundinguniverse.com/company-histories/WL-Gore-amp;-Associates-Inc-Company-History.html, accessed October 1, 2012.
3. M. Gladwell, *The Tipping Point* (Little, Brown & Co., London, 2000, pp. 177–81).
4. Quoted by G. Hamel with B. Breen, *The Future of Management* (Harvard Business School Press, Boston, MA, 2007, p. 87).
5. Reprinted by permission of Harvard Business School Press from the Future of Management by Gary Hamel. Boston, MA 2007, p. 100 Copyright © 2007 by the Harvard Business School Publishing Corporation; all rights reserved.
6. "W. L. Gore & Associates, Inc.: Quality's Different Drummer," *IMPO Magazine*, January 14, 2002, http://www.impomag.com/articles/2002/01/wl-gore-associates-inc-qualitys-different-drummer, accessed June 6, 2012.
7. Reprinted by permission of Harvard Business School Press from the Future of Management by Gary Hamel. Boston, MA 2007, p. 100. Copyright © 2007 by the Harvard Business School Publishing Corporation; all rights reserved.

A video clip relating to this case is available in your interactive e-book at **www.wileyopenpage.com**

GLOSSARY

acquisition (or takeover)   The purchase of one company by another.

activity system   A conceptualization of the firm as a set of inter-related activities.

agency problem   An agency relationship exists when one party (the principal) contracts with another party (the agent) to act on behalf of the principal. The agency problem is the difficulty of ensuring that the agent acts in the principal's interest.

ambidextrous organization   An organization that can simultaneously exploit existing competences while exploring new opportunities for future development.

balanced scorecard   A tool for linking strategic goals to performance indicators. These performance indicators combine performance indicators relating to financial performance, consumer satisfaction, internal efficiency, and learning and innovation.

barriers to entry   Disadvantages that new entrants to an industry face in relation to established firms.

barriers to exit   Costs and other impediments which prevent capacity from leaving an industry.

benchmarking   A systematic process for comparing the practices, processes, resources and capabilities of other organizations with one's own.

blue-ocean strategy   The discovery or creation of uncontested market space.

bottom of the pyramid   This refers to the poorest people in the world: typically the 2 billion people who live on less than $2 per day.

bounded rationality   The principle that the rationality of human beings is constrained ("bounded") by the limits of their cognition and capacity to process information.

business model   The overall logic of a business and the basis upon which it generates revenues and profits.

business strategy (aka competitive strategy)   This refers to how a firm competes within a particular industry or market.

capability   More precisely referred to as *organizational capability*, is an organization's capacity to perform a particular task or function.

causal ambiguity   The difficulty facing any observer of diagnosing the sources of the competitive advantage of a firm with superior performance. It means that potential rivals face the problem of *uncertain imitability.*

comparative advantage   A country's ability to produce a particular product at a lower relative cost than other countries.

competency trap   The barrier to change which results from an organization developing high levels of capability in particular activities.

competitive advantage   A firm possesses a competitive advantage over its direct competitors when it earns (or has the potential to earn) a persistently higher rate of profit.

consumer surplus   The value that a consumer receives from a good or service minus the price that he or she paid.

contingency theory   Postulates that there is no single best way to design and manage an organization. The optimal structure and management systems for any organization are contingent upon its context—in particular, the features of its business environment and the technologies it utilizes.

corporate governance   The system by which companies are directed and controlled.

corporate planning   A systematic approach to resource allocation and strategic decisions within a company over the medium to long-term (typically 4 to 10 years).

corporate restructuring   Radical strategic and organizational change designed to improve performance through cost reduction, employment reduction, divestment of assets, and internal reorganization.

corporate social responsibility (CSR)   The social responsibilities of a business organization.

corporate strategy   A firm's decisions and intentions with regard to the scope of its activities (its choices in relation to the industries, national markets, and vertical activities within which it participates) and the resource allocation among these.

customer relationship management (CRM)   A set of tools, techniques, and methodologies for understanding the needs and characteristics of customers in order to better serve them.

dominant design   A product architecture that defines the look, functionality, and production method for the product and becomes accepted by the industry as a whole.

dynamic capabilities   Organizational capabilities that allow an organization to reconfigure its resources and modify its operating capabilities in order to adapt and change.

economic profit   Pure profit: it is the surplus of revenues over all the costs of producing that revenue inputs (including the costs of capital).

economic value added (EVA)   A measure of economic profit. It is the excess of net operating profit after tax over the cost of the capital used in the business.

economies of scale   These exist when increases in the scale of a firm or plant result in reductions in costs per unit of output.

economies of scope   These exist when using a resource across multiple products or multiple markets uses less of that resource than when the activities are carried out independently.

emergent strategy   The strategy that results from the actions and decisions of different organizational members as they deal with the forces which impinge upon the organization.

first-mover advantage   The competitive advantage that accrues to the firm which is first to occupy a new market or strategic niche, or to exploit a new technology. First-mover advantage is a special case of *early-mover advantage*.

functional structure   Organization around specialized business functions such as accounting, finance marketing, operations, etc.

game theory   This analyzes and predicts the outcomes of competitive (and cooperative) situations where each player's choice of action depends upon the choices made by the other players in the game. Game theory has applications to business, economics, politics, international relations, biology, and social relations.

global strategy   A strategy that treats the world as a single, if segmented, market.

globalization   The process through which differences between countries diminish and the world becomes increasingly integrated.

hypercompetition   Competition that is characterized by rapid and intensive competitive moves where competitive advantage is quickly eroded and firms are continually seeking new sources of competitive advantage.

industry life cycle   The pattern of industry evolution from introduction to growth to maturity to decline.

innovation   The initial commercialization of invention by producing and marketing a new good or service or by using a new method of production.

institutional isomorphism   The tendency for organizations that are subject to common social norms and pressures for legitimacy to develop similar organizational characteristics.

intellectual property   Intangible goods that have no physical presence and which are "creations of the mind." It includes ideas, names, symbols, designs, artwork, and writings.

intended strategy   The strategy conceived by top management with the intention of implementing it within the organization.

invention   The creation of new products and processes through the development of new knowledge or from new combinations of existing knowledge.

isolating mechanisms   Barriers that protect the competitive advantage of firms from imitative competition.

key success factors   Sources of competitive advantage within an industry.

knowledge-based view of the firm   This regards the firm as a pool of knowledge assets. The key challenge of management is to integrate the specialized knowledge of organizational members into the production of goods and services.

matrix structures   Hierarchies that comprise multiple dimensions; these typically include product (or business) units, geographical units, and functions.

merger   The amalgamation of two or more companies to form a new company. In a merger, the owners of the merging companies exchange their shares for shares in the new company.

multidivisional structure   A company structure comprising separate business units, each with significant operational independence, coordinated by a corporate head office that exerts strategic and financial control.

network effects (or network externalities)   Linkages between the users of a product or technology that result in the value of that product or technology being positively related to the number of users.

open innovation   An approach to innovation where a firm seeks solutions from organizations and individuals outside the firm and shares its technologies with other organizations.

organizational culture   An organization's values, traditions, behavioral norms, symbols, and social characteristics.

organizational ecology (aka organizational demography and the population ecology of organizations) This studies the organizational population of industries and the processes of founding and selection that determine entry and exit.

organizational routines Patterns of coordinated activity through which organizations are able to perform tasks on a regular and predictable basis.

path dependency The simple fact that history matters; more specifically, it implies that an organization's strategy and structure and management's options for the future are determined by past decisions.

prisoner's dilemma A simple game theory model which shows how lack of cooperation results in an outcome that is inferior to that which could have been achieved with cooperation.

profit The surplus of revenues over costs available for distribution to the owners of the firm.

real option analysis This identifies and values possibilities for investment in uncertain opportunities. The two major types of real option are investments in flexibility and investment in growth opportunities.

realized strategy The actual strategy that the organization pursues; it is the outcome of the interaction of intended strategy with emergent strategy.

regime of appropriability The conditions that determine the extent to which a firm is able to capture profits from its innovations.

resources The assets of the firm including tangible assets (such as plant, equipment, land, and natural resources), intangible resources (such as technology, brands and other forms of intellectual property) and human resources.

resource-based view of the firm A theoretical perspective on the firm that emphasizes the role of resources and capabilities as the basis of competitive advantage and the foundation for strategy.

scenario analysis A technique for integrating information and ideas on current trends and future developments into a small number of distinctly different future outcomes.

segmentation The process of disaggregating industries and markets into more narrowly defined sub-markets on the basis of product characteristics, customer characteristics or geography.

self-organization The tendency for complex systems, both natural and biological, to spontaneously achieve order and adaptation though decentralized interactions without any centralized direction or control.

seller concentration   This measures the extent to which a market is dominated by a small number of firms. The concentration ratio measures the market share of the largest firms e.g., the four-firm concentration ratio (CR4) is the combined market share of the four biggest firms.

stakeholder approach to the firm   This proposes that the firm operates in the interests of all its stakeholders (owners, employees, customers, suppliers and society). Top management has the task of balancing and integrating these different interests.

strategic fit   The consistency of a firm's strategy with its external environment and with its internal environment, especially with its goals and values, resources and capabilities, and structure and systems.

state capitalism   A market-based economy where a large proportion of leading enterprises are owned by the government.

strategic alliance   A collaborative arrangement between two or more firms involving their pursuit of certain common goals.

strategic group   A group of firms within an industry that follow similar strategies.

strategic intent   The goal of an organization in terms of a desired future strategic position.

SWOT framework   The SWOT framework classifies the factors relevant for a firm's strategic decision making into four categories: strengths, weaknesses, opportunities and threats.

technical standard   A specification or requirement or technical characteristic that becomes a norm for a product or process thereby ensuring compatibility.

transaction costs   The costs incurred in researching, negotiating, monitoring and enforcing market contracts.

value   Within management terminology, value is used to refer to two very different concepts. In its plural form, *values* typically refer to ethical precepts and principles. In its singular form it typically refers to economic value: the monetary worth of a product or asset.

value added   Sales revenue minus the cost of bought-in goods and services; it is equal to all the firm's payments to factors of production (i.e., wages and salaries + interest + rent + royalties and license fees + taxes + dividends + retained profit).

value chain   A sequence of vertically related activities undertaken by a single firm or by a number of vertically-related firms in order to produce a product or service.

vertical integration   A firm's ownership of adjacent vertical activities.

INDEX

Note: Page numbers in *italics* refer to illustrations and tables.